# About the Cover Image

**A Wagon Train on the Plains** American artist Thomas Whittredge, a member of the Hudson River School, was born in 1820 in a log cabin in frontier Ohio. His emerging artistic talent took him first to the East Coast and then to Europe, where he studied with leading painters in Germany. Just after the U.S. Civil War ended, Whittredge found great inspiration in a journey across the Great Plains. This painting, depicting men on horseback with Conestoga wagons and livestock grazing nearby, may have illustrated sheepherders whom Whittredge encountered. Alternatively the artist, observing the Plains at a time when bison herds were vanishing and the first transcontinental railroad was nearly complete, may have used his painting to evoke the great wagon trains that had crossed the Plains in earlier decades. This detail shows the human and animal figures fairly close up; in the full painting, they are dwarfed by an immensity of land and sky.

*A Wagon Train on the Plains* (oil on board), Whittredge, Thomas Worthington (1820–1910)/Private Collection/Photo © Christie's Images/Bridgeman Images.

ARCTIC OCEAN

80°N

Greenland
(Den.)

ICELAND

60°N

Alaska

UNITED
KINGDOM

IRELAND

BEL.

CANADA

FRANCE

SWITZ.

SPAIN

40°N

UNITED STATES

ATLANTIC
OCEAN

PORTUGAL

Azores
(Port.)

ALGERIA

MOROCCO

Canary Is.
(Sp.)

20°N

Hawaii

MEXICO

BAHAMAS

DOMINICAN
REPUBLIC

HAITI

Puerto Rico (U.S.)

Western Sahara
(Mor.)

MAURITANIA

ST. KITTS AND NEVIS

CUBA

JAMAICA

BELIZE

GUATEMALA

EL SALVADOR

HONDURAS

NICARAGUA

COSTA RICA

PANAMA

Guadeloupe (Fr.)

Martinique (Fr.)

ST. LUCIA

ANTIGUA AND BARBUDA

DOMINICA

ST. VINCENT AND THE GRENADINES

BARBADOS

GRENADA

TRINIDAD AND TOBAGO

VENEZUELA

GUYANA

SURINAME

CAPE
VERDE

SENEGAL

GAMBIA

GUINEA-BISSAU

MALI

GUINEA

SIERRA LEONE

LIBERIA

COLOMBIA

French Guiana (Fr.)

CÔTE D'IVOIRE

BURKINA FASO

GHANA

0°

Equator

Galápagos Is.
(Ec.)

ECUADOR

PACIFIC OCEAN

PERU

BRAZIL

SAMOA

20°S

TONGA

BOLIVIA

PARAGUAY

Easter I.
(Chile)

CHILE

URUGUAY

ATLANTIC
OCEAN

N

W        E

S

1,500

3,000 miles

0

1,500

3,000 kilometers

ARGENTINA

40°S

Falkland Is.
(U.K.)

60°S

80°S

160°W      140°W      120°W      100°W      80°W      60°W      40°W      20°W

ARCTIC OCEAN

NORWAY
SWEDEN
FINLAND
ESTONIA
LATVIA
LITHUANIA
DEN.
NETH.
GER. POLAND BELARUS
LUX.
CZ. REP.
UKRAINE
SLK. HUNG. MOLDOVA
ITALY B.H. SER. ROMANIA
MONT. MAC. BULGARIA
KOS. ALB. GREECE
MALTA
TUNISIA

RUSSIAN FEDERATION

KAZAKHSTAN

MONGOLIA

UZBEKISTAN
KYRGYZSTAN
TURKMENISTAN
TAJIKISTAN

GEORGIA
ARMENIA
TURKEY
AZERBAIJAN
CYPRUS
SYRIA LEBANON
ISRAEL
JORDAN
IRAQ
IRAN
AFGHANISTAN
PAKISTAN

CHINA

N. KOREA
S. KOREA
JAPAN

PACIFIC OCEAN

TAIWAN

LIBYA
EGYPT
KUWAIT
BAHRAIN
SAUDI ARABIA
QATAR
UNITED ARAB
EMIRATES
OMAN
YEMEN

NEPAL
BHUTAN

BANGLADESH

INDIA
MYANMAR
(BURMA)

THAILAND
LAOS
VIETNAM
CAMBODIA

PHILIPPINES

Mariana Is.
(U.S.)

Guam
(U.S.)

MARSHALL
IS.

NIGER
CHAD
SUDAN
ERITREA
DJIBOUTI

NIGERIA
BENIN
TOGO CENTRAL
CAMEROON AFRICAN REP.
EQ. SOUTH
GUINEA SUDAN
GABON
RWANDA UGANDA
DEM. REP. OF
SÃO TOMÉ THE CONGO
& PRÍNCIPE BURUNDI TANZANIA

ETHIOPIA

SOMALIA

MALDIVES

SRI
LANKA

BRUNEI

MALAYSIA

PALAU

FEDERATED STATES
OF MICRONESIA

NAURU
KIRIBATI

SINGAPORE

INDONESIA

PAPUA
NEW
GUINEA

EAST TIMOR

SOLOMON
IS.

TUVALU

KENYA

COMOROS
SEYCHELLES

INDIAN OCEAN

ANGOLA
ZAMBIA
MALAWI
ZIMBABWE
MADAGASCAR
NAMIBIA
BOTSWANA

MAURITIUS

VANUATU

FIJI

New Caledonia
(Fr.)

MOZAMBIQUE
SWAZILAND
SOUTH
AFRICA LESOTHO

AUSTRALIA

NEW
ZEALAND

Tasmania
(Aust.)

ANTARCTICA

20°E    40°E    60°E    80°E    100°E    120°E    140°E    160°E

### ABBREVIATIONS

| ALB. | ALBANIA |
| AUS. | AUSTRIA |
| BEL. | BELGIUM |
| B.H. | BOSNIA AND HERZEGOVINA |
| CR. | CROATIA |
| CZ. REP. | CZECH REPUBLIC |
| DEN. | DENMARK |
| GER. | GERMANY |
| HUNG. | HUNGARY |
| KOS. | KOSOVO |
| LUX. | LUXEMBOURG |
| MAC. | MACEDONIA |
| MONT. | MONTENEGRO |
| NETH. | NETHERLANDS |
| SER. | SERBIA |
| SLK. | SLOVAKIA |
| SLN. | SLOVENIA |
| SWITZ. | SWITZERLAND |

# America's History

## VALUE EDITION

VALUE EDITION

# America's History

## Ninth Edition

**Rebecca Edwards**
*Vassar College*

**Eric Hinderaker**
*University of Utah*

**Robert O. Self**
*Brown University*

**James A. Henretta**
*University of Maryland*

bedford/st.martin's
Macmillan Learning

Boston | New York

**FOR BEDFORD/ST. MARTIN'S**

*Vice President, Editorial, Macmillan Learning Humanities:* Edwin Hill
*Program Director for History:* Michael Rosenberg
*Senior Program Manager for History:* William J. Lombardo
*History Marketing Manager:* Melissa Rodriguez
*Director of Content Development:* Jane Knetzger
*Senior Developmental Editor:* Leah Strauss
*Senior Content Project Manager:* Gregory Erb
*Associate Content Project Manager:* Matthew Glazer
*Senior Workflow Project Manager:* Lisa McDowell
*Production Supervisor:* Robert Cherry
*Media Project Manager:* Tess Fletcher
*Composition:* Jouve
*Cartographer:* Mapping Specialists, Ltd.
*Photo Editor:* Sheena Goldstein
*Photo Researcher:* Naomi Kornhauser
*Permissions Editor:* Kalina Ingham
*Permissions Researcher:* Eve Lehmann
*Senior Art Director:* Anna Palchik
*Text Design:* Lumina Datamatics, Inc.
*Cover Design:* William Boardman
*Cover Art: A Wagon Train on the Plains* (oil on board), Whittredge,
    Thomas Worthington (1820–1910)/Private Collection/Photo
    © Christie's Images/Bridgeman Images
*Printing and Binding:* LSC Communications

Manufactured in the United States of America.
2   1   0   9   8
f   e   d   c   b

*For information, write:* Bedford/St. Martin's, 75 Arlington Street, Boston, MA 02116

ISBN 978-1-319-06062-6 (Combined Edition)
ISBN 978-1-319-06056-5 (Volume 1)
ISBN 978-1-319-06054-1 (Loose-leaf Edition, Volume 1)
ISBN 978-1-319-06057-2 (Volume 2)
ISBN 978-1-319-06055-8 (Loose-leaf Edition, Volume 2)

**ACKNOWLEDGMENTS**
*Acknowledgments and copyrights appear on the same page as the text and art selections they cover; these acknowledgments and copyrights constitute an extension of the copyright page.*

# Preface
## Why This Book This Way

We are pleased to publish the Value Edition of *America's History*. The Value Edition provides the same strength of breadth, balance, and the ability to explain not just what happened, but *why* in a two-color, trade-sized format at a low price. Featuring the full narrative of the parent text and select images, maps, and pedagogical tools, the Value Edition continues to incorporate the latest and best scholarship in the field in an accessible, student-friendly manner.

The foundation of our approach lies in a commitment to an integrated history. *America's History, Value Edition* combines traditional "top down" narratives of political and economic history with "bottom up" narratives of the lived experiences of ordinary people. Our goal is to help students achieve a richer understanding of politics, diplomacy, war, economics, intellectual and cultural life, and gender, class, and race relations by exploring how developments in all these areas were interconnected. Our analysis is fueled by a passion for exploring big, consequential questions. How did a colonial slave society settled by people from four continents become a pluralist democracy? How have struggles for liberty, equality, and justice informed the American experience? To whom has the "American Dream" appealed—and who has achieved it, or experienced disillusionment or exclusion? How has the experience of war shaped American politics, society, and culture? Questions like these help students understand what's at stake as we study the past. In *America's History, Value Edition* we provide an integrated historical approach and bring a dedication to *why history matters* to bear on the full sweep of America's past.

One of the most exciting developments in this edition is the attention we have devoted to fresh interpretations of the colonial, early national, and antebellum periods. Since his arrival as a new author on the eighth edition, Eric Hinderaker, an expert in Native American and early American history, has invigorated the chapters on Native, colonial European, and African societies and the revolutionary Atlantic World of the eighteenth century, bringing them in line with the most current historical scholarship. Rebecca Edwards, an expert in women's and gender history and nineteenth-century electoral politics, has done the same for the chapters covering the antebellum decades and the "long Progressive era" of the late nineteenth and early twentieth centuries. These authors have integrated coverage of slavery and the South's economy and society into all the pre–Civil War chapters. They have also consolidated antebellum coverage, enabling teachers to move more efficiently through this material, and have updated coverage of the Civil War. Robert Self, whose work explores the relationship between urban and suburban politics, social movements, and the state, has updated the twentieth- and twenty-first-century chapters, with special attention to Chapter 30, which chronicles the extraordinary events of the most recent decades. Together, we strive to ensure that energy and creativity, as well as our wide experience in the study of history, infuse every page that follows.

In this edition, we bid a fond and deeply appreciative adieu to James Henretta, one of the original authors of *America's History* and its ballast and intellectual leader for eight editions. Professor Emeritus at the University of Maryland, and soon to be an emeritus author, James will use his retirement to pursue a variety of personal and scholarly endeavors. His influence on this book, and his name on the title page, will continue for some time, but he will no longer participate in our cycles of revision. We wish him the best and thank him for sustaining *America's History* for so many years and for his commitment to the highest standards of scholarship and prose.

In our contemporary digital world, facts and data are everywhere. What students crave is analysis. As it has since its inception, *America's History* provides students with a comprehensive explanation and interpretation of events, a guide to why history unfolded as it did and a road map for understanding the world in which we live. The core of a textbook is its narrative, and we have endeavored to make ours clear, accessible, and lively. In it, we focus not only on the marvelous diversity of peoples who came to call themselves Americans, but also on the institutions that have forged a common national identity. More than ever, we daily confront the collision of our past with the demands of the future and the shrinking distance between Americans and others around the globe. To help students meet these challenges, we call attention to connections with the histories of Canada, Latin America, Europe, Africa, and Asia, drawing links between events in the United States and those elsewhere.

Of course, the contents of this book are only helpful if students read and assimilate the material before coming to class. So that students will come to class prepared, they can receive access to **LearningCurve**—an adaptive, online learning tool that helps them master content—when they purchase the **LaunchPad e-Book** (which is free when bundled with the print book). To learn more about the benefits of LearningCurve and LaunchPad, see the "Versions and Supplements" section on page xvii.

## A Nine-Part Framework Highlights Key Developments

One of the greatest strengths of *America's History, Value Edition* is its part structure, which helps students identify the key forces and major developments that shaped each era. A four-page part opener introduces each of the nine parts, using analysis and a **thematic timeline** to orient students to major developments and themes of the period. **Thematic Understanding** questions ask students to consider periodization and make connections among chapters. By organizing U.S. history into nine distinct periods, rather than just thirty successive chapters, we encourage students to trace changes and continuities over time and to grasp connections between political, economic, social, and cultural events.

In this edition, as in earlier ones, we have refined the part structure to reflect the most up-to-date scholarship. Part 4 now focuses more tightly on the history of the emerging republic, ending with the Mexican American War rather than in 1860. Part 5 offers expanded coverage of immigration, while Part 6 gives more emphasis to economic and intellectual debates during the era of industrialization. Part 9 extends to the end of Obama's presidency and the emergence of Donald Trump, linking political upheavals in this era to earlier events and themes.

**Part 1, "Transformations of North America, 1491–1700,"** highlights the diversity and complexity of Native Americans prior to European contact, examines the transformative impact of European intrusions and the Columbian Exchange, and emphasizes the experimental quality of colonial ventures. **Part 2, "British North America and the Atlantic World, 1607–1763,"** explains the diversification of British North America and the rise of the British Atlantic World and emphasizes the importance of contact between colonists and Native Americans and imperial rivalries among European powers. **Part 3, "Revolution and Republican Culture, 1754–1800,"** traces the rise of colonial protest against British imperial reform, outlines the ways that the American Revolution challenged the social order, and explores the processes of conquest, competition, and consolidation that followed it.

**Part 4, "Overlapping Revolutions, 1800–1848,"** traces the transformation of the economy, society, and culture of the new nation; the creation of a democratic polity; and growing sectional divisions. **Part 5, "Consolidating a Continental Union, 1844–1877,"** covers the conflicts generated by America's empire building in the West, including sectional political struggles that led to the Civil War and national consolidation of power during and after Reconstruction. **Part 6, "Industrializing America: Upheavals and Experiments, 1877–1917,"** examines the transformations brought about by the rise of corporations and a powerhouse industrial economy; immigration and a diverse, urbanizing society; and movements for progressive reform.

**Part 7, "Domestic and Global Challenges, 1890–1945,"** explores America's rise to world power, the cultural transformations and political conflicts of the 1920s, the Great Depression, and the creation of the New Deal welfare state. **Part 8, "The Modern State and the Age of Liberalism, 1945–1980,"** addresses the postwar period, including America's new global leadership role during the Cold War; the expansion of federal responsibility during a new "age of liberalism"; and the growth of mass consumption and the middle class. Finally, **Part 9, "Globalization and the End of the American Century, 1980 to the Present,"** discusses the conservative political ascendancy of the 1980s; the end of the Cold War and rising conflict in the Middle East; and globalization and increasing social inequality.

## Helping Students Work with Primary and Secondary Sources

Those using **LaunchPad** will have access to *America's History*'s primary and secondary source program. *America's History* has long emphasized primary sources. In addition to weaving lively quotations throughout the narrative, we offer students substantial excerpts from historical documents — letters, diaries, autobiographies, public testimony, and more — and numerous figures that give students practice working with data. Available in LaunchPad, these documents allow students to experience the past through the words and perspectives of those who lived it, to understand how historians make sense of the past using data, and to gain skill in interpreting historical evidence.

To sharpen the ability of students to think historically, and to expose them to diverse historical views, we have added a new feature called **Interpretations**. The new **Interpretations** feature brings historical argumentation directly into each chapter. Students read short, accessible passages from two scholarly works of history that offer different interpretations of the same event or period. By examining the passages side by side, and responding to the questions we pose, students learn how historians interpret evidence, weigh facts, and arrive at their conclusions. This feature highlights how *history* is a way of thinking and analyzing, rather than an inert set of facts.

Each of the 30 chapters of *America's History* in LaunchPad contains an **Interpretations** feature in addition to three primary-source-based features, continued from the eighth edition.

**Analyzing Voices**, a two-page feature in each chapter, helps students learn to think critically by comparing primary-source texts written or spoken from two or more perspectives. New topics include "Susanna Martin, Accused Witch," "Native Americans and European Empires," "To Secede or Not to Secede?," "The Omaha Platform," "Race and Geography in the Civil Rights Era," and "The Toll of War," about the Vietnam War.

The **America in Global Context** feature, developed for the previous edition, uses primary sources and data to situate U.S. history in a global context while giving students practice in comparison and data analysis. These features appear in every chapter on topics as diverse as the fight for women's rights in France and the United States, an examination of labor laws after emancipation in Haiti and the United States, the loss of human life in World War I, the global protests of 1968, and an analysis of the worldwide economic malaise of the 1970s.

Finally, we are excited to retain and reinvigorate a dynamic feature to aid you in teaching historical thinking skills that we developed for the eighth edition. A **Thinking Like a Historian** feature in every chapter includes five to eight brief primary sources organized around a central theme, such as "Beyond the Proclamation Line," "Making Modern Presidents," and "The Suburban Landscape of Cold War America." Students are asked to analyze the documents and complete a Putting It All Together assignment that asks them to synthesize and use the evidence to create an argument.

Because we understand how important primary sources are to the study of history, we are also pleased to offer for **free**, when packaged, the companion reader, *Sources for America's History*, featuring a wealth of additional documents.

## Helping Students Understand the Narrative

The study aids in the ninth edition have been strengthened to support students in their understanding of the material and in their development of historical thinking skills. **Identify the Big Idea** questions at the start of every chapter guide student reading and focus their attention on identifying not just what happened, but why. A variety of learning tools from the beginning to the end of each chapter support this big idea focus. New **Section Review Questions** help students articulate the main points of each section of a chapter. Where students are likely to stumble over a key concept, we boldface it in the text where it is first mentioned and provide a **glossary** that defines each term.

The **visual program** features over 100 paintings, cartoons, illustrations, photographs, and charts. Informative captions set the illustrations in context and provide students with background for making their own analysis of the images in the book. Keenly aware that students lack geographic literacy, we have included dozens of **maps** that show major developments in the narrative, each with a caption to help students interpret what they see.

The Chapter Review section provides a list of **Key Terms** that include concepts and events and key people students should know, a set of **Review Questions** that restate the individual section review questions, and a chapter **Chronology**.

## Helping Instructors Teach with Digital Resources

As noted, *America's History* is offered in Macmillan's premier learning platform, **LaunchPad**, an intuitive, interactive e-Book and course space. Free when packaged with the print text or available at a low price when used stand-alone, LaunchPad grants students and teachers access to a wealth of online tools and resources built specifically for our text to enhance reading comprehension and promote in-depth study.

Developed with extensive feedback from history instructors and students, *LaunchPad for America's History* includes the complete narrative of the print book, the companion reader, *Sources for America's History,* and **LearningCurve**, an adaptive learning tool that is designed to get students to read before they come to class. With **new source-based questions in the test bank and in LearningCurve** and the ability to **sort test bank questions by chapter learning objectives**, instructors now have more ways to test students on their understanding of sources and narrative in the book.

This edition also includes **Guided Reading Exercises** that prompt students to be active readers of the chapter narrative and auto-graded **primary source quizzes** to test comprehension of written and visual sources. These features, plus **additional primary source documents, video sources and tools for making video assignments, map activities, flash cards,** and **customizable test banks**, make LaunchPad a great asset for any instructor who wants to enliven American history for students.

## New Updates to the Narrative

In the new edition, we continue to offer instructors a bold account of U.S. history that reflects the latest, most exciting scholarship in the field. Throughout the book, we have given increased attention to political culture and political economy, including the history of capitalism, using this analysis to help students understand how society, culture, politics, and the economy informed one another.

The opening chapters incisively analyze the processes by which European colonization transformed the Western Hemisphere. They emphasize the way Native Americans shaped, and were shaped by, the contact experience — a focus that carries through the ninth edition in a continental perspective and sustained coverage of Native Americans, the environment, and the West in every era. These chapters highlight the varied and tenuous nature of experiments in colonization; in doing so, they stress the opportunity, as well as the instability and violence, inherent in the colonial enterprise. And they trace the rise of British North America, the Atlantic World, and the many revolutions — in print, consumption, and politics — that transformed the eighteenth century.

In the early nineteenth-century chapters, coverage of the South and slavery has been integrated throughout, to give more emphasis to the economic and political clout of the "Cotton Kingdom" and its "peculiar institution." Antebellum urban culture and Irish and German immigration also get more attention. The 1850s and the secession crisis receives more extended treatment, showing students that there was no direct or inevitable path from the Kansas-Nebraska Act to war. The Civil War chapter has been extensively revised to reflect recent scholarship, balancing military and technological history with crucial diplomatic and political events, while conveying the experiences of civilians, self-liberated former slaves, refugees, and soldiers.

In the post–Civil War chapters, enhanced coverage of gender, ethnicity, and race includes greater emphasis on gay and lesbian history and Asian and Latino immigration, alongside the entire chapter devoted to the civil rights movement, a major addition to the last edition. Finally, we have kept up with recent developments with an expanded section on the Obama presidency and the election of 2016. Students keen to understand contemporary political developments will find in the post–World War II chapters a strong political and economic narrative that helps them contextualize the very recent past.

## Acknowledgments

We are grateful to the following scholars and teachers who reported on their experiences with the eighth edition or reviewed features of the new edition. Their comments often challenged us to rethink or justify our interpretations and always provided a check on accuracy down to the smallest detail.

Roger Carpenter, *University of Louisiana at Monroe*; Petra DeWitt, *Missouri University of Science and Technology*; Blake Ellis, *Lone Star College–CyFair*; Roger Greenland, *Mineral Area College*; Daniel Haworth, *University of Houston–Clear Lake*; Alan Lehmann, *Blinn College*; Philbert Martin, *San Jacinto College*; Suzanne McCormack, *Community College of Rhode Island*; William Morgan, *Lone Star College–Montgomery*; Daniel Murphree, *University of Central Florida*; Manfred Silva, *El Paso Community College*; Andrew Slap, *East Tennessee State University*; Whitney Snow, *Midwestern State University*; Michael Wise, *University of North Texas*.

As the authors of *America's History*, we know better than anyone else how much this book is the work of other hands and minds. We are especially grateful to Kevin B. Sheets of the State University of New York at Cortland for his peerless help in assembling the material for the new Interpretations feature. We are indebted to the team at Bedford/St. Martin's: Michael Rosenberg, William J. Lombardo, Jane Knetzger, Laura Arcari, Nathan Odell, Blythe Robbins, Leah Strauss, and Kathryn Abbott, who asked the right questions and suggested a multitude of improvements. Greg Erb did a masterful job consulting with the authors and seeing the book through the production process. Melissa Rodriguez and Janie Pierce-Bratcher in the marketing department understood how to communicate our vision to teachers; they and the members of college and high school sales forces did wonderful work in helping this edition reach the classroom. We also thank the rest of our editorial and production team for their dedicated efforts: Media Editor Tess Fletcher; Editorial Assistant Lexi DeConti; copyeditor Susan Zorn; proofreaders Deborah Heimann and Diana George; indexer Rebecca McCorkle; art researchers Naomi Kornhauser and Sheena Goldstein; text permissions researchers Eve Lehmann and Kalina Ingham. Finally, we want to express our appreciation for the assistance of Michelle Whalen and the U.S. historians at Vassar College — Robert Brigham, Miriam Cohen, James Merrell, and Quincy Mills — for their invaluable help and advice. Many thanks to all of you for your contributions to this new edition of *America's History*.

Rebecca Edwards
Eric Hinderaker
Robert O. Self

# Versions and Supplements

Adopters of *America's History* and their students have access to abundant print and digital resources and tools, the acclaimed Bedford Series in History and Culture volumes, and much more. The LaunchPad course space for *America's History* provides access to the narrative as well as a wealth of primary sources and other features, along with assignment and assessment opportunities at the ready. See below for more information, visit the book's catalog site at **macmillanlearning.com**, or contact your local Bedford/St. Martin's sales representative.

## Get the Right Version for Your Class

To accommodate different course lengths and course budgets, *America's History* is available in several different versions and formats to best suit your course needs. The comprehensive *America's History* includes a full-color art program and a robust set of features. The Concise Edition also provides the full narrative, with a streamlined art and feature program, at a lower price. The Value Edition offers a trade-sized two-color option with the full narrative and selected art and maps at a steeper discount. The Value Edition is also offered at the lowest price point in loose-leaf, and all versions are available as e-Books. For the best value of all, package a new print book with LaunchPad at no additional charge to get the best each format offers—a print version for easy portability with a LaunchPad interactive e-Book and course space with LearningCurve and loads of additional assignment and assessment options.

- **Combined Volume** (Chapters 1–30): available in paperback, Concise, Value, and e-Book formats and in LaunchPad
- **Volume 1: To 1877** (Chapters 1–15): available in paperback, Concise, Value, loose-leaf, and e-Book formats and in LaunchPad
- **Volume 2: Since 1865** (Chapters 14–30): available in paperback, Concise, Value, loose-leaf, and e-Book formats and in LaunchPad

As noted below, any of these volumes can be packaged with additional titles for a discount. To get ISBNs for discount packages, visit **macmillanlearning.com** for the comprehensive version or Value Edition or contact your Bedford/St. Martin's representative.

## ⓜ LaunchPad macmillan learning Assign LaunchPad—an Assessment-Ready Interactive e-Book and Course Space

Available for discount purchase on its own or for packaging with new books at no additional charge, LaunchPad is a breakthrough solution for history courses. Intuitive and easy to use for students and instructors alike, LaunchPad is ready to use as is and can be edited, customized with your own material, and assigned quickly. *LaunchPad for America's History* includes Bedford/St. Martin's high-quality content all in one place, including the full interactive e-Book and the companion reader *Sources for America's History*, plus LearningCurve formative quizzing, guided reading activities designed to help students read actively for key concepts, autograded quizzes for each primary source, and chapter summative quizzes. Through a wealth of formative and summative assessments, including the adaptive learning program of LearningCurve (see the full description below), students gain confidence and get into their reading before class. These features, plus additional primary source documents, video sources and tools for making video assignments, map activities, flash cards, and customizable test banks, make LaunchPad an invaluable asset for any instructor.

LaunchPad easily integrates with course management systems, and with fast ways to build assignments, rearrange chapters, and add new pages, sections, or links, it lets teachers build the courses they want to teach and hold students accountable. For more information, visit **launchpadworks.com**, or to arrange a demo, contact us at **history@macmillan.com**.

## ✓ Assign LearningCurve So Your Students Come to Class Prepared

Students using LaunchPad receive access to LearningCurve for *America's History*. Assigning LearningCurve in place of reading quizzes is easy for instructors, and the reporting features help instructors track overall class trends and spot topics that are giving students trouble so they can adjust their lectures and class activities. This online learning tool is popular with students because it was designed to help them rehearse content at their own pace in a nonthreatening, gamelike environment. The feedback for wrong answers provides instructional coaching and sends students back to the book for review. Students answer as many questions as necessary to reach a target score, with repeated chances to revisit material they haven't mastered. When LearningCurve is assigned, students come to class better prepared.

## iClicker, Active Learning Simplified

iClicker offers simple, flexible tools to help you give students a voice and facilitate active learning in the classroom. Students can participate with the devices they already bring to class using our iClicker Reef mobile apps (which work with smart phones, tablets, or laptops) or iClicker remotes. We've now integrated iClicker with Macmillan's LaunchPad to make it easier than ever to synchronize grades and promote engagement — both in and out of class. iClicker Reef access cards can also be packaged with LaunchPad or your textbook at a significant savings for your students. To learn more, talk to your Macmillan Learning representative or visit us at **www.iclicker.com**.

## Take Advantage of Instructor Resources

Bedford/St. Martin's has developed a rich array of teaching resources for this book and for this course. They range from lecture and presentation materials and assessment tools to course management options. Most can be found in LaunchPad or can be downloaded or ordered at **macmillanlearning.com**.

**Bedford Coursepack for Blackboard, Canvas, Brightspace by D2L, or Moodle.** We can help you integrate our rich content into your course management system. Registered instructors can download coursepacks that include our popular free resources and book-specific content for *America's History*. Visit **macmillanlearning.com** to find your version or download your coursepack.

**Instructor's Resource Manual.** The instructor's manual offers both experienced and first-time instructors tools for presenting textbook material in engaging ways. It includes content learning objectives, annotated chapter outlines, and strategies for teaching with the textbook, plus suggestions on how to get the most out of LearningCurve and a survival guide for first-time teaching assistants.

**Guide to Changing Editions.** Designed to facilitate an instructor's transition from the previous edition of *America's History* to this new edition, this guide presents an overview of major changes as well as changes in each chapter.

**Online Test Bank.** The test bank includes a mix of fresh, carefully crafted multiple-choice, matching, short-answer, and essay questions for each chapter. Many of the multiple-choice questions feature a map, an image, or a primary source excerpt as the prompt. All questions appear in Microsoft Word format and in easy-to-use test bank software that allows instructors to add, edit, re-sequence, filter by question type or learning objective, and print questions and answers. Instructors can also export questions into a variety of course management systems. This test bank is tagged to book-specific learning outcomes and to the Texas Higher Education Coordinating Board's Student Learning Outcomes for History 1301 (U.S. History to 1877) and History 1302 (U.S. History Since 1865).

*The Bedford Lecture Kit:* **Lecture Outlines, Maps, and Images.** Look good and save time with *The Bedford Lecture Kit*. These presentation materials include fully customizable multimedia presentations built around chapter outlines that are embedded with maps, figures, and images from the textbook and are supplemented by detailed instructor notes on key points and concepts.

*America in Motion: Video Clips for U.S. History.* Set history in motion with *America in Motion*, an instructor DVD containing dozens of short digital movie files of events in twentieth-century American history. From the wreckage of the battleship *Maine* to FDR's fireside chats, to Ronald Reagan speaking before the Brandenburg Gate, *America in Motion* engages students with dynamic scenes from key events and challenges them to think critically. All files are classroom-ready, edited for brevity, and easily integrated with presentation slides or other software for electronic lectures or assignments. An accompanying guide provides each clip's historical context, ideas for use, and suggested questions.

## Print, Digital, and Custom Options for More Choice and Value

For information on free packages and discounts up to 50%, visit **macmillanlearning .com**, or contact your local Bedford/St. Martin's sales representative.

**NEW** *Sources for America's History,* **Ninth Edition.** This primary source collection provides a revised and expanded selection of sources to accompany *America's History*, Ninth Edition. *Sources for America's History* provides a broad selection of over 225 primary source documents as well as editorial apparatus to help students understand the sources. *To support the structure of the parent text, unique document sets at the end of each part present sources that illustrate the major themes of each section.* This companion reader is an exceptional value for students and offers plenty of assignment options for instructors. Available free when packaged with the print text and included in the LaunchPad e-Book. Also available on its own as a downloadable PDF e-Book.

**NEW Bedford Tutorials for History.** Designed to customize textbooks with resources relevant to individual courses, this collection of brief units, each 16 pages long and loaded with examples, guides students through basic skills such as using historical evidence effectively, working with primary sources, taking effective notes, avoiding plagiarism and citing sources, and more. Up to two tutorials can be added to a Bedford/St. Martin's history survey title at no additional charge, freeing you to spend your class time focusing on content and interpretation. For more information, visit **macmillanlearning.com/historytutorials**.

**NEW Bedford Document Collections for U.S. History.** This source collection provides a flexible and affordable online repository of discovery-oriented primary source projects ready to assign. Each curated project—written by a historian about a favorite topic—poses a historical question and guides students step by step through analysis of primary sources. Examples include What Caused the Civil War?; The California Gold Rush: A Trans-Pacific Phenomenon; and War Stories: Black Soldiers and the Long Civil Rights Movement. For more information, visit **macmillanlearning.com**. Available free when packaged.

**NEW Bedford Document Collections Custom Print Modules.** Choose one or two document projects from the collection (see above) and add them in print to a Bedford/St. Martin's title, or select several to be bound together in a custom reader created specifically for your course. Either way, the modules are affordably priced. For more information, contact your Bedford/St. Martin's representative.

**The Bedford Series in History and Culture.** More than one hundred titles in this highly praised series combine first-rate scholarship, historical narrative, and important primary documents for undergraduate courses. Each book is brief, inexpensive, and focused on a specific topic or period. Revisions of several best-selling titles, such as *The Cherokee Removal: A Brief History with Documents* by Theda Perdue; *Narrative of the Life of Frederick Douglass,* edited by David Blight; and *The Triangle Fire: A Brief History with Documents* by Jo Ann Argersinger, are now available. For a complete list of titles, visit **macmillanlearning.com**. Package discounts are available.

***Rand McNally Atlas of American History.*** This collection of more than eighty full-color maps illustrates key events and eras from early exploration, settlement, expansion, and immigration to U.S. involvement in wars abroad and on U.S. soil. Introductory pages for each section include a brief overview, timelines, graphs, and photos to quickly establish a historical context. Free when packaged.

***The Bedford Glossary for U.S. History.*** This handy supplement for the survey course gives students historically contextualized definitions for hundreds of terms—from *abolitionism* to *zoot suit*—that they will encounter in lectures, reading, and exams. Free when packaged.

**Trade Books.** Titles published by sister companies Hill and Wang; Farrar, Straus and Giroux; Henry Holt and Company; St. Martin's Press; Picador; and Palgrave Macmillan are available at a 50% discount when packaged with Bedford/St. Martin's textbooks. For more information, visit **macmillanlearning.com/tradeup**.

*A Pocket Guide to Writing in History.* Updated to reflect changes made in the 2017 *Chicago Manual of Style* revision, this portable and affordable reference tool by Mary Lynn Rampolla provides reading, writing, and research advice useful to students in all history courses. Concise yet comprehensive advice on approaching typical history assignments, developing critical reading skills, writing effective history papers, conducting research, using and documenting sources, and avoiding plagiarism—enhanced with practical tips and examples throughout—has made this slim reference a best-seller. Package discounts are available.

*A Student's Guide to History.* This complete guide to success in any history course provides the practical help students need to be successful. In addition to introducing students to the nature of the discipline, author Jules Benjamin teaches a wide range of skills, from preparing for exams to approaching common writing assignments, and explains the research and documentation process with plentiful examples. Package discounts are available.

*Going to the Source: The Bedford Reader in American History.* Developed by Victoria Bissell Brown and Timothy J. Shannon, this reader combines a rich diversity of primary and secondary sources with in-depth instructions for how to use each type of source. Mirroring the chronology of the U.S. history survey, each of the main chapters familiarizes students with a single type of source—from personal letters to political cartoons—while focusing on an important historical episode such as the Cherokee Removal or the 1894 Pullman Strike. The reader's wide variety of chapter topics and sources provokes students' interest as it teaches them the skills they need to successfully interrogate historical sources. Package discounts are available.

*America Firsthand.* With its distinctive focus on first-person accounts from ordinary people, this primary documents reader by Anthony Marcus, John M. Giggie, and David Burner offers a remarkable range of perspectives on America's history from those who lived it. Popular Points of View sections expose students to different perspectives on a specific event or topic. Package discounts are available.

# Brief Contents

# Contents

## PART 7

# Domestic and Global Challenges, 1890–1945     578

### CHAPTER 20

## An Emerging World Power, 1890–1918   582

### CHAPTER 21

## Unsettled Prosperity: From War to Depression, 1919–1932   610

# Maps and Figures

**Chapter 30**

# America's History

## VALUE EDITION

# PART 1

Each of the nine parts in *America's History* covers a particular period of time. The choice of beginning and ending dates is called *periodization*: the process of deciding how to break down history into pieces with coherent themes. Throughout this book, each choice of periodization represents a form of historical argument, and we'll explain and explore each periodization choice as we go.

Part 1 of *America's History* is about collisions and experiments. Our choice to begin in 1491 is symbolic: it represents the moment before Columbus's first voyage in 1492 bridged the Atlantic Ocean. At this time North America, Europe, and Africa were home to complex societies with distinctive cultures. But their histories were about to collide, bringing vast changes to all three continents. Sustained contact among Native Americans, Europeans, and Africans was one of the most momentous developments in world history.

No one knew what European colonies in the Americas would be like. Only by experimenting did new societies gradually emerge. These experiments were neither easy nor peaceful. Warfare, mass enslavement, death, and destruction lay at the heart of colonial enterprise. Native Americans, Europeans, and Africans often clashed violently as they struggled to control their fates.

But colonies also created opportunities for new societies to flourish. Across two centuries, five European nations undertook colonial experiments in dozens of places. Some failed miserably; some prospered beyond anyone's imagining. We bring Part 1 to a close in 1700, when the first fruits of these experiments were clear, though colonial societies remained insecure and unstable. Would other concluding dates be possible for this part—for example, 1607? Yes, but to our minds, it's best to consider the early decades of British and French colonization—1607 to 1700—in tandem with a deep exploration of precontact Native American and African societies. Chapters 1 and 2 address three main developments that are central to this period.

## Native American Diversity and Complexity

Native American societies ranged from vast, complex imperial states to small kin-based bands of hunters and gatherers: a spectrum much too broad for the familiar term *tribe* to cover. Native Americans' economic and social systems were adapted to the ecosystems they inhabited. Many were productive farmers, and some hunted bison and deer, while others were expert salmon fishermen who plied coastal waters in large oceangoing boats. Native American religions and cultures also differed, though many had broad characteristics in common.

These variations in Native American societies shaped colonial enterprise. Europeans conquered and co-opted the Native American empires in Mexico and the Andes with relative ease, but smaller societies were harder to exploit. Mobile hunter-gatherers were especially formidable opponents of colonial expansion.

## The Columbian Exchange

European colonization triggered a series of sweeping changes that historians have labeled the Columbian Exchange. Plants, animals, and germs crossed the Atlantic as well as people. European grains and weeds were carried westward, while American foods like potatoes and maize (corn) transformed diets in Europe and Asia. Native Americans had domesticated very few animals; the Columbian Exchange introduced many new creatures to the American landscape. Germs also made the voyage, especially deadly pathogens like smallpox, influenza, and bubonic plague, which took an enormous toll. Having lost on average 90 percent of their populations from disease over the first century of contact, Native American societies were forced to cope with European and African newcomers in a weakened and vulnerable state.

Inanimate materials crossed oceans as well: enough gold and silver traveled from the Americas to Europe and Asia to transform the world's economies, intensifying competition and empire building in Europe.

## Experimentation and Transformation

The collisions of American, European, and African worlds challenged the beliefs and practices of all three groups. Colonization was, above all, a long and tortured process of experimentation. Over time, Europeans carved out three distinct types of colonies in the Americas. Where Native American societies were organized into densely settled empires, Europeans conquered the ruling class and established tribute-based empires of their own. In tropical and subtropical settings, colonizers created plantation societies that demanded large, imported labor forces—a need that was met through the African slave trade. And in temperate regions, colonists came in large numbers hoping to create societies similar to the ones they knew in Europe.

Everywhere, core beliefs were shaken by contact with radically unfamiliar peoples. Native Americans and Africans struggled to maintain autonomy, while Europeans labored to understand—and profit from—their relations with nonwhite peoples. These transformations are the subject of Part 1.

## Thematic Understanding

This timeline arranges some of the important events of this period into themes. Look at the entries for "Culture and Society" from 1450 to 1700. How did the Protestant Reformation and the response of the Catholic Church influence the colonization of the Americas in these years? In the realm of "Work, Exchange, and Technology," how did colonial economies evolve, and what roles did Native American and African labor play in them?

| | AMERICAN AND NATIONAL IDENTITY | POLITICS AND POWER | WORK, EXCHANGE, AND TECHNOLOGY |
|---|---|---|---|
| 1450 | • Castile and Aragon join to create Spain; the Inquisition helps create a sense of a Spanish identity <br> • John Calvin establishes a Protestant commonwealth in Geneva, Switzerland | • Rise of monarchical nation-states in Europe <br> • Aztecs and Incas consolidate their empires <br> • Probable founding of the Iroquois Confederacy <br> • Rise of the Songhai Empire in Africa | • Diversified economies of Native America <br> • Rise of the Ottoman Empire blocks Asian trading routes of the Italian city-states <br> • Europeans fish off North American coast <br> • Portuguese traders explore African coast |
| 1550 | • English conquest and persecution of native Irish <br> • Growing Protestant movement in England | • Elizabeth's "sea dogs" plague Spanish shipping <br> • English monarchs adopt mercantilist policies <br> • Defeat of the Spanish Armada (1588) | • Growth of the outwork system in English textile industry <br> • Spanish *encomienda* system organizes native labor in Mexico <br> • Inca *mita* system is co-opted by the Spanish in the Andes |
| 1600 | • Pilgrims and Puritans seek to create godly commonwealths <br> • Powhatan and Virginia Company representatives attempt to extract tribute from each other | • Virginia's House of Burgesses (1619) <br> • The Powhatan (1620s and 1640s) and Pequot (1630s) Wars <br> • Restoration of the English crown (1660) <br> • English conquer New Netherland (1664) <br> • Native American revolts against New England (1670s) and New Mexico (1680s) <br> • Bacon's Rebellion in Virginia (1675–1676) | • First staple exports from the English mainland colonies: furs and tobacco <br> • Subsistence farms in New England <br> • Transition to sugar plantation system in the Caribbean islands |
| 1700 | • Social mobility for Africans ends with collapse of tobacco trade and increased power of gentry | | • Tobacco trade stagnates <br> • Maturing yeoman economy and emerging Atlantic trade in New England |

| CULTURE AND SOCIETY | MIGRATION AND SETTLEMENT | GEOGRAPHY AND THE ENVIRONMENT | AMERICA IN THE WORLD | |
| --- | --- | --- | --- | --- |
| • Protestant Reformation (1517) sparks century of religious warfare<br>• Henry VIII creates Church of England (1534)<br>• Founding of Jesuit order (1540) | • Christopher Columbus explores the Bahamas and West Indies (1492–1504)<br>• Pedro Alvares Cabral makes landfall in Brazil (1500)<br>• Spanish conquest of Mexico and Peru (1519–1535) | • Native American burning practices alter North American landscapes<br>• Martellus map underestimates distance from Europe to Asia (1489)<br>• Columbian Exchange begins to transform global ecology | • Amerigo Vespucci gives America its name<br>• Spain and Portugal begin to tap American resources | 1450 |
| • Philip II defends the Roman Catholic Church against Protestantism<br>• Elizabeth I adopts Protestant Book of Common Prayer (1559) | • Castilians and Africans arrive in Spanish America in large numbers<br>• English colonies in Newfoundland, Maine, and Roanoke fail | • Plantation complex brings sugarcane agriculture to the Americas<br>• Steep Native American population decline in Hispaniola, Mesoamerica, and the Andes | • Protestant nations challenge Catholic control of the Americas<br>• American gold and silver flow to Europe and Asia | 1550 |
| • Persecuted English Puritans and Catholics migrate to America<br>• Dissenters settle in Rhode Island<br>• Metacom's War in New England (1675–1676)<br>• Bacon's Rebellion calls for removal of Indians and end of elite rule<br>• Salem witchcraft crisis (1692) | • First set of Anglo-Indian wars<br>• African servitude begins in Virginia (1619)<br>• Caribbean islands move from servitude to slavery<br>• White indentured servitude shapes Chesapeake society<br>• Africans defined as property rather than people in the Chesapeake | • Chesapeake colonists suffer from unbalanced sex ratios and subtropical illnesses<br>• New England colonists benefit from balanced sex ratios and healthy climate<br>• Native American burning practices decline in the eastern woodlands | • Opportunities for trade and settlement in America attract European investment<br>• American colonies become a prime destination for bound labor<br>• England's American colonies become a destination for free migrants | 1600 |
| | • Three types of colonies formed in America: tribute, plantation, and neo-European | • French merchants found New Orleans | | 1700 |

# 1

## Colliding Worlds

### 1491–1600

**IDENTIFY THE BIG IDEA**

How did the political, economic, and religious systems of Native Americans, Europeans, and Africans compare, and how did things change as a result of contacts among them?

**IN APRIL 1493, A GENOESE SAILOR OF HUMBLE ORIGINS APPEARED AT** the court of Queen Isabella of Castile and King Ferdinand of Aragon along with six Caribbean natives, numerous colorful parrots, and "samples of finest gold, and many other things never before seen or heard tell of in Spain." The sailor was Christopher Columbus, just returned from his first voyage into the Atlantic. He and his party entered Barcelona's fortress in a solemn procession. The monarchs stood to greet Columbus; he knelt to kiss their hands. They talked for an hour and then adjourned to the royal chapel for a ceremony of thanksgiving. Columbus, now bearing the official title *Admiral of the Ocean Sea*, remained at court for more than a month. The highlight of his stay was the baptism of the six natives, whom Columbus called Indians because he mistakenly believed he had sailed westward all the way to Asia.

•

In the spring of 1540, the Spanish explorer Hernando de Soto met the Lady of Cofachiqui, ruler of a large Native American province in present-day South Carolina. Though an epidemic had carried away many of her people, the lady of the province offered the Spanish expedition as much corn, and as many pearls, as it could carry. As she spoke to de Soto, she unwound "a great rope of pearls as large as hazelnuts" and handed them to the Spaniard; in return he gave her a gold ring set with a ruby. De Soto and his men then visited the temples of Cofachiqui, which were guarded by carved statues and held storehouses of weapons and chest upon chest of pearls. After loading their horses with corn and pearls, they continued on their way.

•

A Portuguese traveler named Duarte Lopez visited the African kingdom of Kongo in 1578. "The men and women are black," he reported, "some approaching olive colour, with black curly hair, and others with red. The men are of middle height, and, excepting the black skin, are like the Portuguese." The royal city of Kongo sat on a high plain that was "entirely cultivated," with a population of more than 100,000. The city included a separate commercial district, a mile around, where Portuguese traders acquired ivory, wax, honey, palm oil, and slaves from the Kongolese.

•

Three glimpses of three lost worlds. Soon these peoples would be transforming one another's societies, often through conflict and exploitation. But at the moment they first met, Europeans, Native Americans, and Africans stood on roughly equal terms. Even a hundred years after Columbus's discovery of the Americas, no one could have foreseen the shape that their interactions would take in the generations to come. To begin, we need to understand the three worlds as distinct places, each home to unique societies and cultures.

# The Native American Experience

When Europeans arrived, perhaps 60 million people occupied the Americas, 7 million of whom lived north of Mexico. In Mesoamerica (present-day Mexico and Guatemala) and the Andes, empires that rivaled the greatest civilizations in world history ruled over millions of people. At the other end of the political spectrum, **hunters and gatherers** were organized into kin-based bands. Between these extremes, **semisedentary societies** planted and tended crops in the spring and summer, fished and hunted, made war, and conducted trade. Though we often see this spectrum as a hierarchy in which the empires are most impressive and important while hunter-gatherers deserve scarcely a mention, this bias toward civilizations that left behind monumental architecture and spawned powerful ruling classes is misplaced. To be fully understood, the Americas must be treated in all their complexity, with an appreciation for their diverse societies and cultures.

## The First Americans

Archaeologists believe that migrants from Asia crossed a 100-mile-wide land bridge connecting Siberia and Alaska during the last Ice Age sometime between 13,000 and 3000 B.C. and thus became the first Americans. The first wave of this migratory stream from Asia lasted from about fifteen thousand to eleven thousand years ago. Then the glaciers melted, and the rising ocean submerged the land bridge beneath the Bering Strait (Map 1.1). Around eight thousand years ago, a second movement

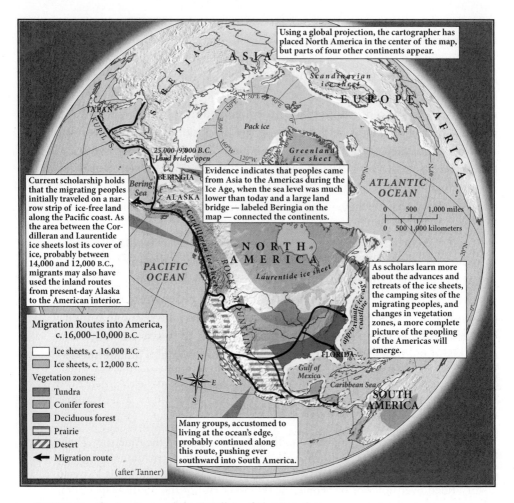

Using a global projection, the cartographer has placed North America in the center of the map, but parts of four other continents appear.

Evidence indicates that peoples came from Asia to the Americas during the Ice Age, when the sea level was much lower than today and a large land bridge — labeled Beringia on the map — connected the continents.

Current scholarship holds that the migrating peoples initially traveled on a narrow strip of ice-free land along the Pacific coast. As the area between the Cordilleran and Laurentide ice sheets lost its cover of ice, probably between 14,000 and 12,000 B.C., migrants may also have used the inland routes from present-day Alaska to the American interior.

As scholars learn more about the advances and retreats of the ice sheets, the camping sites of the migrating peoples, and changes in vegetation zones, a more complete picture of the peopling of the Americas will emerge.

Many groups, accustomed to living at the ocean's edge, probably continued along this route, pushing ever southward into South America.

**Migration Routes into America, c. 16,000–10,000 B.C.**

- ☐ Ice sheets, c. 16,000 B.C.
- ☐ Ice sheets, c. 12,000 B.C.

Vegetation zones:
- Tundra
- Conifer forest
- Deciduous forest
- Prairie
- Desert
- ◀— Migration route

(after Tanner)

**MAP 1.1    The Ice Age and the Settling of the Americas**

Some sixteen thousand years ago, a sheet of ice covered much of Europe and North America. As the ice lowered the level of the world's oceans, a broad bridge of land was created between Siberia and Alaska. Using that land bridge, hunting peoples from Asia migrated to North America as they pursued woolly mammoths and other large game animals and sought ice-free habitats. By 10,000 B.C., the descendants of these migrant peoples had moved south to present-day Florida and central Mexico. In time, they would settle as far south as the tip of South America and as far east as the Atlantic coast of North America.

of peoples, traveling by water across the same narrow strait, brought the ancestors of the Navajos and the Apaches to North America. The forebears of the Aleut and Inuit peoples, the "Eskimos," came in a third wave around five thousand years ago. Then, for three hundred generations, the peoples of the Western Hemisphere were largely cut off from the rest of the world.

Migrants moved across the continents as they hunted and gathered available resources. Most flowed southward, and the densest populations developed in central Mexico—home to some 20 million people at the time of first contact with Europeans—and the Andes Mountains, with a population of perhaps 12 million. In North America, a secondary trickle pushed to the east, across the Rockies and into the Mississippi Valley and the eastern woodlands.

Around 6000 B.C., Native peoples in present-day Mexico and Peru began raising domesticated crops. Mesoamericans cultivated maize (corn) into a nutritious plant with a higher yield per acre than wheat, barley, or rye, the staple cereals of Europe. In Peru they also bred the potato, a root crop of unsurpassed nutritional value. The resulting agricultural surpluses encouraged population growth and laid the foundation for wealthy, urban societies in Mexico and Peru, and later in the Mississippi Valley and the southeastern woodlands of North America (Map 1.2).

## American Empires

In Mesoamerica and the Andes, the two great empires of the Americas—the Aztecs and Incas—dominated the landscape. Dense populations, productive agriculture, and an aggressive bureaucratic state were the keys to their power. Each had an impressive capital city. Tenochtitlán, established in 1325 at the center of the Aztec Empire, had at its height around 1500 a population of about 250,000, at a time when the European cities of London and Seville each had perhaps 50,000. The Aztec state controlled the fertile valleys in the highlands of Mexico, and Aztec merchants forged trading routes that crisscrossed the empire. Trade, along with tribute demanded from subject peoples (comparable to taxes in Europe), brought gold, textiles, turquoise, obsidian, tropical bird feathers, and cacao to Tenochtitlán. The Europeans who first encountered this city in 1519 marveled at its wealth and beauty. "Some of the soldiers among us who had been in many parts of the world," wrote Spanish conquistador Bernal Díaz del Castillo, "in Constantinople, and all over Italy, and in Rome, said that [they had never seen] so large a market place and so full of people, and so well regulated and arranged."

Ruled by priests and warrior-nobles, the Aztecs subjugated most of central Mexico. Captured enemies were brought to the capital, where Aztec priests brutally sacrificed thousands of them. The Aztecs believed that these ritual murders sustained the cosmos, ensuring fertile fields and the daily return of the sun.

Cuzco, the Inca capital located more than 11,000 feet above sea level, had perhaps 60,000 residents. A dense network of roads, storehouses, and administrative centers stitched together this improbable high-altitude empire, which ran down the 2,000-mile-long spine of the Andes Mountains. A king claiming divine status ruled the empire through a bureaucracy of nobles. As with the Aztecs, the empire consisted of subordinate kingdoms that had been conquered by the Incas, and tribute flowed from local centers of power to the imperial core.

## Chiefdoms and Confederacies

Nothing on the scale of the Aztec and Inca empires ever developed north of Mexico, but maize agriculture spread from Mesoamerica across much of North America beginning around A.D. 800, laying a foundation for new ways of life there as well.

**The Mississippi Valley**   The spread of maize to the Mississippi River Valley and the Southeast around A.D. 800 led to the development of a large-scale northern Native

**MAP 1.2   Native American Peoples, 1492**
Having learned to live in many environments, Native Americans populated the entire Western Hemisphere. They created cultures that ranged from centralized empires (the Incas and Aztecs), to societies that combined farming with hunting, fishing, and gathering (the Iroquois and Algonquians), to nomadic tribes of hunter-gatherers (the Micmacs and Shoshones). The great diversity of Native American peoples—in language, tribal identity, and ways of life—and the long-standing rivalries among neighboring peoples usually prevented them from uniting to resist the European invaders.

American culture. The older Adena and Hopewell cultures had already introduced moundbuilding and distinctive pottery styles to the region. Now residents of the Mississippi River Valley experienced the greater urban density and more complex social organization that agriculture encouraged.

The city of Cahokia, in the fertile bottomlands along the Mississippi River, emerged around A.D. 1000 as the foremost center of the new **Mississippian culture**.

At its peak, Cahokia had about 10,000 residents; including satellite communities, the region's population was 20,000 to 30,000. In an area of 6 square miles, archaeologists have found 120 mounds of varying size, shape, and function. Some contain extensive burials; others, known as platform mounds, were used as bases for ceremonial buildings or rulers' homes. Cahokia had a powerful ruling class and a priesthood that worshipped the sun. After peaking in size around 1350, it declined rapidly. Scholars speculate that its decline was caused by a period of ruinous warfare, made worse by environmental changes that made the site less habitable. It had been abandoned by the time Europeans arrived in the area.

Mississippian culture endured, however, and was still in evidence throughout much of the Southeast at the time of first contact with Europeans. The Lady of Cofachiqui encountered by Hernando de Soto in 1540 ruled over a Mississippian community, and others dotted the landscape between the Carolinas and the lower Mississippi River. In Florida, sixteenth-century Spanish explorers encountered the Apalachee Indians, who occupied a network of towns built around mounds and fields of maize.

**Eastern Woodlands**   In the **eastern woodlands**, the Mississippian-influenced peoples of the Southeast interacted with other groups, many of whom adopted maize agriculture but did not otherwise display Mississippian characteristics. **Algonquian** and **Iroquoian** speakers shared related languages and lifeways but were divided into dozens of distinct societies. Most occupied villages built around fields of maize, beans, and squash during the summer months; at other times of the year, they dispersed in smaller groups to hunt, fish, and gather. Throughout the eastern woodlands, as in most of North America, women tended crops, gathered plants, and oversaw affairs within the community, while men were responsible for activities beyond it, especially hunting, fishing, and warfare.

In this densely forested region, Indians regularly set fires—in New England, twice a year, in spring and fall—to clear away underbrush, open fields, and make it easier to hunt big game. The catastrophic population decline accompanying European colonization quickly put an end to seasonal burning, but in the years before Europeans arrived in North America, bison roamed east as far as modern-day New York and Georgia. Early European colonists remarked upon landscapes that "resemble[d] a stately Parke," where men could ride among widely spaced trees on horseback and even a "large army" could pass unimpeded.

Algonquian and Iroquoian peoples had no single style of political organization. Many were chiefdoms, with one individual claiming authority. Some were paramount chiefdoms, in which numerous communities with their own local chiefs banded together under a single, more powerful ruler. For example, the Powhatan Chiefdom, which dominated the Chesapeake Bay region, was made up of more than thirty subordinate chiefdoms, and some 20,000 people, when Englishmen established the colony of Virginia. Powhatan himself, according to the English colonist John Smith, was attended by "a guard of 40 or 50 of the tallest men his Country affords."

Elsewhere, especially in the Mid-Atlantic region, the power of chiefs was strictly local. Along the Delaware and Hudson rivers, Lenni Lenape (or Delaware) and Munsee Indians lived in small, independent communities without overarching political

**The Kincaid Site** Located on the north bank of the Ohio River 140 miles from Cahokia, the Kincaid site was a Mississippian town from c. A.D. 1050 to 1450. It contains at least nineteen mounds topped by large buildings thought to have been temples or council houses. Now a state historic site in Illinois, it has been studied by anthropologists and archaeologists since the 1930s. Artist Herb Roe depicts the town as it may have looked at its peak. Herb Roe, Chromesun Productions.

organizations. Early European maps of this region show a landscape dotted with a bewildering profusion of Indian names. Colonization would soon drive many of these groups into oblivion and force survivors to coalesce into larger groups.

Some Native American groups were not chiefdoms at all but instead granted political authority to councils of sachems, or leaders. This was the case with the **Iroquois Confederacy**. Sometime shortly before the arrival of Europeans, probably around 1500, five nations occupying the region between the Hudson River and Lake Erie — the Mohawks, Oneidas, Onondagas, Cayugas, and Senecas — banded together to form the Iroquois.

These nations had been fighting among themselves for years. Then, according to Iroquois legend, a Mohawk man named Hiawatha lost his family in one of these wars. Stricken by grief, he met a spirit who taught him a series of condolence rituals. He returned to his people preaching a new gospel of peace and power, and the condolence rituals he taught became the foundation for the Iroquois Confederacy. Once bound by these rituals, the Five Nations began acting together as a political confederacy. They made peace among themselves and became one of the most powerful Native American groups in the Northeast.

The Iroquois did not recognize chiefs; instead, councils of sachems made decisions. These were matriarchal societies, with power inherited through female lines of authority. Women were influential in local councils, though men served as sachems, made war, and conducted diplomacy.

Along the southern coast of the region that would soon be called New England, a dense network of powerful chiefdoms—including the Narragansetts, Wampanoags, Mohegans, Pequots, and others—competed for resources and dominance. When the Dutch and English arrived, they were able to exploit these rivalries and pit Indian groups against one another. Farther north, in northern New England and much of present-day Canada, the short growing season and thin, rocky soil were inhospitable to maize agriculture. Here the Native peoples were hunters and gatherers and therefore had smaller and more mobile communities.

**The Great Lakes**   To the west, Algonquian-speaking peoples dominated the **Great Lakes**. The tribal groups recognized by Europeans in this region included the Ottawas, Ojibwas, and Potawatomis. But collectively they thought of themselves as a single people: the Anishinaabe. Clan identities—beaver, otter, sturgeon, deer, and others—crosscut tribal affiliations and were in some ways more fundamental. The result was a social landscape that could be bewildering to outsiders. Here lived, one French official remarked, "an infinity of undiscovered nations."

The extensive network of lakes and rivers, and the use of birchbark canoes, made Great Lakes peoples especially mobile. "They seem to have as many abodes as the year has seasons," wrote one observer. They traveled long distances to hunt and fish, to trade, or to join in important ceremonies or military alliances. Groups negotiated access to resources and travel routes. Instead of an area with clearly delineated tribal territories, it is best to imagine the Great Lakes as a porous region, where "political power and social identity took on multiple forms," as one scholar has written.

**The Great Plains and Rockies**   Farther west lies the vast, arid steppe region known as the **Great Plains**, which was dominated by small, dispersed groups of hunter-gatherers. The world of these Plains Indians was transformed by a European import—the horse—long before Europeans themselves arrived on the plains. Horses were introduced in the Spanish colony of New Mexico in the late sixteenth century and gradually dispersed across the plains. Bison hunters who had previously relied on stealth became much more successful on horseback.

Indians on horseback were also more formidable opponents in war than their counterparts on foot, and some Plains peoples leveraged their control of horses to gain power over their neighbors. The Comanches were a small Shoshonean band on the northern plains that migrated south in pursuit of horses. They became expert raiders, capturing people and horses alike and trading them for weapons, food, clothing, and other necessities. Eventually they controlled a vast territory. Their skill in making war on horseback transformed the Comanches from a small group to one of the region's most formidable peoples.

Similarly, horses allowed the Sioux, a confederation of seven distinct peoples who originated in present-day Minnesota, to move west and dominate a vast territory ranging from the Mississippi River to the Black Hills. The Crow Indians moved from the Missouri River to the eastern slope of the **Rocky Mountains**, where they became nomadic bison hunters. Beginning in the mid-eighteenth century, they became horse breeders and traders as well.

In some places, farming communities were embedded within the much wider territories of hunter-gatherers. The Hidatsa and Mandan Indians, for example, maintained settled agricultural villages along the Missouri River, while the more mobile Sioux dominated the region around them. Similarly, the Caddos, who lived on the edge of the southern plains, inhabited farming communities that were like islands in a sea of more mobile peoples.

Three broad swaths of Numic-speaking peoples occupied the **Great Basin** that separated the Rockies from the Sierra Mountains: Bannocks and Northern Paiutes in the north, Shoshones in the central basin, and Utes and Southern Paiutes in the south. Resources were varied and spread thin on the land. Kin-based bands traveled great distances to hunt bison along the Yellowstone River (where they shared territory with the Crows) and bighorn sheep in high altitudes, to fish for salmon, and to gather pine nuts when they were in season. Throughout the Great Basin, some groups adopted horses and became relatively powerful, while others remained foot-borne and impoverished in comparison with their more mobile neighbors.

**The Arid Southwest**   In the part of North America that appears to be most hostile to agriculture—the canyon-laced country of the arid Southwest—surprisingly large farming settlements developed. Anasazi peoples were growing maize by the first century A.D., earlier than anywhere else north of Mexico, and Pueblo cultures emerged around A.D. 600. By A.D. 1000, the Hohokams, Mogollons, and Anasazis (all Pueblo peoples) had developed irrigation systems to manage scarce water, enabling them to build sizable villages and towns of adobe and rock that were often molded to sheer canyon walls. Chaco Canyon, in modern New Mexico, supported a dozen large Anasazi towns, while beyond the canyon a network of roads tied these settlements together with hundreds of small Anasazi villages.

Extended droughts and soil exhaustion caused the abandonment of Chaco Canyon and other large settlements in the Southwest after 1150, but smaller communities still dotted the landscape when the first Europeans arrived. It was the Spanish who called these groups Pueblos: *pueblo* means "town" in Spanish, and the name refers to their distinctive building style. When Europeans arrived, Pueblo peoples, including the Acomas, Zuñis, Tewas, and Hopis, were found throughout much of modern New Mexico, Arizona, and western Texas.

**The Pacific Coast**   Hunter-gatherers inhabited the Pacific coast. Before the Spanish arrived, California was home to more than 300,000 people, subdivided into dozens of small, localized groups and speaking at least a hundred distinct languages. This diversity of languages and cultures discouraged intermarriage and kept these societies independent. Despite their differences, many groups did share common characteristics,

**Chilkat Tlingit Bowl** This bowl in the form of a brown bear, which dates to the mid-nineteenth century, is made of alder wood and inlaid with snail shells. The brown bear is a Tlingit clan totem. Animal-form bowls like this one, which express an affinity with nonhuman creatures, are a common feature of Tlingit culture. National Museum of the American Indian, Smithsonian Institution 9/7990.

including clearly defined social hierarchies separating elites from commoners. They gathered acorns and other nuts and seeds, caught fish and shellfish, and hunted game.

The Pacific Northwest also supported a dense population that was divided into many distinct groups who controlled small territories — both on land and on the sea — and spoke different languages. Their stratified societies were ruled by wealthy families. To maintain control of their territories, the more powerful nations, including the Chinooks, Coast Salishes, Haidas, and Tlingits, nurtured strong warrior traditions. They developed sophisticated fishing technologies and crafted oceangoing dugout canoes, made from enormous cedar trees, that ranged up to 60 feet in length. Their distinctive material culture included large longhouses that were home to dozens of people and totem poles representing clan lineages or local legends.

## Patterns of Trade

Expansive trade networks tied together regions and carried valuable goods hundreds and even thousands of miles. Trade goods included food and raw materials, tools, ritual artifacts, and decorative goods. Trade enriched diets, enhanced economies, and allowed the powerful to set themselves apart with luxury items.

In areas where Indians specialized in a particular economic activity, regional trade networks allowed them to share resources. Thus nomadic hunters of the southern plains, including the Navajos and Apaches, conducted annual trade fairs with Pueblo farmers, exchanging hides and meat for maize, pottery, and cotton blankets. Similar patterns of exchange occurred throughout the Great Plains, wherever hunters and farmers coexisted. In some parts of North America, a regional trade in war captives who were offered as slaves helped to sustain friendly relations among neighboring groups. One such network developed in the Upper Mississippi River basin, where Plains Indian captives were traded, or given as diplomatic gifts, to Ottawas and other Great Lakes and eastern woodlands peoples.

Rare and valuable objects traveled longer distances. Great Lakes copper, Rocky Mountain mica, jasper from Pennsylvania, obsidian from New Mexico and Wyoming, and pipestone from the Midwest have all been found in archaeological sites hundreds of miles from their points of origin. Seashells — often shaped and polished into beads and other artifacts—were highly prized and widely distributed. Grizzly bear claws and eagle feathers were valuable, high-status objects. After European contact, Indian hunters often traveled long distances to trade for cloth, iron tools, and weapons. Historians debate the extent to which such long-distance connections helped to create deeper cultural ties.

Powerful leaders controlled much of a community's wealth and redistributed it to prove their generosity and strengthen their authority. In small, kin-based bands, the strongest hunters possessed the most food, and sharing it was essential. In chiefdoms, rulers filled the same role, often collecting the wealth of a community and then redistributing it to their followers. Powhatan, the powerful Chesapeake Bay chief, reportedly collected nine-tenths of the produce of the communities he oversaw—"skins, beads, copper, pearls, deer, turkeys, wild beasts, and corn"—and then gave much of it back to his subordinates. His generosity was considered a mark of good leadership. In the Pacific Northwest, the Chinook word *potlatch* refers to periodic festivals in which wealthy residents gave away belongings to friends, family, and followers.

## Sacred Power

Most Native North Americans were animists who believed that the natural world was suffused with spiritual power. They interpreted dreams and visions to understand the world, and their rituals appeased guardian spirits to ensure successful hunts and other forms of good fortune. Although their views were subject to countless local variations, certain patterns were widespread.

Women and men interacted differently with these spiritual forces. In farming communities, women grew crops and maintained hearth, home, and village. Native American ideas about female power linked their bodies' generative functions with the earth's fertility, and rituals like the Green Corn Ceremony—a summer ritual of purification and renewal—helped to sustain the life-giving properties of the world around them.

For men, spiritual power was invoked in hunting and war. To ensure success in hunting, men took care not to offend the spirits of the animals they killed. They performed rituals before, during, and after a hunt to acknowledge the power of those guardian spirits, and they believed that, when an animal had been killed properly, its spirit would rise from the earth unharmed. Success in hunting and prowess in war were both interpreted as signs of sacred protection and power.

Ideas about war varied widely. War could be fought for geopolitical reasons—to gain ground against an enemy—but for many groups, warfare was a crucial rite of passage for young men, and raids were conducted to allow warriors to prove themselves in battle. Motives for war could be highly personal; war was often more like a blood feud between families than a contest between nations. If a community lost warriors in battle, it might retaliate by capturing or killing a like number of warriors in response—a so-called mourning war. Some captives were adopted into new communities, while others were enslaved or tortured.

| **IN YOUR OWN WORDS** | What factors might best explain the variations among Native American societies and cultures? |

# Western Europe: The Edge of the Old World

In 1491, Western Europe lay at the far edge of the Eurasian and African continents. It had neither the powerful centralized empires nor the hunter-gatherer bands and semisedentary societies of the Americas. Western Europe was, instead, a patchwork of roughly equivalent kingdoms, duchies, and republics vying with one another and struggling to reach out effectively to the rest of the world. No one would have predicted that Europeans would soon become overlords of the Western Hemisphere. A thousand years after the fall of the Roman Empire, Europe's populations still relied on subsistence agriculture and were never far from the specter of famine. Moreover, around 1350, a deadly plague was introduced from Central Asia—the Black Death—that killed one-third of Europe's people. The lives of ordinary people were afflicted by poverty, disease, and uncertainty, and the future looked as difficult and dark as the past.

## Hierarchy and Authority

In traditional hierarchical societies—American or European—authority came from above. In Europe, kings and princes owned vast tracts of land, forcibly conscripted men for military service, and lived off the peasantry's labor. Yet monarchs were far from supreme: local nobles also owned large estates and controlled hundreds of peasant families. Collectively, these nobles challenged royal authority with both their military power and their legislative institutions, such as the French *parlements* and the English House of Lords.

Just as kings and nobles ruled society, men governed families. These were patriarchies, in which property and social identity descended in male family lines. Rich or poor, the man was the head of the house, his power justified by the teachings of the Christian Church. As one English clergyman put it, "The woman is a weak creature not embued with like strength and constancy of mind"; law and custom "subjected her to the power of man." Once married, an Englishwoman assumed her husband's surname, submitted to his orders, and surrendered the right to her property.

Men also controlled the lives of their children, who usually worked for their father into their middle or late twenties. Then landowning peasants would give land to their sons and dowries (property or money given by a bride's family to her husband) to their daughters and choose marriage partners of appropriate wealth and status. In many regions, fathers bestowed all their land on their eldest son—a practice known as primogeniture—forcing many younger children to join the ranks of the roaming poor. Few men and even fewer women had much personal freedom.

Powerful institutions—nobility, church, and village—enforced hierarchy and offered ordinary people a measure of security in a violent and unpredictable world. Carried by migrants to America, these security-conscious institutions would shape the character of family and society well into the eighteenth century.

## Peasant Society

Most Europeans were **peasants**, farmworkers who lived in small villages surrounded by fields farmed cooperatively by different families. On manorial lands, farming rights were given in exchange for labor on the lord's estate, an arrangement that turned peasants into serfs. Gradually, obligatory manorial services gave way to paying rent or, as in France, landownership. Once freed from the obligation to labor for their farming rights, European farmers began to produce surpluses and created local market economies.

As with Native Americans, the rhythm of life followed the seasons. In March, villagers began the exhausting work of plowing and then planting wheat, rye, and oats. During the spring, the men sheared wool, which the women washed and spun into yarn. In June, peasants cut hay and stored it as winter fodder for their livestock. During the summer, life was more relaxed, and families repaired their houses and barns. Fall brought the harvest, followed by solemn feasts of thanksgiving and riotous bouts of merrymaking. As winter approached, peasants slaughtered excess livestock and salted or smoked the meat. During the cold months, they threshed grain and wove textiles, visited friends and relatives, and celebrated the winter solstice or the birth of Christ. Just before the cycle began again in the spring, they held carnivals, celebrating with drink and dance the end of the long winter.

For most peasants, survival meant constant labor, and poverty corroded family relationships. Malnourished mothers fed their babies sparingly, calling them "greedy and gluttonous," and many newborn girls were "helped to die" so that their brothers would have enough to eat. Half of all peasant children died before the age of twenty-one, victims of malnourishment and disease. Many peasants drew on strong religious beliefs, "counting blessings" and accepting their harsh existence. Others hoped for a better life. It was the peasants of Spain, Germany, and Britain who would supply the majority of white migrants to the Western Hemisphere.

## Expanding Trade Networks

In the millennium before contact with the Americas, Western Europe was the barbarian fringe of the civilized world. In the Mediterranean basin, Arab scholars carried on the legacy of Byzantine civilization, which had preserved the achievements of the Greeks and Romans in medicine, philosophy, mathematics, astronomy, and geography, while Arab merchants controlled trade in the Mediterranean, Africa, and the Near East. This control gave them access to spices from India and silks, magnetic compasses, water-powered mills, and mechanical clocks from China.

In the twelfth century, merchants from the Italian city-states of Genoa, Florence, Pisa, and especially Venice began to push their way into the Arab-dominated trade routes of the Mediterranean. Trading in Alexandria, Beirut, and other eastern Mediterranean ports, they carried the luxuries of Asia into European markets. At its peak, Venice had a merchant fleet of more than three thousand ships. This enormously profitable commerce created wealthy merchants, bankers, and textile manufacturers who expanded trade, lent vast sums of money, and spurred technological innovation in silk and wool production.

Italian moneyed elites ruled their city-states as **republics**, states that had no prince or king but instead were governed by merchant coalitions. They celebrated civic humanism, an ideology that praised public virtue and service to the state; over time, this tradition profoundly influenced European and American conceptions of government. They sponsored great artists—Michelangelo, Leonardo da Vinci, and others—who produced an unprecedented flowering of genius. Historians have labeled the arts and learning associated with this cultural transformation from 1300 to 1450 the Renaissance.

The economic revolution that began in Italy spread slowly to northern and western Europe. England's principal export was woolen cloth, which was prized in the colder parts of the continent but had less appeal in southern Europe and beyond. Northern Europe had its own trade system, controlled by an alliance of merchant communities called the Hanseatic League. Centered on the Baltic and North seas, it dealt in timber, furs, wheat and rye, honey, wax, and amber.

As trade picked up in Europe, merchants and artisans came to dominate its growing cities and towns. While the Italian city-states ruled themselves without a powerful monarch, in much of Europe the power of merchants stood in tension with that of kings and nobles. In general, the rise of commerce favored the power of kings at the expense of the landed nobility. The kings of Western Europe established royal law courts that gradually eclipsed the manorial courts controlled by nobles; they also built bureaucracies that helped them centralize power while they forged alliances with merchants and urban artisans. Monarchs allowed merchants to trade throughout their realms; granted privileges to guilds, or artisan organizations that regulated trades; and safeguarded commercial transactions, thereby encouraging domestic manufacturing and foreign trade. In return, they extracted taxes from towns and loans from merchants to support their armies and officials.

## Myths, Religions, and Holy Warriors

The oldest European religious beliefs drew on a form of animism similar to that of Native Americans, which held that the natural world — the sun, wind, stones, animals — was animated by spiritual forces. As in North America, such beliefs led ancient European peoples to develop localized cults of knowledge and spiritual practice. Wise men and women created rituals to protect their communities, ensure abundant harvests, heal illnesses, and bring misfortunes to their enemies.

The pagan traditions of Greece and Rome overlaid animism with elaborate myths about gods interacting directly with the affairs of human beings. As the Roman Empire expanded, it built temples to its gods wherever it planted new settlements. Thus peoples throughout Europe, North Africa, and the Near East were exposed to the Roman pantheon. Soon the teachings of Christianity began to flow in these same channels.

**The Rise of Christianity**    **Christianity**, which grew out of Jewish monotheism (the belief in one god), held that Jesus Christ was himself divine. As an institution, Christianity benefitted enormously from the conversion of the Roman emperor Constantine in A.D. 312. Prior to that time, Christians were an underground sect at odds with the Roman Empire. After Constantine's conversion, Christianity became Rome's official religion, temples were abandoned or remade into churches, and noblemen who hoped to retain their influence converted to the new state religion.

For centuries, the Roman Catholic Church was the great unifying institution in Western Europe. The pope in Rome headed a vast hierarchy of cardinals, bishops, and priests. Catholic theologians preserved Latin, the language of classical scholarship, and imbued kingship with divine power. Christian dogma provided a common

***The Beaune Altarpiece*, c. 1445–1450** Fifteenth-century Christians understood their lives to be part of a cosmic drama. Death—and their fate in the afterlife—loomed large in their imaginations, and artists depicted their hopes and fears in vividly rendered scenes. In this massive altarpiece by Dutch painter Rogier van der Weyden, Christ sits in judgment as the world ends and the dead rise from their graves. The archangel Michael weighs the souls of the dead in a balance to determine their final fate: either eternal life with God in heaven or everlasting punishment in hell. Erich Lessing/Art Resource, NY.

understanding of God and human history, and the authority of the Church buttressed state institutions. Every village had a church, and holy shrines served as points of contact with the sacred world. Often those shrines had their origins in older, animist practices, now largely forgotten and replaced with Christian ritual.

Christian doctrine penetrated deeply into the everyday lives of peasants. While animist traditions held that spiritual forces were alive in the natural world, Christian priests taught that the natural world was flawed and fallen. Spiritual power came from outside nature, from a supernatural God who had sent his divine son, Jesus Christ, into the world to save humanity from its sins. The Christian Church devised a religious calendar that transformed animist festivals into holy days. The winter solstice, which had for millennia marked the return of the sun, became the feast of Christmas.

The Church also taught that Satan, a wicked supernatural being, was constantly challenging God by tempting people to sin. People who spread heresies—doctrines that were inconsistent with the teachings of the Church—were seen as the tools of Satan, and suppressing false doctrines became an obligation of Christian rulers.

**The Crusades**   In their work suppressing false doctrines, Christian rulers were also obliged to combat **Islam**, the religion whose followers considered Muhammad to be God's last prophet. Islam's reach expanded until it threatened European Christendom. Following the death of Muhammad in A.D. 632, the newly converted Arab peoples of North Africa used force and fervor to spread the Muslim faith into sub-Saharan Africa, India, and Indonesia, as well as deep into Spain and the Balkan regions of Europe. Between A.D. 1096 and 1291, Christian armies undertook a series of **Crusades** to reverse the Muslim advance in Europe and win back the holy lands where Christ had lived. Under the banner of the pope and led by Europe's Christian monarchs, crusading armies aroused great waves of popular piety as they marched off to combat. New orders of knights, like the Knights Templar and the Teutonic Knights, were created to support them.

The crusaders had some military successes, but their most profound impact was on European society. Religious warfare intensified Europe's Christian identity and prompted the persecution of Jews and their expulsion from many European countries. The Crusades also introduced Western European merchants to the trade routes that stretched from Constantinople to China along the Silk Road and from the Mediterranean Sea through the Persian Gulf to the Indian Ocean. And crusaders encountered sugar for the first time. Returning soldiers brought it back from the Middle East, and as Europeans began to conquer territory in the eastern Mediterranean, they experimented with raising it themselves. These early experiments with sugar would have a profound impact on European enterprise in the Americas—and European involvement with the African slave trade—in the centuries to come. Although Western Europe in 1491 remained relatively isolated from the centers of civilization in Eurasia and Africa, the Crusades and the rise of Italian merchant houses had introduced it to a wider world.

**The Reformation** In 1517, Martin Luther, a German monk and professor at the university in Wittenberg, took up the cause of reform in the Catholic Church. Luther's *Ninety-five Theses* condemned the Church for many corrupt practices. More radically, Luther downplayed the role of the clergy as mediators between God and believers and said that Christians must look to the Bible, not to the Church, as the ultimate authority in matters of faith. So that every literate German could read the Bible, previously available only in Latin, Luther translated it into German.

Meanwhile, in Geneva, Switzerland, French theologian John Calvin established a rigorous Protestant regime. Even more than Luther, Calvin stressed human weakness and God's omnipotence. His *Institutes of the Christian Religion* (1536) depicted God as an absolute ruler. Calvin preached the doctrine of predestination, the idea that God chooses certain people for salvation before they are born and condemns the rest to eternal damnation. In Geneva, he set up a model Christian community ruled by ministers who prohibited frivolity and luxury. "We know," wrote Calvin, "that man is of so perverse and crooked a nature, that everyone would scratch out his neighbor's eyes if there were no bridle to hold them in." Calvin's authoritarian doctrine won converts all over Europe, including the Puritans in Scotland and England.

Luther's criticisms triggered a war between the Holy Roman Empire and the northern principalities in Germany, and soon the controversy between the Roman Catholic Church and radical reformers like Luther and Calvin spread throughout much of Western Europe. The **Protestant Reformation**, as this movement came to be called, triggered a **Counter-Reformation** in the Catholic Church that sought change from within and created new monastic and missionary orders, including the Jesuits (founded in 1540), who saw themselves as soldiers of Christ. The competition between these divergent Christian traditions did much to shape European colonization of the Americas. Roman Catholic powers—Spain, Portugal, and France—sought to win souls in the Americas for the Church, while Protestant nations—England and the Netherlands—viewed the Catholic Church as corrupt and exploitative and hoped instead to create godly communities attuned to the true gospel of Christianity.

| IN YOUR OWN WORDS | How had recent developments changed Western Europe by 1491? |
|---|---|

# West and Central Africa: Origins of the Atlantic Slave Trade

*Homo sapiens* originated in Africa. Numerous civilizations had already risen and fallen there, and contacts with the Near East and the Mediterranean were millennia old, when Western Europeans began sailing down its Atlantic coast. Home to perhaps 100 million in 1400, Africa was divided by the vast expanse of the Sahara Desert. North Africa bordered on the Mediterranean, and its peoples fell under the domination of Christian Byzantium until the seventh century, when Muslim conquests brought the region under Islamic influence. In its coastal seaports, the merchandise of Asia, the Near East, Africa, and Europe converged. South of the Sahara, by contrast, the societies of West and Central Africa bordering on the Atlantic were relatively isolated. After 1400, that would quickly change.

## Empires, Kingdoms, and Ministates

West Africa—the part of the continent that bulges into the Atlantic—can be visualized as a broad horizontal swath divided into three climatic zones. The Sahel is the mostly flat, semiarid zone immediately south of the Sahara. Below it lies the savanna, a grassland region dotted with trees and shrubs. South of the savanna, in a band 200 to 300 miles wide along the West African coast, lies a tropical rain forest. A series of four major watersheds—the Senegal, Gambia, Volta, and Niger—dominate West Africa (Map 1.3).

Sudanic civilization took root at the eastern end of West Africa beginning around 9000 B.C. and traveled westward. Sudanic peoples domesticated cattle (8500–7500 B.C.) and cultivated sorghum and millet (7500–7000 B.C.). Over several thousand years, these peoples developed a distinctive style of pottery, began to grow and weave cotton (6500–3500 B.C.), and invented techniques for working copper and iron (2500–1000 B.C.). Sudanic civilization had its own tradition of monotheism distinct from that of Christians, Muslims, and Jews. Most Sudanic peoples in West Africa lived in stratified states ruled by kings and princes who were regarded as divine.

From these cultural origins, three great empires arose in succession in the northern savanna. The first, the Ghana Empire, appeared sometime around A.D. 800. Ghana capitalized on the recently domesticated camel to pioneer trade routes across the Sahara to North Africa, where Ghana traders carried the wealth of West Africa. The Ghana Empire gave way to the Mali Empire in the thirteenth century, which was eclipsed in turn by the Songhai Empire in the fifteenth century. All three empires were composed of smaller vassal kingdoms, not unlike the Aztec and Inca empires, and relied on military might to control their valuable trade routes.

Gold, abundant in West Africa, was the cornerstone of power and an indispensable medium of international trade. By 1450, West African traders had carried so much

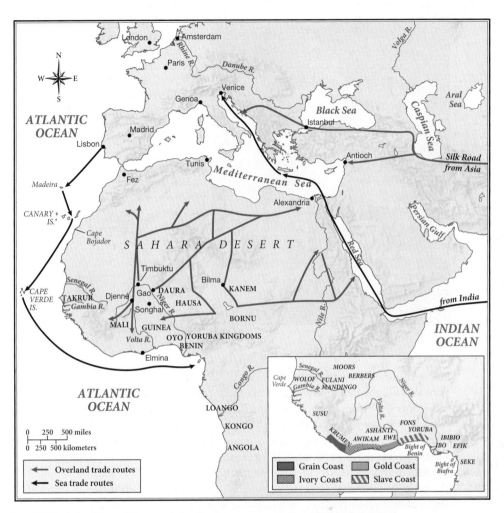

**MAP 1.3**   **West Africa and the Mediterranean in the Fifteenth Century**
Trade routes across the Sahara had long connected West Africa with the Mediterranean region. Gold, ivory, and slaves moved north and east; fine textiles, spices, and the Muslim faith traveled south. Beginning in the 1430s, the Portuguese opened up maritime trade with the coastal regions of West Africa, which were home to many peoples and dozens of large and small states. Over the next century, the movement of gold and slaves into the Atlantic would surpass that across the Sahara.

of it across the Sahara that it constituted one-half to two-thirds of all the gold in circulation in Europe, North Africa, and Asia. Mansa Musa, the tenth emperor of Mali, was a devout Muslim famed for his construction projects and his support of mosques and schools. In 1326, he went on a pilgrimage to Mecca with a vast retinue that crossed the Sahara and passed through Egypt. They spent so much gold along the way that the region's money supply was devalued for more than a decade after their visit.

To the south of these empires, the lower savanna and tropical rain forest of West Africa were home to a complex mosaic of kingdoms that traded among themselves

**Terracotta Figure from Mali**
Dating to the thirteenth or fourteenth century, this terracotta figure came from an archaeological site near Djenné. The rider wears a large, ornate necklace, while the horse has a decorative covering on its head. The Mali Empire relied on a large cavalry to expand and defend its borders, and the horse was an important symbol of Mali's wealth and power. Werner Forman/ Art Resource, NY.

and with the empires to the north. In such a densely populated, resource-rich region, they also fought frequently in a competition for local power. A few of these coastal kingdoms were quite large in size, but most were small enough that they have been termed ministates by historians. Comparable to the city-states of Italy, they were often about the size of a modern-day county in the United States. The tropical ecosystem prevented them from raising livestock, since the tsetse fly (which carries a parasite deadly to livestock) was endemic to the region, as was malaria. In place of the grain crops of the savanna, these peoples pioneered the cultivation of yams; they also gathered resources from the rivers and seacoast.

## Trans-Saharan and Coastal Trade

For centuries, the primary avenue of trade for West Africans passed through the Ghana, Mali, and Songhai empires, whose power was based on the monopoly they enjoyed over the trans-Saharan trade. Their caravans carried West African goods—including gold, copper, salt, and slaves—from the south to the north across the Sahara, then returned with textiles and other products. For the smaller states clustered along the West African coast, merchandise originating in the world beyond the Sahara was scarce and expensive, while markets for their own products were limited.

Beginning in the mid-fifteenth century, a new coastal trade with Europeans offered many West African peoples a welcome alternative. As European sailors made their way along the coast of West and then Central Africa, they encountered a bewilderingly complicated political landscape. Around the mouths of the Senegal and Gambia rivers, numerous Mande-speaking states controlled access to the trade routes into the interior. Proceeding farther along the coast, they encountered the Akan states, a region of several dozen independent but culturally linked peoples. The Akan states had goldfields of their own, and this region soon became known to Europeans as the Gold Coast. East of the Akan states lay the Bight of Benin, which became an early center of the slave trade and thus came to be called the Slave Coast. Bending south, fifteenth-century sailors encountered the Kingdom of Kongo in Central Africa, the largest state on the Atlantic seaboard, with a coastline that ran for some 250 miles. It was here in 1578 that Duarte Lopez visited the capital city of more than 100,000 residents. Wherever they went ashore along this route, European traders had to negotiate contacts on local terms.

## The Spirit World

Some West Africans who lived immediately south of the Sahara — the Fulanis in Senegal, the Mande-speakers in Mali, and the Hausas in northern Nigeria—learned about Islam from Arab merchants and Muslim leaders called imams. Converts to Islam knew the Koran and worshipped only a single God. Some of their cities, like Timbuktu, the legendary commercial center on the Niger River, became centers of Islamic learning and instruction. But most West Africans acknowledged multiple gods, as well as spirits that lived in the earth, animals, and plants.

Like animists in the Americas and Europe, African communities had wise men and women adept at manipulating these forces for good or ill. The Sudanic tradition of divine kingship persisted, and many people believed that their kings could contact the spirit world. West Africans treated their ancestors with great respect, believing that the dead resided in a nearby spiritual realm and interceded in their lives. Most West African peoples had secret societies, such as the Poro for men and the Sande for women, that united people from different lineages and clans. These societies conducted rituals that celebrated male virility and female fertility. "Without children you are naked," said a Yoruba proverb. Happy was the man with a big household, many wives, many children, and many relatives — and, in a not very different vein, many slaves.

| **IN YOUR OWN WORDS** | How was sub-Saharan Africa affected by the arrival of European traders? |
|---|---|

# Exploration and Conquest

Beginning around 1400, the Portuguese monarchy propelled Europe into overseas expansion. Portugal soon took a leading role in the African slave trade, while the newly unified kingdom of Spain undertook Europe's first conquests in the Americas. These two ventures, though not initially linked, eventually became cornerstones in the creation of the "Atlantic World," which connected Europe, Africa, and the Americas.

## Portuguese Expansion

As a young soldier fighting in the Crusades, Prince Henry of Portugal (1394–1460) learned about the trans-Saharan trade in gold and slaves. Seeking a maritime route to the source of this trade in West Africa, Henry founded a center for oceanic navigation. Henry's mariners, challenged to find a way through the treacherous waters off the northwest African coast, designed a better-handling vessel, the caravel, which was rigged with a lateen (triangular) sail that enabled the ship to tack into the wind. This innovation allowed them to sail far into the Atlantic, where they discovered and colonized the Madeira and Azore islands. From there, they sailed in 1435 to sub-Saharan Sierra Leone, where they exchanged salt, wine, and fish for African ivory and gold.

Henry's efforts were soon joined to those of Italian merchants, who were being forced out of eastern Mediterranean trade routes by the rising power of the Ottoman Empire. Cut off from Asia, Genoese traders sought an Atlantic route to the lucrative markets of the Indian Ocean. They began to work with Portuguese and Castilian mariners and monarchs to finance trading voyages, and the African coast and its off-shore islands opened to their efforts. European voyagers discovered the Canaries, the Cape Verde Islands, and São Tomé; all of them became laboratories for the expansion of Mediterranean agriculture.

On these Atlantic islands, planters transformed local ecosystems to experiment with a variety of familiar cash crops: wheat, wine grapes, and woad, a blue dye plant; livestock and honeybees; and, where the climate permitted, sugar. By 1500, Madeira was producing 2,500 metric tons a year, and Madeira sugar was available—in small, expensive quantities—in London, Paris, Rome, and Constantinople. Most of the islands were unpopulated. The Canaries were the exception; it took Castilian adventurers decades to conquer the Guanches who lived there. Once defeated, they were enslaved to labor in the Canaries or on Madeira, where they carved irrigation canals into the island's steep rock cliffs.

Europeans made no such inroads on the continent of Africa itself. The coastal kingdoms were well defended, and yellow fever, malaria, and dysentery quickly struck down Europeans who spent any time in the interior of West Africa. Instead they maintained small, fortified trading posts on offshore islands or along the coast, usually as guests of the local king.

Portuguese sailors continued to look for an Atlantic route to Asia. In 1488, Bartolomeu Dias rounded the Cape of Good Hope, the southern tip of Africa. Vasco da Gama reached East Africa in 1497 and India in the following year; his ships were mistaken for those of Chinese traders, the last pale-skinned men to arrive by sea. Although da Gama's inferior goods—tin basins, coarse cloth, honey, and coral beads—were snubbed by the Arab and Indian merchants along India's Malabar Coast, he managed to acquire a highly profitable cargo of cinnamon and pepper. Da Gama returned to India in 1502 with twenty-one fighting vessels, which outmaneuvered and outgunned the Arab fleets. Soon the Portuguese government set up fortified trading posts for its merchants at key points around the Indian Ocean, in Indonesia, and along the coast of China (Map 1.4). In a transition that sparked

**MAP 1.4   The Eurasian Trade System and European Maritime Ventures, c. 1500 >**
For centuries, the Mediterranean Sea was the meeting point for the commerce of Europe, North Africa, and Asia—via the Silk Road from China and the Spice Route from India. Beginning in the 1490s, Portuguese, Spanish, and Dutch rulers and merchants subsidized Christian maritime explorers who discovered new trade routes around Africa and new sources of wealth in the Americas. These initiatives undermined the commercial primacy of the Arab Muslim–dominated Mediterranean.

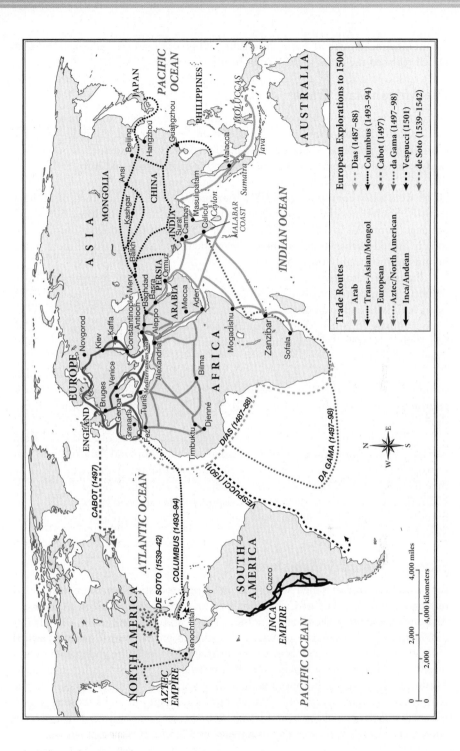

European Explorations to 1500

- Dias (1487–88)
- Columbus (1493–94)
- Cabot (1497)
- da Gama (1497–98)
- Vespucci (1501)
- de Soto (1539–1542)

Trade Routes

- Arab
- Trans-Asian/Mongol
- European
- Aztec/North American
- Inca/Andean

the momentous growth of European wealth and power, the Portuguese and then the Dutch replaced the Arabs as the leaders in Asian commerce.

## The African Slave Trade

Portuguese traders also ousted Arab merchants as the leading suppliers of African slaves. Coerced labor—through slavery, serfdom, or indentured servitude—was the norm in most premodern societies, and in Africa slavery was widespread. Some Africans were held in bondage as security for debts; others were sold into servitude by their kin in exchange for food in times of famine; many others were war captives. Slaves were a key commodity, sold as agricultural laborers, concubines, or military recruits. Sometimes their descendants were freed, but others endured hereditary bondage. Sonni Ali (r. 1464–1492), the ruler of the powerful Songhai Empire, personally owned twelve "tribes" of hereditary agricultural slaves, many of them seized in raids against neighboring peoples.

Slaves were also central to the trans-Saharan trade. When the renowned Tunisian adventurer Ibn Battuta crossed the Sahara from the Kingdom of Mali around 1350, he traveled with a caravan of six hundred female slaves, destined for domestic service or concubinage in North Africa, Egypt, and the Ottoman Empire. Between A.D. 700 and 1900, it is estimated that as many as nine million Africans were sold in the trans-Saharan slave trade.

Europeans initially were much more interested in trading for gold and other commodities than in trading for human beings, but gradually they discovered the enormous value of human trafficking. To exploit and redirect the existing African slave trade, Portuguese merchants established fortified trading posts like those in the Indian Ocean beginning at Elmina in 1482, where they bought gold and slaves from African princes and warlords. First they enslaved a few thousand Africans each year to work on sugar plantations on São Tomé, Cape Verde, the Azores, and Madeira; they also sold slaves in Lisbon, which soon had an African population of 9,000. After 1550, the Atlantic slave trade, a forced diaspora of African peoples, expanded enormously as Europeans set up sugar plantations across the Atlantic, in Brazil and the West Indies.

## Sixteenth-Century Incursions

As Portuguese traders sailed south and east, the Spanish monarchs Ferdinand II of Aragon and Isabella I of Castile financed an explorer who looked to the west. As Renaissance rulers, Ferdinand (r. 1474–1516) and Isabella (r. 1474–1504) saw national unity and foreign commerce as the keys to power and prosperity. Married in an arranged match to combine their Christian kingdoms, the young rulers completed the centuries-long *reconquista*, the campaign by Spanish Catholics to drive Muslim Arabs from the European mainland, by capturing Granada, the last Islamic territory in Western Europe, in 1492. Using Catholicism to build a sense of "Spanishness," they launched the brutal Inquisition against suspected Christian heretics and expelled or forcibly converted thousands of Jews and Muslims.

**Columbus and the Caribbean**    Simultaneously, Ferdinand and Isabella sought trade and empire by subsidizing the voyages of Christopher Columbus, an ambitious and daring mariner from Genoa. Columbus believed that the Atlantic Ocean, long feared by Arab merchants as a 10,000-mile-wide "green sea of darkness," was a much narrower channel of water separating Europe from Asia. After six years of lobbying, Columbus persuaded Genoese investors and Ferdinand and Isabella to accept his dubious theories and finance a western voyage to Asia.

Columbus set sail in three small ships in August 1492. Six weeks later, after a perilous voyage of 3,000 miles, he disembarked on an island in the present-day Bahamas. Believing that he had reached Asia — "the Indies," in fifteenth-century parlance — Columbus called the native inhabitants Indians and the islands the West Indies. He was surprised by the crude living conditions but expected the Native peoples "easily [to] be made Christians." He claimed the islands for Spain and then explored the neighboring Caribbean islands, demanding tribute from the local Taino, Arawak, and Carib peoples. Columbus left forty men on the island of Hispaniola (present-day Haiti and the Dominican Republic) and returned triumphantly to Spain (Map 1.5).

The Spanish monarchs supported three more voyages. Columbus colonized the West Indies with more than 1,000 Spanish settlers — all men — and hundreds of domestic animals. But he failed to find either golden treasures or great kingdoms, and his death in 1506 went virtually unnoticed.

A German geographer soon named the newly found continents "America" in honor of a different explorer. Amerigo Vespucci, a Florentine explorer who had visited the coast of present-day South America around 1500, denied that the region was part of Asia. He called it a *nuevo mundo*, a "new world." The Spanish crown called the two continents *Las Indias* ("the Indies") and wanted to make them a new Spanish world.

**The Spanish Invasion**    After brutally subduing the Arawaks and Tainos on Hispaniola, the Spanish probed the mainland for gold and slaves. In 1513, Juan Ponce de León explored the coast of Florida and gave that peninsula its name. In the same year, Vasco Núñez de Balboa crossed the Isthmus of Darien (Panama) and became the first European to see the Pacific Ocean. Rumors of rich Indian kingdoms encouraged other Spaniards, including hardened veterans of the *reconquista*, to invade the mainland. The Spanish monarchs offered successful conquistadors noble titles, vast estates, and Indian laborers.

With these inducements before him, in 1519 Hernán Cortés (1485–1547) led an army of 600 men to the Yucatán Peninsula. Gathering allies among Native peoples who chafed under Aztec rule, he marched on Tenochtitlán and challenged its ruler, Moctezuma. Awed by the Spanish invaders, Moctezuma received Cortés with great ceremony. But Cortés soon took the emperor captive, and after a long siege he and his men captured the city. The conquerors cut off the city's supply of food and water, causing great suffering for the residents of Tenochtitlán. By 1521, Cortés and his men had toppled the Aztec Empire.

The Spanish had a silent ally: disease. Having been separated from Eurasia for thousands of years, the inhabitants of the Americas had no immunities to common European diseases. After the Spaniards arrived, a massive smallpox epidemic ravaged Tenochtitlán, "striking everywhere in the city," according to an Aztec source, and killing Moctezuma's brother and thousands more. "They could not move, they could not stir. . . . Covered, mantled with pustules, very many people died of them."

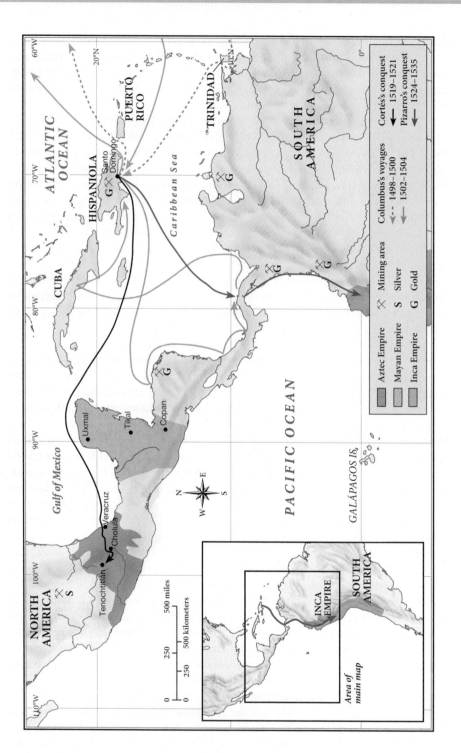

Subsequent outbreaks of smallpox, influenza, and measles killed hundreds of thousands of Indians and sapped the survivors' morale. Exploiting this advantage, Cortés quickly extended Spanish rule over the Aztec Empire. His lieutenants then moved against the Mayan city-states of the Yucatán Peninsula, eventually conquering them as well.

In 1524, Francisco Pizarro set out to accomplish the same feat in Peru. By the time he and his small force of 168 men and 67 horses finally reached their destination in 1532, half of the Inca population had already died from European diseases. Weakened militarily and divided between rival claimants to the throne, the Inca nobility was easy prey. Pizarro killed Atahualpa, the last Inca emperor, and seized his enormous wealth. Although Inca resistance continued for a generation, the conquest was complete by 1535, and Spain was now the master of the wealthiest and most populous regions of the Western Hemisphere.

The Spanish invasion changed life forever in the Americas. Disease and warfare wiped out virtually all of the Indians of Hispaniola — at least 300,000 people. In Peru, the population of 9 million in 1530 plummeted to fewer than 500,000 a century later. Mesoamerica suffered the greatest losses: in one of the great demographic disasters in world history, its population of 20 million Native Americans in 1500 had dwindled to just 3 million in 1650.

**Cabral and Brazil**   At the same time, Portuguese efforts to sail around the southern tip of Africa led to a surprising find. As Vasco da Gama and his contemporaries experimented with winds and currents, their voyages carried them ever farther away from the African coast and into the Atlantic. On one such voyage in 1500, the Portuguese commander Pedro Alvares Cabral and his fleet were surprised to see land loom up in the west. Cabral named his discovery Ihla da Vera Cruz — the Island of the True Cross — and continued on his way toward India. Others soon followed and changed the region's name to Brazil after the indigenous tree that yielded a valuable red dye; for several decades, Portuguese sailors traded with the Tupi Indians for brazilwood. Then in the 1530s, to secure Portugal's claim, King Dom João III sent settlers, who began the long, painstaking process of carving out sugar plantations in the coastal lowlands.

For several decades, Native Americans supplied most of the labor for these operations, but African slaves gradually replaced them. Brazil would soon become the world's leading producer of sugar; it would also devour African lives. By introducing the **plantation system** to the Americas — a form of estate agriculture using slave labor that was pioneered by Italian merchants and crusading knights in the twelfth century and transplanted to the islands off the coast of Africa in the fifteenth

**< MAP 1.5   The Spanish Conquest of America's Great Empires**
The Spanish first invaded the islands of the Caribbean, largely wiping out the Native peoples. Rumors of a gold-rich civilization led to Cortés's invasion of the Aztec Empire in 1519. By 1535, other Spanish conquistadors had conquered the Mayan temple cities and the Inca Empire in Peru, completing one of the great conquests in world history.

century—the Portuguese set in motion one of the most significant developments of the early modern era.

By the end of the sixteenth century, the European colonization of the Americas had barely begun. Yet several of its most important elements were already taking shape. Spanish efforts demonstrated that densely populated empires were especially vulnerable to conquest and were also especially valuable sources of wealth. The Portuguese had discovered the viability of sugar plantations in the tropical regions of the Americas and pioneered the transatlantic slave trade as a way of manning them. And contacts with Native peoples revealed their devastating vulnerabilities to Eurasian diseases—one part of the larger phenomenon of the Columbian Exchange (discussed in Chapter 2).

| IN YOUR OWN WORDS | What motivated Portuguese and Spanish expansion into the Atlantic, and what were its unintended consequences? |
|---|---|

## Summary

Native American, European, and African societies developed independently over thousands of years before they experienced direct contacts with one another. In the Americas, residents of Mesoamerica and the Andes were fully sedentary (with individual ownership of land and intensive agriculture), but elsewhere societies were semisedentary (with central fields and villages that were occupied seasonally) or nonsedentary (hunter-gatherers). West and Central Africa also had a mix of sedentary, semisedentary, and nonsedentary settlements. Western Europe, by contrast, was predominantly sedentary. All three continents had a complex patchwork of political organizations, from empires, to kingdoms and chiefdoms, to principalities, duchies, and ministates; everywhere, rulership was imbued with notions of spiritual power. Ruling classes relied on warfare, trade, and tribute (or taxes) to dominate those around them and accumulate precious goods that helped to set them apart from ordinary laborers, but they also bore responsibility for the well-being of their subjects and offered them various forms of protection.

As sailors pushed into the Atlantic, they set in motion a chain of events whose consequences they could scarcely imagine. From a coastal trade with Africa that was secondary to their efforts to reach the Indian Ocean, from the miscalculations of Columbus and the happy accident of Cabral, developed a pattern of transatlantic exploration, conquest, and exploitation that no one could have foretold or planned. In the tropical zones of the Caribbean and coastal Brazil, invading Europeans enslaved Native Americans and quickly drove them into extinction or exile. The demands of plantation agriculture soon led Europeans to import slaves from Africa, initiating a transatlantic trade that would destroy African lives on both sides of the ocean. And two of the greatest empires in the world—the Aztec and Incan empires—collapsed in response to unseen biological forces that acted in concert with small invading armies.

# Chapter 1 Review

## KEY TERMS

**Identify and explain the significance of each term below.**

hunters and gatherers (p. 7)
semisedentary societies (p. 7)
Mississippian culture (p. 10)
eastern woodlands (p. 11)
Algonquian cultures/languages
　(p. 11)
Iroquoian cultures/languages (p. 11)
Iroquois Confederacy (p. 12)
Great Lakes (p. 13)
Great Plains (p. 13)

Rocky Mountains (p. 14)
Great Basin (p. 14)
peasants (p. 17)
republic (p. 18)
Christianity (p. 19)
Islam (p. 20)
Crusades (p. 21)
Protestant Reformation (p. 21)
Counter-Reformation (p. 21)
plantation system (p. 31)

## REVIEW QUESTIONS

**Answer these questions to demonstrate your understanding of the chapter's main ideas.**

1. What factors might best explain the variations among Native American societies and cultures?

2. How had recent developments changed Western Europe by 1491?

3. How was sub-Saharan Africa affected by the arrival of European traders?

4. What motivated Portuguese and Spanish expansion into the Atlantic, and what were its unintended consequences?

5. Review the events listed under "Work, Exchange, and Technology" and "Migration and Settlement" on the thematic timeline on pages 4–5. How did contacts among Europeans, Native Americans, and Africans alter the economies of the three continents?

## CHRONOLOGY

**As you read, ask yourself why this chapter begins and ends with these dates and then identify the links among related events.**

| | |
|---|---|
| **c. 13,000–3000 B.C.** | • Asian migrants reach North America |
| **c. 6000 B.C.** | • Domestication of maize begins in Mesoamerica |
| **312** | • Roman emperor Constantine converts to Christianity |
| **c. 600** | • Pueblo cultures emerge |

| | |
|---|---|
| **632** | • Death of Muhammad |
| **632–1100** | • Arab people adopt Islam and spread its influence |
| **c. 800** | • Ghana Empire emerges |
| **c. 1000** | • Irrigation developed by Hohokam, Mogollon, and Anasazi peoples |
| **c. 1000–1350** | • Development of Mississippian culture |
| **c. 1050** | • Founding of Cahokia |
| **1096–1291** | • Crusades link Europe with Arab trade routes |
| **c. 1150** | • Chaco Canyon abandoned |
| **c. 1200** | • Mali Empire emerges |
| **c. 1300–1450** | • The Renaissance in Italy |
| **c. 1325** | • Aztecs establish capital at Tenochtitlán |
| **1326** | • Mansa Musa's pilgrimage to Mecca |
| **c. 1350** | • The Black Death sweeps Europe; Cahokia goes into rapid decline |
| **c. 1400** | • Songhai Empire emerges |
| **1435** | • Portuguese trade begins along West and Central African coasts |
| **c. 1450** | • Founding of the Iroquois Confederacy |
| **1492** | • Christopher Columbus makes first voyage to America |
| **1497–1498** | • Portugal's Vasco da Gama reaches East Africa and India |
| **1500** | • Pedro Alvares Cabral encounters Brazil |
| **1513** | • Juan Ponce de León explores Florida |
| **1517** | • Martin Luther sparks Protestant Reformation |
| **1519–1521** | • Hernán Cortés conquers Aztec Empire |
| **1532–1535** | • Francisco Pizarro vanquishes Incas |
| **1536** | • John Calvin publishes *Institutes of the Christian Religion* |
| **1540** | • De Soto meets the Lady of Cofachiqui; founding of the Jesuit order |
| **1578** | • Duarte Lopez visits the Kongo capital |

# 2

# American Experiments

## 1521–1700

**IDENTIFY THE BIG IDEA**

In what ways did European migrants transfer familiar patterns and institutions to their colonies in the Americas, and in what ways did they create new American worlds? How did Native Americans adapt to the growing presence of Europeans among them?

**BEGINNING IN THE 1660S, LEGISLATORS IN VIRGINIA AND MARYLAND** hammered out the legal definition of **chattel slavery**: the ownership of human beings as property. The institution of slavery—which would profoundly affect African Americans and shape much of American history—had been obsolete in England for centuries, and articulating its logic required lawmakers to reverse some of the most basic presumptions of English law. For example, in 1662 a Virginia statute declared, "all children borne in this country shalbe held bond or free only according to the condition of the mother." This idea—that a child's legal status derived from the mother, rather than the father—ran contrary to the patriarchal foundations of English law. The men who sat in Virginia's House of Burgesses would not propose such a thing lightly. Why would they decide that the principle of patriarchal descent, which was so fundamental to their own worlds, was inappropriate for their slaves?

The question needed to be addressed, according to the statute's preamble, since "doubts have arisen whether children got by an Englishman upon a negro woman should be slave or free." One such case involved Elizabeth Key, a woman whose father was a free Englishman and mother was an African slave. She petitioned for her freedom in 1656, based on her father's status. Her lawyer was an Englishman named William Greensted.

He not only took Key's case, but he also fathered two of her children and, eventually, married her. Key won her case and her freedom from bondage. Elizabeth Key escaped her mother's fate—a life in slavery—because her father and her husband were both free Englishmen. The 1662 statute aimed to close Key's avenue to freedom.

The process by which the institution of chattel slavery was molded to the needs of colonial planters is just one example of the way Europeans adapted the principles they brought with them to the unfamiliar demands of their new surroundings. In the showdown between people like Elizabeth Key and William Greensted, on the one hand, and the members of Virginia's House of Burgesses on the other, we see how people in disorienting circumstances—some in positions of power, others in various states of subjection to their social and political superiors—scrambled to make sense of their world and bend its rules to their advantage. Through countless contests of power and authority like this one, the outlines of a new world gradually began to emerge from the collision of cultures.

By 1700, three distinct types of colonies had developed in the Americas. The tribute colonies created in Mexico and Peru relied initially on the wealth and labor of indigenous peoples. Plantation colonies produced sugar and other tropical and subtropical crops with bound labor. Finally, **neo-Europes** sought to replicate, or at least approximate, economies and social structures that colonists knew at home.

# Spain's Tribute Colonies

European interest in the Americas took shape under the influence of Spain's conquest of the Aztec and Inca empires. There, Spanish colonizers capitalized on preexisting systems of tribute and labor discipline to tap the enormous wealth of Mesoamerica and the Andes. Once native rulers were overthrown, the Spanish monarchs transferred their institutions—municipal councils, the legal code, the Catholic Church—to America; the empire was centrally controlled to protect the crown's immensely valuable holdings. The Spanish conquest also set in motion a global ecological transformation through a vast intercontinental movement of plants, animals, and diseases that historians call the Columbian Exchange. And the conquest triggered hostile responses from Spain's European rivals, especially the Protestant Dutch and English.

## A New American World

After Cortés toppled Moctezuma and Pizarro defeated Atahualpa (see Chapter 1), leading conquistadors received *encomiendas* from the crown, which allowed them to claim tribute in labor and goods from Indian communities. Later these grants were repartitioned, but the pattern was set early: prominent men controlled vast resources and monopolized Indian labor. The value of these grants was dramatically enhanced by the discovery of gold and, especially, silver deposits in both Mexico and the Andes. In the decades after the conquest, mines were developed in Zacatecas, in Guanajuato, and — most famously — at Potosí, high in the Andes. There, Spanish officials co-opted the *mita* system, which had made laborers available to the Inca Empire, to force Indian workers into the mines. At its peak, Potosí alone produced 200 tons of silver per year, accounting for half the world's supply.

The two great indigenous empires of the Americas thus became the core of an astonishingly wealthy European empire. Vast amounts of silver poured across the Pacific Ocean to China, where it was minted into money; in exchange, Spain received valuable Chinese silks, spices, and ceramics. In Europe, the gold that had formerly honored Aztec and Inca gods now flowed into the countinghouses of Spain and gilded the Catholic churches of Europe. The Spanish crown benefitted enormously from all this wealth — at least initially. In the long run, it triggered ruinous inflation. As a French traveler noted in 1603, "Everything is dear [expensive] in Spain, except silver."

A new society took shape on the conquered lands. Between 1500 and 1650, at least 350,000 Spaniards migrated to Mesoamerica and the Andes. About two-thirds were males drawn from a cross section of Spanish society, many of them skilled tradesmen. Also arriving were 250,000 to 300,000 Africans. Racial mixture was widespread, and such groups as mestizos (Spaniard-Indian) and mulattos (Spaniard-African) grew rapidly. Zambo (Indian-African) populations developed gradually as well. Over time, a system of increasingly complex racial categories developed — the **casta system** — buttressed by a legal code that differentiated among the principal groups.

Indians were always in the majority in Mexico and Peru, but profound changes came as their numbers declined and peoples of Spanish and mixed-race descent grew in number. Spaniards initially congregated in cities, but gradually they moved into the countryside, creating large estates (known as haciendas) and regional networks of market exchange. Most Indians remained in their Native communities, under the authority of Native rulers and speaking Native languages. However, Spanish priests suppressed religious ceremonies and texts and converted Natives to Christianity *en masse*. Catholicism was transformed in the process: Catholic parishes took their form from Indian communities; indigenous ideas and expectations reshaped Church practices; and new forms of Native American Christianity emerged in both regions.

## The Columbian Exchange

The Spanish invasion permanently altered the natural as well as the human environment. Smallpox, influenza, measles, yellow fever, and other silent killers carried from Europe and Africa ravaged Indian communities, whose inhabitants had never encountered these diseases before and thus had no immunities to them. In the densely populated core areas, populations declined by 90 percent or more in the first century of contact with Europeans. On islands and in the tropical lowlands, the toll was even heavier; Native populations were often wiped out altogether. Syphilis was the only significant illness that traveled in the opposite direction: Columbus's sailors carried a virulent strain of the sexually transmitted disease back to Europe with them.

The movement of diseases and peoples across the Atlantic was part of a larger pattern of biological transformation that historians call the **Columbian Exchange** (Map 2.1). Foods of the Western Hemisphere — especially maize, potatoes, manioc,

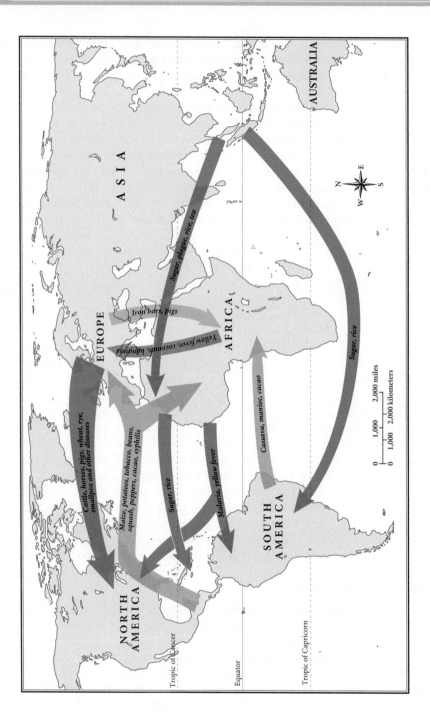

sweet potatoes, and tomatoes—significantly increased agricultural yields and population growth in other continents. Maize and potatoes, for example, reached China around 1700; in the following century, the Chinese population tripled from 100 million to 300 million. At the same time, many animals, plants, and germs were carried to the Americas. European livestock transformed American landscapes. While Native Americans domesticated very few animals—dogs and llamas were the principal exceptions—Europeans brought an enormous Old World bestiary to the Americas, including cattle, swine, horses, oxen, chickens, and honeybees. Eurasian grain crops—wheat, barley, rye, and rice—made the transatlantic voyage along with inadvertent imports like dandelions and other weeds.

## The Protestant Challenge to Spain

Beyond the core regions of its empire, Spain claimed vast American dominions but struggled to hold them. Controlling the Caribbean basin, which was essential for Spain's transatlantic shipping routes, was especially difficult, since the net of tiny islands spanning the eastern Caribbean — the Lesser Antilles — provided many safe harbors for pirates and privateers. Fortified outposts in Havana (Cuba) and St. Augustine (Florida) provided some protection, but they were never sufficient to keep enemies at bay.

And Spain had powerful enemies, their animosity sharpened by the Protestant Reformation and the resulting split in European Christendom (see Chapter 1). In the wake of Martin Luther's attack on the Catholic Church, the Protestant critique of Catholicism broadened and deepened. Gold and silver from Mexico and Peru made Spain the wealthiest nation in Europe, and King Philip II (r. 1556–1598)—an ardent Catholic—its most powerful ruler. Philip was determined to root out challenges to the Catholic Church wherever they appeared. One such place was in the Spanish Netherlands, a collection of Dutch- and Flemish-speaking provinces that had grown wealthy from textile manufacturing and trade with Portuguese outposts in Africa and Asia. To protect their Calvinist faith and political liberties, they revolted against Spanish rule in 1566. After fifteen years of war, the seven northern provinces declared their independence, becoming the Dutch Republic (or Holland) in 1581.

The English king Henry VIII (r. 1509–1547) initially opposed Protestantism. However, when the pope refused to annul his marriage to the Spanish princess Catherine of Aragon in 1534, Henry broke with Rome and placed himself at the head of the new Church of England, which promptly granted an annulment. Although Henry's new church maintained most Catholic doctrines and practices, Protestant

**< MAP 2.1   The Columbian Exchange**
As European traders and adventurers traversed the world between 1430 and 1600, they began what historians call the Columbian Exchange, a vast intercontinental movement of plants, animals, and diseases that changed the course of historical development. The nutritious, high-yielding American crops of corn and potatoes enriched the diets of Europeans, Africans, and Asians. However, the Eurasian and African diseases of smallpox, diphtheria, malaria, and yellow fever nearly wiped out the native inhabitants of the Western Hemisphere and virtually ensured that they would lose control of their lands.

teachings continued to spread. Faced with popular pressure for reform, Henry's daughter and successor, Queen Elizabeth I (r. 1558–1603), approved a Protestant confession of faith. But she also retained the Catholic ritual of Holy Communion and left the Church in the hands of Anglican bishops and archbishops. Elizabeth's compromises angered radical Protestants, but the independent Anglican Church was anathema to the Spanish king, Philip II.

Elizabeth supported a generation of English seafarers who took increasingly aggressive actions against Spanish control of American wealth. The most famous of these Elizabethan "sea dogs" was Francis Drake, a rough-hewn, devoutly Protestant farmer's son from Devon who took to the sea and became a scourge to Philip's American interests. In 1577, he ventured into the Pacific to disrupt Spanish shipping to Manila. Drake's fleet lost three ships and a hundred men, but the survivors captured two Spanish treasure ships and completed the first English circumnavigation of the globe. When Drake's flagship, the *Golden Hind,* returned to England in 1580, it brought enough silver, gold, silk, and spices to bring his investors a 4,700 percent return on their investment.

At the same time, Elizabeth imposed English rule over Gaelic-speaking Catholic Ireland. Calling the Irish "wild savages" who were "more barbarous and more brutish in their customs . . . than in any other part of the world," English soldiers brutally massacred thousands, prefiguring the treatment of Indians in North America.

To meet Elizabeth's challenges, Philip sent a Spanish Armada — 130 ships and 30,000 men — against England in 1588. Philip intended to restore the Roman Church in England and then wipe out Calvinism in Holland. But he failed utterly: a fierce storm and English ships destroyed the Spanish fleet. Philip continued to spend his American gold and silver on religious wars, an ill-advised policy that diverted workers and resources from Spain's fledgling industries. The gold was like a "shewer of Raine," complained one critic, that left "no benefite behind." Oppressed by high taxes on agriculture and fearful of military service, more than 200,000 residents of Castile, once the most prosperous region of Spain, migrated to America. By the time of Philip's death in 1598, Spain was in serious economic decline.

By contrast, England's population soared from 3 million in 1500 to 5 million in 1630. English merchants had long supplied European weavers with high-quality wool; around 1500, they created their own textile industry. Merchants bought wool from the owners of great estates and sent it to landless peasants in small cottages to spin and weave into cloth. The government aided textile entrepreneurs by setting low wage rates and helped merchants by giving them monopolies in foreign markets.

This system of state-assisted manufacturing and trade became known as **mercantilism**. By encouraging textile production, Elizabeth reduced imports and increased exports. The resulting favorable balance of trade caused gold and silver to flow into England and stimulated further economic expansion. Increased trade with Turkey and India also boosted import duties, which swelled the royal treasury and the monarch's power. By 1600, Elizabeth's mercantile policies had laid the foundations for overseas colonization. Now the English had the merchant fleet and wealth needed to challenge Spain's control of the Western Hemisphere.

| **IN YOUR OWN WORDS** | How did Spanish colonization affect people in the Americas and in Europe? |

# Plantation Colonies

As Spain hammered out its American empire and struggled against its Protestant rivals, Portugal, England, France, and the Netherlands created successful plantation settlements in Brazil, Jamestown, Maryland, and the Caribbean islands (Map 2.2). Worldwide demand for sugar and tobacco fueled the growth of these new colonies, and the resulting influx of colonists diminished Spain's dominance in the New World. At the same time, they imposed dramatic new pressures on Native populations, who scrambled to survive and carve out pathways to the future.

## Brazil's Sugar Plantations

Portuguese colonists transformed the tropical lowlands of coastal Brazil into a sugar plantation zone like the ones they had recently created on Madeira, the Azores, the Cape Verdes, and São Tomé. The work proceeded slowly, but by 1590 more than

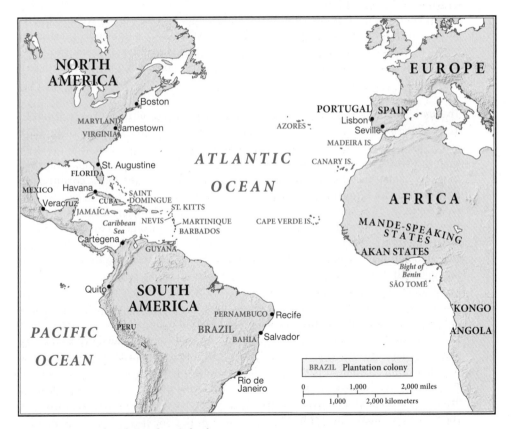

**MAP 2.2 The Plantation Colonies**
The plantation zone in the Americas extended from the tropical coast of Brazil northwestward through the West Indies and into the tropical and subtropical lowlands of southeastern North America. Sugar was the most important plantation crop in the Americas, but where the soil or climate could not support it planters experimented with a wide variety of other possibilities, including tobacco, indigo, cotton, cacao, and rice.

a thousand sugar mills had been established in Pernambuco and Bahia. Each large plantation had its own milling operation: because sugarcane is extremely heavy and rots quickly, it must be processed on site. Thus sugar plantations combined back-breaking agricultural labor with milling, extracting, and refining processes that made them look like Industrial Revolution–era factories.

Initially, Portuguese planters hoped that Brazil's indigenous peoples would supply the labor required to operate their sugar plantations. But, beginning with a small-pox epidemic in 1559, unfamiliar diseases ravaged the coastal Indian population. As a result, planters turned to African slaves in ever-growing numbers; by 1620, the switch was complete. While Spanish colonies in Mexico and Peru took shape with astonishing speed following conquest, Brazil's development required both trial and error and prolonged hard work.

## England's Tobacco Colonies

England was slow to pursue colonization in the Americas. There were fumbling attempts in the 1580s in Newfoundland and Maine, privately organized and poorly funded. Sir Walter Raleigh's three expeditions to North Carolina ended in disaster when 117 settlers on Roanoke Island, left unsupplied for several years, vanished. The fate of Roanoke — the "lost colony" — remains a compelling puzzle for modern historians.

**The Jamestown Settlement**    Merchants then took charge of English expansion. In 1606, King James I (r. 1603–1625) granted to the Virginia Company of London all the lands stretching from present-day North Carolina to southern New York. To honor the memory of Elizabeth I, the never-married "Virgin Queen," the company's directors named the region Virginia (Map 2.3). This was a **joint-stock corporation** that pooled the resources of many investors, spreading the financial risk widely. Influenced by the Spanish example, in 1607 the Virginia Company dispatched an all-male group with no ability to support itself: there were no women, farmers, or ministers among the first arrivals. Instead the first colonists hoped to demand tribute from the region's Indian population while it searched out valuable commodities like pearls and gold. All they wanted, one of them said, was to "dig gold, refine gold, load gold."

But there was no gold, and the men fared poorly in their new environment. Arriving in Virginia after an exhausting four-month voyage, they settled on a swampy peninsula, which they named Jamestown to honor the king. There the adventurers lacked access to fresh water, refused to plant crops, and quickly died off; only 38 of the 120 men were alive nine months later. Death rates remained high: by 1611, the Virginia Company had dispatched 1,200 colonists to Jamestown, but fewer than half remained alive. "Our men were destroyed with cruell diseases, as Swellings, Fluxes, Burning Fevers, and by warres," reported one of the settlement's leaders, "but for the most part they died of meere famine."

Their plan to dominate the local Indian population ran up against the presence of Powhatan, the powerful paramount chief who oversaw some thirty subordinate chiefdoms between the James and Potomac rivers. He was willing to treat the English traders as potential allies who could provide valuable goods, but — just as the Englishmen expected tribute from the Indians — Powhatan expected tribute

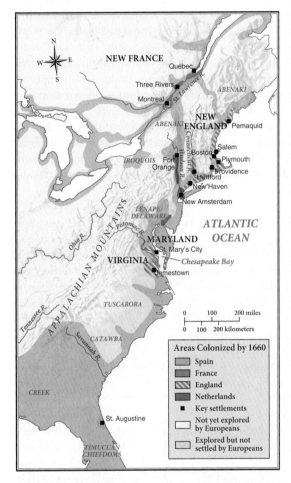

### MAP 2.3 Eastern North America, 1650

By 1650, four European nations had permanent settlements along the eastern coast of North America, but only England had substantial numbers of settlers, some 25,000 in New England and another 15,000 in the Chesapeake region. French, Dutch, Swedish, and English colonists were also trading European manufactures to Native Americans in exchange for animal furs and skins, with far-reaching implications for Indian societies.

from the English. He provided the hungry English adventurers with corn; in return, he demanded "hatchets . . . bells, beads, and copper" as well as "two great guns" and expected Jamestown to become a dependent community within his chiefdom. Subsequently, Powhatan arranged a marriage between his daughter Pocahontas and John Rolfe, an English colonist. But these tactics failed. The inability to decide who would pay tribute to whom led to more than a decade of uneasy relations, followed by a long era of ruinous warfare.

The war was precipitated by the discovery of a cash crop that—like sugar in Brazil—offered colonists a way to turn a profit but required steady expansion onto Indian lands. Tobacco was a plant native to the Americas, long used by Indians as a medicine and a stimulant. John Rolfe found a West Indian strain that could flourish in Virginia soil and produced a small crop—"pleasant, sweet, and strong"—that fetched a high price in England and spurred the migration of thousands of new settlers. The English soon came to crave the nicotine that tobacco contained. James I initially condemned the plant as a "vile Weed" whose "black stinking fumes" were "baleful to the nose, harmful to the brain, and dangerous to the lungs." But the king's attitude changed as taxes on imported tobacco bolstered the royal treasury. Powhatan, however, now accused the English of coming "not to trade but to invade my people and possess my country."

To encourage immigration, the Virginia Company allowed individual settlers to own land, granting 100 acres to every freeman and more to those who imported servants. The company also created a system of representative government: the **House of Burgesses**, first convened in 1619, could make laws and levy taxes, although the governor and the company council in England could veto its acts. By 1622, landownership, self-government, and a judicial system based on "the lawes of the realme of England" had attracted some 4,500 new recruits. To encourage the transition to a settler colony, the Virginia Company recruited dozens of "Maides young and uncorrupt to make wifes to the Inhabitants."

**The Indian War of 1622**   The influx of migrants sparked war with the neighboring Indians. The struggle began with an assault led by Opechancanough, Powhatan's younger brother and successor. In 1607, Opechancanough had attacked some of the first English invaders; subsequently, he "stood aloof" from the English settlers and "would not be drawn to any Treaty." In particular, he resisted English proposals to place Indian children in schools to be "brought upp in Christianytie." Upon becoming the paramount chief in 1621, Opechancanough told the leader of the neighboring Potomack Indians: "Before the end of two moons, there should not be an Englishman in all their Countries."

Opechancanough almost succeeded. In 1622, he coordinated a surprise attack by twelve Indian chiefdoms that killed 347 English settlers, nearly one-third of the population. The English fought back by seizing the fields and food of those they now called "naked, tanned, deformed Savages" and declared "a perpetual war without peace or truce" that lasted for a decade. They sold captured warriors into slavery, "destroy[ing] them who sought to destroy us" and taking control of "their cultivated places."

Shocked by the Indian uprising, James I revoked the Virginia Company's charter and, in 1624, made Virginia a **royal colony**. Now the king and his ministers appointed the governor and a small advisory council, retaining the locally elected House of Burgesses but stipulating that the king's Privy Council (a committee of political advisors) must ratify all legislation. The king also decreed the legal establishment of the Church of England in the colony, which meant that residents had to pay taxes to support its clergy. These institutions — an appointed governor, an elected assembly, a formal legal system, and an established Anglican Church — became the model for royal colonies throughout English America.

**Lord Baltimore Settles Catholics in Maryland**   A second tobacco-growing colony developed in neighboring Maryland. King Charles I (r. 1625–1649), James's successor, was secretly sympathetic toward Catholicism, and in 1632 he granted lands bordering the vast Chesapeake Bay to Catholic aristocrat Cecilius Calvert, Lord Baltimore. Thus Maryland became a refuge for Catholics, who were subject to persecution in England. In 1634, twenty gentlemen, mostly Catholics, and two hundred artisans and laborers, mostly Protestants, established St. Mary's City at the mouth of the Potomac River. To minimize religious confrontations, the proprietor instructed the governor to allow "no scandall nor offence to be given to any of the Protestants" and to "cause All Acts of Romane Catholicque Religion to be done as privately as may be."

Maryland grew quickly because Baltimore imported many artisans and offered ample lands to wealthy migrants. But political conflict threatened the colony's stability. Disputing Baltimore's powers, settlers elected a representative assembly and insisted on the right to initiate legislation, which Baltimore grudgingly granted. Anti-Catholic agitation by Protestants also threatened his religious goals. To protect his coreligionists, Lord Baltimore persuaded the assembly to enact the Toleration Act (1649), which granted all Christians the right to follow their beliefs and hold church services. In Maryland, as in Virginia, tobacco quickly became the main crop, and that similarity, rather than any religious difference, ultimately made the two colonies very much alike in their economic and social systems.

## The Caribbean Islands

Virginia's experiment with a cash crop that created a land-intensive plantation society ran parallel to developments in the Caribbean, where English, French, and Dutch sailors began looking for a permanent toehold. In 1624, a small English party under the command of Sir Thomas Warner established a settlement on St. Christopher (St. Kitts). A year later, Warner allowed a French group to settle the other end of the island so they could better defend their position from the Spanish. Within a few years, the English and French colonists on St. Kitts had driven the native Caribs from the island, weathered a Spanish attack, and created a common set of bylaws for mutual occupation of the island.

After St. Kitts, a dozen or so colonies were founded in the Lesser Antilles, including the French islands of Martinique, Guadeloupe, and St. Bart's; the English outposts of Nevis, Antigua, Montserrat, Anguilla, Tortola, and Barbados; and the Dutch colony of St. Eustatius. In 1655, an English fleet captured the Spanish island of Jamaica — one of the large islands of the Greater Antilles — and opened it to settlement as well. A few of these islands were unpopulated before Europeans settled there; elsewhere, native populations were displaced, and often wiped out, within a decade or so. Only on the largest islands did native populations hold out longer.

Colonists experimented with a wide variety of cash crops, including tobacco, indigo, cotton, cacao, and ginger. Beginning in the 1640s — and drawing on the example of Brazil — planters on many of the islands shifted to sugar cultivation. Where conditions were right, as they were in Barbados, Jamaica, Nevis, and Martinique, these colonies were soon producing substantial crops of sugar and, as a consequence, claimed some of the world's most valuable real estate.

## Plantation Life

In North America and the Caribbean, plantations were initially small **freeholds**, farms of 30 to 50 acres owned and farmed by families or male partners. But the logic of plantation agriculture soon encouraged consolidation: large planters engrossed as much land as they could and experimented with new forms of labor discipline that maximized their control over production. In Virginia, the **headright system**

**A Sugar Mill in the French West Indies, 1655** Making sugar required both hard labor and considerable expertise. Field slaves labored strenuously in the hot tropical sun to cut the sugarcane and carry or cart it to an oxen- or wind-powered mill, where it was pressed to yield the juice. Then skilled slave artisans took over. They carefully heated the juice and, at the proper moment, added ingredients that granulated the sugar and separated it from the molasses, which was later distilled into rum. Sarin Images / Granger, NYC.

guaranteed 50 acres of land to anyone who paid the passage of a new immigrant to the colony; thus, by buying additional indentured servants and slaves, the colony's largest planters also amassed ever-greater claims to land.

European demand for tobacco set off a forty-year economic boom in the Chesapeake. "All our riches for the present do consist in tobacco," a planter remarked in 1630. Exports rose from 3 million pounds in 1640 to 10 million pounds in 1660. After 1650, wealthy migrants from gentry or noble families established large estates along the coastal rivers, then acquired English indentured servants and enslaved Africans to work their lands. At about the same time, the switch to sugar production in Barbados caused the price of land there to quadruple, driving small landowners out.

For rich and poor alike, life in the plantation colonies of North America and the Caribbean was harsh. The scarcity of towns deprived settlers of community (Map 2.4). Families were equally scarce because there were few women, and marriages often ended with the early death of a spouse. Pregnant women were especially vulnerable to malaria, spread by mosquitoes that flourished in tropical and subtropical climates. Many mothers died after bearing a first or second child, so orphaned children (along with unmarried young men) formed a large segment of the society. Sixty percent of the children born in Middlesex County, Virginia, before 1680 lost one or both parents before they were thirteen. Death was pervasive. Although 15,000 English migrants arrived in Virginia between 1622 and 1640, the population rose only from 2,000 to 8,000. It was even harsher in the islands, where yellow fever epidemics killed indiscriminately. On Barbados, burials outnumbered baptisms in the second half of the seventeenth century by 4 to 1.

**Indentured Servitude**   Still, the prospect of owning land continued to lure settlers. By 1700, more than 100,000 English migrants had come to Virginia and Maryland and over 200,000 had migrated to the islands of the West Indies, principally to Barbados; the vast majority to both destinations traveled as indentured servants.

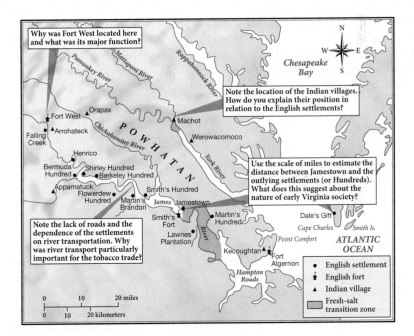

**MAP 2.4   River Plantations in Virginia, c. 1640**
The first migrants settled in widely dispersed plantations along the James River, a settlement pattern promoted by the tobacco economy. From their riverfront plantations wealthy planter-merchants could easily load heavy hogsheads of tobacco onto oceangoing ships and offload supplies that they then sold to smallholding planters. Consequently, few substantial towns or trading centers developed in the Chesapeake region.

Shipping registers from the English port of Bristol reveal the backgrounds of 5,000 servants embarking for the Chesapeake. Three-quarters were young men. They came to Bristol searching for work; once there, merchants persuaded them to sign contracts to labor in America. **Indentured servitude** contracts bound the men — and the quarter who were women — to work for a master for four or five years, after which they would be free to marry and work for themselves.

For merchants, servants were valuable cargo: their contracts fetched high prices from Chesapeake and West Indian planters. For the plantation owners, indentured servants were a bargain if they survived the voyage and their first year in a harsh new disease environment, a process called "seasoning." During the Chesapeake's tobacco boom, a male servant could produce five times his purchase price in a single year. To maximize their gains, many masters ruthlessly exploited servants, forcing them to work long hours, beating them without cause, and withholding permission to marry. If servants ran away or became pregnant, masters went to court to increase the term of their service. Female servants were especially vulnerable to abuse. A Virginia law of 1692 stated that "dissolute masters have gotten their maids with child; and yet claim the benefit of their service." Planters got rid of uncooperative servants by selling their contracts. In Virginia, an Englishman remarked in disgust that "servants were sold up and down like horses."

Few indentured servants escaped poverty. In the Chesapeake, half the men died before completing the term of their contract, and another quarter remained landless. Only one-quarter achieved their quest for property and respectability. Female servants generally fared better. Because men had grown "very sensible of the Misfortune of Wanting Wives," many propertied planters married female servants. Thus a few — very fortunate — men and women escaped early death or a life of landless poverty.

**African Laborers**   The rigors of indentured servitude paled before the brutality that accompanied the large-scale shift to African slave labor. In Barbados and the other English islands, sugar production devoured laborers, and the supply of indentured servants quickly became inadequate to planters' needs. By 1690, blacks outnumbered whites on Barbados nearly 3 to 1, and white slave owners were developing a code of force and terror to keep sugar flowing and maintain control of the black majority that surrounded them. The first comprehensive slave legislation for the island, adopted in 1661, was called an "Act for the better ordering and governing of Negroes."

In the Chesapeake, the shift to slave labor was more gradual. In 1619, John Rolfe noted that "a Dutch man of warre . . . sold us twenty Negars" — slaves originally shipped by the Portuguese from the port of Luanda in Angola. For a generation, the number of Africans remained small. About 400 Africans lived in the Chesapeake colonies in 1649, just 2 percent of the population. By 1670, that figure had reached 5 percent. Most Africans served their English masters for life. However, since English common law did not acknowledge chattel slavery, it was possible for some Africans to escape bondage. Some were freed as a result of Christian baptism; some purchased their freedom from their owners; some — like Elizabeth Key, whose story was related at the beginning of the chapter — won their freedom in the courts. Once free, some ambitious Africans became landowners and purchased slaves or the labor contracts of English servants for themselves.

Social mobility for Africans ended in the 1660s with the collapse of the tobacco boom and the increasing political power of the gentry. Tobacco had once sold for 30 pence a pound; now it fetched less than one-tenth of that. The "low price of Tobacco requires it should bee made as cheap as possible," declared Virginia planter-politician Nicholas Spencer, and "blacks can make it cheaper than whites." As they imported more African workers, the English-born political elite grew more race-conscious. Increasingly, Spencer and other leading legislators distinguished English from African residents by color (white-black) rather than by religion (Christian-pagan). By 1671, the Virginia House of Burgesses had forbidden Africans to own guns or join the militia. It also barred them—"tho baptized and enjoying their own Freedom"—from owning English servants. Being black was increasingly a mark of inferior legal status, and slavery was fast becoming a permanent and hereditary condition. As an English clergyman observed, "These two words, Negro and Slave had by custom grown Homogeneous and convertible."

| IN YOUR OWN WORDS | How did the labor demands of plantation colonies transform the process of colonization? |
|---|---|

# Neo-European Colonies

While Mesoamerica and the Andes emerged at the heart of a tribute-based empire in Latin America, and tropical and subtropical environments were transformed into plantation societies, a series of colonies that more closely replicated European patterns of economic and social organization developed in the temperate zone along North America's Atlantic coast. Dutch, French, and English sailors probed the continent's northern coastline, initially searching for a Northwest Passage through the continent to Asia. Gradually, they developed an interest in the region on its own terms. They traded for furs with coastal Native American populations, fished for cod on the Grand Banks off the coast of Newfoundland, and established freehold family farms and larger manors where they reproduced European patterns of agricultural life. Many migrants also came with aspirations to create godly communities, places of refuge where they could put religious ideals into practice. New France, New Netherland, and New England were the three pillars of neo-European colonization in the early seventeenth century.

## New France

In the 1530s, Jacques Cartier ventured up the St. Lawrence River and claimed it for France. Cartier's claim to the St. Lawrence languished for three-quarters of a century, but in 1608 Samuel de Champlain returned and founded the fur-trading post of Quebec. Trade with the Cree-speaking Montagnais; Algonquian-speaking Micmacs, Ottawas, and Ojibwas; and Iroquois-speaking Hurons gave the French access to furs—mink, otter, and beaver—that were in great demand in Europe. To secure plush beaver pelts from the Hurons, who controlled trade north of the Great Lakes, Champlain provided them with manufactured goods. Selling pelts, an Indian told a French priest, "makes kettles, hatchets, swords, knives, bread." It also made guns, which Champlain sold to the Hurons.

The Hurons also became the first focus of French Catholic missionary activity. Hundreds of priests, most of them Jesuits, fanned out to live in Indian communities. They mastered Indian languages and came to understand, and sometimes respect, Indian values. Many Native peoples initially welcomed the French "Black Robes" as spiritually powerful beings, but when prayers to the Christian god did not protect them from disease, the Indians grew skeptical. A Peoria chief charged that a priest's "fables are good only in his own country; we have our own [beliefs], which do not make us die as his do." When a drought struck, Indians blamed the missionaries. "If you cannot make rain, they speak of nothing less than making away with you," lamented one Jesuit.

While New France became an expansive center of fur trading and missionary work, it languished as a farming settlement. In 1662, King Louis XIV (r. 1643–1714) turned New France into a royal colony and subsidized the migration of indentured servants. French servants labored under contract for three years, received a salary, and could eventually lease a farm — far more generous terms than those for indentured servants in the English colonies.

Nonetheless, few people moved to New France, a cold and forbidding country "at the end of the world," as one migrant put it. And some state policies discouraged migration. Louis XIV drafted tens of thousands of men into military service and barred Huguenots (French Calvinist Protestants) from migrating to New France, fearing they might win converts and take control of the colony. Moreover, the French legal system gave peasants strong rights to their village lands, whereas migrants to New France faced an oppressive, aristocracy- and church-dominated feudal system. In the village of Saint Ours in Quebec, for example, peasants paid 45 percent of their wheat crop to nobles and the Catholic Church. By 1698, only 15,200 Europeans lived in New France, compared to 100,000 in England's North American colonies.

Despite this small population, France eventually claimed a vast inland arc, from the St. Lawrence Valley through the Great Lakes and down the course of the Ohio and Mississippi rivers. Explorers and fur traders drove this expansion. In 1673, Jacques Marquette reached the Mississippi River in present-day Wisconsin; then, in 1681, Robert de La Salle traveled down the majestic river to the Gulf of Mexico. To honor Louis XIV, La Salle named the region Louisiana. By 1718, French merchants had founded the port of New Orleans at the mouth of the Mississippi. Eventually a network of about two dozen forts grew up in the Great Lakes and Mississippi. Soldiers and missionaries used them as bases of operations, while Indians, traders, and their métis (mixed-race) offspring created trading communities alongside them.

## New Netherland

By 1600, Amsterdam had become the financial and commercial hub of northern Europe, and Dutch financiers dominated the European banking, insurance, and textile industries. Dutch merchants owned more ships and employed more sailors than did the combined fleets of England, France, and Spain. Indeed, the Dutch managed much of the world's commerce. During their struggle for independence from Spain and Portugal (ruled by Spanish monarchs, 1580–1640), the Dutch seized Portuguese forts in Africa and Indonesia and sugar plantations in Brazil. These conquests gave the Dutch control of the Atlantic trade in slaves and sugar and the Indian Ocean commerce in East Indian spices and Chinese silks and ceramics (Map 2.5).

In 1609, Dutch merchants sent the English mariner Henry Hudson to locate a navigable route to the riches of the East Indies. What he found as he probed the rivers of northeast America was a fur bonanza. Following Hudson's exploration of the river that now bears his name, the merchants built Fort Orange (Albany) in 1614 to trade for furs with the Munsee and Iroquois Indians. Then, in 1621, the Dutch government chartered the West India Company, which founded the colony of New Netherland, set up New Amsterdam (on Manhattan Island) as its capital, and brought in farmers and artisans to make the enterprise self-sustaining. The new colony did not thrive. The population of the Dutch Republic was too small to support much emigration — just 1.5 million people, compared to 5 million in Britain and 20 million in France — and its migrants sought riches in Southeast Asia rather than fur-trading profits in America. To protect its colony from rival European nations, the West India Company granted huge estates along the Hudson River to wealthy Dutchmen who promised to populate them. But by 1664, New Netherland had only 5,000 residents, and fewer than half of them were Dutch.

Like New France, New Netherland flourished as a fur-trading enterprise. Trade with the powerful Iroquois, though rocky at first, gradually improved. But Dutch settlers had less respect for their Algonquian-speaking neighbors. They seized prime farming land and disrupted Native American trade. In response, in 1643 the Algonquians launched attacks that nearly destroyed the colony. "Almost every place is abandoned," a settler lamented, "whilst the Indians daily threaten to overwhelm us." To defeat the Algonquians, the Dutch waged vicious warfare — maiming, burning, and killing hundreds of men, women, and children — and formed an alliance with the Mohawks, who were no less brutal. The grim progression of Euro-Indian relations — an uneasy welcome, followed by rising tensions and war — afflicted even the Dutch, who had few designs on Indian lands or on their "unregenerate" souls and were only looking to do business.

After the crippling Indian war, the West India Company ignored New Netherland and expanded its profitable trade in African slaves and Brazilian sugar. In New Amsterdam, Governor Peter Stuyvesant ruled in an authoritarian fashion, rejecting demands for a representative system of government and alienating the colony's diverse Dutch, English, and Swedish residents. Consequently, the residents of New Netherland offered little resistance when England invaded the colony in 1664. New Netherland became New York and fell under English control.

## The Rise of the Iroquois

Like other Native groups decimated by European diseases and warfare, the Five Nations of the Iroquois suffered as a result of colonization, but they were able to capitalize on their strategic location in central New York to dominate the region between the French and Dutch colonies. Obtaining guns and goods from Dutch merchants at Fort Orange, Iroquois warriors inflicted terror on their neighbors. Partly in response

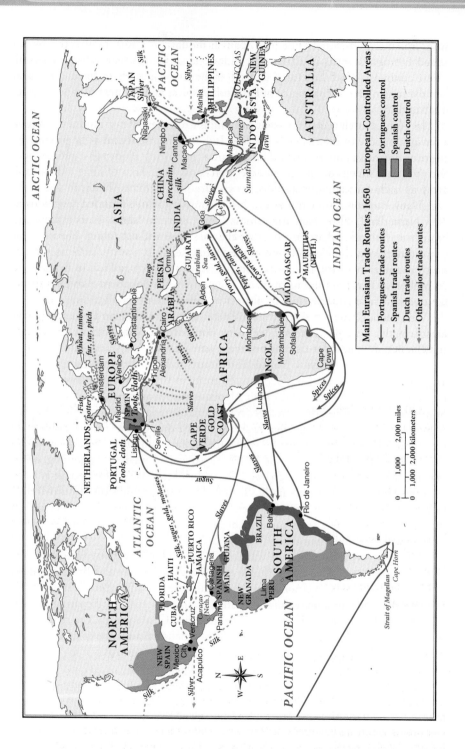

Main Eurasian Trade Routes, 1650

European-Controlled Areas
- Portuguese control
- Spanish control
- Dutch control

- → Portuguese trade routes
- ⇢ Spanish trade routes
- → Dutch trade routes
- ⋯ Other major trade routes

to a virulent smallpox epidemic in 1633, which cut their number by one-third, the Iroquois waged a series of devastating wars against the Hurons (1649), Neutrals (1651), Eries (1657), and Susquehannocks (1660) — all Iroquoian-speaking peoples. They razed villages, killing many residents and taking many more captive. The conquered Hurons ceased to exist as a distinct people; survivors trekked westward with displaced Algonquian peoples and formed a new nation, the Wyandots. Iroquois warriors pressed still farther — eastward into New England, south to the Carolinas, north to Quebec, and west via the Great Lakes to the Mississippi — dominating Indian groups along the way. Collectively known as the Beaver Wars, these Iroquois campaigns dramatically altered the map of northeastern North America.

Many Iroquois raids came at the expense of French-allied Algonquian Indians, and in the 1660s New France committed to all-out war against the Iroquois. In 1667, the Mohawks were the last of the Five Nations to admit defeat. As part of the peace settlement, the Five Nations accepted Jesuit missionaries into their communities. A minority of Iroquois — perhaps 20 percent of the population — converted to Catholicism and moved to the St. Lawrence Valley, where they settled in mission communities near Montreal (where their descendants still live today).

The Iroquois who remained in New York did not collapse, however. Forging a new alliance with the Englishmen who had taken over New Netherland, they would continue to be a dominant force in the politics of the Northeast for generations to come.

## New England

In 1620, 102 English Protestants landed at a place they called Plymouth, near Cape Cod. A decade later, a much larger group began to arrive just north of Plymouth, in the newly chartered Massachusetts Bay Colony. By 1640, the region had attracted more than 20,000 migrants. Unlike the early arrivals in Virginia and Barbados, these were not parties of young male adventurers seeking their fortunes or bound to labor for someone else. They came in family groups to create communities like the ones they left behind, except that they intended to establish them according to Protestant principles, as John Calvin had done in Geneva. Their numbers were small compared to the Caribbean and the Chesapeake, but their balanced sex ratio and organized approach to community formation allowed them to multiply quickly. By distributing land broadly, they built a society of independent farm families. And by establishing a "holy commonwealth," they gave a moral dimension to American history that survives today.

< **MAP 2.5**   **The Eurasian Trade System and European Spheres of Influence, 1650**
Between 1550 and 1650, Spanish, Portuguese, and Dutch merchants took control of the maritime trade routes between Europe and India, Indonesia, and China. They also created two new trading connections. The South Atlantic System carried slaves, sugar, and manufactured goods between Europe, Africa, and the valuable plantation settlements in Brazil and the Caribbean islands. And a transpacific trade carried Spanish American silver to China in exchange for silks, ceramics, and other manufactures. (To trace long-term changes in trade and empires, see Map 1.4 on p. 27 and Map 5.1 on p. 138.)

**The Hurons' Feast of the Dead** Hurons buried their dead in temporary raised tombs so they could easily care for their spirits. When they moved their villages in search of fertile soil and better hunting, the Hurons held a Feast of the Dead and reburied the bones of their own deceased (and often bones from other villages) in a common pit lined with beaver robes. This solemn ceremony united living and dead clan members, strengthening the bonds of the Huron Confederacy. It also was believed to release the spirits of the dead, allowing them to travel to the land where the first Huron, Aataentsic, fell from the sky, "made earth and man," and lived with her son and assistant, Iouskeha. Library of Congress.

**The Pilgrims**    The **Pilgrims** were religious separatists—committed Protestants who had left the Church of England. When King James I threatened to drive them "out of the land, or else do worse," some chose to live among Dutch Calvinists in Holland. Subsequently, 35 of these exiles resolved to maintain their English identity by moving to America. Led by William Bradford and joined by 67 migrants from England, the Pilgrims sailed to America aboard the *Mayflower*. Because they lacked a royal charter, they combined themselves "together into a civill body politick," as their leader explained. This Mayflower Compact used the Pilgrims' self-governing religious congregation as the model for their political structure.

Only half of the first migrant group survived until spring, but thereafter Plymouth thrived; the cold climate inhibited the spread of mosquito-borne disease, and the Pilgrims' religious discipline encouraged a strong work ethic. Moreover, a smallpox epidemic in 1618 had devastated the local Wampanoags, minimizing the danger they posed. By 1640, there were 3,000 settlers in Plymouth. To ensure political stability, they established representative self-government, broad political rights, property ownership, and religious freedom of conscience.

Meanwhile, England plunged deeper into religious turmoil. When King Charles I repudiated certain Protestant doctrines, English Puritans, now powerful in Parliament, accused the king of "popery"—of holding Catholic beliefs. In 1629, Charles dissolved Parliament. When his archbishop, William Laud, began to purge Protestant ministers, thousands of **Puritans**—Protestants who (unlike the Pilgrims) did not separate from the Church of England but hoped to purify it of its ceremony and hierarchy—fled to America.

**John Winthrop and Massachusetts Bay**    The Puritan exodus began in 1630 with the departure of 900 migrants led by John Winthrop, a well-educated country squire who became the first governor of the Massachusetts Bay Colony. Calling England morally corrupt and "overburdened with people," Winthrop sought land for his children and a place in Christian history for his people. "We must consider that we shall be as a City upon a Hill," Winthrop told the migrants. "The eyes of all people are upon us." Like the Pilgrims, the Puritans envisioned a reformed Christian society with "authority in magistrates, liberty in people, purity in the church," as minister John Cotton put it. By their example, they hoped to inspire religious reform throughout Christendom.

Winthrop and his associates governed the Massachusetts Bay Colony from the town of Boston. Like the Virginia Company, the Massachusetts Bay Company was a joint-stock corporation. But the colonists transformed the company into a representative political system with a governor, council, and assembly. To ensure rule by the godly, the Puritans limited the right to vote and hold office to men who were church members. Rejecting the Plymouth Colony's policy of religious tolerance, the Massachusetts Bay Colony established Puritanism as the state-supported religion, barred other faiths from conducting services, and used the Bible as a legal guide. "Where there is no Law," they said, magistrates should rule "as near the law of God as they can." Over the next decade, about 10,000 Puritans migrated to the colony, along with 10,000 others fleeing hard times in England.

Seeing bishops as "traitours unto God," the New England Puritans placed power in the congregation of members—hence the name *Congregationalist* for their churches. Inspired by John Calvin, many Puritans embraced predestination, the idea that God saved only a few chosen people. Church members often lived in great anxiety, worried that God had not placed them among the "elect." Some hoped for a conversion experience, the intense sensation of receiving God's grace and being "born again." Other Puritans relied on "preparation," the confidence in salvation that came from spiritual guidance by their ministers. Still others believed that they were God's chosen people, the new Israelites, and would be saved if they obeyed his laws.

**Roger Williams and Rhode Island**   To maintain God's favor, the Massachusetts Bay magistrates purged their society of religious dissidents. One target was Roger Williams, the Puritan minister in Salem, a coastal town north of Boston. Williams opposed the decision to establish an official religion and praised the Pilgrims' separation of church and state. He advocated **toleration**, arguing that political magistrates had authority over only the "bodies, goods, and outward estates of men," not their spiritual lives. Williams also questioned the Puritans' seizure of Indian lands. The magistrates banished him from the colony in 1636.

Williams and his followers settled 50 miles south of Boston, founding the town of Providence on land purchased from the Narragansett Indians. Other religious dissidents settled nearby at Portsmouth and Newport. In 1644, these settlers obtained a corporate charter from Parliament for a new colony — Rhode Island — with full authority to rule themselves. In Rhode Island, as in Plymouth, there was no legally established church, and individuals could worship God as they pleased.

**Anne Hutchinson**   The Massachusetts Bay magistrates saw a second threat to their authority in Anne Hutchinson. The wife of a merchant and mother of seven, Hutchinson held weekly prayer meetings for women and accused various Boston clergymen of placing undue emphasis on good behavior. Like Martin Luther, Hutchinson denied that salvation could be earned through good deeds. There was no "**covenant of works**" that would save the well-behaved, only a "**covenant of grace**" through which God saved those he predestined for salvation. Hutchinson likewise declared that God "revealed" divine truth directly to individual believers, a controversial doctrine that the Puritan magistrates denounced as heretical.

The magistrates also resented Hutchinson because of her sex. Like other Christians, Puritans believed that both men and women could be saved. But gender equality stopped there. Women were inferior to men in earthly affairs, said leading Puritan divines, who told married women: "Thy desires shall bee subject to thy husband, and he shall rule over thee." Puritan women could not be ministers or lay preachers, nor could they vote in church affairs. In 1637, the magistrates accused Hutchinson of teaching that inward grace freed an individual from the rules of the Church and found her guilty of holding heretical views. Banished, she followed Roger Williams into exile in Rhode Island.

Other Puritan groups moved out from Massachusetts Bay in the 1630s and settled on or near the Connecticut River. For several decades, the colonies of Connecticut, New Haven, and Saybrook were independent of one another; in 1660, they secured a charter from King Charles II (r. 1660–1685) for the self-governing colony of Connecticut. Like Massachusetts Bay, Connecticut had a legally established church and an elected governor and assembly; however, it granted voting rights to most property-owning men, not just to church members as in the original Puritan colony.

**Puritan-Pequot War**   Many rival Indian groups lived in New England before Europeans arrived; by the 1630s, these groups were bordered by the Dutch colony of New Netherland to their west and the various English settlements to the east — Plymouth, Massachusetts Bay, Rhode Island, Connecticut, New Haven, and Saybrook. The region's Indian leaders created various alliances for the purposes of trade and defense: Wampanoags with Plymouth; Mohegans with Massachusetts and Connecticut; Pequots with New Netherland; and Narragansetts with Rhode Island.

Because of their alliance with the Dutch, the Pequots became a thorn in the side of English traders. A series of violent encounters began in July 1636 and escalated until May 1637, when a combined force of Massachusetts and Connecticut militiamen, accompanied by Narragansett and Mohegan warriors, attacked a Pequot village and massacred some five hundred men, women, and children. In the months that followed, the New Englanders drove the surviving Pequots into oblivion and divided their lands.

Believing they were God's chosen people, Puritans considered their presence to be divinely ordained. Initially, they pondered the morality of acquiring Native American lands. "By what right or warrant can we enter into the land of the Savages?" they asked themselves. Responding to such concerns, John Winthrop detected God's hand in a recent smallpox epidemic: "If God were not pleased with our inheriting these parts," he asked, "why doth he still make roome for us by diminishing them as we increase?" Experiences like the Pequot War confirmed New Englanders' confidence in their enterprise. "God laughed at the Enemies of his People," one soldier boasted after the 1637 massacre, "filling the Place with Dead Bodies."

Like Catholic missionaries, Puritans believed that their church should embrace all peoples. However, their strong emphasis on predestination—the idea that God saved only a few chosen people—made it hard for them to accept that Indians could be counted among the elect. "Probably the devil" delivered these "miserable savages" to America, Cotton Mather suggested, "in hopes that the gospel of the Lord Jesus Christ would never come here." A few Puritan ministers committed themselves to the effort to convert Indians. On Martha's Vineyard, Jonathan Mayhew helped to create an Indian-led community of Wampanoag Christians. John Eliot translated the Bible into Algonquian and created fourteen Indian praying towns. By 1670, more than 1,000 Indians lived in these settlements, but relatively few Native Americans were ever permitted to become full members of Puritan congregations.

**The Puritan Revolution in England**   Meanwhile, a religious civil war engulfed England. Archbishop Laud had imposed the Church of England prayer book on Presbyterian Scotland in 1637; five years later, a rebel Scottish army invaded England. Thousands of English Puritans (and hundreds of American Puritans) joined the Scots, demanding religious reform and parliamentary power. After years of civil war, parliamentary forces led by Oliver Cromwell emerged victorious. In 1649, Parliament beheaded King Charles I, proclaimed a republican Commonwealth, and banished bishops and elaborate rituals from the Church of England.

The Puritan triumph in England was short-lived. Popular support for the Commonwealth ebbed after Cromwell took dictatorial control in 1653. Following his death in 1658, moderate Protestants and a resurgent aristocracy restored the monarchy and the hierarchy of bishops. With Charles II (r. 1660–1685) on the throne, England's experiment in radical Protestant government came to an end.

For the Puritans in America, the restoration of the monarchy began a new phase of their "errand into the wilderness." They had come to New England expecting to return to Europe in triumph. When the failure of the English Revolution dashed that sacred mission, ministers exhorted congregations to create a godly republican society in America. The Puritan colonies now stood as outposts of Calvinism and the Atlantic republican tradition.

**Puritanism and Witchcraft**   Like Native Americans, Puritans believed that the physical world was full of supernatural forces. Devout Christians saw signs of God's (or Satan's) power in blazing stars, birth defects, and other unusual events. Noting after a storm that the houses of many ministers "had been smitten with Lightning," Cotton Mather, a prominent Puritan theologian, wondered "what the meaning of God should be in it."

Puritans were hostile toward people who they believed tried to manipulate these forces, and many were willing to condemn neighbors as Satan's "wizards" or "witches." People in the town of Andover "were much addicted to sorcery," claimed one observer, and "there were forty men in it that could raise the Devil as well as any astrologer." Between 1647 and 1662, civil authorities in New England hanged fourteen people for witchcraft, most of them older women accused of being "double-tongued" or of having "an unruly spirit."

The most dramatic episode of witch-hunting occurred in Salem in 1692. Several girls who had experienced strange seizures accused neighbors of bewitching them. When judges at the accused witches' trials allowed the use of "spectral" evidence—visions of evil beings and marks seen only by the girls—the accusations spun out of control. Eventually, Massachusetts Bay authorities tried 175 people for witchcraft and executed 19 of them. The causes of this mass hysteria were complex and are still debated. Some historians point to group rivalries: many accusers were the daughters or servants of poor farmers, whereas many of the alleged witches were wealthier church members or their friends. Because 18 of those put to death were women, other historians see the episode as part of a broader Puritan effort to subordinate women. Still others focus on political instability in Massachusetts Bay in the early 1690s and on fears raised by recent Indian attacks in nearby Maine, which had killed the parents of some of the young accusers. It is likely that all of these causes played some role in the executions.

Whatever the cause, the Salem episode marked a major turning point. Shaken by the number of deaths, government officials now discouraged legal prosecutions for witchcraft. Moreover, many influential people embraced the outlook of the European Enlightenment, a major intellectual movement that began around 1675 and promoted a rational, scientific view of the world. Increasingly, educated men

**MAP 2.6   Settlement Patterns in New England Towns, 1630–1700 >**
Throughout New England, colonists pressed onto desirable Indian lands. Initially, most Puritan towns were compact, or nucleated: families lived close to one another in village centers and traveled daily to work in the surrounding fields. This 1640 map of Wethersfield, Connecticut, a town situated on the broad plains of the Connecticut River Valley, shows this pattern clearly. The first settlers in Andover, Massachusetts, also chose to live in the village center. However, the rugged topography of eastern Massachusetts encouraged the townspeople to disperse. By 1692 (as the varied location of new houses shows), many Andover residents were living on farms distant from the village center.

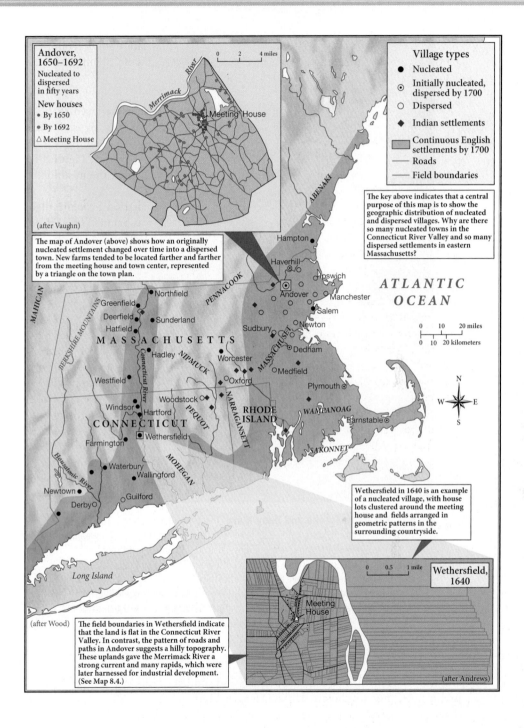

**Andover,
1650–1692**

Nucleated to
dispersed
in fifty years

**New houses**

● By 1650
● By 1692
△ Meeting House

(after Vaughn)

The map of Andover (above) shows how an originally
nucleated settlement changed over time into a dispersed
town. New farms tended to be located farther and farther
from the meeting house and town center, represented
by a triangle on the town plan.

**Village types**

● Nucleated

⊙ Initially nucleated,
   dispersed by 1700

○ Dispersed

◆ Indian settlements

▨ Continuous English
   settlements by 1700

── Roads

── Field boundaries

The key above indicates that a central
purpose of this map is to show the
geographic distribution of nucleated
and dispersed villages. Why are there
so many nucleated towns in the
Connecticut River Valley and so many
dispersed settlements in eastern
Massachusetts?

*ATLANTIC
OCEAN*

Wethersfield in 1640 is an example
of a nucleated village, with house
lots clustered around the meeting
house and fields arranged in
geometric patterns in the
surrounding countryside.

**Wethersfield,
1640**

Meeting
House

(after Andrews)

(after Wood)   The field boundaries in Wethersfield indicate
that the land is flat in the Connecticut River
Valley. In contrast, the pattern of roads and
paths in Andover suggests a hilly topography.
These uplands gave the Merrimack River a
strong current and many rapids, which were
later harnessed for industrial development.
(See Map 8.4.)

*Merrimack River*   Meeting House

Hampton

Haverhill

Ipswich

Andover   Manchester

Salem

Sudbury   Newton

*MASSACHUSETTS*

Northfield

Greenfield
Deerfield
Hatfield   Sunderland

Hadley   *NIPMUCK*   Worcester

Dedham

Westfield   Oxford   Medfield

Woodstock   Plymouth

Windsor   Hartford

*CONNECTICUT*   Wethersfield   *RHODE
ISLAND*   *WAMPANOAG*   Barnstable

Farmington

Waterbury
Wallingford

Newtown   Guilford

Derby

*Long Island*

*MAHICAN*

*BERKSHIRE MOUNTAINS*

*Connecticut River*

*Housatonic River*

*PEQUOT*   *NARRAGANSETT*   *MOHEGAN*   *SAKONNET*

*ABENAKI*

*PENNACOOK*

*MASSACHUSETT*

N
W   E
S

**Mrs. Elizabeth Freake and Baby Mary** This portrait, completed around 1674 by an unknown artist, depicts the wife and youngest daughter of a wealthy Bostonian. Their clothes and surroundings illustrate the growing prosperity of well-to-do households. Mother and child both wear fine linen edged with fine lace. Elizabeth Freake's sleeve is decorated with colorful red and black ribbons and she wears a beaded bracelet on her wrist. They are seated on a chair colorfully upholstered in a style intended to imitate a Turkish carpet. Worcester Art Museum, Massachusetts, USA / Bridgeman Images.

and women explained strange happenings and sudden deaths by reference to "natural causes," not witchcraft. Unlike Cotton Mather (1663–1728), who believed that lightning was a supernatural sign, Benjamin Franklin (1706–1790) and other well-read men of his generation would investigate it as a natural phenomenon.

**A Yeoman Society, 1630–1700**   In building their communities, New England Puritans consciously rejected the feudal practices of English society. Many Puritans came from middling families in East Anglia, a region of pasture lands and few manors, and had no desire to live as tenants of wealthy aristocrats or submit to oppressive taxation by a distant government. They had "escaped out of the pollutions of the world," the settlers of Watertown in Massachusetts Bay declared, and vowed to live "close togither" in self-governing communities. Accordingly, the General Courts of Massachusetts Bay and Connecticut bestowed land on groups of settlers, who then distributed it among the male heads of families.

Widespread ownership of land did not mean equality of wealth or status. "God had Ordained different degrees and orders of men," proclaimed Boston merchant John Saffin, "some to be Masters and Commanders, others to be Subjects, and to be commanded." Town proprietors normally awarded the largest plots to men of high social status who often became selectmen and justices of the peace. However, all families received some land, and most adult men had a vote in the **town meeting**, the main institution of local government (Map 2.6).

In this society of independent households and self-governing communities, ordinary farmers had much more political power than Chesapeake yeomen and European peasants did. Although Nathaniel Fish was one of the poorest men in the town of Barnstable—he owned just a two-room cottage, 8 acres of land, an ox, and a cow—he was a voting member of the town meeting. Each year, Fish and other Barnstable farmers levied taxes; enacted ordinances governing fencing, roadbuilding, and the use of common fields; and chose the selectmen who managed town affairs. The farmers also selected the town's representatives to the General Court, which gradually displaced the governor as the center of political authority. For Fish and thousands of other ordinary settlers, New England had proved to be a new world of opportunity.

| IN YOUR OWN WORDS | What conditions were necessary to establish successful neo-European colonies? |
|---|---|

# Instability, War, and Rebellion

Everywhere in Europe's American colonies, conflicts arose over the control of resources, the legitimacy of colonial leaders' claims to power, and attempts to define social and cultural norms. Periodically, these conflicts flared spectacularly into episodes of violence. Each episode has its own story—its own unique logic and narrative—but taken together, they also illustrate the way that, in their formative stages, colonial societies pressured people to accept new patterns of authority and new claims to power. When these claims were contested, the results could quickly turn deadly.

## Native American Resistance

In the English Northeast and the Spanish Southwest, European claims to power and territory prompted Native American wars of resistance. In New England, Wampanoags and other Indian groups had maintained alliances with neighboring colonies for years. But these relations were unstable, and the potential for violence was never far from the surface. In the Spanish colony of New Mexico, soldiers and missionaries conquered Pueblo communities and ruled by force; there, too, violence was woven into colonial relations, and Native American resistance flared spectacularly.

**Metacom's War, 1675–1676**    By the 1670s, Europeans in New England outnumbered Indians by 3 to 1. The English population had multiplied to 55,000, while Native peoples had diminished from an estimated 120,000 in 1570 to barely 16,000. To the Wampanoag leader Metacom (also known as King Philip), the prospects for coexistence looked dim. When his people copied English ways by raising hogs and selling pork in Boston, Puritan officials accused them of selling at "an under rate" and restricted their trade. When Indians killed wandering hogs that devastated their cornfields, authorities prosecuted them for violating English property rights.

Metacom concluded that the English colonists had to be expelled. In 1675, the Wampanoag leader forged a military alliance with the Narragansetts and Nipmucks and attacked white settlements throughout New England. Almost every day, settler William Harris fearfully reported, he heard new reports of the Indians' "burneing houses, takeing cattell, killing men & women & Children: & carrying others captive." Bitter fighting continued into 1676, ending only when the Indian warriors ran short of gunpowder and the Massachusetts Bay government hired Mohegan and Mohawk warriors, who killed Metacom.

**Metacom's War** of 1675–1676 (which English settlers called King Philip's War) was a deadly affair. Indians destroyed one-fifth of the English towns in Massachusetts and Rhode Island and killed 1,000 settlers, nearly 5 percent of the adult population; for a time the Puritan experiment hung in the balance. But the Natives' losses—from famine and disease, death in battle, and sale into slavery—were much larger: about 4,500 Indians died, one-quarter of an already diminished population. Many of the surviving Wampanoag, Narragansett, and Nipmuck peoples moved west, intermarrying with Algonquian tribes allied to the French. Over the next century, these displaced Indian peoples would take their revenge, joining with French Catholics to attack their Puritan enemies. Metacom's War did not eliminate the presence of Native Americans in southern New England, but it effectively destroyed their existence as independent peoples.

**The Pueblo Revolt**    From the time of their first arrival in Pueblo country in 1540, Spanish soldiers and Franciscan missionaries had attempted to dominate its Indian communities. They demanded tribute, labor, and forced conversions to Catholicism, and they ferociously suppressed resistance. A small minority ruling over a population of some 17,000 people, the Spanish were mistrusted and often hated. A drought beginning in 1660 compounded the Pueblos' misery; one priest wrote, "a great many Indians perished of hunger, lying dead along the roads, in the ravines, and in their huts." In this period of suffering, many Pueblos turned away from Christianity and back to their own holy men and traditional ceremonies. Seeking to suppress these practices, in 1675 Spanish officials hanged three Pueblo priests and whipped dozens of others as punishment for sorcery.

One of the convicted sorcerers was a religious leader from San Juan Pueblo named Popé. Five years later, he organized a complex military offensive against the Spanish that came to be known as the **Pueblo Revolt** (also called Popé's Rebellion). Drawing on warriors from two dozen pueblos spread across several hundred miles and speaking six languages, Popé orchestrated an uprising that liberated the pueblos and culminated in the capture of Santa Fe; 400 Spaniards were killed; the remaining 2,100 fled south. New Mexico was in Pueblo hands. Under the leadership of Diego de Vargas, the Spanish returned and recaptured Santa Fe in 1693; three years later, they had reclaimed most of the pueblos of New Mexico. But Spanish policy was redirected by the revolt. Officials reduced their labor demands on Pueblo communities, and across the Southwest—from Baja California to Tejas y Coahuila—Spain relied on Indian missions to create a defensive perimeter against their Ute, Apache, and Navajo neighbors.

In the century that followed, Jesuit and Franciscan missionaries built a dense network of missions extending north from Mexico along the coast of Baja and Alta (or lower and upper) California. From San José del Cabo in the south to San Francisco in the north, these institutions sought to pacify Native peoples and transform their ways of life. Massive waves of smallpox, typhus, and other diseases drove surviving Indians to the missions; their desperation often accomplished what the faithful labors of missionaries could not. Throughout coastal California, remnant Indian populations gravitated toward mission communities and the sustenance and protection they could offer.

## Bacon's Rebellion

At about the same time that New England fought its war with Metacom and the Pueblos took up arms with Popé, Virginia was wracked by a rebellion that nearly toppled its government. It, too, grew out of a conflict with neighboring Indians, but this one inspired a popular uprising against the colony's royal governor. Like Metacom's War, it highlighted the way that a land-intensive settler colony created friction with Native American populations; in addition, it dramatized the way that ordinary colonists could challenge the authority of a new planter elite to rule over them.

By the 1670s, economic and political power in Virginia was in the hands of a small circle of men who amassed land, slaves, and political offices. Through headrights and royal grants, they controlled nearly half of all the settled land in Virginia. What they could not plant themselves, they leased to tenants. Freed indentured servants found it ever harder to get land of their own; many were forced to lease lands, or even sign new indentures, to make ends meet. To make matters worse, the price of tobacco fell until planters received only a penny a pound for their crops in the 1670s.

At the top of Virginia's narrow social pyramid was William Berkeley, governor between 1642 and 1652 and again after 1660. To consolidate power, Berkeley bestowed large land grants on members of his council. The councilors exempted these lands from taxation and appointed friends as justices of the peace and county judges. To win support in the House of Burgesses, Berkeley bought off legislators with land grants and lucrative appointments as sheriffs and tax collectors. But social unrest erupted when the Burgesses took the vote away from landless freemen, who by now constituted half the adult white men. Although property-holding yeomen retained their voting rights, they were angered by falling tobacco prices, political corruption, and "grievous taxations" that threatened the "utter ruin of us the poor commonalty." Berkeley and his allies were living on borrowed time.

**Frontier War** An Indian conflict ignited the flame of social rebellion. In 1607, when the English intruded, 30,000 Native Americans resided in Virginia; by 1675, the Native population had dwindled to only 3,500. By then, Europeans numbered some 38,000 and Africans another 2,500. Most Indians lived on treaty-guaranteed territory along the frontier, where poor freeholders and landless former servants now wanted to settle, demanding that the Natives be expelled or exterminated. Their demands were ignored by wealthy planters, who wanted a ready supply of tenants and laborers, and by Governor Berkeley and the planter-merchants, who traded with the Occaneechee Indians for beaver pelts and deerskins.

Fighting broke out late in 1675, when a vigilante band of Virginia militiamen murdered 30 Indians. Defying Berkeley's orders, a larger force then surrounded a fortified Susquehannock village and killed 5 leaders who came out to negotiate. The Susquehannocks retaliated by attacking outlying plantations and killing 300 whites. In response, Berkeley proposed a defensive strategy: a series of frontier forts to deter Indian intrusions. The settlers dismissed this scheme as a militarily useless plot by planter-merchants to impose high taxes and take "all our tobacco into their own hands."

**Challenging the Government**   Enter Nathaniel Bacon, a young, well-connected migrant from England who emerged as the leader of the rebels. Bacon held a position on the governor's council, but he was shut out of Berkeley's inner circle and differed with Berkeley on Indian policy. When the governor refused to grant him a military commission, Bacon mobilized his neighbors and attacked any Indians he could find. Condemning the frontiersmen as "rebels and mutineers," Berkeley expelled Bacon from the council and had him arrested. But Bacon's army forced the governor to release their leader and hold legislative elections. The newly elected House of Burgesses enacted far-reaching reforms that curbed the powers of the governor and council and restored voting rights to landless freemen.

These much-needed reforms came too late. Poor farmers and servants resented years of exploitation by wealthy planters, arrogant justices of the peace, and "wicked & pernicious Counsellors." As one yeoman rebel complained, "A poor man who has only his labour to maintain himself and his family pays as much [in taxes] as a man who has 20,000 acres." Backed by 400 armed men, Bacon issued a "Manifesto and Declaration of the People" that demanded the removal of Indians and an end to the rule of wealthy "parasites." "All the power and sway is got into the hands of the rich," Bacon proclaimed as his army burned Jamestown to the ground and plundered the plantations of Berkeley's allies. When Bacon died suddenly of dysentery in October 1676, the governor took revenge, dispersing the rebel army, seizing the estates of well-to-do rebels, and hanging 23 men.

In the wake of Bacon's Rebellion, Virginia's leaders worked harder to appease their humble neighbors. But the rebellion also coincided with the time when Virginia planters were switching from indentured servants, who became free after four years, to slaves, who labored for life. In the eighteenth century, wealthy planters would make common cause with poorer whites, while slaves became the colony's most exploited workers. That fateful change eased tensions within the free population but committed subsequent generations of Americans to a labor system based on racial exploitation. Bacon's Rebellion, like Metacom's War, reminds us that these colonies were unfinished worlds, still searching for viable foundations.

| IN YOUR OWN WORDS | What did these three rebellions—Metacom's War, the Pueblo Revolt, and Bacon's Rebellion—have in common? |

# Summary

During the sixteenth and seventeenth centuries, three types of colonies took shape in the Americas. In Mesoamerica and the Andes, Spanish colonists made indigenous empires their own, capitalizing on preexisting labor systems and using tribute and the discovery of precious metals to generate enormous wealth, which Philip II used to defend the interests of the Catholic Church in Europe. In tropical and subtropical regions, colonizers transferred the plantation complex—a centuries-old form of production and labor discipline—to places suited to growing exotic crops like sugar, tobacco, and indigo. The rigors of plantation agriculture demanded a large supply of labor, which was first filled in English colonies by indentured servants and later supplemented and eclipsed by African slaves. The third type of colony, neo-European settlement, developed in North America's temperate zone, where European migrants adapted familiar systems of social and economic organization in new settings.

Everywhere in the Americas, colonization was, first and foremost, a process of experimentation. As resources from the Americas flowed to Europe, monarchies were strengthened and the competition among them—sharpened by the schism between Protestants and Catholics—gained new force and energy. Establishing colonies demanded political, social, and cultural innovations that threw Europeans, Native Americans, and Africans together in bewildering circumstances, triggered massive ecological change through the Columbian Exchange, and demanded radical adjustments. In the Chesapeake and New England—the two earliest regions of English settlement on mainland North America—the adjustment to new circumstances sparked conflict with neighboring Indians and waves of instability within the colonies. These external and internal crises were products of the struggle to adapt to the rigors of colonization.

## Chapter 2 Review

### KEY TERMS

**Identify and explain the significance of each term below.**

chattel slavery (p. 35)

neo-Europes (p. 36)

*encomienda* (p. 36)

casta system (p. 37)

Columbian Exchange (p. 37)

mercantilism (p. 40)

joint-stock corporation (p. 42)

House of Burgesses (p. 44)

royal colony (p. 44)

freeholds (p. 45)

headright system (p. 45)

indentured servitude (p. 48)

Pilgrims (p. 54)

Puritans (p. 55)

toleration (p. 56)

covenant of works (p. 56)

covenant of grace (p. 56)

town meeting (p. 61)

Metacom's War (p. 62)

Pueblo Revolt (p. 62)

## REVIEW QUESTIONS

Answer these questions to demonstrate your understanding of the chapter's main ideas.

1. How did Spanish colonization affect people in the Americas and in Europe?
2. How did the labor demands of plantation colonies transform the process of colonization?
3. What conditions were necessary to establish successful neo-European colonies?
4. What did these three rebellions—Metacom's War, the Pueblo Revolt, and Bacon's Rebellion—have in common?
5. Review the events listed under "Politics and Power" and "Culture and Society" on the thematic timeline on pages 4–5. How did political developments in seventeenth-century England impact the development of its American colonies?

## CHRONOLOGY

As you read, ask yourself why this chapter begins and ends with these dates and then identify the links among related events.

| | |
|---|---|
| **1521** | • Aztec Empire falls to the Spanish |
| **1550–1630** | • English crown supports mercantilism |
| **1556–1598** | • Reign of Philip II, king of Spain |
| **1558–1603** | • Reign of Elizabeth I, queen of England |
| **1560–1620** | • Growth of English Puritan movement |
| **1577–1580** | • Francis Drake's *Golden Hind* circles the globe, captures Spanish treasure fleet |
| **1588** | • Storms and English ships destroy Spanish Armada |
| **1603–1625** | • Reign of James I, king of England |
| **1607** | • English traders settle Jamestown (Virginia) |
| **1608** | • Samuel de Champlain founds Quebec |
| **1609** | • Henry Hudson explores North America for the Dutch |
| **1614** | • Dutch set up fur-trading post at Fort Orange (Albany) |
| **1619** | • First Africans arrive in Chesapeake region |
| | • House of Burgesses convenes in Virginia |
| **1620** | • Pilgrims found Plymouth Colony |

| 1620–1660 | • Chesapeake colonies enjoy tobacco boom |
| 1621 | • Dutch West India Company chartered |
| 1622 | • Opechancanough's uprising |
| 1624 | • Virginia becomes royal colony |
| 1625–1649 | • Reign of Charles I, king of England |
| 1630 | • Puritans found Massachusetts Bay Colony |
| 1634 | • Colonists arrive in Maryland |
| 1636 | • Beginning of Puritan-Pequot War |
| | • Roger Williams founds Providence |
| 1637 | • Anne Hutchinson banished from Massachusetts Bay |
| 1640s | • Iroquois initiate wars over fur trade |
| 1642–1659 | • Puritan Revolution in England |
| 1660 | • Restoration of the English monarchy |
| | • Tobacco prices fall and remain low |
| 1664 | • English conquer New Netherland |
| 1675–1676 | • Bacon's Rebellion in Virginia |
| | • Metacom's War in New England |
| 1692 | • Salem witchcraft trials |

# PART 2

Between 1607 and 1763, English North America took root and flourished. From its unpromising beginnings in Jamestown, where colonists struggled simply to survive, England's colonies grew quickly in number and then, after 1680, became dramatically more populous and diverse. To begin Part 2, we reach back to 1607, the date when Jamestown was founded and permanent English colonization began. We end Part 2 a century and a half later, in 1763, with Britain's victory in the Great War for Empire. The choice to include the Great War in Part 2—thus ending in 1763 rather than 1754—allows us to understand how imperial rivalry and warfare underlay the colonial North American experience in the eighteenth century. By 1763, Britain became the dominant power in eastern North America, and its colonies contained nearly two million subjects.

The rise of British North America occurred amid great changes. Instead of a barrier to contact, the Atlantic Ocean became a watery highway carrying people, merchandise, and ideas. Trade caused more intensive interactions with Europe that knit together the increasingly diverse societies of British North America. After 1689, Europe plunged into a century of warfare that spilled over into North America. British, French, and Spanish colonies all turned to Indian allies for help, fundamentally changing the character of cross-cultural relations. The Great War for Empire transformed the map of North America, making Great Britain ascendant in eastern North America, while also creating new challenges for everyone living there.

We give particular attention in Part 2 to the following three main concepts.

## The Diversification of British North America

The American colonies of the various European nations gradually diverged from each other in character. The core of Spanish America developed into complex multiracial societies, while Portuguese Brazil was dominated by plantations and mining. The Dutch kept only a few tropical plantation colonies; the French also had valuable plantation colonies but struggled to populate their vast North American holdings. Britain's mainland colonies, by contrast, gradually stabilized and then grew and diversified rapidly. Britain came to dominate the Atlantic slave trade and brought more than two million slaves across the Atlantic. Most went to Jamaica and Barbados, but half a million found their way to the mainland. Slavery was a growing and thriving institution in British North America.

Many non-English Europeans also came to British North America, including more than 200,000 Germans and Scots-Irish. Most immigrated to Pennsylvania, which soon had the most ethnically diverse population of Europeans on the continent. These groups struggled to maintain their identities in a rapidly changing landscape.

# British North America and the Atlantic World 1607–1763

## Rise of the British Atlantic World

These population movements were part of the larger growth and development of the British Atlantic world. Britain's transatlantic shipping networks laid the foundation for rising economic productivity and dramatic cultural transformations. The cultural impact of this change grew out of two further developments: the print revolution, which brought many ideas into circulation; and the consumer revolution, which flooded the Atlantic world with a variety of newly available merchandise.

Four new cultural developments emerged in the British Atlantic world. A transatlantic community interested in science and rationalism shared Enlightenment ideas; Pietists promoted the revival and expansion of Christianity; well-to-do colonists gained access to genteel values and the finery needed to put them into action; and colonial consumers went further into debt than they ever had before.

## Contact and Conflict

In Europe, the period after 1689 has sometimes been called the Second Hundred Years' War, when Britain, France, and their European allies went to war against each other repeatedly. As these conflicts came to the North American theater, they decisively influenced Indian relations. The Columbian Exchange had devastated Native American populations. The rise of imperial warfare encouraged the process of tribalization, whereby Indians regrouped into political structures—called tribes by Europeans—to deal with their colonial neighbors and strike alliances in times of war. Europeans, in turn, used Indian allies as proxy warriors in their conflicts over North American territory.

This pattern culminated in the Great War for Empire, which began in North America and reshaped its map. The Treaty of Paris of 1763 gave Britain control of the entire continent east of the Mississippi. Events would soon show what a mixed blessing that outcome was, for Native Americans, colonists, and British administrators alike.

## Thematic Understanding

This timeline organizes some of the important developments of this period into themes. How did the demographic changes outlined under the theme "Migration and Settlement" impact the developments that are listed under "Work, Exchange, and Technology"?

| | AMERICAN AND NATIONAL IDENTITY | POLITICS AND POWER | WORK, EXCHANGE, AND TECHNOLOGY |
|---|---|---|---|
| **1607** | • English colonies founded<br>• English civil war allows colonial "big men" to govern | • Colonial elites establish their authority<br>• King Charles I beheaded by Parliament (1649) | • Indentured servants provide labor in the Chesapeake<br>• Yeoman society takes root in New England |
| **1660** | • The Glorious Revolution makes England a constitutional monarchy<br>• Massachusetts loses its charter (1684) and gains a new one (1691) | • Dominion of New England (1686–1689)<br>• Glorious Revolution (1688–1689)<br>• Founding of the Restoration Colonies: the Carolinas (1663), New York (1664), New Jersey (1664), Pennsylvania (1681) | • South Atlantic System links plantation and neo-European colonies<br>• English Navigation Acts (1651, 1660, 1663)<br>• African slavery supports sugar, tobacco, and rice plantation systems |
| **1690** | • Colonists gain autonomy in the post–Glorious Revolution era<br>• Tribalization develops among Native American peoples | • Parliament creates Board of Trade (1696)<br>• War of the Spanish Succession (1702–1713) | • New England shipbuilders and merchants dominate the coastal trade<br>• Agricultural labor and artisanal skills in high demand in the Middle colonies |
| **1720** | • African American community forms in the Chesapeake<br>• Planter aristocracy emerges in the Chesapeake and South Carolina<br>• Gentility spreads among well-to-do | • Robert Walpole is prime minister (1720–1742)<br>• Stono Rebellion (1739)<br>• War of Jenkins's Ear (1739–1741) and the Austrian Succession (1740–1748) | • British trade dominates the Atlantic<br>• Opportunity and inequality in the Middle colonies<br>• Ohio Company of Virginia receives 200,000 acres (1749) |
| **1750** | • Great War for Empire sparks pro-British pride in the colonies<br>• Desire for political and economic autonomy grows | • French and Indian War/Seven Years' War (1754–1763)<br>• Treaty of Paris (1763)<br>• Pontiac's War (1763) | • Freehold society in crisis in New England<br>• Conflicts over western lands and political power (1750–1775) |

| CULTURE AND SOCIETY | MIGRATION AND SETTLEMENT | GEOGRAPHY AND THE ENVIRONMENT | AMERICA IN THE WORLD | |
|---|---|---|---|---|
| • Puritan magistrates and tobacco planters govern the colonies | • Male laborers migrate to the Chesapeake<br>• Migration to New England brings intact households | • Tobacco takes root in the Chesapeake | • England intermittently ignores its American colonies | 1607 |
| • Collapse of the Puritan Commonwealth leads to toleration in England<br>• Isaac Newton publishes *Principia Mathematica* (1687) | • The Middle Passage shapes Africans' experiences of arrival<br>• Indian slave trade emerges in South Carolina<br>• First Mennonites arrive in Pennsylvania (1683) | • Native American populations of the eastern woodlands decline catastrophically<br>• African Americans are imported to tropical and semitropical colonies in large numbers | • England's proprietary colonies claim much of the Atlantic coast of North America | 1660 |
| • John Locke publishes *Two Treatises on Government* (1690)<br>• Rise of toleration among colonial Protestants<br>• Print revolution begins | • Quakers emigrate to Pennsylvania and New Jersey<br>• Second wave of Germans arrives in Pennsylvania, Shenandoah Valley | • Rice cultivation begins in the Carolina and Georgia low country<br>• New England fish feed southern Europe and Caribbean slaves | • European wars begin to spill onto American shores<br>• Pennsylvania begins to draw large numbers of Scots-Irish and German migrants | 1690 |
| • George Whitefield's visit to America sparks the Great Awakening (1739)<br>• Benjamin Franklin founds American Philosophical Society (1743) | • Scots-Irish begin migrating to Pennsylvania (c. 1720)<br>• Parliament charters Georgia (1732)<br>• Penns make Walking Purchase from the Delawares (1737) | • The pace of transatlantic shipping accelerates<br>• A road network begins to knit together colonial towns | • The South Atlantic System connects America, Africa, and Europe<br>• Mercantilism shapes England's policies toward its American colonies | 1720 |
| • New colleges, newspapers, and magazines<br>• Neolin promotes nativist revival among Ohio Indians (1763) | • 40,000 Germans and Swiss emigrate to Pennsylvania<br>• Anglo-Americans push onto backcountry lands | • The size of North America challenges European armies in the French and Indian War | • Britain wins the Great War for Empire and claims eastern North America | 1750 |

# 3

# The British Atlantic World

## 1607–1750

**IDENTIFY THE BIG IDEA**

How did the South Atlantic System create an interconnected Atlantic world, and how did this system impact development in the British colonies?

**FOR TWO WEEKS IN JUNE 1744, THE TOWN OF LANCASTER,** Pennsylvania, hosted more than 250 Iroquois men, women, and children for a diplomatic conference with representatives from Pennsylvania, Maryland, and Virginia. Crowds of curious observers thronged Lancaster's streets and courthouse. The conference grew out of a diplomatic system between the colonies and the Iroquois designed to air grievances and resolve conflict: the Covenant Chain. Participants welcomed each other, exchanged speeches, and negotiated agreements in public ceremonies whose minutes became part of the official record of the colonies.

At Lancaster, the colonies had much to ask of their Iroquois allies. For one thing, they wanted them to confirm a land agreement. The Iroquois often began such conferences by resisting land deals; as the Cayuga orator Gachradodon said, "You know very well, when the White people came first here they were poor; but now they have got our Lands, and are by them become rich, and we are now poor; what little we have had for the Land goes soon away, but the Land lasts forever." In the end, however, they had little choice but to accept merchandise in exchange for land, since colonial officials were unwilling to take no for an answer. The colonists also announced that Britain was once again going to war with France, and they requested military support from their Iroquois allies. Canassatego—a tall, commanding Onondaga orator, about sixty years old, renowned for his eloquence—replied, "We shall never forget that you and we have but one

Heart, one Head, one Eye, one Ear, and one Hand. We shall have all your Country under our Eye, and take all the Care we can to prevent any Enemy from coming into it."

The Lancaster conference—and dozens of others like it—demonstrates that the British colonies, like those of France and Spain, relied ever more heavily on alliances with Native Americans as they sought to extend their power in North America. Indian nations remade themselves in these same years, creating political structures—called "tribes" by Europeans—that allowed them to regroup in the face of population decline and function more effectively alongside neighboring colonies. The colonies, meanwhile, were drawn together into an integrated economic sphere—the South Atlantic System—that brought prosperity to British North America, while they achieved a measure of political autonomy that became essential to their understanding of what it meant to be British subjects.

# Colonies to Empire, 1607–1713

Before 1660, England governed its New England and Chesapeake colonies haphazardly. Taking advantage of that laxness and the English civil war, local "big men" (Puritan magistrates and tobacco planters) ran their societies as they wished. Following the restoration of the monarchy in 1660, royal bureaucrats tried to impose order on the unruly settlements and, enlisting the aid of Indian allies, warred with rival European powers.

## Self-Governing Colonies and New Elites, 1607–1660

In the years after its first American colonies were founded, England experienced a wrenching series of political crises. Disagreements between King Charles I and Parliament grew steadily worse until they culminated in the English civil war, which lasted from 1642 to 1651. A parliamentary army led by Oliver Cromwell fought against royalist forces for control of the country. Charles I was captured by Cromwell's army, tried for treason, and beheaded in 1649. Charles II, his son and successor, carried on the war for two more years but was defeated in 1651 and fled to France. England was no longer a monarchy. It was ruled by Parliament as a commonwealth, then fell under the personal rule of Oliver Cromwell, who was known as the Lord Protector. Cromwell's death in 1658 triggered a political crisis that led Parliament to invite Charles II to restore the monarchy and take up the throne.

During the long period of instability and crisis in England, its American colonies largely managed their own affairs. Neither crown nor Parliament devised a consistent system of imperial administration; in these years, England had colonies but no empire. Moreover, these were difficult years for all the colonies, when important decisions about the nature of the economy, the government, and the social system had to be worked out through trial and error (see Chapter 2). In this era of intense experimentation and struggle, emerging colonial elites often had to arrive at their own solutions to pressing problems. Leading men in Virginia, Maryland, the New England colonies, and the islands of the West Indies claimed authority and hammered out political systems that allowed the colonies to be largely self-governing. Even in colonies with crown-appointed governors, such as Sir William Berkeley in Virginia, it soon became apparent that those appointees had to make alliances with local leaders in order to be effective.

The restoration of the crown in 1660 marked a decisive end to this period of near-independence in the colonies. Charles II (r. 1660–1685) and his brother and successor, James II (r. 1685–1688), were deeply interested in England's overseas possessions and dramatically reshaped colonial enterprise. From England's early, prolonged, halting efforts to sponsor overseas activity, an empire finally began to take shape.

## The Restoration Colonies and Imperial Expansion

Charles II expanded English power in Asia and America. In 1662, he married the Portuguese princess Catherine of Braganza, whose dowry included the islands of Bombay (present-day Mumbai, India). Then, in 1663, Charles initiated new outposts in America by authorizing eight loyal noblemen to settle Carolina, an area that had long been claimed by Spain and was populated by thousands of Indians. The following year, he awarded the just-conquered Dutch colony of New Netherland to his brother James, the Duke of York, who renamed the colony New York and then re-granted a portion of it, called New Jersey, to another group of proprietors. Finally, in 1681, Charles granted a vast tract to William Penn — Pennsylvania, or "Penn's Woods." In a great land grab, England had ousted the Dutch from North America, intruded into Spain's northern empire, and claimed all the land in between.

### The Carolinas   In 1660, English settlement was concentrated in New England and the Chesapeake. Five corporate colonies coexisted in New England: Massachusetts Bay, Plymouth, Connecticut, New Haven, and Rhode Island. (Connecticut absorbed New Haven in 1662, while Massachusetts Bay became a royal colony and absorbed Plymouth in 1692.) In the Chesapeake, Virginia was controlled by the crown while Maryland was in the hands of a Lord Proprietor. Like Lord Baltimore's Maryland, the new settlements in Carolina, New York, New Jersey, and Pennsylvania — the Restoration Colonies, as historians call them — were **proprietorships**. The Carolina and Jersey grantees, the Duke of York, and William Penn owned all the land in their new colonies and could rule them as they wished, provided that their laws conformed broadly to those of England. Indeed, in New York, James II refused to allow an elective assembly and ruled by decree. The Carolina proprietors envisioned a traditional European society; they hoped to implement a manorial system, with a mass of serfs governed by a handful of powerful nobles.

The manorial system proved a fantasy. The first North Carolina settlers were a mixture of poor families and runaway servants from Virginia and English Quakers, an equality-minded Protestant sect (also known as the Society of Friends). Quakers "think there is no difference between a Gentleman and a labourer," complained an Anglican clergyman. Refusing to work on large manors, the settlers raised corn, hogs, and tobacco on modest family farms. Inspired by Bacon's Rebellion, they rebelled in

1677 against taxes on tobacco and again in 1708 against taxes to support the Anglican Church. Through their stubborn independence, residents forced the proprietors to abandon their dreams of a manorial society.

In South Carolina, the colonists also went their own way. The leading white settlers there were migrants from overcrowded Barbados. Hoping to re-create that island's hierarchical slave society, they used enslaved workers—both Africans and Native Americans—to raise cattle and food crops for export to the West Indies. Carolina merchants opened a lucrative trade in deerskins and Indian slaves with neighboring peoples. Then, around 1700, South Carolina planters hit upon rice cultivation. The swampy estuaries of the coastal low country could be modified with sluices, floodgates, and check dams to create ideal rice-growing conditions, and slaves could do the backbreaking work. By 1708, white South Carolinians relied upon a few thousand slaves to work their coastal plantations; thereafter, the African population exploded. Blacks outnumbered whites by 1710 and constituted two-thirds of the population by 1740.

**William Penn and Pennsylvania**  In contrast to the Carolinas, which languished for decades with proprietors and colonists at odds, William Penn's colony was marked by unity of purpose: all who came hoped to create a prosperous neo-European settlement similar to the societies they knew at home. Penn, though born to wealth—he owned substantial estates in Ireland and England and lived lavishly—joined the **Quakers**, who condemned extravagance. Penn designed his colony as a refuge for his fellow Quakers, who were persecuted in England because they refused to serve in the military or pay taxes to support the Church of England. Penn himself had spent more than two years in jail in England for preaching his beliefs.

Like the Puritans, the Quakers sought to restore Christianity to its early simple spirituality. But they rejected the Puritans' pessimistic Calvinist doctrines, which restricted salvation to a small elect. The Quakers followed the teachings of two English visionaries, George Fox and Margaret Fell, who argued that God had imbued all men—and women—with an "inner light" of grace or understanding. Reflecting the sect's emphasis on gender equality, 350 Quaker women would serve as ministers in the colonies.

Mindful of the catastrophic history of Indian relations in the Chesapeake and New England, Penn exhorted colonists to "sit downe Lovingly" alongside the Native American inhabitants of the Delaware and Susquehanna valleys. He wrote a letter to the leaders of the Iroquois Confederacy alerting them to his intention to settle a colony, and in 1682 he arranged a public treaty with the Delaware Indians to purchase the lands that Philadelphia and the surrounding settlements would soon occupy.

Penn's Frame of Government (1681) applied the Quakers' radical beliefs to politics. It ensured religious freedom by prohibiting a legally established church, and it promoted political equality by allowing all property-owning men to vote and hold office. Cheered by these provisions, thousands of English Quakers flocked to Pennsylvania. To attract European Protestants, Penn published pamphlets in Germany promising cheap land and religious toleration. In 1683, migrants from Saxony founded Germantown (just outside Philadelphia), and thousands of other Germans soon followed. Ethnic diversity, pacifism, and freedom of conscience made Pennsylvania the most open and democratic of the Restoration Colonies.

## From Mercantilism to Imperial Dominion

As Charles II distributed American land, his ministers devised policies to keep colonial trade in English hands. Since the 1560s, the English crown had pursued mercantilist policies, using government subsidies and charters to stimulate English manufacturing and foreign trade. Now it extended these mercantilist strategies to the American settlements through the **Navigation Acts**.

**The Navigation Acts**    Dutch and French shippers were often buying sugar and other colonial products from English colonies and carrying them directly into foreign markets. To counter this practice, the Navigation Act of 1651 required that goods be carried on ships owned by English or colonial merchants. New parliamentary acts in

PENNS TREATY with the INDIANS, made 1681 without an Oath, and never broken. The foundation of Religious and Civil LIBERTY, in the U.S. of AMERICA.

**Edward Hicks, *Penn's Treaty*, c. 1830–1835**  Edward Hicks was a Pennsylvania-born painter and preacher whose art expressed a religiously infused understanding of early Pennsylvania history. In more than a hundred paintings, Hicks depicted the colony as a "peaceable kingdom," in which lions lay down with lambs and colonists met peacefully with Native Americans. This painting, which features Hicks's characteristic folk art style, depicts William Penn's first meeting with the Lenni-Lenape peoples in 1683. A Quaker pacifist, Penn refused to seize Indian lands by force and instead negotiated their purchase. This spirit of peaceful cooperation eroded in the later colonial era, but Hicks chose to portray Penn's meeting with the Indians as the foundation of religious and civil liberty in America. Private Collection / Bridgeman Images.

1660 and 1663 strengthened the ban on foreign traders: colonists could export sugar and tobacco only to England and import European goods only through England; moreover, three-quarters of the crew on English vessels had to be English. To pay the customs officials who enforced these laws, the Revenue Act of 1673 imposed a "plantation duty" on American exports of sugar and tobacco.

The English government backed these policies with military force. In three wars between 1652 and 1674, the English navy drove the Dutch from New Netherland and contested Holland's control of the Atlantic slave trade by attacking Dutch forts and ships along the West African coast. Meanwhile, English merchants expanded their fleets, which increased in capacity from 150,000 tons in 1640 to 340,000 tons in 1690. This growth occurred on both sides of the Atlantic; by 1702, only London and Bristol had more ships registered in port than did the town of Boston.

Though colonial ports benefitted from the growth of English shipping, many colonists violated the Navigation Acts. Planters continued to trade with Dutch shippers, and New England merchants imported sugar and molasses from the French West Indies. The Massachusetts Bay assembly boldly declared: "The laws of England are bounded within the seas [surrounding it] and do not reach America." Outraged by this insolence, customs official Edward Randolph called for troops to "reduce Massachusetts to obedience." Instead, the Lords of Trade — the administrative body charged with colonial affairs — chose a less violent, but no less confrontational, strategy. In 1679, it denied the claim of Massachusetts Bay to New Hampshire and eventually established a separate royal colony there. Then, in 1684, the Lords of Trade persuaded an English court to annul the Massachusetts Bay charter by charging the Puritan government with violating the Navigation Acts and virtually outlawing the Church of England.

**The Dominion of New England**    The Puritans' troubles had only begun, thanks to the accession of King James II (r. 1685–1688), an aggressive and inflexible ruler. During the reign of Oliver Cromwell, James had grown up in exile in France, and he admired its authoritarian king, Louis XIV. James wanted stricter control over the colonies and targeted New England for his reforms. In 1686, the Lords of Trade revoked the charters of Connecticut and Rhode Island and merged them with Massachusetts Bay and Plymouth to form a new royal province, the **Dominion of New England**. James II appointed Sir Edmund Andros, a hard-edged former military officer, as governor of the Dominion. Two years later, James II added New York and New Jersey to the Dominion, creating a vast colony that stretched from Maine to Pennsylvania (Map 3.1).

The Dominion extended to America the authoritarian model of colonial rule that the English government had imposed on Catholic Ireland. James II ordered Governor Andros to abolish the existing legislative assemblies. In Massachusetts, Andros banned town meetings, angering villagers who prized local self-rule. Andros also advocated public worship in the Church of England, offending Puritan Congregationalists. Even worse, from the colonists' perspective, the governor invalidated all land titles granted under the original Massachusetts Bay charter. Andros offered to provide new deeds, but only if the colonists would pay an annual fee. James's plan for the Dominion of New England made it clear that he intended to rule his overseas possessions as an absolute monarch, rejecting the institutions and rights that colonists had come to expect.

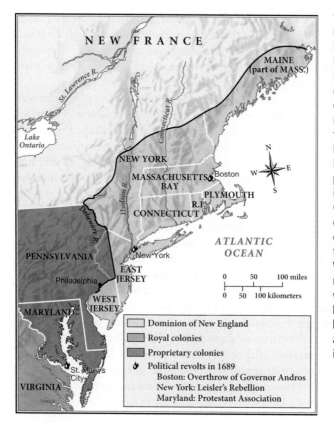

**MAP 3.1    The Dominion of New England, 1686–1689**
In the Dominion, James II created a vast royal colony that stretched nearly 500 miles along the Atlantic coast. During the Glorious Revolution in England, politicians and ministers in Boston and New York City led revolts that ousted Dominion officials and repudiated their authority. King William and Queen Mary replaced the Dominion with governments that balanced the power held by imperial authorities and local political institutions.

## The Glorious Revolution in England and America

Fortunately for the colonists, James II angered English political leaders as much as Andros alienated colonists. The king revoked the charters of English towns, rejected the advice of Parliament, and aroused popular opposition by openly practicing Roman Catholicism. Then, in 1688, James's Spanish Catholic wife gave birth to a son. Faced with a Catholic heir to the English throne, Protestant bishops and parliamentary leaders in the Whig Party invited William of Orange, a staunchly Protestant Dutch prince who was married to James's Protestant daughter, Mary Stuart, to come to England at the head of an invading army. With their support, William led a quick and nearly bloodless coup, and King James II was overthrown in an event dubbed the **Glorious Revolution** by its supporters. Whig politicians forced King William and Queen Mary to accept the Declaration of Rights, creating a constitutional monarchy that enhanced the powers of the House of Commons at the expense of the crown. The Whigs wanted political power, especially the power to levy taxes, to reside in the hands of the gentry, merchants, and other substantial property owners.

To justify their coup, the members of Parliament relied on political philosopher John Locke. In his *Two Treatises on Government* (1690), Locke rejected the divine-right monarchy celebrated by James II, arguing that the legitimacy of government rests on the consent of the governed and that individuals have inalienable natural rights to life, liberty, and property. Locke's celebration of individual rights and representative government had a lasting influence in America, where many political leaders wanted to expand the powers of the colonial assemblies.

**Rebellions in America**   The Glorious Revolution sparked rebellions by Protestant colonists in Massachusetts, Maryland, and New York. When news of the coup reached Boston in April 1689, Puritan leaders and 2,000 militiamen seized Governor Andros and shipped him back to England. Heeding American complaints of authoritarian rule, the new monarchs broke up the Dominion of New England. However, they refused to restore the old Puritan-dominated government of Massachusetts Bay, instead creating in 1692 a new royal colony (which absorbed Plymouth and Maine). The new charter empowered the king to appoint the governor and customs officials, gave the vote to all male property owners (not just Puritan church members), and eliminated Puritan restrictions on the Church of England.

In Maryland, the uprising had economic as well as religious causes. Since 1660, falling tobacco prices had hurt poorer farmers, who were overwhelmingly Protestant, while taxes and fees paid to mostly Catholic proprietary officials continued to rise. When Parliament ousted James II, a Protestant association mustered 700 men and forcibly removed the Catholic governor. The Lords of Trade supported this Protestant initiative: they suspended Lord Baltimore's proprietorship, imposed royal government, and made the Church of England the legal religion in the colony. This arrangement lasted until 1715, when Benedict Calvert, the fourth Lord Baltimore, converted to the Anglican faith and the king restored the proprietorship to the Calvert family.

In New York, a Dutchman named Jacob Leisler led the rebellion against the Dominion of New England. Initially he enjoyed broad support, but he soon alienated many English-speaking New Yorkers and well-to-do Dutch residents. Leisler's heavy-handed tactics made him vulnerable; when William and Mary appointed Henry Sloughter as governor in 1691, Leisler was indicted for treason, hanged, and decapitated.

The Glorious Revolution of 1688–1689 began a new era in the politics of both England and its American colonies. In England, William and Mary ruled as **constitutional monarchs**; overseas, they promoted an empire based on commerce. They accepted the overthrow of James's disastrous Dominion of New England and allowed Massachusetts (under its new charter) and New York to resume self-government. In 1696, Parliament created a new body, the Board of Trade, to oversee colonial affairs. While the Board of Trade continued to pursue the mercantilist policies that made the colonies economically beneficial, it permitted local elites to maintain a strong hand in colonial affairs. As England plunged into a new era of European warfare, its leaders had little choice but to allow its colonies substantial autonomy.

| **IN YOUR OWN WORDS** | Identify three new developments between 1660 and 1690 that helped shape England's American Empire. |

# Imperial Wars and Native Peoples

The price that England paid for bringing William of Orange to the throne was a new commitment to warfare on the continent. England wanted William because of his unambiguous Protestant commitments; William wanted England because of the resources it could bring to bear in European wars. Beginning with the War of the League of Augsburg in 1689, England embarked on an era sometimes called the **Second Hundred Years' War**, which lasted until the defeat of Napoleon at Waterloo in 1815. In that time, England (Britain after 1707) fought in seven major wars; the longest era of peace lasted only twenty-six years.

Imperial wars transformed North America. Prior to 1689, American affairs were distant from those of Europe, but the recurrent wars of the eighteenth century spilled over repeatedly into the colonies. Governments were forced to arm themselves and create new alliances with neighboring Native Americans, who tried to turn the fighting to their own advantage. Although war brought money to the American colonies in the form of war contracts, it also placed new demands on colonial governments to support the increasingly militant British Empire. To win wars in Western Europe, the Caribbean, and far-flung oceans, British leaders created a powerful central state that spent three-quarters of its revenue on military and naval expenses.

## Tribalization

For Native Americans, the rise of war intersected with a process scholars have called **tribalization**: the adaptation of stateless peoples to the demands imposed on them by neighboring states. In North America, tribalization occurred in catastrophic circumstances. Eurasian diseases rapidly killed off broad swaths of Native communities, disproportionately victimizing the old and the very young. In oral cultures, old people were irreplaceable repositories of knowledge, while the young were literally the future. With populations in free fall, many polities disappeared altogether. By the eighteenth century, the groups that survived had all been transformed. Some new tribes, like the Catawbas, had not existed before and were pieced together from remnants of formerly large groups. Other nations, like the Iroquois, declined in numbers but sustained themselves by adopting many war captives. In the Carolina borderlands, a large number of Muskogean-speaking communities came together as a nation known to the British as the "Creek" Indians, so named because some of them lived on Ochese Creek. Similarly, the Cherokees, the Delawares, and other groups that were culturally linked but politically fragmented became coherent "tribes" to deal more effectively with their European neighbors.

The rise of imperial warfare exposed Native American communities to danger, but it also gave them newfound leverage. The Iroquois were radically endangered by imperial conflict. A promised English alliance failed them, and in 1693 a combined force of French soldiers, militiamen, and their Indian allies burned all three Mohawk villages to the ground. Thereafter, the Iroquois devised a strategy for playing French and English interests off against each other. In 1701, they made alliances with both empires, declaring their intention to remain neutral in future conflicts between them. This did not mean that the Iroquois stayed on the sideline. Iroquois warriors often participated in raids during wartime, and Iroquois spokesmen met regularly with representatives of New York and New France to affirm their alliances and receive diplomatic gifts that included guns, powder, lead, clothing, and rum (from the British) or brandy (from the French). Their neutrality, paradoxically, made them more sought after as allies. For example, their alliance with New York, known as the **Covenant Chain**, soon became a model for relations between the British Empire and other Native American peoples.

Imperial warfare also reshaped Indian relations in the Southeast. During the War of the Spanish Succession (1702–1713), which pitted Britain against France and Spain, English settlers in the Carolinas armed the Creeks, whose 15,000 members farmed the fertile lands along the present-day border of Georgia and Alabama. A joint English-Creek expedition attacked Spanish Florida, burning the town of St. Augustine but failing to capture the fort. To protect Havana in nearby Cuba, the Spanish reinforced St. Augustine and unsuccessfully attacked Charleston, South Carolina.

## Indian Goals

The Creeks had their own agenda: to become the dominant tribe in the region, they needed to vanquish their longtime enemies, the pro-French Choctaws to the west and the Spanish-allied Apalachees to the south. Beginning in 1704, a force of Creek and Yamasee warriors destroyed the remaining Franciscan missions in northern Florida, attacked the Spanish settlement at Pensacola, and captured a thousand Apalachees, whom they sold to South Carolinian slave traders for sale in the West Indies. Simultaneously, a Carolina-supported Creek expedition attacked the Iroquois-speaking Tuscarora people of North Carolina, killing hundreds, executing 160 male captives, and sending 400 women and children into slavery. The surviving Tuscaroras joined the Iroquois in New York (who now became the Six Nations of the Iroquois). The Carolinians, having used the Creeks to kill Spaniards, now died at the hands of their former allies: when English traders demanded payment for trade debts in 1715, the Creeks and Yamasees revolted, killing 400 colonists before being overwhelmed by the Carolinians and their new Indian allies, the Cherokees.

Native Americans also joined in the warfare between French Catholics in Canada and English Protestants in New England. With French aid, Catholic Mohawk and Abenaki warriors attacked their Puritan neighbors. They destroyed English settlements in Maine and, in 1704, attacked the western Massachusetts town of Deerfield, where they killed 48 residents and carried 112 into captivity. In response, New England militia attacked French settlements and, in 1710, joined with British naval forces to seize Port Royal in French Acadia (Nova Scotia). However, a major British–New England expedition against the French stronghold at Quebec, inspired in part by the visit of four Indian "kings" to London, failed miserably.

Stalemated militarily in America, Britain won major territorial and commercial concessions through its victories in Europe. In the Treaty of Utrecht (1713), Britain obtained Newfoundland, Acadia, and the Hudson Bay region of northern Canada from France, as well as access through Albany to the western Indian trade. From

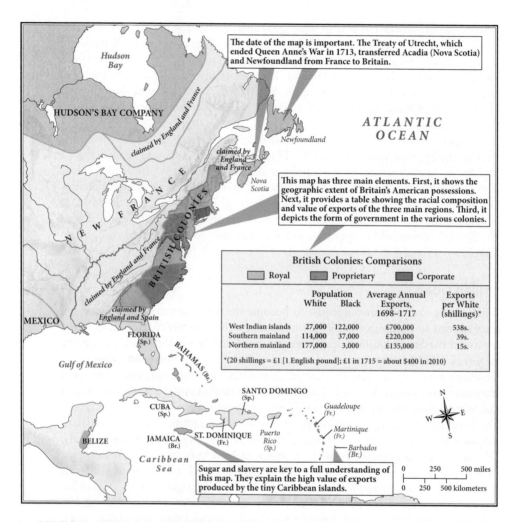

The date of the map is important. The Treaty of Utrecht, which ended Queen Anne's War in 1713, transferred Acadia (Nova Scotia) and Newfoundland from France to Britain.

This map has three main elements. First, it shows the geographic extent of Britain's American possessions. Next, it provides a table showing the racial composition and value of exports of the three main regions. Third, it depicts the form of government in the various colonies.

**British Colonies: Comparisons**

☐ Royal      ▨ Proprietary      ▨ Corporate

|  | Population White | Black | Average Annual Exports, 1698–1717 | Exports per White (shillings)* |
|---|---|---|---|---|
| West Indian islands | 27,000 | 122,000 | £700,000 | 538s. |
| Southern mainland | 114,000 | 37,000 | £220,000 | 39s. |
| Northern mainland | 177,000 | 3,000 | £135,000 | 15s. |

*(20 shillings = £1 [1 English pound]; £1 in 1715 = about $400 in 2010)

Sugar and slavery are key to a full understanding of this map. They explain the high value of exports produced by the tiny Caribbean islands.

**MAP 3.2    Britain's American Empire, 1713**

Many of Britain's possessions in the West Indies were tiny islands, mere dots on the Caribbean Sea. However, in 1713, these small pieces of land were by far the most valuable parts of the empire. Their sugar crops brought wealth to English merchants, commerce to the northern colonies, and a brutal life and early death to the hundreds of thousands of African slaves working on the plantations.

Spain, Britain acquired the strategic fortress of Gibraltar at the entrance to the Mediterranean and a thirty-year contract to supply slaves to Spanish America. These gains advanced Britain's quest for commercial supremacy and brought peace to eastern North America for a generation (Map 3.2).

| IN YOUR OWN WORDS | What was tribalization, and how did it help Native Americans cope with their European neighbors? |
|---|---|

# The Imperial Slave Economy

Britain's focus on America reflected the growth of a new agricultural and commercial order — the **South Atlantic System** — that produced sugar, tobacco, rice, and other tropical and subtropical products for an international market. Its plantation societies were ruled by European planter-merchants and worked by hundreds of thousands of enslaved Africans.

## The South Atlantic System

The South Atlantic System had its center in Brazil and the West Indies, and sugar was its primary product. Before 1500, there were few sweet foods in Europe — mostly honey and fruits — so when European planters developed vast sugarcane plantations in America, they found a ready market for their crop. (The craving for the potent new sweet food was so intense that, by 1900, sugar accounted for an astonishing 20 percent of the calories consumed by the world's people.)

European merchants, investors, and planters garnered the profits of the South Atlantic System. Following mercantilist principles, they provided the plantations with tools and equipment to grow and process the sugarcane and ships to carry it to Europe. But it was the Atlantic slave trade that made the system run. Between 1520 and 1650, Portuguese traders carried about 820,000 Africans across the Atlantic — about 4,000 slaves a year before 1600 and 10,000 annually thereafter. Over the next half century, the Dutch dominated the Atlantic slave trade; then, between 1700 and 1800, the British transported about 2.5 million of the total of 6.1 million Africans carried to the Americas.

**England and the West Indies**   England was a latecomer to the plantation economy, but from the beginning the prospect of a lucrative cash crop drew large numbers of migrants. On St. Kitts, Nevis, Montserrat, and Barbados, most early settlers were small-scale English farmers (and their indentured servants) who exported tobacco and livestock hides; on this basis, they created small but thriving colonies. In 1650, there were more English residents in the West Indies (some 44,000) than in the Chesapeake (20,000) and New England (23,000) colonies combined.

After 1650, sugar transformed Barbados and the other islands into slave-based plantation societies, a change facilitated by English capital combined with the knowledge and experience of Dutch merchants. By 1680, an elite group of 175 planters, described by one antislavery writer of the time as "inhumane and barbarous," dominated Barbados's economy; they owned more than half of the island, thousands of indentured servants, and half of its more than 50,000 slaves. In 1692, exploited Irish servants and island-born African slaves staged a major uprising, which was brutally suppressed. The "leading principle" in a slave society, declared one West Indian planter, was to instill "fear" among workers and a commitment to "absolute coercive" force among masters. As social inequality and racial conflict increased, hundreds of English farmers fled to South Carolina and the large island of Jamaica. But the days of Caribbean smallholders were numbered. English sugar merchants soon invested heavily in Jamaica; by 1750, it had seven hundred large sugar plantations, worked by more than 105,000 slaves, and had become the wealthiest British colony.

Sugar was a rich man's crop because it could be produced most efficiently on large plantations. Scores of slaves planted and cut the sugarcane, which was then processed by expensive equipment—crushing mills, boiling houses, distilling apparatus—into raw sugar, molasses, and rum. The affluent planter-merchants who controlled the sugar industry drew annual profits of more than 10 percent on their investment. As Scottish economist Adam Smith noted in his famous treatise *The Wealth of Nations* (1776), sugar was the most profitable crop grown in America or Europe.

**The Impact on Britain**    The South Atlantic System generated enormous wealth and helped Europeans achieve world economic leadership. Most British West Indian plantations belonged to absentee owners who lived in England, where they spent their profits and formed a powerful sugar lobby. The Navigation Acts kept the British sugar trade in the hands of British merchants, who exported sugar to foreign markets, and by 1750 reshipments of American sugar and tobacco to Europe accounted for half of British exports. Enormous profits also flowed into Britain from the slave trade. The value of the guns, iron, rum, and cloth that were used to buy slaves was only about one-tenth (in the 1680s) to one-third (by the 1780s) of the value of the crops those slaves produced in America, allowing English traders to sell slaves in the West Indies for three to five times what they paid for them in Africa.

These massive profits drove the slave trade. At its height in the 1790s, Britain annually exported three hundred thousand guns to Africa, and a British ship carrying 300 to 350 slaves left an African port every other day. This commerce stimulated the entire British economy. English, Scottish, and American shipyards built hundreds of vessels, and thousands of people worked in trade-related industries: building port facilities and warehouses, refining sugar and tobacco, distilling rum from molasses, and manufacturing textiles and iron products for the growing markets in Africa and America. More than one thousand British merchant ships were plying the Atlantic by 1750, providing a supply of experienced sailors and laying the foundation for the supremacy of the Royal Navy.

## Africa, Africans, and the Slave Trade

As the South Atlantic System enhanced European prosperity, it imposed enormous costs on West and Central Africa. Between 1550 and 1870, the Atlantic slave trade uprooted 11 million Africans, draining lands south of the Sahara of people and wealth and changing African society (Map 3.3). By directing commerce away from the savannas and the Islamic world on the other side of the Sahara, the Atlantic slave trade changed the economic and religious dynamics of the African interior. It also fostered militaristic, centralized states in the coastal areas.

**Africans and the Slave Trade**    Warfare and slaving had been part of African life for centuries, but the South Atlantic System made slaving a favorite tactic of ambitious kings and plundering warlords. "Whenever the King of Barsally wants Goods or Brandy," an observer noted, "the King goes and ransacks some of his enemies' towns, seizing the people and selling them." Supplying slaves became a way of life in the West African state of Dahomey, where the royal house monopolized the sale of slaves

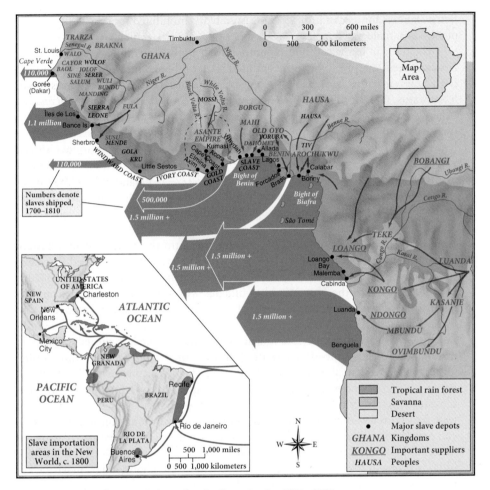

**MAP 3.3 Africa and the Atlantic Slave Trade, 1700–1810**

The tropical rain forest of West Africa was home to scores of peoples and dozens of kingdoms. With the rise of the slave trade, some of these kingdoms became aggressive slavers. Dahomey's army, for example, seized tens of thousands of captives in wars with neighboring peoples and sold them to European traders. About 14 percent of the captives died during the grueling Middle Passage, the transatlantic voyage between Africa and the Americas. Most of the survivors labored on sugar plantations in Brazil and the British and French West Indies.

and used European guns to create a military despotism. Dahomey's army, which included a contingent of 5,000 women, raided the interior for captives; between 1680 and 1730, Dahomey annually exported 20,000 slaves from the ports of Allada and Whydah. The Asante kings likewise used slaving to conquer states along the Gold Coast as well as Muslim kingdoms in the savanna. By the 1720s, they had created a prosperous empire of 3 to 5 million people. Yet participation in the transatlantic slave trade remained a choice for Africans, not a necessity. The powerful kingdom of

Benin, famous for its cast bronzes and carved ivory, prohibited for decades the export of all slaves, male and female.

The trade in humans produced untold misery. Hundreds of thousands of young Africans died, and millions more endured a brutal life in the Americas. In Africa itself, class divisions hardened as people of noble birth enslaved and sold those of lesser status. Gender relations shifted as well. Two-thirds of the slaves sent across the Atlantic were men, partly because European planters paid more for men and "stout men boys" and partly because Africans were more likely to sell enslaved women locally. The resulting sexual imbalance prompted more African men to take several wives. Finally, the expansion of the Atlantic slave trade increased the extent of slavery in Africa. Sultan Mawlay Ismail of Morocco (r. 1672–1727) owned 150,000 black slaves, obtained by trade in Timbuktu and in wars he waged in Senegal. In Africa, as in the Americas, slavery eroded the dignity of human life.

**The Middle Passage and Beyond**    Africans sold into the South Atlantic System suffered the bleakest fate. Torn from their villages, they were marched in chains to coastal ports, their first passage in slavery. Then they endured the perilous **Middle Passage** to the New World in hideously overcrowded ships. The captives had little to eat or drink, and some died from dehydration. The feces, urine, and vomit below decks prompted outbreaks of dysentery, which took more lives. "I was so overcome by the heat, stench, and foul air that I nearly fainted," reported a European doctor. Some slaves jumped overboard to drown rather than endure more suffering. Others staged violent shipboard revolts. Slave uprisings occurred on two thousand voyages, roughly one of every ten Atlantic passages. Nearly 100,000 slaves died in these insurrections, and nearly 1.5 million others—about 14 percent of those who were transported—died of disease or illness on the month-long journey.

For those who survived the Atlantic crossing, things only got worse as they passed into endless slavery. Life on the sugar plantations of northwestern Brazil and the West Indies was one of relentless exploitation. Slaves worked ten hours a day under the hot tropical sun; slept in flimsy huts; and lived on a starchy diet of corn, yams, and dried fish. They were subjected to brutal discipline: "The fear of punishment is the principle [we use] . . . to keep them in awe and order," one planter declared. When punishments came, they were brutal. Flogging was commonplace; some planters rubbed salt, lemon juice, or urine into the resulting wounds.

Planters often took advantage of their power by raping enslaved women. Sexual exploitation was a largely unacknowledged but ubiquitous feature of master-slave relations, something that many slave masters considered to be an unquestioned privilege of their position. "It was almost a constant practice with our clerks, and other whites," Olaudah Equiano wrote, "to commit violent depredations on the chastity of the female slaves." Thomas Thistlewood was a Jamaica planter who kept an unusually detailed journal in which he noted every act of sexual exploitation he committed. In thirty-seven years as a Jamaica planter, Thistlewood recorded 3,852 sex acts with 138 enslaved women.

With sugar prices high and the cost of slaves low, many planters worked their slaves to death and then bought more. Between 1708 and 1735, British planters on Barbados imported about 85,000 Africans; however, in that same time the island's black population increased by only 4,000 (from 42,000 to 46,000). The constant

**Two Views of the Middle Passage** An 1846 watercolor (on the right) shows the cargo hold of a slave ship en route to Brazil, which imported large numbers of African slaves until the 1860s. Painted by a ship's officer, the work minimizes the brutality of the Middle Passage—none of the slaves are in chains—and captures the Africans' humanity and dignity. The illustration on the left, which was printed by England's Abolitionist Society, shows the plan of a Liverpool slave ship designed to hold 482 Africans, packed in with no more respect than that given to hogsheads of sugar and tobacco. Records indicate that the ship actually carried as many as 609 Africans at once. Left: Private Collection © Michael Graham-Stewart/Bridgeman Images. Right: © National Maritime Museum, London/The Image Works.

influx of new slaves kept the population thoroughly "African" in its languages, religions, and culture. "Here," wrote a Jamaican observer, "each different nation of Africa meet and dance after the manner of their own country . . . [and] retain most of their native customs."

## Slavery in the Chesapeake and South Carolina

West Indian–style slavery came to Virginia and Maryland following Bacon's Rebellion. Taking advantage of the expansion of the British slave trade (following the end of the Royal African Company's monopoly in 1698), elite planter-politicians led a "tobacco revolution" and bought more Africans, putting these slaves to work on ever-larger plantations. Scholars continue to debate the relationship between economic considerations and cultural values in their efforts to explain the rise of African slavery. By 1720, Africans made up 20 percent of the Chesapeake population; by 1740, nearly 40 percent. Slavery had become a core institution, no longer just one of several forms of unfree labor. Moreover, slavery was now defined in racial terms. Virginia legislators prohibited sexual intercourse between English and Africans and defined virtually all resident Africans as slaves: "All servants imported or brought into this country by sea or land who were not Christians in their native country shall be accounted and be slaves."

On the mainland as in the islands, slavery was a system of brutal exploitation. Violence was common, and the threat of violence always hung over master-slave relationships. In 1669, Virginia's House of Burgesses decreed that a master who killed a slave in the process of "correcting" him could not be charged with a felony, since it would be irrational to destroy his own property. From that point forward, even the most extreme punishments were permitted by law. Slaves could not carry weapons or gather in large numbers. Slaveholders were especially concerned to discourage slaves from running away. Punishments for runaways commonly included not only brutal whipping but also branding or scarring to make recalcitrant slaves easier to identify. Virginia laws spelled out the procedures for capturing and returning runaway slaves in detail. If a runaway slave was killed in the process of recapturing him, the county would reimburse the slave's owner for his full value. In some cases, slave owners could put runaway slaves up for trial; if they were found guilty and executed, the owner would be compensated for his loss.

Despite the inherent brutality of the institution, slaves in Virginia and Maryland worked under better conditions than those in the West Indies. Many lived relatively long lives. Unlike sugar and rice, which were "killer crops" that demanded strenuous labor in a tropical climate, tobacco cultivation required steadier and less demanding labor in a more temperate environment. Workers planted young tobacco seedlings in spring, hoed and weeded the crop in summer, and in fall picked and hung the leaves to cure over the winter. Nor did diseases spread as easily in the Chesapeake, because plantation quarters were less crowded and more dispersed than those in the West Indies. Finally, because tobacco profits were lower than those from sugar, planters treated their slaves less harshly than West Indian planters did.

Many tobacco planters increased their workforce by buying female slaves and encouraging them to have children. In 1720, women made up more than one-third of the Africans in Maryland, and the black population had begun to increase naturally. "Be kind and indulgent to the breeding wenches," one slave owner told his overseer, "[and do not] force them when with child upon any service or hardship that will be injurious to them." By midcentury, more than three-quarters of the enslaved workers in the Chesapeake were American-born.

Slaves in South Carolina labored under much more oppressive conditions. The colony grew slowly until 1700, when planters began to plant and export rice to southern Europe, where it was in great demand. Between 1720 and 1750, rice production increased fivefold. To expand production, planters imported thousands of Africans, some of them from rice-growing societies. By 1710, Africans formed a majority of the total population, eventually rising to 80 percent in rice-growing areas.

Most rice plantations lay in inland swamps, and the work was dangerous and exhausting. Slaves planted, weeded, and harvested the rice in ankle-deep mud. Pools of stagnant water bred mosquitoes, which transmitted diseases that claimed hundreds of African lives. Other slaves, forced to move tons of dirt to build irrigation works, died from exhaustion. "The labour required [for growing rice] is only fit for slaves," a Scottish traveler remarked, "and I think the hardest work I have seen them engaged in." In South Carolina, as in the West Indies and Brazil, there were many slave deaths and few births, and the arrival of new slaves continually "re-Africanized" the black population.

## An African American Community Emerges

Slaves came from many peoples in West Africa and the Central African regions of Kongo and Angola. White planters welcomed ethnic diversity to deter slave revolts. "The safety of the Plantations," declared a widely read English pamphlet, "depends upon having Negroes from all parts of Guiny, who do not understand each other's languages and Customs and cannot agree to Rebel." By accident or design, most plantations drew laborers of many languages, including Kwa, Mande, and Kikongo. Among Africans imported after 1730 into the upper James River region of Virginia, 41 percent came from ethnic groups in present-day Nigeria, and another 25 percent from West-Central Africa. The rest hailed from the Windward and Gold coasts, Senegambia, and Sierra Leone. In South Carolina, plantation owners preferred laborers from the Gold Coast and Gambia, who had a reputation as hardworking farmers. But as African sources of slaves shifted southward after 1730, more than 30 percent of the colony's workers later came from Kongo and Angola.

Initially, the slaves did not think of themselves as Africans or blacks but as members of a specific family, clan, or people—Wolof, Hausa, Ibo, Yoruba, Teke, Ngola—and they sought out those who shared their language and customs. In the upper James River region, Ibo men and women arrived in equal numbers, married each other, and maintained their Ibo culture. In most places, though, this was impossible. Slaves from varying backgrounds were thrown together and only gradually discovered common ground.

**Building Community**  Through painful trial and error, slaves eventually discovered what limited freedoms their owners would allow them. Those who were not too rebellious or too recalcitrant were able to carve out precarious family lives—though they were always in danger of being disrupted by sale or life-threatening punishment—and build the rudiments of a slave community.

One key to the development of families and communities was a more or less balanced sex ratio that encouraged marriage and family formation. In South Carolina, the high death rate among slaves undermined ties of family and kinship; but in the Chesapeake, after 1725 some slaves, especially on larger plantations, were able to create strong nuclear families and extended kin relations. On one of Charles Carroll's estates in Maryland, 98 of the 128 slaves were members of two extended families. These African American kin groups passed on family names, traditions, and knowledge to the next generation, and thus a distinct culture gradually developed. As one observer suggested, blacks had created a separate world, "a Nation within a Nation."

As slaves forged a new identity, they carried on certain African practices but let others go. Many Africans arrived in America with ritual scars that white planters called "country markings"; these signs of ethnic identity fell into disuse on culturally diverse plantations. (Ironically, on some plantations these African markings were replaced by brands or scars that identified them with their owners.) But other tangible markers of African heritage persisted, including hairstyles, motifs used in wood carvings and pottery, the large wooden mortars and pestles used to hull rice, and the design of houses, in which rooms were arranged from front to back in a distinctive "I" pattern, not side by side as was common in English dwellings. Musical instruments — especially drums, gourd rattles, and a stringed instrument called a "molo," forerunner of the banjo — helped Africans preserve cultural traditions and, eventually, shape American musical styles.

African values also persisted. Some slaves passed down Muslim beliefs, and many more told their children of the spiritual powers of conjurers, called *obeah* or *ifa*, who knew the ways of the African gods. Enslaved Yorubas consulted Orunmila, the god of fate, and other Africans (a Jamaican planter noted) relied on *obeah* "to revenge injuries and insults, discover and punish thieves and adulterers; [and] to predict the future."

**Resistance and Accommodation**     Slaves' freedom of action was always dramatically circumscribed. It became illegal to teach slaves to read and write, and most slaves owned no property of their own. Because the institution of slavery rested on fear, planters had to learn a ferocious form of cruelty. Slaves might be whipped, restrained, or maimed for any infraction, large or small. A female cook in a Virginia household "was cruelly loaded with various kinds of iron machines; she had one particularly on her head, which locked her mouth so fast that she could scarcely speak; and could not eat nor drink." Thomas Jefferson, who witnessed such punishments on his father's Virginia plantation, noted that each generation of whites was "nursed, educated, and daily exercised in tyranny," and he concluded that the relationship "between master and slave is a perpetual exercise of the most unremitting despotism on the one part, and degrading submission on the other." A fellow Virginian, planter George Mason, agreed: "Every Master is born a petty tyrant."

The extent of white violence often depended on the size and density of the slave population. As Virginia planter William Byrd II complained of his slaves in 1736, "Numbers make them insolent." In the northern colonies, where slaves were few, white violence was sporadic. But plantation owners and overseers in the sugar- and rice-growing areas, where Africans outnumbered Europeans 8 or more to 1, routinely whipped assertive slaves. They also prohibited their workers from leaving the plantation without special passes and called on their poor white neighbors to patrol the countryside at night.

Despite the constant threat of violence, some slaves ran away, a very small number of them successfully. In some parts of the Americas — for example, in Jamaica — runaway slaves were able to form large, independent Maroon communities. But on the mainland, planters had the resources necessary to reclaim runaways, and such communities were unusual and precarious. More often, slaves who spoke English and possessed artisanal skills fled to colonial towns, where they tried to pass as free; occasionally they succeeded. Slaves who did not run away were engaged in a constant tug-of-war with their owners over the terms of their enslavement. Some blacks bartered extra work for better food and clothes; others seized a small privilege and dared the master to revoke it. In this way, Sundays gradually became a day of rest—asserted as a right, rather than granted as a privilege. When bargaining failed, slaves protested silently by working slowly or stealing.

Slave owners' greatest fear was that their regime of terror would fail and slaves would rise up to murder them in their beds. Occasionally that fear was realized. In the 1760s, in Amherst County, Virginia, a slave killed four whites; in Elizabeth City County, eight slaves strangled their master in bed. But the circumstances of slavery made any larger-scale uprising all but impossible. To rebel against their masters, slaves would have to be able to communicate secretly but effectively across long distances; choose leaders they could trust; formulate and disseminate strategy; accumulate large numbers of weapons; and ensure that no one betrayed their plans. This was all but impossible: in plantation slavery, the preponderance of force was on the side of the slave owners, and blacks who chose to rise up did so at their peril.

**The Stono Rebellion**    The largest slave uprising in the mainland colonies, South Carolina's **Stono Rebellion** of 1739, illustrates the impossibility of success. The Catholic governor of Spanish Florida instigated the revolt by promising freedom to fugitive slaves. By February 1739, at least 69 slaves had escaped to St. Augustine, and rumors circulated "that a Conspiracy was formed by Negroes in Carolina to rise and make their way out of the province." When war between England and Spain broke out in September, 75 Africans rose in revolt and killed a number of whites near the Stono River. According to one account, some of the rebels were Portuguese-speaking Catholics from the Kingdom of Kongo who hoped to escape to Florida. Displaying their skills as soldiers—decades of brutal slave raiding in Kongo had militarized the society there—the rebels marched toward Florida "with Colours displayed and two Drums beating."

Though their numbers and organization were impressive, the Stono rebels were soon met by a well-armed, mounted force of South Carolina militia. In the ensuing battle, 44 slaves were killed and the rebellion was suppressed, preventing any general uprising. In response, frightened South Carolinians cut slave imports and tightened plantation discipline.

## The Rise of the Southern Gentry

As the southern colonies became full-fledged slave societies, life changed for whites as well as for blacks. Consider the career of William Byrd II (1674–1744). Byrd's father, a successful planter-merchant in Virginia, hoped to marry his children into the English gentry. To smooth his son's entry into landed society, Byrd sent him to England for his education. But his status-conscious classmates shunned young Byrd, calling him a "colonial," a first bitter taste of the gradations of rank in English society.

Other English rejections followed. Lacking aristocratic connections, Byrd was denied a post with the Board of Trade, passed over three times for the royal governorship of Virginia, and rejected as a suitor by a rich Englishwoman. In 1726, at age fifty-two, Byrd finally gave up and moved back to Virginia, where he sometimes felt he was "being buried alive." Accepting his lesser destiny as a member of the colony's elite, Byrd built an elegant brick mansion on the family's estate at

Westover, sat in "the best pew in the church," and won an appointment to the governor's council.

William Byrd II's experience mirrored that of many planter-merchants, trapped in Virginia and South Carolina by their inferior colonial status. They used their wealth to rule over white yeomen families and tenant farmers and relied on violence to exploit enslaved blacks. Planters used Africans to grow food, as well as tobacco; to build houses, wagons, and tobacco casks; and to make shoes and clothes. By making their plantations self-sufficient, the Chesapeake elite survived the depressed tobacco market between 1670 and 1720.

**White Identity and Equality**   To prevent uprisings like Bacon's Rebellion, the Chesapeake gentry found ways to assist middling and poor whites. They gradually lowered taxes; in Virginia, for example, the annual head tax (on each adult man) fell from 45 pounds of tobacco in 1675 to just 5 pounds in 1750. They also encouraged smallholders to improve their economic lot by using slave labor, and many did so. By 1770, 60 percent of English families in the Chesapeake owned at least one slave. On the political front, planters now allowed poor yeomen and some tenants to vote. The strategy of the leading families — the Carters, Lees, Randolphs, and Robinsons — was to bribe these voters with rum, money, and the promise of minor offices in county governments. In return, they expected the yeomen and tenants to elect them to office and defer to their rule. This horse-trading solidified the authority of the planter elite, which used its control of the House of Burgesses to limit the power of the royal governor. Hundreds of yeomen farmers benefitted as well, tasting political power and garnering substantial fees and salaries as deputy sheriffs, road surveyors, estate appraisers, and grand jurymen.

Even as wealthy Chesapeake gentlemen formed political ties with smallholders, they took measures to set themselves apart culturally. As late as the 1720s, leading planters were boisterous, aggressive men who lived much like the common folk — hunting, drinking, gambling on horse races, and demonstrating their manly prowess by forcing themselves on female servants and slaves. As time passed, however, planters like William Byrd II began to model themselves on the English aristocracy, remaining sexual predators but learning from advice books how to act like gentlemen in other regards: "I must not sit in others' places; Nor sneeze, nor cough in people's faces. Nor with my fingers pick my nose, Nor wipe my hands upon my clothes." Cultivating **gentility** — a lifestyle that stressed refinement and self-control — they replaced their modest wooden houses with mansions of brick and mortar. Planters educated their sons in London as lawyers and gentlemen. But unlike Byrd's father, they expected them to return to America, marry local heiresses, and assume their fathers' roles: managing plantations, socializing with fellow gentry, and running the political system.

Wealthy Chesapeake and South Carolina women likewise emulated the English elite. They read English newspapers and fashionable magazines, wore the finest English clothes, and dined in the English fashion, including an elaborate afternoon tea. To enhance their daughters' gentility (and improve their marriage prospects), parents hired English tutors. Once married, planter women deferred to their husbands, reared pious children, and maintained complex social networks, in time creating a new ideal: the southern gentlewoman. Using the profits generated by enslaved

Africans in the South Atlantic System of commerce, wealthy planters formed an increasingly well-educated, refined, and stable ruling class.

| IN YOUR OWN WORDS | How did their ties to Great Britain and Africa change the lives of American planters? |
|---|---|

# The Northern Maritime Economy

The South Atlantic System had a broad geographical reach. As early as the 1640s, New England farmers supplied the sugar islands with bread, lumber, fish, and meat. As a West Indian explained, planters "had rather buy foode at very deare rates than produce it by labour, soe infinite is the profitt of sugar works." By 1700, the economies of the West Indies and New England were closely interwoven. Soon farmers and merchants in New York, New Jersey, and Pennsylvania were also shipping wheat, corn, and bread to the Caribbean. By the 1750s, about two-thirds of New England's exports and half of those from the Middle Atlantic colonies went to the British and French sugar islands.

The sugar economy linked Britain's entire Atlantic empire. In return for the sugar they sent to England, West Indian planters received credit, in the form of bills of exchange, from London merchants. The planters used these bills to buy slaves from Africa and to pay North American farmers and merchants for their provisions and shipping services. The mainland colonists then exchanged the bills for British manufactures, primarily textiles and iron goods.

## The Urban Economy

The West Indian trade created the first American merchant fortunes and the first urban industries. Merchants in Boston, Newport, Providence, Philadelphia, and New York invested their profits in new ships; some set up manufacturing enterprises, including twenty-six refineries that processed raw sugar into finished loaves. Mainland distilleries turned West Indian molasses into rum, producing more than 2.5 million gallons in Massachusetts alone by the 1770s. Merchants in Salem, Marblehead, and smaller New England ports built a major fishing industry by selling salted mackerel and cod to the sugar islands and to southern Europe. Baltimore merchants transformed their town into a major port by developing a bustling export business in wheat, while traders in Charleston shipped deerskins, indigo, and rice to European markets (Map 3.4).

As transatlantic commerce expanded—from five hundred voyages a year in the 1680s to fifteen hundred annually in the 1730s—American port cities grew in size and complexity. By 1750, the populations of Newport and Charleston were nearly 10,000; Boston had 15,000 residents; and New York had almost 18,000. The largest port was Philadelphia, whose population by 1776 had reached 30,000, the size of a large European provincial city. Smaller coastal towns emerged as centers of the lumber and shipbuilding industries. Seventy sawmills lined the Piscataqua River in New Hampshire, providing low-cost wood for homes, warehouses, and especially shipbuilding. Hundreds of shipwrights turned out oceangoing vessels, while other artisans made ropes, sails, and metal fittings for the new fleet. By the 1770s, colonial-built ships made up one-third of the British merchant fleet.

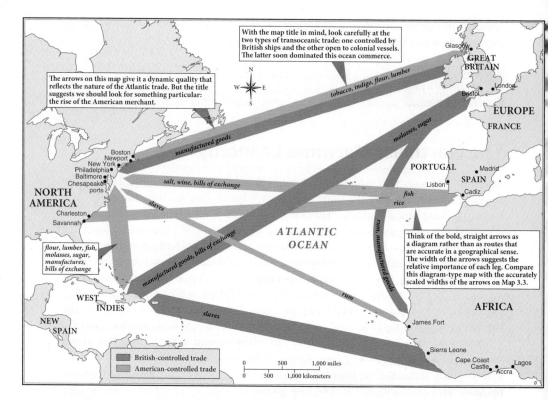

**MAP 3.4   The Growing Power of American Merchants, 1750**
Throughout the colonial era, British merchant houses dominated the transatlantic trade in manufactures, sugar, tobacco, and slaves. However, by 1750, American-born merchants in Boston, New York, and Philadelphia had seized control of the commerce between the mainland and the West Indies. In addition, Newport traders played a small role in the slave trade from Africa, and Boston and Charleston merchants grew rich carrying fish and rice to southern Europe.

The South Atlantic System extended far into the interior. A fleet of small vessels sailed back and forth on the Hudson and Delaware rivers, delivering cargoes of European manufactures and picking up barrels of flour and wheat to carry to New York and Philadelphia for export to the West Indies and Europe. By the 1750s, hundreds of professional teamsters in Maryland were transporting 370,000 bushels of wheat and corn and 16,000 barrels of flour to urban markets each year—more than 10,000 wagon trips. To service this traffic, entrepreneurs and artisans set up taverns, horse stables, and barrel-making shops in towns along the wagon roads. Lancaster (the town that hosted the Iroquois conference described in the chapter opening), in a prosperous wheat-growing area of Pennsylvania, boasted more than 200 German and English artisans and a dozen merchants.

## Urban Society

Wealthy merchants dominated the social life of seaport cities. In 1750, about forty merchants controlled more than 50 percent of Philadelphia's trade. Like the Chesapeake gentry, urban merchants imitated the British upper classes, importing architectural design books from England and building Georgian-style mansions to display their wealth. Their wives strove to create a genteel culture by buying fine furniture and entertaining guests at elegant dinners.

Artisan and shopkeeper families, the middle ranks of seaport society, made up nearly half the population. Innkeepers, butchers, seamstresses, shoemakers, weavers, bakers, carpenters, masons, and dozens of other skilled workers toiled to gain an income sufficient to maintain their families in modest comfort. Wives and husbands often worked as a team and taught the "mysteries of the craft" to their children. Some artisans aspired to wealth and status, an entrepreneurial ethic that prompted them to hire apprentices and expand production. However, most artisans were not well-to-do. During his working life, a tailor was lucky to accumulate £30 worth of property, far less than the £2,000 owned at death by an ordinary merchant or the £300 listed in the probate inventory of a successful blacksmith.

Laboring men and women formed the lowest ranks of urban society. Merchants needed hundreds of dockworkers to unload manufactured goods and molasses from inbound ships and reload them with barrels of wheat, fish, and rice. For these demanding jobs, merchants used enslaved blacks and indentured servants, who together made up 30 percent of the workforce in Philadelphia and New York City until the 1750s; otherwise, they hired unskilled wageworkers. Poor white and black women eked out a living by washing clothes, spinning wool, or working as servants or prostitutes. To make ends meet, laboring families sent their children out to work.

Periods of stagnant commerce threatened the financial security of merchants and artisans alike. For laborers, seamen, and seamstresses — whose household budgets left no margin for sickness or unemployment — depressed trade meant hunger, dependence on public charity, and (for the most desperate) petty thievery or prostitution. The sugar- and slave-based South Atlantic System, and cycles of imperial warfare, brought economic uncertainty as well as opportunity to the people of the northern colonies.

| IN YOUR OWN WORDS | What economic activities drove the northern maritime economy? |

# The New Politics of Empire, 1713–1750

The South Atlantic System also changed the politics of empire. British ministers, pleased with the wealth produced by the trade in slaves, sugar, rice, and tobacco, ruled the colonies with a gentle hand. The colonists took advantage of that leniency to strengthen their political institutions and eventually to challenge the rules of the mercantilist system.

## The Rise of Colonial Assemblies

After the Glorious Revolution, representative assemblies in America copied the English Whigs and limited the powers of crown officials. In Massachusetts during the 1720s, the assembly repeatedly ignored the king's instructions to provide the royal governor with a permanent salary, and legislatures in North Carolina,

New Jersey, and Pennsylvania did the same. Using such tactics, the legislatures gradually took control of taxation and appointments, angering imperial bureaucrats and absentee proprietors. "The people in power in America," complained William Penn during a struggle with the Pennsylvania assembly, "think nothing taller than themselves but the Trees."

Leading the increasingly powerful assemblies were members of the colonial elite. Although most property-owning white men had the right to vote, only men of wealth and status stood for election. In New Jersey in 1750, 90 percent of assemblymen came from influential political families. In Virginia, seven members of the wealthy Lee family sat in the House of Burgesses and, along with other powerful families, dominated its major committees. In New England, affluent descendants of the original Puritans formed a core of political leaders. "Go into every village in New England," John Adams wrote in 1765, "and you will find that the office of justice of the peace, and even the place of representative, have generally descended from generation to generation, in three or four families at most."

However, neither elitist assemblies nor wealthy property owners could impose unpopular edicts on the people. Purposeful crowd actions were a fact of colonial life. An uprising of ordinary citizens overthrew the Dominion of New England in 1689. In New York, mobs closed houses of prostitution; in Salem, Massachusetts, they ran people with infectious diseases out of town; and in New Jersey in the 1730s and 1740s, mobs of farmers battled with proprietors who were forcing tenants off disputed lands. When officials in Boston restricted the sale of farm produce to a single public market, a crowd destroyed the building, and its members defied the authorities to arrest them. "If you touch One you shall touch All," an anonymous letter warned the sheriff, "and we will show you a Hundred Men where you can show one." These expressions of popular discontent, combined with the growing authority of the assemblies, created a political system that was broadly responsive to popular pressure and increasingly resistant to British control.

## Salutary Neglect

British colonial policy during the reigns of George I (r. 1714–1727) and George II (r. 1727–1760) allowed for this rise of American self-government as royal bureaucrats, pleased by growing trade and import duties, relaxed their supervision of internal colonial affairs. In 1775, British political philosopher Edmund Burke would praise this strategy as **salutary neglect**.

Salutary neglect was a by-product of the political system developed by Sir Robert Walpole, the Whig leader in the House of Commons from 1720 to 1742. Walpole relied on **patronage** — the practice of giving offices and salaries to political allies — to create a strong Court Party. Under his leadership, Britain's government achieved a new measure of financial and political stability. But critics — the so-called Country Party — charged that Walpole's policies of high taxes and a bloated royal bureaucracy threatened British liberties.

These arguments were echoed in North America, where colonial legislators complained that royal governors abused their patronage powers. To preserve American liberty, the colonists strengthened the powers of the representative assemblies, unintentionally laying the foundation for the American independence movement.

## Protecting the Mercantile System

In 1732, Walpole provided a parliamentary subsidy for the new colony of Georgia. While Georgia's reform-minded trustees envisioned the colony as a refuge for Britain's poor, Walpole had little interest in social reform; he subsidized Georgia to protect the valuable rice-growing colony of South Carolina. But the new colony had the opposite effect. Britain's expansion into Georgia outraged Spanish officials, who were already angry about the rising tide of smuggled British manufactures in New Spain. To counter Britain's commercial imperialism, Spanish naval forces stepped up their seizure of illegal traders, in the process cutting off the ear of an English sea captain, Robert Jenkins.

Yielding to parliamentary pressure, Walpole declared war on Spain in 1739. The so-called War of Jenkins's Ear (1739–1741) was a fiasco for Britain. In 1740, British regulars failed to capture St. Augustine because South Carolina whites, still shaken by the Stono Rebellion, refused to commit militia units to the expedition. A year later, an assault on the prosperous seaport of Cartagena (in present-day Colombia) also failed; 20,000 British sailors and soldiers and 2,500 colonial troops died in the attack, mostly from tropical diseases.

**The Siege and Capture of Louisbourg, 1745** In 1760, as British and colonial troops moved toward victory in the French and Indian War (1754–1763), the London artist J. Stevens sought to bolster imperial pride by celebrating an earlier Anglo-American triumph. In 1745, a British naval squadron led a flotilla of colonial ships and thousands of New England militiamen in an attack on the French fort at Louisbourg, on Cape Breton Island, near the mouth of the St. Lawrence River. After a siege of forty days, the Anglo-American force captured the fort, long considered impregnable. The victory was bittersweet because the Treaty of Aix-la-Chapelle (1748) returned the island to France. Anne S. K. Brown Military Collection, Brown University Library.

The War of Jenkins's Ear quickly became part of a general European conflict, the War of the Austrian Succession (1740–1748). Massive French armies battled British-subsidized German forces in Europe, and French naval forces roamed the West Indies, vainly trying to conquer a British sugar island. In 1745, three thousand New England militiamen and a British naval squadron captured Louisbourg, the French fort guarding the entrance to the St. Lawrence River. To the dismay of New England Puritans, who feared invasion from Catholic Quebec, the Treaty of Aix-la-Chapelle (1748) returned Louisbourg to France. The treaty made it clear to colonial leaders that England would act in its own interests, not theirs.

## Mercantilism and the American Colonies

Though Parliament prohibited Americans from manufacturing textiles (Woolen Act, 1699), hats (Hat Act, 1732), and iron products such as plows, axes, and skillets (Iron Act, 1750), and also curbed the colonies' ability to print their own paper money (Currency Act, 1751), it could not prevent the colonies from maturing economically. American merchants soon controlled over 75 percent of the transatlantic trade in manufactures and 95 percent of the commerce between the mainland and the British West Indies (see Map 3.4).

Moreover, by the 1720s, the British sugar islands could not absorb all the flour, fish, and meat produced by mainland settlers. So, ignoring Britain's intense rivalry with France, colonial merchants sold their produce to the French sugar islands. When American rum distillers began to buy cheap molasses from the French islands, the West Indian sugar lobby in London persuaded Parliament to pass the Molasses Act of 1733. The act placed a high tariff on French molasses, so high that it would no longer be profitable for American merchants to import it. Colonists protested that the Molasses Act would cripple the distilling industry; cut farm exports; and, by slashing colonial income, reduce the mainland's purchases of British goods. When Parliament ignored these arguments, American merchants smuggled in French molasses by bribing customs officials.

These conflicts angered a new generation of English political leaders. In 1749, Charles Townshend of the Board of Trade charged that the American assemblies had assumed many of the "ancient and established prerogatives wisely preserved in the Crown," and he vowed to replace salutary neglect with more rigorous imperial control.

The wheel of empire had come full circle. In the 1650s, England had set out to create a centrally managed Atlantic empire and, over the course of a century, achieved the military and economic aspects of that goal. Mercantilist legislation, maritime warfare, commercial expansion, and the forced labor of a million African slaves brought prosperity to Britain. However, internal unrest (the Glorious Revolution) and a policy of salutary neglect had weakened Britain's political authority over its American colonies. Recognizing the threat self-government posed to the empire, British officials in the late 1740s vowed to reassert their power in America — an initiative with disastrous results.

| **IN YOUR OWN WORDS** | How could Great Britain maintain its mercantilist policies and permit the "salutary neglect" of its colonies at the same time? |
|---|---|

# Summary

In this chapter, we examined processes of change in politics and society. The political story began in the 1660s as Britain imposed controls on its American possessions. Parliament passed the Acts of Trade and Navigation to keep colonial products and trade in English hands. Then King James II abolished representative institutions in the northern colonies and created the authoritarian Dominion of New England. Following the Glorious Revolution, the Navigation Acts remained in place and tied the American economy to that of Britain. But the uprisings of 1688–1689 overturned James II's policy of strict imperial control, restored colonial self-government, and ushered in an era of salutary political neglect. It also initiated a long era of imperial warfare, in which Native American peoples allied themselves to the colonies and often served as proxy warriors against French- and Spanish-allied peoples, pursuing their own goals in the process.

The social story centers on the development of the South Atlantic System of production and trade, which involved an enormous expansion in African slave raiding; the Atlantic slave trade; and the cultivation of sugar, rice, and tobacco in America. This complex system created an exploited African American labor force in the southern mainland and West Indian colonies, while it allowed European American farmers, merchants, and artisans on the North American mainland to prosper. How would the two stories play out? In 1750, slavery and the South Atlantic System seemed firmly entrenched, but the days of salutary neglect appeared numbered.

## Chapter 3 Review

### KEY TERMS

**Identify and explain the significance of each term below.**

proprietorship (p. 74)
Quakers (p. 75)
Navigation Acts (p. 76)
Dominion of New England (p. 77)
Glorious Revolution (p. 78)
constitutional monarchy (p. 79)
Second Hundred Years' War (p. 80)
tribalization (p. 80)

Covenant Chain (p. 81)
South Atlantic System (p. 83)
Middle Passage (p. 86)
Stono Rebellion (p. 91)
gentility (p. 92)
salutary neglect (p. 96)
patronage (p. 96)

## REVIEW QUESTIONS

Answer these questions to demonstrate your understanding of the chapter's main ideas.

1. Identify three new developments between 1660 and 1690 that helped shape England's American Empire.
2. What was tribalization, and how did it help Native Americans cope with their European neighbors?
3. How did their ties to Great Britain and Africa change the lives of American planters?
4. What economic activities drove the northern maritime economy?
5. How could Great Britain maintain its mercantilist policies and permit the "salutary neglect" of its colonies at the same time?
6. Trace the developments outlined in the section entitled "Politics and Power" from 1660 to 1750 on the thematic timeline on page 70. What pattern of political evolution do you see in colonial interactions with Britain?

## CHRONOLOGY

As you read, ask yourself why this chapter begins and ends with these dates and then identify the links among related events.

| | |
|---|---|
| **1642–1651** | • English civil war |
| **1649** | • Charles I beheaded |
| **1651** | • First Navigation Act |
| **1660–1685** | • Reign of Charles II, king of England |
| **1663** | • Charles II grants Carolina proprietorship |
| **1664** | • English capture New Netherland, rename it New York |
| **1669** | • Virginia law declares that the murder of a slave cannot be treated as a felony |
| **1681** | • William Penn founds Pennsylvania |
| **1685–1688** | • Reign of James II, king of England |
| **1686–1689** | • Dominion of New England |
| **1688–1689** | • Glorious Revolution in England |
| **1689** | • William and Mary ascend throne in England |
| | • Revolts in Massachusetts, Maryland, and New York |

| 1689–1713 | • England, France, and Spain at war |
| 1696 | • Parliament creates Board of Trade |
| 1714–1750 | • British policy of salutary neglect |
| | • American assemblies gain power |
| 1720–1742 | • Robert Walpole leads Parliament |
| 1720–1750 | • African American communities form |
| | • Rice exports from South Carolina soar |
| | • Planter aristocracy emerges |
| | • Seaport cities expand |
| 1732 | • Parliament charters Georgia, challenging Spain |
| | • Hat Act limits colonial enterprise |
| 1733 | • Molasses Act threatens distillers |
| 1739 | • Stono Rebellion in South Carolina |
| 1739–1748 | • War with Spain in the Caribbean and France in Canada and Europe |
| 1750 | • Iron Act restricts colonial iron production |
| 1751 | • Currency Act prohibits land banks and paper money |

# 4

# Growth, Diversity, and Conflict

## 1720–1763

**IDENTIFY THE BIG IDEA**

In what ways were Britain's American colonies affected by events across the Atlantic, and how were their societies taking on a life of their own?

**IN 1736, ALEXANDER MACALLISTER LEFT THE HIGHLANDS OF** Scotland for the backcountry of North Carolina, where his wife and three sisters soon joined him. MacAllister prospered as a landowner and mill proprietor and had only praise for his new home. Carolina was "the best poor man's country," he wrote to his brother Hector, urging him to "advise all poor people . . . to take courage and come." In North Carolina, there were no landlords to keep "the face of the poor . . . to the grinding stone," and so many Highlanders were arriving that "it will soon be a new Scotland." Here, on the far margins of the British Empire, people could "breathe the air of liberty, and not want the necessarys of life." Some 300,000 European migrants—primarily Highland Scots, Scots-Irish, and Germans—heeded MacAllister's advice and helped swell the population of Britain's North American settlements from 400,000 in 1720 to almost 2 million by 1765.

MacAllister's "air of liberty" did not last forever, as the rapid increase in white settlers and the arrival of nearly 300,000 enslaved Africans transformed life throughout mainland British North America. Long-settled towns in New England became overcrowded, and antagonistic ethnic and religious communities jostled uneasily with one another in the Middle Atlantic colonies; in 1748, there were more than a hundred German Lutheran and Reformed congregations in Quaker-led Pennsylvania. By then, the MacAllisters and thousands of other Celtic and German migrants had altered the social landscape and introduced religious conflict into the southern backcountry.

Everywhere, two European cultural movements, the Enlightenment and Pietism, changed the tone of intellectual and spiritual life. Advocates of "rational thought" viewed human beings as agents of moral self-determination and urged Americans to fashion a better social order. Religious Pietists outnumbered them and had more influence. Convinced of the weakness of human nature, evangelical ministers told their followers to seek regeneration through divine grace. Amidst this intellectual and religious ferment, migrants and the landless children of long-settled families moved inland and sparked wars with the Native peoples and with France and Spain. A generation of dynamic growth produced a decade of deadly warfare that would set the stage for a new era in American history.

# New England's Freehold Society

In the 1630s, the Puritans had fled England, where a small elite of nobles and gentry owned 75 percent of the arable land, while **tenants** (renters) and propertyless workers farmed it. In New England, the Puritans created a yeoman society of relatively equal landowning farm families. But by 1750, the migrants' numerous descendants had parceled out the best farmland, threatening the future of the freehold ideal.

## Farm Families: Women in the Household Economy

The Puritans' vision of social equality did not extend to women, and their ideology placed the husband firmly at the head of the household. In *The Well-Ordered Family* (1712), the Reverend Benjamin Wadsworth of Boston advised women, "Since he is thy Husband, God has made him the head and set him above thee." It was a wife's duty "to love and reverence" her husband.

Women learned this subordinate role throughout their lives. Small girls watched their mothers defer to their fathers, and as young women, they were told to be "silent in company." They saw the courts prosecute more women than men for the crime of fornication (sex outside of marriage), and they found that their marriage portions would be inferior to those of their brothers. Thus Ebenezer Chittendon of Guilford, Connecticut, left his land to his sons, decreeing that "Each Daughter [shall] have half so much as Each Son, one half in money and the other half in Cattle."

Throughout the colonies, women assumed the role of dutiful helpmeets (helpmates) to their husbands. In addition to tending gardens, farmwives spun thread and yarn from flax and wool and then wove it into cloth for shirts and gowns. They knitted sweaters and stockings, made candles and soap, churned milk into butter, fermented malt for beer, preserved meats, and mastered dozens of other household tasks. "Notable women" — those who excelled at domestic arts — won praise and high status.

Bearing and rearing children were equally important tasks. Most women in New England married in their early twenties and by their early forties had given birth to six or seven children, delivered with the help of a female neighbor or a midwife. One Massachusetts mother confessed that she had little time for religious activities because "the care of my Babes takes up so large a portion of my time and attention." Yet most Puritan congregations were filled with women: "In a Church of between *Three* and *Four* Hundred *Communicants*," the eminent minister Cotton Mather noted, "there are but few more than *One* Hundred *Men*; all the Rest are Women."

Women's lives remained tightly bound by a web of legal and cultural restrictions. Ministers praised women for their piety but excluded them from an equal role in the church. When Hannah Heaton, a Connecticut farmwife, grew dissatisfied with her Congregational minister, thinking him unconverted and a "blind guide," she sought out equality-minded Quaker and evangelist Baptist churches that welcomed questioning women such as herself and treated "saved" women equally with men. However, by the 1760s, many evangelical congregations had reinstituted men's dominance over women. "The government of Church and State must be . . . family government" controlled by its "king," declared the Danbury (Connecticut) Baptist Association.

## Farm Property: Inheritance

By contrast, European men who migrated to the colonies escaped many traditional constraints, including the curse of landlessness. "The hope of having land of their own & becoming independent of Landlords is what chiefly induces people into America," an official noted in the 1730s. Owning property gave formerly dependent peasants a new social identity.

Unlike the adventurers seeking riches in other parts of the Americas, most New England migrants wanted farms that would provide a living for themselves and ample land for their children. In this way, they hoped to secure a **competency** for their families: the ability to keep their households solvent and independent and to pass that ability on to the next generation. Parents who could not give their offspring land placed these children as indentured servants in more prosperous households. When the indentures ended at age eighteen or twenty-one, propertyless sons faced a decades-long climb up the agricultural ladder, from laborer to tenant and finally to freeholder.

Sons and daughters in well-to-do farm families were luckier: they received a marriage portion when they were in their early twenties. That portion — land, livestock, or farm equipment — repaid them for their past labor and allowed parents to choose their marriage partners. Parents' security during old age depended on a wise choice of son- or daughter-in-law. Although the young people could refuse an unacceptable match, they did not have the luxury of falling in love with and marrying whomever they pleased.

Marriage under eighteenth-century English common law was not a contract between equals. Under the legal principle of **coverture**, which placed married women under the protection and authority of their husbands, a bride relinquished to her husband the legal ownership of all her property. After his death, she received a dower right, the right to use (though not sell) one-third of the family's property. On the widow's death or remarriage, her portion was divided among the children. Thus the widow's property rights were subordinate to those of the family line, which stretched across the generations.

**Prudence Punderson (1758–1784),** *The First, Second and Last Scenes of Mortality* This powerful image reveals both the artistic skills of colonial women in the traditional medium of needlework and the Puritans' continuing cultural concern with the inevitability of death. Prudence Punderson, the Connecticut woman who embroidered this scene, rejected a marriage proposal and followed her Loyalist father into exile on Long Island in 1778. Sometime later, she married a cousin, Timothy Rossiter, and bore a daughter, Sophia, who may well be the baby in the cradle being rocked by "Jenny," a slave owned by Prudence's father. Long worried by "my ill state of health" and perhaps now anticipating her own death, Prudence has inscribed her initials on the coffin — and, in creating this embroidery, transformed her personal experience into a broader meditation on the progression from birth, to motherhood, to death. Embroidery, 1776–1783, Gift of Newton C. Brainard, accession no. 1962.28.4, the Connecticut Historical Society.

A father's duty was to provide inheritances for his children so that one day they could "be for themselves." Men who failed to do so lost status in the community. Some fathers willed the family farm to a single son and provided other children with money, an apprenticeship, or uncleared frontier tracts. Other yeomen moved their families to the frontier, where life was hard but land was cheap and abundant. "The Squire's House stands on the Bank of the Susquehannah," traveler Philip Fithian reported from the Pennsylvania backcountry in the early 1760s. "He tells me that he will be able to settle all his sons and his fair Daughter Betsy on the Fat of the Earth."

## Freehold Society in Crisis

Because of rapid natural increase, New England's population doubled each generation, from 100,000 in 1700, to nearly 200,000 in 1725, to almost 400,000 in 1750. After being divided and then subdivided, farms became so small—50 acres or less—that parents could provide only one child with an adequate inheritance. In the 1740s, the Reverend Samuel Chandler of Andover, Massachusetts, was "much distressed for land for his children," seven of them young boys. A decade later, in nearby Concord, about 60 percent of the farmers owned less land than their fathers had.

Because parents had less to give their sons and daughters, they had less control over their children's lives. The traditional system of arranged marriages broke down, as young people engaged in premarital sex and then used the urgency of pregnancy to win permission to marry. Throughout New England, premarital conceptions rose dramatically, from about 10 percent of firstborn children in the 1710s to more than 30 percent in the 1740s. Given another chance, young people "would do the same again," an Anglican minister observed, "because otherwise they could not obtain their parents' consent to marry."

Even as New England families changed, they maintained the freeholder ideal. Some parents chose to have smaller families and used birth control to do so: abstention, coitus interruptus, or primitive condoms. Other families petitioned the provincial government for frontier land grants and hacked new farms out of the forests of central Massachusetts, western Connecticut, and eventually New Hampshire and Vermont. Still others improved their farms' productivity by replacing the traditional English crops of wheat and barley with high-yielding potatoes and maize (Indian corn). Corn was an especially wise choice: good for human consumption, as well as for feeding cattle and pigs, which provided milk and meat. Gradually, New England changed from a grain to a livestock economy, becoming a major exporter of salted meat to the plantations of the West Indies.

As the population swelled, New England farmers developed the full potential of what one historian has called the "**household mode of production**," in which families swapped labor and goods. Women and children worked in groups to spin yarn, sew quilts, and shuck corn. Men loaned neighbors tools, draft animals, and grazing land. Farmers plowed fields owned by artisans and shopkeepers, who repaid them with shoes, furniture, or store credit. Partly because currency was in short supply, no cash changed hands. Instead, farmers, artisans, and shopkeepers recorded debits and credits and "balanced" the books every few years. This system helped New Englanders to maximize agricultural output and preserve the freehold ideal.

> **IN YOUR OWN WORDS**    What goals and values shaped New England society in the eighteenth century?

# Diversity in the Middle Colonies

The Middle colonies—New York, New Jersey, and Pennsylvania—became home to peoples of differing origins, languages, and religions. Scots-Irish Presbyterians, English and Welsh Quakers, German Lutherans and Moravians, Dutch Reformed

Protestants, and others all sought to preserve their cultural and religious identities as they pursued economic opportunity. At the same time, rapid population growth throughout the region strained public institutions, pressured Indian lands, and created a dynamic but unstable society.

## Economic Growth, Opportunity, and Conflict

Previously home to New Netherland and New Sweden, the Mid-Atlantic region was already ethnically diverse before England gained control of it. The founding of Pennsylvania and New Jersey amplified this pattern. Fertile land seemed abundant, and grain exports to Europe and the West Indies financed the colonies' rapid settlement. Between 1720 and 1770, a growing demand for wheat, corn, and flour doubled their prices and brought people and prosperity to the region. Yet that very growth led to conflict, both within the Middle colonies and in their relations with Native American neighbors.

**Tenancy in New York**   In New York's fertile Hudson River Valley, wealthy Dutch and English families presided over the huge manors created by the Dutch West India Company and English governors. Like Chesapeake planters, the New York landlords aspired to live in the manner of the European gentry but found that few migrants wanted to labor as peasants. To attract tenants, the manorial lords granted long leases, with the right to sell improvements such as houses and barns to the next tenant. They nevertheless struggled to populate their estates.

Most tenant families hoped that with hard work and ample sales they could eventually buy their own farmsteads. But preindustrial technology limited output. A worker with a hand sickle could reap only half an acre of wheat, rye, or oats a day. The cradle scythe, a tool introduced during the 1750s, doubled or tripled the amount of grain one worker could cut. Even so, a family with two adult workers could reap only about 12 acres of grain, or roughly 150 to 180 bushels of wheat. After saving enough grain for food and seed, the surplus might be worth £15 — enough to buy salt and sugar, tools, and cloth, but little else. The road to landownership was not an easy one.

**Conflict in the Quaker Colonies**   In Quaker-dominated Pennsylvania and New Jersey, wealth was initially distributed more evenly than in New York, but the proprietors of each colony, like the manor lords of New York, had enormous land claims. The first migrants lived simply in small, one- or two-room houses with a sleeping loft, a few benches or stools, and some wooden platters and cups. Economic growth brought greater prosperity, along with conflicts between ordinary settlers and the proprietors who tried to control their access to land, resources, and political power.

William Penn's early appeals to British Quakers and continental Protestants led to a boom in immigrants. When these first arrivals reported that Pennsylvania and New Jersey were "the best poor man's country in the world," thousands more followed. Soon the proprietors of both colonies were overwhelmed by the demand for land. By the 1720s, many new migrants were forced to become **squatters**, settling illegally on land they hoped eventually to be able to acquire on legal terms.

Frustration over the lack of land led the Penn family to perpetrate one of the most infamous land frauds of the eighteenth century, the so-called Walking Purchase of 1737, in which they fraudulently exploited an Indian deed to claim more than a million acres of prime farmland north of Philadelphia. This purchase, while opening new lands to settlement, poisoned Indian relations in the colony. Delaware and Shawnee migration to western Pennsylvania and the Ohio Valley, which was already under way, accelerated rapidly in response.

Immigrants flooded into Philadelphia, which grew from 2,000 people in 1700 to 25,000 by 1760. Many families came in search of land; for them, Philadelphia was only a temporary way station. Other migrants came as laborers, including a large number of indentured servants. Some were young, unskilled men, but the colony's explosive growth also created a strong demand for all kinds of skilled laborers, especially in the construction trades.

Pennsylvania and New Jersey grew prosperous but contentious. New Jersey was plagued by contested land titles, and ordinary settlers rioted against the proprietors in the 1740s and the 1760s. By the 1760s, eastern Pennsylvania landowners with large farms were using slaves and poor Scots-Irish migrants to grow wheat. Other ambitious men were buying up land and dividing it into small tenancies, which they lent out on profitable leases. Still others sold farming equipment and manufactured goods or ran mills. These large-scale farmers, rural landlords, speculators, storekeepers, and gristmill operators formed a distinct class of agricultural capitalists. They built large stone houses for their families, furnishing them with four-poster beds and expensive mahogany tables, on which they laid elegant linen and imported Dutch dinnerware.

By contrast, one-half of the Middle colonies' white men owned no land and little personal property. Some were the sons of smallholding farmers and would eventually inherit some land. But many were Scots-Irish or German "inmates"—single men or families, explained a tax assessor, "such as live in small cottages and have no taxable property, except a cow." In the predominantly German township of Lancaster, Pennsylvania, a merchant noted an "abundance of Poor people" who "maintain their Families with great difficulty by day Labour." Although these workers hoped eventually to become landowners, rising land prices prevented many from realizing their dreams.

## Cultural Diversity

The Middle Atlantic colonies were not a melting pot. Most European migrants held tightly to their traditions, creating a patchwork of ethnically and religiously diverse communities. In 1748, a Swedish traveler counted no fewer than twelve religious denominations in Philadelphia, including Anglicans, Baptists, Quakers, Swedish and German Lutherans, Mennonites, Scots-Irish Presbyterians, and Roman Catholics.

Migrants preserved their cultural identity by marrying within their ethnic groups. A major exception was the Huguenots, Calvinists who had been expelled from Catholic France in the 1680s and resettled in Holland, England, and the British colonies. Huguenots in American port cities such as Boston, New York, and Charleston quickly lost their French identities by intermarrying with other Protestants. More typical were the Welsh Quakers in Chester County, Pennsylvania: 70 percent of the children of the original Welsh migrants married other Welsh Quakers, as did 60 percent of the third generation.

In Pennsylvania and western New Jersey, Quakers shaped the culture because of their numbers, wealth, and social cohesion. Most Quakers came from English counties with few landlords and brought with them traditions of local village governance, popular participation in politics, and social equality. But after 1720, the growth of German and Scots-Irish populations challenged their dominance.

**The German Influx**   The Quaker vision of a "peaceable kingdom" attracted 100,000 German migrants who had fled their homelands because of military conscription, religious persecution, and high taxes. First to arrive, in 1683, were the Mennonites, religious dissenters drawn by the promise of freedom of worship. In the 1720s, a larger wave of German migrants arrived from the overcrowded villages of southwestern Germany and Switzerland. "Wages were far better" in Pennsylvania, Heinrich Schnee-beli reported to his friends in Zurich, and "one also enjoyed there a free unhindered exercise of religion." A third wave of Germans and Swiss—nearly 40,000 strong—landed in Philadelphia between 1749 and 1756. To help pay the costs of the expensive trip from the Rhine Valley, German immigrants pioneered the **redemptioner** system, a flexible form of indentured servitude that allowed families to negotiate their own terms upon arrival. Families often indentured one or more children while their parents set up a household of their own.

Germans soon dominated many districts in eastern Pennsylvania, and thousands more moved down the fertile Shenandoah Valley into the western backcountry of Maryland, Virginia, and the Carolinas (Map 4.1). Many migrants preserved their cultural identity by settling in German-speaking Lutheran and Reformed communities that endured well beyond 1800. A minister in North Carolina admonished young people "not to contract any marriages with the English or Irish," arguing that "we owe it to our native country to do our part that German blood and the German language be preserved in America."

These settlers were willing colonial subjects of Britain's German-born and German-speaking Protestant monarchs, George I (r. 1714–1727) and George II (r. 1727–1760). They generally avoided politics except to protect their cultural practices; for example, they insisted that married women have the legal right to hold property and write wills, as they did in Germany.

**Scots-Irish Settlers**   Migrants from Ireland, who numbered about 115,000, were the most numerous of the incoming Europeans. Some were Irish and Catholic, but most were Scots and Presbyterian, the descendants of the Calvinist Protestants sent to Ireland during the seventeenth century to solidify English rule there. Once in Ireland, the Scots faced hostility from both Irish Catholics and English officials and landlords. The Irish Test Act of 1704 restricted voting and office holding to members of the Church of England, English mercantilist regulations placed heavy import duties on linens made by Scots-Irish weavers, and farmers paid heavy taxes. This persecution made America seem desirable. "Read this letter, Rev. Baptist Boyd," a migrant to New York wrote back to his minister, "and tell all the poor folk of ye place that God has opened a door for their deliverance . . . all that a man works for is his own; there are no revenue hounds to take it from us here."

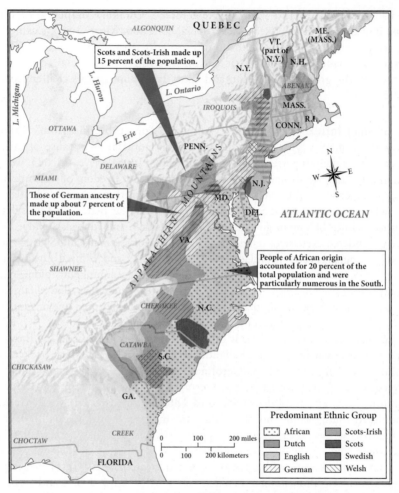

Scots and Scots-Irish made up 15 percent of the population.

Those of German ancestry made up about 7 percent of the population.

People of African origin accounted for 20 percent of the total population and were particularly numerous in the South.

Predominant Ethnic Group

| African | Scots-Irish |
| Dutch | Scots |
| English | Swedish |
| German | Welsh |

**MAP 4.1   Ethnic and Racial Diversity in the British Colonies, 1775**
In 1700, most colonists in British North America were of English origin; by 1775, settlers of English descent constituted only about 50 percent of the total population. African Americans now accounted for one-third of the residents of the South, while tens of thousands of German and Scots-Irish migrants added ethnic and religious diversity in the Middle colonies, the southern backcountry, and northern New England.

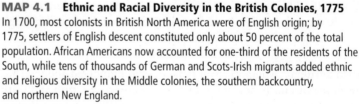

Lured by such reports, thousands of Scots-Irish families sailed for the colonies. By 1720, most migrated to Philadelphia, attracted by the religious tolerance there. Seeking cheap land, they moved to central Pennsylvania and to the fertile Shenandoah Valley to the south. Governor William Gooch of Virginia welcomed the Scots-Irish presence to secure "the Country against the Indians." An Anglican planter, however, thought them as dangerous as "the Goths and Vandals of old" had been to the Roman Empire. Like the Germans, the Scots-Irish retained their culture, living in ethnic communities and holding firm to the Presbyterian Church.

## Religion and Politics

In Western Europe, the leaders of church and state condemned religious diversity. "To tolerate all [religions] without controul is the way to have none at all," declared an Anglican clergyman. Orthodox church officials carried such sentiments to Pennsylvania. "The preachers do not have the power to punish anyone, or to force anyone to go to church," complained Gottlieb Mittelberger, an influential German minister. As a result, "Sunday is very badly kept. Many people plough, reap, thresh, hew or split wood and the like." He concluded: "Liberty in Pennsylvania does more harm than good to many people, both in soul and body."

Mittelberger was mistaken. Although ministers in Pennsylvania could not invoke government authority to uphold religious values, the result was not social anarchy. Instead, religious sects enforced moral behavior through communal self-discipline. Quaker families attended a weekly meeting for worship and a monthly meeting for business; every three months, a committee reminded parents to provide proper religious instruction. The committee also supervised adult behavior; a Chester County meeting, for example, disciplined a member "to reclaim him from drinking to excess and keeping vain company." Significantly, Quaker meetings allowed couples to marry only if they had land and livestock sufficient to support a family. As a result, the children of well-to-do Friends usually married within the sect, while poor Quakers remained unmarried, wed later in life, or married without permission — in which case they were often ousted from the meeting. These marriage rules helped the Quakers build a self-contained and prosperous community.

In the 1740s, the flood of new migrants reduced Quakers to a minority — a mere 30 percent of Pennsylvanians. Moreover, Scots-Irish settlers in central Pennsylvania demanded an aggressive Indian policy, challenging the pacifism of the assembly. To retain power, Quaker politicians sought an alliance with those German religious groups that also embraced pacifism and voluntary (not compulsory) militia service. In response, German leaders demanded more seats in the assembly and laws that respected their inheritance customs.

By the 1750s, politics throughout the Middle colonies roiled with conflict. In New York, a Dutchman declared that he "Valued English Law no more than a Turd," while in Pennsylvania, Benjamin Franklin disparaged the "boorish" character and "swarthy complexion" of German migrants. Yet there was broad agreement on the importance of economic opportunity and liberty of conscience. The unstable balance between shared values and mutual mistrust prefigured tensions that would pervade an increasingly diverse American society in the centuries to come.

| **IN YOUR OWN WORDS** | How were the goals of immigrants to the Middle colonies similar to those of New England colonists, and how did they differ? |
|---|---|

# Commerce, Culture, and Identity

After 1720, transatlantic shipping grew more frequent and Britain and its colonies more closely connected, while a burgeoning print culture flooded the colonies with information and ideas. Two great European cultural movements — the **Enlightenment**, which emphasized the power of human reason to understand and shape the world; and **Pietism**, an evangelical Christian movement that stressed the individual's personal relationship with God — reached America as a result. At the same time, an abundance of imported goods began to reshape material culture, bringing new comforts into the lives of the middling sort while allowing prosperous merchants and landowners to set themselves apart from their neighbors in new ways.

## Transportation and the Print Revolution

In the eighteenth century, improved transportation networks opened Britain's colonies in new ways, and British shipping came to dominate the North Atlantic. In 1700, Britain had 40,000 sailors; by 1750, the number had grown to 60,000, while many more hailed from the colonies. An enormous number of vessels plied Atlantic waters: in the late 1730s, more than 550 ships arrived in Boston annually. About a tenth came directly from Britain or Ireland; the rest came mostly from other British colonies, either on the mainland or in the West Indies.

A road network slowly took shape as well, though roadbuilding was expensive and difficult. In 1704, Sarah Kemble Knight traveled from Boston to New York on horseback. The road was "smooth and even" in some places, treacherous in others; it took eight days of hard riding to cover 200 miles. Forty years later, a physician from Annapolis, Maryland, traveled along much better roads to Portsmouth, New Hampshire, and back — more than 1,600 miles in all. He spent four months on the road, stopping frequently to meet the locals and satisfy his curiosity. By the mid-eighteenth century, the "Great Wagon Road" carried migrating families down the Shenandoah Valley as far as the Carolina backcountry.

All of these water and land routes carried people, produce, and finished merchandise. They also carried information, as letters, newspapers, pamphlets, and crates of books began to circulate widely. The trip across the Atlantic took seven to eight weeks on average, so the news arriving in colonial ports was not fresh by our standard, but compared to earlier years, the colonies were awash in information.

Until 1695, the British government had the power to censor all printed materials. In that year, Parliament let the Licensing Act lapse, and the floodgates opened. Dozens of new printshops opened in London and Britain's provincial cities. They printed newspapers and pamphlets; poetry, ballads, and sermons; and handbills, tradesman's cards, and advertisements. Larger booksellers also printed scientific treatises, histories, travelers' accounts, and novels. The result was a print revolution. In Britain and throughout Europe, print was essential to the transmission of new ideas, and both the Enlightenment and Pietism took shape in part through its growing influence.

All this material crossed the Atlantic and filled the shops of colonial booksellers. The colonies also began printing their own newspapers. In 1704, the *Boston*

*Newsletter* was founded; by 1720, Boston had five printing presses and three newspapers; and by 1776, the thirteen colonies that united in declaring independence had thirty-seven newspapers among them. This world of print was essential to their ability to share grievances and join in common cause.

## The Enlightenment in America

To explain the workings of the natural world, some colonists relied on folk wisdom. Swedish migrants in Pennsylvania attributed magical powers to the great white mullein, a common wildflower, and treated fevers by tying the plant's leaves around their feet and arms. Traditionally, Christians believed that the earth stood at the center of the universe, and God (and Satan) intervened directly and continuously in human affairs. The scientific revolution of the sixteenth and seventeenth centuries challenged these ideas, and educated people—most of them Christians—began to modify their views accordingly.

**The European Enlightenment**   In 1543, the Polish astronomer Copernicus published his observation that the earth traveled around the sun, not vice versa. Copernicus's discovery suggested that humans occupied a more modest place in the universe than Christian theology assumed. In the next century, Isaac Newton, in his *Principia Mathematica* (1687), used the sciences of mathematics and physics to explain the movement of the planets around the sun (and invented calculus in the process). Though Newton was himself profoundly religious, in the long run his work undermined the traditional Christian understanding of the cosmos.

In the century between the *Principia Mathematica* and the French Revolution of 1789, the philosophers of the European Enlightenment used empirical research and scientific reasoning to study all aspects of life, including social institutions and human behavior. Enlightenment thinkers advanced four fundamental principles: the lawlike order of the natural world, the power of human reason, the "natural rights" of individuals (including the right to self-government), and the progressive improvement of society.

English philosopher John Locke was a major contributor to the Enlightenment. In his *Essay Concerning Human Understanding* (1690), Locke stressed the impact of environment and experience on human behavior and beliefs, arguing that the character of individuals and societies was not fixed but could be changed through education, rational thought, and purposeful action. Locke's *Two Treatises of Government* (1690) advanced the revolutionary theory that political authority was not given by God to monarchs, as James II had insisted (see Chapter 3). Instead, it derived from social compacts that people made to preserve their **natural rights** to life, liberty, and property. In Locke's view, the people should have the power to change government policies—or even their form of government.

Some clergymen responded to these developments by devising a rational form of Christianity. Rejecting supernatural interventions and a vengeful Calvinist God, Congregational minister Andrew Eliot maintained that "there is nothing in Christianity that is contrary to reason." The Reverend John Wise of Ipswich, Massachusetts, used Locke's philosophy to defend giving power to ordinary church members. Just as the social compact formed the basis of political society,

Wise argued, so the religious covenant among the lay members of a congregation made them — not the bishops of the Church of England or even ministers like himself — the proper interpreters of religious truth. The Enlightenment influenced Puritan minister Cotton Mather as well. When a measles epidemic ravaged Boston in the 1710s, Mather thought that only God could end it; but when smallpox struck a decade later, he used his newly acquired knowledge of inoculation — gained in part from a slave, who told him of the practice's success in Africa — to advocate this scientific preventive for the disease.

**Franklin's Contributions**   Benjamin Franklin was the exemplar of the American Enlightenment. Born in Boston in 1706 to devout Calvinists, he grew to manhood during the print revolution. Apprenticed to his brother, a Boston printer, Franklin educated himself through voracious reading. At seventeen, he fled to Philadelphia, where he became a prominent printer, and in 1729 he founded the *Pennsylvania Gazette*, which became one of the colonies' most influential newspapers. Franklin also formed a "club of mutual improvement" that met weekly to discuss "Morals, Politics, or Natural Philosophy." These discussions, as well as Enlightenment literature, shaped his thinking. As Franklin explained in his *Autobiography* (1771), "From the different books I read, I began to doubt of Revelation [God-revealed truth]."

Like a small number of urban artisans, wealthy Virginia planters, and affluent seaport merchants, Franklin became a deist. **Deism** was a way of thinking, not an established religion. "My own mind is my own church," said deist Thomas Paine. "I am of a sect by myself," added Thomas Jefferson. Influenced by Enlightenment science, deists such as Jefferson believed that a Supreme Being (or Grand Architect)

**Benjamin Franklin's Rise**  This portrait of Benjamin Franklin, attributed to Robert Feke and executed around 1746, portrays Franklin as a successful businessman. His ruffled collar and cuffs, his fashionably curly wig, and his sober but expensive suit reveal his social ambitions. In later portraits, after he gained fame as an Enlightenment sage, he dispensed with the wig and chose more unaffected poses; but in 1746, he was still establishing his credentials as a young Philadelphia gentleman on the rise.  Fogg Art Museum, Harvard Art Museums, USA/Bridgeman Images.

created the world and then allowed it to operate by natural laws but did not intervene in people's lives. Rejecting the divinity of Christ and the authority of the Bible, deists relied on "natural reason," their innate moral sense, to define right and wrong. Thus Franklin, a onetime slave owner, came to question the morality of slavery, repudiating it once he recognized the parallels between racial bondage and the colonies' political bondage to Britain.

Franklin popularized the practical outlook of the Enlightenment in *Poor Richard's Almanack* (1732–1757), an annual publication that was read by thousands. He also founded the American Philosophical Society (1743–present) to promote "useful knowledge." Adopting this goal in his own life, Franklin invented bifocal lenses for eyeglasses, the Franklin stove, and the lightning rod. His book on electricity, published in England in 1751, won praise as the greatest contribution to science since Newton's discoveries. Inspired by Franklin, ambitious printers in America's seaport cities published newspapers and gentlemen's magazines, the first significant nonreligious periodicals to appear in the colonies. The European Enlightenment, then, added a secular dimension to colonial cultural life, foreshadowing the great contributions to republican political theory by American intellectuals of the Revolutionary era: John Adams, James Madison, and Thomas Jefferson.

## American Pietism and the Great Awakening

As some colonists turned to deism, thousands of others embraced Pietism, a Christian movement originating in Germany around 1700 and emphasizing pious behavior (hence the name). In its emotional worship services and individual striving for a mystical union with God, Pietism appealed to believers' hearts rather than their minds. In the 1720s, German migrants carried Pietism to America, sparking a religious **revival** (or renewal of religious enthusiasm) in Pennsylvania and New Jersey, where Dutch minister Theodore Jacob Frelinghuysen preached passionate sermons to German settlers and encouraged church members to spread the message of spiritual urgency. A decade later, William Tennent and his son Gilbert copied Frelinghuysen's approach and led revivals among Scots-Irish Presbyterians throughout the Middle Atlantic region.

**New England Revivalism**    Simultaneously, an American-born Pietist movement appeared in New England. Revivals of Christian zeal were built into the logic of Puritanism. In the 1730s, Jonathan Edwards, a minister in Northampton, Massachusetts, encouraged a revival there that spread to towns throughout the Connecticut River Valley. Edwards guided and observed the process and then published an account entitled *A Faithful Narrative of the Surprising Work of God*, printed first in London (1737), then in Boston (1738), and then in German and Dutch translations. Its publication history highlights the transatlantic network of correspondents that gave Pietism much of its vitality.

**Whitefield's Great Awakening**    English minister George Whitefield transformed the local revivals of Edwards and the Tennents into a Great Awakening. After Whitefield had his personal awakening upon reading the German Pietists, he became a follower of John Wesley, the founder of English Methodism. In 1739, Whitefield carried Wesley's fervent message to America, where he attracted huge crowds from Georgia to Massachusetts.

Whitefield had a compelling presence. "He looked almost angelical; a young, slim, slender youth . . . cloathed with authority from the Great God," wrote a Connecticut farmer. Like most evangelical preachers, Whitefield did not read his sermons but spoke from memory. More like an actor than a theologian, he gestured eloquently, raised his voice for dramatic effect, and at times assumed a female persona—as a woman in labor struggling to deliver the word of God. When the young preacher told his spellbound listeners that they had sinned and must seek salvation, some suddenly felt a "new light" within them. As "the power of god come down," Hannah Heaton recalled, "my knees smote together . . . [and] it seemed to me I was a sinking down into hell . . . but then I resigned my distress and was perfectly easy quiet and calm . . . [and] it seemed as if I had a new soul & body both." Strengthened and self-confident, these converts, the so-called New Lights, were eager to spread Whitefield's message.

The rise of print intersected with this enthusiasm. "Religion is become the Subject of most Conversations," the *Pennsylvania Gazette* reported. "No books are in Request but those of Piety and Devotion." Whitefield and his circle did their best to answer the demand for devotional reading. As he traveled, Whitefield regularly sent excerpts of his journal to be printed in newspapers. Franklin printed Whitefield's sermons and journals by subscription and found them to be among his bestselling titles. Printed accounts of Whitefield's travels, conversion narratives, sermons, and other devotional literature helped to confirm Pietists in their faith and strengthen the communication networks that sustained them.

## Religious Upheaval in the North

Like all cultural explosions, the Great Awakening was controversial. Conservative ministers—passionless **Old Lights**, according to the evangelists—condemned the "cryings out, faintings and convulsions" in revivalist meetings and the New Lights' claims of "working Miracles or speaking with Tongues." Boston minister Charles Chauncy attacked the Pietist **New Lights** for allowing women to speak in public: it was "a plain breach of that commandment of the lord, where it is said, Let your women keep silence in the churches." In Connecticut, Old Lights persuaded the legislature to prohibit evangelists from speaking to a congregation without the minister's permission. But the New Lights refused to be silenced. Dozens of farmers, women, and artisans roamed the countryside, condemning the Old Lights as "unconverted" and willingly accepting imprisonment: "I shall bring glory to God in my bonds," a dissident preacher wrote from jail.

The Great Awakening undermined legally established churches and their tax-supported ministers. In New England, New Lights left the Congregational Church and founded 125 "separatist" churches that supported their ministers through voluntary contributions. Other religious dissidents joined Baptist congregations, which also condemned government support of churches: "God never allowed any civil state upon earth to impose religious taxes," declared Baptist preacher Isaac Backus. In New York and New Jersey, the Dutch Reformed Church split in two as New Lights refused to accept doctrines imposed by conservative church authorities in Holland.

The Great Awakening also appealed to Christians whose established churches could not serve their needs. By 1740, Pennsylvania's German Reformed and Lutheran congregations suffered from a severe lack of university-trained pastors. In the colony's Dutch Reformed, Dutch and Swedish Lutheran, and even its Anglican congregations, half the pulpits were empty. In this circumstance, itinerant preachers who stressed the power of "heart religion" and downplayed the importance of formal ministerial training found a ready audience.

The Great Awakening challenged the authority of all ministers whose status rested on respect for their education and knowledge of the Bible. In an influential pamphlet, *The Dangers of an Unconverted Ministry* (1740), Gilbert Tennent asserted that ministers' authority should come not from theological knowledge but from the conversion experience. Reaffirming Martin Luther's belief in the priesthood of all Christians, Tennent suggested that anyone who had felt God's redeeming grace could speak with ministerial authority. Sarah Harrah Osborn, a New Light "exhorter" in Rhode Island, refused "to shut up my mouth . . . and creep into obscurity" when silenced by her minister.

As religious enthusiasm spread, churches founded new colleges to educate their young men and to train ministers. New Light Presbyterians established the College of New Jersey (Princeton) in 1746, and New York Anglicans founded King's College (Columbia) in 1754. Baptists set up the College of Rhode Island (Brown) in 1764; two years later, the Dutch Reformed Church subsidized Queen's College (Rutgers) in New Jersey. However, the main intellectual legacy of the Great Awakening was not education for the privileged few but a new sense of authority among the many. A European visitor to Philadelphia remarked in surprise, "The poorest day-laborer . . . holds it his right to advance his opinion, in religious as well as political matters, with as much freedom as the gentleman."

## Social and Religious Conflict in the South

In the southern colonies, where the Church of England was legally established, religious enthusiasm triggered social conflict. Anglican ministers generally ignored the spiritual needs of African Americans and landless whites, who numbered 40 percent and 20 percent of the population, respectively. Middling white freeholders (35 percent of the residents) formed the core of most Church of England congregations. But prominent planters (just 5 percent) held the real power, using their control of parish finances to discipline ministers. One clergyman complained that dismissal awaited any minister who "had the courage to preach against any Vices taken into favor by the leading Men of his Parish."

**The Presbyterian Revival**    Soon, a democratization of religion challenged the dominance of both the Anglican Church and the planter elite. In 1743, bricklayer Samuel Morris, inspired by reading George Whitefield's sermons, led a group of Virginia Anglicans out of their congregation. Seeking a deeper religious experience, Morris invited New Light Presbyterian Samuel Davies to lead their prayer meetings. Davies's sermons, filled with erotic devotional imagery and urging Christians to feel "ardent Passion," sparked Presbyterian revivals across the Tidewater region, threatening the social authority of the Virginia gentry. Traditionally, planters and their well-dressed families arrived at Anglican services in fancy carriages drawn by well-bred horses and flaunted their power by sitting in the front pews. Such ritual displays of the gentry's superiority were meaningless if freeholders attended other churches. Moreover, religious pluralism threatened the tax-supported status of the Anglican Church.

To halt the spread of New Light ideas, Virginia governor William Gooch denounced them as "false teachings," and Anglican justices of the peace closed Presbyterian churches. This harassment kept most white yeomen and poor tenant families in the Church of England.

**The Baptist Insurgency**   During the 1760s, the vigorous preaching and democratic message of New Light Baptist ministers converted thousands of white farm families. The Baptists were radical Protestants whose central ritual was adult (rather than infant) baptism. Once men and women had experienced the infusion of grace—had been "born again"—they were baptized in an emotional public ceremony, often involving complete immersion in water.

Slaves were welcome at Baptist revivals. During the 1740s, George Whitefield had urged Carolina planters to bring their slaves into the Christian fold, but white opposition and the Africans' commitment to their ancestral religions kept the number of converts low. However, in the 1760s, native-born African Americans in Virginia welcomed the Baptists' message that all people were equal in God's eyes. Sensing a threat to the system of racial slavery, the House of Burgesses imposed heavy fines on Baptists who preached to slaves without their owners' permission.

Baptists threatened gentry authority because they repudiated social distinctions and urged followers to call one another "brother" and "sister." They also condemned the planters' decadent lifestyle. As planter Landon Carter complained, the Baptists were "destroying pleasure in the Country; for they encourage ardent Prayer . . . & an intire Banishment of *Gaming, Dancing*, & Sabbath-Day Diversions." The gentry responded with violence. In Caroline County, an Anglican posse attacked Brother John Waller at a prayer meeting. Waller "was violently jerked off the stage; they caught him by the back part of his neck, beat his head against the ground, and a gentleman gave him twenty lashes with his horsewhip."

Despite these attacks, Baptist congregations multiplied. By 1775, about 15 percent of Virginia's whites and hundreds of enslaved blacks had joined Baptist churches. To signify their state of grace, some Baptist men "cut off their hair, like Cromwell's round-headed chaplains." Others forged a new evangelical masculinity, "crying, weeping, lifting up the eyes, groaning" when touched by the Holy Spirit.

The Baptist revival in the Chesapeake challenged customary authority in families and society but did not overturn it. Rejecting the pleas of evangelical women, Baptist men kept church authority in the hands of "free born male members," and Anglican slaveholders retained control of the political system. Still, the Baptist insurgency infused the lives of poor tenant families with spiritual meaning and empowered yeomen to defend their economic interests. Moreover, as Baptist ministers spread Christianity among slaves, the cultural gulf between blacks and whites shrank, undermining one justification for slavery and giving some blacks a new religious identity. Within a generation, African Americans would develop distinctive versions of Protestant Christianity.

| IN YOUR OWN WORDS | How did the accelerating pace of travel and communication affect colonial society and culture? |
| --- | --- |

# The Midcentury Challenge: War, Trade, and Social Conflict, 1750–1763

Between 1750 and 1763, three significant events transformed colonial life. First, Britain went to war against the French in America, sparking a worldwide conflict: the Great War for Empire. Second, a surge in trade boosted colonial consumption but caused Americans to become deeply indebted to British creditors. Third, westward migration sparked warfare with Indian peoples, violent disputes between settlers and land speculators, and backcountry rebellions against eastern-controlled governments.

## The French and Indian War

In 1754, overlapping French and British claims in North America came to a head (Map 4.2). The French maintained their vast claims through a network of forts and trading posts that sustained alliances with neighboring Indians. The soft underbelly of this sprawling empire was the Ohio Valley, where French claims were tenuous. Native peoples were driven out of the valley by Iroquois attacks in the seventeenth century, but after 1720 displaced Indian populations—especially Delawares and Shawnees from Pennsylvania—resettled there in large numbers. In the 1740s, British traders from Pennsylvania began traveling down the Ohio River. They traded with Delawares and Shawnees in the upper valley and began to draw French-allied Indians into their orbit and away from French posts. Then, in 1748, the Ohio Company of Virginia, a partnership of prominent colonial planters and London merchants, received a 200,000-acre grant from the crown to establish a new settlement on the upper Ohio, threatening French claims to the region.

### Conflict in the Ohio Valley
By midcentury, Britain relied on the Iroquois Confederacy as its partner in Indian relations throughout the Northeast. By extending the Covenant Chain, the Iroquois had become a kind of Indian Empire in their own right, claiming to speak for other groups throughout the region based on their seventeenth-century conquests. The Delawares, Shawnees, and other groups who repopulated the Ohio Valley did so in part to escape the Iroquois yoke. To maintain influence on the Ohio, the Iroquois sent two " half-kings," Tanaghrisson (an adopted Seneca) and Scarouady (an Oneida), to the Native settlement of Logstown, a trading town on the upper Ohio, where Britain recognized them as leaders.

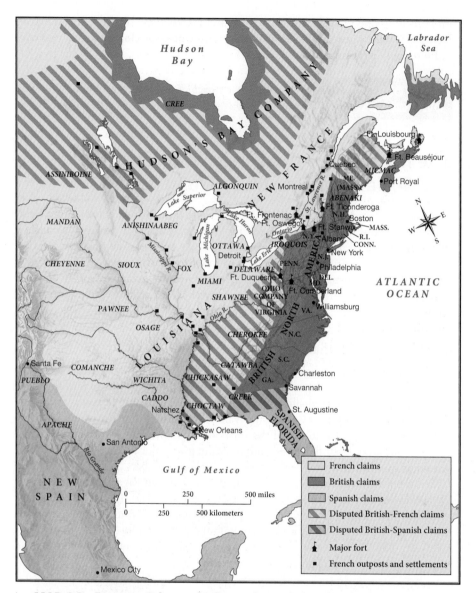

### MAP 4.2   European Spheres of Influence in North America, 1754

In the mid-eighteenth century, France, Spain, and the British-owned Hudson's Bay Company laid claim to the vast areas of North America still inhabited primarily by Indian peoples. British settlers had already occupied much of the land east of the Appalachian Mountains. To safeguard their lands west of the mountains, Native Americans played off one European power against another. As a British official remarked: "To preserve the Ballance between us and the French is the great ruling Principle of Modern Indian Politics." When Britain expelled France from North America in 1763, Indians had to face encroaching Anglo-American settlers on their own.

French authorities, alarmed by British inroads, built a string of forts from Lake Erie to the headwaters of the Ohio, culminating with Fort Duquesne on the site of present-day Pittsburgh. To reassert British claims, Governor Dinwiddie dispatched an expedition led by Colonel George Washington, a twenty-two-year-old Virginian whose half-brothers were Ohio Company stockholders. Washington discovered that most of the Ohio Indians had decided to side with the French; only the Iroquois half-kings and a few of their followers supported his efforts. After Washington's party fired on a French detachment, Tanaghrisson rushed in and killed a French officer to ensure war—a prospect that would force British arms to support Iroquois interests in the valley.

Washington's party was soon defeated by a larger French force. The result was an international incident that prompted Virginian and British expansionists to demand war. But war in North America was a worrisome prospect: the colonies were notoriously incapable of cooperating in their own defense, and the Covenant Chain was badly in need of repair.

**The Albany Congress**   The Iroquois Confederacy was unhappy with its British alliance and believed that the British were neglecting the Iroquois while settlers from New York pressed onto their lands. Moreover, the Ohio Indians, France, and Britain were all acting in the Ohio Valley without consulting them. To mend relations with the Iroquois, the British Board of Trade called a meeting at Albany in June 1754. There, a prominent Mohawk leader named Hendrick Peters

**Hendrick Peters Theyanoguin, Chief of the Mohawks** Great Britain's alliance with the Iroquois Confederacy—the Covenant Chain—was central to its Indian policy in the mid-eighteenth century, and the Mohawk warrior and sachem Hendrick Peters Theyanoguin emerged as its most powerful spokesman. His speech at the Albany Congress of 1754, in which he urged Great Britain toward war, was reported in newspapers in Britain and the colonies and made him a transatlantic celebrity. This print was advertised for sale in London bookstalls just as his death at the Battle of Lake George (1755) was being reported in newspapers there. Hendrick wears a rich silk waistcoat, an overcoat trimmed with gold lace, a ruffled shirt, and a tricorn hat—gifts from his British allies—while he holds a wampum belt in one hand and a tomahawk in the other. Courtesy of the John Carter Brown Library at Brown University.

Original in the John Carter Brown Library at Brown University

Theyanoguin challenged Britain to defend its interests more vigorously, while Benjamin Franklin proposed a "Plan of Union" among the colonies to counter French expansion.

The Albany Plan of Union proposed that "one general government . . . be formed in America, including all the said colonies." It would have created a continental assembly to manage trade, Indian policy, and the colonies' defense. Though it was attractive to a few reform-minded colonists and administrators, the plan would have compromised the independence of colonial assemblies and the authority of Parliament. It never received serious consideration, but that did not stop the push toward war.

**The War Hawks Win**   In Parliament, the fight for the Ohio prompted a debate over war with France. Henry Pelham, the British prime minister, urged calm: "There is such a load of debt, and such heavy taxes already laid upon the people, that nothing but an absolute necessity can justifie our engaging in a new War." But two expansionist-minded war hawks — rising British statesman William Pitt and Lord Halifax, the new head of the Board of Trade — persuaded Pelham to launch an American war. In June 1755, British and New England troops captured Fort Beauséjour in the disputed territory of Nova Scotia (which the French called Acadia). Soldiers from Puritan Massachusetts then forced nearly 10,000 French settlers from their lands, arguing they were "rebels" without property rights, and deported them to France, the West Indies, and Louisiana (where "Acadians" became "Cajuns"). English and Scottish Protestants took over the farms the French Catholics left behind.

This Anglo-American triumph was quickly offset by a stunning defeat. In July 1755, General Edward Braddock advanced on Fort Duquesne with a force of 1,500 British regulars and Virginia militiamen. Braddock and his fellow officers were persuaded that British arms could easily triumph in the American backcountry, but instead they were routed by a French and Indian force. Braddock was killed, and more than half his troops were dead or wounded. "We have been beaten, most shamefully beaten, by a handfull of Men," George Washington complained bitterly as he led the survivors back to Virginia.

## The Great War for Empire

By 1756, the American conflict had spread to Europe, where it was known as the Seven Years' War, and pitted Britain and Prussia against France, Spain, and Austria. When Britain mounted major offensives in India, West Africa, and the West Indies as well as in North America, the conflict became the Great War for Empire.

William Pitt emerged as the architect of the British war effort. Pitt was a committed expansionist with a touch of arrogance. "I know that I can save this country and that I alone can," he boasted. A master strategist, he planned to cripple France by seizing its colonies. In North America, he enjoyed a decisive demographic advantage, since George II's 2 million subjects outnumbered the French 14 to 1. To mobilize the colonists, Pitt paid half the cost of their troops and supplied them with arms and equipment, at a cost of £1 million a year. He also committed a fleet of British ships and 30,000 British soldiers to the conflict in America.

Beginning in 1758, the powerful Anglo-American forces moved from one triumph to the next, in part because they brought Indian allies back into the fold. They forced the French to abandon Fort Duquesne (renamed Fort Pitt) and then captured Fort Louisbourg, the stronghold at the mouth of the St. Lawrence that had been captured in 1745, only to be returned at the close of the previous war. In 1759, an armada led by British general James Wolfe sailed down the St. Lawrence and took Quebec, the heart of France's American Empire. The Royal Navy prevented French reinforcements from crossing the Atlantic, allowing British forces to complete the conquest of Canada in 1760 by capturing Montreal (Map 4.3).

Elsewhere, the British likewise had great success. From Spain, the British won Cuba and the Philippine Islands. Fulfilling Pitt's dream, the East India Company ousted French traders from India, and British forces seized French Senegal in West Africa. They also captured the rich sugar islands of Martinique and Guadeloupe in

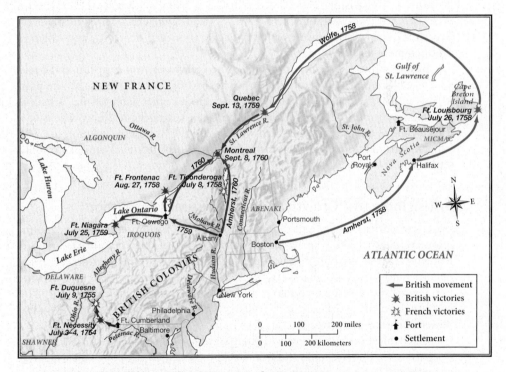

**MAP 4.3  The Anglo-American Conquest of New France**

After full-scale war with France began in 1756, it took almost three years for the British ministry to equip colonial forces and dispatch a sizable army to far-off America. In 1758, British and colonial troops attacked the heartland of New France, capturing Quebec in 1759 and Montreal in 1760. This conquest both united and divided the allies. Colonists celebrated the great victory: "The Illuminations and Fireworks exceeded any that had been exhibited before," reported the *South Carolina Gazette*. However, British officers had little respect for colonial soldiers. Said one, "[They are] the dirtiest, most contemptible, cowardly dogs you can conceive."

the French West Indies, but at the insistence of the West Indian sugar lobby (which wanted to protect its monopoly), the ministry returned the islands to France in the Treaty of Paris of 1763. Despite that controversial decision, the treaty confirmed Britain's triumph. It granted Britain sovereignty over half of North America, including French Canada, all French territory east of the Mississippi River, Spanish Florida, and the recent conquests in Africa and India. Britain had forged a commercial and colonial empire that was nearly worldwide.

Though Britain had won cautious support from some Native American groups in the late stages of the war, its territorial acquisitions alarmed many Native peoples from New York to the Mississippi, who preferred the presence of a few French traders to an influx of thousands of Anglo-American settlers. To encourage the French to return, the Ottawa chief Pontiac declared, "I am French, and I want to die French." Neolin, a Delaware prophet, went further, calling for the expulsion of all white-skinned invaders: "If you suffer the English among you, you are dead men. Sickness, smallpox, and their poison [rum] will destroy you entirely." In 1763, inspired by Neolin's nativist vision, Pontiac led a major uprising at Detroit. Following his example, Indians throughout the Great Lakes and Ohio Valley seized nearly every British military garrison west of Fort Niagara, besieged Fort Pitt, and killed or captured more than 2,000 settlers.

British military expeditions defeated the Delawares near Fort Pitt and broke the siege of Detroit, but it took the army nearly two years to reclaim all the posts it had lost. In the peace settlement, Pontiac and his allies accepted the British as their new political "fathers." The British ministry, having learned how expensive it was to control the trans-Appalachian west, issued the Royal Proclamation of 1763, which confirmed Indian control of the region and declared it off-limits to colonial settlement. It was an edict that many colonists would ignore.

## British Industrial Growth and the Consumer Revolution

Britain owed its military and diplomatic success to its unprecedented economic resources. Since 1700, when it had wrested control of many oceanic trade routes from the Dutch, Britain had become the dominant commercial power in the Atlantic and Indian oceans. By 1750, it was also becoming the first country to use new manufacturing technology and work discipline to expand output. This combination of commerce and industry would soon make Britain the most powerful nation in the world.

Mechanical power was key to Britain's Industrial Revolution. British artisans designed and built water mills and steam engines that efficiently powered a wide array of machines: lathes for shaping wood, jennies and looms for spinning and weaving textiles, and hammers for forging iron. Compared with traditional manufacturing methods, the new power-driven machinery produced woolen and linen textiles, iron tools, furniture, and chinaware in greater quantities—and at lower cost. Moreover, the entrepreneurs running the new workshops drove their employees hard, forcing them to keep pace with the machines and work long hours. To market the abundant factory-produced goods, English and Scottish merchants extended credit to colonial shopkeepers for a full year instead of the traditional six months. Americans soon were purchasing 30 percent of all British exports.

To pay for British manufactures, mainland colonists increased their exports of tobacco, rice, indigo, and wheat. Using credit advanced by Scottish merchants, planters in Virginia bought land, slaves, and equipment to grow tobacco, which they exported to expanding markets in France and central Europe. In South Carolina, rice planters used British government subsidies to develop indigo and rice plantations. New York, Pennsylvania, Maryland, and Virginia became the breadbasket of the Atlantic World, supplying Europe's exploding population with wheat.

Americans used their profits and the generous credit extended from overseas to buy English manufactures. When he was practicing law in Boston, John Adams visited the home of Nicholas Boylston, one of the city's wealthiest merchants, "to view the Furniture, which alone cost a thousand Pounds sterling," he wrote. "[T]he Marble Tables, the rich Beds with Crimson Damask Curtains and Counterpins, the Beautiful Chimny Clock, the Spacious Garden, are the most magnificent of any Thing I have ever seen." Through their possessions, well-to-do colonists set themselves apart from their humbler — or, as they might have said, more vulgar — neighbors.

Although Britain's **consumer revolution** raised living standards, it landed many consumers — and the colonies as a whole — in debt. Even during the wartime boom of the 1750s, exports paid for only 80 percent of British imports. Britain financed the remaining 20 percent — the Americans' trade deficit — through the extension of credit and Pitt's military expenditures. When the military subsidies ended in 1763, the colonies fell into an economic recession. Merchants looked anxiously at their overstocked warehouses and feared bankruptcy. "I think we have a gloomy prospect before us," a Philadelphia trader noted in 1765. The increase in transatlantic trade had made Americans more dependent on overseas credit and markets.

## The Struggle for Land in the East

In good times and bad, the population continued to grow, intensifying the demand for arable land. Consider the experience of Kent, Connecticut. Like earlier generations, Kent's residents had moved inland to establish new farms, but Kent stood at the colony's western boundary. To provide for the next generation, many Kent families joined the Susquehanna Company (1749), which speculated in lands in the Wyoming Valley in present-day northeastern Pennsylvania. As settlers took up farmsteads there, the company urged the Connecticut legislature to claim the region on the basis of Connecticut's "sea-to-sea" royal charter of 1662. However, Charles II had also granted the Wyoming Valley to William Penn, and the Penn family had sold farms there to Pennsylvania residents. By the late 1750s, settlers from Connecticut and Pennsylvania were at war, burning down their rivals' houses and barns. Delawares with their own claim to the valley were caught in the crossfire. In April 1763, the Delaware headman Teedyuscung was burned to death in his cabin; in retaliation, Teedyuscung's son Captain Bull led a war party that destroyed a community of Connecticut settlers.

Simultaneously, three distinct but related land disputes broke out in the Hudson River Valley (Map 4.4). Dutch tenant farmers, Wappinger Indians, and migrants

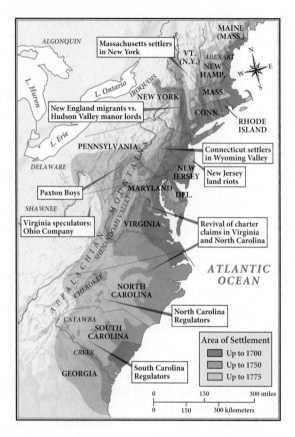

**MAP 4.4   Westward Expansion and Land Conflicts, 1750–1775**

Between 1750 and 1775, the mainland colonial population more than doubled—from 1.2 million to 2.5 million—triggering westward migrations and legal battles over land, which had become increasingly valuable. Violence broke out in eastern areas, where tenant farmers and smallholders contested landlords' property claims based on ancient titles; and in the backcountry, where migrating settlers fought with Indians, rival claimants, and the officials of eastern-dominated governments.

from Massachusetts asserted ownership rights to lands long claimed by manorial families such as the Van Rensselaers and the Livingstons. When the manor lords turned to the legal system to uphold their claims, Dutch and English farmers in Westchester, Dutchess, and Albany counties rioted to close the courts. In response, New York's royal governor ordered British troops to assist local sheriffs and manorial bailiffs: they suppressed the tenant uprisings, intimidated the Wappingers, and evicted the Massachusetts squatters.

Other land disputes erupted in New Jersey and the southern colonies, where landlords and English aristocrats had successfully revived legal claims based on long-dormant seventeenth-century charters. One court decision allowed Lord Granville, the heir of an original Carolina proprietor, to collect an annual tax on land in North Carolina; another decision awarded ownership of the entire northern neck of Virginia (along the Potomac River) to Lord Fairfax.

The revival of these proprietary claims by manorial lords and English nobles testified to the rising value of land along the Atlantic coastal plain. It also underscored the increasing similarities between rural societies in Europe and America. To avoid the status of European peasants, native-born yeomen and tenant families joined the stream of European migrants searching for cheap land near the Appalachian Mountains.

## Western Rebels and Regulators

As would-be landowners moved west, they sparked conflicts over Indian policy, political representation, and debts. During the war with France, Delaware and Shawnee warriors had exacted revenge for Thomas Penn's land swindle of 1737 by destroying frontier farms in Pennsylvania and killing hundreds of residents. Scots-Irish settlers demanded the expulsion of all Indians, but Quaker leaders refused. So in 1763, a group of Scots-Irish frontiersmen called the Paxton Boys massacred twenty Conestoga Indians, an assimilated community that had lived alongside their colonist neighbors peacefully for many years. When Governor John Penn tried to bring the murderers to justice, 250 armed Scots-Irishmen advanced on Philadelphia. Benjamin Franklin intercepted the angry mob at Lancaster and arranged a truce, averting a battle with the militia. Prosecution of the Paxton Boys failed for lack of witnesses, and the episode gave their defenders the opportunity to excoriate Pennsylvania's government for protecting Indians while it neglected the interests of backcountry colonists.

**The South Carolina Regulators**     Violence also broke out in the backcountry of South Carolina, where land-hungry Scottish and Anglo-American settlers clashed repeatedly with Cherokees during the war with France. After the fighting ended in 1763, a group of landowning vigilantes known as the **Regulators** demanded that the eastern-controlled government provide western districts with more courts, fairer taxation, and greater representation in the assembly. "We are *Free-Men* — British Subjects — Not Born *Slaves*," declared a Regulator manifesto. Fearing slave revolts, the lowland rice planters who ran the South Carolina assembly compromised. In 1767, the assembly created western courts and reduced the fees for legal documents; but it refused to reapportion the legislature or lower western taxes. Like the Paxton Boys in Pennsylvania, the South Carolina Regulators won attention to backcountry needs but failed to wrest power from the eastern elite.

**Civil Strife in North Carolina**     In 1766, a more radical Regulator movement arose in North Carolina. When the economic recession of the early 1760s brought a sharp fall in tobacco prices, many farmers could not pay their debts. When creditors sued these farmers for payment, judges directed sheriffs to seize the debtors' property. Many backcountry farmers lost their property or ended up in jail for resisting court orders.

To save their farms, North Carolina's debtors defied the government's authority. Disciplined mobs intimidated judges, closed courts, and freed their comrades from jail. The Regulators proposed a series of reforms, including lower legal fees and tax payments in the "produce of the country" rather than in cash. They also demanded greater representation in the assembly and a just revenue system that would tax each person "in proportion to the profits arising from his estate." All to no avail. In

May 1771, Royal Governor William Tryon mobilized British troops and the eastern militia, which defeated a large Regulator force at the Alamance River. When the fighting ended, thirty men lay dead, and Tryon summarily executed seven insurgent leaders. Not since Bacon's Rebellion in Virginia in 1675 and the colonial uprisings during the Glorious Revolution of 1688 (see Chapters 2 and 3) had a colonial dispute caused so much political agitation.

In 1771, as in 1675 and 1688, colonial conflicts became linked with imperial politics. In Connecticut, the Reverend Ezra Stiles defended the North Carolina Regulators. "What shall an injured & oppressed people do," he asked, "[when faced with] Oppression and tyranny?" Stiles's remarks reflected growing resistance to recently imposed British policies of taxation and control. The American colonies still depended primarily on Britain for their trade and military defense. However, by the 1760s, the mainland settlements had evolved into complex societies with the potential to exist independently. British policies would play a crucial role in determining the direction the maturing colonies would take.

| IN YOUR OWN WORDS | How did midcentury developments reflect Britain's deepening connections to North America? |
| --- | --- |

## Summary

In this chapter, we observed dramatic changes in British North America between 1720 and 1763. An astonishing surge in population — from 400,000 to almost 2 million — was the combined result of natural increase, European migration, and the African slave trade. The print revolution and the rise of the British Atlantic world brought important new influences: the European Enlightenment and European Pietism transformed the world of ideas, while a flood of British consumer goods and the genteel aspirations of wealthy colonists reshaped the colonies' material culture.

Colonists confronted three major regional challenges. In New England, crowded towns and ever-smaller farms threatened the yeoman ideal of independent farming, prompting families to limit births, move to the frontier, or participate in an "exchange" economy. In the Middle Atlantic colonies, Dutch, English, German, and Scots-Irish residents maintained their religious and cultural identities while they competed for access to land and political power. Across the backcountry, new interest in western lands triggered conflicts with Indian peoples, civil unrest among whites, and, ultimately, the Great War for Empire. In the aftermath of the fighting, Britain stood triumphant in Europe and America.

# Chapter 4 Review

## KEY TERMS

**Identify and explain the significance of each term below.**

tenancy (p. 103)
competency (p. 104)
coverture (p. 104)
household mode of production
   (p. 106)
squatters (p. 107)
redemptioner (p. 109)
Enlightenment (p. 112)

Pietism (p. 112)
natural rights (p. 113)
deism (p. 114)
revival (p. 115)
Old Lights (p. 116)
New Lights (p. 116)
consumer revolution (p. 125)
Regulators (p. 127)

## REVIEW QUESTIONS

**Answer these questions to demonstrate your understanding of the chapter's main ideas.**

1. What goals and values shaped New England society in the eighteenth century?
2. How were the goals of immigrants to the Middle colonies similar to those of New England colonists, and how did they differ?
3. How did the accelerating pace of travel and communication affect colonial society and culture?
4. How did midcentury developments reflect Britain's deepening connections to North America?
5. Review the events listed under "American and National Identity" and "Work, Exchange, and Technology" for the period 1720–1750 on the thematic timeline on page 70. How did economic developments in the colonies influence the formation of new cultural identities in this era?

## CHRONOLOGY

As you read, ask yourself why this chapter begins and ends with these dates and then identify the links among related events.

| | |
|---|---|
| **1695** | • Licensing Act lapses in England, triggering the print revolution |
| **1710s–1730s** | • Enlightenment ideas spread from Europe to America |
| | • Germans and Scots-Irish settle in Middle colonies |
| | • Theodore Jacob Frelinghuysen preaches Pietism to German migrants |
| **1720s–1730s** | • William and Gilbert Tennent lead Presbyterian revivals among Scots-Irish |
| | • Jonathan Edwards preaches in New England |
| **1729** | • Benjamin Franklin buys the *Pennsylvania Gazette* |
| **1739** | • George Whitefield sparks Great Awakening |
| **1740s–1760s** | • Conflict between Old Lights and New Lights |
| | • Shortage of farmland in New England threatens freehold ideal |
| | • Growing ethnic and religious pluralism in Middle Atlantic colonies |
| | • Religious denominations establish colleges |
| **1743** | • Benjamin Franklin founds American Philosophical Society |
| | • Samuel Morris starts Presbyterian revivals in Virginia |
| **1748** | • Ohio Company receives grant of 200,000 acres from the crown |
| **1749** | • Connecticut farmers form Susquehanna Company |
| **1750s** | • Industrial Revolution begins in England |
| | • British shipping dominates North Atlantic |
| | • Consumer purchases increase American imports and debt |
| **1754** | • French and Indian War begins |
| | • Iroquois and colonists meet at Albany Congress |
| | • Franklin's Plan of Union |

| **1756** | • Britain begins Great War for Empire |
| **1759–1760** | • Britain completes conquest of Canada |
| **1760s** | • Land conflict along New York and New England border |
| | • Baptist revivals win converts in Virginia |
| **1763** | • Pontiac's Rebellion leads to Proclamation of 1763 |
| | • Treaty of Paris ends Great War for Empire |
| | • Scots-Irish Paxton Boys massacre Indians in Pennsylvania |
| **1771** | • Royal governor puts down Regulator revolt in North Carolina |

# PART 3

Although Part 3 is dominated by the causes and consequences of the War of Independence, it opens in 1754 to capture the changes wrought by the Great War for Empire, which were revolutionary in themselves—Britain had triumphed in the war, only to see its American empire unravel and descend into rebellion. Against all odds, thirteen colonies first united to win their independence, and then formed a federal republic that could claim a place among the nations of the world. "The American war is over," Philadelphia Patriot Benjamin Rush declared in 1787, "but this is far from being the case with the American Revolution. On the contrary, nothing but the first act of the great drama is closed. It remains yet to establish and perfect our new forms of government."

The republican revolution extended far beyond politics. It challenged many of the values and institutions that had prevailed for centuries in Europe and the Atlantic world. After 1776, Americans reconsidered basic assumptions that structured their societies, cultures, families, and communities. These social and cultural effects of the Revolution were only beginning to take shape by 1800, but we end Part 3 there, when the essential characteristics of the United States were becoming clear. (Chapter 7 carries the political story forward to 1820 in order to trace key themes to their conclusion, but Part 4 takes 1800 as its start date.) This periodization—1754 to 1800—captures a critical phase in American history: the transition from imperial rivalry and wars among European powers and Native societies to the founding of a new nation-state and its political institutions. Three principal developments are discussed in Part 3.

## From British North America to the United States of America

To administer the vast new American territory it gained in 1763, Britain had to reform its empire. Until that time, its colonies had been left largely free to manage their own affairs. Now, Parliament hoped to pay the costs of empire by taxing the colonies, while at the same time extending control over its new lands in the continental interior. Colonial radicals resisted these reforms. Calling themselves Patriots, they insisted on preserving local control over taxes. As Britain pressured local communities, colonists created intercolonial institutions and developed a broad critique of British rule that combined older, republican political principles with radical ideas of natural rights and the equality of all men. Their protests grew more strident, eventually resulting in open warfare with Great Britain and a declaration of independence.

# Revolution and Republican Culture 1754–1800

## Experiments in Government

At the same time they fought a war against Great Britain, Patriot leaders in the newly independent states had to create new governments. They drafted constitutions for their states while maintaining a loose confederacy to bind them together. In 1787, reformers put forward a new plan of government: a constitution that would bind the states into a single nation.

The new American republic emerged fitfully. Experiments in government took shape across an entire generation, and it took still longer to decide how much power the federal republic should wield over the states. Political culture was unformed and slow to develop. Political parties, for example, were an unexpected development. At first they were widely regarded as illegitimate, but by 1800 they had become essential to managing political conflict, heightening some forms of competition while blunting others. In the last half of the eighteenth century, American political culture was transformed as newly created governments gained the allegiance of their citizens.

## Conquest, Competition, and Consolidation

One uncontested value of the Revolutionary era was a commitment to economic opportunity. To achieve this, people migrated in large numbers, creating new pressures on the United States to meet the needs of its citizens. The federal government acted against westerners who tried to rebel or secede, fought Indian wars to claim new territory, and turned back challenges from Britain and France to maintain its control over western lands. By 1820, the United States had dramatically expanded its boundaries and extended control far beyond the original seaboard states.

Even as the borders of the United States expanded, its diversity inhibited the effort to define an American culture and identity. Native Americans still lived in their own clans and nations; black Americans were developing a distinct African American culture; and white Americans were enmeshed in vigorous regional ethnic communities. But by 1800, to be an American meant, for many members of the dominant white population, to be a republican, a Protestant, and an enterprising individual.

## Thematic Understanding

This timeline arranges some of the important events of this period into themes. Consider the items listed under the theme "Culture and Society." How did the American Revolution challenge existing social arrangements? Consider the role of religion in American life, the status of women, and the institution of slavery. What tensions developed as a result of those challenges?

| AMERICAN AND NATIONAL IDENTITY | POLITICS AND POWER | WORK, EXCHANGE, AND TECHNOLOGY |
|---|---|---|
| **1763** • Concept of popular sovereignty gains force <br> • Colonists claim rights of Englishmen | • Stamp Act Congress (1765) <br> • First Continental Congress (1774) <br> • Second Continental Congress (1775) | • Merchants defy Sugar and Stamp Acts <br> • Patriots boycott British goods in 1765, 1767, and 1774 <br> • Boycotts spur Patriot women to make textiles |
| **1776** • Thomas Paine's *Common Sense* (1776) causes colonists to rethink political loyalties <br> • New state constitutions rely on property qualifications to define citizenship rights | • The Declaration of Independence (1776) <br> • States adopt republican constitutions (1776 on) <br> • Articles of Confederation ratified (1781) <br> • Treaty of Paris (1783) | • Manufacturing expands during the war <br> • Cutoff of trade and severe inflation threaten economy <br> • War debt grows |
| **1787** • Indians form Western Confederacy (1790) <br> • Second Great Awakening (1790–1860) <br> • Emerging political divide between South and North | • U.S. Constitution drafted (1787) <br> • Conflict over Alexander Hamilton's economic policies <br> • First national parties: Federalists and Republicans | • Bank of the United States founded (1791) <br> • Land speculation increases in the West <br> • War in Europe raises wheat prices <br> • Invention of cotton gin creates boom in cotton production |
| **1800** • Marshall's Supreme Court affirms national over state powers | • Jefferson reduces activism of national government <br> • "Era of Good Feeling" in politics | • Congress cuts off Atlantic slave trade (1808) <br> • Eastern farmers change crop mix and upgrade equipment |

| CULTURE AND SOCIETY | MIGRATION AND SETTLEMENT | GEOGRAPHY AND THE ENVIRONMENT | AMERICA IN THE WORLD | |
|---|---|---|---|---|
| • Patriots call for American unity<br>• The idea of natural rights challenges the institution of chattel slavery | • Migration into the Ohio Valley after Pontiac's Rebellion<br>• Quebec Act (1774) allows Catholicism | • The trans-Appalachian west attracts the interest of settlers and investors<br>• Ohio Indians resist Anglo-American expansion | • France and Spain cede all their territories east of the Mississippi River to Britain in the Treaty of Paris (1763)<br>• Patriots invade Canada (1775) | 1763 |
| • Judith Sargent Murray publishes "On the Equality of the Sexes" (1779)<br>• Emancipation of slaves begins in the North<br>• Virginia enacts religious freedom (1786) | • Declining immigration from Europe (1775–1820) enhances American identity<br>• African American slaves seek freedom through military service | • The vast geographical scale of the American Revolution poses challenges for its combatants | • Thomas Paine's *Common Sense* (1776) assaults monarchy<br>• U.S. alliances with France (1778) and Spain (1779) virtually ensure a Patriot victory | 1776 |
| • Politicians and ministers deny vote to women; praise republican motherhood<br>• Bill of Rights ratified (1791)<br>• Sedition Act limits freedom of the press (1798) | • State cessions, land ordinances, and Indian wars create national domain in the West<br>• The Alien Act makes it harder for immigrants to become citizens and allows deportation (1798) | • The Northwest Ordinance and sham Indian treaties open western land to settlement | • War between Britain and France puts American neutrality at risk<br>• The French Revolution divides Americans | 1787 |
| • Handsome Lake preaches a middle path between Indian and Christian traditions | • Conflicts with Native Americans increase as settlers move west | • The Louisiana Purchase (1803) nearly doubles the size of the U.S.<br>• Lewis and Clark explore the West (1804–1806) | • Jefferson enacts Embargo Act of 1807<br>• Battle of Tippecanoe eliminates threat from Western Confederacy<br>• War of 1812 | 1800 |

# 5

# The Problem of Empire

## 1754–1776

**IDENTIFY THE BIG IDEA**

Was colonial independence inevitable, and was war the only way to achieve it?

**IN JUNE 1775, THE CITY OF NEW YORK FACED A PERPLEXING DILEMMA.**
Word arrived that George Washington, who had just been named commander in chief of the newly formed Continental army, was coming to town. But on the same day, William Tryon, the colony's crown-appointed governor, was scheduled to return from Britain. Local leaders orchestrated a delicate dance. Though the Provincial Congress was operating illegally in the eyes of the crown, it did not wish to offend Governor Tryon. It instructed the city's newly raised volunteer battalion to divide in two. One company awaited Washington's arrival, while another prepared to greet the governor. The "residue of the Battalion" was to be "ready to receive either the General or Governour *Tryon*, which ever shall first arrive." Washington arrived first. He was met by nine companies of the volunteer battalion and a throng of well-wishers, who escorted him to his rooms in a local tavern. Many of this same crowd then crossed town to join the large group assembled to greet the governor, whose ship was just landing. The crowd met him with "universal shouts of applause" and accompanied him home.

This awkward moment in the history of one American city reflects a larger crisis of loyalty that plagued colonists throughout British North America in the years between 1763 and 1776. The outcome of the Great War for Empire left Great Britain the undisputed master of eastern North America. But that success pointed the way to catastrophe. Convinced of the need to reform the empire and tighten its administration, British policymakers imposed a series of new administrative measures on the colonies.

Accustomed as they were to governing their own affairs, colonists could not accept these changes. Yet the bonds of loyalty were strong, and the unraveling of British authority was tortuous and complex. Only gradually — as militancy slowly mounted on both sides — were the ties of empire broken and independence declared.

# An Empire Transformed

The war that began as the French and Indian War in 1754 and culminated in the Great War for Empire of 1756–1763 (Chapter 4) transformed the British Empire in North America. The British ministry could no longer let the colonies manage their own affairs while it minimally oversaw Atlantic trade. Its interests and responsibilities now extended far into the continental interior — a much more costly and complicated proposition than it had ever faced before. And neither its American colonies nor their Native American neighbors were inclined to cooperate in the transformation.

British administrators worried about their American colonists, who, according to former Georgia governor Henry Ellis, felt themselves "entitled to a greater measure of Liberty than is enjoyed by the people of England." Ireland had been closely ruled for decades, and recently the East India Company set up dominion over millions of non-British peoples (Map 5.1). Britain's American possessions were likewise filled with aliens and "undesirables": "French, Dutch, Germans innumerable, Indians, Africans, and a multitude of felons from this country," as one member of Parliament put it. Consequently, declared Lord Halifax, "The people of England" considered Americans "as foreigners."

Contesting that status, wealthy Philadelphia lawyer John Dickinson argued that his fellow colonists were "not [East Indian] Sea Poys, nor Marattas, but *British subjects* who are born to liberty, who know its worth, and who prize it high." Thus was the stage set for a struggle between the conceptions of identity — and empire — held by British ministers, on the one hand, and many American colonists on the other.

## The Costs of Empire

The Great War for Empire imposed enormous costs on Great Britain. The national debt soared from £75 million to £133 million and was, an observer noted, "becoming the alarming object of every British subject." By war's end, interest on the debt alone consumed 60 percent of the nation's budget, and the ministry had to raise taxes. During the eighteenth century, taxes were shifting from land — owned by the gentry and aristocracy — to consumables, and successive ministries became ever more ingenious in devising new ways to raise money. Excise (or sales) taxes were levied on all kinds of ordinary goods — salt and beer, bricks and candles, paper (in the form of a stamp tax) — that were consumed by middling and poor Britons. In the 1760s, the per capita tax burden was 20 percent of income.

To collect the taxes, the government doubled the size of the tax bureaucracy. Customs agents patrolled the coasts of southern Britain, seizing tons of contraband French wines, Dutch tea, and Flemish textiles. Convicted smugglers faced heavy

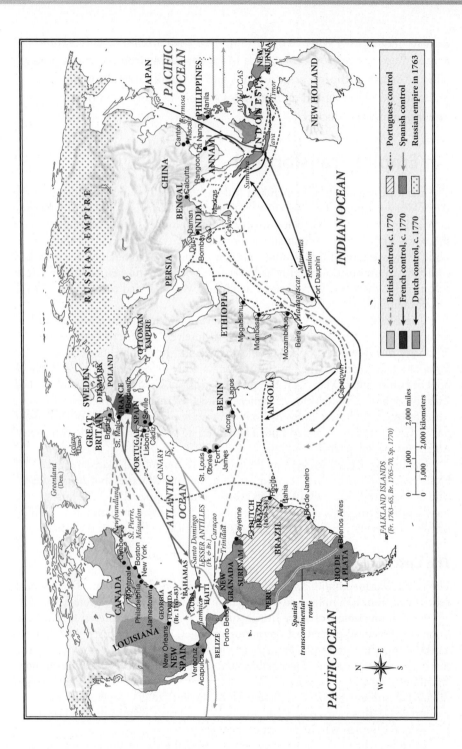

penalties, including death or forced "transportation" to America as indentured servants. (Despite colonial protests, nearly fifty thousand English criminals had already been shipped to America to be sold as indentured servants.)

The price of empire abroad was thus larger government and higher taxes at home. Members of two British opposition parties, the Radical Whigs and the Country Party, complained that the huge war debt placed the nation at the mercy of the "monied interests," the banks and financiers who reaped millions of pounds' interest from government bonds. To reverse the growth of government and the threat to personal liberty and property rights, British reformers demanded that Parliament represent a broader spectrum of the property-owning classes. The Radical Whig John Wilkes condemned rotten boroughs—sparsely populated, aristocratic-controlled electoral districts—and demanded greater representation for rapidly growing commercial and manufacturing cities. The war thus transformed British politics.

The war also revealed how little power Britain wielded in its American colonies. In theory, royal governors had extensive political powers; in reality, they shared power with the colonial assemblies, which outraged British officials. Moreover, colonial merchants had evaded trade duties for decades by bribing customs officials. To end that practice, Parliament passed the Revenue Act of 1762. The ministry also instructed the Royal Navy to seize American vessels carrying food crops from the mainland colonies to the French West Indies. It was absurd, declared a British politician, that French armies attempting "to Destroy one English province . . . are actually supported by Bread raised in another."

Britain's military victory brought another fundamental shift in policy: a new peacetime deployment of 15 royal battalions—some 7,500 troops—in North America. In part the move was strategic. The troops would maintain Britain's hold on its vast new North American territory: they would prevent colonists from defying the Proclamation of 1763 (see Chapter 4), while managing relations with Native Americans and 60,000 French residents of Canada, Britain's newly conquered colony (Map 5.2).

In part, too, the move had financial implications. The cost of supporting these troops was estimated at £225,000 per year, and Parliament expected that the colonies would bear the cost of the troops stationed in America. The king's ministers agreed that Parliament could no longer let them off the hook for the costs of empire. The greatest gains from the war had come in North America, where the specter of French encirclement had finally been lifted, and the greatest new postwar expenses were being incurred in North America as well.

**< MAP 5.1   Eurasian Trade and European Colonies, c. 1770**
By 1770, the Western European nations that had long dominated maritime trade had created vast colonial empires and spheres of influence. Spain controlled the western halves of North and South America, Portugal owned Brazil, and Holland ruled Indonesia. Britain, a newer imperial power, boasted settler societies in North America, rich sugar islands in the West Indies, slave ports in West Africa, and a growing presence on the Indian subcontinent. France had lost its possessions on mainland North America but retained lucrative sugar islands in the Caribbean.

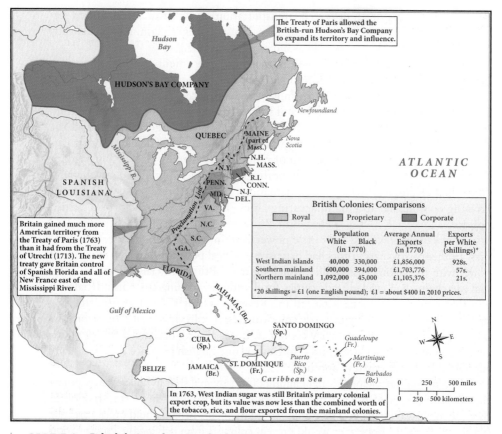

The Treaty of Paris allowed the British-run Hudson's Bay Company to expand its territory and influence.

Britain gained much more American territory from the Treaty of Paris (1763) than it had from the Treaty of Utrecht (1713). The new treaty gave Britain control of Spanish Florida and all of New France east of the Mississippi River.

British Colonies: Comparisons

| | | Royal | | Proprietary | | Corporate |
|---|---|---|---|---|---|---|

| | Population White Black (in 1770) | | Average Annual Exports (in 1770) | Exports per White (shillings)* |
|---|---|---|---|---|
| West Indian islands | 40,000 | 330,000 | £1,856,000 | 928s. |
| Southern mainland | 600,000 | 394,000 | £1,703,776 | 57s. |
| Northern mainland | 1,092,000 | 45,000 | £1,105,376 | 21s. |

*20 shillings = £1 (one English pound); £1 = about $400 in 2010 prices.

In 1763, West Indian sugar was still Britain's primary colonial export crop, but its value was now less than the combined worth of the tobacco, rice, and flour exported from the mainland colonies.

**MAP 5.2  Britain's American Empire in 1763**
The Treaty of Paris gave Britain control of the eastern half of North America and returned a few captured sugar islands in the West Indies to France. To protect the empire's new mainland territories, British ministers dispatched troops to Florida and Quebec. They also sent troops to uphold the terms of the Proclamation of 1763, which prohibited Anglo-American settlement west of the Appalachian Mountains.

## George Grenville and the Reform Impulse

The challenge of raising revenue from the colonies fell first to George Grenville. Widely regarded as "one of the ablest men in Great Britain," Grenville understood the need for far-reaching imperial reform. He first passed the Currency Act of 1764, which banned the American colonies from using paper money as legal tender. Colonial shopkeepers, planters, and farmers had used local currency, which was worth less than British pounds sterling, to pay their debts to British merchants. The Currency Act ensured that merchants would no longer be paid in money printed in the colonies, boosting their profits and British wealth.

**The Sugar Act**   Grenville also won parliamentary approval of the **Sugar Act of 1764** to replace the widely ignored Molasses Act of 1733 (see Chapter 3). The earlier act had set a tax rate of 6 pence per gallon on French molasses, in effect outlawing the trade, since such a high tax made it unprofitable. Rather than pay it, colonial merchants bribed customs officials at the going rate of 1.5 pence per gallon. Grenville intended to allow the trade and settled on a duty of 3 pence per gallon, which merchants could pay and still turn a profit.

This carefully crafted policy garnered little support in America. New England merchants, among them John Hancock of Boston, had made their fortunes smuggling French molasses. In 1754, Boston merchants paid customs duties on a mere 400 hogsheads of molasses, yet they imported 40,000 hogsheads for use by 63 Massachusetts rum distilleries. Publicly, the merchants claimed that the Sugar Act would ruin the distilling industry; privately, they vowed to evade the duty by smuggling or by bribing officials.

**The End of Salutary Neglect**　　More important, colonists raised constitutional objections to the Sugar Act. In Massachusetts, the leader of the assembly argued that the new legislation was "contrary to a fundamental Principall of our Constitution: That all Taxes ought to originate with the people." In Rhode Island, Governor Stephen Hopkins warned: "They who are taxed at pleasure by others cannot possibly have any property, and they who have no property, can have no freedom." The Sugar Act raised other constitutional issues as well. Merchants prosecuted under the act would be tried in **vice-admiralty courts**, tribunals governing the high seas and run by British-appointed judges. Previously, merchants accused of Navigation Acts violations were tried by local common-law courts, where friendly juries often acquitted them. The Sugar Act instead extended the jurisdiction of the vice-admiralty courts to all customs offenses.

The Sugar Act revived old American fears. The influential Virginia planter Richard Bland emphasized that the American colonists "were not sent out to be the Slaves but to be the Equals of those that remained behind." John Adams, the young Massachusetts lawyer defending John Hancock on a charge of smuggling, argued that the vice-admiralty courts diminished this equality by "degrad[ing] every American . . . below the rank of an Englishman."

In fact, accused smugglers in Britain were also tried in vice-admiralty courts, so there was no discrimination against Americans. The real issue was the growing power of the British state. After decades of salutary neglect, Americans saw that the new imperial regime would deprive them "of some of their most essential Rights as British subjects," as a committee of the Massachusetts assembly put it. In response, Royal Governor Francis Bernard replied: "The rule that a British subject shall not be bound by laws or liable to taxes, but what he has consented to by his representatives must be confined to the inhabitants of Great Britain only." To Bernard, Grenville, and other imperial reformers, Americans were second-class subjects of the king, with rights limited by the Navigation Acts, parliamentary laws, and British interests.

## An Open Challenge: The Stamp Act

Another new tax, the **Stamp Act of 1765**, sparked the first great imperial crisis. Grenville hoped the Stamp Act would raise £60,000 per year. The act would require a tax stamp on all printed items, from college diplomas, court documents, land titles, and contracts to newspapers, almanacs, and playing cards. It was ingeniously

**Protesting the Stamp Act in Portsmouth, New Hampshire** Throughout the colonies, disciplined mobs protesting the Stamp Act forced stamp distributors to resign their offices. In this engraving, protesters in the small city of Portsmouth, New Hampshire, stone an effigy of the distributor as other members of the mob carry off a coffin representing the death of American "Liberty." Illustration from "Interesting Events in the History of the U.S." by J. W. Barber, 1829/Picture Research Consultants & Archives.

designed. Like its counterpart in England, it bore more heavily on the rich, since it charged only a penny a sheet for newspapers and other common items but up to £10 for a lawyer's license. It also required no new bureaucracy; stamped paper would be delivered to colonial ports and sold to printers in lieu of unstamped stock.

Benjamin Franklin, agent of the Pennsylvania assembly, proposed a different solution: American representation in Parliament. "If you chuse to tax us," he wrote, "give us Members in your Legislature, and let us be one People." With the exception of William Pitt, British politicians rejected Franklin's idea as too radical. They argued that the colonists already had **virtual representation** in Parliament because some of its members were transatlantic merchants and West Indian sugar planters. Colonial leaders were equally skeptical of Franklin's plan. Americans were "situate at a great Distance from their Mother Country," the Connecticut assembly declared, and therefore "cannot participate in the general Legislature of the Nation."

The House of Commons ignored American opposition and passed the act by an overwhelming majority of 205 to 49. At the request of General Thomas Gage, the British military commander in America, Parliament also passed the **Quartering Act of 1765**, which required colonial governments to provide barracks and food for British troops. Finally, Parliament approved Grenville's proposal that violations of the Stamp Act be tried in vice-admiralty courts.

Using the doctrine of parliamentary supremacy, Grenville had begun to fashion a centralized imperial system in America much like that already in place in Ireland: British officials would govern the colonies with little regard for the local assemblies. Consequently, the prime minister's plan provoked a constitutional confrontation on the specific issues of taxation, jury trials, and military quartering as well as on the general question of representative self-government.

| IN YOUR OWN WORDS | What changes in Britain's imperial policy were triggered by its victory in the Great War for Empire? |

# The Dynamics of Rebellion, 1765–1770

In the name of reform, Grenville had thrown down the gauntlet to the Americans. The colonists had often resisted unpopular laws and aggressive governors, but they had faced an all-out attack on their institutions only once before—in 1686, when James II had unilaterally imposed the Dominion of New England. Now the danger was even greater because both the king and Parliament backed reform. But the Patriots, as the defenders of American rights came to be called, met the challenge posed by Grenville and his successor, Charles Townshend. They organized protests—formal and informal, violent as well as peaceful—and fashioned a compelling ideology of resistance.

## Formal Protests and the Politics of the Crowd

Virginia's House of Burgesses was the first formal body to complain. In May 1765, hotheaded young Patrick Henry denounced Grenville's legislation and attacked George III (r. 1760–1820) for supporting it. He compared the king to Charles I, whose tyranny had led to his overthrow and execution in the 1640s. These remarks, which bordered on treason, frightened the Burgesses; nonetheless, they condemned the Stamp Act's "manifest Tendency to Destroy American freedom." In Massachusetts, James Otis, another republican-minded firebrand, persuaded the House of Representatives to call a meeting of all the mainland colonies "to implore Relief" from the act.

**The Stamp Act Congress**    Nine assemblies sent delegates to the **Stamp Act Congress**, which met in New York City in October 1765. The congress protested the loss of American "rights and liberties," especially the right to trial by jury. It also challenged the constitutionality of both the Stamp and Sugar Acts by declaring that only the colonists' elected representatives could tax them. Still, moderate-minded delegates wanted compromise, not confrontation. They assured Parliament that Americans "glory in being subjects of the best of Kings" and humbly petitioned for repeal of the Stamp Act. Other influential Americans favored active (but peaceful) resistance, organizing a boycott of British goods.

**Crowd Actions**    Popular opposition also took a violent form, however. When the Stamp Act went into effect on November 1, 1765, disciplined mobs demanded the resignation of stamp-tax collectors. In Boston, a group calling itself the **Sons of Liberty** burned an effigy of collector Andrew Oliver and then destroyed Oliver's new brick warehouse. Two weeks later, Bostonians attacked the house of Lieutenant Governor Thomas Hutchinson, Oliver's brother-in-law and a prominent defender of imperial authority, breaking his furniture, looting his wine cellar, and setting fire to his library.

Wealthy merchants and Patriot lawyers, such as John Hancock and John Adams, encouraged the mobs, which were usually led by middling artisans and minor merchants. In New York City, nearly three thousand shopkeepers, artisans, laborers, and seamen marched through the streets breaking windows and crying "Liberty!" Resistance to the Stamp Act spread far beyond the port cities. In nearly every colony, angry crowds — the "rabble," their detractors called them — intimidated royal officials. Near Wethersfield, Connecticut, five hundred farmers seized tax collector Jared Ingersoll and forced him to resign his office in "the Cause of the People."

**The Motives of the Crowd**    Such crowd actions were common in both Britain and America, and protesters had many motives. Roused by the Great Awakening, evangelical Protestants resented arrogant British military officers and corrupt royal bureaucrats. In New England, where rioters invoked the antimonarchy sentiments of their great-grandparents, an anonymous letter sent to a Boston newspaper promising to save "all the Freeborn Sons of America" was signed "Oliver Cromwell," the English republican revolutionary of the 1650s. In New York City, Sons of Liberty leaders Isaac Sears and Alexander McDougall were minor merchants and Radical Whigs who feared that imperial reform would undermine political liberty. The mobs also included apprentices, day laborers, and unemployed sailors: young men with their own notions of liberty who — especially if they had been drinking — were quick to resort to violence.

Nearly everywhere popular resistance nullified the Stamp Act. Fearing an assault on Fort George, New York lieutenant governor Cadwallader Colden called on General Gage to use his small military force to protect the stamps. Gage refused. "Fire from the Fort might disperse the Mob, but it would not quell them," he told Colden, and the result would be "an Insurrection, the Commencement of Civil War." The tax was collected in Barbados and Jamaica, but frightened collectors resigned their offices in all thirteen colonies that would eventually join in the Declaration of Independence. This popular insurrection gave a democratic cast to the emerging Patriot movement. "Nothing is wanting but your own Resolution," declared a New York rioter, "for great is the Authority and Power of the People."

## The Ideological Roots of Resistance

Some Americans couched their resistance in constitutional terms. Many were lawyers or well-educated merchants and planters. Composing pamphlets of remarkable political sophistication, they gave the resistance movement its rationale, its political agenda, and its leaders.

Patriot writers drew on three intellectual traditions. The first was **English common law**, the centuries-old body of legal rules and procedures that protected the lives and property of the monarch's subjects. In the famous *Writs of Assistance* case of 1761, Boston lawyer James Otis invoked English legal precedents to challenge open-ended search warrants. In demanding a jury trial for John Hancock in the late 1760s, John Adams appealed to the Magna Carta (1215), the ancient document that, said Adams, "has for many Centuries been esteemed by Englishmen, as one of the . . . firmest Bulwarks of their Liberties." Other lawyers protested that new strictures violated specific "liberties and privileges" granted in colonial charters or embodied in Britain's "ancient constitution."

Enlightenment rationalism provided Patriots with a second important intellectual resource. Virginia planter Thomas Jefferson and other Patriots drew on the writings of John Locke, who had argued that all individuals possessed certain **natural rights** — life, liberty, and property — that governments must protect (see Chapter 4). And they turned to the works of French philosopher Montesquieu, who had maintained that a "separation of powers" among government departments prevented arbitrary rule.

The republican and Whig strands of the English political tradition provided a third ideological source for American Patriots. Puritan New England had long venerated the Commonwealth era (1649–1660), when England had been a republic (see Chapter 2). After the Glorious Revolution of 1688–1689, many colonists praised the English Whigs for creating a constitutional monarchy that prevented the king from imposing taxes and other measures. Joseph Warren, a physician and a Radical Whig Patriot, suggested that the Stamp Act was part of a ministerial plot "to force the colonies into rebellion" and justify the use of "military power to reduce them to servitude." John Dickinson's *Letters from a Farmer in Pennsylvania* (1768) urged colonists to "remember your ancestors and your posterity" and oppose parliamentary taxes. The letters circulated widely and served as an early call to resistance. If Parliament could tax the colonies without their consent, he wrote, "our boasted liberty is but A sound and nothing else."

Such arguments, widely publicized in newspapers and pamphlets, gave intellectual substance to the Patriot movement and turned a series of impromptu riots, tax protests, and boycotts of British manufactures into a formidable political force.

## Another Kind of Freedom

"We are taxed without our own consent," Dickinson wrote in one of his *Letters*. "We are therefore — SLAVES." As Patriot writers argued that taxation without representation made colonists the slaves of Parliament, many, including Benjamin Franklin in Philadelphia and James Otis in Massachusetts, also began to condemn the institution of chattel slavery itself as a violation of slaves' natural rights. African Americans made the connection as well. In Massachusetts, slaves submitted at least four petitions to the legislature asking that slavery be abolished. As one petition noted, slaves "have in common with other men, a natural right to be free, and without molestation, to enjoy such property, as they may acquire by their industry."

In the southern colonies, where slaves constituted half or more of the population and the economy depended on their servitude, the quest for freedom alarmed slaveholders. In November 1773, a group of Virginia slaves hoped to win their freedom by supporting British troops that, they heard, would soon arrive in the colony. Their plan was uncovered, and, as James Madison wrote, "proper precautions" were taken "to prevent the Infection" from spreading. He fully understood how important it was to defend the colonists' liberties without allowing the idea of natural rights to undermine the institution of slavery. "It is prudent," he wrote, "such things should be concealed as well as suppressed." Throughout the Revolution, the quest for African American rights and liberties would play out alongside that of the colonies, but unlike national independence, the liberation of African Americans would not be fulfilled for many generations.

## Parliament and Patriots Square Off Again

When news of the Stamp Act riots and the boycott reached Britain, Parliament was already in turmoil. Disputes over domestic policy had led George III to dismiss Grenville as prime minister. However, Grenville's allies demanded that imperial reform continue, if necessary at gunpoint. "The British legislature," declared Chief Justice Sir James Mansfield, "has authority to bind every part and every subject, whether such subjects have a right to vote or not."

Yet a majority in Parliament was persuaded that the Stamp Act was cutting deeply into British exports and thus doing more harm than good. "The Avenues of Trade are all shut up," a Bristol merchant told Parliament: "We have no Remittances and are at our Witts End for want of Money to fulfill our Engagements with our Tradesmen." Grenville's successor, the Earl of Rockingham, forged a compromise. He repealed the Stamp Act and reduced the duty on molasses imposed by the Sugar Act to a penny a gallon. Then he pacified imperial reformers and hard-liners with the **Declaratory Act of 1766**, which explicitly reaffirmed Parliament's "full power and authority to make laws and statutes . . . to bind the colonies and people of America . . . in all cases whatsoever." By swiftly ending the Stamp Act crisis, Rockingham hoped it would be forgotten just as quickly.

**Charles Townshend Steps In**    Often the course of history is changed by a small event — an illness, a personal grudge, a chance remark. That was the case in 1767, when George III named William Pitt to head a new government. Pitt, chronically ill and often absent from parliamentary debates, left chancellor of the exchequer Charles Townshend in command. Pitt was sympathetic toward America; Townshend was not. He had strongly supported the Stamp Act, and in 1767 he promised to find a new source of revenue in America.

The new tax legislation, the **Townshend Act of 1767**, had both fiscal and political goals. It imposed duties on colonial imports of paper, paint, glass, and tea that were expected to raise about £40,000 a year. Though Townshend did allocate some of this revenue for American military expenses, he earmarked most of it to pay the salaries of royal governors, judges, and other imperial officials, who had always previously been paid by colonial assemblies. Now, he hoped, royal appointees could better enforce parliamentary laws and carry out the king's instructions. Townshend next devised the Revenue Act of 1767, which created a board of customs commissioners in Boston and vice-admiralty courts in Halifax, Boston, Philadelphia, and Charleston. By using parliamentary taxes to finance imperial administration, Townshend intended to undermine American political institutions.

The Townshend duties revived the constitutional debate over taxation. During the Stamp Act crisis, some Americans, including Benjamin Franklin, distinguished between external and internal taxes. They suggested that external duties on trade (such as those long mandated by the Navigation Acts) were acceptable to Americans, but that direct, or internal, taxes were not. Townshend thought this distinction was "perfect nonsense," but he indulged the Americans and laid duties only on trade.

**A Second Boycott and the Daughters of Liberty**   Even so, most colonial leaders rejected the legitimacy of Townshend's measures. In February 1768, the Massachusetts assembly condemned the Townshend Act, and Boston and New York merchants began a new boycott of British goods. Throughout Puritan New England, ministers and public officials discouraged the purchase of "foreign superfluities" and promoted the domestic manufacture of cloth and other necessities.

American women, ordinarily excluded from public affairs, became crucial to the **nonimportation movement**. They reduced their households' consumption of imported goods and produced large quantities of homespun cloth. Pious farmwives spun yarn at their ministers' homes. In Berwick, Maine, "true Daughters of Liberty" celebrated American products by "drinking rye coffee and dining on bear venison." Other women's groups supported the boycott with charitable work, spinning flax and wool for the needy. Just as Patriot men followed tradition by joining crowd

**Edenton Ladies' Tea Party**   In October 1774, a group of fifty-one women from Edenton, North Carolina, led by Penelope Barker, created a local association to support a boycott of British goods. Patriots in the colonies praised the Edenton Tea Party, which was one of the first formal female political associations in North America, but it was ridiculed in Britain, where this cartoon appeared in March 1775. The women are given a mannish appearance, and the themes of promiscuity and neglect to their female duties are suggested by the presence of a slave and an amorous man, the neglected child, and the urinating dog. Library of Congress.

actions, so women's protests reflected their customary concern for the well-being of the community.

Newspapers celebrated these exploits of the Daughters of Liberty. One Massachusetts town proudly claimed an annual output of 30,000 yards of cloth; East Hartford, Connecticut, reported 17,000 yards. This surge in domestic production did not offset the loss of British imports, which had averaged about 10 million yards of cloth annually, but it brought thousands of women into the public arena.

The boycott mobilized many American men as well. In the seaport cities, the Sons of Liberty published the names of merchants who imported British goods and harassed their employees and customers. By March 1769, the nonimportation movement had spread to Philadelphia; two months later, the members of the Virginia House of Burgesses vowed not to buy duties articles, luxury goods, or imported slaves. Reflecting colonial self-confidence, Benjamin Franklin called for a return to the pre-1763 mercantilist system: "Repeal the laws, renounce the right, recall the troops, refund the money, and return to the old method of requisition."

Despite the enthusiasm of Patriots, nonimportation—accompanied by pressure on merchants and consumers who resisted it—opened fissures in colonial society. Not only royal officials, but also merchants, farmers, and ordinary folk, were subject to new forms of surveillance and coercion—a pattern that would only become more pronounced as the imperial crisis unfolded.

**Troops to Boston**   American resistance only increased British determination. When the Massachusetts assembly's letter opposing the Townshend duties reached London, Lord Hillsborough, the secretary of state for American affairs, branded it "unjustifiable opposition to the constitutional authority of Parliament." To strengthen the "Hand of Government" in Massachusetts, Hillsborough dispatched General Thomas Gage and 2,000 British troops to Boston (Map 5.3). Once in Massachusetts, Gage accused its leaders of "Treasonable and desperate Resolves" and advised the ministry to "Quash this Spirit at a Blow." In 1765, American resistance to the Stamp Act had sparked a parliamentary debate; in 1768, it provoked a plan for military coercion.

## The Problem of the West

At the same time that successive ministries addressed the problem of raising a colonial revenue, they quarreled over how to manage the vast new inland territory—about half a billion acres—acquired in the Treaty of Paris in 1763 (see Chapter 4). The Proclamation Line had drawn a boundary between the colonies and Indian country. The line was originally intended as a temporary barrier. It prohibited settlement "for the present, and until our further Pleasure be known." The Proclamation also created three new mainland colonies—Quebec, East Florida, and West Florida—and thus opened new opportunities at the northern and southern extremities of British North America.

But many colonists looked west rather than north or south. Four groups in the colonies were especially interested in westward expansion. First, gentlemen who had invested in numerous land speculation companies were petitioning the crown for large land grants in the Ohio country. Second, officers who served in the Seven Years' War were paid in land warrants—up to 5,000 acres for field officers—and some, led by George Washington, were exploring possible sites beyond the Appalachians.

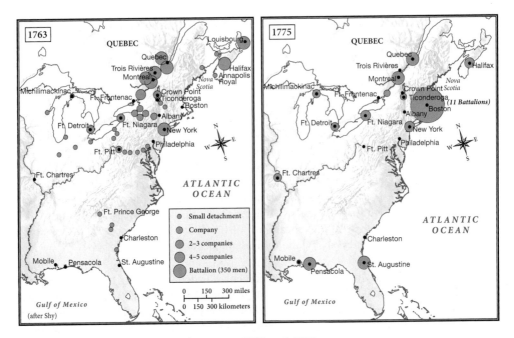

**MAP 5.3   British Troop Deployments, 1763 and 1775**

As the imperial crisis deepened, British military priorities changed. In 1763, most British battalions were stationed in Canada to deter Indian uprisings and French Canadian revolts. After the Stamp Act riots of 1765, the British placed large garrisons in New York and Philadelphia. By 1775, eleven battalions of British regulars occupied Boston, the center of the Patriot movement.

Third, Indian traders who had received large grants from the Ohio Indians hoped to sell land titles. And fourth, thousands of squatters were following the roads cut to the Ohio by the Braddock and Forbes campaigns during the Seven Years' War to take up lands in the hope that they could later receive a title to them. "The roads are . . . alive with Men, Women, Children, and Cattle from Jersey, Pennsylvania, and Maryland," wrote one astonished observer.

All of this activity antagonized the Ohio Indians. In 1770, Shawnees invited hundreds of Indian leaders to gather at the town of Chillicothe on the Scioto River. There they formed the Scioto Confederacy, which pledged to oppose any further expansion into the Ohio country. Some British officers and administrators tried to protect Indian interests, while others encouraged their exploitation, leading to interpretive disagreements among historians.

Meanwhile, in London, the idea that the Proclamation Line was only temporary gave way to the view that it should be permanent. Hillsborough, who became colonial secretary in 1768, adamantly opposed westward expansion, believing it would antagonize the Indians without benefitting the empire. Moreover, he owned vast Irish estates, and he was alarmed by the number of tenants who were leaving Ireland for America. To preserve Britain's laboring class, as well as control costs, Hillsborough wanted to make the Proclamation Line permanent.

For colonists who were already moving west to settle in large numbers, this shift in policy caused confusion and frustration. Eventually, like the Patriots along the seaboard, they would take matters into their own hands.

## Parliament Wavers

In Britain, the colonies' nonimportation agreement was taking its toll. In 1768, the colonies had cut imports of British manufactures in half; by 1769, the mainland colonies had a trade surplus with Britain of £816,000. Hard-hit by these developments, British merchants and manufacturers petitioned Parliament to repeal the Townshend duties. Early in 1770, Lord North became prime minister. A witty man and a skillful politician, North designed a new compromise. Arguing that it was foolish to tax British exports to America (thereby raising their price and decreasing consumption), he persuaded Parliament to repeal most of the Townshend duties. However, North retained the tax on tea as a symbol of Parliament's supremacy.

**The Boston Massacre**    Even as Parliament was debating North's repeal, events in Boston guaranteed that reconciliation between Patriots and Parliament would be hard to achieve. Between 1,200 and 2,000 troops had been stationed in Boston for a year and a half. Soldiers were also stationed in New York, Philadelphia, several towns in New Jersey, and various frontier outposts in these years, with a minimum of conflict or violence. But in Boston—a small port town on a tiny peninsula—the troops numbered 10 percent of the local population, and their presence wore on the locals. On the night of March 5, 1770, a group of nine British redcoats fired into a crowd and killed five townspeople. A subsequent trial exonerated the soldiers, but Boston's Radical Whigs, convinced of a ministerial conspiracy against liberty, labeled the incident a "massacre" and used it to rally sentiment against imperial power.

**Sovereignty Debated**    When news of North's compromise arrived in the colonies in the wake of the Boston Massacre, the reaction was mixed. Most of Britain's colonists remained loyal to the empire, but five years of conflict had taken their toll. In 1765, American leaders had accepted Parliament's authority; the Stamp Act Resolves had opposed only certain "unconstitutional" legislation. By 1770, the most outspoken Patriots—Benjamin Franklin in Pennsylvania, Patrick Henry in Virginia, and Samuel Adams in Massachusetts—repudiated parliamentary supremacy and claimed equality for the American assemblies within the empire. Franklin suggested that the colonies were now "distinct and separate states" with "the same Head, or Sovereign, the King."

Franklin's suggestion outraged Thomas Hutchinson, the American-born royal governor of Massachusetts. Hutchinson emphatically rejected the idea of "two independent legislatures in one and the same state." He told the Massachusetts assembly, "I know of no line that can be drawn between the supreme authority of Parliament and the total independence of the colonies."

There the matter rested. The British had twice imposed revenue acts on the colonies, and American Patriots had twice forced a retreat. If Parliament insisted on a policy of constitutional absolutism by imposing taxes a third time, some Americans were prepared to pursue violent resistance. Nor did they flinch when reminded that George III condemned their agitation. As the Massachusetts House replied to Hutchinson, "There is more reason to dread the consequences of absolute uncontrolled supreme power, whether of a nation or a monarch, than those of total independence." Fearful of civil war, Lord North's ministry hesitated to force the issue.

| | |
|---|---|
| **IN YOUR OWN WORDS** | What was the relationship between formal protests against Parliament and popular resistance in the years between 1765 and 1770? |

# The Road to Independence, 1771–1776

Repeal of the Townshend duties in 1770 restored harmony to the British Empire, but strong feelings and mutual distrust lay just below the surface. In 1773, those emotions erupted, destroying any hope of compromise. Within two years, the Americans and the British clashed in armed conflict. Despite widespread resistance among loyal colonists, Patriot legislators created provisional governments and military forces, the two essentials for independence.

## A Compromise Repudiated

Once aroused, political passions are not easily quieted. In Boston, Samuel Adams and other radical Patriots continued to warn Americans of imperial domination and, late in 1772, persuaded the town meeting to set up a committee of correspondence "to state the Rights of the Colonists of this Province." Soon, eighty Massachusetts towns had similar committees. When British officials threatened to seize the Americans responsible for the burning of the customs vessel *Gaspée* and prosecute them in Britain, the Virginia House of Burgesses and several other assemblies set up their own **committees of correspondence**. These standing committees allowed Patriots to communicate with leaders in other colonies when new threats to liberty occurred. By 1774, among the colonies that would later declare independence, only Pennsylvania was without one.

**The East India Company and the Tea Act**   These committees sprang into action when Parliament passed the **Tea Act of May 1773**. The act provided financial relief for the East India Company, a royally chartered private corporation that served as the instrument of British imperialism. The company was deeply in debt; it also had a huge surplus of tea as a result of high import duties, which led Britons and colonists alike to drink smuggled Dutch tea instead. The Tea Act gave the company a government loan and, to boost its revenue, canceled the import duties on tea the company exported to Ireland and the American colonies. Now even with the Townshend duty of 3 pence a pound on tea, high-quality East India Company tea would cost less than the Dutch tea smuggled into the colonies by American merchants.

Radical Patriots accused the British ministry of bribing Americans with the cheaper East India Company tea so they would give up their principled opposition to the tea tax. As an anonymous woman wrote to the *Massachusetts Spy*, "The use of [British] tea is considered not as a private but as a public evil . . . a handle to introduce a variety of . . . oppressions amongst us." Merchants joined the protest because the East India Company planned to distribute its tea directly to shopkeepers, excluding American wholesalers from the trade's profits. "The fear of an Introduction of a Monopoly in this Country," British general Frederick Haldimand reported from New York, "has induced the mercantile part of the Inhabitants to be very industrious in opposing this Step and added Strength to a Spirit of Independence already too prevalent."

**The Tea Party and the Coercive Acts**    The Sons of Liberty prevented East India Company ships from delivering their cargoes in New York, Philadelphia, and Charleston. In Massachusetts, Royal Governor Hutchinson was determined to land the tea and collect the tax. To foil the governor's plan, artisans and laborers disguised as Indians boarded three ships — the *Dartmouth*, the *Eleanor*, and the *Beaver* — on December 16, 1773, broke open 342 chests of tea (valued at about £10,000, or about $900,000 today), and threw them into the harbor. "This destruction of the Tea . . . must have so important Consequences," John Adams wrote in his diary, "that I cannot but consider it as an Epoch in History."

The king was outraged. "Concessions have made matters worse," George III declared. "The time has come for compulsion." Early in 1774, Parliament passed four **Coercive Acts** to force Massachusetts to pay for the tea and to submit to imperial authority. The Boston Port Bill closed Boston Harbor to shipping; the Massachusetts Government Act annulled the colony's charter and prohibited most town meetings; a new Quartering Act mandated new barracks for British troops; and the Justice Act allowed trials for capital crimes to be transferred to other colonies or to Britain.

Patriot leaders throughout the colonies branded the measures "Intolerable" and rallied support for Massachusetts. In Georgia, a Patriot warned the "Freemen of the Province" that "every privilege you at present claim as a birthright, may be wrested from you by the same authority that blockades the town of Boston." "The cause of Boston," George Washington declared in Virginia, "now is and ever will be considered as the cause of America." The committees of correspondence had created a firm sense of Patriot unity.

In 1774, Parliament also passed the Quebec Act, which allowed the practice of Roman Catholicism in Quebec. This concession to Quebec's predominantly Catholic population reignited religious passions in New England, where Protestants associated Catholicism with arbitrary royal government. Because the act extended Quebec's boundaries into the Ohio River Valley, it also angered influential land speculators in Virginia and Pennsylvania and ordinary settlers by the thousands (Map 5.4). Although the ministry did not intend the Quebec Act as a coercive measure, many colonists saw it as further proof of Parliament's intention to control American affairs.

## The Continental Congress Responds

In response to the Coercive Acts, Patriot leaders convened a new continent-wide body, the **Continental Congress**. Twelve mainland colonies sent representatives. Four recently acquired colonies — Florida, Quebec, Nova Scotia, and

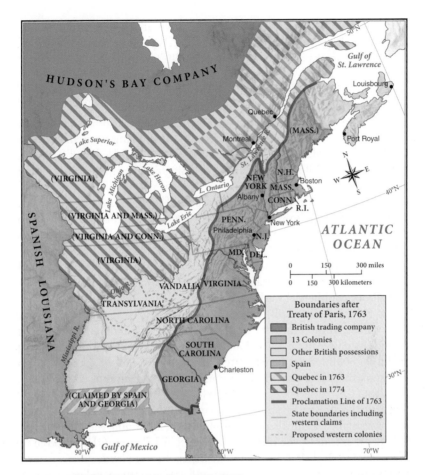

**MAP 5.4   British Western Policy, 1763–1774**

The Proclamation of 1763 prohibited white settlement west of the Appalachian Mountains. Nonetheless, Anglo-American settlers and land speculators proposed the new colonies of Vandalia and Transylvania to the west of Virginia and North Carolina. The Quebec Act of 1774 designated most western lands as Indian reserves and vastly enlarged the boundaries of Quebec, dashing speculators' hopes and eliminating the old sea-to-sea land claims of many seaboard colonies. The act especially angered New England Protestants, who condemned it for allowing French residents to practice Catholicism, and colonial political leaders, who protested its failure to provide Quebec with a representative assembly.

Newfoundland—refused to send delegates, as did Georgia, where the royal governor controlled the legislature. The assemblies of Barbados, Jamaica, and the other sugar islands, although wary of British domination, were even more fearful of revolts by their predominantly African populations and therefore declined to attend.

The delegates who met in Philadelphia in September 1774 had different agendas. Southern representatives, fearing a British plot "to overturn the constitution and introduce a system of arbitrary government," advocated a new economic boycott. Independence-minded representatives from New England demanded political union and defensive military preparations. Many delegates from the Middle Atlantic colonies favored compromise.

Led by Joseph Galloway of Pennsylvania, these men of "loyal principles" proposed a new political system similar to Benjamin Franklin's proposal at the Albany Congress of 1754: each colony would retain its assembly to legislate on local matters, and a new continent-wide body would handle general American affairs. The king would appoint a president-general to preside over a legislative council selected by the colonial assemblies. Galloway's plan failed by a single vote; a bare majority thought it was too conciliatory.

Instead, the delegates demanded the repeal of the Coercive Acts and stipulated that British control be limited to matters of trade. They also approved a program of economic retaliation: Americans would stop importing British goods in December 1774. If Parliament did not repeal the Coercive Acts by September 1775, the Congress vowed to cut off virtually all colonial exports to Britain, Ireland, and the British West Indies. Ten years of constitutional conflict had culminated in a threat of all-out commercial warfare.

A few British leaders still hoped for compromise. In January 1775, William Pitt, now sitting in the House of Lords as the Earl of Chatham, asked Parliament to renounce its power to tax the colonies and to recognize the Continental Congress as a lawful body. In return, he suggested, the Congress should acknowledge parliamentary supremacy and provide a permanent source of revenue to help defray the national debt.

The British ministry rejected Pitt's plan. Twice it had backed down in the face of colonial resistance; a third retreat was impossible. Branding the Continental Congress an illegal assembly, the ministry rejected Lord Dartmouth's proposal to send commissioners to negotiate a settlement. Instead, Lord North set stringent terms: Americans must pay for their own defense and administration and acknowledge Parliament's authority to tax them. To put teeth in these demands, North imposed a

**Lord North** Frederick North, the second earl of Guilford, served as George III's prime minister from 1770 until the end of the American Revolution. He began his term of service by seeking reconciliation with the colonies. In that spirit, he championed the repeal of most of the Townshend duties. After the destruction of the East India Company tea in Boston, however, Lord North pursued a hard line, sponsoring the Coercive Acts and insisting that Boston should pay for the tea it destroyed. In taking this approach, North had the full support of the king, who was appalled by the destruction of the tea and believed that the colonies had to be pressed to acknowledge British authority.
The Granger Collection, NY.

naval blockade on American trade with foreign nations and ordered General Gage to suppress dissent in Massachusetts. "Now the case seemed desperate," the prime minister told Thomas Hutchinson, whom the Patriots had forced into exile in London. "Parliament would not—could not—concede." North predicted that the crisis "must come to violence."

## The Rising of the Countryside

The fate of the urban-led Patriot movement would depend on the colonies' large rural population. Most farmers had little interest in imperial affairs. Their lives were deeply rooted in the soil, and their prime allegiance was to family and community. But imperial policies had increasingly intruded into the lives of farm families by sending their sons to war and raising their taxes. In 1754, farmers on Long Island, New York, had paid an average tax of 10 shillings; by 1756, thanks to the Great War for Empire, their taxes had jumped to 30 shillings.

**The Continental Association**   The boycotts of 1765 and 1768 raised the political consciousness of rural Americans. When the First Continental Congress established the **Continental Association** in 1774 to enforce a third boycott of British goods, it quickly set up a rural network of committees to do its work. In Concord, Massachusetts, 80 percent of the male heads of families and a number of single women signed a "Solemn League and Covenant" supporting nonimportation. In other farm towns, men blacked their faces, disguised themselves in blankets "like Indians," and threatened violence against shopkeepers who traded "in rum, molasses, & Sugar, &c." in violation of the boycott.

Patriots likewise warned that British measures threatened the yeoman tradition of landownership. In Petersham, Massachusetts, the town meeting worried that new British taxes would drain "this People of the Fruits of their Toil." Arable land was now scarce and expensive in older communities, and in new settlements merchants were seizing farmsteads for delinquent debts. By the 1770s, many northern yeomen felt personally threatened by British policies, which, a Patriot pamphlet warned, were "paving the way for reducing the country to lordships."

**Southern Planters Fear Dependency**   Despite their higher standard of living, southern slave owners had similar fears. Many Chesapeake planters were deeply in debt to British merchants. Accustomed to being absolute masters on their slave-labor plantations and seeing themselves as guardians of English liberties, planters resented their financial dependence on British creditors and dreaded the prospect of political subservience to British officials.

That danger now seemed real. If Parliament used the Coercive Acts to subdue Massachusetts, then it might turn next to Virginia, dissolving its representative assembly and assisting British merchants to seize debt-burdened properties. Consequently, the Virginia gentry supported demands by indebted yeomen farmers to close the law courts so that they could bargain with merchants over debts without the threat of legal action. "The spark of liberty is not yet extinct among our people," declared one planter, "and if properly fanned by the Gentlemen of influence will, I make no doubt, burst out again into a flame."

## Loyalists and Neutrals

Yet in many places, the Patriot movement was a hard sell. In Virginia, Patriot leaders were nearly all wealthy planters, and many of their poorer neighbors regarded the movement with suspicion. In regions where great landowners became Patriots—the Hudson River Valley of New York, for example—many tenant farmers supported the king because they hated their landlords. Similar social conflicts prompted some Regulators in the North Carolina backcountry and many farmers in eastern Maryland to oppose the Patriots there.

There were many reasons to resist the Patriot movement. Skeptics believed that Patriot leaders were subverting British rule only to advance their own selfish interests. Peter Oliver wrote of Samuel Adams, for example, "He was so thorough a Machiavilian, that he divested himself of every worthy Principle, & would stick at no Crime to accomplish his Ends." Some "Gentlemen of influence" worried that resistance to Britain would undermine all political institutions and "introduce Anarchy and disorder and render life and property here precarious." Their fears increased when the Sons of Liberty used intimidation and violence to uphold the boycotts. One well-to-do New Yorker complained, "No man can be in a more abject state of bondage than he whose Reputation, Property and Life are exposed to the discretionary violence . . . of the community." As the crisis deepened, such men became Loyalists—so called because they remained loyal to the British crown.

Many other colonists simply hoped to stay out of the fray. Some did so on principle: in New Jersey and Pennsylvania, thousands of pacifist Quakers and Germans resisted conscription and violence out of religious conviction. Others were ambivalent or confused about the political crisis unfolding around them. The delegate elected to New York's Provincial Congress from Queen's County, on Long Island, chose not to attend since "the people [he represented] seemed to be much inclined to remain peaceable and quiet." More than three-fourths of Queen's County voters, in fact, opposed sending any delegate at all. Many loyal or neutral colonists hoped, above all, to preserve their families' property and independence, whatever the outcome of the imperial crisis.

Historians estimate that some 15 to 20 percent of the white population—perhaps as many as 400,000 colonists—were loyal to the crown. Some managed to avoid persecution, but many were pressured by their neighbors to join the boycotts and subjected to violence and humiliation if they refused. As Patriots took over the reins of local government throughout the colonies, Loyalists were driven out of their homes or forced into silence. At this crucial juncture, Patriots commanded the allegiance, or at least the acquiescence, of the majority of white Americans.

> **IN YOUR OWN WORDS**    What actions did the Continental Association take to support the efforts of the Continental Congress?

# Violence East and West

By 1774, British authority was wavering. At the headwaters of the Ohio, the abandonment of Fort Pitt left a power vacuum that was filled by opportunistic men, led by a royally appointed governor acting in defiance of his commission. In Massachusetts, the attempt to isolate and punish Boston and the surrounding countryside backfired as Patriots resisted military coercion. Violence resulted in both places, and with it the collapse of imperial control.

## Lord Dunmore's War

In the years since the end of Pontiac's Rebellion, at least 10,000 people had traveled along Braddock's and Forbes's Roads to the headwaters of the Ohio River, where Fort Pitt had replaced Fort Duquesne during the Great War for Empire, and staked claims to land around Pittsburgh (Map 5.5). They relied for protection on Fort Pitt, which remained one of Britain's most important frontier outposts. But the revenue crisis forced General Gage to cut expenses, and in October 1772, the army pulled down the fort's log walls and left the site to the local population. Settler relations with the neighboring Ohio Indians were tenuous and ill-defined, and the fort's abandonment left them exposed and vulnerable.

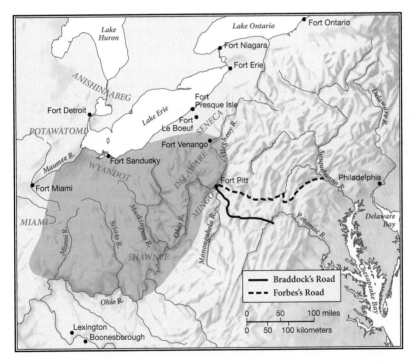

### MAP 5.5 The Ohio Country, 1774–1775

The erosion of British imperial authority caused chaos in the Ohio country. Pennsylvania and Virginia each claimed Pittsburgh and the surrounding countryside, while the Indian communities on the upper Ohio increasingly feared colonist aggression. Their fears were realized in the summer of 1774, when Lord Dunmore led a force of Virginia militia into the valley. After defeating a Shawnee force in the Battle of Point Pleasant, many Virginians began surveying and staking claims to land in the Kentucky bluegrass. In the summer of 1775, perhaps a dozen new towns were settled there, in violation of the Royal Proclamation of 1763 and the Quebec Act of 1774.

In the ensuing power vacuum, Pennsylvania and Virginia both claimed the region. Pennsylvania had the better claim on paper. It had organized county governments, established courts, and collected taxes there. But—in keeping with its pacifist Quaker roots—it did not organize a militia. In this omission, Virginia's royal governor, the Earl of Dunmore, recognized an opportunity. Appointed to his post in 1771, Dunmore was an irascible and unscrupulous man who clashed repeatedly with the House of Burgesses. But when it suited him, he was just as willing to defy the crown. In 1773, he traveled to Pittsburgh, where, he later wrote, "the people flocked about me and beseeched me . . . to appoint magistrates and officers of militia." He organized a local militia; soon, men armed by Virginia were drilling near the ruins of Fort Pitt.

In the summer of 1774, Dunmore took the next step. In defiance of both his royal instructions and the House of Burgesses, he called out Virginia's militia and led a force of 2,400 men against the Ohio Shawnees, who had a long-standing claim to Kentucky as a hunting ground. They fought a single battle, at Point Pleasant; the Shawnees were defeated, and Dunmore and his militia forces claimed Kentucky as their own. A participant justified his actions shortly afterward: "When without a king," he wrote, "[one] doeth according to the freedom of his own will." Years of neglect left many colonists in the backcountry feeling abandoned by the crown. **Dunmore's War** was their declaration of independence.

## Armed Resistance in Massachusetts

Meanwhile, as the Continental Congress gathered in Philadelphia in September 1774, Massachusetts was also defying British authority. In August, a Middlesex County Congress had urged Patriots to close the existing royal courts and to transfer their political allegiance to the popularly elected House of Representatives. Subsequently, armed crowds harassed Loyalists and ensured Patriot rule in most of New England.

In response, General Thomas Gage, now the military governor of Massachusetts, ordered British troops in Boston in September 1774 to seize Patriot armories in nearby Charlestown and Cambridge. An army of 20,000 militiamen quickly mobilized to safeguard other Massachusetts military depots. The Concord town meeting raised a defensive force, the famous **Minutemen**, to "Stand at a minutes warning in Case of alarm." Increasingly, Gage's authority was limited to Boston, where it rested on the bayonets of his 3,500 troops. Meanwhile, the Patriot-controlled Massachusetts assembly met in nearby Salem in open defiance of Parliament, collecting taxes, bolstering the militia, and assuming the responsibilities of government.

In London, the colonial secretary, Lord Dartmouth, proclaimed Massachusetts to be in "open rebellion" and ordered Gage to march against the "rude rabble." On the night of April 18, 1775, Gage dispatched 700 soldiers to capture colonial leaders and supplies at Concord. However, Paul Revere and a series of other riders warned Patriots in many towns, and at dawn, militiamen confronted the British regulars first at Lexington and then at Concord. Those first skirmishes took a handful of lives, but as the British retreated to Boston, militia from neighboring towns repeatedly ambushed them. By the end of the day, 73 British soldiers were dead, 174 wounded, and 26 missing. British fire had killed 49 Massachusetts militiamen and wounded 39. Twelve years of economic and constitutional conflict had ended in violence.

## The Second Continental Congress Organizes for War

A month later, in May 1775, Patriot leaders gathered in Philadelphia for the **Second Continental Congress**. As the Congress opened, 3,000 British troops attacked American fortifications on Breed's Hill and Bunker Hill overlooking Boston. After three assaults and 1,000 casualties, they finally dislodged the Patriot militia. Inspired by his countrymen's valor, John Adams exhorted the Congress to rise to the "defense of American liberty" by creating a continental army. He nominated George Washington to lead it. After bitter debate, the Congress approved the proposals, but, Adams lamented, only "by bare majorities."

**Congress Versus King George**   Despite the bloodshed in Massachusetts, a majority in the Congress still hoped for reconciliation. Led by John Dickinson of Pennsylvania, these moderates won approval of a petition expressing loyalty to George III and asking for repeal of oppressive parliamentary legislation. But Samuel Adams, Patrick Henry, and other zealous Patriots drummed up support for a Declaration of the Causes and Necessities of Taking Up Arms. Americans dreaded the "calamities of civil war," the declaration asserted, but were "resolved to die Freemen rather than to live [as] slaves." George III failed to exploit the divisions among the Patriots; instead, in August 1775, he issued a Proclamation for Suppressing Rebellion and Sedition.

Before the king's proclamation reached America, the radicals in the Congress had won support for an invasion of Canada to prevent a British attack from the north. Patriot forces easily defeated the British at Montreal; but in December 1775, they failed to capture Quebec City and withdrew. Meanwhile, American merchants waged the financial warfare promised at the First Continental Congress by cutting off exports to Britain and its West Indian sugar islands. Parliament retaliated with the Prohibitory Act, which outlawed all trade with the rebellious colonies.

**Fighting in the South**   Skirmishes between Patriot and Loyalist forces now broke out in the southern colonies. In Virginia, Patriots ousted Governor Dunmore and forced him to take refuge on a British warship in Chesapeake Bay. Branding the rebels "traitors," the governor organized two military forces: one white, the Queen's Own Loyal Virginians; and one black, the Ethiopian Regiment, which enlisted 1,000 slaves who had fled their Patriot owners. In November 1775, Dunmore issued a controversial proclamation promising freedom to black slaves and white indentured servants who joined the Loyalist cause. White planters denounced this "Diabolical scheme," claiming it "point[ed] a dagger to their Throats." A new rising of the black and white underclasses, as in Bacon's Rebellion in the 1670s, seemed a possibility. In Fincastle County in southwestern Virginia, Loyalist planter John Hiell urged workers to support the king, promising "a Servant man" that soon "he and all the negroes would get their freedom." Frightened by Dunmore's aggressive tactics, Patriot yeomen and tenants called for a final break with Britain.

In North Carolina, too, military clashes prompted demands for independence. Early in 1776, Josiah Martin, the colony's royal governor, raised a Loyalist force of 1,500 Scottish Highlanders in the backcountry. In response, Patriots mobilized the lowcountry militia and, in February, defeated Martin's army at the Battle of Moore's Creek Bridge, capturing more than 800 Highlanders. Following this victory, radical

Patriots in the North Carolina assembly told its representatives to the Continental Congress to join with "other Colonies in declaring Independence, and forming foreign alliances." In May, the Virginia gentry followed suit: led by James Madison, Edmund Pendleton, and Patrick Henry, the Patriots met in convention and resolved unanimously to support independence.

**Occupying Kentucky**     Beginning in the spring of 1775, in the wake of Dunmore's War, independent parties of adventurers began to occupy the newly won lands of Kentucky. Daniel Boone led one group to the banks of the Kentucky River, where they established the town of Boonesborough; nearby was Lexington, named in honor of the Massachusetts town that had resisted British troops a few months earlier. The Shawnees and other Ohio Indians opposed the settlers, and colonists built their tiny towns in the form of stations to protect themselves — groups of cabins connected by palisades to form small forts.

These western settlers had complex political loyalties. Many had marched under Dunmore and hoped to receive recognition for their claims from the crown. But as the rebellion unfolded, most recognized that the Patriots' emphasis on liberty and equality squared with their view of the world. They soon petitioned Virginia's rebel government, asking it to create a new county that would include the Kentucky settlements. They had "Fought and bled" for the land in Dunmore's War and now wanted to fight against the crown and its Indian allies in the Ohio country. Virginia agreed: in 1776, it organized six new frontier counties and sent arms and ammunition to Kentucky. In July, the Continental Congress followed suit, dispatching troops and arms to the Ohio River as well.

## Thomas Paine's *Common Sense*

As military conflicts escalated, Americans were divided in their opinions of King George III. Many blamed him for supporting oppressive legislation and ordering armed retaliation, but other influential colonists held out the hope that he might mediate their conflict with Parliament. John Dickinson, whose *Letters* did so much to arouse Patriot resistance in 1768, nevertheless believed that war with Great Britain would be folly. In July 1775, he persuaded Congress to send George III the Olive Branch Petition, which pleaded with the king to negotiate. John Adams, a staunch supporter of independence, was infuriated by Dickinson's waffling. But Dickinson had many supporters, both inside and outside of Congress. For example, many of Philadelphia's Quaker and Anglican merchants were neutrals or Loyalists. In response to their passivity, Patriot artisans in the city organized a Mechanics' Association to protect America's "just Rights and Privileges."

With popular sentiment in flux, a single brief pamphlet helped tip the balance. In January 1776, Thomas Paine published *Common Sense*, a rousing call for independence and a republican form of government. Paine had served as a minor customs official in England until he was fired for joining a protest against low wages. In 1774, Paine migrated to Philadelphia, where he met Benjamin Rush and other Patriots who shared his republican sentiments.

In *Common Sense*, Paine assaulted the traditional monarchical order in stirring language. "Monarchy and hereditary succession have laid the world in blood and ashes," Paine proclaimed, leveling a personal attack at George III, "the hard hearted sullen Pharaoh of England." Mixing insults with biblical quotations, Paine blasted the British system of "mixed government" that balanced power among the three estates of king, lords, and commoners. Paine granted that the system "was noble for the dark and slavish times" of the past, but now it yielded only "monarchical tyranny in the person of the king" and "aristocratical tyranny in the persons of the peers."

Paine argued for American independence by turning the traditional metaphor of patriarchal authority on its head: "Is it the interest of a man to be a boy all his life?" he asked. Within six months, *Common Sense* had gone through twenty-five editions and reached hundreds of thousands of people. "There is great talk of independence," a worried New York Loyalist noted, "the unthinking multitude are mad for it. . . . A pamphlet called Common Sense has carried off . . . thousands." Paine urged Americans to create independent republican states: "A government of our own is our natural right, 'tis time to part."

## Independence Declared

Inspired by Paine's arguments and beset by armed Loyalists, Patriot conventions urged a break from Britain. In June 1776, Richard Henry Lee presented Virginia's resolution to the Continental Congress: "That these United Colonies are, and of right ought to be, free and independent states." Faced with certain defeat, staunch Loyalists and anti-independence moderates withdrew from the Congress, leaving committed Patriots to take the fateful step. On July 4, 1776, the Congress approved the **Declaration of Independence** (see Documents, p. D-1).

The Declaration's main author, Thomas Jefferson of Virginia, had mobilized resistance to the Coercive Acts with the pamphlet *A Summary View of the Rights of British America* (1774). Now, in the Declaration, he justified independence and republicanism to Americans and the world by vilifying George III: "He has plundered our seas, ravaged our coasts, burned our towns, and destroyed the lives of our people." Such a prince was a "tyrant," Jefferson concluded, and "is unfit to be the ruler of a free people."

Employing the ideas of the European Enlightenment, Jefferson proclaimed a series of "self-evident" truths: "that all men are created equal"; that they possess the "unalienable rights" of "Life, Liberty, and the pursuit of Happiness"; that government derives its "just powers from the consent of the governed" and can rightly be overthrown if it "becomes destructive of these ends." By linking these doctrines of individual liberty, **popular sovereignty** (the principle that ultimate power lies in the hands of the electorate), and republican government with American independence, Jefferson established them as the defining political values of the new nation.

For Jefferson, as for Paine, the pen proved mightier than the sword. The Declaration won wide support in France and Germany; at home, it sparked celebrations in rural hamlets and seaport cities, as crowds burned effigies and toppled statues of the king. On July 8, 1776, in Easton, Pennsylvania, a "great number of spectators" heard a reading of the Declaration, "gave their hearty assent with three loud huzzahs, and cried out, 'May God long preserve and unite the Free and Independent States of America.'"

| IN YOUR OWN WORDS | How did the colonies' long controversy with Parliament influence the ideals that shaped the independence movement? |
| --- | --- |

## Summary

Chapter 5 has focused on a short span of time—little more than a decade—and outlined the plot of a political drama. Act I of that drama resulted from the Great War for Empire, which prompted British political leaders to implement a program of imperial reform and taxation. Act II is full of dramatic action, as colonial mobs riot, colonists chafe against restrictions on western lands, Patriot pamphleteers articulate ideologies of resistance, and British ministers search for compromise between claims of parliamentary sovereignty and assertions of colonial autonomy. Act III takes the form of tragedy: the once-proud British Empire dissolves into civil war, an imminent nightmare of death and destruction.

Why did this happen? More than two centuries later, the answers still are not clear. Certainly, the lack of astute leadership in Britain was a major factor. But British leaders faced circumstances that limited their actions: a huge national debt and deep commitments to both a powerful fiscal-military state and the absolute supremacy of Parliament. Moreover, in America, decades of salutary neglect strengthened Patriots' demands for political autonomy and economic opportunity. Artisans, farmers, and aspiring western settlers all feared an oppressive new era in imperial relations. The trajectories of their conflicting intentions and ideas placed Britain and its American possessions on course for a disastrous and fatal collision.

# Chapter 5 Review

## KEY TERMS

**Identify and explain the significance of each term below.**

Sugar Act of 1764 (p. 140)
vice-admiralty courts (p. 141)
Stamp Act of 1765 (p. 141)
virtual representation (p. 142)
Quartering Act of 1765 (p. 142)
Stamp Act Congress (p. 143)
Sons of Liberty (p. 144)
English common law (p. 144)
natural rights (p. 145)
Declaratory Act of 1766 (p. 146)
Townshend Act of 1767 (p. 146)
nonimportation movement (p. 147)

committees of correspondence
  (p. 151)
Tea Act of May 1773 (p. 151)
Coercive Acts (p. 152)
Continental Congress (p. 152)
Continental Association (p. 155)
Dunmore's War (p. 158)
Minutemen (p. 158)
Second Continental Congress
  (p. 159)
Declaration of Independence (p. 161)
popular sovereignty (p. 161)

## REVIEW QUESTIONS

**Answer these questions to demonstrate your understanding of the chapter's main ideas.**

1. What changes in Britain's imperial policy were triggered by its victory in the Great War for Empire?

2. What was the relationship between formal protests against Parliament and popular resistance in the years between 1765 and 1770?

3. What actions did the Continental Association take to support the efforts of the Continental Congress?

4. How did the colonies' long controversy with Parliament influence the ideals that shaped the independence movement?

5. Consider the events listed under "Politics and Power" and "Work, Exchange, and Technology" for the period 1763–1776 on the thematic timeline on page 134. How important were the linkages between economic developments and political ones in these years?

## CHRONOLOGY

**As you read, ask yourself why this chapter begins and ends with these dates and then identify the links among related events.**

| | |
|---|---|
| **1763** | • Proclamation Line limits white settlement |
| **1764** | • Sugar Act and Currency Act |
| | • Colonists oppose vice-admiralty courts |
| **1765** | • Stamp Act imposes direct tax |
| | • Quartering Act requires barracks for British troops |
| | • Stamp Act Congress meets |
| | • Americans boycott British goods |
| **1766** | • First compromise: Stamp Act repealed |
| | • Declaratory Act passed |
| **1767** | • Townshend duties |
| **1768** | • Second American boycott |
| **1770** | • Second compromise: partial repeal of Townshend Act |
| | • Boston Massacre |

| 1772 | • Committees of correspondence form |
| 1773 | • Tea Act leads to Boston Tea Party |
| 1774 | • Coercive Acts punish Massachusetts |
| | • Dunmore's War against the Shawnees |
| | • Continental Congress meets |
| | • Third American boycott |
| 1775 | • General Gage marches to Lexington and Concord |
| | • Second Continental Congress creates Continental army |
| | • Lord Dunmore recruits Loyalist slaves |
| | • Patriots invade Canada and skirmish with Loyalists in South |
| | • Western settlers occupy Kentucky |
| 1776 | • Thomas Paine's *Common Sense* |
| | • Declaration of Independence |

# 6

# Making War and Republican Governments

## 1776–1789

**IDENTIFY THE BIG IDEA**

How revolutionary was the American Revolution? What political, social, and economic changes did it produce, and what stayed the same?

**WHEN PATRIOTS IN FREDERICK COUNTY, MARYLAND, DEMANDED HIS** allegiance to their cause in 1776, Robert Gassaway would have none of it. "It was better for the poor people to lay down their arms and pay the duties and taxes laid upon them by King and Parliament than to be brought into slavery and commanded and ordered about [by you]," he told them. The story was much the same in Farmington, Connecticut, where Patriot officials imprisoned Nathaniel Jones and seventeen other men for "remaining neutral." In Pennsylvania, Quakers accused of Loyalism were rounded up, jailed, and charged with treason, and some were hanged for aiding the British cause. Everywhere, the outbreak of fighting in 1776 forced families to choose the Loyalist or the Patriot side.

The Patriots' control of most local governments gave them an edge in this battle. Patriot leaders organized militia units and recruited volunteers for the Continental army, a ragtag force that surprisingly held its own on the battlefield. "I admire the American troops tremendously!" exclaimed a French officer. "It is incredible that soldiers composed of every age, even children of fifteen, of whites and blacks, almost naked, unpaid, and rather poorly fed, can march so well and withstand fire so steadfastly."

Military service created political commitment, and vice versa. Many Patriot leaders encouraged Americans not only to support the war but also to take an active role in government. As more people did so, their political identities changed. Previously, Americans had lived within a social world dominated by the links of family, kinship, and locality. Now, the abstract bonds of citizenship connected them directly to more distant institutions of government. "From subjects to citizens the difference is immense," remarked South Carolina Patriot David Ramsay. By repudiating monarchical rule and raising a democratic army, the Patriots launched the age of republican revolutions.

Soon republicanism would throw France into turmoil and inspire revolutionaries in Spain's American colonies. The independence of the Anglo-American colonies, remarked the Venezuelan political leader Francisco de Miranda, who had been in New York and Philadelphia at the end of the American Revolution, "was bound to be . . . the infallible preliminary to our own [independence movement]." The Patriot uprising of 1776 set in motion a process that gradually replaced an Atlantic colonial system that spanned the Americas with an American system of new nations.

# The Trials of War, 1776–1778

The Declaration of Independence appeared just as the British launched a full-scale military assault. For two years, British troops manhandled the Continental army. A few inspiring American victories kept the rebellion alive, but during the winters of 1776 and 1777, the Patriot cause hung in the balance.

## War in the North

Once the British resorted to military force, few Europeans gave the rebels a chance. The population of Great Britain was 11 million; the colonies, 2.5 million, 20 percent of whom were enslaved Africans. Moreover, the British government had access to the immense wealth generated by the South Atlantic System and the emerging Industrial Revolution. Britain also had the most powerful navy in the world, a standing army of 48,000 Britons plus thousands of German (Hessian) soldiers, and the support of thousands of American Loyalists and powerful Indian coalitions. In the Carolinas, the Cherokees resisted colonists' demands for their lands by allying with the British, as did four of the six Iroquois nations of New York (Map 6.1). In the Ohio country, Shawnees and their allies, armed by the British, attacked the new Kentucky settlements.

By contrast, the Americans were economically and militarily weak. They lacked a strong central government and a reliable source of tax revenue. Their new Continental army, commanded by General George Washington, consisted of 18,000 poorly trained and inexperienced recruits.

To demonstrate Britain's military superiority, Prime Minister Lord North ordered General William Howe to capture New York City. His strategy was to seize control of the Hudson River and thereby isolate the radical Patriots in New England from the colonies to the south. As the Second Continental Congress declared independence in Philadelphia in July 1776, Howe landed 32,000 troops—British regulars

**Joseph Brant** Mohawk chief Thayendanegea, known to whites as Joseph Brant, was a devout member of the Church of England and helped to translate the Bible into the Mohawk language. Brant persuaded four of the six Iroquois nations to support Britain in the war. He received a captain's commission in the British army and led Iroquois warriors and Tory rangers in devastating attacks on American settlements in the Wyoming Valley of Pennsylvania and Cherry Valley in New York. After the war, he was instrumental in resettling Mohawks and other British-allied Indians on the Grand River in Ontario, Canada. Brant was depicted many times by painters and sculptors. In this 1786 portrait, painted during one of his trips to England, Gilbert Stuart depicts his hybrid identity and captures a haunting sense of melancholy. Corbis Historical/Getty Images.

and German mercenaries—outside New York City. In August 1776, Howe defeated the Americans in the **Battle of Long Island** and forced their retreat to Manhattan Island. There, Howe outflanked Washington's troops and nearly trapped them. Outgunned and outmaneuvered, the Continental army again retreated, eventually crossing the Hudson River to New Jersey. By December, the British army had pushed the rebels across New Jersey and over the Delaware River into Pennsylvania.

From the Patriots' perspective, winter came just in time. Following eighteenth-century custom, the British halted their military campaign for the cold months, allowing the Americans to catch them off guard. On Christmas night 1776, Washington crossed the Delaware River and staged a successful surprise attack on Trenton, New Jersey, where he forced the surrender of 1,000 German soldiers. In early January 1777, the Continental army won a small victory at nearby Princeton (Map 6.2). But these minor triumphs could not mask British military superiority. "These are the times," wrote Thomas Paine, "that try men's souls."

## Armies and Strategies

Thanks in part to General Howe, the rebellion survived. Howe had opposed the Coercive Acts of 1774 and still hoped for a political compromise. So he did not try to destroy the American army but instead tried to show its weakness and persuade the Continental Congress to give up the struggle. Howe's restrained tactics cost Britain the opportunity to nip the rebellion in the bud. For his part, Washington acted cautiously to avoid a major defeat: "On our Side the War should be defensive," he told Congress. His strategy was to draw the British away from the seacoast, extend their lines of supply, and sap their morale.

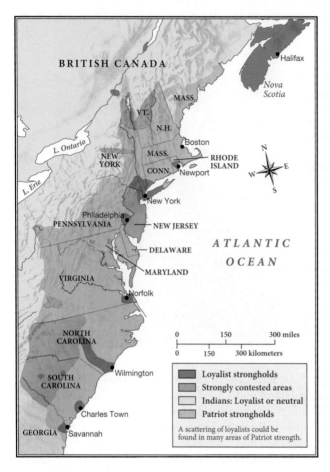

**MAP 6.1  Patriot and Loyalist Strongholds**

Patriots were in the majority in most of the thirteen mainland colonies and used their control of local governments to funnel men, money, and supplies to the rebel cause. Although Loyalists could be found in every colony, their strongholds were limited to Nova Scotia, eastern New York, New Jersey, and certain areas in the South. However, most Native American peoples favored the British cause and bolstered the power of Loyalist militias in central New York (see Map 6.3) and in the Carolina backcountry.

Congress had promised Washington a regular force of 75,000 men, but the Continental army never reached even a third of that number. Yeomen, refusing to be "Haras'd with callouts" that took them away from their families and farms, would serve only in local militias. When the Virginia gentry imposed a military draft and three years of service on propertyless men—the "Lazy fellows who lurk about and are pests to Society"—they resisted so fiercely that the legislature had to pay them substantial bounties and agree to shorter terms of service. The Continental soldiers recruited in Maryland by General William Smallwood were poor American youths and older foreign-born men, often British ex-convicts and former indentured servants. Most enlisted for the $20 cash bonus (about $2,000 today) and the promise of 100 acres of land.

Molding such recruits into an effective fighting force was nearly impossible. Inexperienced soldiers panicked in the face of British attacks; thousands deserted, unwilling to submit to the discipline of military life. The soldiers who stayed resented the contempt their officers had for the "camp followers," the women who made do with the meager supplies provided to feed and care for the troops. General Philip Schuyler of New York complained that his troops were "destitute of provisions, without camp equipage, with little ammunition, and not a single piece of cannon."

## MAP 6.2   The War in the North, 1776–1777

In 1776, the British army drove Washington's forces across New Jersey into Pennsylvania. The Americans counterattacked successfully at Trenton and Princeton and then set up winter headquarters in Morristown. In 1777, British forces stayed on the offensive. General Howe attacked the Patriot capital, Philadelphia, from the south and captured it in early October. Meanwhile, General Burgoyne and Colonel St. Leger launched simultaneous invasions from Canada. With the help of thousands of New England militiamen, American troops commanded by General Horatio Gates defeated Burgoyne in August at Bennington, Vermont, and in October at Saratoga, New York, the military turning point in the war.

The Continental army was not only poorly supplied but was also held in suspicion by Radical Whig Patriots, who believed that a standing army was a threat to liberty. Even in wartime, they preferred militias to a professional fighting force. Given these handicaps, Washington and his army were fortunate to have escaped an overwhelming defeat.

## Victory at Saratoga

After Howe failed to achieve an overwhelming victory, Lord North and his colonial secretary, Lord George Germain, launched another major military campaign in 1777. Isolating New England remained the primary goal. To achieve it, Germain planned a three-pronged attack converging on Albany, New York. General John Burgoyne would lead a large contingent of regulars south from Quebec, Colonel Barry St. Leger and a force of Iroquois would attack from the west, and General Howe would lead troops north from New York City.

Howe instead decided to attack Philadelphia, the home of the Continental Congress, hoping to end the rebellion with a single decisive blow. Howe's troops easily outflanked the American positions along Brandywine Creek in Delaware and, in late September, marched triumphantly into Philadelphia. However, the capture of the rebels' capital did not end the uprising; the Continental Congress, determined to continue the struggle, fled to the countryside.

In the north, Burgoyne's troops had at first advanced quickly, overwhelming the American defenses at Fort Ticonderoga in early July and driving south toward the Hudson River. Then they stalled. Burgoyne — nicknamed "Gentleman Johnny" — was used to high living and had fought in Europe in a leisurely fashion; underestimating the extent of popular support for the rebels, he stopped early each day to pitch comfortable tents and eat elaborate dinners with his officers. The American troops led by General Horatio Gates also slowed Burgoyne's progress by felling huge trees in his path and raiding British supply lines to Canada.

At summer's end, Burgoyne's army of 6,000 British and German troops and 600 Loyalists and Indians was stuck near Saratoga, New York. Desperate for food and horses, in August the British raided nearby Bennington, Vermont, but were beaten back by 2,000 American militiamen. Patriot forces in the Mohawk Valley also threw St. Leger and the Iroquois into retreat. Making matters worse, the British commander in New York City recalled 4,000 troops he had sent toward Albany and ordered them to Philadelphia to bolster Howe's force. While Burgoyne waited in vain for help, thousands of Patriot militiamen from Massachusetts, New Hampshire, and New York joined Gates. The Patriots "swarmed around the army like birds of prey," reported an English sergeant, and in October 1777, they forced Burgoyne to surrender.

The victory at the **Battle of Saratoga** was the turning point of the war. The Patriots captured more than 5,000 British troops and ensured the diplomatic success of American representatives in Paris, who won a military alliance with France.

## The Perils of War

The Patriots' triumph at Saratoga was tempered by wartime difficulties. A British naval blockade cut off supplies of European manufactures and disrupted the New England fishing industry; meanwhile, the British occupation of Boston, New York, and Philadelphia reduced trade. As Patriots, along with unemployed artisans and laborers, moved to the countryside, New York City's population declined from 21,000 to 10,000. The British blockade cut tobacco exports in the Chesapeake, so planters grew grain to sell to the contending armies. All across the land, farmers and artisans adapted to a war economy.

With goods now scarce, governments requisitioned military supplies directly from the people. In 1776, Connecticut officials asked the citizens of Hartford to provide 1,000 coats and 1,600 shirts, and soldiers echoed their pleas. After losing all his shirts "except the one on my back" in the Battle of Long Island, Captain Edward Rogers told his wife that "the making of Cloath . . . must go on." Patriot women responded; in Elizabeth, New Jersey, they promised "upwards of 100,000 yards of linnen and woolen cloth." Other women assumed the burdens of farmwork while their men were away at war and acquired a taste for decision making. "We have sow'd our oats as you desired," Sarah Cobb Paine wrote to her absent husband. "Had I been master I should have planted it to Corn." Their self-esteem boosted by wartime activities, some women expected greater legal rights in the new republican society.

Still, goods remained scarce and pricey. Hard-pressed consumers assailed shopkeepers as "enemies, extortioners, and monopolizers" and called for government regulation. But when the New England states imposed price ceilings in 1777, many farmers and artisans refused to sell their goods. Ultimately, a government official admitted, consumers had to pay the higher market prices "or submit to starving."

The fighting endangered tens of thousands of civilians. A British officer, Lord Rawdon, favored giving "free liberty to the soldiers to ravage [the country] at will, that these infatuated creatures may feel what a calamity war is." As British and American armies marched back and forth across New Jersey, they forced Patriot and Loyalist families to flee their homes to escape arrest — or worse. Soldiers and partisans looted farms, and disorderly troops harassed and raped women and girls. "An army, even a friendly one, are a dreadful scourge to any people," wrote one Connecticut soldier. "You cannot imagine what devastation and distress mark their steps."

The war divided many farm communities. Patriots formed committees of safety to collect taxes and seized the property of those who refused to pay. "Every Body submitted to our Sovereign Lord the Mob," lamented a Loyalist preacher. In parts of Maryland, the number of "nonassociators" — those who refused to join either side — was so large that they successfully defied Patriot mobs. "Stand off you dammed rebel sons of bitches," shouted Robert Davis of Anne Arundel County, "I will shoot you if you come any nearer."

## Financial Crisis

Such defiance exposed the weakness of Patriot governments. Most states were afraid to raise taxes, so officials issued bonds to secure gold or silver from wealthy individuals. When those funds ran out, individual states financed the war by issuing so much paper money — some $260 million all told — that it lost worth, and most people refused to accept it at face value. In North Carolina, even tax collectors eventually rejected the state's currency.

The finances of the Continental Congress collapsed, too, despite the efforts of Philadelphia merchant Robert Morris, the government's chief treasury official. Because the Congress lacked the authority to impose taxes, Morris relied on funds requisitioned from the states, but the states paid late or not at all. So Morris secured loans from France and Holland and sold Continental loan certificates to some thirteen thousand firms and individuals. All the while, the Congress was issuing paper money — some $200 million between 1776 and 1779 — which, like state currencies, quickly fell in value. In 1778, a family needed $7 in Continental bills to buy goods worth $1 in gold or silver. As the exchange rate deteriorated—to 42 to 1 in 1779, 100 to 1 in 1780, and 146 to 1 in 1781—it sparked social upheaval. In Boston, a mob of women accosted merchant Thomas Boyleston, "seazd him by his Neck," and forced him to sell his wares at traditional prices. In rural Ulster County, New York, women told the committee of safety to lower food prices or "their husbands and sons shall fight no more." As morale crumbled, Patriot leaders feared the rebellion would collapse.

### Valley Forge

Fears reached their peak during the winter of 1777. While Howe's army lived comfortably in Philadelphia, Washington's army retreated 20 miles to **Valley Forge**, where 12,000 soldiers and hundreds of camp followers suffered horribly. "The army . . . now begins to grow sickly," a surgeon confided to his diary. "Poor food—hard lodging—cold weather—fatigue—nasty clothes—nasty cookery. . . . Why are we sent here to starve and freeze?" Nearby farmers refused to help. Some were pacifists, Quakers and German sectarians unwilling to support either side. Others looked out for their own families, selling grain for gold from British quartermasters but refusing depreciated Continental currency. "Such a dearth of public spirit, and want of public virtue," lamented Washington. By spring, more than 200 officers had resigned, 1,000 hungry soldiers had deserted, and another 3,000 had died from malnutrition and disease. That winter at Valley Forge took as many American lives as had two years of fighting.

In this dark hour, Baron von Steuben raised the readiness of the American army. A former Prussian military officer, von Steuben was one of a handful of republican-minded foreign aristocrats who joined the American cause. Appointed as inspector general of the Continental army, he instituted a strict drill system and encouraged officers to become more professional. Thanks to von Steuben, the smaller army that emerged from Valley Forge in the spring of 1778 was a much tougher and better-disciplined force.

| IN YOUR OWN WORDS | What challenges did Patriot forces confront in the first two years of the war, and what were their key achievements? |
|---|---|

# The Path to Victory, 1778–1783

Wars are often won by astute diplomacy, and so it was with the War of Independence. The Patriots' prospects improved dramatically in 1778, when the Continental Congress concluded a military alliance with France, the most powerful nation in Europe. The alliance gave the Americans desperately needed money, supplies, and, eventually, troops. And it confronted Britain with an international war that challenged its domination of the Atlantic and Indian oceans.

### The French Alliance

France and America were unlikely partners. France was Catholic and a monarchy; the United States was Protestant and a federation of republics. From 1689 to 1763, the two peoples had been enemies: New Englanders had brutally uprooted the French population from Acadia (Nova Scotia) in 1755, and the French and their Indian allies had raided British settlements. But the Comte de Vergennes, the French foreign minister, was determined to avenge the loss of Canada during the Great War for Empire (see Chapter 4) and persuaded King Louis XVI to provide the rebellious colonies with a secret loan and much-needed gunpowder. When news of the rebel victory at Saratoga reached Paris in December 1777, Vergennes sought a formal alliance.

Benjamin Franklin and other American diplomats craftily exploited France's rivalry with Britain to win an explicit commitment to American independence. The Treaty of Alliance of February 1778 specified that once France entered the war, neither partner would sign a separate peace without the "liberty, sovereignty, and independence" of the United States. In return, the Continental Congress agreed to recognize any French conquests in the West Indies. "France and America," warned Britain's Lord Stormont, were "indissolubly leagued for our destruction."

The alliance gave new life to the Patriots' cause. "There has been a great change in this state since the news from France," a Patriot soldier reported from Pennsylvania. Farmers — "mercenary wretches," he called them — were "as eager for Continental Money now as they were a few weeks ago for British gold." Its confidence bolstered, the Continental Congress addressed the demands of the officer corps. Most officers were gentlemen who equipped themselves and raised volunteers; in return, they insisted on lifetime military pensions at half pay. John Adams condemned the officers for "scrambling for rank and pay like apes for nuts," but General Washington urged the Congress to grant the pensions: "The salvation of the cause depends upon it." The Congress reluctantly granted the officers half pay, but only for seven years.

Meanwhile, the war had become unpopular in Britain. At first, George III was determined to crush the rebellion. If America won independence, he warned Lord North, "the West Indies must follow them. Ireland would soon follow the same plan and be a separate state, then this island would be reduced to itself, and soon would be a poor island indeed." Stunned by the defeat at Saratoga, however, the king changed his mind. To thwart an American alliance with France, he authorized North to seek a negotiated settlement. In February 1778, North persuaded Parliament to repeal the Tea and Prohibitory Acts and, amazingly, to renounce its power to tax the colonies. But the Patriots, now allied with France and committed to independence, rejected North's overture.

## War in the South

The French alliance did not bring a rapid end to the war. When France entered the conflict in June 1778, it hoped to seize all of Britain's sugar islands. Spain, which joined the war against Britain in 1779, aimed to regain Florida and the fortress of Gibraltar at the entrance to the Mediterranean Sea.

**Britain's Southern Strategy**    For its part, the British government revised its military strategy to defend the West Indies and capture the rich tobacco- and rice-growing colonies: Virginia, the Carolinas, and Georgia. Once conquered, the ministry planned to use the Scottish Highlanders in the Carolinas and other Loyalists to hold them. It had already mobilized the Cherokees and Delawares against the land-hungry Americans and knew that the Patriots' fears of slave uprisings weakened them militarily (Map 6.3). As South Carolina Patriots admitted to the Continental Congress, they

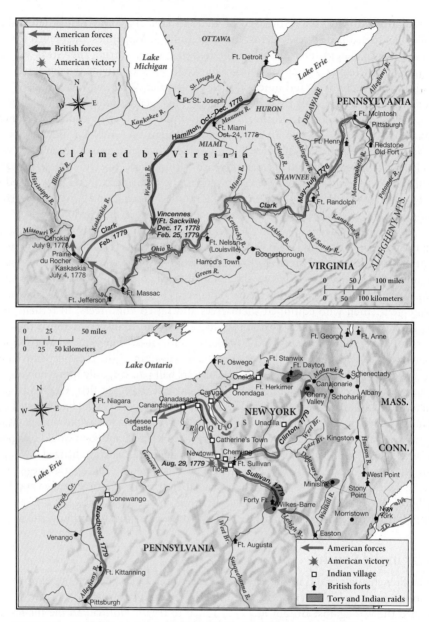

## MAP 6.3   Native Americans and the War in the West, 1778–1779

Many Indian peoples remained neutral, but others, fearing land-hungry Patriot farmers, used British-supplied guns to raid American settlements. To thwart attacks by militant Shawnees, Cherokees, and Delawares, a Patriot militia led by George Rogers Clark captured the British fort and supply depot at Vincennes on the Wabash River in February 1779. To the north, Patriot generals John Sullivan and James Clinton defeated pro-British Indian forces near Tioga (on the New York–Pennsylvania border) in August 1779 and then systematically destroyed villages and crops throughout the lands of the Iroquois.

could raise only a few recruits "by reason of the great proportion of citizens necessary to remain at home to prevent insurrection among the Negroes."

The large number of slaves in the South made the Revolution a "triangular war," in which African Americans constituted a strategic problem for Patriots and a tempting, if dangerous, opportunity for the British. Britain actively recruited slaves to its cause. The effort began with Dunmore's controversial proclamation in November 1775 recruiting slaves to his Ethiopian Regiment (see Chapter 5). In 1779, the **Philipsburg Proclamation** declared that any slave who deserted a rebel master would receive protection, freedom, and land from Great Britain. Together, these proclamations led some 30,000 African Americans to take refuge behind British lines. George Washington initially barred blacks from the Continental army, but he relented in 1777. By war's end, African Americans could enlist in every state but South Carolina and Georgia, and some 5,000 — slave and free — fought for the Patriot cause.

It fell to Sir Henry Clinton — acutely aware of the role slaves might play — to implement Britain's southern strategy. From the British army's main base in New York City, Clinton launched a seaborne attack on Savannah, Georgia. Troops commanded by Colonel Archibald Campbell captured the town in December 1778. Mobilizing hundreds of blacks to transport supplies, Campbell moved inland and captured Augusta early in 1779. By year's end, Clinton's forces and local Loyalists controlled coastal Georgia and had 10,000 troops poised for an assault on South Carolina.

In 1780, British forces marched from victory to victory (Map 6.4). In May, Clinton forced the surrender of Charleston, South Carolina, and its garrison of 5,000 troops. Then Lord Charles Cornwallis assumed control of the British forces and, at Camden, defeated an American force commanded by General Horatio Gates, the hero of Saratoga. Only 1,200 Patriot militiamen joined Gates at Camden, a fifth of the number at Saratoga. Cornwallis took control of South Carolina, and hundreds of African Americans fled to freedom behind British lines. The southern strategy was working.

Then the tide of battle turned. Thanks to another republican-minded European aristocrat, the Marquis de Lafayette, France finally dispatched troops to the American mainland. A longtime supporter of the American cause, Lafayette persuaded King Louis XVI to send General Comte de Rochambeau and 5,500 men to Newport, Rhode Island, in 1780. There, they threatened the British forces holding New York City.

**Guerrilla Warfare in the Carolinas**     Meanwhile, Washington dispatched General Nathanael Greene to recapture the Carolinas, where he found "a country that has been ravaged and plundered by both friends and enemies." Greene put local militiamen, who had been "without discipline and addicted to plundering," under strong leaders and unleashed them on less mobile British forces. In October 1780, Patriot militia defeated a regiment of Loyalists at King's Mountain, South Carolina, taking about one thousand prisoners. American guerrillas commanded by the "Swamp Fox," General Francis Marion, also won a series of small but fierce battles. Then, in January 1781, General Daniel Morgan led an American force to a bloody victory at Cowpens, South Carolina. In March, Greene's soldiers fought Cornwallis's seasoned army to a draw at North Carolina's Guilford Court House. Weakened by this war of attrition, the British general decided to concede the Carolinas to Greene and seek a decisive victory in Virginia. There, many Patriot militiamen had refused to take up arms, claiming that "the Rich wanted the Poor to fight for them."

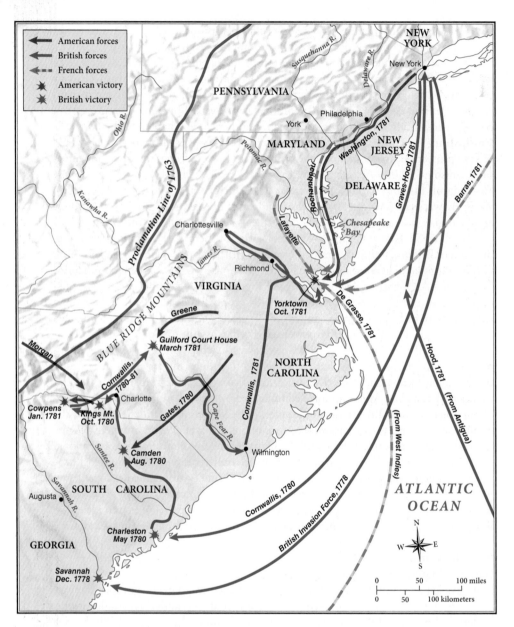

**MAP 6.4   The War in the South, 1778–1781**

Britain's southern military strategy started well. British forces captured Savannah in December 1778, took control of Georgia during 1779, and vanquished Charleston in May 1780. Over the next eighteen months, brutal warfare between the British troops and Loyalist units and the Continental army and militia raged in the interior of the Carolinas and ended in a stalemate. Hoping to break the deadlock, British general Charles Cornwallis carried the battle into Virginia in 1781. A Franco-American army led by Washington and Lafayette, with the help of the French fleet under Admiral de Grasse, surrounded Cornwallis's forces on the Yorktown Peninsula and forced their surrender.

**Francis Marion Crossing the Pedee River** Francis Marion was a master of the ferocious guerrilla fighting that characterized the war in South Carolina. Though Patriot general Horatio Gates had little confidence in him, Marion led an irregular militia brigade in several successful attacks. After chasing Marion into a swamp, British general Banastre Tarleton declared, "As for this damned old fox, the Devil himself could not catch him." Soon Patriots began calling Marion the Swamp Fox. In 1851, William T. Ranney painted Marion (on horseback in a white shirt and blue coat) and his men crossing the Pedee River in flatboats. Ranney included an unidentified (and possibly fictionalized) black oarsman. William T. Ranney, *Marion Crossing the Pedee*, 1850, oil on canvas. Amon Carter Museum, Fort Worth, Texas, 1983.126.

Exploiting these social divisions, Cornwallis moved easily through the Tidewater region of Virginia in the early summer of 1781. Reinforcements sent from New York and commanded by General Benedict Arnold, the infamous Patriot traitor, bolstered his ranks. As Arnold and Cornwallis sparred with an American force led by Lafayette near the York Peninsula, Washington was informed that France had finally sent its powerful West Indian fleet to North America, and he devised an audacious plan. Feigning an assault on New York City, he secretly marched General Rochambeau's army from Rhode Island to Virginia. Simultaneously, the French fleet took control of Chesapeake Bay. By the time the British discovered Washington's scheme, Cornwallis was surrounded, his 9,500-man army outnumbered 2 to 1 on land and cut off from reinforcement or retreat by sea. In a hopeless position, at the conclusion of the **Battle of Yorktown** Cornwallis surrendered in October 1781.

The Franco-American victory broke the resolve of the British government. "Oh God! It is all over!" Lord North exclaimed. Isolated diplomatically in Europe, stymied militarily in America, and lacking public support at home, the British ministry gave up active prosecution of the war on the American mainland.

## The Patriot Advantage

How could mighty Britain, victorious in the Great War for Empire, lose to a motley rebel army? The British ministry pointed to a series of blunders by the military leadership. Why had Howe not ruthlessly pursued Washington's army in 1776? Why had Howe and Burgoyne failed to coordinate their attacks in 1777? Why had Cornwallis marched deep into the Patriot-dominated state of Virginia in 1781?

Historians acknowledge British mistakes, but they also attribute the rebels' victory to French aid and the inspired leadership of George Washington. Astutely deferring to elected officials, Washington won the support of the Continental Congress and the state governments. Confident of his military abilities, he pursued a defensive strategy that minimized casualties and maintained the morale of his officers and soldiers through five difficult years of war. Moreover, the Patriots' control of local governments gave Washington a greater margin for error than the British generals had. Local militiamen provided the edge in the 1777 victory at Saratoga and forced Cornwallis from the Carolinas in 1781.

In the end, it was the American people who decided the outcome, especially the one-third of the white colonists who were zealous Patriots. Tens of thousands of these farmers and artisans accepted Continental bills in payment for supplies, and thousands of soldiers took them as pay, even as the currency literally depreciated in their pockets. Rampant inflation meant that every paper dollar held for a week lost value, imposing a hidden "**currency tax**" on those who accepted the paper currency. Each individual tax was small — a few pennies on each dollar. But as millions of dollars changed hands multiple times, the currency taxes paid by ordinary citizens financed the American military victory.

## Diplomatic Triumph

After Yorktown, diplomats took two years to conclude a peace treaty. Talks began in Paris in April 1782, but the French and Spanish, still hoping to seize a West Indian island or Gibraltar, stalled for time. Their tactics infuriated American diplomats Benjamin Franklin, John Adams, and John Jay. So the Americans negotiated secretly with the British, prepared if necessary to ignore the Treaty of Alliance and sign a separate peace. British ministers were equally eager: Parliament wanted peace, and they feared the loss of a rich sugar island.

Consequently, the American diplomats secured extremely favorable terms. In the **Treaty of Paris of 1783**, signed in September, Great Britain formally recognized American independence and relinquished its claims to lands south of the Great Lakes and east of the Mississippi River. The British negotiators did not insist on a separate territory for their Indian allies. "In endeavouring to assist you," a Wea Indian complained to a British general, "it seems we have wrought our own ruin." The Cherokees were forced to relinquish claims to 5 million acres — three-quarters of their territory — in treaties with Georgia, the Carolinas, and Virginia, while New York and the Continental Congress pressed the Iroquois and Ohio Indians to cede much of their land as well. British officials, like those of other early modern empires, found it easy to abandon allies they had never really understood.

The Paris treaty also granted Americans fishing rights off Newfoundland and Nova Scotia, prohibited the British from "carrying away any negroes or other property," and guaranteed freedom of navigation on the Mississippi to American citizens "forever." In return, the American government allowed British merchants to pursue legal claims for prewar debts and encouraged the state legislatures to return confiscated property to Loyalists and grant them citizenship.

In the Treaty of Versailles, signed simultaneously, Britain made peace with France and Spain. Neither American ally gained very much. Spain reclaimed Florida from Britain, but not the strategic fortress at Gibraltar. France received the Caribbean island of Tobago, small consolation for a war that had sharply raised taxes and quadrupled France's national debt. Just six years later, cries for tax relief and political liberty would spark the French Revolution. Only Americans profited handsomely; the treaties gave them independence and access to the trans-Appalachian west.

| **IN YOUR OWN WORDS** | What were the keys to Patriot victory in the American Revolution? |
|---|---|

# Creating Republican Institutions, 1776–1787

When the Patriots declared independence, they confronted the issue of political authority. "Which of us shall be the rulers?" asked a Philadelphia newspaper. The question was multifaceted. Would power reside in the national government or the states? Who would control the new republican institutions: traditional elites or average citizens? Would women have greater political and legal rights? What would be the status of slaves in the new republic?

## The State Constitutions: How Much Democracy?

In May 1776, the Second Continental Congress urged Americans to reject royal authority and establish republican governments. Most states quickly complied. "Constitutions employ every pen," an observer noted. Within six months, Virginia, Maryland, North Carolina, New Jersey, Delaware, and Pennsylvania had all ratified new constitutions, and Connecticut and Rhode Island had revised their colonial charters to delete references to the king.

Republicanism meant more than ousting the king. The Declaration of Independence stated the principle of popular sovereignty: governments derive "their just powers from the consent of the governed." In the heat of revolution, many Patriots gave this clause a further democratic twist. In North Carolina, the backcountry farmers of Mecklenburg County told their delegates to the state's constitutional convention to "oppose everything that leans to aristocracy or power in the hands of the rich." In Virginia, voters elected a new assembly in 1776 that, an eyewitness remarked, "was composed of men not quite so well dressed, nor so politely educated, nor so highly born" as colonial-era legislatures.

### Pennsylvania's Controversial Constitution    This democratic impulse flowered in Pennsylvania, thanks to a coalition of Scots-Irish farmers, Philadelphia artisans, and Enlightenment-influenced intellectuals. In 1776, these insurgents ousted every officeholder of the Penn family's proprietary government, abolished property ownership as

a qualification for voting, and granted all taxpaying men the right to vote and hold office. The **Pennsylvania constitution of 1776** also created a unicameral (one-house) legislature with complete power; there was no governor to exercise a veto. Other provisions mandated a system of elementary education and protected citizens from imprisonment for debt.

Pennsylvania's democratic constitution alarmed many leading Patriots. From Boston, John Adams denounced the unicameral legislature as "so democratical that it must produce confusion and every evil work." Along with other conservative Patriots, Adams wanted to restrict office holding to "men of learning, leisure and easy circumstances" and warned of oppression under majority rule: "If you give [ordinary citizens] the command or preponderance in the . . . legislature, they will vote all property out of the hands of you aristocrats."

**Tempering Democracy**   To counter the appeal of the Pennsylvania constitution, Adams published *Thoughts on Government* (1776). In that treatise, he adapted the British Whig theory of **mixed government** (a sharing of power among the monarch, the House of Lords, and the Commons) to a republican society. To disperse authority and preserve liberty, he insisted on separate institutions: legislatures would make laws, the executive would administer them, and the judiciary would enforce them. Adams also demanded a bicameral (two-house) legislature with an upper house of substantial property owners to offset the popular majorities in the lower one. As further curbs on democracy, he proposed an elected governor with veto power and an appointed — not elected — judiciary.

Conservative Patriots endorsed Adams's governmental system. In New York's constitution of 1777, property qualifications for voting excluded 20 percent of white men from assembly elections and 60 percent from casting ballots for the governor and the upper house. In South Carolina, elite planters used property rules to disqualify about 90 percent of white men from office holding. The 1778 constitution required candidates for governor to have a debt-free estate of £10,000 (about $700,000 today), senators to be worth £2,000, and assemblymen to own property valued at £1,000. Even in traditionally democratic Massachusetts, the 1780 constitution, authored primarily by Adams, raised property qualifications for voting and office holding and skewed the lower house toward eastern, mercantile interests.

The political legacy of the Revolution was complex. Only in Pennsylvania and Vermont were radical Patriots able to create truly democratic institutions. Yet in all the new states, representative legislatures had acquired more power, and average citizens now had greater power at the polls and greater influence in the halls of government.

## Women Seek a Public Voice

The extraordinary excitement of the Revolutionary era tested the dictum that only men could engage in politics. Men controlled all public institutions — legislatures, juries, government offices — but upper-class women engaged in political debate and, defying men's scorn, filled their letters, diaries, and conversations with opinions on public issues. "The men say we have no business [with politics]," Eliza Wilkinson of South Carolina complained in 1783. "They won't even allow us liberty of thought, and that is all I want."

As Wilkinson's remark suggests, most women did not insist on civic equality with men; many sought only an end to restrictive customs and laws. Abigail Adams demanded equal legal rights for married women, who under common law could not own property, enter into contracts, or initiate lawsuits. The war bonds she purchased had to be held in a trust run by a male relative. "Men would be tyrants" if they continued to hold such power over women, Adams declared to her husband, John, criticizing him and other Patriots for "emancipating all nations" from monarchical despotism while "retaining absolute power over Wives."

Most politicians ignored women's requests, and most men insisted on traditional sexual and political prerogatives. Long-married husbands remained patriarchs who dominated their households, and even young men who embraced the republican ideal of "companionate marriage" did not support legal equality for their wives and daughters. Except in New Jersey, which until 1807 allowed unmarried and widowed female property holders to vote, women remained disenfranchised. In the new American republic, only white men enjoyed full citizenship.

Nevertheless, the republican belief in an educated citizenry created opportunities for some women. In her 1779 essay "On the Equality of the Sexes," Judith Sargent Murray argued that men and women had equal capacities for memory and that women had superior imaginations. She conceded that most women were inferior to men in judgment and reasoning, but only from lack of training: "We can only reason from what we know," she argued, and most women had been denied "the opportunity of acquiring knowledge." That situation changed in the 1790s, when the attorney general of Massachusetts declared that girls had an equal right to schooling under the state constitution. By 1850, the literacy rates of women and men in the northeastern states were equal, and educated women again challenged their subordinate legal and political status.

## The War's Losers: Loyalists, Native Americans, and Slaves

The success of republican institutions was assisted by the departure of as many as 100,000 Loyalists, many of whom suffered severe financial losses. Some Patriots demanded revolutionary justice: the seizure of all Loyalist property and its distribution to needy Americans. But most officials were unwilling to go so far. When state governments did seize Loyalist property, they often auctioned it to the highest bidders; only rarely did small-scale farmers benefit. In the cities, Patriot merchants replaced Loyalists at the top of the economic ladder, supplanting a traditional economic elite — who often invested profits from trade in real estate — with republican entrepreneurs who tended to promote new trading ventures and domestic manufacturing. This shift facilitated America's economic development in the years to come.

Though the Revolution did not result in widespread property redistribution, it did encourage yeomen, middling planters, and small-time entrepreneurs to believe that their new republican governments would protect their property and ensure widespread access to land. In western counties, former Regulators demanded that the new governments be more responsive to their needs; beyond the Appalachians, thousands of squatters who had occupied lands in Kentucky and Tennessee expected their claims to be recognized and lands to be made available on easy terms. If the

United States were to secure the loyalty of westerners, it would have to meet their needs more effectively than the British Empire had.

This meant, among other things, extinguishing Native American claims to land as quickly as possible. At war's end, George Washington commented on the "rage for speculating" in Ohio Valley lands. "Men in these times, talk with as much facility of fifty, a hundred, and even 500,000 Acres as a Gentleman formerly would do of 1000 acres." "If we make a right use of our natural advantages," a Fourth of July orator observed, "we soon must be a truly great and happy people." Native American land claims stood as a conspicuous barrier to the "natural advantages" he imagined.

For southern slaveholders, the Revolution was fought to protect property rights, and any sentiment favoring slave emancipation met with violent objections. When Virginia Methodists called for general emancipation in 1785, slaveholders used Revolutionary principles to defend their right to human property. They "risked [their] Lives and Fortunes, and waded through Seas of Blood" to secure "the Possession of [their] Rights of Liberty and Property," only to hear of "a very subtle and daring Attempt" to "dispossess us of a very important Part of our Property." Emancipation would bring "Want, Poverty, Distress, and Ruin to the Free Citizen." The liberties coveted by ordinary white Americans bore hard on the interests of Native Americans and slaves.

## The Articles of Confederation

As Patriots embraced independence in 1776, they envisioned a central government with limited powers. Carter Braxton of Virginia thought the Continental Congress should "regulate the affairs of trade, war, peace, alliances, &c." but "should by no means have authority to interfere with the internal police [governance] or domestic concerns of any Colony."

That idea informed the **Articles of Confederation**, which were approved by the Continental Congress in November 1777. The Articles provided for a loose union in which "each state retains its sovereignty, freedom, and independence." As an association of equals, each state had one vote regardless of its size, population, or wealth. Important laws needed the approval of nine of the thirteen states, and changes in the Articles required unanimous consent. Though the Confederation had significant powers on paper — it could declare war, make treaties with foreign nations, adjudicate disputes between the states, borrow and print money, and requisition funds from the states "for the common defense or general welfare" — it had major weaknesses as well. It had neither a chief executive nor a judiciary. Though it could make treaties, it could not enforce their provisions, since the states remained sovereign. Most important, it lacked the power to tax either the states or the people.

Although the Congress exercised authority from 1776 — raising the Continental army, negotiating the treaty with France, and financing the war — the Articles won formal ratification only in 1781. The delay stemmed from conflicts over western lands. The royal charters of Virginia, Massachusetts, Connecticut, and other states set boundaries stretching to the Pacific Ocean. States without western lands — Maryland and Pennsylvania — refused to accept the Articles until the land-rich states relinquished these claims to the Confederation. Threatened by Cornwallis's army in 1781, Virginia gave up its claims, and Maryland, the last holdout, finally ratified the Articles (Map 6.5).

### MAP 6.5   The Confederation and Western Land Claims, 1781–1802

The Congress formed by the Articles of Confederation had to resolve conflicting state claims to western lands. For example, the territories claimed by New York and Virginia on the basis of their royal charters overlapped extensively. Beginning in 1781, the Confederation Congress and, after 1789, the U.S. Congress persuaded all of the states to cede their western claims, creating a "national domain" open to all citizens. In the Northwest Ordinance (1787), the Congress divided the domain north of the Ohio River into territories and set up democratic procedures by which they could eventually join the Union as states. South of the Ohio River, the Congress allowed the existing southern states to play a substantial role in settling the ceded lands.

**Continuing Fiscal Crisis**   By 1780, the central government was nearly bankrupt, and General Washington called urgently for a national tax system; without one, he warned, "our cause is lost." Led by Robert Morris, who became superintendent of finance in 1781, nationalist-minded Patriots tried to expand the Confederation's authority. They persuaded Congress to charter the Bank of North America, a private institution in Philadelphia, arguing that its notes would stabilize the inflated Continental currency. Morris also created a central bureaucracy to manage the Confederation's finances and urged Congress to enact a 5 percent import tax. Rhode Island and New York rejected the tax proposal. His state had opposed British import duties, New York's representative declared, and it would not accept them from Congress. To raise revenue, Congress looked to the sale of western lands. In 1783, it asserted that the recently signed Treaty of Paris had extinguished the Indians' rights to those lands and made them the property of the United States.

**The Northwest Ordinance**   By 1784, more than 30,000 settlers had already moved to Kentucky and Tennessee, despite the uncertainties of frontier warfare, and after the war their numbers grew rapidly. In that year, the residents of what is now eastern Tennessee organized a new state, called it Franklin, and sought admission to the Confederation. To preserve its authority over the West, Congress refused to recognize Franklin. Subsequently, Congress created the Southwest and Mississippi Territories (the future states of Tennessee, Alabama, and Mississippi) from lands ceded by North Carolina and Georgia. Because these cessions carried the stipulation that "no regulation . . . shall tend to emancipate slaves," these states and all those south of the Ohio River allowed human bondage.

However, the Confederation Congress banned slavery north of the Ohio River. Between 1784 and 1787, it issued three important ordinances organizing the "Old Northwest." The Ordinance of 1784, written by Thomas Jefferson, established the principle that territories could become states as their populations grew. The Land Ordinance of 1785 mandated a rectangular-grid system of surveying and specified a minimum price of $1 an acre. It also required that half of the townships be sold in single blocks of 23,040 acres each, which only large-scale speculators could afford, and the rest in parcels of 640 acres each, which restricted their sale to well-to-do farmers (Map 6.6).

Finally, the **Northwest Ordinance of 1787** created the territories that would eventually become the states of Ohio, Indiana, Illinois, Michigan, and Wisconsin. The ordinance prohibited slavery and earmarked funds from land sales for the support of schools. It also specified that Congress would appoint a governor and judges to administer each new territory until the population reached 5,000 free adult men, at which point the citizens could elect a territorial legislature. When the population reached 60,000, the legislature could devise a republican constitution and apply to join the Confederation.

The land ordinances of the 1780s were a great and enduring achievement of the Confederation Congress. They provided for orderly settlement and the admission of new states on the basis of equality; there would be no politically dependent "colonies" in the West. But they also extended the geographical division between slave and free areas that would haunt the nation in the coming decades. And they implicitly invalidated Native American claims to an enormous swath of territory—a corollary that would soon lead the newly independent nation, once again, into war.

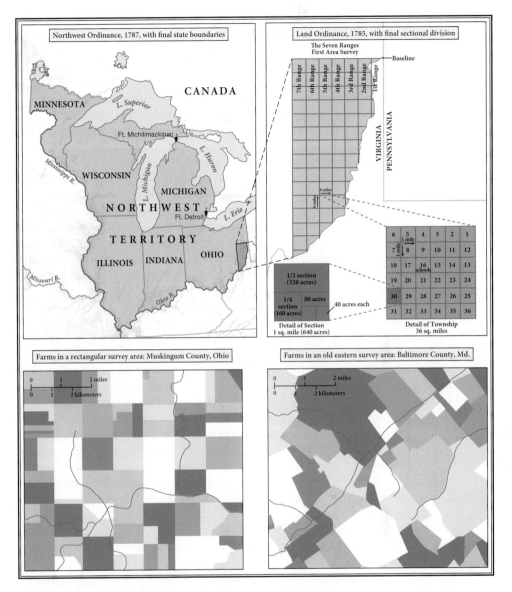

## MAP 6.6 Land Division in the Northwest Territory

Throughout the Northwest Territory, government surveyors imposed a rectangular grid on the landscape, regardless of the local topography, so that farmers bought neatly defined tracts of land. The right-angled property lines in Muskingum County, Ohio (lower left), contrasted sharply with those in Baltimore County, Maryland (lower right), where—as in most of the eastern and southern states—boundaries followed the contours of the land.

## Shays's Rebellion

Though many national leaders were optimistic about the long-term prospects of the United States, postwar economic conditions were grim. The Revolution had crippled American shipping and cut exports of tobacco, rice, and wheat. The British Navigation Acts, which had nurtured colonial commerce, now barred Americans from legal trade with the British West Indies. Moreover, low-priced British manufactures (and some from India as well) were flooding American markets, driving urban artisans and wartime textile firms out of business.

The fiscal condition of the state governments was dire, primarily because of war debts. Well-to-do merchants and landowners (including Abigail Adams) had invested in state bonds during the war; others had speculated in debt certificates, buying them on the cheap from hard-pressed farmers and soldiers. Now creditors and speculators demanded that the state governments redeem the bonds and certificates quickly and at full value, a policy that would require tax increases and a decrease in the amount of paper currency. Most legislatures—now including substantial numbers of middling farmers and artisans—refused. Instead they authorized new issues of paper currency and allowed debtors to pay private creditors in installments. Although wealthy men deplored these measures as "intoxicating Draughts of Liberty" that destroyed "the just rights of creditors," such political intervention prevented social upheaval.

In Massachusetts, however, the new constitution placed power in the hands of a mercantile elite that owned the bulk of the state's war bonds. Ignoring the interests of ordinary citizens, the legislature increased taxes fivefold to pay off wartime debts—and it stipulated that they be paid in hard currency. Even for substantial farmers, this was a crushing burden. When cash-strapped farmers could not pay both their taxes and their debts, creditors threatened lawsuits. Debtor Ephraim Wetmore heard a rumor that merchant Stephan Salisbury "would have my Body Dead or Alive in case I did not pay." To protect their livelihoods, farmers called extralegal conventions to protest high taxes and property seizures. Then mobs of angry farmers, including men of high status, closed the courts by force. "[I] had no Intensions to Destroy the Publick Government," declared Captain Adam Wheeler, a former town selectman; his goal was simply to prevent "Valuable and Industrious members of Society [being] dragged from their families to prison" because of their debts. These crowd actions grew into a full-scale revolt led by Captain Daniel Shays, a Continental army veteran.

As a revolt against taxes imposed by an unresponsive government, **Shays's Rebellion** resembled American resistance to the British Stamp Act. Consciously linking themselves to the Patriot movement, Shays's men placed pine twigs in their hats just as Continental troops had done. "The people have turned against their teachers the doctrines which were inculcated to effect the late revolution," complained Fisher Ames, a conservative Massachusetts lawmaker. Some of the radical Patriots of 1776 likewise condemned the Shaysites: "[Men who] would lessen the Weight of Government lawfully exercised must be Enemies to our happy Revolution and Common Liberty," charged Samuel Adams. To put down the rebellion, the Massachusetts legislature passed the Riot Act, and wealthy bondholders equipped a formidable fighting force, which Governor James Bowdoin used to disperse Shays's ragtag army during the winter of 1786–1787.

Although Shays's Rebellion failed, it showed that many middling Patriot families felt that American oppressors had replaced British tyrants. Massachusetts voters turned Governor Bowdoin out of office, and debt-ridden farmers in New York, northern Pennsylvania, Connecticut, and New Hampshire closed courthouses and forced their governments to provide economic relief. British officials in Canada predicted the imminent demise of the United States; and American leaders urged purposeful action to save their republican experiment. Events in Massachusetts, declared nationalist Henry Knox, formed "the strongest arguments possible" for the creation of "a strong general government."

| IN YOUR OWN WORDS | What were the most important challenges facing governments in the 1780s? |
|---|---|

# The Constitution of 1787

These issues ultimately led to the drafting of a national constitution. From its creation, the U.S. Constitution was a controversial document, both acclaimed for solving the nation's woes and condemned for perverting its republican principles. Critics charged that republican institutions worked only in small political units — the states. Advocates replied that the Constitution extended republicanism by adding another level of government elected by the people. In the new two-level political federation created by the Constitution, the national government would exercise limited, delegated powers, and the existing state governments would retain authority over all other matters.

## The Rise of a Nationalist Faction

Money questions — debts, taxes, and tariffs — dominated the postwar political agenda. Americans who had served the Confederation as military officers, officials, and diplomats viewed these issues from a national perspective and advocated a stronger central government. George Washington, Robert Morris, Benjamin Franklin, John Jay, and John Adams wanted Congress to control foreign and interstate trade and tariff policy. However, lawmakers in Massachusetts, New York, and Pennsylvania — states with strong commercial traditions — insisted on controlling their own tariffs, both to protect their artisans from low-cost imports and to assist their merchants. Most southern states opposed tariffs because planters wanted to import British textiles and ironware at the lowest possible prices.

Nonetheless, some southern leaders became nationalists because their state legislatures had cut taxes and refused to redeem state war bonds. Such policies, lamented wealthy bondholder Charles Lee of Virginia, led taxpayers to believe they would "never be compelled to pay" the public debt. Creditors also condemned state laws that "stayed" (delayed) the payment of mortgages and other private debts. "While men are madly accumulating enormous debts, their legislators are making provisions for their nonpayment," complained a South Carolina merchant. To undercut the democratic majorities in the state legislatures, creditors joined the movement for a stronger central government.

Delegates from five states met in Annapolis, Maryland, in September 1786 to consider solutions to the confederation's economic problems. They recommended that another convention, with representatives from all the states, meet in Philadelphia in 1787. Spurred on by Shays's Rebellion, nationalists in Congress secured a resolution calling for such a convention to revise the Articles of Confederation. Only an "efficient plan from the Convention," a fellow nationalist wrote to James Madison, "can prevent anarchy first & civil convulsions afterwards."

## The Philadelphia Convention

In May 1787, fifty-five delegates arrived in Philadelphia. They came from every state except Rhode Island, where the legislature opposed increasing central authority. Most were strong nationalists; forty-two had served in the Confederation Congress. They were also educated and propertied: merchants, slaveholding planters, and "monied men." There were no artisans, backcountry settlers, or tenants, and only a single yeoman farmer.

Some influential Patriots missed the convention. John Adams and Thomas Jefferson were serving as American ministers to Britain and France, respectively. The Massachusetts General Court rejected Samuel Adams as a delegate because he opposed a stronger national government, and his fellow firebrand from Virginia, Patrick Henry, refused to attend because he "smelt a rat." Just as politically engaged citizens disagreed in 1787 whether a new form of government was needed, historians have argued ever since about whether the Constitution was necessary.

**James Madison, Statesman** Throughout his long public life, Madison kept the details of his private life to himself. His biography, he believed, should be a record of his public accomplishments, not his private affairs. Future generations celebrated him not as a great man (like Hamilton or Jefferson) or as a great president (like Washington), but as an original and incisive political thinker. The chief architect of the U.S. Constitution and the Bill of Rights, Madison was the preeminent republican political theorist of his generation. Mead Art Museum, Amherst College, MA, USA/ Bequest of Herbert L. Pratt (Class of 1895)/Bridgeman Images.

The absence of experienced leaders and contrary-minded delegates allowed capable younger nationalists to set the agenda. Declaring that the convention would "decide for ever the fate of Republican Government," James Madison insisted on increased national authority. Alexander Hamilton of New York likewise demanded a strong central government to protect the republic from "the imprudence of democracy."

**The Virginia and New Jersey Plans**    The delegates elected George Washington as their presiding officer and voted to meet behind closed doors. Then — momentously — they decided not to revise the Articles of Confederation but rather to consider the so-called **Virginia Plan**, a scheme for a powerful national government devised by James Madison. Just thirty-six years old, Madison was determined to fashion national political institutions run by men of high character. A graduate of Princeton, he had read classical and modern political theory and served in both the Confederation Congress and the Virginia assembly. Once an optimistic Patriot, Madison had grown discouraged because of the "narrow ambition" and outlook of state legislators.

Madison's Virginia Plan differed from the Articles of Confederation in three crucial respects. First, the plan rejected state sovereignty in favor of the "supremacy of national authority," including the power to overturn state laws. Second, it called for the national government to be established by the people (not the states) and for national laws to operate directly on citizens of the various states. Third, the plan proposed a three-tier election system in which ordinary voters would elect only the lower house of the national legislature. This lower house would then select the upper house, and both houses would appoint the executive and judiciary.

From a political perspective, Madison's plan had two fatal flaws. First, most state politicians and citizens resolutely opposed allowing the national government to veto state laws. Second, the plan based representation in the lower house on population; this provision, a Delaware delegate warned, would allow the populous states to "crush the small ones whenever they stand in the way of their ambitious or interested views."

So delegates from Delaware and other small states rallied behind a plan devised by William Paterson of New Jersey. The **New Jersey Plan** gave the Confederation the power to raise revenue, control commerce, and make binding requisitions on the states. But it preserved the states' control of their own laws and guaranteed their equality: as in the Confederation Congress, each state would have one vote in a unicameral legislature. Delegates from the more populous states vigorously opposed this provision. After a month-long debate on the two plans, a bare majority of the states agreed to use Madison's Virginia Plan as the basis of discussion.

This decision raised the odds that the convention would create a more powerful national government. Outraged by this prospect, two New York delegates, Robert Yates and John Lansing, accused their colleagues of exceeding their mandate to revise the Articles and left the convention. The remaining delegates met six days a week during the summer of 1787, debating both high principles and practical details. Experienced politicians, they looked for a plan that would be acceptable to most citizens and existing political interests. Pierce Butler of South Carolina invoked a classical Greek precedent: "We must follow the example of Solon, who gave the Athenians not the best government he could devise but the best they would receive."

**The Great Compromise**  As the convention grappled with the central problem of the representation of large and small states, the Connecticut delegates suggested a possible solution. They proposed that the national legislature's upper chamber (the Senate) have two members from each state, while seats in the lower chamber (the House of Representatives) be apportioned by population (determined every ten years by a national census). After bitter debate, delegates from the populous states reluctantly accepted this "Great Compromise."

Other state-related issues were quickly settled by restricting (or leaving ambiguous) the extent of central authority. Some delegates opposed a national system of courts, predicting that "the states will revolt at such encroachments" on their judicial authority. This danger led the convention to vest the judicial power "in one supreme Court" and allow the new national legislature to decide whether to establish lower courts within the states. The convention also refused to set a property requirement for voting in national elections. "Eight or nine states have extended the right of suffrage beyond the freeholders," George Mason of Virginia pointed out. "What will people there say if they should be disfranchised?" Finally, the convention specified that state legislatures would elect members of the upper house, or Senate, and the states would select the electors who would choose the president. By allowing states to have important roles in the new constitutional system, the delegates hoped that their citizens would accept limits on state sovereignty.

**Negotiations over Slavery**  The shadow of slavery hovered over many debates, and Gouverneur Morris of New York brought it into view. To safeguard property rights, Morris wanted life terms for senators, a property qualification for voting in national elections, and a strong president with veto power. Nonetheless, he rejected the legitimacy of two traditional types of property: the feudal dues claimed by aristocratic landowners and the ownership of slaves. An advocate of free markets and personal liberty, Morris condemned slavery as "a nefarious institution."

Many slave-owning delegates from the Chesapeake region, including Madison and George Mason, recognized that slavery contradicted republican principles and hoped for its eventual demise. They supported an end to American participation in the Atlantic slave trade, a proposal the South Carolina and Georgia delegates angrily rejected. Unless the importation of African slaves continued, these rice planters and merchants declared, their states "shall not be parties to the Union." At their insistence, the convention denied Congress the power to regulate immigration—and so the slave trade—until 1808.

The delegates devised other slavery-related compromises. To mollify southern planters, they wrote a "fugitive clause" that allowed masters to reclaim enslaved blacks (or white indentured servants) who fled to other states. But in acknowledgment of the antislavery sentiments of Morris and other northerners, the delegates excluded the words *slavery* and *slave* from the Constitution; it spoke only of citizens and "all other Persons." Because slaves lacked the vote, antislavery delegates wanted their census numbers excluded when apportioning seats in Congress. Southerners— ironically, given that they considered slaves property—demanded that slaves be counted in the census the same as full citizens, to increase the South's representation. Ultimately, the delegates agreed that each slave would count as three-fifths of a free person for purposes of representation and taxation, a compromise that helped southern planters dominate the national government until 1860.

**National Authority**   Having addressed the concerns of small states and slave states, the convention created a powerful national government. The Constitution declared that congressional legislation was the "supreme" law of the land. It gave the new government the power to tax, raise an army and a navy, and regulate foreign and interstate commerce, with the authority to make all laws "necessary and proper" to implement those and other provisions. To assist creditors and establish the new government's fiscal integrity, the Constitution required the United States to honor the existing national debt and prohibited the states from issuing paper money or enacting "any Law impairing the Obligation of Contracts."

The proposed constitution was not a "perfect production," Benjamin Franklin admitted, as he urged the delegates to sign it in September 1787. But the great statesman confessed his astonishment at finding "this system approaching so near to perfection." His colleagues apparently agreed; all but three signed the document.

## The People Debate Ratification

The procedure for ratifying the new constitution was as controversial as its contents. Knowing that Rhode Island (and perhaps other states) would reject it, the delegates did not submit the Constitution to the state legislatures for their unanimous consent, as required by the Articles of Confederation. Instead, they arbitrarily—and cleverly—declared that it would take effect when ratified by conventions in nine of the thirteen states. Moreover, they insisted that the conventions could only approve or disapprove the plan; they could not suggest alterations. As George Mason put it, the conventions would "take this or take nothing."

As the constitutional debate began in early 1788, the nationalists seized the initiative with two bold moves. First, they called themselves **Federalists**, suggesting that they supported a federal union—a loose, decentralized system—and obscuring their commitment to a strong national government. Second, they launched a coordinated campaign in pamphlets and newspapers to explain and justify the Philadelphia constitution.

**The Antifederalists**   The opponents of the Constitution, called by default the **Antifederalists**, had diverse backgrounds and motives. Some, like Governor George Clinton of New York, feared that state governments would lose power. Rural democrats protested that the proposed document, unlike most state constitutions, lacked a declaration of individual rights; they also feared that the central government would be run by wealthy men. "Lawyers and men of learning and monied men expect to be managers of this Constitution," worried a Massachusetts farmer. "[T]hey will swallow up all of us little folks . . . just as the whale swallowed up Jonah." Giving political substance to these fears, Melancton Smith of New York argued that the large electoral districts prescribed by the Constitution would restrict office holding to wealthy men, whereas the smaller districts used in state elections usually produced legislatures "composed principally of respectable yeomanry." John Quincy Adams agreed: if only "*eight* men" would represent Massachusetts, "they will infallibly be chosen from the aristocratic part of the community."

Smith summed up the views of Americans who held traditional republican values. To keep government "close to the people," they wanted the states to remain small sovereign republics tied together only for trade and defense—not the "United States" but the "States United." Citing the French political philosopher Montesquieu, Antifederalists argued that republican institutions were best suited to small polities. "No extensive empire can be governed on republican principles," declared James Winthrop of Massachusetts. Patrick Henry worried that the Constitution would re-create British rule: high taxes, an oppressive bureaucracy, a standing army, and a "great and mighty President . . . supported in extravagant munificence." As another Antifederalist put it, "I had rather be a free citizen of the small republic of Massachusetts than an oppressed subject of the great American Empire." Many Americans found themselves somewhere in the middle, supporting a stronger central government in principle but worried about countless details that made the Constitution appear flawed.

**Federalists Respond**   In New York, where ratification was hotly contested, James Madison, John Jay, and Alexander Hamilton defended the proposed constitution in a series of eighty-five essays written in 1787 and 1788, collectively titled *The Federalist*. This work influenced political leaders throughout the country and subsequently won acclaim as an important treatise of practical republicanism. Its authors denied that a centralized government would lead to domestic tyranny. Drawing on Montesquieu's theories and John Adams's *Thoughts on Government*, Madison, Jay, and Hamilton pointed out that authority would be divided among the president, a bicameral legislature, and a judiciary. Each branch of government would "check and balance" the others and so preserve liberty.

In "**Federalist No. 10**," Madison challenged the view that republican governments only worked in small polities, arguing that a large state would better protect republican liberty. It was "sown in the nature of man," Madison wrote, for individuals to seek power and form factions. Indeed, "a landed interest, a manufacturing interest, a mercantile interest, a moneyed interest, with many lesser interests, grow up of necessity in civilized nations." A free society should welcome all factions but keep any one of them from becoming dominant—something best achieved in a large republic. "Extend the sphere and you take in a greater variety of parties and interests," Madison concluded, inhibiting the formation of a majority eager "to invade the rights of other citizens."

**The Constitution Ratified**   The delegates debating these issues in the state ratification conventions included untutored farmers and middling artisans as well as educated gentlemen. Generally, backcountry delegates were especially skeptical, while those from coastal areas were more likely to support the new constitution. In Pennsylvania, a coalition of Philadelphia merchants and artisans and commercial farmers ensured its ratification. Other early Federalist successes came in four less populous states—Delaware, New Jersey, Georgia, and Connecticut—where delegates hoped that a strong national government would offset the power of large neighboring states (Map 6.7).

The Constitution's first real test came in January 1788 in Massachusetts, a hotbed of Antifederalist sentiment. Influential Patriots, including Samuel Adams and Governor John Hancock, opposed the new constitution, as did many followers of Daniel Shays. But Boston artisans, who wanted tariff protection from British imports, supported ratification. To win over other delegates, Federalist leaders

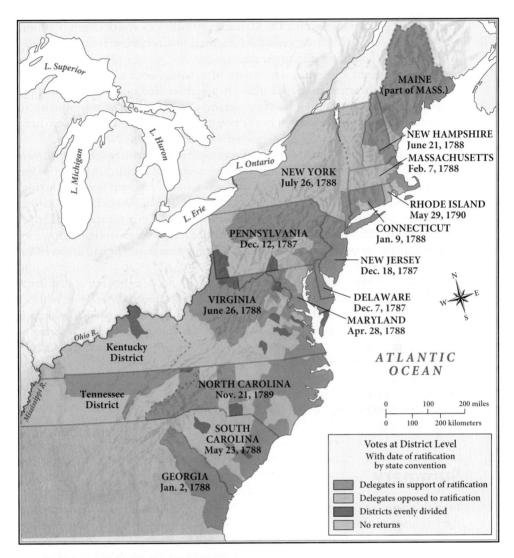

**MAP 6.7   Ratifying the Constitution of 1787**

In 1907, geographer Owen Libby mapped the votes of members of the state conventions that ratified the Constitution. His map showed that most delegates from seaboard or commercial farming districts (which sent many delegates to the conventions) supported the Constitution, while those from sparsely represented, subsistence-oriented backcountry areas opposed it. Subsequent research has confirmed Libby's socioeconomic interpretation of the voting patterns in North and South Carolina and in Massachusetts. However, other states' delegates were influenced by different factors. For example, in Georgia, delegates from all regions voted for ratification.

suggested nine amendments that the Massachusetts delegation would submit to the new Congress for consideration once the Constitution was ratified. By a close vote of 187 to 168, the Federalists carried the day.

Spring brought Federalist victories in Maryland, South Carolina, and New Hampshire, reaching the nine-state quota required for ratification. But it took the powerful arguments advanced in *The Federalist* and more talk of amendments to secure the Constitution's adoption in the essential states of Virginia and New York. The votes were again close: 89 to 79 in Virginia and 30 to 27 in New York.

Testifying to their respect for popular sovereignty and majority rule, most Americans accepted the verdict of the ratifying conventions. "A decided majority" of the New Hampshire assembly had opposed the "new system," reported Joshua Atherton, but now they said, "It is adopted, let us try it." In Virginia, Patrick Henry vowed to "submit as a quiet citizen" and fight for amendments "in a constitutional way." And during the first session of Congress, James Madison set to work drafting a set of amendments to satisfy some of the most pressing concerns that had arisen in the ratification process (see Chapter 7).

Unlike in France, where the Revolution of 1789 divided the society into irreconcilable factions for generations, the American Constitutional Revolution of 1787 created a national republic that enjoyed broad popular support. Federalists celebrated their triumph by organizing great processions in the seaport cities. By marching in an orderly fashion — in conscious contrast to the riotous Revolutionary mobs — Federalist-minded citizens affirmed their allegiance to a self-governing but elite-ruled republican nation.

| IN YOUR OWN WORDS | What were the most important compromises struck in the Philadelphia convention of 1787? |
|---|---|

# Summary

In this chapter, we examined the unfolding of two related sets of events. The first was the war between Britain and its rebellious colonies that began in 1776 and ended in 1783. The two great battles of Saratoga (1777) and Yorktown (1781) determined the outcome of that conflict. Surprisingly, given the military might of the British Empire, both were American victories. These triumphs testify to the determination of George Washington, the resilience of the Continental army, and support for the Patriot cause from hundreds of local militias and tens of thousands of taxpaying citizens.

This popular support reflected the Patriots' second success: building effective institutions of republican government. These elected institutions of local and state governance evolved out of colonial-era town meetings and representative assemblies. They were defined in the state constitutions written between 1776 and 1781, and their principles informed the first national constitution, the Articles of Confederation. Despite the challenges posed by conflicts over suffrage, women's rights, and fiscal policy, these self-governing political institutions carried the new republic successfully through the war-torn era and laid the foundation for the Constitution of 1787, the national charter that endures today.

# Chapter 6 Review

## KEY TERMS

**Identify and explain the significance of each term below.**

Battle of Long Island (1776) (p. 167)
Battle of Saratoga (1777) (p. 170)
Valley Forge (p. 172)
Philipsburg Proclamation (p. 175)
Battle of Yorktown (1781) (p. 177)
currency tax (p. 178)
Treaty of Paris of 1783 (p. 178)
Pennsylvania constitution of 1776
　(p. 180)

mixed government (p. 180)
Articles of Confederation (p. 182)
Northwest Ordinance of 1787 (p. 184)
Shays's Rebellion (p. 186)
Virginia Plan (p. 189)
New Jersey Plan (p. 189)
Federalists (p. 191)
Antifederalists (p. 191)
Federalist No. 10 (p. 192)

## REVIEW QUESTIONS

**Answer these questions to demonstrate your understanding of the chapter's main ideas.**

**1.** What challenges did Patriot forces confront in the first two years of the war, and what were their key achievements?

**2.** What were the keys to Patriot victory in the American Revolution?

**3.** What were the most important challenges facing governments in the 1780s?

**4.** What were the most important compromises struck in the Philadelphia convention of 1787?

**5.** Consider the events listed under "Politics and Power" and "Work, Exchange, and Technology" for the period 1776–1787 on the thematic timeline on page 134. How did war debt and inflation influence the development of political institutions during these years?

## CHRONOLOGY

**As you read, ask yourself why this chapter begins and ends with these dates and then identify the links among related events.**

**1776**
- Second Continental Congress declares independence
- Howe forces Washington to retreat from New York and New Jersey
- Pennsylvania approves democratic state constitution
- John Adams publishes *Thoughts on Government*

| 1777 | • Articles of Confederation create central government |
| | • Howe occupies Philadelphia (September) |
| | • Gates defeats Burgoyne at Saratoga (October) |
| 1778 | • Franco-American alliance (February) |
| | • Lord North seeks political settlement |
| | • Congress rejects negotiations |
| | • British adopt southern strategy |
| | • British capture Savannah (December) |
| 1778–1781 | • Severe inflation of Continental currency |
| 1779 | • British and American forces battle in Georgia |
| 1780 | • Clinton seizes Charleston (May) |
| | • French troops land in Rhode Island |
| 1781 | • Cornwallis invades Virginia (April), surrenders at Yorktown (October) |
| | • States finally ratify Articles of Confederation |
| 1783 | • Treaty of Paris (September 3) officially ends war |
| 1784–1785 | • Congress enacts political and land ordinances for new states |
| 1786 | • Nationalists hold convention in Annapolis, Maryland |
| | • Shays's Rebellion roils Massachusetts |
| 1787 | • Congress passes Northwest Ordinance |
| | • Constitutional Convention in Philadelphia |
| 1787–1788 | • Jay, Madison, and Hamilton write *The Federalist* |
| | • Eleven states ratify U.S. Constitution |

# 7

# Hammering Out a Federal Republic

## 1787–1820

**IDENTIFY THE BIG IDEA**

What was required to make the United States a viable independent republic, and how did debates over the Constitution shape relations between the national government and the states?

**LIKE AN EARTHQUAKE, THE AMERICAN REVOLUTION SHOOK THE** European monarchical order, and its aftershocks reverberated for decades. By "creating a new republic based on the rights of the individual, the North Americans introduced a new force into the world," the eminent German historian Leopold von Ranke warned the king of Bavaria in 1854, a force that might cost the monarch his throne. Before 1776, "a king who ruled by the grace of God had been the center around which everything turned. Now the idea emerged that power should come from below [from the people]."

Other republican-inspired upheavals—England's Puritan Revolution of the 1640s and the French Revolution of 1789—ended in political chaos and military rule. Similar fates befell many Latin American republics that won independence from Spain in the early nineteenth century. But the American states escaped both anarchy and dictatorship. Having been raised in a Radical Whig political culture that viewed standing armies and powerful generals as instruments of tyranny, General George Washington left public life in 1783 to manage his plantation, astonishing European observers but bolstering the authority of elected Patriot leaders. "'Tis a Conduct so novel," American painter John Trumbull reported from London, that it is "inconceivable to People [here]."

The great task of fashioning representative republican governments absorbed the energy and intellect of an entire generation and was rife with conflict. Seeking to perpetuate the elite-led polity of the colonial era, Federalists celebrated "natural aristocrats" such as Washington and condemned the radical republicanism of the French Revolution. In response, Jefferson and his Republican followers claimed the Fourth of July as their holiday and "we the people" as their political language. "There was a grand democrat procession in Town on the 4th of July," came a report from Baltimore: "All the farmers, tanners, black-smiths, shoemakers, etc. were there . . . and afterwards they went to a grand feast."

Many people of high status worried that the new state governments were too attentive to the demands of such ordinary workers and their families. When considering a bill, Connecticut conservative Ezra Stiles grumbled, every elected official "instantly thinks how it will affect his constituents" rather than how it would enhance the general welfare. What Stiles criticized as irresponsible, however, most Americans welcomed. The concerns of ordinary citizens were now paramount, and traditional elites trembled.

# The Political Crisis of the 1790s

The final decade of the eighteenth century brought fresh challenges for American politics. The Federalists split into two factions over financial policy and the French Revolution, and their leaders, Alexander Hamilton and Thomas Jefferson, offered contrasting visions of the future. Would the United States remain an agricultural nation governed by local officials, as Jefferson hoped? Or would Hamilton's vision of a strong national government and an economy based on manufacturing become reality?

## The Federalists Implement the Constitution

The Constitution expanded the dimensions of political life by allowing voters to choose national leaders as well as local and state officials. The Federalists swept the election of 1788, winning forty-four seats in the House of Representatives; only eight Antifederalists won election. As expected, members of the electoral college chose George Washington as president. John Adams received the second-highest number of electoral votes and became vice president.

**Devising the New Government**   Once the military savior of his country, Washington now became its political father. At age fifty-seven, the first president possessed great personal dignity and a cautious personality. To maintain continuity, he adopted many of the administrative practices of the Confederation and asked Congress to reestablish the existing executive departments: Foreign Affairs (State), Finance (Treasury), and War. To head the Department of State, Washington chose Thomas Jefferson, a fellow Virginian and an experienced diplomat. For secretary of the treasury, he turned to Alexander Hamilton, a lawyer and his former military aide. The president designated Jefferson, Hamilton, and Secretary of War Henry Knox as his cabinet, or advisory body.

The Constitution mandated a supreme court, but the Philadelphia convention gave Congress the task of creating a national court system. The Federalists wanted strong national institutions, and the **Judiciary Act of 1789** reflected their vision. The act established a federal district court in each state and three circuit courts to hear appeals from the districts, with the Supreme Court having the final say. The Judiciary Act also specified that cases arising in state courts that involved federal laws could be appealed to the Supreme Court. This provision ensured that federal judges would determine the meaning of the Constitution.

**The Bill of Rights**   The Federalists kept their promise to consider amendments to the Constitution. James Madison, now a member of the House of Representatives, submitted nineteen amendments to the First Congress; by 1791, ten had been approved by Congress and ratified by the states. These ten amendments, known as the **Bill of Rights**, safeguard fundamental personal rights, including freedom of speech and religion, and mandate legal procedures, such as trial by jury. By protecting individual citizens, the amendments eased Antifederalists' fears of an oppressive national government and secured the legitimacy of the Constitution. They also addressed the issue of federalism: the proper balance between the authority of the national and state governments. But that question was constantly contested until the Civil War and remains important today.

## Hamilton's Financial Program

George Washington's most important decision was choosing Alexander Hamilton as secretary of the treasury. An ambitious self-made man of great intelligence, Hamilton married into the Schuyler family, influential Hudson River Valley landowners, and was a prominent lawyer in New York City. At the Philadelphia convention, he condemned the "democratic spirit" and called for an authoritarian government and a president with near-monarchical powers.

As treasury secretary, Hamilton devised bold policies to enhance national authority and to assist financiers and merchants. He outlined his plans in three pathbreaking reports to Congress: on public credit (January 1790), on a national bank (December 1790), and on manufactures (December 1791). These reports outlined a coherent program of national mercantilism—government-assisted economic development. Hamilton's system was controversial at the time, and historians continue to debate whether the powers they gave the national government were necessary or excessive.

**Public Credit: Redemption and Assumption**   The financial and social implications of Hamilton's "**Report on the Public Credit**" made it instantly controversial. Hamilton asked Congress to redeem at face value the $55 million in Confederation securities held by foreign and domestic investors. His reasons were simple: as an underdeveloped nation, the United States needed good credit to secure loans from Dutch and British financiers. However, Hamilton's redemption plan would give enormous profits to speculators, who had bought up depreciated securities. For example, the Massachusetts firm of Burrell & Burrell had paid $600 for Confederation notes with a face value of $2,500; it stood to reap a profit of $1,900. Such windfall gains offended a majority of Americans, who condemned the speculative practices of capitalist financiers. Equally controversial was Hamilton's proposal to pay the Burrells and other note holders with new interest-bearing securities, thereby creating a permanent national debt and tying the interests of wealthy creditors to the survival of the new nation.

Patrick Henry condemned this plan "to erect, and concentrate, and perpetuate a large monied interest" and warned that it would prove "fatal to the existence of American liberty." James Madison demanded that Congress recompense those who originally owned Confederation securities: the thousands of shopkeepers, farmers, and soldiers who had bought or accepted them during the dark days of the war. However, it would have been difficult to trace the original owners; moreover, nearly half the members of the House of Representatives owned Confederation securities and would profit personally from Hamilton's plan. Melding practicality with self-interest, the House rejected Madison's suggestion.

Hamilton then proposed that the national government further enhance public credit by assuming the war debts of the states. This assumption plan, costing $22 million, also favored well-to-do creditors such as Abigail Adams, who had bought depreciated Massachusetts government bonds with a face value of $2,400 for only a few hundred dollars and would reap a windfall profit. Still, Adams was a long-term investor, not a speculator like Assistant Secretary of the Treasury William Duer. Knowing Hamilton's intentions in advance, Duer and his associates secretly bought up $4.6 million of the war bonds of southern states at bargain rates. Congressional critics condemned Duer's speculation. They also pointed out that some states had already paid off their war debts; in response, Hamilton promised to reimburse those states. To win the votes of congressmen from Virginia and Maryland, the treasury chief arranged another deal: he agreed that the permanent national capital would be built along the Potomac River, where suspicious southerners could easily watch its operations. Such astute bargaining gave Hamilton the votes he needed to enact his redemption and assumption plans.

**Creating a National Bank**   In December 1790, Hamilton asked Congress to charter the **Bank of the United States**, which would be jointly owned by private stockholders and the national government. Hamilton argued that the bank would provide stability to the specie-starved American economy by making loans to merchants, handling government funds, and issuing bills of credit — much as the Bank of England had done in Great Britain. These potential benefits persuaded Congress to grant Hamilton's bank a twenty-year charter and to send the legislation to the president for his approval.

At this critical juncture, Secretary of State Thomas Jefferson joined with James Madison to oppose Hamilton's financial initiatives. Jefferson charged that Hamilton's national bank was unconstitutional. "The incorporation of a Bank," Jefferson told President Washington, was not a power expressly "delegated to the United States by the Constitution." Jefferson's argument rested on a *strict* interpretation of the Constitution. Hamilton preferred a *loose* interpretation; he told Washington that Article 1, Section 8, empowered Congress to make "all Laws which shall be necessary and proper" to carry out the provisions of the Constitution. Agreeing with Hamilton, the president signed the legislation.

**Raising Revenue Through Tariffs**   Hamilton now sought revenue to pay the annual interest on the national debt. At his insistence, Congress imposed excise taxes, including a duty on whiskey distilled in the United States. These taxes would yield $1 million a year. To raise another $4 million to $5 million, the treasury secretary proposed higher tariffs on foreign imports. Although Hamilton's "**Report on Manufactures**" (1791) urged the expansion of American manufacturing, he did not support high protective tariffs that would exclude foreign products. Rather, he advocated moderate revenue tariffs that would pay the interest on the debt and other government expenses.

Hamilton's scheme worked brilliantly. As American trade increased, customs revenue rose steadily and paid down the national debt. Controversies notwithstanding, the treasury secretary had devised a strikingly modern and successful fiscal system; as entrepreneur Samuel Blodget Jr. declared in 1801, "the country prospered beyond all former example."

## Jefferson's Agrarian Vision

Hamilton paid a high political price for his success. As Washington began his second four-year term in 1793, Hamilton's financial measures had split the Federalists into bitterly opposed factions. Most northern Federalists supported the treasury secretary, while most southern Federalists joined a group headed by Madison and Jefferson. By 1794, the two factions had acquired names. Hamiltonians remained Federalists; the allies of Madison and Jefferson called themselves Democratic Republicans or simply Republicans.

Thomas Jefferson spoke for southern planters and western farmers. Well-read in architecture, natural history, agricultural science, and political theory, Jefferson embraced the optimism of the Enlightenment. He believed in the "improvability of the human race" and deplored the corruption and social divisions that threatened its progress. Having seen the poverty of laborers in British factories, Jefferson doubted that wageworkers had the economic and political independence needed to sustain a republican polity.

Jefferson therefore set his democratic vision of America in a society of independent yeomen farm families. "Those who labor in the earth are the chosen people of God," he wrote. The grain and meat from their homesteads would feed European nations, which "would manufacture and send us in exchange our clothes and other comforts." Jefferson's notion of an international division of labor resembled that proposed by Scottish economist Adam Smith in *The Wealth of Nations* (1776).

Turmoil in Europe brought Jefferson's vision closer to reality. The French Revolution began in 1789; four years later, the First French Republic (1792–1804) went to war against a British-led coalition of monarchies. As fighting disrupted European farming, wheat prices leaped from 5 to 8 shillings a bushel and remained high for twenty years, bringing substantial profits to Chesapeake and Middle Atlantic farmers. "Our farmers have never experienced such prosperity," remarked one observer. Simultaneously, a boom in the export of raw cotton, fueled by the invention of the cotton gin and the mechanization of cloth production in Britain, boosted the economies of Georgia and South Carolina. As Jefferson had hoped, European markets brought prosperity to American agriculture.

## The French Revolution Divides Americans

American merchants profited even more handsomely from the European war. In 1793, President Washington issued a **Proclamation of Neutrality**, allowing U.S. citizens to trade with all belligerents. As neutral carriers, American merchant ships claimed a right to pass through Britain's naval blockade of French ports, and American firms quickly took over the lucrative sugar trade between France and its West Indian islands. Commercial earnings rose spectacularly, averaging $20 million annually in the 1790s — twice the value of cotton and tobacco exports. As the American merchant fleet increased from 355,000 tons in 1790 to 1.1 million tons in 1808, northern shipbuilders and merchants provided work for thousands of shipwrights, sailmakers, dockhands, and seamen. Carpenters, masons, and cabinetmakers in Boston, New York, and Philadelphia easily found work building warehouses and fashionable "Federal-style" town houses for newly affluent merchants.

**Ideological Politics**   As Americans profited from Europe's struggles, they argued passionately over its ideologies. Most Americans had welcomed the **French Revolution** (1789–1799) because it abolished feudalism and established a constitutional monarchy. The creation of the First French Republic was more controversial. Many applauded the end of the monarchy and embraced the democratic ideology of the radical **Jacobins**. Like the Jacobins, they formed political clubs and began to address one another as "citizen." However, Americans with strong religious beliefs condemned the new French government for closing Christian churches and promoting a rational religion based on "natural morality." Fearing social revolution at home, wealthy Americans condemned revolutionary leader Robespierre and his followers for executing King Louis XVI and three thousand aristocrats.

Their fears were well founded, because Hamilton's economic policies quickly sparked a domestic insurgency. In 1794, western Pennsylvania farmers mounted the so-called **Whiskey Rebellion** to protest Hamilton's excise tax on spirits. This tax had cut demand for the corn whiskey the farmers distilled and bartered for eastern manufactures. Like the Sons of Liberty in 1765 and the Shaysites in 1786, the Whiskey Rebels assailed the tax collectors who sent the farmers' hard-earned money to a distant government. Protesters waved banners proclaiming the French revolutionary slogan "Liberty, Equality, Fraternity!" To deter popular rebellion and uphold national authority, President Washington raised a militia force of 12,000 troops and dispersed the Whiskey Rebels.

**Jay's Treaty**   Britain's maritime strategy intensified political divisions in America. Beginning in late 1793, the British navy seized 250 American ships carrying French sugar and other goods. Hoping to protect merchant property through diplomacy, Washington dispatched John Jay to Britain. But Jay returned with a controversial treaty that ignored the American claim that "free ships make free goods" and accepted Britain's right to stop neutral ships. The treaty also required the U.S. government to make "full and complete compensation" to British merchants for pre–Revolutionary War debts owed by American citizens. In return, the agreement allowed Americans to submit claims for illegal seizures and required the British to remove their troops and Indian agents from the Northwest Territory. Despite Republican charges that

**Jay's Treaty** was too conciliatory, the Senate ratified it in 1795, but only by the two-thirds majority required by the Constitution. As long as the Federalists were in power, the United States would have a pro-British foreign policy.

**The Haitian Revolution**   The French Revolution inspired a revolution closer to home that would also impact the United States. The wealthy French plantation colony of Saint-Domingue in the West Indies was deeply divided: a small class of elite planters stood atop the population of 40,000 free whites and dominated the island's half million slaves. In between, some 28,000 *gens de couleur*—free men of color—were excluded from most professions, forbidden from taking the names of their white relatives, and prevented from dressing like whites. The French Revolution intensified conflict between planters and free blacks, giving way to a massive slave uprising in 1791 that aimed to abolish slavery. The uprising touched off years of civil war, along with Spanish and British invasions. In 1798, black Haitians led by Toussaint L'Ouverture—himself a former slave-owning planter—seized control of the country. After five more years of fighting, in 1803 Saint-Domingue became the independent nation of Haiti: the first black republic in the Atlantic world.

The **Haitian Revolution** profoundly impacted the United States. In 1793, thousands of refugees—planters, slaves, and free blacks alike—fled the island and traveled to Charleston, Norfolk, Baltimore, Philadelphia, and New York, while newspapers detailed the horrors of the unfolding war. Many slaveholders panicked, fearful that the "contagion" of black liberation would undermine their own slave regimes. U.S. policy toward the rebellion presented a knotty problem. The first

**Toussaint L'Ouverture, Haitian Revolutionary and Statesman**   The American Revolution of 1776 constituted a victory for republicanism; the Haitian revolt of the 1790s represented a triumph of liberty over slavery and a demand for racial equality. After leading the black army that ousted French planters and British invaders from Haiti, Toussaint formed a constitutional government in 1801. A year later, when French troops invaded the island, he negotiated a treaty that halted Haitian resistance in exchange for a pledge that the French would not reinstate slavery. Subsequently, the French seized Toussaint and imprisoned him in France, where he died in 1803. This image, engraved in France in 1802, places Toussaint on horseback to emphasize his military prowess. Photo12/UIG/Getty Images.

instinct of the Washington administration was to supply aid to the island's white population. Adams — strongly antislavery and no friend of France — changed course, aiding the rebels and strengthening commercial ties. Jefferson, though sympathetic to moral arguments against slavery, was himself a southern slaveholder; he was, moreover, an ardent supporter of France. When he became president, he cut off aid to the rebels, imposed a trade embargo, and refused to recognize an independent Haiti. For many Americans, an independent nation of liberated citizen-slaves was a horrifying paradox, a perversion of the republican ideal.

## The Rise of Political Parties

The appearance of Federalists and Republicans marked a new stage in American politics — what historians call the First Party System. Colonial legislatures had factions based on family, ethnicity, or region, but they did not have organized political parties. Nor did the new state and national constitutions make any provision for political societies. Indeed, most Americans believed that parties were dangerous because they looked out for themselves rather than serving the public interest.

But a shared understanding of the public interest collapsed in the face of sharp conflicts over Hamilton's fiscal policies. Most merchants and creditors supported the Federalist Party, as did wheat-exporting slaveholders in the Tidewater districts of the Chesapeake. The emerging Republican coalition included southern tobacco and rice planters, debt-conscious western farmers, Germans and Scots-Irish in the southern backcountry, and subsistence farmers in the Northeast.

Party identity crystallized in 1796. To prepare for the presidential election, Federalist and Republican leaders called caucuses in Congress and conventions in the states. They also mobilized popular support by organizing public festivals and processions: the Federalists held banquets in February to celebrate Washington's birthday, and the Republicans marched through the streets on July 4 to honor the Declaration of Independence.

In the election, voters gave Federalists a majority in Congress and made John Adams president. Jefferson, narrowly defeated, became vice president. Adams continued Hamilton's pro-British foreign policy and strongly criticized French seizures of American merchant ships. When the French foreign minister Talleyrand solicited a loan and a bribe from American diplomats to stop the seizures, Adams charged that Talleyrand's agents, whom he dubbed X, Y, and Z, had insulted America's honor. In response to the **XYZ Affair**, Congress cut off trade with France in 1798 and authorized American privateering (licensing private ships to seize French vessels). This undeclared maritime war curtailed American trade with the French West Indies and resulted in the capture of nearly two hundred French and American merchant vessels.

**The Naturalization, Alien, and Sedition Acts of 1798**    As Federalists became more hostile to the French Republic, they also took a harder line against their Republican critics. When Republican-minded immigrants from Ireland vehemently attacked Adams's policies, a Federalist pamphleteer responded in kind: "Were I president, I would hang them for otherwise they would murder me." To silence the critics, the Federalists enacted three coercive laws limiting individual rights and threatening the fledgling party system. The **Naturalization Act** lengthened the residency requirement for American citizenship from five to fourteen years, the **Alien Act** authorized the deportation of foreigners, and the **Sedition Act** prohibited the publication of insults or malicious attacks on the president or members of Congress. "He that is not for us is against us," thundered the Federalist *Gazette of the United States*. Using the Sedition Act, Federalist prosecutors arrested more than twenty Republican newspaper editors and politicians, accused them of sedition, and convicted and jailed a number of them.

This repression sparked a constitutional crisis. Republicans charged that the Sedition Act violated the First Amendment's prohibition against "abridging the freedom of speech, or of the press." However, they did not appeal to the Supreme Court because the Court's power to review congressional legislation was uncertain and because most of the justices were Federalists. Instead, Madison and Jefferson looked to the state legislatures. At their urging, the Kentucky and Virginia legislatures issued resolutions in 1798 declaring the Alien and Sedition Acts to be "unauthoritative, void, and of no force." The

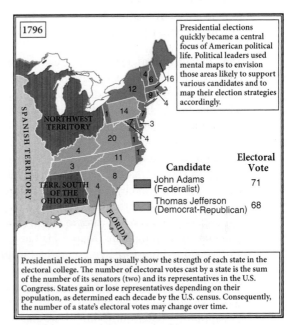

Presidential elections quickly became a central focus of American political life. Political leaders used mental maps to envision those areas likely to support various candidates and to map their election strategies accordingly.

| Candidate | Electoral Vote |
|---|---|
| John Adams (Federalist) | 71 |
| Thomas Jefferson (Democrat-Republican) | 68 |

Presidential election maps usually show the strength of each state in the electoral college. The number of electoral votes cast by a state is the sum of the number of its senators (two) and its representatives in the U.S. Congress. States gain or lose representatives depending on their population, as determined each decade by the U.S. census. Consequently, the number of a state's electoral votes may change over time.

### MAP 7.1  The Presidential Elections of 1796 and 1800

Both elections pitted Federalist John Adams of Massachusetts against Republican Thomas Jefferson of Virginia, and both saw voters split along regional lines. Adams carried every New England state and, reflecting Federalist strength in maritime and commercial areas, the eastern districts of the Middle Atlantic states; Jefferson won most of the agricultural-based states of the South and West (Kentucky and Tennessee). New York was the pivotal swing state. It gave its 12 electoral votes to Adams in 1796 and, thanks to the presence of Aaron Burr on the Republican ticket, bestowed them on Jefferson in 1800.

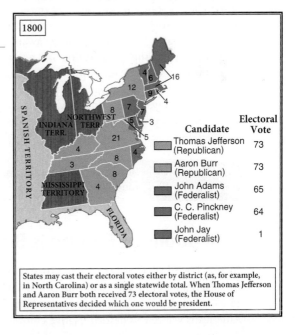

| Candidate | Electoral Vote |
|---|---|
| Thomas Jefferson (Republican) | 73 |
| Aaron Burr (Republican) | 73 |
| John Adams (Federalist) | 65 |
| C. C. Pinckney (Federalist) | 64 |
| John Jay (Federalist) | 1 |

States may cast their electoral votes either by district (as, for example, in North Carolina) or as a single statewide total. When Thomas Jefferson and Aaron Burr both received 73 electoral votes, the House of Representatives decided which one would be president.

**Virginia and Kentucky Resolutions** set forth a states' rights interpretation of the Constitution, asserting that the states had a "right to judge" the legitimacy of national laws.

The conflict over the Sedition Act set the stage for the presidential election of 1800. Jefferson, once opposed on principle to political parties, now asserted that they could "watch and relate to the people" the activities of an oppressive government. Meanwhile, John Adams reevaluated his foreign policy. Rejecting Hamilton's advice to declare war against France (and benefit from the resulting upsurge in patriotism), Adams put country ahead of party and used diplomacy to end the maritime conflict.

### The "Revolution of 1800"

The campaign of 1800 was a bitter, no-holds-barred contest. The Federalists launched personal attacks on Jefferson, branding him an irresponsible pro-French radical and, because he opposed state support of religion in Virginia, "the arch-apostle of irreligion and free thought." Both parties changed state election laws to favor their candidates, and rumors circulated of a Federalist plot to stage a military coup.

The election did not end these worries. Thanks to a surprising Republican victory in New York, low Federalist turnout in Virginia and Pennsylvania, and the three-fifths rule (which boosted electoral votes in the southern states), Jefferson won a narrow 73-to-65 victory over Adams in the electoral college. However, the Republican electors also gave 73 votes to Aaron Burr of New York, who was Jefferson's vice-presidential running mate (Map 7.1). The Constitution specified that in the case of a tie vote, the House of Representatives would choose between the candidates. For thirty-five rounds of balloting, Federalists in the House blocked Jefferson's election, prompting rumors that Virginia would raise a military force to put him into office.

Ironically, arch-Federalist Alexander Hamilton ushered in a more democratic era by supporting Jefferson. Calling Burr an "embryo Caesar" and the "most unfit man in the United States for the office of president," Hamilton persuaded key Federalists to allow Jefferson's election. The Federalists' concern for political stability also played a role. As Senator James Bayard of Delaware explained, "It was admitted on all hands that we must risk the Constitution and a Civil War or take Mr. Jefferson."

Jefferson called the election the "Revolution of 1800," and so it was. The bloodless transfer of power showed that popularly elected governments could be changed in an orderly way, even in times of bitter partisan conflict. In his inaugural address in 1801, Jefferson praised this achievement, declaring, "We are all Republicans, we are all Federalists."

| IN YOUR OWN WORDS | What were the most important differences between Federalists and Republicans in the 1790s? |

# A Republican Empire Is Born

In the Treaty of Paris of 1783, Great Britain gave up its claims to the trans-Appalachian region and, said one British diplomat, left the Indian nations "to the care of their [American] neighbours." *Care* was hardly the right word: many white Americans wanted to destroy Native communities. "Cut up every Indian Cornfield and burn every Indian town," proclaimed Congressman William Henry Drayton of South Carolina, so that their "nation be extirpated and the lands become the property of the public." Other leaders, including Henry Knox, Washington's first secretary of war, favored assimilating Native peoples into Euro-American society. Knox proposed the division of tribal lands among individual Indian families, who would become citizens of the various states. Indians resisted both forms of domination and fought to retain control of their lands and cultures. In the ensuing struggle, the United States emerged as an expansive power, determined to control the future of the continent.

## Sham Treaties and Indian Lands

As in the past, the major struggle between Natives and Europeans centered on land rights. Invoking the Paris treaty and regarding Britain's Indian allies as conquered peoples, the U.S. government asserted both sovereignty over and ownership of the trans-Appalachian west. Indian nations rejected both claims, pointing out they had not been conquered and had not signed the Paris treaty. "Our lands are our life and our breath," declared Creek chief Hallowing King; "if we part with them, we part with our blood." Brushing aside such objections and threatening military action, U.S. commissioners forced the pro-British Iroquois peoples — Mohawks, Onondagas, Cayugas, and Senecas — to cede huge tracts in New York and Pennsylvania in the Treaty of Fort Stanwix (1784). New York land speculators used liquor and bribes to take a million more acres, confining the once powerful Iroquois to reservations — essentially colonies of subordinate peoples.

American negotiators used similar tactics to grab Ohio Valley lands. At the Treaties of Fort McIntosh (1785) and Fort Finney (1786), they pushed the Chippewas, Delawares, Ottawas, Wyandots, and Shawnees to cede most of the future state of Ohio. The tribes quickly repudiated the agreements, justifiably claiming they were made under duress. Recognizing the failure of these agreements, American negotiators arranged for a comprehensive agreement at Fort Harmar (1789), but it, too, failed. To defend their lands, these tribes joined with the Miami and Potawatomi Indians to form the Western Confederacy. Led by Miami chief Little Turtle, confederacy warriors crushed American expeditionary forces sent by President Washington in 1790 and 1791.

**The Treaty of Greenville** Fearing an alliance between the Western Confederacy and the British in Canada, Washington doubled the size of the U.S. Army and ordered General "Mad Anthony" Wayne to lead a new expedition. In August 1794, Wayne defeated the confederacy in the Battle of Fallen Timbers (near present-day Toledo, Ohio). However, continuing Indian resistance forced a compromise. In the **Treaty of Greenville** (1795), American negotiators acknowledged Indian ownership of the land, and, in return for various payments, the Western Confederacy ceded most of Ohio (Map 7.2). The Indian peoples also agreed to accept American sovereignty, placing themselves "under the protection of the United States, and no other Power whatever." These American advances caused Britain to agree, in Jay's Treaty (1795), to reduce its trade and military aid to Indians in the trans-Appalachian region.

The Greenville treaty sparked a wave of white migration. Kentucky already had a population of 73,000 in 1790, and in 1792 it was admitted to the Union as the fifteenth state (Vermont entered a year earlier). Tennessee, Kentucky's neighbor to the

**MAP 7.2    Indian Cessions and State Formation, 1776–1840**
By virtue of the Treaty of Paris (1783) with Britain, the United States claimed sovereignty over the entire trans-Appalachian west. The Western Confederacy contested this claim, but the U.S. government upheld it with military force. By 1840, armed diplomacy had forced most Native American peoples to move west of the Mississippi River. White settlers occupied their lands, formed territorial governments, and eventually entered the Union as members of separate — and equal — states. By 1860, the trans-Appalachian region constituted an important economic and political force in American national life.

south, was admitted in 1796. By 1800, more than 375,000 people had moved into the Ohio and Tennessee valleys; in 1805, the new state of Ohio alone had more than 100,000 residents. Thousands more farm families moved into the future states of Indiana and Illinois, sparking new conflicts with Native peoples over land and hunting rights. Between 1790 and 1810, farm families settled as much land as they had during the entire colonial period. The United States "is a country in flux," a visiting French aristocrat observed in 1799, and "that which is true today as regards its population, its establishments, its prices, its commerce will not be true six months from now."

**Assimilation Rejected**   To dampen further conflicts, the U.S. government encouraged Native Americans to assimilate into white society. The goal, as one Kentucky Protestant minister put it, was to make the Indian "a farmer, a citizen of the United States, and a Christian." Most Indians rejected wholesale assimilation; even those who joined Christian churches retained many ancestral values and religious beliefs. To think of themselves as individuals or members of a nuclear family, as white Americans were demanding, meant repudiating the clan, the very essence of Indian life. To preserve "the old Indian way," many Native communities expelled white missionaries and forced Christianized Indians to participate in tribal rites. As a Munsee prophet declared, "There are two ways to God, one for the whites and one for the Indians."

A few Indian leaders sought a middle path in which new beliefs overlapped with old practices. Among the Senecas, the prophet Handsome Lake encouraged traditional animistic rituals that gave thanks to the sun, the earth, water, plants, and animals. But he included Christian elements in his teachings—the concepts of heaven and hell and an emphasis on personal morality—to deter his followers from alcohol, gambling, and witchcraft. Handsome Lake's teachings divided the Senecas into hostile factions. Led by Chief Red Jacket, traditionalists condemned European culture as evil and demanded a complete return to ancestral ways.

Most Indians also rejected the efforts of American missionaries to turn warriors into farmers and women into domestic helpmates. Among eastern woodland peoples, women grew corn, beans, and squash—the mainstays of the Indians' diet—and land cultivation rights passed through the female line. Consequently, women exercised considerable political influence, which they were eager to retain. Nor were Indian men interested in becoming farmers. When war raiding and hunting were no longer possible, many turned to grazing cattle and sheep.

## Migration and the Changing Farm Economy

Native American resistance slowed the advance of white settlers but did not stop it. Nothing "short of a Chinese Wall, or a line of Troops," Washington declared, "will restrain . . . the Incroachment of Settlers, upon the Indian Territory." During the 1790s, two great streams of migrants moved out of the southern states.

**Southern Migrants**   One stream, composed primarily of white tenant farmers and struggling yeomen families, flocked through the Cumberland Gap into Kentucky and Tennessee. "Boundless settlements open a door for our citizens to run off and leave us," a worried Maryland landlord lamented, "depreciating all our landed property and disabling us from paying taxes." In fact, many migrants were fleeing from this planter-controlled society. They wanted more freedom and hoped to prosper by growing cotton and hemp, which were in great demand.

Many settlers in Kentucky and Tennessee lacked ready cash to buy land. Like the North Carolina Regulators in the 1770s, poorer migrants claimed a customary right to occupy "back waste vacant Lands" sufficient "to provide a subsistence to themselves and their Posterity." Virginia legislators, who administered the Kentucky Territory, had a more elitist vision. Although they allowed poor settlers to buy up to 1,400 acres of land at reduced prices, they sold or granted huge tracts of 100,000 acres to twenty-one groups of speculators and leading men. In 1792, this landed elite owned one-fourth of the state, while half the white men owned no land and lived as quasi-legal squatters or tenant farmers.

Widespread landlessness—and opposition to slavery—prompted a new migration across the Ohio River into the future states of Ohio, Indiana, and Illinois. In a free community, thought Peter Cartwright, a Methodist lay preacher from southwestern Kentucky who moved to Illinois, "I would be entirely clear of the evil of slavery . . . [and] could raise my children to work where work was not thought a degradation." Yet land distribution in Ohio was almost exactly as unequal as in Kentucky: in 1810, a quarter of its real estate was owned by 1 percent of the population, while more than half of its white men were landless.

Meanwhile, a second stream of southern planters and slaves from the Carolinas moved along the coastal plain toward the Gulf of Mexico. Some set up new estates in the interior of Georgia and South Carolina, while others moved into the future states of Alabama, Mississippi, and Louisiana. "The Alabama Feaver rages here with great violence," a North Carolina planter remarked, "and has carried off vast numbers of our Citizens."

Cotton was the key to this migratory surge. Around 1750, the demand for raw wool and cotton increased dramatically as water-powered spinning jennies, weaving mules, and other technological innovations of the Industrial Revolution boosted textile production in England. South Carolina and Georgia planters began growing cotton, and American inventors, including Connecticut-born Eli Whitney, built machines (called gins) that efficiently extracted seeds from its strands. To grow more cotton, white planters imported about 115,000 Africans between 1776 and 1808, when Congress cut off the Atlantic slave trade. The cotton boom financed the rapid settlement of Mississippi and Alabama—in a single year, a government land office in Huntsville, Alabama, sold $7 million of uncleared land—and the two states entered the Union in 1817 and 1819, respectively.

### Exodus from New England

As southerners moved across the Appalachians and along the Gulf Coast, a third stream of migrants flowed out of the overcrowded communities of New England. Previous generations of Massachusetts and Connecticut farm families had moved north and east, settling New Hampshire, Vermont, and Maine. Now New England farmers moved west. Seeking land for their children, thousands of parents migrated to New York. "The town of Herkimer," noted one traveler, "is entirely populated by families come from Connecticut." By 1820, almost 800,000 New Englanders lived in a string of settlements stretching from Albany to Buffalo, and many others had traveled on to Ohio and Indiana. Soon, much of the Northwest Territory consisted of New England communities that had moved inland.

In New York, as in Kentucky and Ohio, well-connected speculators snapped up much of the best land, leasing farms to tenants for a fee. Imbued with the "homestead" ethic, many New England families preferred to buy farms. They signed contracts with the Holland Land Company, a Dutch-owned syndicate of speculators, that allowed settlers to pay for their farms as they worked them, or moved west again in an elusive search for land on easy terms.

### Innovation on Eastern Farms

The new farm economy in New York, Ohio, and Kentucky forced major changes in eastern agriculture. Unable to compete with lower-priced western grains, farmers in New England switched to potatoes, which were high yielding and nutritious. To make up for the labor of sons and daughters who had moved inland, Middle Atlantic farmers bought more efficient farm equipment. They replaced metal-tipped wooden plows with cast-iron models that dug deeper and required a single yoke of oxen instead of two. Such changes in crop mix and technology kept production high.

Easterners also adopted the progressive farming methods touted by British agricultural reformers. "Improvers" in Pennsylvania doubled their average yield per acre by rotating their crops. Yeomen farmers raised sheep and sold the wool to textile manufacturers. Many farmers adopted a year-round planting cycle, sowing corn in the spring for animal fodder and then planting winter wheat in September for market sale. Women and girls milked the family cows and made butter and cheese to sell in the growing towns and cities.

Whether hacking fields out of western forests or carting manure to replenish eastern soils, farmers now worked harder and longer, but their increased productivity brought them a better standard of living. European demand for American produce was high in these years, and westward migration — the settlement and exploitation of Indian lands — boosted the farming economy throughout the country.

## The Jefferson Presidency

From 1801 to 1825, three Republicans from Virginia — Thomas Jefferson, James Madison, and James Monroe — each served two terms as president. Supported by farmers in the South and West and strong Republican majorities in Congress, this "Virginia Dynasty" completed what Jefferson had called the Revolution of 1800. It reversed many Federalist policies and actively supported westward expansion.

When Jefferson took office in 1801, he inherited an old international conflict. Beginning in the 1780s, the Barbary States of North Africa had raided merchant ships in the Mediterranean, and like many European nations, the United States had paid an annual bribe — massive in relation to the size of the federal budget — to protect its vessels. Initially Jefferson refused to pay this "tribute" and ordered the U.S. Navy to attack the pirates' home ports. After four years of intermittent fighting, in which the United States bombarded Tripoli and captured the city of Derna, the Jefferson administration cut its costs. It signed a peace treaty that included a ransom for returned prisoners, and Algerian ships were soon taking American sailors hostage again. Finally, in 1815, President Madison sent a fleet of ten warships to the Barbary Coast under the command of Commodore Stephen Decatur, which forced leaders in Algiers, Tunis, and Tripoli to sign a treaty respecting American sovereignty.

At home, Jefferson inherited a national judiciary filled with Federalist appointees, including the formidable John Marshall of Virginia, the new chief justice of the Supreme Court. To add more Federalist judges, the outgoing Federalist Congress had passed the Judiciary Act of 1801. The act created sixteen new judgeships and various other positions, which President Adams filled at the last moment with "midnight appointees." The Federalists "have retired into the judiciary as a stronghold," Jefferson complained, "and from that battery all the works of Republicanism are to be beaten down and destroyed."

**America in the Middle East, 1804**  To protect American merchants from capture and captivity in the Barbary States, President Thomas Jefferson sent in the U.S. Navy. This 1846 lithograph, created by the famous firm of Currier & Ives, depicts one of the three attacks on the North African port of Tripoli by Commodore Edward Preble in August 1804. As the USS *Constitution* and other large warships lob shells into the city, small American gunboats defend the fleet from Tripolitan gunboats. "Our loss in Killed & Wounded has been considerable," Preble reported, and "the Enemy must have suffered very much . . . among their Shipping and on shore." The Granger Collection, New York.

Jefferson's fears were soon realized. When Republican legislatures in Kentucky and Virginia repudiated the Alien and Sedition Acts as unconstitutional, Marshall declared that only the Supreme Court held the power of constitutional review. The Court claimed this authority for itself when James Madison, the new secretary of state, refused to deliver the commission of William Marbury, one of Adams's midnight appointees. In ***Marbury v. Madison* (1803)**, Marshall asserted that Marbury had the right to the appointment but that the Court did not have the constitutional power to enforce it. In defining the Court's powers, Marshall voided a section of the Judiciary Act of 1789, in effect asserting the Court's authority to review congressional legislation and interpret the Constitution. "It is emphatically the province and duty of the judicial department to say what the law is," the chief justice declared, directly challenging the Republican view that the state legislatures had that power.

Ignoring this setback, Jefferson and the Republicans reversed other Federalist policies. When the Alien and Sedition Acts expired in 1801, Congress branded them unconstitutional and refused to extend them. It also amended the Naturalization Act, restoring the original waiting period of five years for resident aliens to become citizens. Charging the Federalists with grossly expanding the national government's size and power, Jefferson had the Republican Congress shrink it. He abolished all internal taxes, including the excise tax that had sparked the Whiskey Rebellion of 1794. To quiet Republican fears of a military coup, Jefferson reduced the size of the permanent army. He also secured repeal of the Judiciary Act of 1801, ousting forty of Adams's midnight appointees. Still, Jefferson retained competent Federalist officeholders, removing only 69 of 433 properly appointed Federalists during his eight years as president.

Jefferson likewise governed tactfully in fiscal affairs. He tolerated the economically important Bank of the United States, which he had once condemned as unconstitutional. But he chose as his secretary of the treasury Albert Gallatin, a fiscal conservative who believed that the national debt was "an evil of the first magnitude." By limiting expenditures and using customs revenue to redeem government bonds, Gallatin reduced the debt from $83 million in 1801 to $45 million in 1812. With Jefferson and Gallatin at the helm, the nation's fiscal affairs were no longer run in the interests of northeastern creditors and merchants.

## Jefferson and the West

Jefferson had long championed settlement of the West. He celebrated the yeoman farmer in *Notes on the State of Virginia* (1785); wrote one of the Confederation's western land ordinances; and supported Pinckney's Treaty (1795), the agreement between the United States and Spain that reopened the Mississippi River to American trade and allowed settlers to export crops via the Spanish-held port of New Orleans.

As president, Jefferson pursued policies that made it easier for farm families to acquire land. In 1796, a Federalist-dominated Congress had set the price of land in the national domain at $2 per acre; by the 1830s, Jefferson-inspired Republican Congresses had enacted more than three hundred laws that cut the cost to $1.25, eased credit terms, and allowed illegal squatters to buy their farms. Eventually, in the Homestead Act of 1862, Congress gave farmsteads to settlers for free.

**The Louisiana Purchase**    International events challenged Jefferson's vision of westward expansion. In 1799, Napoleon Bonaparte seized power in France and sought to reestablish France's American Empire. In 1801, he coerced Spain into signing a secret treaty that returned Louisiana to France and restricted American access to New Orleans, violating Pinckney's Treaty. Napoleon also launched an invasion to restore French rule in Saint-Domingue. It was once the richest sugar colony in the Americas, but its civil war had ruined the economy and cost France a fortune. Napoleon wanted to crush the rebellion and restore its planter class.

Napoleon's actions in Haiti and Louisiana prompted Jefferson to question his pro-French foreign policy. "The day that France takes possession of New Orleans, we must marry ourselves to the British fleet and nation," the president warned, dispatching James Monroe to Britain to negotiate an alliance. To keep the Mississippi River open to western farmers, Jefferson told Robert Livingston, the American minister in Paris, to negotiate the purchase of New Orleans.

Jefferson's diplomacy yielded a magnificent prize: the entire territory of Louisiana. By 1802, the French invasion of Saint-Domingue was faltering in the face of disease and determined black resistance, a new war threatened in Europe, and Napoleon feared an American invasion of Louisiana. Acting with characteristic decisiveness, the French ruler offered to sell the entire territory of Louisiana for $15 million (about

$500 million today). "We have lived long," Livingston remarked to Monroe as they concluded the **Louisiana Purchase** in 1803, "but this is the noblest work of our lives."

The Louisiana Purchase forced Jefferson to reconsider his strict interpretation of the Constitution. He had long believed that the national government possessed only the powers expressly delegated to it in the Constitution, but there was no provision for adding new territory. So Jefferson pragmatically accepted a loose interpretation of the Constitution and used its treaty-making powers to complete the deal with France. The new western lands, Jefferson wrote, would be "a means of tempting all our Indians on the East side of the Mississippi to remove to the West."

**Secessionist Schemes**    The acquisition of Louisiana brought new political problems. Some New England Federalists, fearing that western expansion would hurt their region and party, talked openly of leaving the Union and forming a confederacy of northeastern states. The secessionists won the support of Aaron Burr, the ambitious vice president. After Alexander Hamilton accused Burr of planning to destroy the Union, the two fought an illegal pistol duel that led to Hamilton's death.

This tragedy propelled Burr into another secessionist scheme, this time in the Southwest. When his term as vice president ended in 1805, Burr moved west to avoid prosecution. There, he conspired with General James Wilkinson, the military governor of the Louisiana Territory, either to seize territory in New Spain or to establish Louisiana as a separate nation. But Wilkinson, himself a Spanish spy and incipient traitor, betrayed Burr and arrested him. In a highly politicized trial presided over by Chief Justice John Marshall, the jury acquitted Burr of treason.

The Louisiana Purchase had increased party conflict and generated secessionist schemes in both New England and the Southwest. Such sectional differences would continue, challenging Madison's argument in "Federalist No. 10" that a large and diverse republic was more stable than a small one.

**Lewis and Clark Meet the Mandans and Sioux**    A scientist as well as a statesman, Jefferson wanted information about Louisiana: its physical features, plant and animal life, and Native peoples. He was also worried about intruders: the British-run Hudson's Bay Company and Northwest Company were actively trading for furs on the upper Missouri River. So in 1804, Jefferson sent his personal secretary, Meriwether Lewis, to explore the region with William Clark, an army officer. From St. Louis, Lewis, Clark, and their party of American soldiers and frontiersmen traveled up the Missouri for 1,000 miles to the fortified, earth-lodge towns of the Mandan and Hidatsa peoples (near present-day Bismarck, North Dakota), where they spent the winter.

The Mandans lived primarily by horticulture, growing corn, beans, and squash. They had acquired horses by supplying food to nomadic Plains Indians and secured guns, iron goods, and textiles by selling buffalo hides and dried meat to European traders. However, the Mandans (and neighboring Arikaras) had been hit hard by the smallpox epidemics that swept across the Great Plains in 1779–1781 and 1801–1802. Now they were threatened by Sioux peoples: Tetons, Yanktonais, and Oglalas. Originally, the Sioux had lived in the prairie and lake region of northern Minnesota. As their numbers rose and fish and game grew scarce, the Sioux moved westward, acquired horses, and hunted buffalo, living as nomads in portable skin tepees. The Sioux became ferocious fighters who tried to reduce the Mandans and

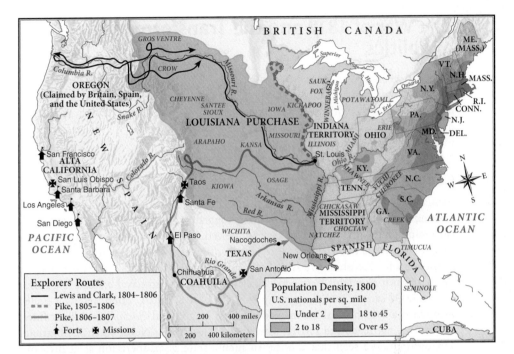

**MAP 7.3   U.S. Population Density in 1803 and the Louisiana Purchase**
When the United States purchased Louisiana from France in 1803, much of the land to its east—the vast territory between the Appalachian Mountains and the Mississippi River—remained in Indian hands. The equally vast lands beyond the Mississippi were virtually unknown to Anglo-Americans, even after the epic explorations of Meriwether Lewis and William Clark. Still, President Jefferson predicted quite accurately that the huge Mississippi River Valley "from its fertility . . . will ere long yield half of our whole produce, and contain half of our whole population."

other farming tribes to subject peoples. According to Lewis and Clark, they were the "pirates of the Missouri." Soon the Sioux would dominate the buffalo trade throughout the upper Missouri region.

In the spring of 1805, Lewis and Clark began an epic 1,300-mile trek into unknown country. Their party now included Toussaint Charbonneau, a French Canadian fur trader, and his Shoshone wife, Sacagawea, who served as a guide and translator. After following the Missouri River to its source on the Idaho-Montana border, they crossed the Rocky Mountains, and—venturing far beyond the Louisiana Purchase—traveled down the Columbia River to the Pacific Ocean. Nearly everywhere, Indian peoples asked for guns so they could defend themselves from other armed tribes. In 1806, Lewis and Clark capped off their pathbreaking expedition by providing Jefferson with the first maps of the immense wilderness and a detailed account of its natural resources and inhabitants (Map 7.3). Their report prompted some Americans to envision a nation that would span the continent.

| IN YOUR OWN WORDS | How were the principles of the Jeffersonian Republicans reflected in this era of dramatic growth and development? |

# The War of 1812 and the Transformation of Politics

The Napoleonic Wars that ravaged Europe after 1802 brought new attacks on American merchant ships. American leaders struggled desperately to protect the nation's commerce while avoiding war. When this effort finally failed, it sparked dramatic political changes that destroyed the Federalist Party and split the Republicans into National and Jeffersonian factions.

## Conflict in the Atlantic and the West

As Napoleon conquered European countries, he cut off their commerce with Britain and seized American merchant ships that stopped in British ports. The British ministry responded with a naval blockade and seized American vessels carrying sugar and molasses from the French West Indies. The British navy also searched American merchant ships for British deserters and used these raids to replenish its crews, a practice known as impressment. Between 1802 and 1811, British naval officers impressed nearly 8,000 sailors, including many U.S. citizens. In 1807, American anger boiled over when a British warship attacked the U.S. Navy vessel *Chesapeake*, killing three, wounding eighteen, and seizing four alleged deserters. "Never since the battle of Lexington have I seen this country in such a state of exasperation as at present," Jefferson declared.

**The Embargo of 1807**    To protect American interests, Jefferson pursued a policy of peaceful coercion. The **Embargo Act of 1807** prohibited American ships from leaving their home ports until Britain and France stopped restricting U.S. trade. A drastic maneuver, the embargo overestimated the reliance of Britain and France on American shipping and underestimated the resistance of merchants, who feared the embargo would ruin them. In fact, the embargo cut the American gross national product by 5 percent and weakened the entire economy. Exports plunged from $108 million in 1806 to $22 million in 1808, hurting farmers as well as merchants. "All was noise and bustle" in New York City before the embargo, one visitor remarked; afterward, everything was closed up as if "a malignant fever was raging in the place."

Despite popular discontent over the embargo, voters elected Republican James Madison to the presidency in 1808. A powerful advocate for the Constitution, the architect of the Bill of Rights, and a prominent congressman and party leader, Madison had served the nation well. But John Beckley, a loyal Republican, worried that Madison would be "too timid and indecisive as a statesman," and events proved him right. Acknowledging the embargo's failure, Madison replaced it with new economic restrictions, which also failed to protect American commerce.

**Western War Hawks**    Republican congressmen from the West were certain that Britain was the primary offender. They pointed to its trade with Indians in the Ohio River Valley in violation of the Treaty of Paris and Jay's Treaty. Bolstered by British guns and supplies, the Shawnee war chief Tecumseh revived the Western Confederacy in 1809. His brother, the prophet Tenskwatawa, provided the confederacy with a powerful nativist ideology. He urged Indian peoples to shun Americans, "the children of the Evil Spirit . . . who have taken away your lands"; renounce alcohol; and return to traditional ways. The Shawnee leaders found their greatest support among Kickapoo, Potawatomi, Winnebago, Ottawa, and Chippewa warriors: Indians of the western Great Lakes who had so far been largely shielded from the direct effects of U.S. westward expansion. They flocked to Tenskwatawa's holy village, Prophetstown, in the Indiana Territory.

As Tecumseh mobilized the western Indian peoples for war, William Henry Harrison, the governor of the Indiana Territory, decided on a preemptive strike. In November 1811, when Tecumseh went south to seek support from the Chickasaws, Choctaws, and Creeks, Harrison took advantage of his absence and attacked Prophetstown. The governor's 1,000 troops and militiamen traded heavy casualties with the confederacy's warriors at the **Battle of Tippecanoe** and then destroyed the holy village.

With Britain assisting Indians in the western territories and seizing American ships in the Atlantic, Henry Clay of Kentucky, the new Speaker of the House of Representatives, and John C. Calhoun, a rising young congressman from South Carolina, pushed Madison toward war. Like other Republican "war hawks" from the West and South, they wanted to seize territory in British Canada and Spanish Florida. With national elections approaching, Madison issued an ultimatum to Britain. When Britain failed to respond quickly, the president asked Congress for a declaration of war. In June 1812, a sharply divided Senate voted 19 to 13 for war, and the House of Representatives concurred, 79 to 49.

The causes of the War of 1812 have been much debated. Officially, the United States went to war because Britain had violated its commercial rights as a neutral nation. But the Federalists in Congress who represented the New England and Middle Atlantic merchants voted against the war; and in the election of 1812, those regions cast their 89 electoral votes for the Federalist presidential candidate, De Witt Clinton of New York. Madison amassed most of his 128 electoral votes in the South and West, where voters and congressmen strongly supported the war. Many historians therefore argue that the conflict was actually "a western war with eastern labels."

## The War of 1812

The War of 1812 was a near disaster for the United States. An invasion of British Canada in 1812 quickly ended in a retreat to Detroit. Nonetheless, the United States stayed on the offensive in the West. In 1813, American raiders burned the Canadian capital of York (present-day Toronto), Commodore Oliver Hazard Perry defeated a small British flotilla on Lake Erie, and General William Henry Harrison overcame a British and Indian force at the Battle of the Thames, taking the life of Tecumseh, now a British general.

In the East, political divisions prevented a wider war. New England Federalists opposed the war and prohibited their states' militias from attacking Canada. Boston merchants and banks refused to lend money to the federal government, making the

**Tenskwatawa, "The Prophet," 1830** Tenskwatawa added a spiritual dimension to Native American resistance by urging a holy war against the invading whites and calling for a return to sacred ancestral ways. His dress reflects his teachings: note the animal-skin shirt and the heavily ornamented ears. However, some of Tenskwatawa's religious rituals reflected the influence of French Jesuits; he urged his followers to finger a sacred string of beads (such as those in his left hand) that were similar to the Catholic rosary, thereby "shaking hands with the Prophet." Whatever its origins, Tenskwatawa's message transcended the cultural differences among Indian peoples and helped his brother Tecumseh create a formidable political and military alliance. Smithsonian American Art Museum, Washington, DC/Art Resource, NY.

war difficult to finance. In Congress, Daniel Webster, a dynamic young politician from New Hampshire, led Federalists opposed to higher tariffs and national conscription of state militiamen.

Gradually, the tide of battle turned in Britain's favor. When the war began, American privateers had captured scores of British merchant vessels, but by 1813 British warships were disrupting American commerce and threatening seaports along the Atlantic coast. In 1814, a British fleet sailed up the Chesapeake Bay, and troops stormed ashore to attack Washington City. Retaliating for the destruction of York, the invaders burned the U.S. Capitol and government buildings. After two years of fighting, the United States was stalemated along the Canadian frontier and on the defensive in the Atlantic, and its new capital city lay in ruins. The only U.S. victories came in the Southwest. There, a rugged slave-owning planter named Andrew Jackson and a force of Tennessee militiamen defeated British- and Spanish-supported Creek Indians in the Battle of Horseshoe Bend (1814) and forced the Indians to cede 23 million acres of land (Map 7.4).

**Federalists Oppose the War**　American military setbacks increased opposition to the war in New England. In 1814, Massachusetts Federalists called for a convention "to lay the foundation for a radical reform in the National Compact." When New England Federalists met in Hartford, Connecticut, some delegates proposed secession, but most wanted to revise the Constitution. To end Virginia's domination of the presidency, the Hartford Convention proposed a constitutional amendment limiting the office to a single four-year term and rotating it among citizens from different states. The convention also suggested amendments restricting commercial embargoes to sixty days and requiring a two-thirds majority in Congress to declare war, prohibit trade, or admit a new state to the Union.

As a minority party, the Federalists could prevail only if the war continued to go badly—a very real prospect. The war had cost $88 million, raising the national debt to $127 million. And now, as Albert Gallatin warned Henry Clay in May 1814, Britain's triumph over Napoleon in Europe meant that a "well organized and large army is [now ready] . . . to act immediately against us." When an attack from Canada came in the late summer of 1814, only an American naval victory on Lake Champlain stopped the British from marching down the Hudson River Valley. A few months later, thousands of seasoned British troops landed outside New Orleans, threatening American control of the Mississippi River. With the nation politically divided and under attack from north and south, Gallatin feared that "the war might prove vitally fatal to the United States."

**Peace Overtures and a Final Victory**　Fortunately for the young American republic, by 1815 Britain wanted peace. The twenty-year war with France had sapped its wealth and energy, so it began negotiations with the United States in Ghent, Belgium. At first, the American commissioners—John Quincy Adams, Gallatin, and Clay—demanded territory in Canada and Florida, while British diplomats sought an Indian buffer state between the United States and Canada. Both sides quickly realized that these objectives were not worth the cost of prolonged warfare. The **Treaty of Ghent**, signed on Christmas Eve 1814, retained the prewar borders of the United States.

That result hardly justified three years of war, but before news of the treaty reached the United States, a final military victory lifted Americans' morale. On January 8, 1815, General Jackson's troops crushed the British forces attacking New Orleans. Fighting from carefully constructed breastworks, the Americans rained "grapeshot and cannister bombs" on the massed British formations. The British lost 700 men, and 2,000 more were wounded or taken prisoner; just 13 Americans died,

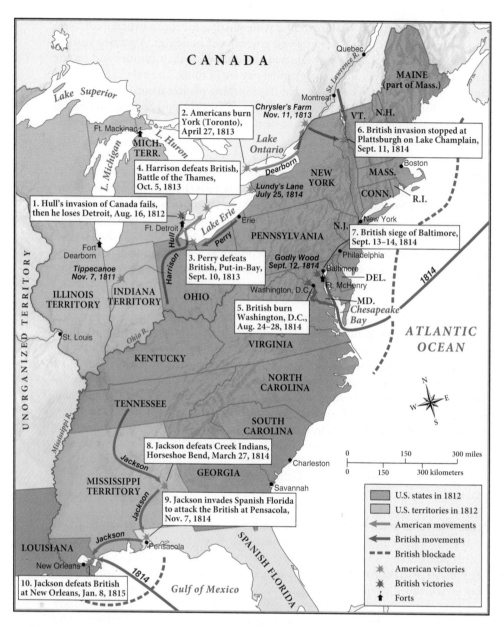

**MAP 7.4  The War of 1812**

Unlike the War of Independence, the War of 1812 had few large-scale military campaigns. In 1812 and 1813, most of the fighting took place along the Canadian border, as small American military forces attacked British targets with mixed success (nos. 1–4). The British took the offensive in 1814, launching a successful raid on Washington, but their attack on Baltimore failed, and they suffered heavy losses when they invaded the United States along Lake Champlain (nos. 5–7). Near the Gulf of Mexico, American forces moved from one success to another: General Andrew Jackson defeated the pro-British Creek Indians at the Battle of Horseshoe Bend, won a victory in Pensacola, and, in the single major battle of the war, routed an invading British army at New Orleans (nos. 8–10).

and only 58 suffered wounds. A newspaper headline proclaimed: "Almost Incredible Victory!! Glorious News." The victory made Jackson a national hero, redeemed the nation's battered pride, and undercut the Hartford Convention's demands for constitutional revision.

## The Federalist Legacy

The War of 1812 ushered in a new phase of the Republican political revolution. Before the conflict, Federalists had strongly supported Alexander Hamilton's program of national mercantilism—a funded debt, a central bank, and tariffs—while Jeffersonian Republicans had opposed it. After the war, the Republicans split into two camps. Led by Henry Clay, National Republicans pursued Federalist-like policies. In 1816, Clay pushed legislation through Congress creating the Second Bank of the United States and persuaded President Madison to sign it. In 1817, Clay won passage of the Bonus Bill, which created a national fund for roads and other internal improvements. Madison vetoed it. Reaffirming traditional Jeffersonian Republican principles, he argued that the national government lacked the constitutional authority to fund internal improvements.

Meanwhile, the Federalist Party crumbled. As one supporter explained, the National Republicans in the eastern states had "destroyed the Federalist party by the adoption of its principles" while the favorable farm policies of Jeffersonians maintained the Republican Party's dominance in the South and West. "No Federal character can run with success," Gouverneur Morris of New York lamented, and the election of 1818 proved him right: Republicans outnumbered Federalists 37 to 7 in the Senate and 156 to 27 in the House. Westward expansion and the success of Jefferson's Revolution of 1800 had shattered the First Party System.

**Marshall's Federalist Law**   However, Federalist policies lived on thanks to John Marshall's long tenure on the Supreme Court. Appointed chief justice by President John Adams in January 1801, Marshall had a personality and intellect that allowed him to dominate the Court until 1822 and strongly influence its decisions until his death in 1835.

Three principles informed Marshall's jurisprudence: judicial authority, the supremacy of national laws, and traditional property rights. Marshall claimed the right of judicial review for the Supreme Court in *Marbury v. Madison* (1803), and the Court frequently used that power to overturn state laws that, in its judgment, violated the Constitution.

**Asserting National Supremacy**   The important case of ***McCulloch v. Maryland* (1819)** involved one such law. When Congress created the Second Bank of the United States in 1816, it allowed the bank to set up state branches that competed with state-chartered banks. In response, the Maryland legislature imposed a tax on notes issued by the Baltimore branch of the Second Bank. The Second Bank refused to pay, claiming that the tax infringed on national powers and was therefore unconstitutional. The state's lawyers then invoked Jefferson's argument: that Congress lacked the constitutional authority to charter a national bank. Even if a national bank was legitimate, the lawyers argued, Maryland could tax its activities within the state.

Marshall and the nationalist-minded Republicans on the Court firmly rejected both arguments. The Second Bank was constitutional, said the chief justice, because it was "necessary and proper," given the national government's control over currency and credit, and Maryland did not have the power to tax it.

The Marshall Court again asserted the dominance of national over state statutes in *Gibbons v. Ogden* (1824). The decision struck down a New York law granting a monopoly to Aaron Ogden for steamboat passenger service across the Hudson River to New Jersey. Asserting that the Constitution gave the federal government authority over interstate commerce, the chief justice sided with Thomas Gibbons, who held a federal license to run steamboats between the two states.

### Upholding Vested Property Rights

Finally, Marshall used the Constitution to uphold Federalist notions of property rights. During the 1790s, Jefferson Republicans had celebrated "the will of the people," prompting Federalists to worry that popular sovereignty would result in a "tyranny of the majority." If state legislatures enacted statutes infringing on the property rights of wealthy citizens, Federalist judges vowed to void them.

Marshall was no exception. Determined to protect individual property rights, he invoked the contract clause of the Constitution to do it. The contract clause (in Article I, Section 10) prohibits the states from passing any law "impairing the obligation of contracts." Economic conservatives at the Philadelphia convention had inserted the clause to prevent "stay" laws, which kept creditors from seizing the lands and goods of delinquent debtors. In *Fletcher v. Peck* (1810), Marshall greatly expanded its scope. The Georgia legislature had granted a huge tract of land to the Yazoo Land Company. When a new legislature cancelled the grant, alleging fraud and bribery, speculators who had purchased Yazoo lands appealed to the Supreme Court to uphold their titles. Marshall did so by ruling that the legislative grant was a contract that could not be revoked. His decision was controversial and far-reaching. It limited state power; bolstered vested property rights; and, by protecting out-of-state investors, promoted the development of a national capitalist economy.

The Court extended its defense of vested property rights in *Dartmouth College v. Woodward* (1819). Dartmouth College was a private institution created by a royal charter issued by King George III. In 1816, New Hampshire's Republican legislature enacted a statute converting the school into a public university. The Dartmouth trustees opposed the legislation and hired Daniel Webster to plead their case. A renowned constitutional lawyer and a leading Federalist, Webster cited the Court's decision in *Fletcher v. Peck* and argued that the royal charter was an unalterable contract. The Marshall Court agreed and upheld Dartmouth's claims.

### The Diplomacy of John Quincy Adams

Even as John Marshall incorporated important Federalist principles into the American legal system, voting citizens and political leaders embraced the outlook of the Republican Party. The political career of John

Quincy Adams was a case in point. Although he was the son of Federalist president John Adams, John Quincy Adams had joined the Republican Party before the War of 1812. He came to national attention for his role in negotiating the Treaty of Ghent, which ended the war.

Adams then served brilliantly as secretary of state for two terms under James Monroe (1817–1825). Ignoring Republican antagonism toward Great Britain, in 1817 Adams negotiated the Rush-Bagot Treaty, which limited American and British naval forces on the Great Lakes. In 1818, he concluded another agreement with Britain setting the forty-ninth parallel as the border between Canada and the lands of the Louisiana Purchase. Then, in the **Adams-Onís Treaty** of 1819, Adams persuaded Spain to cede the Florida territory to the United States (Map 7.5). In return,

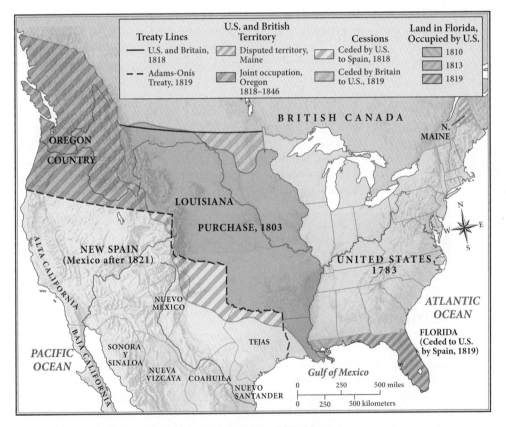

### MAP 7.5   Defining the National Boundaries, 1800–1820

After the War of 1812, American diplomats negotiated treaties with Great Britain and Spain that defined the boundaries of the Louisiana Purchase, with British Canada to the north and New Spain (which in 1821 became the independent nation of Mexico) to the south and west. These treaties eliminated the threat of border wars with neighboring states for a generation, giving the United States a much-needed period of peace and security.

the American government accepted Spain's claim to Texas and agreed to a compromise on the western boundary for the state of Louisiana, which had entered the Union in 1812.

Finally, Adams persuaded President Monroe to declare American national policy with respect to the Western Hemisphere. At Adams's behest, Monroe warned Spain and other European powers to keep their hands off the newly independent republics in Latin America. The American continents were not "subject for further colonization," the president declared in 1823—a policy that thirty years later became known as the **Monroe Doctrine**. In return, Monroe pledged that the United States would not "interfere in the internal concerns" of European nations. Thanks to John Quincy Adams, the United States had successfully asserted its diplomatic leadership in the Western Hemisphere and won international acceptance of its northern and western boundaries.

The appearance of political consensus after two decades of bitter party conflict prompted observers to dub James Monroe's presidency (1817–1825) the "Era of Good Feeling." This harmony was real but transitory. The Republican Party was now split between the National faction, led by Clay and Adams, and the Jeffersonian faction, soon to be led by Martin Van Buren and Andrew Jackson. The two groups differed sharply over federal support for roads and canals and many other issues. As the aging Jefferson himself complained, "You see so many of these new [National] republicans maintaining in Congress the rankest doctrines of the old federalists." This division in the Republican Party would soon produce the Second Party System, in which national-minded Whigs and state-focused Democrats would confront each other. By the early 1820s, one cycle of American politics and economic debate had ended, and another was about to begin.

> **IN YOUR OWN WORDS**    What elements of Federalist political philosophy survived the end of the First Party System?

# Summary

In this chapter, we traced three interrelated themes: public policy, westward expansion, and party politics. We began by examining the contrasting public policies advocated by Alexander Hamilton and Thomas Jefferson. A Federalist, Hamilton supported a strong national government and created a fiscal infrastructure (the national debt, tariffs, and a national bank) to spur trade and manufacturing. By contrast, Jefferson wanted to preserve the authority of state governments, and he envisioned an America enriched by farming rather than industry.

Jefferson and the Republicans promoted a westward movement that transformed the agricultural economy and sparked new wars with Indian peoples. Expansion westward also shaped American diplomatic and military policy, leading to the Louisiana Purchase, the War of 1812, and the treaties negotiated by John Quincy Adams.

Finally, there was the unexpected rise of the First Party System. As Hamilton's policies split the political elite, the French Revolution divided Americans into hostile ideological groups. The result was two decades of bitter conflict and controversial measures: the Federalists' Sedition Act, the Republicans' Embargo Act, and Madison's decision to go to war with Britain. Although the Federalist Party faded away, it left as its enduring legacy Hamilton's financial innovations and John Marshall's constitutional jurisprudence.

# Chapter 7 Review

## KEY TERMS

**Identify and explain the significance of each term below.**

Judiciary Act of 1789 (p. 199)
Bill of Rights (p. 199)
Report on the Public Credit (p. 199)
Bank of the United States (p. 200)
Report on Manufactures (p. 201)
Proclamation of Neutrality (p. 202)
French Revolution (p. 202)
Jacobins (p. 202)
Whiskey Rebellion (p. 202)
Jay's Treaty (p. 203)
Haitian Revolution (p. 203)
XYZ Affair (p. 204)

Naturalization, Alien, and Sedition Acts (p. 205)
Virginia and Kentucky Resolutions (p. 206)
Treaty of Greenville (p. 207)
*Marbury v. Madison* (1803) (p. 212)
Louisiana Purchase (p. 214)
Embargo Act of 1807 (p. 216)
Battle of Tippecanoe (p. 217)
Treaty of Ghent (p. 219)
*McCulloch v. Maryland* (1819) (p. 221)
Adams-Onís Treaty (p. 223)
Monroe Doctrine (p. 224)

## REVIEW QUESTIONS

**Answer these questions to demonstrate your understanding of the chapter's main ideas.**

1. What were the most important differences between Federalists and Republicans in the 1790s?

2. How were the principles of the Jeffersonian Republicans reflected in this era of dramatic growth and development?

3. What elements of Federalist political philosophy survived the end of the First Party System?

4. Look at the events listed under "Politics and Power" and "Work, Exchange, and Technology" for the period 1787–1800 on the thematic timeline on page 134. What was the relationship in these years between disagreements over the national government and developments in the American economy?

## CHRONOLOGY

As you read, ask yourself why this chapter begins and ends with these dates and then identify the links among related events.

| | |
|---|---|
| **1784–1789** | • Contested Indian treaties: Fort Stanwix (1784), Fort McIntosh (1785), Fort Finney (1786), and Fort Harmar (1789) |
| **1789–1799** | • French Revolution |
| **1789** | • Judiciary Act establishes federal courts |
| **1790** | • Hamilton's public credit system approved |
| **1790–1791** | • Western Confederacy defeats U.S. armies |
| **1791–1803** | • Haitian Revolution |
| **1791** | • Bill of Rights ratified<br>• Bank of the United States chartered |
| **1792** | • Kentucky joins Union |
| **1793** | • War between Britain and France |
| **1794** | • Madison and Jefferson found Republican Party<br>• Whiskey Rebellion<br>• Battle of Fallen Timbers |
| **1795** | • Jay's Treaty with Great Britain<br>• Pinckney's Treaty with Spain<br>• Treaty of Greenville accepts Indian land rights |
| **1796** | • Tennessee joins Union |
| **1798** | • XYZ Affair<br>• Alien, Sedition, and Naturalization Acts<br>• Virginia and Kentucky Resolutions |
| **1800** | • Jefferson elected president |
| **1801–1812** | • Gallatin reduces national debt |
| **1803** | • Louisiana Purchase<br>• *Marbury v. Madison* asserts judicial review |
| **1804–1806** | • Lewis and Clark explore West |
| **1807** | • Embargo Act cripples American shipping |

| | |
|---|---|
| **1808** | • Madison elected president |
| **1809** | • Tecumseh and Tenskwatawa revive Western Confederacy |
| **1812–1815** | • War of 1812 |
| **1817–1825** | • Era of Good Feeling |
| **1819** | • Adams-Onís Treaty |
| | • *McCulloch v. Maryland; Dartmouth College v. Woodward* |

# PART 4

We begin Part 4 in 1800 because important structural changes were reshaping American life at the beginning of the new century. They included new banking, credit, and transportation systems; the invention of the cotton gin and the transformation of American slavery; innovations in political structures and practices; and new religious and cultural expressions. We have chosen 1848 as a useful end point for this period because that was the year that the U.S.-Mexico War ended and the continental ambitions of the new American nation were fully realized.

Historians often call these decades the antebellum (prewar) era because, looking back, we know that in 1861 the Civil War pitted North against South. But many of the developments of this era worked to unite northern and southern interests. Policymakers and entrepreneurs built canals and banks, expanded the reach of plantation slavery, opened textile factories in the North to process slave-grown cotton from the South, hired wageworkers to tend the water-powered looms, and sold northern products back to southern planters. By the 1830s, a few radical abolitionists criticized this system for binding "Lords of the Loom and Lords of the Lash" in one vast cycle of exploitative enterprise.

Four transformations marked the United States in the early nineteenth century. One was economic: the expansion of commercial agriculture, the rise of manufacturing, and development of the cotton complex triggered unprecedented economic growth. Another was political, as new democratic political forms took shape. A third transformation was the emergence of evangelical Christianity, reform movements, and utopian experiments that remade American culture and society. Finally, the geographical boundaries of the United States expanded enormously in these years. Part 4 of *America's History* explains how these momentous changes happened and shows how closely intertwined they were. Building on these transformations, three principal developments are discussed in Part 4.

## A Commercial Slaveholding Republic

The economic revolution of the early 1800s rested on innovations in transportation and technology, from the cotton gin to the steam-powered loom. It also relied on steady acquisitions of frontier lands, where farmers specialized in agricultural products that could be shipped to an increasingly industrial Northeast.

The rise of the "cotton complex" vastly expanded slavery in the South. It also sharpened social and economic class divisions among business elites, planters, middle-class merchants and professionals, artisans, wageworkers, and the urban poor. At first, Americans hoped manufacturing would increase prosperity for all, but by the end of the period some desperate immigrants from Ireland, and others who labored in low-skill jobs, lived in shocking poverty. Like many other transformations, the commercial revolution had unintended consequences.

## Democratic Citizenship and Culture

Americans celebrated the expansion of political rights and the rise of mass political parties, starting with the Democrats under the charismatic leadership of Andrew Jackson. Jacksonian Democrats cut federal and state government aid to financiers, merchants, and corporations. Beginning in the 1830s, the Democrats faced challenges from the Whigs, who devised a competing program that stressed state-sponsored economic development, moral reform, and individual social mobility. The parties wrestled over such issues as Jackson's Indian Removal Act of 1830 and high protective tariffs on manufactured goods, the latter of which many farmers and planters opposed.

New democratic forms flourished in culture as well as politics. The expanding urban middle class created a distinct religious culture and an ideal of domesticity or "separate spheres" for women, as well as an array of reform movements, from temperance to moral reform. Wage-earning workers in the growing cities, including poor immigrants from Germany and Ireland, participated in a vibrant popular culture of their own. New England intellectuals launched the distinctly American movement of transcendentalism, while utopians founded cooperative experiments and religious communities such as those of the Shakers and Mormons.

## Claiming an Empire

Territorial expansion between 1800 and 1848 was vast and violent. Moving into Texas at the behest of Mexican authorities, who were struggling to populate Mexico's northern areas, southern cotton planters brought slavery and a spirit of independence that soon triggered the Texas revolution for separation from Mexico. Other Americans, especially on the midwestern frontier, pushed ardently for annexation of Oregon and by the 1840s began a drive to the Pacific. Most decisive was the election in 1844 of James K. Polk, an expansionist Democrat who promised to claim all of Oregon from the United States's chief rival—Britain—and to annex Texas even if it precipitated war with Mexico. Though the former conflict was arbitrated, the latter triggered a war that brought in not only Texas but also a vast new domain including California and the Southwest—acquisitions that would lead to sectional crisis.

## Thematic Understanding

This timeline arranges some of the important events of this period into themes. How did economic, political, and cultural developments influence one another in this era?

| | AMERICAN AND NATIONAL IDENTITY | POLITICS AND POWER | WORK, EXCHANGE, AND TECHNOLOGY |
|---|---|---|---|
| 1800 | • Neomercantilist policies support banking, transportation, and communication systems | • Jefferson reduces activism of national government<br>• Chief Justice Marshall asserts federal judicial powers | • Cotton output and demand for African labor expands<br>• Congress approves funds for a National Road (1806) |
| 1810 | • Emma Willard founds Middlebury Female Seminary for young women (1814)<br>• American Colonization Society founded (1817) | • Expansion of white male political rights<br>• Martin Van Buren creates first statewide political machine<br>• Missouri crisis (1819–1821) over slavery | • Construction on National Road begins (1811)<br>• First American textile factory opens in Waltham, Massachusetts (1814) |
| 1820 | • Public schools, female academies strengthen civic engagement<br>• Domesticity and ideal of "separate spheres" emerge in middle class | • Rise of Andrew Jackson and Democratic Party<br>• Anti-Masonic and Working Men's parties rise and decline | • Erie Canal completed (1825)<br>• Henry Clay proposes "American System" of government-assisted development |
| 1830 | • Middle-class and working-class identities emerge<br>• Nat Turner's uprising in Virginia (1831)<br>• American Anti-Slavery Society founded (1833)<br>• Abolitionist Grimké sisters defend public roles for women | • Tariff battles and nullification crisis<br>• Whig Party forms<br>• Jackson destroys Second National Bank, expands executive power<br>• Congress adopts "gag rule" to block antislavery petitions | • U.S. textiles compete with British goods<br>• Canal systems expand trade in eastern United States<br>• Cotton complex expands<br>• Financial panic of 1837 begins six-year depression |
| 1840 | • Margaret Fuller publishes *Woman in the Nineteenth Century* (1844)<br>• Seneca Falls Convention seeks women's equal rights (1848) | • Heyday of Second Party System (Democrats vs. Whigs)<br>• Liberty Party runs James G. Birney for president (1844)<br>• U.S.-Mexico War (1846–1848) | • American machine tool industry expands |

| CULTURE AND SOCIETY | MIGRATION AND SETTLEMENT | GEOGRAPHY AND THE ENVIRONMENT | AMERICA IN THE WORLD | |
|---|---|---|---|---|
| • Rural white Americans share a common culture | • Congress outlaws Atlantic slave trade (1808) | • Louisiana Purchase nearly doubles the land mass of the United States (1803)<br>• Lewis and Clark explore the West | • Embargo Act prohibits trade with Great Britain (1807) | 1800 |
| • African Methodist Episcopal Church founded (1816) | • Andrew Jackson forces Creeks to relinquish millions of acres during War of 1812 | • Road and turnpike construction facilitate travel<br>• The cotton frontier moves inland | • Africans from Congo region influence black culture for decades<br>• U.S. and Great Britain agree to joint control of Oregon Country (1818) | 1810 |
| • Second Great Awakening; Charles Finney begins Protestant revival campaigns (1823) | • Internal slave trade forces thousands of African Americans west in cotton boom<br>• Rise of migration from rural areas to cities | • Canals and steamboats shrink space<br>• Major Stephen H. Long labels the Great Plains the "Great American Desert" | • Mexico gains independence from Spain (1821) | 1820 |
| • Emerson champions transcendentalism<br>• Benevolent Empire of reform movements<br>• Popularity of blackface minstrel shows<br>• Joseph Smith founds Mormon church (Latter-day Saints) (1830) | • Indian Removal Act (1830) forces Native peoples west<br>• Cherokee Trail of Tears (1838) | • U.S. immigration into Texas accelerates<br>• Emergence of commercial cities in the Old Northwest<br>• Indian Removal Act (1830) leads to mass relocation | • Emerson and others draw on European romanticism in developing transcendentalist ideas<br>• Texas declares its independence from Mexico (1836) | 1830 |
| • Dorothea Dix promotes hospitals for the mentally ill (1841)<br>• Henry Thoreau spends a year at Walden Pond<br>• John Humphrey Noyes establishes cooperative experiment at Oneida | • Brigham Young leads Mormons to Salt Lake (1846)<br>• Increased immigration from Ireland and Germany | • Immigration to the Oregon Country increases dramatically | • United States declares war on Mexico (1846)<br>• Treaty with Britain divides Oregon Country (1846)<br>• American troops capture Mexico City (1847) | 1840 |

# 8

# Economic Transformations

## 1800–1848

### IDENTIFY THE BIG IDEA

How did the economic transformations of the first half of the nineteenth century reshape northern and southern society and culture?

**IN 1804, LIFE TURNED GRIM FOR ELEVEN-YEAR-OLD CHAUNCEY JEROME.** His father died suddenly, and Jerome became an indentured servant on a Connecticut farm. Quickly learning that few farmers "would treat a poor boy like a human being," Jerome bought out his indenture by making dials for clocks and then found a job with clockmaker Eli Terry. A manufacturing wizard, Terry used water power to drive precision saws and woodworking lathes. Soon his shop, and dozens of outworkers, were turning out thousands of tall clocks with wooden works. Then, in 1816, Terry patented an enormously popular desk clock with brass parts, an innovation that turned Waterbury, Connecticut, into the clockmaking center of the United States.

In 1822, Chauncey Jerome set up his own clock factory. By organizing work more efficiently and using new machines that stamped out interchangeable metal parts, he drove down the price of a simple clock from $20 to $5 and then to less than $2. By the 1840s, Jerome was selling his clocks in England, the hub of the Industrial Revolution; a decade later, his workers were turning out 400,000 clocks a year. By 1860, the United States was not only the world's leading exporter of cotton and wheat but also the third-ranked manufacturing nation behind Britain and France.

"Business is the very soul of an American: the fountain of all human felicity," author Francis Grund observed shortly after arriving from Europe. Stimulated by America's entrepreneurial culture, thousands of artisan-inventors like Chauncey Jerome propelled the country into the Industrial Revolution, a new system of production based on water and steam power and machine technology. To bring their products to market, they relied on important innovations in travel and communication. By 1848, northern entrepreneurs—and their southern counterparts who invested in cotton planting—had created a new economic order.

Not all Americans embraced the new business-dominated society, and many failed to share in the new prosperity. The increase in manufacturing, commerce, and finance created class divisions that challenged the founders' vision of an agricultural republic with few distinctions of wealth. As the philosopher Ralph Waldo Emerson warned in 1839: "The invasion of Nature by Trade with its Money, its Credit, its Steam, [and] its Railroad threatens to . . . establish a new, universal Monarchy."

# Foundations of a New Economic Order

The emerging economic order was based on core principles grounded in republican ideals. Private property, market exchange, and individual opportunity were widely shared values, and throughout the nation, activist state governments pursued **neomercantilist** policies to help achieve them. New systems of banking and credit, often supported by state charters, increased the money supply and made capital more widely available to American entrepreneurs. State legislatures also issued charters to turnpike and canal companies, whose new roads and waterways reduced the cost of transportation and stimulated economic activity. As a result, beginning around 1800 the average per capita income of Americans increased by more than 1 percent a year—more than 30 percent in a single generation.

## Credit and Banking

America was "a Nation of Merchants," a British visitor reported from Philadelphia in 1798, "keen in the pursuit of wealth in all the various modes of acquiring it." Acquire it they did, making spectacular profits as the wars of the French Revolution and Napoleon (1793–1815) crippled European firms. Merchants John Jacob Astor and Robert Oliver became the nation's first millionaires. After working for an Irish-owned linen firm in Baltimore, Oliver struck out on his own, achieving affluence by trading West Indian sugar and coffee. Astor, who migrated from Germany to New York in 1784, began by selling dry-goods and became wealthy carrying furs from the Pacific Northwest to China and investing in New York City real estate.

To finance their ventures, Oliver, Astor, and other merchants needed capital, from either their own savings or loans. Before the American Revolution, colonial merchants often relied on credit from British suppliers. In 1781, the Confederation Congress chartered the Bank of North America in Philadelphia, and traders in Boston and New York soon founded similar institutions to raise and loan money. "Our monied capital has so much increased from the Introduction of Banks, &

**The China Trade** Following the Revolution, New England merchants traded actively with the major Asian manufacturing centers of China and India. In this painting by George Chinnery (1774–1852), the American flag flies prominently, alongside other national banners, in front of the warehouse district in Canton (modern Guangzhou). There, merchants exchanged bundles of American furs for cargoes of Chinese tea, silks, and porcelain plates, cups, and serving dishes. © Peabody Essex Museum, Salem, Massachusetts, USA/Bridgeman Images.

the Circulation of the Funds," Philadelphia merchant William Bingham boasted in 1791, "that the Necessity of Soliciting Credits from England will no longer exist."

That same year, Federalists in Congress chartered the Bank of the United States (Chapter 7). By 1805, the bank had branches in eight seaport cities, profits that averaged a handsome 8 percent annually, and clients with easy access to capital. As trader Jesse Atwater noted, "the foundations of our [merchant] houses are laid in bank paper."

But Jeffersonians attacked the bank as an unconstitutional expansion of federal power "supported by public creditors, speculators, and other insidious men." When the bank's charter expired in 1811, the Jeffersonian Republican–dominated Congress refused to renew it. Merchants, artisans, and farmers quickly persuaded state legislatures to charter banks — in Pennsylvania, no fewer than 41. By 1816, when Congress (now run by National Republicans) chartered a new national bank (the Second Bank of the United States), there were 246 state-chartered banks with tens of thousands of stockholders and $68 million in banknotes in circulation. These state banks were often shady operations that issued notes without adequate specie reserves, made loans to insiders, and lent generously to farmers buying overpriced land.

Bad banking policies helped bring on the **Panic of 1819** (just as they caused the financial crisis of 2008), but broader forces were equally important. As the

Napoleonic Wars ended in 1815, American imports of English woolen and cotton goods spiked. Then, in 1818, farmers and planters faced an abrupt 30 percent drop in world agricultural prices. As farmers' income declined, they could not pay debts owed to stores and banks, many of which went bankrupt. "A deep shadow has passed over our land," lamented one New Yorker, as land prices dropped by 50 percent. The panic gave Americans their first taste of a business cycle, the periodic boom and bust inherent to an unregulated market economy.

## Transportation and the Market Revolution

Economic expansion also depended on improvements in transportation, where governments once again played a crucial role. As with bank charters, legislative charters for turnpikes and canal companies reflected the ideology of mercantilism—government-assisted economic development. Just as Parliament had used the Navigation Acts to spur British prosperity, so American legislatures enacted laws "of great public utility" to increase the "common wealth." Following Jefferson's embargo of 1807, which cut off goods and credit from Europe, the New England states awarded charters to two hundred iron-mining, textile-manufacturing, and banking companies, while Pennsylvania granted more than eleven hundred. By 1820, state governments had created a republican political economy: a **Commonwealth System** that funneled state aid to private businesses whose projects would improve the general welfare.

Transportation projects were among the greatest beneficiaries of the Commonwealth System. Between 1793 and 1812, for example, the Massachusetts legislature granted charters to more than one hundred private turnpike corporations. These charters gave the companies special legal status and often included monopoly rights to a transportation route. Pennsylvania issued fifty-five charters, including one to the Lancaster Turnpike Company, which built a 65-mile graded and graveled toll road to Philadelphia. The road quickly boosted the regional economy. A farm woman noted, "The turnpike is finished and we can now go to town at all times and in all weather." New turnpikes soon connected dozens of inland market centers to seaport cities. Westward migration beyond the seaboard states created a rapidly growing demand for new transportation routes.

The vital precondition for westward migration was the dispossession of Native American peoples. In the War of 1812, the United States defeated the confederation of Great Lakes and Ohio Indians led by Tecumseh and Tenskwatawa and claimed their lands, along with 23 million acres ceded by the Creeks after the Battle of Horseshoe Bend. Subsequent treaties with the Creeks, Cherokees, Chickasaws, and Choctaws in the South and with the Miamis, Ottawas, Sauks, Fox, and other nations in the North brought millions more acres into the public domain (see Map 7.2, p. 208).

For farmers, artisans, and merchants to capitalize on these new lands, however, they needed access to transportation routes. Farmers in Kentucky, Tennessee, southern Ohio, Indiana, and Illinois settled near the Ohio River and its many tributaries, so they could easily get goods to market. Similarly, speculators hoping to capitalize on the expansion of commerce bought up property in the cities along the banks of major rivers: Cincinnati, Louisville, Chattanooga, and St. Louis. Farmers and merchants built barges to carry cotton, grain, and meat downstream to New

Orleans, which by 1815 was exporting about $5 million in agricultural products yearly.

But natural waterways were not enough, by themselves, to connect east and west. To link westward migrants to the seaboard states, Congress approved funds for a National Road constructed of compacted gravel. The project began in 1811 at Cumberland in western Maryland, at the head of navigation of the Potomac River; reached Wheeling, Virginia (now West Virginia), on the Ohio River in 1818; and ended in Vandalia, Illinois, in 1839. As migrants traveled west on the National Road and other interregional highways, they passed livestock herds heading in the opposite direction, destined for eastern markets.

**Shrinking Space: Canals**    Even on well-built gravel roads, overland travel was slow and expensive. As U.S. territory expanded and artisans, farmers, and manufacturers produced an ever expanding array of goods, legislators and businessmen created faster and cheaper ways to get those products to consumers. To carry people, crops, and manufactures to and from the great Mississippi River basin, public money and private businesses developed a water-borne transportation system of unprecedented size, complexity, and cost. State governments and private entrepreneurs dredged shallow rivers and constructed canals to bypass waterfalls and rapids. Around 1820, they began constructing a massive system of canals and roads linking states along the Atlantic coast with new states in the trans-Appalachian west.

This transportation system set in motion a mass migration of people to the Greater Mississippi River basin. This huge area, drained by six river systems (the Missouri, Arkansas, Red, Ohio, Tennessee, and Mississippi), contains the largest and most productive contiguous acreage of arable land in the world. By 1860, nearly one-third of the nation's citizens lived in eight of its states — the "Midwest," consisting of the five states carved out of the Northwest Territory (Ohio, Indiana, Illinois, Michigan, and Wisconsin) along with Missouri, Iowa, and Minnesota. There they created a rich agricultural economy and an industrializing society.

The key event was the New York legislature's 1817 financing of the **Erie Canal**, a 364-mile waterway connecting the Hudson River and Lake Erie. Previously, the longest canal in the United States was just 28 miles long — reflecting the huge capital cost of canals and the lack of American engineering expertise. New York's ambitious project had three things working in its favor: the vigorous support of New York City's merchants, who wanted access to western markets; the backing of New York's governor, De Witt Clinton, who proposed to finance the waterway from tax revenues, tolls, and bond sales to foreign investors; and the relatively gentle terrain west of Albany. Even so, the task was enormous. Workers — many of them Irish immigrants — dug out millions of cubic yards of soil, quarried thousands of tons of rock for the huge locks that raised and lowered the boats, and constructed vast reservoirs to ensure a steady supply of water.

The first great engineering project in American history, the Erie Canal altered the ecology of an entire region. As farming communities and market towns sprang up along the waterway, settlers cut down millions of trees to provide wood for houses and barns and to open the land for growing crops and grazing animals. Cows and sheep foraged in pastures that had recently been forests occupied by deer and bears, and spring rains caused massive erosion of the denuded landscape.

Whatever its environmental consequences, the Erie Canal was an instant economic success. The first 75-mile section opened in 1819 and quickly yielded enough revenue to repay its construction cost. When workers finished the canal in 1825, a 40-foot-wide ribbon of water stretched from Buffalo, on the eastern shore of Lake Erie, to Albany, where it joined the Hudson River for the 150-mile trip to New York City. The canal's water "must be the most fertilizing of all fluids," suggested novelist Nathaniel Hawthorne, "for it causes towns with their masses of brick and stone, their churches and theaters, their business and hubbub, their luxury and refinement, their gay dames and polished citizens, to spring up."

The Erie Canal brought prosperity to the farmers of central and western New York and the entire Great Lakes region. Northeastern manufacturers shipped clothing, boots, and agricultural equipment to farm families; in return, farmers sent grain, cattle, hogs, and raw materials (leather, wool, and hemp, for example) to eastern cities and foreign markets. Two horses pulling a wagon overland could tow 4 tons of freight; now, those same two horses working the towpaths of the Erie Canal could pull 100-ton freight barges at a steady 30 miles a day, cutting transportation costs and accelerating the flow of goods. In 1818, the mills in Rochester, New York, processed 26,000 barrels of flour for export. Ten years later their output soared to 200,000 barrels, and by 1840 it was at 500,000 barrels.

The spectacular benefits of the Erie Canal prompted a national canal boom. Civic and business leaders in Philadelphia and Baltimore proposed waterways to link their cities to the Midwest. Copying New York's fiscal innovations, they persuaded their state legislatures to invest directly in canal companies or to force state-chartered banks to do so, and to offer guarantees that encouraged British and Dutch investors. Soon, artificial waterways connected Philadelphia and Baltimore, via the Pennsylvania Canal and the Chesapeake and Ohio Canal, to the Great Lakes region. The Michigan and Illinois Canal (finished in 1848), which linked Chicago to the Mississippi River, completed an inland all-water route from New York City to New Orleans, the two most important port cities in North America (Map 8.1). Historians have labeled the economic boom resulting from these new banking and transportation systems the **Market Revolution**. Americans had greater access to capital, more financial liquidity, and more opportunities to buy and sell products over long distances, than they had ever had before.

**Shrinking Space: Steamboats**　　The steamboat, another product of the industrial age, added crucial flexibility to the Mississippi basin's river-based transportation system. In 1807, engineer-inventor Robert Fulton piloted the first American steamboat, the *Clermont*, up the Hudson River. To navigate shallow western rivers, engineers broadened steamboats' hulls to reduce their draft and enlarge their cargo capacity. These vessels halved the cost of upstream river transport and dramatically increased the flow of goods, people, and news. In 1830, a traveler or a letter from New York could reach Buffalo or Pittsburgh by water in less than a week and Detroit, Chicago, or St. Louis in two weeks. In 1800, the same journeys had taken twice as long.

Slave-owning planters from the Lower South settled in Missouri (admitted to the Union in 1821) and pushed on to Arkansas (admitted in 1836). Simultaneously, yeomen families from the Upper South joined migrants from New England and New York in farming the fertile lands near the Great Lakes. Once Indiana and Illinois

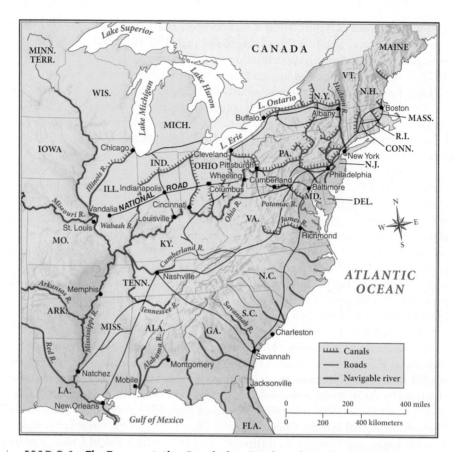

**MAP 8.1   The Transportation Revolution: Roads and Canals, 1820–1850**

By 1850, the United States had an efficient system of water-borne transportation with three distinct parts. Short canals and navigable rivers carried cotton, tobacco, and other products from the countryside of the southern seaboard states into the Atlantic commercial system. A second system, centered on the Erie, Chesapeake and Ohio, and Pennsylvania Mainline canals, linked northeastern seaports to the vast trans-Appalachian region. Finally, a set of regional canals in the Midwest connected most of the Great Lakes region to the Ohio and Mississippi rivers and the port of New Orleans.

were settled, American-born farmers poured into Michigan (1837), Iowa (1846), and Wisconsin (1848)—where they resided among tens of thousands of hardworking immigrants from Germany. To meet the demand for cheap farmsteads, Congress in 1820 reduced the price of federal land from $2.00 an acre to $1.25. For $100, a farmer could buy 80 acres, the minimum required under federal law. By the 1840s, this generous policy had enticed about 5 million people to states and territories west of the Appalachians (Map 8.2).

While state legislatures subsidized canals, the national government created a vast postal system, the first network for the exchange of information. Thanks to the Post Office Act of 1792, there were more than eight thousand post offices by 1830, and

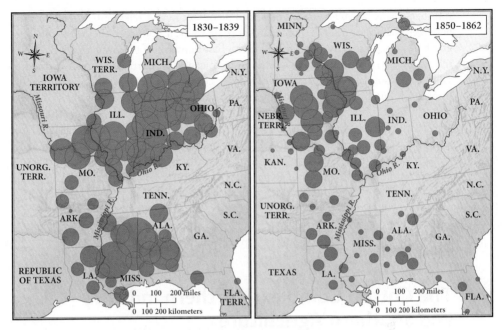

**MAP 8.2   Western Land Sales, 1830–1839 and 1850–1862**

The federal government set up local offices to sell land in the national domain to settlers. During the 1830s, the offices sold huge amounts of land in the corn and wheat belt of the Midwest (Ohio, Indiana, Illinois, and Michigan) and the cotton belt to the south (especially Alabama and Mississippi). As settlers moved westward in the 1850s, most sales were in the upper Mississippi River Valley (particularly Iowa and Wisconsin). Each circle indicates the relative amount of land sold at a local office.

the postal service had more employees than all the rest of the government's civilian employees combined. They safely delivered thousands of letters and banknotes worth millions of dollars, along with newspapers that carried information from the Atlantic seaboard to the Mississippi basin. The U.S. Supreme Court, headed by John Marshall, likewise encouraged interstate trade by firmly establishing federal authority over interstate commerce (Chapter 7). In *Gibbons v. Ogden* (1824), the Court voided a New York law that created a monopoly on steamboat travel into New York City. That decision prevented local or state monopolies — or tariffs — from impeding the flow of goods, people, and news across the nation.

**Shrinking Space: The Telegraph**   An efficient postal service was a great boon to merchants and manufacturers doing business across long distances. But for decades, inventors who were familiar with the properties of electricity dreamed of a much faster form of communication: electrical telegraphy. Across Europe, scientists experimented with various methods of using electrical impulses to send messages, but they struggled to devise a practical way to represent the alphabet. In 1837, a Massachusetts painter-turned-inventor, Samuel F. B. Morse, devised a telegraph capable of sending signals through miles of wire. Of equal importance, Morse and his collaborator, machinist and inventor Alfred Vail, invented a code for transmitting letters and numbers along a single wire by means of a contact key. A telegraph line was strung between Washington, D.C., and Baltimore in 1844; a year later, the Magnetic Telegraph Company was founded to create the first network of telegraph lines. By 1848, telegraph wires connected New York and Chicago. Western Union was formed in 1856 to consolidate the operations of smaller companies, and in 1861 it completed a transcontinental telegraph line connecting New York with San Francisco.

All these innovations — roads and turnpikes, canals and steamboats, the postal service and the telegraph — helped to shrink the vast spaces of North America. They enabled farmers and merchants to sell goods in distant markets, helped entrepreneurs to coordinate business activity, aided immigrants as they relocated, and created a network of information that shaped politics and culture on a national scale. Together, they constituted the foundation of a new social order.

| **IN YOUR OWN WORDS** | What was the relationship between government support and private enterprise in economic development? |

# The Cotton Complex: Northern Industry and Southern Agriculture

In 1800, the economy of the United States remained overwhelmingly agricultural and manufacturing was still in its infancy. Nevertheless, in the first half of the nineteenth century the **Industrial Revolution** came to the United States. At its center was the **cotton complex**: the relationship between northern industry and southern agriculture that drove a major economic transformation. In the Northeast, merchants and manufacturers invested in new textile mills that relied on the labor of young women drawn from nearby farms. These northeastern mills, and many more like them in Great Britain, created vast demand for cotton, which transformed the southern economy as well. As northern merchants and manufacturers reorganized work routines and increased output, goods that were once luxury items became part of everyday life. Southern planters poured capital into land and slaves, revolutionizing agricultural production and sentencing additional generations of African American slaves to the miseries of plantation life.

## The American Industrial Revolution

The Industrial Revolution had its roots in Great Britain, where textile manufacturing had undergone major changes in the last half of the eighteenth century. Clothmaking was an ancient enterprise common to Asia, Africa, Europe, and the Americas, but until this time it was driven by small-scale production. For millennia, spinning and weaving — whether wool, cotton, linen, or silk — were crafts that were plied in the home, using technology that had been very slow to change. Strands of fiber were spun into thread and yarn by hand or using foot-driven spinning wheels, while yarn was woven into cloth on foot-powered looms.

A series of technical innovations in Britain in the eighteenth century made clothmaking increasingly efficient. The flying shuttle, invented in 1733, made it possible to weave cloth much more rapidly than yarn could be spun. Then, beginning in the 1760s, a series of devices for spinning fibers into yarn were invented: first a spinning jenny, then a water frame, and then a mule. Because the water frame and the mule were machines that relied on water or steam power, spinning moved out of households and into factories built alongside rivers that could drive the apparatus. Water-powered spinning mills could now produce abundant yarn, and cloth production soared. In India, it took 50,000 hours of labor to spin 100 pounds of raw cotton. In Britain in 1790, workers using a spinning mule could do the same work in 1,000 hours; by 1825, it took only 135 hours. This was a revolution in productivity.

To protect its textile industry from American competition, Great Britain prohibited the export of textile machinery and the emigration of the skilled craftsmen who could replicate the mills. But the promise of higher wages brought thousands of these skilled **mechanics** to the United States illegally.

Samuel Slater, the most important émigré mechanic, came to America in 1789 after working for Richard Arkwright, who had invented the most advanced British machinery for spinning cotton. A year later, Slater reproduced Arkwright's innovations in merchant Moses Brown's cotton mill in Providence, Rhode Island — the first in North America. The fast-flowing rivers that cascaded down from the Appalachian foothills to the coastal plain provided a cheap source of energy. From Massachusetts to Delaware, these waterways were soon lined with industrial villages and textile mills as large as 150 feet long, 40 feet wide, and four stories high (Map 8.3). The Industrial Revolution had arrived on American shores.

**American and British Advantages**    British textile manufacturers nevertheless easily undersold their American competitors, for two reasons. First, they enjoyed the benefit of efficient shipping networks, which brought raw cotton to Britain at bargain prices, and low interest rates, which enabled mill owners to borrow money cheaply to support and expand their operations. Second, Britain had cheap labor: it had a larger population — about 12.6 million in 1810 compared to 7.3 million Americans — and thousands of landless laborers prepared to accept low-paying factory jobs, while in the United States labor was scarce and well paid.

To offset these advantages, American entrepreneurs relied on help from the federal government: in 1816, 1824, and 1828, Congress passed tariff bills that placed high taxes on imported cotton and woolen cloth. However, in the 1830s, Congress reduced tariffs because southern planters, western farmers, and urban consumers demanded inexpensive imports.

**Better Machines, Cheaper Workers**    American producers used two other strategies to compete with their British rivals. First, they improved on British technology. In 1811, Francis Cabot Lowell, a wealthy Boston merchant, toured British textile mills, secretly making detailed drawings of their power machinery. Paul Moody, an experienced American mechanic, then copied the machines and improved their design. In 1814, Lowell joined with merchants Nathan Appleton and Patrick Tracy Jackson to form the Boston Manufacturing Company. Having raised the staggering sum of $400,000, they built a textile plant in Waltham, Massachusetts — the first American factory to perform all clothmaking operations under one roof. Thanks to Moody's improvements, Waltham's power looms operated at higher speeds than British looms and needed fewer workers.

**MAP 8.3   New England's Dominance in Cotton Spinning, 1840**

Although the South grew the nation's cotton, it did not process it. Prior to the Civil War, entrepreneurs in Massachusetts and Rhode Island built most of the factories that spun and wove raw cotton into cloth. Their factories made use of the abundant water power available in New England and the region's surplus labor force. Initially, factory managers hired young farmwomen to work the machines; later, they relied on immigrants from Ireland and the French-speaking Canadian province of Quebec.

The second strategy was to tap a cheaper source of labor. In the 1820s, the Boston Manufacturing Company recruited thousands of young women from farm families, providing them with rooms in boardinghouses and with evening lectures and other cultural activities. To reassure parents about their daughters' moral welfare, the mill owners enforced strict curfews, prohibited alcoholic beverages, and required regular church attendance. At Lowell (1822), Chicopee (1823), and other sites in Massachusetts and New Hampshire, the company built new factories that used this labor system, known as the **Waltham-Lowell System**.

By the early 1830s, more than 40,000 New England women were working in textile mills. As an observer noted, the wages were "more than could be obtained by the hitherto ordinary occupation of housework," the living conditions were better than those in crowded farmhouses, and the women had greater independence. Lucy

Larcom became a Lowell textile operative at age eleven to avoid being "a trouble or burden or expense" to her widowed mother. Other women operatives used wages to pay off their father's farm mortgages, send brothers to school, or accumulate a marriage dowry for themselves.

Some operatives just had a good time. Susan Brown, who worked as a Lowell weaver for eight months, spent half her earnings on food and lodging and the rest on plays, concerts, lectures, and a two-day excursion to Boston. Like most textile workers, Brown soon tired of the rigors of factory work and the never-ceasing clatter of the machinery, which ran twelve hours a day, six days a week. After she quit, she lived at home for a time and then moved to another mill. Whatever the hardships, waged work gave young women a sense of freedom. "Don't I feel independent!" a woman mill worker wrote to her sister. "The thought that I am living on no one is a happy one indeed to me." The owners of the Boston Manufacturing Company were even happier. By combining tariff protection with improved technology and cheap female labor, they could undersell their British rivals. Their textiles were also cheaper than those made in New York and Pennsylvania, where farmworkers were paid more than in New England and textile wages consequently were higher. Manufacturers in those states garnered profits by using advanced technology to produce higher-quality cloth. Even Thomas Jefferson, the great champion of yeoman farming, was impressed. "Our manufacturers are now very nearly on a footing with those of England," he boasted in 1825.

## Origins of the Cotton South

As its industrial capacity grew in the eighteenth century, Great Britain began to import cotton in larger quantities. But the world supply was relatively small because cotton production was immensely labor-intensive. A revolution in cotton cloth production would require a revolution in cotton agriculture, based on new forms of cheap labor. The black belt of the American Southeast — an arc of fertile soil stretching from western South Carolina through central Georgia, Alabama, and Mississippi — provided a landscape that was ideal for cotton cultivation, and the slave plantation complex offered a system of labor discipline that could bring cotton to world markets on an entirely new scale.

**The Decline of Slavery, 1776–1800**   The possibility that cotton production would lead to a boom in African slavery would have come as a surprise to the generation that lived through the American Revolution, because in that era slavery was in a steep decline. Whites and blacks alike perceived a contradiction between the colonies' pursuit of liberty and the institution of slavery. "I wish most sincerely there was not a Slave in the province," Abigail Adams confessed to her husband, John. "It always appeared a most iniquitous Scheme to me — to fight ourselves for what we are daily robbing and plundering from those who have as good a right to freedom as we do."

**The North Ends Slavery — Slowly**   Beginning in the 1750s, Quaker evangelist John Woolman urged Friends to free their slaves, and many did so. In 1780, antislavery activists in Pennsylvania passed the first **gradual emancipation** law in the United States. Though it freed no one, the law set an important precedent. In subsequent years, legislators in Connecticut (1784), Rhode Island (1784), New York (1799), and New Jersey (1804) adopted gradual emancipation statutes as well (Map 8.4). These laws recognized white property rights by requiring slaves to buy their freedom by years—even decades—of additional labor. For example, the New York Emancipation Act of 1799 allowed slavery to continue until 1828 and freed slave children only at the age of twenty-five. Consequently, as late as 1810, almost 30,000

This simple map illustrates a complex process: the abolition of slavery in the United States up to 1800. The political boundaries are those of the states and territories in 1800.

Some areas marked "free" on the map, the Indiana Territory, for example, actually had slaves dating from the French colonial days.

In 1800, the free black population of the United States numbered about 100,000, roughly 10 percent of those of African ancestry. Half of these free blacks lived in states in which slavery remained legal until the end of the Civil War.

Free (date when slavery eliminated)
Gradual abolition
Slave

The three colors show areas where slavery was legally abolished, where it continued to exist, and where it was in the process of being eliminated.

(after Paullin)

0     100     200 miles
0     100     200 kilometers

### MAP 8.4 The Status of Slavery, 1800

In 1775, racial slavery was legal in all of the British colonies in North America. By the time the confederated states achieved their independence in 1783, the New England region was mostly free of slavery. By 1800, all of the states north of Maryland had provided for the gradual abolition of slavery except New Jersey, whose legislature finally acted in 1804, but the process of gradual emancipation dragged on until the 1830s. Some slave owners in the Chesapeake region manumitted a number of their slaves, leaving only the whites of the Lower South firmly committed to racial bondage.

blacks in the northern states—nearly one-fourth of the African Americans living there—were still enslaved.

Freed blacks faced severe prejudice from whites who feared job competition and racial melding. When Massachusetts judges abolished slavery through case law in 1784, the legislature reenacted an old statute that prohibited whites from marrying blacks, mulattos, or Indians. For African Americans in the North, freedom meant second-class citizenship; nevertheless, the institution of slavery was being ushered slowly out of existence.

**Manumission in the Chesapeake**    The coming of war encouraged many southern slaves to expect that the Revolution would bring their freedom. A black preacher in Georgia told his fellow slaves that King George III "was about to alter the World, and set the Negroes free." Similar rumors, prompted in part by Royal Governor Lord Dunmore's proclamation of 1775 and the Philipsburg Proclamation of 1779 (see Chapters 5 and 6), led thousands of African Americans to flee behind British lines. Two neighbors of Virginia Patriot Richard Henry Lee lost "every slave they had in the world," as did many other planters. In 1781, when the British army evacuated Charleston, more than 6,000 former slaves went with them; another 4,000 left from Savannah. All told, about 30,000 blacks fled their owners.

Yet thousands of African Americans supported the Patriot cause as well. In Maryland, some slaves took up arms for the rebels in return for the promise of freedom. Enslaved Virginians struck informal bargains with their Patriot owners, trading loyalty in wartime for the hope of liberty. Following the Virginia legislature's passage of a **manumission** act in 1782, allowing owners to free their slaves, 10,000 slaves won their freedom.

The southern states faced the most glaring contradiction between liberty and property rights because enslaved blacks represented a huge financial investment. But in the Chesapeake, slavery was in decline for three reasons. First, the tobacco economy was chronically depressed, and many tobacco planters were shifting to wheat and livestock production, a less labor-intensive form of farming that gave them an oversupply of slaves. Second, many leading planters were committed to the principle of human liberty and saw, in the institution of slavery, the same contradiction that their northern counterparts did. Third, evangelical Christianity encouraged some planters to regard their slaves as spiritual equals. In 1784, a conference of Virginia Methodists declared that slavery was "contrary to the Golden Law of God on which hang all the Law and the Prophets." Under these influences, many Chesapeake slave owners manumitted their slaves or allowed them to buy their freedom by working as artisans or laborers. In 1785 a Powhatan planter named Joseph Mayo manumitted all of his slaves, 150 to 170 in number; in the 1790s, Robert "Councillor" Carter manumitted more than 500 slaves and provided them with land. John Randolph of Roanoke manumitted hundreds of slaves in his will, and also left money to buy them land. Widespread manumission gradually brought freedom to one-third of the African Americans in Maryland.

**Slavery Resurgent**    But slavery still had powerful advocates. In Virginia, slave owners pushed back against the wave of manumissions. Fearing the possibility of total emancipation, hundreds of slave owners petitioned the Virginia legislature to repeal the manumission act and thereby protect "the most valuable and indispensible Article of our Property, our Slaves." In 1792, legislators forbade further manumissions. Following the lead of Thomas Jefferson, who owned more than a hundred slaves, political leaders now argued that slavery was a "necessary evil" required to maintain white supremacy and the luxurious planter lifestyle. In North Carolina, legislators condemned private Quaker manumissions as "highly criminal and reprehensible."

Farther south, in the rice-growing states of South Carolina and Georgia, slavery was even more deeply entrenched. Yet rice plantations were confined to the seaboard; at the time of the Revolution, there was no cash crop that could support plantation agriculture farther inland. Cotton was about to change that. In 1786, responding to rising prices resulting from Great Britain's mechanized processing, Georgia planters on the Sea Islands harvested their first crop of long-staple cotton. Its silky fibers produced a high grade of cotton, but—like rice and indigo—Sea Island cotton would not grow in the uplands. Hardier varieties of short-staple cotton could thrive in rich inland soils, but their bolls, with tightly packed fibers, required machine processing. American inventors immediately put their minds to the problem. In 1793, Massachusetts native Eli Whitney devised a machine, called a cotton engine (or cotton "gin" for short), that could quickly separate the seeds of a short-staple cotton boll from their delicate fibers, an innovation that increased the speed of cotton processing fiftyfold. The cotton rush was on.

## The Cotton Boom and Slavery

In the early nineteenth century, slave plantations pushed into the interior of North America in two directions at once: westward, from the coastal states of South Carolina and Georgia; and northward from New Orleans up the Mississippi (Map 8.5). In the lower Mississippi Valley, sugar was a viable crop; thus, a combination of sugar and cotton drove the development of formerly French Louisiana (admitted as a state in 1812) and Mississippi (admitted in 1817). After crossing the Appalachians, westward-moving cotton planters settled in southern Tennessee (admitted 1796) and Alabama (1819), then pushed into Missouri (1821), Arkansas (1836), and Texas (1845). These migratory streams converged in the rich alluvial soils of the black belt, which stretched from western South Carolina all the way to east Texas. Between 1800 and 1848, the new cotton-growing lands of the American Southeast became some of the most valuable real estate in the world.

The cotton boom immediately tripled the value of good southern farmland. As Creeks, Choctaws, and Chickasaws ceded land, the federal government made it

**MAP 8.5   Distribution of the Slave Population in 1790 and 1830 >**
The cotton boom shifted the African American population to the South and West. In 1790, most slaves lived and worked on Chesapeake tobacco and Carolina rice and indigo plantations. By 1830, those areas were still heavily populated by black families, but hundreds of thousands of slaves also labored on the cotton and sugar lands of the lower Mississippi Valley and on cotton plantations in Georgia, northern Florida, and Alabama. In the decades to come, the cotton frontier would push across Mississippi and Louisiana and into Texas.

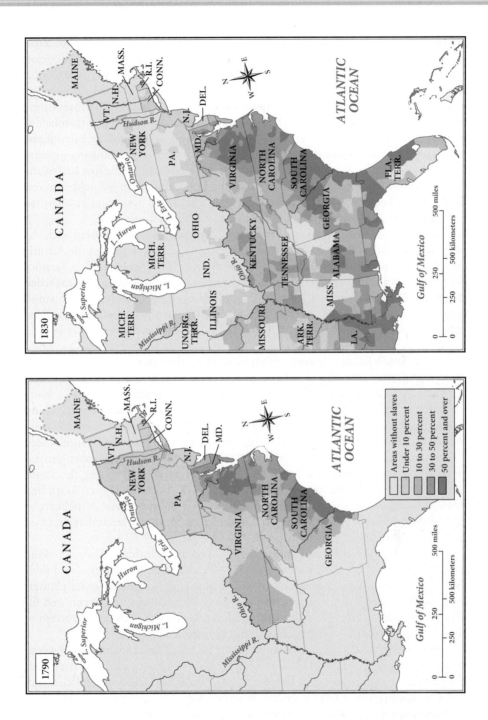

available to southern planters as quickly as possible. Capital investments from overseas helped to speed the process, as wealthy British investors like banker and cotton merchant Thomas Baring loaned money to bring the lands under cultivation. Cotton was wildly profitable; in 1807, a Mississippi cotton plantation returned 22.5 percent a year on its investment. As cotton cultivation expanded, it became the cornerstone of the nation's economy: between 1815 and 1860, it accounted for more than half of all U.S. exports. By 1840, the South produced and exported 1.5 million bales of raw cotton a year, over two-thirds of the world's supply. The cotton-producing capacity of the South dwarfed the industrial capacity of the Northeast. In the first half of the nineteenth century, more than 85 percent of the U.S. cotton crop was sold in Liverpool to be processed in Great Britain, while only a small fraction could be absorbed by American mills. "Cotton is King," boasted the *Southern Cultivator*.

To plant this vast new inland frontier, white planters first imported enslaved laborers from Africa. Between 1776 and 1808, when Congress outlawed the Atlantic slave trade, planters purchased about 115,000 Africans. "The Planter will . . . Sacrifice every thing to attain Negroes," declared one slave trader. But demand far exceeded the supply. Planters also imported new African workers illegally, through the Spanish colony of Florida until 1819 and then through the Mexican province of Texas. Yet these Africans—about 50,000 between 1810 and 1865—did not satisfy the demand either.

**The Upper South Exports Slaves**    Planters seeking labor also looked to the Chesapeake region, where the African American population was growing by natural increase at an average of 27 percent a decade, creating a surplus of enslaved workers on many plantations. The result was a growing domestic trade in slaves. Between 1818 and 1829, planters in just one Maryland tobacco-growing county—Frederick—sold at least 952 slaves to traders or cotton planters. Plantation owners in Virginia sold 75,000 slaves during the 1810s and again during the 1820s. That number jumped to nearly 120,000 during the 1830s and then averaged 85,000 during the 1840s and 1850s. By 1860, the "mania for buying negroes" from the Upper South had resulted in a massive transplantation of more than 1 million slaves. A majority of African Americans now lived and worked in the Deep South, the lands that stretched from Georgia to Texas.

This African American migration took two forms: transfer and sale. Looking for new opportunities, thousands of Chesapeake and Carolina planters sold their existing plantations and moved their slaves to the Southwest. Many other planters gave slaves to sons and daughters who moved west. Such transfers accounted for about 40 percent of the African American migrants. The rest—about 60 percent of the 1 million migrants—were sold south through traders.

One set of trading routes ran to the Atlantic coast and sent thousands of slaves to rapidly developing sugar plantations in Louisiana. As sugar output soared, slave traders scoured the countryside near the port cities of Baltimore, Alexandria, Richmond, and Charleston—searching, as one of them put it, for "likely young men such as I think would suit the New Orleans market." Because this **coastal trade** in laborers was highly visible, it elicited widespread condemnation by northern abolitionists. Sugar was a "killer" crop, and Louisiana (like the eighteenth-century West Indies) soon had a well-deserved reputation among African Americans "as a place of slaughter." Maryland farmer John Anthony Munnikhuysen refused to allow his daughter

**The Inland Slave Trade** Mounted whites escort a convoy of slaves from Virginia to Tennessee in Lewis Miller's *Slave Trader, Sold to Tennessee* (1853). For white planters, the interstate trade in slaves was lucrative; it pumped money into the declining Chesapeake economy and provided young workers for the expanding plantations of the cotton belt. For blacks, it was a traumatic journey, a new Middle Passage that broke up their families and communities. "Arise! Arise! and weep no more, dry up your tears, we shall part no more," the slaves sing sorrowfully as they journey to new lives in Tennessee. The Colonial Williamsburg Foundation. Gift of Dr. Richard M. Kain in memory of George Hay Kain.

Priscilla to marry a Louisiana sugar planter, declaring: "Mit has never been used to see negroes flayed alive and it would kill her."

The **inland system** that fed slaves to the Cotton South was less visible than the coastal trade but more extensive. Professional slave traders went from one rural village to another buying "young and likely Negroes." The traders marched their purchases in coffles—columns of slaves bound to one another—to Alabama, Mississippi, and Missouri in the 1830s and to Arkansas and Texas in the 1850s.

Chesapeake and Carolina planters provided the human cargo. Some planters sold slaves when they ran into debt. "Trouble gathers thicker and thicker around me," Thomas B. Chaplin of South Carolina lamented in his diary. "I will be compelled to send about ten prime Negroes to Town on next Monday, to be sold." Many more planters doubled as slave traders, earning substantial profits by traveling south to sell some of their slaves and those of their neighbors. Colonel E. S. Irvine, a member of the South Carolina legislature and "a highly respected gentleman" in white circles, traveled frequently "to sell a drove of Negroes." Prices marched in step with those for cotton; during a boom year in the 1850s, a planter noted that a slave "will fetch $1000, cash, quick."

The domestic slave trade was crucial to the prosperity of the fast-developing Cotton South. Equally important, it sustained the wealth of slave owners in the East.

By selling surplus black workers, planters in the Chesapeake and Carolinas added about 20 percent to their income. As a Maryland newspaper remarked in 1858, "[The trade serves as] an almost universal resource to raise money. A prime able-bodied slave is worth three times as much to the cotton or sugar planter as to the Maryland agriculturalist."

**The Impact on Blacks**    For African American families, the domestic slave trade was a personal disaster that underlined their status—and vulnerability—as chattel slaves. In law, they were the movable personal property of the whites who owned them. As Lewis Clark, a fugitive from slavery, noted: "Many a time i've had 'em say to me, 'You're my property.'" "The being of slavery, its soul and its body, lives and moves in the **chattel principle**, the property principle, the bill of sale principle," declared former slave James W. C. Pennington. As a South Carolina master put it, "[The slave's earnings] belong to me because I bought him."

Slave property underpinned the entire southern economic system. Whig politician Henry Clay noted that the "immense amount of capital which is invested in slave property . . . is owned by widows and orphans, by the aged and infirm, as well as the sound and vigorous. It is the subject of mortgages, deeds of trust, and family settlements."

As a slave owner, Clay also knew that property rights were key to slave discipline. "I govern them . . . without the whip," another master explained, "by stating . . . that I should sell them if they do not conduct themselves as I wish." The threat was effective. "The Negroes here dread nothing on earth so much as this," a Maryland observer noted. "They regard the south with perfect horror, and to be sent there is considered as the worst punishment." Thousands of slaves suffered that fate, which destroyed about one in every four slave marriages. "Why does the slave ever love?" asked black abolitionist Harriet Jacobs in her autobiography, *Incidents in the Life of a Slave Girl*, when her partner "may at any moment be wrenched away by the hand of violence?" After being sold, one Georgia slave lamented, "My Dear wife for you and my Children my pen cannot Express the griffe I feel to be parted from you all."

The interstate slave trade often focused on young adults. In northern Maryland, planters sold away boys and girls at an average age of seventeen years. "Dey sole my sister Kate," Anna Harris remembered decades later, "and I ain't seed or heard of her since." The trade also separated almost a third of all slave children under the age of fourteen from one or both of their parents. Sarah Grant remembered, "Mamma used to cry when she had to go back to work because she was always scared some of us kids would be sold while she was away."

Despite these sales, 75 percent of slave marriages remained unbroken, and the majority of children lived with one or both parents until puberty. Consequently, the sense of family among African Americans remained strong. Sold from Virginia to Texas in 1843, Hawkins Wilson carried with him a mental picture of his family. Twenty-five years later and now a freedman, Wilson set out to find his "dearest relatives" in Virginia. "My sister belonged to Peter Coleman in Caroline County and her name was Jane. . . . She had three children, Robert, Charles and Julia, when I left—Sister Martha belonged to Dr. Jefferson. . . . Sister Matilda belonged to Mrs. Botts."

During the decades between sale and freedom, Hawkins Wilson and thousands of other African Americans constructed new lives for themselves in the Mississippi Valley. Undoubtedly, many did so with a sense of foreboding, knowing from personal experience that their owners could disrupt their lives at any moment. Like Charles Ball, some "longed to die, and escape from the bonds of my tormentors." The darkness of slavery shadowed even moments of joy. Knowing that sales often ended slave marriages, a white minister blessed one couple "for so long as God keeps them together."

**The Ideology and Reality of "Benevolence"**    The planter aristocracy flourished around the periphery of the South's booming Cotton Belt—in Virginia, South Carolina, and Louisiana—and took the lead in defending slavery. Within a generation after the Revolution, southern apologists rejected the view that slavery was, at best, a "necessary evil." In 1837, South Carolina Senator John C. Calhoun argued that the institution was a **"positive good"** because it subsidized an elegant lifestyle for a white elite and provided tutelage for genetically inferior Africans. "As a race, the African is inferior to the white man," declared Alexander Stephens, the future vice president of the Confederacy. "Subordination to the white man is his normal condition." Apologists depicted planters and their wives as aristocratic models of "disinterested benevolence," who provided food and housing for their workers and cared for them in old age. One wealthy Georgian declared, "Plantation government should be eminently patriarchal. . . . The paterfamilias, or head of the family, should, in one sense, be the father of the whole concern, negroes and all."

Those planters who embraced Christian stewardship tried to shape the religious lives of their chattel. They built churches on their plantations, welcomed evangelical preachers, and required their slaves to attend services. A few encouraged African Americans with spiritual "gifts" to serve as exhorters and deacons. Most of these planters acted from sincere Christian belief, but they also hoped to counter abolitionist criticism and to use religious teachings to control their workers.

Indeed, slavery's defenders increasingly used religious justifications for human bondage. Protestant ministers in the South pointed out that the Hebrews, God's chosen people, had owned slaves and that Jesus Christ had never condemned slavery. As James Henry Hammond told a British abolitionist in 1845: "What God ordains and Christ sanctifies should surely command the respect and toleration of man." In making their case, slavery's advocates rarely acknowledged its day-to-day brutality and exploitation. "I was at the plantation last Saturday and the crop was in fine order," a son wrote to his absentee father, "but the negroes are most brutally scarred & several have run off."

Despite the violence inherent in the chattel principle, many white planters considered themselves benevolent masters, committed to the welfare of "my family, black and white." Historians have labeled this idea **paternalism**. Some masters gave substance to the paternalist ideal by treating kindly "loyal and worthy" slaves—black overseers, the mammy who raised their children, and trusted house servants. By preserving the families of these slaves, many planters could believe that they "sold south" only "coarse" troublemakers who had "little sense of family." Other owners were more honest about the human cost of their pursuit of wealth. "Tomorrow the negroes are to get off [to Kentucky]," a slave-owning woman in Virginia wrote to a friend, "and I expect there will be great crying and moaning, with children Leaving there mothers, mothers there children, and women there husbands."

Whether or not they acknowledged the slaves' pain, few southern whites questioned the morality of the slave trade. Responding to abolitionists' criticism, the city council of Charleston, South Carolina, declared that "the removal of slaves from place to place, and their transfer from master to master, by gift, purchase, or otherwise" was completely consistent "with moral principle and with the highest order of civilization."

| IN YOUR OWN WORDS | How were industrial development in the North and the expansion of cotton agriculture in the South connected? |
| --- | --- |

# Technological Innovation and Labor

The technical advances that spurred the rise of cotton mills in the North were part of a larger pattern of economic innovation and change. Americans became inventive, seeking countless ways to improve and simplify production. Machines were at the center of many of these improvements, and American mechanics led the world in creating devices that worked faster and better than before. But workers did not always benefit. Skilled laborers formed unions to strengthen their bargaining position with employers. Lower-skilled workers in factory jobs, who often performed repetitive labor under close supervision, tried to organize as well, but they often faced legal obstacles. In the first half of the nineteenth century, many Americans struggled to understand their place in an increasingly complex social order. Urban growth was one sign of change, as wageworkers swelled the size of older cities and prompted the creation of many new ones.

## The Spread of Innovation

By the 1820s, American-born artisans had replaced British immigrants at the cutting edge of technological innovation. In the Philadelphia region, the remarkable Sellars family produced the most important inventors. Samuel Sellars Jr. invented a machine for twisting worsted woolen yarn to give it an especially smooth surface. His son John improved the efficiency of the waterwheels powering the family's sawmills and built a machine to weave wire sieves. John's sons and grandsons ran machine shops that turned out riveted leather fire hoses, papermaking equipment, and eventually locomotives. In 1824, the Sellars and other mechanics founded the Franklin Institute in Philadelphia. Named after Benjamin Franklin, whom the mechanics admired for his work ethic and scientific accomplishments, the institute published a journal; provided high-school-level instruction in chemistry, mathematics, and mechanical design; and organized exhibits of new products. Craftsmen in Ohio and other states established similar institutes to disseminate technical knowledge and encourage innovation. Between 1820 and 1860, the number of patents issued by the U.S. Patent Office rose from two hundred to four thousand a year.

American craftsmen pioneered the development of **machine tools** — machines that made parts for other machines. Eli Whitney was a key innovator. At the age of fourteen, Whitney began fashioning nails and knife blades; later, he made women's hatpins. Aspiring to wealth and status, Whitney won admission to Yale College and subsequently worked as a tutor on a Georgia cotton plantation. He capitalized on his expertise in making hatpins to design his cotton gin. Although Whitney patented the machine, other manufacturers improved on his design and captured the market.

Still seeking his fortune, Whitney decided in 1798 to manufacture military weapons. He eventually designed and built machine tools that could rapidly produce interchangeable musket parts, bringing him the wealth and fame he had long craved. After Whitney's death in 1825, his partner John H. Hall built an array of metalworking machine tools, such as turret lathes, milling machines, and precision grinders.

Technological innovation now swept through American manufacturing. Mechanics in the textile industry invented lathes, planers, and boring machines that turned out standardized parts for new spinning jennies and weaving looms. Despite being mass-produced, these jennies and looms were precisely made and operated at higher speeds than British equipment. Richard Garsed nearly doubled the speed of the power looms in his father's Delaware factory and patented a cam-and-harness device that allowed damask and other elaborately designed fabrics to be machine-woven. Meanwhile, the mechanics employed by Samuel W. Collins built a machine for pressing and hammering hot metal into dies (cutting forms). Using this machine, a worker could make three hundred ax heads a day—compared to twelve using traditional methods. In Richmond, Virginia, Welsh- and American-born mechanics at the Tredegar Iron Works produced low-cost parts for complicated manufacturing equipment. As a group of British observers noted admiringly, many American products were made "with machinery applied to almost every process . . . all reduced to an almost perfect system of manufacture."

As mass production spread, the American Industrial Revolution came of age. Reasonably priced products such as Remington rifles, Singer sewing machines, and Yale locks became household names in the United States and abroad. After winning praise at the Crystal Palace Exhibition in London in 1851—the first major international display of industrial goods—Remington, Singer, and other American firms became multinational businesses, building factories in Great Britain and selling goods throughout Europe. By 1877, the Singer Manufacturing Company controlled 75 percent of the world market for sewing machines.

## Wageworkers and the Labor Movement

As the Industrial Revolution gathered momentum, it changed the nature of workers' lives. Following the American Revolution, many craft workers espoused **artisan republicanism**, an ideology of production based on liberty and equality. They saw themselves as small-scale producers, equal to one another and free to work for themselves. The poet Walt Whitman summed up their outlook: "Men must be masters, under themselves."

**Free Workers Form Unions**    However, as the outwork and factory systems spread, more and more workers became wage earners who labored under the control of an employer. Unlike young women, who embraced factory work because it freed them from parental control and domestic service, men bridled at their status as supervised wageworkers. To assert their independence, male wageworkers rejected the traditional terms of *master* and *servant* and used the Dutch word *boss* to refer to their employer. Likewise, lowly apprentices refused to allow masters to control their private (non-work) lives and joined their mates in building a robust plebeian culture. Still, as hired hands, they received meager wages and had little job security. The artisan-republican ideal of "self-ownership" confronted the harsh reality of waged work in an industrializing capitalist society. Labor had become a commodity, to be bought and sold.

Some wage earners worked in carpentry, stonecutting, masonry, and cabinet-making—traditional crafts that required specialized skills. Their strong sense of identity, or trade consciousness, enabled these workers to form **unions** and bargain with their master-artisan employers. They resented low wages and long hours, which restricted their family life and educational opportunities. In Boston, six hundred carpenters went on strike in 1825. That protest failed, but in 1840, craft workers in St. Louis secured a ten-hour day, and President Van Buren issued an executive order setting a similar workday for federal workers.

Artisans in other occupations were less successful in preserving their pay and working conditions. As aggressive entrepreneurs and machine technology took command, shoemakers, hatters, printers, furniture makers, and weavers faced low-paid factory work. In response, some artisans in these trades moved to small towns, while in New York City, 800 highly skilled cabinetmakers made fashionable furniture. In status and income, these cabinetmakers outranked a group of 3,200 semitrained, wage-earning workers who made cheaper tables and chairs in factories. Thus the new industrial system split the traditional artisan class into self-employed craftsmen and wage-earning workers.

When wage earners banded together to form unions, they faced a legal hurdle: English and American common law branded such groups as illegal "combinations." As a Philadelphia judge put it, unions interfered with a "master's" authority over his "servant." Other lawsuits accused unions of "conspiring" to raise wages and thereby injure employers. "It is important to the best interests of society that the price of labor be left to regulate itself," the New York Supreme Court declared in 1835, while excluding

**Woodworker, c. 1850** Skilled makers took great pride in their furniture, which was often intricately designed and beautifully executed. To underline the dignity of his occupation, this woodworker poses in formal dress and proudly displays the tools of his craft. A belief in the value of their labor was an important ingredient of the artisan-republican ideology held by many workers. Library of Congress.

employers from this rule. Clothing manufacturers in New York City collectively agreed to set wage rates and to dismiss members of the Society of Journeymen Tailors.

**Labor Ideology**   Despite such obstacles, during the 1830s journeymen shoemakers founded mutual benefit societies in Lynn, Massachusetts, and other shoemaking centers. As the workers explained, "The capitalist has no other interest in us, than to get as much labor out of us as possible." To exert more pressure on their employers, in 1834 local unions from Boston to Philadelphia formed the National Trades Union, the first regional union of different trades.

Workers found considerable popular support for their cause. When a New York City court upheld a conspiracy verdict against their union, tailors warned that the "Freemen of the North are now on a level with the slaves of the South," and organized a mass meeting of 27,000 people to denounce the decision. In 1836, local juries hearing conspiracy cases acquitted shoemakers in Hudson, New York; carpet makers in Thompsonville, Connecticut; and plasterers in Philadelphia. Then, in *Commonwealth v. Hunt* (1842), Chief Justice Lemuel Shaw of the Massachusetts Supreme Judicial Court upheld the right of workers to form unions and call strikes to enforce closed-shop agreements that limited employment to union members. But many judges continued to resist unions by forbidding strikes.

Union leaders expanded artisan republicanism to include wageworkers. Arguing that wage earners were becoming "slaves to a monied aristocracy," they condemned the new factory system in which "capital and labor stand opposed." To create a just society in which workers could "live as comfortably as others," they advanced a **labor theory of value**. Under this theory, the price of goods should reflect the labor required to make them, and the income from their sale should go primarily to the producers, not to factory owners, middlemen, or storekeepers. "The poor who perform the work, ought to receive at least half of that sum which is charged" to the consumer, declared minister Ezra Stiles Ely. Union activists agreed, organizing nearly fifty strikes for higher wages in 1836. Appealing to the spirit of the American Revolution, which had destroyed the aristocracy of birth, they called for a new revolution to demolish the aristocracy of capital.

Women textile operatives were equally active. Competition in the woolen and cotton textile industries was fierce because mechanization caused output to grow faster than consumer demand. As textile prices fell, manufacturers' revenues declined. To maintain profits, employers reduced workers' wages and imposed tougher work rules. In 1828 and again in 1834, women mill workers in Dover, New Hampshire, went on strike and won some relief. In Lowell, two thousand women operatives backed a strike by withdrawing their savings from an employer-owned bank. "One of the leaders mounted a pump," the *Boston Transcript* reported, "and made a flaming . . . speech on the rights of women and the iniquities of the 'monied aristocracy.'" Increasingly, young New England women refused to enter the mills, and impoverished Irish (and later French Canadian) immigrants took their places.

## The Growth of Cities and Towns

The expansion of industry and trade dramatically increased America's urban population. In 1820, there were 58 towns with more than 2,500 inhabitants; by 1840, there were 126 such towns, located mostly in the Northeast and Midwest.

During those two decades, the total number of city dwellers grew more than fourfold, from 443,000 to 1,844,000 (Map 8.6).

The fastest growth occurred in the new industrial towns that sprouted along the "fall line," where rivers descended rapidly from the Appalachian Mountains to the coastal plain. In 1822, the Boston Manufacturing Company built a complex of mills in a sleepy Merrimack River village that quickly became the bustling textile factory town of Lowell, Massachusetts. The towns of Hartford, Connecticut; Trenton, New Jersey; and Wilmington, Delaware, also became urban centers as mill owners exploited the water power of their rivers and recruited workers from the countryside.

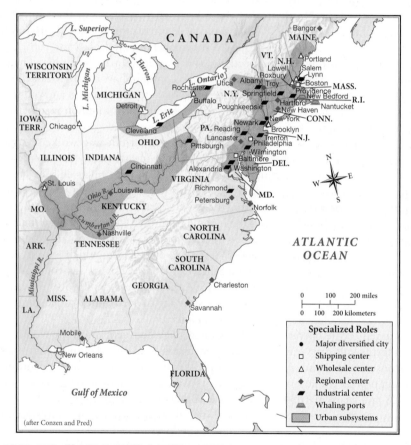

**MAP 8.6   The Nation's Major Cities, 1840**
By 1840, the United States boasted three major conglomerations of cities. The long-settled ports on the Atlantic — from Boston to Baltimore — served as centers for import merchants, banks, insurance companies, and manufacturers of ready-made clothing, and their financial reach extended far into the interior — nationwide in the case of New York City. A second group of cities stretched along the Great Lakes and included the commercial hubs of Buffalo, Detroit, and Chicago, as well as the manufacturing center of Cleveland. A third urban system extended along the Ohio River, comprising the industrial cities of Pittsburgh and Cincinnati and the wholesale centers of Louisville and St. Louis.

Western commercial cities such as Pittsburgh, Cincinnati, and New Orleans grew almost as fast. They began as transit centers, where workers transferred goods from farmers' rafts and wagons to flatboats or steamboats. As the midwestern population grew during the 1830s and 1840s, St. Louis, Detroit, and especially Buffalo and Chicago also emerged as dynamic centers of commerce. "There can be no two places in the world," journalist Margaret Fuller wrote from Chicago in 1843, "more completely thoroughfares than this place and Buffalo. . . . The life-blood [of commerce] rushes from east to west, and back again from west to east." Chicago's merchants and bankers developed the marketing, provisioning, and financial services essential to farmers and small-town shopkeepers in its vast hinterland. "There can be no better [market] any where in the Union," declared a farmer in Paw Paw, Illinois.

These midwestern hubs quickly became manufacturing centers. Capitalizing on the cities' links to rivers and canals, entrepreneurs built warehouses, flour mills, packing plants, and machine shops, creating work for hundreds of artisans and factory laborers. In 1846, Cyrus McCormick moved his reaper factory from western Virginia to Chicago to be closer to his midwestern customers.

The old Atlantic seaports — Boston, Philadelphia, Baltimore, Charleston, and especially New York City — remained important for their foreign commerce and, increasingly, as centers of finance and small-scale manufacturing. New York City and nearby Brooklyn grew at a phenomenal rate: between 1820 and 1860, their combined populations increased nearly tenfold to 1 million people, thanks to the arrival of hundreds of thousands of German and Irish immigrants. Drawing on these workers, New York became a center of the readymade clothing industry, which relied on thousands of low-paid seamstresses. "The wholesale clothing establishments are . . . absorbing the business of the country," a "Country Tailor" complained to the *New York Tribune*, "casting many an honest and hardworking man out of employment [and helping] . . . the large cities to swallow up the small towns."

New York City had the best harbor in the United States and, thanks to the Erie Canal, was the best gateway to the Midwest and the best outlet for western grain. Recognizing the city's advantages, in 1818 four English Quaker merchants founded the Black Ball Line to carry cargo, people, and mail between New York and London, Liverpool, and Le Havre, establishing the first regularly scheduled transatlantic shipping service. By 1840, its port handled almost two-thirds of foreign imports into the United States, almost half of all foreign trade, and much of the immigrant traffic. New York likewise monopolized trade with the newly independent South American nations of Brazil, Peru, and Venezuela, and its merchants took over the trade in cotton by offering finance, insurance, and shipping to southern planters and merchants.

| **IN YOUR OWN WORDS** | How did technological innovation improve the lives of ordinary people, and what challenges did it present to them? |

# New Social Classes and Cultures

The economic changes of the early nineteenth century improved the lives of many Americans, who now lived in larger houses, cooked on iron stoves, and wore better-made clothes, but they also created a more stratified society. In 1800, white

Americans thought of their society in terms of rank: "notable" families had higher status than those from the "lower orders." Yet in rural areas, people of different ranks often shared a common culture. Gentlemen farmers talked easily with yeomen about crop yields, while their wives conversed about the art of quilting. In the South, humble tenants and aristocratic slave owners enjoyed the same amusements: gambling, cockfighting, and horse racing. Rich and poor attended the same Quaker meetinghouse or Presbyterian church. "Almost everyone eats, drinks, and dresses in the same way," a European visitor to Hartford, Connecticut, reported in 1798, "and one can see the most obvious inequality only in the dwellings."

The rise of the cotton complex heightened economic inequality. In the South, the cotton boom sharpened distinctions between poorer and wealthier whites and concentrated slaves on larger plantations. In the booming cities, the new economic order spawned distinct social classes: a small but wealthy business elite, a substantial middle class, and a mass of propertyless wage earners. By creating a class-divided society, industrialization posed a momentous challenge to America's republican ideals.

## Planters, Yeomen, and Slaves

By the time of the American Revolution, tobacco and rice planting in the South had already created a three-tiered slave society. Large planters who owned dozens, or even hundreds, of slaves dominated the life of the Chesapeake and the Carolina lowcountry, while poorer whites with less land and fewer slaves deferred to their wealthy neighbors' leadership. African American slaves possessed little or nothing of their own and lived at the mercy of their owners. After 1800, South Carolina rice planters remained at the apex of the seaboard plantation aristocracy. In 1860, the fifteen proprietors of the vast plantations in All Saints Parish in South Carolina owned 4,383 slaves—nearly 300 apiece—who annually grew and processed 14 million pounds of rice. As inexpensive Asian rice entered the world market in the 1820s, the Carolina rice planters sold some slaves and worked the others harder to maintain their lifestyle.

In tobacco-growing regions, the planter aristocracy followed a different path. Slave ownership had always been more widely diffused: in the 1770s, about 60 percent of white families in the Chesapeake owned at least one slave. As wealthy tobacco planters moved their estates and slaves to the Cotton South, middling whites (who owned between five and twenty slaves) came to dominate the Chesapeake economy. The descendants of the old tobacco aristocracy remained influential, but increasingly as slave-owning grain farmers, lawyers, merchants, industrialists, and politicians. They hired out surplus slaves, sold them south, or allowed them to purchase their freedom.

In the Cotton South, ambitious planters worked their slaves ferociously as they sought to establish themselves. A Mississippi planter put it plainly: "Everything has to give way to large crops of cotton." It was a demanding crop. Frederick Law Olmsted, the future architect of New York's Central Park, noted during his travels that slaves in the Cotton South worked "much harder and more unremittingly" than those in the tobacco regions. To increase output, profit-seeking cotton planters began during the 1820s to use a rigorous **gang-labor system**. Previously, many planters had supervised workers only sporadically, or had assigned them tasks to complete at their own pace. Now masters with twenty or more slaves organized disciplined teams, or "gangs," supervised by black drivers and white overseers. They worked the gangs at a steady pace, clearing and plowing land or hoeing and picking cotton.

The gang-labor system enhanced profits by increasing productivity. Because slaves in gangs finished tasks in thirty-five minutes that took a white yeoman planter an hour to complete, gang labor became ever more prevalent. As the price of raw cotton surged after 1846, the wealth of the planter class skyrocketed. And no wonder: nearly 2 million enslaved African Americans now labored on the plantations of the Cotton South and annually produced 4 million bales of the valuable fiber.

On the eve of the Civil War, southern slave owners accounted for nearly two-thirds of all American men with wealth of $100,000 or more. Other white southerners — backcountry yeoman farmers and cotton-planting tenants in particular — occupied some of the lowest rungs of the nation's social order. The expansion of southern slavery, like the flowering of northern capitalism, increased inequalities of wealth and status.

## The Northern Business Elite

In the North, the Industrial Revolution altered the older agrarian social order. The urban economy made a few city residents — the merchants, manufacturers, bankers, and landlords who made up the business elite — very rich. In 1800, the richest 10 percent of the nation's families owned about 40 percent of the wealth; by 1860, they held nearly 70 percent. In New York, Chicago, Baltimore, and New Orleans, the superrich — the top 1 percent — owned more than 40 percent of the land, buildings, and other tangible property and an even higher share of intangible property, such as stocks and bonds.

Government tax policies facilitated the accumulation of wealth. There were no federal taxes on individual and corporate income. Rather, the U.S. Treasury raised most of its revenue from tariffs: regressive taxes on textiles and other imported goods purchased mostly by ordinary citizens. State and local governments also favored the wealthy. They taxed real estate (farms, city lots, and buildings) and tangible personal property (furniture, tools, and machinery), but almost never taxed stocks and bonds or the inheritances the rich passed on to their children.

As cities expanded in size and wealth, affluent families set themselves apart. They dressed in well-tailored clothes, rode in fancy carriages, and bought expensively furnished houses tended by butlers, cooks, and other servants. The women no longer socialized with those of lesser wealth, and the men no longer labored side by side with their employees. Instead, they became managers and directors and relied on trusted subordinates to supervise their employees. Merchants, manufacturers, and bankers placed a premium on privacy and lived in separate neighborhoods, often in exclusive central areas or at the city's edge. The geographic isolation of privileged families and the massive flow of immigrants into separate districts divided cities spatially along lines of class, race, and ethnicity.

## The Middle Class

Standing between wealthy owners and propertyless wage earners was a growing **middle class** — the social product of increased commerce. The "middling class," a

Boston printer explained, was made up of "the farmers, the mechanics, the manufacturers, the traders, who carry on professionally the ordinary operations of buying, selling, and exchanging merchandize." Professionals with other skills—building contractors, lawyers, surveyors, and so on—were suddenly in great demand and well compensated, as were middling business owners and white-collar clerks. In the Northeast, men with these qualifications numbered about 30 percent of the population in the 1840s. But they also could be found in small towns of the agrarian Midwest and South. In 1854, the cotton boomtown of Oglethorpe, Georgia (population 2,500), boasted eighty "business houses" and eight hotels.

The emergence of the middle class reflected a dramatic rise in prosperity. Between 1830 and 1857, the per capita income of Americans increased by about 2.5 percent a year, a remarkable rate that has never since been matched. This surge in income, along with an abundance of inexpensive mass-produced goods, fostered a distinct middle-class urban culture. Middle-class husbands earned enough to save about 15 percent of their income, which they used to buy well-built houses in a "respectable part of town." Middle-class wives became purveyors of genteel culture, buying books, pianos, lithographs, and comfortable furniture for their front parlors. Upper-middle-class families hired Irish or African American domestic servants, while less prosperous folk enjoyed the comforts provided by new industrial goods. For their homes they acquired furnaces (to warm the entire house and heat water for bathing), cooking stoves with ovens, and Singer's treadle-operated sewing machines. Some urban families now kept their perishable food in iceboxes, which ice-company wagons periodically refilled.

If material comfort was one distinguishing mark of the middle class, moral and mental discipline was another. Middle-class writers denounced raucous carnivals and festivals as a "chaos of sin and folly, of misery and fun" and, by the 1830s, had largely suppressed them. Ambitious parents were equally concerned with their children's moral and intellectual development, providing a high school education (in an era when most white children received only five years of schooling) and stressing the importance of discipline and hard work. American Protestants had long believed that diligent work in an earthly "calling" was a duty owed to God. Now the business elite and the middle class gave this idea a secular twist by celebrating work as the key to individual social mobility and national prosperity.

Young, middle-class men saved their money, adopted temperate habits, and aimed to rise in the world. There was an "almost universal ambition to get forward," observed Hezekiah Niles, editor of *Niles' Weekly Register*. Warner Myers, a Philadelphia housepainter, rose from poverty by saving his wages, borrowing from his family and friends, and becoming a builder, eventually constructing and selling sixty houses. Countless children's books, magazine stories, self-help manuals, and novels recounted the tales of similar individuals. The **self-made man** became a central theme of American popular culture. Just as the yeoman ethic had served as a unifying ideal in pre-1800 agrarian America, so the gospel of personal achievement linked the middle and business classes of the new industrializing society.

## Urban Workers and the Poor

As thoughtful business leaders surveyed their society, they concluded that the yeoman farmer and artisan-republican ideal—a social order of independent producers—was no longer possible. "Entire independence ought not to be wished for," Ithamar A. Beard, the paymaster of the Hamilton Manufacturing Company (in Lowell, Massachusetts), told a mechanics' association in 1827. "In large manufacturing towns, many more must fill subordinate stations and must be under the immediate direction and control of a master or superintendent, than in the farming towns."

Beard had a point. In 1840, all of the nation's slaves, some 2.5 million people, and about half of its adult white workers, another 3 million (of a total population of 17 million), were laboring for others. The bottom 10 percent of white wage earners consisted of casual workers hired on a short-term basis for arduous jobs. Poor women washed clothes; their husbands and sons carried lumber and bricks for construction projects, loaded ships, and dug out dirt and stones to build canals. Even when they could find jobs, they could never save enough "to pay rent, buy fire wood and eatables" when the job market or the harbor froze up. During business depressions, casual laborers suffered and died; in good times, their jobs were temporary and dangerous.

Other laborers had greater security of employment, but few were prospering. In Massachusetts in 1825, an unskilled worker earned about two-thirds as much as a mechanic did; two decades later, it was less than half as much. A journeyman carpenter in Philadelphia reported that he was about "even with the World" after several years of work but that many of his coworkers were in debt. Only the most fortunate working-class families could afford to educate their children, buy apprenticeships for their sons, or accumulate small dowries for their daughters. Most families sent ten-year-old children out to work, and the death of a parent often threw the survivors into dire poverty. As a charity worker noted, "What can a bereaved widow do, with 5 or 6 little children, destitute of every means of support but what her own hands can furnish (which in a general way does not amount to more than 25 cents a day)?"

Impoverished workers congregated in dilapidated housing in bad neighborhoods. Single men and women lived in crowded boardinghouses, while families jammed themselves into tiny apartments in the basements and attics of small houses. As immigrants poured in after 1840, urban populations soared, and developers squeezed more and more dwellings and foul-smelling outhouses onto a single lot. By 1848, America's largest cities were deeply divided between the genteel dwellings of the middle and upper classes and the impoverished neighborhoods of the working poor.

| **IN YOUR OWN WORDS** | How was the structure of American society different in 1848 than it had been in 1800? |

# Summary

This chapter examined the causes of the economic transformation of the first half of the nineteenth century. The Market Revolution enabled long-distance travel, trade, and communication, while a revolution in productivity—the Industrial Revolution in the North and the expansion of cotton production in the South—dramatically increased economic output. Water, steam, and minerals such as coal and iron were essential to this transformation; so, too, were technological innovation and labor discipline. Together they helped the United States to master and exploit its vast new territory.

We also explored the consequences of that transformation. In the South, the institution of slavery expanded its geographical reach, with millions of new laborers exploited more intensively than ever before. In the North, where new urban centers developed and older cities grew, workers struggled to control the terms of their employment. The Northeast and the Midwest shared important cultural affinities, while the resurgence of slavery in the South set it apart, but in every region the social order was growing more divided by race and class. As the next chapter suggests, Americans looked to their political system, which was becoming increasingly democratic, to address these social divisions. In fact, the tensions among economic inequality, cultural diversity, and political democracy became a troubling—and enduring—part of American life.

## Chapter 8 Review

### KEY TERMS

**Identify and explain the significance of each term below.**

neomercantilism (p. 233)
Panic of 1819 (p. 234)
Commonwealth System (p. 235)
Erie Canal (p. 236)
Market Revolution (p. 237)
Industrial Revolution (p. 240)
cotton complex (p. 240)
mechanics (p. 241)
Waltham-Lowell System (p. 242)
gradual emancipation (p. 243)
manumission (p. 245)
coastal trade (p. 248)

inland system (p. 249)
chattel principle (p. 250)
"positive good" (p. 251)
paternalism (p. 251)
machine tools (p. 252)
artisan republicanism (p. 253)
unions (p. 254)
labor theory of value (p. 255)
gang-labor system (p. 258)
middle class (p. 259)
self-made man (p. 260)

### REVIEW QUESTIONS

**Answer these questions to demonstrate your understanding of the chapter's main ideas.**

1. What was the relationship between government support and private enterprise in economic development?

2. How were industrial development in the North and the expansion of cotton agriculture in the South connected?

3. How did technological innovation improve the lives of ordinary people, and what challenges did it present to them?

4. How was the structure of American society different in 1848 than it had been in 1800?

5. Review the events listed under "Work, Exchange, and Technology" on the thematic timeline on page 230. What were the most important changes in the economy between 1800 and 1848, and how did they affect people's lives?

## CHRONOLOGY

As you read, ask yourself why this chapter begins and ends with these dates and then identify the links among related events.

| | |
|---|---|
| **1790** | • Samuel Slater reproduces Arkwright's inventions in Providence, Rhode Island |
| **1792** | • Congress passes Post Office Act |
| **1793** | • Eli Whitney devises cotton gin |
| **1800s** | • Natural increase produces surplus of slaves in Old South |
| | • Domestic slave trade expands, disrupting black family life |
| **1807** | • Embargo Act prohibits trade with Great Britain |
| **1808** | • African slave trade abolished by Congress |
| **1812** | • Louisiana becomes a state and its sugar output increases |
| **1814** | • Boston Manufacturing Company opens factory in Waltham, Massachusetts |
| **1816–1828** | • Congress levies protective tariffs |
| **1817** | • Erie Canal begun (completed in 1825) |
| | • Mississippi becomes a state; Alabama follows (1819) |
| **1820–1840** | • Urban population surges in Northeast and Midwest; shoe entrepreneurs adopt division of labor |
| **1820s** | • New England women take textile jobs |
| | • Entrepreneurial planters in Cotton South turn to gang labor |
| **1824** | • *Gibbons v. Ogden* promotes interstate trade |
| **1830s** | • Emergence of western commercial cities |
| | • Boom in cotton production |
| | • Labor movement gains strength |
| | • Middle-class culture emerges |
| **1837** | • South Carolina Senator John C. Calhoun argues that slavery is a "positive good" |
| **1840s** | • Gradual emancipation completed in North |
| | • Maturation of machine-tool industry |
| **1842** | • *Commonwealth v. Hunt* legitimizes trade unions |

# 9

# A Democratic Revolution

## 1800–1848

**IDENTIFY THE BIG IDEA**

What were the main features of the Democratic Revolution, and what role did Andrew Jackson play in its outcome?

**EUROPEANS WHO VISITED THE UNITED STATES IN THE 1830S MOSTLY** praised its republican society but not its political parties and politicians. "The gentlemen spit, talk of elections and the price of produce, and spit again," Frances Trollope reported in *Domestic Manners of the Americans* (1832). In her view, American politics was the sport of self-serving party politicians who reeked of "whiskey and onions." Other Europeans lamented the low intellectual level of American political debate. The "clap-trap of praise and pathos" from a Massachusetts politician "deeply disgusted" Harriet Martineau, while the shallow arguments advanced by the inept "farmers, shopkeepers, and country lawyers" who sat in the New York assembly astonished Basil Hall.

The negative verdict was nearly unanimous. "The most able men in the United States are very rarely placed at the head of affairs," French aristocrat Alexis de Tocqueville concluded in *Democracy in America* (1835). The reason, said Tocqueville, lay in the character of democracy itself. Most citizens ignored important policy issues, jealously refused to elect their intellectual superiors, and listened in awe to "the clamor of a mountebank [a charismatic fraud] who knows the secret of stimulating their tastes."

These Europeans were witnessing the American Democratic Revolution. Before 1815, men of ability had sat in the seats of government, and the prevailing ideology had been republicanism, or rule by "men of TALENTS and VIRTUE," as a newspaper put it. Many of those leaders feared popular rule, so they wrote constitutions with Bills of Rights, bicameral legislatures, and independent judiciaries, and they criticized overambitious men who campaigned for public office. But history took a different course. By the 1820s and 1830s, the watchwords were *democracy* and *party politics*, a system run by men who avidly sought office and rallied supporters through newspapers, broadsides, and great public processions. Politics became a sport—a competitive contest for the votes of ordinary men. "That the majority should govern was a fundamental maxim in all free governments," declared Martin Van Buren, the most talented of the new breed of professional politicians. By encouraging ordinary Americans to burn with "election fever" and support party principles, he and other politicians redefined the meaning of democratic government and made it work.

# The Rise of Popular Politics

Expansion of the **franchise** (the right to vote) dramatically symbolized the Democratic Revolution. By the 1830s, most states allowed nearly all white men to vote. Nowhere else in the world did ordinary farmers and wage earners exercise such political influence; in England, the Reform Bill of 1832 extended the vote to only 600,000 out of 6 million men—a mere 10 percent. Equally important, political parties provided voters with the means to express their preferences. At the same time, state legislatures barred women and free African Americans from exercising the franchise. As political democracy took shape in the United States, participation was restricted to white men.

## The Decline of the Notables and the Rise of Parties

The American Revolution weakened the elite-run society of the colonial era but did not overthrow it. Only two states—Pennsylvania and Vermont—gave the vote to all male taxpayers, and many families of low rank continued to defer to their social "betters." Consequently, wealthy **notables**—northern landlords, slave-owning planters, and seaport merchants—dominated the political system in the new republic. And rightly so, said John Jay, the first chief justice of the Supreme Court: "Those who own the country are the most fit persons to participate in the government of it." Jay and other notables managed local elections by building up an "interest": lending money to small farmers, giving business to storekeepers, and treating their tenants to rum. An outlay of $20 for refreshments, remarked one poll watcher, "may produce about 100 votes." This gentry-dominated system kept men who lacked wealth and powerful family connections from seeking office.

**The Rise of Democracy**　To broaden voting rights, Maryland reformers in the 1810s invoked the equal rights rhetoric of republicanism. They charged that property qualifications for voting were a "tyranny" because they endowed "one class of men with privileges which are denied to another." In response, legislators in Maryland and other seaboard states grudgingly expanded the franchise. The new voters often rejected candidates who wore "top boots, breeches, and shoe buckles," their hair in "powder and queues." Instead, they elected men who dressed simply and endorsed popular rule.

Farmers and laborers in the Midwest and Southwest also challenged the old order. The constitutions of the new states of Indiana (1816), Illinois (1818), and Alabama (1819) prescribed a broad male franchise, and voters usually elected middling men to local and state offices. A well-to-do migrant in Illinois was surprised to learn that the man who plowed his fields "was a colonel of militia, and a member of the legislature." Once in public office, men from modest backgrounds restricted imprisonment for debt, kept taxes low, and allowed farmers to claim squatters' rights to unoccupied land.

By 1830, most state legislatures had given the vote to all white men or to all men who paid taxes or served in the militia. Only two—North Carolina and Rhode Island—still required the possession of freehold property (Map 9.1). Equally significant,

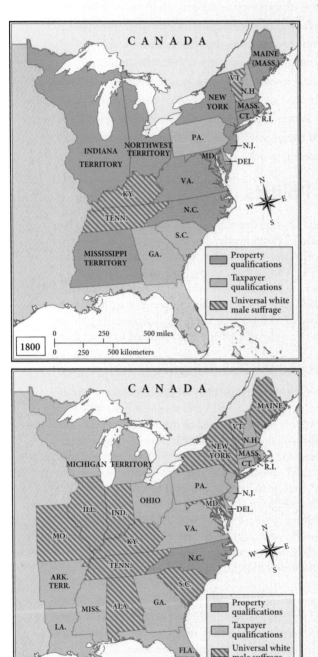

**MAP 9.1  The Expansion of Voting Rights for White Men, 1800 and 1830**

Between 1800 and 1830, the United States moved steadily toward political equality for white men. Many existing states revised their constitutions and replaced a property qualification for voting with less restrictive criteria, such as paying taxes or serving in the militia. Some new states in the West extended the suffrage to all adult white men. As parties sought votes from a broader electorate, the tone of politics became more open and competitive—swayed by the interests and values of ordinary people.

between 1818 and 1821, Connecticut, Massachusetts, and New York wrote more democratic constitutions that reapportioned legislative districts on the basis of population and stipulated that judges and justices of the peace would be elected rather than appointed.

Democratic politics was contentious and, because it attracted ambitious men, often corrupt. Powerful entrepreneurs and speculators — both notables and self-made men — demanded government assistance and paid bribes to get it. Speculators won land grants by paying off the members of important committees, and bankers distributed shares of stock to key legislators. When the Seventh Ward Bank of New York City received a legislative charter in 1833, the bank's officials set aside one-third of the 3,700 shares of stock for themselves and their friends and almost two-thirds for state legislators and bureaucrats, leaving just 40 shares for public sale.

**Parties Take Command**    The appearance of political parties encouraged vigorous debates over government policy. Revolutionary-era Americans had condemned political "factions" as antirepublican, and the new state and national constitutions made no mention of political parties. However, as the power of notables waned in the 1820s, disciplined political parties appeared in a number of states. Usually they were run by professional politicians, often middle-class lawyers and journalists. One observer called the new parties **political machines** because, like the new power-driven textile looms, they efficiently wove together the interests of diverse social and economic groups.

Martin Van Buren of New York was the chief architect of the emerging system of party government. The ambitious son of a Jeffersonian tavern keeper, Van Buren grew up in the landlord-dominated society of the Hudson River Valley. Trained as a lawyer, he sought an alternative to the system of deferring to local notables. He wanted to create a political order based on party identity, not family connections. Van Buren rejected the traditional republican belief that political factions were dangerous and claimed that the opposite was true. In his autobiography he wrote, "All men of sense know that political parties are inseparable from free government," because they restrain an elected official's inherent "disposition to abuse power."

Between 1817 and 1821 in New York, Van Buren turned his "Bucktail" supporters (who wore a deer's tail on their hats) into the first statewide political machine. He purchased a newspaper, the *Albany Argus*, and used it to promote his policies and get out the vote. Patronage was an even more important tool. When Van Buren's Bucktails won control of the New York legislature in 1821, they acquired the power to appoint some six thousand of their friends to positions in New York's legal bureaucracy of judges, justices of the peace, sheriffs, deed commissioners, and coroners. Critics called this ruthless distribution of offices a **spoils system**, but Van Buren argued it was fair, operating "sometimes in favour of one party, and sometimes of another." Party government was thoroughly republican, he added, because it reflected the preferences of a majority of the citizenry. To ensure the passage of the party's legislative program, Van Buren insisted on disciplined voting as determined by a **caucus**, a meeting of party leaders. On one crucial occasion, the "Little Magician" — a nickname reflecting Van Buren's short stature and political dexterity — honored seventeen New York legislators for sacrificing "individual preferences for the general good" of the party.

## Racial Exclusion and Republican Motherhood

The rise of a more democratic political system did not lead to universal voting rights. Old cultural rules — and new laws — denied the vote to most women and free African American men. When women and free blacks asked for voting rights, legislators wrote explicit race and gender restrictions into the law. In 1802, Ohio disenfranchised African Americans, and the New York constitution of 1821 imposed a property-holding requirement on black voters. A striking case of sexual discrimination occurred in New Jersey, where the state constitution of 1776 had granted the voting franchise to all property holders. As Federalists and Republicans competed for power, they ignored customary gender rules and urged property-owning single women and widows to vote. Sensing a threat to men's monopoly on politics, the New Jersey legislature in 1807 invoked both biology and custom to limit voting to men only: "Women, generally, are neither by nature, nor habit, nor education, nor by their necessary condition in society fitted to perform this duty with credit to themselves or advantage to the public."

**Republican Motherhood**    The controversy over women's political rights mirrored a debate over authority within the household. Traditionally, most American women had spent their active adult years working as farmwives and bearing and nurturing children. However, after 1800, the birthrate in the northern states dropped significantly. In the farming village of Sturbridge in central Massachusetts, women now bore an average of six children; their grandmothers had usually given birth to eight or nine. In the growing seaport cities, native-born white women now bore an average of only four children.

The United States was among the first nations to experience this sharp decline in the birthrate — what historians call the **demographic transition**. There were several causes. Thousands of young men migrated to the trans-Appalachian west, which increased the number of never-married women in the East and delayed marriage for many more. Women who married in their late twenties had fewer children. In addition, white urban middle-class couples deliberately limited the size of their families. Fathers wanted to leave children an adequate inheritance, while mothers, influenced by new ideas of individualism and self-achievement, refused to spend their entire adulthood rearing children. After having four or five children, these couples used birth control or abstained from sexual intercourse.

Even as women bore fewer children, they accepted greater responsibility for the welfare of the family. In his *Thoughts on Female Education* (1787), Philadelphia physician Benjamin Rush argued that young women should ensure their husbands' "perseverance in the paths of rectitude" and called for loyal "republican mothers" who would instruct "their sons in the principles of liberty and government."

Christian ministers readily embraced this idea of **republican motherhood**. "Preserving virtue and instructing the young are not the fancied, but the real 'Rights of Women,'" the Reverend Thomas Bernard told the Female Charitable Society of Salem, Massachusetts. He urged his audience to dismiss public roles for women, such as voting or serving on juries, that English feminist Mary Wollstonecraft had advocated in *A Vindication of the Rights of Woman* (1792). Instead, women should care for their children, a responsibility that gave them "an extensive power over the fortunes

**The Wedding, 1805** Bride and groom stare intently into each other's eyes as they exchange vows, suggesting that their union was a love match, not an arranged marriage based on economic calculation. The plain costumes of the guests and the sparse furnishings of the room suggest that the unknown artist may have provided us with a picture of a rural Quaker wedding. The Granger Collection, New York.

of man in every generation." As ordinary white men voted in unprecedented num-bers, their wives were expected to exercise influence in their homes, not in public.

**Debates over Education** Although families provided most moral and intellectual training, republican ideology encouraged publicly supported schooling. Bostonian Caleb Bingham, an influential textbook author, called for "an equal distribution of knowledge to make us emphatically a 'republic of letters.'" Farmers, artisans, and laborers wanted elementary schools that would instruct their children in the "three Rs"—reading, 'riting, and 'rithmetic—and make them literate enough to read the Bible. In New England, locally funded public schools offered basic instruction to most boys and some girls. In other regions, there were few publicly supported schools, and only 25 percent of the boys and perhaps 10 percent of the girls attended private institutions or had personal tutors.

Although many state constitutions encouraged support for education, few leg-islatures acted until the 1820s. Then a new generation of educational reformers established statewide standards. To encourage students, the reformers chose text-books such as Parson Mason Weems's *The Life of George Washington* (c. 1800), which praised honesty and hard work and condemned gambling, drinking, and laziness. To bolster patriotism and shared cultural ideals, reformers required the study of American history. As a New Hampshire schoolboy, Thomas Low recalled: "We were taught every day and in every way that ours was the freest, the happiest, and soon to be the greatest and most powerful country of the world."

**Slavery and National Politics**   As the northern states ended human bondage, the South's commitment to slavery became a political issue. At the Philadelphia convention in 1787, northern delegates had reluctantly accepted clauses allowing slave imports for twenty years and guaranteeing the return of fugitive slaves (Chapter 6). Seeking even more protection for their "peculiar institution," southerners in the new national legislature won approval of James Madison's resolution that "Congress have no authority to interfere in the emancipation of slaves, or in the treatment of them within any of the States."

Nonetheless, slavery remained a contested issue. When Congress outlawed the Atlantic slave trade in 1808, some northern representatives demanded an end to the trade in slaves between states. Southern leaders responded with a forceful defense of their labor system. "A large majority of people in the Southern states do not consider slavery as even an evil," declared one congressman. The South's political clout — its domination of the presidency and the Senate — ensured that the national government would protect slavery.

**African Americans Speak Out**   Heartened by the end of the Atlantic slave trade, black abolitionists spoke out. In speeches and pamphlets, Henry Sipkins and Henry Johnson pointed out that slavery — "relentless tyranny," they called it — was a central legacy of America's colonial history. For inspiration, they looked to the Haitian Revolution; for collective support, they joined in secret societies, such as Prince Hall's African Lodge of Freemasons in Boston. Initially, black (and white) antislavery advocates hoped that slavery would die out naturally as the tobacco economy declined. The cotton boom ended that hope.

As some Americans campaigned against slavery, a group of prominent citizens founded the **American Colonization Society** in 1817. Its leaders argued for gradual emancipation plans such as the ones adopted in northern states after the Revolution. Most believed that emancipation should include compensation to masters and that freedpeople, conceived as alien "Africans," should be deported from the United States. According to Henry Clay — a society member, Speaker of the House of Representatives, and a slave owner — racial bondage hindered economic progress, but emancipation without removal would cause "a civil war that would end in the extermination or subjugation of the one race or the other." Few slave owners responded to the society's plea. It resettled only about 6,000 African Americans in Liberia, its colony on the west coast of Africa.

Most free blacks strongly opposed such colonization schemes because they saw themselves as Americans. As the African American minister Richard Allen put it, "This land which we have watered with our tears and our blood is now our mother country." Allen spoke from experience. Born into slavery in Philadelphia in 1760 and sold to a farmer in Delaware, Allen grew up in bondage. In 1777, Freeborn Garretson, an itinerant preacher, converted Allen to Methodism and convinced Allen's owner that on Judgment Day, slaveholders would be "weighted in the balance, and . . . found wanting." Allowed to buy his freedom, Allen became a Methodist minister in Philadelphia. In 1795, Allen formed a separate black congregation, the Bethel Church; in 1816, he became the first bishop of a new denomination: the African Methodist Episcopal Church (Chapter 10). Two years later, 3,000 African Americans met in Allen's church to condemn colonization and to claim American citizenship. Sounding the principles of democratic republicanism, they vowed to defy racial prejudice and advance in American society using "those opportunities . . . which the Constitution and the laws allow to all."

## The Missouri Crisis, 1819–1821

The abject failure of colonization set the stage for a major battle over slavery. In 1818, Congressman Nathaniel Macon of North Carolina warned that radical members of the "bible and peace societies" intended to place "the question of emancipation" on the national political agenda. When Missouri applied for admission to the Union in 1819, Congressman James Tallmadge of New York did just that: he declared that he would support statehood for Missouri only if its constitution banned the entry of new slaves and provided for the emancipation of existing bonds-people. Missouri whites rejected Tallmadge's proposals, and the northern majority in the House of Representatives blocked the territory's admission.

White southerners were horrified. "It is believed by some, & feared by others," Alabama senator John Walker reported from Washington, that Tallmadge's amendment was "merely the entering wedge and that it points already to a total emancipation of the blacks." Underlining their commitment to slavery, southerners used their power in the Senate—where they held half the seats—to withhold statehood from Maine, which was seeking to separate itself from Massachusetts.

**Constitutional Issues**  In the ensuing debate, southerners advanced three constitutional arguments. First, they invoked the principle of "equal rights," arguing that Congress could not impose conditions on Missouri that it had not imposed on other territories. Second, they maintained that the Constitution guaranteed a state's sovereignty with respect to its internal affairs and domestic institutions, such as slavery and marriage. Finally, they insisted that Congress had no authority to infringe on the property rights of individual slaveholders. Southern leaders began to justify slavery on religious grounds. "Christ himself gave a sanction to slavery," declared Senator William Smith of South Carolina.

Controversy raged in Congress and the press for two years before Henry Clay devised a series of political agreements known collectively as the **Missouri Compromise**. Faced with unwavering southern opposition to Tallmadge's amendment, a group of northern congressmen deserted the antislavery coalition. They accepted a deal that allowed Maine to enter the Union as a free state in 1820 and Missouri to follow as a slave state in 1821. This bargain preserved a balance in the Senate between North and South and set a precedent for future admissions to the Union. For their part, southern senators accepted the prohibition of slavery in most of the Louisiana Purchase, all the lands north of latitude 36°30′ except for the state of Missouri (Map 9.2).

As they had in the Philadelphia convention of 1787, white politicians preserved the Union by compromising over slavery. However, the delegates in Philadelphia had

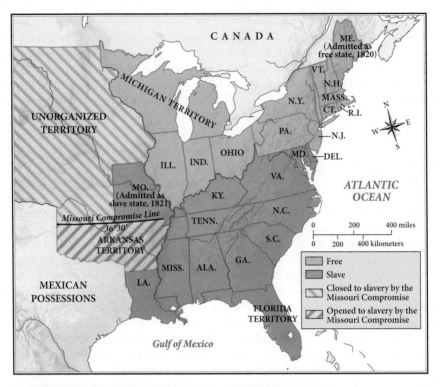

**MAP 9.2   The Missouri Compromise, 1820–1821**
The Missouri Compromise resolved for a generation the issue of slavery in the lands of the Louisiana Purchase. The agreement prohibited slavery north of the Missouri Compromise line (36°30′ north latitude), with the exception of the state of Missouri. To maintain an equal number of senators from free and slave states in the U.S. Congress, the compromise provided for the nearly simultaneous admission to the Union of Missouri and Maine.

resolved their differences in two months; it took Congress two years to work out the Missouri Compromise, which even then did not command universal support. "[B]eware," the *Richmond Enquirer* protested sharply as southern representatives agreed to exclude slavery from most of the Louisiana Purchase: "What is a territorial restriction to-day becomes a state restriction tomorrow." The fate of western lands, enslaved blacks, and the Union itself were now intertwined, raising the specter of civil war and the end of the American experiment. As the aging Thomas Jefferson exclaimed during the Missouri crisis, "This momentous question, like a fire-bell in the night, awakened and filled me with terror."

## The Election of 1824

These pressing political concerns came to the fore as the structure of national politics fractured, bringing the "era of good feeling" to an abrupt end. The advance of political democracy had led to the demise of the Federalist Party, while the

Republican Party splintered into competing factions (Chapter 7). Now, as the election of 1824 approached, five Republican candidates campaigned for the presidency. Three were veterans of President James Monroe's cabinet: Secretary of State John Quincy Adams, the son of former president John Adams; Secretary of War John C. Calhoun; and Secretary of the Treasury William H. Crawford. The other candidates were Henry Clay of Kentucky, the hard-drinking, dynamic Speaker of the House of Representatives; and General Andrew Jackson, now a senator from Tennessee. When the Republican caucus in Congress selected Crawford as the party's official nominee, the other candidates took their case to the voters. Thanks to democratic reforms, eighteen of the twenty-four states required popular elections (rather than a vote of the state legislature) to choose their representatives to the electoral college.

Each candidate had strengths. John Quincy Adams enjoyed national recognition for his diplomatic successes as secretary of state, and his family's prestige in Massachusetts ensured him the electoral votes of New England. Henry Clay based his candidacy on the **American System**, his integrated mercantilist program of national economic development. Clay wanted to strengthen the Second Bank of the United States, raise tariffs, and use tariff revenues to finance **internal improvements**, that is, public works such as roads and canals. His nationalistic program won praise in the Northwest, which needed better transportation, but elicited sharp criticism in the South, which relied on rivers to market its cotton and had few manufacturing industries to protect. William Crawford of Georgia, an ideological heir of Thomas Jefferson, denounced Clay's American System as a scheme to "consolidate" political power in Washington. Concluding that he could not defeat Crawford, John C. Calhoun of South Carolina withdrew from the race and endorsed Andrew Jackson.

As the hero of the Battle of New Orleans, Jackson benefitted from the surge of patriotism after the War of 1812. Born in the Carolina backcountry, Jackson settled in Nashville, Tennessee, where he formed ties to influential families through marriage and a career as an attorney and a slave-owning cotton planter. His rise from common origins symbolized the new democratic age, and his reputation as a "plain solid republican" attracted voters in all regions. Still, Jackson's strong showing in the electoral college surprised most political leaders. The Tennessee senator received 99 electoral votes; Adams, 84 votes; Crawford, struck down by a stroke during the campaign, won 41; and Clay finished with 37 (Map 9.3).

Because no candidate received an absolute majority, the Twelfth Amendment to the Constitution (ratified in 1804) set the rules: the House of Representatives would choose the president from among the three highest vote-getters. This procedure hurt Jackson because many congressmen feared that the rough-hewn "military chieftain" might become a tyrant. Excluded from the race, Henry Clay used his influence as Speaker of the House to thwart Jackson's election. Clay assembled a coalition of representatives from New England and the Ohio River Valley that voted Adams into the presidency in 1825. Adams showed his gratitude by appointing Clay his secretary of state, the traditional stepping-stone to the presidency. Clay's appointment was politically fatal for both men: Jackson's supporters accused Clay and Adams of making a **corrupt bargain**, and they vowed to oppose Adams's policies and to prevent Clay's rise to the presidency.

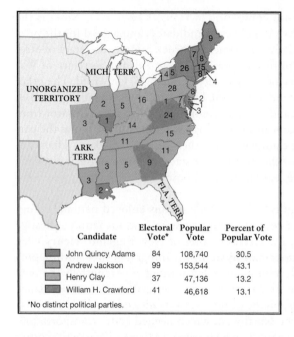

| Candidate | Electoral Vote* | Popular Vote | Percent of Popular Vote |
|---|---|---|---|
| John Quincy Adams | 84 | 108,740 | 30.5 |
| Andrew Jackson | 99 | 153,544 | 43.1 |
| Henry Clay | 37 | 47,136 | 13.2 |
| William H. Crawford | 41 | 46,618 | 13.1 |

*No distinct political parties.

**MAP 9.3  The Presidential Election of 1824**
Regional voting was the dominant pattern in 1824. John Quincy Adams captured every electoral vote in New England and most of those in New York; Henry Clay carried Ohio and Kentucky, the most populous trans-Appalachian states, as well as Missouri; and William Crawford took the southern states of Virginia and Georgia. Only Andrew Jackson claimed a national constituency, winning Pennsylvania and New Jersey in the East, Indiana and most of Illinois in the Midwest, and much of the South. Only 356,000 Americans voted, about 27 percent of the eligible electorate.

## The Last Notable President: John Quincy Adams

As president, Adams called for bold national action. "The moral purpose of the Creator," he told Congress, was to use the president to "improve the conditions of himself and his fellow men." Adams called for the establishment of a national university in Washington, scientific explorations in the Far West, and a uniform standard of weights and measures. Most important, he endorsed Henry Clay's American System and its three key elements: protective tariffs to stimulate manufacturing, federally subsidized roads and canals to facilitate commerce, and a national bank to control credit and provide a uniform currency.

**The Demise of the American System**   Manufacturers, entrepreneurs, and farmers in the Northeast and Midwest welcomed Adams's proposals. However, his policies won little support in the South, where planters opposed protective tariffs because these taxes raised the price of manufactures. Southern smallholders also feared powerful banks that could force them into bankruptcy. From his deathbed, Thomas Jefferson condemned Adams for promoting the rule of a monied "aristocracy" over "the plundered ploughman and beggared yeomanry."

Other politicians objected to the American System on constitutional grounds. In 1817, President Madison had vetoed the Bonus Bill, which proposed using the national government's income from the Second Bank of the United States to fund improvement projects in the states. Such projects, Madison argued, were the sole responsibility of the states, a sentiment shared by the Republican followers of Thomas Jefferson. In 1824, Martin Van Buren likewise declared his allegiance to the constitutional "doctrines of the Jefferson School" and his opposition to "consolidated government," a powerful and potentially oppressive national administration. Now a member of the U.S. Senate, Van Buren helped to defeat most of Adams's proposed subsidies for roads and canals.

**The Tariff Battle**    The major battle of the Adams administration came over tariffs. The Tariff of 1816 had placed relatively high duties on imports of cheap English cotton cloth, allowing New England textile producers to control that segment of the market. In 1824, Adams and Clay secured a new tariff that protected New England and Pennsylvania manufacturers from more expensive woolen and cotton textiles and also English iron goods. Without these tariffs, British imports would have dominated the market and slowed American industrial development.

Recognizing the appeal of tariffs, Van Buren and his Jacksonian allies hopped on the bandwagon. By increasing duties on wool, hemp, and other imported raw materials, they hoped to win the support of farmers in New York, Ohio, and Kentucky for Jackson's presidential candidacy in 1828. The tariff had become a political weapon. "I fear this tariff thing," remarked Thomas Cooper, the president of the College of South Carolina and an advocate of free trade. "By some strange mechanical contrivance [it has become] . . . a machine for manufacturing Presidents, instead of broadcloths, and bed blankets." Disregarding southern protests, northern Jacksonians joined with supporters of Adams and Clay to enact the Tariff of 1828, which raised duties significantly on raw materials, textiles, and iron goods.

The new tariff cost southerners about $100 million a year. Planters had to buy either higher-cost American textiles and iron goods, thus enriching northeastern businesses and workers, or highly taxed British imports, thus paying the expenses of the national government. The new tariff was "little less than legalized pillage," an Alabama legislator declared, calling it a **Tariff of Abominations**. Ignoring the Jacksonians' support for the Tariff of 1828, most southerners heaped blame on President Adams.

Southern governments also criticized Adams's Indian policy. A deeply moral man, the president supported the treaty-guaranteed land rights of Native Americans against expansion-minded whites. In 1825, U.S. commissioners had secured a treaty from one faction of Creeks ceding its lands in Georgia to the United States for eventual sale to the state's citizens. When the Creek National Council claimed the treaty was fraudulent, Adams called for new negotiations. In response, Georgia governor George M. Troup attacked the president as a "public enemy . . . the unblushing ally of the savages." Mobilizing Georgia's congressional delegation, Troup persuaded Congress to extinguish the Creeks' land titles, forcing most Creeks to leave the state.

Elsewhere, Adams's primary weakness was his out-of-date political style. He was aloof, inflexible, and paternalistic. When Congress rejected his economic policies, Adams accused its members of following the whims of public opinion and told them not to be enfeebled "by the will of our constituents." Rather than "run" for reelection in 1828, Adams "stood" for it, telling friends, "If my country wants my services, she must ask for them."

## "The Democracy" and the Election of 1828

Martin Van Buren and the politicians handling Andrew Jackson's campaign for the presidency had no reservations about running for office. To put Jackson in the White House, Van Buren revived the political coalition created by Thomas Jefferson, championing policies that appealed to both southern planters and northern farmers and artisans, the "plain Republicans of the North." John C. Calhoun, Jackson's running mate, brought his South Carolina allies into Van Buren's party, and Jackson's close friends in Tennessee rallied voters throughout the Old Southwest. The Little Magician hoped that a national party would reconcile the diverse "interests" that, as James Madison suggested in "Federalist No. 10" (Chapter 6), inevitably existed in a large republic. Equally important, added Jackson's ally Duff Green, it would put the "antislave party in the North . . . to sleep for twenty years to come."

Van Buren and the Jacksonians orchestrated a massive publicity campaign. In New York, fifty Democrat-funded newspapers declared their support for Jackson. Elsewhere, Jacksonians used mass meetings, torchlight parades, and barbecues to celebrate the candidate's frontier origin and rise to fame. They praised "Old Hickory" as a "natural" aristocrat, a self-made man.

The Jacksonians called themselves Democrats or "the Democracy" to convey their egalitarian message. As Thomas Morris told the Ohio legislature, Democrats were fighting for equality: the republic had been corrupted by legislative charters that gave "a few individuals rights and privileges not enjoyed by the citizens at large." Morris promised that the Democracy would destroy such "artificial distinction." Jackson himself declared that "equality among the people in the rights conferred by government" was the "great radical principle of freedom."

Jackson's message appealed to many social groups. His hostility to corporations and to Clay's American System won support from northeastern artisans and workers who felt threatened by industrialization. Jackson captured the votes of Pennsylvania ironworkers and New York farmers who had benefitted from the controversial Tariff of Abominations. Yet, by astutely declaring his support for a "judicious" tariff that would balance regional interests, Jackson remained popular in the South. In the Southeast and Midwest, Jackson's well-known hostility toward Native Americans reassured white farmers seeking Indian removal.

The Democrats' celebration of popular rule carried Jackson into office. In 1824, about one-quarter of the electorate had voted; in 1828, more than one-half went to the polls, and 56 percent voted for the Tennessee senator — the first president from a trans-Appalachian state (Map 9.4). Jackson's popularity and sharp temper frightened men of wealth. Senator Daniel Webster of Massachusetts, a former Federalist and now a corporate lawyer, warned his clients that the new president would "bring a breeze with him. Which way it will blow, I cannot tell [but] . . . my fear is stronger than my hope." Supreme Court justice Joseph Story shared Webster's apprehensions. Watching an unruly Inauguration Day crowd climb over the elegant White House furniture to congratulate Jackson, Story lamented that "the reign of King 'Mob' seemed triumphant."

| IN YOUR OWN WORDS | How did Jackson and the new Democratic Party overcome sectional differences? |
|---|---|

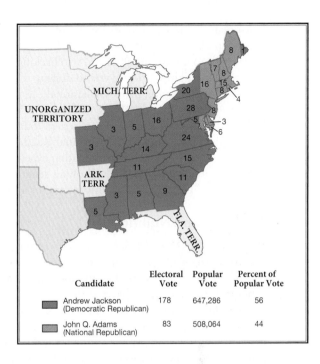

**MAP 9.4 The Presidential Election of 1828**

As in 1824, John Quincy Adams carried all of New England and some of the Mid-Atlantic states. However, Andrew Jackson swept the rest of the nation and won a resounding victory in the electoral college. Over 1.1 million American men cast ballots in 1828, more than three times the number who voted in 1824.

| Candidate | Electoral Vote | Popular Vote | Percent of Popular Vote |
|---|---|---|---|
| Andrew Jackson (Democratic Republican) | 178 | 647,286 | 56 |
| John Q. Adams (National Republican) | 83 | 508,064 | 44 |

# Jackson in Power, 1829–1837

American-style political democracy—a broad franchise, a disciplined political party, and policies favoring specific interests—ushered Andrew Jackson into office. Jackson used his popular mandate to transform the national government. During his two terms, he enhanced presidential authority, destroyed the mercantilist and nationalist American System, established a new ideology of limited government, and supported Indian removal. An Ohio supporter summed up Jackson's vision: "the Sovereignty of the People, the Rights of the States, and a Light and Simple Government."

## Jackson's Agenda: Rotation and Decentralization

To make policy, Jackson relied primarily on his so-called Kitchen Cabinet. Its most influential members were two Kentuckians, Francis Preston Blair, who edited the *Washington Globe*, and Amos Kendall, who wrote Jackson's speeches; Roger B. Taney (pronounced "tawny") of Maryland, who became attorney general, treasury secretary, and then chief justice of the Supreme Court; and Martin Van Buren, whom Jackson named secretary of state.

Following Van Buren's example in New York, Jackson used patronage to create a disciplined national party. He rejected the idea of "property in office" (that a qualified official held a position permanently) and insisted on a rotation of officeholders when a new administration took power. Rotation would not lessen expertise, Jackson insisted, because public duties were "so plain and simple that men of intelligence may readily qualify themselves for their performance." William L. Marcy, a New York

Jacksonian, offered a more realistic explanation for rotation: government jobs were like the spoils of war, and "to the victor belong the spoils of the enemy." Jackson used those spoils to reward his allies and win backing for his policies.

Jackson's highest priority was to destroy the American System. He believed that government-sponsored plans for national economic development were unconstitutional. Declaring that the "voice of the people" called for "economy in the expenditures of the Government," Jackson vetoed four internal improvement bills in 1830, including an extension of the National Road, arguing that they infringed on "the reserved powers of states." By eliminating expenses, these vetoes also undermined the case for protective tariffs. As Jacksonian senator William Smith of South Carolina pointed out, "Destroy internal improvements and you leave no motive for the tariff."

## The Tariff and Nullification

The Tariff of 1828 had helped Jackson win the presidency, but it saddled him with a major political crisis. There was fierce opposition to high tariffs throughout the South and especially in South Carolina. That state was the only one with an African American majority — 56 percent of the population in 1830 — and its slave owners, like the white sugar planters in the West Indies, feared a black rebellion. Even more, they worried about the legal abolition of slavery. The British Parliament had declared that slavery in its West Indian colonies would end in 1833; South Carolina planters, vividly recalling northern efforts to end slavery in Missouri, worried that the U.S. Congress would follow the British lead. So they attacked the tariff, both to lower rates and to discourage the use of federal power to attack slavery.

The crisis began in 1832, when Congress reenacted the Tariff of Abominations. In response, leading South Carolinians called a state convention that boldly adopted an Ordinance of Nullification declaring the tariffs of 1828 and 1832 to be null and void. The ordinance prohibited the collection of those duties in South Carolina after February 1, 1833, and threatened secession if federal officials tried to collect them.

South Carolina's act of **nullification** — the argument that a state has the right to void, within its borders, a law passed by Congress — rested on the constitutional arguments developed in *The South Carolina Exposition and Protest* (1828). Written anonymously by Vice President John C. Calhoun, the *Exposition* contended that protective tariffs and other national legislation that operated unequally on the various states lacked fairness and legitimacy. "Constitutional government and the government of a majority," Calhoun concluded, "are utterly incompatible."

Calhoun's argument echoed the claims made by Jefferson and Madison in the Kentucky and Virginia Resolutions of 1798. Those resolutions asserted that, because state-based conventions had ratified the Constitution, sovereignty lay in the states, not in the people. Beginning from this premise, Calhoun argued that a state convention could declare a congressional law to be void within the state's borders. Replying to this **states' rights** interpretation of the Constitution, which had little support in the text of the document, Senator Daniel Webster of Massachusetts presented a nationalist interpretation that celebrated popular sovereignty and Congress's responsibility to secure the "general welfare."

Jackson hoped to find a middle path between Webster's strident nationalism and Calhoun's radical doctrine of localist federalism. Jackson declared that South

Carolina's Ordinance of Nullification violated the letter of the Constitution and was "destructive of the great object for which it was formed." At his request, Congress in early 1833 passed a military Force Bill, authorizing the president to compel South Carolina's obedience to national laws. At the same time, Jackson addressed the South's objections to high import duties with a new tariff act that, over the course of a decade, reduced rates to the modest levels of 1816. Export-hungry midwestern wheat farmers joined southern planters in advocating low duties to avoid retaliatory tariffs by foreign nations. "Illinois wants a market for her agricultural products," declared Senator Sidney Breese in 1846. "[S]he wants the market of the world."

Having won the political battle by securing a tariff reduction, the South Carolina convention did not press its constitutional stance on nullification. Jackson was satisfied. He had assisted the South economically while upholding the constitutional principle of national authority—a principle that Abraham Lincoln would embrace to defend the Union during the secession crisis of 1861.

## The Bank War

In the midst of the tariff crisis, Jackson faced a major challenge from politicians who supported the **Second Bank of the United States**. Founded in Philadelphia in 1816 (Chapter 7), the bank was privately managed and operated under a twenty-year charter from the federal government, which owned 20 percent of its stock. The bank's most important role was to stabilize the nation's money supply, which consisted primarily of paper money issued by state-chartered banks. The state banks promised to redeem the notes on demand with "hard" money (or "specie")—that is, gold or silver coins minted by the U.S. or foreign governments—but there were few coins in circulation. By collecting those notes and regularly demanding specie, the Second Bank kept the state banks from issuing too much paper money and depreciating its value.

This cautious monetary policy pleased creditors—the bankers and entrepreneurs in Boston, New York, and Philadelphia, whose capital investments were underwriting economic development. However, expansion-minded bankers, including friends of Jackson's in Nashville, demanded an end to central oversight. Moreover, many ordinary Americans worried that the Second Bank would force weak banks to close, leaving them holding worthless paper notes. Many politicians resented the arrogance of the bank's president, Nicholas Biddle. "As to mere power," Biddle boasted, "I have been for years in the daily exercise of more personal authority than any President habitually enjoys."

**Jackson's Bank Veto** Although the Second Bank had many enemies, a political miscalculation by its friends brought its downfall. In 1832, Henry Clay and Daniel Webster persuaded Biddle to seek an early extension of the bank's charter (which still had four years to run). They had the votes in Congress to enact the required legislation and hoped to lure Jackson into a veto that would split the Democrats just before the 1832 elections.

Jackson turned the tables on Clay and Webster. He vetoed the rechartering bill with a masterful message that blended constitutional arguments with class rhetoric and patriotic fervor. Adopting the position taken by Thomas Jefferson in 1793, Jackson declared that Congress had no constitutional authority to charter a national bank. He condemned the bank as "subversive of the rights of the States," "dangerous to the liberties of the people," and a privileged monopoly that promoted "the advancement of the few at the expense of . . . farmers, mechanics, and laborers." Finally, the president noted that British aristocrats owned much of the bank's stock. Such a powerful institution should be "purely American," Jackson declared with patriotic zeal.

Jackson's attack on the bank carried him to victory in 1832. Old Hickory and Martin Van Buren, his new running mate, overwhelmed Henry Clay, who headed the National Republican ticket, by 219 to 49 electoral votes. Jackson's most fervent supporters were eastern workers and western farmers, who blamed the Second Bank for high prices and stagnant farm income. Other Jackson supporters had prospered during a decade of strong economic growth. Thousands of middle-class Americans — lawyers, clerks, shopkeepers, and artisans — had used the opportunity to rise in the world and cheered Jackson's attack on privileged corporations.

**The Bank Destroyed**   Early in 1833, Jackson met their wishes by appointing Roger B. Taney, a strong opponent of corporate privilege, as head of the Treasury Department. Taney promptly transferred the federal government's gold and silver from the Second Bank to various state banks, which critics labeled Jackson's "pet banks." To justify this abrupt (and probably illegal) transfer, Jackson declared that his reelection represented "the decision of the people against the bank" and gave him a mandate to destroy it. This sweeping claim of presidential power was new and radical. Never before had a president claimed that victory at the polls allowed him to pursue a controversial policy or to act independently of Congress.

The "bank war" escalated into an all-out political battle. In March 1834, Jackson's opponents in the Senate passed a resolution composed by Henry Clay that censured the president and warned of executive tyranny: "We are in the midst of a revolution, hitherto bloodless, but rapidly descending towards a total change of the pure republican character of the Government, and the concentration of all power in the hands of one man." The censure did not deter Jackson. "The Bank is trying to kill me but I will kill it," he vowed to Van Buren. And so he did. When the Second Bank's national charter expired in 1836, Jackson prevented its renewal.

Jackson had destroyed both national banking — the handiwork of Alexander Hamilton — and the American System of protective tariffs and public works created by Henry Clay and John Quincy Adams. The result was a profound check on economic activism and innovative policymaking by the national government. "All is gone," observed a Washington newspaper correspondent. "All is gone, which the General Government was instituted to create and preserve."

## Indian Removal

The status of Native American peoples posed an equally complex political problem. By the late 1820s, white voices throughout the South and Midwest demanded the resettlement of Indian peoples west of the Mississippi River. Many whites who were sympathetic to Native Americans also favored resettlement. Removal to the West seemed the only way to protect Indians from alcoholism, financial exploitation, and cultural decline.

However, most Indians did not want to leave their ancestral lands. For centuries, Cherokees and Creeks had lived in Georgia, Tennessee, and Alabama; Chickasaws and Choctaws in Mississippi and Alabama; and Seminoles in Florida. During the War of 1812, Andrew Jackson had forced the Creeks to relinquish millions of acres, but Indian nations still controlled vast tracts and wanted to keep them.

**Cherokee Resistance**   But on what terms? Some Indians had adopted white ways. An 1825 census revealed that various Cherokees owned 33 gristmills, 13 sawmills, 2,400 spinning wheels, 760 looms, and 2,900 plows. Many of these owners were mixed-race, the offspring of white traders and Indian women. They had grown up in a bicultural world, knew the political and economic ways of whites, and often favored assimilation into white society. Indeed, some of these mixed-race people were indistinguishable from southern planters. At his death in 1809, Georgia Cherokee James Vann owned one hundred black slaves, two trading posts, and a gristmill. Three decades later, forty other mixed-blood Cherokee families each owned ten or more African American workers.

Prominent mixed-race Cherokees believed that integration into American life was the best way to protect their property and the lands of their people. In 1821, Sequoyah, a part-Cherokee silversmith, perfected a system of writing for the Cherokee language; six years later, mixed-race Cherokees devised a new charter of Cherokee government modeled directly on the U.S. Constitution. "You asked us to throw off the hunter and warrior state," Cherokee John Ridge told a Philadelphia audience in 1832. "We did so. You asked us to form a republican government: We did so. . . . You asked us to learn to read: We did so. You asked us to cast away our idols, and worship your God: We did so." Full-blood Cherokees, who made up 90 percent of the population, resisted many of these cultural and political innovations but were equally determined to retain their ancestral lands. "We would not receive money for land in which our fathers and friends are buried," one full-blood chief declared. "We love our land; it is our mother."

What the Cherokees did or wanted carried no weight with the Georgia legislature. In 1802, Georgia had given up its western land claims in return for a federal promise to extinguish Indian landholdings in the state. Now it demanded fulfillment of that pledge. Having spent his military career fighting Indians and seizing their lands, Andrew Jackson gave full support to Georgia. On assuming the presidency, he withdrew the federal troops that had protected Indian enclaves there and in Alabama and Mississippi. The states, he declared, were sovereign within their borders.

**The Removal Act and Its Aftermath**   Jackson then pushed the **Indian Removal Act of 1830** through Congress over the determined opposition of evangelical Protestant men — and women. To block removal, Catharine Beecher and Lydia Sigourney composed a Ladies Circular that urged "benevolent ladies" to use "prayers and exertions to avert the calamity of removal." Women from across the nation flooded Congress with petitions. Nonetheless, Jackson's bill squeaked through the House of Representatives by a vote of 102 to 97.

The Removal Act created the Indian Territory on national lands acquired in the Louisiana Purchase and located in present-day Oklahoma and Kansas. It promised money and reserved land to Native American peoples who would give up their ancestral holdings east of the Mississippi River. Government officials promised the Indians that they could live on their new land, "they and all their children, as long as grass grows and water runs." However, as one Indian leader noted, on the Great Plains "water and timber are scarcely to be seen." When Chief Black Hawk and his Sauk and Fox followers refused to leave rich, well-watered farmland in western Illinois in 1832, Jackson sent troops to expel them by force. Eventually, the U.S. Army pursued Black Hawk into the Wisconsin Territory and, in the brutal eight-hour Bad Axe Massacre, killed 850 of his 1,000 warriors. Over the next five years, American diplomatic pressure and military power forced 70 Indian peoples to sign treaties and move west of the Mississippi (Map 9.5).

In the meantime, the Cherokees had carried the defense of their lands to the Supreme Court, where they claimed the status of a "foreign nation." In *Cherokee Nation v. Georgia* (1831), Chief Justice John Marshall denied that claim and declared

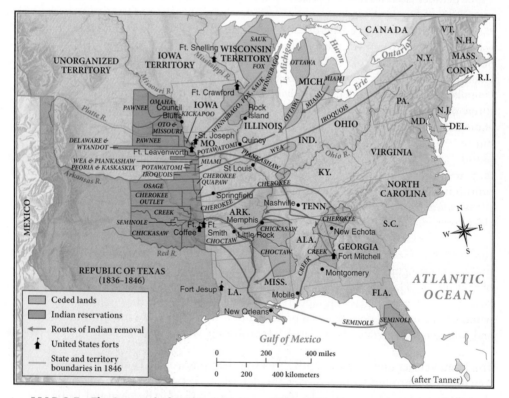

**MAP 9.5    The Removal of Native Americans, 1820–1846**

As white settlers moved west, the U.S. government forced scores of Native American communities to leave their ancestral lands. Andrew Jackson's Indian Removal Act of 1830 formalized this policy. Subsequently, many Indian peoples signed treaties that exchanged their lands in the East, Midwest, and Southeast for money and designated reservations in an Indian Territory west of the Mississippi River. When the Sauk, Fox, Cherokees, and Seminoles resisted resettlement, the government used the U.S. Army to enforce the removal policy.

that Indian peoples were "domestic dependent nations." However, in *Worcester v. Georgia* (1832), Marshall and the Court sided with the Cherokees against Georgia. Voiding Georgia's extension of state law over the Cherokees, the Court held that Indian nations were "distinct political communities, having territorial boundaries, within which their authority is exclusive [and is] guaranteed by the United States."

Instead of guaranteeing the Cherokees' territory, the U.S. government took it from them. In 1835, American officials and a minority Cherokee faction negotiated the Treaty of New Echota, which specified that Cherokees would resettle in Indian Territory. When only 2,000 of 17,000 Cherokees had moved by the May 1838 deadline, President Martin Van Buren ordered General Winfield Scott to enforce the treaty. Scott's army rounded up 14,000 Cherokees (including mixed-race African Cherokees) and marched them 1,200 miles, an arduous journey that became known as the **Trail of Tears**. Along the way, 3,000 Indians died of starvation and exposure. Once in Oklahoma, the Cherokees excluded anyone of "negro or mulatto parentage" from governmental office, thereby affirming that full citizenship in their nation was racially defined. Just as the United States was a "white man's country," so Indian Territory would be a "red man's country."

Pressed by their white neighbors, the Creeks, Chickasaws, and Choctaws accepted grants of land west of the Mississippi, leaving the Seminoles in Florida as the only numerically significant Indian people remaining in the Southeast. Government pressure persuaded about half of the Seminoles to migrate to Indian Territory, but families whose ancestors had intermarried with runaway slaves feared the emphasis on

**Andrew Jackson as the Great Father, 1835** Jackson championed the Indian Removal Act of 1830, which created the Indian Territory on lands obtained in the Louisiana Purchase and forced dozens of Native American nations throughout the eastern United States to move across the Mississippi. Jackson professed a concern for Native American welfare, prompting this sarcastic portrayal as the "Great Father" tending to the needs of his diminutive Native American "children." Jackson is portrayed unflatteringly, with dark skin that seems to suggest his own racial ambiguity. William L. Clements Library, University of Michigan.

"blood purity" there. During the 1840s, they fought a successful guerrilla war against the U.S. Army and retained their lands in central Florida. These Seminoles were the exception: the Jacksonians had forced the removal of most eastern Indian peoples.

## Jackson's Impact

Jackson's legacy is complex. He expanded the authority of the nation's chief executive: as Jackson put it, "The President is the direct representative of the American people." Assuming that role during the nullification crisis, he upheld national authority by threatening the use of military force, laying the foundation for Lincoln's defense of the Union a generation later. At the same time (and somewhat contradictorily), Jackson curbed the reach of the national government. By undermining Henry Clay's American System of national banking, protective tariffs, and internal improvements, Jackson reinvigorated the Jeffersonian tradition of a limited and frugal central government.

**The Taney Court**    Jackson also undermined the constitutional jurisprudence of John Marshall by appointing Roger B. Taney as his successor in 1835. During his long tenure as chief justice (1835–1864), Taney partially reversed the nationalist and vested-property-rights decisions of the Marshall Court and gave constitutional legitimacy to Jackson's policies of states' rights and free enterprise. In the landmark case *Charles River Bridge Co. v. Warren Bridge Co.* (1837), Taney declared that a legislative charter—in this case, to build and operate a toll bridge—did not necessarily bestow a monopoly, and that a legislature could charter a competing bridge to promote the general welfare: "While the rights of private property are sacredly guarded, we must not forget that the community also has rights." This decision directly challenged Marshall's interpretation of the contract clause of the Constitution in *Dartmouth College v. Woodward* (1819), which had stressed the binding nature of public charters and the sanctity of "vested rights" (Chapter 7). By limiting the property claims of existing canal and turnpike companies, Taney's decision allowed legislatures to charter competing railroads that would provide cheaper and more efficient transportation.

The Taney Court also limited Marshall's nationalistic interpretation of the commerce clause by enhancing the regulatory role of state governments. For example, in *Mayor of New York v. Miln* (1837), the Taney Court ruled that New York State could use its "police power" to inspect the health of arriving immigrants. The Court also restored to the states some of the economic powers they had exercised prior to the Constitution of 1787. In *Briscoe v. Bank of Kentucky* (1837), the justices allowed a bank owned by the state of Kentucky to issue currency, despite the wording of Article 1, Section 10 of the Constitution, which prohibits states from issuing "bills of credit."

**States Revise Their Constitutions**    Inspired by Jackson and Taney, Democrats in the various states mounted their own constitutional revolutions. Between 1830 and 1860, twenty states called conventions that furthered democratic principles by reapportioning state legislatures on the basis of population and giving the vote to all white men. Voters also had more power because the new documents mandated the election, rather than the appointment, of most public officials, including sheriffs, justices of the peace, and judges.

The new constitutions also embodied the principles of **classical liberalism, or laissez-faire**, by limiting the government's role in the economy. (Twenty-first-century social-welfare liberalism endorses the opposite principle: that government should intervene in economic and social life.) As president, Jackson had destroyed the American System, and his disciples now attacked the state-based Commonwealth System (see Chapter 8), which used chartered corporations and state funds to promote economic development. Most Jackson-era constitutions prohibited states from granting special charters to corporations and extending loans and credit guarantees to private businesses. "If there is any danger to be feared in . . . government," declared a New Jersey Democrat, "it is the danger of associated wealth, with special privileges." The revised constitutions also protected taxpayers by setting strict limits on state debt. Said New York reformer Michael Hoffman, "We will not trust the legislature with the power of creating indefinite mortgages on the people's property."

"The world is governed too much," the Jacksonians proclaimed as they embraced a small-government, laissez-faire outlook and celebrated the power of ordinary people to make decisions in the voting booth and the marketplace.

| IN YOUR OWN WORDS | What were the constitutional arguments for and against internal improvements, the tariff, and nullification? |
|---|---|

# Class, Culture, and the Second Party System

The rise of the Democracy and Jackson's tumultuous presidency sparked the creation in the mid-1830s of a second national party: the **Whigs**. For the next two decades, Whigs and Democrats competed fiercely for votes and appealed to different cultural groups. Many evangelical Protestants became Whigs, while most Catholic immigrants and traditional Protestants joined the Democrats. By debating issues of economic policy, class power, and moral reform, party politicians offered Americans a choice between competing programs and political leaders. The First Party System in United States politics, pitting Federalists against Jeffersonian Republicans, had ended with the collapse of the Federalist Party and the "era of good feeling." The Second Party System, pitting Whigs against Democrats, persisted until the Whig Party fractured in the 1850s.

## The Whig Worldview

The Whig Party arose in 1834, when a group of congressmen contested Andrew Jackson's policies and his high-handed, "kinglike" conduct. They took the name *Whigs* to identify themselves with the pre-Revolutionary American and British parties—also called Whigs—that had opposed the arbitrary actions of British monarchs. The Whigs accused "King Andrew I" of violating the Constitution by creating a spoils system and undermining elected legislators, whom they saw as the true representatives of the sovereign people. One Whig accused Jackson of ruling in a manner "more absolute than that of any absolute monarchy of Europe."

Initially, the Whigs consisted of political factions with distinct points of view. However, guided by Senators Webster of Massachusetts, Clay of Kentucky, and

Calhoun of South Carolina, they gradually coalesced into a party with a distinctive stance and coherent ideology. The Whigs celebrated the entrepreneur and the enterprising individual: "This is a country of self-made men," they boasted, pointing to the relative absence of permanent distinctions of class and status among white citizens. Embracing the Industrial Revolution, northern Whigs welcomed the investments of "moneyed capitalists," which provided workers with jobs and "bread, clothing and homes." Whig congressman Edward Everett championed a "holy alliance" among laborers, owners, and governments and called for a return to Henry Clay's American System. Many New England and Pennsylvania textile and iron workers shared Everett's vision because they benefitted directly from protective tariffs.

**Calhoun's Dissent**    Support for the Whigs in the South — less widespread than that in the North — rested on the appeal of specific policies and politicians. Some southern Whigs were wealthy planters who invested in railroads and banks or sold their cotton to New York merchants. But the majority were poorer whites who resented the power and policies of low-country planters, most of whom were Democrats.

Southern Whigs rejected their party's enthusiasm for high tariffs and social mobility, and John C. Calhoun was their spokesman. Extremely conscious of class divisions in society, Calhoun believed that northern Whigs' rhetoric of equal opportunity was contradicted not only by slavery, which he considered a fundamental American institution, but also by the wage-labor system of industrial capitalism. "There is and always has been in an advanced state of wealth and civilization a conflict between labor and capital," Calhoun declared in 1837. He urged slave owners and factory owners to unite against their common foe: the working class of enslaved blacks and propertyless whites.

Most northern Whigs denied Calhoun's class-conscious social ideology. "A clear and well-defined line between capital and labor" might fit the slave South or class-ridden Europe, Daniel Webster conceded, but in the North "this distinction grows less and less definite as commerce advances." Ignoring the ever-increasing numbers of propertyless immigrants and native-born wageworkers, Webster focused on the growing size of the middle class, whose members generally favored Whig candidates. In the election of 1834, the Whigs took control of the House of Representatives by appealing to evangelical Protestants and upwardly mobile families — prosperous farmers, small-town merchants, and skilled industrial workers in New England, New York, and the new communities along the Great Lakes.

**Anti-Masons Become Whigs**    Many Whig voters in 1834 had previously supported the Anti-Masons, a powerful but short-lived party that formed in the late 1820s. As its name implies, Anti-Masons opposed the Order of Freemasonry. Freemasonry began in Europe as an organization of men seeking moral improvement by promoting the welfare and unity of humanity. Many Masons espoused republicanism, and the Order spread rapidly in America after the Revolution. Its ideology, mysterious symbols, and semisecret character gave the Order an air of exclusivity that attracted ambitious businessmen and political leaders, including George Washington, Henry Clay, and Andrew Jackson. In New York State alone by the mid-1820s, there were more than 20,000 Masons, organized into 450 local lodges. However, after the kidnapping and murder in 1826 of William Morgan, a New York Mason who had threatened to reveal the Order's secrets, the Freemasons fell into disrepute. Thurlow Weed, a newspaper editor in Rochester, New York, spearheaded an Anti-Masonic Party, which condemned the Order as a secret aristocratic fraternity. The new party quickly ousted Freemasons from local and state offices, and just as quickly ran out of political steam.

Because many Anti-Masons espoused temperance, equality of opportunity, and evangelical morality, they gravitated to the Whig Party. Throughout the Northeast and Midwest, Whig politicians won election by proposing legal curbs on the sale of alcohol and local ordinances that preserved Sunday as a day of worship. The Whigs also secured the votes of farmers, bankers, and shopkeepers, who favored Henry Clay's American System. For these citizens of the growing Midwest, the Whigs' program of government subsidies for roads, canals, and bridges was as important as their moral agenda.

In the election of 1836, the Whig Party faced Martin Van Buren, the architect of the Democratic Party and Jackson's handpicked successor. Like Jackson, Van Buren denounced the American System and warned that its revival would create a "consolidated government." Positioning himself as a defender of individual rights, Van Buren also condemned the efforts of Whigs and moral reformers to enact state laws imposing temperance and national laws abolishing slavery. "The government is best which governs least" became his motto in economic, cultural, and racial matters.

To oppose Van Buren, the Whigs ran four candidates, each with a strong regional reputation. They hoped to garner enough electoral votes to throw the contest into the House of Representatives. However, the Whig tally—73 electoral votes collected by William Henry Harrison of Ohio, 26 by Hugh L. White of Tennessee, 14 by Daniel Webster of Massachusetts, and 11 by W. P. Mangum of Georgia—fell far short of Van Buren's 170 votes. Still, the four Whigs won 49 percent of the popular vote, showing that the party's message of economic and moral improvement had broad appeal.

## Labor Politics and the Depression of 1837–1843

As the Democrats battled Whigs on the national level, they faced challenges from urban artisans and workers. Between 1828 and 1833, artisans and laborers in fifteen states formed Working Men's Parties. "Past experience teaches us that we have nothing to hope from the aristocratic orders of society," declared the New York Working Men's Party. It vowed "to send men of our own description, if we can, to the Legislature at Albany."

The new parties' agenda reflected the values and interests of ordinary urban workers. The Philadelphia Working Men's Party set out to secure "a just balance of power . . . between all the various classes." It called for the abolition of private banks, chartered monopolies, and debtors' prisons, and it demanded universal public education and a fair system of taxation. It won some victories, electing a number of assemblymen and persuading the Pennsylvania legislature in 1834 to authorize tax-supported schools. Elsewhere, Working Men's candidates won office in many cities, but their parties' weakness in statewide contests soon took a toll. By the mid-1830s, most politically active workers had joined the Democratic Party.

The Working Men's Parties left a mixed legacy. They mobilized craft workers and gave political expression to their ideology of artisan republicanism. As labor intellectual Orestes Brownson defined their distinctive vision, "All men will be independent proprietors, working on their own capitals, on their own farms, or in their own shops." However, this emphasis on proprietorship inhibited alliances between the artisan-based Working Men's Parties and the rapidly increasing class of dependent wage earners. As Joseph Weydemeyer, a close friend of Karl Marx, reported from New York in the early 1850s, many American craft workers "are incipient bourgeois, and feel themselves to be such."

The **Panic of 1837** threw the American economy — and the workers' movement — into disarray. The panic began when the Bank of England tried to boost the faltering British economy by sharply curtailing the flow of money and credit to the United States. Since 1822, British manufacturers had extended credit to southern planters to expand cotton production, and British investors had purchased millions of dollars of the canal bonds from the northern states. Suddenly deprived of British funds, American planters, merchants, and canal corporations had to withdraw gold from domestic banks to pay their foreign debts. Moreover, British textile mills drastically reduced their purchases of raw cotton, causing its price to plummet from 20 cents a pound to 10 cents or less.

Falling cotton prices and the drain of specie to Britain set off a financial panic. On May 8, the Dry Dock Bank of New York City ran out of specie, prompting worried depositors to withdraw gold and silver coins from other banks. Within two weeks, every American bank had stopped trading specie and called in its loans, turning a financial panic into an economic crisis. "This sudden overthrow of the commercial credit" had a "stunning effect," observed Henry Fox, the British minister in Washington. "The conquest of the land by a foreign power could hardly have produced a more general sense of humiliation and grief."

To stimulate the economy, state governments increased their investments in canals and railroads. However, as governments issued (or guaranteed) more bonds to finance these ventures, they were unable to pay the interest charges, sparking a severe financial crisis on both sides of the Atlantic in 1839. Nine state governments defaulted on their debts, and hard-pressed European lenders cut the flow of new capital to the United States.

The American economy fell into a deep depression. By 1843, canal construction had dropped by 90 percent, prices and wages had fallen by 50 percent, and unemployment in seaports and industrial centers had reached 20 percent. Bumper crops drove down cotton prices, pushing hundreds of planters and merchants into bankruptcy. Minister Henry Ward Beecher described a land "filled with lamentation . . . its inhabitants wandering like bereaved citizens among the ruins of an earthquake, mourning for children, for houses crushed, and property buried forever."

By creating a surplus of unemployed workers, the depression finished off the union movement and the Working Men's Parties. In 1837, six thousand masons, carpenters, and other building-trades workers lost their jobs in New York City, destroying their unions' bargaining power. By 1843, most local unions, all the national labor organizations, and all the workers' parties had disappeared.

## "Tippecanoe and Tyler Too!"

Many Americans blamed the Democrats for the depression of 1837–1843. They criticized Jackson for destroying the Second Bank and directing the Treasury Department in 1836 to issue the **Specie Circular**, an executive order that required the Treasury Department to accept only gold and silver in payment for lands in the national domain. Critics charged—mistakenly—that the Circular drained so much specie from the economy that it sparked the Panic of 1837.

The public turned its anger on Van Buren, who took office just before the panic struck. Ignoring the pleas of influential bankers, the new president refused to revoke the Specie Circular or take actions to stimulate the economy. Holding to his philosophy of limited government, Van Buren advised Congress that "the less government interferes with private pursuits the better for the general prosperity." As the depression deepened in 1839, this laissez-faire outlook commanded less and less political support. Worse, Van Buren's major piece of fiscal legislation, the Independent Treasury Act of 1840, delayed recovery by pulling federal specie out of Jackson's pet banks (where it had backed loans) and placing it in government vaults, where it had little economic impact.

**The Log Cabin Campaign** The Whigs exploited Van Buren's weakness. In 1840, they organized their first national convention and nominated William Henry Harrison of Ohio for president and John Tyler of Virginia for vice president. A military hero of the Battle of Tippecanoe and the War of 1812, Harrison was well advanced in age (sixty-eight) and had little political experience. However, the Whig leaders in Congress, Henry Clay and Daniel Webster, wanted a president who would rubber-stamp their program for protective tariffs and a national bank. An unpretentious, amiable man, Harrison told voters that Whig policies were "the only means,

**Harrison's Log Cabin and Cider Campaign** To boost the chances that William Henry Harrison would be elected president in 1840, Whig political strategists promoted him as the "log cabin and hard cider" candidate, in contrast to the aristocratic Martin Van Buren. On this patriotic cotton banner, Harrison, coming out the door of his cabin in shirtsleeves, greets a veteran who has lost a leg in service to his country. A third man bends down before a keg of hard cider, presumably intending to offer the visitor a drink. Despite Harrison's well-to-do background—the son of a prominent Virginia slaveowner, he had served as territorial governor of Indiana and in both the House and the Senate—the campaign presented him as a simple Ohio farmer. The populist appeal of the Whig campaign was misleading, but it succeeded in elevating Harrison to the White House. © Collection of the New-York Historical Society, USA/Bridgeman Images.

under Heaven, by which a poor industrious man may become a rich man without bowing to colossal wealth."

The depression stacked the political cards against Van Buren, but the election turned as much on style as on substance. It became the great "log cabin campaign"—the first time two well-organized parties competed for votes through a new style of campaigning. Whig songfests, parades, and mass meetings drew new voters into politics. Whig speakers assailed "Martin Van Ruin" as a manipulative politician with aristocratic tastes—a devotee of fancy wines, elegant clothes, and polite refinement, as indeed he was. Less truthfully, they portrayed Harrison as a self-made man who lived contentedly in a log cabin and quaffed hard cider, a drink of the common people. In fact, Harrison's father was a wealthy Virginia planter who had signed the Declaration of Independence, and Harrison himself lived in a series of elegant mansions.

The Whigs boosted their electoral hopes by welcoming women to campaign festivities—a "first" for American politics. Many Jacksonian Democrats had long embraced an ideology of aggressive manhood, likening politically minded females to "public" women, prostitutes who plied their trade in theaters and other public places. Whigs took a more restrained view of masculinity and recognized that Christian women had already entered American public life through the temperance movement and other benevolent activities. In October 1840, Daniel Webster celebrated moral reform to an audience of twelve hundred women and urged them to back Whig candidates. "This way of making politicians of their women is something new under the sun," exclaimed one Democrat, worried that it would bring more Whig men to the polls. And it did: more than 80 percent of the eligible male voters cast ballots in 1840, up from fewer than 60 percent in 1832 and 1836. Heeding the Whigs' campaign slogan "Tippecanoe and Tyler Too," they voted Harrison into the White House with 53 percent of the popular vote and gave the party a majority in Congress.

**Tyler Subverts the Whig Agenda**     Led by Clay and Webster, the Whigs in Congress prepared to reverse the Jacksonian revolution. Their hopes were short-lived; barely a month after his inauguration in 1841, Harrison died of pneumonia, and the nation got "Tyler Too." But in what capacity: as acting president or as president? The Constitution was vague on the issue. Ignoring his Whig associates in Congress, who wanted a weak chief executive, Tyler took the presidential oath of office and declared his intention to govern as he pleased. As it turned out, that would not be like a Whig.

Tyler had served in the House and the Senate as a Jeffersonian Democrat, firmly committed to slavery and states' rights. He had joined the Whigs only to protest Jackson's stance against nullification. On economic issues, Tyler shared Jackson's hostility to the Second Bank and the American System. He therefore vetoed Whig bills that would have raised tariffs and created a new national bank. Outraged by this betrayal, most of Tyler's cabinet resigned in 1842, and the Whigs expelled Tyler from their party. "His Accidency," as he was called by his critics, was now a president without a party.

The split between Tyler and the Whigs allowed the Democrats to regroup. The party vigorously recruited small farmers in the North, smallholding planters in the South, and former members of the Working Men's Parties in the cities. It also won support among Irish and German Catholic immigrants—whose numbers had increased during the 1830s—by backing their demands for religious and cultural liberty, such as the freedom to drink beer and whiskey. A pattern of ethnocultural politics, as historians refer to the practice of voting along ethnic and religious lines, now became a prominent feature of American life. Thanks to these urban and rural recruits, the Democrats remained the majority party in most parts of the nation. Their program of equal rights, states' rights, and cultural liberty was attractive to more white Americans than the Whig platform of economic nationalism, moral reform, temperance laws, and individual mobility.

| IN YOUR OWN WORDS | What principles united the Whig Party, and why did the Tyler presidency fail to fulfill its leaders' wishes? |

## Summary

In this chapter, we examined the causes and the consequences of the democratic political revolution. We saw that the expansion of the franchise weakened the political system run by notables of high status and encouraged the transfer of power to professional politicians—men like Martin Van Buren, who were mostly of middle-class origin.

We also witnessed a revolution in government policy, as Andrew Jackson and his Democratic Party dismantled the mercantilist economic system of government-supported economic development. On the national level, Jackson destroyed Henry Clay's American System; on the state level, Democrats wrote new constitutions that ended the Commonwealth System of government charters and subsidies to private businesses. Jackson's treatment of Native Americans was equally revolutionary; the Removal Act of 1830 forcefully resettled eastern Indian peoples west of the Mississippi River, opening their ancestral lands to white settlement.

Finally, we watched the emergence of the Second Party System. Following the split in the Republican Party during the election of 1824, two new parties—the Democrats and the Whigs—developed on the national level and eventually absorbed the members of the Anti-Masonic and Working Men's Parties. The new party system established universal suffrage for white men and a mode of representative government that was responsive to ordinary citizens. In their scope and significance, these political innovations matched the economic advances of both the Industrial Revolution and the Market Revolution.

## Chapter 9 Review

### KEY TERMS

**Identify and explain the significance of each term below.**

franchise (p. 265)

notables (p. 265)

political machine (p. 267)

spoils system (p. 267)

caucus (p. 267)

demographic transition (p. 268)

republican motherhood
  (p. 268)

American Colonization Society (p. 270)

Missouri Compromise (p. 271)

American System (p. 273)

internal improvements (p. 273)

corrupt bargain (p. 273)

Tariff of Abominations (p. 275)

nullification (p. 278)

states' rights (p. 278)

Second Bank of the United States (p. 279)

Indian Removal Act of 1830 (p. 281)

Trail of Tears (p. 283)

classical liberalism, or laissez-faire (p. 285)

Whigs (p. 285)

Panic of 1837 (p. 288)

Specie Circular (p. 288)

## REVIEW QUESTIONS

**Answer these questions to demonstrate your understanding of the chapter's main ideas.**

1. How did Jackson and the new Democratic Party overcome sectional differences?

2. What were the constitutional arguments for and against internal improvements, the tariff, and nullification?

3. What principles united the Whig Party, and why did the Tyler presidency fail to fulfill its leaders' wishes?

4. Review the events listed under "Politics and Power" on the thematic timeline on page 230. As the timeline indicates, the Working Men's and Anti-Masonic Parties rose and declined between 1827 and 1834, and then the Whig Party emerged. How do you explain the timing of these events?

## CHRONOLOGY

**As you read, ask yourself why this chapter begins and ends with these dates and then identify the links among related events.**

| | |
|---|---|
| **1810s** | • States expand white male voting rights |
| | • Martin Van Buren creates disciplined party in New York |
| **1825** | • House of Representatives selects John Quincy Adams as president |
| | • Adams endorses Henry Clay's American System |
| **1828** | • Working Men's Parties win support |
| | • Tariff of Abominations raises duties |
| | • Andrew Jackson elected president |
| | • John C. Calhoun's *South Carolina Exposition and Protest* |

| **1830** | • Jackson vetoes National Road bill |
| | • Congress enacts Jackson's Indian Removal Act |
| **1831** | • *Cherokee Nation v. Georgia* denies Indians' independence, but *Worcester v. Georgia* (1832) upholds their political autonomy |
| **1832** | • Massacre of 850 Sauk and Fox warriors at Bad Axe |
| | • Jackson vetoes renewal of Second Bank |
| | • South Carolina adopts Ordinance of Nullification |
| **1833** | • Congress enacts compromise tariff |
| **1834** | • Whig Party formed by Clay, Calhoun, and Daniel Webster |
| **1835** | • Roger Taney named Supreme Court chief justice |
| **1836** | • Van Buren elected president |
| **1837** | • *Charles River Bridge* case weakens chartered monopolies |
| | • Panic of 1837 derails economy and labor movement |
| **1838** | • Many Cherokees die in Trail of Tears march to Indian Territory |
| **1839–1843** | • Defaults on bonds by state governments spark international financial crisis and depression |
| **1840** | • Whigs win "log cabin campaign" |
| **1841** | • John Tyler succeeds William Henry Harrison as president |

# 10

# Religion, Reform, and Culture

## 1820–1848

### IDENTIFY THE BIG IDEA

What changes and conflicts emerged as Americans developed a national culture?

**AMID A WILD THUNDERSTORM IN THE SUMMER OF 1830, AN AFRICAN** American seamstress in Philadelphia woke to hear God speaking. "I rose up and walked the floor wringing my hands and crying under great fear," Rebecca Cox Jackson wrote later. She prayed for hours, plunged in "the chamber of death." Suddenly she felt ecstasy: "my spirit was light, my heart filled with love for God and all mankind. . . . I ran downstairs and opened the door to let the lightning in the house, for it was like sheets of glory to my soul." God had told her, Jackson believed, that sexual relations caused sin: she should leave her husband. Sharing this news with her astonished spouse, Jackson was reportedly so full of spiritual power that she placed her hands on a hot stove over and over and removed them unhurt.

Jackson left home and became a traveling preacher. In upstate New York she discovered the communal movement of Shakers, or United Society of Believers in Christ's Second Appearing, whose popular nickname came from their ecstatic dances in worship. Like Jackson, Shakers practiced sexual abstinence. They also recognized women as religious and community leaders. Inspired by visions of a "mother spirit," Jackson returned to Philadelphia and built her own African American Shaker community, which endured for decades after her death in 1871.

Like Rebecca Cox Jackson, many Americans of the 1830s and 1840s discovered new identities and callings. Influenced by the era's economic and political transformations, they believed they could perfect their lives and society as a whole. Mainstream reformers, especially in the emerging northeastern middle class, advocated church attendance and a strict moral code. Their efforts were driven in part by growing fears of disorder, as they watched the rise of urban saloons, prostitution, and a boisterous working-class street culture. Soon, more radical reformers promoted a bewildering assortment of ideas: rejection of church institutions, common ownership of property, immediate emancipation of slaves, and sexual equality. These activists challenged social hierarchies and provoked horrified opposition. As one fearful southerner argued, radicals favored a world with "No-Marriage, No-Religion, No-Private Property, No-Law and No-Government."

Such fears were not exaggerated. Rapid economic growth and geographical expansion had weakened traditional institutions, forcing individuals to fend for themselves. In 1835, Alexis de Tocqueville coined the word *individualism* to describe the result. Native-born white Americans were "no longer attached to each other by any tie of caste, class, association, or family," the French aristocrat lamented, and so lived in social isolation. But while Tocqueville mourned the loss of social ties, Americans built new movements for community, worship, and reform.

# Spiritual Awakenings

At the time of the American Revolution, every state except Pennsylvania and Rhode Island had a legally established church that claimed everyone as a member and collected compulsory religious taxes. In the years that followed, the combined pressure of Enlightenment principles and religious dissent eliminated most state support for religion and allowed voluntary church membership. Americans in large numbers joined evangelical Methodist and Baptist churches that preached spiritual equality and developed egalitarian cultures marked by communal singing and emotional services.

From the 1790s through the 1830s, the country experienced powerful waves of religious revival. One of the largest frontier camp meetings, at Cane Ridge in Kentucky in 1801, lasted for nine electrifying days and attracted almost 20,000 people. Similar religious excitement swept all regions of the country. Known to historians as the **Second Great Awakening**, this upheaval stimulated an array of long-lasting reform movements. By the time the Awakening subsided, New England intellectuals led by Ralph Waldo Emerson were developing a radical individualist theology known as transcendentalism. Other spiritual seekers, like Rebecca Cox Jackson, joined utopian communities to remake the world.

## The Second Great Awakening

In the South, evangelical religion was initially a disruptive force because many ministers spoke of spiritual equality and criticized slavery. Husbands and planters grew angry when wives became more assertive and blacks joined evangelical congregations. To retain white men in their churches, Methodist and Baptist preachers gradually adapted their religious message to justify the authority of yeomen patriarchs and slave-owning planters. Man was naturally at "the head of the woman," declared one Baptist minister, while a Methodist conference told Christian slaves to be "submissive, faithful, and obedient." African Americans, both free and enslaved, developed a theology of their own (see Chapter 11).

**The Second Great Awakening in the North**   Many New Englanders rejected Calvinists' emphasis on human depravity and celebrated reason and free will. A new sect of Universalists, who preached universal salvation, gained tens of thousands of converts. Congregationalists discarded the concept of the Trinity—Father, Son, and Holy Spirit—and, taking the name *Unitarians*, emphasized reason. "The ultimate reliance of a human being is, and must be, on his own mind," argued William Ellery Channing, a famous Unitarian minister. A children's catechism conveyed the denomination's optimistic message: "If I am good, God will love me, and make me happy." Reflecting this optimism, ministers and popular writers linked individual salvation to religious benevolence. The mark of a true church, declared Christian social reformer Lydia Maria Child, is when members' "heads and hearts unite in working for the welfare of the human race."

By the 1820s, many Protestant Christians embraced that goal. Unlike the First Great Awakening, which split churches into warring factions, the second fostered cooperation among denominations. Between 1815 and 1826, religious leaders founded five interdenominational societies: the American Education Society, Bible Society, Sunday School Union, Tract Society, and Home Missionary Society. Based in northeastern cities, these societies dispatched hundreds of missionaries to the West and distributed thousands of Bibles and religious pamphlets.

One of the Awakening's most successful leaders was Presbyterian minister Charles Grandison Finney. Born into a poor farming family in Connecticut, Finney planned to become a lawyer before he underwent an intense religious experience in 1823 and chose the ministry. Beginning in towns along the Erie Canal, the young minister conducted emotional revival meetings. Finney's central message was that "God has made man a moral free agent" who could choose salvation. This doctrine of free will was particularly attractive to members of the new middle class, who emphasized self-discipline, sought to improve their material condition, and welcomed Finney's assurance that heaven was also in their grasp.

Finney's greatest triumph came in 1830, when he moved his revivals to Rochester, New York, a new commercial city on the Erie Canal. Preaching every day for six months and promoting group prayer in family homes, Finney converted influential merchants and manufacturers of Rochester. They promised to attend church, give up intoxicating beverages, and work hard. To encourage their employees to do the same, wealthy businessmen founded a Free Presbyterian Church—"free" because members did not have to pay for pew space. Other evangelicals founded churches to serve transient canal laborers, while pious businessmen set up a savings bank to encourage thrift among workers. Finney's wife, Lydia, and other middle-class women carried the evangelical message to the wives of the unconverted, set up Sunday schools for poor children, and formed the Female Charitable Society to assist the unemployed.

Finney's efforts were not completely successful. Skilled workers in strong craft organizations—boot makers, carpenters, stonemasons, and boatbuilders—protested that they needed higher wages and better schools more urgently than sermons and prayers. Most poor people ignored Finney's revival, as did Irish Catholic immigrants, many of whom hated Protestants as religious heretics and political oppressors.

Nonetheless, revivalists from New England to the Midwest copied Finney's message and techniques. In New York City, wealthy silk merchants Arthur and Lewis Tappan founded the *Journal of Commerce* to promote business enterprise while advocating Finney's evangelical and reform ideas. Revivals swept through Pennsylvania, North Carolina, Tennessee, and Indiana, where, a convert reported, "you could not go upon the street and hear any conversation, except upon religion." The success of the revivals "has been so general and thorough," concluded a Presbyterian general assembly, "that the whole customs of society have changed."

**The Benevolent Empire**　　The reform impulse sweeping through Protestant denominations found fertile ground in America's growing cities. Members of the rising middle classes wanted to save the world; they also wanted safe cities and a disciplined workforce. By the 1820s, led by Congregational and Presbyterian ministers, upwardly mobile reformers created a network of organizations that historians call the **Benevolent Empire**. Their goal was to restore "the moral government of God" by reducing consumption of alcohol and other vices that they believed resulted in poverty. Reform-minded individuals had regulated their own behavior; now they tried to control the lives of working people—by persuasion if possible, by law if necessary.

The Benevolent Empire targeted age-old evils such as drunkenness, adultery, prostitution, and crime, but its methods were new. Instead of relying on church sermons, reformers created large-scale organizations such as the Prison Discipline Society and the General Union for Promoting the Observance of the Christian Sabbath. Each organization had a managing staff, a network of hundreds of chapters, thousands of volunteer members, and a newspaper. Often acting in concert, these groups encouraged people to exercise self-control and acquire "regular habits." They persuaded local governments to ban public carnivals of drink and dancing, such as Negro Election Day (festivities in which African Americans symbolically took control of the government), which had been enjoyed by whites as well as blacks. Reformers created homes for abandoned children and asylums for the insane, who previously had often been confined by their families in attics and cellars.

Temperance advocates built the most successful movement. Beer and rum had long been a standard part of American holidays and everyday life. Grogshops dotted almost every block in working-class districts and became centers of disorder. During the 1820s and 1830s, alcohol consumption reached new heights, even among the elite; alcoholism, for example, killed Daniel Tompkins, vice president under James Monroe. Heavy drinking was devastating for wage earners, who could ill afford its costs. Though Methodist artisans and ambitious craftsmen swore off liquor to protect their skills, health, and finances, other workers drank heavily on the job—and not just during the traditional 11 a.m. and 4 p.m. "refreshers." A baker recalled how "one man was stationed at the window to watch, while the rest drank."

The evangelical Protestants who took over the American Temperance Society in 1832 set out to curb consumption of alcohol. The society grew quickly to two thousand chapters and more than 200,000 members. Its campaigns relied on revivalist methods — group confession and prayer, and using women as spiritual guides — and were a stunning success. On one day in New York City in 1841, more than 4,000 people took the temperance pledge. Annual consumption of spirits fell dramatically, from an average of 5 gallons per person in 1830 to 2 gallons in 1845.

Despite this trend, temperance advocates were frustrated that thousands of Americans — especially working-class men — refused to join the cause. By the early 1850s they turned from the goal of individual persuasion toward prohibition — laws to forbid the manufacture and sale of alcohol. In 1851, the Maine legislature passed a statute outlawing sale of alcoholic beverages in the state. The Maine Supreme Court upheld the statute, arguing that the legislature had the "right to regulate by law the sale of any article, the use of which would be detrimental of the morals of the people." The success of this **Maine Law** shaped the reformers' goals for decades to come (Chapter 17).

Temperance met resistance among workers who enjoyed their "refreshers" and Sunday beer. Even more controversial was Sabbatarianism, a movement to require business closings on the Christian Sabbath. As the Market Revolution spread, merchants and storekeepers conducted business on Sundays. Sabbatarians pressured state legislatures to halt such practices and urged Congress to repeal an 1810 law allowing mail to be transported — though not delivered — on Sundays. Members boycotted shipping companies that did business on the Sabbath and campaigned for municipal laws forbidding games and festivals on the Lord's day.

Provoking opposition from workers and freethinkers, these efforts had limited success. Men who labored twelve to fourteen hours a day, six days a week, wanted the freedom to spend their one day of leisure as they wished. To keep goods moving, shipping company managers demanded that the Erie Canal provide lockkeepers on Sundays. Using laws to enforce a particular set of moral beliefs, they said, was "contrary to the free spirit of our institutions."

## Ralph Waldo Emerson and Transcendentalism

Influential New England philosopher Ralph Waldo Emerson ranged far beyond benevolent reform. He celebrated the overthrow of old hierarchies and the spiritual power of individuals, influencing thousands of ordinary Americans and a generation of writers in the **American Renaissance**, a mid-nineteenth-century flourishing of literature and philosophy. Its roots lay with Unitarian ministers from well-to-do New England families who questioned the constraints of their Puritan heritage. For inspiration, they turned to European **romanticism**, a new conception of self and society. Romantic thinkers, such as German philosopher Immanuel Kant and English poet Samuel Taylor Coleridge, rejected the ordered, rational world of the eighteenth-century Enlightenment. They embraced human passion and sought deeper insight into the mysteries of existence. Through spiritual quest and self-knowledge, young Unitarians believed, each individual could experience the infinite and eternal.

### Emerson's Individualism.
As a Unitarian, Emerson already stood outside the mainstream of American Protestantism. In 1832, Emerson took a more radical step by resigning his Boston pulpit and rejecting organized religion. He moved to Concord,

**The Founder of Transcendentalism** As this painting of Ralph Waldo Emerson by an unknown artist indicates, the young philosopher was an attractive man, his face brimming with confidence and optimism. With his radiant personality and incisive intellect, Emerson deeply influenced dozens of influential writers, artists, and scholars and enjoyed great success as a lecturer to the emerging middle class. Stock Montage/Getty Images.

Massachusetts, and wrote influential essays probing what he called "the infinitude of the private man," the radically free person. In doing so, Emerson was launching the intellectual movement of **transcendentalism**. He argued that people needed to shake off inherited customs and institutions and discover their "original relation with Nature," in order to enter a mystical union with the "currents of Universal Being."

Transcendentalists' message of self-realization reached hundreds of thousands of people through Emerson's writings and lectures. Beginning in 1826, the lyceum movement — modeled on the public forum of the ancient Greek philosopher Aristotle — arranged speaking tours by poets, preachers, scientists, and reformers. The lyceum became an important cultural institution in the North and Midwest, though not in the South, where the middle class was smaller and popular education had a lower priority. Emerson became the most popular speaker in America, eventually delivering fifteen hundred lectures in more than three hundred towns in twenty states.

Emerson's individualistic ethos spoke to the experiences of many middle-class Americans, who had left family farms to make their way in the urban world. His pantheistic, nature-centered view of God encouraged Unitarians in Boston to create Mount Auburn Cemetery, a beautiful landscape with burial markers for the dead of all faiths. Despite his own rejection of organized religion, Emerson's optimism also inspired many Protestant leaders of the Second Great Awakening, such as Finney, who urged believers to reject old doctrines and seek direct experiences of God's power.

**Thoreau, Fuller, and Whitman** New England intellectual Henry David Thoreau heeded Emerson's call to seek inspiration from the natural world. In 1845, depressed by his beloved brother's death, Thoreau built a cabin near Walden Pond in Concord, Massachusetts, and lived alone there for two years. In 1854, he published *Walden, or Life in the Woods*, an account of his search for meaning beyond the artificiality of civilized society:

> I went to the woods because I wished to live deliberately, to front only the essential facts of life, and see if I could not learn what it had to teach, and not, when I came to die, discover that I had not lived.

*Walden's* most famous metaphor provides an enduring justification for independent thinking: "If a man does not keep pace with his companions, perhaps it is because he hears a different drummer." Beginning from this premise, Thoreau urged readers to avoid unthinking conformity and peacefully resist unjust laws.

As Thoreau sought self-realization for men, Margaret Fuller explored the possibilities of freedom for women. Born into a wealthy Boston family, Fuller mastered six languages and read broadly. Embracing Emerson's ideas, she started a transcendental discussion group for educated Boston women in 1839. While editing *The Dial*, the leading transcendentalist journal, Fuller also published *Woman in the Nineteenth Century* (1844). In it, Fuller endorsed the transcendental principle that all people could develop a life-affirming mystical relationship with God. Every woman therefore deserved psychological and social independence: the ability "to grow, as an intellect to discern, as a soul to live freely and unimpeded." She also called for equality in education and work: "We would have every arbitrary barrier thrown down [and] every path laid open to Woman as freely as to Man." Fuller traveled to Italy to report on the Revolution of 1848, only to drown in a shipwreck on her way home to the United States. Her life and writings inspired a rising generation of women writers and reformers.

Emerson issued a declaration of literary independence, urging American authors to reject European influences and find inspiration in everyday life: "the ballad in the street; the news of the boat; the glance of the eye; the form and gait of the body." No one responded to that call more vibrantly than poet Walt Whitman. While working as a printer, teacher, journalist, and publicist for the Democratic Party, Whitman recalled that he had been "simmering, simmering"; Emerson "brought me to a boil." Poetry was the "direction of his dreams." In *Leaves of Grass*, a collection of wild, exuberant poems first published in 1855 and constantly revised and expanded, Whitman recorded in verse his efforts to transcend various "invisible boundaries": between solitude and community, between prose and poetry, even between the living and the dead. At the center of *Leaves of Grass* is the individual: "I celebrate myself, and sing myself." Through his Emersonian "original relation" with nature, Whitman claims perfect communion with others: "Every atom belonging to me as good belongs to you." For Emerson, Thoreau, and Fuller, the individual had a divine spark; for Whitman, America's collective democracy assumed a sacred character.

**Limits of Transcendentalism**     Like many others, transcendentalists worried that the new market society—focused on work, profits, and consumption—was debasing Americans' spiritual lives. "Things are in the saddle," Emerson wrote, "and ride mankind." Seeking to revive intellectual life, transcendentalists created communal experiments. The most important was Brook Farm, just outside Boston, where Emerson, Thoreau, and Fuller were residents or frequent visitors. Members recalled that they "inspired the young with a passion for study, and the middle-aged with deference and admiration." But Brook Farm was an economic failure. The residents planned to produce their own food and exchange surplus milk, vegetables, and hay for manufactures. However, most members had few farming skills; only cash from affluent residents kept the enterprise afloat for five years. After a devastating fire in 1846, the community disbanded and sold the farm. With this failure, transcendentalists abandoned their quest for new social institutions. They accepted the emerging commercial order but tried to reform it, especially through the education of workers and the movement to abolish slavery.

In the meantime, Emerson's writings influenced two great novelists, Nathaniel Hawthorne and Herman Melville, with more pessimistic worldviews. Both sounded powerful warnings about the dangers of individualism when it became unfettered egoism. The main characters of Hawthorne's novel *The Scarlet Letter* (1850), Hester Prynne and Arthur Dimmesdale, blatantly challenge their seventeenth-century New England community by committing adultery and producing a child. Their decision to ignore social restraints results not in liberation but in degradation: a profound sense of guilt and condemnation by the community.

Melville explored the limits of individualism in even more extreme and tragic terms and became a scathing critic of transcendentalism. His most powerful work, *Moby-Dick* (1851), tells the story of Captain Ahab's obsessive hunt for a mysterious white whale, which ends in the destruction of Ahab and almost his entire crew. Here, the quest for spiritual meaning in nature brings death, not transcendence, because Ahab lacks discipline and self-restraint. *Moby-Dick* was a commercial failure. Middle-class readers who devoured sentimental American fiction refused to follow Melville into the dark, dangerous realm of individualism gone mad. They emphatically preferred the optimistic views of Emerson or Finney.

## Utopian Experiments

Like the founders of Brook Farm, thousands of less affluent Americans rejected life in America's emerging market society and sought to create ideal communities, or **utopias**, in rural parts of the Northeast and Midwest (Map 10.1). They hoped to build models for different ways of living. Many rural communalists were farmers and artisans seeking refuge from the economic depression of 1837–1843. Others were religious idealists. By advocating common ownership of property (socialism) and unconventional forms of family life, communalists challenged traditional property rights and gender roles.

The first successful American communal movement was the one that attracted Rebecca Cox Jackson: Shakerism. In 1770, Ann Lee Stanley (Mother Ann Lee), a young cook in Manchester, England, had a vision that she was an incarnation of Christ. Four years later, she led a few disciples to America and established a church near Albany, New York. After her death in 1784, her followers formed disciplined religious communities. Members embraced common ownership of property; accepted strict oversight by church leaders; and pledged to abstain from alcohol, tobacco, politics, and war. Shakers' repudiation of sexual pleasure and marriage followed Mother Ann's teaching that "lustful gratifications of the flesh" were "the foundation of human corruption." Holding that God was "a dual person, male and female," Shakers placed community governance in the hands of both women and men — Elderesses and Elders.

Shakers founded twenty communities, mostly in New England, New York, and Ohio. Their agriculture and crafts, especially furniture making, acquired a reputation for quality that made them self-sustaining and even comfortable. Because the Shakers disdained sexual intercourse, they relied on conversions and the adoption of thousands of young orphans to increase their numbers. During the 1830s, 3,000

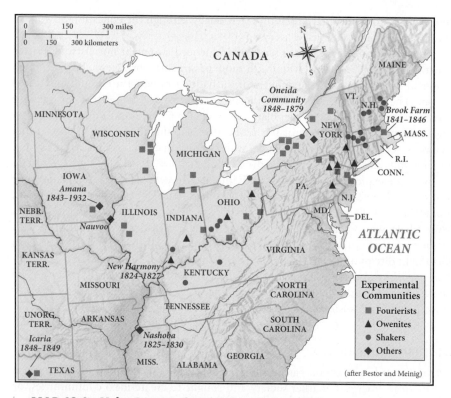

**MAP 10.1    Major Communal Experiments Before 1860**
Some experimental communities settled along the frontier, but the vast majority chose rural areas in settled regions of the North and Midwest. Because they opposed slavery, communalists usually avoided the South. Most secular experiments failed within a few decades, as conflicts arose within the communities, or as founders lost their reformist enthusiasm or died off; some tightly knit religious communities, such as the Shakers and the Mormons, were longer-lived.

adults, mostly women, joined the Shakers, attracted by their communal intimacy and sexual equality. However, as the Benevolent Empire expanded public and private orphanages during the 1840s and 1850s, Shaker communities began to decline and, by 1900, virtually disappeared.

Other Americans championed the ideas of French reformer Charles Fourier, who devised an eight-stage theory of social evolution that predicted the imminent decline of individual property rights and capitalism, through the creation of cooperative communities whose members shared work and property. Fourier's leading disciple in America, Albert Brisbane, argued that **Fourierist socialism** would liberate workers from low wages and servitude to capitalist employers. Fourierists also called for "associated households" in which both sexes shared domestic labor, emancipating women from "slavish domestic duties."

Following the Panic of 1837, Fourierism found a receptive audience among educated farmers and craftsmen who yearned for economic stability and communal solidarity. In the 1840s, Fourierists started nearly one hundred cooperative communities, mostly in western New York and the Midwest. Members worked in cooperative groups and owned property in common, including stores, banks, schools, and libraries. Most communities quickly collapsed as members fought over work responsibilities and social policies. Fourierism's rapid decline revealed the difficulty of maintaining a utopian community in the absence of a charismatic leader or a compelling religious vision.

John Humphrey Noyes ascribed the Fourierists' failure to their secular outlook and praised Shakers as the true "pioneers of modern Socialism." Noyes was a well-to-do graduate of Dartmouth College who joined the ministry after hearing a sermon by Charles Grandison Finney. Dismissed as a pastor for holding unorthodox beliefs, Noyes turned to perfectionism, an evangelical Protestant movement of the 1830s that attracted thousands of New Englanders who had migrated to New York and Ohio. Perfectionists believed Christ had already returned to earth (the Second Coming) and therefore people could aspire to sinless perfection. Unlike most perfectionists, who lived conventional personal lives, Noyes rejected marriage. But instead of Shaker-style celibacy, Noyes embraced "complex marriage," in which all members of the community married one another. He rejected monogamy partly to free women from their status as the property of their husbands.

In 1839, Noyes set up a perfectionist community near his hometown of Putney, Vermont. Local outrage, however, forced Noyes to relocate in 1848 to an isolated site near Oneida, New York. To give women time and energy to participate fully in community affairs, Noyes urged them to avoid multiple pregnancies. He instructed men to help by avoiding orgasm during intercourse. Less positively, he encouraged sexual relations at a very early age and used his position of power to manipulate the sexual lives of his followers. Eventually dissenters reported on such practices to outsiders. When Noyes fled to Canada in 1879 to avoid prosecution for adultery, the community abandoned complex marriage but remained a successful cooperative silverware venture until the mid-twentieth century.

The historical significance of the Shaker, Fourierist, and Oneida projects does not lie in their numbers, which were small, or in their fine crafts. Rather, it stems from their radical questioning of traditional sexual norms and of the capitalist values and class divisions of the emerging market society. Their utopian communities stood as countercultural blueprints for a more egalitarian social and economic order.

**Joseph Smith and Mormonism**   The era's most successful religious utopian movement emerged, like several others, from religious ferment among families of Puritan descent who lived along the Erie Canal — heirs to religious beliefs in supernatural powers and visions of the divine. The founder of Mormonism, Joseph Smith, was born in Vermont to a poor farming and shop-keeping family who migrated to Palmyra in central New York. In 1820, Smith began to have religious experiences: "A pillar of light above the brightness of the sun at noonday came down from above and rested upon me and I was filled with the spirit of God." Smith believed God had singled him out for special revelations. In 1830, he published *The Book of Mormon*, which he claimed to have translated from ancient hieroglyphics on gold plates shown to him by an angel named Moroni. *The Book of Mormon* told the story of ancient Jews from the Middle East who had migrated to the Western Hemisphere and were

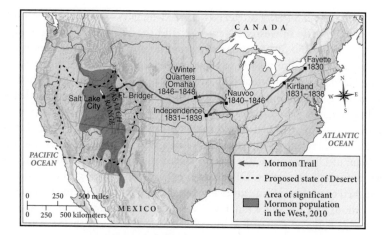

**MAP 10.2   The Mormon Trek, 1830–1848**

Because of their unorthodox religious views and communal solidarity, Mormons faced hostility first in New York and then in Missouri and Illinois. After the murder of church founder Joseph Smith in 1844, Brigham Young led the majority of Latter-day Saints from Illinois westward to Omaha, Nebraska. From Omaha the migrants followed the path of the Oregon Trail to Fort Bridger and then struck off to the southwest to settle in the basin of the Great Salt Lake, along the Wasatch Range in what is now Utah. At the time, this land was part of northern Mexico and was occupied by Utes, Paiutes, and Shoshones. The United States's victory in the U.S.-Mexico War (Chapter 11) turned Deseret into U.S. territory only two years later.

visited by Jesus Christ soon after his Resurrection. Smith's account explained the presence of Native peoples in the Americas and integrated the New World into the Judeo-Christian tradition.

Smith organized the **Church of Jesus Christ of Latter-day Saints, or Mormons**. Seeing himself as a prophet in a sinful, excessively individualistic society, he emphasized the family as the heart of religious and social life. Like many Protestants, Smith encouraged practices that led to individual success in the age of capitalist markets and factories: frugality, hard work, and enterprise. But Smith also stressed communal discipline. His goal was a church-directed society that would restore primitive Christianity and encourage moral perfection.

Constantly harassed by violent threats, Smith struggled to find a secure place to settle. At one point he identified Jackson County in Missouri as the site of the "City of Zion," and his followers began to move there. But they met extreme hostility: Mormons were "enemies of mankind and ought to be destroyed," said one cleric, and Missouri's governor agreed, issuing an order for Mormons to be "exterminated or driven out." Smith and his growing congregation eventually settled in Nauvoo, Illinois, a town they founded on the Mississippi River. By the early 1840s Nauvoo had 30,000 residents. Mormons' prosperity and their secret rituals and rigid discipline — including bloc voting in Illinois elections — fueled resentment among their neighbors. Antagonism increased when Smith asked Congress to make Nauvoo a separate federal territory and declared himself a candidate for president of the United States.

In secret, Smith also preached a new revelation justifying polygamy, the practice of a man having multiple wives. Smith pointed to biblical precedent for this practice of patriarchal or **plural marriage**. The revelation caused some of Smith's followers to break with him; when word got out, polygamy enraged church enemies. In 1844, Illinois officials arrested Smith and charged him with treason for allegedly conspiring to create a Mormon colony in Mexican territory. An anti-Mormon mob stormed the jail in Carthage, Illinois, where Smith and his brother Hyrum were being held and murdered them.

Some Mormons who rejected polygamy remained in the Midwest, led by Smith's son, Joseph Smith III. About 6,500 Mormons, however, fled the United States under the guidance of Brigham Young, Smith's leading disciple. Beginning in 1846, they crossed the Great Plains into Mexican territory and settled the Great Salt Lake Valley in present-day Utah (Map 10.2). Using cooperative labor and an irrigation system based on communal water rights, Mormon pioneers quickly built successful agricultural communities.

> **IN YOUR OWN WORDS**
> To what extent did antebellum intellectual and religious movements draw on the values of individualism, on the one hand, and of communal cooperation, on the other?

# Urban Cultures and Conflicts

As utopians organized communities in the countryside, rural migrants and foreign immigrants plunged into the exciting and risky world of the growing cities. In 1800, American cities had been overgrown towns: New York had only 60,000 residents; Philadelphia, 41,000. Then urban growth accelerated as a huge in-migration outweighed the high death rates that persisted for city dwellers (especially infants and children). By 1850, New York's population had ballooned to over half a million. Five other cities — Baltimore, Boston, Philadelphia, New Orleans, and Cincinnati — had more than 100,000 each. In the Northeast, by this time, the arrival of thousands of desperate immigrants fleeing the Irish famine (Chapter 12) made the working class seem even more alien and threatening. Cities generated new cultural practices that drew newcomers while also scandalizing middle-class reformers.

## Sex in the City

Thousands of young men and women flocked to the city searching for adventure and fortune, but many found only a hard life. Young men labored for meager wages building tenements, warehouses, and workshops. Others worked as low-paid clerks or operatives in mercantile and manufacturing firms. Young women had an even harder time. Thousands toiled as live-in domestic servants, ordered about by the mistress of the household and often sexually exploited by the master. Others scraped out a bare living as needlewomen in New York City's booming ready-made clothes industry.

Unwilling to endure domestic service or subsistence wages, many young girls turned to prostitution. Dr. William Sanger's careful survey, commissioned in 1855 by worried city officials, found that six thousand women engaged in commercial sex. Three-fifths were native-born whites; the rest were foreign immigrants; most were between fifteen and twenty years old. Half were or had been domestic servants, half had children, and half were infected with syphilis.

Commercialized sex—and sex in general—became one of the allures of urban life for men. "Sporting men" boasted of their sexual conquests in racy journals like *Flash*. Otherwise respectable husbands kept mistresses in handy apartments, and working men frequented bawdy houses. New York City had two hundred brothels in the 1820s and five hundred by the 1850s. Prostitutes—so-called public women—openly advertised their wares on Broadway, the city's most fashionable thoroughfare, and welcomed clients on the infamous third tier of theaters. Many men considered illicit sex a right. "Man is endowed by nature with passions that must be gratified," declared *Sporting Whip*. Even Reverend William Berrian, pastor of the ultra-respectable Trinity Episcopal Church, admitted from the pulpit that he had resorted ten times to "a house of ill-fame."

Not all urban sex was commercial. Freed from family oversight, men formed homoerotic relationships; as early as 1800, the homosexual "fop" was an acknowledged character in Philadelphia. Heterosexual young people moved from partner to partner until they chanced on an ideal mate. Middle-class youth strolled Broadway in the latest fashions: elaborate bonnets and silk dresses for young women; flowing capes, leather boots, and silver-plated walking sticks for young men. Rivaling the elegance on Broadway were the colorful costumes of the working-class Bowery, the broad avenue that ran along the east side of lower Manhattan. By day, Bowery Boys worked as apprentices or journeymen. By night, they prowled the streets as "dandies," hair cropped at the back of the head "as close as scissors could cut," with long front locks "matted by a lavish application of *bear's grease*, the ends tucked under so as to form a roll and brushed until they shone like glass bottles." The "B'hoy," as he was called, cut a dashing figure as he walked along with a "Bowery Gal" in a bright dress and shawl. To some shocked observers, however, such couples represented disorder and disrespect for middle-class values of respectability and piety.

## Popular Fiction and the Penny Press

Fostered by high literacy rates and advances in technology, publishing became one of the American city's most lucrative industries. By 1850 the United States had over six hundred magazines in publication. Boston and Philadelphia specialized in religious devotionals, sentimental and reform literature, and magazines for the growing middle class. Most Protestant denominations communicated with followers through monthly publications, as did homeopathic doctors, leaders of the Sunday School movement, and temperance advocates. For affluent women, *Godey's Lady's Book* depicted the latest Paris fashions and offered uplifting stories, poems, and advice on wifely and motherly duties. By publishing novels in serial form, magazines became an important springboard for popular fiction. America's expanding print culture also provided a forum for newly arrived groups to assert their American identities. Jewish authors included poet Penina Moïse of Charleston, South Carolina, and Reform

Rabbi Isaac Mayer Wise, editor of *The Israelite* and author of historical novels such as *The Jewish Heroine* (1855).

Print culture helped Americans navigate the chaotic, unstable world of the market economy. Advice books told aspiring young men how to dress and comport themselves and how to recognize deception and fraud. Other guidebooks counseled women and men on how to choose marriage partners and manage their domestic lives, by limiting family size, for example, to provide more nurture and education for each child. Despite repeated indictments for "obscenity," Massachusetts physician Charles Knowlton sold thousands of copies of *The Fruits of Philosophy* (1832), the first American guide to contraceptive practices.

Knowlton's sales were modest, however, in comparison with urban newspapers, which won huge audiences as the cost of printing fell and entrepreneurs developed new models for marketing and delivery. By the 1830s, young boys in New York hawked daily newspapers on the streets; four major **penny papers** had a combined circulation of 50,000, reaching many more readers as copies passed from hand to hand in tenements, workshops, and saloons. Within two years of its first issue in 1835, the *New York Herald* was selling 11,500 copies a day, the largest circulation of any American newspaper.

The *Herald*'s editor was colorful and controversial James Gordon Bennett, a brilliant businessman adept at attracting advertising revenue. Bennett pitched his paper to "the great masses of the community — the merchant, mechanic, working people — the private family as well as the public hotel — the journeyman and his employer." Unabashedly racist and strongly proslavery, Bennett won loyalty through his ardent support for building an "Empire in the West." The *Herald* also featured gossip, exposés, and above all, lurid and sensational accounts of violent crime, often falsified for dramatic effect. Disgusted, Walt Whitman denounced Bennett as a "reptile marking his path with slime wherever he goes. . . . A midnight ghoul, preying on rottenness and repulsive filth." Undeterred, Bennett built the *Herald* into a political force that exerted national influence by the time of the Civil War.

Fascinated by the urban underworld of crime, author Edgar Allan Poe drew on such sensational journalism to develop a new genre of popular fiction. Deserted by his father and orphaned at age three, Poe had a tumultuous relationship with the Richmond, Virginia, family who adopted him. He found a position at *The Southern Literary Messenger* before moving north to edit a series of gentlemen's magazines in Philadelphia and New York, quarreling all the time with owners and coworkers. Disdaining those who wrote for small literary audiences, Poe sought to represent and reach what he called "the popular mind." Despite his tormented career and early death from complications of alcoholism, Poe's dark stories of supernatural terror and secret crime, like "The Murders in the Rue Morgue," helped establish the genres of mystery and detective fiction.

## Urban Entertainments

City pastimes extended far beyond the printed page. In New York, working men could partake of traditional rural blood sports — rat and terrier fights, boxing matches — at Sportsmen's Hall, or they could seek drink and fun in billiard and bowling saloons. Other workers crowded the pit of the Bowery Theatre to see the

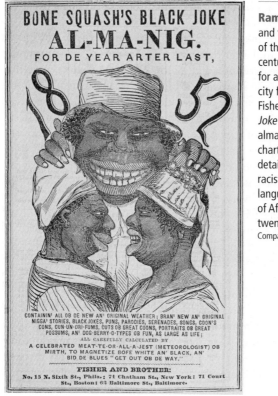

**Rampant Racism** Minstrel shows and their music were just two facets of the racist culture of mid-nineteenth-century America. Exploiting the market for almanacs among farmers and city folk alike, the publishing firm of Fisher and Brother produced the *Black Joke Al-Ma-Nig* for 1852. Like other almanacs, it provided astrological charts, weather predictions, and a detailed calendar of events. Such racist caricatures of black faces and language influenced white views of African Americans well into the twentieth century. Courtesy: The Library Company of Philadelphia, www.librarycompany.org.

"Mad Tragedian," Junius Brutus Booth, perform Shakespeare's *Richard III*. Reform-minded couples enjoyed evenings at the huge Broadway Tabernacle, where they could hear an abolitionist lecture or see the renowned Hutchinson Family Singers lead a roof-raising rendition of their antislavery anthem, "Get Off the Track." Families could visit the museum of oddities (and hoaxes) created by P. T. Barnum, the great cultural entrepreneur and founder of Barnum & Bailey Circus.

The most popular theatrical entertainments were **minstrel shows**, which featured white actors in blackface presenting comic routines that combined racist caricature and social criticism. Minstrelsy began around 1830, when a few actors put on blackface and performed song-and-dance routines. The most famous was John Dartmouth Rice, whose "Jim Crow" blended a shuffle-dance-and-jump with unintelligible lyrics delivered in "Negro dialect." By the 1840s hundreds of minstrel troupes toured the country. Minstrel players used African musical instruments, including banjos and castanets.

At least one traveling group, Gavitt's Original Ethiopian Serenaders, was actually composed of black musicians. But in the vast majority of shows, white performers used rambling lyrics and vicious stereotypes to depict African Americans as lazy, sensual, and irresponsible. Minstrel singers simultaneously criticized white society: their songs ridiculed the alleged drunkenness of Irishmen, parodied the halting English of German immigrants, denounced women's demands for political rights, and mocked the arrogance of upper-class men. Still, minstrelsy declared white supremacy most of all. The racial stereotypes of minstrelsy—which can be traced up through the era of radio and television and beyond—had an immense and enduring impact on American popular culture.

| IN YOUR OWN WORDS | What new working-class cultural practices emerged in large antebellum cities, and why? |

# African Americans and the Struggle for Freedom

Between 1820 and 1840, in northern states that abolished slavery, free African American communities found their political voice. Chief among their goals was abolition of slavery. By the 1830s they began to work with white allies, who like other reformers drew on the religious enthusiasm of the Second Great Awakening. After the American Revolution, white antislavery activists had assailed human bondage as contrary to republicanism and liberty, but most had called for gradual emancipation with compensation to slave owners. Three decades later, white and black abolitionists built the nation's first interracial movement for justice, demanding immediate, uncompensated emancipation: an uncompromising stance that met with fierce denunciations and violence.

## Free Black Communities, North and South

The free black population in the slave states lived primarily in coastal cities—Mobile, Memphis, New Orleans—and in the Upper South. Partly because skilled Europeans avoided the South, free blacks formed the backbone of the urban artisan workforce, laboring as carpenters, blacksmiths, barbers, butchers, and shopkeepers. Whatever their skills, free blacks faced many dangers. White officials often denied jury trials to free blacks accused of crimes; sometimes they forced people charged with vagrancy back into slavery. Some free blacks were simply kidnapped and sold.

Seeking opportunity and protection, some free blacks distanced themselves from plantation slaves and assimilated white culture and values. Indeed, mixed-race individuals sometimes joined the planter class. David Barland, one of twelve children born to a white Mississippi planter and his black slave Elizabeth, himself owned no fewer than 18 slaves. But such men and women were rare. Most free African Americans identified with the great mass of slaves, some of whom were their relatives. Calls by white planters in the 1840s to re-enslave free African Americans reinforced black unity.

Almost half of free blacks in the United States in 1840 (some 170,000) lived in the free states of the North. However, few enjoyed unfettered freedom. In rural areas, blacks worked as farm laborers or tenant farmers; in towns and cities, they toiled as domestic servants, laundresses, or day laborers. Only a small number owned land. "You do not see one out of a hundred . . . that can make a comfortable living, own a cow, or a horse," a traveler in New Jersey noted. In most states, law or custom prohibited northern blacks from voting or attending public schools. They could testify in court against whites only in Massachusetts. The federal government did not allow African Americans to work for the postal service, claim public lands, or hold a passport. Furthermore, the Fugitive Slave Law (1793) allowed owners and hired slave catchers to seize suspected runaways and return them to bondage. As black activist Martin Delaney remarked in 1852: "We are slaves in the midst of freedom."

Of the few African Americans able to make full use of their talents, several achieved great distinction. Mathematician and surveyor Benjamin Banneker published an almanac and helped lay out the new capital in the District of Columbia; Joshua Johnston won praise for his portraiture. More impressive and enduring were the community institutions created by free blacks. Throughout the North, largely unknown men and women founded schools, mutual-benefit organizations, and fellowship groups, often called **Free African Societies**. Discriminated against by white Protestants, they formed their own congregations and a new religious denomination — the **African Methodist Episcopal Church**. Founded in 1816, it spread across the Northeast and Midwest and even founded a few congregations in the slave states of Missouri, Kentucky, Louisiana, and South Carolina.

Leading African Americans in the North advocated a strategy of social uplift, encouraging free blacks to "elevate" themselves through education, temperance, and hard work. By securing "respectability," they argued, blacks could become the social equals of whites. To promote that goal, black businessmen and ministers founded an array of churches, schools, and self-help associations. Capping this effort, John Russwurm and Samuel D. Cornish of New York published the first African American newspaper, *Freedom's Journal*, in 1827.

## The Rise of Abolitionism

Free blacks' quest for respectability elicited a violent response in Boston, Pittsburgh, and other northern cities among whites who refused to accept African Americans as social equals. Motivated by racial contempt, white mobs terrorized black communities. White workers in northern towns laid waste to taverns and brothels where blacks and whites mixed and vandalized African American churches, temperance halls, and orphanages.

Responding to such attacks, David Walker published a stirring pamphlet, *An Appeal . . . to the Colored Citizens of the World* (1829), protesting black "wretchedness in this Republican Land of Liberty!!!!!" Walker was a free black from North Carolina who had moved to Boston, where he sold secondhand clothes and copies of *Freedom's Journal*. Self-educated, Walker ridiculed the religious pretensions of slaveholders and in biblical language warned of a slave revolt if justice were delayed. "We must and shall be free," he told white Americans. "And woe, woe, will be it to you if we have to obtain our freedom by fighting." Walker's call represented a radical challenge to the beliefs of white citizens, both North and South, including those who led the American Colonization Society (Chapter 9). Walker's *Appeal* quickly went through three printings and, carried by black merchant seamen, reached free African Americans in the South.

**Nat Turner's Revolt**   While David Walker called for a violent rebellion, Nat Turner, a slave in Southampton County, Virginia, staged one — a chronological coincidence that had far-reaching consequences. As a child, Turner had taught himself to read and hoped for emancipation, but one master forced him into the fields, while another separated him from his wife. Becoming deeply spiritual, Turner had a religious vision in which "the Spirit" explained that "Christ had laid down the yoke he had borne for the sins of men, and that I should take it on and fight against the Serpent, for the time was fast approaching when the first should be last and the last should be first." In August 1831, Turner and a group of relatives and friends rose in rebellion and killed at least 55 white men, women, and children. Turner, apparently seeking to seize weapons from a nearby armory and take up a defensive position in the Great Dismal Swamp, hoped hundreds of slaves would rally to his cause, but he mustered only 60. The white militia quickly dispersed his poorly armed force and took their revenge. One company of cavalry killed 40 blacks in two days. They put 15 of the severed heads on poles to warn "all those who should undertake a similar plot." Turner died by hanging, still identifying his mission with that of his Savior. "Was not Christ crucified?" he asked.

Turner's Rebellion sowed terror across the South. For a brief moment, the American Colonization Society became wildly popular as Americans debated remedies for the violence inherent in the slave system. Deeply shaken, Virginia's legislature debated a law providing for gradual emancipation and colonization abroad. When the bill failed by a vote of 73 to 58, the possibility that southern planters would voluntarily end slavery ended forever. Instead, the southern states toughened their slave codes, limited black movement, banned independent slave preaching, and prohibited anyone from teaching slaves to read. Blaming northern "agitation," they met Walker's radical *Appeal* with radical measures of their own.

**The American Anti-Slavery Society**   Rejecting Turner's and Walker's strategy of armed rebellion, a cadre of northern white Protestants launched a moral crusade to abolish the slave regime by pacifist means. If planters did not allow blacks their God-given status as free moral agents, these radicals warned, they faced eternal damnation at the hands of a just God. The most determined white advocate of **abolitionism** was William Lloyd Garrison. A Massachusetts-born printer, Garrison had worked during the 1820s in Baltimore on an antislavery newspaper, the *Genius of Universal Emancipation*. In 1830 he went to jail, convicted of libeling a New England merchant engaged in the domestic slave trade. After his release Garrison moved to Boston and started his own weekly, *The Liberator* (1831–1865). Inspired by a bold pamphlet written by English Quaker Elizabeth Coltman Heyrick, Garrison demanded immediate abolition without compensation to slaveholders. "I will not retreat a single inch," he declared, "AND I WILL BE HEARD."

Garrison accused the American Colonization Society of perpetuating slavery. He assailed the U.S. Constitution as "a covenant with death and an agreement with Hell" because it implicitly accepted racial bondage. In 1833, Garrison and sixty other religious abolitionists, black and white, established the **American Anti-Slavery Society** (AA-SS). It won financial support from the influential New York merchants and editors Arthur and Lewis Tappan. Women abolitionists established separate groups, including the Philadelphia Female Anti-Slavery Society, founded by Lucretia Mott in 1833.

AA-SS leaders launched a three-pronged attack. Using new steam-powered presses to print a million pamphlets, they first carried out a "great postal campaign" in 1835, flooding the nation, including the South, with antislavery literature. More publications followed, including Theodore Weld's *The Bible Against Slavery* (1837). Two years later, Weld teamed up with the Grimké sisters—Angelina, whom he married, and Sarah. The Grimkés had left their father's plantation in South Carolina, converted to Quakerism, and taken up the abolitionist cause. In *American Slavery as It Is: Testimony of a Thousand Witnesses* (1839), Weld and the Grimkés addressed a simple question: "What is the actual condition of the slaves in the United States?" Using evidence from southern newspapers and firsthand testimony, they showed slavery's inherent violence. Angelina Grimké told of a whipping house used by South Carolina slave owners: "One poor girl, [who was] sent there to be flogged, and who was accordingly stripped naked and whipped, showed me the deep gashes on her back—I might have laid my whole finger in them—large pieces of flesh had actually been cut out by the torturing lash." Filled with such images of suffering, the book sold more than 100,000 copies in a single year.

Abolitionists' second tactic was to aid fugitive slaves. They provided lodging and jobs for escaped blacks in free states and helped build the **Underground Railroad**, an informal network of blacks and whites who assisted fugitives. In Baltimore, a free African American sailor loaned his identification papers to future abolitionist Frederick Douglass, who used them to escape to New York. Harriet Tubman and other runaways risked re-enslavement or death by returning repeatedly to the South to help others escape. "I should fight for . . . liberty as long as my strength lasted," Tubman explained, "and when the time come for me to go, the Lord let them take me." Thanks to the Railroad, about a thousand African Americans reached freedom in the North each year.

A petition campaign was the final element of abolitionists' program. Between 1835 and 1838, the AA-SS bombarded Congress with nearly 500,000 signatures of citizens demanding abolition of slavery in the District of Columbia, an end to the interstate slave trade, and a ban on admission of new slave states. Along with many free blacks, thousands of deeply religious white farmers and small-town proprietors supported these efforts. The number of local abolitionist societies grew from two hundred in 1835 to two thousand by 1840, with nearly 200,000 members. The transcendentalist thinker Emerson condemned Americans for supporting slavery, while Thoreau, viewing the U.S.-Mexico War as a naked scheme to extend slavery, refused to pay taxes and submitted to arrest. In 1848, he published "Resistance to Civil Government," a foundational text for later advocates of civil disobedience. African American minister Henry Highland Garnet went further; his *Address to the Slaves of the United States of America* (1841) urged "Resistance! Resistance!" Still, abolitionists remained a small minority in the North, at most perhaps 10 percent of northerners and midwesterners.

### Hostility to Abolitionism

**Hostility to Abolitionism**   The rhetoric of Walker and the AA-SS, combined with the shock of Turner's Rebellion, alarmed white Americans. Abolitionist agitation, ministers warned, risked "setting friend against friend" and "embittering one portion of the land against the other." Northern merchants and textile manufacturers supported southern planters who supplied them with cotton, as did hog farmers in Ohio, Indiana, and Illinois and pork packers in Cincinnati and Chicago who profited from lucrative sales in the South. Wealthy men feared that attacks on slave property might become an assault on all property rights. Conservative clergymen condemned the public roles assumed by abolitionist women. Northern working men feared freed blacks would work for lower wages and take their jobs. Finally, whites almost universally opposed "amalgamation," the racial mixing and intermarriage that Garrison seemed to support by holding meetings of blacks and whites of both sexes together.

Racial fears and hatreds led to violent mob actions. In 1829, working-class whites in Cincinnati drove over a thousand African Americans from the city—enforcing, through vigilantism, an 1807 law that had banned all blacks from Ohio. Four years later, a mob of 1,500 New Yorkers stormed a church in search of Garrison and Arthur Tappan. Another white mob swept through Philadelphia's African American neighborhoods, clubbing and stoning residents and destroying homes and churches. In 1835, "gentlemen of property and standing"—lawyers, merchants, and bankers—broke up an abolitionist convention in Utica, New York. Two years later, a mob in Alton, Illinois, shot and killed Elijah P. Lovejoy, editor of the abolitionist *Alton Observer*. By pressing for emancipation and equality, abolitionists had revealed the extent of racial prejudice.

In the South, racial solidarity increased and whites banned all abolitionist writings, sermons, and lectures. Georgia's legislature offered a $5,000 reward to anyone who would kidnap Garrison and bring him to the South to be tried (or lynched) for inciting rebellion. In Nashville, vigilantes whipped a northern college student for distributing abolitionist pamphlets; in Charleston, a mob attacked the post office and destroyed sacks of abolitionist mail. After 1835, southern postmasters simply refused to deliver mail suspected to be of abolitionist origin. By that time, politicians joined the fray. President Andrew Jackson, a longtime slave owner, asked Congress to restrict use of the mails by abolitionist groups. Congress refused, but in 1836, the House of Representatives adopted the so-called **gag rule**. Under this informal agreement, which remained in force until 1844, the House automatically tabled abolitionist petitions, refusing even to discuss the explosive issue of slavery.

Assailed from the outside, abolitionists also divided internally over gender issues and political strategy. Many antislavery clergymen opposed public roles for women, but Garrison championed women's rights: "Our object is universal emancipation, to redeem women as well as men from a servile to an equal condition." In 1840, this issue split the movement. Women's rights advocates remained in the AA-SS, while opponents founded a new organization, the American and Foreign Anti-Slavery Society.

At the same time, dissenters from Garrison's strategy of "moral suasion" focused their energies on electoral politics. Led by key African Americans who had escaped from slavery, this group broke with Garrison and argued that slavery would never end except through electoral action. They organized the **Liberty Party**, the first antislavery political party. In 1840, they nominated James G. Birney, a former Alabama slave owner, for president. Birney won few votes, but his campaign began to open the way for further electoral action against slavery. In 1844, Birney's second run for president would have a far-ranging impact (Chapter 11). Political abolitionists would, over the next two decades, transform the political system.

| **IN YOUR OWN WORDS** | How did free African American communities shape American life and culture, and how did black civic leadership transform debates over slavery and race? |
|---|---|

# The Women's Rights Movement

The controversial role of abolitionist women reflected a broad shift in American culture. The post-Revolutionary ideal of republican motherhood (Chapter 9) recognized a limited civic role for women. By the 1830s and 1840s, republican motherhood was shaped by religious revivals and rapid expansion of the middle class. The result was **domesticity**, a set of ideals that emerged first among middle-class and elite families in the Northeast. Advocates of domesticity hailed "Woman's Sphere of Influence," celebrating women's special role as mothers and homemakers. Some even praised women's charitable efforts—as long as they didn't go too far. Almost all Americans believed married women should remain under their husbands' authority and that women should stay in the "separate sphere" of the home, away from politics. As one minister put it, women had no place in "the markets of trade, the scenes of politics and popular agitation, the courts of justice and the halls of legislation." But women's education and reform work raised questions about these long-standing norms of marriage and family authority. By the 1840s, a small group of northern women began to advocate women's equal rights.

## Origins of the Women's Rights Movement

Women formed a crucial part of the Second Great Awakening and the Benevolent Empire. After 1800, more than 70 percent of the members of New England Congregational churches were women. The predominance of women prompted Congregational ministers to end traditional gender-segregated prayer meetings, and evangelical Methodist and Baptist preachers actively promoted mixed-sex praying. "Our prayer meetings have been one of the greatest means of the conversion of souls," a minister in central New York reported in the 1820s, "especially those in which brothers and sisters have prayed together."

Far from leading to sexual promiscuity, as critics feared, mixing men and women in religious activities promoted greater self-discipline. Believing in female virtue, young women and the men who courted them postponed sexual intercourse until after marriage—previously a much rarer form of self-restraint. In many New England towns, more than 30 percent of the women who married between 1750 and 1800 bore a child within eight months of their wedding day; by the 1820s, the rate had dropped to 15 percent.

As women claimed spiritual authority, men tried to curb their power. In both the North and the South, evangelical Baptist churches that had once advocated spiritual equality now prevented women from voting on church matters or offering public testimonies of faith. Testimonies by women, one layman declared, were "directly opposite to the apostolic command in [Corinthians] xiv, 34, 35, 'Let your women learn to keep silence in the churches.'" Such injunctions merely changed the focus of women's religious activism. Embracing the ideal of republican motherhood, Christian women throughout the United States founded maternal associations to encourage proper child rearing. By the 1820s, journals such as *Mother's Magazine*, widely read in hundreds of towns and villages, gave women a sense of shared identity and purpose. Women also undertook missionary fund-raising, Sunday School teaching, and other religious activities. The ideal of domesticity justified such work, since it celebrated women as more pious, caring, patient, and self-sacrificing than men could be. In towns and on prosperous farms in the Northeast and Midwest, women drew on domesticity to claim new roles.

**Domesticity and Education**    Outside the South — where literacy lagged for white women and was banned altogether for enslaved women — a post-Revolutionary surge in women's education gave the rising generation tools and confidence to pursue reform. Religious activism also advanced female education, as churches sponsored academies for girls from the middling classes. Emma Willard, the first American advocate of higher education for women, opened the Middlebury Female Seminary in Vermont in 1814 and later founded girls' academies in Waterford and famously at Troy, New York, in 1821.

The intellectual leader of the new women educators was Catharine Beecher, whose *Treatise on Domestic Economy* (1841) advised women on how to make their homes examples of middle-class efficiency and domesticity. Though Beecher largely upheld woman's "separate sphere," she made an exception for teaching, arguing that "energetic and benevolent women" were better qualified than men to instruct the young.

By the 1820s, women educated in the nation's growing female seminaries and academies participated in a remarkable expansion of public education. From Maine to Wisconsin, women vigorously supported the movement led by reformer Horace Mann to increase elementary schooling and improve the quality of instruction. As secretary of the Massachusetts Board of Education from 1837 to 1848, Mann lengthened the school year, established standards in key subjects, and recruited well-educated women as teachers. By the 1850s, a majority of teachers were women, both because local school boards heeded Beecher's arguments and because they discovered they could hire women at much lower wages than men. A female teacher earned $12 to $14 a month with room and board — less than a male farm laborer. But among the employments open to women, teaching became a respectable and relatively well-paid option, as well as a route into public life.

**Moral Reform**    Keenly aware of the dangers around them, women in the growing cities made particularly bold efforts at reform. In 1834, middle-class women in New York City founded the **Female Moral Reform Society** and elected Lydia Finney, wife of revivalist Charles Grandison Finney, as its president. Rejecting the sexual double standard, its members demanded chaste behavior by men. Employing only women as agents, society members provided moral guidance for young female factory operatives, seamstresses, and servants. They visited brothels, where they sang hymns, searched for runaway girls, and pointedly recorded the names of clients. By 1840, the society had blossomed into a national association with 555 chapters and 40,000 members throughout the North and Midwest. Many local chapters founded homes of refuge for prostitutes; in New York and Massachusetts they won passage of laws that made seduction a crime.

Dorothea Dix became a model for women who set out to improve public institutions. Dix's paternal grandparents were prominent Bostonians, but her father, a Methodist minister, ended up an impoverished alcoholic. Emotionally abused as a child, Dix grew into a compassionate young woman with a strong sense of moral purpose. She used money from her grandparents to set up charity schools to "rescue some of America's miserable children from vice." By 1832, she had published seven popular books, including *Conversations on Common Things* (1824), an enormously successful treatise on natural science and moral improvement.

In 1841, Dix took up a new cause. Discovering that insane women were jailed alongside male criminals, she persuaded Massachusetts lawmakers to enlarge the state hospital to house indigent mental patients. Exhilarated by that success, Dix began a national movement to establish public asylums for the mentally ill. By 1854, she had traveled more than 30,000 miles and had visited eighteen state penitentiaries, three hundred county jails, and more than five hundred almshouses and hospitals. Dix's reports and agitation prompted many states to improve their prisons and public hospitals. Like women's entry into education, Dix's career showed that ideas about women's "natural" maternalism and self-sacrifice did not necessarily confine them at home.

## From Antislavery to Women's Rights

Women joined the antislavery movement, in part, because they understood the special horrors of slavery for women. In her autobiography, *Incidents in the Life of a Slave Girl*, former slave Harriet Jacobs described how enslaved women were sexually coerced and raped by masters. "I cannot tell how much I suffered in the presence of these wrongs," she wrote. She reported that such sexual assaults incited additional cruelty by slave owners' wives, who were enraged by their husbands' promiscuity. Jacobs and others made pointed gender-based appeals to northern women. Angelina Grimké denounced the slave system in which "women are degraded and brutalized, . . . forcibly plundered of their virtue and their offspring." "*They are our sisters,*" she wrote, "and to us, as women, they have a right to look for sympathy with their sorrows, and effort and prayer for their rescue."

As Garrisonian women attacked slavery, they frequently violated social taboos by speaking publicly. Maria W. Stewart, an African American, spoke to mixed crowds in Boston in the early 1830s. Soon scores of women were delivering lectures condemning slavery. When Congregationalist clergymen in New England assailed Angelina and Sarah Grimké for such activism in a pastoral letter in 1837, Sarah Grimké turned to the Bible for justification: "The Lord Jesus defines the duties of his followers . . . without any reference to sex or condition," she observed. "Men and women were created equal; both are moral and accountable beings."

In a pamphlet debate with Catharine Beecher, Angelina Grimké pushed the argument beyond religion by invoking Enlightenment principles to claim equal civic rights: "It is a woman's right to have a voice in all the laws and regulations by which she is governed, whether in Church or State." By 1840, female abolitionists were asserting that traditional gender roles resulted in the domestic slavery of women. They focused particularly on the laws of coverture (Chapter 4), which gave husbands all rights of property and child custody and even declared a wife's body to belong to her husband. Having acquired a public voice and political skills in the crusade for African American freedom, thousands of northern women now advocated greater rights for themselves.

Unlike radical utopians, women's rights advocates of the 1840s did not reject the institution of marriage or conventional divisions of labor within the family. Instead, they tried to strengthen the legal rights of married women by seeking legislation that permitted them to own property. This initiative won crucial support from affluent men, who feared bankruptcy in the volatile market economy and wanted to protect family assets by putting them in their wives' names. Fathers also desired their married daughters to have property rights to shield them (and their paternal inheritances) from financially irresponsible husbands. Such motives prompted legislatures in three states — Mississippi, Maine, and Massachusetts — to enact **married women's property laws** between 1839 and 1845. Then, in 1848, women activists in New York won a comprehensive statute that gave women full legal control over any property they brought to a marriage. This law became the model for similar laws in fourteen other states.

Also in 1848, Elizabeth Cady Stanton and Lucretia Mott organized a gathering of women's rights activists in the small New York town of Seneca Falls. Seventy women and thirty men attended the **Seneca Falls Convention**, which issued a rousing manifesto extending to women the egalitarian republican ideology of the Declaration of Independence. "All men and women are created equal," the Declaration of Sentiments declared. It denounced coverture and asserted that no man had the right to tell a woman what her "sphere" should be — a decision that belonged to "her conscience and her God." The Declaration called for women's higher education, access to property rights and the professions, rights of divorce, and an end to the sexual double standard. It also claimed women's "right to the elective franchise." The authors acknowledged that their struggle would be difficult, because society worked to "destroy [woman's] confidence in her own powers, to lessen her self-respect." But they called Americans to work for gender equality.

Most Americans — both male and female — dismissed the Seneca Falls declaration as nonsense. In her diary, one small-town mother lashed out at the female reformer who "talks of her wrongs in harsh tone, who struts and strides, and thinks that she proves herself superior to the rest of her sex." Still, the women's rights movement grew. In 1850, delegates to the first national women's rights convention in Worcester, Massachusetts, called on churches to eliminate theological notions of female inferiority. Addressing state legislatures, they proposed laws to allow married women to institute lawsuits and testify in court. After 1850 the movement held annual national conventions — though few southern-born women attended. Women's rights continued to have a strong abolitionist bent. Passionate speeches by African American women, in particular, reminded convention delegates of the continued plight of women in slavery.

Legislative campaigns for women's rights required talented organizers and speakers. The most prominent was Susan B. Anthony, a Quaker who had acquired political skills in the temperance and antislavery movements. Those experiences, Anthony reflected, taught her "the great evil of woman's utter dependence on man." Joining the women's rights movement, she worked closely with Elizabeth Cady Stanton, an elite New Yorker who wrote some of the movement's most eloquent manifestos. Anthony created an activist network of political "captains," all women, who relentlessly lobbied state legislatures. In 1860, her efforts secured a New York law

No. VI.—*SOMETHING MORE OF BLOOMERISM.*

(BEHIND THE COUNTER THERE IS ONE OF THE "INFERIOR ANIMALS.")

**Attacking the Women's Rights Movement**  Amelia Jenks Bloomer (1818–1894) wrote for her husband's newspaper, the *County Courier* of Seneca Falls, New York. In 1848 she attended the women's convention there and began her own biweekly newspaper, *The Lily*, focusing on temperance and women's rights. In 1851, Bloomer enthusiastically promoted — and serendipitously gave her name to — the comfortable women's costume devised by another temperance activist: loose trousers gathered at the ankles topped by a short skirt. Fearing women's quest for equal dress and equal rights, humorists such as John Leech ridiculed the new female attire. Here, bloomer-attired women smoke away and belittle the male proprietor as "one of the 'inferior animals,' " a thinly veiled effort by Leech to reassert men's "natural" claim as the dominant sex. From *Punch* 1851, John Leech Archive/Picture Research Consultants & Archives.

granting women the right to control their own wages; to own property acquired by "trade, business, labors, or services"; and, if widowed, to assume sole guardianship of her children. Genuine individual equality for women, the dream of transcendentalist Margaret Fuller, had advanced a small step closer to reality. In ways large and small, new thinkers and reform movements had altered the character of American culture.

| **IN YOUR OWN WORDS** | What new rights did women gain in the early nineteenth century, and which women most benefitted from these changes? What rights remained out of reach? |
|---|---|

# Summary

Between the 1820s and the 1840s, Americans developed new republican ideas and practices. A sweeping series of Protestant revivals, known to historians as the Second Great Awakening, inspired thousands of Americans to evangelize and reform the world. In doing so they built movements to shelter orphans, reform prisons, combat prostitution, discourage alcohol consumption, and close businesses on the Christian Sabbath. Many of these efforts were aimed at the urban working classes, whom middle-class reformers viewed as undisciplined and sinful. Urban workers, however, often ignored reformers and built their own vibrant cultures of leisure and entertainment, including such enduring institutions as minstrel shows and the penny press.

Some reformers took more radical directions. Critics of the emerging market economy, ranging from pious Shakers to Fourierist socialists, founded utopian communities to experiment with different ways of organizing labor and family life. The most successful of these, the Mormons, met such hostility and violence from non-Mormons that they eventually trekked west to resettle in what is now Utah. New England intellectuals, led by Ralph Waldo Emerson, articulated transcendentalism, a romantic movement that emphasized spiritual connections with nature and the individual autonomy of each human soul. Transcendentalist thinkers joined the growing movement for immediate abolition of slavery, which originated in free African American communities in the North and also found support among some white northern evangelicals and Quakers. Some whites responded to abolitionist ideas—and to African American business success and political activism—with threats and riots. But the antislavery movement survived external pressures and internal disagreements. By the 1840s a small group of northern abolitionist women, inspired by ideals of equality and by the growth of women's education and reform activism, argued for women's rights.

# Chapter 10 Review

## KEY TERMS

**Identify and explain the significance of each term below.**

individualism (p. 295)

Second Great Awakening (p. 295)

Benevolent Empire (p. 297)

Maine Law (p. 298)

American Renaissance (p. 298)

romanticism (p. 298)

transcendentalism (p. 299)

utopias (p. 301)

Fourierist socialism (p. 302)

Church of Jesus Christ of Latter-day Saints, or Mormons (p. 304)

plural marriage (p. 305)

penny papers (p. 307)

minstrel shows (p. 308)

Free African Societies (p. 310)

African Methodist Episcopal Church
  (p. 310)

abolitionism (p. 311)

American Anti-Slavery Society
  (p. 311)

Underground Railroad (p. 312)

gag rule (p. 313)

Liberty Party (p. 313)

domesticity (p. 314)

Female Moral Reform Society (p. 315)

married women's property laws
  (p. 317)

Seneca Falls Convention (p. 317)

## REVIEW QUESTIONS

**Answer these questions to demonstrate your understanding of the chapter's main ideas.**

1. To what extent did antebellum intellectual and religious movements draw on the values of individualism, on the one hand, and of communal cooperation, on the other?

2. What new working-class cultural practices emerged in large antebellum cities, and why?

3. How did free African American communities shape American life and culture, and how did black civic leadership transform debates over slavery and race?

4. What new rights did women gain in the early nineteenth century, and which women most benefitted from these changes? What rights remained out of reach?

5. Review the events listed under "Culture and Society" on the thematic timeline on page 231, paying particular attention to the entries related to individualism and rights on the one hand and to various communal and religious movements on the other. What was the relationship between these somewhat contradictory cultural impulses? How were these two movements related to the social and economic changes in America in the decades after 1800?

## CHRONOLOGY

**As you read, ask yourself why this chapter begins and ends with these dates and identify the links among related events.**

| | |
|---|---|
| **1816** | • African Methodist Episcopal Church founded |
| **1821** | • Emma Willard founds Troy Female Seminary for young women |
| **1823** | • Charles Grandison Finney begins Protestant revival campaigns |
| **1827** | • *Freedom's Journal*, first African American newspaper, published in New York |

| | |
|---|---|
| **1829** | • Violence drives over a thousand African Americans out of Cincinnati |
| | • David Walker's *Appeal . . . to the Colored Citizens of the World* |
| **1830** | • Joseph Smith publishes *The Book of Mormon* |
| **1830s** | • Emergence of minstrel shows |
| | • Peak membership of Shaker communities |
| **1831** | • William Lloyd Garrison founds *The Liberator* |
| | • Nat Turner's uprising in Virginia |
| **1832** | • Ralph Waldo Emerson turns to transcendentalism |
| | • American Temperance Society founded |
| | • Charles Knowlton publishes first American birth control guide |
| **1833** | • American Anti-Slavery Society founded |
| **1834** | • New York activists create Female Moral Reform Society |
| **1835** | • James Gordon Bennett founds *New York Herald* |
| | • Abolitionists launch great postal campaign |
| **1836** | • House of Representatives adopts gag rule barring antislavery petitions |
| **1837** | • Horace Mann begins public school expansion in Massachusetts |
| | • Grimké sisters defend public roles for women |
| | • Abolitionist Elijah Lovejoy killed by a mob in Illinois |
| **1839–1845** | • First wave of married women's property laws |
| **1840** | • Liberty Party first runs James G. Birney for president |
| **1840s** | • Fourierist communities arise in Midwest |
| **1841** | • Dorothea Dix promotes hospitals for mentally ill |
| | • Catharine Beecher publishes *Treatise on Domestic Economy* |
| **1844** | • Margaret Fuller publishes *Woman in the Nineteenth Century* |
| **1845** | • Henry David Thoreau goes to Walden Pond |
| **1846** | • Brigham Young leads Mormons to Salt Lake |
| **1848** | • Seneca Falls Convention proposes women's equality |
| | • John Humphrey Noyes establishes cooperative experiment at Oneida |
| **1851** | • Herman Melville publishes *Moby-Dick* |
| **1855** | • Dr. William Sanger surveys sex trade in New York City |
| | • Walt Whitman publishes *Leaves of Grass* |

# 11

## Imperial Ambitions

### 1820–1848

**IDENTIFY THE BIG IDEA**

How did the ideology of Manifest Destiny shape U.S. government policies and the experiences of ordinary people?

**SINCE THE NATION'S FOUNDING IN 1776, VISIONARIES BELIEVED THAT** it would become both a republic and an empire, predicting a glorious expansion across the continent. "It belongs of right to the United States to regulate the future destiny of North America," declared the *New-York Evening Post* in 1803. Politicians soon took up the refrain. "Our natural boundary is the Pacific Ocean," asserted Massachusetts congressman Francis Baylies in 1823. "The swelling tide of our population must and will roll on until that mighty ocean interposes its waters." Missouri senator Thomas Hart Benton concurred. "All obey the same impulse—*that of going to the West*," he wrote, "which, from the beginning of time has been the course of heavenly bodies, of the human race, and of science, civilization, and national power following in their train." Northerners and southerners alike viewed westward expansion as the durable foundation of American identity.

But in the 1820s, the United States was only one of the imperial powers vying for control of western North America. Mexico, which gained its independence from Spain in 1821, claimed a broad swath of the Southwest that stretched from Coahuila y Tejas on the Gulf coast to Alta California on the Pacific, and France, Mexico's principal creditor, had an interest in helping it to defend that claim. North of Alta California, Great Britain and the United States competed for control of a vast region known as the Oregon Country. Still farther north, Russia laid claim to a coastal strip stretching north to the arctic circle and west to the Bering Strait. And throughout these lands, Native American groups controlled access to resources. In particular, U.S. expansion directly threatened the sovereignty and independence of the Plains Indians, many of whom were formidable and well armed. Despite the confidence of politicians, U.S. control of the North American West was far from assured (Map 11.1).

President James Polk, an ardent imperialist, willingly assumed the risks associated with expansion. "I would meet the war which either England or France . . . might wage and fight until the last man," he told Secretary of State James Buchanan in 1846. Polk's aggressive expansionism sparked conflict. A war with Mexico intended to be "brief, cheap, and bloodless" became "long, costly, and sanguinary," complained Senator Benton. Polk oversaw massive territorial acquisitions—New Mexico, California, and the Oregon Country—but, in so doing, set the stage for a bitter debate over slavery.

# The Expanding South

For southerners, imperial ambitions meant territorial expansion and a commitment to the slave plantation system. With slavery's resurgence in the early nineteenth century, the social and political order of the South settled into new patterns. A small minority of planter elites came to dominate southern society, while a larger number of middling planters and aspiring slaveholders supported their ambitions. But the growing number of propertyless whites separated themselves from the plantation economy by moving onto marginal lands. Southern expansionists pushed into east Texas in the 1820s, while the planters of the Cotton South who dominated state legislatures adapted their aristocratic ideals to the demands of a democratic political order.

## Planters, Small Freeholders, and Poor Freemen

Although the South was a **slave society**—a society in which the institution of slavery affected all aspects of life—most white southerners did not own slaves. The percentage of white families who held blacks in bondage steadily decreased—from 36 percent in 1830, to 31 percent in 1850, to about 25 percent a decade later. However, slave ownership varied by region. In some cotton-rich counties, 40 percent of the white families owned slaves; in the hill country near the Appalachian Mountains, the proportion dropped to 10 percent.

**Planter Elites**   A privileged minority of 395,000 southern families owned slaves in 1860, their ranks divided into a strict hierarchy. The top one-fifth of these families owned twenty or more slaves. This elite—just 5 percent of the South's white population—dominated the economy, owning over 50 percent of the entire slave population of 4 million and growing 50 percent of the South's cotton crop (Map 11.2). The average wealth of these planters was $56,000 (about $1.6 million in purchasing power today);

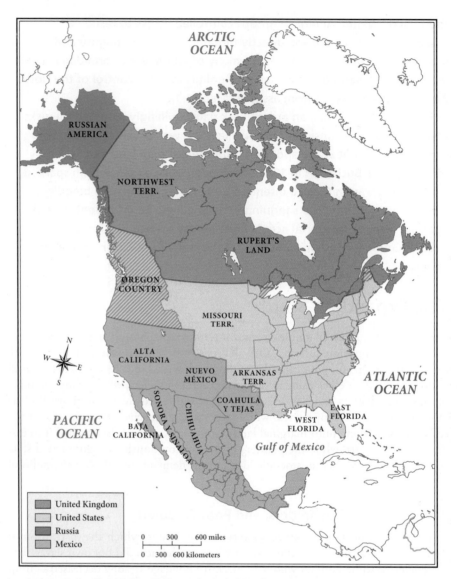

## MAP 11.1   Nonnative Claims to North America, 1821

In 1821, North America was a complex patchwork. Louisiana and Missouri were the first two states west of the Mississippi. Beyond the states' borders, the Michigan, Missouri, Arkansas, and East and West Florida Territories extended U.S. claims. To the south, the newly independent nation of Mexico claimed nearly as much territory as the United States did, while British Canada included a vast landscape to the north. Russia controlled the northern Pacific coast, while Mexico claimed Alta and Baja California. In between, Great Britain and the United States vied for the Oregon Country, which held the key to each nation's desire for an outlet to the Pacific. Underlying all these claims, a large and diverse population of Native Americans considered their own claims to be sovereign.

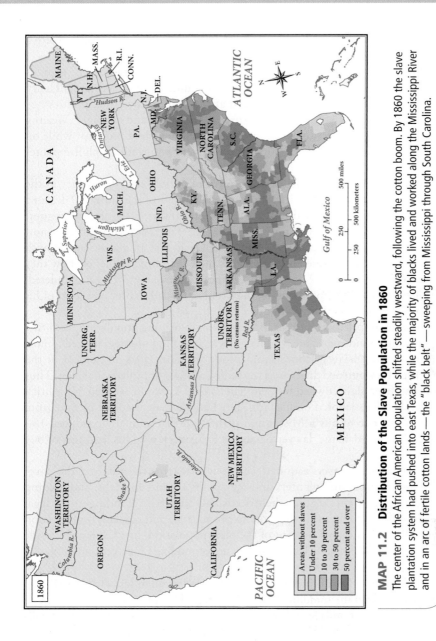

**MAP 11.2   Distribution of the Slave Population in 1860**

The center of the African American population shifted steadily westward, following the cotton boom. By 1860 the slave plantation system had pushed into east Texas, while the majority of blacks lived and worked along the Mississippi River and in an arc of fertile cotton lands — the "black belt" — sweeping from Mississippi through South Carolina.

by contrast, a prosperous southern yeoman or northern farmer owned property worth a mere $3,200.

Wealthy southerners cast themselves as a **republican aristocracy**. "The planters here are essentially what the nobility are in other countries," declared James Henry Hammond of South Carolina. "They stand at the head of society & politics . . . [and form] an aristocracy of talents, of virtue, of generosity and courage." Wealthy planters feared federal government interference with their slave property, while on the state level, they worried about populist politicians who would mobilize poorer whites.

Many southern leaders criticized the growth of middle-class democracy in the Northeast and Midwest. "Inequality is the fundamental law of the universe," declared one planter. Others condemned professional politicians as "a set of demagogues" and questioned the legitimacy of universal suffrage. "Times are sadly different now to what they were when I was a boy," lamented David Gavin, a prosperous South Carolinian. Then, the "Sovereign people, alias mob" had little influence; now they vied for power with the elite. "[How can] I rejoice for a freedom," Gavin thundered, "which allows every bankrupt, swindler, thief, and scoundrel, traitor and seller of his vote to be placed on an equality with myself?"

Substantial proprietors, another fifth of the slave-owning population, held title to six to twenty bondsmen and -women. These middling planters owned almost 40 percent of the enslaved laborers and produced more than 30 percent of the cotton. Often they pursued dual careers as skilled artisans or professional men. Thus some of the fifteen slaves owned by Georgian Samuel L. Moore worked in his brick factory, while others labored on his farm. Dr. Thomas Gale used the income from his medical practice to buy a Mississippi plantation that annually produced 150 bales of cotton. In Alabama, lawyer Benjamin Fitzpatrick used his legal fees to buy ten slaves.

Like Fitzpatrick, lawyers acquired wealth by managing the affairs of the slave-owning elite, representing planters and merchants in suits for debt, and helping smallholders and tenants register their deeds and contracts. Standing at the legal crossroads of their small towns, they rose to prominence and regularly won election to public office. Less than 1 percent of the male population, in 1828 lawyers made up 16 percent of the Alabama legislature and an astounding 26 percent in 1849.

**Small Freeholders**    Smallholding slave owners were much less visible than the wealthy grandees and the middling lawyer-planters. These planters held from one to five black laborers in bondage and owned a few hundred acres of land. Some small-holders were well-connected young men who would rise to wealth when their father's death blessed them with more land and slaves. Others were poor but ambitious men trying to pull themselves up by their bootstraps, often encouraged by elite planters and proslavery advocates. "Ours is a proslavery form of Government, and the pro-slavery element should be increased," declared a Georgia newspaper. "We would like to see every white man at the South the owner of a family of negroes." Some aspiring planters achieved modest prosperity. A German settler reported from Alabama in 1855 that "nearly all his countrymen" who emigrated with him were slaveholders. "They were poor on their arrival in the country; but no sooner did they realize a little money than they invested it in slaves."

Bolstered by the patriarchal ideology of the planter class, middling farmers ruled with a firm hand. The male head of the household had legal authority over all the dependents—wives, children, and slaves—and, according to one South Carolina judge, the right on his property "to be as churlish as he pleases." Their wives had little power; like women in the North, under the laws of coverture, they lost their legal identity when they married (Chapter 10). To express their concerns, many southern women joined churches, where they usually outnumbered men by a margin of two to one. Women especially welcomed the message of spiritual equality preached in evangelical Baptist and Methodist churches, and they hoped that the church community would hold their husbands to the same standards of Christian behavior to which they conformed. However, most churches supported patriarchal rule and told female members to remain in "wifely obedience" to their husbands.

Whatever their authority within the household, most southern freeholders lived and died as hardscrabble farmers. They worked alongside their slaves in the fields, struggled to make ends meet as their families grew, and moved regularly in search of opportunity. In 1847, James Buckner Barry left North Carolina with his new wife and two slaves to settle in Bosque County, Texas. There he worked part-time as an Indian fighter while his slaves toiled on a drought-ridden farm that barely kept the family in food. In South Carolina, W. J. Simpson struggled for years as a smallholding cotton planter and then gave up. He hired out one of his two slaves and went to work as an overseer on his father's farm.

**Poor Freemen** Less fortunate smallholders fell from the privileged ranks of the slave-owning classes. Selling their land and slaves to pay off debts, they joined the mass of propertyless tenants who farmed the estates of wealthy landlords. In 1860, in Hancock County, Georgia, there were 56 slave-owning planters and 300 propertyless white farm laborers and factory workers; in nearby Hart County, 25 percent of the white farmers were tenants. Across the South, about 40 percent of the white population worked as tenants or farm laborers. As the *Southern Cultivator* observed, they had "no legal right nor interest in the soil [and] no homes of their own."

Propertyless whites suffered the ill consequences of living in a slave society that accorded little respect to hardworking white laborers. Nor could they hope for a better life for their children, because slave owners refused to pay taxes to fund public schools. Moreover, wealthy planters bid up the price of slaves, depriving white laborers and tenants of easy access to the labor required to accumulate wealth. Finally, planter-dominated legislatures forced all white men, whether they owned slaves or not, to serve in the patrols and militias that deterred black uprisings. After touring the South, the future architect of New York's Central Park, Frederick Law Olmsted, concluded that the majority of white southerners "are poor. They . . . have little—very little—of the common comforts and consolations of civilized life. Their destitution is not material only; it is intellectual and it is moral."

Marking this moral destitution, poor whites enjoyed the psychological satisfaction that they ranked above blacks. As Alfred Iverson, a U.S. senator from Georgia, explained: a white man "walks erect in the dignity of his color and race, and feels that he is a superior being, with the more exalted powers and privileges than others." To reinforce that sense of racial superiority, planter James Henry Hammond told his poor white neighbors, "In a slave country every freeman is an aristocrat."

**North Carolina Emigrants:** *Poor White Folks*  Completed in 1845, James Henry Beard's (1811–1893) painting depicts a family moving north to Ohio. Unlike many optimistic scenes of emigration, the picture conveys a sense of resigned despair. The family members, led by a sullen, disheveled father, pause at a water trough while their cow drinks and their dog chews a bone. The mother looks apprehensively toward the future as she cradles a child; two barefoot older children listlessly await their father's command. New York writer Charles Briggs interpreted the painting as an "eloquent sermon on Anti-Slavery . . . , the blight of Slavery has paralyzed the strong arm of the man and destroyed the spirit of the woman." Although primarily a portrait painter, Beard questioned the ethics and optimism of American culture in *Ohio Land Speculator* (1840) and *The Last Victim of the Deluge* (1849), as well as in *Poor White Folks.* Cincinnati Art Museum, Ohio, USA/Gift of the Proctor & Gamble Company/Bridgeman Images.

Rejecting that half-truth, many southern whites fled planter-dominated counties in the 1830s and sought farms in the Appalachian hill country and beyond—in western Virginia, Kentucky, Tennessee, the southern regions of Illinois and Indiana, and Missouri. Living as small farmers, they used family labor to grow foodstuffs for sustenance. To obtain cash or store credit to buy agricultural implements, cloth, shoes, salt, and other necessities, farm families sold their surplus crops, raised hogs for market sale, and—when the price of cotton rose sharply—grew a few bales. Their goals were modest: on the family level, they wanted to preserve their holdings and buy enough land to set up their children as small-scale farmers. As citizens, smallholders wanted to control their local government and elect men of their own kind to public office. But most understood that the slave-based cotton economy sentenced family farmers to a subordinate place in the social order. They could hope for a life of independence and dignity only by moving north or farther west, where labor was "free" and hard work was respected.

By the 1830s, settlers from the South had carried both small farming and plantation slavery into Arkansas and Missouri. Between those states and the Rocky Mountains stretched great grasslands. An army explorer, Major Stephen H. Long, thought the plains region "almost wholly unfit for cultivation" and in 1820 labeled it the **Great American Desert**. The label stuck. Americans looking for land turned south, to Mexican territory. At the same time, elite planters struggled to control state governments in the Cotton South.

## The Settlement of Texas

After winning independence from Spain in 1821, the Mexican government pursued an activist settlement policy. To encourage migration to the newly reconfigured state of Coahuila y Tejas, it offered sizable land grants both to its own citizens and to American emigrants. Moses Austin, an American land speculator, settled smallholding farmers on his large grant, and his son, Stephen F. Austin, acquired even more land—some 180,000 acres—which he sold to newcomers. By 1835, about 27,000 white Americans and their 3,000 African American slaves were raising cotton and cattle in the well-watered plains and hills of eastern and central Texas. They far outnumbered the 3,000 Mexican residents, who lived primarily near the southwestern Texas towns of Goliad and San Antonio.

When Mexico in 1835 adopted a new constitution creating a stronger central government and dissolving state legislatures, the Americans split into two groups. The "war party," led by Sam Houston and recent migrants from Georgia, demanded independence for Texas. Members of the "peace party," led by Stephen Austin, negotiated with the central government in Mexico City for greater political autonomy. They believed Texas could flourish within a decentralized Mexican republic, a "federal" constitutional system favored by the Liberal Party in Mexico (and advocated in the United States by Jacksonian Democrats). Austin won significant concessions for the Texans, including an exemption from a law ending slavery, but in 1835 Mexico's president, General Antonio López de Santa Anna, nullified them. Santa Anna wanted to impose national authority throughout Mexico. Fearing central control, the war party provoked a rebellion that most of the American settlers ultimately supported. On March 2, 1836, the American rebels proclaimed the independence of Texas and adopted a constitution legalizing slavery.

To put down the rebellion, President Santa Anna led an army that wiped out the Texan garrison defending the **Alamo** in San Antonio and then captured Goliad, executing about 350 prisoners of war (see Map 11.3). Santa Anna thought that he had crushed the rebellion, but New Orleans and New York newspapers romanticized the deaths at the Alamo of folk heroes Davy Crockett and Jim Bowie. Drawing on anti-Catholic sentiment aroused by Irish immigration and the massacre at Goliad, they urged Americans to "Remember the Alamo" and depicted the Mexicans as tyrannical butchers in the service of the pope. American adventurers, lured by offers of land grants, flocked to Texas to join the rebel forces. Commanded by General Sam Houston, the Texans routed Santa Anna's overconfident army in the Battle of San Jacinto in April 1836, winning de facto independence. The Mexican government refused to recognize the Texas Republic but, for the moment, did not seek to conquer it.

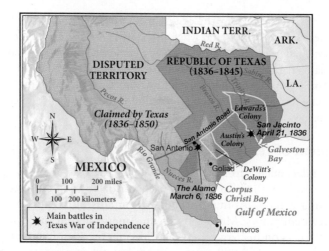

**MAP 11.3   American Settlements, Texas War of Independence, and Boundary Disputes**

During the 1820s the Mexican government encouraged Americans to settle in the sparsely populated state of Coahuila y Tejas. By 1835 the nearly 30,000 Americans far outnumbered Mexican residents. To put down an American-led revolt, General Santa Anna led 6,000 soldiers into Tejas in 1836. After overwhelming the rebels at the Alamo in March, Santa Anna set out to capture the Texas Provisional Government, which had fled to Galveston. But the Texans' victory at San Jacinto in April ended the war and secured de facto independence for the Republic of Texas (1836–1845). However, the annexation of Texas to the United States sparked a war with Mexico in 1846, and the state's boundaries remained in dispute until the Compromise of 1850.

The Texans voted for annexation by the United States, but President Martin Van Buren refused to bring the issue before Congress. As a Texas diplomat reported, the cautious Van Buren and other party politicians feared that annexation would spark a war with Mexico and, beyond that, a "desperate death-struggle . . . between the North and the South [over the extension of slavery]; a struggle involving the probability of a dissolution of the Union."

## The Politics of Democracy

As national leaders refused admission to Texas, elite planters faced political challenges in the Cotton South. Unlike the planter-aristocrats who ruled the colonial world, they lived in a republican society with a democratic ethos. The Alabama Constitution of 1819 granted suffrage to all white men; it also provided for a **secret ballot** (rather than voice-voting); apportionment of legislative seats based on population; and the election of county supervisors, sheriffs, and clerks of court. Given these democratic provisions, political factions in Alabama had to compete for votes. When a Whig newspaper sarcastically asked whether the state's policies should "be governed and controlled by the whim and caprice of the majority of the people," Democrats hailed the power of the common folk. They called on "Farmers, Mechanics, laboring men" to repudiate Whig "aristocrats . . . the soft handed and soft headed gentry."

**Taxation Policy**   Whatever the electioneering rhetoric, most Whig and Democrat political candidates were men of means. In the early 1840s, nearly 90 percent of Alabama's legislators owned slaves, testimony to the political power of the slave-owning minority. Still, relatively few lawmakers — only about 10 percent — were rich planters, a group voters by and large distrusted. "A rich man cannot sympathize with the poor," declared one candidate. Consequently, the majority of state and county officials in the Cotton South came from the ranks of middle-level planters and planter-lawyers. Astute politicians, they refrained from laying "oppressive" taxes on the people, particularly the white majority who owned no slaves. Between 1830 and 1860, the Alabama legislature obtained about 70 percent of the state's revenue from taxes on slaves and land. Another 10 to 15 percent came from levies on carriages, gold watches, and other luxury goods and on the capital invested in banks, transportation companies, and manufacturing enterprises.

To win the votes of taxpaying slave owners, Alabama Democrats advocated limited government and low taxes. They attacked their Whig opponents for favoring higher taxes and for providing government subsidies for banks, canals, railroads, and other internal improvements. "Voting against appropriations is the safe and popular side," one Democratic legislator declared, and his colleagues agreed; until the 1850s, they rejected most of the bills that would have granted subsidies to transportation companies or banks.

If tax policy in Alabama had a democratic thrust, elsewhere in the South it did not. In some states, wealthy planters used their political muscle to exempt slave property from taxation. Or they shifted the burden to backcountry freeholders, who owned low-quality pasturelands, by taxing farms according to acreage rather than value. Planter-legislators also spared themselves the cost of building fences around their fields by requiring small farmers to "fence in" their livestock. And, during the 1850s, wealthy legislators throughout the South used public funds to subsidize the canals and railroads in which they had invested, ignoring the protests of yeoman-backed legislators.

**The Paradox of Southern Prosperity**   Even without these internal improvements, the South had a strong economy. Indeed, it ranked fourth in the world in 1860, with a per capita income among whites higher than that of France and Germany. As a contributor to a Georgia newspaper argued in the 1850s, planters and yeomen should not complain about "tariffs, and merchants, and manufacturers" because "the most highly prosperous people now on earth, are to be found in these very [slave] States." Such arguments tell only part of the story. Nearly all African Americans — 40 percent of the population — lived in dire and permanent poverty. And, although the average southern white man was 80 percent richer than the average northerner in 1860, the southerner's *nonslave* wealth was only 60 percent of the northern average. Moreover, the wealth of the industrializing Northeast was increasing at a faster pace than that of the South. Between 1820 and 1860, slave-related trade across the Atlantic declined from 12.6 percent of world trade to 5.3 percent.

Influential southerners blamed the shortcomings of their plantation-based economy on outsiders: "Purely agricultural people," intoned slave-owning planter-politician James Henry Hammond, "have been in all ages the victims of rapacious tyrants grinding them down." And they steadfastly defended their way of life.

***Colonel and Mrs. James A. Whiteside, Son Charles and Servants*** James A. Whiteside (1803–1861) was a Tennessee lawyer, politician, land speculator, and entrepreneur, with investments in iron manufacturing, banking, steamboats, and railroads. In 1857, he became vice president of the Nashville, Chattanooga, and St. Louis Railroad. The following year, Whiteside persuaded the Scottish-born painter James Cameron (1817–1882) to move to Chattanooga, where Cameron completed this ambitious portrait of the colonel; his second wife, Harriet; their youngest child, Charles; and two enslaved "servants." The painting shows the family at home, with a view of Chattanooga and of Lookout Mountain, where the colonel had built a hotel. Whiteside died from pneumonia in 1861 after returning home from Virginia with his son James, who had fallen ill while serving in the Confederate army. Hunter Museum of American Art, Chattanooga, Tennessee. Oil on canvas, c. 1858–1859. Gift of Mr. & Mrs. Thomas B. Whiteside, 1975.7.

"We have no cities — we don't want them," boasted U.S. senator Louis Wigfall of Texas in 1861. "We want no manufactures: we desire no trading, no mechanical or manufacturing classes. . . . As long as we have our rice, our sugar, our tobacco, and our cotton, we can command wealth to purchase all we want." So wealthy southerners continued to buy land and slaves, a strategy that neglected investments in the great technological innovations of the nineteenth century — water- and steam-powered factories, machine tools, steel plows, and crushed-gravel roads — that would have raised the South's productivity and wealth.

Urban growth, the key to prosperity in Europe and the North, occurred primarily in the commercial cities around the periphery of the South: New Orleans, St. Louis, and Baltimore. Factories — often staffed by slave labor — appeared primarily in the Chesapeake region, which had a diverse agricultural economy and a surplus of enslaved workers. Within the Cotton South, wealthy planters invested in railroads primarily to grow and sell more cotton; when the Western & Atlantic Railroad reached the Georgia upcountry, the cotton crop there quickly doubled. Cotton and agriculture remained king.

Slavery also deterred Europeans from migrating to the South, because they feared competition from bound labor. Their absence deprived the region of skilled artisans and of hardworking laborers to drain swamps, dig canals, smelt iron, and work on railroads. When entrepreneurs tried to hire slaves for these dangerous tasks, planters replied that "a negro's life is too valuable to be risked." Slave owners also feared that hiring out would make their slaves too independent. As a planter told Frederick Law Olmsted, such workers "had too much liberty . . . and got a habit of roaming about and taking care of themselves."

Thus, despite its increasing size and booming exports, the South remained an economic colony: Great Britain and the North bought its staple crops and provided its manufactures, financial services, and shipping facilities. In 1860, some 84 percent of southerners — more than double the percentage in the northern states — still worked in agriculture, and southern factories turned out only 10 percent of the nation's manufactures. The South's fixation on an "exclusive and exhausting" system of cotton monoculture and slave labor filled South Carolina textile entrepreneur William Gregg with "dark forebodings": "It has produced us such an abundant supply of all the luxuries and elegances of life, with so little exertion on our part, that we have become enervated, unfitted for other and more laborious pursuits."

> **IN YOUR OWN WORDS**    What were the strengths and limitations of the South's economy and social structure?

# The African American World

By the 1820s, the cultural life of most slaves reflected both the values and customs of their West African ancestors and the language, laws, and religious beliefs of the South's white population. This mix of African- and European-derived cultural values persisted for decades because whites discouraged blacks from assimilating and because slaves prized their diverse African heritages.

## Evangelical Black Protestantism

The emergence of black Christianity illustrated the synthesis of African and European cultures. From the 1790s to the 1840s, the Second Great Awakening swept over the South, and evangelical Baptist and Methodist preachers converted thousands of white families and hundreds of enslaved blacks. Until that time, African-born blacks, often identifiable by their ritual scars, had maintained the religious practices of their homelands.

**African Religions and Christian Conversion**    Africans carried their traditional religious practices to the United States. Some practiced Islam, but the majority relied on African gods and spirits. As late as 1842, Charles C. Jones, a Presbyterian minister, noted that the blacks on his family's plantation in Georgia believed "in second-sight, in apparitions, charms, witchcraft . . . [and other] superstitions brought from Africa." Fearing for their own souls if they withheld "the means of salvation" from African Americans, Jones and other zealous Protestant preachers and planters set out to convert slaves.

Other Protestant crusaders came from the ranks of pious black men and women who had become Christians in the Chesapeake. Swept to the Cotton South by the domestic slave trade, they carried with them the evangelical message of emotional conversion, ritual baptism, and communal spirituality. Equally important, these crusaders adapted Protestant doctrines to black needs. Enslaved Christians pointed out that blacks as well as whites were "children of God" and should be treated accordingly. **Black Protestantism** generally ignored the doctrines of original sin and predestination, and preachers didn't use biblical passages that encouraged unthinking obedience to authority. A white minister in Liberty County, Georgia, reported that when he urged slaves to obey their masters, "one half of my audience deliberately rose up and walked off."

**Black Worship**    Indeed, some African American converts envisioned the deity as the Old Testament warrior who had liberated the Jews and so would liberate them. Inspired by a vision of Christ, Nat Turner led his bloody rebellion against slavery in Virginia (see Chapter 10). Other black Christians saw themselves as Chosen People: "de people dat is born of God." Charles Davenport, a Mississippi slave, recalled black preachers "exhort[ing] us dat us was de chillun o' Israel in de wilderness an' de Lawd done sont us to take dis lan' o' milk an' honey."

Still, African Americans expressed their Christianity in distinctive ways. The thousands of blacks who joined the Methodist Church respected its ban on profane dancing but praised the Lord in what minister Henry George Spaulding called the "religious dance of the Negroes." Spaulding described the African-derived "ring shout" this way: "Three or four, standing still, clapping their hands and beating time with their feet, commence singing in unison one of the peculiar shout melodies, while the others walk around in a ring, in single file, joining also in the song." The songs themselves were usually collective creations, devised spontaneously from bits of old hymns and tunes. Recalled an ex-slave:

> We'd all be at the "prayer house" de Lord's day, and de white preacher he'd splain de word and read whar Esekial done say—Dry bones gwine ter lib ergin. And, honey, de Lord would come a-shinin' thoo dem pages and revive dis ole nigger's heart, and I'd jump up dar and den and holler and shout and sing and pat, and dey would all cotch de words and I'd sing it to some ole shout song I'd heard 'em sing from Africa, and dey'd all take it up and keep at it, and keep a-addin' to it, and den it would be a spiritual.

By such African-influenced means, black congregations devised a distinctive and joyous brand of Protestant worship to sustain them on the long journey to emancipation and the Promised Land. "O my Lord delivered Daniel," the slaves sang. "O why not deliver me too?"

## Forging Families and Communities

Black Protestantism was one facet of an increasingly homogeneous African American culture in the rural South. Even in South Carolina—a major point of entry for imported slaves—only 20 percent of the black residents in 1820 had been born in Africa. The domestic slave trade mingled blacks from many states, erased regional differences, and prompted the emergence of a core culture in the Lower Mississippi

Valley. A prime example was the fate of the **Gullah dialect**, which combined words from English and a variety of African languages in an African grammatical structure. Spoken by blacks in the Carolina lowcountry well into the twentieth century, Gullah did not take root on the cotton plantations of Alabama and Mississippi. There, slaves from Carolina were far outnumbered by migrants from the Chesapeake, who spoke black English. Like Gullah, black English used double negatives and other African grammatical forms, but it consisted primarily of English words rendered with West African pronunciation (for example, with *th* pronounced as *d*—"de preacher").

Nonetheless, African influences remained significant. At least one-third of the slaves who entered the United States between 1776 and 1809 came from the Congo region of West-Central Africa, and they brought their cultures with them. As traveler Isaac Holmes reported in 1821: "In Louisiana, and the state of Mississippi, the slaves . . . dance for several hours during Sunday afternoon. The general movement is in what they call the Congo dance." Similar descriptions of blacks who "danced the Congo and sang a purely African song to the accompaniment of . . . a drum" appeared as late as 1890.

African Americans also continued to respect African incest taboos by shunning marriages between cousins. On the Good Hope Plantation in South Carolina, nearly half of the slave children born between 1800 and 1857 were related by blood to one another; yet when they married, only one of every forty-one unions took place between cousins. White planters were not the source of this taboo: cousin marriages were frequent among the 440 South Carolina men and women who owned at least 100 slaves in 1860, in part because such unions kept wealth within an extended family.

Unlike white marriages, slave unions were not legally binding. According to a Louisiana judge, "slaves have no legal capacity to assent to any contract . . . because slaves are deprived of all civil rights." Nonetheless, many African Americans took marriage vows before Christian ministers or publicly marked their union in ceremonies that included the West African custom of jumping over a broomstick together. Once married, newly arrived young people in the Cotton South often chose older people in their new communities as fictive "aunts" and "uncles." The slave trade had destroyed their family but not their family values.

The creation of fictive kinship ties was part of a community-building process, a partial substitute for the family ties that sustained whites during periods of crisis. Naming children was another. Recently imported slaves frequently gave their children African names. Males born on Friday, for example, were often called Cuffee—the name of that day in several West African languages. Many American-born parents chose names of British origin, but they usually named sons after fathers, uncles, or grandfathers and daughters after grandmothers. Those transported to the Cotton South often named their children for relatives left behind. Like incest rules and marriage rituals, this intergenerational sharing of names evoked memories of a lost world and bolstered kin ties in the new one.

## Negotiating Rights

By forming stable families and communities, African Americans gradually created a sense of order in the harsh and arbitrary world of slavery. In a few regions, slaves won substantial control over their lives.

**Working Lives**    During the Revolutionary era, blacks in the rice-growing lowlands of South Carolina successfully asserted the right to labor by the "task." Under the **task system**, workers had to complete a precisely defined job each day—for example, digging up a quarter-acre of land, hoeing half an acre, or pounding seven mortars of rice. By working hard, many finished their tasks by early afternoon, a Methodist preacher reported, and had "the rest of the day for themselves, which they spend in working their own private fields . . . planting rice, corn, potatoes, tobacco &c. for their own use and profit."

Slaves on sugar and cotton plantations led more regimented lives, thanks to the gang-labor system. As one field hand put it, there was "no time off [between] de change of de seasons. . . . Dey was allus clearin' mo' lan' or sump'." Many slaves faced bans on growing crops on their own. "It gives an excuse for trading," explained one owner, and that encouraged roaming and independence. Still, many masters hired out surplus workers as teamsters, drovers, steamboat workers, turpentine gatherers, and railroad builders; in 1856, no fewer than 435 hired slaves laid track for the Virginia & Tennessee Railroad. Many owners regretted the result. As an overseer remarked about a slave named John, "He is not as good a hand as he was before he went to Alabamy."

The planters' greatest fear was that enslaved African Americans—a majority of the population in most cotton-growing counties—would rise in rebellion. Legally speaking, owners had virtually unlimited power over their slaves. "The power of the master must be absolute," intoned Justice Thomas Ruffin of the North Carolina Supreme Court in 1829. But absolute power required brutal coercion, and only hardened or sadistic masters had the stomach for such violence. "These poor negroes, receiving none of the fruits of their labor, do not love work," explained one woman who worked her own farm; "if we had slaves, we should have to . . . beat them to make use of them."

Moreover, passive resistance by African Americans seriously limited their owners' power. Slaves slowed the pace of work by feigning illness and losing or breaking tools. One Maryland slave, faced with transport to Mississippi and separation from his wife, flatly refused "to accompany my people, or to be exchanged or sold," his owner reported. Masters ignored such feelings at their peril. A slave (or a relative) might retaliate by setting fire to the master's house and barns, poisoning his food, or destroying his crops. Fear of resistance, as well as critical scrutiny by abolitionists, prompted many masters to reduce their reliance on the lash and use positive incentives such as food and special privileges. Noted Frederick Law Olmsted: "Men of sense have discovered that it was better to offer them rewards than to whip them." Nonetheless, owners could always resort to violence, and countless masters regularly asserted their power by demanding sex from their female slaves. As ex-slave Bethany Veney lamented in her autobiography, from "the unbridled lust of the slave-owner . . . the law holds . . . no protecting arm" over black women.

**Survival Strategies**    Slavery remained an exploitative system grounded in fear and coercion. Over the decades, hundreds of individual slaves responded by attacking their masters and overseers. But only a few blacks—among them Gabriel and Martin Prosser (1800) and Nat Turner (1831) (Chapter 10)—plotted mass uprisings. Most slaves recognized that revolt would be futile. The tasks of planning, organizing, and assembling weapons for such an action were all but impossible under the constraints of slavery. Whites, by contrast, were readily mobilized, well armed, and determined to maintain their position of racial superiority.

Escape was equally problematic. Blacks in the Upper South could flee to the North, but only by leaving their families and kin. Slaves in the Lower South escaped to sparsely settled regions of Florida, where some intermarried with the Seminole Indians. Elsewhere in the South, escaped slaves eked out a meager existence in inhospitable marshy areas or mountain valleys. Consequently, most African Americans remained on plantations; as Frederick Douglass put it, they were "pegged down to one single spot, and must take root there or die."

"Taking root" meant building the best possible lives for themselves. Over time, enslaved African Americans pressed their owners for a greater share of the product of their labor, much like unionized workers in the North were doing. Thus slaves insisted on getting paid for "overwork" and on the right to cultivate a garden and sell its produce. "De menfolks tend to de gardens round dey own house," recalled a Louisiana slave. "Dey raise some cotton and sell it to massa and git li'l money dat way." Enslaved women raised poultry and sold chickens and eggs. An Alabama slave remembered buying "Sunday clothes with dat money, sech as hats and pants and shoes and dresses." By the 1850s, thousands of African Americans were reaping the small rewards of this underground economy, and some accumulated sizable property. Enslaved Georgia carpenter Alexander Steele owned four horses, a mule, a silver watch, two cows, a wagon, and large quantities of fodder, hay, and corn.

Whatever their material circumstances, few slaves accepted the legitimacy of their status. Although he was fed well and never whipped, a former slave told an English traveler, "I was cruelly treated because I was kept in slavery." In an address to a white audience on the Fourth of July, the escaped slave and abolitionist Frederick Douglass asked, "What, to the American slave, is your Fourth of July? I answer: a day that reveals to him, more than all other days in the year, the gross injustice and cruelty to which he is the constant victim."

| **IN YOUR OWN WORDS** | What resources and strategies gave African American slaves a measure of control over their lives? |
|---|---|

# Manifest Destiny, North and South

The institution of slavery cast a pall over national politics. The Missouri crisis of 1819–1821 (Chapter 9) frightened the nation's leaders. For the next two decades, the professional politicians who ran the Second Party System avoided policies, such as the annexation of the slaveholding Republic of Texas, that would prompt regional strife. Then, during the 1840s, many citizens embraced an ideology of expansion and proclaimed a God-given duty to extend American republicanism to the Pacific Ocean. But whose republican institutions: the hierarchical slave system of the South or the more egalitarian, reform-minded, capitalist-managed society of the North and Midwest? Or both? Ultimately, the failure to find a political solution to this question would rip the nation apart.

## The Push to the Pacific

As expansionists developed continental ambitions, the term *Manifest Destiny* captured those dreams. John L. O'Sullivan, editor of the *Democratic Review*, coined the phrase in 1845: "Our manifest destiny is to overspread the continent allotted by Providence for the free development of our yearly multiplying millions." Underlying the rhetoric of Manifest Destiny was a sense of Anglo-American cultural and racial superiority: the "inferior" peoples who lived in the Far West—Native Americans and Mexicans—would be subjected to American dominion, taught republicanism, and converted to Protestantism.

Long before American politicians became interested in the Far West, however, the region was enmeshed in trade systems that connected Pacific coast settlements with Asia, Europe, and eastern North America. Russian traders made contact with Aleut and Tlingit communities in Alaska in the late eighteenth century and developed a lucrative trade in sea otter pelts, which was controlled after 1799 by the Russian-American Company. British explorer James Cook mapped the Pacific coast in 1778 and learned of the great demand for sea otter pelts in China, prompting a series of British trading voyages to the Pacific Northwest. Between 1788 and 1814, American traders based in Boston overtook their British rivals and dominated the region's maritime trade. Then, in the nineteenth century, overland traders from the Pacific Fur Company of John Jacob Astor, the North West Company based in Montreal, and the Hudson's Bay Company all pushed westward to establish footholds in the region. Thus, the Native peoples of the Pacific Northwest had had sustained contact with Europeans for two generations before the United States became interested in settlement there.

**Oregon**    As a result of their overlapping trading activities, Britain and the United States agreed in 1818 to joint control of the Oregon Country, which allowed settlement by people from both nations. Under its terms, the British-run Hudson's Bay Company developed a lucrative fur business and oversaw Indian relations north of the Columbia River, while Methodist missionaries and a few hundred American farmers settled to the south, in the Willamette Valley (Map 11.4).

In 1842, American interest in Oregon increased dramatically. The U.S. Navy published a glowing report of fine harbors in the Puget Sound, which New England merchants trading with China were already using. Simultaneously, a party of one hundred farmers journeyed along the Oregon Trail, which fur traders and explorers had blazed from Independence, Missouri, across the Great Plains and the Rocky Mountains (Map 11.5). Their letters from Oregon told of a mild climate and rich soil.

"Oregon fever" suddenly raged. A thousand men, women, and children—with a hundred wagons and five thousand oxen and cattle—gathered in Independence in April 1843. As the spring mud dried, they began their six-month trek, hoping to miss the winter snows. Another 5,000 settlers, mostly farm families from the southern border states (Missouri, Kentucky, and Tennessee), set out over the next two years. These pioneers overcame floods, dust storms, livestock deaths, and a few armed encounters with Native peoples before reaching Oregon, a journey of 2,000 miles.

By 1860, about 250,000 Americans had braved the **Oregon Trail**, with 65,000 heading for Oregon, 185,000 to California, and others staying in Wyoming, Idaho,

**MAP 11.4 Territorial Conflict in Oregon, 1819–1846**
As thousands of American settlers poured into the Oregon Country in the early 1840s, British authorities tried to keep them south of the Columbia River. However, the migrants—and fervent expansionists—asserted that Americans could settle anywhere in the territory, raising the prospect of armed conflict. In 1846, British and American diplomats resolved the dispute by dividing most of the region at the forty-ninth parallel while giving both nations access to fine harbors (Vancouver and Seattle) through the Strait of Juan de Fuca.

and Montana. More than 34,000 migrants died, mostly from disease and exposure; fewer than 500 deaths resulted from Indian attacks. The walking migrants wore paths 3 feet deep, and their wagons carved 5-foot ruts across sandstone formations in southern Wyoming—tracks that are visible today. Women found the trail especially difficult; in addition to their usual chores and the new work of driving wagons and animals, they lacked the support of female kin and the security of their domestic space. About 2,500 women endured pregnancy or gave birth during the long journey, and some did not survive. "There was a woman died in this train yesterday," Jane Gould Tortillott noted in her diary. "She left six children, one of them only two days old."

The 10,000 migrants who made it to Oregon in the 1840s mostly settled in the Willamette Valley. Many families squatted on 640 acres and hoped Congress would legalize their claims so that they could sell surplus acreage to new migrants. The settlers quickly created a race- and gender-defined polity by restricting voting to a "free male descendant of a white man."

**California** About 3,000 other early migrants ended up in the Mexican province of California. They left the Oregon Trail along the Snake River, trudged down the California Trail, and mostly settled in the interior along the Sacramento River, where there were few Mexicans. A remote outpost of Spain's American empire, California had few nonnative residents until the 1770s, when Spanish authorities built a chain of forts and religious missions along the Pacific coast. When Mexico achieved independence in 1821, its government took over the Franciscan-run missions and freed the 20,000 Indians whom the monks had persuaded or coerced into working on them. Some mission Indians rejoined their tribes, but many intermarried with mestizos (Mexicans of mixed Spanish and Indian ancestry). They worked on

**MAP 11.5    The Great Plains: Settler Trails, Indian Raiders, and Traders**

By the 1850s, the Mormon, Oregon, and Santa Fe trails ran across "Indian Country," the semiarid, bison-filled Great Plains west of the ninety-fifth meridian, and then through the Rocky Mountains. Tens of thousands of Americans set out on these trails to found new communities in Utah, Oregon, New Mexico, and California. This mass migration exposed sedentary Indian peoples to American diseases, guns, and manufactures. However, raids by Comanches and Sioux affected their lives even more significantly, as did the Euro-American traders who provided a ready market for Indian horses and mules, dried meat, and bison skins.

huge ranches—the 450 estates created by Mexican officials and bestowed primarily on their families and political allies. The owners of these vast properties (averaging 19,000 acres) mostly raised Spanish cattle, prized for their hides and tallow.

The ranches soon linked California to the American economy. New England merchants dispatched dozens of agents to buy leather for the booming Massachusetts boot and shoe industry and tallow to make soap and candles. Many agents married the daughters of the elite Mexican ranchers — the **Californios** — and adopted their manners, attitudes, and Catholic religion. A crucial exception was Thomas Oliver Larkin, a successful merchant in the coastal town of Monterey. Although Larkin worked closely with Mexican politicians and landowners, he remained strongly American in outlook.

Like Larkin, the American migrants in the Sacramento River Valley did not assimilate into Mexican society. Some hoped to emulate the Americans in Texas by colonizing the country and then seeking annexation. However, in the early 1840s, these settlers numbered only about 1,000, far outnumbered by the 7,000 Mexicans who lived along the coast.

## The Plains Indians

As the Pacific-bound wagon trains rumbled across Nebraska along the broad Platte River, the migrants encountered the unique ecology of the Great Plains. A vast sea of wild grasses stretched from Texas to Saskatchewan in Canada, and west from the Missouri River to the Rocky Mountains. Tall grasses flourished in the eastern regions of the future states of Kansas, Nebraska, and the Dakotas, where there was moderate rainfall. To the west, in the semiarid region beyond the ninety-fifth meridian, the migrants found short grasses that sustained a rich wildlife dominated by buffalo and grazing antelopes. Nomadic buffalo-hunting Indian peoples roamed the western plains, while the eastern river valleys were home to semisedentary tribes and, since the 1830s, the Indian peoples whom Andrew Jackson had "removed" to the west. A line of military forts — stretching from Fort Jesup in Louisiana to Fort Snelling, then in the Wisconsin Territory — policed the boundary between white settlements and what Congress in 1834 designated as Permanent Indian Territory.

For centuries, the Indians who lived on the eastern edge of the plains, such as the Pawnees and the Mandans on the Upper Missouri River, subsisted primarily on corn and beans, supplemented by buffalo meat. They hunted buffalo on foot, driving them over cliffs or into canyons for the kill. To the south, the nomadic Apaches acquired horses from Spanish settlers in New Mexico and ranged widely across the plains. The Comanches, who migrated down the Arkansas River from the Rocky Mountains around 1750, developed both a horse-based culture and imperial ambitions. Skilled buffalo hunters and fierce warriors, the Comanches slowly pushed the Apaches to the southern edge of the plains. They also raided Spanish settlements in New Mexico, incorporating captured women and children into their society.

After 1800, the Comanches gradually built up a pastoral economy, raising horses and mules and selling them to northern Indian peoples and to Euro-American farmers in Missouri and Arkansas. Many Comanche families owned thirty to thirty-five horses or mules, far more than the five or six required for hunting buffalo and fighting neighboring peoples. The Comanches also exchanged goods with merchants and travelers along the Santa Fe Trail, which cut through their territory as it connected Missouri and New Mexico. By the early 1840s, goods worth nearly $1 million moved along the trail each year.

By the 1830s, the Kiowas, Cheyennes, and Arapahos had also adopted this horse culture and, allied with the Comanches, dominated the plains between the Arkansas and Red rivers. The new culture brought sharper social divisions. Some Kiowa men owned hundreds of horses and had several "chore wives" and captive children who worked for them. Poor men, who owned only a few horses, had difficulty finding marriage partners and often had to work for their wealthy kinsmen.

While European horses made Plains Indians wealthier and more mobile, European diseases and guns thinned their ranks. A devastating smallpox epidemic spread northward from New Spain in 1779–1781 and killed half of the Plains peoples. Twenty years later, another smallpox outbreak left dozens of deserted villages along the Missouri River. Smallpox struck the northern plains again from 1837 to 1840, killing half of the Assiniboines and Blackfeet and nearly a third of the Crows, Pawnees, and Cheyennes. "If I could see this thing, if I knew where it came from, I would go there and fight it," exclaimed a distressed Cheyenne warrior.

European weapons also altered the geography of Native peoples. Around 1750, the Crees and Assiniboines, who lived on the far northern plains, acquired guns by trading wolf pelts and beaver skins to the British-run Hudson's Bay Company. Once armed, they drove the Blackfoot peoples westward into the Rocky Mountains and took control of the Saskatchewan and Upper Missouri River basins. When the Blackfeet obtained guns and horses around 1800, they emerged from the mountains and pushed the Shoshones and Crows to the south. Because horses could not easily find winter forage in the snow-filled plains north of the Platte River, Blackfoot families kept only five to ten horses and remained hunters rather than pastoralists.

The powerful Lakota Sioux, who acquired guns and ammunition from French, Spanish, and American traders along the Missouri River, also remained buffalo hunters. A nomadic war-prone people who lived in small groups, the Lakotas largely avoided major epidemics. They kept some sedentary peoples, such as the Arikaras, in subjection and raided others for their crops and horses. By the 1830s, the Lakotas were the dominant tribe on the central as well as the northern plains. "Those lands once belonged to the Kiowas and the Crows," boasted the Oglala Sioux chief Black Hawk, "but we whipped those nations out of them, and in this we did what the white men do when they want the lands of the Indians."

The Sioux's prosperity also came at the expense of the bison, which provided them with a diet rich in protein and with hides and robes to sell. The number of hides and robes shipped down the Missouri River each year by the American Fur Company and the Missouri Fur Company increased from 3,000 in the 1820s, to 45,000 in the 1830s, and to 90,000 annually after 1840. North of the Missouri, the story was much the same. The 24,000 Indians of that region—Blackfeet, Crees, and Assiniboines—annually killed about 160,000 bison. The women dried the meat to feed their people and to sell to white traders and soldiers. The women also undertook the arduous work of skinning and tanning the hides, which they fashioned into tepees, robes, and sleeping covers. Over time, Indian hunters increased the kill and traded surplus hides and robes—about 40,000 annually by the 1840s—for pots, knives, guns, and other Euro-American manufactures. As among the Kiowas, trade increased social divisions. "It is a fine sight," a traveler noted around 1850, "to see one of those big men among the Blackfeet, who has two or three lodges, five or six wives, twenty or thirty children, fifty to a hundred head of horses; for his trade amounts to upward of $2,000 per year."

Although the Blackfeet, Kiowas, and Lakotas contributed bison hides to the national economy, they did not fully grasp their market value as winter clothes, leather accessories, and industrial drive belts. Consequently, they could not demand the best price. Moreover, the increasing size of the kill diminished the bison herds. Between 1820 and 1870, the northern herd shrank from 5 million to less than 2 million. When the Assiniboines' cultural hero Inkton'mi had taught his people how to kill the bison, he told them that the animals "will live as long as your people. There will be no end of them until the end of time." Meant as a perpetual guarantee, by the 1860s Inkton'mi's words prefigured the end of time — the demise of traditional bison hunting and, perhaps, of the Assiniboines as well.

## The Fateful Election of 1844

The election of 1844 changed the American government's policy toward the Great Plains, the Far West, and Texas. Since 1836, southern leaders had supported the annexation of Texas, but cautious party politicians, pressured by northerners who opposed the expansion of slavery, had rebuffed them. Now rumors swirled that Great Britain was encouraging Texas to remain independent; wanted California as payment for the Mexican debts owed to British investors; and had designs on Spanish Cuba, which some slave owners wanted to add to the United States. To thwart such imagined schemes, southern expansionists demanded the immediate annexation of Texas.

At this crucial juncture, Oregon fever altered the political landscape in the North. In 1843, Americans in the Ohio River Valley and the Great Lakes states organized "Oregon conventions," and Democratic and Whig politicians alike called for American sovereignty over the entire Oregon Country, from Spanish California to Russian Alaska (which began at 54°40′ north latitude). With northerners demanding Oregon, President John Tyler, a proslavery zealot, called for the annexation of Texas. Disowned by the Whigs because he thwarted Henry Clay's nationalist economic program, Tyler hoped to win reelection in 1844 as a Democrat. To curry favor among northern expansionists, Tyler supported claims to all of Oregon.

In April 1844, Tyler and John C. Calhoun, his proslavery, expansionist-minded secretary of state, sent the Senate a treaty to bring Texas into the Union. However, the two major presidential hopefuls, Democrat Martin Van Buren and Whig Henry Clay, opposed Tyler's initiative. Fearful of raising the issue of slavery, they persuaded the Senate to reject the treaty.

Nonetheless, expansion into Texas and Oregon became the central issue in the election of 1844. Most southern Democrats favored Texas annexation and refused to support Van Buren's candidacy. The party also passed over Tyler, whom they did not trust. Instead, the Democrats selected Governor James K. Polk of Tennessee, a slave owner and an avowed expansionist. Known as "Young Hickory" because he was a protégé of Andrew Jackson, Polk shared his mentor's iron will, boundless ambition, and determination to open up lands for American settlement. Accepting the false claim in the Democratic Party platform that both areas already belonged to the United States, Polk campaigned for the "Re-occupation of Oregon and the Re-annexation of Texas." He insisted that the United States defy British claims and occupy "the whole of the territory of Oregon" to the Alaskan border. **"Fifty-four forty or fight!"** became his jingoistic cry.

The Whigs nominated Henry Clay, who again advocated his American System of high tariffs, internal improvements, and national banking. Clay initially dodged the issue of Texas but, seeking southern votes, ultimately supported annexation. Northern Whigs who opposed the admission of a new slave state refused to vote for Clay and cast their ballots for James G. Birney of the Liberty Party (Chapter 10). Birney garnered less than 3 percent of the national vote but took enough Whig votes in New York to cost Clay that state—and the presidency.

Following Polk's narrow victory, congressional Democrats called for immediate Texas statehood. However, they lacked the two-thirds majority in the Senate needed to ratify a treaty of annexation. So the Democrats admitted Texas using a joint resolution of Congress, which required just a majority vote in each house, and Texas became the twenty-eighth state in December 1845. Polk's strategy of linking Texas and Oregon had put him in the White House and Texas in the Union. Shortly, it would make the expansion of the South—and its system of slavery—the central topic of American politics.

| IN YOUR OWN WORDS | Did the idea of Manifest Destiny cause westward migration and political support for territorial expansion, or did it only justify actions taken for other reasons? |
| --- | --- |

# The U.S.-Mexico War, 1846–1848

In the Southwest, as in the Oregon Country, dramatic change came quickly in the 1840s. Comanches, Kiowas, Apaches, and Navajos who had traded peacefully with northern Mexicans for decades began, instead, to make war on their ranches and towns, ruining the region's economy and devastating many of its settlements. The Mexican government proved unable to suppress these attacks. Recognizing an opportunity to gain even more territory, Polk determined to go to war if necessary to acquire all the Mexican lands between Texas and the Pacific Ocean. What he and many Democrats consciously ignored was the domestic crisis that a war of conquest to expand slavery would unleash.

## The "War of a Thousand Deserts"

Since gaining independence in 1821, Mexico had not prospered. Its federal system of government tended to serve the northern frontier states poorly, while two decades of political instability resulted in a stagnant economy and modest tax revenues, which debt payments to European bankers quickly devoured. In the 1830s and 1840s, Comanche warriors conducted dozens of campaigns against the settlements of the Mexican north. Mexico's central government lacked the resources to respond effectively, and the northern territories were devastated. Always sparsely settled—California and New Mexico had a Spanish-speaking population of only 75,000 in 1840—many northern ranches and communities were abandoned in what one historian has called the "War of a Thousand Deserts." Nevertheless, Mexican officials vowed to preserve their nation's historic boundaries. When its breakaway province of Texas prepared to join the American Union, Mexico suspended diplomatic relations with the United States.

## Polk's Expansionist Program

President Polk moved quickly to acquire Mexico's other northern provinces. He hoped to foment a revolution in California that, like the 1836 rebellion in Texas, would lead to annexation. In October 1845, Secretary of State James Buchanan told merchant Thomas Oliver Larkin, now the U.S. consul for the Mexican province, to encourage influential Californios to seek independence and union with the United States. To add military muscle to this scheme, Polk ordered American naval commanders to seize San Francisco Bay and California's coastal towns in case of war with Mexico. The president also instructed the War Department to dispatch Captain John C. Frémont and an "exploring" party of soldiers into Mexican territory. By December 1845, Frémont's force had reached California's Sacramento River Valley.

With these preparations in place, Polk launched a secret diplomatic initiative: he sent Louisiana congressman John Slidell to Mexico, telling him to secure the Rio Grande boundary for Texas and to buy the provinces of California and New Mexico for $30 million. Insulted by U.S. disregard for Mexico's sovereignty, government officials refused to meet with Slidell.

Events now moved quickly toward war. Polk ordered General Zachary Taylor and an American army of 2,000 soldiers to occupy disputed lands between the Nueces River (the historic southern boundary of Spanish Texas) and the Rio Grande, which the Republic of Texas had claimed as its border with Mexico. "We were sent to provoke a fight," recalled Ulysses S. Grant, then a young officer serving with Taylor, "but it was essential that Mexico should commence it." When the armies clashed near the Rio Grande in May 1846, Polk delivered the war message he had drafted long before. Taking liberties with the truth, the president declared that Mexico "has passed the boundary of the United States, has invaded our territory, and shed American blood upon the American soil." Ignoring pleas by some Whigs for a negotiated settlement, an overwhelming majority in Congress voted for war—a decision greeted with great popular acclaim. To avoid a simultaneous war with Britain, Polk retreated from his demand for "fifty-four forty or fight" and in June 1846 accepted British terms that divided the Oregon Country at the forty-ninth parallel.

## American Military Successes

American forces in Texas quickly established their military superiority. Zachary Taylor's army crossed the Rio Grande; occupied the Mexican city of Matamoros; and, after a fierce six-day battle in September 1846, took the interior Mexican town of Monterrey. Two months later, a U.S. naval squadron in the Gulf of Mexico seized Tampico, Mexico's second most important port. By the end of 1846, the United States controlled much of northeastern Mexico (Map 11.6).

Fighting also broke out in California. In June 1846, naval commander John Sloat landed 250 marines in Monterey and declared that California "henceforward will be a portion of the United States." Simultaneously, American settlers in the Sacramento River Valley staged a revolt and, supported by Frémont's force, captured the town of Sonoma, where they proclaimed the independence of the "**Bear Flag Republic**." To

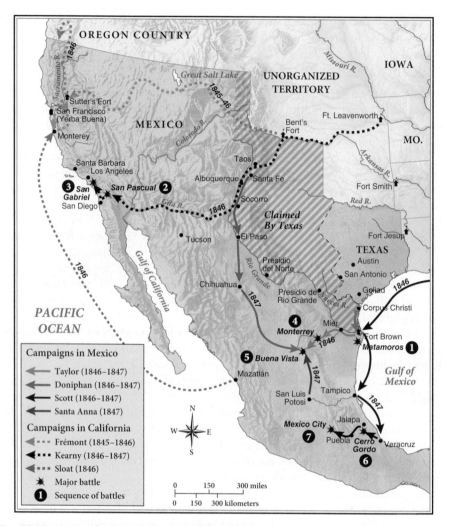

**MAP 11.6   The U.S.-Mexico War, 1846–1848**
After moving west from Fort Leavenworth in present-day Kansas, American forces commanded by Captain John C. Frémont and General Stephen Kearny defeated Mexican armies in California in 1846 and early 1847. Simultaneously, U.S. troops under General Zachary Taylor and Colonel Alfred A. Doniphan won victories over General Santa Anna's forces south of the Rio Grande. In mid-1847, General Winfield Scott mounted a successful seaborne attack on Veracruz and Mexico City, ending the war.

cement these victories, Polk ordered army units to capture Santa Fe in New Mexico and then march to southern California. Despite stiff Mexican resistance, American forces secured control of California early in 1847.

Polk expected these victories to end the war, but he underestimated the Mexicans' national pride and the determination of President Santa Anna. In February 1847 in the Battle of Buena Vista, Santa Anna nearly defeated Taylor's army in northeastern Mexico. With most Mexican troops deployed in the north, Polk approved General

**Street Fighting in the Calle de Iturbide, 1846** Monterrey, which had resisted Spanish troops during Mexico's war for independence (1820–1821), was captured by the Americans only after bloody house-to-house fighting in the U.S.-Mexico War (1846–1848). Protected by thick walls and shuttered windows, Mexican defenders pour a withering fire on the dark-uniformed American troops and buckskin-clad frontier fighters. A large Catholic cathedral looms in the background, its foundations obscured by the smoke from the Mexicans' cannons. West Point Museum, United States Military Academy, West Point, NY.

Winfield Scott's plan to capture the port of Veracruz and march 260 miles to Mexico City. An American army of 14,000 seized the Mexican capital in September 1847. That American victory cost Santa Anna his presidency, and a new Mexican government made a forced peace with the United States.

| IN YOUR OWN WORDS | What were the roles of Plains Indians, Anglo-American immigrants to Texas, the Mexican government, the U.S. government, and the American public in sparking the U.S.-Mexico War? |
| --- | --- |

## Summary

This chapter explored the imperial ambitions of the United States and the competition among nations for control of western North America. It began by tracing the contours of the southern social order that emerged with the expansion of slave plantation agriculture. It followed the migration of ambitious slaveholders into the Mexican state of Coahuila y Tejas, considered the challenges that aristocratic planters faced in a democratic political order, and analyzed the patterns of work, family, community life, and culture that structured African American experience.

The American ideology of Manifest Destiny, which held that God intended that the dominion of the United States should extend across the entire North American continent, informed U.S. efforts to claim the Oregon Country and California and shaped the country's interactions with the independent Plains Indians, many of whom were formidable powers in their own right. Finally, the chapter examined the aftermath of the presidential election of 1844, which brought James K. Polk to power and set the nation's course toward war with Mexico. In Chapter 12, we will consider the effects of that war on American society and politics.

# Chapter 11 Review

## KEY TERMS

**Identify and explain the significance of each term below.**

slave society (p. 323)
republican aristocracy (p. 326)
Great American Desert (p. 329)
Alamo (p. 329)
secret ballot (p. 330)
black Protestantism (p. 334)
Gullah dialect (p. 335)

task system (p. 336)
Manifest Destiny (p. 338)
Oregon Trail (p. 338)
Californios (p. 341)
"Fifty-four forty or fight!" (p. 344)
Bear Flag Republic (p. 345)

## REVIEW QUESTIONS

**Answer these questions to demonstrate your understanding of the chapter's main ideas.**

1. What were the strengths and limitations of the South's economy and social structure?

2. What resources and strategies gave African American slaves a measure of control over their lives?

3. Did the idea of Manifest Destiny cause westward migration and political support for territorial expansion, or did it only justify actions taken for other reasons?

4. What were the roles of Plains Indians, Anglo-American immigrants to Texas, the Mexican government, the U.S. government, and the American public in sparking the U.S.-Mexico War?

5. Review the events listed under "Migration and Settlement" on the thematic timeline on page 231, and then discuss how southern expansion, the end of the Atlantic slave trade in 1808, and the subsequent rise of the internal slave trade affected the experiences and identities of the African American population.

## CHRONOLOGY

**As you read, ask yourself why this chapter begins and ends with these dates and then identify the links among related events.**

| | |
|---|---|
| **1810s** | • Africans from Congo region influence black culture for decades |
| **1818** | • United States and Great Britain agree to joint control of Oregon Country |
| **1820s** | • Mexican government encourages migration to Coahuila y Tejas |
| | • African Americans increasingly adopt Christian beliefs |
| **1820** | • Major Stephen H. Long labels the Great Plains the "Great American Desert" |
| **1821** | • Mexico gains independence from Spain |
| **1830s** | • Percentage of slave-owning white families falls |
| | • Yeomen farm families retreat to hill country |
| | • Lawyers become influential in southern politics |
| **1835** | • Mexico creates stronger central government, outlaws slavery |
| **1836** | • Texas declares its independence from Mexico |
| **1842–1843** | • Immigration to the Oregon Country increases dramatically |
| **1844** | • James K. Polk elected president |
| **1845** | • John L. O'Sullivan coins the phrase *Manifest Destiny* |
| | • Texas admitted into Union |
| **1846** | • United States declares war on Mexico |
| | • Treaty with Britain divides Oregon Country |
| | • California's "Bear Flag Republic" declares independence |
| **1847** | • American troops capture Mexico City |

# PART 5

S hould historians of the United States call the mid-nineteenth century the Civil War era? Many do, but in *America's History* we choose a slightly different emphasis. Like other scholars, we argue that the Civil War and the end of slavery brought extraordinary changes in U.S. politics, law, society, and culture. We devote a full chapter to the political crisis of the 1850s; one to the Civil War itself; one to the turmoil of Reconstruction, the postwar struggle over power and policy in the ex-Confederacy and nationwide; and one to the consolidation of the West, a process that began before the Civil War and continued after the end of Reconstruction.

The first Republican president, Abraham Lincoln, engineered the triumph of the Union, but on terms few expected when the war began. Instead of a short, heroic conflict between white northerners and southerners, the Civil War turned into an agonizing "hard war" that lasted four weary years. Emancipation, which few white Unionists expected at the start, proved essential to winning the war, as did the participation and sacrifice of African Americans, 180,000 of whom served in the U.S. Army for the first time.

Union victory ended slavery—a momentous achievement. It did not, however, resolve the bitter disagreements that had caused the war in the first place. In fact, conflicting points of view only multiplied in the decades after Confederate defeat. That's why, in Part 5, we place the Civil War in broader context. In one of history's astonishing upsets, the Republican Party—which did not exist until 1854—not only won national power by 1860 but, because of the South's secession, wielded it freely to remake federal policies. Those policies increased U.S. control over the trans-Mississippi West, transformed economic and political relationships among the nation's regions, and set the stage for U.S. global power.

## Sectional Conflict and Civil War

The U.S.-Mexico War prompted a decade-long debate over whether slavery should expand into the newly conquered lands. The Compromise of 1850, a complex legislative agreement designed to solve the conflict, won little support in either North or South, and the Kansas-Nebraska Act of 1854 precipitated even further conflict. Southern Whigs abandoned their party for the Democrats, while northern Whigs became Republicans or anti-immigrant Know-Nothings. By 1860 Democrats also split on sectional lines, enabling the election of Republican president Abraham Lincoln.

Starting with South Carolina, eleven southern states seceded in response to Lincoln's election and created the Confederate States of America. Elsewhere, citizens

# Consolidating a Continental Union 1844–1877

rallied to preserve the Union. In the long Civil War that followed, the military forces of the Union and Confederacy were at first evenly matched. However, as neither side proved able to crush the other, the North's superior financial and industrial resources gradually gave it the advantage, as did Lincoln's proclamation of emancipation in 1863. Linking Union victory to the end of slavery undermined European support for the Confederacy and added thousands of African Americans to the northern armies, helping Union forces sweep across the South and end the war.

## Expanding Federal Power

The Civil War created a powerful American state, as the Union government mobilized millions of men and billions of dollars. Republicans created an elaborate network of national banks and — for the first time in U.S. history — a significant federal bureaucracy. Congress intervened forcefully to integrate the national economy and promote industrialization. These policies, along with the nation's dynamic postwar economy, set the nation on a course toward global power.

The Civil War increased federal authority in other ways. Three Republican-sponsored constitutional amendments limited the powers of the states and imposed new definitions of citizenship — prohibiting slavery, enfranchising black men, and forbidding state actions that denied people equal protection under the law. The U.S. Army, which occupied parts of the ex-Confederacy as late as 1877, also suppressed Indian resistance and extended national control in the West.

## A Continental Empire

The United States claimed large swaths of western territory in the 1840s, through victory in the U.S.-Mexico War and the California gold rush that followed. But it was post–Civil War railroad building and economic expansion that truly brought the West into the orbit of federal authority. This expansion intensified conflicts between Native peoples, Mexican Americans, and Anglo newcomers. By 1890, most Native peoples had been forced onto reservations, while thousands of Mexicans also found themselves dispossessed. The legacies of the Civil War, therefore, were as significant in the West as in the former Confederacy. Western minerals, lumber, cattle, wheat, and oil proved essential to the transformation we will discuss in Part 6: the United States's economic transformation and rise to global economic power.

## Thematic Understanding

This timeline arranges some of the important events of this period into themes. Which events reflect the causes and consequences of the Civil War, as well as Union and Confederate actions during the war itself? Which events show how the U.S. asserted control over the trans-Mississippi West, and who resisted that process and why? Which events in each set of conflicts were military, economic, or legal and constitutional? How would you compare and contrast these different modes of nation-building?

| | AMERICAN AND NATIONAL IDENTITY | POLITICS AND POWER | WORK, EXCHANGE, AND TECHNOLOGY |
|---|---|---|---|
| 1840 | • Free Soil Party forms (1848)<br>• Foreign Miner's Tax enacted in California (1850) | • James K. Polk elected president (1844)<br>• Wilmot Proviso approved by House but not by Senate (1846) | • Gold discovered in California (1848) |
| 1850 | • American Party forms (1851)<br>• *Dred Scott v. Sandford* (1857)<br>• John Brown raid at Harpers Ferry (1859) | • Compromise of 1850<br>• Kansas-Nebraska Act tests popular sovereignty (1854)<br>• Republican Party forms (1854) | • Comstock silver lode discovered in Nevada (1859) |
| 1860 | • Preliminary emancipation proclamation (1862)<br>• Union initiates draft, sparking riots in New York City (1863)<br>• Ex-Confederate states pass Black Codes (1865)<br>• Wyoming Territory grants women suffrage (1869) | • Lincoln elected president (1860)<br>• Deep South states secede (1860–1861)<br>• Robert E. Lee surrenders (1865)<br>• Lincoln assassinated (1865)<br>• Impeachment of Andrew Johnson (1868)<br>• Fourteenth Amendment (1868)<br>• Grant elected (1868) | • Legal Tender Act authorizes greenback currency (1862)<br>• Explosion kills munitions workers in Pittsburgh (1862)<br>• Long Drive of Texas longhorns begins (1865)<br>• Transcontinental railroad completed (1869) |
| 1870 | • Utah Territory grants women suffrage (1870)<br>• *Minor v. Happersett* (1875)<br>• Sioux, Cheyennes, and Arapahos win Battle of Little Big Horn (1876) | • Enforcement Laws to suppress Klan (1870)<br>• Fifteenth Amendment (1870)<br>• Crédit Mobilier scandal (1872)<br>• *Slaughter-House Cases* (1873)<br>• *Munn v. Illinois* (1877) | • Panic of 1873 ushers in severe economic depression (1873)<br>• United States begins to move to gold standard (1873) |
| 1880 | • Dawes Severalty Act (1887) | | |
| 1890 | • Massacre of Sioux Ghost Dancers at Wounded Knee (1890) | | |

| CULTURE AND SOCIETY | MIGRATION AND SETTLEMENT | GEOGRAPHY AND THE ENVIRONMENT | AMERICA IN THE WORLD | |
|---|---|---|---|---|
| | • Great Irish famine prompts mass immigration to U.S. (1845–1851)<br>• California gold rush begins (1849) | | • United States declares war on Mexico (1846)<br>• Treaty of Guadalupe Hidalgo transfers Mexican lands to United States (1848) | 1840 |
| • Harriet Beecher Stowe publishes *Uncle Tom's Cabin* (1852) | | | • Treaty of Kanagawa (1854)<br>• President Buchanan seeks to annex Cuba as a slave state (1858) | 1850 |
| • U.S. Sanitary Commission formed (1861)<br>• Morrill Act funds public state universities (1862) | • African Americans escape slavery and become "contrabands" behind Union lines (1861–1865) | • Homestead Act passed (1862)<br>• Sherman's army devastates Georgia and South Carolina (1864–1865) | • Britain and France refuse recognition to the Confederacy (1863)<br>• Burlingame Treaty with China (1868) | 1860 |
| • Ku Klux Klan at peak of power (1870)<br>• Beecher-Tilton scandal dominates headlines (1875) | • Nez Perces forcibly removed from homelands (1877)<br>• Exoduster migration to Kansas (1879) | • Yellowstone National Park created (1872)<br>• John Wesley Powell presents *Report on . . . Arid Region of the United States* (1879) | | 1870 |
| • Sitting Bull tours with Buffalo Bill's Wild West (1885) | • Chiricahua Apache leader Geronimo surrenders (1886) | • Dry cycle begins on the Great Plains (1886) | | 1880 |
| | | | | 1890 |

# 12

# Sectional Conflict and Crisis

## 1844–1861

### IDENTIFY THE BIG IDEA

What caused the political turmoil that led to the rise of the Republican Party, Democratic division, and southern secession?

**THE U.S.-MEXICO WAR WAS IMMENSELY POPULAR WITH MILLIONS** of Americans. Those who opposed it took big risks, as young Abraham Lincoln discovered to his dismay. In December 1847, as a freshman Whig congressman from Illinois, Lincoln introduced a bill demanding that President Polk identify the exact geographical spot where the war had begun, which Polk claimed had been in U.S. territory. Lincoln, like other critics, believed U.S. troops had been trespassing on Mexican soil. But Lincoln's "spot resolution" went nowhere. Ridiculing the young congressman, a newspaper in his home state nicknamed him "Spotty Lincoln" and a Democrat defeated him in the next election. Lincoln went back to his law practice in Springfield.

Soon afterward, in 1849, tales of California gold generated great excitement over the riches waiting in newly won territories. Thousands of American men rushed west, joining counterparts from Mexico, Chile, Hawaii, Britain, and elsewhere to gather gold from the beds of California's rivers and streams. San Francisco became an overnight boomtown. Alas, few struck it rich, and the chaotic quest for gold led to vigilantism, ugly racial conflicts, and the deliberate near-extermination of California's Native peoples.

Like the lure of California gold, U.S. dreams of territorial expansion gave way to harsher truths in the 1850s. The process of incorporating the **Mexican cession**—lands the United States had acquired in the war—reignited fierce debates over the expansion of slavery. Though only a small minority of white northerners were abolitionists, by the 1850s many feared the "slave power" of southern interests and wanted western territories reserved as "free soil" for white farmers. Rising politicians—among them Lincoln, who returned to politics to help found the Illinois Republican Party—vowed to block the expansion of slavery, pointing out that the Northwest Ordinance of 1787 barred slavery in the Midwest. Southerners, in turn, insisted that the Constitution protected slaveholders' property rights throughout the nation. As early as 1850, some radicals called for secession while others launched military expeditions into Latin America to add territory to slavery's empire. As conflict accelerated, violence erupted in California, Kansas, Virginia, and even on the Senate floor. The dispute shattered old alliances, ultimately fragmenting both major parties. By 1861 it ignited a political firestorm that engulfed the Union.

# A Divisive War, 1844–1850

"The United States will conquer Mexico," Ralph Waldo Emerson had predicted as the war began, but "Mexico will poison us." He was right. The U.S.-Mexico War roused bitter sectional conflict, even while it was being fought. Some northern Whigs—among them Charles Francis Adams of Massachusetts (son of John Quincy Adams) and Chancellor James Kent of New York—opposed the war on moral grounds, calling it "causeless & wicked & unjust." These **conscience Whigs** accused Polk of waging the war to add new slave states and increase slave-owning Democrats' control of the federal government. Swayed by such arguments, troops deserted in droves (leading to the highest desertion rate of any American war), and antiwar activists denounced enlistees as "murderers and robbers."

## "Free Soil" in Politics

When voters repudiated Polk's war policy in the election of 1846, Whigs took control of the House. They called for a congressional pledge that the United States would not seek any land from the Mexican republic. Polk's expansionist policies also split the Democrats. As early as 1839, Ohio Democrat Thomas Morris had warned that "the power of slavery is aiming to govern the country." In 1846, David Wilmot, an antislavery Democratic congressman from Pennsylvania, took up that refrain and proposed the **Wilmot Proviso**, a ban on slavery in any territories gained from the war with Mexico. Whigs and antislavery Democrats in the House of Representatives quickly passed the bill, dividing Congress along sectional lines. Fearful that southern voters would heed radical calls for secession, a few proslavery northern senators joined their southern colleagues to kill the proviso. But the dispute had just begun.

**Slavery in the Mexican Cession**    At the war's end, President Polk, Secretary of State Buchanan, and Senators Stephen A. Douglas of Illinois and Jefferson Davis of Mississippi called for annexation of a huge swath of Mexican territory south of the Rio

Grande. John C. Calhoun and others, however, feared this would require the assimilation of many mixed-race people. They favored only annexation of sparsely settled New Mexico and California. "Ours is a government of the white man," proclaimed Calhoun; it should never welcome "any but the Caucasian race." To unify the Democratic Party, Polk and Buchanan accepted Calhoun's policy. In 1848, Polk signed, and the Senate ratified, the Treaty of Guadalupe Hidalgo, in which the United States agreed to pay Mexico $15 million in return for more than one-third of its territory (Map 12.1).

Congress also created the Oregon Territory in 1848 and, two years later, passed the Oregon Donation Land Claim Act, which granted farm-sized plots of land to settlers who took up residence before 1854. Soon, treaties with Native peoples erased Indian titles to much of the new territory. With the claiming of Oregon, New Mexico, and California, American conquest of the Far West rapidly advanced.

Commentators debated whether the arid lands of the Southwest were suitable for slavery or cotton culture. Debates over expansion dominated the election of 1848. The Senate's rejection of the Wilmot Proviso revived charges that southern politicians were leading a **"slave power" conspiracy** to dominate the federal government. They pointed out that the Constitution allowed slaveholding states to count each slave as three-fifths of a person for purposes of electoral representation, though

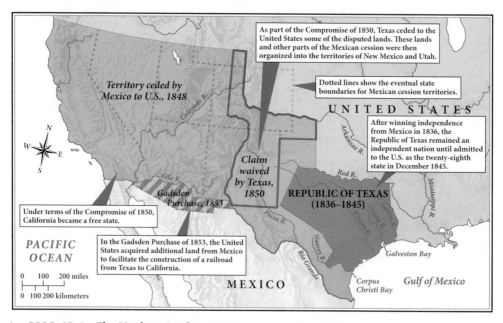

As part of the Compromise of 1850, Texas ceded to the United States some of the disputed lands. These lands and other parts of the Mexican cession were then organized into the territories of New Mexico and Utah.

*Territory ceded by Mexico to U.S., 1848*

Dotted lines show the eventual state boundaries for Mexican cession territories.

UNITED STATES

After winning independence from Mexico in 1836, the Republic of Texas remained an independent nation until admitted to the U.S. as the twenty-eighth state in December 1845.

*Claim waived by Texas, 1850*

**REPUBLIC OF TEXAS (1836–1845)**

*Gadsden Purchase, 1853*

Under terms of the Compromise of 1850, California became a free state.

PACIFIC OCEAN

In the Gadsden Purchase of 1853, the United States acquired additional land from Mexico to facilitate the construction of a railroad from Texas to California.

0    100    200 miles
0  100 200 kilometers

MEXICO

*Galveston Bay*

*Corpus Christi Bay*    *Gulf of Mexico*

### MAP 12.1   The Mexican Cession, 1848

In the Treaty of Guadalupe Hidalgo (1848), Mexico ceded to the United States its vast northern territories—the present-day states of California, Nevada, Utah, Arizona, New Mexico, and half of Colorado. These new territories, President Polk boasted to Congress, "constitute of themselves a country large enough for a great empire, and the acquisition is second in importance only to that of Louisiana in 1803."

of course slaves did not vote; thus, whites in areas with large numbers of slaves had disproportionate political power. Northerners also argued that Democrats were favoring southern interests in their appointments and policies.

To protest this perceived bias, thousands of ordinary northerners, such as farmer Abijah Beckwith of Herkimer County, New York, joined the **free soil movement**. Slavery, Beckwith wrote in his diary, was an "aristocratic" institution, a danger to "the great mass of the people [because it] . . . threatens the general and equal distribution of our lands into convenient family farms." Free soil ideas drew on a popular movement for access to public lands that had been growing since the 1820s. Increasingly, frontier congressmen pressured the U.S. government to give land to poor farmers — a demand ultimately fulfilled by the Homestead Act of 1862.

Free soilers quickly organized for the election of 1848. Compared with abolitionists, the new Free Soil Party placed less emphasis on slavery as a sin. Instead, like Beckwith, the new party's leaders depicted slavery as a threat to republicanism and the Jeffersonian ideal of a freeholder society, arguments that won broad support among aspiring white farmers. Hundreds of men and women in the Great Lakes states joined free soil organizations formed by the American and Foreign Anti-Slavery Society. So, too, did Frederick Douglass, the foremost black abolitionist, who attended the first Free Soil Party convention in the summer of 1848 and endorsed its strategy. Douglass believed Free Soilers could achieve far more political clout than abolitionists could, ultimately undermining slavery. William Lloyd Garrison and other abolitionists, however, condemned the new party's stress on the rights of freeholders as racist "whitemanism."

**The Election of 1848**   The conflict over slavery took a toll on Polk and the Democratic Party. Scorned by Whigs and Free Soilers and exhausted by his rigorous dawn-to-midnight work regime, Polk declined to run for a second term and died just three months after leaving office. In his place, Democrats nominated Senator Lewis Cass of Michigan, an avid expansionist who had advocated buying Cuba, annexing Mexico's Yucatán Peninsula, and taking all of Oregon. To maintain party unity, Cass promoted a new idea — squatter sovereignty. Under this plan, Congress would allow settlers in each territory to determine its status as free or slave. Cass's doctrine failed to persuade those northern Democrats who opposed any expansion of slavery. They joined the Free Soil Party, as did former Democratic president Martin Van Buren, who became its candidate for president. To attract Whig votes, the new party chose conscience Whig Charles Francis Adams for vice president.

Whigs nominated General Zachary Taylor, a Louisiana slave owner firmly committed to defending slavery in the South but not in the territories, a position that won him support in the North. The general's military exploits in the U.S.-Mexico War had made him a popular hero, known affectionately to his troops as "Old Rough and Ready." In 1848, as in 1840 with the candidacy of William Henry Harrison, running a military hero worked for the Whigs. Taylor took 47 percent of the popular vote to Cass's 42 percent. However, Taylor won in part because Van Buren and the Free Soil ticket took away enough Democratic votes in New York to block Cass's victory there. Although their numbers were small, antislavery voters in New York had denied the presidency to Clay in 1844 and to Cass in 1848. Bitter debates over slavery were changing the dynamics of national politics.

## California Gold and Racial Warfare

Even before Taylor took office, events in California took center stage. In January 1848, workers building a milldam for John A. Sutter in the Sierra Nevada foothills came across flakes of gold. Sutter was a Swiss immigrant who had come to California in 1839, become a Mexican citizen, and accumulated land in the Sacramento Valley. He tried to hide the discovery, but by mid-1848 indigenous Californians, Mexican Californios, and Anglo-Americans from Monterey and San Francisco poured into the foothills, along with scores of Mexicans and Chileans. By January 1849, sixty-one crowded ships had left New York and other northeastern ports to sail around Cape Horn to San Francisco; by May, twelve thousand wagons had crossed the Missouri River bound for the goldfields. Forty-niners from South America, Europe, China, and Australia also converged on California to seek their fortunes.

**Forty-Niners**  The mining prospectors—almost all men—lived in crowded, chaotic towns and camps amid gamblers, saloonkeepers, and prostitutes. They set up "claims clubs" to settle mining disputes and cobbled together a system of legal rules based on practice "back East." Anglo-American miners usually treated alien whites fairly, but they ruthlessly expelled Indians, Mexicans, and Chileans from the goldfields or confined them to marginal diggings. When substantial numbers of Chinese miners arrived in 1850, often in the employ of Chinese companies, whites called for laws to expel them from California. Chilean immigrant Vicente Pérez Rosales reported sardonically on affairs in San Francisco: the leading official was "a Yankee, more or less drunk"; in disputes "between a Yankee and someone who speaks Spanish, his job is to declare the Spaniard guilty and make him pay the court costs." A **Foreign Miner's Tax**, implemented in 1850, charged a prohibitive fee that drove out many Latino and Asian miners.

The first miners to exploit a site often met success, scooping up easily reached deposits and leaving small pickings for later arrivals. "High hopes" wrecked, one latecomer saw himself and most other forty-niners as little better than "convicts condemned to exile and hard labor." They faced disease and death as well: "Diarrhea was so general during the fall and winter months" and so often fatal, a Sacramento doctor remarked, that it was called "the disease of California."

By the mid-1850s almost as many people were sailing from San Francisco each year as were arriving to seek their fortune. But thousands of disillusioned forty-niners were too ashamed, exhausted, broke, or ambitious to go home. Some became wageworkers for companies that engaged in hydraulic or underground mining; others turned to farming. "Instead of going to the mines where fortune hangs upon the merest chance," one frustrated miner advised emigrants, "commence the cultivation of the soil."

**Racial Warfare and Land Rights**  Farming required arable land, and Mexican grantees and Native peoples occupied much of it. American migrants brushed aside both groups, brutally eliminating the Indians and wearing down Mexican claimants with legal tactics and political pressure.

Subjugation of Native peoples came first. When the gold rush began in 1848, California Indians numbered about 150,000; by 1861, there were only 30,000. As elsewhere in the Americas, European diseases took the lives of thousands. Some miners sexually assaulted Native women and forced them into virtual slavery as domestic workers. White settlers also undertook systematic campaigns of extermination, which local leaders did little to stop. "A war of extermination will continue to be waged . . . until the Indian race becomes extinct," predicted Governor Peter Burnett in 1851.

Congress abetted these assaults. At the bidding of white Californians, it repudiated treaties that federal agents had negotiated with 119 tribes and that had allotted the state's Indians 7 million acres of land. Instead, in 1853, Congress authorized five reservations of only 25,000 acres each and refused to provide Indians with military protection. Consequently, some settlers simply murdered Indians to push them off nonreservation lands.

The Yuki people, who lived in the Round Valley in northern California, were one target. As the *Petaluma Journal* reported nonchalantly in April 1857: "Within the past three weeks, from 300 to 400 bucks, squaws and children have been killed by whites." Other white Californians turned to slave trading: "Hundreds of Indians have been stolen and carried into the settlements and sold," the state's Indian Affairs superintendent reported in 1856. Labor-hungry farmers quickly put them to work. Expelled from their lands and widely dispersed, many Indian peoples could no longer sustain distinct communities. Those tribal communities that survived were devastated by population loss. In 1854, at least 5,000 Yukis lived in the Round Valley; a decade later, only 85 men and 215 women remained.

Mexicans and Californios who held grants to thousands of acres were harder to dislodge. The Treaty of Guadalupe Hidalgo guaranteed that property owned by Mexicans would be "inviolably respected." Though many of the eight hundred grants made by Spanish and Mexican authorities in California were poorly documented or in some cases fraudulent, a Land Claims Commission created by Congress eventually upheld the validity of 75 percent of them. In the meantime, however, hundreds of Anglo-Americans set up farms on the sparsely settled grants. Having come of age in the antimonopoly Jacksonian era, these squatters rejected the legitimacy of Californios' claims to "unimproved" land and successfully pressured local land commissioners and judges to void or reduce the size of many grants. Indeed, Anglos' clamor for land was so intense and their numbers so large that many Californio claimants gave up and sold off their properties at bargain prices.

In northern California, farmers found that they could grow most eastern crops: corn and oats to feed work horses, pigs, and chickens; potatoes, beans, and peas for the farm table; and refreshing grapes, apples, and peaches. Ranchers gradually replaced Spanish cattle with American breeds that yielded more milk and meat, which found a ready market as California's population shot up to 380,000 by 1860 and 560,000 by 1870. Using the latest agricultural machinery and scores of hired workers, California farmers produced huge crops of wheat and barley, which San Francisco merchants exported to Europe at high prices. The gold rush turned into a wheat boom.

## 1850: Crisis and Compromise

When British miner William Shaw arrived in California in 1849, he brought a Chinese carpenter and a young Malaysian man as his employees. He reported that a posse of armed Anglo-Americans immediately confronted him, demanding to know whether the workers were "in a state of slavery or vassalage to us." Shaw assured them that his men were paid, but he found his group shunned and denied medical care because it included Asians. The Chinese and Malaysian men ended up dying of fever.

As this group's experience suggested, Americans carried the burning issue of slavery with them to the Pacific coast. Recognizing these tensions and hoping to avoid an extended debate over slavery, President Taylor advised Californians to skip the territorial phase and immediately apply for statehood. Early in the gold rush, in November 1849, voters ratified a state constitution prohibiting slavery; Taylor urged Congress to admit California as a free state.

**Constitutional Conflict**   California's bid for admission produced passionate debate in Congress and four distinct responses. On the verge of death, John C. Calhoun reiterated his deep resentment of the North's "long-continued agitation of the slavery question." He proposed a constitutional amendment to create a dual presidency, permanently dividing executive power between North and South. Calhoun also advanced the radical argument that Congress had no constitutional authority to regulate slavery in the territories. Slaves were property, Calhoun insisted, and the Constitution restricted Congress's power to abrogate or limit property rights. That argument ran counter to a half century of practice: Congress had prohibited slavery in the Northwest Territory in 1787 and had extended that ban to most of the Louisiana Purchase in the Missouri Compromise of 1820. But Calhoun's position—that planters could by right take slave property into new territories—won growing support in the Deep South.

Other southerners favored a more moderate proposal to extend the Missouri Compromise line to the Pacific Ocean. This plan won the backing of Pennsylvanian James Buchanan and other influential northern Democrats. It would guarantee slave owners access to some western territory, including a separate state in southern California.

A third alternative was Lewis Cass's idea of squatter sovereignty—allowing newcomers in a territory to decide the status of slavery. Democratic senator Stephen Douglas of Illinois now championed this approach, renaming it **popular sovereignty** to link it to republican ideology, which placed ultimate power in the hands of voters. Douglas's idea had considerable appeal. Politicians hoped it would relieve Congress from having to make explosive decisions about slavery, and men on the frontier welcomed the power it would give them. However, popular sovereignty was a slippery concept. Could residents accept or ban slavery when a territory was first organized, or must they delay their decision until a territory had enough people to frame a constitution and apply for statehood? Douglas did not say.

For their part, free soilers and opponents of slavery refused to accept any proposal for California or other territories that allowed slavery. Senator Salmon P. Chase of Ohio, elected by a Democratic–Free Soil coalition, and Senator William H. Seward, a New York Whig, urged a fourth plan: federal laws to restrict slavery within its existing boundaries and eventually end it completely. Condemning slavery as "morally unjust, politically unwise, and socially pernicious" and invoking "a higher law than the Constitution," Seward demanded bold action to advance freedom, "the common heritage of mankind."

**Resolving the Crisis of 1850** By 1850, Whig Henry Clay had been in Congress for nearly four decades. Now in partnership with fellow Whig Daniel Webster and Democrat Stephen Douglas, Clay fashioned a complex—and controversial—compromise that preserved the Union. In this engraving, he addresses a crowded Senate chamber, with Webster sitting immediately to his left. Clay addresses his remarks to his prime antagonist, southern advocate John C. Calhoun, the man with the long white hair at the far right of the picture. Library of Congress.

**A Complex Compromise**   Faced with bitter and potentially disastrous political divisions, senior Whig and Democratic politicians worked desperately to draft bills that could pass Congress. Aided by Millard Fillmore, who became president in 1850 after Zachary Taylor's sudden death, Whig leaders Henry Clay and Daniel Webster and Democrat Stephen A. Douglas managed to win passage of five separate laws known collectively as the **Compromise of 1850**. To mollify southern planters, the compromise included a new Fugitive Slave Act strengthening federal aid to slave catchers. To satisfy various groups of northerners, the legislation admitted California as a free state, resolved a boundary dispute between New Mexico and Texas in favor of New Mexico, and abolished the slave trade (but not slavery) in the District of Columbia. Finally, the compromise organized the rest of the conquered Mexican lands into the territories of New Mexico and Utah and, invoking popular sovereignty, left the issue of slavery in the hands of their residents (Map 12.2).

The Compromise of 1850 preserved national unity by accepting once again the stipulation advanced by the South since 1787: no Union without slavery. Still,

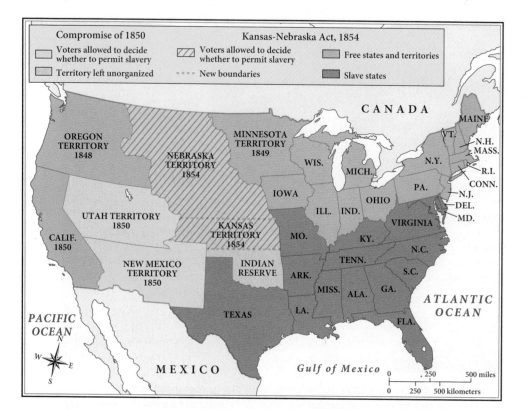

**MAP 12.2　The Compromise of 1850 and the Kansas-Nebraska Act of 1854**

The contest over the expansion of slavery involved vast territories. The Compromise of 1850 peacefully resolved the status of the Far West: California would be a free state, and settlers in the Utah and New Mexico territories would vote for or against slavery (the doctrine of popular sovereignty). However, the Kansas-Nebraska Act of 1854 voided the Missouri Compromise (1820) and instituted popular sovereignty in those territories. That decision sparked a bitter local war and revealed a fatal flaw in the doctrine.

southerners feared for the future and threatened secession. Militant activists (or "fire-eaters") in South Carolina, Georgia, Mississippi, and Alabama organized a special convention to safeguard "southern rights." Georgia congressman Alexander H. Stephens called on delegates to this Nashville Convention to prepare "men and money, arms and munitions, etc. to meet the emergency." Passage of the compromise deflated the secessionist bubble, however: when the convention reconvened for a second meeting, only a small group showed up. Most southerners continued to support the Union, but the convention had spelled out conditions for that support: Congress must protect slavery where it existed and grant statehood to any territory that ratified a proslavery constitution.

| **IN YOUR OWN WORDS** | What political conflicts were triggered by U.S. acquisition of lands in the U.S.-Mexico War? |

# The End of the Second Party System, 1850–1858

The Missouri Compromise had endured for a generation, and architects of the Compromise of 1850 hoped their agreement would have an even longer life. Religious leaders, businessmen, and leading judges called on citizens to support the compromise to preserve "government and civil society." Their hopes quickly faded. Demanding freedom for fugitive slaves and free soil in the West, antislavery northerners refused to accept the legitimacy of the compromise, while proslavery southerners plotted to extend slavery into the West, the Caribbean, northern Mexico, and Central America. At the same time, the arrival of millions of Irish and German immigrants triggered another set of political upheavals. The resulting disputes fragmented both parties and precipitated a crisis.

## The Abolitionist Movement Grows

The Fugitive Slave Act of 1850 proved the most controversial element of the compromise. To mollify slaveholders, who found it increasingly difficult to capture escaped fugitives in the North, the act set up special federal courts to determine the legal status of alleged runaways. An owner's sworn affidavit was considered proof, while defendants could not receive a jury trial or even the right to testify. U.S. marshals and clerks were paid $10 for each person remanded to slavery and only $5 when they set a captive free.

Under the act's provisions, southern owners located and re-enslaved about 200 fugitives, as well as some free blacks. The plight of runaways and the presence of slave catchers aroused popular hostility in the North and Midwest, broadening support for the abolitionist cause. Ignoring the threat of prison sentences and $1,000 fines, free blacks and white abolitionists protected fugitives. In October 1850, Boston abolitionists helped two slaves escape from Georgia slave catchers. Rioters in Syracuse, New York, broke into a courthouse, freed a fugitive and spirited him to Canada, and then tried to charge the U.S. marshal with kidnapping. Abandoning nonviolence, Frederick Douglass declared that "the only way to make a Fugitive Slave Law a dead letter is to make half a dozen or more dead kidnappers." Precisely such a deadly result occurred in Christiana, Pennsylvania, in September 1851, when twenty African Americans exchanged gunfire with Maryland slave catchers, killing two of them. Federal authorities indicted thirty-six blacks and four whites for treason and other crimes, but a Pennsylvania jury acquitted one defendant, and the government dropped charges against the rest.

The following year, an electrifying novel helped strengthen abolitionist sentiment in the North. Harriet Beecher Stowe's *Uncle Tom's Cabin* (1852) conveyed the moral principles of abolitionism by depicting heartrending personal situations: the barbarity of whippings and sexual abuse; the cruel separation of enslaved husbands and wives, mothers and children; and the sin and guilt of white Christian men and women who could not escape the slave system. Touching a nerve, Stowe's book quickly sold 310,000 copies in the United States and double that number in Britain, where it prompted an antislavery petition signed by 560,000 English women.

Promoters soon created theatrical versions of *Uncle Tom's Cabin*—including, improbably, a musical that drew on some of the tropes of minstrel shows. These introduced broad popular audiences to characters such as Uncle Tom, who endures unspeakable cruelties with Christian patience and hope, and Little Eva, an angelic slaveholder's child who, on her deathbed, begs in vain for Tom's freedom. When white southerners indignantly challenged Stowe's portrayal of slavery, she published a *Key to Uncle Tom's Cabin* presenting the evidence she had used, including autobiographies and other testimony from those who had escaped slavery.

As Stowe's novel sparked outrage, northern legislators protested that the Fugitive Slave Act violated state sovereignty. Many states passed **personal liberty laws** that guaranteed to all residents, including alleged escapees from slavery, the right to a jury trial. In 1857, the Wisconsin Supreme Court went further, ruling in *Ableman v. Booth* that the Fugitive Slave Act was unconstitutional because it violated the rights of Wisconsin's citizens. Taking a states' rights stance—traditionally a southern position—the Wisconsin court denied the federal judiciary's authority to review its decision. In 1859, Chief Justice Roger B. Taney led a unanimous Supreme Court in affirming the supremacy of federal courts—a position that has withstood the test of time—and upholding the constitutionality of the Fugitive Slave Act.

But popular opposition made the law difficult to enforce. Some African Americans fled temporarily to Canada. Others formed vigilance committees, vowing to defend themselves and their families to the death. Even in far-off San Francisco, networks of abolitionists organized to help local freedom seekers after an 1852 California law authorized southerners who had arrived before statehood, bringing their slaves, to take them back in bondage when they departed the state. The resulting Underground Railroad activity showed the complexity of U.S. racial identities: under the law, an African American named Charlotte Gomez was arrested for having rescued an indigenous nine-year-old Yuki girl who had been forced into servitude in a white family. The slavery question now touched every corner of the country.

## The Whig Party's Demise

Hoping to unify their party in 1852, Whigs ran yet another war hero, General Winfield Scott, as their presidential candidate. Among Democrats, southerners demanded a candidate who embraced Calhoun's constitutional argument that all territories were open to slavery. However, northern and midwestern Democrats stood behind the three leading candidates—Lewis Cass of Michigan, Stephen Douglas of Illinois, and James Buchanan of Pennsylvania—who advocated popular sovereignty. Ultimately, the party settled on Franklin Pierce of New Hampshire, a congenial man who was sympathetic to the South. The Whigs floundered: as the Free Soil Party ran another spirited campaign, many northerners demanded that Whigs take a stronger stand against slavery expansion, while Democrats strengthened their base in the South by arguing that the Whigs were not doing enough to protect slavery. Pierce swept to victory.

**Proslavery Initiatives**   As president, Pierce pursued an expansionist foreign policy. With California and Oregon now firmly in U.S. hands, northern merchants wanted a trans-Pacific commercial empire, and Pierce moved to support them. For centuries, since unpleasant encounters with Portuguese traders in the 1600s, Japan's leaders had adhered to a policy of strict isolation. Americans, who wanted coal stations in Japan, argued that trade would extend what one missionary called "commerce, knowledge, and Christianity, with their multiplied blessings." Whether or not Japan wanted these blessings was irrelevant. In 1854, Commodore Matthew Perry succeeded in getting Japanese officials to sign the **Treaty of Kanagawa**, allowing U.S. ships to refuel at two ports. The Pierce administration rejected Perry's bid to annex more Pacific territories, including Formosa (now Taiwan). But by 1858 the United States and Japan had commenced trade, and a U.S. consul took up residence in Japan's capital, Edo (now known as Tokyo).

Pierce did far more to satisfy southern expansionists. The president and his aggressive secretary of state, William Marcy, first sought to buy extensive Mexican lands south of the Rio Grande. Ultimately, Pierce settled for a smaller slice of territory — the Gadsden Purchase of 1853, now part of Arizona and New Mexico — that opened the way for his negotiator, James Gadsden, to build a transcontinental rail line from New Orleans to Los Angeles.

Pierce's most controversial initiatives came in the Caribbean and Central America. Southern expansionists had long urged Cuban slave owners to declare independence from Spain and join the United States. To assist the expansionists and American traders who still supplied enslaved Africans to Cuba, Pierce threatened war with Spain and covertly supported **filibustering** (private military) expeditions. In 1853 John Quitman, a fabulously wealthy cotton planter and former governor of Mississippi, organized a not-so-secret expedition to take Cuba. Volunteers and offers of aid poured in from across the South. A Texan hailed Quitman's plan as the "paramount enterprise of the age," while a Mississippian reported that in his area "the desire that Cuba should be acquired as a Southern conquest is almost unanimous."

In 1854, Marcy arranged for American diplomats in Europe to compose the **Ostend Manifesto**, urging Pierce to seize Cuba by force. When the document was exposed, however, Whigs, northern Democrats, and Free Soilers all denounced it, calling it new evidence of southern "slave power" machinations. Pierce saw the political risks of supporting filibusters and withdrew his support for Quitman, who eventually cancelled his plan.

That did not stop William Walker, a Tennessee-born adventurer who had failed as a California forty-niner. Gathering other disappointed gold-seekers, Walker first tried to capture Sonora, in northern Mexico. After that failed, he organized three separate expeditions to Central America between 1855 and 1860. In 1856, after being hired as mercenaries to help a faction in a civil war in Nicaragua, Walker and 300 men overthrew the country's government and established their own (with some help from New York shipping magnate Cornelius Vanderbilt, who operated a U.S.-Nicaragua steamship line). Walker's new government declared slavery legal in Nicaragua and received immediate recognition from the United States. But Walker could not hold on to power. He fled Nicaragua and then returned to Central America twice more before being captured and shot and killed, apparently by Honduran forces, in 1860. Combined with the expeditions of other filibusters, Walker's exploits confirmed many northerners' belief that the "slave power" would stop at nothing to expand.

## Immigrants and Know-Nothings

While conflict over slavery intensified, another issue vied for center stage in politics. Outside the South, where the slave-labor system discouraged poor immigrants from settling, foreign immigration rose sharply in the 1840s and 1850s. Newcomers arrived almost entirely from northern Europe—England, Ireland, the German states, and Scandinavia—and their circumstances varied widely. German-speaking migrants were a mix of Protestants, Catholics, and Jews, and they included many skilled workers who came in family groups. Often bringing funds they had saved, more than half settled on farms or in small towns. Not so Irish Catholics, who came from an overwhelmingly rural island that was not an independent nation but a colony of Britain. Thus when a catastrophe hit Ireland in the late 1840s, it forced millions to flee or die.

**The Irish Famine**   Ireland's population had grown rapidly during the Napoleonic Wars. Most Irish farmers, working as tenants for English landlords, were required to send their grain crops to England. The poorest third of households ate little but potatoes. Ireland was thus terribly vulnerable to a potato blight in 1845 that destroyed almost the whole crop the following year. Forced to eat their seed potatoes to avoid starvation, and with very little aid offered by the British government, millions of Irish were soon desperate. *An Gorta Mór*—Celtic for "The Great Hunger"—had descended.

The results were horrific. Between 1845 and 1851 over one million people died of malnutrition or diseases that preyed on the hungry, including dysentery and cholera. "Famine and pestilence are sweeping away hundreds," reported a journalist from Bantry on the southwest coast. "The number of deaths is beyond counting." Those who could gathered their meager possessions and took passage: over 1.5 million—one-sixth of Ireland's people—emigrated, mostly to the United States.

In the 1820s and 1830s, Irish immigrants had largely been poor, unskilled men who came alone and found "heavy, rough work" in northeastern cities and towns, repairing streets or digging canals. The famine refugees came, instead, largely in family groups. Since the famine struck hardest against children and the elderly, the refugees tended to be young, healthy adults—tenant farmers, although not the very poorest. But the Atlantic voyage held new dangers: shipboard conditions in cheap steerage berths were terrible, and typhus and other diseases turned many vessels into "coffin ships." In 1853, when a cholera epidemic raged, 10 percent of Irish immigrants died at sea.

Those Irish who landed in the United States made up more than a third of all American immigrants in the 1850s. Unable to afford land, they clustered in urban areas. By 1860, a third of Irish-born Americans lived in just ten cities. Finding employment as laborers, factory workers, and domestic servants, the new arrivals faced great hardship. Some, however, through thrift and determination, managed to find their way into the ranks of shopkeepers, policemen, or farmers. Many formed mutual aid groups to support their communities. They also found support through the American Catholic Church, which soon became an Irish-dominated institution.

As early as the 1850s, some Irish began to send positive reports to kin back home. Like many later groups, the Irish developed a pattern of **chain migration**. Once a newcomer settled in, he or she saved carefully and arranged to send for neighbors and family members. As a result, steady streams of immigrants arrived long after the famine had passed. Between 1860 and 1910, more than 2.6 million Irish would arrive—far more than during the famine itself.

**Hostility Toward Immigrants**   Already by 1850, immigrants were a major presence throughout the Northeast. Like other immigrant groups, Irish and Germans boosted the American economy. Factories expanded on low-wage Irish labor. Thousands of elite and middle-class women hired "Bridgets"—Irishwomen—for domestic labor. German-language shop signs filled entire neighborhoods; Irish pubs sprang up all over Boston, while German foods (sausages, hamburgers, sauerkraut) became part of New York culture.

But the scale of immigration prompted a political backlash. Native-born Americans looked with dismay on the crowded tenement districts that sprang up to house low-paid Irish factory workers. They feared the erosion of wages—with some justification, since employers repeatedly used immigrants to break strikes and reduce pay. Advocates of the growing temperance movement condemned Irishmen's tendency to frequent the neighborhood saloon and German families' Sunday afternoons at the *biergarten*. One German observer complained that everywhere three Germans settled together, "one opened a saloon so that the other two might have a place to argue." Some English speakers also resented the tendency of proud Germans to continue speaking their own language and patronize their own newspapers, businesses, and clubs.

Perhaps the most significant factor in this era's **nativism**—hostility toward immigrants—was anti-Catholicism. Almost all the newly arrived Irish and perhaps a third of Germans were Catholics. Viewing the pope as authoritarian, some Protestants argued that Catholics could not develop the independent judgment that would make them good citizens. They would instead expect the pope to tell them how to vote. Northerners who mistrusted the "slave power" made such arguments with particular forcefulness. "Slavery and priestcraft," declared one Republican leader in 1854, "have a common purpose: they seek [to add to the United States] Cuba and Hayti and the Mexican States together, because they will be Catholic and Slave. I say they are in alliance by the necessity of their nature—for one denies the right of a man to his body, and the other the right of a man to his soul." Other nativists, believing vows of celibacy were unnatural, provoked hysteria over the alleged secret crimes of Catholic priests and nuns. *The Awful Disclosures of Maria Monk*, a popular exposé originally published in 1836, alleged that sexual debauchery and infanticide went on behind the closed doors of a Montreal convent. Though its claims were debunked, the book circulated for decades, stoking anti-Catholic prejudice.

The actions of some working-class Irish immigrants intensified these fears. In urban areas, groups of Irish men became notorious for organizing mob violence against African Americans, temperance parades, and abolitionist meetings. A much larger number devoted themselves to electoral politics. Most urban Irish forged loyalties with the Democratic Party, which gave them a foothold in the political process. This fueled, in turn, allegations that Irish voters and politicians were corrupt and clannish.

A small number of German immigrants provoked anger in the opposite direction. As radicals who were fleeing oppressive governments after the failed European revolutions of 1848, they brought socialist ideals, and some enrolled in the abolitionist cause. Abraham Lincoln, resuming his political career in the 1850s after his early defeat as a Whig, discovered that many German Americans in Illinois were eager to prevent slavery's expansion onto "free soil." Lincoln greeted one group in Chicago as "*German*

*Fellow-Citizens*" who were "true to Liberty, not *selfishly*, but upon *principle*." Among whites who supported slavery, though — including many Irish immigrants — the anti-slavery views of these German immigrants made them politically suspect.

As early as the mid-1830s, nativists called for a halt to immigration and mounted a cultural and political assault on foreign-born residents. Gangs of nativists assaulted Irish youths in the streets. In 1844, a new group called the American Republican Party won the endorsement of local Whigs and swept New York City's elections by stressing temperance, anti-Catholicism, and nativism. Rather than trying to stop immigration, they sought to deny voting and office-holding rights to noncitizens, especially by delaying the waiting period before immigrants could naturalize.

By 1850, with immigration swelling, various local nativist societies banded together as the Order of the Star-Spangled Banner. The following year they formed the **American, or Know-Nothing, Party**. When questioned, the party's secrecy-conscious members often replied, "I know nothing" — hence the nickname given by their opponents. The American Party's program was far from secret, however; supporters wanted to mobilize native-born Protestants against the "alien menace" of Irish and German Catholics, discourage further immigration, and institute literacy tests for voting. The new party drew primarily from former Whigs in the South, and about equally from Whigs and Democrats in the North. Many northern Know-Nothings had an antislavery or free soil outlook. By the mid-1850s, it was clear that these voters were hostile both to immigrants and to the expansion of slavery. What was unclear, yet, was whether a new national party would take up both of these issues, or which one party leaders would prioritize.

In 1854, voters elected dozens of American Party candidates to the House of Representatives and gave the party control of the state governments of Massachusetts and Pennsylvania. The emergence of a Protestant-based nativist party to replace the Whigs became a real possibility. At that same moment, Illinois Democrat Stephen Douglas proposed a new application of his idea of popular sovereignty, furthering the Whig Party's collapse and sending the Union spinning toward disaster.

## The West and the Fate of the Union

Since the Missouri Compromise prohibited new slave states in the Louisiana Purchase north of 36°30′, southern senators had long prevented the creation of new territories there. It remained Permanent Indian Territory. But Douglas wanted to open it up to allow a transcontinental railroad to link Chicago to California. In 1854 he proposed to extinguish Native American rights on the Great Plains and create a large free territory called Nebraska.

Southern politicians opposed Douglas's initiative. They hoped to extend slavery throughout the Louisiana Purchase and have a southern city — New Orleans, Memphis, or St. Louis — serve as the eastern terminus of a transcontinental railroad. To win their support, Douglas amended his bill so that it explicitly repealed the Missouri Compromise, potentially enabling slavery to extend farther west in new areas. He also agreed to the formation of two territories, Nebraska and Kansas, raising the prospect that settlers in the southern one, Kansas, would choose slavery. Knowing the revised bill would "raise a hell of a storm," Douglas insisted to northerners that Kansas, even though it lay next door to the slave state of Missouri, was not suited to plantation agriculture and would become a free state. After weeks of bitter debate, the Senate passed the **Kansas-Nebraska Act** (see Map 12.2, p. 362). With petitions opposed to the bill flooding the House of Representatives, the measure barely squeaked through.

**Emergence of the Republican Party**    The Kansas-Nebraska Act of 1854 jolted the political system. It galvanized thousands of northerners, especially Whigs, to stand up against the "slave power." Cotton textile magnate Amos Lawrence lamented, "We went to bed one night old fashioned, conservative Union Whigs and waked up stark mad abolitionists." In northeastern cities where nativism had been strong, renewed controversy over slavery's expansion in the West deflected attention from immigration. The Kansas-Nebraska Act also crippled the Democratic Party, with northern "anti-Nebraska Democrats" denouncing it as "part of a great scheme for extending and perpetuating supremacy of the slave power." In 1854, these former Democrats joined ex-Whigs and Free Soil supporters to form the Republican Party.

The new party was a coalition of "strange, discordant and even hostile elements," one Republican observed. Many abolitionists refused to join, arguing that the Republicans compromised too much on the need for immediate abolition. However, almost all Republicans disliked and wished to limit slavery, which, they argued, drove down the wages of free workers and degraded the dignity of manual labor. Like Thomas Jefferson, Republicans praised a society based on "the middling classes who own the soil and work it with their own hands." Abraham Lincoln, now a Republican, conveyed the new party's vision of social mobility. "There is no permanent class of hired laborers among us," he declared, ignoring growing economic and social divisions in the industrializing North and Midwest. Lincoln and his fellow Republicans envisioned a society of independent farmers, artisans, and proprietors, and they celebrated middle-class values: domesticity and respectability, religious commitment, and capitalist enterprise.

Meanwhile, thousands of settlers rushed into the Kansas Territory, putting Douglas's concept of popular sovereignty to the test. On the side of slavery, Missouri senator David R. Atchison encouraged residents of his state to cross temporarily into Kansas to vote in crucial elections there. Opposing Atchison was the abolitionist New England Emigrant Aid Society, which dispatched its supporters to Kansas. Adding to the tension, in 1855 the Pierce administration accepted the legitimacy of a proslavery legislature in Lecompton, Kansas, that had been elected with aid from border-crossing Missourians. The majority of Kansas residents favored free soil and refused allegiance to the Lecompton government.

In 1856, both sides turned to violence, prompting Horace Greeley of the *New York Tribune* to label the territory "Bleeding Kansas." A proslavery force, seven hundred strong, looted and burned the antislavery town of Lawrence. The attack enraged John Brown, a fifty-six-year-old abolitionist from New York who commanded a free-state militia. Brown was a complex man with a record of failed businesses, but his intellectual and moral intensity won the trust of influential people. Avenging the sack of Lawrence, Brown and his followers murdered five proslavery settlers at Pottawatomie. Abolitionists must "fight fire with fire" and "strike terror in the hearts of the proslavery people," Brown declared. The attack on Lawrence and the Pottawatomie killings started a guerrilla war in Kansas that took nearly two hundred lives.

In Washington, leaders of the new Republican Party distanced themselves from Brown and from radical abolitionists but took the lead in denouncing proslavery

**Armed Abolitionists in Kansas, 1859** The confrontation between North and South in Kansas took many forms. In the spring of 1859, Dr. John Doy (seated) slipped across the border into Missouri and tried to lead thirteen escaped slaves to freedom in Kansas, only to be captured and jailed in St. Joseph, Missouri. The serious-looking men standing behind Doy, well armed with guns and Bowie knives, attacked the jail and carried Doy back to Kansas. The photograph celebrated and memorialized their successful exploit. Kansas State Historical Society.

maneuvers. In May 1856, in a speech called "The Crime Against Kansas," Massachusetts Republican senator Charles Sumner accused his South Carolina colleague Andrew P. Butler of having taken "the harlot slavery" as his mistress. Butler's cousin Preston Brooks, also a southern congressman, decided to avenge his kinsman, but he disdained to fight a gentleman's duel with any "Black Republican." Instead, he found Sumner working at his desk on the Senate floor and beat him unconscious with a walking cane. Sumner, gravely injured, did not resume his seat for many months. The attack shocked northerners, providing further evidence of the arrogance and outrageousness of proslavery political leaders. Massachusetts voters reelected Sumner even while he remained disabled and could not serve. Brooks, at the same time, resigned his seat as a matter of honor but was reelected by a large margin. He received replacement canes and notes of congratulation from allies across the South.

**Buchanan's Failed Presidency**    The violence in Kansas dominated the presidential election of 1856. The new Republican Party stoked anger over Bleeding Kansas. Its platform denounced the Kansas-Nebraska Act and demanded that the federal government prohibit slavery in all the territories. Linking Mormon plural marriage with slavery, it used the language of domesticity and civilization to denounce "those twin relics of barbarism, polygamy and slavery." Republicans also called for federal subsidies to build transcontinental railroads, reviving a Whig economic proposal popular among midwestern Democrats. For president, the Republicans nominated Colonel John C. Frémont, a free soiler who had won fame in the conquest of Mexican California.

The American Party entered the election with equally high hopes, but like the Whigs, it split along sectional lines over slavery. The party's southern faction nominated former Whig president Millard Fillmore, while the northern contingent endorsed Frémont. During the campaign, Republicans won the votes of many northern Know-Nothings by demanding legislation banning foreign immigrants and imposing high tariffs on foreign manufactures. As a Pennsylvania Republican put it, "Let our motto be, protection to everything American, against everything foreign." In New York, Republicans campaigned on a reform platform designed to unite "all of the Anti-Slavery, Anti-Popery, and Anti-Whiskey" voters.

Democrats reaffirmed their support for popular sovereignty and the Kansas-Nebraska Act and nominated James Buchanan of Pennsylvania. A tall, dignified, and experienced politician, Buchanan was staunchly prosouthern. He won the three-way race with 1.8 million popular votes (45.3 percent) and 174 electoral votes. A dramatic restructuring of politics was becoming apparent: with the splintering of the American Party, Republicans replaced the Whigs as the second major party (see Map 12.3, p. 376). However, Frémont had not won a single vote in the South; had he triumphed, a North Carolina newspaper warned, the result would have been "a separation of the states." The fate of the republic hinged on President Buchanan's ability to quiet the passions of the past decade and hold the Democratic Party—the only remaining national party—together. In the end, he could not.

**Dred Scott: Petitioner for Freedom**   Events—and his own values and weaknesses—conspired against Buchanan. Early in 1857, the Supreme Court handed down the ***Dred Scott* decision,** which sought to clarify Congress's constitutional authority over slavery. Dred Scott was an enslaved African American who had lived for almost five years with his owner, an army surgeon, in the free state of Illinois and in Wisconsin Territory, both places where the Missouri Compromise (1820) prohibited slavery. Scott argued that residence in a free state and territory had made him free. Buchanan opposed Scott's appeal and, hoping to resolve the slavery controversy, secretly pressured two justices from Pennsylvania to side with their southern colleagues.

Seven of the nine justices declared that Scott was still a slave, but they disagreed on the legal rationale. Chief Justice Roger B. Taney of Maryland, a slave owner himself, wrote the most influential opinion. He declared that Negroes, whether enslaved or free, could not be citizens of the United States; he added, notoriously, that they had "no rights that a white man was bound to respect." Therefore, no African American could sue in federal court—a controversial argument, given that free blacks were citizens in many northern states. Taney then made two even more radical claims. First, he endorsed John C. Calhoun's argument that the Fifth Amendment, which prohibited "taking" of property without due process, meant that Congress could not prevent southern citizens from moving slave property into the territories. Consequently, the chief justice concluded, the provisions of the Northwest Ordinance and Missouri Compromise that prohibited slavery had *never* been constitutional. Second, Taney declared that Congress could not give to territorial governments any powers that it did not possess, such as the authority to prohibit slavery. Taney thereby endorsed Calhoun's interpretation of popular sovereignty: only when settlers wrote a constitution and requested statehood could they prohibit slavery.

In a single stroke, Taney had declared Republicans' proposals to restrict the expansion of slavery through legislation to be unconstitutional. Republicans could never accept the legitimacy of Taney's constitutional arguments, which indeed had significant flaws. Led by Senator Seward of New York, they accused the chief justice and President Buchanan of participating in the slave power conspiracy.

Buchanan then added fuel to the raging constitutional fire. Ignoring pleas from his advisers, who saw that antislavery residents held a clear majority in Kansas, he refused to allow a popular vote on the proslavery Lecompton constitution and in 1858 strongly urged Congress to admit Kansas as a slave state. Angered by Buchanan's machinations, Stephen Douglas, the most influential Democratic senator and architect of the Kansas-Nebraska Act, broke with the president and persuaded Congress to deny Kansas statehood. (Kansas would enter the Union as a free state in 1861.) Still determined to aid the South, Buchanan resumed negotiations to buy Cuba in December 1858. By pursuing an open proslavery agenda—first in *Dred Scott* and then in Kansas and Cuba—Buchanan widened the split in his party and the nation.

**The Mormon War**    The president's policies in the West did nothing to stem the growing controversy. When the United States had acquired Mexico's northern territories in 1848, Salt Lake Mormons had petitioned Congress to create a vast new state, Deseret, stretching from Utah to the Pacific coast. Instead, grudgingly, Congress set up the much smaller Utah Territory in 1850, and President Pierce appointed Mormon leader Brigham Young as governor. Tensions between Mormons and federal authorities simmered in the early 1850s. Pressured by Protestant leaders to end polygamy and angered by Mormons' threat to nullify federal laws, Buchanan dispatched a small army to Utah in 1858. He and other Democrats apparently sought to deflect attention from the slavery question. "I believe," one of the president's advisers wrote him privately, "we can supersede the Negro-Mania with the almost universal excitements of an Anti-Mormon Crusade." Buchanan backed down, however; he decided that forced abolition of polygamy might be a risky precedent for ending slavery, and he offered a pardon to Utah citizens who acknowledged federal authority. The Mormon War ended quietly, turning the nation's attention once again to the question of slavery's expansion.

| IN YOUR OWN WORDS | Why did Democrats and Whigs fail in their attempts to keep the issue of slavery in the federal territories from creating a sectional rift? |
| --- | --- |

# Abraham Lincoln and the Republican Triumph, 1858–1860

While Democrats divided along sectional lines, Republicans gained support in the North and Midwest, and Abraham Lincoln emerged as one of the party's most eloquent and politically astute candidates. However, few southerners trusted Lincoln, and his presidential candidacy in 1860 revived secessionist agitation.

## Lincoln's Political Career

The middle-class world of storekeepers, lawyers, and entrepreneurs in the small towns of the Ohio River Valley shaped Lincoln's early career. He came from a hardscrabble yeoman farm family that was continually on the move—from Kentucky, where Lincoln was born in 1809, to Indiana and then Illinois. In 1831, Lincoln rejected his father's life as a subsistence farmer and became a store clerk in New Salem, Illinois. Socially ambitious, he won entry to the middle class by mastering its culture; he joined the New Salem Debating Society, read Shakespeare, and studied law. Admitted to the bar in 1837, Lincoln moved to Springfield, the new state capital. There he met Mary Todd, the cultured daughter of a Kentucky banker; they married in 1842. Her tastes were aristocratic; his were humble. She was volatile; he was easygoing but suffered bouts of depression that tried her patience and tested his character.

**An Ambitious Politician**   Lincoln became a dexterous party politician, adept in the use of patronage and passage of legislation. As a Whig in the Illinois legislature, he promoted education, banks, canals, and railroads. During his single term in Congress during the U.S.-Mexico War, he took a middle ground by voting for military appropriations but also endorsing the Wilmot Proviso's ban on slavery in any acquired territories. Lincoln also introduced legislation that would require the gradual, compensated emancipation of slaves in the District of Columbia. To avoid future racial strife, he favored the colonization of freed blacks in Africa or South America.

After his defeat in 1848, Lincoln returned to Illinois and focused on his growing law practice representing railroads and manufacturers. The Kansas-Nebraska Act propelled him back into politics as a Republican. Shocked by the act's repeal of the Missouri Compromise and Senator Douglas's advocacy of popular sovereignty, Lincoln reaffirmed his opposition to slavery in the territories. Although he believed Congress had no power under the Constitution to interfere with slavery in states where it already existed, he likened slavery to a cancer that had to be cut out if the nation's republican ideals and moral principles were to endure.

**The Lincoln-Douglas Debates**   In 1858, Lincoln ran for the U.S. Senate seat held by Douglas. Lincoln claimed that the proslavery Supreme Court might soon declare that the Constitution "does not permit a state to exclude slavery," just as it had decided in *Dred Scott* that "neither Congress nor the territorial legislature" could ban slavery in a territory. In that event, he warned, "we shall awake to the reality . . . that the Supreme Court has made Illinois a slave state." This prospect informed Lincoln's famous House Divided speech. Quoting the biblical adage "A house divided against itself cannot stand," he predicted that American society "cannot endure permanently half slave and half free. . . . It will become all one thing, or all the other."

The Senate race in Illinois attracted national interest because of Douglas's prominence and Lincoln's reputation as a formidable speaker. During a series of seven debates, Douglas declared his support for white supremacy: "This government was made by our fathers, by white men for the benefit of white men," he said, attacking Lincoln for supporting "negro equality." Lincoln parried Douglas's racist attacks by arguing that free blacks should have equal economic opportunities but not equal political rights. Taking the offensive, he asked how Douglas could accept the *Dred*

*Scott* decision (which protected slave property in the territories) yet advocate popular sovereignty (which allowed settlers to exclude slavery). Douglas responded that a territory's residents could exclude slavery by not adopting laws to protect it. That position pleased neither proslavery nor antislavery advocates. Nonetheless, when Democrats won a narrow majority in the state legislature, they reelected Douglas to the U.S. Senate.

## The Union Under Siege

The debates with Douglas gave Lincoln a national reputation, and in the election of 1858, the Republican Party won control of the U.S. House of Representatives. Shaken by Republicans' advance, southern Democrats divided again. Moderates, who included Senator Jefferson Davis of Mississippi, strongly defended "southern rights" and demanded ironclad political or constitutional protections for slavery. The so-called fire-eaters—powerful orators such as Robert Barnwell Rhett of South Carolina and William Lowndes Yancey of Alabama—repudiated the Union and actively promoted secession. President Buchanan's secessionist secretary of war, John B. Floyd, quietly sold ten thousand federal muskets to South Carolina.

Antislavery northerners likewise took a strong stance. Senator Seward of New York declared that freedom and slavery were locked in "an irrepressible conflict." Ruthless abolitionist John Brown, who had perpetrated the Pottawatomie massacre, showed what that might mean. In October 1859, Brown led eighteen heavily armed black and white men in a raid on the federal arsenal at Harpers Ferry, Virginia. Brown hoped to arm slaves with the arsenal's weapons and mount a major rebellion to end slavery.

The raid was a failure, and Brown was quickly captured. But though he was a poor military strategist, Brown made an excellent martyr. As Virginia rushed to convict and execute him, the wounded Brown came to the courtroom on a stretcher. From the gallows he declared that the New Testament

> teaches me that all things whatsoever I would that men should do to me, I should do even so to them. It teaches me, further, to remember them that are in bonds as bound with them. I endeavored to act up to that instruction. . . . If it is deemed necessary that I should forfeit my life for the furtherance of the ends of justice, and mingle my blood further with the blood of my children and with the blood of millions in this slave country . . . I say, let it be done.

As had happened after the caning of Senator Sumner, onlookers' reactions divided the nation even more than the acts of Brown himself. Southerners were shocked to find that a group of abolitionists—the "Secret Six"—had funded Brown's raid. They were equally outraged to read that northern churchbells tolled on the day of Brown's hanging. "The lesson of the hour is insurrection," thundered abolitionist Wendell Phillips. In Virginia, the *Richmond Enquirer* reported that "the Harpers Ferry invasion has advanced the cause of disunion more than any other event." Republican leaders denounced Brown's plot, but Democrats called it "a natural, logical, inevitable result of the doctrines and teachings of the Republican party." One southern Democratic paper warned that Republicans planned to "put the torch to our dwellings and the knife to our throats."

## The Election of 1860

Within months, southern Democrats decided they could no longer count on their northern allies. At the party's convention in April 1860, northern Democrats rejected Jefferson Davis's proposal to protect slavery in the territories. Delegates from eight southern states quit the meeting. At a second Democratic convention, northern and midwestern delegates nominated Stephen Douglas for president. Meeting separately, southern Democrats nominated the sitting vice president, John C. Breckinridge of Kentucky. Democrats—the only remaining party with strong bases in both North and South—had split in half.

With Democrats divided, Republicans sensed victory. They courted white voters with a free soil platform that opposed both slavery and racial equality: "Missouri for white men and white men for Missouri," declared that state's Republican platform. The national

## THE NATIONAL GAME. THREE "OUTS" AND ONE "RUN".
### ABRAHAM WINNING THE BALL.

**Lincoln on Home Base** Beginning in the 1820s and 1830s, the language and imagery of sports saturated politics, cutting across the lines of class and party. Wielding a long, bat-like rail labeled "Equal Rights and Free Territory," Abraham Lincoln holds a baseball and appears ready to score a victory in the election. His three opponents—from left to right, John Bell (the candidate of a new Constitutional Union Party), Stephen A. Douglas, and John C. Breckinridge—will soon be "out." Indeed, according to the pro-Lincoln cartoonist, they were about to be "skunk'd." As Douglas laments, their attempt to put a "short stop" to Lincoln's presidential ambitions had failed. Library of Congress.

Republican convention chose Lincoln as its presidential candidate because he was more moderate on slavery than the best-known Republicans, Senators William Seward of New York and Salmon Chase of Ohio. Lincoln also conveyed a compelling egalitarian image that appealed to smallholding farmers, wage earners, and midwestern voters.

The Republican strategy worked. Although Lincoln was not on the ballot in any Deep South state, and though he received less than 1 percent of the popular vote in the South and only 40 percent of the national vote, he won every northern and western state except New Jersey, giving him 180 (of 303) electoral votes and thus a majority in the electoral college. Breckinridge took 72 electoral votes by sweeping the Deep South and picking up Delaware, Maryland, and North Carolina. Douglas won 30 percent of the popular ballot but secured only 51 electoral votes, winning in Missouri and New Jersey. Republicans had united voters in the Northeast and Midwest behind free soil. To his surprise, Lincoln also won California and Oregon by the barest of margins, apparently due in part to public outrage over a duel in which a proslavery California Democrat killed an antislavery rival (Map 12.3).

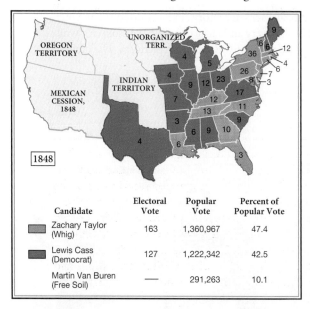

| Candidate | Electoral Vote | Popular Vote | Percent of Popular Vote |
|---|---|---|---|
| Zachary Taylor (Whig) | 163 | 1,360,967 | 47.4 |
| Lewis Cass (Democrat) | 127 | 1,222,342 | 42.5 |
| Martin Van Buren (Free Soil) | — | 291,263 | 10.1 |

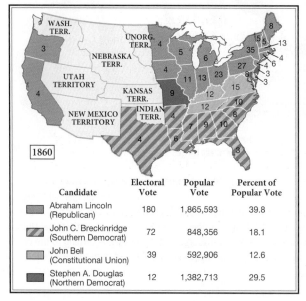

| Candidate | Electoral Vote | Popular Vote | Percent of Popular Vote |
|---|---|---|---|
| Abraham Lincoln (Republican) | 180 | 1,865,593 | 39.8 |
| John C. Breckinridge (Southern Democrat) | 72 | 848,356 | 18.1 |
| John Bell (Constitutional Union) | 39 | 592,906 | 12.6 |
| Stephen A. Douglas (Northern Democrat) | 12 | 1,382,713 | 29.5 |

**MAP 12.3  Political Realignment, 1848 and 1860**

In the presidential election of 1848, both the Whig and Democratic candidates won electoral votes throughout the nation. Subsequently, the political conflict over slavery and the Compromise of 1850 destroyed the Whig Party in the South. As the only nationwide party, the Democrats won easily over the Whigs in 1852 and, with the opposition split between the Republican and American parties, triumphed in 1856 as well. However, a new region-based party system appeared by 1860 and persisted for the next seventy years—with Democrats dominant in the South and Republicans usually controlling the Northeast, Midwest, and Far West.

A revolution was in the making. "Oh My God!!! This morning heard that Lincoln was elected," Keziah Brevard, a widowed South Carolina plantation mistress and owner of two hundred slaves, scribbled in her diary. "Lord save us." Slavery had long been part of the American constitutional order — an order many southerners now believed was under siege. Fearful of a massive slave uprising, Chief Justice Taney recalled "the horrors of St. Domingo [Haiti]." At the very least, warned John Townsend of South Carolina, a Republican administration in Washington would suppress "the inter-State slave trade" and thereby "cripple this vital Southern institution of slavery." To many slaveholders, it seemed time to think carefully about Lincoln's 1858 statement that the Union must "become all one thing, or all the other."

| **IN YOUR OWN WORDS** | What factors led to the rise of the Republican Party and Lincoln's election in 1860? |
|---|---|

# Secession Winter, 1860–1861

Following Lincoln's election, secessionist fervor swept through the Deep South. The Union collapsed first in South Carolina, home of John C. Calhoun and nullification. Robert Barnwell Rhett and other fire-eaters had demanded secession since the Compromise of 1850, and their goal was now within reach. "Our enemies are about to take possession of the Government," warned one South Carolinian. Frightened by that prospect, a state convention voted unanimously on December 20, 1860, to dissolve "the union now subsisting between South Carolina and other States."

Fire-eaters elsewhere in the Deep South quickly called similar conventions and organized mobs to attack local Union supporters. In early January, white Mississippians enacted a secession ordinance. Florida and Louisiana followed, while fierce controversy raged in other states. Holding out to the end of a bitter debate, over a third of delegates to Alabama's secession convention voted to oppose leaving the Union. In early February, Texans ousted Unionist governor Sam Houston, ignoring his warning that "the North . . . will overwhelm the South." Georgia's prosecession governor waited a month before announcing that a secession referendum had won by 57 percent; returns were never released, and historians now suspect the vote was much closer and a majority may even have opposed secession.

Nevertheless, when the smoke cleared, the Deep South states had all seceded. In February, jubilant secessionists met in Montgomery, Alabama, to proclaim a new nation, the Confederate States of America. Adopting a provisional constitution, the delegates named Mississippian Jefferson Davis, a former U.S. senator and secretary of war, as the Confederacy's president and Georgia congressman Alexander Stephens as vice president.

Secessionist fervor was less intense in four states of the Upper South (Virginia, North Carolina, Tennessee, and Arkansas), where there were fewer slaves. White opinion was especially divided in the four border slave states (Maryland, Delaware, Kentucky, and Missouri), where yeomen farmers held greater political power, and over whose ground any resulting civil war would likely be fought. The legislatures of Virginia and Tennessee refused to join the secessionist movement and urged a compromise.

Meanwhile, President Buchanan's administration floundered. Buchanan declared secession illegal but, in line with his states' rights outlook, claimed that the federal government lacked authority to restore the Union by force. Buchanan's timidity prompted South Carolina's new government to demand the surrender of Fort Sumter (a federal garrison in Charleston Harbor) and to cut off its supplies. The president again backed down, refusing to use the navy to supply the fort.

Instead, the outgoing president urged Congress to find a compromise. The plan proposed by Senator John J. Crittenden of Kentucky received the most support. His proposal had two parts. The first, which Congress approved, called for a constitutional amendment to protect slavery from federal interference in any state where it already existed. Crittenden's second provision called for the westward extension of the Missouri Compromise line (36°30′ north latitude) to the California border. The provision would have banned slavery north of the line and allowed it to the south, including any territories "hereafter acquired," raising the prospect of expansion into Cuba or Central America.

Congressional Republicans rejected Crittenden's second proposal on strict instructions from president-elect Lincoln. With good reason, Lincoln feared it would unleash new imperialist adventures. "On the territorial question, I am inflexible," he wrote; restoring the Missouri Compromise line would simply invite southerners to keep "filibustering to expand slavery." In 1787, 1821, and 1850, the North and South had resolved their differences over slavery. In 1861, there would be no compromise.

In his March 1861 inaugural address, Lincoln carefully outlined his positions. He promised to safeguard slavery where it existed but vowed to prevent its expansion. Equally important, the Republican president declared that the Union was "perpetual"; consequently, the secession of the Confederate states was illegal. Lincoln asserted his intention to "hold, occupy, and possess" federal property in the seceded states and "to collect duties and imposts" there. If military force was necessary to preserve the Union, Lincoln—like Democrat Andrew Jackson during the nullification crisis—would use it. The choice was the South's: return to the Union or face war.

The South's decision came quickly (Map 12.4). When Lincoln dispatched an unarmed ship to resupply Fort Sumter, Jefferson Davis and his associates in the Provisional Government of the Confederate States decided to seize the fort. Their forces opened fire on April 12, with ardent fire-eater Edmund Ruffin supposedly firing the first cannon. Two days later, the Union defenders capitulated. On April 15, Lincoln called 75,000 state militiamen into federal service for ninety days to put down an insurrection "too powerful to be suppressed by the ordinary course of judicial proceedings."

Northerners responded to Lincoln's call to arms with wild enthusiasm. In western Pennsylvania, a group of lumbermen organized themselves into a regiment, built rafts, and floated down to Harrisburg before the state governor had even requested volunteers. Asked to provide thirteen regiments, Republican governor William Dennison of Ohio sent twenty. Most northern Democrats lent their support. Despite his past differences with Lincoln, Stephen Douglas toured the North urging citizens to

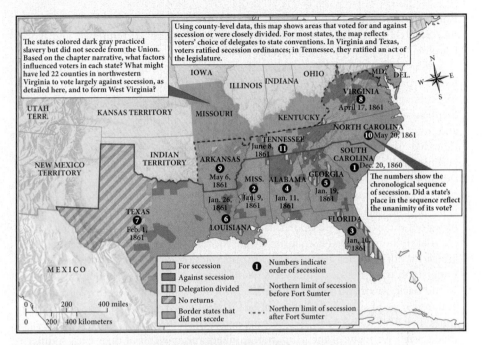

The states colored dark gray practiced slavery but did not secede from the Union. Based on the chapter narrative, what factors influenced voters in each state? What might have led 22 counties in northwestern Virginia to vote largely against secession, as detailed here, and to form West Virginia?

Using county-level data, this map shows areas that voted for and against secession or were closely divided. For most states, the map reflects voters' choice of delegates to state conventions. In Virginia and Texas, voters ratified secession ordinances; in Tennessee, they ratified an act of the legislature.

The numbers show the chronological sequence of secession. Did a state's place in the sequence reflect the unanimity of its vote?

Legend:
- For secession
- Against secession
- Delegation divided
- No returns
- Border states that did not secede
- ❶ Numbers indicate order of secession
- — Northern limit of secession before Fort Sumter
- ···· Northern limit of secession after Fort Sumter

**MAP 12.4   The Process of Secession, 1860–1861**

The states of the Lower South had the highest concentration of slaves, and they led the secessionist movement. After the attack on Fort Sumter in April 1861, the states of the Upper South joined the Confederacy. Yeomen farmers in Tennessee and the backcountry of Alabama, Georgia, and Virginia opposed secession but, except in the future state of West Virginia, initially rallied to the Confederate cause. Consequently, the South entered the Civil War with its white population relatively united.

support the government. "Every man must be for the United States or against it," he declared. "There can be no neutrals in this war, only patriots — or traitors."

Voters in the Middle and Border South now faced a new situation: war was imminent. Those eight states accounted for two-thirds of whites in the slaveholding states, three-fourths of their industrial production, and well over half of their food. They were home to many of the nation's best military leaders, including Colonel Robert E. Lee of Virginia, a career officer whom veteran General Winfield Scott recommended to Lincoln to lead the new Union army. Those states were also geographically strategic. Kentucky, with its 500-mile border on the Ohio River, was essential to the movement of troops and supplies. Maryland was vital to the Union's security because it bordered the nation's capital on three sides.

The weight of its history as a slave-owning society decided the outcome in Virginia. On April 17, 1861, a convention approved secession by a vote of 88 to 55, with dissenters concentrated in the state's yeoman-dominated northwestern counties. Elsewhere, Virginia whites embraced the Confederate cause. "The North was the aggressor," declared Richmond lawyer William Poague as he enlisted. "The South resisted her invaders." Refusing General Scott's offer of the Union command,

Robert E. Lee resigned from the U.S. Army. "Save in defense of my native state," Lee told Scott, "I never desire again to draw my sword." Arkansas, Tennessee, and North Carolina quickly joined Virginia in the Confederacy.

Whatever their prior views, the citizens of eleven southern states now committed to separate nationhood on a basis already determined by the Deep South. Two weeks after Lincoln's inauguration, the Confederacy's new vice president, Alexander Stephens of Georgia, outlined its goals in his famous "cornerstone" speech. Jefferson and other founders, he wrote, had considered slavery an "evil" — an institution they inherited and practiced reluctantly, believing it "wrong in principle, socially, morally, and politically." The new Confederacy, Stephens declared, "is founded upon exactly the opposite idea; its foundations are laid, its corner-stone rests, upon the great truth that the negro is not equal to the white man; that subordination to the superior race is his natural and normal condition. This, our new government, is the first, in the history of the world, based upon this great physical, philosophical, and moral truth."

For millions of loyal Unionists outside the South, secession and the Confederate attack on Fort Sumter automatically meant war. Yet on both sides, few Americans understood what the next four years would bring. At first many thought the South would back down and return to the Union if Republicans stood firm. Republican congressman Thaddeus Stevens scoffed, "They have tried it fifty times, and fifty times they have found weak and recreant tremblers in the north." If war came, northerners were confident of their superior numbers and power. For their part, southerners argued that cotton was "King" and would give them extraordinary economic and political leverage, including likely aid from Britain and France. Many southerners also claimed that "the Yankees are cowards and will not fight," as one put it. A South Carolina congressman promised to drink all the blood that would be shed as a result of the Confederacy's founding.

But others expected something different. When Fort Sumter fell, a former army officer and banker named William Tecumseh Sherman was serving as superintendent of a military school in Louisiana. Upon hearing that Lincoln had called up 75,000 troops for three months, Sherman was sure it would not be enough: "You might as well attempt to put out the flames of a burning house with a squirt-gun." He left Louisiana and rejoined the U.S. Army. As volunteers began to mobilize, an enslaved woman in Mississippi named Dora Franks overheard a conversation between her master and his wife: "He feared all the slaves 'ud be took away. She say if dat was true she feel lak jumpin' in de well." Franks added, "I hate to hear her say dat, but from dat minute I started prayin' for freedom."

| **IN YOUR OWN WORDS** | After South Carolina's secession, why were Unionists and Confederates unable to avoid war? |

# Summary

U.S. victory in the U.S.-Mexico War set off bitter political conflicts over whether Congress could or should allow slavery in lands taken from Mexico. Some northerners, both Democrats and Whigs, opposed slavery in the new territories. Southern

Democrats responded angrily, claiming the constitutional right to carry slave property into all U.S. territories. Senior congressmen engineered the Compromise of 1850, hoping to placate all sides. But this series of bills, which included a controversial new Fugitive Slave Act, settled little.

The discovery of gold led to rapid settlement of California; though few got rich, an array of gold-seekers pushed out Mexican landholders and waged a war of extermination on Native peoples. Abolitionist sentiment grew; even more broadly popular was the free soil movement, which by 1848 became a political party advocating that western lands be reserved for free white families. As antislavery activists protested the injustice of the Fugitive Slave Act, and with evidence emerging that southerners were working to annex slave Cuba, abolitionists began to warn that southern Democrats' "slave power" conspiracy controlled federal power. In response, some radical southerners began to advocate secession.

Northern Democratic efforts to implement popular sovereignty in the territories, through the Kansas-Nebraska Act, proved disastrous: increasing violence in Kansas led coalitions of former Democrats, Whigs, and Free Soilers in the North to form the Republican Party. Amid massive immigration from Ireland, it appeared for a while that nativism might eclipse slavery as a key national issue. But by 1856 the Republican Party emerged as the main challenger to Democrats in the North. In 1860 the Democratic Party also fragmented on sectional lines, leading to a four-way race in which Republican Abraham Lincoln emerged victorious. South Carolina seceded almost immediately, arguing that southern slavery could no longer be protected in the Union. Though thousands of white southerners opposed secession, majorities in the Deep South voted to leave the Union. After Confederate forces fired on federal Fort Sumter, Lincoln called up troops to suppress rebellion. Four more states in the Upper South then seceded, leading by April 1861 to civil war.

# Chapter 12 Review

## KEY TERMS

**Identify and explain the significance of each term below.**

Mexican cession (p. 354)
conscience Whigs (p. 355)
Wilmot Proviso (p. 355)
"slave power" conspiracy (p. 356)
free soil movement (p. 357)
Foreign Miner's Tax (p. 358)
popular sovereignty (p. 360)
Compromise of 1850 (p. 361)
personal liberty laws (p. 364)

Treaty of Kanagawa (p. 365)
filibustering (p. 365)
Ostend Manifesto (p. 365)
chain migration (p. 366)
nativism (p. 367)
American, or Know-Nothing, Party (p. 368)
Kansas-Nebraska Act (p. 369)
*Dred Scott* decision (p. 371)

## REVIEW QUESTIONS

**Answer these questions to demonstrate your understanding of the chapter's main ideas.**

1. What political conflicts were triggered by U.S. acquisition of lands in the U.S.-Mexico War?

2. Why did Democrats and Whigs fail in their attempts to keep the issue of slavery in the federal territories from creating a sectional rift?

3. What factors led to the rise of the Republican Party and Lincoln's election in 1860?

4. After South Carolina's secession, why were Unionists and Confederates unable to avoid war?

5. Chapter 12 revisits the years between 1844 and 1848, which have already been explored in earlier chapters. Review the timelines in Part 4 (pp. 230–231) and Part 5 (pp. 352–353), and consider what events occurred in those years. Why do you think they were included in both Parts 4 and 5? If you were making your own timeline of the events and trends that led to the Civil War, would you begin in 1844, 1848, or another date? What causes of sectional crisis would your timeline emphasize?

## CHRONOLOGY

**As you read, ask yourself why this chapter begins and ends with these dates and identify the links among related events.**

| | |
|---|---|
| **1844** | • James K. Polk elected president |
| **1845–1851** | • Great Irish famine prompts mass immigration to United States |
| **1846** | • Congress supports Polk's recommendation and declares war against Mexico |
| **1846** | • Wilmot Proviso approved by House but not by Senate |
| **1848** | • Gold found in California; gold rush begins |
| | • Treaty of Guadalupe Hidalgo transfers Mexican lands to United States |
| | • Free Soil Party forms |
| **1850** | • Compromise of 1850 passes, including Fugitive Slave Act |
| | • Foreign Miner's Tax enacted in California |
| **1851** | • American (Know-Nothing) Party forms |
| **1852** | • Harriet Beecher Stowe publishes *Uncle Tom's Cabin* |
| **1854** | • Treaty of Kanagawa opens U.S. coaling stations in Japan |
| | • Ostend Manifesto urges U.S. seizure of Cuba |
| | • Kansas-Nebraska Act tests policy of popular sovereignty |
| | • Republican Party forms |

| | |
|---|---|
| **1856** | • Rep. Preston Brooks canes Sen. Charles Sumner on Senate floor |
| | • William Walker deposes Nicaraguan government, sets up "filibuster" regime |
| **1857** | • *Dred Scott v. Sandford* allows slavery in all U.S. territories |
| **1858** | • President James Buchanan urges Congress to admit Kansas under the proslavery Lecompton constitution |
| | • Buchanan seeks to buy and annex Cuba as a slave state |
| | • United States fights brief "Mormon War" for federal control of Utah |
| **1859** | • John Brown raids federal arsenal at Harpers Ferry |
| **1860** | • Abraham Lincoln elected president in four-way contest |
| | • South Carolina secedes (December) |
| **1861** | • Mississippi, Florida, Alabama, Georgia, Louisiana, and Texas secede before February 1 |
| | • Confederate States of America formed (February) |
| | • Lincoln inaugurated (March) |
| | • Confederate forces fire on Fort Sumter when Lincoln administration directs an attempted food resupply (April) |
| | • Lincoln calls for three-month volunteer troops to suppress rebellion |
| | • Four Upper South states (Virginia, Arkansas, North Carolina, Tennessee) secede |

# 13

# Bloody Ground: The Civil War

## 1861–1865

**IDENTIFY THE BIG IDEA**

How and why did the Union win the Civil War?

**IN FEBRUARY 1865, AS U.S. TROOPS UNDER GENERAL WILLIAM** Tecumseh Sherman completed their destructive march through Georgia and crossed into South Carolina, their pace quickened. They were approaching the state capital, Columbia, where four years earlier South Carolina legislators had passed the ordinance of secession. "Hail Columbia, happy land," some of the soldiers sang, "If we don't burn you, I'll be damned." "The whole army," wrote Sherman, "is burning with an insatiable desire to wreak vengeance upon South Carolina. I almost tremble at her fate, but feel that she deserves all that seems in store for her."

As the Union army approached, many white residents of Columbia fled. Terrified of slave revolt, others set up a new whipping post in town, where one enslaved man received a hundred lashes for communicating with federal prisoners held nearby. Local officials dithered: one wanted to defend Columbia house by house, but at the last moment Confederate commanders abandoned the city. Even before Sherman arrived, looting began. Things got worse when arriving Union soldiers discovered 120 barrels of whiskey. One regiment entered the capitol building, voted to revoke secession, and plundered trophies from the senate chamber. More sober soldiers remembered being greeted with glares and curses from whites and shouts of "God bless you" from African Americans. One woman, freed from slavery, gave birth three days later to a son she named Liberty Sherman.

The Union army destroyed all targets of military importance in the city—warehouses, rail stations, machinery. Stacks of cotton bales left on the streets caught fire, and a stiff breeze carried the flames from house to house. One well-dressed southern lady managed to locate Lt. Col. Jeremiah Jenkins, the Union provost marshal, as he hurried around trying to stamp out fires. She begged him to protect her home, but Jenkins replied, "The women of the South kept the war alive—and it is only by making them suffer that we can subdue the men."

The burning of Columbia showed that the Civil War unfolded in ways no one expected at the start. In 1861 both Unionists and Confederates had believed they were embarking on a quick and limited conflict. Each side argued they would quickly win. Both proved wrong. Such is often the case at the outset of wars that become long, agonizing, and terrible, and the Civil War was no exception. As each side hung on fiercely, determined to win, the scale of conflict escalated on battlefields and home fronts. The result, in President Lincoln's words, was "fundamental and astounding": unprecedented political and civilian mobilization; hundreds of thousands dead; the Confederacy's crushing defeat; and the end of slavery.

**Ruins of Richmond** A street scene in Richmond, Virginia, capital of the Confederacy, in 1865. The women's black dresses indicate that they have recently lost husbands, sons, or other close relatives. On the left, the camera's long exposure caught the ghostly image of a man walking by—possibly a veteran in Confederate gray. The Granger Collection, New York.

# War Begins, 1861–1862

With hindsight we know that the Civil War lasted four years, the Union won, and the war abolished slavery. But if any of these outcomes had been apparent in 1861, the South would not likely have seceded. Southern leaders banked on cotton's centrality to the national and world economy in achieving Confederate independence. They viewed slavery as an asset to the war effort and argued that southern soldiers would be braver and more effective than northern immigrants and urban workers, whom one disdainfully referred to as "mongrel hordes of Yankees." Events on the battlefield, however, proved neither quick nor decisive. By fall 1862, both the Union and the Confederacy were forced to adopt new military and political strategies.

## Early Expectations

In 1861, patriotic fervor filled both Union and Confederate armies with eager young volunteers. One Union recruit wrote that "if a fellow wants to go with a girl now he had better enlist. The girls sing 'I am bound to be a Soldier's Wife or Die an Old Maid.' " Even men of sober minds joined up. "I don't think a young man ever went over all the considerations more carefully than I did," reflected William Saxton of Cincinnatus, New York. "It might mean sickness, wounds, loss of limb, and even life itself. . . . But my country was in danger." The southern call for volunteers was even more successful, thanks to the region's strong military tradition and culture of masculine honor. Confederate soldiers emphasized their duty to protect hearth and home as well as northerners' opposition to slavery. If it had not been for "Psalm singing 'brethren' and 'sistern' . . . preaching abolitionism from every northern pulpit," one Alabama infantryman wrote to his wife, "I would never have been soldiering."

Speaking as provisional president of the Confederacy in April 1861, Jefferson Davis identified the Confederate cause with that of Patriots in 1776: like their grandfathers, white southerners were fighting for the "sacred right of self-government." That right included slaveholding. Secessionists did not believe Lincoln when he promised not to interfere "directly or indirectly . . . with the institution of slavery in the States where it exists." Soon, one southern senator warned, "cohorts of Federal office-holders, Abolitionists, may be sent into [our] midst" to encourage slave revolts of the kind John Brown had attempted. Slave rebellion raised the prospect of racial mixture, or amalgamation — by which, of course, white southerners meant sexual relations between white *women* and black *men*, given that white masters had already fathered untold thousands of children by enslaved black women. "Better, far better! [to] endure all horrors of civil war," insisted a Confederate recruit, "than to see the dusky sons of Ham leading the fair daughters of the South to the altar." To preserve black subordination and white supremacy, radical southerners chose the dangerous enterprise of secession.

Lincoln responded in a speech to Congress on July 4, 1861, portraying secession as an attack on representative government, America's great contribution to world history. The issue, Lincoln declared, was "whether a constitutional republic" had the will and means to "maintain its territorial integrity against a domestic foe." Living in a world still ruled by monarchies, northern leaders believed that the collapse of the American Union would destroy the possibility of republican governments.

## Campaigns East and West

Confederates had the advantage of defense: they only needed to preserve their new national boundaries to achieve independence. Moreover, with 9 million people, the Confederacy could mobilize enormous armies. Enslaved blacks, one-third of the population, produced food for the army and raw cotton for export. Southerners counted on sales of **King Cotton**—the leading American export and an essential global commodity—to purchase clothes, boots, blankets, and weapons from abroad. Confederate leaders believed Britain and France, with their large textile industries, were too dependent on cotton not to recognize and assist the Confederacy. Their hopes were boosted in November 1861 when a hot-headed U.S. naval captain intercepted a British steamer, the *Trent*, to seize and detain two Confederate diplomats en route from Cuba to London. The incident nearly precipitated war between the United States and Britain, until the Lincoln administration wisely released the prisoners and the crisis subsided.

In contrast to the Confederacy's defensive stance, the Union had the more difficult job of bringing the rebels back into the Union. U.S. commanding general Winfield Scott proposed a strategy of peaceful persuasion through economic sanctions, combined with a naval blockade of southern ports. Lincoln agreed to the blockade, which was organized with impressive efficiency through the navy's purchase and charter of merchant vessels. By the start of 1862, over 260 ships were on blockade duty and another 100 under construction. But Lincoln, determined to crush the rebellion, insisted also on an aggressive military campaign to restore the Union.

**Failed Attempts to Take Richmond and Washington**    Lincoln hoped a quick strike against the Confederate capital of Richmond, Virginia, would end the rebellion. Many northerners were equally optimistic. "What a picnic," thought one New York volunteer, "to go down South for three months and clean up the whole business." In July 1861, Lincoln ordered General Irvin McDowell's army of 30,000 men to attack General P. G. T. Beauregard's force of 20,000 troops at Manassas (Bull Run), a Virginia rail junction 30 miles southwest of Washington. McDowell launched a strong assault near Bull Run, but panic swept his troops when the Confederate soldiers counterattacked, shouting the hair-raising "rebel yell." McDowell's troops—and many civilians who had come to observe the battle—retreated in disarray. Suddenly, Washington, D.C., seemed threatened, the first of several times during the war that federal officials and residents made preparations to flee.

The Confederate victory at Bull Run showed the rebellion's strength. Lincoln replaced McDowell with General George McClellan and enlisted a million men to serve for three years in the new Army of the Potomac. A cautious military engineer, McClellan spent the winter of 1861–1862 training the recruits and launched his first major offensive in March 1862. With great logistical skill, the Union general ferried 100,000 troops down the Potomac River to the Chesapeake Bay and landed them on the peninsula between the York and James rivers (Map 13.1). Ignoring Lincoln's advice to "strike a blow" quickly, McClellan advanced slowly toward Richmond, allowing Confederates to mount a counterstrike. Thomas J. "Stonewall" Jackson marched a Confederate force rapidly northward through the Shenandoah Valley in western Virginia and threatened Washington. When Lincoln recalled 30,000 troops

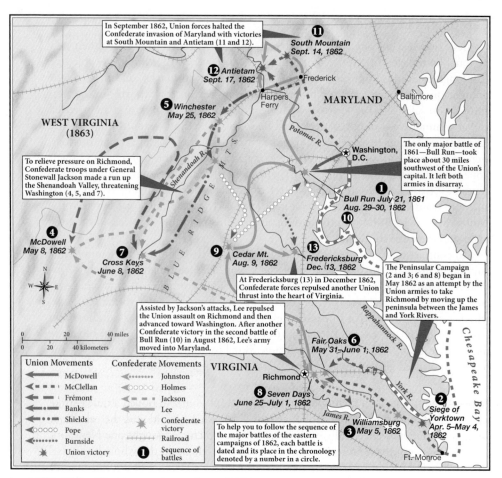

In September 1862, Union forces halted the Confederate invasion of Maryland with victories at South Mountain and Antietam (11 and 12).

⑪ South Mountain Sept. 14, 1862

⑫ Antietam Sept. 17, 1862

⑤ Winchester May 25, 1862

Frederick

Harpers Ferry

MARYLAND

Baltimore

WEST VIRGINIA (1863)

Potomac R.

Washington, D.C.

The only major battle of 1861—Bull Run—took place about 30 miles southwest of the Union's capital. It left both armies in disarray.

To relieve pressure on Richmond, Confederate troops under General Stonewall Jackson made a run up the Shenandoah Valley, threatening Washington (4, 5, and 7).

① Bull Run July 21, 1861 Aug. 29–30, 1862

⑩

④ McDowell May 8, 1862

⑦ Cross Keys June 8, 1862

⑨ ⑬ Cedar Mt. Aug. 9, 1862

Fredericksburg Dec. 13, 1862

The Peninsular Campaign (2 and 3; 6 and 8) began in May 1862 as an attempt by the Union armies to take Richmond by moving up the peninsula between the James and York Rivers.

At Fredericksburg (13) in December 1862, Confederate forces repulsed another Union thrust into the heart of Virginia.

Assisted by Jackson's attacks, Lee repulsed the Union assault on Richmond and then advanced toward Washington. After another Confederate victory in the second battle of Bull Run (10) in August 1862, Lee's army moved into Maryland.

Fair Oaks ⑥ May 31–June 1, 1862

Rappahannock R.

Chesapeake Bay

Union Movements
- McDowell
- McClellan
- Frémont
- Banks
- Shields
- Pope
- Burnside
- ✳ Union victory

Confederate Movements
- Johnston
- Holmes
- Jackson
- Lee
- ✳ Confederate victory
- ┼┼┼ Railroad
- ① Sequence of battles

VIRGINIA

Richmond ☆

⑧ Seven Days June 25–July 1, 1862

To help you to follow the sequence of the major battles of the eastern campaigns of 1862, each battle is dated and its place in the chronology denoted by a number in a circle.

James R. Williamsburg ③ May 5, 1862

York R.

② Siege of Yorktown Apr. 5–May 4, 1862

Ft. Monroe

## MAP 13.1    The Eastern Campaigns of 1862

Many of the great battles of the Civil War took place in the 125 miles separating the Union capital, Washington, D.C., and the Confederate capital, Richmond, Virginia. During 1862, Confederate generals Thomas Jonathan "Stonewall" Jackson and Robert E. Lee won battles that defended the Confederate capital (3, 6, 8, and 13) and launched offensive strikes against Union forces guarding Washington (1, 4, 5, 7, 9, and 10). They also suffered a defeat—at Antietam (12), in Maryland—that was almost fatal to the Confederate cause. As was often the case in the Civil War, the victors in these battles were either too bloodied or too timid to exploit their advantage.

from McClellan's army to protect the Union capital, Jackson returned quickly to Richmond to bolster General Robert E. Lee's army. In late June, Lee launched a ferocious six-day attack that cost 20,000 casualties to the Union's 10,000. When McClellan failed to exploit the Confederates' losses, Lincoln ordered a withdrawal. Richmond remained secure.

**Border Wars**    In addition to taking the Confederate capital, Lincoln's second major goal was to hold on to strategic border areas where relatively few whites owned slaves. To secure the railroad connecting Washington to the Ohio River Valley,

Lincoln ordered General McClellan to take control of northwestern Virginia. In October 1861, Unionist-leaning voters in that area chose overwhelmingly to create a breakaway territory, West Virginia. Unwilling to "cut our own throats merely to sustain . . . a most unwarrantable rebellion," as one put it, West Virginians formed their own state in 1863. Unionists also carried the day in Delaware.

In Maryland, where slavery remained entrenched, a pro-Confederate mob attacked Massachusetts troops traveling through Baltimore in late April 1861, causing some of the war's first combat deaths: three soldiers and nine civilians. When Maryland secessionists destroyed railroad bridges and telegraph lines, Lincoln ordered Union troops to occupy the state and arrest Confederate sympathizers, including legislators, releasing them only in November 1861, after Unionists had secured control of Maryland's government. Lincoln's actions provoked bitter debate over this suspension of **habeas corpus** — a legal instrument that protects citizens from arbitrary arrest. The president's opponents pointed to Article I, Section 9 of the U.S. Constitution, which states that "the privilege of the Writ of Habeas Corpus shall not be suspended"; Lincoln argued that the same clause continues, "unless when in Cases of Rebellion or Invasion the public Safety may require it." To ardent Unionists, a rebellion was clearly under way. Lincoln continued to use occasional habeas corpus suspensions throughout the war when he deemed them essential; Republicans and Democrats continued to disagree bitterly over his actions.

In Kentucky, where secessionist and Unionist sentiment was evenly balanced, Lincoln moved cautiously. He allowed Kentucky's thriving trade with the Confederacy to continue until August 1861, when Unionists took over the state government. After the Confederacy unwisely responded to the trade cutoff by invading Kentucky in September, Illinois volunteers commanded by Ulysses S. Grant drove them out, and Kentucky public opinion swung against the Confederacy. Mixing military force with political persuasion, Lincoln had kept three border states (Delaware, Maryland, and Kentucky) and the northwestern portion of Virginia in the Union.

But how far west did "border regions" extend? As the territorial conflicts of the 1850s had revealed, the answer was not clear. Lincoln's election roused deep suspicion among many westerners, from Utah Mormons — whom Republicans had alienated by seeking to abolish polygamy — to gold-rush Californians, nearly 40 percent of whom were southern-born. In Oregon, a former U.S. senator praised the "gallant South" and claimed that "the Republican Party will have war enough at home." In Indian Territory (now Oklahoma), many slave-owning Choctaws, Chickasaws, and Cherokees cast their lot with the Confederacy, hoping to secure more autonomy than the Union had allowed them. Thus, the war bitterly divided Native peoples in Indian Territory. It was a Confederate Cherokee, General Stand Watie, who became the war's highest-ranking Native American.

Meanwhile, Texas coveted New Mexico, and enterprising Confederates argued that they could bolster their economy if they captured the gold mines of Colorado, seized Nevada's fabulously rich Comstock silver lode, and perhaps even took San Francisco. In autumn 1861, therefore, an expedition of 3,500 Texans marched west and succeeded in capturing Albuquerque and Santa Fe. But the following March, as the Confederates headed north, Union forces turned them back at the Battle of Glorieta Pass (Map 13.2). Henceforth Union control of the Far West remained secure. Among the victorious troops were Colorado volunteers whose massacre of friendly Cheyennes at Sand Creek, soon after, embroiled the West in a new round of Indian wars (Chapter 15).

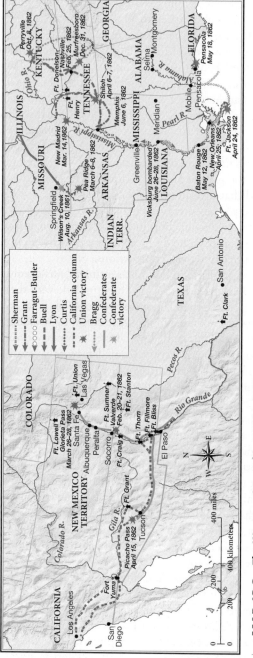

## MAP 13.2  The Western Campaigns, 1861–1862

As the Civil War intensified in 1862, Union and Confederate military and naval forces sought control of the great valleys of the Ohio, Tennessee, and Mississippi rivers, as well as the trans-Mississippi west. In fall 1861, a Confederate force marched west from Texas, hoping to seize the rich mining areas of Nevada and Colorado, but they were turned back in March 1862 at the Battle of Glorieta Pass. From February through April 1862, Union armies moved south through western Tennessee. By the end of June, Union naval forces controlled the Mississippi River north of Memphis and from the Gulf of Mexico to Vicksburg. These military and naval victories gave the Union control of crucial transportation routes, kept Missouri in the Union, and carried the war to the states of the Lower South.

**The Struggle to Control the Mississippi**  Union commanders in Tennessee also won key victories, dividing the Confederacy and reducing the mobility of its armies. Because Kentucky did not join the rebellion, the Union already dominated the Ohio River Valley. In February 1862, the Union army used an innovative tactic to extend control to the south and west. General Grant used riverboats clad with iron plates to capture Fort Donelson on the Cumberland River and Fort Henry on the Tennessee River. When Grant moved south to seize critical railroad lines, Confederate troops led by Albert Sidney Johnston and P. G. T. Beauregard caught his army by surprise near a small log church at Shiloh, Tennessee. However, Grant relentlessly committed troops and forced a Confederate withdrawal.

When it ended on April 7, the Battle of Shiloh left 20,000 men dead or wounded—a shocking total, larger than most of the war's prior battles combined. A Tennessee private wrote of hearing the cries of "the wounded begging piteously for help," while Grant's second in command, General William Tecumseh Sherman, described "piles of dead soldiers' mangled bodies . . . without heads or legs." Grant surveyed a large field "so covered with dead that it would have been possible to walk over the clearing in any direction, stepping on dead bodies, without a foot touching the ground." Ambrose Bierce, an Indiana sergeant, was haunted afterward by the hideous sight of charred bodies of Illinois men, too wounded to flee the battlefield, who had burned to death when the woodland caught fire. Some lay in "postures of agony that told of the tormenting flame." Those who survived Shiloh had few illusions about the war's supposed romance and glory.

Further north and west, the Union barely maintained control of the crucial border slave state of Missouri. At the war's start Lincoln had mobilized the state's German American militia, most of whom strongly opposed slavery. In July 1861 they defeated a force of Confederate sympathizers commanded by the state's governor. In March 1862, at the battle of Pea Ridge, Arkansas, a small Union army defeated a Confederate force that had hoped to capture St. Louis and attack Grant from behind. The Union victory at Pea Ridge secured Missouri for the Union, though it did not end violent local conflicts that continued through the war.

Meanwhile, Union naval forces commanded by David G. Farragut struck the Confederacy from the Gulf of Mexico. They captured New Orleans, the Deep South's financial center and largest city. The Union army also took control of fifteen hundred plantations and 50,000 slaves in the surrounding region, striking a strong blow against slavery. Workers on some plantations looted their owners' mansions; in order to harvest cotton and sugar, planters were forced to pay wages. "[Slavery there] is forever destroyed and worthless," declared a northern reporter. The taking of New Orleans, combined with other Union victories, significantly undermined Confederate strength in the Mississippi River Valley.

## Antietam and Its Consequences

In the east, hoping for victories that would humiliate Lincoln's government, Lee went on the offensive. Joining with Jackson in northern Virginia, he routed Union troops in August 1862, in the Second Battle of Bull Run, and then struck north through western Maryland. There, he nearly met disaster. When the Confederate commander divided his force, sending Jackson to capture Harpers Ferry in West Virginia, a copy of Lee's orders fell into McClellan's hands. But the Union general again failed to exploit his advantage, delaying an attack against Lee's depleted army and thereby allowing it to secure a strong defensive position west of Antietam Creek, near Sharpsburg, Maryland. Outnumbered 87,000 to 50,000, Lee desperately fought off McClellan's attacks until Jackson's troops arrived and saved the Confederates from a major defeat. Appalled by the Union casualties, McClellan allowed Lee to retreat to Virginia.

The fighting at Antietam was savage. A Wisconsin officer described his men "loading and firing with demoniacal fury." A sunken road—nicknamed Bloody Lane—was filled with Confederate bodies two and three deep, and the advancing Union troops knelt on this "ghastly flooring" to shoot at retreating Confederates. The day of the battle, September 17, 1862, remains the bloodiest single day in U.S. military history. Together, the Confederate and Union dead numbered 4,800 and the wounded 18,500, of whom 3,000 soon died. (By comparison, American troops suffered 6,000 casualties on D-Day, which began the invasion of Nazi-occupied France in World War II.)

In public, Lincoln claimed Antietam as a Union victory; privately, he criticized McClellan for not pursuing Lee to seek a full Confederate surrender. A masterful organizer of men and supplies, McClellan refused to risk his troops, fearing heavy casualties would undermine public support for the war. Lincoln worried more about the danger of a lengthy war. He dismissed McClellan and began a long search for an aggressive commanding general. At the same time, he began laying the groundwork for ending slavery.

**Calls for Emancipation**    From the war's beginning, northern abolitionists called for slavery's end. Because slave-grown crops sustained the Confederacy, activists justified black emancipation on military grounds. As Frederick Douglass put it, "Arrest that hoe in the hands of the Negro, and you smite the rebellion in the very seat of its life."

In the South, enslaved African Americans exploited wartime chaos to seize freedom for themselves. When three slaves reached the camp of Union general Benjamin Butler in Virginia in May 1861, he labeled them "contraband of war" (enemy property that can be legitimately seized, according to international law) and refused to return them. Butler's term captured the imagination of northerners. Soon thousands of so-called **"contrabands"** were camping with Union armies. Near Fredericksburg, Virginia, an average of 200 blacks appeared every day, "with their packs on their backs and handkerchiefs tied over their heads—men, women, little children, and babies." The influx created a humanitarian crisis. Abolitionist Harriet Jacobs reported that hundreds of refugees were "packed together in the most miserable quarters," where many died from smallpox and dysentery. To provide legal status to the refugees—some 400,000 by war's end—in August 1861 Congress passed the Confiscation Act, which authorized the seizure of all property, including slave property, used to support the rebellion.

With the Confiscation Act, **Radical Republicans**—members of the party who had bitterly opposed the "slave power" since the mid-1850s—began to use wartime legislation to destroy slavery. Their leaders were Treasury Secretary Salmon Chase, Senator Charles Sumner of Massachusetts, and Representative Thaddeus Stevens of Pennsylvania. A longtime member of Congress, Stevens was skilled at fashioning legislation that could win majority support. In April 1862, Radicals persuaded Congress to end slavery in the District of Columbia by providing compensation for owners; in June, Congress outlawed slavery in the federal territories (finally enacting the Wilmot Proviso of 1846); in July, it passed a second Confiscation Act, which declared "forever free" the thousands of refugee slaves and all slaves captured by the Union army. Emancipation had become an instrument of war.

**The Emancipation Proclamation**   Initially, Lincoln rejected emancipation as a war aim. In August 1861, when Union general John C. Frémont (who had been the Republican presidential candidate in 1856) issued a field order freeing the slaves of Missouri Confederates, Lincoln promptly revoked it. But he faced rising Radical Republican pressure and, from his field commanders, reports of overwhelming throngs of African American refugees, most of whom risked their lives to reach Union lines and expressed strong support for the Union. Secretly, the president drafted a general proclamation of emancipation in July 1862. He began to test the waters in his public statements. "If I could save the Union without freeing any slave, I would do it," he wrote to Horace Greeley of the *New York Tribune*, "and if I could save it by freeing all the slaves, I would do it." With this statement Lincoln reassured white Americans, fearful of Radical goals, that his paramount goal was to save the Union — while also planting the idea that emancipation might be the best way to accomplish that aim.

Secretary of State William Seward, fearful that the Union would look desperate if it threatened emancipation after a string of military losses, advised Lincoln to wait for a Union victory. Lincoln took his advice. Considering the Battle of Antietam "an indication of the Divine Will," Lincoln issued a preliminary proclamation of emancipation on September 22, 1862, basing its legal authority on his duty as commander in chief to suppress rebellion. The proclamation warned that the president would abolish slavery in all states that remained out of the Union on January 1, 1863. Rebel states could preserve slavery by renouncing secession. None chose to do so.

The proclamation was politically astute. Lincoln conciliated slave owners in the Union-controlled border states, such as Maryland and Missouri, by leaving slavery intact there. He also permitted slavery to continue in areas occupied by Union armies: western and central Tennessee, western Virginia, and southern Louisiana. Consequently, the **Emancipation Proclamation** did not immediately free a single slave. Yet, as abolitionist Wendell Phillips argued, Lincoln's proclamation had moved slavery to "the edge of Niagara," ready to sweep it over the brink. Advancing Union troops became agents of slavery's destruction. "I became free in 1863, in the summer, when the yankees come by and said I could go work for myself," recalled Jackson Daniel of Maysville, Alabama. On South Carolina's Sea Islands, which were under Union control and largely abandoned by Confederate land owners, an idealistic group of northern abolitionists arrived to bring aid to freedpeople, open schools, and recruit the First South Carolina U.S. Regiment (Colored). As Lincoln now saw it, "the old South is to be destroyed and replaced by new propositions and ideas."

Hailed by reformers in Europe, emancipation helped persuade Britain and France to refrain from recognizing the Confederacy, in a war now being fought between slavery and freedom. Though Britain never recognized the Confederacy as an independent nation, it treated the rebel government as a belligerent power, with the right under international law to borrow money and purchase weapons. However, British manufacturers had stockpiled cotton and began to develop new sources of the commodity in Egypt and India.

Confederate president Jefferson Davis labeled the Emancipation Proclamation the "most execrable measure recorded in the history of guilty man." In the Union, the measure was hardly less controversial. In the 1862 midterm elections, Democrats denounced emancipation as unconstitutional, warned of slave uprisings, and predicted that freed blacks would take white jobs. Every freed slave, suggested one nativist New Yorker, should "shoulder an Irishman and leave the Continent." Such sentiments propelled Democrat Horatio Seymour into the governor's office in New York; if abolition was a war goal, Seymour argued, the South should not be conquered. In the election, Democrats swept to victory in Pennsylvania, Ohio, and Illinois and gained 34 seats in Congress. However, Republicans still held a 25-seat majority in the House and gained 5 seats in the Senate. Lincoln refused to retreat. Calling emancipation an "act of justice," he signed the final proclamation on New Year's Day 1863. "If my name ever goes into history," he said, "it was for this act."

The proclamation meant little, however, without victory on the battlefield to enforce it. Lincoln's first choice to replace McClellan, Ambrose E. Burnside, proved to be more daring but woefully incompetent. In December, after heavy losses in futile attacks against well-entrenched Confederate forces at Fredericksburg, Virginia, Burnside resigned his command, and Lincoln replaced him with Joseph "Fighting Joe" Hooker. As 1862 ended, Confederates were optimistic: the outcome at Fredericksburg demonstrated that the Union still lacked effective generals, and the South had won a stalemate in the East.

| **IN YOUR OWN WORDS** | What early political and military strategies did Confederate and Union leaders adopt, and which were most successful? |
| --- | --- |

# Toward "Hard War," 1863

The military carnage in 1862 made clear that the war would be long and costly. Grant later remarked that, after Shiloh, he "gave up all idea of saving the Union except by complete conquest." Lincoln committed the Union to mobilizing all its resources — economic, political, and cultural — in support of the North's military effort and to end slavery in the South. Aided by the Republican Party and a talented cabinet, Lincoln gradually organized an effective central government that adopted new strategies to pursue victory. In the Confederacy, despite the doctrine of states' rights, Jefferson Davis also exerted centralized authority to harness resources for the fight. Both North and South implemented military drafts — a dramatic change from the all-volunteer forces of 1861. The Union availed itself, also, of a fresh and determined body of volunteers: African American soldiers. What emerged from these developments, and out of the logic of the struggle itself, was a far more ruthless and systemic war.

## Politics North and South

With nearly two-thirds of the nation's population, the North was far better equipped than the South to sustain the prolonged, large-scale conflict that the Civil War became by 1863. Its economy also lent itself better to wartime needs—largely because of recent innovations. In 1852, canals carried twice as much tonnage as the nation's newly emerging railroads. But by 1860, after capitalists in Boston, New York, and London secured state charters and invested heavily, railroads had become the major carriers of wheat and freight from the Midwest to northeastern Atlantic ports, returning with machine tools, hardware, and furniture manufactured in the Northeast. Served by a vast network of locomotive and freight-car repair shops, railroads also hauled lumber from Michigan to the prairie states and livestock to Chicago's rapidly growing slaughterhouses.

The Union was thus investing in a state-of-the-art transportation system, and entrepreneurs were also modernizing agricultural technology. After 1847, John Deere operated a steel plow factory in Moline, Illinois. Far better than older cast-iron plows manufactured in New York, Deere plows enabled farmers to cut through deep, tough roots of prairie grasses and open new regions for farming. Other midwestern companies, such as McCormick and Hussey, mass-produced self-raking reapers that harvested 12 acres of grain a day, rather than the 2 acres an adult worker could cut by hand. Such innovations proved to be substantial advantages when the Civil War became long and resource-intensive. Without "reapers, mowers, separators, sowers, drills &c," wrote the *Cincinnati Gazette*, "the wheat, oats, and hay of Ohio, in 1862, could not have been got in safely." "We have seen," one journalist reported in the 1863 harvest season, "a stout matron whose sons are in the army, with her team cutting hay at seventy-five cents per acre, and she cut seven acres with ease in a day, riding leisurely upon her cutter. . . . War occupations, even on a most gigantic scale, do not seem to check the supply of food."

**Republican Economic and Fiscal Policies** To mobilize northern resources, the Republican-dominated Congress enacted a program of government-assisted economic development. It imposed high tariffs, averaging nearly 40 percent, on various foreign goods, thereby encouraging domestic industries. To boost agricultural output, it offered free land to farmers through the Homestead Act of 1862. Republicans also created an integrated network of national banks and implemented Clay's program for a nationally financed transportation system, chartering the Union Pacific and Central Pacific companies to build a transcontinental railroad and granting them substantial land subsidies to complete the difficult work (see Chapter 15). This economic program won the allegiance of farmers, workers, and entrepreneurs while bolstering the Union's ability to fight a long war.

New industries sprang up to provide the Union's 1.5 million soldiers with guns, clothes, and food. Over the course of the war, soldiers consumed more than half a billion pounds of pork and other packed meats. To meet this demand, Chicago railroads built new lines to carry thousands of hogs and cattle to the city's stockyards and slaughterhouses. By 1862, Chicago had passed Cincinnati as the meatpacking capital of the nation, bringing prosperity to thousands of midwestern farmers and great wealth to Philip D. Armour and other meatpacking entrepreneurs.

Bankers and financiers likewise found themselves pulled into the war effort. Annual U.S. government spending shot up from $63 million in 1860 to more than $865 million in 1864. To raise that enormous sum, Republicans created a modern system of public finance that raised money in three ways. First, the government raised money directly by increasing tariffs, placing high duties on alcohol and tobacco, and imposing taxes on business corporations, large inheritances, and the incomes of wealthy citizens. These levies paid about 20 percent of the war's cost. Interest-paying bonds issued by the U.S. Treasury financed another 65 percent. The National Banking Acts of 1863 and 1864 forced most banks to buy those bonds, and Philadelphia banker and Treasury Department agent Jay Cooke used newspaper ads and 2,500 subagents to persuade a million northern families to buy them.

The Union paid the remaining 15 percent by printing paper money. The Legal Tender Act of 1862 authorized $150 million in paper currency — soon known as **greenbacks** — and required the public to accept them as legal tender. Like the Continental currency of the Revolutionary era, greenbacks could not be exchanged for specie; however, the Treasury issued a limited amount of paper money, so it lost only a small part of its face value.

By 1863, the Lincoln administration had created an efficient war machine and a set of strategic priorities. Henry Adams, the grandson of John Quincy Adams and a future novelist and historian, noted the change from his diplomatic post in London: "Little by little, one began to feel that, behind the chaos in Washington power was taking shape; that it was massed and guided as it had not been before." The short-term results contributed substantially to Union victory. In the longer term, immense concentrations of capital in many industries — meatpacking, steel, coal, railroads, textiles, shoes — gave a few men "command of millions of money," setting up new political conflicts in the postwar era.

**Confederate Policies and Conflicts**    Economic demands on the South were equally great, but, true to its states' rights philosophy, the Confederacy initially left most matters to the state governments. However, as the scale and length of the conflict became clear, Jefferson Davis's administration took extraordinary measures. It built and operated shipyards, armories, foundries, and textile mills; commandeered food and scarce raw materials such as coal, iron, copper, and lead; set prices; requisitioned slaves to work on fortifications; and directly controlled foreign trade.

The Confederate Congress, dominated by slaveholders, opposed many of Davis's initiatives, particularly taxes. It refused to tax cotton exports and slaves, the most valuable property held by wealthy planters. Consequently, the Confederacy covered less than 10 percent of its expenditures through taxation. The government paid another 30 percent by borrowing, but as Union forces secured control of more and more southern territory, wealthy planters and foreign bankers grew reluctant to provide loans, fearing they would never be repaid. Consequently, the Confederacy paid 60 percent of its war costs by printing paper money. This flood of currency created spectacular inflation: by 1865, prices had risen to ninety-two times their 1861 level.

Conflicts over government impressment, or borrowing, of slaves also revealed weaknesses in the Confederacy. Many planters were reluctant to lend their slaves to work on military fortifications, rightly fearing that if these enslaved men found themselves near the battlefront, they would try to flee to Union lines. As a result, wealthy southerners used their political pull to keep slaves in private use. "The planter," wrote the *Mobile Register* angrily in 1863, "is more ready to contribute his sons than his slaves to the war."

Poor whites had no such luxury. The Confederate **one-tenth tax**, adopted in April 1863, required all farmers to turn over a tenth of their crops and livestock to the government for military use. Applied to poor families with husbands and fathers in the army, the policy pushed thousands of civilians to the brink of starvation. In letters and petitions to state officials, women pleaded desperately for help, designating themselves proudly as "S.W.," Soldiers' Wives. "The rich is all at home making great fortunes," wrote an outraged group of Georgia women, "and don't care what becomes of the poor class of people [as long as] they can save there neggroes."

As food prices soared, riots erupted in more than a dozen southern cities and towns. In Richmond, several hundred women broke into bakeries, crying, "our children are starving." In Randolph County, Alabama, women confiscated grain from a government warehouse "to prevent starvation of themselves and their families." As inflation spiraled upward, many southerners refused to accept paper money. When South Carolina storekeeper Jim Harris refused the depreciated currency presented by Confederate soldiers, they raided his storehouse and, he claimed, "robbed it of about five thousand dollars worth of goods." Army supply officers likewise seized goods from merchants and offered payment in worthless IOUs. Facing a public that feared strong government and high taxation, the Confederacy could sustain the war effort only by seizing its citizens' property.

Still, after two years of war, the Confederate position was far from weak. Virginia, North Carolina, and Tennessee deployed their substantial industrial capacity. Richmond, with its Tredegar Iron Works, served as an important manufacturing center. The purchase of Enfield rifles from Britain and the capture of 100,000 Union guns at Harpers Ferry near the start of the war helped the Confederacy provide every infantryman with a modern rifle-musket by 1863. Even though life had become difficult, the Confederate military was hardly ready to surrender.

**Conscription**   With battles proving more and more deadly and no end in sight, the supply of volunteers for the armies soon dried up. Still, both the Union and the Confederacy needed more men. The South acted first. In April 1862, following the bloodshed at Shiloh, the Confederate Congress imposed the first legally binding **draft (conscription)** in American history. New laws required existing soldiers to serve for the duration of the war and mandated three years of military service from all men between the ages of eighteen and thirty-five. In September 1862, after heavy casualties at Antietam, the age limit jumped to forty-five.

The Confederate draft had two loopholes, both controversial. First, it exempted one white man—the planter, a son, or an overseer—for each twenty slaves, allowing some whites on large plantations to avoid military service. This **twenty-Negro rule**, a Mississippi legislator warned Jefferson Davis, "has aroused a spirit of rebellion in some places." Second, wealthier draftees could hire substitutes. By the time the Confederate Congress closed this loophole in 1864, the price of a substitute had soared to $300 in gold, three times the annual wage of a skilled worker. Laborers and poor farmers angrily complained that both these measures made the war a "poor man's fight."

Some southerners refused to serve. Because the Confederate constitution vested sovereignty in individual states, the government in Richmond could not compel military service. Independent-minded governors such as Joseph Brown of Georgia and Zebulon Vance of North Carolina simply ignored President Davis's first draft call in early 1862. Elsewhere, state judges issued writs of habeas corpus and ordered the Confederate army to release reluctant draftees. The Confederate Congress, however, overrode judges' authority to free conscripted men, keeping substantial armies in the field well into 1864. Confederate militia also scoured areas that harbored large groups of deserters, like Jones County and surrounding areas of southeast Mississippi, using bloodhounds to track resisters and hanging those they could catch.

The Union's draft or Enrollment Act, introduced in March 1863, provoked equally dramatic opposition. Some recent German and Irish immigrants refused to serve; it was not their war, they said. Northern Democrats used the furor to bolster support for their party, which increasingly criticized Lincoln's policies. They accused Lincoln of drafting poor whites to liberate enslaved blacks, who would then flood northern cities. In July 1863, as conscription went into effect, immigrants' hostility toward the draft and toward blacks sparked virulent **draft riots** in New York City. For five days working-class men ran rampant, burned draft offices, sacked the homes of influential Republicans, and attacked the police. The rioters lynched and mutilated a dozen African Americans, drove hundreds of black families from their homes, and burned down the Colored Orphan Asylum. To suppress the mobs, Lincoln rushed in Union troops who had just fought at Gettysburg; they killed more than a hundred rioters. The war on the battlefield was eroding peace at home.

In contested areas, the Union government treated draft resisters and enemy sympathizers ruthlessly. Union commanders in Missouri and other border states levied special taxes on southern supporters. Lincoln went further, suspending habeas corpus and, over the course of the war, temporarily imprisoning about 15,000 southern sympathizers without trial. He also gave military courts jurisdiction over civilians who discouraged enlistments or resisted the draft, preventing acquittals by sympathetic local juries. However, most Union states used incentives to lure recruits. To meet local quotas set by the Militia Act of 1862, towns, counties, and states offered cash bounties of as much as $600 (about $11,000 today) and signed up nearly a million men.

## The Impact of Emancipation

Facing controversy and violent resistance, the Lincoln administration pursued a novel strategy: enlisting African American soldiers. As early as 1861, free African Americans and fugitive slaves had volunteered, hoping to end slavery and secure citizenship rights. Yet many northern whites refused to serve with blacks. "I am as much opposed to slavery as any of them," a New York soldier told his local newspaper, "but I am not willing to be put on a level with the negro and fight with them." Union generals also opposed military service by African Americans, doubting they would make good soldiers. Nonetheless, as the war unfolded, free and contraband blacks formed volunteer regiments in New England, South Carolina, Louisiana, and Kansas.

The Emancipation Proclamation changed military policy and popular sentiment. It invited former slaves to serve in the Union army. Northern whites, having suffered thousands of casualties, now accepted that African Americans should share in the fighting and dying. A heroic and costly attack by the black troops of the 54th Massachusetts Infantry on Fort Wagner, South Carolina, in 1863 convinced Union officers that African American soldiers could fight bravely. Commentators observed that black soldiers from the seceded states could have a triple impact: in addition to strengthening the Union army, their liberation demoralized white southerners and robbed the Confederacy of much-needed labor.

Military service did not end racial discrimination. Black Union soldiers initially earned less than white soldiers ($10 a month versus $13). They served in segregated regiments under white commissioned officers and they died, mostly from disease, at higher rates than white soldiers. Nonetheless, over 180,000 African Americans volunteered by 1865, fighting for emancipation and often their own freedom. "Hello, Massa," said one black soldier to his former master, who had been taken prisoner, "bottom rail on top dis time." Raiding a South Carolina town for supplies, a Union colonel took pleasure in introducing a plantation mistress to Corporal Robert Sutton of his regiment, saying he believed they had been "previously acquainted." When the woman recognized the corporal, her former slave, she "drew herself up, and dropped out the monosyllables of her answer as if they were so many drops of nitric acid: . . . '*we* called him Bob!' " The worst fears of secessionists had come true. Through the disciplined agency of the Union army, African Americans had risen in a successful rebellion against slavery.

Lincoln, among others, believed the Union could not have won the war without black troops. At the same time, southern responses to the new soldiers upped the stakes in the conflict. Furious Confederate officials vowed to treat black Union prisoners as runaway slaves and execute their officers for inciting slave rebellion. Colonel Thomas

**African American Soldiers Strengthen the Union Army**
Determined to end racial slavery, tens of thousands of African Americans volunteered for service in the Union army in 1864 and 1865, boosting the northern war effort at a critical moment. This unknown soldier posed for his studio portrait at Benton Barracks, Saint Louis, Missouri, proudly displaying his weapons while backed by the American flag. Library of Congress.

Wentworth Higginson, an abolitionist who went south to lead the First South Carolina Regiment (Colored), wrote that his men "fought with ropes round their necks." Confederate threats gave them "grim satisfaction . . . [and] a peculiar sense of self-respect. . . . The First South Carolina must fight it out or be re-enslaved." Faced with southern intransigence, General Grant suggested that the Union retaliate by shooting Confederate prisoners, man for man. Lincoln declined to carry out this policy, but race warfare nonetheless erupted on the battlefield. At Fort Pillow in Tennessee, in April 1864, Confederate cavalry under Nathan Bedford Forrest (future founder of the Ku Klux Klan) gunned down African American troops as they tried to surrender. After a subsequent battle in Mississippi, one Union lieutenant wrote, "We did not take many prisoners. The Negroes remembered 'Fort Pillow.'"

Confederates' refusal to exchange African American prisoners precipitated a new Union policy: suspending prisoner exchanges, which had taken place regularly since the war's start. As a result, by late 1863 both sides accumulated large numbers of prisoners of war, who suffered horrific conditions in crowded prison camps. Particularly notorious was the Confederacy's prison at Andersonville, Georgia, where over 13,000 of 45,000 Union prisoners died of disease or malnutrition. Amid public outrage, both Lee and Grant tried to reopen prisoner exchanges, but they could not agree on the treatment of black Union troops. Lee warned that "negroes belonging to our citizens" could not be "considered subjects of exchange." Grant responded that his government had a duty "to secure to all persons received into her armies the rights due to soldiers." The effort to renew exchanges failed.

Grant was guided in these discussions by the Union's **Lieber Code**, an innovative statement of the laws of war drafted by German immigrant law professor Francis Lieber, who had sons serving in both the Union and Confederate armies. Issued in April 1863, the code declared that the "law of nations and of nature" had never recognized slavery and knew "no distinction of color." Anyone who escaped a slaveholding locality was therefore free, and African American soldiers must be treated exactly as whites were. Arguing that the most humane war was one that ended quickly, Lieber defined "military necessity" liberally, permitting many military actions, from shooting spies to starving civilians, if they would "hasten surrender." At the same time, Lieber's code spelled out protections for prisoners of war, outlawed use of torture for any reason, and forbade "the infliction of suffering for the sake of suffering or for revenge." Widely admired in Europe, the code provided a foundation for later international agreements on the laws of war, including the Geneva Conventions.

## Citizens and the Work of War

Lieber was among tens of thousands of civilians who contributed in distinctive ways to the Union war effort, from buying bonds to sewing banners. Unlike the rural Confederacy, northern states had an increasingly urban population and stronger infrastructure of schools, press, and reform groups that provided a base for innovative forms of civilian mobilization. On both sides, however, the conflict was a "people's war" marked by intensive citizen participation.

**Medicine and Nursing**  In 1861, prominent New Yorkers established the **U.S. Sanitary Commission** to provide Union troops with clothing, food, and medical services. While paid agents and spokesmen were male, over 200,000 women supported the commission as volunteers, working through seven thousand local auxiliaries. "I almost weep," reported one agent, "when these plain rural people come to send their simple offerings to absent sons and brothers." The commission also recruited battlefield nurses and doctors for the Union army.

Despite these efforts, dysentery, typhoid, and malaria spread through the camps, as did mumps and measles, viruses that were often deadly to rural recruits. Diseases and infections killed about 250,000 Union soldiers, nearly twice the 135,000 who died in combat. These numbers would have been far higher if the Sanitary Commission had not, for example, persuaded key military leaders that their troops should dig latrines for proper waste disposal. The internationally acclaimed U.S. ambulance corps, authorized by Congress in 1864, developed efficient procedures to evacuate wounded soldiers from the battlefield. As a result of such efforts, one historian estimates that 25 percent of wounded Union soldiers died in 1861 but only 10 percent by 1864.

Confederate troops were less fortunate because the Confederate army's health system was poorly organized. Scurvy was a special problem for southern soldiers; lacking vitamin C in their diets, they suffered muscle ailments and had low resistance to camp diseases. Confederate women created dozens of local or state-level relief societies, and thousands volunteered as nurses. "The war is certainly ours as well as that of the men," wrote Kate Cumming, a Scottish-born immigrant to Alabama who served for four years at Confederate hospitals in Georgia. In her diary Cumming recorded the horrors of hospital service, with wounded soldiers groaning in agony among piles of amputated limbs. "I daily witness the same sad scenes—men dying all around me. I do not know who they are, nor have I time to learn."

**Women and the War**   Far more than Cumming and her fellow Confederate nurses, northern women had a strong base of antebellum public and reform activism on which to build. Freedmen's aid societies, which sent supplies and teachers to black refugees in the South, attracted the energies of religious congregations and of African American abolitionists such as Harriet Tubman and Sojourner Truth. In 1863, women's rights advocates founded the **Woman's Loyal National League**, hoping energetic war service would bring recognition and voting rights.

The war also drew women into the wage-earning workforce as clerks and factory operatives. Thousands of educated Union women became government clerks in offices such as the Treasury Department—the first women hired to work for the U.S. government. White southern women staffed the efficient Confederate postal service. In both North and South, millions of women took over farm tasks, filled jobs in hospitals and schools, and worked in factories.

Working-class women did some of the war's most grueling, dangerous work in munitions factories, where gunpowder caused over thirty explosions during the war. One of the most horrific occurred in Pittsburgh, Pennsylvania, on September 17, 1862, the same day as the battle of Antietam. With the Allegheny Arsenal's largely female, Irish immigrant employees under pressure to increase production of rifle cartridges, a spark triggered a series of explosions that destroyed the building and left seventy-eight dead. The arsenal grounds became an outdoor morgue. One Pittsburgh paper described the "agonizing screams of relatives and friends upon discovering the remains of some loved one whose humble earnings contributed to their comfort." Most were burned beyond recognition.

A few daring women worked as spies and scouts, and at least five hundred disguised themselves as men in order to serve in the Union or Confederate armies. Those who made it through the trauma of battle without being discovered were often accepted afterward by fellow soldiers who kept their secret. More frequently, women who adhered to the rules of domesticity contributed as writers, penning patriotic songs, poems, editorials, and fiction. Eventually, even the most reluctant Unionist and Confederate men were forced to recognize women's value to the cause. As Union nurse Clara Barton, who later founded the American Red Cross, recalled, "At the war's end, woman was at least fifty years in advance of the normal position which continued peace would have assigned her."

**The War at Home**    In contested border regions such as Tennessee, North Carolina, and Missouri, few boundaries existed between home and battlefield. There, civilians found themselves trapped between ruthless guerrilla or irregular bands of soldiers, such as William Quantrill's notorious Confederate raiders. Operating often as near-bandits, such guerrillas on both sides raided, plundered, tortured civilians for information, and carried out revenge killings. In 1863, after a Union commander detained a group of wives and sisters of Quantrill's men, five of the women were killed in a federal building collapse. In retaliation, Quantrill and his men burned the "Free State" town of Lawrence, Kansas, and summarily executed 183 men and boys. The Union responded by evacuating ten thousand people from four Missouri counties that bordered Kansas—while Quantrill continued to wreak destruction in other parts of the state.

As casualties mounted to shocking levels, civilians in both North and South became more and more familiar with the rituals of mourning. The rising tide of death created new industries: embalmers, for example, devised a zinc chloride fluid to preserve soldiers' bodies, allowing them to be shipped home for burial, an innovation that began modern funeral practices. Military cemeteries with hundreds of crosses in neat rows replaced the landscaped "rural cemeteries" that had been in vogue in American cities before the Civil War. As thousands of mothers, wives, and sisters mourned the deaths of fallen soldiers, they faced changed lives. Even the poorest bereaved women often dyed a dress black so they could mark the loss of a husband, son, or father. Middle-class women, with greater financial resources, might purchase black-bordered stationery, onyx jewelry, or other tokens of grief. The destructive war, in concert with America's emerging consumer culture and ethic of domesticity, produced a new "cult of mourning" among the middle and upper classes.

## Vicksburg and Gettysburg

Confederate hopes ran high in the spring of 1863. In the Union, Democrats had made significant gains in 1862, and popular support was growing for a negotiated peace. Two brilliant victories in Virginia by General Robert E. Lee, at Fredericksburg (December 1862) and Chancellorsville (May 1863), further eroded northern support for the war. At this critical juncture, General Ulysses Grant mounted a major offensive to split the Confederacy in two. Grant drove south along the west bank of the Mississippi in Arkansas and then crossed the river near Vicksburg, Mississippi. There, he defeated two Confederate armies and laid siege to the city. After repelling Union assaults for six weeks, the exhausted and starving Vicksburg garrison surrendered on July 4, 1863.

Five days later, Union forces took Port Hudson, Louisiana, near Baton Rouge, and seized control of the entire Mississippi River. Grant had cut off Louisiana, Arkansas, and Texas from the rest of the Confederacy and prompted thousands of slaves to desert their plantations. Confederate troops responded by targeting refugees for re-enslavement and massacre. "The battlefield was sickening," a Confederate officer reported from Arkansas, "no orders, threats or commands could restrain the men from vengeance on the negroes, and they were piled in great heaps about the wagons, in the tangled brushwood, and upon the muddy and trampled road." Partly due to the undercounting of civilian casualties on occasions such as this, historians have revised upward their reckoning of the war's total deaths: not 620,000, as was previously thought, but over 750,000.

As Grant had advanced toward Vicksburg in May, Confederate leaders had argued over the best strategic response. President Davis and other politicians wanted to send an army to Tennessee to relieve the Union pressure along the Mississippi River. General Lee, buoyed by his recent victories, favored a new invasion of the North. That strategy, Lee suggested, would either draw Grant's forces to the east or give the Confederacy a major victory that would destroy the North's will to fight.

Lee won out. In June 1863, he maneuvered his army north through Maryland into Pennsylvania. The Army of the Potomac moved along with him, positioning itself between Lee and Washington, D.C. On July 1, the two great armies met by accident at Gettysburg, Pennsylvania, in what became a decisive confrontation (Map 13.3). On the first day of battle, Lee drove the Union's advance guard to the south of town. There, Union commander George G. Meade placed his troops in well-defended hilltop positions and called for reinforcements. By the morning of July 2, Meade had 90,000 troops to Lee's 75,000. Lee knew he was outnumbered but was determined not to give up; he ordered assaults on Meade's flanks, which failed.

On July 3, Lee decided on a dangerous frontal assault against the center of the Union line. After the heaviest artillery barrage of the war, Lee sent General George E. Pickett and his 14,000 men to take Cemetery Ridge. When Pickett's men charged across a mile of open terrain, they faced deadly fire from artillery and massed riflemen. Thousands suffered death, wounds, or capture. As the three-day battle ended, the Confederates counted 28,000 casualties—one-third of Lee's Army of Northern Virginia—while 23,000 of Meade's soldiers lay killed or wounded. Shocked by the bloodletting, Meade allowed the Confederate units to escape. Lincoln was furious at Meade's caution, perceiving that "the war will be prolonged indefinitely."

Still, Gettysburg was a major Union victory and, together with the simultaneous triumph at Vicksburg, marked a military and political turning point. In his **Gettysburg Address**, dedicating a national cemetery at the battlefield, Lincoln dared to hope that the Union might win. Such a victory, he argued, would extend the promise of the Declaration of Independence that "all men are created equal."

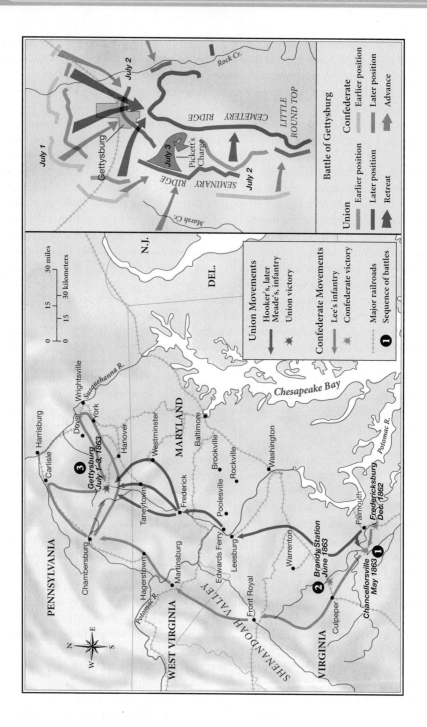

Without mentioning slavery by name, Lincoln suggested that Americans could draw "from these honored dead" the determination not only to preserve the Union, but also to bring about "a new birth of freedom" in the United States.

As southern citizens grew increasingly critical of their government, Confederate elections of 1863 went sharply against politicians who supported Jefferson Davis. Meanwhile, northern citizens rallied to the Union, and Republicans swept state elections in Pennsylvania, Ohio, and New York. In Europe, the victories boosted the leverage of the Union's diplomats. Since 1862, a British-built ironclad cruiser, the CSS *Alabama,* had sunk or captured more than a hundred Union merchant ships, and the Confederacy was about to accept delivery of two more ironclads. With a Union victory increasingly likely, the British government decided to impound the warships. British workers and reformers had long condemned slavery and praised emancipation. Moreover, because of poor grain harvests, Britain depended on imports of wheat and flour from the American Midwest. King Cotton diplomacy had failed and King Wheat stood triumphant. "Rest not your hopes in foreign nations," President Jefferson Davis advised his people. "This war is ours; we must fight it ourselves."

| **IN YOUR OWN WORDS** | In what ways did the scope and direction of the Civil War change in 1863, and why? |
|---|---|

# The Road to Union Victory, 1864–1865

The Union victories of 1863 made it less and less likely that the South would win independence through a decisive military triumph. Confederate leaders, however, still hoped for a battlefield stalemate and a negotiated peace. To keep the Union in Republican hands, Lincoln faced the daunting task of conquering the South. By the time his new generals finally succeeded, the war's impact had devastated the South.

## Grant and Sherman Take Command

Lincoln finally found a ruthless commanding general in March 1864, when he placed Ulysses S. Grant in charge of all Union armies. From then on, the president determined overall strategy and Grant implemented it. Lincoln wanted a simultaneous advance against the major Confederate armies, a strategy Grant had long favored, in order to achieve a decisive victory before the election of 1864.

**< MAP 13.3  Lee Invades the North, 1863**
After Lee's victories at Chancellorsville (1) in May and Brandy Station (2) in June, the Confederate forces moved northward, constantly shadowed by the Union army. On July 1, the two armies met accidentally near Gettysburg, Pennsylvania. In the ensuing battle (3), the Union army, commanded by General George Meade, emerged victorious, primarily because it was much larger than the Confederate force and held well-fortified positions along Cemetery Ridge, which gave its units a major tactical advantage.

Grant knew how to fight a war that relied on industrial technology and targeted the enemy's infrastructure. At Vicksburg in July 1863, he had besieged the whole city and forced its surrender. Then, in November, he had used railroads to rescue an endangered Union army near Chattanooga, Tennessee. Grant believed the cautious tactics of previous Union commanders had prolonged the war. He was willing to accept heavy casualties, a stance that earned him a reputation as a butcher. But he followed the tenets of Lieber's code: whatever "military necessity" he might need to invoke, Grant would bring the war to its end.

In May 1864, Grant ordered two major offensives. Personally taking charge of the 115,000-man Army of the Potomac, he set out to destroy Lee's force of 75,000

**Grant Planning a Strategic Maneuver** On May 21, 1864, the day this photograph was taken, Grant pulled his forces from Spotsylvania Court House, where a bitter two-week battle (May 8–21) resulted in 18,000 Union and 10,000 Confederate casualties. He moved his army to the southeast, seeking to outflank Lee's forces. Photographer Timothy H. O'Sullivan caught up to the Union army's high command at Massaponax Church, Virginia, and captured this image of Grant (to the left) leaning over a pew and reading a map held by General George H. Meade. As Grant plots the army's movement, his officers smoke their pipes and read reports of the war in newspapers that had just arrived from New York City. Intercepting Grant's forces, Lee took up fortified positions first at the North Anna River and then at Cold Harbor, where the Confederates scored their last major victory of the war (May 31–June 3). Library of Congress.

troops in Virginia. Grant instructed General William Tecumseh Sherman, who shared his harsh outlook, to invade Georgia and take Atlanta. "All that has gone before is mere skirmish," Sherman wrote as he prepared for battle. "The war now begins." As a young military officer stationed in the South, Sherman had sympathized with the planter class and felt that slavery upheld social stability. However, secession meant "anarchy," he told his southern friends in early 1861: "If war comes . . . I must fight your people whom I best love." Sherman, more than anyone else, developed the philosophy and tactics of **hard war**. When Confederate guerrillas fired on a boat carrying Unionist civilians near Randolph, Tennessee, Sherman had sent a regiment to destroy the town, asserting, "We are justified in treating all inhabitants as combatants."

Grant advanced toward Richmond, hoping to force Lee to fight in open fields, where the Union's superior manpower and artillery would prevail. Remembering his tactical errors at Gettysburg, Lee remained in strong defensive positions and attacked only when he held an advantage. The Confederate general seized such opportunities twice in May 1864, winning costly victories at the battles of the Wilderness and Spotsylvania Court House. At Spotsylvania, troops fought at point-blank range; an Iowa recruit recalled "lines of blue and grey [firing] into each other's faces; for an hour and a half." Despite heavy losses in these battles and then at Cold Harbor, Grant drove on (Map 13.4). His attacks severely eroded Lee's forces, which suffered 31,000 casualties, but Union losses were even higher: 55,000 killed or wounded.

**Stalemate**    The fighting took a heavy psychological toll. "Many a man has gone crazy since this campaign began from the terrible pressure on mind and body," observed a Union captain. In June 1864, Grant laid siege to Petersburg, an important railroad center near Richmond. As the siege continued, Union and Confederate soldiers built complex networks of trenches, tunnels, and artillery emplacements stretching 40 miles along the eastern edge of Richmond and Petersburg, foreshadowing the devastating trench warfare that would emerge in France during World War I. Invoking the intense imagery of the Bible, an officer described the continuous artillery barrages and sniping as "living night and day within the 'valley of the shadow of death.'" The stress was especially great for the outnumbered Confederates, who spent months in the muddy, hellish trenches without rotation to the rear.

As time passed, Lincoln and Grant felt pressures of their own. The enormous casualties and military stalemate threatened Lincoln with defeat in the November election. Republicans' outlook worsened in July, when a body of almost 3,000 Confederate cavalry raided and burned the town of Chambersburg, in southern Pennsylvania, and threatened Washington. To punish farmers in the Shenandoah Valley who had aided the Confederate raiders, Grant ordered General Philip H. Sheridan to turn the region into "a barren waste." Sheridan's troops conducted a scorched-earth campaign, destroying grain, barns, and gristmills and any other resource useful to the Confederates. Hard war had become hard indeed.

## The Election of 1864 and Sherman's March

As the siege at Petersburg dragged on, General William Tecumseh Sherman's 90,000 Union men moved methodically toward Atlanta, a railway hub at the heart of the Confederacy. General Joseph E. Johnson's Confederate army of 60,000 stood

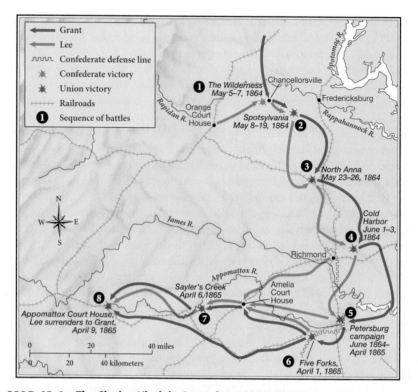

**MAP 13.4   The Closing Virginia Campaign, 1864–1865**

Beginning in May 1864, General Ulysses S. Grant launched an all-out campaign against Richmond, trying to lure General Robert E. Lee into open battle. Lee avoided a major test of strength. Instead, he retreated to defensive positions and inflicted heavy casualties on Union attackers at the Wilderness, Spotsylvania Court House, North Anna, and Cold Harbor (1–4). From June 1864 to April 1865, the two armies faced each other across defensive fortifications outside Richmond and Petersburg (5). Grant finally broke this ten-month siege by a flanking maneuver at Five Forks (6). Lee's surrender followed shortly.

in Sherman's way and, in June 1864, inflicted heavy casualties on his forces near Kennesaw Mountain, Georgia. By late July, the Union army was poised on the northern outskirts of Atlanta, but the next month brought little gain. Like Grant, Sherman seemed bogged down in a hopeless campaign.

Both Unionists and Confederates pinned their hopes on the election of 1864. In June, the Republican convention rebuffed attempts to prevent Lincoln's renomination. It endorsed the president's war strategy, demanded unconditional Confederate surrender, and called for a constitutional amendment to abolish slavery. Delegates likewise embraced Lincoln's political strategy. To attract border-state and Democratic voters, the Republicans took a new name, the National Union Party, and chose Andrew Johnson, a Tennessee slave owner and Unionist Democrat, as Lincoln's running mate.

The Democratic Party met in August and nominated George McClellan for president. Lincoln had twice removed McClellan from military commands: first for an excess of caution and then for his opposition to emancipation. Like McClellan, Democratic delegates rejected emancipation and condemned Lincoln's repression of domestic dissent, particularly his suspension of habeas corpus and use of military courts to prosecute civilians. However, they split into two camps over war policy. War Democrats vowed to continue fighting until the rebellion ended, while Peace Democrats called for a "cessation of hostilities" and a constitutional convention to negotiate a peace settlement. Although personally a War Democrat, McClellan promised if elected to recommend to Congress an immediate armistice and a peace convention. Hearing this news, Confederate vice president Alexander Stephens celebrated "the first ray of real light I have seen since the war began." He predicted that if Atlanta and Richmond held out, Lincoln would be defeated and McClellan would eventually accept an independent Confederacy.

**The Fall of Atlanta and Lincoln's Victory**   Stephens's hopes collapsed on September 2, 1864, as Atlanta fell to Sherman's army. In a stunning move, the Union general pulled his troops from the trenches, swept around the city, and destroyed its rail links to the south. Fearing that Sherman would encircle his army, Confederate general John B. Hood abandoned the city. "Atlanta is ours, and fairly won," Sherman telegraphed Lincoln, sparking hundred-gun salutes and wild Republican celebration. "We are gaining strength," Lincoln warned Confederate leaders, "and may, if need be, maintain the contest indefinitely."

A deep pessimism settled over the Confederacy. Mary Chesnut, a South Carolina plantation mistress and general's wife, wrote in her diary, "I felt as if all were dead within me, forever," and foresaw the end of the Confederacy: "We are going to be wiped off the earth." Recognizing the dramatically changed military situation, McClellan repudiated the Democratic peace platform. Democrats' fall campaign focused heavily instead on the alleged dangers of emancipation. Cartoonists caricatured Lincoln as an ape; parade floats featured "Negroes"—white men in blackface makeup—dancing with white women. An anonymous Democratic pamphlet warned of the dangers of race mixing, coining the term **miscegenation** to denounce interracial marriage and claim that it would result from Republican policies.

The National Union Party went on the offensive, attacking McClellan's inconsistency and attacking Peace Democrats as traitors. Boosted by Sherman's victories in Georgia, Lincoln won a clear-cut victory in November. He received 55 percent of the popular vote and won 212 of 233 electoral votes. Republicans and National Unionists captured 145 of the 185 seats in the House of Representatives and increased their Senate majority to 42 of 52 seats. Republicans owed their victory in part to the votes of Union troops.

Legal emancipation was already underway at the edges of the South. In 1864, Maryland and Missouri amended their constitutions to end slavery, and the three Confederate states occupied by the Union army—Tennessee, Arkansas, and Louisiana—followed suit. Still, abolitionists worried that the Emancipation Proclamation, based legally on the president's wartime powers, would lose its force at the end of the war. It took three attempts, but urged on by Lincoln and the National Equal Rights

League, Congress finally approved the Thirteenth Amendment in January 1865. Once ratified by two-thirds of the states, in December 1865, the amendment officially ended slavery in the United States.

**Sherman Crosses Georgia**   Thanks to Sherman, the Confederacy was also reaching its end. After capturing Atlanta, Sherman advocated a bold strategy. Instead of pursuing a retreating Confederate army northward into Tennessee, he proposed to move south, live off the land, and "cut a swath through to the sea." To persuade Lincoln and Grant to approve his unconventional plan, Sherman argued that his march would be "a demonstration to the world, foreign and domestic, that we have a power [Jefferson] Davis cannot resist." The general lived up to his pledge (Map 13.5). "We are not only fighting hostile armies," Sherman wrote, "but a hostile people, and must make old and young, rich and poor, feel the hard hand of war." He left Atlanta in

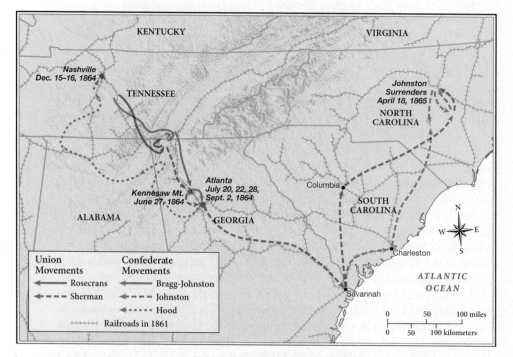

**MAP 13.5    Sherman's March Through the Confederacy, 1864–1865**
The Union victory in November 1863 at Chattanooga, Tennessee, was almost as critical as the victories in July at Gettysburg and Vicksburg, because it opened up a route of attack into the heart of the Confederacy. In mid-1864, General William Tecumseh Sherman advanced on the railway hub of Atlanta. After taking the city in September 1864, Sherman relied on other Union armies to stem an invasion of Tennessee by Confederate General John Bell Hood, while Sherman began a devastating march across Georgia. By December Sherman's army reached Savannah, and from there they cut a swath through the Carolinas. Note how Sherman's march followed key rail lines: his troops ripped up, heated, and twisted sections of track to disrupt Confederate transport and communications.

flames, and during his 300-mile March to the Sea his army consumed or demolished everything in its path. Though Sherman's army focused on damaging property, not murdering civilians, the havoc so demoralized Confederate soldiers that many deserted their units and returned home. When Sherman reached Savannah in mid-December, the city's 10,000 defenders left without a fight.

Georgia's African Americans treated Sherman as a savior. "They flock to me, old and young," he wrote. "They pray and shout and mix up my name with Moses . . . as well as 'Abram Linkom,' the Great Messiah of 'Dis Jubilee.'" To provide for the hundreds of African American families now following his army, Sherman issued **Special Field Order No. 15**, which set aside 400,000 acres of prime rice-growing land for the exclusive use of freedpeople. By June 1865, about 40,000 African Americans were cultivating "Sherman lands." Many expected the lands were to be theirs forever, a form of payment for generations of unpaid labor: "All the land belongs to the Yankees now and they gwine divide it out among de coloured people." By March, after his destructive march through South Carolina, Sherman was ready to link up with Grant and crush Lee's army.

## The Confederacy Collapses

Grant's war of attrition in Virginia had already exposed a weakness in the Confederacy: rising class resentment among poor whites. Angered by slave owners' exemptions from military service and fearing that the Confederacy was doomed, ordinary southern farmers now repudiated the draft. "All they want is to git you . . . to fight for their infurnal negroes," grumbled an Alabama hill farmer. More and more soldiers fled their units. "I am now going to work instead of to the war," vowed David Harris, another backcountry yeoman. By 1865, at least 100,000 men had deserted from Confederate armies, prompting reluctant Confederate leaders to approve the enlistment of black soldiers and promising them freedom. It was a hollow offer: tens of thousands were already proving excellent soldiers for the Union.

The symbolic end of the war took place in Virginia. In April 1865, Grant finally gained control of the crucial railroad junction at Petersburg and forced Lee to abandon Richmond. As Lincoln visited the ruins of the Confederate capital, greeted by joyful freedmen and women, Grant cut off Lee's escape route to North Carolina. It was one of Lincoln's last acts: on April 14, a pro-Confederate actor named John Wilkes Booth assassinated the president, shouting "Sic semper tyrannis"—Virginia's state motto, *thus always to tyrants*. Lincoln's murder plunged the Union into mourning and opened disturbing questions about the postwar political order (Chapter 14).

Before his death Lincoln had received, with weary satisfaction, news that the Union had won. On April 9, almost four years to the day after the attack on Fort Sumter, Lee had surrendered at Appomattox Court House, Virginia. In return for their promise not to fight again, Grant allowed Confederate officers and men to take their horses and personal weapons and go home. By late May, all the secessionist armies and governments had surrendered or melted away.

## The World the War Made

The brutal conflict was finally over. The North had won, to a large degree, because the Confederacy had not won quickly. Southern leaders' hopes for European aid, based on the power of King Cotton, turned out to be misplaced, and the Union proved far better equipped to fight a grueling four-year war of attrition. The Union could not have won, however, without impressive wartime innovations in policy, strategy, and technology. These ranged from the adoption of greenback dollars and steam-powered gunboats to the Lieber Code and the hard war tactics of Grant and Sherman. The Confederacy had innovated, also, exerting strong centralized powers to marshal men and resources for the conflict. But the Union had ultimately proven bolder and stronger. "As our case is new," Lincoln had told Congress in 1863, "so we must think anew, and act anew." Northerners had done so, most notably by abolishing slavery and recruiting African American soldiers, and had persevered to maintain the Union.

Over 700,000 people were dead. Delivering his second inaugural address in March 1865, Lincoln sought to explain the carnage by eloquently suggesting that the war's purpose had not been to preserve the Union but to end slavery. That purpose, however ignored or disavowed by Union leaders, had been a divine plan. "If we shall suppose," Lincoln said,

> that American slavery is one of those offenses which, in the providence of God, must needs come, but which, having continued through His appointed time, He now wills to remove, and that He gives to both North and South this terrible war as the woe due to those by whom the offense came, shall we discern therein any departure from those divine attributes which the believers in a living God always ascribe to Him? Fondly do we hope, fervently do we pray, that this mighty scourge of war may speedily pass away. Yet, if God wills that it continue until all the wealth piled by the bondsman's two hundred and fifty years of unrequited toil shall be sunk, and until every drop of blood drawn with the lash shall be paid by another drawn with the sword, as was said three thousand years ago, so still it must be said, the judgments of the Lord are true and righteous altogether.

For the first time, Lincoln had named the sin of slavery as the central cause of the war—and proposed, remarkably, that both the Union and Confederacy shared guilt for that sin. Abolitionist Frederick Douglass, who heard the address, told Lincoln afterward that it was a "sacred effort." Yet at the same time, Lincoln's second inaugural depicted the catastrophe of war as visited only on *whites*—as if enslaved African Americans had been passive victims and bystanders, rather than participants in the war who, as "contrabands," scouts, soldiers, and refugees, had suffered terribly as well, and had played decisive roles in Union victory. Even Lincoln's most powerful antislavery speech, then, revealed unresolved political problems that would arise with peace. As southern states returned to the Union, what kind of nation would emerge? Former Confederates wanted a "reunion" of the white North and South, a nation adhering as nearly as possible to prewar principles. African Americans and Radical Republicans wanted revolution—a complete transformation of the South. Neither would get their wish.

As for the future of the United States, an optimistic New York census-taker suggested that the conflict had had an "equalizing effect." In some ways he was right. Slavery was dead: in a transformation of immense significance, no American could ever again legally claim to own another human being. The official also reflected that, in the North, "military men from the so called 'lower classes' now lead society, having been elevated by real merit and valor." However perceptive these remarks, they ignored the wartime emergence of the new financial aristocracy that soon presided over what Mark Twain labeled the Gilded Age. As early as 1863, a journalist warned that when the war was over, "there will be the same wealth in the country, but it will be in fewer hands; we shall have . . . more merchant princes and princely bankers."

Astonishing its European rivals, the United States did emerge from the Civil War with the "same wealth," and relatively unscathed. High tariffs put in place by Republicans, for example, paid off the nation's war debt with remarkable speed. And however devastated the South's economy might be, the United States had started on the path to global economic power. In the postwar period, Republicans would wrestle with the limits of that power at home and on the world stage.

| **IN YOUR OWN WORDS** | How did Union objectives appear different to Lincoln at the end of the Civil War than they had at the beginning? |
| --- | --- |

# Summary

As the Civil War began, both the Union and the Confederacy hoped for a quick, decisive victory, but none was forthcoming. Union commander George B. McClellan proved unable to crush his daring southern equivalent, Robert E. Lee, but as attempts to invade the West and North failed, Confederates proved unable to move the theater of war outside their own territory. From the beginning, also, thousands of African Americans fled to Union lines, undermining Confederates' war effort. Congress soon authorized use of these "contrabands" as scouts, spies, and paid workers.

By 1862 and 1863, new strategies were needed. First the Confederacy and then the Union instituted military conscription. This unprecedented move, along with new taxes and inflation, caused considerable civilian unrest, especially in the South, as Union forces made inroads into occupying Confederate land and resources. Even more important was the Emancipation Proclamation, which Lincoln issued after the Union victory at Antietam and put into effect on January 1, 1863. African American troops soon enlisted for the Union, hardening Confederate attitudes but playing a crucial role in Union victory. Two decisive battles in the summer of 1863, Gettysburg and Vicksburg, began to turn the tide toward Union victory. Lincoln then chose an effective commander, Ulysses Grant, to lead U.S. forces, but it took almost two years of grueling, brutal campaigns to defeat the South.

In the fall of 1864, exhausted and shocked by the war's magnitude, Confederates pinned their last hopes on Lincoln's defeat in his campaign for reelection, anticipating that his Democratic opponent would sue for peace and reinstate slavery. But General William T. Sherman's brilliant campaigns helped bolster Union morale and ensure Lincoln's reelection. In the war's final months, as the Confederacy began to collapse, Congress passed the Thirteenth Amendment abolishing slavery.

# Chapter 13 Review

## KEY TERMS

**Identify and explain the significance of each term below.**

King Cotton (p. 387)
habeas corpus (p. 389)
"contrabands" (p. 392)
Radical Republicans (p. 392)
Emancipation Proclamation (p. 393)
greenbacks (p. 396)
one-tenth tax (p. 397)
draft (conscription) (p. 397)
twenty-Negro rule (p. 397)

draft riots (p. 398)
Lieber Code (p. 400)
U.S. Sanitary Commission (p. 400)
Woman's Loyal National League
(p. 401)
Gettysburg Address (p. 403)
hard war (p. 407)
miscegenation (p. 409)
Special Field Order No. 15 (p. 411)

## REVIEW QUESTIONS

**Answer these questions to demonstrate your understanding of the chapter's main ideas.**

1. What early political and military strategies did Confederate and Union leaders adopt, and which were most successful?
2. In what ways did the scope and direction of the Civil War change in 1863, and why?
3. How did Union objectives appear different to Lincoln at the end of the Civil War than they had at the beginning?
4. The thematic timeline for Part 5 (pp. 352–353) lists events or developments in the 1860s relating directly to the South's secession and the Civil War. Does that list capture the war's overwhelming importance to the history of nineteenth-century America? If not, is this deficiency inherent to timelines, or does it reflect a faulty construction of this specific timeline? How would you address this problem?

## CHRONOLOGY

**As you read, ask yourself why this chapter begins and ends with these dates and identify the links among related events.**

**1861**
- General Butler declares refugee slaves "contraband of war" (May)
- Confederates win First Battle of Bull Run (July 21)
- First Confiscation Act (August)
- West Virginia created and remains with the Union (October)
- U.S. Sanitary Commission formed

**1862**    • Legal Tender Act authorizes greenbacks (February)

• Confederate Far West campaign turned back at Glorieta Pass (March)

• Union victory at Pea Ridge, Arkansas (March)

• Union victory at Shiloh (April 6–7)

• Confederacy introduces military draft (April)

• Union halts Confederates at Antietam (September 17)

• Explosion kills munitions workers in Pittsburgh (September 17)

• Lincoln issues preliminary emancipation proclamation (September 22)

**1863**    • Britain and France refuse recognition to the Confederacy; Britain impounds Confederate ships being built in British shipyards

• Lincoln signs final Emancipation Proclamation (January 1)

• Union wins battles at Gettysburg (July 1–3) and Vicksburg (July 4)

• Union initiates draft (March), sparking riots in New York City (July)

• Women's rights activists form Woman's Loyal National League

• Lincoln delivers Gettysburg Address (November)

**1864**    • Ulysses S. Grant named commander of all Union forces (March)

• William Tecumseh Sherman takes Atlanta (September 2)

• Lincoln reelected (November 8)

• Sherman's army devastates Georgia and South Carolina

**1865**    • Robert E. Lee surrenders to Grant (April 9)

• Lincoln assassinated (April 14)

• Thirteenth Amendment ratified (December 6)

# 14

# Reconstruction

## 1865–1877

**IDENTIFY THE BIG IDEA**

What goals did Republican policymakers, ex-Confederates, and freedpeople pursue during Reconstruction? To what degree did each succeed?

**ON THE LAST DAY OF APRIL 1866, BLACK SOLDIERS IN MEMPHIS,** Tennessee, turned in their weapons as they mustered out of the Union army. The next day, whites who resented the soldiers' presence provoked a clash. At a street celebration where African Americans shouted "Hurrah for Abe Lincoln," a white policeman responded, "Your old father, Abe Lincoln, is dead and damned." The scuffle that followed precipitated three days of white violence and rape that left forty-eight African Americans dead and dozens more wounded. Mobs burned black homes and churches and destroyed all twelve of the city's black schools.

Unionists were appalled. They had won the Civil War, but where was the peace? Ex-Confederates murdered freedmen and flagrantly resisted federal control. After the Memphis attacks, Republicans in Congress proposed a new measure that would protect African Americans by defining and enforcing U.S. citizenship rights. Eventually this bill became the most significant law to emerge from Reconstruction, the Fourteenth Amendment to the Constitution.

Andrew Johnson, however—the Unionist Democrat who became president after Abraham Lincoln's assassination—refused to sign the bill. In May 1865, while Congress was adjourned, Johnson had implemented his own Reconstruction plan. It extended amnesty to all southerners who took a loyalty oath, except for a few high-ranking Confederates. It also allowed states to reenter the Union as soon as they revoked secession, abolished

416

slavery, and relieved their new state governments of financial burdens by repudiating Confederate debts. A year later, at the time of the Memphis carnage, all ex-Confederate states had met Johnson's terms. The president rejected any further intervention.

Johnson's vetoes, combined with ongoing violence in the South, angered Unionist voters. In the political struggle that ensued, congressional Republicans seized the initiative from the president and enacted a sweeping program that became known as Radical Reconstruction. One of its key achievements, the Fifteenth Amendment, would have been unthinkable a few years earlier: voting rights for African American men.

Black southerners, though, had additional, urgent priorities. "We have toiled nearly all our lives as slaves [and] have made these lands what they are," a group of South Carolina petitioners declared. They pleaded for "some provision by which we as Freedmen can obtain a Homestead." Though northern Republicans and freedpeople agreed that black southerners must have physical safety and the right to vote, former slaves also wanted economic independence. Northerners sought, instead, to revive cash-crop plantations with wage labor. Reconstruction's eventual failure stemmed from the conflicting goals of lawmakers, freedpeople, and relentlessly hostile ex-Confederates.

# The Struggle for National Reconstruction

Congress clashed with President Johnson, in part, because the framers of the Constitution did not anticipate a civil war or provide for its aftermath. Had Confederate states legally left the Union when they seceded? If so, then their reentry required action by Congress. If not—if even during secession they had retained U.S. statehood—then restoring them might be an administrative matter, best left to the president. Lack of clarity on this fundamental question made for explosive politics.

## Presidential Approaches: From Lincoln to Johnson

As wartime president, Lincoln had offered a plan similar to Johnson's. It granted amnesty to most ex-Confederates and allowed each rebellious state to return to the Union as soon as 10 percent of its voters had taken a loyalty oath and the state had approved the Thirteenth Amendment, abolishing slavery. But even amid defeat, Confederate states rejected this **Ten Percent Plan**—an ominous sign for the future. In July 1864, Congress proposed a tougher substitute, the **Wade-Davis Bill**, that required an oath of allegiance by a majority of each state's adult white men, new governments formed only by those who had never taken up arms against the Union, and permanent disenfranchisement of Confederate leaders. Lincoln defeated the Wade-Davis Bill with a pocket veto, leaving it unsigned when Congress adjourned. At the same time, he opened talks with key congressmen, aiming for a compromise.

On April 14, 1865, Lincoln was shot by John Wilkes Booth while watching a play at Ford's Theatre. We will never know what would have happened had Lincoln lived. His death precipitated grief and political turmoil. As a special train bore the president's flag-draped coffin home to Illinois, thousands of Americans lined the railroad tracks in mourning. Furious and grief-stricken, many Unionists blamed all Confederates for the acts of southern sympathizer John Wilkes Booth and his accomplices in the murder. At the same time, Lincoln's death left the presidency in the hands of Andrew Johnson, a man utterly lacking in Lincoln's moral sense and political judgment.

Johnson was a self-styled "common man" from the hills of eastern Tennessee. Trained as a tailor, he built his political career on the support of farmers and laborers. Loyal to the Union, Johnson had refused to leave the U.S. Senate when Tennessee seceded. After federal forces captured Nashville in 1862, Lincoln appointed Johnson as Tennessee's military governor. In the election of 1864, placing Lincoln and this War Democrat on the ticket together had seemed a smart move, designed to promote unity. But after Lincoln's death, Johnson's disagreement with Republicans, combined with his belligerent and contradictory actions, wreaked political havoc.

The new president and Congress confronted a set of problems that would have challenged even Lincoln. During the war, Unionists had insisted that rebel leaders were a small minority and most white southerners wanted to rejoin the Union. With even greater optimism, Republicans hoped the defeated South would accept postwar reforms. Ex-Confederates, however, contested that plan through both violence and political action. New southern state legislatures, created under Johnson's limited Reconstruction plan, moved to restore slavery in all but name. In 1865, they enacted **Black Codes**, designed to force former slaves back to plantation labor. Like similar laws passed in other places after slavery ended, the codes reflected plantation owners' economic interests. They imposed severe penalties on blacks who did not hold full-year labor contracts and also set up procedures for taking black children from their parents and apprenticing them to former slave masters.

Faced with these developments, Johnson gave all the wrong signals. He had long talked tough against southern planters. But in practice, Johnson allied himself with ex-Confederate leaders, forgiving them when they appealed for pardons. White southern leaders were delighted. "By this wise and noble statesmanship," wrote a Confederate legislator, "you have become the benefactor of the Southern people." Northerners and freedmen were disgusted. The president had left Reconstruction "to the tender mercies of the rebels," wrote one Republican. An angry Union veteran in Missouri called Johnson "a traitor to the loyal people of the Union." Emboldened by Johnson's indulgence, ex-Confederates began to filter back into the halls of power. When Georgians elected Alexander Stephens, former vice president of the Confederacy, to represent them in Congress, many outraged Republicans saw this as the last straw.

## Congress Versus the President

Under the Constitution, Congress is "the judge of the Elections, Returns and Qualifications of its own Members" (Article 1, Section 5). Using this power, Republican majorities in both houses had refused to admit southern delegations when Congress convened in December 1865, effectively blocking Johnson's program. Hoping to mollify Congress, some southern states dropped the most objectionable provisions from their Black Codes. But at the same time, antiblack violence erupted in various parts of the South.

Congressional Republicans concluded that the federal government had to intervene. Back in March 1865, Congress had established the **Freedmen's Bureau** to aid displaced blacks and other war refugees. In early 1866, Congress voted to extend the bureau, gave it direct funding for the first time, and authorized its agents to investigate southern abuses. Even more extraordinary was the **Civil Rights Act of 1866**, which declared formerly enslaved people to be citizens and granted them equal protection and rights of contract, with full access to the courts.

These bills provoked bitter conflict with Johnson, who vetoed them both. Johnson's racism, hitherto publicly muted, now blazed forth: "This is a country for white men, and by God, as long as I am president, it shall be a government for white men." Galvanized, Republicans in Congress gathered two-thirds majorities and overrode both vetoes, passing the Civil Rights Act in April 1866 and the Freedmen's Bureau law four months later. Their resolve was reinforced by continued upheaval in the South. In addition to the violence in Memphis, twenty-four black political leaders and their allies in Arkansas were murdered and their homes burned.

Anxious to protect freedpeople and reassert Republican power in the South, Congress took further measures to sustain civil rights. In what became the **Fourteenth Amendment** (1868), it declared that "all persons born or naturalized in the United States" were citizens. No state could abridge "the privileges or immunities of citizens of the United States"; deprive "any person of life, liberty, or property, without due process of law"; or deny anyone "equal protection." In a stunning increase of federal power, the Fourteenth Amendment declared that when people's essential rights were at stake, national citizenship henceforth took priority over citizenship in a state.

Johnson opposed ratification, but public opinion had swung against him. In the 1866 congressional elections, voters gave Republicans a 3-to-1 majority in Congress. Power shifted to the so-called Radical Republicans, who sought sweeping transformations in the defeated South. The Radicals' leader in the Senate was Charles Sumner of Massachusetts, the fiery abolitionist who in 1856 had been nearly beaten to death by South Carolina congressman Preston Brooks. Radicals in the House followed Thaddeus Stevens of Pennsylvania, a passionate advocate of freedmen's political and economic rights. With such men at the fore, and with congressional Republicans now numerous and united enough to override Johnson's vetoes on many questions, Congress proceeded to remake Reconstruction.

## Radical Reconstruction

The **Reconstruction Act of 1867**, enacted in March, divided the conquered South into five military districts, each under the command of a U.S. general (Map 14.1). To reenter the Union, former Confederate states had to grant the vote to freedmen and deny it to leading ex-Confederates. Each military commander was required to register all eligible adult males, black as well as white; supervise state constitutional conventions; and ensure that new constitutions guaranteed black suffrage. Congress

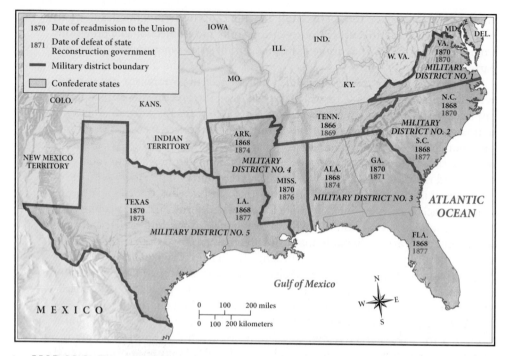

**MAP 14.1 Reconstruction**

The federal government organized the Confederate states into five military districts during congressional Reconstruction. For the states shown in this map, the first date indicates when that state was readmitted to the Union; the second date shows when Republicans lost control of the state government. All the ex-Confederate states rejoined the Union between 1868 and 1870, but the periods of Radical government varied widely. Republicans lasted only a few months in Virginia; they held on until the end of Reconstruction in Louisiana, Florida, and South Carolina.

would readmit a state to the Union once these conditions were met and the new state legislature ratified the Fourteenth Amendment. Johnson vetoed the Reconstruction Act, but Congress overrode his veto.

**The Impeachment of Andrew Johnson** In August 1867, Johnson fought back by "suspending" Secretary of War Edwin M. Stanton, a Radical, and replacing him with Union general Ulysses S. Grant, believing Grant would be a good soldier and follow orders. Johnson, however, had misjudged Grant, who publicly objected to the president's machinations. When the Senate overruled Stanton's suspension, Grant—now an open enemy of Johnson—resigned so Stanton could resume his place as secretary of war. On February 21, 1868, Johnson formally dismissed Stanton. The feisty secretary of war responded by barricading himself in his office, precipitating a crisis.

Three days later, for the first time in U.S. history, legislators in the House of Representatives introduced articles of impeachment against the president, employing their constitutional power to charge high federal officials with "Treason, Bribery, or other high Crimes and Misdemeanors." The House serves, in effect, as the prosecutor in such cases, and the Senate serves as the court. The Republican majority brought eleven counts of misconduct against Johnson, most relating to infringement of the powers of Congress. After an eleven-week trial in the Senate, thirty-five senators voted for conviction—one vote short of the two-thirds majority required. Twelve Democrats and seven Republicans voted for acquittal. The dissenting Republicans felt that removing a president for defying Congress was too damaging to the constitutional system of checks and balances. But despite the president's acquittal, Congress had shown its power. For the brief months remaining in his term, Johnson was largely irrelevant.

**Election of 1868 and the Fifteenth Amendment**    The impeachment controversy made Grant, already the Union's greatest war hero, a Republican idol as well. He easily won the party's presidential nomination in 1868. Although he supported congressional Reconstruction, Grant also urged sectional reconciliation. His Democratic opponent, former New York governor Horatio Seymour, almost declined the

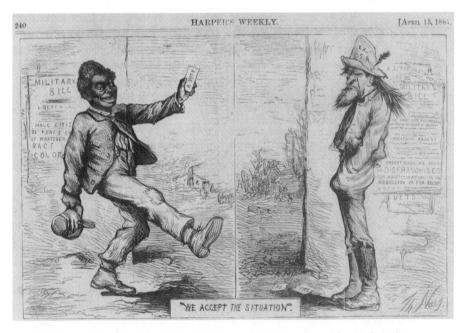

**"We Accept the Situation"** This 1867 *Harper's Weekly* cartoon refers to the Military Reconstruction Act of 1867, which instructed ex-Confederate states to hold constitutional conventions and stipulated that the resulting constitutions must provide voting rights for black men. The two images here suggest white northerners' views of both ex-Confederates and emancipated slaves. How is each depicted? What does this suggest about the troubles that lay ahead for Reconstruction policy? The cartoonist was Thomas Nast (1840–1902), one of the most influential artists of his era. Nast first drew "Santa Claus" in his modern form, and it was he who began depicting the Democratic Party as a kicking donkey and Republicans as an elephant—suggesting (since elephants are supposed to have good memories) their long remembrance of the Civil War and emancipation. Library of Congress.

nomination because he understood that Democrats could not yet overcome the stain of disloyalty. Grant won by an overwhelming margin, receiving 214 out of 294 electoral votes. Republicans retained two-thirds majorities in both houses of Congress.

In February 1869, following this smashing victory, Republicans produced the era's last constitutional amendment, the Fifteenth. It protected male citizens' right to vote irrespective of race, color, or "previous condition of servitude." Despite Radical Republicans' protests, the amendment left room for a poll tax (paid for the privilege of voting) and literacy requirements. Both were concessions to northern and western states that sought such provisions to keep immigrants and the "unworthy" poor from the polls. Congress required the four states remaining under federal control to ratify the measure as a condition for readmission to the Union. A year later, the **Fifteenth Amendment** became law.

Passage of the Fifteenth Amendment, despite its limitations, was an astonishing feat. Elsewhere in the Western Hemisphere, lawmakers had left emancipated slaves in a condition of semi-citizenship, with no voting rights. But, like almost all Americans, congressional Republicans had extraordinary faith in the power of the vote. Many African Americans agreed. "The colored people of these Southern states have cast their lot with the Government," declared a delegate to Arkansas's constitutional convention, "and with the great Republican Party. . . . The ballot is our only means of protection." In the election of 1870, hundreds of thousands of African Americans voted across the South, in an atmosphere of collective pride and celebration.

## Women's Rights Denied

Passage of the Fifteenth Amendment was a bittersweet victory for national women's rights leaders, who had campaigned for the ballot since the Seneca Falls Convention of 1848. They hoped to secure voting rights for women and African American men at the same time. As Elizabeth Cady Stanton put it, women could "avail ourselves of the strong arm and the blue uniform of the black soldier to walk in by his side." The protected categories for voting in the Fifteenth Amendment could have read "race, color, *sex*, or previous condition of servitude." But that word proved impossible to obtain.

Enfranchising black men had clear benefits for the authors of Reconstruction. It punished ex-Confederates and ensured Republican support in the South. But women's party loyalties were more divided, and a substantial majority of northern voters — all men, of course — opposed women's enfranchisement. Even Radicals feared that this "side issue" would overburden their program. Influential abolitionists such as Wendell Philips refused to campaign for women's suffrage, fearing it would detract from the focus on black men. Philips criticized women's leaders for being "selfish." "Do you believe," Stanton hotly replied, "the African race is entirely composed of males?"

By May 1869, the former allies were at an impasse. At a convention of the Equal Rights Association, black abolitionist and women's rights advocate Frederick Douglass pleaded for white women to consider the situation in the South and allow black male suffrage to take priority. "When women, because they are women, are hunted down, . . . dragged from their homes and hung upon lamp posts," Douglass said, "then they will have an urgency to obtain the ballot equal to our own." Some women's suffrage leaders joined Douglass in backing the Fifteenth Amendment without the word *sex*. But many, especially white women, rejected Douglass's plea. One African American woman remarked that they "all go for sex, letting race occupy a minor position." Embittered, Elizabeth Cady Stanton lashed out against "Patrick and Sambo and Hans and Ung Tung," maligning uneducated freedmen and immigrants who could vote while educated white women could not. Douglass's resolution in support of the Fifteenth Amendment failed, and the convention broke up.

A rift thus opened in the women's movement. The majority, led by Lucy Stone, reconciled themselves to disappointment. Organized into the **American Woman Suffrage Association**, they remained loyal to the Republican Party in hopes that once Reconstruction had been settled, it would be women's turn. A group led by Elizabeth Cady Stanton and Susan B. Anthony struck out in a new direction. They saw that, once the Reconstruction amendments had passed, women's suffrage was unlikely in the near future. Stanton declared that woman "must not put her trust in man." The new organization she headed, the **National Woman Suffrage Association** (NWSA), focused exclusively on women's rights and took up the battle for a federal suffrage amendment.

In 1873, NWSA members decided to test the new constitutional amendments. Suffragists all over the United States, including some black women in the South, tried to register and vote. Most were turned away. In an ensuing lawsuit, suffrage advocate Virginia Minor of Missouri argued that the registrar who denied her a ballot had violated her rights under the Fourteenth Amendment. In ***Minor v. Happersett*** (1875), the Supreme Court dashed such hopes. It ruled that suffrage rights were not inherent in citizenship; women were citizens, but state legislatures could deny women the vote if they wished.

Women's rights advocates began to focus narrowly on suffrage as their movement suffered backlash from controversies over sexual freedom. After Victoria Woodhull, a flamboyant young woman from Ohio, became the nation's first female stockbroker on Wall Street, she won notoriety by denouncing marriage as a form of tyranny. She urged that women be "trained like men," for independent thought and economic self-sufficiency. Particularly sensational was Woodhull's insistence, in a speech in New York in 1871, that "I am a free lover. I have an inalienable, constitutional, and natural right to love whom I may, to love as long or as short a period as I can; to change that love every day if I please."

Woodhull helped trigger the **Beecher-Tilton scandal**, a sensational trial that dominated headlines in the mid-1870s. She accused Brooklyn Congregationalist minister Henry Ward Beecher, a staunch Republican and abolitionist from a famous reform family, of secretly being a free lover himself. For making allegations of adultery, Woodhull was tried on obscenity charges, briefly jailed, and released. Beecher was then sued by the husband of a congregant with whom he had allegedly had an affair. The results of the trial were inconclusive, but the relentless publicity, including the publication of intimate letters, damaged the reputation of everyone involved. Many Americans concluded that Radical Republicans wanted to go too far, and that, in private, former abolitionists like Beecher and his congregants were behaving immorally. Social conservatives, including ex-Confederates in the South, gleefully watched leading abolitionists get their come-uppance. Women's rights advocates, who had welcomed Victoria Woodhull as an ally, soon distanced themselves from her free love proclamations. Leaders such as Susan B. Anthony decided that the only way to win the vote was to practice and advocate strict sexual respectability.

Despite these defeats and embarrassments, Radical Reconstruction had created the conditions for a nationwide women's rights movement. Some argued for suffrage as part of a broader expansion of democracy. Others, on the contrary, saw white women's votes as a possible counterweight to the votes of African American or Chinese men (while opponents pointed out that black and immigrant women would likely be enfranchised, too). When Wyoming Territory gave women full voting rights in 1869, its governor received telegrams of congratulation from around the world. Afterward, contrary to dire predictions, female voters in Wyoming did not appear to neglect their homes, abandon their children, or otherwise "unsex" themselves. Women's suffrage could no longer be dismissed as the absurd notion of a tiny minority. It had become a serious issue for national debate.

| **IN YOUR OWN WORDS** | What factors explain how Reconstruction policies unfolded between 1865 and 1870, and what was the impact on different groups of Americans? |

# The Meaning of Freedom

While political leaders wrangled in Washington, emancipated slaves acted on their own ideas about freedom. Emancipation meant many things: the end of punishment by the lash; the ability to move around; reunion of families; and opportunities to build schools and churches and to publish and read newspapers. Foremost among freedpeople's demands were voting rights and economic autonomy. Former Confederates opposed these goals. Most southern whites believed the proper place for blacks was as "servants and inferiors," as a Virginia planter testified to Congress. Mississippi's governor, elected under President Johnson's plan, vowed that "ours is and it shall ever be, a government of white men." Meanwhile, as Reconstruction unfolded, it became clear that on economic questions, southern blacks and northern Republican policymakers did not see eye to eye.

## The Quest for Land

During the Civil War, wherever Union forces had conquered portions of the South, rural black workers had formed associations that agreed on common goals and even practiced military drills. After the war, when resettlement became the responsibility of the Freedmen's Bureau, thousands of rural blacks hoped for land distributions. But Johnson's amnesty plan, which allowed pardoned Confederates to recover property seized during the war, blasted such hopes. In October 1865, for example, Johnson ordered General Oliver O. Howard, head of the Freedmen's Bureau, to restore plantations on South Carolina's Sea Islands to white property holders. Dispossessed blacks protested: "Why do you take away our lands? You take them from us who have always been true, always true to the Government! You give them to our all-time enemies! That is not right!" Former slaves resisted efforts to evict them. Led by black Union veterans, they fought pitched battles with former slaveholders and bands of ex-Confederate soldiers. But white landowners, sometimes aided by federal troops, generally prevailed.

**Freed Slaves and Northerners: Conflicting Goals** On questions of land and labor, freedmen in the South and Republicans in Washington seriously differed. The economic revolution of the antebellum period had transformed New England and the Mid-Atlantic states. Believing similar development could revolutionize the South, most congressional leaders sought to restore cotton as the country's leading export, and they envisioned former slaves as wageworkers on cash-crop plantations, not independent farmers. Only a handful of Republican leaders, like Thaddeus Stevens, argued that freed slaves had earned a right to land grants, through what Lincoln had referred to as "four hundred years of unrequited toil." Stevens proposed that southern plantations be treated as "forfeited estates of the enemy" and broken up into small farms for former slaves. "Nothing will make men so industrious and moral," Stevens declared, "as to let them feel that they are above want and are the owners of the soil which they till."

Today, most historians of Reconstruction agree with Stevens: policymakers did not do enough to ensure freedpeople's economic security. Without land, former slaves were left poor and vulnerable. At the time, though, Stevens had few allies. A deep veneration for private property lay at the heart of his vision, but others interpreted the same principle differently: they defined ownership by legal title, not by labor invested. Though often accused of harshness toward the defeated Confederacy, most Republicans—even Radicals—could not imagine "giving" land to former slaves. The same congressmen, of course, had no difficulty giving away homesteads on the frontier that had been taken from Indians. But they were deeply reluctant to confiscate white-owned plantations.

Some southern Republican state governments did try, without much success, to use tax policy to break up large landholdings and get them into the hands of poorer whites and blacks. In 1869, South Carolina established a land commission to buy property and resell it on easy terms to the landless; about 14,000 black families acquired farms through the program. But such initiatives were the exception, not the rule. Over time, some rural blacks did succeed in becoming small-scale landowners, especially in Upper South states such as Virginia, North Carolina, and Tennessee. But it was an uphill fight, and policymakers provided little aid.

**Wage Labor and Sharecropping** Without land, most freedpeople had few options but to work for former slave owners. Landowners wanted to retain the old gang-labor system, with wages replacing the food, clothing, and shelter that slaves had once received. Southern planters—who had recently scorned the North for the cruelties of wage labor—now embraced waged work with apparent satisfaction. Maliciously comparing black workers to free-roaming pigs, landowners told them to "root, hog, or die." Former slaves found themselves with rock-bottom wages; it was a shock to find that emancipation and "free labor" did not prevent a hardworking family from nearly starving.

African American workers used a variety of tactics to fight back. As early as 1865, alarmed whites across the South reported that former slaves were holding mass meetings to agree on "plans and terms for labor." Such meetings continued through the Reconstruction years. Facing limited prospects at home, some workers left the fields and traveled long distances to seek better-paying jobs on the railroads or in turpentine and lumber camps. Others—from rice cultivators to laundry workers—organized strikes.

At the same time, struggles raged between employers and freedpeople over women's work. In slavery, African American women's bodies had been the sexual property of white men. Protecting black women from such abuse, as much as possible, was a crucial priority for freedpeople. When planters demanded that black women go back into the fields, African Americans resisted resolutely. "I seen on some plantations," one freedman recounted, "where the white men would . . . tell colored men that their wives and children could not live on their places unless they work in the fields. The colored men [answered that] whenever they wanted their wives to work they would tell them themselves."

There was a profound irony in this man's definition of freedom: it designated a wife's labor as her husband's property. Some black women asserted their independence and headed their own households, though this was often a matter of necessity rather than choice. For many freedpeople, the opportunity for a stable family life was one of the greatest achievements of emancipation. Many enthusiastically accepted the northern ideal of domesticity. Missionaries, teachers, and editors of black newspapers urged men to work diligently and support their families, and they told women (though many worked for wages) to devote themselves to motherhood and the home.

Even in rural areas, former slaves refused to work under conditions that recalled slavery. There would be no gang work, they vowed: no overseers, no whippings, no regulation of their private lives. Across the South, planters who needed labor were forced to yield to what one planter termed the "prejudices of the freedmen, who desire to be masters of their own time." In a few areas, waged work became the norm — for example, on the giant sugar plantations of Louisiana financed by northern capital. But cotton planters lacked money to pay wages, and sometimes, in lieu of a wage, they offered a share of the crop. Freedmen, in turn, paid their rent in shares of the harvest.

Thus the Reconstruction years gave rise to a distinctive system of cotton agriculture known as **sharecropping**, in which freedmen worked as renters, exchanging their labor for the use of land, house, implements, and sometimes seed and fertilizer. Sharecroppers typically turned over half of their crops to the landlord (Map 14.2). In a credit-starved agricultural region that grew crops for a world economy, sharecropping was an effective strategy, enabling laborers and landowners to share risks and returns. But it was a very unequal relationship. Starting out penniless, sharecroppers had no way to make it through the first growing season without borrowing for food and supplies.

Country storekeepers stepped in. Bankrolled by northern suppliers, they furnished sharecroppers with provisions and took as collateral a lien on the crop,

**MAP 14.2   The Barrow Plantation, 1860 and 1881 >**

This map is a modern redrawing of one that first appeared in the popular magazine *Scribner's Monthly* in April 1881, accompanying an article about the Barrow plantation. Comparing the 1860 map of this central Georgia plantation with the 1881 map reveals the impact of sharecropping on patterns of black residence. In 1860, the slave quarters were clustered near the planter's house. In contrast, by 1881 the sharecroppers were scattered across the plantation's 2,000 acres, having built cabins on the ridges between the low-lying streams. The surname *Barrow* was common among the sharecropping families, which means almost certainly that they had been slaves who, years after emancipation, still had not moved on. For sharecroppers, freedom meant not only their individual lots and cabins but also the school and church shown on the map.

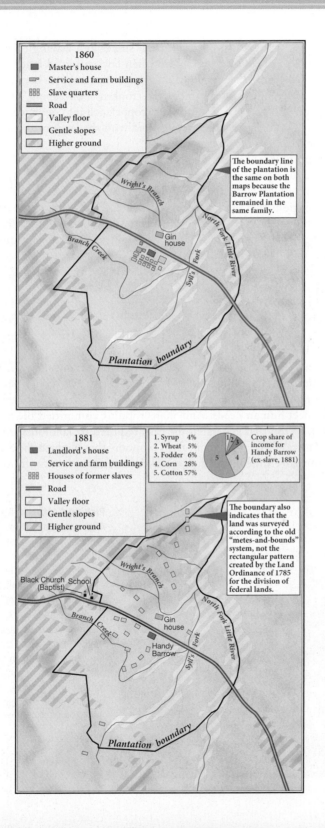

**1860**

- ◼ Master's house
- ◻━ Service and farm buildings
- ▦ Slave quarters
- ═══ Road
- ▢ Valley floor
- ▢ Gentle slopes
- ▨ Higher ground

Wright's Branch

Branch Creek

Gin house

Syll's Fork

North Fork Little River

The boundary line of the plantation is the same on both maps because the Barrow Plantation remained in the same family.

Plantation boundary

**1881**

- ◼ Landlord's house
- ◻ Service and farm buildings
- ▦ Houses of former slaves
- ═══ Road
- ▢ Valley floor
- ▢ Gentle slopes
- ▨ Higher ground

1. Syrup 4%
2. Wheat 5%
3. Fodder 6%
4. Corn 28%
5. Cotton 57%

Crop share of income for Handy Barrow (ex-slave, 1881)

Wright's Branch

Black Church (Baptist)   School

Branch Creek

Gin house

Handy Barrow

Syll's Fork

North Fork Little River

The boundary also indicates that the land was surveyed according to the old "metes-and-bounds" system, not the rectangular pattern created by the Land Ordinance of 1785 for the division of federal lands.

Plantation boundary

effectively assuming ownership of croppers' shares and leaving them only what remained after debts had been paid. Crop-lien laws enforced lenders' ownership rights to the crop share. Once indebted at a store, sharecroppers became easy targets for exorbitant prices, unfair interest rates, and crooked bookkeeping. As cotton prices declined in the 1870s, more and more sharecroppers fell into permanent debt. If the merchant was also the landowner or conspired with the landowner, debt became a pretext for forced labor, or peonage.

Sharecropping arose in part because it was a good fit for cotton agriculture. Cotton, unlike sugarcane, could be raised efficiently by small farmers (provided they had the lash of indebtedness always on their backs). We can see this in the experience of other regions that became major producers in response to the global cotton shortage set off by the Civil War. In India, Egypt, Brazil, and West Africa, variants of the sharecropping system emerged. Everywhere international merchants and bankers, who put up capital, insisted on passage of crop-lien laws. Indian and Egyptian villagers ended up, like their American counterparts, permanently under the thumb of furnishing merchants.

By 1890, three out of every four black farmers in the South were tenants or sharecroppers; among white farmers, the ratio was one in three. For freedmen, sharecropping was not the worst choice, in a world where former masters threatened to impose labor conditions that were close to slavery. But the costs were devastating. With farms leased on a year-to-year basis, neither tenant nor owner had much incentive to improve the property. The crop-lien system rested on expensive interest payments — money that might otherwise have gone into agricultural improvements or to meet human needs. And sharecropping committed the South inflexibly to cotton, a crop that generated the cash required by landlords and furnishing merchants. The result was a stagnant farm economy that blighted the South's future. As Republican governments tried to remake the region, they confronted not only

**Picking Cotton in Mississippi**
After emancipation most African Americans in the South, lacking land or capital, continued to work in agriculture. Through sharecropping and other arrangements, they sought as much autonomy and control over their work as they could obtain. Many families made it a priority for women to work in the home and children to attend school. At harvest time, however, everyone was needed in the fields.
The Granger Collection, New York.

wartime destruction but also the failure of their hopes that free labor would create a modern, prosperous South, built in the image of the industrializing North. Instead, the South's rural economy remained mired in widespread poverty and based on an uneasy compromise between landowners and laborers.

## Republican Governments in the South

Between 1868 and 1871, all the former Confederate states met congressional stipulations and rejoined the Union. Protected by federal troops, Republican administrations in these states retained power for periods ranging from a few months in Virginia to nine years in South Carolina, Louisiana, and Florida. These governments remain some of the most misunderstood institutions in all U.S. history. Ex-Confederates never accepted their legitimacy. Many other whites agreed, focusing particularly on the role of African Americans who began to serve in public office. "It is strange, abnormal, and unfit," declared one British visitor to Louisiana, "that a *negro* Legislature should deal . . . with the gravest commercial and financial interests." During much of the twentieth century, historians echoed such critics, condemning Reconstruction leaders as ignorant and corrupt. These historians shared the racial prejudices of the British observer: black men were simply unfit to govern.

In fact, Reconstruction governments were ambitious. They were hated, in part, because they undertook impressive reforms in public education, family law, social services, commerce, and transportation. Like their northern allies, southern Republicans admired the economic and social transformations that had occurred in the North before the Civil War and worked energetically to import them.

The southern Republican Party included former Whigs, a few former Democrats, black and white newcomers from the North, and southern African Americans. From the start, its leaders faced the dilemma of racial prejudice. In the upcountry, white Unionists were eager to join the party but sometimes reluctant to work with black allies. In most areas, the Republicans also desperately needed African Americans, who constituted a majority of registered voters in Alabama, Florida, South Carolina, and Mississippi.

For a brief moment in the late 1860s, black and white Republicans joined forces through the Union League, a secret fraternal order. Formed in border states and northern cities during the Civil War, the league became a powerful political association that spread through the former Confederacy. Functioning as a grassroots wing of Radical Republicanism, it pressured Congress to uphold justice for freedmen. After blacks won voting rights, the league organized meetings at churches and schoolhouses to instruct freedmen on political issues and voting procedures. League clubs held parades and military drills, giving a public face to the new political order.

The Freedmen's Bureau also supported grassroots Reconstruction efforts. Though some bureau officials sympathized with planters, most were dedicated, idealistic men who tried valiantly to reconcile opposing interests. Bureau men kept a sharp eye out for unfair labor contracts and often forced landowners to bargain with workers and tenants. They advised freedmen on economic matters; provided direct payments to desperate families, especially women and children; and helped establish schools. In cooperation with northern aid societies, the bureau played a key role in founding African American colleges and universities such as Fisk, Tougaloo, and the Hampton Institute. These institutions, in turn, focused on training teachers. By 1869, there were more than three thousand teachers instructing freedpeople in the South. More than half were themselves African Americans.

Ex-Confederates viewed the Union League, Freedmen's Bureau, and Republican Party as illegitimate forces in southern affairs, and they resented the political education of freedpeople. They referred to southern whites who supported Reconstruction as scalawags — an ancient Scots-Irish term for worthless animals — and denounced northern whites as carpetbaggers, self-seeking interlopers who carried all their property in cheap suitcases called carpetbags. Such labels glossed over the actual diversity of white Republicans. Many arrivals from the North, while motivated by personal profit, also brought capital and skills. Interspersed with ambitious schemers were reformers hoping to advance freedmen's rights. So-called scalawags were even more varied. Some southern Republicans were former slave owners; others were ex-Whigs or even ex-Democrats who hoped to attract northern capital. But most hailed from the backcountry and wanted to rid the South of its slaveholding aristocracy, believing slavery had victimized whites as well as blacks.

Southern Democrats' contempt for black politicians, whom they regarded as ignorant field hands, was just as misguided as their stereotypes about white Republicans. Many African American leaders in the South came from the ranks of antebellum free blacks. Others were skilled men like Robert Smalls of South Carolina, who as a slave had worked for wages that he turned over to his master. Smalls, a steamer pilot in Charleston harbor, had become a war hero when he escaped with his family and other slaves and brought his ship to the Union navy. Buying property in Beaufort after the war, Smalls became a state legislator and later a congressman. Blanche K. Bruce, another former slave, had been tutored on a Virginia plantation by his white father; during the war, he escaped and established a school for freedmen in Missouri. In 1869, he moved to Mississippi and became, five years later, Mississippi's second black U.S. senator. Political leaders such as Smalls and Bruce were joined by northern blacks — including ministers, teachers, and Union veterans — who moved south to support Reconstruction.

During radical Reconstruction, such men fanned out into plantation districts and recruited former slaves to participate in politics. Literacy helped freedman Thomas Allen, a Baptist minister and shoemaker, win election to the Georgia legislature. "The colored people came to me," Allen recalled, "and I gave them the best instructions I could. I took the *New York Tribune* and other papers, and in that way I found out a great deal, and I told them whatever I thought was right." Though never proportionate to their numbers in the population, blacks became officeholders across the South. In South Carolina, African Americans constituted a majority in the lower house of the legislature in 1868. Over the course of Reconstruction, twenty African Americans served in state administrations as governor, lieutenant governor, secretary of state, or lesser offices. More than six hundred became state legislators, and sixteen were congressmen.

Both white and black Republicans had big plans. Their southern Reconstruction governments eliminated property qualifications for the vote and abolished Black Codes. Their new state constitutions expanded the rights of married women, enabling them to own their own property and wages — "a wonderful reform," one white woman in Georgia wrote, for "the cause of Women's Rights." Like their counterparts in the North, southern Republicans also believed in using government to foster economic growth. Seeking to diversify the economy beyond cotton agriculture, they poured money into railroads and other projects.

In myriad ways, Republicans brought southern state and city governments up to date. They outlawed corporal punishments such as whipping and branding. They established hospitals and asylums for orphans and the disabled. South Carolina offered free public health services, while Alabama provided free legal representation for defendants who could not pay. Some municipal governments paved streets and installed streetlights. Petersburg, Virginia, established a board of health that offered free medical care during the smallpox epidemic of 1873. Nashville, Tennessee, created soup kitchens for the poor.

Most impressive of all were achievements in public education, where the South had lagged woefully. Republicans viewed education as the foundation of a true democratic order. By 1875, over half of black children were attending school in Mississippi, Florida, and South Carolina. African Americans of all ages rushed to the newly established schools, even when they had to pay tuition. They understood why slaveholders had criminalized slave literacy: the practice of freedom rested on the ability to read newspapers, labor contracts, history books, and the Bible. A school official in Virginia reported that freedpeople were "*crazy* to learn." One Louisiana man explained why he was sending his children to school, even though he needed their help in the field. It was "better than leaving them a fortune; because if you left them even five hundred dollars, some man having more education than they had would come along and cheat them out of it all." Thousands of white children, particularly girls and the sons of poor farmers and laborers, also benefitted from new public education systems. Young white women's graduation from high school, an unheard-of occurrence before the Civil War, became a celebrated event in southern cities and towns.

Southern Reconstruction governments also had their flaws—flaws that would become more apparent as the 1870s unfolded. In the race for economic development, for example, state officials allowed private companies to hire out prisoners to labor in mines and other industries, in a notorious system known as **convict leasing**. Corruption was rife and conditions horrific. In 1866, Alabama's governor leased 200 state convicts to a railroad construction company for the grand total of $5. While they labored to build state-subsidized lines such as the Alabama and Chattanooga, prisoners were housed at night in open, rolling cages. Physical abuse was common and medical care nonexistent. At the start of 1869, Alabama counted 263 prisoners available for leasing; by the end of the year, a staggering 92 of them had died. While convict leasing expanded in later decades, it began during Reconstruction, supported by both Republicans and Democrats.

## Building Black Communities

Enslaved African Americans had built networks of religious worship and mutual aid, but these operated largely in secret. After emancipation, southern blacks could engage in open community building. In doing so, they cooperated with northern missionaries and teachers, both black and white, who came to help in the great work of freedom. "Ignorant though they may be, on account of long years of oppression, they exhibit a desire to hear and to learn, that I never imagined," reported African

THE FISK UNIVERSITY COLLEGE AND JUBILEE HALL, NASHVILLE, TENNESSEE.

THE JUBILEE SINGERS FOR THE FISK UNIVERSITY COLLEGE.

**Fisk Jubilee Singers, 1873** Fisk University in Nashville, Tennessee, was established in 1865 to provide higher education for African Americans from across the South. When funds ran short in 1871, enterprising students formed the Jubilee Singers choral group (bottom) and toured to raise money for the school. They performed African American spirituals and folk songs, such as "Swing Low, Sweet Chariot," arranged in ways that appealed to white audiences, making this music nationally popular for the first time. In 1872, the group performed for President Grant at the White House. Money raised by this acclaimed group saved Fisk from bankruptcy and built the university's imposing Jubilee Hall (top). Private Collection/© Look and Learn/Illustrated Papers Collection/ Bridgeman Images.

American minister Reverend James Lynch, who traveled from Maryland to the Deep South. "Every word you say while preaching, they drink down and respond to, with an earnestness that sets your heart all on fire."

Independent churches quickly became central community institutions, as blacks across the South left white-dominated congregations, where they had sat in segregated balconies, and built churches of their own. These churches joined their counterparts in the North to become national denominations, including, most prominently, the National Baptist Convention and the African Methodist Episcopal Church. Black churches served not only as sites of worship but also as schools, social centers, and meeting halls. Ministers were often political spokesmen as well. As Charles H. Pearce, a black Methodist pastor in Florida, declared, "A man in this State cannot do his whole duty as a minister except he looks out for the political interests of his people." Religious leaders articulated the special destiny of freedpeople as the new "Children of Israel."

The flowering of black churches, schools, newspapers, and civic groups was one of the most enduring initiatives of the Reconstruction era. Dedicated teachers and charity leaders embarked on a project of "race uplift" that never ceased thereafter,

while black entrepreneurs were proud to build businesses that served their communities. The issue of desegregation — sharing public facilities with whites — was a trick-
ier one. Though some black leaders pressed for desegregation, they were keenly aware
of the backlash this was likely to provoke. Others made it clear that they preferred
their children to attend all-black schools, especially if they encountered hostile or
condescending white teachers and classmates. Many had pragmatic concerns. Asked
whether she wanted her boys to attend an integrated school, one woman in New
Orleans said no: "I don't want my children to be pounded by . . . white boys. I don't
send them to school to fight, I send them to learn."

At the national level, congressmen wrestled with similar issues as they debated
an ambitious civil rights bill championed by Radical Republican senator Charles
Sumner. Sumner first introduced his bill in 1870, seeking to enforce, among other
things, equal access to schools, public transportation, hotels, and churches. Due
to a series of defeats and delays, the bill remained on Capitol Hill for five years.
Opponents charged that shared public spaces would lead to race mixing and intermarriage. Some sympathetic Republicans feared a backlash, while others questioned whether, because of the First Amendment, the federal government had the
right to regulate churches. On his deathbed in 1874, Sumner exhorted a visitor to
remember the civil rights bill: "Don't let it fail." In the end, the Senate removed
Sumner's provision for integrated churches, and the House removed the clause
requiring integrated schools. But to honor the great Massachusetts abolitionist,
Congress passed the **Civil Rights Act of 1875**. The law required "full and equal"
access to jury service and to transportation and public accommodations, irrespective
of race. It was the last such act for almost a hundred years — until the Civil Rights
Act of 1964.

| **IN YOUR OWN WORDS** | What goals were southern freedmen and freedwomen able to achieve in the post–Civil War years, and why? What goals were they not able to achieve, and why not? |
|---|---|

# The Undoing of Reconstruction

Sumner's death marked the waning of Radical Reconstruction. That movement
had accomplished more than anyone dreamed a few years earlier. But a chasm had
opened between the goals of freedmen, who wanted autonomy, and policymakers,
whose first priorities were to reincorporate ex-Confederates into the nation and
build a powerful national economy. Meanwhile, the North was flooded with one-
sided, racist reports such as James M. Pike's influential book *The Prostrate State*
(1873), which claimed South Carolina was in the grip of "black barbarism." Events
of the 1870s deepened the northern public's disillusionment. Scandals rocked the
Grant administration, and an economic depression curbed both private investment
and public spending. At the same time, northern resolve was worn down by continued ex-Confederate resistance and violence. Only full-scale military intervention
could reverse the situation in the South, and by the mid-1870s the North had no
political willpower to renew the occupation.

## The Republicans Unravel

Republicans had banked on economic growth to underpin their ambitious program, but their hopes were dashed in 1873 by the sudden onset of a severe worldwide depression. In the United States, the initial panic was triggered by the bankruptcy of the Northern Pacific Railroad, backed by leading financier Jay Cooke. Cooke's supervision of Union finances during the Civil War had made him a national hero; his downfall was a shock, and since Cooke was so well connected in Washington, it raised suspicions that Republican financial manipulation had caused the depression. Officials in the Grant administration deepened public resentment toward their party when they rejected pleas to increase the money supply and provide relief from debt and unemployment.

The impact of the depression varied in different parts of the United States. Farmers suffered a terrible plight as crop prices plunged, while industrial workers faced layoffs and sharp wage reductions. Within a year, 50 percent of American iron manufacturing had stopped. By 1877, half the nation's railroad companies had filed for bankruptcy. Rail construction halted. With hundreds of thousands thrown out of work, people took to the road. Wandering "tramps," who camped by railroad tracks and knocked on doors to beg for work and food, terrified prosperous Americans.

In addition to discrediting Republicans, the depression directly undercut their policies, most dramatically in the South. The ex-Confederacy was still recovering from the ravages of war, and its new economic and social order remained fragile. The bold policies of southern Republicans — for education, public health, and grants to railroad builders — cost a great deal of money. Federal support, through programs like the Freedmen's Bureau, had begun to fade even before 1873. Republicans had banked on major infusions of northern and foreign investment capital; for the most part, these failed to materialize. Investors who had sunk money into Confederate bonds, only to have those repudiated, were especially wary. The South's economy grew more slowly than Republicans had hoped, and after 1873, growth screeched to a halt. State debts mounted rapidly, and as crushing interest on bonds fell due, public credit collapsed.

Not only had Republican officials failed to anticipate a severe depression; during the era of generous spending, considerable funds had also been wasted or had ended up in the pockets of corrupt officials. Two swindlers in North Carolina, one of them a former Union general, were found to have distributed more than $200,000 in bribes and loans to legislators to gain millions in state funds for rail construction. Instead of building railroads, they used the money to travel to Europe and speculate in stocks and bonds. Not only Republicans were on the take. "You are mistaken," wrote one southern Democrat to a northern friend, "if you suppose that all the evils . . . result from the carpetbaggers and negroes. The Democrats are leagued with them when anything is proposed that promises to pay." In South Carolina, when African American congressman Robert Smalls was convicted of taking a bribe, the Democratic governor pardoned him in exchange for an agreement that federal officials would drop an investigation of Democratic election fraud.

One of the depression's most tragic results was the failure of the Freedman's Savings and Trust Company. This private bank, founded in 1865, had worked closely with the Freedmen's Bureau and Union army across the South. Former slaves associated it with the party of Lincoln, and thousands responded to northerners' call for thrift and savings by bringing their small deposits to the nearest branch. African American farmers, entrepreneurs, churches, and charitable groups opened accounts at the bank. But in the early 1870s, the bank's directors sank their money into risky loans and speculative investments. In June 1874, the bank failed.

Some Republicans believed that, because the bank had been so closely associated with the U.S. Army and federal agencies, Congress had a duty to step in. Even one southern Democrat argued that the government was "morally bound to see to it that not a dollar is lost." But in the end, Congress refused to compensate the 61,000 depositors. About half recovered small amounts—averaging $18.51—but the others received nothing. The party of Reconstruction was losing its moral gloss.

**The Disillusioned Liberals**    As a result of the depression and rising criticism of postwar activist government, a revolt emerged in the Republican Party. It was led by influential intellectuals, journalists, and businessmen who believed in **classical liberalism**: free trade, small government, low property taxes, and limitation of voting rights to men of education and property. Liberals responded to the massive increase in federal power, during the Civil War and Reconstruction, by urging a policy of *laissez faire*, in which government "let alone" business and the economy. In the postwar decades, laissez faire advocates never succeeded in ending federal policies such as the protective tariff and national banking system (Chapter 16), but their arguments helped roll back Reconstruction. Unable to block Grant's renomination for the presidency in 1872, the dissidents broke away and formed a new party under the name Liberal Republican. Their candidate was Horace Greeley, longtime publisher of the *New York Tribune* and veteran reformer and abolitionist. The Democrats, still in disarray, also nominated Greeley, notwithstanding his editorial diatribes against them. A poor campaigner, Greeley was assailed so severely that, as he said, "I hardly knew whether I was running for the Presidency or the penitentiary."

Grant won reelection overwhelmingly, capturing 56 percent of the popular vote and every electoral vote. Yet Liberal Republicans had shifted the terms of debate. The agenda they advanced—smaller government, restricted voting rights, and reconciliation with ex-Confederates—resonated with Democrats, who had long advocated limited government and were working to reclaim their status as a legitimate national party. Liberalism thus crossed party lines, uniting disillusioned conservative Republicans with Democrats who denounced government activism. E. L. Godkin of *The Nation* and other classical liberal editors played key roles in turning northern public opinion against Reconstruction. With unabashed elitism, Godkin and others claimed that freedmen were unfit to vote. They denounced universal suffrage, which "can only mean in plain English the government of ignorance and vice."

The second Grant administration gave liberals plenty of ammunition. The most notorious scandal involved **Crédit Mobilier**, a sham corporation set up by shareholders in the Union Pacific Railroad to secure government grants at an enormous profit. Organizers of the scheme protected it from investigation by providing gifts of Crédit Mobilier stock to powerful members of Congress. Controversy over this railroad scandal arose even before Grant's reelection; by 1875 another scandal emerged involving the so-called "Whiskey Ring," a network of liquor distillers and treasury agents who defrauded the government of millions of dollars of excise taxes on whiskey. The ringleader was Grant's private secretary, Orville Babcock. Others went to prison, but Grant stood by Babcock, possibly perjuring himself to save his secretary from jail. The stench of scandal permeated the White House.

## Counterrevolution in the South

While northerners became preoccupied with scandals and the shock of economic depression, ex-Confederates seized power in the South. Most believed (as northern liberals had also begun to argue) that southern Reconstruction governments were illegitimate "regimes." Led by the planters, ex-Confederates staged a massive insurgency to take back the South.

When they could win at the ballot box, southern Democrats took that route. They got ex-Confederate voting rights restored and campaigned against "negro rule." But when force was necessary, southern Democrats used it. Present-day Americans, witnessing political violence in other countries, seldom remember that our own history includes the overthrow of elected governments by paramilitary groups. But this is exactly how Reconstruction ended in many parts of the South. Ex-Confederates terrorized Republicans, especially in districts with large proportions of black voters. Black political leaders were shot, hanged, beaten to death, and in one case even beheaded. Many Republicans, both black and white, went into hiding or fled for their lives. Southern Democrats called this violent process "Redemption"—a heroic name that still lingers today, even though this seizure of power was murderous and undemocratic.

No one looms larger in this bloody story than Nathan Bedford Forrest, a decorated Confederate general. Born in poverty in 1821, Forrest had risen to become a big-time slave trader and Mississippi planter. A fiery secessionist, Forrest had formed a Tennessee Confederate cavalry regiment, fought bravely at the battle of Shiloh, and won fame as a daring raider. On April 12, 1864, his troops perpetrated one of the war's worst atrocities, the massacre at Fort Pillow, Tennessee, of black Union soldiers who were trying to surrender.

After the Civil War, Forrest's determination to uphold white supremacy altered the course of Reconstruction. William G. Brownlow, elected as Tennessee's Republican governor in 1865, was a tough man, a former prisoner of the Confederates who was not shy about calling his enemies to account. Ex-Confederates struck back with a campaign of terror, targeting especially Brownlow's black supporters. Amid the mayhem, ex-Confederates formed the first **Ku Klux Klan** group in late 1865 or early 1866. As it proliferated across the state, the Klan turned to Forrest, who had been trying, unsuccessfully, to rebuild his prewar fortune. Late in 1866, at a secret meeting in Nashville, Forrest donned the robes of Grand Wizard. His activities are mostly cloaked in mystery, but there is no mistake about his goals: the Klan would strike blows against the despised Republican government of Tennessee.

In many towns, the Klan became virtually identical to the Democratic Party. Klan members—including Forrest—dominated Tennessee's delegation to the Democratic national convention of 1868. At home, the Klan unleashed a murderous campaign of terror, and though Governor Brownlow responded resolutely, in the end Republicans cracked. The Klan and similar groups—organized under such names as the White League and Knights of the White Camelia—arose in other states.

Vigilantes burned freedmen's schools, beat teachers, attacked Republican gatherings, and murdered political opponents. By 1870, Democrats had seized power in Georgia and North Carolina and were making headway across the South. Once they took power, they slashed property taxes and passed other laws favorable to landowners. They terminated Reconstruction programs and cut funding for schools, especially those teaching black students.

In responding to the Klan between 1869 and 1871, the federal government showed it could still exert power effectively in the South. Determined to end Klan violence, Congress held extensive hearings and in 1870 passed laws designed to protect freedmen's rights under the Fourteenth and Fifteenth Amendments. These so-called **Enforcement Laws** authorized federal prosecutions, military intervention, and martial law to suppress terrorist activity. Grant's administration made full use of these new powers. In South Carolina, where the Klan was deeply entrenched, U.S. troops occupied nine counties, made hundreds of arrests, and drove as many as 2,000 Klansmen from the state.

This assault on the Klan, while raising the spirits of southern Republicans, revealed how dependent they were on Washington. "No such law could be enforced by state authority," one Mississippi Republican observed, "the local power being too weak." But northern Republicans were growing disillusioned with Reconstruction, while in the South, prosecuting Klansmen was an uphill battle against all-white juries and unsympathetic federal judges. After 1872, prosecutions dropped off. Meanwhile, the Texas government fell to the Democrats in 1873 and Alabama and Arkansas fell in 1874.

## Reconstruction Rolled Back

As divided Republicans debated how to respond, voters in the congressional election of 1874 handed them one of the most stunning defeats of the nineteenth century. Responding especially to the severe depression that gripped the nation, they removed almost half of the party's 199 representatives in the House. Democrats, who had held 88 seats, now commanded an overwhelming majority of 182. "The election is not merely a victory but a revolution," exulted a Democratic newspaper in New York.

After 1874, with Democrats in control of the House, Republicans who tried to shore up their southern wing had limited options. Bowing to election results, the Grant administration began to reject southern Republicans' appeals for aid. Events in Mississippi showed the outcome. As state elections neared there in 1875, paramilitary groups such as the Red Shirts operated openly. Mississippi's Republican governor, Adelbert Ames, a Union veteran from Maine, appealed for U.S. troops, but Grant refused. "The whole public are tired out with these annual autumnal outbreaks in the South," complained a Grant official, who told southern Republicans that they were responsible for their own fate. Facing a rising tide of brutal murders, Governor Ames—realizing that only further bloodshed could result—urged his allies to give up the fight. Brandishing guns and stuffing ballot boxes, Democratic "Redeemers" swept the 1875 elections and took control of Mississippi. By 1876, Reconstruction was largely over. Republican governments, backed by token U.S. military units, remained in only three southern states: Louisiana, South Carolina, and Florida. Elsewhere, former Confederates and their allies took power.

**The Supreme Court Rejects Equal Rights**    Though ex-Confederates seized power in southern states, new landmark constitutional amendments and federal laws remained in force. If the Supreme Court had left these intact, subsequent generations of civil rights advocates could have used the federal courts to combat racial discrimination and violence. Instead, the Court closed off this avenue for the pursuit of justice, just as it dashed the hopes of women's rights advocates.

As early as 1873, in a group of decisions known collectively as the ***Slaughter-House Cases***, the Court began to undercut the power of the Fourteenth Amendment. In *Slaughter-House* and a related ruling, *U.S. v. Cruikshank* (1876), the justices argued that the Fourteenth Amendment offered only a few, rather trivial federal protections to citizens (such as access to navigable waterways). In *Cruikshank*—a case that emerged from a gruesome killing of African American farmers by ex-Confederates in Colfax, Louisiana, followed by a Democratic political coup—the Court ruled that voting rights remained a state matter unless the state itself violated those rights. If former slaves' rights were violated by individuals or private groups (including the Klan), that lay beyond federal jurisdiction. The Fourteenth Amendment did not protect citizens from armed vigilantes, even when those vigilantes seized political power. The Court thus gutted the Fourteenth Amendment. In the ***Civil Rights Cases*** (1883), the justices also struck down the Civil Rights Act of 1875, paving the way for later decisions that sanctioned segregation. The impact of these decisions endured well into the twentieth century.

## The Political Crisis of 1877

After the grim election results of 1874, Republicans faced a major battle in the presidential election of 1876. Abandoning Grant, they nominated Rutherford B. Hayes, a former Union general who was untainted by corruption and—even more important—hailed from the key swing state of Ohio. Hayes's Democratic opponent was New York governor Samuel J. Tilden, a Wall Street lawyer with a reform reputation. Tilden favored home rule for the South, but so, more discreetly, did Hayes. With enforcement on the wane, Reconstruction did not figure prominently in the campaign, and little was said about the states still led by Reconstruction governments: Florida, South Carolina, and Louisiana.

Once returns started coming in on election night, however, those states loomed large. Tilden led in the popular vote and seemed headed for victory until sleepless politicians at Republican headquarters realized that the electoral vote stood at 184 to 165, with the 20 votes from Florida, South Carolina, and Louisiana still uncertain. If Hayes took those votes, he would win by a margin of 1. Citing ample evidence of Democratic fraud and intimidation, Republican officials certified all three states for Hayes. "Redeemer" Democrats who had taken over the states' governments submitted their own electoral votes for Tilden. When Congress met in early 1877, it confronted two sets of electoral votes from those states.

The Constitution does not provide for such a contingency. All it says is that the president of the Senate (in 1877, a Republican) opens the electoral certificates before the House (Democratic) and the Senate (Republican) and "the Votes shall then be counted" (Article 2, Section 1). Suspense gripped the country. There was talk of inside deals or a new election—even a violent coup. Finally, Congress appointed an electoral commission to settle the question. The commission included seven Republicans, seven Democrats, and, as the deciding member, David Davis, a Supreme Court justice not known to have fixed party loyalties. Davis, however, disqualified himself by accepting an Illinois Senate seat. He was replaced by Republican justice Joseph P. Bradley, and by a vote of 8 to 7, on party lines, the commission awarded the election to Hayes.

In the House of Representatives, outraged Democrats vowed to stall the final count of electoral votes so as to prevent Hayes's inauguration on March 4. But in the end, they went along, partly because Tilden himself urged that they do so. Hayes had publicly indicated his desire to offer substantial patronage to the South, including federal funds for education and internal improvements. He promised "a complete change of men and policy," naively hoping he could count on support from old-line southern Whigs and protect black voting rights. Hayes was inaugurated on schedule. He expressed hope in his inaugural address that the federal government could serve "the interests of both races carefully and equally." But, setting aside the U.S. troops who were serving on border duty in Texas, only 3,000 Union soldiers remained in the South. As soon as the new president ordered them back to their barracks, the last Republican administrations in the South collapsed. Reconstruction had ended.

## Lasting Legacies

In the short run, the political events of 1877 had little impact on most southerners. Much of the work of "Redemption" had already been done. What mattered was the long, slow decline of Radical Republican power and the corresponding rise of Democrats in the South and nationally. It was obvious that so-called Redeemers in the South had assumed power through violence. But many Americans, including prominent classical liberals who shaped public opinion, believed the Democrats had overthrown corrupt, illegitimate governments. Thus the end justified the means. After 1874, those who deplored the results had little political traction. The only remaining question was how far Reconstruction would be rolled back.

The South never went back to the antebellum status quo. Sharecropping, for all its flaws and injustices, was not slavery. Freedmen and freedwomen managed to resist gang labor and work on their own terms. They also established their right to marry, read and write, worship as they pleased, and travel in search of a better life—rights that were not easily revoked. Across the South, black farmers overcame great odds to buy and work their own land. African American businessmen built thriving enterprises. Black churches and community groups sustained networks of mutual aid. Parents sacrificed to send their children to school, and a few proudly watched their sons and daughters graduate from college.

Reconstruction had also shaken, if not fully overturned, the legal and political framework that had made the United States a white man's country. This was a stunning achievement, and though hostile courts and political opponents undercut it, no one ever repealed the Thirteenth, Fourteenth, or Fifteenth Amendments. They remained in the Constitution, and the civil rights movement of the twentieth century would return and build on this framework (Chapter 26).

Still, in the final reckoning, Reconstruction failed. The majority of freedpeople remained in poverty, and by the late 1870s their political rights were also eroding. Vocal advocates of smaller government argued that Reconstruction had been a mistake; pressured by economic hardship, northern voters abandoned their southern

Unionist allies. One of the enduring legacies of this process was the way later Americans remembered Reconstruction itself. After "Redemption," generations of schoolchildren were taught that ignorant, lazy blacks and corrupt whites had imposed illegitimate Reconstruction "regimes" on the South. White southerners won national support for their celebration of a heroic Confederacy.

One of the first historians to challenge these views was the great African American intellectual W. E. B. Du Bois. In *Black Reconstruction in America* (1935), Du Bois meticulously documented the history of African American struggle, white vigilante violence, and national policy failure. If Reconstruction, he wrote, "had been conceived as a major national program . . . whose accomplishment at any price was well worth the effort, we should be living today in a different world." His words still ring true, but in 1935 historians ignored him. Not a single scholarly journal reviewed Du Bois's important book. Ex-Confederates had lost the war, but they won control over the nation's memory of Reconstruction.

Meanwhile, though their programs failed in the South, Republicans carried their nation-building project into the West, where their policies helped consolidate a continental empire. There, the federal power that had secured emancipation created the conditions for the United States to become an industrial power and a major leader on the world stage.

> **IN YOUR OWN WORDS**    Why and how did federal Reconstruction policies falter in the South?

## Summary

Postwar Republicans faced two tasks: restoring rebellious states to the Union and defining the role of emancipated slaves. After Lincoln's assassination, his successor, Andrew Johnson, hostile to Congress, unilaterally offered the South easy terms for reentering the Union. Exploiting this opportunity, southerners adopted oppressive Black Codes and put ex-Confederates back in power. Congress impeached Johnson and, though failing to convict him, seized the initiative and placed the South under military rule. In this second, or radical, phase of Reconstruction, Republican state governments tried to transform the South's economic and social institutions. Congress passed innovative civil rights acts and funded new agencies like the Freedmen's Bureau. The Fourteenth Amendment defined U.S. citizenship and asserted that states could no longer supersede it, and the Fifteenth Amendment gave voting rights to formerly enslaved men. Debate over this amendment precipitated a split among women's rights advocates, since women did not win inclusion.

Freedmen found that their goals conflicted with those of Republican leaders, who counted on cotton to fuel economic growth. Like southern landowners, national lawmakers envisioned former slaves as wageworkers, while freedmen wanted their own land. Sharecropping, which satisfied no one completely, emerged as a compromise suited to the needs of the cotton market and an impoverished, credit-starved region.

Nothing could reconcile ex-Confederates to Republican government, and they staged a violent counterrevolution in the name of white supremacy and "Redemption." Meanwhile, struck by a massive economic depression, northern voters handed

Republicans a crushing defeat in the election of 1874. By 1876, Reconstruction was dead. Rutherford B. Hayes's narrow victory in the presidential election of that year resulted in withdrawal of the last Union troops from the South. A series of Supreme Court decisions also undermined the Fourteenth Amendment and civil rights laws, setting up legal parameters through which, over the long term, disenfranchisement and segregation would flourish.

## Chapter 14 Review

### KEY TERMS

**Identify and explain the significance of each term below.**

Ten Percent Plan (p. 417)

Wade-Davis Bill (p. 417)

Black Codes (p. 418)

Freedmen's Bureau (p. 419)

Civil Rights Act of 1866 (p. 419)

Fourteenth Amendment (p. 419)

Reconstruction Act of 1867 (p. 419)

Fifteenth Amendment (p. 422)

American Woman Suffrage
    Association (p. 423)

National Woman Suffrage Association
    (p. 423)

*Minor v. Happersett* (p. 423)

Beecher-Tilton scandal (p. 423)

sharecropping (p. 426)

convict leasing (p. 431)

Civil Rights Act of 1875 (p. 433)

classical liberalism (p. 435)

Crédit Mobilier (p. 435)

Ku Klux Klan (p. 436)

Enforcement Laws (p. 437)

*Slaughter-House Cases* (p. 438)

*Civil Rights Cases* (p. 438)

### REVIEW QUESTIONS

**Answer these questions to demonstrate your understanding of the chapter's main ideas.**

1. What factors explain how Reconstruction policies unfolded between 1865 and 1870, and what was the impact on different groups of Americans?

2. What goals were southern freedmen and freedwomen able to achieve in the post–Civil War years, and why? What goals were they not able to achieve, and why not?

3. Why and how did federal Reconstruction policies falter in the South?

4. Look again at the events listed under "American and National Identity" on the thematic timeline on page 352. Some historians have argued that, during this era, the United States moved, politically and socially, from being a loose union of states to being a more unified and inclusive *nation*. To what extent do you agree? Use the events of Reconstruction as evidence in making your case.

## CHRONOLOGY

As you read, ask yourself why this chapter begins and ends with these dates and try to identify the links among related events.

| | |
|---|---|
| **1864** | • Wade-Davis Bill passed by Congress but killed by Lincoln's pocket veto |
| **1865** | • Freedmen's Bureau established |
| | • Lincoln assassinated; Andrew Johnson succeeds him as president |
| | • Johnson implements restoration plan |
| | • Ex-Confederate states pass Black Codes to limit freedpeople's rights |
| **1866** | • Civil Rights Act passes over Johnson's veto |
| | • Major Republican gains in congressional elections |
| **1867** | • Reconstruction Act |
| **1868** | • Impeachment of Andrew Johnson |
| | • Fourteenth Amendment ratified |
| | • Ulysses S. Grant elected president |
| **1870** | • Ku Klux Klan at peak of power |
| | • Congress passes Enforcement Laws to suppress Klan |
| | • Fifteenth Amendment ratified |
| | • Victoria Woodhull declares her support for "free love" |
| **1872** | • Grant reelected; Crédit Mobilier scandal emerges |
| **1873** | • Panic of 1873 ushers in severe economic depression |
| | • Supreme Court severely curtails Reconstruction in *Slaughter-House Cases* |
| **1874** | • Sweeping Democratic gains in congressional elections |
| **1875** | • Whiskey Ring and other scandals undermine Grant administration |
| | • *Minor v. Happersett*: Supreme Court rules that Fourteenth Amendment does not extend voting rights to women |
| | • Beecher-Tilton scandal dominates headlines |
| **1877** | • Rutherford B. Hayes becomes president |
| | • Federal Reconstruction ends |

# 15

# Conquering a Continent

## 1860–1890

### IDENTIFY THE BIG IDEA

How did U.S. policymakers seek to stimulate the economy and integrate the trans-Mississippi west into the nation, and how did this affect people living there?

**ON MAY 10, 1869, AMERICANS POURED INTO THE STREETS FOR A GIANT** party. In big cities, the racket was incredible. Cannons boomed and train whistles shrilled. New York fired a hundred-gun salute at City Hall. Congregations sang anthems, while the less religious gathered in saloons to celebrate with whiskey. Philadelphia's joyful throngs reminded an observer of the day, four years earlier, when news had arrived of Lee's surrender. The festivities were prompted by a long-awaited telegraph message: executives of the Union Pacific and Central Pacific railroads had driven a golden spike at Promontory Point, Utah, linking up their lines. Unbroken track now stretched from the Atlantic to the Pacific. A journey across North America could be made in less than a week.

The first **transcontinental railroad** meant jobs and money. San Francisco residents got right to business: after firing a salute, they loaded Japanese tea on a train bound for St. Louis, marking California's first overland delivery to the East. In coming decades, trade and tourism fueled tremendous growth west of the Mississippi. San Francisco, which in 1860 had handled $7.4 million in imports, increased that figure to $49 million over thirty years. The new railroad would, as one speaker predicted in 1869, "populate our vast territory" and make America "the highway of nations."

The railroad was also a political triumph. Victorious in the Civil War, Republicans saw themselves as heirs to the American System envisioned by antebellum Whigs. They believed government intervention in the economy was the key to nation building. But unlike Whigs, whose plans had met stiff Democratic opposition, Republicans enjoyed a decade of unparalleled federal power. They used it vigorously: U.S. government spending per person, after skyrocketing in the Civil War, remained well above earlier levels. Republicans believed that national economic integration was the best guarantor of lasting peace. As a New York minister declared, the federally supported transcontinental railroad would "preserve the Union."

The minister was wrong on one point. He claimed the railroad was a peaceful achievement, in contrast to military battles that had brought "devastation, misery, and woe." In fact, creating a continental empire caused plenty of woe. Regions west of the Mississippi could only be incorporated if the United States subdued Native peoples and established favorable conditions for international investors—often at great domestic cost. And while conquering the West helped make the United States into an industrial power, it also deepened America's rivalry with European empires and created new patterns of exploitation.

# The Republican Vision

Reshaping the former Confederacy was only part of Republicans' plan for a reconstructed nation. They remembered the era after Andrew Jackson's destruction of the Second National Bank as one of economic chaos, when the United States had become vulnerable to international creditors and market fluctuations. Land speculation on the frontier had provoked extreme cycles of boom and bust. Failure to fund a transcontinental railroad had left different regions of the country disconnected. This, Republicans believed, had helped trigger the Civil War, and they were determined to set a new direction.

Even while the war raged, Congress made vigorous use of federal power, launching the transcontinental rail project and a new national banking system. Congress also raised the **protective tariff** on a range of manufactured goods, from textiles to steel, and on some agricultural products, like wool and sugar. At federal customhouses in each port, foreign manufacturers who brought merchandise into the United States had to pay import fees. These tariff revenues gave U.S. manufacturers, who did not pay the fees, a competitive advantage in America's vast domestic market.

The economic depression that began in 1873 set limits on Republicans' economic ambitions, just as it hindered their Reconstruction plans in the South. But their policies continued to shape the economy. Though some historians argue that the late nineteenth century was an era of *laissez faire* or unrestrained capitalism, in which government sat passively by, the industrial United States was actually the product of a massive public-private partnership in which government played critical roles.

## The New Union and the World

The United States emerged from the Civil War with new leverage in its negotiation with European countries, especially Great Britain, whose navy dominated the seas. Britain, which had allowed Confederate raiding ships such as the CSS *Alabama* to be built in its shipyards, submitted afterward to arbitration and paid the United States $15.5 million in damages. Flush with victory, many Americans expected more British and Spanish territories to drop into the Union's lap. Senator Charles Sumner proposed, in fact, that Britain settle the *Alabama* claims by handing over Canada.

Such dreams were a logical extension of pre–Civil War conquests, especially in the U.S.-Mexico War. With the coasts now linked by rail, merchants and manufacturers looked across the Pacific, hungry for trade with Asia.

Union victory also increased U.S. economic influence in Latin America. While the United States was preoccupied with its internal war, France had deposed Mexico's government and installed an emperor. On May 5, 1867, Mexico overthrew the French invaders and executed Emperor Maximilian. But while Mexico regained independence, it lay open to the economic designs of its increasingly powerful northern neighbor.

A new model emerged for asserting U.S. power in Latin America and Asia: not by direct conquest, but through trade. The architect of this vision was William Seward, secretary of state from 1861 to 1869 under presidents Abraham Lincoln and Andrew Johnson. A New Yorker of grand ambition and ego, Seward believed, like many contemporaries, that Asia would become "the chief theatre of [world] events" and that commerce there was key to America's prosperity. He urged the Senate to purchase sites in both the Pacific and the Caribbean for naval bases and refueling stations. When Japan changed policy and tried to close its ports to foreigners, Seward dispatched U.S. naval vessels to join those of Britain, France, and the Netherlands in reopening trade by force. At the same time, Seward urged annexation of Hawaii. He also predicted that the United States would one day claim the Philippines and build a Panama canal.

Seward's short-term achievements were modest. Exhausted by civil war, Americans had little enthusiasm for further military exploits. Seward achieved only two significant victories. In 1868, he secured congressional approval for the **Burlingame Treaty** with China, which guaranteed the rights of U.S. missionaries in China and set official terms for the emigration of Chinese laborers, some of whom were already clearing farmland and building railroads in the West. That same year, Seward negotiated the purchase of Alaska from Russia. After the Senate approved the deal, Seward waxed poetic:

> Our nation with united interests blest
> Not now content to poise, shall sway the rest;
> Abroad our empire shall no limits know,
> But like the sea in endless circles flow.

Many Americans scoffed at the purchase of Alaska, a frigid arctic tract that skeptics nicknamed "Seward's Icebox." But the secretary of state mapped out a path his Republican successors would follow thirty years later in an aggressive bid for global power.

## Integrating the National Economy

Closer to home, Republicans focused on transportation infrastructure. Railroad development in the United States began well before the Civil War, with the first locomotives arriving from Britain in the early 1830s. Unlike canals or roads, railroads offered the promise of year-round, all-weather service. Locomotives could run in the dark and never needed to rest, except to take on coal and water. Steam engines crossed high mountains and rocky gorges where pack animals could find no fodder and canals could never reach. West of the Mississippi, railroads opened vast regions for farming, trade, and tourism. A transcontinental railroad executive was only half-joking when he said, "The West is purely a railroad enterprise."

Governments could choose to build and operate railroads themselves or promote construction by private companies. Unlike most European countries, the United States chose the private approach. The federal government, however, provided essential loans, subsidies, and grants of public land. States and localities also lured railroads with offers of financial aid, mainly by buying railroad bonds. Without this aid, rail networks would have grown much more slowly and would probably have concentrated in urban regions. With it, railroads enjoyed an enormous — and reckless — boom. By 1900, virtually no corner of the country lacked rail service (Map 15.1). At the same time, U.S. railroads built across the border into Mexico.

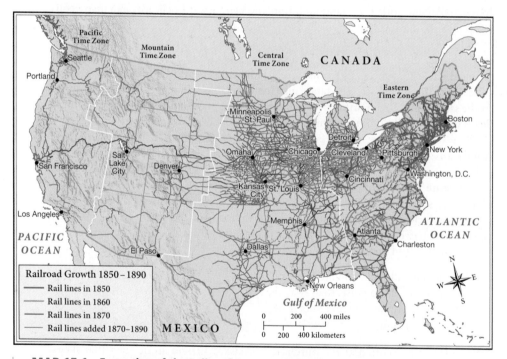

**MAP 15.1   Expansion of the Railroad System, 1850–1890**
In 1850, the United States had 9,000 miles of rail track; by 1890, it had 167,000 miles, including transcontinental lines terminating in San Francisco, Los Angeles, and Seattle. The tremendous burst of construction during the last twenty years of that period essentially completed the nation's rail network, although there would be additional expansion for the next two decades. The main areas of growth were in the South and in lands west of the Mississippi. Time zones — an innovation introduced not by government entities, but by railroad corporations in 1883 — are marked by the white lines.

Railroad companies transformed American capitalism. They adopted a legal form of organization, the corporation, that enabled them to raise private capital in prodigious amounts. In earlier decades, state legislatures had chartered corporations for specific public purposes, binding these creations to government goals and oversight. But over the course of the nineteenth century, legislatures gradually began to allow any business to become a corporation by simply applying for a state charter. Among the first corporations to become large interstate enterprises, private railroads were much freer than earlier companies to do as they pleased. After the Civil War, they received lavish public aid with few strings attached. Their position was like that of American banks in late 2008 after the big federal bailout: even critics acknowledged that public aid to these giant companies was good for the economy, but they observed that it also lent government support to fabulous accumulations of private wealth.

**Tariffs and Economic Growth**    Along with the transformative power of railroads, Republicans' protective tariffs helped build other U.S. industries, including textiles and steel in the Northeast and Midwest and, through tariffs on imported sugar and wool, sugar beet farming and sheep ranching in the West. Tariffs also funded government itself. In an era when the United States did not levy income taxes, tariffs provided the bulk of treasury revenue. The Civil War had left the Union with a staggering debt of $2.8 billion. Tariff income erased that debt and by the 1880s generated huge budget *surpluses*—a circumstance hard to imagine today.

As Reconstruction faltered, tariffs came under political fire. Democrats argued that tariffs taxed American consumers by denying them access to low-cost imported goods and forcing them to pay subsidies to U.S. manufacturers. Republicans claimed, conversely, that tariffs benefitted workers because they created jobs, blocked

**Building the Central Pacific Railroad**  In 1865, Chinese workers had labored to build the 1,100-foot-long, 90-foot-high trestle over the divide between the American and Bear rivers at Secret Town in the Sierra Nevada Mountains. In 1877, the Chinese workers shown in this photograph by Carleton Watkins were again at work on the site, burying the trestle to avoid replacement of the aging timbers, which had become a fire hazard. Copyright © Phoebe A. Hearst Museum of Anthropology and the Regents of the University of California, Photography by unknown (Catalog No. 13-1304ee).

low-wage foreign competition, and safeguarded America from the kind of indus-trial poverty that had arisen in Europe. According to this argument, tariffs helped American men earn enough to support their families; wives could devote themselves to homemaking, and children could go to school, not the factory. For protectionist Republicans, high tariffs were akin to the abolition of slavery: they protected and uplifted the most vulnerable workers.

In these fierce debates, both sides were partly right. Protective tariffs did play a powerful role in economic growth. They helped transform the United States into a global industrial power. Eventually, though, even protectionist Republicans had to admit that Democrats had a point: tariffs had not prevented industrial poverty in the United States. Corporations accumulated massive benefits from tariffs but failed to pass them along to workers, who often toiled long hours for low wages. Furthermore, tariffs helped foster trusts, corporations that dominated whole sectors of the econ-omy and wielded near-monopoly power. The rise of large private corporations and trusts generated enduring political problems.

**The Role of Courts**   While fostering growth, most historians agree, Republicans did not give government enough regulatory power over the new corporations. State legislatures did pass hundreds of regulatory laws after the Civil War, but inter-state companies challenged them in federal courts. In ***Munn v. Illinois*** (1877), the Supreme Court affirmed that states could regulate key businesses, such as railroads and grain elevators, that were "clothed in the public interest." However, the justices feared that too many state and local regulations would impede business and fragment the national marketplace. Starting in the 1870s, they interpreted the "due process" clause of the new Fourteenth Amendment — which dictated that no state could "deprive any person of life, liberty, or property, without due process of law" — as shielding corporations from excessive regulation. Ironically, the Court refused to use the same amendment to protect the rights of African Americans.

In the Southwest as well, federal courts promoted economic development at the expense of racial justice. Though the United States had taken control of New Mexico and Arizona after the U.S.-Mexico War, much land remained afterward in the hands of Mexican farmers and ranchers. Many lived as *peónes*, under long-standing agree-ments with landowners who held large tracts originally granted by the Spanish crown. The post–Civil War years brought railroads and an influx of land-hungry Anglos. New Mexico's governor reported indignantly that Mexican shepherds were often "asked" to leave their ranges "by a cowboy or cattle herder with a brace of pis-tols at his belt and a Winchester in his hands."

Existing land claims were so complex that Congress eventually set up a special court to rule on land titles. Between 1891 and 1904, the court invalidated most traditional claims, including those of many New Mexico *ejidos*, or villages owned collectively by their communities. Mexican Americans lost about 64 percent of the contested lands. In addition, much land was sold or appropriated through legal machinations like those of a notorious cabal of politicians and lawyers known as the Santa Fe Ring. The result was displacement of thousands of Mexican American villagers and farmers. Some found work as railroad builders or mine workers; others, moving into the sparse high country of the Sierras and Rockies where cattle could not survive, developed sheep raising into a major enterprise.

**Silver and Gold**   In an era of nation building, U.S. and European policymakers sought new ways to rationalize markets. Industrializing nations, for example, tried to develop an international system of standard measurements and even a unified currency. Though these proposals failed as each nation succumbed to self-interest, governments did increasingly agree that, for "scientific" reasons, money should be based on gold, which was thought to have an intrinsic worth above other metals. Great Britain had long held to the **gold standard**, meaning that paper notes from the Bank of England could be backed by gold held in the bank's vaults. During the 1870s and 1880s, the United States, Germany, France, and other countries also converted to gold.

Beforehand, these nations had been on a bimetallic standard: they issued both gold and silver coins, with respective weights fixed at a relative value. The United States switched to the gold standard in part because treasury officials and financiers were watching developments out west. Geologists accurately predicted the discovery of immense silver deposits, such as Nevada's Comstock Lode, without comparable new gold strikes. A massive influx of silver would clearly upset the long-standing ratio. Thus, with a law that became infamous to later critics as the **"Crime of 1873,"** Congress chose gold. It directed the U.S. Treasury to cease minting silver dollars and, over a six-year period, retire Civil War–era greenbacks (paper dollars) and replace them with notes from an expanded system of national banks. After this process was complete in 1879, the treasury exchanged these notes for gold on request. (Advocates of bimetallism did achieve one small victory: the Bland-Allison Act of 1878 required the U.S. Mint to coin a modest amount of silver.)

By adopting the gold standard, Republican policymakers sharply limited the nation's money supply, to the level of available gold. The amount of money circulating in the United States had been $30.35 per person in 1865; by 1880, it fell to only $19.36 per person. Today, few economists would sanction such a plan, especially for an economy growing at breakneck speed. They would recommend, instead, increasing money supplies to keep pace with development. But at the time, policymakers remembered rampant antebellum speculation and the hardships of inflation during the Civil War. The United States, as a developing country, also needed to attract investment capital from Britain, Belgium, and other European nations that were on the gold standard. Making it easy to exchange U.S. bonds and currency for gold encouraged European investors to send their money to the United States.

Republican policies fostered exuberant growth and a breathtakingly rapid integration of the economy. Railroads and telegraphs tied the nation together. U.S. manufacturers amassed staggering amounts of capital and built corporations of national and even global scope. With its immense, integrated marketplace of workers, consumers, raw materials, and finished products, the United States was poised to become a mighty industrial power.

| **IN YOUR OWN WORDS** | What federal policies contributed to the rise of America's industrial economy, and what were their results? |

# Incorporating the West

Republicans wanted farms as well as factories. As early as 1860, popular lyrics hailed the advent of "Uncle Sam's Farm":

> A welcome, warm and hearty, do we give the sons of toil,
> To come west and settle and labor on Free Soil;
> We've room enough and land enough, they needn't feel alarmed—
> Oh! Come to the land of Freedom and vote yourself a farm.

The **Homestead Act** (1862) gave 160 acres of federal land to any applicant who occupied and improved the property. Republicans hoped the bill would help build up the interior West, which was inhabited by Indian peoples but remained "empty" on U.S. government survey maps.

Implementing this plan required innovative policies. The same year it passed the Homestead Act, Congress also created the federal Department of Agriculture and, through the Morrill Act, set aside 140 million federal acres that states could sell to raise money for public universities. The goal of these **land-grant colleges** was to broaden educational opportunities and foster technical and scientific expertise. After the Civil War, Congress also funded a series of geological surveys, dispatching U.S. Army officers, scientists, and photographers to chart unknown western terrain and catalog resources.

To a large extent, these policies succeeded in incorporating lands west of the Mississippi. The United States began to exploit its western empire for minerals, lumber, and other raw materials. But for ordinary Americans who went west, dreams often outran reality. Well-financed corporations, not individual prospectors, reaped most of the profits from western mines, while the Great Plains environment proved resistant to ranching and farming.

## Mining Empires

In the late 1850s, as easy pickings in the California gold rush diminished, prospectors scattered in hopes of finding riches elsewhere. They found gold at many sites, including Nevada, the Colorado Rockies, and South Dakota's Black Hills (Map 15.2). As news of each strike spread, remote areas turned overnight into mob scenes of prospectors, traders, prostitutes, and saloon keepers. At community meetings, white prospectors made their own laws, often using them as an instrument for excluding Mexicans, Chinese, and blacks.

The silver from Nevada's **Comstock Lode**, discovered in 1859, built the boomtown of Virginia City, which soon acquired fancy hotels, a Shakespearean theater, and even its own stock exchange. In 1870, a hundred saloons operated in Virginia City, brothels lined D Street, and men outnumbered women 2 to 1. In the 1880s, however, as the Comstock ore gave out, Virginia City suffered the fate of many mining camps: it became a ghost town. What remained was a ravaged landscape with mountains of debris, poisoned water sources, and surrounding lands stripped of timber.

In hopes of encouraging development of western resources, Congress passed the General Mining Act of 1872, which allowed those who discovered

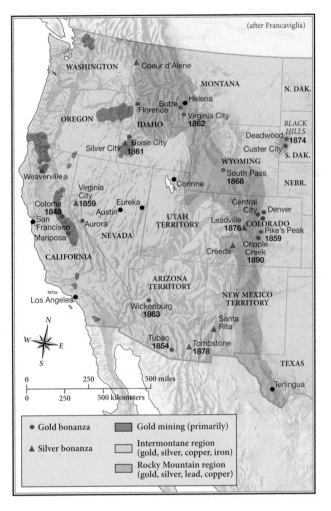

**MAP 15.2  Mining Frontiers, 1848–1890**
The Far West was America's gold country because of its geological history. Veins of gold and silver form when molten material from the earth's core is forced up into fissures caused by the tectonic movements that create mountain ranges, such as the ones that dominate the far western landscape. It was these veins, the product of mountain-forming activity many thousands of years earlier, that prospectors began to discover after 1848 and furiously exploit. Although widely dispersed across the Far West, the lodes that they found followed the mountain ranges bisecting the region and bypassing the great plateaus not shaped by the ancient tectonic activity.

minerals on federally owned land to work the claim and keep all the proceeds. (The law—including the $5-per-acre fee for filing a claim—remains in force today.) Americans idealized the notion of the lone, hardy mining prospector with his pan and his mule, but digging into deep veins of underground ore required big money. Consortiums of powerful investors, bringing engineers and advanced equipment, generally extracted the most wealth. This was the case for the New York trading firm Phelps Dodge, which invested in massive copper mines and smelting operations on both sides of the U.S.-Mexico border. The mines created jobs in new towns like Bisbee and Morenci, Arizona—but with dangerous conditions and low pay, especially for those who received the segregated "Mexican wage." Anglos, testified one Mexican mine worker, "occupied decorous residences . . . and had large amounts of money," while "the Mexican population and its economic condition offered a pathetic contrast." He protested this affront to "the most elemental principles of justice."

The rise of western mining created an insatiable market for timber and produce from the Pacific Northwest. Seattle and Portland grew rapidly as supply centers, especially during the great gold rushes of California (after 1848) and the Klondike in Canada's Yukon Territory (after 1897). Residents of Tacoma, Washington, claimed theirs was the "City of Destiny" when it became the Pacific terminus for the Northern Pacific, the nation's third transcontinental railroad, in 1887. But rival businessmen in Seattle succeeded in promoting their city as the gateway to Alaska and the Klondike. Seattle, a town with 1,000 residents in 1870, grew over the next forty years to a population of a quarter million.

## Cattlemen on the Plains

While boomtowns arose across the West, hunters began transforming the plains. As late as the Civil War years, great herds of bison still roamed this region. But overhunting and the introduction of European animal afflictions, like the bacterial disease brucellosis, were already decimating the herds. In the 1870s, hide hunters finished them off so thoroughly that at one point fewer than two hundred bison remained in U.S. territory. Hunters hidden downwind, under the right conditions, could kill four dozen at a time without moving from the spot. They took hides but left the meat to rot, an act of vast wastefulness that shocked Native peoples.

Removal of the bison opened opportunities for cattle ranchers. South Texas provided an early model for their ambitious plans. By the end of the Civil War, about five million head of longhorn cattle grazed on Anglo ranches there. In 1865, the Missouri Pacific Railroad reached Sedalia, Missouri, far enough west to be accessible as Texas reentered the Union. A longhorn worth $3 in Texas might command $40 at Sedalia. With this incentive, ranchers inaugurated the Long Drive, hiring cowboys to herd cattle hundreds of miles north to the new rail lines, which soon extended into Kansas. At Abilene and Dodge City, Kansas, ranchers sold their longhorns and trail-weary cowboys crowded into saloons. These cow towns captured the nation's imagination as symbols of the Wild West, but the reality was much less exciting. Cowboys, many of them African Americans and Latinos, were really farmhands on horseback who worked long, harsh hours for low pay.

North of Texas, public grazing lands drew investors and adventurers eager for a taste of the West. By the early 1880s, as many as 7.5 million cattle were overgrazing the plains' native grasses. A cycle of good weather postponed disaster, which arrived in 1886: record blizzards and bitter cold. An awful scene of rotting carcasses greeted cowboys as they rode onto the range that spring. Further hit by a severe drought the following summer, the cattle boom collapsed.

Thanks to new strategies, however, cattle ranching survived and became part of the integrated national economy. As railroads reached Texas and ranchers there abandoned the Long Drive, the invention of barbed wire—which enabled ranchers and farmers to fence large areas cheaply and easily on the plains, where wood was scarce and expensive—made it easier for northern cattlemen to fence small areas and feed animals on hay. Stockyards appeared beside the rapidly extending railroad tracks, and trains took these gathered cattle to giant slaughterhouses in cities like Chicago, which turned them into cheap beef for customers back east.

**Cowboys, Real and Mythic** As early as the 1860s, popular dime novels such as this one (right) celebrated the alleged ruggedness, individual freedoms, and gun-slinging capabilities of western cowboys. (Note that this 1888 story, like most dime novels, was published in New York.) Generations of young Americans grew up on stories of frontier valor and "Cowboys versus Indians." In fact, cowboys like the ones depicted in the photograph were really wageworkers on horseback. An ethnically diverse group, including many blacks and Hispanics, they earned perhaps $25 a month, plus meals and a bed in the bunkhouse, in return for long hours of grueling, lonesome work. Left: Getty Images. Right: Denver Public Library, Western History Collection/Bridgeman Images.

## Homesteaders

Republicans envisioned the Great Plains dotted with small farms, but farmers had to be persuaded that crops would grow there. Powerful interests worked hard to overcome the popular idea that the grassland was the Great American Desert. Railroads, eager to sell land the government had granted them, advertised aggressively. Land speculators, transatlantic steamship lines, and western states and territories joined the campaign.

Newcomers found the soil beneath the native prairie grasses deep and fertile. Steel plows enabled them to break through the tough roots, while barbed wire provided cheap, effective fencing against roaming cattle. European immigrants brought strains of hard-kernel wheat that tolerated the extreme temperatures of the plains. As if to confirm promoters' optimism, a wet cycle occurred between 1878 and 1886, increasing rainfall in the arid regions east of the Rockies. Americans decided that **"rain follows the plow"**: settlement and farming of the plains was increasing rainfall. Some attributed the rain to soil cultivation and tree planting, while others credited God. One Harvard professor proposed that steel railroad tracks attracted moisture. Such optimists would soon learn their mistake.

The motivation for most settlers, American or immigrant, was to better themselves economically. Union veterans, who received favorable terms in staking homestead claims, played a major role in settling Kansas and other plains states. When severe depression hit northern Europe in the 1870s, Norwegians and Swedes joined German emigrants in large numbers. At the peak of "American fever" in 1882, more than 105,000 Scandinavians left for the United States. Swedish and Norwegian became the primary languages in parts of Minnesota and the Dakotas.

For some African Americans, the plains represented a promised land of freedom. In 1879, a group of black communities left Mississippi and Louisiana in a quest to escape poverty and white violence. Some 6,000 blacks departed together, most carrying little but the clothes on their backs and faith in God. They called themselves **Exodusters**, participants in a great exodus to Kansas. The 1880 census reported 40,000 blacks there, by far the largest African American concentration in the West aside from Texas, where the expanding cotton frontier attracted hundreds of thousands of black migrants.

For newcomers, taming the plains differed from pioneering in antebellum Iowa or Oregon. Dealers sold big new machines to help with plowing and harvesting. Western wheat traveled by rail to giant grain elevators and traded immediately on world markets. Hoping frontier land values would appreciate rapidly, many farmers planned to profit from selling acres as much as (or more than) from their crops. In boom times, many rushed into debt to acquire more land and better equipment. All these enthusiasms—for cash crops, land speculation, borrowed money, and new technology—bore witness to the conviction that farming was, as one agricultural journal remarked, a business "like all other business."

**Women in the West**    Early miners, lumbermen, and cowboys were overwhelmingly male, but homesteading was a family affair. The success of a farm depended on the work of wives and children who tended the garden and animals, preserved food, and helped out at harvest time. Some women struck out on their own: a study of North Dakota found between 5 and 20 percent of homestead claims filed by single women, often working land adjacent to that of sisters, brothers, and parents. Family members thus supported one another in the difficult work of farming, while easing the loneliness many newcomers felt. Looking back with pride on her homesteading days, one Dakota woman said simply, "It was a place to stay and it was mine."

While promoting farms in the West, Republicans clashed with the distinctive religious group that had already settled Utah: Mormons, or members of the Church of Jesus Christ of Latter-day Saints (LDS). After suffering persecution in Missouri and Illinois, Mormons had moved west to Utah in the 1840s, attracting many working-class converts from England as well. Most Americans at the time were deeply hostile to Mormonism, especially the LDS practice of plural marriage—sanctioned by church founder Joseph Smith—through which some Mormon men married more than one wife.

Mormons had their own complex view of women's role, illustrated by the career of Mormon leader Emmeline Wells. Born Emmeline Woodward in New Hampshire, Wells converted to Mormonism at age thirteen along with her mother and joined the exodus to Utah in 1848. After her first husband abandoned her when he left the church, Wells became the seventh wife of church elder Daniel Wells. In 1870, due in part to organized pressure from Wells and other Mormon women, the Utah legislature granted full voting rights to women, becoming the second U.S. territory to do so (after Wyoming, in 1869). The measure increased LDS control, since most Utah women were Mormons, while non-Mormons in mining camps were predominantly male. It also recognized the central role of women in Mormon life.

Amid the constitutional debates of Reconstruction, polygamy and women's voting rights became intertwined issues. Encouraged by other plural wives, Wells began in 1877 to write for a Salt Lake City newspaper, the *Woman's Exponent*. She served as editor for forty years and led local women's rights groups. At first, Utah's legislature blocked Wells's candidacy in a local election, based on her sex. But when Utah won statehood in 1896, Wells had the pleasure of watching several women win seats in the new legislature, including Dr. Martha Hughes Cannon, a physician and Mormon plural wife who became the first American woman to serve in a state senate. Like their counterparts in other western states, Utah's women experienced a combination of severe frontier hardships and striking new opportunities.

**Environmental Challenges**   Homesteaders faced a host of challenges, particularly the natural environment of the Great Plains. Clouds of grasshoppers could descend and destroy a crop in a day; a prairie fire or hailstorm could do the job in an hour. In spring, homesteaders faced sudden, terrifying tornados, while their winter experiences in the 1870s added the word *blizzard* to America's vocabulary. On the plains, also, water and lumber were hard to find. Newly arrived families often cut dugouts into hillsides and then, after a season or two, erected houses made of turf cut from the ground.

Over the long term, homesteaders discovered that the western grasslands did not receive enough rain to grow wheat and other grains. As the cycle of rainfall shifted from wet to dry, farmers as well as ranchers suffered. "A wind hot as an oven's fury . . . raged like a pestilence," reported one Nebraskan, leaving "farmers helpless, with no weapon against this terrible and inscrutable wrath of nature." By the late 1880s, some recently settled lands emptied as homesteaders fled in defeat—50,000 from the Dakotas alone. It became obvious that farming in the arid West required methods other than those used east of the Mississippi.

Clearly, 160-acre homesteads were the wrong size for the West: farmers needed either small irrigated plots or immense tracts for dry farming, which involved deep planting to bring subsoil moisture to the roots and quick harrowing after rainfalls to slow evaporation. Dry farming developed most fully on huge corporate farms in the Red River Valley of North Dakota. But even family farms, the norm elsewhere, could not survive on less than 300 acres of grain. Crop prices were too low, and the climate too unpredictable, to allow farmers to get by on less.

In this struggle, settlers regarded themselves as nature's conquerors, striving, as one pioneer remarked, "to get the land subdued and the wilde nature out of it." Much about its "wilde nature" was hidden to the newcomers. They did not know that destroying biodiversity, which was what farming the plains really meant, opened pathways for exotic, destructive pests and weeds, and that removing native grasses left the soil vulnerable to erosion. By the turn of the twentieth century, about half the nation's cattle and sheep, one-third of its cereal crops, and nearly three-fifths of its wheat came from the Great Plains. But in the drier parts of the region, it was not a sustainable achievement. This renowned breadbasket was later revealed to be, in the words of one historian, "the largest, longest-run agricultural and environmental miscalculation in American history."

John Wesley Powell, a one-armed Union veteran, predicted the catastrophe from an early date. Powell, employed by the new U.S. Geological Survey, led a famous expedition in the West in which his team navigated the rapids of the Colorado River through the Grand Canyon in wooden boats. In his *Report on the Lands of the Arid Region of the United States* (1879), Powell told Congress bluntly that 160-acre homesteads would not work in dry regions. Impressed with the success of Mormon irrigation projects in Utah, Powell urged the United States to follow their model. He proposed that the government develop the West's water resources, building dams and canals and organizing landowners into local districts to operate them. Doubting that rugged individualism would succeed in the West, Powell proposed massive cooperation under government control.

After heated debate, Congress rejected Powell's plan. Critics accused him of playing into the hands of large ranching corporations; boosters were not yet willing to give up the dream of small homesteads. But Powell turned out to be right. Though environmental historians do not always agree with Powell's proposed solutions, they point to his *Report on Arid Lands* as a cogent critique of what went wrong on the Great Plains. Later, federal funding paid for dams and canals that supported intensive agriculture in many parts of the West.

## The First National Park

Powell was not the only one rethinking land use. The West's incorporation into the national marketplace occurred with such speed that some Americans began to fear rampant overdevelopment. Perhaps the federal government should not sell off all its public land, but instead hold and manage some of it. Amid the heady initiatives of Reconstruction, Congress began to preserve sites of unusual natural splendor. As early as 1864, Congress gave 10 square miles of the Yosemite Valley to California for "public use, resort, and recreation." (In 1890, Yosemite reverted to federal control.) In 1872, Congress set aside 2 million acres of Wyoming's Yellowstone Valley as the world's first national park: preserved as a public holding, it would serve as "a public park or pleasuring ground for the benefit and enjoyment of the people."

Railroad tourism, which developed side by side with other western industries, was an important motive for the creation of **Yellowstone National Park**. The Northern Pacific Railroad lobbied Congress vigorously to get the park established. Soon, luxury Pullman cars ushered visitors to Yellowstone's hotel, operated by the railroad itself. But creation of the park was fraught with complications. Since no one knew exactly what a "national park" was or how to operate it, the U.S. Army was dispatched to take charge; only in the early 1900s, when Congress established many more parks in the West, did consistent management policies emerge. In the meantime, soldiers spent much of their time arresting Native peoples who sought to hunt on Yellowstone lands.

The creation of Yellowstone was an important step toward an ethic of respect for land and wildlife. So was the 1871 creation of a **U.S. Fisheries Commission**, which made recommendations to stem the decline in wild fish; by the 1930s, it merged with other federal wildlife bureaus to become the U.S. Fish and Wildlife Service. At the same time, eviction of Indians showed that defining small preserves of "uninhabited wilderness" was part of conquest itself. In 1877, for example, the federal government forcibly removed the Nez Perce tribe from their ancestral land in what is now Idaho, Washington, and Oregon. Under the leadership of young Chief Joseph, the Nez Perce tried to flee to Canada. After a journey of 1,100 miles, they were forced to surrender just short of the border. During their trek, five bands crossed Yellowstone; as a Nez Perce named Yellow Wolf recalled, they "knew that country well." For thirteen days, Nez Perce men raided the valley for supplies, waylaying several groups of tourists. The conflict made national headlines. Easterners, proud of their new "pleasuring ground," were startled to find that it remained a site of Native resistance. Americans were not settling an empty West. They were *un*settling it by taking it from Native peoples who already lived there.

| IN YOUR OWN WORDS | What factors led to transformation of the trans-Mississippi west after the Civil War? |
|---|---|

# A Harvest of Blood: Native Peoples Dispossessed

Before the Civil War, when most Americans believed the prairie could not be farmed, Congress reserved the Great Plains for Indian peoples. But in the era of steel plows and railroads, policymakers suddenly had the power and desire to incorporate the whole region. The U.S. Army fought against the loosely federated Sioux—the major power on the northern grasslands—as well as other peoples who had agreed to live on reservations but found conditions so desperate that they fled (Map 15.3). These "reservation wars," caused largely by local violence and confused federal policies, were messy and bitter. Pointing to failed military campaigns, army atrocities, and egregious corruption in the Indian Bureau, reformers called for new policies that would destroy Native peoples' traditional lifeways and "civilize" them—or, as one reformer put it, "kill the Indian and save the man."

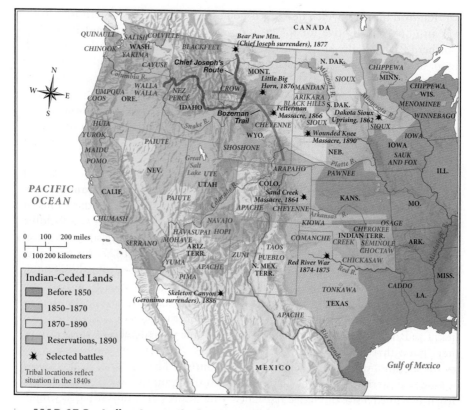

**MAP 15.3   Indian Country in the West, to 1890**

As settlement pushed onto the Great Plains after the Civil War, Native peoples put up bitter resistance but ultimately to no avail. Over a period of decades, they ceded most of their lands to the federal government, and by 1890 they were confined to scattered reservations.

## The Civil War and Indians on the Plains

In August 1862, the attention of most Unionists and Confederates was riveted on General George McClellan's failing campaign in Virginia. But in Minnesota, the Dakota Sioux were increasingly frustrated. In 1858, the year Minnesota secured statehood, they had agreed to settle on a strip of land reserved by the government, in exchange for receiving regular payments and supplies. But Indian agents, contractors, and even Minnesota's territorial governor pocketed most of the funds. When the Dakotas protested that their children were starving, state officials dismissed their appeals. Corruption was so egregious that one leading Minnesotan, Episcopal bishop Henry Whipple, wrote an urgent appeal to President James Buchanan. "A nation which sows robbery," he warned, "will reap a harvest of blood."

Whipple's prediction proved correct. During the summer of 1862, a decade of anger boiled over. In a surprise attack, Dakota fighters fanned out through the Minnesota countryside, killing immigrants and burning farms. They planned to sweep eastward to St. Paul but were stopped at Fort Ridgely. In the end, more than four hundred whites lay dead, including women and children from farms and small towns. Thousands fled; panicked officials telegraphed for aid, spreading hysteria from Wisconsin to Colorado.

Minnesotans' ferocious response to the uprising set the stage for further conflict. A hastily appointed military court, bent on revenge, sentenced 307 Dakotas to death, making it clear that rebellious Indians would be treated as criminals rather than warriors. President Abraham Lincoln reviewed the trial records and commuted most of the sentences but authorized the deaths of 38 Dakota men. They were hanged just after Christmas 1862 in the largest mass execution in U.S. history. Two months later, Congress canceled all treaties with the Dakotas, revoked their annuities, and expelled them from Minnesota. The scattered bands fled west to join nonreservation allies.

As the uprising showed, the Civil War created two dangerous conditions in the West, compounding the problems already caused by corruption. With the Union army fighting the Confederacy, western whites felt vulnerable to Indian attacks. They also discovered they could fight Indians with minimal federal oversight. In the wake of the Dakota uprising, worried Coloradans favored a military campaign against the Cheyennes — allies of the Sioux — even though the Cheyennes had shown little evidence of hostility. Colorado militia leader John M. Chivington, an aspiring politician, determined to quell public anxiety and make his career.

In May 1864, Cheyenne chief Black Kettle, fearing his band would be attacked, consulted with U.S. agents, who instructed him to settle along Sand Creek in eastern Colorado until a treaty could be signed. On November 29, 1864, Chivington's Colorado militia attacked the camp while most of the men were out hunting, slaughtering more than a hundred women and children. "I killed all I could," one officer testified later. "I think and earnestly believe the Indian to be an obstacle to civilization and should be exterminated." Captain Silas Soule, who served under Chivington but refused to give his men the order to fire, dissented. "It was hard to see little children on their knees," he wrote later, "having their brains beat out by men professing to be civilized." Chivington's men rode back for a celebration in Denver, where they hung Cheyenne scalps (and women's genitals) from the rafters of the Apollo Theater.

The northern plains exploded in conflict. Infuriated by the **Sand Creek massacre**, Cheyennes carried war pipes to the Arapahos and Sioux, who attacked and burned white settlements along the South Platte River. Ordered to subdue these peoples, the U.S. Army failed miserably: officers could not even locate the enemy, who traveled rapidly in small bands and knew the country well. A further shock occurred in December 1866 when 1,500 Sioux warriors executed a perfect ambush, luring Captain William Fetterman and 80 soldiers from a Wyoming fort and wiping them out. With the **Fetterman massacre**, the Sioux succeeded in closing the Bozeman Trail, a private road under army protection that had served as the main route into Montana.

General William Tecumseh Sherman, now commanding the army in the West, swore to defeat defiant Indians. But the Union hero met his match on the plains. Another year of fighting proved expensive and inconclusive. In 1868, the Sioux, led by the Oglala band under Chief Red Cloud, told a peace commission they would not sign any treaty unless the United States pledged to abandon all its forts along the Bozeman Trail. The commission agreed. Red Cloud had won.

In the wake of these events, eastern public opinion turned against the Indian wars, which seemed at best ineffective, at worst brutal. Congress held hearings on the slaughter at Sand Creek. Though Chivington, now a civilian, was never prosecuted, the massacre became an infamous example of western vigilantism. By the time Ulysses Grant entered the White House in 1869, the authors of Reconstruction in the South also began to seek solutions to what they called the "Indian problem."

## Grant's Peace Policy

Grant inherited an Indian policy in disarray. Federal incompetence was highlighted by yet another mass killing of friendly Indians in January 1870, this time on the Marias River in Montana, by an army detachment that shot and burned to death 173 Piegans (Blackfeet). Having run out of other options, Grant introduced a peace policy, based on recommendations from Christian advisors. He offered selected appointments to the reformers—including many former abolitionists—who had created such groups as the Indian Rights Association and the Women's National Indian Association.

Rejecting the virulent anti-Indian stance of many westerners, reformers argued that Native peoples had the innate capacity to become equal with whites. They believed, however, that Indians could achieve this only if they embraced Christianity and white ways. Reformers thus aimed to destroy indigenous languages, cultures, and religions. Despite humane intentions, their condescension was obvious. They ignored dissenters like Dr. Thomas Bland of the National Indian Defense Association, who suggested that instead of an "Indian problem" there might be a "white problem"—refusal to permit Indians to follow their own lifeways. To most nineteenth-century Americans, such a notion was shocking and uncivilized. Increasingly dismissive of blacks' capacity for citizenship and hostile toward "heathen" Chinese immigrants, white Americans were even less willing to understand and respect Indian cultures. They believed that in the modern world, Native peoples were fated for extinction.

**Indian Boarding Schools**    Reformers focused their greatest energy on educating the next generation. Realizing that acculturation—adoption of white ways—was difficult when children lived at home, agents and missionaries created off-reservation schools. Native families were exhorted, bullied, and bribed into sending their children to these schools, where, in addition to school lessons, boys learned farming skills and girls practiced housekeeping. "English only" was the rule; students were punished if they spoke their own languages. Mourning Dove, a Salish girl from what is now Washington State, remembered that her school "ran strictly. We never talked during meals without permission, given only on Sunday or special holidays. Otherwise there was silence—a terrible silent silence. I was used to the freedom of the forest, and it was hard to learn this strict discipline. I was punished many times before I learned." The Lakota boy Plenty Kill, who at boarding school received the new name Luther, remembered his loneliness and fear upon arrival: "The big boys would sing brave songs, and that would start the girls to crying. . . . The girls' quarters were about a hundred and fifty yards from ours, so we could hear them." After having his hair cut short, Plenty Kill felt a profound change in his identity. "None of us slept well that night," he recalled. "I felt that I was no more Indian, but would be an imitation of a white man."

Even in the first flush of reform zeal, Grant's policies faced major hurdles. Most Indians had been pushed off traditional lands and assigned to barren ground that would have defeated the most enterprising farmer. Poverty and dislocation left Indians especially vulnerable to the ravages of infectious diseases like measles and scarlet fever. At the same time, Quaker, Presbyterian, and Methodist reformers fought turf battles among themselves and with Catholic missionaries. Many traders and agents also continued to steal money and supplies from people they were supposed to protect. In the late 1870s, Rutherford B. Hayes's administration undertook more housecleaning at the Bureau of Indian Affairs, but corruption lingered.

From the Indians' point of view, reformers often became just another interest group in a crowded field of whites sending hopelessly mixed messages. The attitudes of individual army representatives, agents, and missionaries ranged from courageous and sympathetic to utterly ruthless. Many times, after chiefs thought they had reached a face-to-face agreement, they found it drastically altered by Congress or Washington bureaucrats. Nez Perce leader Joseph observed that "white people have too many chiefs. They do not understand each other. . . . I cannot understand why so many chiefs are allowed to talk so many different ways, and promise so many different things." A Kiowa chief agreed: "We make but few contracts, and them we remember well. The whites make so many they are liable to forget them. The white chief seems not to be able to govern his braves."

Native peoples were nonetheless forced to accommodate, as independent tribal governance and treaty making came to an end. Back in the 1830s, the U.S. Supreme Court had declared Indians no longer sovereign but rather "domestic dependent nations." On a practical basis, however, both the U.S. Senate and agents in the field continued to negotiate treaties as late as 1869. Two years later, the House of Representatives, jealous of Senate privileges, passed a bill to abolish all treaty making with Indians. The Senate agreed, provided that existing treaties remained in force. It was one more step in a long, torturous erosion of Native rights. Eventually, the U.S. Supreme Court ruled in **Lone Wolf v. Hitchcock** (1903) that Congress could make whatever Indian policies it chose, ignoring all existing treaties. That same year, in *Ex Parte Crow Dog*, the Court ruled that no Indian was a citizen unless Congress designated him so. Indians were henceforth wards of the government. These rulings remained in force until the New Deal of the 1930s.

**Breaking Up Tribal Lands**   Reformers' most sweeping effort to assimilate Indians was the **Dawes Severalty Act** (1887), the dream of Senator Henry L. Dawes of Massachusetts, a leader in the Indian Rights Association. Dawes saw the reservation system as an ugly relic of the past. Through severalty — division of tribal lands — he hoped to force Indians onto individual landholdings, partitioning reservations into homesteads, just like those of white farmers. Supporters of the plan believed that landownership would encourage Indians to assimilate. It would lead, as Dawes wrote, to "a personal sense of independence." Individual property, echoed another reformer, would make the Indian man "intelligently selfish, . . . with a *pocket that aches to be filled with dollars!*"

The Dawes Act was a disaster. It played into the hands of whites who coveted Indian land and who persuaded the government to sell them land that was not needed for individual allotments. In this and other ways, the Bureau of Indian Affairs (BIA) implemented the law carelessly, to the outrage of Dawes. In Indian Territory, a commission seized more than 15 million "surplus" acres from Native tribes by 1894, opening the way for whites to convert the last federal territory set aside for Native peoples into the state of Oklahoma. In addition to catastrophic losses of collectively held property, Native peoples lost 66 percent of their individually allotted lands between the 1880s and the 1930s, through fraud, BIA mismanagement, and pressure to sell to whites.

## The End of Armed Resistance

As the nation consolidated control of the West in the 1870s, Americans hoped that Grant's peace policy was solving the "Indian problem." In the Southwest, such formidable peoples as the Kiowas and Comanches had been forced onto reservations. The Diné or Navajo nation, exiled under horrific conditions during the Civil War but permitted to reoccupy their traditional land, gave up further military resistance. An outbreak among California's Modoc people in 1873 — again, humiliating to the army — was at last subdued. Only Sitting Bull, a leader of the powerful Lakota Sioux on the northern plains, openly refused to go to a reservation. When pressured by U.S. troops, he repeatedly crossed into Canada, where he told reporters that "the life of white men is slavery. . . . I have seen nothing that a white man has, houses or railways or clothing or food, that is as good as the right to move in open country and live in our own fashion."

In 1874, the Lakotas faced direct provocation. Lieutenant Colonel George Armstrong Custer, a brash self-promoter who had graduated last in his class at West Point, led an expedition into South Dakota's Black Hills and loudly proclaimed the discovery of gold. Amid the severe depression of the 1870s, prospectors rushed in. The United States, wavering on its 1868 treaty, pressured Sioux leaders to sell the Black Hills. The chiefs said no. Ignoring this answer, the government demanded in 1876 that all Sioux gather at the federal agencies. The policy backfired: not only did Sitting Bull refuse to report, but other Sioux, Cheyennes, and Arapahos slipped away from reservations to join him. Knowing they might face military attack, they agreed to live together for the summer in one great village numbering over seven thousand people. By June, they were camped on the Little Big Horn River in what is now southeastern Montana. Some of the young men wanted to organize raiding parties, but elders counseled against it. "We [are] within our treaty rights as hunters," they argued. "We must keep ourselves so."

The U.S. Army dispatched a thousand cavalry and infantrymen to drive the Indians back to the reservation. Despite warnings from experienced scouts — including Crow Indian allies — most officers thought the job would be easy. Their greatest fear was that the Indians would manage to slip away. But amid the nation's centennial celebration on the Fourth of July 1876, Americans received dreadful news. On June 26 and 27, Lieutenant Colonel Custer, leading the 7th Cavalry as part of a three-pronged effort to surround the Indians, had led 210 men

**Little Plume and Yellow Kidney** Photographer Edward S. Curtis took this photograph of the Piegan (Blackfeet) leader Little Plume and his son Yellow Kidney. Curtis's extensive collection of photographs of Native Americans remains a valuable resource for historians. However, Curtis altered his images to make his Native subjects seem more "authentic": though Indians made widespread use of nonnative furniture, clothes, and other consumer goods (such as Singer sewing machines), Curtis removed those from the frame. He also retouched photographs to remove items such as belts and watches. Note the circular "shadow" here, against the lodge wall, near Little Plume's right arm: the original photograph included a clock. Library of Congress.

in an ill-considered assault on Sitting Bull's camp. The Sioux and their allies had killed the attackers to the last man. "The Indians," one Oglala woman remembered, "acted just like they were driving buffalo to a good place where they could be easily slaughtered."

As retold by the press in sensational (and often fictionalized) accounts, the story of Custer's "last stand" quickly served to justify American conquest of Indian "savages." Long after Americans forgot the massacres of Cheyenne women and children at Sand Creek and of Piegan people on the Marias River, prints of the **Battle of Little Big Horn** hung in barrooms across the country. William F. "Buffalo Bill" Cody, in his traveling Wild West performances, enacted a revenge killing of a

Cheyenne man named Yellow Hand in a tableau Cody called "first scalp for Custer." Notwithstanding that the tableau featured a white man scalping a Cheyenne, Cody depicted it as a triumph for civilization.

Little Big Horn proved to be the last military victory of Plains Indians against the U.S. Army. Pursued relentlessly after Custer's death and finding fewer and fewer bison to sustain them, Sioux parents watched their children starve through a bitter winter. Slowly, families trickled into the agencies and accommodated themselves to reservation life (Map 15.4). The next year, the Nez Perces, fleeing for the Canadian border, also surrendered. The final holdouts fought in the Southwest with Chiricahua Apache leader Geronimo. Like many others, Geronimo had accepted reservation life but found conditions unendurable. Describing the desolate land the tribe had been

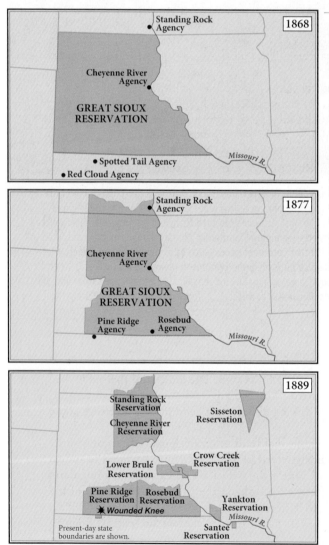

**MAP 15.4   The Sioux Reservations in South Dakota, 1868–1889**
In 1868, when they bent to the demand that they move onto the reservation, the Sioux thought they had gained secure rights to a substantial part of their ancestral hunting grounds. But harsh conditions on reservations led to continuing military conflicts. Land-hungry whites exerted continuous local pressure, and officials in Washington repeatedly changed the terms of Sioux landholdings—always eroding Native claims.

allotted, one Apache said it had "nothing but cactus, rattlesnakes, heat, rocks, and insects. . . . Many, many of our people died of starvation." When Geronimo took up arms in protest, the army recruited other Apaches to track him and his band into the hills; in September 1886, he surrendered for the last time. The Chiricahua Apaches never returned to their homeland. The United States had completed its military conquest of the West.

## Strategies of Survival

Though the warpath closed, many Native peoples continued secretly to practice traditional customs. Away from the disapproving eyes of agents and teachers, they passed on their languages, histories, and traditional arts and medicine to younger generations. Frustrated missionaries often concluded that little could be accomplished because bonds of kinship and custom were so strong. Parents also hated to relinquish their children to off-reservation boarding schools. Thus more and more Indian schools ended up on or near reservations; white teachers had to accept their pupils' continued participation in the rhythms of Indian community life.

Selectively, most indigenous peoples adopted some white ways. Many parents urged their sons and daughters to study hard, learn English, and develop skills to help them succeed in the new world they confronted. Even Sitting Bull announced in 1885 that he wanted his children "to be educated like the white children are." Some Indian students grew up to be lawyers, doctors, and advocates for their people, including writers and artists who interpreted Native experiences for national audiences. One of the most famous was a Santee Sioux boy named Ohiyesa, who became Dr. Charles Eastman. Posted to the Pine Ridge Reservation in South Dakota, Eastman practiced medicine side by side with traditional healers, whom he respected, and wrote popular books under his Sioux name. He remembered that when he left for boarding school, his father had said, "We have now entered upon this life, and there is no going back. . . . Remember, my boy, it is the same as if I sent you on your first war-path. I shall expect you to conquer."

Nothing exemplified this syncretism, or cultural blending, better than the **Ghost Dance movement** of the late 1880s and early 1890s, which fostered American Indian peoples' hope that they could, through sacred dances, resurrect the bison and call a great storm to drive whites back across the Atlantic. The Ghost Dance drew on Christian elements as well as Native ones. As the movement spread from reservation to reservation — Paiutes, Arapahos, Sioux — indigenous peoples developed new forms of pan-Indian identity and cooperation.

White responses to the Ghost Dance showed continued misunderstanding and lethal exertion of authority. In 1890, when a group of Lakota Sioux Ghost Dancers left their South Dakota reservation, they were pursued by the U.S. Army, who feared that further spread of the religion would provoke war. On December 29, at **Wounded Knee**, the 7th Cavalry caught up with fleeing Lakotas and killed at least 150 — perhaps as many as 300. Like other massacres, this one could have been avoided. The deaths at Wounded Knee stand as a final indictment of decades of relentless U.S. expansion, white ignorance and greed, chaotic and conflicting policies, and bloody mistakes.

## Western Myths and Realities

The post–Civil War frontier produced mythic figures who have played starring roles in America's national folklore ever since: "savage" Indians, brave pioneers, rugged cowboys, and gun-slinging sheriffs. Far from being invented by Hollywood in the twentieth century, these oversimplified characters emerged in the era when the nation incorporated the West. Pioneers helped develop the mythic ideal. As one Montana woman claimed, they had come west "at peril of their lives" and faced down "scalp dances" and other terrors; in the end, they "conquered the wilderness and transformed it into a land of peace and plenty." Some former cowboys, capitalizing on the popularity of dime novel Westerns, spiced up their memoirs for sale. Eastern readers were eager for stories like *The Life and Adventures of Nat Love* (1907), written by a Texas cowhand who had been born in slavery in Tennessee and who, as a rodeo star in the 1870s, had won the nickname "Deadwood Dick."

No myth-maker proved more influential than Buffalo Bill Cody. Unlike those who saw the West as free or empty, Bill understood that the United States had taken it by conquest. Ironically, his famous Wild West, which he insisted was not a "show" but an authentic representation of frontier experience, provided one of the few employment options for Plains Indians. To escape harsh reservation conditions, Sioux and Cheyenne men signed on with Bill and demonstrated their riding skills for cheering audiences across the United States and Europe, chasing buffalo and attacking U.S. soldiers and pioneer wagons in the arena. Buffalo Bill proved to be a good employer to Native men, including Lakota Sioux leader Sitting Bull, who toured with Bill's Wild West in 1885. Black Elk, another Lakota Sioux man who joined Cody's operation, recalled that Bill was generous and "had a strong heart." But Black Elk had a mixed reaction to the Wild West. "I liked the part of the show we made," he told an interviewer, "but not the part the Wasichus [white people] made." As he observed, the Wild West of the 1880s was at its heart a celebration of U.S. military conquest.

At this same moment of transition, a young historian named Frederick Jackson Turner reviewed recent census data and proclaimed the end of the frontier. Up to 1890, he wrote, a clear, westward-moving line had existed between "civilization and savagery." The frontier experience, Turner argued, shaped Americans' national character. It left them a heritage of "coarseness and strength, combined with acuteness and inquisitiveness," as well as "restless, nervous energy."

Today, historians reject Turner's depiction of Indian "savagery"—and his contradictory idea that white pioneers in the West claimed empty "free land." Many scholars have noted that frontier conquest was both violent and incomplete. The Dust Bowl of the 1930s, as well as more recent cycles of drought, have repeated late-nineteenth-century patterns of hardship and depopulation on the plains. During the 1950s and 1960s, also, uranium mining rushes in the West mimicked earlier patterns of boom and bust, leaving ghost towns in their wake. Turner himself acknowledged that the frontier had both good and evil elements. He noted that in the West, "frontier liberty was sometimes confused with absence of all effective government." But in 1893, when Turner first published "The Significance of the Frontier in American History," eager listeners heard only the positives. They saw pioneering in the West as evidence of American exceptionalism: of the nation's unique history and destiny. They claimed that "peaceful" American expansion was the opposite of European empires—ignoring the many military and economic similarities. Although politically the American West became a set of states rather than a colony, historians today emphasize the legacy of conquest that is central to its (and America's) history.

Less than two months after the massacre at Wounded Knee, General William T. Sherman died in New York. As the nation marked his passing with pomp and oratory, commentators noted that his career reflected a great era of conquest and consolidation of national power. Known primarily for his role in defeating the Confederacy, Sherman's first military exploits had been against Seminoles in Florida. Later, during the U.S.-Mexico War, he had gone west with the U.S. Army to help claim California. After the Civil War, the general went west again, supervising the forced removal of Sioux and Cheyennes to reservations.

When Sherman graduated from West Point in 1840, the United States had counted twenty-six states, none of them west of Missouri. At his death in 1891, the nation boasted forty-four states, stretching to the Pacific coast. The United States now rivaled Britain and Germany as an industrial giant, and its dynamic economy was drawing immigrants from around the world. Over the span of Sherman's career, the United States had become a major player on the world stage. It had done so through the kind of fierce military conquest that Sherman made famous, as well as through bold expansions of federal authority to foster economic expansion. From the wars and policies of Sherman's lifetime, the children and grandchildren of Civil War heroes inherited a vast empire. In the coming decades, it would be up to them to decide how they would use the nation's new power.

| IN YOUR OWN WORDS | In the late nineteenth century, what strategies did Native peoples in the West pursue in response to dispossession of their lands and efforts to assimilate them? |
| --- | --- |

## Summary

Between 1861 and 1877, the United States completed its conquest of the continent. After the Civil War, expansion of railroads fostered integration of the national economy. Republican policymakers promoted this integration through protective tariffs, while federal court rulings facilitated economic growth and strengthened corporations. To attract foreign investment, Congress placed the nation on the gold standard. Federal officials also pursued a vigorous foreign policy, acquiring Alaska and asserting U.S. power indirectly through control of international trade in Latin America and Asia.

An important result of economic integration was incorporation of the Great Plains. Cattlemen built an industry linked to the integrated economy, in the process nearly driving the native bison to extinction. Homesteaders confronted harsh environmental conditions as they converted the grasslands for agriculture. Republicans championed homesteader families as representatives of domesticity, an ideal opposed to Mormon plural marriage in Utah. Homesteading accelerated the rapid, often violent, transformation of western environments. Perceiving this transformation, federal officials began setting aside natural preserves such as Yellowstone, often clashing with Native Americans who wished to hunt there.

Conflicts led to the dispossession of Native American lands. During the Civil War, whites clashed with the Sioux and their allies. Grant's peace policy sought to end this conflict by forcing Native Americans to acculturate to European-style practices. Indian armed resistance continued through the 1880s, ending with Geronimo's surrender in 1886. Thereafter, Native Americans survived by secretly continuing their traditions and selectively adopting white ways. Due in part to the determined military conquest of this period, the United States claimed a major role on the world stage. Frontier myths shaped Americans' view of themselves as rugged individualists with a unique national destiny.

# Chapter 15 Review

## KEY TERMS

**Identify and explain the significance of each term below.**

transcontinental railroad (p. 443)
protective tariff (p. 444)
Burlingame Treaty (p. 445)
*Munn v. Illinois* (p. 448)
gold standard (p. 449)
"Crime of 1873" (p. 449)
Homestead Act (p. 450)
land-grant colleges (p. 450)
Comstock Lode (p. 450)
"rain follows the plow" (p. 454)

Exodusters (p. 454)
Yellowstone National Park (p. 457)
U.S. Fisheries Commission (p. 457)
Sand Creek massacre (p. 459)
Fetterman massacre (p. 459)
*Lone Wolf v. Hitchcock* (p. 461)
Dawes Severalty Act (p. 461)
Battle of Little Big Horn (p. 463)
Ghost Dance movement (p. 465)
Wounded Knee (p. 465)

## REVIEW QUESTIONS

**Answer these questions to demonstrate your understanding of the chapter's main ideas.**

1. What federal policies contributed to the rise of America's industrial economy, and what were their results?

2. What factors led to transformation of the trans-Mississippi west after the Civil War?

3. In the late nineteenth century, what strategies did Native peoples in the West pursue in response to dispossession of their lands and efforts to assimilate them?

4. Review the events listed under "American and National Identity" and "Migration and Settlement" on the thematic timeline on pages 352–353. Between the 1840s and the 1870s, what distinctive patterns of racial and ethnic conflict occurred in the West? What were the results for different ethnic and racial groups?

## CHRONOLOGY

As you read, ask yourself why this chapter begins and ends with these dates and identify the links among related events.

| | |
|---|---|
| **1859** | • Comstock silver lode discovered in Nevada |
| **1862** | • Homestead Act |
| | • Dakota Sioux uprising in Minnesota |
| | • Morrill Act funds public state universities |
| **1864** | • Sand Creek massacre of Cheyennes in Colorado |
| | • Yosemite Valley reserved as public park |
| **1865** | • Long Drive of Texas longhorns begins |
| **1866** | • Fetterman massacre |
| **1868** | • Burlingame Treaty with China |
| **1869** | • Transcontinental railroad completed |
| | • Wyoming women's suffrage |
| **1870** | • Utah women's suffrage |
| **1872** | • General Mining Act |
| | • Yellowstone National Park created |
| **1873** | • United States begins to move to gold standard |
| **1876** | • Battle of Little Big Horn |
| **1877** | • Nez Perce forcibly removed from ancestral homelands in Northwest |
| | • *Munn v. Illinois* Supreme Court decision |
| **1879** | • Exoduster migration to Kansas |
| | • John Wesley Powell presents *Report on the Lands of the Arid Region of the United States* |
| **1880s** | • Rise of the Ghost Dance movement |
| **1885** | • Sitting Bull tours with Buffalo Bill's Wild West |
| **1886** | • Dry cycle begins on the plains |
| | • Chiricahua Apache leader Geronimo surrenders |
| **1887** | • Dawes Severalty Act |
| **1890** | • Massacre of Sioux Ghost Dancers at Wounded Knee, South Dakota |

# PART 6

Touring the United States around 1900, a Hungarian Catholic abbot named Count Péter Vay visited the steel mills of Pittsburgh. "Fourteen-thousand tall chimneys . . . discharge their burning sparks and smoke incessantly," he reported. He was moved by the plight of fellow Hungarians, laboring "wherever the heat is most insupportable, the flames most scorching." One worker had just been killed in a foundry accident. Vay, attending the funeral, worried that immigration was "of no use except to help fill the moneybags of the insatiable millionaires."

Vay witnessed America's emergence as an industrial power, the subject of Part 6 of *America's History*. We begin Part 6 in 1877 because the transformations wrought by capitalism drove the nation's most urgent controversies after the end of the Civil War and Reconstruction. Key working-class reform and protest movements developed new strategies and arguments in the four decades that followed the end of Reconstruction. The Democratic Party, traditionally hostile to strong central government but pressured in new directions by grassroots groups like the People's Party of the 1890s, began to advocate for new measures to address poverty and rein in growing corporate power. By 1910, thousands of middle-class and elite Americans had adopted their own reform visions. As ex-president Theodore Roosevelt declared, American citizens needed to "control the mighty commercial forces which they have called into being."

Part 6 ends in 1917 because we, like many other historians, see U.S. participation in World War I as a key turning point that helped bring about some measures that progressives had sought for decades, such as national women's suffrage, prohibition, and government ownership of railroads. As we shall see in Part 7, the aftermath of World War I also revealed the limits of those reforms.

## Corporations and Conflicts

Giant corporations developed global networks of production, marketing, and finance by innovating technically and developing ruthless tactics such as predatory pricing. Corporations' complex structures opened new careers for managers and "pink-collar workers," but wageworkers, including African Americans and millions of newly arrived immigrants, endured low pay, health hazards, and frequent unemployment. In addition to creating labor unions to protest such conditions, workers forged political alliances with farmers, who also found themselves economically vulnerable. Along with an eight-hour day and union recognition, workers agitated for, and won, Chinese exclusion.

470

# Industrializing America: Upheavals and Experiments 1877–1917

## A Diverse, Urban Society

The values of thrift, piety, and domesticity faced challenges in the era of industrialization. Women took prominent roles in public life, while Charles Darwin's theory of evolution prompted some thinkers to justify economic inequality as a law of nature. Writers and artists experimented with realism and abstraction. People of religious faith had diverse reactions to these upheavals.

The nation's fast-growing cities offered enticing consumer pleasures, while also housing millions of impoverished immigrants. Cities proved challenging to govern, and reformers denounced the immigrant-supported political machines that controlled them. By 1900, however, some machine leaders helped lead urban progressive experiments.

## Reform Initiatives

Progressive reformers—a diverse group who were not at all united—sought to enhance democracy, limit corporate power, ameliorate poverty, and protect the environment. Though Republican President Theodore Roosevelt championed landmark legislation (1901–1909), much reform energy passed to other parties. During the presidency of Woodrow Wilson (1913–1921), Democrats enacted an impressive slate of laws, including new recognition of labor rights. Meanwhile, the Populist, Socialist, and Progressive parties proposed more radical responses to poverty and concentrated wealth. While none of these parties won national power, their ideas helped influence the shape of the emerging modern state.

## Thematic Understanding

This timeline arranges some of the important events of this period into themes. What was the relationship of the two severe economic depressions listed under "Work, Exchange, and Technology" to political reform? Did reform tend to come during or after periods of economic crisis? Why do you think this was the case? In what ways did Americans respond politically to the depression of the 1870s? What continuities and changes do you see in their responses to the next severe depression, in the 1890s?

| | AMERICAN AND NATIONAL IDENTITY | POLITICS AND POWER | WORK, EXCHANGE, AND TECHNOLOGY |
|---|---|---|---|
| 1870 | • Farmers' Alliances form (1875)<br>• San Francisco mob attacks Chinatown (1877) | • Greenback-Labor Party elects fifteen congressmen (1878) | • Economic depression (1873–1879)<br>• Great Railroad Strike (1877) |
| 1880 | • Knights of Labor peaks (1884)<br>• Haymarket Square violence (1886)<br>• American Federation of Labor founded (1886) | • Pendleton Act (1883)<br>• Peak of Woman's Christian Temperance Union (1880s)<br>• Interstate Commerce Act (1887)<br>• Hull House founded (1889) | • John D. Rockefeller creates Standard Oil trust (1882)<br>• American Federation of Labor founded (1886) |
| 1890 | • Lockout at Homestead, Pennsylvania (1892)<br>• Sierra Club founded (1892) | • Disfranchisement in South (1890–1905)<br>• People's Party founded (1890)<br>• *Plessy v. Ferguson* (1896)<br>• William McKinley elected (1896) | • Severe depression hits (1893)<br>• Corporate mergers in key industries<br>• Birth of modern advertising |
| 1900 | • Women's Trade Union League founded (1903)<br>• Industrial Workers of the World founded (1905)<br>• National Association for the Advancement of Colored People founded (1909) | • McKinley assassinated; Theodore Roosevelt assumes presidency (1901)<br>• Food and Drug Administration established (1906)<br>• Hepburn Act (1906) | • J. P. Morgan creates U.S. Steel (1901)<br>• Women's Trade Union League founded (1903)<br>• *Muller v. Oregon* (1908) |
| 1910 | | • Woodrow Wilson wins presidency (1912)<br>• Sixteenth and Seventeenth Amendments (1913)<br>• Federal Reserve created (1913) | • Triangle Fire at Triangle Shirtwaist Company, New York (1911)<br>• Supreme Court orders Standard Oil divided (1911) |

| CULTURE AND SOCIETY | MIGRATION AND SETTLEMENT | GEOGRAPHY AND THE ENVIRONMENT | AMERICA IN THE WORLD | |
|---|---|---|---|---|
| • Comstock Act (1873)<br>• Baseball's National League founded (1876) | | • First national park created at Yellowstone (1872)<br>• Yellow fever epidemic devastates Memphis, Tennessee (1878) | • Social Darwinism gains acceptance<br>• Hostility to Chinese immigrants grows | 1870 |
| • William Dean Howells calls for realism in literature<br>• Booker T. Washington founds Tuskegee Institute (1881)<br>• Birth of American football | • Congress passes Chinese Exclusion Act (1882)<br>• Mass immigration of Russian Jews (1880s) | • Hatch Act (1887)<br>• Industrialization and urban growth cause rising pollution | • Rapid industrialization draws immigrants from around the world<br>• Chinese Exclusion Act (1882–1943) | 1880 |
| • Jacob Riis publishes *How the Other Half Lives* (1890)<br>• World's Columbian Exposition in Chicago (1893) | • New York's Ellis Island opens (1892) | • John Muir founds Sierra Club (1892)<br>• "Bicycle craze" and rise of hiking and camping | • Ellis Island opens (1892)<br>• *Plessy v. Ferguson* (1896) | 1890 |
| • First World Series (1903)<br>• Robert Hunter publishes *Poverty* (1904)<br>• Upton Sinclair's *The Jungle* published (1906) | • Migration of African Americans to northern cities increases<br>• New York passes Tenement House Law (1901)<br>• Mutual aid societies form to help immigrants | • Antiquities Act (1906)<br>• National Audubon Society forms (1901)<br>• Newlands Reclamation Act (1902)<br>• U.S. Forest Service created (1905) | • Rising immigration from Eastern and Southern Europe<br>• Height of eugenics (1900s–1920s)<br>• Japanese immigrants barred from becoming U.S. citizens (1906) | 1900 |
| • Armory Show of modern art held in New York City (1913) | | • National Park Service created (1916) | • Peak of foreign missions activity by American Protestant churches (1915) | 1910 |

# 16

# Industrial America: Corporations and Conflicts

## 1877–1911

### IDENTIFY THE BIG IDEA

What new opportunities and risks did industrialization bring, and how did it reshape American society?

**FOR MILLIONS OF HIS CONTEMPORARIES, ANDREW CARNEGIE** exemplified American success. Arriving from Scotland as a poor twelve-year-old in 1848, Carnegie found work as an errand boy for the Pennsylvania Railroad and rapidly scaled the managerial ladder. In 1865, he struck out on his own as an iron manufacturer, selling to friends in the railroad business. Encouraged by Republican tariffs to enter the steel industry, he soon built a massive steel mill outside Pittsburgh where a state-of-the-art Bessemer converter made steel refining dramatically more efficient. With Carnegie leading the way, steel became a major U.S. industry, reaching annual production of 10 million metric tons by 1900—almost as much as the *combined* output of the world's other top producers, Germany (6.6 million tons) and Britain (4.8 million).

At first, skilled workers at Carnegie's mill in Homestead, Pennsylvania, earned good wages. They had a strong union, and Carnegie affirmed workers' right to organize. But Carnegie—confident that new machinery enabled him to replace many skilled laborers—eventually decided that collective bargaining was too expensive. In the summer of 1892, he withdrew to his estate in Scotland, leaving his partner Henry Clay Frick in command. A former coal magnate and veteran foe of labor, Frick was well qualified to do the dirty work. He announced that after July 1, members of the Amalgamated Association of Iron and Steel Workers would be locked out of the Homestead mill. If they wanted to return to work, they would have to abandon the union and sign new individual contracts. Frick fortified the mill and prepared to hire replacement workers. The battle was on.

At dawn on July 6, barges chugging up the Monongahela River brought dozens of private armed guards from the Pinkerton Detective Agency, hired by Carnegie to defend the plant. Locked-out workers opened fire, starting a gunfight that left seven workers and three Pinkertons dead. Frick appealed to Pennsylvania's governor, who sent the state militia to arrest labor leaders on charges of riot and murder. Most of the locked-out workers lost their jobs. The union was dead.

As the **Homestead lockout** showed, industrialization was a controversial and often bloody process. During the half century after the Civil War, more and more Americans worked not as independent farmers or artisans but as employees of large corporations. Conditions of work changed for people of all economic classes. Drawn by the dynamic economy, immigrants arrived from around the globe. These transformations provoked working people, including farmers as well as industrial workers, to organize and defend their interests.

# The Rise of Big Business

In the late 1800s, industrialization in Europe and the United States revolutionized the world economy. It brought large-scale commercial agriculture to many parts of the globe and prompted millions of migrants—both skilled workers and displaced peasants—to cross continents and oceans in search of jobs. Industrialization also created a production glut. The immense scale of agriculture and manufacturing caused a long era of deflation, when prices dropped worldwide (Figure 16.1).

Falling prices normally signal low demand for goods and services, and thus stagnation. In England, a mature industrial power, the late nineteenth century did bring economic decline. But in the United States, production expanded. Between 1877 and 1900, Americans' average real per capita income increased from $388 to $573. In this sense, Andrew Carnegie was right when he argued that, even though industrialization increased the gap between rich and poor, everyone's standard of living rose. In his famous 1889 essay "Wealth"—later called the **Gospel of Wealth**—he observed that "the poor enjoy what the rich could not before afford. What were the luxuries have become the necessaries of life."

Technological and business efficiencies allowed American firms to grow, invest in new equipment, and earn profits even as prices for their products fell. Growth depended, in turn, on America's large and growing population, expansion into the West, and an integrated national marketplace. In many fields, large corporations became the dominant form of business.

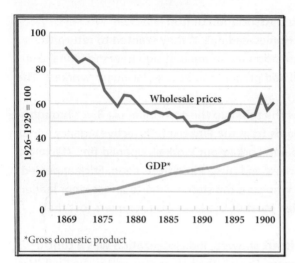

**FIGURE 16.1 Business Activity and Wholesale Prices, 1869–1900**
This graph shows the key feature of the performance of the late-nineteenth-century economy: while output was booming, wholesale prices were, on the whole, falling. Thus, while workers often struggled with falling wages — especially during decades of severe economic crisis — consumer products also became cheaper to buy.

## Innovators in Enterprise

As rail lines stretched westward between the 1850s and 1880s, operators faced a crisis. As one Erie Railroad executive noted, a superintendent on a 50-mile line could personally attend to every detail. But supervising a 500-mile line was impossible; trains ran late, communications failed, and trains crashed. Managers gradually invented systems to solve these problems. They distinguished top executives from those responsible for day-to-day operations. They departmentalized operations by function — purchasing, machinery, freight traffic, passenger traffic — and established clear lines of communication. They perfected cost accounting, which allowed an industrialist like Carnegie to track expenses and revenues carefully and thus follow his Scottish mother's advice: "Take care of the pennies, and the pounds will take care of themselves." This **management revolution** created the internal structure adopted by many large, complex corporations.

During these same years, the United States became an industrial power by tapping North America's vast natural resources, particularly in the West. Industries that had once depended on water power began to use prodigious amounts of coal. Steam engines replaced human and animal labor, and kerosene replaced whale oil and wood. By 1900, America's factories and urban homes were converting to electric power. With new management structures and dependency on fossil fuels (oil, coal, natural gas), corporations transformed both the economy and the country's natural and built environments.

**Production and Sales** After Chicago's Union Stock Yards opened in 1865, middlemen shipped cows by rail from the Great Plains to Chicago and from there to eastern cities, where slaughter took place in local butchertowns. Such a system — a national livestock market with local processing — could have lasted, as it did in Europe. But Gustavus Swift, a shrewd Chicago cattle dealer, saw that local slaughterhouses lacked the scale to utilize waste by-products and cut labor costs. To improve productivity, Swift invented the assembly line, where each wageworker repeated the same slaughtering task over and over.

Swift also pioneered **vertical integration**, a model in which a company controlled all aspects of production from raw materials to finished goods. Once his engineers designed a cooling system, Swift invested in a fleet of refrigerator cars to keep beef fresh as he shipped it eastward, priced below what local butchers could afford. In cities that received his chilled meat, Swift built branch houses and fleets of delivery wagons. He also constructed factories to make fertilizer and chemicals from the by-products of slaughter, and he developed marketing strategies for those products as well. Other Chicago packers followed Swift's lead. By 1900, five firms, all vertically integrated, produced nearly 90 percent of the meat shipped in interstate commerce.

Big packers invented new sales tactics. For example, Swift & Company periodically slashed prices in certain markets to below production costs, driving independent distributors to the wall. With profits from its sales elsewhere, a large firm like Swift could survive temporary losses in one locality until competitors went under. Afterward, Swift could raise prices again. This technique, known as predatory pricing, helped give a few firms unprecedented market control.

**Standard Oil and the Rise of the Trusts**  No one used ruthless business tactics more skillfully than the king of petroleum, John D. Rockefeller. After inventors in the 1850s figured out how to extract kerosene—a clean-burning fuel for domestic heating and lighting—from crude oil, enormous oil deposits were discovered at Titusville, Pennsylvania. Just then, the Civil War severely disrupted whaling, forcing whale-oil customers to look for alternative lighting sources. Overnight, a forest of oil wells sprang up around Titusville. Connected to these Pennsylvania oil fields by rail in 1863, Cleveland, Ohio, became a refining center. John D. Rockefeller was then an up-and-coming Cleveland grain dealer. (He, like Carnegie and most other budding tycoons, hired a substitute to fight for him in the Civil War.) Rockefeller had strong nerves, a sharp eye for able partners, and a genius for finance. He went into the kerosene business and borrowed heavily to expand. Within a few years, his firm— Standard Oil of Ohio—was Cleveland's leading refiner.

Like Carnegie and Swift, Rockefeller succeeded through vertical integration: to control production and sales all the way from the oil well to the kerosene lamp, he took a big stake in the oil fields, added pipelines, and developed a vast distribution network. Rockefeller allied with railroad executives, who, like him, hated the oil market's boom-and-bust cycles. What they wanted was predictable, high-volume traffic, and they offered Rockefeller secret rebates that gave him a leg up on competitors.

Rockefeller also pioneered a strategy called **horizontal integration**. After driving competitors to the brink of failure through predatory pricing, he invited them to merge their local companies into his conglomerate. Most agreed, often because they had no choice. Through such mergers, Standard Oil wrested control of 95 percent of the nation's oil refining capacity by the 1880s. In 1882, Rockefeller's lawyers created a new legal form, the **trust**. It organized a small group of associates—the board of trustees—to hold stock from a group of combined firms, managing them as a single entity. Rockefeller soon invested in Mexican oil fields and competed in world markets against Russian and Middle Eastern producers.

Other companies followed Rockefeller's lead, creating trusts to produce such products as linseed oil, sugar, and salt. Many expanded sales and production overseas.

As early as 1868, Singer Manufacturing Company established a factory in Scotland to produce sewing machines. By World War I, such brands as Ford and General Electric had become familiar around the world.

Distressed by the development of near monopolies, reformers began to denounce "the trusts," a term that in popular usage referred to any large corporation that seemed to wield excessive power. Some states outlawed trusts as a legal form. But in an effort to attract corporate headquarters to its state, New Jersey broke ranks in 1889, passing a law that permitted the creation of holding companies and other combinations. Delaware soon followed, providing another legal haven for consolidated corporations. A wave of mergers further concentrated corporate power during the depression of the 1890s, as weaker firms succumbed to powerful rivals. By 1900, America's largest one hundred companies controlled a third of the nation's productive capacity. Purchasing several steel companies in 1901, including Carnegie Steel, J. P. Morgan created U.S. Steel, the nation's first billion-dollar corporation. Such familiar firms as DuPont and Eastman Kodak assumed dominant places in their respective industries.

**Assessing the Industrialists**   The work of men like Swift, Rockefeller, and Carnegie was controversial in their lifetimes and has been ever since. Carnegie, in his "Wealth" essay, argued that corporate titans attained their wealth through talent, proving they deserved their success. He also declared, however, that wealth was a "public trust" and that every elite man, after providing for his family, had a patriotic obligation to give away his millions to benefit education and other worthy causes. Carnegie advocated a near 100 percent inheritance tax on privately held wealth: inheriting large sums, he believed, discouraged young people's initiative, just as "handouts" of food or shelter to the poor discouraged them from working. Carnegie rejected both, viewing Social Darwinism, or "survival of the fittest," as the key principle of the new order (see Chapter 17).

Historians' opinions of the first industrial titans have tended to be harsh in eras of economic crisis, when the shortcomings of corporate America appear in stark relief. During the Great Depression of the 1930s, a historian coined the term *robber barons*, which is still used today. In periods of prosperity, both scholars and the public have tended to view early industrialists more favorably, calling them *industrial statesmen*.

Some scholars have argued that industrialists benefitted the economy by replacing the chaos of market competition with a "visible hand" of planning and expert management. But one recent study of railroads asserts that the main skills of early tycoons (as well as those of today) were cultivating political "friends," defaulting on loans, and lying to the public. Whether we consider the industrialists heroes, villains, or something in between, it is clear that the corporate economy was not the creation of just a few individuals, however famous or influential. It was a systemic transformation of the economy.

**A National Consumer Culture**   As they integrated vertically and horizontally, corporations innovated in other ways. Companies such as Bell Telephone and Westinghouse set up research laboratories. Steelmakers invested in chemistry and materials science to make their products cheaper, better, and stronger. Mass markets brought an appealing array of goods to consumers who could afford them. Railroads whisked Florida oranges and other fresh produce to the shelves of grocery stores. Retailers such as F. W. Woolworth and the Great Atlantic and Pacific Tea Company (A&P) opened chains of stores that soon stretched nationwide.

The department store was pioneered in 1875 by John Wanamaker in Philadelphia. These megastores displaced small retail shops, tempting customers with large show windows and Christmas displays. Like industrialists, department store magnates developed economies of scale that enabled them to slash prices. An 1898 newspaper advertisement for Macy's Department Store urged shoppers to "read our books, cook in our saucepans, dine off our china, wear our silks, get under our blankets, smoke our cigars, drink our wines — Shop at Macy's — and Life will Cost You Less and Yield You More Than You Dreamed Possible."

While department stores became urban fixtures, Montgomery Ward and Sears built mail-order empires. Rural families from Vermont to California pored over the companies' annual catalogs, making wish lists of tools, clothes, furniture, and toys. Mail-order companies used money-back guarantees to coax wary customers to buy products they could not see or touch. "Don't be afraid to make a mistake," the Sears catalog counseled. "Tell us what you want, in your own way." By 1900, America counted more than twelve hundred mail-order companies.

The active shaping of consumer demand became, in itself, a new enterprise. Outdoors, advertisements appeared everywhere: in New York's Madison Square, the Heinz Company installed a 45-foot pickle made of green electric lights. Tourists had difficulty admiring Niagara Falls because billboards obscured the view. By 1900, companies were spending more than $90 million a year ($2.3 billion today) on print advertising, as the press itself became a mass-market industry. Rather than charging subscribers the cost of production, magazines began to cover their costs by selling ads. Cheap subscriptions built a mass readership, which in turn attracted more advertisers. In 1903, the *Ladies' Home Journal* became the first magazine with a million subscribers.

## The Corporate Workplace

Before the Civil War, most American boys had hoped to become farmers, small-business owners, or independent artisans. Afterward, more and more Americans — both male and female — began working for someone else. Because they wore white shirts with starched collars, those who held professional positions in corporations became known as white-collar workers, a term differentiating them from blue-collar employees, who labored with their hands. For a range of employees — managers and laborers, clerks and salespeople — the rise of corporate work had wide-ranging consequences.

**Managers and Salesmen**    As the managerial revolution unfolded, the headquarters of major corporations began to house departments handling specific activities such as purchasing and accounting. These departments were supervised by middle managers, something not seen before in American industry. Middle managers took on entirely new tasks, directing the flow of goods, labor, and information throughout the enterprise. They were key innovators, counterparts to the engineers in research laboratories who, in the same decades, worked to reduce costs and improve efficiency.

Corporations also needed a new kind of sales force. In post–Civil War America, the drummer, or traveling salesman, became a familiar sight on city streets and in remote country stores. Riding rail networks from town to town, drummers introduced merchants to new products, offered incentives, and suggested sales displays. They built nationwide distribution networks for such popular consumer products as cigarettes and Coca-Cola. By the late 1880s, the leading manufacturer of cash registers produced a sales script for its employees' conversations with local merchants. "Take for granted that he will buy," the script directed. "Say to him, 'Now, Mr. Blank, what color shall I make it?' . . . Handing him your pen say, 'Just sign here where I have made the cross.'"

With such companies in the vanguard, sales became systematized. Managers set individual sales quotas and awarded prizes to top salesmen, while those who sold too little were singled out for remedial training or dismissal. Executives embraced the ideas of business psychologist Walter Dill Scott, who published *The Psychology of Advertising* in 1908. Scott's principles — which included selling to customers based on their presumed "instinct of escape" and "instinct of combat" — were soon taught at Harvard Business School. Others also promised that a "scientific attitude" would "attract attention" and "create desire."

**Women in the Corporate Office**    Beneath the ranks of managers emerged a new class of female office workers. Before the Civil War, most clerks at small firms had been young men who expected to rise through the ranks. In a large corporation, secretarial work became a dead-end job, and employers began assigning it to women. By the turn of the twentieth century, 77 percent of all stenographers and typists were female; by 1920, women held half of all low-level office jobs.

For white working-class women, clerking and office work represented new opportunities. In an era before most families had access to day care, mothers most often earned money at home, where they could tend children while also taking in laundry, caring for boarders, or doing piecework (sewing or other assembly projects, paid on a per-item basis). Unmarried daughters could enter domestic service or factory work, but clerking and secretarial work were cleaner and better paid.

New technologies provided additional opportunities for women. The rise of the telephone, introduced by inventor Alexander Graham Bell in 1876, was a notable example. Originally intended for business use on local exchanges, telephones were eagerly adopted by residential customers. Thousands of young women found work as telephone operators. By 1900, more than 4 million women worked for wages. About a third worked in domestic service; another third in industry; the rest in office work, teaching, nursing, or sales. As new occupations arose, the percentage of wage-earning women in domestic service dropped dramatically, a trend that continued in the twentieth century.

## On the Shop Floor

Despite the managerial revolution at the top, skilled craft workers — almost all of them men — retained considerable autonomy in many industries. A coal miner, for example, was not an hourly wageworker but essentially an independent contractor, paid by the amount of coal he produced. He provided his own tools, worked at his own pace, and knocked off early when he chose. The same was true for puddlers and rollers in ironworks; molders in stove making; and machinists, glass blowers, and skilled workers in many other industries. Such workers abided by the stint, a self-imposed limit on how much they would produce each day. This informal system of restricting output infuriated efficiency-minded engineers, but to the workers it signified personal dignity, manly pride, and brotherhood with fellow employees.

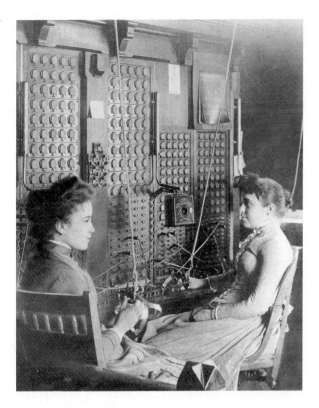

**Telephone Operators, 1888** Like other women office workers, these switchboard operators enjoyed relatively high pay and comfortable working conditions—especially in the early years of the telephone industry, before operators' work routines speeded up. These young women worked for the Central Union Telephone Company in Canton, Ohio. Courtesy of the Ohio History Connection, AL00129.

One shop in Lowell, Massachusetts, posted regulations requiring all employees to be at their posts by the time of the opening bell and to remain, with the shop door locked, until the closing bell. A machinist promptly packed his tools, declaring that he had not "been brought up under such a system of slavery."

Skilled workers—craftsmen, inside contractors, and foremen—enjoyed a high degree of autonomy. But those who paid helpers from their own pocket could also exploit them. Subcontracting arose, in part, to enable manufacturers to distance themselves from the consequences of shady labor practices. In Pittsburgh steel mills, foremen were known as "pushers," notorious for driving their gangs mercilessly. On the other hand, industrial labor operated on a human scale, through personal relationships that could be close and enduring. Striking craft workers would commonly receive the support of helpers and laborers, and labor gangs would sometimes walk out on behalf of a popular foreman.

As industrialization advanced, however, workers increasingly lost the independence characteristic of craft work. The most important cause of this was the **deskilling** of labor under a new system of mechanized manufacturing that men like meatpacker Gustavus Swift had pioneered and that automobile maker Henry Ford would soon call mass production. Everything from typewriters to automobiles came to be assembled from standardized parts, using machines that increasingly operated with little human oversight. A machinist protested in 1883 that the sewing machine industry was so "subdivided" that "one man may make just a particular part of a machine and may not know anything whatever about another part of the same machine." Such a worker, noted an observer, "cannot be master of a craft, but only master of a fragment." Employers, who originally favored automatic machinery because it increased output, quickly found that it also helped them control workers and cut labor costs. They could pay unskilled workers less and replace them easily.

By the early twentieth century, managers sought to further reduce costs through a program of industrial efficiency called **scientific management**. Its inventor, a metal-cutting expert named Frederick W. Taylor, recommended that employers eliminate all brain work from manual labor, hiring experts to develop rules for the shop floor. Workers must be required to "do what they are told promptly and without asking questions or making suggestions." In its most extreme form, scientific management called for engineers to time each task with a stopwatch; companies would pay workers more if they met the stopwatch standard. Taylor assumed that workers would respond automatically to the lure of higher earnings. But scientific management was not, in practice, a great success. Implementing it proved to be expensive, and workers stubbornly resisted. Corporate managers, however, adopted bits and pieces of Taylor's system, and they enthusiastically agreed that decisions should lie with "management alone." Over time, in comparison with businesses in other countries, American corporations created a particularly wide gap between the roles of managers and those of the blue-collar workforce.

Blue-collar workers had little freedom to negotiate, and their working conditions deteriorated markedly as deskilling and mass production took hold. At the same time, industrialization brought cheaper products that enabled many Americans to enjoy new consumer products—if they could avoid starvation. From executives down to unskilled workers, the hierarchy of corporate employment contributed to sharper distinctions among three economic classes: the wealthy elite; an emerging, self-defined "middle class"; and a struggling class of workers, who bore the brunt of the economy's new risks and included many Americans living in dire poverty. As it wrought these changes, industrialization prompted intense debate over inequality.

**Health Hazards and Pollution**    Industrialized labor also damaged workers' health. In 1884, a study of the Illinois Central Railroad showed that, over the previous decade, one in twenty of its workers had been killed or permanently disabled by an accident on the job. For brakemen—one of the most dangerous jobs—the rate was one in seven. Due to lack of regulatory laws and inspections, mining was 50 percent more dangerous in the United States than in Germany; between 1876 and 1925, an average of over two thousand U.S. coal miners died each year from cave-ins and explosions. Silver, gold, and copper mines were also not immune from such tragedies, but mining companies resisted demands for safety regulation.

Extractive industries and factories also damaged nearby environments and the people who lived there. In big cities, poor residents suffered from polluted air and the dumping of noxious by-products into the water supply. Mines like those in Leadville, Colorado, contaminated the land and water with mercury and lead. Alabama convicts, forced to work in coal mines, faced brutal working conditions and fatal illnesses caused by the mines' contamination of local water. At the time, people were well aware of many of these dangers, but workers had an even more urgent priority: work. Pittsburgh's belching smokestacks meant coughing and lung damage, but they also meant running mills and paying jobs.

**Unskilled Labor and Discrimination**   As managers deskilled production, the ranks of factory workers came to include more and more women and children, who were almost always unskilled and low paid. Men often resented women's presence in factories, and male labor unions often worked to exclude women—especially wives, who they argued should remain in the home. Women vigorously defended their right to work. On hearing accusations that married women worked only to buy frivolous luxuries, one female worker in a Massachusetts shoe factory wrote a heated response to the local newspaper: "When the husband and father cannot provide for his wife and children, it is perfectly natural that the wife and mother should desire to work. . . . Don't blame married women if the land of the free has become a land of slavery and oppression."

In 1900, one of every five children under the age of sixteen worked outside the home. Child labor was most widespread in the ex-Confederacy. Here, a low-wage industrial sector emerged after Reconstruction, leading commentators to hail the region as a more economically diversified **New South** (Map 16.1). Textile mills

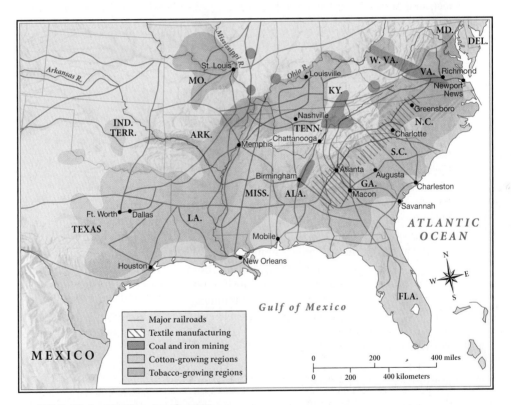

**MAP 16.1   The New South, 1900**
The economy of the Old South focused on raising staple crops, especially cotton and tobacco. In the New South, staple agriculture continued to dominate, but industrial regions also evolved, producing textiles, coal, and iron. By 1900, the South's industrial pattern was well defined, though the region still served—like the West—as a major producer of raw materials for the industrial region that stretched from New England to Chicago.

sprouted in the Carolinas and Georgia, recruiting workers from surrounding farms; whole families often worked in the mills. Many children also worked in Pennsylvania coal fields, where death and injury rates were high. State law permitted children as young as twelve to labor with a family member, but turn-of-the-century investigators estimated that about 10,000 additional boys, at even younger ages, were illegally employed in the mines.

Also at the bottom of the pay scale were most African Americans. Corporations and industrial manufacturers widely discriminated against them on the basis of race, and such prejudice was hardly limited to the South. After the Civil War, African American women who moved to northern cities were largely barred from office work and other new employment options; instead, they remained heavily concentrated in domestic service, with more than half employed as cooks or servants. African American men confronted similar exclusion. America's booming vertically integrated corporations turned black men away from all but the most menial jobs. In 1890, almost a third of black men worked in personal service. Employers in the North and West recruited, instead, a different kind of low-wage labor: newly arrived immigrants.

> **IN YOUR OWN WORDS**
>
> What new business practices arose in the late-nineteenth-century United States, and what impact did they have on employees, consumers, and the environment?

# Immigrants, East and West

Across the globe, industrialization set people in motion with the lure of jobs. Between the Civil War and World War I, over 25 million immigrants entered the United States. The American working class became truly global, including not only people of African and Western European descent but also Southern and Eastern Europeans, Mexicans, and Asians. In 1900, census-takers found that more than 75 percent of San Francisco and New York City residents had at least one parent who was foreign-born.

In the new industrial order, immigrants made an ideal labor supply. They took the worst jobs at low pay, and during economic downturns tens of thousands returned to their home countries, reducing the shock of unemployment in the United States. But many native-born Americans viewed immigrants with hostility, through the lens of racial, ethnic, and religious prejudices. They also feared that immigrants would take more coveted jobs and erode white men's wages. For immigrants themselves, America could be disorienting, liberating, and disappointing.

## Newcomers from Europe

Mass migration from Western Europe had started in the 1840s, when more than one million Irish fled a terrible famine. In the following decades, as Europe's population grew rapidly and agriculture became commercialized, peasant economies suffered, first in Germany and Scandinavia, then across Austria-Hungary, Russia, Italy, and the Balkans. This upheaval displaced millions of rural people. Some went to Europe's mines and factories; others headed for South America and the United States (Map 16.2).

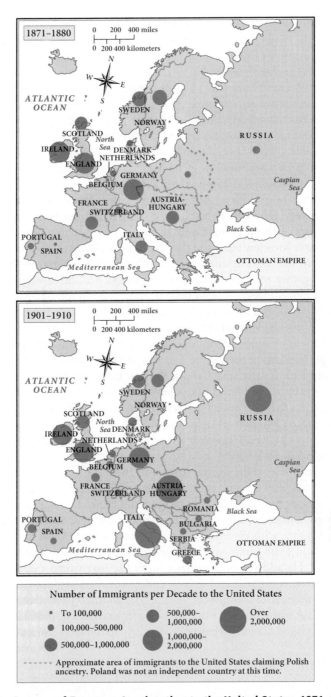

### MAP 16.2  Sources of European Immigration to the United States, 1871–1910

Around 1900, Americans began to speak of the "new" immigration. They meant the large numbers of immigrants arriving from Eastern and Southern Europe—Poles, Slovaks and other Slavic peoples, Yiddish-speaking Jews, Greeks, and Italians—who overwhelmed the still substantial number of immigrants from the British Isles and Northern Europe.

"America was known to foreigners," remembered one Jewish woman from Lithuania, "as the land where you'd get rich." But the reality was much harsher. Even in the age of steam, a transatlantic voyage was grueling. For ten to twenty days, passengers in steerage class crowded below decks, eating terrible food and struggling with seasickness. An investigator who traveled with immigrants from Naples asked, "How can a steerage passenger remember that he is a human being when he must first pick the worms from his food?" After 1892, European immigrants were routed through the enormous receiving station at New York's Ellis Island.

Some immigrants brought skills. Many Welshmen, for example, arrived in the United States as experienced tin-plate makers; Germans came as machinists and carpenters, Scandinavians as sailors. But industrialization required, most of all, increasing quantities of unskilled labor. As poor farmers from Italy, Greece, and Eastern Europe arrived in the United States, heavy, low-paid labor became their domain.

In an era of cheap railroad and steamship travel, many immigrants expected to work and save for a few years and then head home. More than 800,000 French Canadians moved to New England in search of textile jobs, many families with hopes of scraping together enough savings to return to Quebec and buy a farm. Thousands of men came alone, especially from Ireland, Italy, and Greece. Many single Irishwomen also immigrated. But some would-be sojourners ended up staying a lifetime, while immigrants who had expected to settle permanently found themselves forced to leave by an accident or sudden economic depression. One historian has estimated that a third of immigrants to the United States in this era returned to their home countries.

Along with Italians and Greeks, Eastern European Jews were among the most numerous arrivals. The first American Jews, who numbered around 50,000 in 1880, had been mostly of German Jewish descent. In the next four decades, more than 3 million poverty-stricken Jews arrived from Russia, Ukraine, Poland, and other parts of Eastern Europe, transforming the Jewish presence in the United States. Like other immigrants, they sought economic opportunity, but they also came to escape religious repression.

Wherever they came from, immigrants took a considerable gamble in traveling to the United States. Some prospered quickly, especially if they came with education, money, or well-placed business contacts. Others, by toiling many years in harsh conditions, succeeded in securing a better life for their children or grandchildren. Still others met with catastrophe or early death. One Polish man who came with his parents in 1908 summed up his life over the next thirty years as "a mere struggle for bread." He added: "Sometimes I think life isn't worth a damn for a man like me. . . . Look at my wife and kids—undernourished, seldom have a square meal." But an Orthodox Russian Jewish woman told an interviewer that she "thanked God for America," where she had married, raised three children, and made a good life. She "liked everything about this country, especially its leniency toward the Jews."

## Asian Americans and Exclusion

Compared with Europeans, newcomers from Asia faced even harsher treatment. The first Chinese immigrants had arrived in the late 1840s during the California gold rush. After the Civil War, the Burlingame Treaty between the United States and China opened the way for increasing numbers to emigrate. Fleeing poverty and upheaval in southern China, they, like European immigrants, filled low-wage jobs in the American economy. The Chinese confronted threats and violence. "We kept indoors after dark for fear of being shot in the back," remembered one Chinese immigrant to California. During the depression of the 1870s, a rising tide of racism was especially extreme in the Pacific coast states, where the majority of Chinese immigrants lived. "The Chinese must go!" railed Dennis Kearney, leader of the California Workingmen's Party, who referred to Asians as "almond-eyed lepers." Incited by Kearney in July 1877, a mob burned San Francisco's Chinatown and beat up residents. In the 1885 Rock Springs massacre in Wyoming, white men burned the local Chinatown and murdered at least twenty-eight Chinese miners.

Despite such atrocities, some Chinese managed to build profitable businesses and farms. Many did so by filling the only niches native-born Americans left open to them: running restaurants and laundries. Facing intense political pressure, Congress in 1882 passed the **Chinese Exclusion Act**, specifically barring Chinese laborers from entering the United States. Each decade thereafter, Congress renewed the law and tightened its provisions; it was not repealed until 1943. Exclusion barred almost all Chinese women, forcing husbands and wives to spend many years apart when men took jobs in the United States.

Asian immigrants made vigorous use of the courts to try to protect their rights. In a series of cases brought by Chinese and later Japanese immigrants, the U.S. Supreme Court ruled that all persons born in the United States had citizenship rights that could not be revoked, even if their parents had been born abroad. Nonetheless, well into the twentieth century, Chinese immigrants (as opposed to native-born Chinese Americans) could not apply for citizenship. Meanwhile, Japanese and a few Korean immigrants also began to arrive; by 1909, there were 40,000 Japanese immigrants working in agriculture, 10,000 on railroads, and 4,000 in canneries. In 1906, the U.S. attorney general ruled that Japanese and Koreans, like Chinese immigrants, were barred from citizenship.

**Anti-Chinese Racism**  This cartoon from the magazine *Puck*, drawn by James A. Wales during the 1880 presidential campaign, offers vivid evidence of the widespread and virulent American prejudice against Chinese immigrants. Republican candidate James Garfield, on the left, and Democratic candidate Winfield Scott Hancock, on the right, both nail up their party's "planks" in favor of restricting Chinese immigration. Asian immigrants were not permitted to apply for naturalization as U.S. citizens; they thus had no vote and no power in politics. Congress passed the Chinese Exclusion Act, with bipartisan support, soon after Garfield's victory. Library of Congress.

The Chinese Exclusion Act created the legal foundations on which far-reaching exclusionary policies would be built in the 1920s and after (Chapter 21). To enforce the law, Congress and the courts gave sweeping new powers to immigration officials, transforming the Chinese into America's first illegal immigrants. Drawn, like others, by the promise of jobs in America's expanding economy, Chinese men stowed away on ships or walked across the borders. Disguising themselves as Mexicans — who at that time could freely enter the United States — some perished in the desert as they tried to reach California.

Some would-be immigrants, known as paper sons, relied on Chinese residents in the United States, who generated documents falsely claiming the newcomers as American-born children. Paper sons memorized pages of information about their supposed relatives and hometowns. The San Francisco earthquake of 1906 helped their cause by destroying all the port's records. "That was a big chance for a lot of Chinese," remembered one immigrant. "They forged themselves certificates saying they could go back to China and bring back four or five sons, just like that!" Such persistence ensured that, despite the harsh policies of Chinese exclusion, the flow of Asian immigrants never fully ceased.

| IN YOUR OWN WORDS | What factors encouraged immigrants to seek entry into the United States, and how did their experiences differ? |

# Labor Gets Organized

In the American political system, labor has typically been weak. Industrial workers cluster in cities, near factories and jobs; compared with small towns and rural areas, urban areas have been underrepresented in bodies such as the U.S. Senate and the presidential electoral college, in which representation is calculated by state, rather than (or in addition to) individuals. This problem became acute in the era of industrialization, and it has lingered. Even today, the twenty-two U.S. senators elected from Alaska, Idaho, Iowa, Maine, Mississippi, Montana, New Mexico, North Dakota, Vermont, West Virginia, and Wyoming represent a smaller number of people, *combined*, than the two U.S. senators who represent heavily urban California.

Faced with this obstacle, labor advocates could adopt one of two strategies. First, they could try to make political alliances with sympathetic rural voters who shared their problems. Second, they could reject politics and create narrowly focused trade unions to negotiate directly with employers. In general, labor advocates emphasized the first strategy between the 1870s and the early 1890s, and the latter in the early twentieth century. Across this era, while industrialization made America increasingly rich and powerful, it also brought large-scale conflict between labor and capital.

## The Emergence of a Labor Movement

The problem of industrial labor entered Americans' consciousness dramatically with the **Great Railroad Strike of 1877**. Protesting steep wage cuts amid the depression that had begun in 1873, thousands of railroad workers walked off the job. Broader issues were at stake. "The officers of the road," reported strike leader Barney

Donahue in upstate New York, "were bound to break the spirit of the men, and any or all organizations they belonged to." He believed railroad companies wanted to block workers from "all fellowship for mutual aid." The strike brought rail travel and commerce to a halt. Thousands of people poured into the streets of Buffalo, Pittsburgh, and Chicago to protest the economic injustice wrought by railroads—as well as fires caused by stray sparks from locomotives and injuries and deaths on train tracks in urban neighborhoods. When Pennsylvania's governor sent state militia to break the strike, Pittsburgh crowds reacted by burning railroad property and over-turning locomotives. Similar clashes between police and protesters occurred in other cities across the country, from Galveston, Texas, to San Francisco.

The 1877 strike left more than fifty people dead and caused $40 million worth of damage, primarily to railroad property. "It seemed as if the whole social and polit-ical structure was on the very brink of ruin," wrote one journalist. For their role in the strike, many railroad workers were fired and blacklisted: railroad companies cir-culated their names on a "do not hire" list to prevent them from getting any work in the industry. In the aftermath of the strike, the U.S. government created the National Guard, intended not to protect Americans against foreign invasion but to enforce order at home.

Watching the upheavals of industrialization, some radical thinkers pointed out its impact on workers. Among the most influential was Henry George, whose book *Progress and Poverty* (1879) was a best-seller for decades after publication. George warned that Americans had been too optimistic about the impact of railroads and man-ufacturing, which they hoped would—after an initial period of turmoil—bring pros-perity to all. George believed the emerging industrial order meant permanent poverty. Industrialization, he wrote, was driving a wedge through society, lifting the fortunes of professionals and the middle class but pushing the working class down by forcing them into deskilled, dangerous, and low-paid labor. George's proposed solution, a federal "single tax" on landholdings, did not win widespread support, but his insightful diag-nosis of the problem helped encourage radical movements for economic reform.

Many rural people believed they faced the same problems as industrial work-ers. In the new economy, they found themselves at the mercy of large corporations, from equipment dealers who sold them harvesters and plows to railroads and grain elevators that shipped and stored their products. Though farmers appeared to have more independence than corporate employees, many felt trapped in a web of mid-dlemen who chipped away at their profits while international forces robbed them of decision-making power.

Farmers denounced not only corporations but also the previous two decades of government efforts to foster economic development—policies that now seemed wrongheaded. Farmers' advocates argued that high tariffs forced rural families to pay too much for basic necessities while failing to protect America's great export crops, cotton and wheat. At the same time, they charged, Republican financial policies ben-efitted banks, not borrowers. Farmers blamed railroad companies for taking govern-ment grants and subsidies to build but then charging unequal rates that privileged big manufacturers. From the farmers' point of view, public money had been used to build giant railroad companies that turned around and exploited ordinary people.

The most prominent rural protest group of the early postwar decades was the National Grange of the Patrons of Husbandry, founded in 1867. Like industrial workers, Grange farmers sought to counter the rising power of corporate middle-men through cooperation and mutual aid. Local Grange halls brought farm families together for recreation and conversation. The Grange set up its own banks, insurance companies, and grain elevators, and, in Iowa, even a farm implement factory. Many Grange members also advocated political action, building independent local parties that ran on anticorporate platforms.

During the 1870s depression, Grangers, labor advocates, and local workingmen's parties forged a national political movement, the **Greenback-Labor Party**. In the South, Greenbackers protested the collapse of Reconstruction and urged that every man's vote be protected. Across the country, Greenbackers advocated laws to regu-late corporations and enforce an eight-hour workday to reduce long, grueling work hours. They called for the federal government to print more greenback dollars and increase the amount of money in circulation; this, they argued, would stimulate the economy, create jobs, and help borrowers by allowing them to pay off debts in dollars that, over time, slowly decreased in value. Greenbackers, like many industrial labor leaders, subscribed to the ideal of **producerism**: they dismissed middlemen, bankers, lawyers, and investors as idlers who lived off the sweat of people who worked with their hands. As a Pittsburgh worker put it in an 1878 poem, it was not the money-handlers or executives at the top but the "noble sons of Labor . . . who with bone, and brain, and fiber make the nation's wealth."

The Greenback movement radicalized thousands of farmers, miners, and indus-trial workers. In Alabama's coal-mining regions, black and white miners cooperated in the party. Texas boasted seventy African American Greenback clubs. In 1878, Greenback-Labor candidates won more than a million votes, and the party elected fifteen congressmen nationwide. In the Midwest, Greenback pressure helped trigger a wave of economic regulatory actions known as **Granger laws**. By the early 1880s, twenty-nine states had created railroad commissions to supervise railroad rates and policies; others appointed commissions to regulate insurance and utility companies. Such early regulatory efforts were not always effective, but they were crucial starting points for reform. While short-lived, the Greenback movement created the founda-tion for more sustained efforts to regulate big business.

## The Knights of Labor

The most important union of the late nineteenth century, the **Knights of Labor**, was founded in 1869 as a secret society of garment workers in Philadelphia. In 1878, as the Greenback movement reached its height, some Knights served as delegates to Greenback-Labor conventions. Like Grangers, Knights believed that ordinary people needed control over the enterprises in which they worked. They proposed to set up shops owned by employees, transforming America into what they called a cooper-ative commonwealth. In keeping with this broad-based vision, the order practiced open membership, irrespective of race, gender, or field of employment—though, like other labor groups, the Knights excluded Chinese immigrants.

The Knights had a strong political bent. They believed that only electoral action could bring about many of their goals, such as government regulation of corporations and laws that required employers to negotiate during strikes. Their 1878 platform denounced the "aggressiveness of great capitalists and corporations." "If we desire to enjoy the full blessings of life," the Knights warned, "a check [must] be placed upon unjust accumulation, and the power for evil of aggregated wealth." Among their demands were workplace safety laws, prohibition of child labor, a federal tax on the nation's highest incomes, public ownership of telegraphs and railroads, and government recognition of workers' right to organize. The Knights also advocated personal responsibility and self-discipline. Their leader, Terence Powderly, warned that the abuse of liquor robbed as many workers of their wages as did ruthless employers.

Growing rapidly in the 1880s, the Knights' union was sprawling and decentralized. It included not only skilled craftsmen such as carpenters, ironworkers, and beer brewers but also textile workers in Rhode Island, domestic workers in Georgia, and tenant farmers in Arkansas. Knights organized workingmen's parties to advocate a host of reforms, ranging from an eight-hour workday to cheaper streetcar fares and better garbage collection in urban areas. One of their key innovations was hiring a full-time women's organizer, Leonora Barry. An Irish American widow who was forced into factory work after her husband's death, Barry became a labor advocate out of horror at the conditions she experienced on the job. To the discomfort of some male Knights, she investigated and exposed widespread evidence of sexual harassment on the job.

The Knights' growth in the 1880s showed the grassroots basis of labor activism. Powderly tried to avoid strikes, which he saw as costly and risky. But the organization's greatest growth resulted from spontaneous, grassroots striking. In 1885, thousands of workers on the Southwest Railroad walked off the job to protest wage cuts; afterward, they telegraphed the Knights and asked to be admitted as members. The strike enhanced the Knights' reputation among workers and built membership to 750,000. By the following year, local assemblies had sprung up in every state and almost every county in the United States.

Just as the Knights reached this pinnacle of influence, an episode of violence brought them down. In 1886, a protest at the McCormick reaper works in Chicago led to a clash with police that left four strikers dead. (Three unions, including a Knights of Labor assembly, had struck, but the Knights had reached an agreement and returned to work. Only the machinists' union remained on strike when the incident occurred.) Chicago was a hotbed of **anarchism**, the revolutionary advocacy of a stateless society. Local anarchists, many of them German immigrants, called a protest meeting the next day, May 4, 1886, at **Haymarket Square**. When police tried to disperse the crowd, someone threw a bomb that killed several policemen. Officers responded with gunfire. In the trial that followed, eight anarchists were found guilty of murder and criminal conspiracy. All were convicted, not on any definitive evidence that one of them threw the bomb (the bomber's identity remains unknown) but on the basis of their antigovernment speeches. Four of the eight were executed by hanging, one committed suicide in prison, and the others received long sentences.

The Haymarket violence profoundly damaged the American labor movement. Seizing on resulting antiunion hysteria, employers took the offensive. They broke strikes with mass arrests, tied up the Knights in expensive court proceedings, and forced workers to sign contracts pledging not to join labor organizations. The Knights of Labor never recovered. In the view of the press and many prosperous Americans, they were tainted by their alleged links with anarchism. Struggles between industrialists and workers had created bitter divides.

## Farmers and Workers: The Cooperative Alliance

In the aftermath of Haymarket, the Knights' cooperative vision did not entirely fade. A new rural movement, the **Farmers' Alliance**, arose to take up many of the issues that Grangers and Greenbackers had earlier sought to address. Founded in Texas during the depression of the 1870s, the Farmers' Alliance spread across the plains states and the South, becoming by the late 1880s the largest farmer-based movement in American history. A separate Colored Farmers' Alliance arose to represent rural African Americans. The harsh conditions farmers were enduring—including drought in the West and plunging global prices for corn, cotton, and wheat—intensified the movement's appeal. Traveling Alliance lecturers exhorted farmers to "stand as a great conservative body against . . . the growing corruption of wealth and power."

Like earlier movements, Alliance leaders pinned their initial hopes on cooperative stores and exchanges that would circumvent middlemen. Cooperatives gathered farmers' orders and bought in bulk at wholesale prices, passing the savings

**Industrial Violence: A Dynamited Mine, 1894** Strikes in the western mining regions pitted ruthless owners, bent on control of their property and workforce, against fiercely independent miners who knew how to use dynamite. Some of the bloodiest conflicts occurred in Colorado mining towns, where the Western Federation of Miners (WFM) had strong support and a series of Republican governors sent state militia to back the mine owners. Violence broke out repeatedly between the early 1890s and the 1910s. At Victor, Colorado, in May 1894, as dozens of armed sheriffs' deputies closed in on angry WFM members occupying the Strong Mine in protest, the miners blew up the mine's shaft house and boiler. Showered with debris, the deputies boarded the next train out of town. Because Colorado then had a Populist governor, Davis Waite, who sympathized with the miners and ordered the deputies to disband, this strike was one of the few in which owners and miners reached a peaceful settlement—a temporary victory for the union. Library of Congress.

along. Alliance cooperatives achieved notable victories in the late 1880s. The Dakota Alliance, for example, offered members cheap hail insurance and low prices on machinery and farm supplies. The Texas Alliance established a huge cooperative enterprise to market cotton and provide farmers with cheap loans. When cotton prices fell further in 1891, however, the Texas exchange failed. Other cooperatives also suffered from chronic underfunding and lack of credit, and they faced hostility from merchants and lenders they tried to circumvent.

The Texas Farmers' Alliance thus proposed a federal price-support system for farm products, modeled on the national banks. Under this plan, the federal government would hold crops in public warehouses and issue loans on their value until they could be profitably sold. When Democrats — still wary of big-government schemes — declared the idea too radical, Alliances in Texas, Kansas, South Dakota, and elsewhere decided to create a new political party, the Populists (see Chapter 19). In this venture, the Alliance cooperated with the weakened Knights of Labor, seeking to use rural voters' substantial clout on behalf of urban workers who shared their vision.

By this time, farmer-labor coalitions had made a considerable impact on state politics. But state laws and commissions were proving ineffective against corporations of national and even global scope. It was difficult for Wisconsin, for instance, to enforce new laws against a railroad company whose lines might stretch from Chicago to Seattle and whose corporate headquarters might be in Minnesota. Militant farmers and labor advocates demanded federal action.

In 1887, responding to this pressure, Congress and President Grover Cleveland passed two landmark laws. The Hatch Act provided federal funding for agricultural research and education, meeting farmers' demands for government aid to agriculture. The **Interstate Commerce Act** counteracted a Supreme Court decision of the previous year, *Wabash v. Illinois* (1886), that had struck down states' authority to regulate railroads. The act created the Interstate Commerce Commission (ICC), charged with investigating interstate shipping, forcing railroads to make their rates public, and suing in court when necessary to make companies reduce "unjust or unreasonable" rates.

Though creation of the ICC was a direct response to farmer-labor demands, its final form represented a compromise. Radical leaders wanted Congress to establish a direct set of rules under which railroads must operate. If a railroad did not comply, any citizen could take the company to court; if the new rules triggered bankruptcy, the railroad could convert to public ownership. But getting such a plan through Congress proved impossible. Lawmakers more sympathetic to business called instead for an expert commission to oversee the railroad industry. In a pattern that repeated frequently over the next few decades, the commission model proved more acceptable to the majority of congressmen.

The ICC faced formidable challenges. Though the new law forbade railroads from reaching secret rate-setting agreements, evidence was difficult to gather and secret "pooling" continued. A hostile Supreme Court also undermined the commission's powers. In a series of sixteen decisions over the two decades after the ICC was created, the Court sided with railroads fifteen times. The justices delivered a particularly hard blow in 1897 when they ruled that the ICC had no power to interfere with shipping rates. Nonetheless, the ICC's existence was a major achievement.

In the early twentieth century, Congress would strengthen the commission's powers, and the ICC would become one of the most powerful federal agencies charged with overseeing private business.

## Another Path: The American Federation of Labor

While the Knights of Labor exerted political pressure, other workers pursued a different strategy. In the 1870s, printers, ironworkers, bricklayers, and other skilled workers organized nationwide trade unions. These "brotherhoods" focused on the everyday needs of workers in skilled occupations. Trade unions sought a closed shop — with all jobs reserved for union members — that kept out lower-wage workers. Union rules specified terms of work, sometimes in minute detail. Many unions emphasized mutual aid. Because working on the railroads was a high-risk occupation, for example, brotherhoods of engineers, brakemen, and firemen pooled contributions into funds that provided accident and death benefits. Above all, trade unionism asserted craft workers' rights as active decision-makers in the workplace, not just cogs in a management-run machine.

In the early 1880s, many trade unionists joined the Knights of Labor coalition. But the aftermath of the Haymarket violence persuaded them to leave and create the separate **American Federation of Labor** (AFL). The man who led them was Samuel Gompers, a Dutch-Jewish cigar maker whose family had immigrated to New York in 1863. Gompers headed the AFL for nearly forty years. He believed the Knights relied too much on electoral politics, where victories were likely to be limited, and he did not share their sweeping critique of capitalism. The AFL, made up of relatively skilled and well-paid workers, was less interested in challenging the corporate order than in winning a larger share of its rewards.

Having gone to work at age ten, Gompers always contended that what he missed at school he more than made up for in the shop, where cigar makers paid one of their members to read to them while they worked. As a young worker-intellectual, Gompers gravitated to New York's radical circles, where he participated in lively debates about which strategies workingmen should pursue. Partly out of these debates, and partly from his own experience in the Cigar Makers Union, Gompers hammered out a doctrine that he called pure-and-simple unionism. *Pure* referred to membership: strictly limited to workers, organized by craft and occupation, with no reliance on outside advisors or allies. *Simple* referred to goals: only those that immediately benefitted workers — better wages, hours, and working conditions. Pure-and-simple unionists distrusted politics. Their aim was collective bargaining with employers.

On one level, pure-and-simple unionism worked. The AFL was small at first, but by 1904 its membership rose to more than two million. In the early twentieth century, it became the nation's leading voice for workers, lasting far longer than movements like the Knights of Labor. The AFL's strategy — personified by Gompers — was well suited to an era when Congress and the courts were hostile to labor. By the 1910s, the political climate would become more responsive; at that later moment, Gompers would soften his antipolitical stance and join the battle for new labor laws (Chapter 19).

What Gompers gave up most crucially, in the meantime, was the inclusiveness of the Knights. By comparison, the AFL was far less welcoming to women and blacks; it included mostly skilled craftsmen. There was little room in the AFL for department-store clerks and other service workers, much less the farm tenants and domestic servants whom the Knights had organized. Despite the AFL's success among skilled craftsmen, the narrowness of its base was a problem that would come back to haunt the labor movement later on. Gompers, however, saw that corporate titans and their political allies held tremendous power, and he advocated what he saw as the most practical defensive plan. In the meantime, the upheaval wrought by industrialization spread far beyond the workplace, transforming every aspect of American life.

| IN YOUR OWN WORDS | How did the key institutions and goals of the labor movement change between 1877 and 1900, and what gains and losses resulted from these shifts? |
|---|---|

## Summary

The end of the Civil War ushered in the era of American big business. Exploiting the continent's vast resources, vertically integrated corporations emerged as the dominant business form, and giant companies built near monopolies in some sectors of the economy. Corporations devised new modes of production, distribution, and marketing, extending their reach through the department store, the mail-order catalog, and the new advertising industry. These developments laid the groundwork for mass consumer culture. They also offered emerging jobs in management, sales, and office work.

Rapid industrialization drew immigrants from around the world. Until the 1920s, most European and Latin American immigrants were welcome to enter the United States, though they often endured harsh conditions after they arrived. Asian immigrants, by contrast, faced severe discrimination. The Chinese Exclusion Act blocked all Chinese laborers from coming to the United States; it was later extended to other Asians, and it built the legal framework for broader forms of exclusion.

Nationwide movements for workers' rights arose in response to industrialization. During the 1870s and 1880s, coalitions of workers and farmers, notably the Knights of Labor and the Farmers' Alliance, sought political solutions to what they saw as large corporations' exploitation of working people. Pressure from such movements led to the first major attempts to regulate corporations, such as the federal Interstate Commerce Act. Radical protest movements were weakened, however, after public condemnation of anarchist violence in 1886 at Chicago's Haymarket Square. Meanwhile, trade unions such as the American Federation of Labor organized skilled workers and negotiated directly with employers, becoming the most popular form of labor organization in the early twentieth century.

# Chapter 16 Review

## KEY TERMS

**Identify and explain the significance of each term below.**

Homestead lockout (p. 475)
Gospel of Wealth (p. 475)
management revolution (p. 476)
vertical integration (p. 477)
horizontal integration (p. 477)
trust (p. 477)
deskilling (p. 481)
scientific management (p. 482)
New South (p. 483)
Chinese Exclusion Act (p. 487)
Great Railroad Strike of 1877 (p. 488)

Greenback-Labor Party (p. 490)
producerism (p. 490)
Granger laws (p. 490)
Knights of Labor (p. 490)
anarchism (p. 491)
Haymarket Square (p. 491)
Farmers' Alliance (p. 492)
Interstate Commerce Act (p. 493)
American Federation of Labor
   (p. 494)

## REVIEW QUESTIONS

**Answer these questions to demonstrate your understanding of the chapter's main ideas.**

1. What new business practices arose in the late-nineteenth-century United States, and what impact did they have on employees, consumers, and the environment?

2. What factors encouraged immigrants to seek entry into the United States, and how did their experiences differ?

3. How did the key institutions and goals of the labor movement change between 1877 and 1900, and what gains and losses resulted from these shifts?

4. Review the events listed under "Politics and Power," "Migration and Settlement," and "Work, Exchange, and Technology" on the thematic timeline on pages 472–473. How did industrialization as an *economic* process transform American society and politics?

## CHRONOLOGY

**As you read, ask yourself why this chapter begins and ends with these dates and identify the links among related events.**

| 1863 | • Cleveland, Ohio, becomes nation's petroleum refining center |
| 1865 | • Chicago's Union Stock Yards opens |
| 1867 | • National Grange of the Patrons of Husbandry founded |

| | |
|---|---|
| **1869** | • Knights of Labor founded |
| **1873** | • Panic followed by severe economic depression |
| **1875** | • John Wanamaker opens nation's first department store in Philadelphia |
| **1876** | • Alexander Graham Bell invents the telephone |
| **1877** | • San Francisco mob attacks Chinatown |
| | • Great Railroad Strike |
| | • First Farmers' Alliances form in South and West |
| **1878** | • Greenback-Labor Party elects fifteen congressmen |
| **1879** | • Henry George publishes *Progress and Poverty* |
| **1880s** | • Violence in Russia and Eastern Europe prompts mass immigration of Jews to United States |
| **1882** | • John D. Rockefeller creates Standard Oil trust |
| | • Congress passes Chinese Exclusion Act |
| **1884** | • Knights of Labor at peak of membership |
| **1885** | • Rock Springs massacre of Chinese miners |
| **1886** | • Haymarket Square violence |
| | • American Federation of Labor (AFL) founded |
| **1887** | • Hatch Act |
| | • Interstate Commerce Act |
| **1889** | • New Jersey passes law enabling trusts to operate in the state |
| **1892** | • Homestead lockout |
| **1893** | • Severe depression hits, causes mass unemployment and wave of corporate mergers |
| **1901** | • J. P. Morgan creates U.S. Steel, America's first billion-dollar corporation |
| **1908** | • Walter Dill Scott publishes *The Psychology of Advertising* |
| | • Marianna, Pennsylvania, mine disaster |

# 17

# Making Modern American Culture

## 1880–1917

### IDENTIFY THE BIG IDEA

How did the changes wrought by industrialization shape Americans' identities, beliefs, and culture?

**BETWEEN 1888 AND 1900, AMERICAN ARCHAEOLOGISTS CONDUCTED** their first explorations in what is now Iraq, at the site of the ancient city of Nippur. Leaders of the expedition included Protestant ministers and the editor of the national *Sunday-School Times*. Their goal was to practice biblical archaeology: to confirm the truth of Old Testament accounts of Babylon. As one participant wrote, they sought to blend a "spirit of Christian enlightenment" with modern "scientific inquiry." The expeditions unearthed thousands of cuneiform tablets, which Jewish and Christian linguists and anthropologists used to reveal much about ancient Assyrian society. Some investigators found that these discoveries strengthened their faith in biblical truth. Others were not so sure.

As shown by the Babylonian expeditions, a passion for scientific inquiry swept the late-nineteenth-century United States, often inspired by religious teachings but ultimately calling into question many tenets of faith. Between the 1870s and the 1910s, a stunning series of scientific discoveries—from dinosaur fossils to telescopic observations of nebulae—challenged long-held beliefs. Biological theories of evolution prompted fierce debate, but so did the effects of technological innovations such as medical vaccines and electric chairs. While science gained popularity, religion hardly faded. In fact, religious diversity grew, as immigrants brought new faiths to the United States and Protestants responded with innovations of their own.

At the same time, industrialization reshaped class identities and generated an alluring consumer culture. Lavish urban department stores catered to middle-class customers, while working-class men and women enjoyed vaudeville shows. Americans of all backgrounds and classes mingled at baseball games and summer amusement parks. An older ethos of duty, self-restraint, and moral uplift gave way to expectations of leisure and fun. As African Americans and women claimed a right to education and public space—the opportunity to shop, dine, and travel freely—they built powerful reform movements. At the same time, the pressures of the industrial workplace led to aggressive calls for masculine fitness, exemplified by the rise of sports. Here, too, scientific research sparked debates over the body, gender, and race. Americans found themselves living in a modern world—one in which many of their grandparents' beliefs and practices might no longer apply.

# Science and Faith

In the early nineteenth century, most Americans believed the world was about six thousand years old. No one knew what lay beyond the solar system. By the 1910s, paleontologists were classifying Jurassic dinosaurs, astronomers had identified distant galaxies, and physicists were beginning to measure the speed of light. Many scientists and ordinary Americans accepted Charles Darwin's theory of evolution, though exactly how natural selection worked—and its implications for religious belief—remained contested.

Scientific discoveries received widespread publicity through a series of great world's fairs, most famously Chicago's 1893 World's Columbian Exposition, held (a year late) to mark the four-hundredth anniversary of Columbus's first voyage to America. At the fairgrounds, visitors strolled through enormous buildings that displayed the latest inventions in industry, machinery, and transportation. They marveled over steam engines, weather-forecasting equipment, and moving sidewalks. At dusk they gathered to watch the fair buildings illuminated with strings of electric lights. One observer called the exposition "a vast and wonderful university of the arts and sciences."

It is hardly surprising, amid these achievements, that "fact worship" became a central feature of American intellectual life. Researchers in many fields argued that one could rely only on hard facts to understand the "laws of life." In their enthusiasm, some economists and sociologists rejected all social reform as sentimental. Fiction writers and artists kept a more humane emphasis, but they made use of similar methods—close observation and attention to real-life experience—to create works of realism. Meanwhile, other Americans struggled to reconcile scientific discoveries with religious faith.

## Darwinism and Its Critics

Evolution—the idea that species are not fixed, but ever changing—was not a simple idea on which all scientists agreed. In his immensely influential 1859 book, *On the Origin of Species*, British naturalist Charles Darwin argued that all creatures struggle to survive. When individual members of a species are born with random genetic mutations that better suit them for their environment—for example, camouflage coloring for a moth—these characteristics, since they are genetically transmissible, become dominant in future generations. Many scientists rejected this theory of natural selection. They followed a line of thinking laid out by French biologist Jean Baptiste Lamarck, who argued, unlike Darwin, that individual animals or plants could acquire transmittable traits within a single lifetime. A rhinoceros that fought fiercely, in Lamarck's view, could build up a stronger horn; its offspring would then be born with that trait.

**Evolution and Capitalism**   Darwin himself disapproved of the word *evolution* (which does not appear in his book) because it implied upward progress. In his view, natural selection was blind: environments and species changed randomly. Others were less scrupulous about drawing sweeping conclusions from Darwin's work. In the 1870s, British philosopher Herbert Spencer spun out an elaborate theory of how human society advanced through ruthless competitive struggle, resulting in "survival of the fittest." He applied this particularly to capitalism and industry.

The doctrine of **Social Darwinism**, as Spencer's idea became (confusingly) known, found its American champion in William Graham Sumner, a sociology professor at Yale. Competition, said Sumner, was a law of nature, like gravity. Who were the fittest? "Millionaires," Sumner declared. Their success showed they were "naturally selected." Sumner's views bolstered the pride and self-justification of industrial titans such as Andrew Carnegie, who loved Herbert Spencer's works and invited him to tour Pittsburgh. (Spencer was not impressed.) "The concentration of capital is necessary for meeting the demands of our day," was the message Carnegie took from Spencer. Similarly, John D. Rockefeller of Standard Oil declared that "the growth of a large business is merely a survival of the fittest. This is not an evil tendency of business. It is merely the working out of a law of nature and a law of God."

Even in the heyday of Social Darwinism, Spencer and Sumner's views were controversial. Many thinkers objected to the application of biological findings to the realm of economics and society. They pointed out that Darwin had observed finches and tortoises, not human institutions. Sociologist Lester Frank Ward argued that humanity "progresses through the *protection* of the weak," not through ruthless competition. "Man," he wrote, "through his intelligence, has labored successfully to resist the law of nature." Ward suggested, tongue in cheek, that if Americans subscribed to a doctrine of "survival of the fittest," they should abolish police and fire departments, irrigation works, and flood control. Social Darwinism, such critics argued, was simply an excuse for the worst excesses of industrialization. By the early twentieth century, intellectuals revolted against Sumner and his allies.

**Eugenics**   Meanwhile, though, some of the most dubious applications of evolutionary ideas were codified into new reproductive laws based on **eugenics**, a so-called science of human breeding. Eugenicists argued that mentally deficient people should be prevented from reproducing. They proposed to sterilize those deemed "unfit," especially residents of state asylums for the insane or mentally disabled. In early-twentieth-century America, almost half of the states enacted eugenics laws. By the time eugenics subsided in the 1930s, tens of thousands of people had been sterilized, with California and Virginia taking the lead. Women in Puerto Rico and other U.S. imperial possessions (see Chapter 20) also suffered from eugenic policies.

Advocates of eugenics had a broad impact. Because they associated mental unfitness with "lower races" — including people of African, Asian, and Native American descent — their arguments lent support to Jim Crow segregation laws and racial discrimination. In a wave of legislation beginning in the 1870s and peaking in the 1910s, most states in the South and West passed laws prohibiting interracial marriage, claiming that only separation of the races could foster human advancement. By warning that immigrants from Eastern and Southern Europe would dilute white Americans' racial purity, eugenicists helped win passage of immigration restriction in the 1920s.

## Religion: Diversity and Innovation

By the turn of the twentieth century, emerging scientific and cultural paradigms posed a significant challenge to religious faith. Some Americans argued that science and modernity would sweep away religion altogether. Contrary to such predictions, American religious practice remained vibrant. Protestants developed creative new responses to the challenges of industrialization, while millions of newcomers built institutions for worship and religious education.

**Immigrant Faiths**    Arriving in the United States in large numbers, Catholics and Jews wrestled with similar questions. To what degree should they adapt to Protestant-dominated American society? Should the education of clergy be changed? Should children attend religious or public schools? What happened if they married outside the faith? Among Catholic leaders, Bishop John Ireland of Minnesota argued that "the principles of the Church are in harmony with the interests of the Republic." But traditionalists, led by Archbishop Michael A. Corrigan of New York, disagreed. They sought to insulate Catholics from the pluralistic American environment. Indeed, by 1920, almost two million children attended Catholic elementary schools nationwide, and Catholic dioceses operated fifteen hundred high schools. Catholics as well as Jews feared some of the same threats that distressed Protestants: industrial poverty and overwork kept working-class people away from worship services, while new consumer pleasures enticed many of them to go elsewhere.

Faithful immigrant Catholics were anxious to preserve familiar traditions from Europe, and they generally supported the Church's traditional wing. But they also wanted religious life to express their ethnic identities. Italians, Poles, and other new arrivals wanted separate parishes where they could celebrate their customs, speak their languages, and establish their own parochial schools. When they became numerous enough, they also demanded their own bishops. Since the demand for ethnic parishes implied local control of church property, the Catholic hierarchy, dominated by Irish Americans, felt that the integrity of the Church was at stake. With some strain, however, the Catholic Church managed to satisfy the diverse needs of the immigrant faithful. It met the demand for representation, for example, by appointing immigrant priests as auxiliary bishops within existing dioceses.

In the same decades, many prosperous native-born Jews embraced Reform Judaism, abandoning such religious practices as keeping a kosher kitchen and conducting services in Hebrew. This was not the way of Yiddish-speaking Jews from Eastern Europe, who arrived in large numbers after the 1880s. Generally much poorer and eager to preserve their own traditions, they founded Orthodox synagogues, often in vacant stores, and practiced Judaism as they had at home.

But in Eastern Europe, Judaism had been an entire way of life, one not easily replicated in a large American city. "The very clothes I wore and the very food I ate had a fatal effect on my religious habits," confessed the hero of Abraham Cahan's novel *The Rise of David Levinsky* (1917). "If you . . . attempt to bend your religion to the spirit of your surroundings, it breaks. It falls to pieces." Levinsky shaved off his beard and plunged into the Manhattan clothing business. Orthodox Judaism survived the transition to America, but like other immigrant religions, it had to renounce its claims to some of the faithful.

**Protestant Innovations**     One of the era's dramatic religious developments — facilitated by global steamship and telegraph lines — was the rise of Protestant foreign missions. From a modest start before the Civil War, this movement peaked around 1915, a year when American religious organizations sponsored more than nine thousand overseas missionaries, supported at home by armies of volunteers, including more than three million women. A majority of Protestant missionaries served in Asia, with smaller numbers posted to Africa and the Middle East. Most saw American-style domesticity as a central part of evangelism, and missionary societies sent married couples into the field. Many unmarried women also served overseas as missionary teachers, doctors, and nurses, though almost never as ministers. "American woman," declared one Christian reformer, has "the exalted privilege of extending over the world those blessed influences, that are to renovate degraded man."

Protestant missionaries won converts, in part, by providing such modern services as medical care and women's education. Some missionaries developed deep bonds of respect with the people they served. Others showed considerable condescension toward the "poor heathen," who in turn bristled at their assumptions. One Presbyterian, who found Syrians uninterested in his gospel message, angrily denounced all Muslims as "corrupt and immoral." By imposing their views of "heathen races" and attacking those who refused to convert, Christian missionaries sometimes ended up justifying Western imperialism.

Cultural imperialism abroad reflected attitudes at home. Starting in Iowa in 1887, militant Protestants created a powerful political organization, the **American Protective Association** (APA), which for a brief period in the 1890s counted more than two million members. This virulently nativist group expressed outrage at the existence of separate Catholic schools while demanding, at the same time, that all public school teachers be Protestants. The APA called for a ban on Catholic officeholders, arguing that they were beholden to an "ecclesiastic power" that was "not created and controlled by American citizens." In its virulent anti-Catholicism and calls for restrictions on immigrants, the APA prefigured the revived Ku Klux Klan of the 1920s (Chapter 21).

The APA arose, in part, because Protestants found their dominance challenged. Millions of Americans, especially in the industrial working class, were now Catholics or Jews. Overall, in 1916, Protestants still constituted about 60 percent of Americans affiliated with a religious body. But they faced formidable rivals: the number of practicing Catholics in 1916 — 15.7 million — was greater than the number of Baptists, Methodists, and Presbyterians combined.

Some Protestants responded to the urban, immigrant challenge by evangelizing among the unchurched. They provided reading rooms, day nurseries, vocational classes, and other services. The goal of renewing religious faith through dedication to justice and social welfare became known as the **Social Gospel**. Its goals were epitomized by Charles Sheldon's novel *In His Steps* (1896), which told the story of a congregation that resolved to live by Christ's precepts for one year. "If church members were all doing as Jesus would do," Sheldon asked, "could it remain true that armies of men would walk the streets for jobs, and hundreds of them curse the church, and thousands of them find in the saloon their best friend?"

The Salvation Army, which arrived from Great Britain in 1879, also spread a gospel message among the urban poor, offering assistance that ranged from soup kitchens to shelters for former prostitutes. When all else failed, down-and-outers knew they could count on the Salvation Army, whose bell ringers became a familiar sight on city streets. The group borrowed up-to-date marketing techniques and used the latest business slang in urging its Christian soldiers to "hustle."

The Salvation Army succeeded, in part, because it managed to bridge an emerging divide between Social Gospel reformers and Protestants who were taking a different theological path. Disturbed by what they saw as rising secularism, conservative ministers and their allies held a series of Bible Conferences at Niagara Falls between 1876 and 1897. The resulting "Niagara Creed" reaffirmed the literal truth of the Bible and the certain damnation of those not born again in Christ. By the 1910s, a network of churches and Bible institutes had emerged from these conferences. They called their movement **fundamentalism**, based on their belief in the fundamental truth of the Bible.

Fundamentalists and their allies made particularly effective use of revival meetings. Unlike Social Gospel advocates, revivalists said little about poverty or earthly justice, focusing not on the matters of the world, but on heavenly redemption. The pioneer modern evangelist was Dwight L. Moody, a former Chicago shoe salesman and YMCA official who won fame in the 1870s. Eternal life could be had for the asking, Moody promised. His listeners needed only "to come forward and take, TAKE!" Moody's successor, Billy Sunday, helped bring evangelism into the modern era. More often than his predecessors, Sunday took political stances based on his Protestant beliefs. Condemning the "booze traffic" was his greatest cause. Sunday also denounced unrestricted immigration and labor radicalism. "If I had my way with these ornery wild-eyed Socialists," he once threatened, "I would stand them up before a firing squad." Sunday supported some progressive reform causes; he opposed child labor, for example, and advocated voting rights for women. In other ways, his views anticipated the nativism and antiradicalism that would dominate American politics after World War I.

## Realism in the Arts

Inspired by the quest for facts, American authors rejected nineteenth-century romanticism and what they saw as its unfortunate product, sentimentality. Instead, they took up literary **realism**. In the 1880s, editor and novelist William Dean Howells called for writers "to picture the daily life in the most exact terms possible." By the 1890s, a younger generation of writers pursued this goal. Theodore Dreiser dismissed unrealistic novels that always had "a happy ending." In *Main-Travelled Roads* (1891), based on the struggles of his midwestern farm family, Hamlin Garland turned the same unsparing eye on the hardships of rural life. Stephen Crane's *Maggie: A Girl of the Streets* (1893), privately printed because no publisher would touch it, described the seduction, abandonment, and death of a slum girl.

Some authors believed realism did not go far enough to overturn sentimentalism. Jack London spent his teenage years as a factory worker, sailor, and tramp. In stories such as "The Law of Life" (1901), he dramatized what he saw as the harsh reality of an uncaring universe. American society, he said, was "a jungle wherein wild beasts eat and are eaten." Similarly, Stephen Crane tried to capture "a world full of fists." London and Crane suggested that human beings were not so much rational shapers of their own destinies as blind victims of forces beyond their control — including their own subconscious impulses.

America's most famous writer, Samuel Langhorne Clemens, who took the pen name of Mark Twain, came to an equally bleak view. Though he achieved enormous success with such lighthearted books as *The Adventures of Tom Sawyer* (1876), Clemens courted controversy with *The Adventures of Huckleberry Finn* (1884), notable for its indictment of slavery and racism. In his novel *A Connecticut Yankee in King Arthur's Court* (1889), which ends with a bloody, technology-driven slaughter of Arthur's knights, Mark Twain became one of the bitterest critics of America's idea of progress. Afterward, Clemens was devastated by the loss of his wife and two daughters, as well as by failed investments and bankruptcy. An outspoken critic of imperialism and foreign missions, Twain eventually denounced Christianity itself as a hypocritical delusion. Like his friend the industrialist Andrew Carnegie, Clemens "got rid of theology."

By the time Clemens died in 1910, American artists had laid the groundwork for **modernism**, which rejected traditional canons of artistic taste. Questioning the whole idea of progress and order, modernists focused on the subconscious and "primitive" mind. Above all, they sought to overturn convention and tradition. Poet Ezra Pound exhorted, "Make it new!" Modernism became the first great literary and artistic movement of the twentieth century.

In the visual arts, new technologies influenced aesthetics. By 1900, some photographers argued that their "true" representations made painting obsolete. But painters invented their own forms of realism. Nebraska-born artist Robert Henri became fascinated with life in the great cities. "The backs of tenement houses are living documents," he declared, and he set out to put them on canvas. Henri and his followers, notably John Sloan and George Bellows, called themselves the New York Realists. Critics derided them as the Ash Can school because they chose subjects that were not conventionally beautiful.

In 1913, realists participated in one of the most controversial events in American art history, the Armory Show. Housed in an enormous National Guard building in New York, the exhibit introduced America to modern art. Some painters whose work appeared at the show were experimenting with cubism, characterized by abstract, geometric forms. Along with works by Henri, Sloan, and Bellows, organizers featured paintings by European rebels such as Pablo Picasso. America's academic art world was shocked. One critic called cubism "the total destruction of the art of painting."

But as the exhibition went on to Boston and Chicago, more than 250,000 people crowded to see it.

A striking feature of both realism and modernism, as they developed, was that many leading writers and artists were men. In making their work strong and modern, they also strove to assert their masculinity. Paralleling Theodore Roosevelt's call for "manly sports," they denounced nineteenth-century culture as hopelessly feminized. Stephen Crane called for "virility" in literature. Jack London described himself as a "man's man, . . . lustfully roving and conquering." Artist Robert Henri banned small brushes as "too feminine." In their own ways, these writers and artists contributed to a broad movement to masculinize American culture.

| **IN YOUR OWN WORDS** | How did Charles Darwin's theory of evolution and other scientific ideas impact American culture and intellectual life in the late nineteenth century? What uses did nonscientists make of such ideas? |
|---|---|

# Commerce and Culture

Debates over faith, science, and society affected Americans in widely different ways, partly because divisions between rural and urban life, and between affluent and poor Americans, were growing. As the United States industrialized, the terms *middle class* and *working class* came widely into use. Americans adopted these broad identities not only in the workplace but also in their leisure time. As professionals and corporate managers prospered, they and their families enjoyed rising income and an array of tempting ways to spend their dollars. Celebrating these new technological wonders, Americans hailed inventors as heroes. The most famous, Thomas Edison, operated an independent laboratory rather than working for a corporation. Edison, like many of the era's businessmen, was a shrewd entrepreneur who focused on commercial success. He and his colleagues helped introduce such lucrative products as the incandescent light bulb and the phonograph.

Even working-class Americans enjoyed cheaper products delivered by global trade and mass production, from bananas and cigarettes to colorful dime novels and magazines. Edison's moving pictures, for example, first found popularity among the urban working class. Consumer culture appeared, at least, to be democratic: anyone could eat at a restaurant or buy a rail ticket for the "ladies' car"—as long as she or he could pay. In practice, though, well-to-do Americans enjoyed new amenities at much higher rates. Consumer culture thus became a site of struggle over class inequality, race privilege, and proper male and female behavior.

## Consumer Spaces

America's public spaces—from election polls to saloons and circus shows—had long been boisterous and male-centered. A woman who ventured there without a male chaperone risked damaging her reputation (or worse). But the rise of new businesses encouraged change. To attract an eager public, purveyors of consumer culture invited women and families, especially those of the middle class, to linger in department stores and enjoy new amusements.

No one promoted commercial domesticity more successfully than showman P. T. Barnum, who used the country's expanding rail network to develop his famous traveling circus. Barnum condemned earlier circus managers who had opened their tents to "the rowdy element." Proclaiming children as his key audience, he created family entertainment for diverse audiences (though in the South, black audiences sat in segregated seats or attended separate shows). He promised middle-class parents that his circus would teach children courage and promote the benefits of exercise. To encourage women's attendance, Barnum emphasized the respectability and refinement of his female performers.

Department stores also lured middle-class women by offering tearooms, children's play areas, and clerks to wrap and carry every purchase. Store credit plans enabled well-to-do women to shop without handling money in public. Such tactics succeeded so well that New York's department store district became known as Ladies' Mile. Boston department store magnate William Filene called the department store an "Adamless Eden."

These Edens were reserved for the elite and middle classes. Though bargain basements and neighborhood stores served working-class families, big department stores used vagrancy laws and police to discourage the "wrong kind" from entering. Working-class women gained access primarily as clerks, cashiers, and cash girls, who at age twelve or younger served as internal store messengers, carrying orders and change for $1.50 a week. The department store was no Eden for these women, who worked long hours on their feet, often dealing with difficult customers. Nevertheless, many clerks claimed their own privileges as shoppers, making enthusiastic use of employee discounts and battling employers for the right to wear their fashionable purchases while they worked in the store.

In similar ways, class status was marked by the ways technology entered American homes. The rise of electricity, in particular, marked the gap between affluent urban consumers and rural and working-class families. In elite houses, domestic servants began to use—or find themselves replaced by—an array of new devices, from washing machines to vacuum cleaners. When Alexander Graham Bell invented the telephone in 1876, entrepreneurs introduced the device for business use, but it soon found eager residential customers, especially among the affluent. Telephones changed etiquette and social relations for middle-class suburban women—while providing their working-class counterparts with new employment as operators or "hello girls."

Railroads also reflected the emerging privileges of professional families. Finding prosperous Americans eager for excursions, railroad companies, like department stores, made things comfortable for middle-class women and children. Boston's South Station boasted of its modern amenities, including "everything that the traveler needs down to cradles in which the baby may be soothed." Rail cars manufactured by the famous Pullman Company of Chicago set a national standard for taste and elegance. Part of their appeal was the chance for people of modest means to emulate the rich. An experienced train conductor observed that the wives of grocers, not millionaires, were the ones most likely to "sweep . . . into a parlor car as if the very carpet ought to feel highly honored by their tread."

First-class "ladies' cars" soon became sites of struggle for racial equality. For three decades after the end of the Civil War, state laws and railroad regulations varied, and African Americans often succeeded in securing seats. One reformer noted, however, "There are few ordeals more nerve-wracking than the one which confronts a colored woman when she tries to secure a Pullman reservation in the South and even in some parts of the North." When they claimed first-class seats, black women often faced confrontations with conductors, resulting in numerous lawsuits in the 1870s and 1880s. Riding the Chesapeake & Ohio line in 1884, young African American journalist Ida B. Wells was told to leave. "I refused," she wrote later, "saying that the [nearest alternative] car was a smoker, and as I was in the ladies' car, I proposed to stay." Wells resisted, but the conductor and a baggage handler threw her bodily off the train. Returning home to Memphis, Wells sued and won in local courts, but Tennessee's supreme court reversed the ruling.

In 1896, the U.S. Supreme Court settled such issues decisively, but not justly. The case, **Plessy v. Ferguson**, was brought by civil rights advocates on behalf of Homer Plessy, a New Orleans resident who was one-eighth black. Ordered to leave a first-class car and move to the "colored" car of a Louisiana train, Plessy refused and was arrested. The Court ruled that such segregation did not violate the Fourteenth Amendment as long as blacks had access to accommodations that were "separate but equal" to those of whites. "Separate but equal" was a myth: segregated facilities in the South were flagrantly inferior. **Jim Crow** segregation laws, named for a stereotyped black character who appeared in minstrel shows, clearly discriminated, but the Court allowed them to stand.

Jim Crow laws applied to public schools and parks and also to emerging commercial spaces—hotels, restaurants, streetcars, trains, and eventually sports stadiums and movie theaters. Placing a national stamp of approval on segregation, the *Plessy* decision remained in place until 1954, when the Court's *Brown v. Topeka Board of Education* ruling finally struck it down (Chapter 26). Until then, blacks' exclusion from first-class "public accommodations" was one of the most painful marks of racism. The *Plessy* decision, like the rock-bottom wages earned by twelve-year-old girls at Macy's, showed that consumer culture could be modern and innovative without being politically progressive. Business and consumer culture were shaped by, and themselves shaped, racial and class injustices.

## Masculinity and the Rise of Sports

Industrialization changed expectations in the workplace. Traditionally, the mark of a successful American man was economic independence: he was his own boss. Now, tens of thousands worked for other men in big companies and in offices, rather than using their muscles. Would the professional American male, through his concentration on "brain work," become "weak, effeminate, [and] decaying," as one editor warned? How could well-to-do men assert their independence if work no longer required them to prove themselves physically? How could they develop toughness and strength? One answer was athletics.

**"Muscular Christianity"**    The **Young Men's Christian Association** (YMCA) was one of the earliest and most successful promoters of athletic fitness. Introduced in

**Horatio Alger Jr.** In dozens of popular boys' books published between 1867 and 1917, Horatio Alger Jr. assured young readers that if they were honest, worked hard, and cultivated good character, they could succeed in the new competitive economy. His heroes, such as the famous "Ragged Dick," often grew up in poverty on the streets of big cities. *Brave and Bold* (1874) tells the story of a small-town boy forced to work in a factory; he is unfairly fired, but through persistence and courage he wins a good job and recovers an inheritance for his mother. Alger's books were republished often, as in this boys' magazine from 1911, and many remain in print today. Courtesy of the Department of Special Collections, Stanford University Libraries.

Boston in 1851, the group promoted muscular Christianity, combining evangelism with gyms and athletic facilities where men could make themselves "clean and strong." Focusing first on white-collar workers, the YMCA developed a substantial industrial program after 1900. Railroad managers and other corporate titans hoped YMCAs would foster a loyal and contented workforce, discouraging labor unrest. Business leaders also relied on sports to build physical and mental discipline and help men adjust their bodies to the demands of the industrial clock. Sports honed men's competitive spirit, they believed; employer-sponsored teams instilled teamwork and company pride.

Working-class men had their own ideas about sports and leisure, and YMCAs quickly became a site of negotiation. Could workers come to the "Y" to play billiards or cards? Could they smoke? At first, YMCA leaders said no, but to attract working-class men they had to make concessions. As a result, the "Y" became a place where middle-class and working-class customs blended—or existed in uneasy tension. At the same time, YMCA leaders innovated. Searching for winter activities in the 1890s, YMCA instructors invented the new indoor games of basketball and volleyball.

For elite Americans, meanwhile, country clubs flourished; both men and women could enjoy tennis, golf, and swimming facilities as well as social gatherings. By the turn of the century—perhaps because country club women were encroaching on their athletic turf—elite men took up even more aggressive physical sports, including boxing, weightlifting, and martial arts. As early as 1890, future president Theodore Roosevelt argued that such "virile" activities were essential to "maintain and defend this very civilization." "Most masterful nations," he claimed, "have shown a strong taste for manly sports." Roosevelt, son of a wealthy New York family, became one of the first American devotees of jujitsu. During his presidency (1901–1909), he designated a judo room in the White House and hired an expert Japanese instructor. Roosevelt also wrestled and boxed, urging other American men—especially among the elite—to increase their leadership fitness by pursuing the "strenuous life."

**America's Game**　Before the 1860s, the only distinctively American game was Native American lacrosse, and the most popular team sport among European Americans was cricket. After the Civil War, however, team sports became a fundamental part of American manhood, none more successfully than baseball. A derivative of cricket, the game's formal rules had begun to develop in New York in the 1840s and 1850s; its popularity spread in military camps during the Civil War. Afterward, the idea that baseball "received its baptism in the bloody days of our Nation's direst danger," as one promoter put it, became part of the game's mythology.

Until the 1870s, most amateur players were clerks and white-collar workers who had the leisure time to play and the income to buy their own uniforms. Business frowned on baseball and other sports as a waste of time, especially for working-class men. But late-nineteenth-century employers came to see baseball, like other athletic pursuits, as a benefit for workers. It provided fresh air and exercise, kept men out of saloons, and promoted discipline and teamwork. Players on company-sponsored teams, wearing uniforms emblazoned with their employers' names, began to compete on paid work time. Baseball thus set a pattern for how other American sports developed. Begun among independent craftsmen, it was taken up by elite men anxious to prove their strength and fitness. Well-to-do Americans then decided the sport could benefit the working class.

Big-time professional baseball arose with the launching of the National League in 1876. The league quickly built more than a dozen teams in large cities, from the Brooklyn Trolley Dodgers to the Cleveland Spiders. Team owners were, in their own right, profit-minded entrepreneurs who shaped the sport to please consumers. Wooden grandstands soon gave way to concrete and steel stadiums. By 1900, boys collected lithographed cards of their favorite players, and the baseball cap came into fashion. In 1903, the Boston Americans defeated the Pittsburgh Pirates in the first World Series. American men could now adopt a new consumer identity—not as athletes, but as fans.

**Rise of the Negro Leagues**　Baseball stadiums, like first-class rail cars, were sites of racial negotiation and conflict. In the 1880s and 1890s, major league managers hired a few African American players. As late as 1901, the Baltimore Orioles succeeded in signing Charlie Grant, a light-skinned black player from Cincinnati, by renaming him Charlie Tokohoma and claiming he was Cherokee. But as this subterfuge suggested, black players were increasingly barred. A Toledo team received a threatening note before one game in Richmond, Virginia: if their "negro catcher" played, he would be lynched. Toledo put a substitute on the field, and at the end of the season the club terminated the black player's contract.

Shut out of white leagues, players and fans turned to all-black professional teams, where black men could showcase athletic ability and race pride. Louisiana's top team, the New Orleans Pinchbacks, pointedly named themselves after the state's black Reconstruction governor. By the early 1900s, such teams organized into separate **Negro Leagues**. Though players suffered from erratic pay and rundown ball fields, the leagues thrived until the desegregation of baseball after World War II. In an era of stark discrimination, they celebrated black manhood and talent. "I liked the way their uniform fit, the way they wore their cap," wrote an admiring fan of the Newark Eagles. "They showed a style in almost everything they did."

**American Football**   The most controversial sport of the industrializing era was football, which began at elite colleges during the 1880s. The great powerhouse was the Yale team, whose legendary coach Walter Camp went on to become a watch manufacturer. Between 1883 and 1891, under Camp's direction, Yale scored

**Football Practice, Chilocco Indian School, 1911**  Football became widely popular, spreading from Ivy League schools and state universities to schools like this one, built on Cherokee land in Oklahoma. The uniforms of this team, typical of the day, show very limited padding and protection—a factor that contributed to high rates of injury and even death on the field. As they practiced in 1911, these Chilocco students had an inspiring model to look up to: in that year Jim Thorpe, a fellow Oklahoman and a member of the Sac and Fox tribe, was winning national fame by leading the all-Indian team at Pennsylvania's Carlisle School to victory against Harvard. Thorpe, one of the finest athletes of his generation, went on to win gold medals in the pentathlon and decathlon at the 1912 Olympics in Stockholm, Sweden. National Archives.

4,660 points; its opponents scored 92. Drawing on the workplace model of scientific management, Camp emphasized drill and precision. He and other coaches argued that football offered perfect training for the competitive world of business. The game was violent: six players' deaths in the 1908 college season provoked a public outcry. Eventually, new rules protected quarterbacks and required coaches to remove injured players from the game. But such measures were adopted grudgingly, with supporters arguing that they ruined football's benefits in manly training.

Like baseball and the YMCA, football attracted sponsorship from business leaders hoping to divert workers from labor activism. The first professional teams emerged in western Pennsylvania's steel towns, soon after the defeat of the steelworkers' union. Carnegie Steel executives organized teams in Homestead and Braddock; the first league appeared during the anthracite coal strike of 1902. Other teams arose in the midwestern industrial heartland. The Indian-Acme Packing Company sponsored the Green Bay Packers; the future Chicago Bears, first known as the Decatur Staleys, were funded by a manufacturer of laundry starch. Like its baseball equivalent, professional football encouraged men to buy in as spectators and fans.

## The Great Outdoors

As the rise of sports suggests, by the 1890s elite and middle-class Americans began to see Victorian culture as stuffy and claustrophobic. They revolted by heading outdoors. A craze for bicycling swept the country; in 1890, at the height of the mania, U.S. manufacturers sold an astonishing ten million bikes. Women were not far behind men in taking up athletics. By the 1890s, even elite women, long confined to corsets and heavy clothes that restricted their movement, donned lighter dresses and pursued archery and golf. Artist Charles Gibson became famous for his portraits of the Gibson Girl, an elite beauty depicted on the tennis court or swimming at the beach. The Gibson Girl personified the ideal of "New Women," more educated, athletic, and independent than their mothers.

Those with money and leisure time used railroad networks to get to the national parks of the West, which, as one senator put it, became a "breathing-place for the national lungs." People of more modest means began to take up camping. As early as 1904, California's Coronado Beach offered tent rentals for $3 a week. A decade later, campgrounds and cottages in many parts of the country catered to a working-class clientele. In an industrial society, the outdoors became associated with leisure and renewal rather than danger and hard work. One journalist, reflecting on urban life from the vantage point of a western vacation, wrote, "How stupid it all seems: the mad eagerness of money-making men, the sham pleasures of conventional society." In the wilderness, he wrote, "your blood clarifies; your brain becomes active. You get a new view of life."

As Americans searched for such renewal in remnants of unexploited land, the nation's first environmental movement arose. John Muir, who fell in love with the Yosemite Valley in 1869, became the most famous voice for wilderness. Raised in a stern Scots Presbyterian family on a Wisconsin farm, Muir knew much of the Bible by heart. He was a keen observer who developed a deeply spiritual relationship with the natural world. His contemporary Mary Austin, whose book *Land of Little Rain* (1905) celebrated the austere beauty of the California desert, called him "a devout man." In cooperation with his editor at *Century* magazine, Muir founded the **Sierra Club** in 1892. Like the earlier Appalachian Mountain Club, founded in Boston in 1876, the Sierra Club dedicated itself to preserving and enjoying America's great mountains.

Encouraged by such groups, national and state governments set aside more public lands for preservation and recreation. The United States substantially expanded its park system and, during Theodore Roosevelt's presidency, extended the reach of national forests. Starting in 1872 with the preservation of Yellowstone in Wyoming, Congress had begun to set aside land for national parks. In 1916, President Woodrow Wilson provided comprehensive oversight of these national parks, signing an act creating the **National Park Service** (Map 17.1). A year later, the system numbered thirteen parks—including Maine's Acadia, the first east of the Mississippi River.

Environmentalists also worked to protect wildlife. By the 1890s, several state Audubon Societies, named in honor of antebellum naturalist John James Audubon, banded together to advocate broader protections for wild birds, especially herons and egrets, which were being slaughtered by the thousands for their plumes. They succeeded in winning the Lacey Act (1900), which established federal penalties for selling specified birds, animals, and plants. Soon afterward, state organizations joined together to form the National Audubon Society. Women played prominent roles in the movement, promoting boycotts of hats with plumage. In 1903, President Theodore Roosevelt created the first National Wildlife Refuge at Pelican Island, Florida.

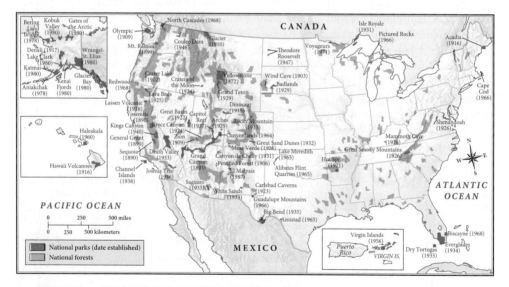

**MAP 17.1  National Parks and Forests, 1872–1980**
Yellowstone, the first national park in the United States, dates from 1872. In 1893, the federal government began to intervene to protect national forests. Without Theodore Roosevelt, however, the national forest program might have languished; during his presidency, he added 125 million acres to the forest system, plus six national parks in addition to several that had already been created during the 1890s. America's national forest and park systems remain one of the most visible and beloved legacies of federal policy innovation in the decades between the Civil War and World War I.

Roosevelt also expanded preservation under the **Antiquities Act** (1906), which enabled the U.S. president, without congressional approval, to set aside "objects of historic and scientific interest" as national monuments. Two years later, Roosevelt used these powers to preserve 800,000 acres at Arizona's magnificent Grand Canyon. The act proved a mixed blessing for conservation. Monuments received weaker protection than national parks did; many fell under the authority of the U.S. Forest Service, which permitted logging and grazing. Business interests thus lobbied to have coveted lands designated as monuments rather than national parks so they could more easily exploit resources. Nonetheless, the creation of national monuments offered some protection, and many monuments (such as Alaska's Katmai) later obtained park status. The expanding network of parks and monuments became popular places to hike, camp, and contemplate natural beauty.

The great outdoors provided new opportunities for women with the means to travel. One writer, advising women to enjoy mountain hikes, hinted at liberating possibilities: "For those loving freedom and health," he recommended "short skirts, pantlets, stout shoes, tasty hat." And like other leisure venues, "wilderness" did not remain in the hands of elite men and women. As early as the late 1880s, the lakes and hiking trails of the Catskill Mountains became so thronged with working-class tourists from nearby New York City, including many Jewish immigrants, that elite visitors began to segregate themselves into gated summer communities. They thus preserved the "seclusion and privacy" that they snobbishly claimed as the privilege of those who could demonstrate "mental and personal worth."

At the state level, meanwhile, new game laws triggered conflicts between elite conservationists and the poor. Shifting from year-round subsistence hunting to a limited, recreational hunting season brought hardship to poor rural families who depended on game for food. Regulation brought undeniable benefits: it suppressed such popular practices as songbird hunting and the use of dynamite to kill fish. Looking back on the era before game laws, one Alabama hunter remembered that "the slaughter was terrific." But while game laws prevented further extinctions like that of the passenger pigeon, which vanished around 1900, they made it harder for rural people to support themselves through subsistence hunting and fishing.

| **IN YOUR OWN WORDS** | How did industrialization change Americans' ideas about appropriate leisure activities for men and women of various social classes? |
|---|---|

# Women, Men, and the Solitude of Self

Speaking to Congress in 1892, women's rights advocate Elizabeth Cady Stanton described what she called the "solitude of self." Stanton rejected the claim that women did not need equal rights because they enjoyed men's protection. "The talk of sheltering woman from the fierce storms of life is the sheerest mockery," she declared. "They beat on her from every point of the compass, just as they do on man, and with more fatal results, for he has been trained to protect himself."

Stanton's argument captured one of the dilemmas of industrialization: the marketplace of labor brought both freedom and risk, and working-class women were particularly vulnerable. At the same time, middle-class women — expected to engage in selfless community service — often saw the impact of industrialization more clearly than fathers, brothers, and husbands did. In seeking to address alcoholism, poverty, and other social and economic ills, they gained a new sense of their own collective power. Women's protest and reform work thus helped lay the foundations for progressivism (Chapter 19) and modern women's rights.

## Changing Families

The average American family, especially in the middle class, decreased in size during the industrial era. In 1800, white women who survived to menopause had borne an average of 7.0 children; by 1900, the average was 3.6. On farms and in many working-class families, youngsters counted as assets on the family balance sheet: they worked in fields or factories. But parents who had fewer sons and daughters could concentrate their resources, educating and preparing each child for success in the new economy. Among the professional classes, education became a necessity, while limiting family size became, more broadly, a key to upward mobility.

Several factors limited childbearing. Americans married at older ages, and many mothers tried to space pregnancies more widely — as their mothers and grandmothers had — by nursing children for several years, which suppressed fertility. By the late nineteenth century, as vulcanized rubber became available, couples also had access to a range of other contraceptive methods, such as condoms and diaphragms. With pressure for family limitation rising, these methods were widely used and apparently effective. But couples rarely wrote about them. Historians' evidence comes from the occasional frank diary and from the thriving success of the mail-order contraceptive industry, which advertised prominently and shipped products — wrapped in discreet brown paper packages — to customers nationwide.

Reluctance to talk about contraceptives was understandable, since information about them was stigmatized and, after 1873, illegal to distribute. During Reconstruction, Anthony Comstock, crusading secretary of the New York Society for the Suppression of Vice, secured a federal law banning "obscene materials" from the U.S. mail. The **Comstock Act** (1873) prohibited circulation of almost any information about sex and birth control — even in private letters. Comstock won support for the law, in part, by appealing to parents' fears that young people were receiving sexual information through the mail, promoting the rise of "secret vice." Though critics charged Comstock with high-handed interference in private matters, others supported his work, fearful of the rising tide of pornography, sexual information, and contraceptives made available by industrialization. A committee of the New York legislature declared Comstock's crusade "wholly essential to the safety and decency of the community." It appears, however, that Comstock had little success in stopping the lucrative and popular trade in contraceptives.

## Education

In the industrial economy, the watchword for young people who hoped to secure good jobs was *education*. A high school diploma — now a gateway to a college degree — was valuable for boys who hoped to enter professional or managerial work. Daughters attended in even larger numbers than their brothers. Parents of the Civil War generation, who had witnessed the plight of war widows and orphans, encouraged girls to prepare themselves for teaching or office jobs, work before marriage, and gain skills they could fall back on, "just in case." By 1900, 71 percent of Americans between the ages of five and eighteen attended school. That figure rose further in the early twentieth century, as public officials adopted laws requiring school attendance.

Most high schools were coeducational, and almost every high school featured athletics. Recruited first as cheerleaders for boys' teams, girls soon established field hockey and other sports of their own. Boys and girls engaged in friendly—and sometimes not-so-friendly—rivalry in high school. In 1884, a high school newspaper in Concord, New Hampshire, published this poem from a disgruntled boy who caricatured his female classmates:

> We know many tongues of living and dead,
> In science and fiction we're very well read,
> But we cannot cook meat and cannot make bread
> And we've wished many times that we were all dead.

A female student shot back a poem of her own, denouncing male students' smoking habit:

> But if boys will smoke cigarettes
> Although the smoke may choke them,
> One consolation still remains —
> *They kill the boys that smoke them.*

The rate of Americans attending college had long hovered around 2 percent; driven by public universities' expansion, the rate rose in the 1880s, reaching 8 percent by 1920. Much larger numbers attended a growing network of business and technical schools. "GET A PLACE IN THE WORLD," advertised one Minneapolis business college in 1907, "where your talents can be used to the best advantage." Typically, such schools offered both day and night classes in subjects such as bookkeeping, typewriting, and shorthand.

The needs of the new economy also shaped the curriculum at more traditional collegiate institutions. State universities emphasized technical training and fed the growing professional workforce with graduates trained in fields such as engineering. Many private colleges distanced themselves from such practical pursuits; their administrators argued that students who aimed to be leaders needed broad-based knowledge. But they modernized course offerings, emphasizing French and German, for example, rather than Latin and Greek. Harvard, led by dynamic president Charles W. Eliot from 1869 to 1909, pioneered the liberal arts. Students at the all-male college chose from a range of electives, as Eliot called for classes that developed each young man's "individual reality and creative power."

In the South, one of the most famous educational projects was Booker T. Washington's Tuskegee Institute, founded in 1881. Washington both taught and exemplified the goal of self-help; his autobiography, *Up from Slavery* (1901), became a best-seller. Because of the deep poverty in which most southern African Americans lived, Washington concluded that "book education" for most "would be almost a waste of time." He focused instead on industrial education. Students, he argued, would "be sure of knowing how to make a living after they had left us." Tuskegee sent female graduates into teaching and nursing; men more often entered the industrial trades or farmed by the latest scientific methods.

Washington gained national fame in 1895 with his **Atlanta Compromise** address, delivered at the Cotton States Exposition in Atlanta, Georgia. For the exposition's white organizers, the racial "compromise" was inviting Washington to speak at all. It was a move intended to show racial progress in the South. Washington, in turn, delivered an address that many interpreted as approving racial segregation. Stating that African Americans had, in slavery days, "proved our loyalty to you," he assured whites that "in our humble way, we shall stand by you . . . ready to lay down our lives, if need be, in defense of yours." The races could remain socially detached: "In all things that are purely social we can be as separate as the fingers, yet one as the hand in all things essential to mutual progress." Washington urged, however, that whites join him in working for "the highest intelligence and development of all."

Whites greeted this address with enthusiasm, and Washington became the most prominent black leader of his generation. His soothing rhetoric and style of leadership, based on avoiding confrontation and cultivating white patronage and private influence, was well suited to the difficult years after Reconstruction. Washington believed that money was color-blind, that whites would respect economic success. He represented the ideals of millions of African Americans who hoped education and hard work would erase white prejudice. That hope proved tragically overoptimistic. As the tide of disfranchisement and segregation rolled in, Washington would come under fire from a younger generation of race leaders who argued that he accommodated too much to white racism.

In addition to African American education, women's higher education expanded notably. In the Northeast and South, women most often attended single-sex institutions, including teacher-training colleges. For affluent families, private colleges offered an education equivalent to men's—for an equally high price. Vassar College started the trend when it opened in 1861; Smith, Wellesley, and others followed. Anxious doctors warned that these institutions were dangerous: intensive brain work would unsex young women and drain energy from their ovaries, leading them to bear weak children. But as thousands of women earned degrees and suffered no apparent harm, fears faded. Single-sex higher education for women spread from private to public institutions, especially in the South, where the Mississippi State College for Women (1885) led the way.

Coeducation was more prevalent in the Midwest and West, where many state universities opened their doors to female students after the Civil War. Women were also admitted to most African American colleges founded during Reconstruction. By 1910, 58 percent of America's colleges and universities were coeducational. While students at single-sex institutions forged strong bonds with one another, women also gained benefits from learning with men. When male students were friendly, they built comfortable working relationships; when men were hostile, women learned coping skills that served them well in later employment or reform work. One doctor who studied at the University of Iowa remembered later that he and his friends mercilessly harassed the first women who entered the medical school. But when the women showed they were good students, the men's attitudes changed to "wholesome respect."

Whether or not they got a college education, more and more women recognized, in the words of Elizabeth Cady Stanton, their "solitude of self." In the changing economy, they could not always count on fathers and husbands. Women who needed to support themselves could choose from dozens of guidebooks such as *What Girls*

**Class of 1896, Radcliffe College** When Harvard University, long a bastion of male privilege, created an "Annex" for women's instruction in 1879, it was a sure sign of growing support for women's higher education. The Annex became Radcliffe College in 1894. Two years later, this graduating class of thirty posed for their portrait. Among them was Alice Sterling of Bridgeport, Connecticut, who went on to marry Harvard graduate Frank Cook and devote herself to Protestant foreign missions. On two trips around the world, Alice Sterling Cook visited all the women's colleges that missionaries had founded in India, China, and Japan. Cook's energetic public activities typified those of many women's college alumnae. Schlesinger Library, Radcliffe Institute, Harvard University/Bridgeman Images.

*Can Do* (1880) and *How to Make Money Although a Woman* (1895). The Association for the Advancement of Women, founded in 1873 by women's college graduates, defended women's higher education and argued that women's paid employment was a positive good.

Today, many economists argue that education and high-quality jobs for women are keys to reducing poverty in the developing world. In the United States, that process also led to broader gains in women's political rights. As women began to earn advanced degrees, work for wages and salaries, and live independently, it became harder to argue that women were "dependents" who did not need to vote.

## Toward Women's Emancipation

As the United States confronted industrialization, middle-class women steadily expanded their place beyond the household, building reform movements and taking political action. Starting in the 1880s, women's clubs sprang up and began to study such problems as pollution, unsafe working conditions, and urban poverty. So many formed by 1890 that their leaders created a nationwide umbrella organization, the General Federation of Women's Clubs. Women justified such work through the ideal of **maternalism**, appealing to their special role as mothers. Maternalism was an intermediate step between domesticity and modern arguments for women's equality. "Women's place is Home," declared the journalist Rheta Childe Dorr. But she added, "Home is the community. The city full of people is the Family. . . . Badly do the Home and Family need their mother."

**Women's Temperance Activism**    One maternalist goal was to curb alcohol abuse by prohibiting liquor sales. The **Woman's Christian Temperance Union** (WCTU), founded after a series of women's grassroots campaigns in 1874, spread rapidly after 1879, when charismatic Frances Willard became its leader. More than any other group of the late nineteenth century, the WCTU launched women into reform. Willard knew how to frame political demands in the language of feminine self-sacrifice. "Womanliness first," she advised her followers; "afterward, what you will." WCTU members vividly described the plight of abused wives and children when men suffered in the grip of alcoholism. Willard's motto was "Home Protection," and though it placed all the blame on alcohol rather than other factors, the WCTU became the first organization to identify and combat domestic violence.

The prohibitionist movement drew activists from many backgrounds. Middle-class city dwellers worried about the link between alcoholism and crime, especially in the growing immigrant wards. Rural citizens equated liquor with big-city sins such as prostitution and political corruption. Methodists, Baptists, Mormons, and members of other denominations condemned drinking for religious reasons. Immigrants passionately disagreed, however: Germans and Irish Catholics enjoyed their Sunday beer and saw no harm in it. Saloons were a centerpiece of working-class leisure and community life, offering free lunches, public toilets, and a place to share neighborhood news. Thus, while some labor unions advocated voluntary temperance, attitudes toward prohibition divided along ethnic, religious, and class lines.

WCTU activism led some leaders to raise radical questions about the shape of industrial society. As she investigated alcohol abuse, Willard increasingly confronted poverty, hunger, unemployment, and other industrial problems. Across the United States, WCTU locals founded soup kitchens and free libraries. They introduced a German educational innovation, the kindergarten. They investigated prison conditions. Though she did not persuade most prohibitionists to follow her lead, Willard declared herself a Christian Socialist and urged more attention to workers' plight. She advocated laws establishing an eight-hour workday and abolishing child labor.

Willard also called for women's voting rights, lending powerful support to the independent suffrage movement that had emerged during Reconstruction. Controversially, the WCTU threw its energies behind the Prohibition Party, which exercised considerable clout during the 1880s. Women worked in the party as speakers, convention delegates, and even local candidates. Liquor was big business, and powerful interests mobilized to block antiliquor legislation. In many areas — particularly the cities — prohibition simply did not gain majority support. Willard retired to England, where she died in 1898, worn and discouraged by many defeats. But her legacy was powerful. Other groups took up the cause, eventually winning national prohibition after World War I.

Through its emphasis on human welfare, the WCTU encouraged women to join the national debate over poverty and inequality of wealth. Some became active in the People's Party of the 1890s, which welcomed women as organizers and stump speakers. Others led groups such as the National Congress of Mothers, founded in 1897, which promoted better child-rearing techniques in rural and working-class families. The WCTU had taught women how to lobby, raise money, and even run for office. Willard wrote that "perhaps the most significant outcome" of the movement was women's "knowledge of their own power."

**Women, Race, and Patriotism**   As in temperance work, women played central roles in patriotic movements and African American community activism. Members of the Daughters of the American Revolution (DAR), founded in 1890, celebrated the memory of Revolutionary War heroes. Equally influential was the United Daughters of the Confederacy (UDC), founded in 1894 to extol the South's "Lost Cause." The UDC's elite southern members shaped Americans' memory of the Civil War by constructing monuments, distributing Confederate flags, and promoting school textbooks that defended the Confederacy and condemned Reconstruction. The UDC's work helped build and maintain support for segregation and disfranchisement.

African American women did not sit idle in the face of this challenge. In 1896, they created the **National Association of Colored Women**. Through its local clubs, black women arranged for the care of orphans, founded homes for the elderly, advocated temperance, and undertook public health campaigns. Such women shared with white women a determination to carry domesticity into the public sphere. Journalist Victoria Earle Matthews hailed the American home as "the foundation upon which nationality rests, the pride of the citizen, and the glory of the Republic." She and other African American women used the language of domesticity and respectability to justify their work.

One of the most radical voices was Ida B. Wells, who as a young Tennessee schoolteacher sued the Chesapeake & Ohio Railroad for denying her a seat in the ladies' car (see p. 507). In 1892, a white mob in Memphis invaded a grocery store owned by three of Wells's friends, angry that it competed with a nearby white-owned store. When the black store owners defended themselves, wounding several of their attackers, all three were lynched. Grieving their deaths, Wells left Memphis and urged other African Americans to join her in boycotting the city's white businesses. As a journalist, she launched a one-woman campaign against lynching. Wells's investigations demolished the myth that lynchers were reacting to the crime of rape; she showed that the real cause was more often economic competition, a labor dispute, or a consensual relationship between a white woman and a black man. Settling in Chicago, Wells became a noted and accomplished reformer, but in an era of increasing racial injustice, few whites supported her cause.

The largest African American women's organization arose within the National Baptist Church (NBC), which by 1906 represented 2.4 million black churchgoers. Founded in 1900, the Women's Convention of the NBC funded night schools, health clinics, kindergartens, day care centers, and prison outreach programs. Adella Hunt Logan, born in Alabama, exemplified how such work could lead women to demand political rights. Educated at Atlanta University, Logan became a women's club leader, teacher, and suffrage advocate. "If white American women, with all their mutual and acquired advantage, need the ballot," she declared, "how much more do

Black Americans, male and female, need the strong defense of a vote to help secure them their right to life, liberty, and the pursuit of happiness?"

**Women's Rights**   Though it had split into two rival organizations during Reconstruction (Chapter 14), the movement for women's suffrage reunited in 1890 in the **National American Woman Suffrage Association** (NAWSA). Soon afterward, suffragists built on earlier victories in the West, winning full ballots for women in Colorado (1893), Idaho (1896), and Utah (1896, reestablished as Utah gained statehood). Afterward, movement leaders were discouraged by a decade of state-level defeats and Congress's refusal to consider a constitutional amendment. But suffrage again picked up momentum after 1911 (Map 17.2). By 1913, most

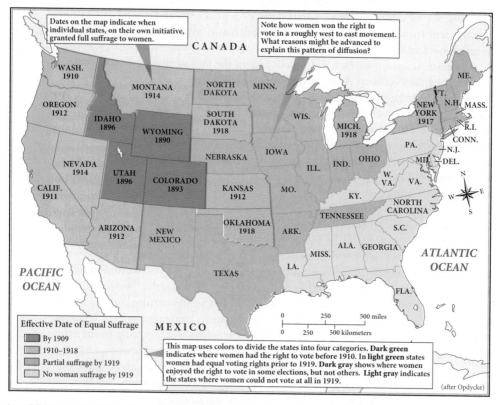

### MAP 17.2   Women's Suffrage, 1890–1919

By 1909, after more than sixty years of agitation, only four lightly populated western states had granted women full voting rights. A number of other states offered partial suffrage, limited to voting for school boards and such issues as taxes and local referenda on whether or not to permit the sale of liquor licenses (the so-called local option). Between 1910 and 1918, as the effort shifted to the struggle for a constitutional amendment, eleven states joined the list granting full suffrage. The West remained the most progressive region in granting women's voting rights; the most stubborn resistance lay in the ex-Confederacy.

women living west of the Mississippi River had the ballot. In other localities, women could vote in municipal elections, school elections, or liquor referenda.

The rising prominence of the women's suffrage movement had an ironic result: it prompted some women—and men—to organize against it, in groups such as the National Association Opposed to Woman Suffrage (1911). Antisuffragists argued that it was expensive to add so many voters to the rolls; wives' ballots would just "double their husbands' votes" or worse, cancel them out, subjecting men to "petticoat rule." Some antisuffragists also argued that voting would undermine women's special roles as disinterested reformers: no longer above the fray, they would be plunged into the "cesspool of politics." In short, women were "better citizens without the ballot." Such arguments helped delay passage of national women's suffrage until after World War I.

By the 1910s, some women moved beyond suffrage to take a public stance for what they called **feminism**—women's full political, economic, and social equality. A famous site of sexual rebellion was New York's Greenwich Village, where radical intellectuals, including many gays and lesbians, created a vibrant community. Among other political activities, women there founded the Heterodoxy Club (1912), open to any woman who pledged not to be "orthodox in her opinions." The club brought together intellectuals, journalists, and labor organizers. Almost all supported suffrage, but they had a more ambitious view of what was needed for women's liberation. "I wanted to belong to the human race, not to a ladies' aid society," wrote one divorced journalist who joined Heterodoxy. Feminists argued that women should not simply fulfill expectations of feminine self-sacrifice; they should work on their own behalf. As the United States entered the modern era, then, greater advocacy for women's rights proved to be—like new consumer spaces, literary realism, and appreciation for wilderness—another unexpected transformation wrought by industrialization.

> **IN YOUR OWN WORDS**    How did women's public activism impact American politics and society?

# Summary

In the era of industrialization, new intellectual currents, including Darwinism, challenged nineteenth-century certainties. Debates over evolution, especially its implications for the human species, proved particularly intense and long-lasting. "Survival of the fittest"—a term invented not by Charles Darwin, but by Herbert Spencer—was cited to justify ruthless business practices and inequalities of wealth. Eugenic "science" underlay such discriminatory practices as forced sterilization and laws against interracial marriage.

Science and modernism did not, however, displace religion. Newly arrived Catholics and Jews, as well as old-line Protestants, adapted their faiths to the conditions of modern life. Foreign missions spread the Christian gospel around the world, with mixed results for those receiving the message.

In the arts, realist and naturalist writers rejected both romanticism and the tenets of domesticity. Many Americans were shocked by the results, including Theodore Dreiser's scandalous novel *Sister Carrie*, Mark Twain's rejection of Christian faith, and the boldly modernist paintings displayed at New York's Armory Show.

Industrialization and new consumer practices created foundations for modern American culture. While middle-class families sought to preserve the Victorian domestic ideal, a variety of factors transformed family life. Families had fewer children, and a substantial majority of young people achieved more education than their parents had obtained. Across class and gender lines, Americans enjoyed athletics and the outdoors, fostering the rise of environmentalism.

Among an array of women's reform movements, the Woman's Christian Temperance Union sought prohibition of liquor, but it also addressed issues such as domestic violence, poverty, and education. Members of women's clubs pursued a variety of social and economic reforms, while other women organized for race uplift and patriotic work. Gradually, the Victorian ideal of female moral superiority gave way to modern claims for women's equal rights.

# Chapter 17 Review

## KEY TERMS

**Identify and explain the significance of each term below.**

Social Darwinism (p. 500)
eugenics (p. 500)
American Protective Association (p. 502)
Social Gospel (p. 503)
fundamentalism (p. 503)
realism (p. 503)
modernism (p. 504)
*Plessy v. Ferguson* (p. 507)
Jim Crow (p. 507)
Young Men's Christian Association (p. 507)
Negro Leagues (p. 510)

Sierra Club (p. 512)
National Park Service (p. 512)
Antiquities Act (p. 513)
Comstock Act (p. 514)
Atlanta Compromise (p. 516)
maternalism (p. 517)
Woman's Christian Temperance Union (p. 518)
National Association of Colored Women (p. 519)
National American Woman Suffrage Association (p. 520)
feminism (p. 521)

## REVIEW QUESTIONS

**Answer these questions to demonstrate your understanding of the chapter's main ideas.**

1. How did Charles Darwin's theory of evolution and other scientific ideas impact American culture and intellectual life in the late nineteenth century? What uses did nonscientists make of such ideas?

2. How did industrialization change Americans' ideas about appropriate leisure activities for men and women of various social classes?

3. How did women's public activism impact American politics and society?

4. On the Part 6 thematic timeline (p. 473), review developments in "Culture and Society" and "Geography and the Environment." How did industrialization change Americans' relationship to the outdoors—to natural environments? What connections do you see between those changes and other, broader shifts in American society and culture?

## CHRONOLOGY

As you read, ask yourself why this chapter begins and ends with these dates and identify the links among related events.

| | |
|---|---|
| **1870s** | • Social Darwinism gains growing acceptance |
| **1873** | • Comstock Act |
| **1874** | • Woman's Christian Temperance Union founded |
| **1876** | • Baseball's National League founded |
| | • Appalachian Mountain Club founded |
| **1879** | • Salvation Army established in the United States |
| **1881** | • Tuskegee Institute founded |
| **1885** | • Mississippi State College for Women founded |
| **1887** | • American Protective Association founded to oppose immigration |
| **1890** | • National American Woman Suffrage Association founded |
| | • Daughters of the American Revolution founded |
| **1892** | • Elizabeth Cady Stanton delivers "solitude of self" speech to Congress |
| | • John Muir founds Sierra Club |
| **1893** | • Chicago World's Columbian Exposition |
| **1894** | • United Daughters of the Confederacy founded |
| **1895** | • Booker T. Washington delivers Atlanta Compromise address |
| **1896** | • National Association of Colored Women founded |
| | • Charles Sheldon publishes *In His Steps* |
| | • *Plessy v. Ferguson* legalizes "separate but equal" doctrine |
| **1900** | • Lacey Act protects wildlife |

**1903**
- First World Series
- First National Wildlife Refuge established

**1906**
- Antiquities Act

**1913**
- Armory Show of modern art held in New York City

**1915**
- Peak of foreign missions activity by American Protestant churches

**1916**
- National Park Service created

# 18

# "Civilization's Inferno": The Rise and Reform of Industrial Cities

## 1880–1917

**IDENTIFY THE BIG IDEA**

How did the rise of big cities shape American society and politics?

**CLARENCE DARROW, A SUCCESSFUL LAWYER FROM ASHTABULA, OHIO,** felt isolated and overwhelmed when he moved to Chicago in the 1880s. "There is no place so lonely to a young man as a great city," Darrow later wrote. "When I walked along the street I scanned every face I met to see if I could not perchance discover someone from Ohio." Instead, he saw a "sea of human units, each intent upon hurrying by." At one point, Darrow felt near despair. "If it had been possible I would have gone back to Ohio," he wrote, "but I didn't want to borrow the money, and I dreaded to confess defeat." Yet Darrow stayed in Chicago and eventually prospered, becoming one of the nation's most famous defense attorneys.

In the era of industrialization, more and more Americans had experiences like Darrow's. In 1860, the United States was rural: less than 20 percent of Americans lived in an urban area, defined by census-takers as a place with more than 2,500 inhabitants. By 1910, more Americans lived in cities (42.1 million) than had lived in the entire nation on the eve of the Civil War (31.4 million). The country now had three of the world's ten largest cities. Though the Northeast remained by far the most urbanized region, the industrial Midwest was catching up. Seattle, San Francisco, and soon Los Angeles became hubs on the Pacific coast. Even the South boasted of thriving Atlanta and Birmingham. As journalist Frederic C. Howe declared in 1905, "Man has entered on an urban age."

525

The scale of industrial cities encouraged experiments that ranged from the amusement park to the art museum, the skyscraper to the subway. Yet the city's complexity also posed problems, some of them far worse than Clarence Darrow's loneliness. Brothels flourished, as did slums, pollution, disease, and corrupt political machines. Fast-talking hucksters enjoyed prime opportunities to fleece newcomers; homeless men slept in the shadows of the mansions of the superrich. One African American observer called the city "Civilization's Inferno." The locus of urgent problems, industrial cities became important sites of political innovation and reform.

# The New Metropolis

Mark Twain, arriving in New York in 1867, remarked, "You cannot accomplish anything in the way of business, you cannot even pay a friendly call without devoting a whole day to it. . . . [The] distances are too great." But new technologies allowed engineers and planners to reorganize urban geographies. Specialized districts began to include not only areas for finance, manufacturing, wholesaling, and warehousing but also immigrant wards, shopping districts, and business-oriented downtowns. It was an exciting and bewildering world.

## The Shape of the Industrial City

Before the Civil War, cities served the needs of commerce and finance, not industry. Early manufacturing sprang up mostly in the countryside, where mill owners could draw water power from streams, find plentiful fuel and raw materials, and recruit workers from farms and villages. The nation's largest cities were seaports; urban merchants bought and sold goods for distribution into the interior or to global markets.

As industrialization developed, though, cities became sites for manufacturing as well as finance and trade. Steam engines played a central role in this change. With them, mill operators no longer had to depend on less reliable water power. Steam power also vastly increased the scale of industry. A factory employing thousands of workers could instantly create a small city such as Aliquippa, Pennsylvania, which belonged body and soul to the Jones and Laughlin Steel Company. Older commercial cities also industrialized. Warehouse districts converted to small-scale manufacturing. Port cities that served as immigrant gateways offered abundant cheap labor, an essential element in the industrial economy.

**Mass Transit**   New technologies helped residents and visitors negotiate the industrial city. Steam-driven cable cars appeared in the 1870s. By 1887, engineer Frank Sprague designed an electric trolley system for Richmond, Virginia. Electricity from a central generating plant was fed to trolleys through overhead power lines, which each trolley touched with a pole mounted on its roof. Trolleys soon became the primary mode of transportation in most American cities. Congestion and frequent accidents, however, led to demands that trolley lines be moved off streets. The "el" or elevated railroad, which began operation as early as 1871 in New York City, became a safer alternative. Other

**Downtown St. Louis, c. 1890**
This photograph suggests how new technologies transformed urban spaces. Architects built up; streetcars carried pedestrians from home to work and play; and telegraph and telephone wires began to crisscross streets, causing some to complain that they were dangerous eyesores. The unusual cleanliness of this street also suggests the impact of streetcars, subways, and other modern forms of transport: horses and their manure gradually disappeared from cities, replaced by fossil fuels. Library of Congress.

urban planners built down, not up. Boston opened a short underground line in 1897; by 1904, a subway running the length of Manhattan demonstrated the full potential of high-speed underground trains.

Even before the Civil War, the spread of railroads led to growth of outlying residential districts for the well-to-do. The high cost of transportation effectively segregated these wealthy districts. In the late nineteenth century, the trend accelerated. Businessmen and professionals built homes on large, beautifully landscaped lots in outlying towns such as Riverside, Illinois, and Tuxedo Park, New York. In such places, affluent wives and children enjoyed refuge from the pollution and perceived dangers of the city.

Los Angeles entrepreneur Henry Huntington, nephew of a wealthy Southern Pacific Railroad magnate, helped foster an emerging suburban ideal as he pitched the benefits of southern California sunshine. Huntington invested his family fortune in Los Angeles real estate and transportation. Along his trolley lines, he subdivided property into lots and built rows of bungalows, planting the tidy yards with lush trees and tropical fruits. Middle-class buyers flocked to purchase Huntington's houses. One exclaimed, "I have apparently found a Paradise on Earth." Anticipating twentieth-century Americans' love for affordable single-family homes near large cities, Huntington had begun to invent southern California sprawl.

**Skyscrapers** By the 1880s, the invention of steel girders, durable plate glass, and passenger elevators began to revolutionize urban building methods. Architects invented the skyscraper, a building supported by its steel skeleton. Its walls bore little weight, serving instead as curtains to enclose the structure. Although expensive to build, skyscrapers allowed downtown landowners to profit from small plots of land. By investing in a skyscraper, a landlord could collect rent for ten or even twenty floors of space. Large corporations commissioned these striking designs as symbols of business prowess.

The first skyscraper was William Le Baron Jenney's ten-story Home Insurance Building (1885) in Chicago. Though unremarkable in appearance—it looked just like other downtown buildings—Jenney's steel-girder construction inspired the creativity of American architects. A **Chicago school** sprang up, dedicated to the design of buildings whose form expressed, rather than masked, their structure and function. The presiding genius of this school was architect Louis Sullivan, whose "vertical aesthetic" of set-back windows and strong columns gave skyscrapers a "proud and soaring" presence and offered plentiful natural light for workers inside. Chicago pioneered skyscraper construction, but New York, with its unrelenting demand for prime downtown space, took the lead by the late 1890s. The fifty-five-story Woolworth Building, completed in 1913, marked the beginning of Manhattan's modern skyline.

**The Electric City**    One of the most dramatic urban amenities was electric light. Gaslight, produced from coal gas, had been used for residential light since the early nineteenth century, but gas lamps were too dim to brighten streets and public spaces. In the 1870s, as generating technology became commercially viable, electricity proved far better. Electric arc lamps, installed in Wanamaker's department store in Philadelphia in 1878, astonished viewers with their brilliant illumination. Electric streetlights soon replaced gaslights on city streets.

Before it had a significant effect on industry, electricity gave the city its modern tempo. It lifted elevators, illuminated department store windows, and above all, turned night into day. Electric streetlights made residents feel safer; as one magazine put it in 1912, "A light is as good as a policeman." Nightlife became less risky and more appealing. One journalist described Broadway in 1894: "All the shop fronts are lighted, and the entrances to the theaters blaze out on the sidewalk." At the end of a long working day, city dwellers flocked to this free entertainment. Nothing, declared an observer, matched the "festive panorama" of Broadway "when the lights are on."

## Newcomers and Neighborhoods

Explosive population growth made cities a world of new arrivals, including many young women and men arriving from the countryside. Traditionally, rural daughters had provided essential labor for spinning and weaving cloth, but industrialization relocated those tasks from the household to the factory. Finding themselves without a useful household role, many farm daughters sought paid employment. In an age of declining rural prosperity, many sons also left the farm and—like immigrants arriving from other countries—set aside part of their pay to help the folks at home. Explaining why she moved to Chicago, an African American woman from Louisiana declared, "A child with any respect about herself or hisself wouldn't like to see their mother and father work so hard and earn nothing. I feel it my duty to help."

America's cities also became homes for millions of overseas immigrants. Most numerous in Boston were the Irish; in Minneapolis, Swedes; in other northern cities, Germans. Arriving in a great metropolis, immigrants confronted many difficulties. One Polish man, who had lost the address of his American cousins, felt utterly alone after disembarking at New York's main immigration facility, Ellis Island, which opened in 1892. Then he heard a kindly voice in Polish, offering to help.

"From sheer joy," he recalled, "tears welled up in my eyes to hear my native tongue." Such experiences suggest why immigrants stuck together, relying on relatives and friends to get oriented and find jobs. A high degree of ethnic clustering resulted, even within a single factory. At the Jones and Laughlin steelworks in Pittsburgh, for example, the carpentry shop was German, the hammer shop Polish, and the blooming mill Serbian. "My people . . . stick together," observed a son of Ukrainian immigrants. But he added, "We who are born in this country . . . feel this country is our home."

Patterns of settlement varied by ethnic group. Many Italians, recruited by *padroni*, or labor bosses, found work in northeastern and Mid-Atlantic cities. Their urban concentration was especially marked after the 1880s, as more and more laborers arrived from southern Italy. The attraction of America was obvious to one young man, who had grown up in a poor southern Italian farm family. "I had never gotten any wages of any kind before," he reported after settling with his uncle in New Jersey. "The work here was just as hard as that on the farm; but I didn't mind it much because I would receive what seemed to me like a lot." Amadeo Peter Giannini, who started off as a produce merchant in San Francisco, soon turned to banking. After the San Francisco earthquake in 1906, his Banca d'Italia was the first financial institution to reopen in the Bay area. Expanding steadily across the West, it eventually became Bank of America.

Like Giannini's bank, institutions of many kinds sprang up to serve ethnic urban communities. Throughout America, Italian speakers avidly read the newspaper *Il Progresso Italo-Americano*; Jews read the Yiddish-language *Jewish Daily Forward*, also published in New York. Bohemians gathered in singing societies, while New York Jews patronized a lively Yiddish theater. By 1903, Italians in Chicago had sixty-six **mutual aid societies**, most composed of people from a particular province or town. These societies collected dues from members and paid support in case of death or disability on the job. Mutual benefit societies also functioned as fraternal clubs. "We are strangers in a strange country," explained one member of a Chinese *tong*, or mutual aid society, in Chicago. "We must have an organization (*tong*) to control our country fellows and develop our friendship."

Sharply defined ethnic neighborhoods such as San Francisco's Chinatown, Italian North Beach, and Jewish Hayes Valley grew up in every major city, driven by both discrimination and immigrants' desire to stick together (Map 18.1). In addition to patterns of ethnic and racial segregation, residential districts in almost all industrial cities divided along lines of economic class. Around Los Angeles's central plaza, Mexican neighborhoods diversified, incorporating Italians and Jews. Later, as the plaza became a site for business and tourism, immigrants were pushed into working-class neighborhoods like Belvedere and Boyle Heights, which sprang up to the east. Though ethnically diverse, East Los Angeles was resolutely working class; middle-class white neighborhoods grew up predominantly in West Los Angeles.

African Americans also sought urban opportunities. In 1900, almost 90 percent of American blacks still lived in the South, but increasing numbers had moved to cities such as Baton Rouge, Jacksonville, Montgomery, and Charleston, all of whose populations were more than 50 percent African American. Blacks also settled in northern cities, albeit not in the numbers that would arrive during the Great Migration of World War I. Though blacks constituted only 2 percent of New York City's population in 1910, they already numbered more than 90,000.

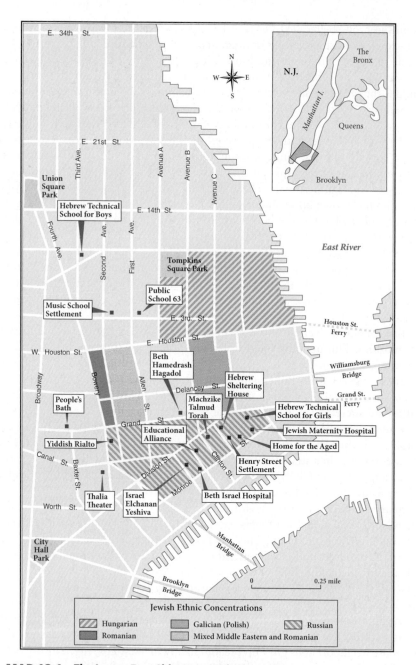

**MAP 18.1   The Lower East Side, New York City, 1900**

As this map shows, the Jewish immigrants dominating Manhattan's Lower East Side preferred to live in neighborhoods populated by those from their home regions of Eastern Europe. Their sense of a common identity made for a remarkable flowering of educational, cultural, and social institutions on the Jewish East Side. Ethnic neighborhoods became a feature of almost every American city.

These newcomers confronted conditions even worse than those for foreign-born immigrants. Relentlessly turned away from manufacturing jobs, most black men and women took up work in the service sector, becoming porters, laundrywomen, and domestic servants.

Blacks faced another urban danger: the so-called **race riot**, an attack by white mobs triggered by street altercations or rumors of crime. One of the most virulent episodes occurred in Atlanta, Georgia, in 1906. The violence was fueled by a nasty political campaign that generated sensational false charges of "negro crime." Roaming bands of white men attacked black Atlantans, invading middle-class black neighborhoods and in one case lynching two barbers after seizing them in their shop. The rioters killed at least twenty-four blacks and wounded more than a hundred. The disease of hatred was not limited to the South. Race riots broke out in New York City's Tenderloin district (1900); Evansville, Indiana (1903); and Springfield, Illinois (1908). By then, one journalist observed, "In every important Northern city, a distinct race-problem already exists which must, in a few years, assume serious proportions."

Whether they arrived from the South or from Europe, Latin America, or Asia, working-class city residents needed cheap housing near their jobs. They faced grim choices. As urban land values climbed, speculators tore down houses that were vacated by middle-class families moving away from the industrial core. In their place, they erected five- or six-story **tenements**, buildings that housed twenty or more

**The Cherry Family, 1906** Wiley and Fannie Cherry migrated in 1893 from North Carolina to Chicago, settling in the small African American community that had established itself on the city's West Side. The Cherrys apparently prospered. By 1906, when this family portrait was taken, they had entered the black middle class. When migration intensified after 1900, longer-settled urban blacks like the Cherrys often became uncomfortable, and relations with needy rural newcomers were sometimes tense. Collection of Lorraine Heflin/ Picture Research Consultants & Archives.

families in cramped, airless apartments (Figure 18.1). Tenements fostered rampant disease and horrific infant mortality. In New York's Eleventh Ward, an average of 986 persons occupied each acre. One investigator in Philadelphia described twenty-six people living in nine rooms of a tenement. "The bathroom at the rear of the house was used as a kitchen," she reported. "One privy compartment in the yard was the sole toilet accommodation for the five families living in the house." African Americans often suffered most. A study of Albany, Syracuse, and Troy, New York, noted, "The colored people are relegated to the least healthful buildings."

Denouncing these conditions, reformers called for model tenements financed by public-spirited citizens willing to accept a limited return on their investment. When private philanthropy failed to make a dent, cities turned to housing codes. The most advanced was New York's Tenement House Law of 1901, which required interior courts, indoor toilets, and fire safeguards for new structures. The law, however, had no effect on the 44,000 tenements that already existed in Manhattan and the Bronx.

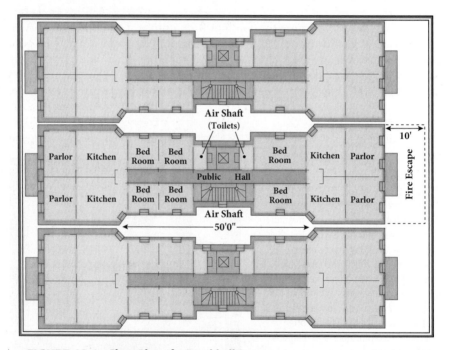

**FIGURE 18.1   Floor Plan of a Dumbbell Tenement**

In a contest for a design that met an 1879 requirement for every room to have a window, the dumbbell tenement won. The interior indentation, which created an airshaft between adjoining buildings, gave the tenement its "dumbbell" shape. But what was touted as a model tenement demonstrated instead the futility of trying to reconcile maximum land usage with decent housing. Each floor contained four apartments of three or four rooms, the largest only 10 by 11 feet. The two toilets in the hall became filthy or broke down under daily use by forty or more people. The narrow airshaft provided almost no light for the interior rooms and served mainly as a dumping ground for garbage. So deplorable were these tenements that they became the stimulus for the next wave of New York housing reform.

Reformers were thwarted by the economic facts of urban development. Industrial workers could not afford transportation and had to live near their jobs; commercial development pushed up land values. Only high-density, cheaply built housing earned landlords a significant profit.

## City Cultures

Despite their dangers and problems, industrial cities could be exciting places to live. In the nineteenth century, white middle-class Protestants had set the cultural standard; immigrants and the poor were expected to follow cues from their betters, seeking "uplift" and respectability. But in the cities, new mass-based entertainments emerged among the working classes, especially youth. These entertainments spread from the working class to the middle class — much to the distress of many middle-class parents. At the same time, cities became stimulating centers for intellectual life.

**Urban Amusements**    One enticing attraction was **vaudeville theater**, which arose in the 1880s and 1890s. Vaudeville customers could walk in anytime and watch a continuous sequence of musical acts, skits, magic shows, and other entertainment. First popular among the working class, vaudeville quickly broadened its appeal to include middle-class audiences. By the early 1900s, vaudeville faced competition from early movie theaters, or nickelodeons, which offered short films for a nickel entry fee. With distaste, one reporter described a typical movie audience as "mothers of bawling infants" and "newsboys, bootblacks, and smudgy urchins." By the 1910s, even working girls who refrained from less respectable amusements might indulge in a movie once or twice a week.

More spectacular were the great amusement parks that appeared around 1900, most famously at New York's Coney Island. These parks had their origins in world's fairs, whose paid entertainment areas had offered giant Ferris wheels and camel rides through "a street in Cairo." Entrepreneurs found that such attractions were big business. Between 1895 and 1904, they installed them at several rival amusement parks near Coney Island's popular beaches. The parks offered New Yorkers a chance to come by ferry, escape the hot city, and enjoy roller coasters, lagoon plunges, and "hootchy-kootchy" dance shows. Among the amazed observers was Cuban revolutionary José Martí, working as a journalist in the United States. "What facilities for every pleasure!" Martí wrote. "What absolute absence of any outward sadness or poverty! . . . The theater, the photographers' booth, the bathhouses!" He concluded that Coney Island epitomized America's commercial society, driven not by "love or glory" but by "a desire for gain." Similar parks grew up around the United States. By the summer of 1903, Philadelphia's Willow Grove counted three million visitors annually; so did two amusement parks outside Los Angeles.

**Ragtime and City Blues**    Music also became a booming urban entertainment. By the 1890s, Tin Pan Alley, the nickname for New York City's song-publishing district, produced such national hit tunes as "A Bicycle Built for Two" and "My Wild Irish Rose." The most famous sold more than a million copies of sheet music, as well as audio recordings for the newly invented phonograph. To find out what would sell, publishers had musicians play at New York's working-class beer gardens and dance halls. One publishing agent, who visited "sixty joints a week" to test new songs, declared that "the best songs came from the gutter."

African American musicians brought a syncopated beat that began, by the 1890s, to work its way into mainstream hits like "A Hot Time in the Old Town Tonight." Black performers became stars in their own right with the rise of ragtime. This music, apparently named for its ragged rhythm, combined a steady beat in the bass (played with the left hand on the piano) with syncopated, off-beat rhythms in the treble (played with the right). Ragtime became wildly popular among audiences of all classes and races who heard in its infectious rhythms something exciting — a decisive break with Victorian hymns and parlor songs.

For the master of the genre, composer Scott Joplin, ragtime was serious music. Joplin, the son of former slaves, grew up along the Texas-Arkansas border and took piano lessons as a boy from a German teacher. He and other traveling performers introduced ragtime to national audiences at the Chicago World's Fair in 1893. Seeking to elevate African American music and secure a broad national audience, Joplin warned pianists, "It is never right to play 'Ragtime' fast." But his instructions were widely ignored. Young Americans embraced ragtime.

They also embraced each other, as ragtime ushered in an urban dance craze. By 1910, New York alone had more than five hundred dance halls. In Kansas City, shocked guardians of morality counted 16,500 dancers on the floor on a Saturday night; Chicago had 86,000. Some young Polish and Slovak women chose restaurant jobs rather than domestic service so they would have free time to visit dance halls "several nights a week." New dances like the Bunny Hug and Grizzly Bear were overtly sexual: they called for close body contact and plenty of hip movement. In fact, many of these dances originated in brothels. Despite widespread denunciation, dance mania quickly spread from the urban working classes to rural and middle-class youth.

By the 1910s, black music was achieving a central place in American popular culture. African American trumpet player and bandleader W. C. Handy, born in Alabama, electrified national audiences by performing music drawn from the cotton fields of the Mississippi Delta. Made famous when it reached the big city, this music became known as the **blues**. Blues music spoke of hard work and heartbreak, as in Handy's popular hit "St. Louis Blues" (1914):

> Got de St. Louis Blues jes blue as I can be,
> Dat man got a heart lak a rock cast in the sea,
> Or else he wouldn't gone so far from me.

Blues spoke to the emotional lives of young urbanites who were far from home, experiencing dislocation, loneliness, and bitter disappointment along with the thrills of city life. Like Coney Island and other leisure activities, ragtime and blues helped forge new collective experiences in a world of strangers.

Ragtime and blues spread quickly and had a profound influence on twentieth-century American culture. By the time Handy published "St. Louis Blues," composer Irving Berlin, a Russian Jewish immigrant, was introducing altered ragtime pieces into musical theater — which eventually transferred to radio and film. Lyrics often featured sexual innuendo, as in the title of Berlin's hit song "If You Don't Want My Peaches (You'd Better Stop Shaking My Tree)." The popularity of such music marked the arrival of modern youth culture. Its enduring features included "crossover" music that originated in the black working class and a commercial music industry that brazenly appropriated African American musical styles.

**New Sexual Freedoms**    In the city, many young people found parental oversight weaker than it had been before. Amusement parks and dance halls helped foster the new custom of dating, which like other cultural innovations emerged first among the working class. Gradually, it became acceptable for a young man to escort a young woman out on the town for commercial entertainments rather than spending time at home under a chaperone's watchful eye. Dating opened a new world of pleasure, sexual adventure, and danger. Young women headed to dance halls alone to meet men; the term *gold digger* came into use to describe a woman who wanted a man's money more than the man himself.

But young women, not men, proved most vulnerable in the system of dating. Having less money to spend because they earned half or less of men's wages, working-class girls relied on the **"treat."** Some tried to maintain strict standards of respectability, keenly aware that their prospects for marriage depended on a virtuous reputation. Others became so-called charity girls, eager for a good time. Such young women, one investigator reported, "offer themselves to strangers, not for money, but for presents, attention and pleasure." For some women, sexual favors were a matter of practical necessity. "If I did not have a man," declared one waitress, "I could not get along on my wages." In the anonymous city, there was not always a clear line between working-class treats and casual prostitution.

Dating and casual sex were hallmarks of an urban world in which large numbers of residents were young and single. The 1900 census found that more than 20 percent of women in Detroit, Philadelphia, and Boston lived as boarders and lodgers, not in family units; the percentage topped 30 percent in St. Paul and Minneapolis. Single men also found social opportunities in the city. One historian has called the late nineteenth century the Age of the Bachelor, a time when being an unattached male lost its social stigma. With boardinghouses, restaurants, and abundant personal services, the city afforded bachelors all the comforts of home and, on top of that, an array of men's clubs, saloons, and sporting events.

Many industrial cities developed robust gay subcultures. New York's gay underground, for example, included an array of drinking and meeting places, as well as clubs and drag balls. Middle-class men, both straight and gay, frequented such venues for entertainment or to find companionship. One medical student remembered being taken to a ball at which he was startled to find five hundred gay and lesbian couples waltzing to "a good band." By the 1910s, the word *queer* had come into use as slang for *homosexual*. Though harassment was frequent and moral reformers like Anthony Comstock issued regular denunciations of sexual "degeneracy," arrests were few. Gay sex shows and saloons were lucrative for those who ran them (and for police, who took bribes to look the other way, just as they did for brothels). The exuberant gay urban subculture offered a dramatic challenge to Victorian ideals.

**High Culture**    For elites, the rise of great cities offered an opportunity to build museums, libraries, and other cultural institutions that could flourish only in major metropolitan centers. Millionaires patronized the arts partly to advance themselves socially but also out of a sense of civic duty and national pride. As early as the 1870s, symphony orchestras emerged in Boston and New York. Composers and conductors soon joined Europe in new experiments. The Metropolitan Opera, founded in 1883 by wealthy businessmen, drew enthusiastic crowds to hear the innovative work of Richard Wagner. In 1907, the Met shocked audiences by presenting Richard Strauss's sexually scandalous opera *Salome.*

Art museums and natural history museums also became prominent new institutions in this era. The nation's first major art museum, the Corcoran Gallery of Art, opened in Washington, D.C., in 1869, while New York's Metropolitan Museum of Art settled into its permanent home in 1880. In the same decades, public libraries grew from modest collections into major urban institutions. The greatest library benefactor was steel magnate Andrew Carnegie, who announced in 1881 that he would build a library in any town or city that was prepared to maintain it. By 1907, Carnegie had spent more than $32.7 million to establish over a thousand libraries throughout the United States.

**Urban Journalism**   Patrons of Carnegie's libraries could read, in addition to books, an increasing array of mass-market newspapers. Joseph Pulitzer, owner of the *St. Louis Post-Dispatch* and *New York World,* led the way in building his sales base with sensational investigations, human-interest stories, and targeted sections covering sports and high society. By the 1890s, Pulitzer faced a challenge from William Randolph Hearst. The arrival of Sunday color comics featuring the "Yellow Kid" gave such publications the name **yellow journalism**, a derogatory term for mass-market newspapers. Hearst's and Pulitzer's sensational coverage was often irresponsible. In the late 1890s, for example, their papers helped whip up frenzied pressure for the United States to declare war against Spain (Chapter 20). But Hearst and Pulitzer also exposed scandals and injustices. They believed their papers should challenge the powerful by speaking to and for ordinary Americans.

Along with Hearst's and Pulitzer's stunt reporters, other urban journalists also worked to promote reform. New magazines such as *McClure's* introduced national audiences to reporters such as Ida Tarbell, who exposed the machinations of John D. Rockefeller, and David Graham Phillips, whose "Treason of the Senate," published in *Cosmopolitan* in 1906, documented the deference of U.S. senators—especially Republicans—to wealthy corporate interests. Theodore Roosevelt dismissed such writers as **muckrakers** who focused too much on the negative side of American life. The term stuck, but muckrakers' influence was profound. They inspired thousands of readers to get involved in reform movements and tackle the problems caused by industrialization.

| IN YOUR OWN WORDS | How did American cities change in the late nineteenth century? |
|---|---|

## Governing the Great City

One of the most famous muckrakers was Lincoln Steffens, whose book *The Shame of the Cities* (1904), first published serially in *McClure's* magazine, denounced the corruption afflicting America's urban governments. Steffens used dramatic language to expose "swindling" politicians. He claimed, for example, that the mayor of Minneapolis had turned his city over to "outlaws." In St. Louis, "bribery was a joke," while Pittsburgh's Democratic Party operated a private company that handled most of the city's street-paving projects—at a hefty profit. Historians now believe that Steffens and other middle-class crusaders took a rather extreme view of urban politics; the reality was more complex. But charges of corruption could hardly be denied. As industrial cities grew with breathtaking speed, they posed a serious problem of governance.

## Urban Machines

In the United States, cities relied largely on private developers to build streetcar lines and provide urgently needed water, gas, and electricity. This preference for business solutions gave birth to what one urban historian calls the "private city"—an urban environment shaped by individuals and profit-seeking businesses. Private enterprise, Americans believed, spurred great innovations—trolley cars, electric lighting, skyscrapers—and drove urban real estate development. Investment opportunities looked so tempting, in fact, that new cities sprang up almost overnight from the ruins of a catastrophic Chicago fire in 1871 and a major San Francisco earthquake in 1906. Real estate interests were often instrumental in encouraging streetcar lines to build outward from the central districts.

When contractors sought city business, or saloonkeepers needed licenses, they turned to **political machines**: local party bureaucracies that kept an unshakable grip on both elected and appointed public offices. A machine like New York's infamous Tammany Society—known by the name of its meeting place, Tammany Hall—consisted of layers of political functionaries. At the bottom were precinct captains who knew every city neighborhood and block; above them were ward bosses and, at the top, powerful citywide leaders, who had usually started at the bottom and worked their way up. Machines dispensed jobs and patronage, arranged for urban services, and devoted their energies to staying in office, which they did, year after year, on the strength of their political clout and popularity among urban voters.

For constituents, political machines acted as a rough-and-ready social service agency, providing jobs for the jobless or a helping hand for a bereaved family. Tammany ward boss George Washington Plunkitt, for example, reported that he arranged housing for families after their apartments burned, "fix[ing] them up until they get things runnin' again." Plunkitt was an Irishman, and so were most Tammany Hall leaders. But by the 1890s, Plunkitt's Fifteenth District was filling up with Italians and Russian Jews. On a given day (as recorded in his diary), he might attend an Italian funeral in the afternoon and a Jewish wedding in the evening. Wherever he went, he brought gifts, listened to his constituents' troubles, and offered a helping hand.

The favors dispensed by men like Plunkitt came via a system of boss control that was, as Lincoln Steffens charged, corrupt. Though rural, state, and national politics were hardly immune to such problems, cities offered flagrant opportunities for bribes and kickbacks. The level of corruption, as Plunkitt observed, was greater in cities, "accordin' to the opportunities." When politicians made contracts for city services, some of the money ended up in their pockets. In the 1860s, William Marcy Tweed, known as Boss Tweed, had made Tammany Hall a byword for corruption, until he was brought down in 1871 by flagrant overpricing of contracts for a lavish city courthouse. Thereafter, machine corruption became more surreptitious. Plunkitt declared that he had no need for outright bribes. He favored what he called "honest graft" — the profits that came to savvy insiders who knew where and when to buy land. Plunkitt made most of his money building wharves on Manhattan's waterfront.

Middle-class reformers condemned immigrants for supporting machines. But urban immigrants believed that few middle-class Americans cared about the plight of poor city folk like themselves. Machines were hardly perfect, but immigrants could rely on them for jobs, emergency aid, and the only public services they could hope to obtain. Astute commentators saw that bosses dominated city government because they provided what was needed, with no condescending moral judgments. As reformer Jane Addams put it, the ward boss was a "stalking survival of village kindness." Voters knew he was corrupt, but on election day they might say, "Ah, well, he has a big Irish heart. He is good to the widow and the fatherless," or, "he knows the poor." Addams concluded that middle-class reformers would only make headway if they set aside their prejudices, learned to "stand by and for and with the people," and did a better job of it than the machine bosses did.

Machine-style governments achieved some notable successes. They arranged (at a profit) for companies to operate streetcars, bring clean water and gaslight, and remove garbage. Nowhere in the world were there more massive public projects — aqueducts, sewage systems, bridges, and spacious parks — than in the great cities of the United States. The nature of this achievement can be grasped by comparing Chicago, Illinois, with Berlin, the capital of Germany, in 1900. At that

**A Hint to Boards of Health**
In 1884, *Frank Leslie's Illustrated Newspaper* urged municipal and state boards of health to work harder to protect urban children. When this cartoon appeared, New Yorkers were reading shocking reports of milk dealers who diluted milk with borax and other chemicals. Note the range of health threats that the cartoonist identifies. Rutherford B. Hayes Presidential Center.

time, Chicago's waterworks pumped 500 million gallons of water a day, providing 139 gallons per resident; Berliners made do with 18 gallons each. Flush toilets, a rarity in Berlin, could be found in 60 percent of Chicago homes. Chicago lit its streets with electricity, while Berlin still relied mostly on gaslight. Chicago had twice as many parks as the German capital, and it had just completed an ambitious sanitation project that reversed the course of the Chicago River, carrying sewage into Lake Michigan, away from city residents.

These achievements were remarkable, because American municipal governments labored under severe political constraints. Judges did grant cities some authority: in 1897, for example, New York's state supreme court ruled that New York City was entirely within its rights to operate a municipally owned subway. Use of private land was also subject to whatever regulations a city might impose. But, starting with an 1868 ruling in Iowa, the American legal system largely classified the city as a "corporate entity" subject to state control. In contrast to state governments, cities had only a limited police power, which they could use, for example, to stop crime but not to pass more ambitious measures for public welfare. States, not cities, held most taxation power and received most public revenues. Machines and their private allies flourished, in part, because cities were starved for legitimate cash.

Thus money talked; powerful economic interests warped city government. Working-class residents — even those loyal to their local machines — knew that the newest electric lights and best trolley lines served affluent neighborhoods, where citizens had the most clout. Hilda Satt, a Polish immigrant who moved into a poor Chicago neighborhood in 1893, recalled garbage-strewn streets and filthy backyard privies. "The streets were paved with wooden blocks," she later wrote, "and after a heavy rainfall the blocks would become loose and float about in the street." She remembered that on one such occasion, local pranksters posted a sign saying, "The Mayor and the Aldermen are Invited to Swim Here." As cities expanded, the limitations of political machines became increasingly clear.

## The Limits of Machine Government

The scale of urban problems became dramatically evident in the depression of the 1890s, when unemployment reached a staggering 25 percent in some cities. Homelessness and hunger were rampant; newspapers nationwide reported on cases of starvation, desperation, and suicide. To make matters worse, most cities had abolished the early-nineteenth-century system of outdoor relief, which provided public support for the indigent. Fearing the system promoted laziness among the poor, middle-class reformers had insisted on private, not public, charity. Even cities that continued to provide outdoor relief in the 1890s were overwhelmed by the magnitude of the crisis. Flooded with "tramps," police stations were forced to end the long-standing practice of allowing homeless individuals to sleep inside.

Faced with this crisis, many urban voters proved none too loyal to the machines when better alternatives arose. Cleveland, Ohio, for example, experienced eighty-three labor strikes between 1893 and 1898. Workers' frustration centered on corrupt businesses with close ties to municipal officials. The city's Central Labor Union, dissatisfied with Democrats' failure to address its concerns, worked with middle-class allies to build a thriving local branch of the People's Party (Chapter 19). Their demands for stronger government measures, especially to curb corporate power, culminated in citywide protests in 1899 during a strike against the hated streetcar company. That year, more than eight thousand workers participated in the city's annual Labor Day parade. As they passed the mayor's reviewing stand, the bands fell silent and the unions furled their flags in a solemn protest against the mayor's failure to support their cause.

To recapture support from working-class Clevelanders, Democrats made a dramatic change in 1901, nominating Tom Johnson for mayor. Johnson, a reform-minded businessman, advocated municipal ownership of utilities and a tax system in which "monopoly and privilege" bore the main burdens. (Johnson once thanked Cleveland's city appraisers for raising taxes on his own mansion.) Johnson's comfortable victory transformed the Democrats into Cleveland's leading reform party. While the new mayor did not fulfill the whole agenda of the Central Labor Union and its allies, he became an advocate of publicly owned utilities and one of the nation's most famous and innovative reformers.

Like Johnson, other mayors began to oust machines and launch ambitious programs of reform. Some modeled their municipal governments on those of Glasgow, Scotland; Düsseldorf, Germany; and other European cities on the cutting edge of innovation. In Boston, Mayor Josiah Quincy built public baths, gyms, swimming pools, and playgrounds and provided free public concerts. Like other mayors, he battled streetcar companies to bring down fares. The scope of such projects varied. In 1912, San Francisco managed to open one small municipally owned streetcar line to compete with private companies. Milwaukee, Wisconsin, on the other hand, elected socialists who experimented with a sweeping array of measures, including publicly subsidized medical care and housing.

Republican Hazen Pingree, mayor of Detroit from 1890 to 1897, was a particularly noted reformer who worked for better streets and public transportation. During the depression, Pingree opened a network of vacant city-owned lots as community vegetable gardens. Though some people ridiculed "Pingree's Potato Patches," the gardens helped feed thousands of Detroit's working people during the harsh depression years. By 1901, a coalition of reformers who campaigned against New York's Tammany Hall began to borrow ideas from Pingree and other mayors. In the wealthier wards of New York, they promised to reduce crime and save taxpayer dollars. In working-class neighborhoods, they vowed to provide affordable housing and municipal ownership of gas and electricity. They defeated Tammany's candidates, and though they did not fulfill all of their promises, they did provide more funding for overcrowded public schools.

Reformers also experimented with new ways of organizing municipal government itself. After a devastating hurricane in 1900 killed an estimated six thousand people in Galveston, Texas, and destroyed much of the city, rebuilders adopted a commission system that became a nationwide model for efficient government. Leaders of the **National Municipal League** advised cities to elect small councils and hire professional city managers who would direct operations like a corporate executive. The league had difficulty persuading politicians to adopt its business-oriented model; it won its greatest victories in young, small cities like Phoenix, Arizona, where the professional classes held political power. Other cities chose, instead, to enhance democratic participation. As part of the Oregon System, which called for direct voting on key political questions, Portland voters participated in 129 municipal referendum votes between 1905 and 1913.

| IN YOUR OWN WORDS | What problems did big cities pose for those who ran them, and how did political leaders try to meet those challenges? |
| --- | --- |

## Crucibles of Progressive Reform

The challenges posed by urban life presented rich opportunities for experimentation and reform. As happened in Cleveland with Tom Johnson's election as mayor, working-class radicals and middle-class reformers often mounted simultaneous challenges to political machines, and these combined pressures led to dramatic change. Many reformers pointed to the plight of the urban poor, especially children. Thus it is not surprising that **progressivism**, an overlapping set of movements to combat the ills of industrialization (Chapter 19), had important roots in the city. In the slums and tenements of the metropolis, reformers invented new forms of civic participation that shaped the course of national politics.

### Fighting Dirt and Vice

As early as the 1870s and 1880s, news reporters drew attention to corrupt city governments, the abuse of power by large corporations, and threats to public health. Researcher Helen Campbell reported on tenement conditions in such exposés as *Prisoners of Poverty* (1887). Making innovative use of the invention of flash photography, Danish-born journalist Jacob Riis included photographs of tenement interiors in his famous 1890 book, *How the Other Half Lives*. Riis had a profound influence on Theodore Roosevelt when the future president served as New York City's police commissioner. Roosevelt asked Riis to lead him on tours around the tenements, to help him better understand the problems of poverty, disease, and crime.

**Cleaning Up Urban Environments**   One of the most urgent problems of the big city was disease. In the late nineteenth century, scientists in Europe came to understand the role of germs and bacteria. Though researchers could not yet cure epidemic diseases, they could recommend effective measures for prevention. Following up on New York City's victory against cholera in 1866 — when government officials instituted an effective quarantine and prevented large numbers of deaths — city and state officials began to champion more public health projects. With a major clean-water initiative for its industrial cities in the late nineteenth century, Massachusetts demonstrated that it could largely eliminate typhoid fever. After a horrific yellow fever epidemic in 1878 that killed perhaps 12 percent of its population, Memphis, Tennessee, invested in state-of-the-art sewage and drainage. Though the new system did not eliminate yellow fever, it unexpectedly cut death rates from typhoid and cholera, as well as infant deaths from water-borne disease. Other cities followed suit. By 1913, a nationwide survey of 198 cities found that they were spending an average of $1.28 per resident for sanitation and other health measures.

The public health movement became one of the era's most visible and influential reforms. In cities, the impact of pollution was obvious. Children played on piles of garbage, breathed toxic air, and consumed poisoned food, milk, and water. Infant mortality rates were shocking: in the early 1900s, a baby born to a Slavic woman in an American city had a 1 in 3 chance of dying in infancy. Outraged, reformers mobilized to demand safe water and better garbage collection. Hygiene reformers taught hand-washing and other techniques to fight the spread of tuberculosis.

Americans worked in other ways to make industrial cities healthier and more beautiful to live in. Many municipalities adopted smoke-abatement laws, though they had limited success with enforcement until the post–World War I adoption of natural gas, which burned cleaner than coal. Recreation also received attention. Even before the Civil War, urban planners had established sanctuaries like New York's Central Park, where city people could stroll, rest, and contemplate natural landscapes. By the turn of the twentieth century, the **"City Beautiful" movement** arose to advocate more and better urban park spaces. Though most parks still featured flower gardens and tree-lined paths, they also made room for skating rinks, tennis courts, baseball fields, and swimming pools. Many included play areas with swing sets and seesaws, promoted by the National Playground Association as a way to keep urban children safe and healthy.

### Closing Red Light Districts

Distressed by the commercialization of sex, reformers also launched a campaign against urban prostitution. They warned, in dramatic language, of the threat of white slavery, alleging (in spite of considerable evidence to the contrary) that large numbers of young white women were being kidnapped and forced into prostitution. In *The City's Perils* (1910), author Leona Prall Groetzinger wrote that young women arrived from the countryside "burning with high hope and filled with great resolve, but the remorseless city takes them, grinds them, crushes them, and at last deposits them in unknown graves."

Practical investigators found a more complex reality: women entered prostitution as a result of many factors, including low-wage jobs, economic desperation, abandonment, and often sexual and domestic abuse. Women who bore a child out of wedlock were often shunned by their families and forced into prostitution. Some working women and even housewives undertook casual prostitution to make ends meet. For decades, female reformers had tried to "rescue" such women and retrain them for more respectable employments, such as sewing. Results were, at best, mixed. Efforts to curb demand—that is, to focus on arresting and punishing men who employed prostitutes—proved unpopular with voters.

Nonetheless, with public concern mounting over "white slavery" and the payoffs machine bosses exacted from brothel keepers, many cities appointed vice commissions in the early twentieth century. A wave of brothel closings crested between 1909 and 1912, as police shut down red light districts in cities nationwide. Meanwhile, Congress passed the Mann Act (1910) to prohibit the transportation of prostitutes across state lines.

The crusade against prostitution accomplished its main goal, closing brothels, but in the long term it worsened the conditions under which many prostitutes worked. Though conditions in some brothels were horrific, sex workers who catered to wealthy clients made high wages and were relatively protected by madams, many of whom set strict rules for clients and provided medical care for their workers. In the wake of brothel closings, such women lost control of the prostitution business. Instead, almost all sex workers became "streetwalkers" or "call girls," more vulnerable to violence and often earning lower wages than they had before the antiprostitution crusade began.

## The Movement for Social Settlements

Some urban reformers focused their energies on building a creative new institution, the **social settlement**. These community welfare centers investigated the plight of the urban poor, raised funds to address urgent needs, and helped neighborhood residents advocate on their own behalf. At the movement's peak in the early twentieth century, dozens of social settlements operated across the United States. The most famous, and one of the first, was **Hull House** on Chicago's West Side, founded in 1889 by Jane Addams and her companion Ellen Gates Starr. Their dilapidated mansion, flanked by saloons in a neighborhood of Italian and Eastern European immigrants, served as a spark plug for community improvement and political reform.

The idea for Hull House came partly from Toynbee Hall, a London settlement that Addams and Starr had visited while touring Europe. Social settlements also drew inspiration from U.S. urban missions of the 1870s and 1880s. Some of these, like the Hampton Institute, had aided former slaves during Reconstruction; others, like Grace Baptist in Philadelphia, arose in northern cities. To meet the needs of urban residents, missions offered employment counseling, medical clinics, day care centers, and sometimes athletic facilities in cooperation with the Young Men's Christian Association (YMCA).

Jane Addams, a daughter of the middle class, first expected Hull House to offer art classes and other cultural programs for the poor. But Addams's views quickly changed as she got to know her new neighbors and struggled to keep Hull House open during the depression of the 1890s. Addams's views were also influenced by conversations with fellow Hull House resident Florence Kelley, who had studied in Europe and returned a committed socialist. Dr. Alice Hamilton, who opened a pediatric clinic at Hull House, wrote that Addams came to see her settlement as "a bridge between the classes. . . . She always held that this bridge was as much of a help to the well-to-do as to the poor." Settlements offered idealistic young people "a place where they could live as neighbors and give as much as they could of what they had."

Addams and her colleagues believed that working-class Americans already *knew* what they needed. What they lacked were resources to fulfill those needs, as well as a political voice. These, settlement workers tried to provide. Hull House was typical in offering a bathhouse, playground, kindergarten, and day care center. Some settlements opened libraries and gymnasiums; others operated penny savings banks and cooperative kitchens where tired mothers could purchase a meal at the end of the day. (Addams humbly closed the Hull House kitchen when she found that her bland New England cooking had little appeal for Italians; her coworker, Dr. Alice Hamilton, soon investigated the health benefits of garlic.) At the Henry Street Settlement in New York, Lillian Wald organized visiting nurses to improve health in tenement wards. Addams, meanwhile, encouraged local women to inspect the neighborhood and bring back a list of dangers to health and safety. Together, they prepared a complaint to city council. The women, Addams wrote, had shown "civic enterprise and moral conviction" in carrying out the project themselves.

Social settlements took many forms. Some attached themselves to preexisting missions and African American colleges. Others were founded by energetic college graduates. Catholics ran St. Elizabeth Center in St. Louis; Jews, the Boston Hebrew Industrial School. Whatever their origins, social settlements were, in Addams's words, "an experimental effort to aid in the solution of the social and industrial problems which are engendered by the modern condition of life in a great city."

Settlements served as a springboard for many other projects. Settlement workers often fought city hall to get better schools and lobbied state legislatures for new workplace safety laws. At Hull House, Hamilton investigated lead poisoning and other health threats at local factories. Her colleague Julia Lathrop investigated the plight of teenagers caught in the criminal justice system. She drafted a proposal for separate juvenile courts and persuaded Chicago to adopt it. Pressuring the city to experiment with better rehabilitation strategies for juveniles convicted of crime, Lathrop created a model for juvenile court systems across the United States.

Another example of settlements' long-term impact was the work of Margaret Sanger, a nurse who moved to New York City in 1911 and volunteered with a Lower East Side settlement. Horrified by women's suffering from constant pregnancies — and remembering her devout Catholic mother, who had died young after bearing eleven children — Sanger launched a crusade for what she called birth control. Her newspaper column, "What Every Girl Should Know," soon garnered an indictment for violating obscenity laws. The publicity that resulted helped Sanger launch a national birth control movement.

Settlements were thus a crucial proving ground for many progressive experiments, as well as for the emerging profession of social work, which transformed the provision of public welfare. Social workers rejected the older model of private Christian charity, dispensed by well-meaning middle-class volunteers to those in need. Instead, social workers defined themselves as professional caseworkers who served as advocates of social justice. Like many reformers of the era, they allied themselves with the new social sciences, such as sociology and economics, and undertook statistical surveys and other systematic methods for gathering facts. Social work proved to be an excellent opportunity for educated women who sought professional careers. By 1920, women made up 62 percent of U.S. social workers.

## Cities and National Politics

Despite reform efforts, the problems wrought by industrialization continued to cause suffering in urban workplaces and environments. In 1906, journalist Upton Sinclair exposed some of the most extreme forms of labor exploitation in his novel *The Jungle*, which described appalling conditions in Chicago meatpacking plants. What caught the nation's attention was not Sinclair's account of workers' plight, but his descriptions of rotten meat and filthy packing conditions. With constituents up in arms, Congress passed the **Pure Food and Drug Act** (1906) and created the federal Food and Drug Administration to oversee compliance with the new law.

The impact of *The Jungle* showed how urban reformers could affect national politics. Even more significant was the work of Josephine Shaw Lowell, a Civil War widow from a prominent family. After years of struggling to aid poverty-stricken individuals in New York City, Lowell concluded that charity was not enough. In 1890, she helped found the New York Consumers' League to improve wages and working conditions for female store clerks. The league encouraged shoppers to patronize only stores where wages and working conditions were known to be fair. By 1899, the organization had become the **National Consumers' League** (NCL). At its head stood the outspoken and skillful Florence Kelley, a Hull House worker and former chief factory inspector of Illinois. Kelley believed that only government oversight could protect exploited workers. Under her crusading leadership, the NCL became one of the most powerful progressive organizations advocating worker protection laws.

Many labor organizations also began in a single city and then grew to national stature. One famous example was the **Women's Trade Union League**, founded in New York in 1903. Financed by wealthy women who supported its work, the league trained working-class leaders like Rose Schneiderman, who organized unions among garment workers. Although often frustrated by the patronizing attitude of elite sponsors, trade-union women joined together in the broader struggle for women's rights. When New York State held referenda on women's suffrage in 1915 and 1917, strong support came from Jewish and Italian precincts where unionized garment workers lived. Working-class voters hoped, in turn, that enfranchised women would use their ballots to help industrial workers.

Residents of industrial cities, then, sought allies in state and national politics. The need for broader action was made clear in New York City by a shocking event on March 25, 1911. On that Saturday afternoon, just before quitting time, a fire broke out at the Triangle Shirtwaist Company. The **Triangle Fire** quickly spread through the three floors the company occupied at the top of a ten-story building. Panicked workers discovered that, despite fire safety laws, employers had locked the emergency doors to prevent theft. Dozens of Triangle workers, mostly young immigrant women, were trapped in the flames. Many leaped to their deaths; the rest never reached the windows. The average age of the 146 people who died was just nineteen.

Shocked by this horrific event, New Yorkers responded with an outpouring of anger and grief that crossed ethnic, class, and religious boundaries. Many remembered that, only a year earlier, shirtwaist workers had walked off the job to protest abysmal safety and working conditions—and that the owners of Triangle, among other employers, had broken the strike. Facing demands for action, New York State appointed a factory commission that developed a remarkable program of labor reform: fifty-six laws dealing with such issues as fire hazards, unsafe machines, and wages and working hours for women and children. The chairman and vice chairman of the commission were Robert F. Wagner and Alfred E. Smith, both Tammany Hall politicians then serving in the state legislature. They established the commission, participated fully in its work, and marshaled party regulars to pass the proposals into law—all with the approval of Tammany. The labor code that resulted was the most advanced in the United States.

Tammany's response to the Triangle Fire showed that it was acknowledging its need for help. The social and economic problems of the industrial city had outgrown the power of party machines; only stronger state and national laws could bar industrial firetraps, alleviate sweatshop conditions, and improve slums. Politicians like Wagner and Smith saw that Tammany had to change or die. The fire had unforeseen further consequences. Frances Perkins, a Columbia University student who witnessed the horror of Triangle workers leaping from the windows to their deaths, decided she would devote her efforts to the cause of labor. Already active in women's reform organizations, Perkins went to Chicago, where she volunteered for several years at Hull House. In 1929, she became New York State's first commissioner of labor; four years later, during the New Deal (Chapter 22), Franklin D. Roosevelt appointed her as U.S. secretary of labor—the first woman to hold a cabinet post.

The political aftermath of the Triangle Fire demonstrated how challenges posed by industrial cities pushed politics in new directions, transforming urban government and initiating broader movements for reform. The nation's political and cultural standards had long been set by native-born, Protestant, middle-class Americans. By 1900, the people who thronged to the great cities helped build America into a global industrial power—and in the process, created an electorate that was far more ethnically, racially, and religiously diverse.

In the era of industrialization, some rural and native-born commentators warned that immigrants were "inferior breeds" who would "mongrelize" American culture. But urban political leaders defended cultural pluralism, expressing appreciation—even admiration—for immigrants, including Catholics and Jews, who sought a better life in the United States. At the same time, urban reformers worked to improve conditions of life for the diverse residents of American cities. Cities, then, and the innovative solutions proposed by urban leaders, held a central place in America's consciousness as the nation took on the task of progressive reform.

| IN YOUR OWN WORDS | Why and how did large cities become what one commentator called "seedbeds for reform"? |

## Summary

After 1865, American cities grew at an unprecedented rate, and urban populations swelled with workers from rural areas and abroad. To move their burgeoning populations around, cities pioneered innovative forms of mass transit. Skyscrapers came to mark urban skylines, and new electric lighting systems encouraged nightlife. Neighborhoods divided along class and ethnic lines, with the working class inhabiting crowded, shoddily built tenements. Immigrants developed new ethnic cultures in their neighborhoods, while racism followed African American migrants from the country to the city. At the same time, new forms of popular urban culture bridged class and ethnic lines, challenging traditional sexual norms and gender roles. Popular journalism rose to prominence and helped build rising sympathy for reform.

Industrial cities confronted a variety of new political challenges. Despite notable achievements, established machine governments could not address urban problems through traditional means. Forward-looking politicians took the initiative and implemented a range of political, labor, and social reforms. Urban reformers also launched campaigns to address public health, morals, and welfare. They did so through a variety of innovative institutions, most notably social settlements, which brought affluent Americans into working-class neighborhoods to learn, cooperate, and advocate on behalf of their neighbors. Such projects began to increase Americans' acceptance of urban diversity and their confidence in government's ability to solve the problems of industrialization.

# Chapter 18 Review

## KEY TERMS

**Identify and explain the significance of each term below.**

Chicago school (p. 528)
mutual aid society (p. 529)
race riot (p. 531)
tenement (p. 531)
vaudeville theater (p. 533)
blues (p. 534)
"treat" (p. 535)
yellow journalism (p. 536)
muckrakers (p. 536)
political machines (p. 537)

National Municipal League (p. 540)
progressivism (p. 541)
"City Beautiful" movement (p. 542)
social settlement (p. 543)
Hull House (p. 543)
Pure Food and Drug Act (p. 544)
National Consumers' League (p. 545)
Women's Trade Union League (p. 545)
Triangle Fire (p. 545)

## REVIEW QUESTIONS

**Answer these questions to demonstrate your understanding of the chapter's main ideas.**

1. How did American cities change in the late nineteenth century?

2. What problems did big cities pose for those who ran them, and how did political leaders try to meet those challenges?

3. Why and how did large cities become what one commentator called "seed-beds for reform"?

4. Using the thematic timeline on pages 472–473, consider some of the ways in which mass migrations of people—both from other countries and from places within the United States—shaped industrial cities. How did this influence American society, culture, and national identity?

## CHRONOLOGY

**As you read, ask yourself why this chapter begins and ends with these dates and identify the links among related events.**

| 1871 | • First elevated railroad begins operation in New York |
| 1878 | • Yellow fever epidemic in Memphis, Tennessee |
| 1883 | • Metropolitan Opera opens in New York |
| 1885 | • First skyscraper completed in Chicago |
| 1887 | • First electric trolley system built in Richmond, Virginia |

| | |
|---|---|
| **1889** | • Jane Addams and Ellen Gates Starr found Hull House in Chicago |
| **1890** | • Jacob Riis publishes *How the Other Half Lives* |
| **1892** | • New York's Ellis Island opens |
| **1893** | • Ragtime introduced to national audiences at Chicago World's Columbian Exposition |
| **1897** | • First subway line opened in Boston |
| **1899** | • Central Labor Union protests in Cleveland |
| | • National Consumers' League founded |
| **1901** | • New York passes Tenement House Law |
| **1903** | • Women's Trade Union League founded |
| **1906** | • Upton Sinclair publishes *The Jungle* |
| | • Food and Drug Administration established |
| | • Atlanta race riot |
| **1910** | • Mann Act prohibits transportation of prostitutes across state lines |
| **1911** | • Triangle Fire at Triangle Shirtwaist Company in New York |

# 19

# Whose Government? Politics, Populists, and Progressives

## 1880–1917

**IDENTIFY THE BIG IDEA**

How and why did Progressive Era reformers seek to address the problems of industrial America, and to what extent did they succeed?

**"WE ARE LIVING IN A GRAND AND WONDERFUL TIME," DECLARED KANSAS** political organizer Mary E. Lease in 1891. "Men, women and children are in commotion, discussing the mighty problems of the day." This "movement among the masses," she said, was based on the words of Jesus: "Whatsoever ye would that men should do unto you, do ye even so unto them." Between the 1880s and the 1910s, thousands of reformers like Lease confronted the problems of industrialization. Lease herself stumped not only for the People's Party, which sought more government regulation of the economy, but also for the Knights of Labor and Woman's Christian Temperance Union (WCTU), as well as for women's suffrage and public health.

Between the end of Reconstruction and the start of World War I, political reformers focused on four main goals: cleaning up politics, limiting the power of big business, reducing poverty, and promoting social justice. Historians call this period of agitation and innovation the Progressive Era. In the 1880s and 1890s, labor unions and farm groups took the lead in critiquing the industrial order and demanding change. But over time, more and more middle-class and elite Americans took up the call, earning the name *progressives*. On the whole, they proposed more limited measures than farmer-labor advocates did, but since they had more political clout, they often had greater success in winning new laws. Thus both radicals and progressives played important roles in advancing reform.

No single group defined the Progressive Era. On the contrary, reformers took opposite views on such questions as immigration, racial justice, women's rights, and imperialism. Leaders such as Theodore Roosevelt and Woodrow Wilson, initially hostile to the sweeping critiques of capitalism offered by radicals, gradually adopted bolder ideas. Dramatic political changes influenced the direction of reform. Close party competition in the 1880s gave way to Republican control between 1894 and 1910, followed by a period of Democratic leadership during Wilson's presidency (1913–1919). Progressives gave the era its name, not because they acted as a unified force, but because they engaged in diverse, energetic movements to improve America.

# Reform Visions, 1880–1892

In the 1880s, radical farmers' groups and the Knights of Labor provided a powerful challenge to industrialization (Chapter 16). At the same time, groups such as the WCTU (Chapter 17) and urban settlements (Chapter 18) laid the groundwork for progressivism, especially among women. Though they had different goals, these groups confronted similar dilemmas upon entering politics. Should they work through existing political parties? Create new ones? Or generate pressure from the outside? Reformers tried all these strategies.

## Electoral Politics After Reconstruction

The end of Reconstruction ushered in a period of fierce partisan conflict. Republicans and Democrats traded control of the Senate three times between 1880 and 1894, and the House majority five times. Causes of this tight competition included northerners' disillusionment with Republican policies and the resurgence of southern Democrats, who regained a strong base in Congress. Dizzying population growth also changed the size and shape of the House of Representatives. In 1875, it counted 243 seats; two decades later, that had risen to 356. Between 1889 and 1896, entry of seven new western states—Montana, North and South Dakota, Washington, Idaho, Wyoming, and Utah—contributed to political instability.

Heated competition and the legacies of the Civil War drew Americans into politics. Union veterans donned their uniforms to march in Republican parades, while ex-Confederate Democrats did the same in the South. When politicians appealed to war loyalties, critics ridiculed them for "waving the bloody shirt": whipping up old animosities that ought to be set aside. For those who had fought or lost beloved family members in the conflict, however—as well as those struggling over African American rights in the South—war issues remained crucial. Many voters also had strong views on economic policies, especially Republicans' high protective tariffs. Proportionately more voters turned out in presidential elections from 1876 to 1892 than at any other time in American history.

The presidents of this era had limited room to maneuver in a period of narrow victories, when the opposing party often held one or both houses of Congress. Republicans Rutherford B. Hayes and Benjamin Harrison both won the electoral

**Coxey's Army on the March, 1894** During the severe depression of the 1890s, Ohio businessman Jacob Coxey organized unemployed men for a peaceful march to the U.S. Capitol to plead for an emergency jobs program. They called themselves the Commonweal of Christ but won the nickname "Coxey's Army." Though it failed to win sympathy from Congress, the army's march on Washington — one of the nation's first — inspired similar groups to set out from many cities. Here, Coxey's group nears Washington, D.C. The man on horseback is Carl Browne, one of the group's leaders and a flamboyant publicist. As the marchers entered Washington, Coxey's seventeen-year-old daughter Mamie, dressed as the "Goddess of Peace," led the procession on a white Arabian horse. Library of Congress.

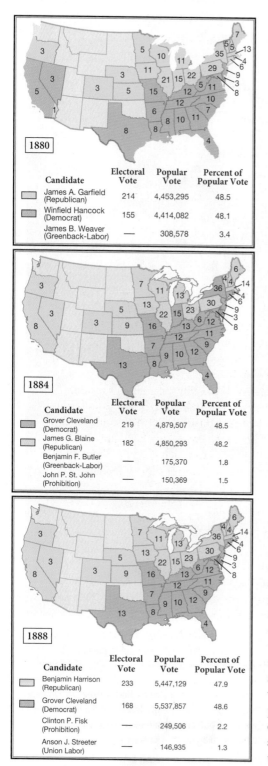

| Candidate | Electoral Vote | Popular Vote | Percent of Popular Vote |
|---|---|---|---|
| James A. Garfield (Republican) | 214 | 4,453,295 | 48.5 |
| Winfield Hancock (Democrat) | 155 | 4,414,082 | 48.1 |
| James B. Weaver (Greenback-Labor) | — | 308,578 | 3.4 |

**1884**

| Candidate | Electoral Vote | Popular Vote | Percent of Popular Vote |
|---|---|---|---|
| Grover Cleveland (Democrat) | 219 | 4,879,507 | 48.5 |
| James G. Blaine (Republican) | 182 | 4,850,293 | 48.2 |
| Benjamin F. Butler (Greenback-Labor) | — | 175,370 | 1.8 |
| John P. St. John (Prohibition) | — | 150,369 | 1.5 |

**1888**

| Candidate | Electoral Vote | Popular Vote | Percent of Popular Vote |
|---|---|---|---|
| Benjamin Harrison (Republican) | 233 | 5,447,129 | 47.9 |
| Grover Cleveland (Democrat) | 168 | 5,537,857 | 48.6 |
| Clinton P. Fisk (Prohibition) | — | 249,506 | 2.2 |
| Anson J. Streeter (Union Labor) | — | 146,935 | 1.3 |

**MAP 19.1 The Presidential Elections of 1880, 1884, and 1888**
The anatomy of hard-fought, narrowly won presidential campaigns is evident in this trio of electoral maps. First, note the equal division of the popular vote between Republicans and Democrats. Second, note the persistent pattern of electoral votes, as states overwhelmingly went to the same party in all three elections. Here, we can identify who determined the outcomes—voters in swing states, such as New York and Indiana, whose vote shifted every four years and always in favor of the winning candidate.

college but lost the popular vote. In 1884, Democrat Grover Cleveland won only 29,214 more votes than his opponent, James Blaine, while almost half a million voters rejected both major candidates (Map 19.1). With key states decided by razor-thin margins, both Republicans and Democrats engaged in vote buying and other forms of fraud. The fierce struggle for advantage also prompted innovations in political campaigning.

Some historians have characterized this period as a Gilded Age, when politics was corrupt and stagnant and elections centered on "meaningless hoopla." The term *Gilded Age*, borrowed from the title of an 1873 novel cowritten by Mark Twain, suggested that America had achieved a glittery outer coating of prosperity and lofty rhetoric, but underneath suffered from moral decay. Economically, the term *Gilded Age* seems apt: as we have seen in previous chapters, a handful of men made spectacular fortunes, and their triumphs belied a rising crisis of poverty, pollution, and erosion of workers' rights. But political leaders were not blind to these problems, and the political scene was hardly idle or indifferent. Rather, Americans bitterly disagreed about what to do. Nonetheless, as early as the 1880s, Congress passed important new federal measures to clean up corruption and rein in corporate power. That decade deserves to be considered an early stage in the emerging Progressive Era.

**New Initiatives**　One of the first reforms resulted from tragedy. On July 2, 1881, only four months after entering the White House, James Garfield was shot at a train station in Washington, D.C. ("Assassination," he had told a friend, "can no more be guarded against than death by lightning, and it is best not to worry about either.") After lingering for several agonizing months, Garfield died. Most historians now believe the assassin, Charles Guiteau, suffered from mental illness. But reformers then blamed the spoils system, arguing that Guiteau had murdered Garfield out of disappointment in the scramble for patronage, the granting of government jobs to party loyalists.

In the wake of Garfield's death, Congress passed the **Pendleton Act** (1883), establishing a nonpartisan Civil Service Commission to fill federal jobs by examination. Initially, civil service applied to only 10 percent of such jobs, but the act laid the groundwork for a sweeping transformation of public employment. By the 1910s, Congress extended the act to cover most federal positions; cities and states across the country enacted similar laws.

Civil service laws had their downside. In the race for government jobs, they tilted the balance toward middle-class applicants who could perform well on tests. "Firemen now must know equations," complained a critic, "and be up on Euclid too." But the laws put talented professionals in office and discouraged politicians from appointing unqualified party hacks. The civil service also brought stability and consistency to government, since officials did not lose their jobs every time their party lost power. In the long run, civil service laws markedly reduced corruption.

Leaders of the civil service movement included many classical liberals (Chapter 14): former Republicans who became disillusioned with Reconstruction and advocated smaller, more professionalized government. Many had opposed President Ulysses S. Grant's reelection in 1872. In 1884, they again left the Republican Party because they could not stomach its scandal-tainted candidate, James Blaine. Liberal Republicans — ridiculed by their enemies as Mugwumps (fence-sitters who had their "mugs" on one side and their "wumps" on the other) — helped elect Democrat Grover Cleveland. They believed he shared their vision of smaller government.

As president, Cleveland showed that he largely did share their views. He vetoed, for example, thousands of bills providing pensions for individual Union veterans. But in 1887, responding to pressure from farmer-labor advocates in the Democratic Party who demanded action to limit corporate power, he signed the Interstate Commerce Act (Chapter 16). At the same time, municipal and state-level initiatives were showing how expanded government could help solve industrial problems. In the 1870s and early 1880s, many states created Bureaus of Labor Statistics to investigate workplace safety and unemployment. Some appointed commissions to oversee key industries, from banking to dairy farming. By later standards, such commissions were underfunded, but even when they lacked legal power, energetic commissioners could serve as public advocates, exposing unsafe practices and generating pressure for further laws.

**Republican Activism**　In 1888, after a decade of divided government, Republicans gained control of both Congress and the White House. They pursued an ambitious agenda they believed would meet the needs of a modernizing nation. In 1890,

Congress extended pensions to all Union veterans and yielded to growing public outrage over trusts by passing a law to regulate interstate corporations. Though it proved difficult to enforce and was soon weakened by the Supreme Court, the **Sherman Antitrust Act** (1890) was the first federal attempt to forbid any "combination, in the form of trust or otherwise, or conspiracy, in restraint of trade."

President Benjamin Harrison also sought to protect black voting rights in the South. Warned during his campaign that the issue was politically risky, Harrison vowed that he would not "purchase the presidency by a compact of silence upon this question." He found allies in Congress. Massachusetts representative Henry Cabot Lodge drafted the Federal Elections Bill of 1890, or **Lodge Bill**, proposing that whenever one hundred citizens in any district appealed for intervention, a bipartisan federal board could investigate and seat the rightful winner.

Despite cries of outrage from southern Democrats, who warned that it meant "Negro supremacy," the House passed the measure. But it met resistance in the Senate. Northern classical liberals, who wanted the "best men" to govern through professional expertise, thought it provided too much democracy, while machine bosses feared the threat of federal interference in the cities. Unexpectedly, many western Republicans also opposed the bill—and with the entry of ten new states since 1863, the West had gained enormous clout. Senator William Stewart of Nevada, who had southern family ties, claimed that federal oversight of elections would bring "monarchy or revolution." He and his allies killed the bill by a single vote.

The defeat was a devastating blow to those seeking to defend black voting rights. In the verdict of one furious Republican leader who supported Lodge's proposal, the episode marked the demise of the party of emancipation. "Think of it," he fumed. "Nevada, barely a respectable *county*, furnished two senators to betray the Republican Party and the rights of citizenship."

Other Republican initiatives also proved unpopular—at the polls as well as in Congress. In the Midwest, swing voters reacted against local Republican campaigns to prohibit liquor sales and end state funding for Catholic schools. Blaming high consumer prices on protective tariffs, other voters rejected Republican economic policies. In a major shift in the 1890 election, Democrats captured the House of Representatives. Two years later, by the largest margin in twenty years, voters reelected Democrat Grover Cleveland to the presidency for a nonconsecutive second term. Republican congressmen abandoned any further attempt to enforce fair elections in the South.

## The Populist Program

As Democrats took power in Washington, they faced rising pressure from rural voters in the South and West who had organized the Farmers' Alliance. Savvy politicians responded quickly. Iowa Democrats, for example, took up some of the farmers' demands, forestalling creation of a separate farmer-labor party in that state. But other politicians listened to Alliance pleas and did nothing. It was a response they came to regret.

Republicans utterly dominated Kansas, a state chock-full of Union veterans and railroad boosters. But politicians there treated the Kansas Farmers' Alliance with contempt. In 1890, the Kansas Alliance joined with the Knights of Labor to create a People's Party. They then stunned the nation by capturing four-fifths of the lower house of the Kansas legislature and most of the state's congressional seats. The victory electrified labor and agrarian radicals nationwide. In July 1892, delegates from these groups met at Omaha, Nebraska, and formally created the national People's Party. Nominating former Union general and Greenback-Labor leader James B. Weaver for president, the Populists, as they became known, captured a million votes in November. They returned to Washington with three representatives in the U.S. Senate and eleven in the House (Map 19.2). By 1896 they would double those totals—still only a sliver of congressional offices, but enough to make them one of the most successful insurgent parties in U.S. history.

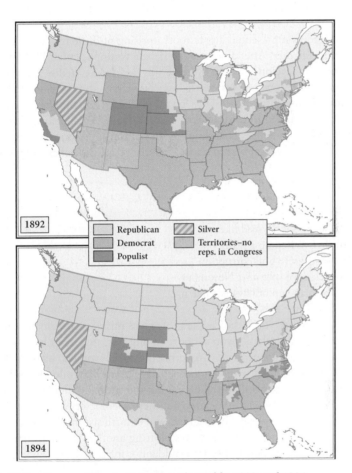

**MAP 19.2   House of Representatives Elected in 1892 and 1894**
Americans focus intensive effort and attention on presidential elections, but midterm congressional elections can be key turning points, as well. In response to the severe economic depression that began in 1893, American voters turned sharply away from the Democrats and toward the Republicans. That dramatic shift was first obvious not in 1896, with the election of President William McKinley, but in the midterm election that transformed Congress. These maps show the number of Democrats, Republicans, and Populists in the House of Representatives after the elections of 1892 (top) and 1894 (bottom). Where did Republicans make the biggest gains? How would the parties' strength in Congress have differed if Southern Populists in states such as Alabama, Arkansas, and Georgia had not been defeated through fraud?

In recognizing an "irrepressible conflict between capital and labor," Populists split from the mainstream parties, calling for stronger government to protect ordinary Americans. Their **Omaha Platform** called for public ownership of railroad and telegraph systems, protection of land from monopoly and foreign ownership, a federal income tax on the rich, and a looser monetary policy to help borrowers. Some Populist allies went further to make their point: in New Mexico, the Gorras Blancas, a vigilante group of small-scale Mexican American farmers, protested exploitative railroads and "land grabbers" by intimidating railroad workers and cutting fences on large Anglo farms.

Populist leaders represented a grassroots uprising of ordinary farmers, and some won colorful nicknames. After a devastating debate triumph, James H. Davis of Texas became known as "Cyclone." Mary E. Lease was derided as "Yellin' Mary Ellen"; her fellow Kansan Jerry Simpson was called "Sockless Jerry" after he ridiculed a wealthy opponent for wearing "fine silk hosiery," boasting that he himself wore no socks at all. The national press, based in northeastern cities, ridiculed such "hayseed politicians," but farmers insisted on being taken seriously. In the run-up to one election, a Populist writer encouraged party members to sing these lyrics to the tune of an old gospel hymn:

> I once was a tool of oppression,
>      As green as a sucker could be
> And monopolies banded together
>      To beat a poor hayseed like me. . . .
> But now I've roused up a little,
>      And their greed and corruption I see,
> And the ticket we vote next November
>      Will be made up of hayseeds like me.

Driven by farmers' votes, the People's Party had mixed success in attracting other constituencies. Its labor planks won support among Alabama steelworkers and Rocky Mountain miners, but not among many other industrial workers, who stuck with the major parties. Prohibitionist and women's suffrage leaders attended Populist conventions, hoping their issues would be taken up, but they were disappointed. The legacies of the Civil War also hampered the party. Southern Democrats warned that Populists were really Radical Republicans in disguise, while northeastern Republicans claimed the southern "Pops" were ex-Confederates plotting another round of treason. Amid these heated debates, the political system suddenly confronted an economic crisis.

| IN YOUR OWN WORDS | How did the political goals of Populists differ from those of Democrats and Republicans? |
|---|---|

## The Political Earthquakes of the 1890s

In 1893, a severe economic depression hit the United States. Though it was a global shock, and the agriculture sector had already lagged for years, Republicans blamed Grover Cleveland, who had just reentered the White House. "On every hand can be seen evidences of Democratic times," declared one Republican. "The deserted farm, the silent factory."

Apparently receptive to such appeals, voters outside the South abandoned the Democrats in 1894 and 1896. Republicans, promising prosperity, gained control of the White House and both chambers of Congress for the next sixteen years. This development created both opportunities and challenges for progressive reformers. A different pattern emerged in the South: Democrats deployed fraud, violence, and race-based appeals for white solidarity to defeat the Populist revolt.

## Depression and Reaction

When Cleveland took the oath of office in March 1893, hard times were prompting European investors to pull money out of the United States; farm foreclosures and railroad bankruptcies signaled economic trouble. A few weeks later, a Pennsylvania railroad went bankrupt, followed by several other companies. Investors panicked; the stock market crashed. By July, major banks had drained their reserves and "suspended" withdrawals, unable to give depositors access to their money. By

**Lynching in Texas** Lynchings peaked between 1890 and 1910; while most common in the South, they occurred in almost every state, from Oregon to Minnesota to New York. After many lynchings—such as this one in the town of Center, Texas, in 1920—crowds posed to have their pictures taken. Commercial photographers often, as in this case, produced photographic postcards to sell as souvenirs. What do we make of these gruesome rituals? Who is in the crowd, and who is not? What do we learn from the fact that this group of white men, some of whom may have been responsible for the lynching, felt comfortable having their photographs recorded with the body? The victim in this photograph, a young man named Lige Daniels, was seized from the local jail by a mob that broke down the prison door to kidnap and kill him. The inscription on the back of the postcard includes information about the killing, along with the instructions "Give this to Bud From Aunt Myrtle." Picture Research Consultants & Archives.

year's end, five hundred banks and thousands of other businesses had gone under. "Boston," one man remembered, "grew suddenly old, haggard, and thin." The unemployment rate in industrial cities soared above 20 percent.

For Americans who had lived through the terrible 1870s, conditions looked grimly familiar. Even fresher in the public mind were recent labor uprisings, including the 1886 Haymarket violence and the 1892 showdown at Homestead—followed, during the depression's first year, by a massive Pennsylvania coal strike and a Pullman railroad boycott that ended with bloody clashes between angry crowds and the U.S. Army. Prosperous Americans, fearful of Populism, were even more terrified that workers would embrace socialism or Marxism. Reminding Americans of upheavals such as the Paris Commune of 1871 and its bloody aftermath, conservative commentators of the 1890s launched America's first "Red Scare"—a precursor to similar episodes of hysteria in the 1920s and 1950s.

In the summer of 1894, a further protest jolted affluent Americans. Radical businessman Jacob Coxey of Ohio proposed that the U.S. government hire the unemployed to fix America's roads. In 1894, he organized hundreds of jobless men—nicknamed Coxey's Army—to march peacefully to Washington and appeal for the program. Though public employment of the kind Coxey proposed would become central to the New Deal in the 1930s, many Americans in the 1890s viewed Coxey as a dangerous extremist. Public alarm grew when more protesters, inspired by Coxey, started out from Los Angeles, Seattle, and other cities. As they marched east, these men found warm support and offers of aid in Populist-leaning cities and towns. In other places, police and property owners drove marchers away at gunpoint. Coxey was stunned by what happened when he reached Capitol Hill: he was jailed for trespassing on the grass. Some of his men, arrested for vagrancy, ended up in Maryland chain gangs. The rest went home hungry.

As this response suggested, President Grover Cleveland's administration was increasingly out of step with rural and working-class demands. Any president would have been hard-pressed to cope with the depression, but Cleveland was particularly inept. He steadfastly resisted pressure to loosen the money supply by expanding federal coinage to include silver as well as gold. Advocates of this **free silver** policy ("free" because, under this plan, the U.S. Mint would not charge a fee for minting silver coins) believed the policy would encourage borrowing and stimulate industry. But Cleveland clung to the gold standard. However dire things became, he believed, the money supply must remain tied to the nation's reserves of gold.

As the 1894 midterm elections loomed, Democratic candidates tried to distance themselves from the president. But on election day, large numbers of voters chose Republicans, who promised to support business, put down social unrest, and bring back prosperity. Western voters turned many Populists out of office. In the next congressional session, Republicans controlled the House by a margin of 245 to 105 (see Map 19.2).

## Democrats and the "Solid South"

In the South, the only region where Democrats gained strength in the 1890s, the People's Party lost ground for distinctive reasons. After the end of Reconstruction, African Americans in most states had continued to vote in significant numbers. As long as Democrats competed for (and sometimes bought) black votes, the possibility remained that other parties could win them away. Populists proposed new measures to help farmers and wage earners—an appealing message for poverty-stricken people of both races. Some white Populists went out of their way to build cross-racial ties. "The accident of color can make no difference in the interest of farmers, croppers, and laborers," argued Georgia Populist Tom Watson. "You are kept apart that you may be separately fleeced of your earnings."

Such appeals threatened the foundations of southern politics. Democrats struck back, calling themselves the "white man's party" and denouncing Populists for advocating "Negro rule." From Georgia to Texas, many poor white farmers, tenants, and wage earners ignored such appeals and continued to support the Populists in large numbers. Democrats found they could put down the Populist threat only through fraud and violence. After using such tactics, Pitchfork Ben Tillman of South Carolina openly bragged that he and other southern whites had "done our level best" to block "every last" black vote. "We stuffed ballot boxes," he said in 1900. "We shot them. We are not ashamed of it." "We had to do it," a Georgia Democrat later argued. "Those damned Populists would have ruined the country."

Having suppressed the political revolt, Democrats looked for new ways to enforce white supremacy. In 1890, a constitutional convention in Mississippi had adopted a key innovation: an "understanding clause" that required would-be voters to interpret parts of the state constitution, with local Democratic officials deciding who met the standard. After the Populist uprising, such measures spread to other southern states. Louisiana's grandfather clause, which denied the ballot to any man whose grandfather had been unable to vote in slavery days, was struck down by the U.S. Supreme Court. But in *Williams v. Mississippi* (1898), the Court allowed poll taxes and literacy tests to stand. By 1908, every southern state had adopted such measures.

The impact of disfranchisement can hardly be overstated (Map 19.3). Across the South, voter turnout plunged, from above 70 percent to 34 percent or even lower. Not only blacks but also many poor whites ceased to vote. Since Democrats faced virtually no opposition, action shifted to the "white primaries," where Democratic candidates competed for nominations. Some former Populists joined the Democrats in openly advocating white supremacy. The racial climate hardened. Segregation laws proliferated. Lynchings of African Americans increasingly occurred in broad daylight, with crowds of thousands gathered to watch.

The convict lease system, which had begun to take hold during Reconstruction, also expanded. Blacks received harsh sentences for crimes such as "vagrancy," often when they were traveling to find work or if they could not produce a current employment contract. By the 1890s, Alabama depended on convict leasing for 6 percent of its total revenue. Prisoners were overwhelmingly black: a 1908 report showed that almost 90 percent of Georgia's leased convicts were black; out of a white population of 1.4 million, only 322 were in prison. Calling attention to the torture and deaths of prisoners, as well as the damaging economic effect of their unpaid labor, reformers, labor unions, and Populists protested the situation strenuously. But "reforms" simply replaced convict leasing with the chain gang, in which prisoners worked directly for the state on roadbuilding and other

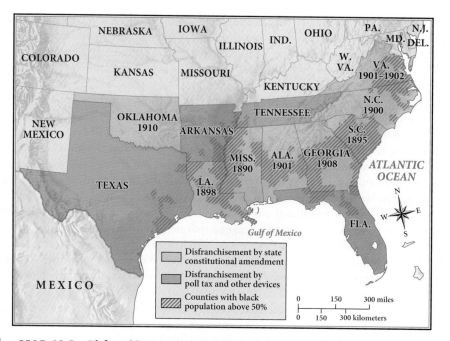

**MAP 19.3   Disfranchisement in the New South**

In the midst of the Populist challenge to Democratic one-party rule in the South, a movement to deprive blacks of the right to vote spread from Mississippi across the South. By 1910, every state in the region except Tennessee, Arkansas, Texas, and Florida had made constitutional changes designed to prevent blacks from voting, and these four states accomplished much the same result through poll taxes and other exclusionary methods. For the next half century, the political process in the South would be for whites only.

projects, under equally cruel conditions. All these developments depended on a political "Solid South" in which Democrats exercised almost complete control.

The impact of the 1890s counterrevolution was dramatically illustrated in Grimes County, a cotton-growing area in east Texas where blacks comprised more than half of the population. African American voters kept the local Republican Party going after Reconstruction and regularly sent black representatives to the Texas legislature. Many local white Populists dismissed Democrats' taunts of "negro supremacy," and a Populist-Republican coalition swept the county elections in 1896 and 1898. But after their 1898 defeat, Democrats in Grimes County organized a secret brotherhood and forcibly prevented blacks from voting in town elections, shooting two in cold blood. The Populist sheriff proved unable to bring the murderers to justice. Reconstituted in 1900 as the White Man's Party, Democrats carried Grimes County by an overwhelming margin. Gunmen then laid siege to the Populist sheriff's office, killed his brother and a friend, and drove the wounded sheriff out of the county. The White Man's Party ruled Grimes County for the next fifty years.

## New National Realities

While their southern racial policies were abhorrent, the national Democrats simultaneously amazed the country in 1896 by embracing parts of the Populists' radical farmer-labor program. They did so in defiance of President Cleveland, whose decisions continued to alienate him from his party's agrarian and labor base. Despite the worsening economic depression, collapsing prices, and a hemorrhage of gold to Europe, the president refused to budge from his defense of the gold standard. With gold reserves dwindling in 1895, he made a secret arrangement with a syndicate of bankers led by J. P. Morgan to arrange purchases to replenish the treasury. Morgan helped maintain America's gold supply—preserving the gold standard—and turned a tidy profit by earning interest on the bonds he provided. Cleveland's deal, once discovered, enraged fellow Democrats. South Carolina governor Ben Tillman vowed to go to Washington and "poke old Grover with a pitchfork," earning the nickname "Pitchfork Ben."

In 1896, amid such outrage, Democrats rejected Cleveland and nominated a young Nebraska congressman, free silver advocate William Jennings Bryan, who passionately defended farmers and workers and attacked the gold standard. "Burn down your cities and leave our farms," Bryan declared in his famous convention speech, "and your cities will spring up again as if by magic; but destroy our farms and the grass will grow in the streets of every city in the country." He ended with a vow: "You shall not crucify mankind on a cross of gold." Cheering delegates endorsed a platform calling for free silver and a federal income tax on the wealthy that would replace tariffs as a source of revenue. Democrats, long defenders of limited government, were moving toward a more activist stance.

Populists, reeling from recent defeats, endorsed Bryan in the campaign, but their power was waning. Populist leader Tom Watson, who wanted a separate program that was more radical than Bryan's, observed that Democrats in 1896 had cast the Populists as "Jonah while they play whale." The People's Party never recovered from its electoral losses in 1894 and from Democrats' ruthless opposition in the South. By 1900, rural voters pursued reform elsewhere, particularly through the new Bryan wing of the Democratic Party.

Meanwhile, horrified Republicans denounced Bryan's platform as anarchistic. Their nominee, the Ohio congressman and tariff advocate William McKinley, chose a brilliant campaign manager, Ohio coal and shipping magnate Marcus Hanna, who orchestrated an unprecedented corporate fund-raising campaign. Under his guidance, the party backed away from moral issues such as prohibition of liquor and reached out to new immigrants. Though the popular vote was closer, McKinley won big: 271 electoral votes to Bryan's 176 (Map 19.4).

Nationwide, as in the South, the realignment of the 1890s prompted new measures to exclude voters. Influenced by classical liberals' denunciations of "unfit voters," many northern states imposed literacy tests and restrictions on immigrant voting. Leaders of both major parties, determined to prevent future Populist-style

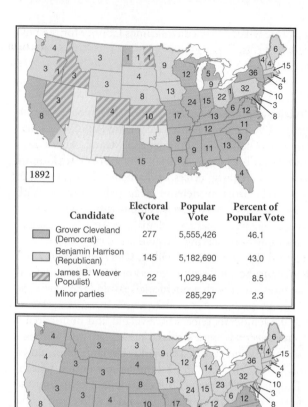

| Candidate | Electoral Vote | Popular Vote | Percent of Popular Vote |
|---|---|---|---|
| Grover Cleveland (Democrat) | 277 | 5,555,426 | 46.1 |
| Benjamin Harrison (Republican) | 145 | 5,182,690 | 43.0 |
| James B. Weaver (Populist) | 22 | 1,029,846 | 8.5 |
| Minor parties | — | 285,297 | 2.3 |

1892

| Candidate | Electoral Vote | Popular Vote | Percent of Popular Vote |
|---|---|---|---|
| William McKinley (Republican) | 271 | 7,102,246 | 51.1 |
| William J. Bryan (Democrat) | 176 | 6,492,559 | 47.7 |

1896

**MAP 19.4 The Presidential Elections of 1892 and 1896**
In the 1890s, the age of political stalemate came to an end. Compare the 1892 map with Map 19.1 (p. 552) and note especially Cleveland's breakthrough in the normally Republican states of the Upper Midwest. In 1896, the pendulum swung in the opposite direction, with McKinley's consolidation of Republican control over the Northeast and Midwest far overbalancing the Democratic advances in the thinly populated western states. The 1896 election marked the beginning of sixteen years of Republican dominance in national politics.

threats, made it more difficult for new parties to get candidates listed on the ballot. In the wake of such laws, voter turnout declined, and the electorate narrowed in ways that favored the native-born and wealthy.

Antidemocratic restrictions on voting helped, paradoxically, to foster certain democratic innovations. Having excluded or reduced the number of poor, African American, and immigrant voters, elite and middle-class reformers felt more comfortable increasing the power of the voters who remained. Both major parties increasingly turned to the direct primary, asking voters (in most states, registered party members) rather than party leaders to choose nominees. Another measure that enhanced democratic participation was the Seventeenth Amendment to the Constitution (1913), requiring that U.S. senators be chosen not by state legislatures, but by popular vote.

Though many states had adopted the practice well before 1913, southern states had resisted, since Democrats feared that it might give more power to their political opponents. After disfranchisement, such objections faded and the measure passed. Thus disfranchisement enhanced the power of remaining voters in multiple, complicated ways.

At the same time, the Supreme Court proved hostile to many proposed reforms. In 1895, for example, it struck down a recently adopted federal income tax on the wealthy. The Court ruled that unless this tax was calculated on a per-state basis, rather than by the wealth of individuals, it could not be levied without a constitutional amendment. It took progressives nineteen years to achieve that goal.

Labor organizations also suffered in the new political regime, as federal courts invalidated many regulatory laws passed to protect workers. As early as 1882, in the case of *In re Jacobs*, the New York State Court of Appeals struck down a public-health law that prohibited cigar manufacturing in tenements, arguing that such regulation exceeded the state's police powers. In **Lochner v. New York** (1905), the U.S. Supreme Court told New York State it could not limit bakers' workdays to ten hours because that violated bakers' rights to make contracts. Judges found support for such rulings in the due process clause of the Fourteenth Amendment, which prohibited states from depriving "any person of life, liberty, or property, without due process of law." Though the clause had been intended to protect former slaves, courts used it to shield contract rights, with judges arguing that they were protecting workers' freedom *from* government regulation. Interpreted in this way, the Fourteenth Amendment was a major obstacle to regulation of private business.

Farmer and labor advocates, along with urban progressives who called for more government regulation, disagreed with such rulings. They believed judges, not state legislators, were overreaching. While courts treated employers and employees as equal parties, critics dismissed this as a legal fiction. "Modern industry has reduced 'freedom of contract' to a paper privilege," declared one labor advocate, "a mere figure of rhetoric." Supreme Court justice Oliver Wendell Holmes Jr., dissenting in the *Lochner* decision, agreed. If the choice was between working and starving, he observed, how could bakers "choose" their hours of work? Holmes's view, known as legal realism, eventually won judicial favor, but only after years of progressive and labor activism.

| IN YOUR OWN WORDS | How did the depression of the 1890s impact federal politics and policy? |
| --- | --- |

# Reform Reshaped, 1901–1912

William McKinley, a powerful presence in the White House, was no reformer. His victory was widely understood as a triumph for business and especially for industrial titans who had contributed heavily to his campaign. But the depression of the 1890s, by subjecting millions to severe hardship, had dramatically illustrated the problems of industrialization. At the same time, the success of McKinley's campaign managers — who spent more than $3.5 million, versus Bryan's $300,000 — raised unsettling questions about corporate power. Once the crisis of the 1890s passed, many middle-class Americans proved ready to embrace progressive ideas. The rise of such ideas was aided by historical chance, when a shocking assassination put a reformer in the White House.

## Theodore Roosevelt as President

On September 14, 1901, only six months after William McKinley won his second face-off against Democrat William Jennings Bryan, the president was shot as he attended the Pan-American Exposition in Buffalo, New York. He died eight days later. The murderer, Leon Czolgosz, was influenced by anarchists who had carried out recent assassinations in Europe. Though Czolgosz was American-born, many feared that McKinley's violent death was another warning of the threat posed by radical immigrants. As the nation mourned its third murdered president in less than four decades, Vice President Theodore Roosevelt was sworn into office.

Roosevelt, from a prominent family, had chosen an unconventional path. After graduating from Harvard, he plunged into politics, winning a seat as a Republican New York assemblyman. Disillusioned by his party's resistance to reform, he left politics in the mid-1880s and moved to a North Dakota ranch. But his cattle herd was wiped out in the blizzards of 1887. He returned east, winning appointments as a U.S. Civil Service commissioner, head of the New York City Police Commission, and McKinley's assistant secretary of the navy. An energetic presence in all these jobs, Roosevelt gained broad knowledge of the problems America faced at the municipal, state, and federal levels.

After serving in the War of 1898 (Chapter 20), Roosevelt was elected as New York's governor. In this job, he pushed through civil service reform and a tax on corporations. Seeking to neutralize this progressive and rather unpredictable political star, Republican bosses chose Roosevelt as McKinley's running mate in 1900, hoping the vice-presidency would be a political dead end. Instead, they suddenly found Roosevelt in the White House. The new president, who called for vigorous reform, represented a major shift for the Republicans.

**Antitrust Legislation**    Roosevelt blended reform with the needs of private enterprise, but on occasion he challenged corporations in new ways. During a bitter 1902 coal strike, for example, he threatened to nationalize the big coal companies if their owners refused to negotiate with the miners' union. The owners hastily came to the table. Roosevelt also sought better enforcement of the Interstate Commerce Act and Sherman Antitrust Act. He pushed through the Elkins Act (1903), which prohibited discriminatory railway rates that favored powerful customers. That same year, he created the Bureau of Corporations, empowered to investigate business practices and bolster the Justice Department's capacity to mount antitrust suits. The department had already filed such a suit against the Northern Securities Company, arguing that this combination of northwestern railroads had created a monopoly in violation of the Sherman Antitrust Act. In a landmark decision in 1904, the Supreme Court ordered Northern Securities dissolved.

That year, calling for every American to get what he called a Square Deal, Roosevelt handily defeated Democratic candidate Alton B. Parker. Now president in his own right, Roosevelt stepped up his attack on trusts. He regarded large-scale enterprise as the natural tendency of modern industry, but he hoped to identify and punish "malefactors of great wealth" who abused their power. After much wrangling in Congress, Roosevelt won a major victory with the passage of the **Hepburn Act** (1906), which strengthened the Interstate Commerce Commission, authorizing it to set shipping rates when it found evidence of railroad collusion to fix prices.

At the time Roosevelt acted, trusts had partially protected themselves with the help of two friendly states, New Jersey and Delaware, whose legislatures had loosened regulations and invited trusts to incorporate under their new state laws. With its Northern Securities ruling, however, the Supreme Court began to recognize federal authority to dissolve the most egregious monopolies. Roosevelt left a powerful legacy to his successor, William Howard Taft. In its **Standard Oil decision** (1911), the Supreme Court agreed with Taft's Justice Department that John D. Rockefeller's massive oil monopoly should be broken up into several competing companies. After this ruling, Taft's attorney general undertook antitrust actions against other giant companies.

**Environmental Conservation**    Roosevelt was an ardent outdoorsman and hunter. It was after the president went bear hunting in Mississippi in 1902, in fact, that a Russian Jewish immigrant couple in New York began to sell stuffed "Teddy's bears," which became an American childhood tradition. After John Muir gave Roosevelt a tour of Yosemite Valley, the president described the transcendent experience of camping in the open air under the giant sequoias. "The majestic trunks, beautiful in color and in symmetry," he wrote, "rose round us like the pillars of a mightier cathedral than ever was conceived."

Roosevelt translated his love of nature into environmental action. By the end of his presidency, he had issued fifty-one executive orders creating wildlife refuges and signed a number of bills advocated by environmentalists. He also oversaw creation of three national parks, including Colorado's Mesa Verde, the first to "protect the works of man": American Indian archaeological sites. Also notable was his vigorous use of the Antiquities Act, through which he set aside such beautiful sites as Arizona's Grand Canyon and Washington's Mt. Olympus.

Some of Roosevelt's conservation policies, however, had a probusiness bent. He increased the amount of land held in federal forest reserves and turned their management over to the new, independent U.S. Forest Service, created in 1905. But his forestry chief, Gifford Pinchot, insisted on fire suppression to maximize logging potential. In addition, Roosevelt lent support to the **Newlands Reclamation Act** (1902), which had much in common with earlier Republican policies to promote economic development in the West. Under the act, the federal government sold public lands to raise money for irrigation projects that expanded agriculture on arid lands. The law, interestingly, fulfilled one of the demands of the unemployed men who had marched with Coxey's Army.

**Roosevelt's Legacies**    Like the environmental laws enacted during his presidency, Theodore Roosevelt was full of contradictions. An unabashed believer in what he called "Anglo-Saxon" superiority, Roosevelt nonetheless incurred the wrath of white supremacists by inviting Booker T. Washington to dine at the White House. Roosevelt called for elite "best men" to enter politics, but he also defended the dignity of labor.

In 1908, Roosevelt chose to retire, bequeathing the Republican nomination to talented administrator William Howard Taft. Taft portrayed himself as Roosevelt's man, though he maintained a closer relationship than his predecessor with probusiness Republicans in Congress. In 1908, Taft faced off against Democrat William Jennings Bryan, who, eloquent as ever, attacked Republicans as the party of "plutocrats": men who used their wealth to buy political influence. Bryan outdid Taft in urging tougher antitrust and prolabor legislation, but Taft won comfortably.

In the wake of Taft's victory, however, rising pressure for reform began to divide Republicans. Conservatives dug in, while militant progressives within the party thought Roosevelt and his successor had not gone far enough. Reconciling these conflicting forces was a daunting task. For Taft, it spelled disaster. Through various incidents, he found himself on the opposite side of progressive Republicans, who began to call themselves "Insurgents" and to plot their own path.

## Diverse Progressive Goals

The revolt of Republican Insurgents signaled the strength of grassroots demands for change. No one described these emerging goals more eloquently than Jane Addams, who famously declared in *Democracy and Social Ethics* (1902), "The cure for the ills of Democracy is more Democracy." It was a poignant statement, given the sharply antidemocratic direction American politics had taken since the 1890s. What, now, should more democracy look like? Various groups of progressives—women, antipoverty reformers, African American advocates—often disagreed about priorities and goals. Some, frustrated by events in the United States, traveled abroad to study inspiring experiments in other nations, hoping to bring ideas home.

States also served as seedbeds of change. Theodore Roosevelt dubbed Wisconsin a "laboratory of democracy" under energetic Republican governor Robert La Follette (1901–1905). La Follette promoted what he called the **Wisconsin Idea**—greater government intervention in the economy, with reliance on experts, particularly progressive economists, for policy recommendations. Like Addams, La Follette combined respect for expertise with commitment to "more Democracy." He won battles to restrict lobbying and to give Wisconsin citizens the right of recall—voting to remove unpopular politicians from office—and referendum—voting directly on a proposed law, rather than leaving it in the hands of legislators. Continuing his career in the U.S. Senate, La Follette, like Roosevelt, advocated increasingly aggressive measures to protect workers and rein in corporate power.

**Protecting the Poor**   The urban settlement movement called attention to poverty in America's industrial cities. In the emerging social sciences, experts argued that unemployment and crowded slums were not caused by laziness and ignorance, as elite Americans had long believed. Instead, as journalist Robert Hunter wrote in his landmark study, *Poverty* (1904), such problems resulted from "miserable and unjust social conditions." Charity work was at best a limited solution. "How vain to waste our energies on single cases of relief," declared one reformer, "when *society* should aim at removing the prolific sources of all the woe."

By the early twentieth century, reformers placed particular emphasis on labor conditions for women and children. The **National Child Labor Committee**, created in 1907, hired photographer Lewis Hine to record brutal conditions in mines and mills where children worked. Impressed by the committee's investigations, Theodore Roosevelt sponsored the first White House Conference on Dependent Children in 1909, bringing national attention to child welfare issues. In 1912, momentum from the conference resulted in creation of the Children's Bureau in the U.S. Labor Department.

Those seeking to protect working-class women scored a major triumph in 1908 with the Supreme Court's decision in **Muller v. Oregon**, which upheld an Oregon law limiting women's workday to ten hours. Given the Court's ruling three years earlier in *Lochner v. New York*, it was a stunning victory. To win the case, the National Consumers' League (Chapter 18) recruited Louis Brandeis, a son of Jewish immigrants who was widely known as "the people's lawyer" for his eagerness to take on vested interests. Brandeis's legal brief in the *Muller* case devoted only two pages to the constitutional issue of state police powers. Instead, Brandeis rested his arguments on data gathered by the NCL describing the toll that long work hours took on women's health. The "Brandeis brief" cleared the way for use of social science research in court decisions. Sanctioning a more expansive role for state governments, the *Muller* decision encouraged women's organizations to lobby for further reforms. Their achievements included the first law providing public assistance for single mothers with dependent children (Illinois, 1911) and the first minimum wage law for women (Massachusetts, 1912).

*Muller* had drawbacks, however. Though men as well as women suffered from long work hours, the *Muller* case did not protect men. Brandeis's brief treated all women as potential mothers, focusing on the state's interest in protecting future children. Brandeis and his allies hoped this would open the door to broader regulation of working hours. The Supreme Court, however, seized on motherhood as the key issue, asserting that the female worker, because of her maternal function, was "in a class by herself, and legislation for her protection may be sustained, even when like legislation is not necessary for men." This conclusion dismayed labor advocates and divided female reformers for decades afterward.

Male workers did benefit, however, from new workmen's compensation measures. Between 1910 and 1917, all the industrial states enacted insurance laws covering on-the-job accidents, so workers' families would not starve if a breadwinner was injured or killed. Some states also experimented with so-called **mothers' pensions**, providing state assistance after a breadwinner's desertion or death. Mothers, however, were subjected to home visits to determine whether they "deserved" government aid; injured workmen were not judged on this basis, a pattern of gender discrimination that reflected the broader impulse to protect women, while also holding them to different standards than men. Mothers' pensions reached relatively small numbers of women, but they laid foundations for the national program Aid to Families with Dependent Children, an important component of the Social Security Act of 1935.

While federalism gave the states considerable freedom to innovate, it hampered national reforms. In some states, for example, opponents of child labor won laws barring young children from factory work and strictly regulating hours and conditions for older children's labor. In the South, however, and in coal-mining states like Pennsylvania, companies fiercely resisted such laws — as did many working-class parents who relied on children's income to keep the family fed. A proposed U.S. constitutional amendment to abolish child labor never won ratification; only four states passed it. Tens of thousands of children continued to work in low-wage jobs, especially in the South. The same decentralized power that permitted innovation in Wisconsin hampered the creation of national minimum standards for pay and job safety.

**The Birth of Modern Civil Rights**    Reeling from disfranchisement and the sanction of racial segregation in the Supreme Court's 1896 *Plessy v. Ferguson* decision (Chapter 17), African American leaders faced distinctive challenges. Given the obvious deterioration of African American rights, a new generation of black leaders proposed bolder approaches than those popularized earlier by Booker T. Washington. Harvard-educated sociologist W. E. B. Du Bois called for a **talented tenth** of educated blacks to develop new strategies. "The policy of compromise has failed," declared William Monroe Trotter, pugnacious editor of the *Boston Guardian*. "The policy of resistance and aggression deserves a trial."

In 1905, Du Bois and Trotter called a meeting at Niagara Falls — on the Canadian side, because no hotel on the U.S. side would admit blacks. The resulting Niagara Principles called for full voting rights; an end to segregation; equal treatment in the justice system; and equal opportunity in education, jobs, health care, and military service. These principles, based on African American pride and an uncompromising demand for full equality, guided the civil rights movement throughout the twentieth century.

In 1908, a bloody race riot broke out in Springfield, Illinois. Appalled by the white mob's violence in the hometown of Abraham Lincoln, New York settlement worker Mary White Ovington called together a group of sympathetic progressives to formulate a response. Their meeting led in 1909 to creation of the **National Association for the Advancement of Colored People (NAACP)**. Most leaders of the Niagara Movement soon joined; W. E. B. Du Bois became editor of the NAACP journal, *The Crisis*. The fledgling group found allies in many African American women's clubs and churches. It also cooperated with the National Urban League (1911), a union of agencies that assisted black migrants in the North. Over the coming decades, these groups grew into a powerful force for racial justice.

**The Problem of Labor**    Samuel Gompers and other leaders of the nation's dominant union, the American Federation of Labor, were slow to ally with progressives. They had long believed workers should improve their situation through strikes and direct negotiation with employers, not through politics. But by the 1910s, as progressive reformers came forward with solutions, labor leaders in state after state began to press for political action.

The nation also confronted a daring wave of radical labor militancy. In 1905, the Western Federation of Miners (WFM), led by fiery leaders such as William "Big Bill" Haywood, helped create a new movement, the **Industrial Workers of the World** (IWW). The Wobblies, as they were called, fervently supported the Marxist class struggle. As syndicalists, they believed that by resisting in the workplace and ultimately launching a general strike, workers could overthrow capitalism. A new society would emerge, run directly by workers. At its height, around 1916, the IWW had about 100,000 members. Though divided by internal conflicts, the group helped spark a number of local protests during the 1910s, including strikes of rail

**The Ludlow Massacre, 1914** This cover illustration for the popular socialist magazine *The Masses* demonstrates John Sloan's outrage at social injustice in progressive America. The drawing memorializes a tragic episode during a coal miners' strike at Ludlow, Colorado — the asphyxiation of women and children when vigilantes torched the tent city of evicted miners — and the aftermath, an armed revolt by enraged miners. Picture Research Consultants & Archives.

car builders in Pennsylvania, textile operatives in Massachusetts, rubber workers in Ohio, and miners in Minnesota.

Meanwhile, after midnight on October 1, 1910, an explosion ripped through the *Los Angeles Times* headquarters, killing twenty employees and wrecking the building. It turned out that John J. McNamara, a high official of the American Federation of Labor's Bridge and Structural Iron Workers Union, had planned the bombing against the fiercely antiunion *Times*. McNamara's brother and another union member had carried out the attack. The bombing created a sensation, as did the terrible Triangle Shirtwaist fire (Chapter 18) and the IWW's high-profile strikes. What should be done? As the election of 1912 approached, labor issues moved high on the nation's agenda.

## The Election of 1912

Retirement did not sit comfortably with Theodore Roosevelt. Returning from a yearlong safari in Africa in 1910 and finding Taft wrangling with the Insurgents, Roosevelt itched to jump in. In a speech in Osawatomie, Kansas, in August 1910, he called for a **New Nationalism**. In modern America, he argued, private property had to be controlled "to whatever degree the public welfare may require it." He proposed a federal child labor law, more recognition of labor rights, and a national minimum wage for women. Pressed by friends like Jane Addams, Roosevelt also endorsed women's suffrage. Most radical was his attack on the legal system. Insisting that courts blocked reform, Roosevelt proposed sharp curbs on their powers.

Early in 1912, Roosevelt announced himself as a Republican candidate for president. A battle within the party ensued. Roosevelt won most states that held primary elections, but Taft controlled party caucuses elsewhere. Dominated by regulars, the Republican convention chose Taft. Roosevelt then led his followers into what became known as the Progressive Party, offering his New Nationalism directly to the people. Though Jane Addams harbored private doubts (especially about Roosevelt's mania for battleships), she seconded his nomination, calling the Progressive Party "the American exponent of a world-wide movement for juster social conditions." In a nod to Roosevelt's combative stance, party followers called themselves "Bull Mooses."

Roosevelt was not the only rebel on the ballot: the major parties also faced a challenge from charismatic socialist Eugene V. Debs. In the 1890s, Debs had founded the American Railway Union (ARU), a broad-based group that included both skilled and unskilled workers. In 1894, amid the upheavals of depression and popular protest, the ARU had boycotted luxury Pullman sleeping cars, in support of a strike by workers at the Pullman Company. Railroad managers, claiming the strike obstructed the U.S. mail, persuaded Grover Cleveland's administration to intervene against the union. The strike failed, and Debs served time in prison along with other ARU leaders. The experience radicalized him, and in 1901 he launched the Socialist Party of America. Debs translated socialism into an American idiom, emphasizing the democratic process as a means to defeat capitalism. By the early 1910s, his party had secured a minor but persistent role in politics. Both the Progressive and Socialist parties drew strength from the West, a region with vigorous urban reform movements and a legacy of farmer-labor activism.

Watching the rise of the Progressives and Socialists, Democrats were keen to build on dramatic gains they had made in the 1910 midterm election. Among their younger leaders was Virginia-born Woodrow Wilson, who as New Jersey's governor had compiled an impressive reform record, including passage of a direct primary, workers' compensation, and utility regulation. In 1912, he won the Democrats' nomination. Wilson possessed, to a fault, the moral certainty that characterized many elite progressives. He had much in common with Roosevelt. "The old time of individual competition is probably gone by," he admitted, agreeing for more federal measures to restrict big business. But his goals were less sweeping than Roosevelt's, and only gradually did he hammer out a reform program, calling it the New Freedom. "If America is not to have free enterprise," Wilson warned, "then she can have freedom of no sort whatever." He claimed Roosevelt's program represented collectivism, whereas the New Freedom would preserve political and economic liberty.

With four candidates in the field — Taft, Roosevelt, Wilson, and Debs — the 1912 campaign generated intense excitement. Democrats continued to have an enormous blind spot: their opposition to African American rights. But Republicans, despite plentiful opportunities, had also conspicuously failed to end segregation or pass antilynching laws. Though African American leaders had high hopes for the Progressive Party, they were crushed when the new party refused to seat southern black delegates or take a stand for racial equality. W. E. B. Du Bois considered voting for Debs, calling the Socialists the only party "which openly recognized Negro

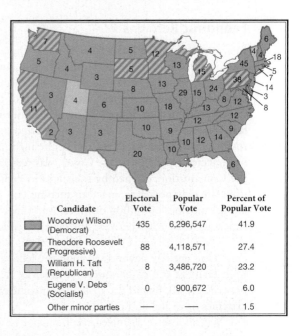

**MAP 19.5   The Presidential Election of 1912**

The 1912 election reveals why the two-party system is so strongly rooted in American politics—especially in presidential elections. The Democrats, though a minority party, won an electoral landslide because the Republicans divided their vote between Roosevelt and Taft. This result indicates what is at stake when major parties splinter. The Socialist Party candidate, Eugene V. Debs, despite a record vote of 900,000, received no electoral votes.

| Candidate | Electoral Vote | Popular Vote | Percent of Popular Vote |
|---|---|---|---|
| Woodrow Wilson (Democrat) | 435 | 6,296,547 | 41.9 |
| Theodore Roosevelt (Progressive) | 88 | 4,118,571 | 27.4 |
| William H. Taft (Republican) | 8 | 3,486,720 | 23.2 |
| Eugene V. Debs (Socialist) | 0 | 900,672 | 6.0 |
| Other minor parties | — | — | 1.5 |

manhood." But he ultimately endorsed Wilson. Across the North, in a startling shift, thousands of African American men and women worked and voted for Wilson, hoping Democrats' reform energy would benefit Americans across racial lines. The change helped lay the foundations for Democrats' New Deal coalition of the 1930s.

Despite the intense campaign, Republicans' division between Taft and Roosevelt made the result fairly easy to predict. Wilson won, though he received only 42 percent of the popular vote and almost certainly would have lost if Roosevelt had not been in the race (Map 19.5). In comparison with Roosevelt and Debs, Wilson appeared to be a rather old-fashioned choice. But with labor protests cresting and progressives gaining support, Wilson faced intense pressure to act.

**IN YOUR OWN WORDS**    What factors transformed national politics between 1900 and 1912?

# Wilson and the New Freedom, 1913–1917

In his inaugural address, Wilson acknowledged that industrialization had precipitated a crisis. "There can be no equality of opportunity," he said, "if men and women and children be not shielded . . . from the consequences of great industrial and social processes which they cannot alter, control, or singly cope with." Wilson was a Democrat, and labor interests and farmers—some previously radicalized in the People's Party—were important components of his base. In the South, many of those voters also upheld strong support for white supremacy. Despite many northern African Americans' support for Wilson, his administration did little for those constituents. But he undertook bold economic reforms.

## Economic Reforms

In an era of rising corporate power, many Democrats believed workers needed stronger government to intervene on their behalf, and they began to transform themselves into a modern, state-building party. The Wilson administration achieved a series of landmark measures—at least as significant as those enacted during earlier administrations, and perhaps more so. The most enduring was the federal progressive income tax. "Progressive," by this definition, referred to the fact that it was not a flat tax but rose progressively toward the top of the income scale. The tax, passed in the 1890s but rejected by the Supreme Court, was reenacted as the Sixteenth Amendment to the Constitution, ratified by the states in February 1913. The next year, Congress used the new power to enact an income tax of 1 to 7 percent on Americans with annual incomes of $4,000 or more. At a time when white male wageworkers might expect to make $800 per year, the tax affected less than 5 percent of households.

Three years later, Congress followed this with an inheritance tax. These measures created an entirely new way to fund the federal government, replacing Republicans' high tariff as the chief source of revenue. Over subsequent decades, especially between the 1930s and the 1970s, the income tax system markedly reduced America's extremes of wealth and poverty.

Wilson also reorganized the financial system to address the absence of a central bank. At the time, the main function of national central banks was to back up commercial banks in case they could not meet their obligations. In the United States, the great private banks of New York (such as J. P. Morgan's) assumed this role; if they weakened, the entire system could collapse. This had nearly happened in 1907, when the Knickerbocker Trust Company failed, precipitating a panic. The **Federal Reserve Act** (1913) gave the nation a banking system more resistant to such crises. It created twelve district reserve banks funded and controlled by their member banks, with a central Federal Reserve Board to impose regulation. The Federal Reserve could issue currency—paper money based on assets held in the system—and set the interest rate that district reserve banks charged to their members. It thereby regulated the flow of credit to the general public. The act strengthened the banking system and, to a modest degree, discouraged risky speculation on Wall Street.

Wilson and the Democratic Congress turned next to the trusts. In doing so, Wilson relied heavily on Louis D. Brandeis, the celebrated people's lawyer. Brandeis denied that monopolies were efficient. On the contrary, he believed the best source of efficiency was vigorous competition in a free market. The trick was to prevent trusts from unfairly using their power to curb such competition. In the **Clayton Antitrust Act** (1914), which amended the Sherman Act, the definition of illegal practices was left flexible, subject to the test of whether an action "substantially lessen[ed] competition." The new Federal Trade Commission received broad powers to decide what was fair, investigating companies and issuing "cease and desist" orders against anticompetitive practices.

Labor issues, meanwhile, received attention from a blue-ribbon U.S. Commission on Industrial Relations, appointed near the end of Taft's presidency and charged with investigating the conditions of labor. In its 1913 report, the commission summed up the impact of industrialization on low-skilled workers. Many earned $10 or less a week and endured regular episodes of unemployment; some faced long-term poverty and hardship. Workers held "an almost universal conviction" that they were "denied justice." The commission concluded that a major cause of industrial violence was the ruthless antiunionism of American employers. In its key recommendation, the report called for federal laws protecting workers' right to organize and engage in collective bargaining. Though such laws were, in 1915, too radical to win passage, the commission helped set a new national agenda that would come to fruition in the 1930s.

Guided by the commission's revelations, President Wilson warmed up to labor. In 1915 and 1916, he championed a host of bills to benefit American workers. They included the Adamson Act, which established an eight-hour day for railroad workers; the Seamen's Act, which eliminated age-old abuses of merchant sailors; and a workmen's compensation law for federal employees. Wilson, despite initial modest goals, presided over a major expansion of federal authority, perhaps the most significant since Reconstruction. The continued growth of U.S. government offices during Wilson's term reflected a reality that transcended party lines: corporations had grown in size and power, and Americans increasingly wanted federal authority to grow, too.

Wilson's reforms did not extend to the African Americans who had supported him in 1912. In fact, the president rolled back certain Republican policies, such as selected appointments of black postmasters. "I tried to help elect Wilson," W. E. B. Du Bois reflected gloomily, but "under Wilson came the worst attempt at Jim Crow legislation and discrimination in civil service that we had experienced since the Civil War." Wilson famously praised the film *Birth of a Nation* (1915), which depicted the Reconstruction-era Ku Klux Klan in heroic terms. In this way, Democratic control of the White House helped set the tone for the Klan's return in the 1920s.

## Progressive Legacies

In the industrial era, millions of Americans decided that their political system needed to adjust to new conditions. Whatever their specific goals — and whether they were rural, working-class, or middle-class — reformers faced fierce opposition from powerful business interests. When they managed to win key regulatory laws, they often found these struck down by hostile courts and were forced to try again by different means. Thus the Progressive Era in the United States should be understood partly by its limitations. Elitism and racial prejudice, embodied in new voting restrictions, limited working-class power at the polls; African Americans, their plight ignored by most white reformers, faced segregation and violence. Divided power in a federalist system blocked passage of uniform national policies on such key issues as child labor. Key social welfare programs that became popular in Europe during these decades, including national health insurance and old-age pensions, scarcely made it onto the American agenda until the 1930s.

An international perspective suggests several reasons for American resistance to such programs. Business interests in the United States were exceptionally successful and powerful, flush with recent expansion. At the time, also, voters in countries with older, more native-born populations tended to support government regulation and welfare spending to a greater extent than their counterparts in countries with younger populations and large numbers of immigrants. Younger voters, understandably, seem to have been less concerned than older voters about health insurance and old-age security. Divisions in the American working class also played a role. Black, immigrant, and native-born white laborers often viewed one another as enemies or strangers rather than as members of a single class with common interests. This helps explain why the Socialist Party drew, at peak, less than 6 percent of the U.S. vote at a time when its counterparts in Finland, Germany, and France drew 40 percent or more. Lack of pressure from a strong, self-conscious workingmen's party contributed to more limited results in the United States.

But it would be wrong to underestimate progressive achievements. Over several decades, in this period, more and more prosperous Americans began to support stronger economic regulations. Even the most cautious, elite progressives recognized that the United States had entered a new era. Multinational corporations overshadowed small businesses; in vast cities, old support systems based on village and kinship melted away. Outdated political institutions—from the spoils system to urban machines—would no longer do. Walter Lippmann, founding editor of the progressive magazine *New Republic*, observed in 1914 that Americans had "no precedents to guide us, no wisdom that wasn't made for a simpler age." Progressives created new wisdom. By 1917, they had drawn blueprints for a modern American state, one whose powers more suited the needs of an industrial era.

| IN YOUR OWN WORDS | What caused Woodrow Wilson to become a reformer once he entered the White House? |
| --- | --- |

# Summary

The Progressive Era emerged from the political turmoil of the 1880s and 1890s. In the 1880s, despite the limits imposed by close elections, federal and state governments managed to achieve important administrative and economic reforms. After 1888, Republican leaders undertook more sweeping efforts, including the Sherman Antitrust Act, but failed in a quest to protect black voting rights. In the South and West, the People's Party called for much stronger government intervention in the economy, but its radical program drew bitter Republican and Democratic resistance.

The depression of the 1890s brought a wave of reaction. Labor unrest threw the nation into crisis, and Cleveland's intransigence over the gold standard cost the Democrats dearly in the 1894 and 1896 elections. While Republicans took over the federal government, southern Democrats restricted voting rights in the Solid South. Federal courts struck down regulatory laws and supported southern racial discrimination.

After McKinley's assassination, Roosevelt launched a program that balanced reform and private enterprise. At both the federal and state levels, progressive reformers made extensive use of elite expertise. At the grassroots, black reformers battled racial discrimination, women reformers worked on issues ranging from public health to women's working conditions, and labor activists tried to address the problems that fueled persistent labor unrest. The election of 1912 split the Republicans, giving victory to Woodrow Wilson, who launched a Democratic program of economic and labor reform. Despite the limits of the Progressive Era, the reforms of this period laid the foundation for a modern American state.

# Chapter 19 Review

## KEY TERMS

**Identify and explain the significance of each term below.**

Pendleton Act (p. 553)

Sherman Antitrust Act (p. 554)

Lodge Bill (p. 554)

Omaha Platform (p. 556)

free silver (p. 558)

*Williams v. Mississippi* (p. 559)

*Lochner v. New York* (p. 563)

Hepburn Act (p. 565)

Standard Oil decision (p. 565)

Newlands Reclamation Act (p. 565)

Wisconsin Idea (p. 566)

National Child Labor Committee (p. 566)

*Muller v. Oregon* (p. 567)

mothers' pensions (p. 567)

talented tenth (p. 568)

National Association for the Advancement of Colored People (NAACP) (p. 568)

Industrial Workers of the World (p. 568)

New Nationalism (p. 569)

Federal Reserve Act (p. 572)

Clayton Antitrust Act (p. 572)

## REVIEW QUESTIONS

**Answer these questions to demonstrate your understanding of the chapter's main ideas.**

1. How did the political goals of Populists differ from those of Democrats and Republicans?

2. How did the depression of the 1890s impact federal politics and policy?

3. What factors transformed national politics between 1900 and 1912?

4. What caused Woodrow Wilson to become a reformer once he entered the White House?

**5.** Look at the events on the thematic timeline on pages 472–473. Historians often call the later decades of this period (1890 to 1920) the Progressive Era. Given the limitations and new problems that emerged during this time, as well as the achievements of progressive policymaking, do you think the name is warranted? What other names might we suggest for this era?

## CHRONOLOGY

As you read, ask yourself why this chapter begins and ends with these dates and identify the links among related events.

| | |
|---|---|
| **1881** | • President James Garfield assassinated |
| **1883** | • Pendleton Act establishes the Civil Service Commission |
| **1890** | • Sherman Antitrust Act |
| | • People's Party created in Kansas |
| **1893** | • Economic depression begins |
| **1894** | • Coxey's Army marches on Washington, D.C. |
| **1895** | • John Pierpont Morgan arranges gold purchases to rescue U.S. Treasury |
| **1896** | • William McKinley wins presidency |
| **1898** | • *Williams v. Mississippi* allows poll taxes and literacy tests for voters |
| **1900** | • William McKinley reelected |
| **1901** | • Eugene Debs founds the Socialist Party of America |
| | • McKinley assassinated; Theodore Roosevelt assumes presidency |
| **1902** | • Newlands Reclamation Act |
| **1903** | • Elkins Act |
| **1904** | • Robert Hunter publishes *Poverty* |
| **1905** | • Industrial Workers of the World founded |
| | • Niagara Principles articulated |
| **1906** | • Hepburn Act |
| **1908** | • *Muller v. Oregon* limits women's work hours |
| **1909** | • NAACP created |

**1911**      • Supreme Court orders Standard Oil divided to overturn its monopoly
              power

**1912**      • Four-way election gives presidency to Woodrow Wilson

**1913**      • Sixteenth Amendment

              • Seventeenth Amendment

              • Federal Reserve Act

**1914**      • Clayton Antitrust Act

# PART 7

W hat should be the role of the United States in the world, and what is the proper relationship between government and society? If these seem like monumental questions, they are indeed. In Part 7, we show how these two pressing questions came to the fore in a tumultuous period of global warfare and domestic strife and reform. Globally, the United States expanded its empire overseas and fought on the winning side in two world wars. Domestically, the reform impulse retreated during and immediately after World War I but surged back to the center of national life during the crisis of the Great Depression, when Americans once more debated the responsibilities and limits of their government.

As the chapters in this part show, on the world stage the United States acted both in calculated self-interest and to protect democratic nations and institutions. By acquiring the Philippines, Hawaii, Guam, and Puerto Rico, the United States behaved as a traditional empire, securing important strategic assets and protecting American investments abroad. In joining its European allies in the two world wars, the United States embraced a broad international partnership against the threat of autocracy and fascism. In his famous speech in 1918 outlining his Fourteen Points for international peace, made amid the horrors of World War I, President Woodrow Wilson argued that as responsible global citizens Americans "cannot be separated in interest or divided in purpose."

Fifteen years later, President Franklin Delano Roosevelt made a similar call for solidarity during the Great Depression. "We face the arduous days that lie before us," he said, "in the warm courage of national unity." During the crises of the depression and World War II, American voters called for—and got—what Roosevelt called "action and action now." We conclude Part 7 in 1945, when the United States emerged from World War II with unprecedented global power and the federal government with a broad mandate for sustaining the new welfare state, a major turning point in modern American history.

## America's Rise to World Power

The United States became a major international power beginning in the 1890s, first in the Western Hemisphere and by the 1940s across the world, renewing debates at home about America's global role. After the War of 1898, the United States claimed overseas colonies and asserted control over the Caribbean basin. And although President Wilson attempted to maintain neutrality at the start of World War I, trade ties and old alliances drew the U.S. into the conflict on the Allied side. Wilson sought to influence the peace, but Allied leaders ignored his proposals and the Senate rejected the Treaty of Versailles. By war's end, the U.S. position on the world stage remained uncertain.

# Domestic and Global Challenges 1890–1945

The 1920s was an era of dollar diplomacy and U.S. business expansion abroad. In the 1930s, faced with isolationist sentiment at home and the rise of fascist powers in Europe and Japan, the Roosevelt administration steered a middle course. In the late 1930s, it began to send aid to its traditional ally Great Britain without committing U.S. forces to the conflict. When the United States entered World War II in 1941, it did so as part of an alliance with both England and the Soviet Union against Germany, Japan, and Italy. The United States emerged from the war as the dominant global power.

## Modernity and Its Discontents

World War I had a powerful domestic impact in the United States, producing a sharp political right turn in the postwar years. A Red Scare, rollback of labor and immigrant rights, race riots against African Americans, and a resurgent nationwide Ku Klux Klan marked the political scene between 1919 and the late 1920s. A full-blown modern consumer culture also emerged in the decade as radio, automobiles, and Hollywood movies transformed leisure pastimes. Prosperity did not prevent conflict over an emerging secular, diverse, and modern society, however, as Americans battled over immigration, race, and religion in the 1920s.

During the Great Depression, the U.S. government deported hundreds of thousands of people of Mexican descent, including American citizens. During World War II, the government temporarily imprisoned Japanese Americans in a mass relocation policy, turned away most Jewish refugees fleeing Hitler, and segregated African Americans in a Jim Crow military. Yet many Americans celebrated the New Deal and the war effort as evidence of what a united country could accomplish. These events, too, represented battles over what a diverse, modern nation would look like.

## Creation of the Welfare State

Republican policymakers of the 1920s believed in hands-off government. Their policies likely helped trigger the Great Depression and deepened its impact after it arrived. President Franklin Roosevelt's New Deal programs (1933–1938) expanded federal responsibility for the welfare of ordinary citizens, breaking dramatically with the *laissez faire* individualism of the previous decade. Though the New Deal faced considerable challenges on the political right—especially from business and corporate leaders and a hostile Supreme Court—the popularity of its programs, such as Social Security, established a broad consensus that the United States needed a modern welfare state to regulate the economy and provide a basic safety net for the nation's citizens.

## Thematic Understanding

This timeline arranges some of the important events of this period into seven themes. Consider the entries under each theme. What connections do you see between events on the world stage and developments within the United States? What impact did World War I, the Great Depression, and World War II have on American politics, society, and culture?

| | AMERICAN AND NATIONAL IDENTITY | POLITICS AND POWER | WORK, EXCHANGE, AND TECHNOLOGY |
|---|---|---|---|
| 1890 | • "American exceptionalism" and rise of imperialism<br>• Alfred Mahan, *The Influence of Sea Power upon History* | • Republicans sweep congressional elections (1894)<br>• William McKinley elected (1896) | • Depression of 1890s increases pressure to secure foreign markets |
| 1900 | • *Insular Cases* establish noncitizenship status for new territories (1901) | • McKinley reelected on pro-imperialist platform (1900)<br>• McKinley assassinated (1901) | • Root-Takahira Agreement (1908)<br>• Ford Motor Company introduces Model T |
| 1910 | • New Ku Klux Klan founded (1915)<br>• Post–World War I race riots | • Woodrow Wilson elected president (1912)<br>• Red Scare (1919) | • Assembly-line production of automobiles begins |
| 1920 | • Harlem Renaissance artists emphasize black pride<br>• National Origins Act limits immigration (1924) | • Nineteenth Amendment grants women's suffrage (1920)<br>• Prohibition (1920–1933) | • Economic prosperity (1922–1929)<br>• Rise of automobile loans and consumer credit |
| 1930 | • Bonus Army (1932)<br>• Indian Reorganization Act (1934)<br>• Social Security created (1935) | • Franklin Roosevelt elected president (1932)<br>• First New Deal (1933)<br>• Second New Deal (1935) | • Great Depression (1929–1941)<br>• Rise of CIO and organized labor |
| 1940 | • Internment of Japanese Americans (1942)<br>• Segregation in armed services until 1948 | • Roosevelt dies and Harry Truman becomes president (1945) | • War spending ends depression<br>• Married women take war jobs |

| CULTURE AND SOCIETY | MIGRATION AND SETTLEMENT | GEOGRAPHY AND THE ENVIRONMENT | AMERICA IN THE WORLD | |
|---|---|---|---|---|
| • "Remember the *Maine*" campaign fuels surge in nationalism | • Josiah Strong encourages overseas Christian missionaries | • Americans debate overseas expansion and empire<br>• Teller Amendment (1898) | • U.S. wins War of 1898 against Spain; claims Hawaii, Puerto Rico, Guam, and Philippines | 1890 |
| • Social Darwinism used to justify U.S. imperialism (1898–1910s) | • Rising immigration from Southern and Eastern Europe<br>• U.S. bars Japanese immigration (1907) | • Congress authorizes funds to purchase land in Colombia for future canal | • Platt Amendment (1902)<br>• Roosevelt Corollary to Monroe Doctrine (1904) | 1900 |
| • Moviemaking industry moves to southern California<br>• Radio Corporation of America created (1919) | • African American Great Migration<br>• St. Louis (1917) and Chicago (1919) race riots | • Panama Canal construction<br>• Panama Canal opens (1914) and links Atlantic and Pacific Oceans | • Wilson intervenes in Mexico (1914)<br>• United States enters World War I (1917) | 1910 |
| • Rise of Hollywood<br>• Harlem Renaissance<br>• Scopes trial (1925) | • Rise of nativism<br>• National Origins Act (1924) imposes immigration restriction | • Suburban housing boom<br>• First suburban shopping center opens outside Kansas City, Missouri (1924) | • Rise of "dollar diplomacy" | 1920 |
| • Documentary impulse in arts<br>• Federal Writers' Project established (1935) | • Migrants ("Okies") leave drought-struck Midwest for California<br>• U.S. deports Mexican immigrants and Mexican Americans | • "Dust Bowl" drought strikes Midwest<br>• Works Progress Administration builds parks, zoos, trails (1935–1943) | • Rise of European fascist powers<br>• Japan invades China (1937) | 1930 |
| • Film industry aids war effort | • Migration to California and major cities<br>• Bracero program increases immigration from Mexico | • Temporary encampments imprison Japanese Americans in inland states (1942) | • United States enters World War II (1941)<br>• Atomic bombing of Japan and end of World War II (1945) | 1940 |

# 20

## An Emerging World Power

### 1890–1918

**IDENTIFY THE BIG IDEA**

As the United States became a major power on the world stage, what ideas and interests did policymakers promote in international affairs?

**ACCEPTING THE DEMOCRATIC PRESIDENTIAL NOMINATION IN 1900,** William Jennings Bryan delivered a famous speech denouncing U.S. military occupations overseas. "God Himself," Bryan declared, "placed in every human heart the love of liberty. . . . He never made a race of people so low in the scale of civilization or intelligence that it would welcome a foreign master." At the time, Republican president William McKinley was leading an ambitious and popular plan of overseas expansion. The United States had asserted control over the Caribbean, claimed Hawaii, and sought to annex the Philippines. Bryan failed to convince a majority of voters that imperialism—the exercise of military, political, and economic power overseas—was the wrong direction. He lost the election by a landslide.

By the 1910s, however, American enthusiasm for overseas involvement cooled. Despite efforts to stay neutral, the United States got caught up in the global catastrophe of World War I, which killed 8 million combatants, including over 50,000 U.S. soldiers. By the war's end, European powers' grip on their colonial empires was weakening. The United States also ceased acquiring overseas territories and pursued a different path. It did so in part because the war brought dramatic changes at home, leaving Americans a postwar legacy of economic upheaval and political disillusionment.

President Woodrow Wilson, who in 1913 appointed Bryan as his secretary of state, tried to steer a middle course between revolutionary socialism and European-style imperialism. In Wilson's phrase, America would "make the world safe for democracy" while unapologetically working to advance U.S. economic interests. The U.S. Senate, however, rejected the 1919 Treaty of Versailles and with it Wilson's vision, leaving the nation's foreign policy in doubt. Should the United States try to promote democracy abroad? If so, how? To what degree should the federal government seek to promote American business interests? Under what conditions was overseas military action justified? When, on the contrary, did it impinge on others' sovereignty, endanger U.S. soldiers, and invite disaster? Today's debates over foreign policy still center to a large degree on questions that Americans debated in the era of McKinley, Bryan, and Wilson, when the nation first asserted itself as a major world power.

**The Great White Fleet** The U.S. Navy's newest battle fleet, nicknamed the "Great White Fleet" and celebrated proudly by President Theodore Roosevelt, took a world tour between 1907 and 1909, demonstrating to the world that the U.S. now had naval power rivaling Britain and Germany. Here, the USS *Connecticut* leads the fleet of sixteen battleships on its way out of Hampton Roads, Virginia, at the start of the voyage. By 1900, global economic and military power brought the United States new prestige — and new problems. Bettmann/Getty Images.

# From Expansion to Imperialism

Historians used to describe turn-of-the-twentieth-century U.S. imperialism as something new and unprecedented. Now they stress continuities between foreign policy in this era and the nation's earlier, relentless expansion across North America. Wars against Native peoples had occurred almost continuously since the country's founding; in the 1840s, the United States had annexed a third of Mexico. The United States never administered a large colonial empire, as did European powers like Spain, England, and Germany, partly because it had a plentiful supply of natural resources in the American West. But policymakers undertook a determined quest for global markets. Events in the 1890s opened opportunities to pursue this goal in new ways.

## Foundations of Empire

American empire builders around 1900 fulfilled a vision laid out earlier by William Seward, secretary of state under presidents Abraham Lincoln and Andrew Johnson, who saw access to global markets as the key to power (Chapter 15). Seward's ideas had won only limited support at the time, but the severe economic depression of the 1890s brought Republicans into power and Seward's ideas back into vogue. Confronting high unemployment and mass protests, policymakers feared American workers would embrace socialism or Marxism. The alternative, they believed, was to create jobs and prosperity at home by selling U.S. products in overseas markets.

Intellectual trends also favored imperialism. As early as 1885, in his popular book *Our Country*, Congregationalist minister Josiah Strong urged Protestants to proselytize overseas. He predicted that the American "Anglo-Saxon race," which represented "the largest liberty, the purest Christianity, the highest civilization," would "spread itself over the earth." Such arguments were grounded in **American exceptionalism**, the idea that the United States had a unique destiny to foster democracy and civilization.

As Strong's exhortation suggested, imperialists also drew on the popular racial theory that people of "Anglo-Saxon" descent — English and often German — were superior to all others. "Anglo-Saxon" rule over foreign people of color made sense in an era when, at home, the United States denied most American Indians and Asian immigrants citizenship and southern states disfranchised blacks. Imperialists argued that "free land" on the western frontier was dwindling, and thus new outlets needed to be found for American energy and enterprise. Responding to critics of U.S. occupation of the Philippines, Theodore Roosevelt scoffed: if Filipinos should control their own islands, he declared, then America was "morally bound to return Arizona to the Apaches."

Imperialists also justified their views through racialized Social Darwinism (Chapter 17). Josiah Strong, for example, predicted that with the globe fully occupied, a "competition of races" would ensue, with victory based on "survival of the fittest." Fear of ruthless competition drove the United States, like European nations, to invest in the latest weapons. Policymakers saw that European powers were amassing steel-plated battleships and carving up Africa and Asia among themselves. In his book *The Influence of Sea Power upon History* (1890), U.S. naval officer Alfred

Mahan urged the United States to enter the fray, observing that naval power had been essential to past empires. As early as 1886, Congress ordered construction of two steel-hulled battleships, the USS *Texas* and USS *Maine*; in 1890, it appropriated funds for three more, a program that expanded over the next two decades.

During Grover Cleveland's second term (1893–1897), his secretary of state, Richard Olney, turned to direct confrontation. He warned Europe to stay away from Latin America, which he saw as the United States's rightful sphere of influence. Without consulting the nation of Venezuela, Olney suddenly demanded in 1895 that Britain resolve a long-standing border dispute between Venezuela and Britain's neighboring colony, British Guiana. Invoking the Monroe Doctrine, which stated that the Western Hemisphere was off-limits to further European colonization, Olney warned that the United States would brook no challenge to its interests. Startled, Britain agreed to arbitrate. U.S. power was on the rise.

## The War of 1898

Events in the Caribbean presented the United States with far greater opportunities. In 1895, Cuban patriots mounted a major guerrilla war against Spain, which had lost most of its other New World territories. The Spanish commander responded by rounding up Cuban civilians into concentration camps, where as many as 200,000 died of starvation, exposure, or dysentery. In the United States, "yellow journalists" such as William Randolph Hearst turned their plight into a cause célèbre. Hearst's coverage of Spanish atrocities fed a surge of nationalism, especially among those who feared that industrialization was causing American men to lose physical strength and valor. The government should not pass up this opportunity, said Indiana senator Albert Beveridge, to "manufacture manhood." Congress called for Cuban independence.

President Cleveland had no interest in supporting the Cuban rebellion but worried over Spain's failure to end it. The war disrupted trade and damaged American-owned sugar plantations on the island. Moreover, an unstable Cuba was incompatible with U.S. strategic interests, including a proposed canal whose Caribbean approaches had to be safeguarded. Taking office in 1897, President William McKinley took a tough stance. In September, a U.S. diplomat informed Spain that it must ensure an "early and certain peace" or the United States would step in. At first, this hard line seemed to work: Spain's conservative regime fell, and a liberal government, taking office in October 1897, offered Cuba limited self-rule. But Spanish loyalists in Havana rioted against this proposal, while Cuban rebels held out for full independence.

In February 1898, Hearst's *New York Journal* published a private letter in which a Spanish minister to the United States belittled McKinley. The minister, Dupuy de Lôme, resigned, but exposure of the de Lôme letter intensified Americans' indignation toward Spain. The next week brought shocking news: the U.S. battle cruiser *Maine* had exploded and sunk in Havana harbor, with 260 seamen lost. "Whole Country Thrills with the War Fever," proclaimed the *New York Journal*. "Remember the *Maine*" became a national chant. Popular passions were now a major factor in the march toward war.

McKinley assumed the sinking of the *Maine* had been accidental. Improbably, though, a naval board of inquiry blamed an underwater mine, fueling public outrage. (Later investigators disagreed: the more likely cause was a faulty ship design that placed explosive munitions too close to coal bunkers, which were prone to fire.) No evidence linked Spain to the purported mine, but if a mine sank the *Maine*, then Spain was responsible for not protecting the ship.

Business leaders became impatient, believing war was preferable to an unending Cuban crisis. On March 27, McKinley cabled an ultimatum to Madrid: an immediate ceasefire in Cuba for six months and, with the United States mediating, peace negotiations with the rebels. Spain, while desperate to avoid war, balked at the added demand that mediation must result in Cuban independence. On April 11, McKinley asked Congress for authority to intervene in Cuba "in the name of civilization, [and] in behalf of endangered American interests."

Historians long referred to the ensuing fight as the Spanish-American War, but because that name ignores the central role of Cuban revolutionaries, many historians now call the three-way conflict the War of 1898. Though Americans widely admired Cubans' aspirations for freedom, the McKinley administration defeated a congressional attempt to recognize the rebel government. In response, Senator Henry M. Teller of Colorado added an amendment to the war bill disclaiming any intention by the United States to occupy Cuba. The **Teller Amendment** reassured Americans that their country would uphold democracy abroad as well as at home. McKinley's expectations differed. He wrote privately, "We must keep all we get; when the war is over we must keep what we want."

On April 24, 1898, Spain declared war on the United States. The news provoked full-blown war fever. Across the country, young men enlisted for the fight. Theodore Roosevelt, serving in the War Department, resigned to become lieutenant colonel of a cavalry regiment. Recruits poured into makeshift bases around Tampa, Florida, where confusion reigned. Rifles failed to arrive; food was bad, sanitation worse. No provision had been made for getting troops to Cuba, so the government hastily collected a fleet of yachts and commercial boats. Fortunately, the regular army was a disciplined, professional force; its 28,000 seasoned troops provided a nucleus for 200,000 volunteers. The navy was in better shape: Spain had nothing to match America's seven battleships and armored cruisers. The Spanish admiral bitterly predicted that his fleet would "like Don Quixote go out to fight windmills and come back with a broken head."

The first, decisive military engagement took place in the Pacific. This was the handiwork of Theodore Roosevelt, who, in his government post, had gotten the intrepid Commodore George Dewey appointed commander of the Pacific fleet. In the event of war, Dewey had instructions to sail immediately for the Spanish-owned Philippines. When war was declared, Roosevelt confronted his surprised superior and pressured him into validating Dewey's instructions. On May 1, 1898, American ships cornered the Spanish fleet in Manila Bay and destroyed it. Manila, the Philippine capital, fell on August 13. "We must on no account let the [Philippines] go," declared Senator Henry Cabot Lodge. McKinley agreed. The United States now had a major foothold in the western Pacific.

Dewey's victory directed policymakers' attention to Hawaii. Nominally independent, these islands had long been subject to U.S. influence, including a horde of resident American sugarcane planters. An 1876 treaty between the United States and the island's monarch gave Hawaiian sugar free access to the American market, without tariff payments, and Hawaii pledged to sign no such agreement with any other power. When this treaty was renewed in 1887, Hawaii also granted a long-coveted lease for a U.S. naval base at Pearl Harbor. Four years later, succeeding her brother as Hawaii's monarch, Queen Liliuokalani made known her frustration with these treaties. In response, an Annexation Club of U.S.-backed planters organized secretly and in 1892, with the help of U.S. Marines, overthrew the queen. They then negotiated a treaty of annexation, but Grover Cleveland rejected it when he entered office in 1893. Cleveland declared that it would violate America's "unbroken tradition" against acquiring territory overseas.

Dewey's victory in Manila, however, delivered what the planters wanted: Hawaii acquired strategic value as a halfway station to the Philippines. In July 1898, Congress voted for annexation, over the protests of Hawaii's deposed queen. "Oh, honest Americans," she pleaded, "as Christians hear me for my down-trodden people! Their form of government is as dear to them as yours is precious to you. Quite as warmly as you love your country, so they love theirs." But to the great powers, Hawaii was not a country. One congressman dismissed Hawaii's monarchy as "absurd, grotesque, tottering"; the "Aryan race," he declared, would "rescue" the islands from it.

Further U.S. annexations took on their own logic. The navy pressed for another coaling base in the central Pacific; that meant Guam, a Spanish island in the Marianas. A strategic base was needed in the Caribbean; that meant Puerto Rico. By early summer, before U.S. troops had fired a shot in Cuba, McKinley's broader war aims were crystallizing.

In Cuba, Spanish forces were depleted by the long guerrilla war. Though poorly trained and equipped, American forces had the advantages of a demoralized foe and knowledgeable Cuban allies. The main battle occurred on July 1 at San Juan Hill, near Santiago, where the Spanish fleet was anchored. Roosevelt's Rough Riders took the lead, but four African American regiments bore the brunt of the fighting. Observers credited much of the victory to the "superb gallantry" of these soldiers. Spanish troops retreated to a well-fortified second line, but U.S. forces were spared the test of a second assault. On July 3, the Spanish fleet in Santiago harbor tried a desperate run through the American blockade and was destroyed. Days later, Spanish forces surrendered. American combat casualties had been few; most U.S. soldiers' deaths had resulted from malaria and yellow fever.

## Spoils of War

The United States and Spain quickly signed a preliminary peace agreement in which Spain agreed to liberate Cuba and cede Puerto Rico and Guam to the United States. But what would happen to the Philippines, an immense archipelago that lay more than 5,000 miles from California? Initially, the United States aimed to keep only Manila, because of its fine harbor. Manila was not defensible, however, without the whole island of Luzon, on which it sat. After deliberating, McKinley found a justification for annexing all of the Philippines. He decided that "we could not leave [the Filipinos] to themselves—they were unfit for self-rule."

This declaration provoked heated debate. Under the Constitution, as Republican senator George F. Hoar argued, "no power is given to the Federal Government to acquire territory to be held and governed permanently as colonies" or "to conquer alien people and hold them in subjugation." Leading citizens and peace advocates, including Jane Addams and Mark Twain, enlisted in the anti-imperialist cause. Steel king Andrew Carnegie offered $20 million to purchase Philippine independence. Labor leader Samuel Gompers warned union members about the threat of competition from low-wage Filipino immigrants. Anti-imperialists, however, were a diverse lot. Some argued that Filipinos were perfectly capable of self-rule; others warned about the dangers of annexing eight million Filipinos of an "inferior race." "No matter whether they are fit to govern themselves or not," declared a Missouri congressman, "they are not fit to govern us."

Beginning in late 1898, anti-imperialist leagues sprang up around the country, but they never sparked a mass movement. On the contrary, McKinley's "splendid little war" proved immensely popular. Confronted with that reality, Democrats waffled. Their standard-bearer, William Jennings Bryan, decided not to stake Democrats' future on opposition to a policy that he believed to be irreversible. He threw his party into turmoil by declaring last-minute support for McKinley's proposed treaty. Having met military defeat, Spanish representatives had little choice. In the Treaty of Paris, Spain ceded the Philippines to the United States for $20 million.

Annexation was not as simple as U.S. policymakers had expected. On February 4, 1899, two days before the Senate ratified the treaty, fighting broke out between American and Filipino patrols on the edge of Manila. Confronted by annexation, rebel leader Emilio Aguinaldo asserted his nation's independence and turned his guns on occupying American forces. Though Aguinaldo found it difficult to organize a mass-based resistance movement, the ensuing conflict between Filipino nationalists and U.S. troops far exceeded in length and ferocity the war just concluded with Spain. Fighting tenacious guerrillas, the U.S. Army resorted to the same tactics Spain had employed in Cuba: burning crops and villages and rounding up civilians. Atrocities became commonplace on both sides. In three years of warfare, 4,200 Americans and an estimated 200,000 Filipinos died; many of the latter were dislocated civilians, particularly children, who succumbed to malnutrition and disease.

McKinley's convincing victory over William Jennings Bryan in 1900 suggested popular satisfaction with America's overseas adventures, even in the face of dogged Filipino resistance to U.S. rule. The fighting ended in 1902, and William Howard Taft, appointed as governor-general of the Philippines, sought to make the territory a model of roadbuilding and sanitary engineering. Yet misgivings lingered as Americans confronted the brutality of the war. Philosopher William James noted that the United States had destroyed "these islanders by the thousands, their villages and cities. . . . Could there be any more damning indictment of that whole bloated ideal termed 'modern civilization'?"

Constitutional issues also remained unresolved. The treaty, while guaranteeing freedom of religion to inhabitants of ceded Spanish territories, withheld any promise of citizenship. It was up to Congress to decide Filipinos' "civil rights and political status." In 1901, the Supreme Court upheld this provision in a set of decisions known as the **_Insular Cases_**. The Constitution, declared the Court, did not automatically extend citizenship to people in acquired territories; Congress could decide. Puerto Rico, Guam, and the Philippines were thus marked as colonies, not future states.

The next year, as a condition for withdrawing from Cuba, the United States forced the newly independent island to accept a proviso in its constitution called the **Platt Amendment** (1902). This blocked Cuba from making a treaty with any country except the United States and gave the United States the right to intervene in Cuban affairs if it saw fit. Cuba also granted the United States a lease on Guantánamo Bay (still in effect), where the U.S. Navy built a large base. Cubans' hard-fought independence was limited; so was that of Filipinos. Eventually, the Jones Act of 1916 committed the United States to Philippine independence but set no date. (The Philippines at last achieved independence in 1946.) Though the war's carnage had rubbed off some of the moralizing gloss, America's global aspirations remained intact.

| IN YOUR OWN WORDS | Explain the steps by which the late-nineteenth-century U.S. government began to exert military influence in different regions of the world. |
|---|---|

# A Power Among Powers

No one appreciated America's emerging influence more than the man who, after William McKinley's assassination, became president in 1901. Theodore Roosevelt was an avid student of world affairs who called on "the civilized and orderly powers to insist on the proper policing of the world." He meant, in part, directing the affairs of "backward peoples." For Roosevelt, imperialism went hand in hand with domestic progressivism. He argued that a strong federal government, asserting itself both at home and abroad, would enhance economic stability and political order. Overseas, Roosevelt sought to arbitrate disputes and maintain a global balance of power, but he also asserted U.S. interests.

## The Open Door in Asia

U.S. officials and business leaders had a burning interest in East Asian markets, but they were entering a crowded field (Map 20.1). In the late 1890s, following Japan's victory in the Sino-Japanese War of 1894–1895, Japan, Russia, Germany, France, and Britain divided coastal China into spheres of influence. Fearful of being shut out, U.S. Secretary of State John Hay sent these powers a note in 1899, claiming the right of equal trade access—an **"open door" policy**—for all nations seeking to do business in China. The United States lacked leverage in Asia, and Hay's note elicited only noncommittal responses. But he chose to interpret this as acceptance of his position.

When a secret society of Chinese nationalists, known outside China as "Boxers" because of their pugnacious political stance, rebelled against foreign occupation in 1900, the United States sent 5,000 troops to join a multinational campaign to break the nationalists' siege of European offices in Beijing. Hay took this opportunity to assert a second open door principle: China must be preserved as a "territorial and administrative entity." As long as the legal fiction of an independent China survived, Americans could claim equal access to its market.

**MAP 20.1 The Great Powers in East Asia, 1898–1910**

European powers established dominance over China by way of "treaty ports," where the powers based their naval forces, and through "spheres of influence" that extended from the ports into the hinterland. This map reveals why the United States had a weak hand: it lacked a presence on this colonized terrain. An uprising of Chinese nationalists in 1900 gave the United States a chance to insert itself on the Chinese mainland by sending an American expeditionary force. American diplomats made the most of the opportunity to defend U.S. commercial interests in China. As noted in the key, all place names in this map are those in use in 1910: Modern *Beijing*, for example, is shown as *Peking*.

European and American plans were, however, unsettled by Japan's emergence as East Asia's dominant power. A decade after its victory over China, Japan responded to Russia's bids for control of both Korea and Manchuria, in northern China, by attacking Russia's fleet at its leased Chinese port. In a series of brilliant victories, the Japanese smashed the Russian forces. Westerners were shocked: for the first time, a European power had been defeated by a non-Western nation. Conveying both admiration and alarm, American cartoonists sketched Japan as a martial artist knocking down the Russian giant. Roosevelt mediated a settlement to the war in 1905, receiving for his efforts the first Nobel Peace Prize awarded to an American.

Though he was contemptuous of other Asians, Roosevelt respected the Japanese, whom he called "a wonderful and civilized people." More important, he understood Japan's rising military might and aligned himself with the mighty. The United States approved Japan's "protectorate" over Korea in 1905 and, six years later, its seizure of full control. With Japan asserting harsh authority over Manchuria, energetic Chinese diplomat Yüan Shih-k'ai tried to encourage the United States to intervene. But Roosevelt reviewed America's weak position in the Pacific and declined. He conceded that Japan had "a paramount interest in what surrounds the Yellow Sea." In 1908, the United States and Japan signed the **Root-Takahira Agreement**, confirming principles of free oceanic commerce and recognizing Japan's authority over Manchuria.

William Howard Taft entered the White House in 1909 convinced that the United States had been shortchanged in Asia. He pressed for a larger role for American investors, especially in Chinese railroad construction. Eager to promote U.S. business interests abroad, he hoped that infusions of American capital would offset Japanese power. When the Chinese Revolution of 1911 toppled the Manchu dynasty, Taft supported the victorious Nationalists, who wanted to modernize their country and liberate it from Japanese domination. The United States had entangled itself in China and entered a long-term rivalry with Japan for power in the Pacific, a competition that would culminate thirty years later in World War II.

## The United States and Latin America

Roosevelt famously argued that the United States should "speak softly and carry a big stick." By "big stick," he meant naval power, and rapid access to two oceans required a canal. European powers conceded the United States's "paramount interest" in the Caribbean. Freed by Britain's surrender of canal-building rights in the Hay-Pauncefote Treaty (1901), Roosevelt persuaded Congress to authorize $10 million, plus future payments of $250,000 per year, to purchase from Colombia a six-mile strip of land across Panama, a Colombian province.

Furious when Colombia rejected this proposal, Roosevelt contemplated outright seizure of Panama but settled on a more roundabout solution. Panamanians, long separated from Colombia by remote jungle, chafed under Colombian rule. The United States lent covert assistance to an independence movement, triggering a bloodless revolution. On November 6, 1903, the United States recognized the new nation of Panama; two weeks later, it obtained a perpetually renewable lease on a canal zone. Roosevelt never regretted the venture, though in 1922 the United States paid Colombia $25 million as a kind of conscience money.

To build the canal, the U.S. Army Corps of Engineers hired 60,000 laborers, who came from many countries to clear vast swamps, excavate 240 million cubic yards of earth, and construct a series of immense locks. The project, a major engineering feat, took eight years and cost thousands of lives among the workers who built it. Opened in 1914, the **Panama Canal** gave the United States a commanding position in the Western Hemisphere.

Meanwhile, arguing that instability invited European intervention, Roosevelt announced in 1904 that the United States would police all of the Caribbean

**Panama Canal Workers, 1910** The 51-mile-long Panama Canal includes seven sets of locks that can raise and lower fifty large ships in a twenty-four-hour period. Building the canal took eight years and required tens of thousands of workers, including immigrants from Spain and Italy and many West Indians such as these men, who accomplished some of the worst-paid, most dangerous labor. Workers endured the horrors of rockslides, explosions, and a yellow fever epidemic that almost halted the project. But American observers hailed the canal as a triumph of modern science and engineering — especially in medical efforts to eradicate the yellow fever and malaria that had stymied earlier canal-building efforts. Theodore Roosevelt insisted on making a personal visit in November 1906. "He made the men that were building there feel like they were special people," recalled the descendant of one canal worker. "Give them pride of what they were doing for the United States." Library of Congress.

(Map 20.2). This so-called **Roosevelt Corollary** to the Monroe Doctrine actually turned that doctrine upside down: instead of guaranteeing that the United States would protect its neighbors from Europe and help preserve their independence, it asserted the United States's unrestricted right to regulate Caribbean affairs. The Roosevelt Corollary was not a treaty but a unilateral declaration sanctioned only

**MAP 20.2 Policeman of the Caribbean**
After the War of 1898, the United States vigorously asserted its interest in the affairs of its neighbors to the south. As the record of interventions shows, the United States truly became the "policeman" of the Caribbean and Central America.

by America's military and economic might. Citing it, the United States intervened regularly in Caribbean and Central American nations over the next three decades.

Entering office in 1913, Democratic president Woodrow Wilson criticized his predecessors' foreign policy. He pledged that the United States would "never again seek one additional foot of territory by conquest." This stance appealed to anti-imperialists in the Democratic base, including longtime supporters of William Jennings Bryan. But the new president soon showed that, when American interests called for it, his actions were not so different from those of Roosevelt and Taft.

Since the 1870s, Mexican dictator Porfirio Díaz had created a friendly climate for American companies that purchased Mexican plantations, mines, and oil fields. By the early 1900s, however, Díaz feared the extraordinary power of these foreign interests and began to nationalize — reclaim — key resources. American investors who faced the loss of Mexican holdings began to back Francisco Madero, an advocate of constitutional government who was friendly to U.S. interests. In 1911, Madero forced Díaz to resign and proclaimed himself president. Thousands of poor Mexicans took this opportunity to mobilize rural armies and demand more radical change. Madero's position was weak, and several strongmen sought to overthrow him; in 1913, he was deposed and murdered by a leading general. Immediately, several other military men vied for control.

Wilson, fearing that the unrest threatened U.S. interests, decided to intervene in the emerging Mexican Revolution. On the pretext of a minor insult to the navy, he ordered U.S. occupation of the port of Veracruz on April 21, 1914, at the cost of 19 American and 126 Mexican lives. Though the intervention helped Venustiano Carranza, the revolutionary leader whom Wilson most favored, Carranza protested it as illegitimate meddling in Mexican affairs. Carranza's forces, after nearly engaging the Americans themselves, entered Mexico City in triumph a few months later. Though Wilson had supported this outcome, his interference caused lasting mistrust.

Carranza's victory did not subdue revolutionary activity in Mexico. In 1916, General Francisco "Pancho" Villa—a thug to his enemies, but a heroic Robin Hood to many poor Mexicans—crossed the U.S.-Mexico border, killing sixteen American civilians and raiding the town of Columbus, New Mexico. Wilson sent 11,000 troops to pursue Villa, a force that soon resembled an army of occupation in northern Mexico. Mexican public opinion demanded withdrawal as armed clashes broke out between U.S. and Mexican troops. At the brink of war, both governments backed off and U.S. forces departed. But policymakers in Washington had shown their intention to police not only the Caribbean and Central America but also Mexico when they deemed it necessary.

> **IN YOUR OWN WORDS** Compare and contrast the factors that influenced U.S. actions in Asia and in Latin America in this period.

# The United States in World War I

While the United States staked claims around the globe, a war of unprecedented scale was brewing in Europe. The military buildup of Germany, a rising power, terrified its neighbors. To the east, the disintegrating Ottoman Empire was losing its grip on the Balkans. Out of these conflicts, two rival power blocs emerged: the Triple Alliance (Germany, Austria-Hungary, and Italy) and Triple Entente (Britain, France, and Russia). Within each alliance, national governments pursued their own interests but were bound to one another by both public and secret treaties.

Americans had no obvious stake in these developments. In 1905, when Germany suddenly challenged French control of Morocco, Theodore Roosevelt arranged an international conference to defuse the crisis. Germany got a few concessions, but France—with British backing—retained Morocco. Accomplished in the same year that Roosevelt brokered peace between Russia and Japan, the conference seemed another diplomatic triumph. One U.S. official boasted that America had kept peace by "the power of our detachment." It was not to last.

## From Neutrality to War

The spark that ignited World War I came in the Balkans, where Austria-Hungary and Russia competed for control. Austria's 1908 seizure of Ottoman provinces, including Bosnia, angered the nearby Slavic nation of Serbia and its ally, Russia. Serbian revolutionaries recruited Bosnian Slavs to resist Austrian rule. In June 1914, in the city of Sarajevo, university student Gavrilo Princip assassinated Archduke Franz Ferdinand, heir to the Austro-Hungarian throne.

Like dominos falling, the system of European alliances pushed all the powers into war. Austria-Hungary blamed Serbia for the assassination and declared war on July 28. Russia, tied by secret treaty to Serbia, mobilized against Austria-Hungary. This prompted Germany to declare war on Russia and its ally France. As a preparation for attacking France, Germany launched a brutal invasion of the neutral country of Belgium, which caused Great Britain to declare war on Germany. Within a week, most of Europe was at war, with the major Allies — Great Britain, France, and Russia — confronting the Central Powers of Germany and Austria-Hungary. Two military zones emerged. On the Western Front, Germany battled the British and French; on the Eastern Front, Germany and Austria-Hungary fought Russia. Because most of the warring nations held colonial empires, the conflict soon spread to the Middle East, Africa, and Asia.

The so-called Great War wreaked terrible devastation. New technology, some of it devised in the United States, made warfare deadlier than ever before. Every soldier carried a long-range, high-velocity rifle that could hit a target at 1,000 yards — a vast technical advancement over the 300-yard range of rifles used in the U.S. Civil War. The machine gun was even more lethal. Its American-born inventor, Hiram Maxim, had moved to Britain in the 1880s to follow a friend's advice: "If you want to make your fortune, invent something which will allow those fool Europeans to kill each other more quickly." Elaborate trenches, familiar from the Civil War era, were now enhanced with barbed wire to protect soldiers in defensive positions. Once advancing Germans ran into French fortifications, they stalled. Across a swath of Belgium and northeastern France, millions of soldiers on both sides hunkered down in fortified trenches. During 1916, repeatedly trying to break through French lines at Verdun, Germans suffered 450,000 casualties. The French fared even worse, with 550,000 dead or wounded. It was all to no avail. From 1914 to 1918, the Western Front barely moved.

At the war's outbreak, President Wilson called on Americans to be "neutral in fact as well as in name." If the United States remained out of the conflict, Wilson reasoned, he could influence the postwar settlement, much as Theodore Roosevelt had done after previous conflicts. Even if Wilson had wished to, it would have been nearly impossible in 1914 to unite Americans behind the Allies. Many Irish immigrants viewed Britain as an enemy — based on its continued occupation of Ireland — while millions of German Americans maintained ties to their homeland. Progressive-minded Republicans, such as Senator Robert La Follette of Wisconsin, vehemently opposed taking sides in a European fight, as did socialists, who condemned the war as a conflict among greedy capitalist empires. Two giants of American industry, Andrew Carnegie and Henry Ford, opposed the war. In December 1915, Ford sent a hundred men and women to Europe on a "peace ship" to urge an end to the war. "It would be folly," declared the *New York Sun*, "for the country to sacrifice itself to . . . the clash of ancient hatreds which is urging the Old World to destruction."

**The Struggle to Remain Neutral**   The United States, wishing to trade with all the warring nations, might have remained neutral if Britain had not held commanding power at sea. In September 1914, the British imposed a naval blockade on the Central Powers to cut off vital supplies of food and military equipment. Though the Wilson administration protested this infringement of the rights of neutral carriers, commerce with the Allies more than made up for the economic loss. Trade with Britain and France grew fourfold over the next two years, to $3.2 billion in 1916; by 1917, U.S. banks had lent the Allies $2.5 billion. In contrast, American trade and loans to Germany stood then at a mere $56 million. This imbalance undercut U.S. neutrality. If Germany won and Britain and France defaulted on their debts, American companies would suffer catastrophic losses.

To challenge the British navy, Germany launched a devastating new weapon, the U-boat (short for *Unterseeboot*, "undersea boat," or submarine). In April 1915, Germany issued a warning that all ships flying flags of Britain or its allies were liable to destruction. A few weeks later, a U-boat torpedoed the British luxury liner *Lusitania* off the coast of Ireland, killing 1,198 people, including 128 Americans. The attack on the passenger ship (which was later revealed to have been carrying munitions) incensed Americans. The following year, in an agreement known as the Sussex pledge, Germany agreed not to target passenger liners or merchant ships unless an inspection showed the latter carried weapons. But the *Lusitania* sinking prompted Wilson to reconsider his options. After quietly trying to mediate in Europe but finding neither side interested in peace, he endorsed a $1 billion U.S. military buildup.

American public opinion still ran strongly against entering the war, a fact that shaped the election of 1916. Republicans rejected the belligerently prowar Theodore Roosevelt in favor of Supreme Court justice Charles Evans Hughes, a progressive former governor of New York. Democrats renominated Wilson, who campaigned on his domestic record and as the president who "kept us out of war." Wilson eked out a narrow victory; winning California by a mere 4,000 votes, he secured a slim majority in the electoral college.

**America Enters the War**    Despite Wilson's campaign slogan, events pushed him toward war. In February 1917, Germany resumed unrestricted submarine warfare, a decision dictated by the impasse on the Western Front. In response, Wilson broke off diplomatic relations with Germany. A few weeks later, newspapers published an intercepted dispatch from German foreign secretary Arthur Zimmermann to his minister in Mexico. The **Zimmermann telegram** urged Mexico to join the Central Powers, promising that if the United States entered the war, Germany would help Mexico recover "the lost territory of Texas, New Mexico, and Arizona." With Pancho Villa's border raids still fresh in Americans' minds, this threat jolted public opinion. Meanwhile, German U-boats attacked U.S. ships without warning, sinking three on March 18 alone.

On April 2, 1917, Wilson asked Congress for a declaration of war. He argued that Germany had trampled on American rights and imperiled U.S. trade and citizens' lives. "We desire no conquest," Wilson declared, "no material compensation for the sacrifices we shall freely make." Reflecting his progressive idealism, Wilson promised that American involvement would make the world "safe for democracy." On April 6, the United States declared war on Germany. Reflecting the nation's divided views, the vote was far from unanimous. Six senators and fifty members of the House voted against entry, including Representative Jeannette Rankin of Montana, the first woman elected to Congress. "You can no more win a war than you can win an earthquake," Rankin said. "I want to stand by my country, but I cannot vote for war."

## "Over There"

To Americans, Europe seemed a great distance away. Many assumed the United States would simply provide munitions and economic aid. "Good Lord," exclaimed one U.S. senator to a Wilson administration official, "you're not going to send soldiers over there, are you?" But when General John J. Pershing asked how the United States could best support the Allies, the French commander put it bluntly: "Men, men, and more men." Amid war fever, thousands of young men prepared to go "over there," in the words of George M. Cohan's popular song: "Make your Daddy glad to have had such a lad. / Tell your sweetheart not to pine, / To be proud her boy's in line."

**Americans Join the War**    In 1917, the U.S. Army numbered fewer than 200,000 soldiers; needing more men, Congress instituted a military draft in May 1917. In contrast to the Civil War, when resistance was common, conscription went smoothly, partly because local, civilian-run draft boards played a central role in the new system. Still, draft registration demonstrated government's increasing power over ordinary citizens. On a single day — June 5, 1917 — more than 9.5 million men between the ages of twenty-one and thirty registered at local voting precincts for possible military service.

President Wilson chose General Pershing to head the American Expeditionary Force (AEF), which had to be trained, outfitted, and carried across the submarine-plagued Atlantic. This required safer shipping. When the United States entered the war, German U-boats were sinking 900,000 tons of Allied ships each month. By sending merchant and troop ships in armed convoys, the U.S. Navy cut that monthly rate to 400,000 tons by the end of 1917. With trench warfare grinding on, Allied commanders pleaded for American soldiers to fill their depleted units, but Pershing waited until the AEF reached full strength. As late as May 1918, the brunt of the fighting fell to the French and British.

The Allies' burden increased when the Eastern Front collapsed following the Bolshevik (Communist) Revolution in Russia in November 1917. To consolidate power at home, the new Bolshevik government, led by Vladimir Lenin, sought peace with the Central Powers. In a 1918 treaty, Russia surrendered its claims over vast parts of its territories in exchange for peace. Released from war against Germany, the Bolsheviks turned their attention to a civil war at home. Terrified by communism, Japan and several Allied countries, including the United States, later sent troops to fight the Bolsheviks and aid forces loyal to the deposed tsar. But after a four-year civil war, Lenin's forces established full control over Russia and reclaimed Ukraine and other former possessions.

Peace with Russia freed Germany to launch a major offensive on the Western Front. By May 1918, German troops had advanced to within 50 miles of Paris. Pershing at last committed about 60,000 U.S. soldiers to support the French defense. With American soldiers engaged in massive numbers, Allied forces brought the Germans to a halt in July; by September, they forced a retreat. Pershing then pitted more than one million American soldiers against an outnumbered and exhausted German army in the Argonne forest. By early November, this attack broke German defenses at a crucial rail hub, Sedan. The cost was high: 26,000 Americans killed and 95,000 wounded (Map 20.3). But the flood of U.S. troops and supplies determined the outcome. Recognizing inevitable defeat and facing popular uprisings at home, Germany signed an armistice on November 11, 1918. The Great War was over.

**The American Fighting Force**    By the end of World War I, almost 4 million American men — popularly known as "doughboys" — wore U.S. uniforms, as did several thousand female nurses. The recruits reflected America's heterogeneity: one-fifth

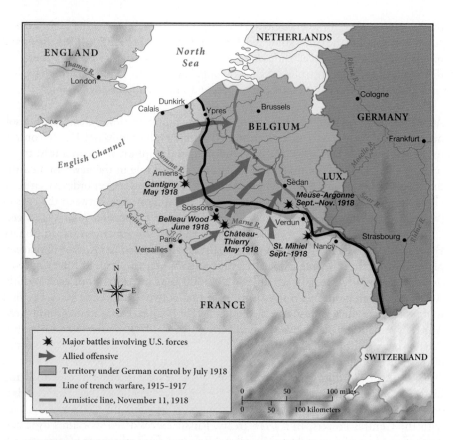

**MAP 20.3  U.S. Participation on the Western Front, 1918**
When American troops reached the European front in significant numbers in 1918, the Allies and Central Powers had been fighting a deadly war of attrition for almost four years. The influx of American troops and supplies helped break the stalemate. Successful offensive maneuvers by the American Expeditionary Force included those at Belleau Wood and Château-Thierry and the Meuse-Argonne campaign.

had been born outside the United States, and soldiers spoke forty-nine different languages. Though ethnic diversity worried some observers, most predicted that military service would promote Americanization.

Over 400,000 African American men enlisted, accounting for 13 percent of the armed forces. Their wartime experiences were often grim: serving in segregated units, they were given the most menial tasks. Racial discrimination hampered military efficiency and provoked violence at several camps. The worst incident occurred in August 1917, when, after suffering a string of racial attacks, black members of the 24th Infantry's Third Battalion rioted in Houston, killing 15 white civilians and police officers. The army tried 118 of the soldiers in military courts for mutiny and riot, hanged 19, and sentenced 63 to life in prison.

Unlike African Americans, American Indians served in integrated combat units. Racial stereotypes about Native Americans' prowess as warriors enhanced their military reputations, but it also prompted officers to assign them hazardous duties as scouts and snipers. About 13,000, or 25 percent, of the adult male American Indian population served during the war; roughly 5 percent died, compared to 2 percent for the military as a whole.

Most American soldiers escaped the horrors of sustained trench warfare. Still, during the brief period of U.S. participation, over 50,000 servicemen died in action; another 63,000 died from disease, mainly the devastating influenza pandemic that began early in 1918 and, over the next two years, killed 50 million people world-wide. The nation's military deaths, though substantial, were only a tenth as many as the 500,000 American civilians who died of this terrible epidemic—not to mention the staggering losses of Europeans in the war.

## War on the Home Front

In the United States, opponents of the war were a minority. Helping the Allies triggered an economic boom that benefitted farmers and working people. Many progressives also supported the war, hoping Wilson's ideals and wartime patriotism would renew Americans' attention to reform. But the war bitterly disappointed them. Rather than enhancing democracy, it chilled the political climate as government agencies tried to enforce "100 percent loyalty."

**Mobilizing the Economy**    American businesses made big bucks from World War I. As grain, weapons, and manufactured goods flowed to Britain and France, the United States became a creditor nation. Moreover, as the war drained British financial reserves, U.S. banks provided capital for investments around the globe.

Government powers expanded during wartime, with new federal agencies overseeing almost every part of the economy. The **War Industries Board** (WIB), established in July 1917, directed military production. After a fumbling start that showed the limits of voluntarism, the Wilson administration reorganized the board and placed Bernard Baruch, a Wall Street financier and superb administrator, at its head. Under his direction, the WIB allocated scarce resources among industries, ordered factories to convert to war production, set prices, and standardized procedures. Though he could compel compliance, Baruch preferred to win voluntary cooperation. A man of immense charm, he usually succeeded—helped by the lucrative military contracts at his disposal. Despite higher taxes, corporate profits soared, as military production sustained a boom that continued until 1920.

Some federal agencies took dramatic measures. The **National War Labor Board** (NWLB), formed in April 1918, established an eight-hour day for war workers with time-and-a-half pay for overtime, and it endorsed equal pay for women. In return for a no-strike pledge, the NWLB also supported workers' right to organize—a major achievement for the labor movement. The Fuel Administration, meanwhile, introduced daylight saving time to conserve coal and oil. In December 1917, the Railroad Administration seized control of the nation's hodgepodge of private railroads, seeking to facilitate rapid movement of troops and equipment—an experiment that had, at best, mixed results.

Perhaps the most successful wartime agency was the Food Administration, created in August 1917 and led by engineer Herbert Hoover. With the slogan "Food will win the war," Hoover convinced farmers to nearly double their acreage of grain. This increase allowed a threefold rise in food exports to Europe. Among citizens, the Food Administration mobilized a "spirit of self-denial" rather than mandatory rationing. Female volunteers went from door to door to persuade housekeepers to observe "Wheatless" Mondays and "Porkless" Thursdays. Hoover, a Republican, emerged from the war as one of the nation's most admired public figures.

**Promoting National Unity**    Suppressing wartime dissent became a near obsession for President Wilson. In April 1917, Wilson formed the Committee on Public Information (CPI), a government propaganda agency headed by journalist George Creel. Professing lofty goals—educating citizens about democracy, assimilating immigrants, and ending the isolation of rural life—the committee set out to mold Americans into "one white-hot mass" of war patriotism. The CPI touched the lives of nearly all civilians. It distributed seventy-five million pieces of literature and enlisted thousands of volunteers—**Four-Minute Men**—to deliver short prowar speeches at movie theaters.

The CPI also pressured immigrant groups to become "One Hundred Percent Americans." German Americans bore the brunt of this campaign. With posters exhorting citizens to root out German spies, a spirit of conformity pervaded the home front. A quasi-vigilante group, the American Protective League, mobilized about 250,000 "agents," furnished them with badges issued by the Justice Department, and trained them to spy on neighbors and coworkers. In 1918, members of the league led violent raids against draft evaders and peace activists. Government propaganda helped rouse a nativist hysteria that lingered into the 1920s.

Congress also passed new laws to curb dissent. Among them was the **Sedition Act of 1918**, which prohibited any words or behavior that might "incite, provoke, or encourage resistance to the United States, or promote the cause of its enemies." Because this and an earlier Espionage Act (1917) defined treason loosely, they led to the conviction of more than a thousand people. The Justice Department prosecuted members of the Industrial Workers of the World, whose opposition to militarism threatened to disrupt war production of lumber and copper. When a Quaker pacifist teacher in New York City refused to teach a prowar curriculum, she was fired. Socialist Party leader Eugene V. Debs was sentenced to ten years in jail for the crime of arguing that wealthy capitalists had started the conflict and were forcing workers to fight.

Federal courts mostly supported the acts. In *Schenck v. United States* (1919), the Supreme Court upheld the conviction of a socialist who was jailed for circulating pamphlets that urged army draftees to resist induction. The justices followed this with a similar decision in *Abrams v. United States* (1919), ruling that authorities could prosecute speech they believed to pose "a clear and present danger to the safety of the country." In an important dissent, however, Justices Oliver Wendell Holmes Jr. and Louis Brandeis objected to the *Abrams* decision. Holmes's probing questions about the definition of "clear and present danger" helped launch twentieth-century legal battles over free speech and civil liberties.

**Great Migrations**    World War I created tremendous economic opportunities at home. Jobs in war industries drew thousands of people to the cities. With so many men in uniform, jobs in heavy industry opened for the first time to African Americans, accelerating the pace of black migration from South to North. During World War I, more than 400,000 African Americans moved to such cities as St. Louis, Chicago, New York, and Detroit, in what became known as the **Great Migration**. The rewards were great, and taking war jobs could be a source of patriotic pride. "If it hadn't been for the negro," a Carnegie Steel manager later recalled, "we could hardly have carried on our operations."

Blacks in the North encountered discrimination in jobs, housing, and education. But in the first flush of opportunity, most celebrated their escape from the repressive racism and poverty of the South. "It is a matter of a dollar with me and I feel that God made the path and I am walking therein," one woman reported to her sister back home. "Tell your husband work is plentiful here." "I just begin to feel like a man," wrote another migrant to a friend in Mississippi. "My children are going to the same school with the whites. . . . Will vote the next election and there isn't any 'yes sir' and 'no sir' — it's all yes and no and Sam and Bill."

Wartime labor shortages prompted Mexican Americans in the Southwest to leave farmwork for urban industrial jobs. Continued political instability in Mexico, combined with increased demand for farmworkers in the United States, also encouraged more Mexicans to move across the border. Between 1917 and 1920, at least 100,000 Mexicans entered the United States; despite discrimination, large numbers stayed. If asked why, many might have echoed the words of an African American man who left New Orleans for Chicago: they were going "north for a better chance." The same was true for Puerto Ricans such as Jésus Colón, who also confronted racism. "I came to New York to poor pay, long hours, terrible working conditions, discrimination even in the slums and in the poor paying factories," Colón recalled, "where the bosses very dexterously pitted Italians against Puerto Ricans and Puerto Ricans against American Negroes and Jews."

Women were the largest group to take advantage of wartime job opportunities. About 1 million women joined the paid labor force for the first time, while another 8 million gave up low-wage service jobs for higher-paying industrial work. Americans soon got used to the sight of female streetcar conductors, train engineers, and defense workers. Though most people expected these jobs to return to men in peacetime, the war created a new comfort level with women's employment outside the home—and with women's suffrage.

**Women's Voting Rights**   The National American Woman Suffrage Association (NAWSA) threw the support of its 2 million members wholeheartedly into the war effort. Its president, Carrie Chapman Catt, declared that women had to prove their patriotism to win the ballot. NAWSA members in thousands of communities promoted food conservation and distributed emergency relief through organizations such as the Red Cross.

Alice Paul and the **National Woman's Party** (NWP) took a more confrontational approach. Paul was a Quaker who had worked in the settlement movement and earned a PhD in political science. Finding as a NAWSA lobbyist that congressmen dismissed her, Paul founded the NWP in 1916. Inspired by militant British suffragists, the group began in July 1917 to picket the White House. Standing silently with their banners, Paul and other NWP activists faced arrest for obstructing traffic

**Wagon Decorated for the Labor Day Parade, San Diego, California, 1910**  As the woman suffrage movement grew stronger in the years before and during World War I, working-class women played increasingly prominent and visible roles in its leadership. This Labor Day parade float, created by the Women's Union Label League of San Diego, showed that activists championed equal pay for women in the workplace as well as women's voting rights. "Union Label Leagues" urged middle-class shoppers to purchase only clothing with a union label, certifying that the item had been manufactured under safe conditions and the workers who made it had received a fair wage. San Diego Historical Society.

and were sentenced to seven months in jail. They protested by going on a hunger strike, which prison authorities met with forced feeding. Public shock at the women's treatment drew attention to the suffrage cause.

Impressed by NAWSA's patriotism and worried by the NWP's militancy, the antisuffrage Wilson reversed his position. In January 1918, he urged support for woman suffrage as a "war measure." The constitutional amendment quickly passed the House of Representatives; it took eighteen months to get through the Senate and another year to win ratification by the states. On August 26, 1920, when Tennessee voted for ratification, the Nineteenth Amendment became law. The state thus joined Texas as one of two ex-Confederate states to ratify it. In most parts of the South, the measure meant that *white* women began to vote: in this Jim Crow era, African American women's voting rights remained restricted along with men's.

In explaining suffragists' victory, historians have debated the relative effectiveness of Catt's patriotic strategy and Paul's militant protests. Both played a role in persuading Wilson and Congress to act, but neither might have worked without the extraordinary impact of the Great War. Across the globe, before 1914, the only places where women had full suffrage were New Zealand, Australia, Finland, and Norway. After World War I, many nations moved to enfranchise women. The new

Soviet Union acted first, in 1917, with Great Britain and Canada following in 1918; by 1920, the measure had passed in Germany, Austria, Poland, Czechoslovakia, and Hungary as well as the United States. (Major exceptions were France and Italy, where women did not gain voting rights until after World War II, and Switzerland, which held out until 1971.) Thus, while World War I introduced modern horrors on the battlefield — machine guns and poison gas — it brought some positive results at home: economic opportunity and women's political participation.

| | |
|---|---|
| **IN YOUR OWN WORDS** | What changes did U.S. participation in World War I bring about on the home front? |

# Catastrophe at Versailles

The idealistic Wilson argued that no victor should be declared after World War I: only "peace among equals" could last. Having won at an incredible price, Britain and France showed zero interest in such a plan. But the devastation wrought by the war created popular pressure for a just and enduring outcome. At the peace conference held at Versailles, near Paris, in 1919, Wilson scored a diplomatic victory when the Allies chose to base the talks on his **Fourteen Points**, a blueprint for peace that he had presented a year earlier in a speech to Congress.

Wilson's Points embodied an important strand in progressivism. They called for open diplomacy; "absolute freedom of navigation upon the seas"; arms reduction; removal of trade barriers; and national self-determination for peoples in the Austro-Hungarian, Russian, and German empires. Essential to Wilson's vision was the creation of an international regulatory body — eventually called the **League of Nations** — that would guarantee each country's "independence and territorial integrity." The League would mediate disputes, supervise arms reduction, and — according to its crucial Article X — curb aggressor nations through collective military action. Wilson hoped the League would "end all wars." But his ideals had marked limits, and in negotiations he confronted harsh realities.

## The Fate of Wilson's Ideas

The peace conference included ten thousand representatives from around the globe, but leaders of France, Britain, and the United States dominated the proceedings. When the Japanese delegation proposed a declaration for equal treatment of all races, the Allies rejected it. Similarly, the Allies ignored a global Pan-African Congress, organized by W. E. B. Du Bois and other black leaders; they snubbed Arab representatives who had been military allies during the war. Even Italy's prime minister — included among the influential "Big Four" because in 1915 Italy had switched to the Allied side — withdrew from the conference, aggrieved at the way British and French leaders marginalized him. The Allies excluded two key players: Russia, because they distrusted its communist leaders, and Germany, because they planned to dictate terms to their defeated foe. For Wilson's "peace among equals," it was a terrible start.

Prime Minister David Lloyd George of Britain and Premier Georges Clemenceau of France imposed harsh punishments on Germany. Unbeknownst to others at the time, they had already made secret agreements to divide up Germany's African colonies and take them as spoils of war. At Versailles, they also forced the defeated nation to pay $33 billion in reparations and surrender coal supplies, merchant ships, valuable patents, and even territory along the French border. These terms caused keen resentment and economic hardship in Germany, and over the following two decades they helped lead to World War II.

Given these conditions, it is remarkable that Wilson influenced the **Treaty of Versailles** as much as he did. He intervened repeatedly to soften conditions imposed on Germany. In accordance with the Fourteen Points, he worked with the other Allies to fashion nine new nations, stretching from the Baltic to the Mediterranean (Map 20.4 and Map 20.5). These were intended as a buffer to protect Western Europe from communist Russia; the plan also embodied Wilson's principle of self-determination for European states. Elsewhere in the world, the Allies dismantled their enemies' empires but did not create independent nations, keeping colonized people subordinate to European power. France, for example, refused to give up its long-standing occupation of Indochina; Clemenceau's snub of future Vietnamese leader Ho Chi Minh, who sought representation at Versailles, had grave long-term consequences for both France and the United States.

The establishment of a British mandate in Palestine (now Israel) also proved crucial. During the war, British foreign secretary Sir Arthur Balfour had stated that his country would work to establish there a "national home for the Jewish people," with the condition that "nothing shall be done which may prejudice the civil and religious rights of existing non-Jewish communities in Palestine." Under the British mandate, thousands of Jews moved to Palestine and purchased land, in some cases evicting Palestinian tenants. As early as 1920, riots erupted between Jews and Palestinians — a situation that, even before World War II, escalated beyond British control.

The Versailles treaty thus created conditions for horrific future bloodshed, and it must be judged one of history's great catastrophes. Balfour astutely described Clemenceau, Lloyd George, and Wilson as "all-powerful, all-ignorant men, sitting there and carving up continents." Wilson, however, remained optimistic as he returned home, even though his health was beginning to fail. The president hoped the new

**MAP 20.4 AND MAP 20.5   Europe and the Middle East Before and After World War I >**
World War I and its aftermath dramatically altered the landscape of Europe and the Middle East. Before the war, the most powerful nations belonged to two alliances: the Central Powers (Germany, Austria-Hungary, and Italy) and the Entente (Great Britain, France, and Russia). The latter's victory, along with the 1917 communist revolution in Russia, dramatically reshaped power relations. Collapse of the German, Austro-Hungarian, and Russian empires allowed reconstitution of Poland and creation of a string of new states along the Baltic Sea and in Eastern Europe, based on the principle of national (ethnic) self-determination. The demise of the Ottoman Empire prompted creation of four quasi-independent territories, or "mandates": Iraq, Syria, Lebanon, and Palestine. The League of Nations stipulated that their affairs would be supervised by one of the victorious Allied powers.

League of Nations, authorized by the treaty, would moderate the settlement and secure peaceful resolutions of other disputes. For this to occur, U.S. participation was crucial.

## Congress Rejects the Treaty

The outlook for U.S. ratification was not promising. Though major opinion makers and religious denominations supported the treaty, openly hostile Republicans held a majority in the Senate. One group, called the "irreconcilables," consisted of western progressive Republicans such as Hiram Johnson of California and Robert La Follette of Wisconsin, who opposed U.S. involvement in European affairs. Another group, led by Senator Henry Cabot Lodge of Massachusetts, worried that Article X — the provision for collective security — would prevent the United States from pursuing an independent foreign policy. Was the nation, Lodge asked, "willing to have the youth of America ordered to war" by an international body? Wilson refused to accept any amendments, especially to placate Lodge, a hated rival. "I shall consent to nothing," the president told the French ambassador. "The Senate must take its medicine."

To mobilize support, Wilson embarked on an exhausting speaking tour. His impassioned defense of the League of Nations brought audiences to tears, but the strain proved too much for the president. While visiting Colorado in September 1919, Wilson collapsed. A week later, back in Washington, he suffered a stroke that left one side of his body paralyzed. Wilson still urged Democratic senators to reject all Republican amendments. When the treaty came up for a vote in November 1919, it failed to win the required two-thirds majority. A second attempt, in March 1920, fell seven votes short.

The treaty was dead, and so was Wilson's leadership. The president never fully recovered from his stroke. During the last eighteen months of his administration, the government drifted as Wilson's physician, his wife, and various cabinet heads secretly took charge. The United States never ratified the Versailles treaty or joined the League of Nations. In turn, the League was weak. When Wilson died in 1924, his dream of a just and peaceful international order lay in ruins.

The impact of World War I can hardly be overstated. Despite bids for power by Britain and France, Europe's hold on its colonial empires never recovered. The United States, now a major world power, appeared to turn its back on the world when it rejected the Versailles treaty. But in laying claim to Hawaii and the Philippines, asserting power in Latin America, and intervening in Asia, the United States had entangled itself deeply in global politics. By 1918, the nation had gained too much diplomatic clout — and was too dependent on overseas trade — for isolation to be a realistic long-term option.

On the home front, the effects of World War I were no less dramatic. Wartime jobs and prosperity ushered in an era of exuberant consumerism, while the achievements of women's voting rights seemed to presage a new progressive era. But as peace returned, it became clear that the war had not advanced reform. Rather than embracing government activism, Americans of the 1920s proved eager to relinquish it.

| IN YOUR OWN WORDS | What arguments did U.S. political leaders make for and against ratification of the Versailles treaty? |

# Summary

Between 1877 and 1918, the United States rose as a major economic and military power. Justifications for overseas expansion emphasized access to global markets, the importance of sea power, and the need to police international misconduct and trade. These justifications shaped U.S. policy toward European powers in Latin America, and victory in the War of 1898 enabled the United States to take control of former Spanish colonies in the Caribbean and Pacific. Victory, however, also led to bloody conflict in the Philippines as the United States struggled to suppress Filipino resistance to American rule.

After 1899, the United States aggressively asserted its interests in Asia and Latin America. In China, the United States used the so-called Boxer Rebellion to make good its claim to an "open door" to Chinese markets. Later, President Theodore Roosevelt strengthened relations with Japan, and his successor, William Howard Taft, supported U.S. business interests in China. In the Caribbean, the United States constructed the Panama Canal and regularly exercised the right, claimed under the Roosevelt Corollary, to intervene in the affairs of states in the region. President Woodrow Wilson publicly disparaged the imperialism of his predecessors but repeatedly used the U.S. military to "police" Mexico.

At the outbreak of World War I, the United States asserted neutrality, but its economic ties to the Allies rapidly undercut that claim. In 1917, German submarine attacks drew the United States into the war on the side of Britain and France. Involvement in the war profoundly transformed the economy, politics, and society of the nation, resulting in an economic boom, mass migrations of workers to industrial centers, and the achievement of national voting rights. At the Paris Peace Conference, Wilson attempted to implement his Fourteen Points. However, the designs of the Allies in Europe undermined the Treaty of Versailles, while Republican resistance at home prevented ratification of the treaty. Although Wilson's dream of a just international order failed, the United States had taken its place as a major world power.

# Chapter 20 Review

## KEY TERMS

**Identify and explain the significance of each term below.**

American exceptionalism (p. 584)
Teller Amendment (p. 586)
*Insular Cases* (p. 588)
Platt Amendment (p. 589)
"open door" policy (p. 589)
Root-Takahira Agreement (p. 591)
Panama Canal (p. 591)
Roosevelt Corollary (p. 592)
Zimmermann telegram (p. 596)

War Industries Board (p. 599)
National War Labor Board (p. 599)
Four-Minute Men (p. 600)
Sedition Act of 1918 (p. 600)
Great Migration (p. 601)
National Woman's Party (p. 601)
Fourteen Points (p. 603)
League of Nations (p. 603)
Treaty of Versailles (p. 604)

## REVIEW QUESTIONS

**Answer these questions to demonstrate your understanding of the chapter's main ideas.**

1. Explain the steps by which the late-nineteenth-century U.S. government began to exert military influence in different regions of the world.
2. Compare and contrast the factors that influenced U.S. actions in Asia and in Latin America in this period.
3. What changes did U.S. participation in World War I bring about on the home front?
4. What arguments did U.S. political leaders make for and against ratification of the Versailles treaty?
5. Review the events listed under "America in the World" on the thematic timeline on page 581. By the end of World War I, what influence did the United States exercise in European affairs and in the Caribbean, Latin America, the Pacific, and China? How, and to what extent, had its power in each region expanded over the previous four decades? Compare and contrast the role of the United States to the roles of other powers in each region.

## CHRONOLOGY

**As you read, ask yourself why this chapter begins and ends with these dates and then identify the links among related events.**

| | |
|---|---|
| **1886** | • United States begins building modern battleships |
| **1892** | • U.S.-backed planters overthrow Hawaii's Queen Liliuokalani |
| **1895** | • United States arbitrates border dispute between Britain and Venezuela |
| | • Guerrilla war against Spanish rule begins in Cuba |

| | |
|---|---|
| **1898** | • War between United States and Spain |
| | • United States annexes Hawaii, Puerto Rico, and Guam |
| **1899–1902** | • U.S.-Philippine War, ending in U.S. occupation of Philippines |
| | • United States pursues open door policy in China |
| **1900** | • United States helps suppress nationalist rebellion in China ("Boxer Rebellion") |
| **1901** | • Hay-Pauncefote Treaty |
| **1902** | • Platt Amendment gives United States exclusive role in Cuba |
| **1903** | • United States recognizes Panama's independence from Colombia |
| **1905** | • Russo-Japanese War; Roosevelt mediates peace |
| **1908** | • Root-Takahira Agreement |
| **1914** | • Panama Canal opens |
| | • U.S. military action in Veracruz, Mexico |
| | • World War I begins in Europe |
| **1916** | • Jones Act commits United States to future Philippine independence |
| **1917** | • United States declares war on Germany and its allies, creates new agencies to mobilize economy and promote national unity |
| | • Espionage Act |
| **1918** | • Sedition Act |
| | • World War I ends |
| | • Beginning of two-year influenza pandemic that kills 50 million people worldwide |
| **1919** | • *Schenck v. United States* and *Abrams v. United States* |
| | • Wilson promotes Fourteen Points at Paris Peace Conference |
| | • Senate rejects the Treaty of Versailles |
| **1920** | • Nineteenth Amendment grants women suffrage |

# 21

# Unsettled Prosperity: From War to Depression

## 1919–1932

### IDENTIFY THE BIG IDEA

What conflicts in culture and politics arose in the 1920s, and how did economic developments in that decade help cause the Great Depression?

**FOR THE UNITED STATES, WORLD WAR I WAS NEITHER THE GHASTLY** and devastating experience that it was for Europe nor the profoundly disillusioning one it was in many other parts of the world. Yet the war years marked a crucial historical divide for Americans, and the country entered a distinctly new era after 1919. Progressivism flagged and gave way to a business-centered philosophy of government. The manufacturing economy surged and delivered a cornucopia of consumer goods to a grow-ing middle class. In the halls of government and in the streets, Americans clashed over what a pluralist, modern society should look like—who got to define what it meant to be "American"? In the complex and turbulent years between World War I and the coming of a new era of reform in 1933, these were the defining themes: limited government, consumerism, and cultural warfare.

In this decade and a half, economic growth and cultural conflict revealed patterns in American life that would hold for the remainder of the twentieth century. The nation had become urban. Mass media and Hollywood shaped popular culture. The automobile became an affordable mass commodity, even a necessity, changing forever the way people lived. Many Americans celebrated the dawning of what they called a "new era," defined by freer individual lifestyles, convenient consumer technologies, and "modern" ways of thinking. Others saw this emerging modernity as a threat to their own social and cultural influence. Groups of native-born, Protestant Americans, for instance, battled with immigrants to define the meaning of race, religion, and national belonging. Many white Americans lashed out at black Americans—in often deadly ways—over economic opportunity. And Catholic, Protestant, Jewish, and secular Americans clashed over everything from the prohibition of alcohol to the teaching of evolution.

By the end of the 1920s, political and cultural divides had hardened, and economic abundance proved short-lived, as the nation slid from consumer boom to Great Depression bust in 1929. The United States had grown more affluent, but it was an unsettled affluence. If the question in the decades of populist and progressive insurgent movements had been "whose government?" in the 1920s the question took on a broader cast: "whose country?"

# Resurgent Conservatism

World War I brought an end to the long period of reform stretching from the 1880s to the 1910s (Chapter 19). A resurgent political conservatism emerged in the war's aftermath. Progressivism survived, but limited government was the dominant motif of national political life from 1919 to the election of Franklin D. Roosevelt in 1932. In place of progressives' call for economic regulation, business priorities now came to the fore. President Calvin Coolidge declared, "The man who builds a factory builds a temple. The man who works there worships there." The same theme prevailed in continued U.S. foreign policy: American business needs were the top priority. The single year of 1919 set the tone for this resurgent conservatism. An antiradical Red Scare, a massive strike wave, and white violence against African Americans together roiled the country and slowed the pace of social change.

## The Red Scare

The war effort, overseen by a Democratic administration sympathetic to organized labor, had increased the size and power of labor unions. Membership in the American Federation of Labor (AFL) grew by a third during World War I, reaching more than 3 million by war's end. Workers' expectations also rose as the war economy brought higher pay and better working conditions. To extend these gains, in the first year after the armistice, 1919, more than 4 million wage laborers—one in every five—went on strike, a proportion never since equaled. A walkout of shipyard workers in Seattle sparked a general strike that shut down the entire city. Another strike disrupted the steel industry, as 350,000 workers demanded union recognition and an end to twelve-hour shifts. Most strikes were about basic economic issues—pay and hours—rather than revolution, but the bold exercise of worker power fueled dire warnings of rising radicalism from labor's opponents.

That same year, when the Soviet Union's new Bolshevik leaders founded the Third International with the intent to foster revolutions abroad, some Americans raised fears that the U.S. harbored dangerous radicals. Wartime hatred of Germans was replaced by hostility toward Bolsheviks (labeled "Reds," after the color of communist flags). In a telling example, Ole Hanson, Seattle's mayor during the general strike, wrote a book called *Americanism Versus Bolshevism* and toured the country lecturing about the threat of revolution. Under the banner of "one hundred percent Americanism," groups such as the newly formed American Legion decried socialists, communists, and the Industrial Workers of the World (IWW) as un-American. Ironically, American communists remained few in number and had little political influence. Of the 63 million adults in the United States in 1920, no more than 13,000 belonged to either the fledgling U.S. Communist Party or the Communist Labor Party.

The strike wave combined with anti-Bolshevism to create fertile conditions for repression. When alert postal workers discovered thirty-four mail bombs addressed to government officials in April 1919, and in June a bomb detonated outside the Washington town house of Attorney General A. Mitchell Palmer, the repression came. Palmer escaped unharmed, but he used the incident to fan public fears, precipitating a convulsive **Red Scare**. He set up an antiradicalism division in the Justice Department and appointed his assistant J. Edgar Hoover to direct it; in 1935, it became the Federal Bureau of Investigation (FBI). In November, Palmer's agents stormed the headquarters of radical organizations. The dragnet captured thousands

**Fear of "Bolshevism," 1919** This cartoon from the *Cleveland Plain Dealer* in Cleveland, Ohio, reflects nationwide panic over the general strike by 110 unions that paralyzed Seattle in February 1919. Opponents of radical labor unrest had a deeper fear: the Bolshevik Revolution in Russia, resulting in creation of the USSR, had brought into existence the world's first enduring communist state. By crushing unions in Seattle with a club of "Law and Order," this image suggests that Uncle Sam could beat back the global communist threat. This aspect of the 1919 Red Scare prefigured, at an early date, the anxieties of the Cold War era. Ohio Historical Society Red Dawn RD8A.

of immigrants who had committed no crimes but who held anarchist or revolutionary beliefs. Lacking the protection of U.S. citizenship, many were deported without indictment or trial. The **Palmer raids** peaked on a notorious night in January 1920, when federal agents invaded homes and meeting halls, arrested six thousand citizens and aliens (immigrants without U.S. citizenship), and denied the prisoners access to legal counsel.

The Red Scare's fusion of antiradicalism and anti-immigrant sentiment had dire consequences in the case of Sacco and Vanzetti. In May 1920, at the height of the Red Scare, police arrested Nicola Sacco, a shoemaker, and Bartolomeo Vanzetti, a fish peddler, for the murder of two men during a robbery of a shoe company in South Braintree, Massachusetts. Sacco and Vanzetti were Italian immigrants and self-proclaimed anarchists who had evaded the draft. Convicted of the murders, Sacco and Vanzetti sat in jail for six years while supporters appealed their verdicts. In 1927, Judge Webster Thayer denied a motion for a new trial and sentenced them to death. Scholars still debate their guilt or innocence. But the case was clearly biased by prosecutors' emphasis on their ties to radical groups and perhaps on their foreign birth. The execution of Sacco and Vanzetti was one of the ugly scars left by the hostilities of the Red Scare.

## Racial Backlash

Other forms of repression escalated during and after World War I. The Great Migration drew hundreds of thousands of African Americans from the South to northern and midwestern industrial cities, where they secured wartime jobs and found they could vote and use their new economic clout to build community institutions and work for racial justice. The arrival of these southern migrants during the war deepened existing racial tensions, as African Americans competed with whites—including recent immigrants from Europe—for jobs and scarce housing.

Racism turned such conflicts into violent confrontations during the war. One of the deadliest riots in American history occurred in 1917 in East St. Louis, Illinois, where rampaging whites burned more than 300 black homes and murdered between 50 and 150 black men, women, and children (the exact death toll remains unknown). "This is a crime against the laws of humanity," said Marcus Garvey, the influential black leader of the Universal Negro Improvement Association.

Tensions also increased after the war because African Americans emerged from the conflict determined to achieve citizenship rights. Millions had loyally supported the war effort, and 370,000 had served in uniform. Returning veterans, empowered by their military service, often refused to accept second-class treatment at the hands of whites, whether North or South. The black man, one observer wrote, "realized that he was part and parcel of the great army of democracy. . . . With this realization came the consciousness of pride in himself as a man, and an American citizen."

These developments sparked white violence. In what became known as **Red Summer** because of bloody battles in more than twenty-four cities, Chicago endured five days of rioting in July 1919 after white youths stoned a black teenager to death on a Lake Michigan beach. By September, the national death toll from racial violence that year reached 120. There were also 78 lynchings in 1919, up from 48 in 1917. That number included several murders of returning black soldiers in uniform.

Attacks on African Americans continued after 1919. The oil boomtown of Tulsa, Oklahoma, was the site of a horrific incident in June 1921. Sensational, false reports of an alleged rape helped incite white mobs who resented growing black prosperity. Anger focused on the 8,000 residents of Tulsa's prosperous Greenwood district, locally known as "the black Wall Street." The mobs—helped by National Guardsmen, who arrested African Americans who resisted—burned thirty-five blocks of Greenwood and killed several dozen people. The city's leading paper acknowledged that "semi-organized bands of white men systematically applied the torch, while others shot on sight men of color." It took a decade for black residents to rebuild Greenwood. And in the January 1923 Rosewood Massacre, mobs of furious whites in a small Florida town torched houses and hunted down African Americans, killing at least six. Police and state authorities refused to intervene, and the town of Rosewood vanished from the map.

## The Business of America

African Americans were not the only ones who faced challenges to their hard-won gains. So did labor unions. Following the strike wave of 1919, business leaders and their political allies fought back against organized labor, which entered a decade of decline. Across the country, employers advocated what they called the **American Plan** of employment—refusing to negotiate with unions. Facing a strike of Boston's police force, Massachusetts governor Calvin Coolidge illustrated this defiant approach by declaring, "There is no right to strike against the public safety by anybody, anywhere, anytime." A majority of the public supported the governor, and Republicans rewarded Coolidge by nominating him for the vice-presidency in 1920.

Decisions by the Supreme Court were an additional factor in organized labor's decline. In *Coronado Coal Company v. United Mine Workers of America* (1925), the Court ruled that a striking union could be penalized for illegal restraint of trade. Such decisions, along with the aggressive antiunion campaigns under the American Plan, caused membership in labor unions to fall from 5.1 million in 1920 to 3.6 million in 1929—just 10 percent of the nonagricultural workforce. Labor's long-sought goal of organizing the nation's workforce retreated further from realization.

In place of unions, the 1920s marked the heyday of **welfare capitalism**, a system of labor relations that stressed a company's responsibility for its employees' well-being. Employers hoped this would build a loyal workforce and head off labor unrest. Automaker Henry Ford, among others, pioneered this system before World War I, famously paying $5 a day. Ford also offered a profit-sharing plan to employees who met the standards of its Sociological Department, which investigated to ensure that workers' private lives met the company's moral standards. At a time when government unemployment compensation and Social Security did not exist, General Electric and U.S. Steel provided health insurance and old-age pensions. Other employers built athletic facilities and selectively offered paid vacations. Such plans covered only about 5 percent of the industrial workforce, however, and when faced with new financial pressures in the late 1920s, even Henry Ford cut back his $5 day. In the tangible benefits it offered workers, welfare capitalism had distinct limitations.

**Dollar Diplomacy**  American business interests shaped foreign affairs as well. The thrust of U.S. foreign policy after World War I continued to be in Latin America. There, under a policy initiated by Taft and continued under Wilson, presidents worked to advance U.S. business interests, especially by encouraging private banks to make foreign loans. Policymakers hoped loans would stimulate growth and increase demand for U.S. products in developing markets. Bankers, for their part, wanted government guarantees of repayment in countries they perceived as weak or unstable.

Officials provided such assurance. In 1922, for example, when American banks offered an immense loan to Bolivia (at a hefty profit), State Department officials pressured the South American nation to accept it. A similar arrangement was reached with El Salvador's government in 1923. In other cases, the United States intervened militarily, often to force repayment of debt. To implement such policies, the U.S. Marines occupied Nicaragua almost continuously from 1912 to 1933, the Dominican Republic from 1916 to 1924, and Haiti from 1915 to 1934. White Americans viewed these nations through demeaning racial stereotypes. They regarded Haitians as primitive savages or childlike people who needed U.S. guidance and supervision. One commander testified that his troops saw themselves as "trustees of a huge estate that belonged to minors. . . . The Haitians were our wards."

At home, critics denounced loan guarantees and military interventions as **dollar diplomacy**. The term was coined in 1924 by Samuel Guy Inman, a Disciples of Christ missionary who toured U.S.-occupied Haiti and the Dominican Republic. "The United States," Inman declared, "cannot go on destroying with impunity the sovereignty of other peoples, however weak." African American leaders also denounced the Haitian occupation. On behalf of the International Council of Women of the Darker Races and the Women's International League for Peace and Freedom, a delegation conducted a fact-finding tour of Haiti in 1926. Their report exposed, among other things, the sexual exploitation of Haitian women by U.S. soldiers.

Inman and other critics put dollar diplomacy on the defensive by the late 1920s. The poor results spoke for themselves. Loans got repaid, securing bankers' profits, but the proceeds often ended up in the pockets of local elites; U.S. policies failed to build broad-based prosperity overseas. Military intervention had even worse results. In Haiti, for example, the marines crushed peasant protests and helped the Haitian elite consolidate power. U.S. occupation thus contributed to the harsh dictatorships that Haitians endured through the rest of the twentieth century. President Franklin Roosevelt initiated the "Good Neighbor" policy with respect to Latin America in 1933 in an effort to reverse these ill effects.

Dollar diplomacy guided U.S. interests in Latin America, but behind the scenes many diplomats considered East Asia more critical to long-term American foreign policy. To ease growing tensions there, the United States signed a major treaty in 1922, known as the Four Powers Act, with Japan, Great Britain, and France, limiting naval strength in the Pacific. A diplomatic triumph for President Harding, the treaty failed to address underlying East-West international rivalries because it reinforced European and American naval superiority over Japan. That island nation would gradually come to see the United States, not the traditional European powers, as its principal adversary for dominance in Asia.

## Politics of Normalcy

The postwar conservative turn was particularly evident in national politics. With President Woodrow Wilson ailing from a stroke, in 1920 Democrats nominated Ohio governor James M. Cox for president, on a platform calling for U.S. participation in the League of Nations and continuation of Wilson's progressivism. Republicans, led by their probusiness wing, tapped genial Ohio senator Warren G. Harding. In a dig at Wilson's idealism, Harding promised "not nostrums but normalcy." On election day, he won in a landslide, beginning an era of Republican political dominance that lasted until 1932.

Harding's most energetic appointee was Secretary of Commerce Herbert Hoover, well known as head of the wartime Food Administration. Under Hoover's direction, the Commerce Department helped create two thousand trade associations representing companies in almost every major industry. Government officials worked closely with the associations, providing statistical research, suggesting industry-wide standards, and promoting stable prices and wages. Hoover hoped that through voluntary business cooperation with government — an **associated state** — he could achieve what progressives had sought through governmental regulation.

Other changes were afoot in Washington, D.C. The practice of lobbying Congress was a long-standing tradition among businesses, trade unions, and other organized interests. That practice grew in scale and became more formal and systematic in the 1920s. Noting the change, one observer joked that "the lobbyists were so thick they were constantly falling over one another." Hundreds of groups set up offices to lobby members of Congress — from religious and civic organizations to the Anti-Saloon League — but business took the lead. The National Association of Manufacturers, the Chamber of Commerce, and public utilities (water and electric companies), among many other business organizations, assumed an ever-larger role in the legislative process.

More malign links between government and corporate interests were soon revealed. When President Harding died suddenly of a heart attack in August 1923, evidence was just emerging that parts of his administration were riddled with corruption. The worst scandal concerned secret leasing of government oil reserves in **Teapot Dome**, Wyoming, and Elk Hills, California, to private companies. Secretary of the Interior Albert Fall was eventually convicted of taking over $300,000 in bribes and became the first cabinet officer in U.S. history to serve a prison sentence.

Vice President Calvin Coolidge became president upon Harding's death. He maintained Republican dominance, calling for limited government and tax cuts for business while campaigning for election in his own right in 1924. Rural and urban Democrats, deeply divided over such issues as prohibition and immigration restriction, deadlocked at their national convention; after 102 ballots, delegates finally nominated John W. Davis, a Wall Street lawyer. Coolidge easily defeated Davis and staved off a challenge from Senator Robert M. La Follette of Wisconsin, who tried to resuscitate the Progressive Party. The 1924 Progressive platform called for stronger government regulation at home and international efforts to reduce weapons production and prevent war. "Free men of every generation," La Follette had once declared in a speech, "must combat the renewed efforts of organized force and greed." In the end, Coolidge received 15.7 million votes to Davis's 8.4 million and La Follette's 4.9 million.

As the progressive reform ethos faded and a conservative impulse grew stronger, the formative period between 1919 and 1932 revealed important tendencies in national political life. Antiradicalism became more pervasive. Business and government became more cooperative. Lobbying surged as a feature of the legislative process. Each development would remain important throughout the remainder of the twentieth century.

| IN YOUR OWN WORDS | How and why did the United States take a conservative turn in the 1920s? |
|---|---|

# Making a Modern Consumer Economy

Spurred by rapid expansion during the war, and benefitting from earlier innovations in mass production such as the assembly line, American business thrived in the 1920s. Corporations expanded more and more into overseas markets, while at home a truly national consumer culture — emphasizing convenience, leisure, and fun — took shape. The years between 1922 and 1929 mark a crucial turning point in the emergence of a mass consumer economy in the United States.

## Postwar Abundance

Productivity proved to be the key. Manufacturing efficiencies accumulated since the turn of the century — the assembly line, mechanization, electrification — made possible enormous increases in productivity. If an American worker who made 6 toasters a day in 1920 fell asleep and woke up in 1929, she or he could now make 10 toasters a day — an incredible 66 percent more. Also, national per capita income rose an impressive 24 percent in that period. Productivity gains and rising incomes, especially among the middle class, meant an explosion of consumer goods. From toasters and radios to telephones, vacuum cleaners, and automobiles, a vast array of consumer products became more affordable. Americans bought them in droves, spurring an economic boom that lasted until the onset of the Great Depression in 1929.

Large-scale corporations continued to replace small business in many sectors of the economy. By 1929, through successive waves of consolidation, the two hundred largest businesses had come to control almost half of the country's nonbanking corporate wealth. The greatest number of mergers occurred in rising industries such as chemicals (with DuPont in the lead) and electrical appliances (General Electric), as well as among Wall Street banks. Aided by Washington's dollar diplomats, U.S. companies exercised growing global power. Seeking cheaper livestock, giant American meatpackers opened plants in Argentina; the United Fruit Company developed plantations in Costa Rica, Honduras, and Guatemala; General Electric set up production facilities in Latin America, Asia, and Australia.

Despite the boom, the U.S. economy had areas of significant weakness throughout the 1920s. Agriculture, which still employed one-fourth of all American workers, never fully recovered from the postwar recession. Once Europe's economy revived, its farmers flooded world markets with grain and other farm products, causing agricultural prices to fall. Other industries, including coal and textiles, languished for similar reasons. As a consequence, many rural Americans shared little of the decade's prosperity. The bottom 40 percent of American families earned an average annual income of only $725 (about $10,000 today). Many, especially rural tenants and sharecroppers, languished in poverty and malnutrition.

## Consumer Culture

In middle-class homes, Americans of the 1920s embraced a consumer ethos. They sat down to a breakfast of Kellogg's corn flakes before getting into Ford Model T's to work or shop at Safeway. On weekends, they might head to the local theater to see the newest Charlie Chaplin film. By 1929, electric refrigerators and vacuum cleaners came into use in affluent homes; 40 percent of American households owned a radio. The advertising industry reached new levels of ambition, entering what one historian calls the era of the "aggressive hard sell." The 1920s gave birth, for example, to fashion modeling and style consulting. "Sell them their dreams," one radio announcer urged advertisers in 1923. "People don't buy things to have things. . . . They buy hope—hope of what your merchandise will do for them."

Many poor and affluent families shared one thing in common: they stretched their incomes, small or large, through new forms of borrowing such as auto loans and installment plans. "Buy now, pay later," said the ads, and millions did. Anyone, no matter how rich, could get into debt, but **consumer credit** was particularly perilous for those living on the economic margins. In Chicago, one Lithuanian man described his neighbor's situation: "She ain't got no money. Sure she buys on credit, clothes for the children and everything." Such borrowing brought consumer merchandise within reach of more and more Americans, but the accumulated debt also turned out to be a factor in the bust of 1929.

**Hollywood**   Movies became a centerpiece of consumer culture. In the 1910s, the moviemaking industry had begun relocating to southern California to take advantage of cheap land, sunshine, and varied scenery within easy reach. The large studios—United Artists, Paramount, and Metro-Goldwyn-Mayer—were run mainly by Eastern European Jewish immigrants like Adolph Zukor, who arrived from Hungary in the 1880s. Starting with fur sales, Zukor and a partner then set up five-cent theaters in Manhattan. "I spent a good deal of time watching the faces of the audience," Zukor recalled. "With a little experience I could see, hear, and 'feel' the reaction to each melodrama and comedy." Founding Paramount Pictures, Zukor signed emerging stars and produced successful feature-length films.

By 1920, **Hollywood** reigned as the world's movie capital, producing nearly 90 percent of all films. Large, ornate movie palaces attracted both middle-class and working-class audiences. Idols such as Rudolph Valentino, Mary Pickford, and Douglas Fairbanks set national trends in style. Thousands of young women followed the lead of actress Clara Bow, Hollywood's famous **flapper**, who flaunted her boyish figure. Decked out in knee-length skirts, flappers shocked the older generation by smoking and wearing makeup. They represented only a tiny minority of women, but thanks to the movies and advertising, flappers became influential symbols of women's sexual and social emancipation. In cities, young immigrant women eagerly bought makeup and the latest flapper fashions. Jazz stars helped popularize the style among working-class African Americans. Mexican American teenagers joined the trend in major cities such as San Antonio and Los Angeles.

Politicians quickly grasped the publicity value of American radio and film to foreign relations. In 1919, with government support, General Electric spearheaded the creation of Radio Corporation of America (RCA) to expand U.S. presence in foreign radio markets. RCA — which had a federal appointee on its board of directors — emerged as a major provider of radio transmission in Latin America and East Asia. Meanwhile, by 1925, American films made up 95 percent of the movies screened in Britain, 80 percent in Latin America, and 70 percent in France. The United States was experimenting with what historians call **soft power** — the exercise of popular cultural influence — as radio and film exported the American standard of consumption to the world.

## The Automobile and Suburbanization

No possession proved more popular than the automobile, a showpiece of modern consumer capitalism that revolutionized American life. The Ford Motor Company introduced the first widely affordable automobile, the Model T, in 1908, but the industry experienced its most dramatic growth in the 1920s. Car sales played a major role in the decade's economic boom: in one year, 1929, Americans spent $2.58 billion on automobiles. By the end of the decade, they owned 26 million cars — about 80 percent of the world's automobiles — or an average of one for every five people (it was one for every forty in France). The number of cars on American roads tripled in ten years.

The auto industry's exuberant expansion rippled through the economy. It stimulated steel, petroleum, chemical, rubber, and glass production and, directly or indirectly, created 3.7 million jobs. Highway construction became a billion-dollar-a-year enterprise, financed by federal subsidies and state gasoline taxes. Car ownership spurred urban sprawl and, in 1924, the first suburban shopping center: Country Club Plaza outside Kansas City, Missouri. But cars were expensive, and most Americans bought them on credit. Alfred Sloan, the president of General Motors and Henry Ford's primary competitor, founded the first national consumer credit agency to help Americans buy more Chevrolets. Other car companies followed. Amid the boom of the 1920s, few worried whether purchasing such expensive items on credit was a good idea. When asked why her family purchased a car before installing indoor plumbing, one woman replied simply, "Why, you can't go to town in a bathtub."

Cars changed the way Americans spent their leisure time, as proud drivers took their machines on the road. An infrastructure of gas stations, motels, and drive-in restaurants soon catered to drivers. Railroad travel faltered. The American Automobile Association, founded in 1902, estimated that by 1929 almost a third of the population took vacations by car. "I had a few days after I got my wheat cut," reported one Kansas farmer, "so I just loaded my family . . . and lit out." An elite Californian complained that automobile travel was no longer "aristocratic." "The clerks and their wives and sweethearts," observed a reporter, "driving through the Wisconsin lake country, camping at Niagara, scattering tin cans and pop bottles over the Rockies, made those places taboo for bankers."

Rising middle-class incomes, new forms of borrowing, and the automobile combined powerfully in the 1920s to produce a major suburban housing boom. Cars were key. The nineteenth-century "streetcar suburbs" allowed the nation's affluent to live outside central cities, but in communities narrowly built along the tracks. After World War I, automobile suburbs grew like the crabgrass of suburban lawns — fast and everywhere. "Cities are spreading out," *National Geographic* announced in a 1923 special feature. Long Island's Nassau County, a major suburb of New York City, tripled in population, and the fifteen fastest-growing towns in Connecticut were all suburbs.

Spreading out happened everywhere — from New York to Chicago, St. Louis to Seattle — but the growth of Los Angeles epitomized the new role of automobiles in American cities. Housing subdivisions opened monthly across a vast expanse of southern California, and the automobile gave birth to an explosive metropolis. Its population more than doubled in the 1920s alone, and Los Angeles went from the tenth largest American city to the fifth in just ten years. Southern California became identified with what historians call "automobility," and Los Angeles led the way in defining American car culture.

| IN YOUR OWN WORDS | What were the primary characteristics of the American economy in the 1920s? |
| --- | --- |

# The Politics and Culture of a Diversifying Nation

At the dawn of the 1920s, public life in the United States had grown immeasurably more diverse. Women could now vote. More than 24 million immigrants — hailing primarily from Europe but also from Latin America and East Asia — called the country home. They spoke different languages, practiced a variety of religions, and followed unique cultural traditions. The Great Migration brought more than one million African Americans from all parts of the South to northern cities such as Chicago, New York, and Philadelphia. Cities grew at the expense of rural areas. Such dramatic changes led to social tensions and pronounced conflict over how the nation would be defined.

## Women in a New Age

At the start of the 1920s, many progressives hoped the attainment of women's voting rights would offer new leverage to tackle poverty. They created organizations like the Women's Joint Congressional Committee, a Washington-based advocacy group. The committee's greatest accomplishment was the first federally funded health-care legislation, the **Sheppard-Towner Federal Maternity and Infancy Act** (1921). Sheppard-Towner provided federal funds for medical clinics, prenatal education programs, and visiting nurses, improving health care for the poor and significantly lowering infant mortality rates. It also marked the first time that Congress designated federal funds for the states to encourage them to administer a social-welfare program. But other reforms stalled, and the decade proved not to be a watershed of welfare legislation.

Other activist women focused on securing legal equality with men. In 1923, Alice Paul, founder of the National Woman's Party, persuaded congressional allies to consider an Equal Rights Amendment (ERA) to the U.S. Constitution. It stated simply that "men and women shall have equal rights throughout the United States." Advocates were hopeful; Wisconsin had passed a similar law two years earlier, and it helped women fight gender discrimination. But opponents pointed out that the ERA would threaten recent labor laws that protected women from workplace abuses. Such laws recognized women's vulnerable place in a heavily sex-segregated labor market. Would a theoretical statement of "equality" help poor and working women more than existing protections did? This question divided women's rights advocates. Introduced repeatedly in Congress over the next five decades, the ERA was debated again and again until the bitter ratification struggle of the 1970s (Chapter 28).

**African American Women**   African American women had distinct priorities. Groups such as the National Association of Colored Women (NACW) fought for suffrage in the 1910s, just as white women had. But the constitutional right of black women to vote was meaningless in the South, where disfranchisement was law. Black women sought racial, not just gender, equality. When Addie Hunton, field secretary of the National Association for the Advancement of Colored People, and sixty black women from the NACW urged the National Woman's Party to take up their cause, Paul refused, declaring disfranchisement to be a racial not a gender injustice. Hunton countered that "five million women in the United States cannot be denied their rights without all women of the United States feeling the effect of that denial. No women are free until all women are free."

Other challenges remained. Women proved to be effective lobbyists for a variety of causes, but the Republican and Democratic parties endured as largely male domains. Finding that women did not vote as a bloc, politicians in both parties began to accord their votes less weight. New reforms failed to gain support, and others were rolled back. Many congressmen, for example, had supported the Sheppard-Towner Act because they feared the voting power of women, but Congress ended the program in the late 1920s.

**New Woman**   Magazines, advertisements, and Hollywood movies crafted an idealized image of the American "new woman" in the 1920s. She had thrown off Victorian modesty and claimed a place for herself alongside men in a new culture of consumption and fun. Such images, used primarily to sell products to the middle class, exaggerated reality. But that did not mean women's lives remained unchanged. The nineteenth-century notion of separate spheres for men and women had eroded considerably by 1930. More women attended college than ever before. Female athletes such as the golfer Glenna Collett, adventurers such as the celebrated pilot Amelia Earhart, and performers such as the brilliant jazz singer Josephine Baker carved out new, more liberated roles for women in public life.

Social change takes time, however, and for the majority of American women in the 1920s ordinary life was far less glamorous. In some professions, such as medicine, women actually declined as a percentage of the workforce: only 3 percent of lawyers and 4 percent of physicians were women in the decade. Women's wages lagged far behind those of men, and women remained confined to strictly gendered occupations: sales clerks in the new department stores, secretaries in the growing corporate world, and low-paid assembly-line workers in industry, alongside their traditional roles as domestic servants. African American and Latino women could not even get jobs as clerks and secretaries. Thus although American women in this era, especially the young, left behind the Victorian prescriptions of feminine modesty and confinement to a female-only separate sphere, they had yet to fully transform women's second-class standing.

## Culture Wars

By 1929, ninety-three U.S. cities had populations of more than 100,000. New York City's population exceeded 7 million; Los Angeles's had exploded to 1.2 million. The 1920 census marked the first time there were more urban than rural Americans. The lives and beliefs of urban Americans, however, often differed dramatically from those in small towns and farming areas. One sharp critic, the writer Sinclair Lewis, wrote three satirical novels—*Main Street* (1920), *Babbitt* (1922), and *Elmer Gantry* (1927)—that mocked small-town life for its religiosity and, as Lewis saw it, hypocrisy and lack of sophistication.

In a decade of conflict between traditional and modern worldviews, the urban-rural split embodied by Lewis represented one line of conflict among many. Others that came to the fore included Protestant versus Catholic and Jewish; religious versus secular; native born versus immigrant; and white versus black. A series of cultural battles in the 1920s revealed a stark conflict over the kinds of values, beliefs, and even people deemed "American."

**Prohibition**    Rural and native-born Protestants started the decade with the achievement of a longtime goal: national prohibition of liquor (Chapter 17). The two principal antialcohol organizations, the Woman's Christian Temperance Union and the Anti-Saloon League, had long hailed temperance as good for health and Christian virtue. In the 1910s, some progressives joined the campaign, convinced that alcohol kept immigrant workers in poverty and the saloon was a source of political corruption. World War I, too, spurred the cause. Mobilizing the economy for war, Congress limited brewers' and distillers' use of barley and other scarce grains, causing consumption to decline. Moreover, anti-German hysteria identified the many German breweries in American cities, like Pabst and Anheuser-Busch, with the wartime enemy. The decades-long prohibition campaign culminated with Congress's passage of the **Eighteenth Amendment** in 1917. Ratified over the next two years by nearly every state and taking effect in January 1920, the amendment prohibited "manufacture, sale, or transportation of intoxicating liquors" anywhere in the United States. It was enforced by the federal government under the 1920 **Volstead Act**.

Defenders of prohibition, especially native-born Protestants in small towns, celebrated prohibition as a victory over sin and vice. In urban areas, though, thousands flagrantly ignored the law, many mocking prohibition as old-fashioned Puritanism. Patrons flocked to urban speakeasies, or illegal drinking sites, which flourished in almost every major city; one raid on a Chicago speakeasy yielded 200,000 gallons of alcohol. Profits from the secret clubs enriched notorious gangsters such as Chicago's Al Capone and New York's Jack Diamond. Immigrants saw prohibition as an attack on the working-class saloon and also resisted the ban, but as the price of alcohol soared on the illegal market it often proved out of reach for the laboring classes.

Prohibition's most ardent supporters were native-born, small-town Protestants, and its greatest opponents were middle-class urbanites and immigrants.

The national ban on alcohol was a prolonged social experiment that fizzled. Alcohol consumption declined in 1921 and 1922 but then began climbing again—though it did not reach pre-1920 levels until after repeal in 1933. Among the middle class, which could afford higher prices, alcohol consumption declined hardly at all in these years. The fact that only the *sale* and not the *possession* of alcohol was illegal made prohibition exceedingly difficult to enforce. And yet the Eighteenth Amendment's most important legacy might well have been the growing influence of the Federal Bureau of Investigation (FBI), the federal agency tasked with enforcing the Volstead Act. Under the shrewd direction of J. Edgar Hoover, the FBI used the Red Scare and prohibition to increase its resources, enlarge its investigative domain, and become a fixture of federal police power. Difficult to enforce, associated with organized crime, and increasingly politically unpopular, prohibition was repealed in 1933.

**Evolution in the Schools**　In another episode of the clash between modern and traditionalist worldviews, controversy erupted as fundamentalist Protestants sought to mandate school curricula based on the biblical account of creation. In 1925, Tennessee's legislature outlawed the teaching of "any theory that denies the story of the Divine creation of man as taught in the Bible, [and teaches] instead that man has descended from a lower order of animals." The **American Civil Liberties Union** (ACLU), formed during the Red Scare to protect free speech rights, challenged the law's constitutionality. The ACLU intervened in the trial of John T. Scopes, a high school biology teacher who taught the theory of evolution to his class and faced a jail sentence for doing so. The case attracted national attention because Clarence Darrow, a famous criminal lawyer, defended Scopes, while William Jennings Bryan, the three-time Democratic presidential candidate, spoke for the prosecution.

Journalists dubbed the **Scopes trial** "the monkey trial." This label referred both to Darwin's argument that human beings and other primates share a common ancestor and to the circus atmosphere at the trial, which was broadcast live over a Chicago radio station. (Proving that urbanites had their own prejudices, acerbic critic H. L. Mencken dismissed antievolutionists as "gaping primates of the upland valleys," implying that they had not evolved.) The jury took only eight minutes to deliver its verdict: guilty. Though the Tennessee Supreme Court later overturned Scopes's conviction, the law remained on the books for more than thirty years.

**Nativism**　Some native-born Protestants pointed to immigration as the primary cause of what they saw as America's moral decline. A nation of 105 million people had added more than 24 million immigrants over the previous four decades; the newcomers included many Catholics and Jews from Southern and Eastern Europe, whom one Maryland congressman referred to as "indigestible lumps" in the "national stomach." Such attitudes recalled hostility toward Irish and Germans in the 1840s and 1850s. In this case, they fueled a momentous shift in immigration policy.

"America must be kept American," President Coolidge declared in 1924. Congress had banned Chinese immigration in 1882, and Theodore Roosevelt had negotiated a so-called gentleman's agreement that limited Japanese immigration in 1907. Now nativists charged that there were also too many European arrivals, some of whom, they claimed, undermined Protestantism and imported anarchism, socialism, and other radical doctrines. Responding to this pressure, Congress passed emergency immigration restrictions in 1921 and a permanent measure three years later. The **National Origins Act** (1924) used backdated census data to establish a baseline: in the future, annual immigration from each country could not exceed 2 percent of that nationality's percentage of the U.S. population as it had stood in 1890. Since only small numbers of Italians, Greeks, Poles, Russians, and other Southern and Eastern European immigrants had arrived before 1890, the law drastically limited immigration from those places. In 1929, Congress imposed even more restrictive quotas, setting a cap of 150,000 immigrants per year from Europe and continuing to ban most immigrants from Asia.

The new law, however, permitted unrestricted immigration from the Western Hemisphere. As a result, Latin Americans arrived in increasing numbers, finding jobs that had gone to other immigrants before exclusion. More than 1 million Mexicans entered the United States between 1900 and 1930, including many fleeing the instability caused by the Mexican Revolution. Nativists lobbied Congress to cut this flow; so did labor leaders, who argued that impoverished migrants lowered wages for other American workers. But Congress heeded the pleas of employers, especially farmers in Texas and California, who wanted cheap labor.

Other anti-immigrant measures emerged at the state level. In 1913, by an overwhelming majority, California's legislature had passed a law declaring that "aliens ineligible to citizenship" could not own "real property." The aim was to prevent

**The U.S. Border Patrol, Laredo, Texas, 1926** In 1926, San Antonio photographer Eugene O. Goldbeck took this photograph of U.S. Border Patrol officers in Laredo. Since 1917, Mexicans, like other immigrants, had been subject to a head tax and literacy test. The U.S. government had not enforced these provisions, however, because of pressure from southwestern employers eager for cheap Mexican labor. Following passage of the National Origins Act in 1924, the United States established the Border Patrol. Its increasing efforts to police the border slowed the casual movement of Mexican workers in and out of the United States. Why do you think the Border Patrol posed in this way for Goldbeck's picture? Notice that some of the officers depicted here were dressed as civilians. What might this signify? Photography Collection, Harry Ransom Center, The University of Texas at Austin.

Asians, especially Japanese immigrants, from owning land, though some had lived in the state for decades and built up prosperous farms. In the wake of World War I, California tightened these laws, making it increasingly difficult for Asian families to establish themselves. California, Washington, and Hawaii also severely restricted any school that taught Japanese language, history, or culture. Denied both citizenship and land rights, Japanese Americans would be in a vulnerable position at the outbreak of World War II, when anti-Japanese hysteria swept the United States.

**The National Klan**    The 1920s brought a nationwide resurgence of the **Ku Klux Klan** (KKK), the white supremacist group formed in the post–Civil War South. Soon after the premiere of *Birth of a Nation* (1915), a popular film glorifying the Reconstruction-era Klan, a group of southerners gathered on Georgia's Stone Mountain to revive the organization. With its blunt motto, "Native, white, Protestant supremacy," the Klan recruited supporters across the country. KKK members did not limit their harassment to African Americans but targeted immigrants, Catholics, and Jews as well, with physical intimidation, arson, and economic boycotts.

At the height of its influence in the early 1920s, the Klan counted more than 3 million members and wielded considerable political clout, particularly at the local level. A typical example was the small town of Monticello, Arkansas, where in the first half of the decade the mayor, city marshall, half the city council, the sheriff, the county clerk, tax assessor, and treasurer, and eleven of fifteen male teachers were all Klan members. From small-town mayors to President Woodrow Wilson, who effusively praised *Birth of a Nation*, the Klan enjoyed broad support among native-born white Protestant Americans for a decade. Klan activism lent a menacing cast to political issues, as its members defined "one hundred percent Americanism" to include white racial purity, Protestantism, prohibition of alcohol, conservative sexual mores, and immigration restriction—the Klan avidly supported both the Eighteenth Amendment and the Immigration Act of 1924.

The Klan declined rapidly after 1925, but its rise was part of an ugly trend that began before World War I and extended into subsequent decades. The rise of the national Klan helped prepare the way for white supremacist movements of the 1930s, such as the Los Angeles–based Silver Legion, a fringe paramilitary group aligned with Hitler's Nazis. Far more influential were major figures such as industrialist Henry Ford, whose *Dearborn Independent* railed against immigrants and warned that members of "the proud Gentile race" must arm themselves against a Jewish conspiracy aimed at world domination. Challenged by critics, Ford issued an apology in 1927 and admitted that his allegations had been based on "gross forgeries." But with his paper's editorials widely circulated by the Klan and other groups, considerable long-term damage had been done.

**The Election of 1928**    Conflicts over race, religion, and ethnicity created the climate for a stormy presidential election in 1928. Democrats had traditionally drawn strength from white voters in the South and immigrants in the North: groups that divided over prohibition, immigration restriction, and the Klan. By 1928, the northern urban wing gained firm control. Democrats nominated Governor Al Smith of New York, the first presidential candidate to reflect the aspirations of the urban working class. A grandson of Irish peasants, Smith had risen through New York

City's Democratic machine to become a dynamic reformer. But he offended many small-town and rural Americans with his heavy New York accent and brown derby hat, which highlighted his ethnic working-class origins. Middle-class reformers questioned his ties to Tammany Hall; temperance advocates opposed him as a "wet." But the governor's greatest handicap was his religion. Although Smith insisted that his Catholic beliefs would not affect his duties as president, many Protestants opposed him. "No Governor can kiss the papal ring and get within gunshot of the White House," vowed one Methodist bishop.

Smith proved no match for the Republican nominee, Secretary of Commerce Herbert Hoover, who embodied the technological promise of the modern age. An organizational genius and a dedicated public servant, Hoover won fame during World War I for successfully managing huge food relief and refugee projects before energizing and reorganizing the Treasury Department as secretary of commerce under President Harding. Riding on eight years of Republican prosperity, Hoover credited business with the country's rising affluence and embraced, updated for a more technocratic age, the American tradition of individualism. He won overwhelmingly, with 444 electoral votes to Smith's 87 (Map 21.1). Because many southern Protestants refused to vote for a Catholic, Hoover carried five ex-Confederate states, breaking the Democratic "Solid South" for the first time since Reconstruction. Smith, though,

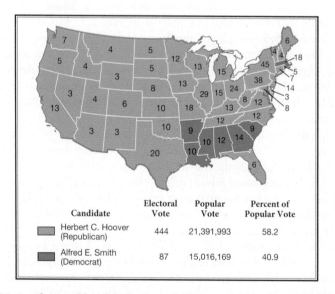

| Candidate | Electoral Vote | Popular Vote | Percent of Popular Vote |
|---|---|---|---|
| Herbert C. Hoover (Republican) | 444 | 21,391,993 | 58.2 |
| Alfred E. Smith (Democrat) | 87 | 15,016,169 | 40.9 |

**MAP 21.1    The Presidential Election of 1928**

Historians still debate the extent to which 1928 was a critical election—an election that produced a significant realignment in voting behavior. Although Republican Herbert Hoover swept the popular and the electoral votes, Democrat Alfred E. Smith won majorities not only in the South, his party's traditional stronghold, but also in Rhode Island, Massachusetts, and (although it is not evident on this map) all of the large cities of the North and Midwest. In subsequent elections, the Democrats won even more votes among African Americans and European ethnic groups and, until 1980, were the nation's dominant political party.

carried industrialized Massachusetts and Rhode Island as well as the nation's twelve largest cities, suggesting that urban voters were moving into the Democrats' camp.

## The Harlem Renaissance

Amidst these clashes over religion, morality, and Americanism, black artists and intellectuals claimed a voice for themselves. They questioned long-standing assumptions about civilization, progress, and the alleged superiority of Western cultures over so-called primitive people. Based in New York City, where the Great Migration had tripled the black population in the decade after 1910 (Map 21.2), a vibrant new black cultural movement took shape. Harlem stood as "the symbol of liberty and the Promised Land to Negroes everywhere," as one minister put it. Talented African Americans flocked to the district, where they created bold new art forms and asserted ties to Africa.

**Black Writers and Artists**    Poet Langston Hughes captured the upbeat spirit of the **Harlem Renaissance** when he asserted, "I am a Negro — and beautiful." Other writers and artists also championed race pride. Claude McKay and Jean Toomer represented in fiction what philosopher Alain Locke called, in an influential 1925 book, the "New Negro." Painter Jacob Lawrence, who had grown up in crowded tenement districts of the urban North, used bold shapes and vivid colors to portray the daily life, aspirations, and suppressed anger of African Americans.

**Augusta Fells Savage, African American Sculptor**  Born in Florida in 1892, Augusta Fells Savage arrived in New York in 1921 to study and remained to take part in the Harlem Renaissance. Widowed at a young age and struggling to support her parents and young daughter, Savage faced both racism and poverty. Much of her work has been lost because she sculpted in clay and could not afford to cast in bronze. Savage began to speak out for racial justice after she was denied, on the basis of her race, a fellowship to study in Paris. In 1923, she married a close associate of UNIA leader Marcus Garvey.  Augusta Savage with her sculpture *Realization*, c. 1938/Andrew Herman, photographer. Federal Art Project, Photographic Division collection, c. 1920–1965, bulk 1935–1942. Archives of American Art, Smithsonian Institution.

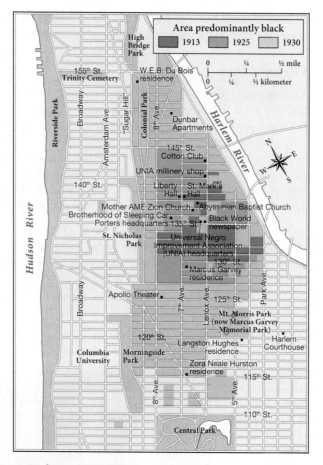

**MAP 21.2   Harlem, 1913–1930**

African Americans had lived in New York City since its founding in 1624 as part of the Dutch settlement of New Amsterdam. A small number lived in Harlem, in the northern part of Manhattan Island until the early 1900s. Then in 1904, a subway line connecting 145th Street in Harlem to lower Manhattan and Brooklyn opened, and black tenants and homeowners began to come in larger numbers. During and after World War I, large numbers of southern migrants joined established black families there, bringing with them the food, music, and folkways of the South, and Harlem increasingly became a center of black life in New York City. By 1930, 165,000 African Americans, almost 75 percent of Manhattan's black population, were concentrated in Harlem.

No one embodied the energy and optimism of the Harlem Renaissance more than Zora Neale Hurston. Born in the prosperous black community of Eatonville, Florida, Hurston had been surrounded as a child by examples of achievement, though she struggled later with poverty and isolation. In contrast to some other black thinkers, Hurston believed African American culture could be understood without heavy emphasis on the impact of white oppression. After enrolling at Barnard College and studying with anthropologist Franz Boas, Hurston traveled through the South and the Caribbean for a decade, documenting folklore, songs, and religious beliefs. She incorporated this material into her short stories and novels, celebrating the humor and spiritual strength of ordinary black men and women. Like other work of the Harlem Renaissance, Hurston's stories and novels sought to articulate what it meant, as black intellectual W. E. B. Du Bois wrote, "to be both a Negro and an American."

**Jazz**　To millions of Americans, the most famous product of the Harlem Renaissance was **jazz**. Though the origins of the word are unclear, many historians believe it was a slang term for sex — an etymology that makes sense, given the music's early association with urban vice districts. As a musical form, jazz coalesced in New Orleans and other parts of the South before World War I. Borrowing from blues, ragtime, and other popular forms, jazz musicians developed an ensemble style in which performers, keeping a rapid ragtime beat, improvised around a basic melodic line. The majority of early jazz musicians were black, but white performers, some of whom had more formal training, injected elements of European concert music.

In the 1920s, as jazz spread nationwide, musicians developed its signature mode, the improvised solo. The key figure in this development was trumpeter Louis Armstrong. A native of New Orleans, Armstrong learned his craft playing in the saloons and brothels of the city's vice district. Like tens of thousands of other African Americans, he moved north, settling in Chicago in 1922. Armstrong showed an inexhaustible capacity for melodic invention, and his dazzling solos inspired other musicians. By the late 1920s, soloists became the celebrities of jazz, thrilling audiences with their improvisational skill.

As jazz spread, it followed the routes of the Great Migration from the South to northern and midwestern cities, where it met consumers primed to receive it. Most cities had plentiful dance halls where jazz could be featured. Radio also helped popularize jazz, with the emerging record industry marketing the latest tunes. As white listeners flocked to ballrooms and clubs to hear Duke Ellington and other stars, Harlem became the hub of this commercially lucrative jazz. Those who hailed "primitive" black music, however, rarely suspended their racial condescension: visiting a mixed-race club became known as "slumming."

The recording industry soon developed so-called race records specifically aimed at urban working-class African Americans. The breakthrough came in 1920, when Otto K. E. Heinemann, a producer who sold immigrant records in Yiddish, Swedish, and other languages, recorded singer Mamie Smith performing "Crazy Blues." This smash hit prompted big recording labels like Columbia and Paramount to copy Heinemann's approach. Yet, while its marketing reflected the segregation of American society, jazz brought black music to the center stage of American culture. It became the era's signature music, so much so that novelist F. Scott Fitzgerald dubbed the 1920s the "Jazz Age."

**Marcus Garvey and the UNIA**　Harlem's creative energy generated broad political aspirations. The Harlem-based **Universal Negro Improvement Association** (UNIA), led by charismatic Jamaican-born Marcus Garvey, arose in the 1920s to mobilize African American workers and champion black nationalism. Garvey urged followers to move to Africa, arguing that people of African descent would never be treated justly in white-run countries.

The UNIA soon claimed 4 million followers, including many recent migrants to northern cities. It published a newspaper, *Negro World*, and solicited funds for the Black Star steamship company, which Garvey created as an enterprise that would foster trade with the West Indies and carry black Americans to Africa. But the UNIA declined as quickly as it had risen. In 1925, Garvey was imprisoned for mail fraud because of his solicitations for the Black Star Line. President Coolidge commuted his sentence but ordered his deportation to Jamaica. Without Garvey's leadership, the movement collapsed.

However, the UNIA left a legacy of activism, especially among the working class. Garvey and his followers represented an emerging **pan-Africanism**. They argued that people of African descent, in all parts of the world, had a common destiny and should cooperate in political action. Several developments contributed to this ideal: black men's military service in Europe during World War I, the Pan-African Congress that had sought representation at the Versailles treaty table, and protests against U.S. occupation of Haiti. One African American historian wrote in 1927, "The grandiose schemes of Marcus Garvey gave to the race a consciousness such as it had never possessed before. The dream of a united Africa, not less than a trip to France, challenged the imagination."

| IN YOUR OWN WORDS | What were the main causes of cultural conflict in the 1920s? |
|---|---|

## The Coming of the Great Depression

By 1927, strains on the economy showed that the mass consumer society that had emerged after World War I was in trouble. Americans of all sorts were overleveraged—that is, sinking in debt. Consumer lending had become the tenth largest business in the country, topping $7 billion that year. Millions of farmers were, like their nineteenth-century forebears, trapped in an annual cycle of debt. Increasing numbers of Americans bought into the stock market, often with borrowed money ("on margin") and usually with unrealistic expectations. An investor might, for example, spend $20 of his own money and borrow $80 to buy a $100 share of stock, expecting to pay back the loan as the stock rose quickly in value. This worked as long as the economy grew and the stock market climbed.

But those conditions did not last. Americans who worried over the rapid economic growth and easy credit that fueled the Roaring Twenties proved right: the "Roar" ended in the Great Depression. Taking into account the recession of 1921, the economic boom lasted only a brief seven years, from 1922 to 1929.

### From Boom to Bust

When the stock market fell, in a series of plunges between October 25 and November 13, 1929, few onlookers understood the magnitude of the crisis. Cyclical downturns had been a familiar part of the industrializing economy since the panic of the

1830s; they tended to follow periods of rapid growth and speculation. The market rose again in late 1929 and early 1930, and while a great deal of money had been lost, most Americans hoped the aftermath of the crash would be brief. In fact, the nation had entered the Great Depression, the most severe economic downturn to that point in the nation's history. Over the next four years, industrial production fell 37 percent. Construction plunged 78 percent. Prices for crops and other raw materials, already low, fell by half. By 1932, unemployment had reached a staggering 24 percent (Figure 21.1).

A precipitous drop in consumer spending deepened the crisis. Facing hard times and unemployment, Americans cut back dramatically, creating a vicious cycle of falling demand and forfeited loans. If buying homes, cars, and appliances on credit seemed like a good deal in 1925, by 1930 the deal turned sour. That year, several major banks went under, victims of overextended credit and reckless management. The following year, as industrial production slowed, a much larger wave of bank failures occurred, causing an even greater shock. Since the government did not insure bank deposits, accounts in failed banks simply vanished. Some people who had had steady jobs and comfortable savings found themselves broke and out of work.

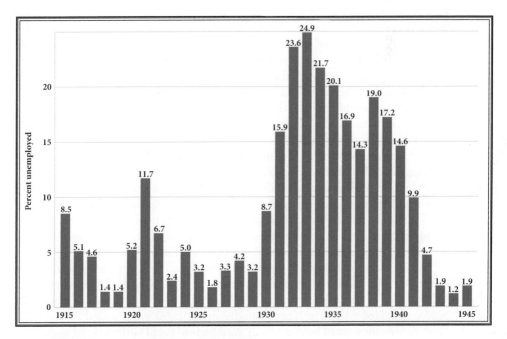

**FIGURE 21.1 Unemployment, 1915–1945**
During the 1920s, business prosperity and low rates of immigration resulted in historically low unemployment levels. The Great Depression threw millions of people out of work; by 1933, one in four American workers was unemployed, and the rate remained high until 1941, when the nation mobilized for World War II.

## Early Depression Years

Not all Americans were devastated by the depression; the middle class did not disappear and the rich lived in accustomed luxury. But incomes plummeted even among workers who kept their jobs. Salt Lake City went bankrupt in 1931. Barter systems developed, as barbers traded haircuts for onions and potatoes and laborers worked for payment in eggs or pork. "We do not dare to use even a little soap," reported one jobless Oregonian, "when it will pay for an extra egg, a few more carrots for our children." "I would be only too glad to dig ditches to keep my family from going hungry," wrote a North Carolina man.

Where did desperate people turn for aid? Their first hope lay in private charity, especially churches and synagogues. But by the winter of 1931, these institutions were overwhelmed, unable to keep pace with the extraordinary need. Only eight states provided even minimal unemployment insurance. There was no public support for the elderly, statistically among the poorest citizens. Few Americans had any retirement savings, and many who had saved watched their accounts erased by failing banks.

Even those who were not wiped out had to adapt to depression conditions. Couples delayed marriage and reduced the number of children they conceived. As a result, the marriage rate fell to a historical low, and by 1933 the birthrate dropped from 97 births per 1,000 women to 75. Often the responsibility for birth control fell to women. It was "one of the worst problems of women whose husbands were out of work," a Californian told a reporter. Campaigns against hiring married women were common, on the theory that available jobs should go to male breadwinners. Three-quarters of the nation's school districts banned married women from working as teachers—ignoring the fact that many husbands were less able to earn than ever before. Despite restrictions, female employment increased, as women expanded their financial contributions to their families in hard times.

The depression crossed regional boundaries, though its severity varied from place to place. Bank failures clustered heavily in the Midwest and plains, while areas dependent on timber, mining, and other extractive industries suffered catastrophic declines. Although southern states endured less unemployment because of their smaller manufacturing base, farm wages plunged. In many parts of the country, unemployment rates among black men stood at double that of white men; joblessness among African American women was triple that of white women.

By 1932, comprehending the magnitude of the crisis, Americans went to the ballot box and decisively rejected the probusiness, antiregulatory policies of the 1920s. A few years earlier, with business booming, politics had been so placid that people chuckled when President Coolidge disappeared on extended fishing trips. Now, Americans wanted bold action in Washington. Faced with the cataclysm of the Great Depression, Americans would transform their government and create a modern welfare state.

| IN YOUR OWN WORDS | What domestic economic factors helped cause the Great Depression? |

# Summary

Involvement in World War I strengthened the United States economically and diplomatically, but it left the nation profoundly unsettled. Racial tensions exploded after the war as African Americans pursued new opportunities and asserted their rights. Meanwhile, labor unrest grew as employers cut wages and sought to break unions, while anxieties over radicalism and immigration prompted a nationwide Red Scare.

The politics of the 1920s brought a backlash against prewar progressivism and a series of clashes over religion, morality, and national belonging. The agenda of women reformers met very limited success. Republican administrations pursued pro-business "normalcy" at home and "dollar diplomacy" abroad. Prohibition and the Scopes trial demonstrated the influence religion could exert on public policy, while rising nativism fueled a resurgent Ku Klux Klan and led to sweeping new restrictions on immigration. Meanwhile, black artists and intellectuals of the Harlem Renaissance, including many inspired by pan-African ideas, explored the complexities of African American life.

Business thrived and a booming consumer culture, exemplified by the radio, the automobile, and Hollywood films, created new forms of leisure, influencing daily life and challenging older sexual norms. However, the risky speculation and easy credit of the 1920s undermined the foundations of the economy. After the 1929 crash, these factors, along with a range of interconnected global conditions to be discussed in Chapter 22, plunged the United States into the Great Depression.

## Chapter 21 Review

### KEY TERMS

**Identify and explain the significance of each term below.**

Red Scare (p. 612)

Palmer raids (p. 613)

Red Summer (p. 613)

American Plan (p. 614)

welfare capitalism (p. 614)

dollar diplomacy (p. 615)

associated state (p. 616)

Teapot Dome (p. 616)

consumer credit (p. 618)

Hollywood (p. 618)

flapper (p. 618)

soft power (p. 619)

Sheppard-Towner Federal
   Maternity and Infancy Act
   (p. 620)

Eighteenth Amendment (p. 622)

Volstead Act (p. 622)

American Civil Liberties Union
   (p. 623)

Scopes trial (p. 623)

National Origins Act (p. 624)

Ku Klux Klan (p. 625)

Harlem Renaissance (p. 627)

jazz (p. 629)

Universal Negro Improvement
   Association (p. 629)

pan-Africanism (p. 630)

## REVIEW QUESTIONS

Answer these questions to demonstrate your understanding of the chapter's main ideas.

1. How and why did the United States take a conservative turn in the 1920s?
2. What were the primary characteristics of the American economy in the 1920s?
3. What caused the cultural conflict of the 1920s?
4. What domestic and global factors helped cause the Great Depression?
5. Between 1917 and 1945, the "Roaring Twenties" were the only years when the United States did not face a major economic or international crisis. Review the categories of "America in the World," "Politics and Power," and "American and National Identity" on the thematic timeline on pages 580–581. In what ways do they suggest that the prosperous 1920s were a politically distinctive era? What continuities do you see in politics and foreign policy?

## CHRONOLOGY

As you read, ask yourself why this chapter begins and ends with these dates and identify the links among related events.

| | |
|---|---|
| **1915** | • New Ku Klux Klan founded |
| | • United States occupies Haiti |
| **1916** | • United States occupies Dominican Republic |
| **1917** | • Race riot in East St. Louis, Illinois |
| **1919** | • Race riot in Chicago |
| | • Boston police strike |
| | • Palmer raids |
| **1920** | • Height of Red Scare |
| | • Eighteenth Amendment (prohibition) takes effect |
| | • Warren Harding wins presidency |
| **1921** | • Race riot in Tulsa, Oklahoma |
| | • Sheppard-Towner Federal Maternity and Infancy Act |

**1923**
- President Harding dies
- Calvin Coolidge assumes presidency
- Race riot in Rosewood, Florida
- Teapot Dome scandal
- Equal Rights Amendment first introduced in Congress

**1924**
- National Origins Act
- Coolidge wins presidential election against Democrats and La Follette's Progressive Party
- First suburban shopping center opens outside Kansas City, Missouri

**1925**
- Scopes "monkey trial"
- Alain Locke's *The New Negro*

**1927**
- Sacco and Vanzetti executed

**1928**
- Herbert Hoover wins presidency

**1929**
- Stock market crashes precipitate Great Depression

# 22

# Managing the Great Depression, Forging the New Deal

## 1929–1938

### IDENTIFY THE BIG IDEA

What new roles did the American government take on during the New Deal, and how did these roles shape the economy and society?

**IN HIS INAUGURAL ADDRESS IN MARCH 1933, PRESIDENT FRANKLIN** Delano Roosevelt did not hide the country's precarious condition. "A host of unemployed citizens face the grim problem of existence," he said, "and an equally great number toil with little return. Only a foolish optimist can deny the dark realities of the moment." Roosevelt, his demeanor sincere and purposeful, saw both despair and determination in the nation's citizens. "This nation asks for action, and action now." From Congress he would request "broad Executive power to wage a war against the emergency, as great as the power that would be given to me if we were in fact invaded by a foreign foe." With these words, Roosevelt launched a program of federal activism—which he called the New Deal—that would change the nature of American government.

The New Deal represented a new form of liberalism, a fresh interpretation of the ideology of individual rights that had long shaped the character of American society and politics. Classical nineteenth-century liberals believed that, to protect those rights, government should be small and relatively weak. However, the progressives of the early twentieth century believed individual freedom and opportunity were best safeguarded by strengthening state and federal control over large businesses and monopolies. New Deal activists went much further: their social-welfare liberalism expanded individual rights to include economic security.

Beginning in the 1930s and continuing through the 1960s, they increased the responsibility of the national government for the welfare of ordinary citizens. Their efforts did not go unchallenged. Conservative critics of the New Deal charged that its "big government" programs were paternalistic and dangerous, undermining individual responsibility and constraining personal freedom. This division between the advocates and the critics of the New Deal shaped American politics for the next half century.

Before Roosevelt was elected president, between the onset of the depression in 1929 and November 1932, the "dark realities of the moment" wore down American society. Rising unemployment, shuttered businesses, failing banks, and home foreclosures tore at the nation's social fabric. As crisis piled upon crisis and the federal government's initiatives under President Hoover proved ineffectual, Americans had to reconsider more than the role of government in economic life: they had to rethink many of the principles of individualism and free enterprise that had guided so much of the nation's history.

# Early Responses to the Depression, 1929–1932

The American economy collapsed between 1929 and 1932, by virtually any measurement. U.S. gross domestic product fell almost by half, from $103 billion to $58 billion. Consumption dropped by 18 percent, construction by 78 percent, and private investment by 88 percent. Nearly 9,000 banks closed their doors, and 100,000 businesses failed. Corporate profits fell from $10 billion to $1 billion. Unemployment rose to 25 percent. Fifteen million people were out of work by 1933. "Hoover made a souphound outa me!" sang jobless harvest hands in the Southwest.

The depression respected no national boundaries. Germany had preceded the United States into economic contraction in 1928, and its economy, burdened by heavy World War I reparations payments, was brought to its knees by 1929. France, Britain, Argentina, Brazil, Poland, and Canada were hard hit as well. Recovery proved difficult because the international gold standard constrained economic policymaking. The United States and most European nations had tied the value of their currencies to the price of gold, and the amount of gold held in reserves, since the late nineteenth century. This system had worked fairly well for a few decades, but it was vulnerable during economic downturns, when large financiers withdrew their investments and demanded gold payments. The gold standard rendered the international monetary system inflexible at precisely the moment when maximum flexibility was needed.

## Enter Herbert Hoover

President Herbert Hoover and Congress responded to the downturn by drawing on two influential American traditions. The first was the belief that economic outcomes were the product of individual character: people's fate was in their own hands, and success went to those who deserved it. The second tradition held that through voluntary action, the business community could right itself and recover from economic downturns without relying on government assistance or, worse, submitting to government regulation. Following these principles, Hoover asked Americans to tighten their belts and work hard. After the stock market crash, he cut federal taxes in an attempt to boost private spending and corporate investment. "Any lack of confidence in the economic future or the strength of business in the United States is foolish," Hoover assured the country in late 1929. Treasury secretary Andrew Mellon suggested that the downturn would help Americans "work harder" and "live a more moral life."

While many factors caused the Great Depression, Hoover's adherence to the gold standard was a major reason for its length and severity in the United States. Faced with economic catastrophe, both Britain and Germany abandoned the gold standard in 1931; when they did so, their economies recovered modestly. But the Hoover administration feared that such a move would weaken the value of the dollar. In reality, an inflexible money supply discouraged investment and therefore prevented growth. The Roosevelt administration would ultimately remove the United States from the burdens of the gold standard in 1933. By that time, however, the crisis had achieved catastrophic dimensions. Billions had been lost in business and bank failures, and the economy had stalled completely.

Along with adherence to the gold standard, Hoover and many congressional Republicans believed in another piece of economic orthodoxy that had protected American manufacturing in good economic times but that proved damaging during the downturn: high tariffs (taxes on imported goods designed to stimulate American manufacturing). In 1930, Republicans enacted the **Smoot-Hawley Tariff**. Despite receiving a letter from more than a thousand economists urging him to veto it, Hoover approved the legislation. What served American interests in earlier eras now undermined them. Smoot-Hawley triggered retaliatory tariffs in other countries, which further hindered global trade and worsened economic contraction throughout the industrialized world.

The president recognized that individual initiative, business voluntarism, and high tariffs might not be enough, given the depth of the crisis, so he proposed government action as well. He called on state and local governments to provide jobs by investing in public projects. And in 1931, he secured an unprecedented increase of $700 million in federal spending for public works. Hoover's most innovative program was the Reconstruction Finance Corporation (RFC), which provided federal loans to railroads, banks, and other businesses. But the RFC lent money too cautiously, and by the end of 1932 it had loaned out only 20 percent of its $1.5 billion in funds. Like most federal initiatives under Hoover, the RFC was not nearly aggressive enough given the severity of the depression.

Few chief executives could have survived the downward economic spiral of 1929–1932, but Hoover's reluctance to break with the philosophy of limited government and his insistence that recovery was just around the corner contributed to his unpopularity. By 1932, Americans perceived Hoover as insensitive to the depth of economic suffering. The nation had come a long way since the depressions of the 1870s and 1890s, when no one except the most radical figures, such as Jacob Coxey, called for direct federal aid to the unemployed (Chapter 19). Compared with previous chief executives—and in contrast to his popular image as a "do-nothing"

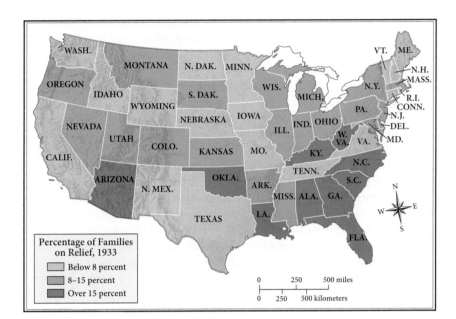

**MAP 22.1   The Great Depression: Families on Relief**

Although the Great Depression was a nationwide crisis, some regions were hit harder than others. Economic hardship was widespread in the agricultural South, the rural Appalachian states, and the industrial states of the Northeast and Midwest. As the depression worsened in 1931 and 1932, local and state governments, as well as charitable organizations, could not keep up with the demand for relief. After Franklin D. Roosevelt assumed the presidency in 1933, the national government began a massive program of aid through the Federal Emergency Relief Administration (FERA).

president—Hoover had responded to the national emergency with unprecedented government action. But the nation's needs were even more unprecedented, and Hoover's programs failed to meet them (Map 22.1).

## Rising Discontent

As the depression deepened, the American vocabulary now included the terms *Hoovervilles* (shantytowns where people lived in packing crates) and *Hoover blankets* (newspapers). Bankrupt farmers banded together to resist the bank agents and sheriffs who tried to evict them from their land. To protest low prices for their goods, in the spring of 1932 thousands of midwestern farmers joined the Farmers' Holiday Association, which cut off supplies to urban areas by barricading roads and dumping milk, vegetables, and other foodstuffs onto the roadways. Agricultural prices were so low that the group advocated a government-supported farm program—drawing on Populist ideas from the 1890s (Chapter 19).

In the industrial sector, layoffs and wage cuts led to violent strikes. When coal miners in Harlan County, Kentucky, went on strike over a 10 percent wage cut in 1931, the mine owners called in the state's National Guard, which crushed the union. A 1932 confrontation between workers and security forces at the Ford Motor Company's giant River Rouge factory outside Detroit left five workers dead and fifty with serious injuries. A news photographer had his camera shot from his hands, and fifteen policemen were beaten. Whether on farms or in factories, those who produced the nation's food and goods had begun to agitate, protest, and organize in the face of mounting economic troubles.

Veterans staged the most publicized—and most tragic—protest. In the summer of 1932, the **Bonus Army**, a determined group of between fifteen thousand and twenty thousand unemployed World War I veterans, piled into cars, hitchhiked, and even walked to Washington to demand immediate payment of pension awards that were due to be paid in 1945. "We were heroes in 1917, but we're bums now," one veteran complained bitterly. While their leaders unsuccessfully lobbied Congress, the Bonus Army set up camps near the Capitol building. Hoover deployed regular army troops under the command of General Douglas MacArthur, who forcefully evicted the marchers and burned their encampment to the ground. When newsreel footage showing the U.S. Army attacking and injuring veterans reached movie theaters across

**Hooverville** The depression cast hundreds of thousands of Americans out of their homes. Most found shelter with relatives, but those with little choice had to make do as they could. Encampments such as this one south of downtown Seattle, Washington—places where the homeless crafted makeshift lodging out of whatever materials were at hand—became known as Hoovervilles. The name reflected Americans' attitudes toward President Hoover, whose popularity plummeted as the depression deepened. AP Photo.

the nation, Hoover's popularity plunged even further. In another measure of how the country had changed since the 1890s, what Americans had applauded when done to Coxey in 1894 was condemned in 1932.

## The 1932 Election

Amidst rising discontent as the 1932 election approached, most Americans believed that something altogether new had to be tried—whatever that might be. The Republicans, reluctant to dump an incumbent president, unenthusiastically renominated Hoover. The Democrats turned to New York governor Franklin Delano Roosevelt, whose state had initiated innovative relief and unemployment programs.

Roosevelt, born into a wealthy New York family, was a distant cousin to former president Theodore Roosevelt, whose career he emulated. After attending Harvard College and Columbia University, Franklin Roosevelt served as assistant secretary of the navy during World War I (as Theodore Roosevelt had done before the War of 1898). Then, in 1921, a crippling attack of polio left both of his legs permanently paralyzed. Supported by his wife, Eleanor, he slowly returned to public life and campaigned successfully for the governorship of New York in 1928 and again in 1930. Running for the presidency in 1932, Roosevelt pledged vigorous action but gave no indication what that action might be, arguing simply that "the country needs and, unless I mistake its temper, the country demands bold, persistent experimentation." He won easily, receiving 22.8 million votes to Hoover's 15.7 million.

Elected in November, Roosevelt would not begin his presidency until March 1933. (The Twentieth Amendment, ratified in 1933, set subsequent inaugurations for January 20.) Meanwhile, Americans suffered through the worst winter of the depression. Unemployment continued to climb nationwide. In a measure of the depth of woe, in three major industrial cities in Ohio, the jobless rate shot to staggering levels: 50 percent in Cleveland, 60 percent in Akron, and 80 percent in Toledo. Private charities and public relief agencies reached only a fraction of the needy. The nation's banking system was so close to collapse that many state governors closed banks temporarily to avoid further withdrawals. Several states were approaching bankruptcy, their tax revenues too low to pay for basic services. By March 1933, the nation had hit rock bottom.

| IN YOUR OWN WORDS | How did Americans, from ordinary citizens to political leaders, respond to the Great Depression? |

# The New Deal Arrives, 1933–1935

The ideological differences between Herbert Hoover and Franklin Roosevelt were not vast. Both leaders wished to maintain the nation's economic institutions and preserve its social structure, to save capitalism while easing its worst downturns. Both believed in a balanced government budget and extolled the values of hard work, cooperation, and sacrifice. But Roosevelt's personal charm, political savvy, and willingness to experiment made him far more effective and popular than Hoover. Most Americans felt a kinship with their new president, calling him simply FDR. His New Deal would put people to work and restore hope in the nation's future.

## Roosevelt and the First Hundred Days

A wealthy patrician, Roosevelt was an unlikely figure to inspire millions of ordinary Americans. But his close rapport with the American people was critical to his political success. More than 450,000 letters poured into the White House in the week after his inauguration. The president's masterful use of the new medium of radio, especially his evening radio addresses to the American public known as **fireside chats**, made him an intimate presence in people's lives. Thousands of citizens felt a personal relationship with FDR, saying, "He gave me a job" or "He saved my home."

Citing the national economic emergency, Roosevelt further expanded the presidential powers that Theodore Roosevelt and Woodrow Wilson had increased previously. To draft legislation and policy, he relied heavily on financier Bernard Baruch and a "Brains Trust" of professors from Columbia, Harvard, and other leading universities. Roosevelt also turned to his talented cabinet, which included Harold L. Ickes, secretary of the interior; Frances Perkins at the Labor Department; Henry A. Wallace at Agriculture; and Henry Morgenthau Jr., secretary of the treasury. These intellectuals and administrators attracted hundreds of highly qualified recruits to Washington. Inspired by New Deal idealism, many of them would devote their lives to public service and the principles of social-welfare liberalism.

Roosevelt could have done little, however, without a sympathetic Congress. The 1932 election had swept Democratic majorities into both the House and Senate, giving the new president the lawmaking allies he needed. The first months of FDR's administration produced a whirlwind of activity on Capitol Hill. In a legendary session, known as the **Hundred Days**, Congress enacted fifteen major bills that focused primarily on four problems: banking failures, agricultural overproduction, the business slump, and soaring unemployment. Derided by some as an "alphabet soup" because of their many abbreviations (CCC, WPA, AAA, etc.), the new policies and agencies represented the emergence of a new American state.

**Banking Reform**   The collapsing banking system hobbled the entire economy, curtailing consumer spending and business investment. Widespread bank failures had reduced the savings of nearly nine million families, and panicked account holders raced to withdraw their funds. On March 5, 1933, the day after his inauguration, FDR declared a national "bank holiday"—closing all the banks—and called Congress into special session. Four days later, Congress passed the Emergency Banking Act, which permitted banks to reopen if a Treasury Department inspection showed they had sufficient cash reserves.

In his first Sunday night fireside chat, to a radio audience of sixty million, the president reassured citizens that their money was safe. When the banks reopened on March 13, calm prevailed and deposits exceeded withdrawals, restoring stability to the nation's basic financial institutions. "Capitalism was saved in eight days," quipped Roosevelt's advisor Raymond Moley. Four thousand banks had failed in the months prior to Roosevelt's inauguration; only sixty-one closed their doors in all of 1934. A second banking law, the **Glass-Steagall Act**, further restored public confidence by creating the Federal Deposit Insurance Corporation (FDIC), which insured deposits up to $2,500 (and now insures them up to $250,000). The act also prohibited banks from making risky, unsecured investments with the deposits of ordinary people.

And in a profoundly important economic and symbolic gesture, Roosevelt removed the U.S. Treasury from the gold standard in June 1933, which allowed the Federal Reserve to lower interest rates; since 1931, it had been raising rates, which had only deepened the downturn.

**Agriculture and Manufacturing**    Roosevelt and the New Deal Congress next turned to agriculture and manufacturing. In those sectors, a seeming paradox was evident: the depression led to overproduction in agriculture and underproduction in manufacturing. Reversing both problematic trends was critical. The **Agricultural Adjustment Act** (AAA) began direct governmental regulation of the farm economy for the first time. To solve the problem of overproduction, which lowered prices, the AAA provided cash subsidies to farmers who cut production of seven major commodities: wheat, cotton, corn, hogs, rice, tobacco, and dairy products. Policymakers hoped that farm prices would rise as production fell.

By dumping cash in farmers' hands, the AAA briefly stabilized the farm economy. But the act's benefits were not evenly distributed. Subsidies went primarily to the owners of large and medium-sized farms, who often cut production by reducing the amount of land they rented to tenants and sharecroppers. In Mississippi, one plantation owner received $26,000 from the federal government, while thousands of black sharecroppers living in the same county received only a few dollars in relief payments.

In manufacturing, the New Deal attacked declining production with the National Industrial Recovery Act. A new government agency, the **National Recovery Administration** (NRA), set up separate self-governing private associations in six hundred industries. Each industry—ranging from large corporations producing coal, cotton textiles, and steel to small businesses making pet food and costume jewelry—regulated itself by agreeing on prices and production quotas.

The AAA and the NRA were designed to rescue the nation's productive industries and stabilize the economy. The measures had positive effects in some regions, but most historians agree that, overall, they did little to end the depression.

**Unemployment Relief**    The Roosevelt administration next addressed the massive unemployment problem. By 1933, local governments and private charities had exhausted their resources and were looking to Washington for assistance. Although Roosevelt wanted to avoid a budget deficit, he asked Congress to provide relief for millions of unemployed Americans. In May, Congress established the Federal Emergency Relief Administration (FERA). Directed by Harry Hopkins, a hard-driving social worker from New York, the FERA provided federal funds for state relief programs.

Roosevelt and Hopkins had strong reservations about the "dole," the nickname for government welfare payments. As Hopkins put it, "I don't think anybody can go year after year, month after month, accepting relief without affecting his character." To support the traditional values of individualism, the New Deal put people to work. Early in 1933, Congress established the **Public Works Administration** (PWA), a construction program, and several months later, Roosevelt created the Civil Works Administration (CWA) and named Hopkins its head. At its peak in 1934, the CWA provided jobs for 4 million Americans, repairing bridges, building highways, and constructing public buildings. A stopgap measure to get the country through the winter of 1933–1934, the CWA lapsed in the spring, when Republican opposition compelled New Dealers to abandon it. A longer-term program, the **Civilian Conservation Corps** (CCC), mobilized 250,000 young men to do reforestation and conservation work. Over the course of the 1930s, the "CCC boys" built thousands of bridges, roads, trails, and other structures in state and national parks, bolstering the national infrastructure (Map 22.2).

**Housing Crisis**    Millions of Americans also faced the devastating prospect of losing their homes. The economic expansion of the 1920s had produced the largest inflationary housing bubble in American history to that point, a scenario in which home prices rose rapidly, fueled by widespread borrowing. In the early 1930s, home prices collapsed, banks closed, and the jobless could not afford mortgage payments. More than half a million Americans lost their homes between 1930 and 1932. In response, Congress created the Home Owners Loan Corporation (HOLC) to refinance home mortgages. In just two years, the HOLC helped more than a million Americans retain their homes. The Federal Housing Act of 1934 would extend this program under a new agency, the **Federal Housing Administration** (FHA). Together, the HOLC, the FHA, and the subsequent Housing Act of 1937 permanently changed

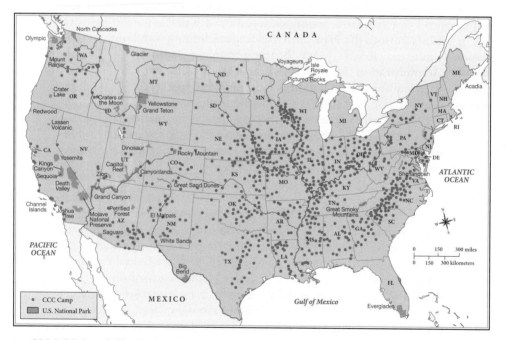

**MAP 22.2   Civilian Conservation Corps Camps**

The Civilian Conservation Corps (CCC) gave hope to unemployed young men during the Great Depression. The first camp opened in Big Meadows, Virginia, in July 1933, and by the end of the decade CCC camps had appeared across the length of the country, located in rural, mountainous, and forested regions alike. Young men constructed bridges and roads, built hiking trails, erected public campgrounds, and performed other improvements. By the early 1940s, the CCC had planted three billion trees, among its many other contributions to the national infrastructure.

the mortgage system and set the foundation for the broad expansion of home owner-ship in the post–World War II decades (Chapter 24).

When an exhausted Congress recessed in June 1933, at the end of the Hundred Days, it had enacted Roosevelt's agenda: banking reform, recovery programs for agri-culture and industry, public works, and unemployment relief. Few presidents had won the passage of so many measures in so short a time. The new federal agencies were far from perfect and had their critics on both the radical left and the conserva-tive right. But the vigorous actions taken by Roosevelt and Congress had halted the downward economic spiral of the Hoover years, stabilized the financial sector, and sent a message of hope from the nation's political leaders. For all that, however, the New Deal did not break the grip of the depression.

## The New Deal Under Attack

As New Dealers waited anxiously for the economy to revive, Roosevelt turned his attention to the reform of Wall Street, where reckless speculation and overleveraged buying of stocks had helped trigger the financial panic of 1929. In 1934, Congress established the **Securities and Exchange Commission** (SEC) to regulate the stock market. The commission had broad powers to determine how stocks and bonds were sold to the public, to set rules for margin (credit) transactions, and to prevent stock sales by those with inside information about corporate plans. The Banking Act of 1935 authorized the president to appoint a new Board of Governors of the Federal Reserve System, placing control of interest rates and other money-market policies in a federal agency based in Washington rather than in the hands of private bankers around the country.

**Critics on the Right**    Such measures exposed the New Deal to attack from economic conservatives — also known as the political right. A man of wealth, Roosevelt saw himself as the savior of American capitalism, declaring simply, "To preserve we had to reform." Many bankers and business executives disagreed. To them, FDR became "That Man," a traitor to his class. In 1934, Republican business leaders joined with conservative Democrats in the **American Liberty League** to fight what they called the "reckless spending" and "socialist" reforms of the New Deal. Herbert Hoover condemned the NRA as "tyranny, not liberalism."

The **National Association of Manufacturers** (NAM) was a more lasting opponent of the New Deal — its influence stretched far into the post–World War II decades. Sparked by a new generation of corporate leaders who launched a probusiness publicity campaign to "serve the purposes of business salvation," the NAM promoted free enterprise and unfettered capitalism. In response to what many conservatives perceived as Roosevelt's antibusiness policies, the NAM produced radio programs, motion pictures, billboards, and direct mail campaigns carrying its message. After World War II, the NAM emerged as a staunch critic of liberalism and forged alliances with influential conservative politicians such as Barry Goldwater and Ronald Reagan.

Based on conservative legal doctrine dating to the late nineteenth century, the Supreme Court repudiated several cornerstones of the early New Deal. In May 1935, in *Schechter v. United States*, the Court unanimously ruled the National Industrial Recovery Act unconstitutional because it delegated Congress's lawmaking power

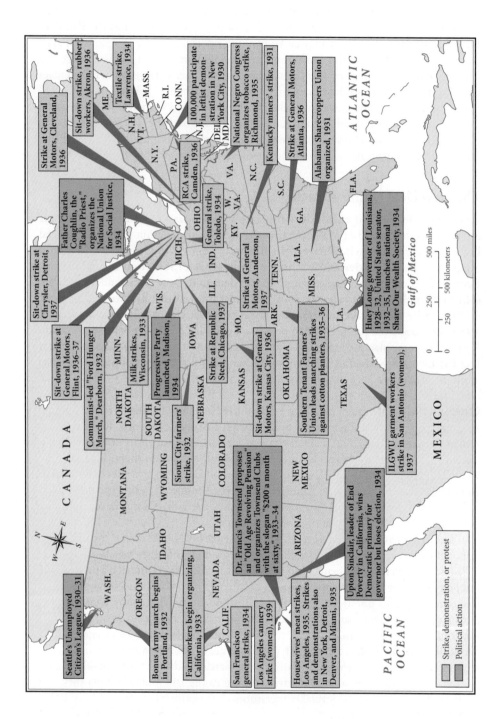

to the executive branch and extended federal authority to intrastate (in contrast to interstate) commerce. Roosevelt protested but watched helplessly as the Court struck down more New Deal legislation: the Agricultural Adjustment Act, the Railroad Retirement Act, and a debt-relief law known as the Frazier-Lemke Act.

**Critics on the Populist Left**   If business leaders and the Supreme Court thought that the New Deal had gone too far, other Americans believed it had not gone far enough. Among these were public figures who, in the tradition of American populism, sought to place government on the side of ordinary citizens against corporations and the wealthy. Francis Townsend, a doctor from Long Beach, California, spoke for the nation's elderly, most of whom had no pensions and feared poverty. In 1933, Townsend proposed the Old Age Revolving Pension Plan, which would give $200 a month (about $3,600 today) to citizens over the age of sixty. To receive payments, the elderly would have to retire and open their positions to younger workers. Townsend Clubs sprang up across the country in support of the **Townsend Plan**, mobilizing mass support for old-age pensions.

The most direct political threat to Roosevelt came from Louisiana senator Huey Long. As the Democratic governor of Louisiana from 1928 to 1932, the flamboyant Long had achieved stunning popularity. He increased taxes on corporations, lowered the utility bills of consumers, and built new highways, hospitals, and schools. To push through these measures, Long seized almost dictatorial control of the state government. A U.S. senator by 1934, Long broke with the New Deal and, like Townsend, established a national movement. According to his Share Our Wealth Society, inequalities in the distribution of wealth prohibited millions of ordinary families from buying the goods that kept factories humming. Long's society advocated a tax of 100 percent on all income over $1 million and on all inheritances over $5 million. He hoped that this populist program would carry him into the White House. Roosevelt himself feared that Long and Townsend, along with the popular "Radio Priest," Father Charles Coughlin, might join forces to form a third party. He had to respond or risk the political unity of the country's liberal forces (Map 22.3).

| IN YOUR OWN WORDS | What were the major components of the Hundred Days, and what was their purpose? |

**< MAP 22.3   Popular Protest in the Great Depression, 1933–1939**
The depression forced Americans to look closely at their society, and many of them did not like what they saw. Some citizens expressed their discontent through popular movements, and this map suggests the geography of discontent. The industrial Midwest witnessed union movements, strikes, and "Radio Priest" Charles Coughlin's demands for social reform. Simultaneously, farmers' movements—tenants in the South, smallholders in the agricultural Midwest—engaged in strikes and dumping campaigns and rallied behind the ideas of progressives in Wisconsin and Huey Long in the South. Protests took diverse forms in California, which was home to strikes by farmworkers, women, and—in San Francisco—all wageworkers. The West was also the seedbed of two important reform proposals: Upton Sinclair's End Poverty in California (EPIC) movement and Francis Townsend's Old Age Revolving Pension clubs.

# The Second New Deal and the Redefining of Liberalism, 1935–1938

As attacks on the New Deal proliferated, Roosevelt and his advisors moved politically to the left. Historians have labeled this shift in policy the Second New Deal. Roosevelt now openly criticized the "money classes," proudly stating, "We have earned the hatred of entrenched greed." He also decisively countered the rising popularity of Townsend, Long, and Coughlin by adopting parts of their programs. The administration's Revenue Act of 1935 proposed a substantial tax increase on corporate profits and higher income and estate taxes on the wealthy. When conservatives attacked this legislation as an attempt to "soak the rich," Congress moderated its taxation rates. But FDR was satisfied. He had met the Share Our Wealth Society's proposal with a tax plan of his own.

## The Welfare State Comes into Being

The Revenue Act symbolized the administration's new outlook. Unlike the First New Deal, which focused on economic recovery, the Second New Deal emphasized social justice and the creation of a safety net: the use of the federal government to assist working people and to provide economic security for the old, the disabled, and the unemployed. The resulting **welfare state**—a term applied to industrial democracies that adopted various government-guaranteed social-welfare programs—fundamentally changed American society.

**The Wagner Act and Social Security**   The first beneficiary of Roosevelt's Second New Deal was the labor movement. Section 7(a) of the National Industrial Recovery Act (NIRA) had given workers the right to organize unions, producing a dramatic growth in rank-and-file militancy and leading to a strike wave in 1934. When the Supreme Court voided the NIRA in 1935, labor unions called for new legislation that would allow workers to organize and bargain collectively with employers. Named for its sponsor, Senator Robert F. Wagner of New York, the **Wagner Act** (1935) established the right of industrial workers to join unions. The act outlawed many practices that employers had used to suppress unions, such as firing workers for organizing activities. A new federal agency, the National Labor Relations Board (NLRB), had the authority to protect workers from employer coercion and would guarantee collective bargaining.

A second initiative, the **Social Security Act** of 1935, had an equally widespread impact. Other industrialized societies, such as Germany and Britain, had created national old-age pension systems at the turn of the century, but American reformers had failed to secure a similar program. The Townsend and Long movements now pressed Roosevelt to act, giving political leverage to pension proponents within the administration. Children's welfare advocates, concerned about the fate of fatherless families, also pressured the president. The resulting Social Security Act had three main provisions: old-age pensions for workers; a joint federal-state system of compensation for unemployed workers; and a program of payments to widowed mothers and the blind, deaf, and disabled. Roosevelt, however, limited the reach of the legislation. Knowing that compulsory pension and unemployment legislation alone would be controversial, he dropped a provision for national health insurance, fearing it would doom the entire bill.

The Social Security Act was a milestone in the creation of an American welfare state. Never before had the federal government assumed such responsibility for the well-being of so many citizens. Social Security, as old-age pensions were known, became one of the most popular government programs in American history. On the other hand, the assistance program for widows and children known as Aid to Dependent Children (ADC) became one of its most controversial measures. ADC covered only 700,000 youngsters in 1939; by 1994, its successor, Aid to Families with Dependent Children (AFDC), enrolled 14.1 million Americans. A minor program during the New Deal, AFDC grew enormously in the 1960s and remained an often maligned cornerstone of the welfare state until it was eliminated under President Bill Clinton in 1996.

**New Deal Liberalism**   The Second New Deal created what historians call New Deal liberalism. **Classical liberalism** held individual liberty to be the foundation of a democratic society, and the word *liberal* had traditionally denoted support for free-market policies and weak government. Roosevelt and his advisors, along with intellectuals such as British economist John Maynard Keynes, disagreed. They countered that, to preserve individual liberty, government must assist the needy and guarantee the basic welfare of citizens. This liberal welfare state was opposed by inheritors of the nineteenth-century ideology of *laissez faire* capitalism, who gradually became known as conservatives. These two visions of liberty and government—with liberals on one side and conservatives on the other—would shape American politics for the remainder of the twentieth century.

## From Reform to Stalemate

Roosevelt's first term had seen an extraordinary expansion of the federal state. The great burst of government action between 1933 and 1935 was unequaled in the nation's history, though Congress and President Lyndon Johnson nearly matched it in 1965 and 1966 (Chapter 27). Roosevelt's second term, however, was characterized by a series of political entanglements and economic bad news that stifled further reform.

**The 1936 Election**   FDR was never enthusiastic about public relief programs. But with the election of 1936 on the horizon and 10 million Americans still out of work, he won funding for the **Works Progress Administration** (WPA). Under the energetic direction of Harry Hopkins, the WPA employed 8.5 million Americans between 1935, when it was established, and 1943. The agency's workers constructed or repaired 651,087 miles of road, 124,087 bridges, 125,110 public buildings, 8,192 parks, and 853 airports. The WPA was an extravagant operation by 1930s standards, yet it reached only about one-third of the nation's unemployed.

As the 1936 election approached, new voters joined the Democratic Party. Many had personally benefitted from New Deal programs such as the WPA or knew people who had. One was Jack Reagan, a down-on-his-luck shoe salesman (and the father of future president Ronald Reagan), who took a job as a federal relief administrator in Dixon, Illinois, and became a strong supporter of the New Deal. In addition to voters such as Reagan, Roosevelt could count on a powerful coalition of organized labor, midwestern farmers, white ethnic groups, northern African Americans, and middle-class families concerned about unemployment and old-age security. He also commanded the support of intellectuals and progressive Republicans. With difficulty, the Democrats held on to the votes of their white southern constituency as well.

Republicans recognized that the New Deal was too popular to oppose directly, so they chose as their candidate the progressive governor of Kansas, Alfred M. Landon. Landon accepted the legitimacy of many New Deal programs but criticized their inefficiency and expense. He also pointed to authoritarian regimes in Italy and Germany and hinted that FDR harbored similar dictatorial ambitions. These charges fell on deaf ears. Roosevelt's victory in 1936 was one of the most lopsided in American history. The assassination of Huey Long by a Louisiana political rival in September 1935 had eliminated the threat of a serious third-party challenge. Roosevelt received 60 percent of the popular vote and carried every state except Maine and Vermont. The *New Republic*, a liberal publication, boasted that "it was the greatest revolution in our political history."

"I see one-third of a nation ill-housed, ill-clad, ill-nourished," the president declared in his second inaugural address in January 1937, pointing to the depression's persistent social costs. But any hopes that FDR had for expanding the liberal welfare state were quickly dashed. Within a year, staunch opposition to Roosevelt's initiatives arose in Congress, and a sharp recession undermined confidence in his economic leadership.

**Court Battle and Economic Recession**     Roosevelt's first setback in 1937 came when he surprised the nation by seeking fundamental changes to the Supreme Court. In 1935, the Court had struck down a series of New Deal measures by the narrow margin of 5 to 4. With the Wagner Act, the Tennessee Valley Authority, and Social Security all slated to come before the Court, the future of the New Deal rested in the hands of a few elderly, conservative-minded judges. To diminish their influence, the president proposed adding a new justice to the Court for every member over the age of seventy, a scheme that would have brought six new judges to the bench at the time the legislation was proposed. Roosevelt's opponents protested that he was trying to "pack" the Court. After a bitter, months-long debate, Congress rejected this blatant attempt to alter the judiciary to the president's advantage.

If Roosevelt lost the battle, he went on to win the war. Swayed in part by the president's overwhelming electoral victory in the 1936 election, the Court upheld the Wagner and Social Security Acts. Moreover, a series of timely resignations allowed Roosevelt to reshape the Supreme Court after all. His new appointees—who included the liberal-leaning and generally pro–New Deal Hugo Black, Felix Frankfurter, and William O. Douglas—viewed the Constitution as a "living document" that had to be interpreted in the light of present conditions.

The so-called **Roosevelt recession** of 1937–1938 dealt another blow to the president. From 1933 to 1937, gross domestic product had grown at a yearly rate of about 10 percent, bringing industrial output back to 1929 levels. Unemployment had declined from 25 percent to 14 percent. "The emergency has passed," declared Senator James F. Byrnes of South Carolina. Acting on this assumption, Roosevelt slashed the federal budget. Following the president's lead, Congress cut the WPA's funding in half, causing layoffs of about 1.5 million workers, and the Federal Reserve, fearing inflation, raised interest rates. These measures halted recovery. The stock market dropped sharply, and unemployment jumped to 19 percent. Quickly reversing course, Roosevelt began once again to spend his way out of the recession by boosting funding for the WPA and resuming public works projects.

Although improvised, this spending program accorded with the theories of John Maynard Keynes, a visionary British economist. Keynes transformed economic thinking in capitalist societies in the 1920s by arguing that government intervention could smooth out the highs and lows of the business cycle through deficit spending and the manipulation of interest rates, which determined the money supply. This view was sharply criticized by Republicans and conservative Democrats in the 1930s, who opposed government management of the economy. But **Keynesian economics** gradually won wider acceptance as World War II defense spending finally ended the Great Depression.

In the midst of boosting WPA spending, Roosevelt achieved a final legislative victory for the New Deal. In 1938, Congress passed the **Fair Labor Standards Act**, which outlawed child labor, made the 40-hour workweek the national standard, mandated overtime pay, and established a federal minimum wage. FDR considered it nearly as important as the Social Security Act because of its implications for how Americans worked and what they earned. But it would be the last major reform of his presidency.

A reformer rather than a revolutionary, Roosevelt had preserved capitalism and liberal individualism — even as he transformed them in significant ways. But the president stopped well short of more radical measures, such as the seizure of private property, that some world leaders considered. At the same time, conservatives had reclaimed a measure of power in Congress, and those who believed the New Deal had created an intrusive federal bureaucracy kept reform in check after 1938. Throughout Roosevelt's second term, a conservative coalition of southern Democrats, rural Republicans, and industrial interests in both parties worked to block or impede social legislation. By 1938, the era of change was over.

| IN YOUR OWN WORDS | How did the Second New Deal reshape American government, and what political differences did it highlight? |
|---|---|

# The New Deal and American Society

Whatever its limits, the New Deal had a tremendous impact on American society. Its ideology of social-welfare liberalism fundamentally altered Americans' relationship to their government and provided assistance to a wide range of ordinary people: the unemployed, the elderly, workers, and the poor. In doing so, New Dealers created a sizable federal bureaucracy: the number of civilian federal employees increased by 80 percent between 1929 and 1940, reaching a total of 1 million. The expenditures — and deficits — of the federal government grew at an even faster rate. In 1930, the Hoover administration spent $3.1 billion and had a surplus of almost $1 billion; in 1939, New Dealers expended $9.4 billion and ran a deficit of nearly $3 billion (still small by later standards). But the New Deal represented more than figures on a balance sheet. Across the country, it inspired new visions of democracy among ordinary citizens.

## A People's Democracy

In 1939, writer John La Touche and musician Earl Robinson produced the patriotic song "Ballad for Americans." The lyrics called for uniting "everybody who's nobody . . . Irish, Negro, Jewish, Italian, French, and English, Spanish, Russian, Chinese, Polish, Scotch, Hungarian, Litvak, Swedish, Finnish, Canadian, Greek, and Turk, and Czech and double Czech American." The song captured the democratic aspirations that the New Deal had awakened. Millions of ordinary people believed that the nation could, and should, become more egalitarian, and Americans from all walks of life seized the chance to work toward that goal.

**Organized Labor**   Demoralized and shrinking during the 1920s, labor unions increased their numbers and clout during the New Deal, thanks to the Wagner Act. "The era of privilege and predatory individuals is over," the fiery and outspoken labor leader John L. Lewis declared. By the end of the decade, the number of unionized

**United Auto Workers Strike**   Trade unions were among the most active and vocal organizations of the 1930s. Organized labor led a number of major strikes between 1934 and 1937 in various industries. None was more important to the future of trade unions than the sit-down strikes at major automobile plants, including General Motors and Chevrolet in Flint, Michigan, in 1936 and 1937. These strikes, in which workers stopped the assembly lines but refused to leave the factories, compelled GM to recognize the United Auto Workers (UAW), which became one of the strongest trade unions in American history. Bettmann/Getty Images.

workers had more than doubled to an unprecedented 23 percent of the nonagricultural workforce. A new union movement, led by the Congress of Industrial Organizations (CIO), promoted "industrial unionism" — organizing all the workers in an industry, from skilled machinists to unskilled janitors, into a single union. The American Federation of Labor (AFL), representing the other major group of unions, favored organizing workers on a craft-by-craft basis. Both federations dramatically increased their membership in the second half of the 1930s.

Labor's new vitality translated into political action and a long-lasting alliance with the Democratic Party. The CIO backed Democratic candidates in 1936, and its political action committee became a major Democratic ally during the 1940s. These successes were real but limited. Unions never enrolled a majority of American wageworkers, and antiunion employer groups such as the National Association of Manufacturers and the Chamber of Commerce remained powerful forces in American business life. After a decade of gains, organized labor remained an important, but still secondary, force in American industry.

**Women and the New Deal**　Because policymakers saw the depression primarily as a crisis of male breadwinners, the New Deal did not directly challenge gender inequities. New Deal measures generally enhanced women's welfare, but few addressed their specific needs and concerns. However, Roosevelt welcomed women into the ranks of government in greater numbers than any previous president. Frances Perkins, the first woman named to a cabinet post, served as secretary of labor throughout Roosevelt's presidency. Josephine Roche was FDR's assistant secretary of the treasury, and the president appointed female ambassadors and the first women to the U.S. Court of Appeals. While still relatively few, female appointees often worked to open up other opportunities in government for other talented women.

The most prominent woman in American politics was the president's wife, Eleanor Roosevelt. In the 1920s, she had worked to expand positions for women in political parties, labor unions, and education. A tireless advocate for women's rights, during her years in the White House Mrs. Roosevelt emerged as an independent public figure and the most influential First Lady in the nation's history. Descending into coal mines to view working conditions, meeting with African Americans seeking antilynching laws, and talking to people on breadlines, she became the conscience of the New Deal, pushing her husband to do more for the disadvantaged. "I sometimes acted as a spur," Mrs. Roosevelt later reflected, "even though the spurring was not always wanted or welcome."

Without the intervention of Eleanor Roosevelt, Frances Perkins, and other prominent women, New Deal policymakers would have largely ignored the needs of women. A fourth of the National Recovery Act's employment rules set a lower minimum wage for women than for men performing the same jobs, and only 7 percent of the workers hired by the Civil Works Administration were female. The Civilian Conservation Corps excluded women entirely. Women fared better under the Works Progress Administration; at its peak, 440,000 women were on the payroll. Most Americans agreed with such policies. When Gallup pollsters in 1936 asked people whether wives should work outside the home when their husbands had jobs, 82 percent said no. Such sentiment reflected a persistent belief in women's subordinate status in American economic life.

**African Americans and the New Deal**   Across the nation, but especially in the South, African Americans held the lowest-paying jobs and faced harsh social and political discrimination. Though FDR did not fundamentally change this fact, he was the most popular president among African Americans since Abraham Lincoln. African Americans held 18 percent of WPA jobs, although they constituted 10 percent of the population. The Resettlement Administration, established in 1935 to help small farmers and tenants buy land, actively protected the rights of black tenant farmers. Black involvement in the New Deal, however, could not undo centuries of racial subordination, nor could it change the disproportionate power of segregationist southern whites in the Democratic Party.

Nevertheless, black Americans received significant benefits from New Deal relief programs and believed that the White House cared about their plight, which caused a momentous shift in their political allegiance. Since the Civil War, black voters had staunchly supported the Republican Party, the party of Lincoln, who was known as the Great Emancipator. Even in the depression year of 1932, they overwhelmingly supported Republican candidates. But in 1936, as part of the tidal wave of national support for FDR, northern African Americans gave Roosevelt 71 percent of their votes and have remained solidly Democratic ever since.

African Americans supported the New Deal partly because the Roosevelt administration appointed a number of black people to federal office, and an informal "black cabinet" of prominent black intellectuals advised New Deal agencies. Among the most important appointees was Mary McLeod Bethune. Born in 1875 in South Carolina to former slaves, Bethune founded Bethune-Cookman College and served during the 1920s as president of the National Association of Colored Women. She joined the New Deal in 1935, confiding to a friend that she "believed in the democratic and humane program" of FDR. Americans, Bethune observed, had to become "accustomed to seeing Negroes in high places." Bethune had access to the White House and pushed continually for New Deal programs to help African Americans.

But the New Deal was limited in its approach to race. Roosevelt did not go further in support of black rights, because of both his own racial conservatism and his need for the votes of the white southern Democrats in Congress — including powerful southern senators, many of whom held influential committee posts in Congress. Most New Deal programs reflected prevailing racial attitudes. Civilian Conservation Corps camps segregated blacks, and most NRA rules did not protect black workers from discrimination. Both Social Security and the Wagner Act explicitly excluded the domestic and agricultural jobs held by most African Americans in the 1930s. Roosevelt also refused to support legislation making lynching a federal crime, which was one of the most pressing demands of African Americans in the 1930s. Between 1882 and 1930, more than 2,500 African Americans were lynched by white mobs in the southern states, which means that statistically, one man, woman, or child was murdered every week for fifty years. But despite pleas from black leaders, and from Mrs. Roosevelt herself, FDR feared that southern white Democrats would block his other reforms in retaliation for such legislation.

If lynching embodied southern lawlessness, southern law was often not much better. In an infamous 1931 case in Scottsboro, Alabama, nine young black men were accused of rape by two white women hitching a ride on a freight train. The women's stories contained many inconsistencies, but within weeks a white jury had convicted all nine defendants; eight received the death sentence. After the U.S. Supreme Court overturned the sentences because the defendants had been denied adequate legal counsel, five of the men were again convicted and sentenced to long prison terms. Across the country, the Scottsboro Boys, as they were known, inspired solidarity within African American communities. Among whites, the Communist Party took the lead in publicizing the case — and was one of the only white organizations to do so — helping to support the Scottsboro Defense Committee, which raised money for legal efforts on the defendants' behalf.

In southern agriculture, where many sharecroppers were black while landowners and government administrators were white, the Agricultural Adjustment Act hurt rather than helped the poorest African Americans. White landowners collected government subsidy checks but refused to distribute payments to their sharecroppers. Such practices forced 200,000 black families off the land. Some black farmers tried to protect themselves by joining the Southern Tenant Farmers Union (STFU), a biracial organization founded in 1934. "The same chain that holds you holds my people, too," an elderly black farmer reminded his white neighbors. But landowners had such economic power and such support from local sheriffs that the STFU could do little.

A generation of African American leaders came of age inspired by the New Deal's democratic promise. But it remained just a promise. From the outset, New Dealers wrestled with potentially fatal racial politics. Roosevelt and the Democratic Party depended heavily on white voters in the South, who wished to maintain racial segregation and white supremacy. But many Democrats in the North and West — centers of New Deal liberalism — would come to oppose racial discrimination. This meant, ironically, that the nation's most liberal political forces and some of its most conservative political forces existed side by side in the same political party. Another thirty years would pass before black Americans would gain an opportunity to reform U.S. racial laws and practices.

**Indian Policy** New Deal reformers seized the opportunity to implement their vision for the future of Native Americans, with mixed results. Indian peoples had long been one of the nation's most disadvantaged and powerless groups. In 1934, the average individual Indian income was only $48 per year, and the Native American unemployment rate was three times the national average. The plight of Native Americans won the attention of the progressive commissioner of the Bureau of Indian Affairs (BIA), John Collier, a critic of past BIA practices. Collier understood what Native Americans had long known: that the government's decades-long policy of forced assimilation, prohibition of Indian religions, and confiscation of Indian lands had left most tribes poor, isolated, and without basic self-determination.

Collier helped to write and push through Congress the **Indian Reorganization Act** of 1934, sometimes called the Indian New Deal. On the positive side, the law reversed the Dawes Act of 1887 (Chapter 15) by promoting Indian self-government through formal constitutions and democratically elected tribal councils. A majority of Indian peoples — some 181 tribes — accepted the reorganization policy, but 77 declined to participate, primarily because they preferred the traditional way of making decisions by consensus rather than by majority vote. Through the new law, Indians won a degree of religious freedom, and tribal governments regained their status as semisovereign dependent nations. When the latter policy was upheld by the courts, Indian people gained a measure of leverage that would have major implications for Native rights in the second half of the twentieth century.

Like so many other federal Indian policies, however, the "Indian New Deal" was a mixed blessing. For some peoples, the act imposed a model of self-government that proved incompatible with tribal traditions and languages. The Papagos of southern Arizona, for instance, had no words for *budget* or *representative*, and they made no linguistic distinctions among *law*, *rule*, *charter*, and *constitution*. In another case, the nation's largest tribe, the Navajos, rejected the BIA's new policy, largely because the government was simultaneously reducing Navajo livestock to make room for the Boulder Dam project. In theory, the new policy gave Indians a much greater degree of self-determination. In practice, however, although some tribes did benefit, the BIA and Congress continued to interfere in internal Indian affairs and retained financial control over reservation governments.

**Struggles in the West**    By the 1920s, agriculture in California had become a big business — intensive, diversified, and export-oriented. Large-scale corporate-owned farms produced specialty crops — lettuce, tomatoes, peaches, grapes, and cotton — whose staggered harvests allowed the use of transient laborers. Thousands of workers, immigrants from Mexico and Asia and white migrants from the midwestern states, trooped from farm to farm and from crop to crop during the long picking season. Some migrants settled in the rapidly growing cities along the West Coast, especially the sprawling metropolis of Los Angeles. Under both Hoover and FDR, the federal government promoted the "repatriation" of Mexican citizens — their deportation to Mexico. Between 1929 and 1937, approximately half a million people of Mexican descent were deported. But historians estimate that more than 60 percent of these were legal U.S. citizens, making the government's actions constitutionally questionable.

Despite the deportations, many Mexican Americans benefitted from the New Deal and generally held Roosevelt and the Democratic Party in high regard. People of Mexican descent, like other Americans, took jobs with the WPA and the CCC, or received relief in the worst years of the depression. The National Youth Administration (NYA), which employed young people from families on relief and sponsored a variety of school programs, was especially important among Mexican Americans in southwestern cities. Even though New Deal programs did not fundamentally improve the migrant farm labor system under which so many people of Mexican descent labored, the New Deal coalition attracted Mexican Americans in large numbers because of the Democrats' commitment to ordinary people. "Franklin D. Roosevelt's name was the spark that started thousands of Spanish-speaking persons to the polls," noted one Los Angeles activist.

Men and women of Asian descent — mostly from China, Japan, and the Philippines — formed a small minority of the American population but were a significant presence in some West Coast cities. Immigrants from Japan and China had long faced discrimination. A 1913 California law prohibited them from owning land. Japanese farmers, who specialized in fruit and vegetable crops, circumvented this restriction by putting land titles in the names of their American-born children. As the depression cut farm prices and racial discrimination excluded young Japanese Americans from nonfarm jobs, about 20 percent of the immigrants returned to Japan.

Chinese Americans were less prosperous than their Japanese American counterparts. Only 3 percent of Chinese Americans worked in professional and technical positions, and discrimination barred them from most industrial jobs. In San Francisco, the majority of Chinese worked in small businesses: restaurants, laundries, and firms that imported textiles and ceramics. During the depression, they turned for assistance to Chinese social organizations such as *huiguan* (district associations) and to the city government; in 1931, about one-sixth of San Francisco's Chinese population was receiving public aid. But few Chinese benefitted from the New Deal. Until the repeal of the Exclusion Act in 1943, Chinese immigrants were classified as "aliens ineligible for citizenship" and therefore were excluded from most federal programs.

Because Filipino immigrants came from a U.S. territory, they were not affected by the ban on Asian immigration enacted in 1924. During the 1920s, their numbers swelled to about 50,000, many of whom worked as laborers on large corporate-owned farms. As the depression cut wages, Filipino immigration slowed to a trickle, and it was virtually cut off by the **Tydings-McDuffie Act** of 1934. The act granted independence to the Philippines (which since 1898 had been an American colony), classified all Filipinos in the United States as aliens, and restricted immigration from the Philippines to fifty people per year.

## Reshaping the Environment

Attention to natural resources was a consistent theme of the New Deal, and the shaping of the landscape was among its most visible legacies. Franklin Roosevelt and Interior Secretary Harold Ickes saw themselves as conservationists in the tradition of FDR's cousin, Theodore Roosevelt. In an era before environmentalism, FDR practiced what he called the "gospel of conservation." The president cared primarily about making the land — and other natural resources, such as trees and water — better serve human needs. National policy stressed scientific land management and ecological balance. Under Roosevelt, the federal government both responded to environmental crises and reshaped the use of natural resources, especially water, in the United States.

**The Dust Bowl**    Among the most hard-pressed citizens during the depression were farmers fleeing the "**dust bowl**" of the Great Plains. Between 1930 and 1941, a severe drought afflicted the semiarid states of Oklahoma, Texas, New Mexico, Colorado, Arkansas, and Kansas. Farmers in these areas had stripped the land of its native vegetation, which destroyed the delicate ecology of the plains. To grow wheat and other crops, they had pushed agriculture beyond the natural limits of the soil, making their land vulnerable, in times of drought, to wind erosion of the topsoil (Map 22.4). When the winds came, huge clouds of thick dust rolled over the land, turning the day into night. This ecological disaster prompted a mass exodus. At least 350,000 "Okies" (so called whether or not they were from Oklahoma) loaded their belongings into cars and trucks and headed to California. John Steinbeck's novel *The Grapes of Wrath* (1939) immortalized them, and New Deal photographer Dorothea Lange's haunting images of California migrant camps made them the public face of the depression's human toll.

Roosevelt and Ickes believed that poor land practices made for poor people. Under their direction, government agencies tackled the dust bowl's human causes.

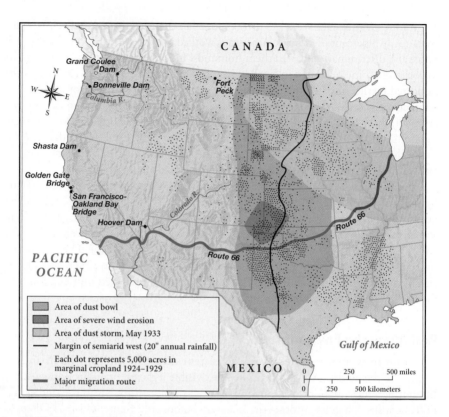

**MAP 22.4   The Dust Bowl and Federal Building Projects in the West, 1930–1941**
A U.S. Weather Bureau scientist called the drought of the 1930s "the worst in the climatological history of the country." Conditions were especially severe in the southern plains, where farming on marginal land threatened the environment even before the drought struck. As farm families migrated west on U.S. Route 66, the federal government began a series of massive building projects that provided flood control, irrigation, electric power, and transportation facilities to residents of the states of the Far West.

Agents from the newly created Soil Conservation Service, for instance, taught farmers to prevent soil erosion by tilling hillsides along the contours of the land. They also encouraged (and sometimes paid) farmers to take certain commercial crops out of production and plant soil-preserving grasses instead. One of the U.S. Forest Service's most widely publicized programs was the Shelterbelts, the planting of 220 million trees running north along the 99th meridian from Abilene, Texas, to the Canadian border. Planted as a windbreak, the trees also prevented soil erosion. A variety of government agencies, from the CCC to the U.S. Department of Agriculture, lent their expertise to establishing sound farming practices in the plains.

**Tennessee Valley Authority**   The most extensive New Deal environmental undertaking was the **Tennessee Valley Authority** (TVA), which Roosevelt saw as the first step in modernizing the South. Funded by Congress in 1933, the TVA integrated flood control, reforestation, electricity generation, and agricultural and industrial development. The dams and their hydroelectric plants provided cheap electric power for homes and factories as well as ample recreational opportunities for the valley's residents. The massive project won praise around the world (Map 22.5).

The TVA was an integral part of the Roosevelt administration's effort to keep farmers on the land by enhancing the quality of rural life. The **Rural Electrification Administration** (REA), established in 1935, was also central to that goal. Fewer than one-tenth of the nation's 6.8 million farms had electricity. The REA addressed this problem by promoting nonprofit farm cooperatives that offered loans to farmers to install power lines. By 1940, 40 percent of the nation's farms had electricity; a decade later, 90 percent did. Electricity brought relief from the drudgery and isolation of farm life. Electric irons, vacuum cleaners, and washing machines eased women's burdens, and radios brightened the lives of the entire family. Along with the automobile and the movies, electricity broke down the barriers between urban and rural life.

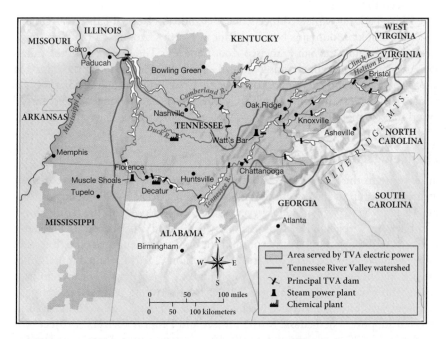

#### MAP 22.5   The Tennessee Valley Authority, 1933–1952

The Tennessee Valley Authority was one of the New Deal's most far-reaching environmental projects. Between 1933 and 1952, the TVA built twenty dams and improved five others, taming the flood-prone Tennessee River and its main tributaries. The cheap hydroelectric power generated by the dams brought electricity to industries as well as hundreds of thousands of area residents, and artificial lakes provided extensive recreational facilities. Widely praised at the time, the TVA came under attack in the 1970s for its practice of strip mining and the pollution caused by its power plants and chemical factories.

**Grand Coulee**    As the nation's least populated but fastest-growing region, the West benefitted enormously from the New Deal's attention to the environment. With the largest number of state and federal parks in the country, the West gained countless trails, bridges, cabins, and other recreational facilities, laying the groundwork for the post–World War II expansion of western tourism. On the Colorado River, Boulder Dam (later renamed Hoover Dam) was completed in 1935 with Public Works Administration funds; the dam generated power for the region's growing cities such as Las Vegas, Los Angeles, and Phoenix.

The largest project in the West, however, took shape in an obscure corner of Washington State, where the PWA and the Bureau of Reclamation built the Grand Coulee Dam on the Columbia River. When it was completed in 1941, Grand Coulee was the largest electricity-producing structure in the world, and its 150-mile lake provided irrigation for the state's major crops: apples, cherries, pears, potatoes, and wheat. Inspired by the dam and the modernizing spirit of the New Deal, folk singer Woody Guthrie wrote a song about the Columbia. "Your power is turning our darkness to dawn," he sang, "so roll on, Columbia, roll on!"

New Deal projects that enhanced people's enjoyment of the natural environment can be seen today throughout the country. CCC and WPA workers built the famous Blue Ridge Parkway, which connects the Shenandoah National Park in Virginia with the Great Smoky Mountains National Park in North Carolina. In the West, government workers built the San Francisco Zoo, Berkeley's Tilden Park, and the canals of San Antonio. The Civilian Conservation Corps helped to complete the East Coast's Appalachian Trail and the West Coast's Pacific Crest Trail through the Sierra Nevada. In state parks across the country, cabins, shelters, picnic areas, lodges, and observation towers stand as monuments to the New Deal ethos of recreation coexisting with nature.

## The New Deal and the Arts

In response to the Great Depression, many American writers and artists redefined their relationship to society. Never had there been a decade, critic Malcolm Cowley suggested in 1939, "when literary events followed so closely on the flying coat-tails of social events." New Deal administrators encouraged artists to create projects that would be of interest to the entire community, not just the cultured elite. Encouraged by the popular New Deal slogan "art for the millions," artists painted murals in hundreds of public buildings. The WPA's Federal Art Project gave work to many young artists who would become the twentieth century's leading painters, muralists, and sculptors. Jackson Pollock, Alice Neel, Willem de Kooning, and Louise Nevelson all received support. The Federal Music Project and **Federal Writers' Project** (FWP) employed 15,000 musicians and 5,000 writers, respectively. Among the latter were Saul Bellow, Ralph Ellison, and John Cheever, who became great American writers. The FWP also collected oral histories, including two thousand narratives by former slaves. The black folklorist and novelist Zora Neale Hurston finished three novels while in the Florida FWP, among them her best-known work, *Their Eyes Were Watching God* (1937). Richard Wright won the 1938 *Story* magazine prize for the best tale by a WPA writer and went on to complete *Native Son* (1940), a searing novel about white racism. Similarly, the Federal Theatre Project (FTP) nurtured such talented directors, actors, and playwrights as Orson Welles, John Huston, and Arthur Miller.

## The Legacies of the New Deal

The New Deal addressed the Great Depression by restoring hope and promising security. FDR and Congress created a powerful social-welfare state that took unprecedented responsibility for the well-being of American citizens. During the 1930s, millions of people began to pay taxes directly to the Social Security Administration, and more than one-third of the population received direct government assistance from federal programs. New legislation regulated the stock market, reformed the Federal Reserve System, and subjected business corporations to federal regulation. The New Deal's pattern of government involvement in social life would persist for the rest of the twentieth century. In the 1960s, Lyndon Johnson and the "Great Society" Congress dramatically expanded social-welfare programs—by creating Medicare and Medicaid, for instance—most of which remained intact in the wake of the "Reagan Revolution" of the 1980s (Chapter 29).

Like all other major social transformations, the New Deal was criticized both by those who thought it did too much and by those who believed it did too little. Conservatives, who prioritized limited government and individual freedom, pointed out that the New Deal state intruded deeply into the personal and financial lives of citizens and the affairs of business. Conversely, advocates of social-welfare liberalism complained that the New Deal's safety net had too many holes: no national health-care system, welfare programs that excluded domestic workers and farm laborers,

**Grand Coulee Dam** This extraordinary photo from a *Life* magazine essay shows workers hitching a ride on a 13-ton conduit as it is lowered into place on the Grand Coulee Dam in Washington State. Dozens of dams were constructed across the country under the auspices of various New Deal programs, but none were more majestic than two in the West: Boulder Dam (renamed Hoover Dam in 1947) and Grand Coulee. Built to harness the awesome power of the Columbia River as it rushed to the Pacific, Grand Coulee would ultimately provide electric power to Seattle, Portland, and other West Coast cities and new irrigation waters for Washington's apple and cherry orchards, among many other crops. Library of Congress.

and state governments that often limited the benefits distributed under New Deal programs.

Whatever the merits of its critics, the New Deal unquestionably transformed the American political landscape. From 1896 to 1932, the Republican Party had commanded the votes of a majority of Americans. That changed as Franklin Roosevelt's magnetic personality and innovative programs brought millions of voters into the Democratic fold. Democratic recruits included first- and second-generation immigrants from southern and central Europe — Italians, Poles, Russians, and Slavs, among others, most of them Catholic or Jewish — as well as African American migrants to northern cities. Organized labor aligned itself with a Democratic administration that had recognized unions as a legitimate force in modern industrial life. The elderly and the unemployed, assisted by the Social Security Act, likewise supported FDR. This New Deal coalition of ethnic groups, city dwellers, organized labor, African Americans, and a cross section of the middle class formed the nucleus of the northern Democratic Party and supported additional liberal reforms in the decades to come.

| **IN YOUR OWN WORDS** | In what ways did the New Deal promote change in American society? In what ways did it not? |

# Summary

We have seen how Franklin Delano Roosevelt's First New Deal focused on stimulating recovery, providing relief to the unemployed, and regulating banks and other financial institutions. The Second New Deal was different. Influenced by the persistence of the depression and the growing popularity of Huey Long's Share Our Wealth proposals, Roosevelt promoted social-welfare legislation that provided Americans with economic security.

We also explored the impact of the New Deal on various groups of citizens, especially African Americans, women, and unionized workers. Our survey paid particular attention to the lives of the Mexicans, Asians, and Okies who worked in the farms and factories of California. Because of New Deal assistance, the members of those groups gravitated toward the Democratic Party. The party's coalition of ethnic workers, African Americans, farmers, parts of the middle classes, and white southerners gave FDR and other Democrats a landslide victory in 1936.

Finally, we examined the accomplishments of the New Deal. In 1933, New Deal programs resolved the banking crisis while preserving capitalist institutions. Subsequently, these programs expanded the federal government and, through the Social Security system, farm subsidy programs, and public works projects, launched federal policies that were important to nearly every American. Great dams and electricity projects sponsored by the Tennessee Valley Authority, the Works Progress Administration in the West, and the Rural Electrification Administration permanently improved the quality of life for the nation's citizens.

# Chapter 22 Review

## KEY TERMS

**Identify and explain the significance of each term below.**

Smoot-Hawley Tariff (p. 638)
Bonus Army (p. 640)
fireside chats (p. 642)
Hundred Days (p. 642)
Glass-Steagall Act (p. 642)
Agricultural Adjustment Act (p. 643)
National Recovery Administration
  (p. 643)
Public Works Administration (p. 643)
Civilian Conservation Corps (p. 644)
Federal Housing Administration
  (p. 644)
Securities and Exchange Commission
  (p. 645)
American Liberty League (p. 645)
National Association of Manufacturers
  (p. 645)

Townsend Plan (p. 647)
welfare state (p. 648)
Wagner Act (p. 648)
Social Security Act (p. 648)
classical liberalism (p. 649)
Works Progress Administration
  (p. 649)
Roosevelt recession (p. 650)
Keynesian economics (p. 651)
Fair Labor Standards Act (p. 651)
Indian Reorganization Act (p. 655)
Tydings-McDuffie Act (p. 657)
dust bowl (p. 657)
Tennessee Valley Authority (p. 658)
Rural Electrification Administration
  (p. 659)
Federal Writers' Project (p. 660)

## REVIEW QUESTIONS

**Answer these questions to demonstrate your understanding of the chapter's main ideas.**

1. How did Americans, from ordinary citizens to political leaders, respond to the Great Depression?
2. What were the major components of the Hundred Days, and what was their purpose?
3. How did the Second New Deal reshape American government, and what political differences did it highlight?
4. In what ways did the New Deal promote change in American society? In what ways did it not?
5. Review the events listed under "American and National Identity," "Politics and Power," and "Culture and Society" on the thematic timeline on pages 580–581. Some historians have seen the New Deal as a natural evolution of progressive reforms from earlier in the century. Others have argued that it represented a revolution in social values and government institutions. Do you view the New Deal as an extension of progressivism, or a radical break with the past? Provide evidence for your argument.

## CHRONOLOGY

**As you read, ask yourself why this chapter begins and ends with these dates and identify the links among related events.**

| | |
|---|---|
| **1929** | • Stock market crash |
| **1930** | • Smoot-Hawley Tariff |
| **1931–1937** | • Scottsboro case: trials and appeals |
| **1932** | • Bonus Army marches on Washington, D.C. (May–July) |
| | • Franklin Delano Roosevelt elected president (November) |
| **1933** | • FDR's inaugural address and first fireside chats |
| | • Emergency Banking Act launches the Hundred Days |
| | • FDR takes United States off the gold standard |
| | • Civilian Conservation Corps (CCC) created |
| | • Agricultural Adjustment Act (AAA) |
| | • National Industrial Recovery Act (NIRA) |
| | • Tennessee Valley Authority (TVA) established |
| | • Townsend Clubs promote Old Age Revolving Pension Plan |
| **1934** | • Securities and Exchange Commission (SEC) created |
| | • Southern Tenant Farmers Union (STFU) founded |
| | • Indian Reorganization Act |
| | • Senator Huey Long promotes Share Our Wealth Society |
| **1935** | • Supreme Court voids NIRA in *Schechter v. United States* |
| | • National Labor Relations (Wagner) Act |
| | • Social Security Act creates old-age pension system |
| | • Works Progress Administration (WPA) created |
| | • Rural Electrification Administration (REA) established |
| | • Supreme Court voids Agricultural Adjustment Act |
| | • Congress of Industrial Organizations (CIO) formed |
| **1936** | • Landslide reelection of FDR marks peak of New Deal |
| **1937** | • FDR's Supreme Court plan fails |
| **1937–1938** | • "Roosevelt recession" raises unemployment |
| **1938** | • Fair Labor Standards Act |

# 23

## The World at War

### 1937–1945

**IDENTIFY THE BIG IDEA**

How did World War II transform the United States domestically and change its relationship with the world?

**THE SECOND WORLD WAR WAS THE DEFINING INTERNATIONAL EVENT** of the twentieth century. Battles raged across three continents and all of the world's oceans. It killed between 50 and 80 million people and wounded hundreds of millions more. When it was over, the industrial economies and much of the infrastructure of Europe and East Asia lay in ruins. Waged with both technologically advanced weapons and massive armies, the war involved every industrialized power in Europe, North America, and Asia, as well as dozens of other nations, many of them colonies of the industrialized countries.

The military conflict began on two continents: in Asia with Japan's 1937 invasion of China across the Sea of Japan, and in Europe with the 1939 blitzkrieg (lightning war) by Germany against Poland. It ended in 1945 after American planes dropped two atomic bombs, the product of stunning yet ominous scientific breakthroughs, on the Japanese cities of Hiroshima and Nagasaki. In between these demonstrations of technological prowess and devastating power, huge armies confronted and destroyed one another in the fields of France, the forests and steppes of Russia, the river valleys of China, the volcanic islands of the Pacific, and the deserts of North Africa.

"Armed defense of democratic existence is now being gallantly waged in four continents," President Franklin Delano Roosevelt told the nation in January 1941. After remaining neutral for several years, the United States would commit to that "armed defense." Both FDR and British prime minister Winston Churchill came to see the war as a defense of democratic values from the threat posed by German, Italian, and Japanese fascism. For them, the brutal conflict was the "good war." When the grim reality of the Jewish Holocaust came to light, U.S. participation in the war seemed even more just. But as much as it represented a struggle between democracy and fascism, it was also inescapably a war to maintain British, French, and Dutch control of colonies in Africa, India, the Middle East, and Southeast Asia. By 1945, democracy in the industrialized world had been preserved, and a new alliance between Western Europe and the United States had taken hold; the future of the vast European colonial empires, however, remained unresolved.

On the U.S. domestic front, World War II ended the Great Depression, hastened profound social changes, and expanded the scope and authority of the federal government. Racial politics and gender roles shifted under the weight of wartime migration and labor shortages. The pace of urbanization increased as millions of Americans uprooted themselves and moved hundreds or thousands of miles to join the military or to take a war job. A stronger, more robust federal government, the product of a long, hard-fought war, would remain in place to fight an even longer, more expensive, and potentially more dangerous Cold War in the ensuing years. These developments, which accelerated transformations already under way, would have repercussions far into the postwar decades.

# The Road to War

The Great Depression disrupted economic life around the world and led to the collapse of traditional political institutions. In response, an antidemocratic movement known as fascism, which had originated in Italy during the 1920s, developed in Germany, Spain, and Japan. By the mid-1930s, these nations had instituted authoritarian, militaristic governments led by powerful dictators: Benito Mussolini in Italy, Adolf Hitler in Nazi Germany, Francisco Franco in Spain, and, after 1940, Hideki Tojo in Japan. As early as 1936, President Roosevelt warned that other nations had "sold their heritage of freedom" and urged Americans to work for "the survival of democracy" both at home and abroad. Constrained by strong isolationist sentiment, by 1940 FDR was cautiously leading the nation toward war against the fascist powers.

## The Rise of Fascism

World War II had its roots in the settlement of World War I. Germany struggled under the harsh terms of the Treaty of Versailles, and Japan and Italy had their desire for overseas empires thwarted by the treaty makers. Faced with the expansive ambitions and nationalist resentments of those countries, the League of Nations, the collective security system established at Versailles, proved unable to maintain the existing international order.

**Fascism**, as instituted in Germany by Hitler, combined a centralized, authoritarian state, a doctrine of Aryan racial supremacy, and fervent nationalism in a call for the spiritual reawakening of the German people. Fascist leaders worldwide disparaged parliamentary government, independent labor movements, and individual rights. They opposed both the economic collectivism of the Soviet Union — where, in theory, the state managed the economy to ensure social equality — and the competitive capitalist economies of the United States and Western Europe. Fascist movements arose around the world in the 1930s but managed to achieve power in only a handful of countries. Those countries were at the center of global war making in that decade.

**Japan and Italy**　The first challenge came from Japan. To become an industrial power, Japan required raw materials and overseas markets. Like the Western European powers and the United States before it, Japan embraced an expansionary foreign policy in pursuit of colonial possessions and overseas influence. In 1931, its troops occupied Manchuria, an industrialized province in northern China, and in 1937 the Japanese launched a full-scale invasion of China. In both instances, the League of Nations condemned Japan's actions but did nothing to stop them.

Japan's defiance of the League encouraged a fascist leader half a world away: Italy's Benito Mussolini, who had come to power in 1922. Il Duce (The Leader), as Mussolini was known, had long denounced the Versailles treaty, which denied Italy's colonial claims in Africa and the Middle East after World War I. As in Japan, the Italian fascists desired overseas colonies for raw materials, markets, and national prestige. In 1935, Mussolini invaded Ethiopia, one of the few remaining independent countries in Africa. Ethiopian emperor Haile Selassie appealed to the League of Nations, but the League's verbal condemnation and limited sanctions, its only real leverage, did not stop Italy from taking control of Ethiopia in 1936.

**Hitler's Germany**　Germany, however, posed the gravest threat to the existing world order. Huge World War I reparation payments, economic depression, fear of communism, labor unrest, and rising unemployment fueled the ascent of Adolf Hitler and his **National Socialist (Nazi) Party**. When Hitler became chancellor of Germany in 1933, the Reichstag (the German legislature) granted him dictatorial powers to deal with the economic crisis. Hitler promptly outlawed other political parties, arrested many of his political rivals, and declared himself führer (leader). Under Nazi control, the Reichstag invested all legislative power in Hitler's hands.

Hitler's goal was nothing short of European domination and world power, as he had made clear in his 1925 book *Mein Kampf* (*My Struggle*). The book outlined his plans to overturn the territorial settlements of the Versailles treaty, unite Germans living throughout central Europe in a great German fatherland, and annex large areas of Eastern Europe. The "inferior races" who lived in these regions — Jews, Gypsies, and Slavs — would be removed or subordinated to the German "master race." These territories would provide Germany with what Hitler called "lebensraum" (living space) — a new region of settlement and farming and a source of natural resources. A virulent anti-Semite, Hitler had long blamed Jews for Germany's problems. Once in power, he began a sustained and brutal persecution of Jews, which expanded into a campaign of extermination in the early 1940s.

In 1935, Hitler began to rearm Germany, in violation of the Versailles treaty. No nation stopped him. In 1936, he sent troops into the Rhineland, a demilitarized zone under the terms of Versailles. Again, France and Britain took no action. Later that year, Hitler and Mussolini formed the **Rome-Berlin Axis**, a political and military alliance between the two fascist nations. Also in 1936, Germany signed a pact to create a military alliance with Japan against the Soviet Union. With these alliances in place, and with France and Great Britain reluctant to oppose him, Hitler had seized the military advantage in Europe by 1937.

## War Approaches

As Hitler pushed his initiatives in Europe, which was as deeply mired in economic depression as the United States, the Roosevelt administration faced widespread isolationist sentiment among Americans. In part, this desire to avoid European entanglements reflected disillusion with American participation in World War I. In 1934, Gerald P. Nye, a progressive Republican senator from North Dakota, launched an investigation into the profits of munitions makers during that war. Nye's committee alleged that arms manufacturers (popularly labeled "merchants of death") had maneuvered President Wilson into World War I.

Although Nye's committee failed to prove its charge against weapon makers, its factual findings prompted an isolationist-minded Congress to pass a series of acts to prevent the nation from being drawn into another overseas war. The **Neutrality Act of 1935** imposed an embargo on selling arms to warring countries and declared that Americans traveling on the ships of belligerent nations did so at their own risk. In two subsequent Neutrality Acts, Congress banned loans to

**Charles Lindbergh Cartoon**
Charles Lindbergh, the first person to fly solo nonstop across the Atlantic Ocean, was an American hero in the 1930s. In 1941, he had become the public face of the America First Committee, which was determined to keep the United States from entering the wars raging in Europe and Asia. In this political cartoon from October 1941, Lindbergh is shown standing on a soapbox labeled "Fascism," looking up at the figure of "Democracy." The implication is that Lindbergh had been fooled by German propaganda into taking its side. Less than two months after the cartoon appeared, Japan attacked Pearl Harbor, and isolationist sentiment all but disappeared in the United States. Library of Congress.

belligerents (1936), and then, in 1937, imposed a "cash-and-carry" requirement: if a warring country wanted to purchase nonmilitary goods from the United States, it had to pay cash and carry them in its own ships, keeping the United States out of potentially dangerous naval warfare (a fourth Neutrality Act, in 1939, permitted military goods to be purchased under the same terms).

Americans for the most part had little enthusiasm for war, and a wide variety of groups and individuals espoused isolationism. Many isolationists looked to Republican Ohio senator Robert Taft, who distrusted both Roosevelt and European nations with equal conviction, or to the aviator hero Charles A. Lindbergh, who delivered impassioned speeches against intervention in Europe. Some isolationists, such as the conservative National Legion of Mothers of America, combined anticommunism, Christian morality, and even anti-Semitism. Isolationists were primarily conservatives, but a contingent of progressives (or liberals) opposed America's involvement in the war on pacifist or moral grounds. Whatever their philosophies, ardent isolationists forced Roosevelt to approach the brewing war cautiously.

**The Popular Front**   Other Americans responded to the rise of European fascism by advocating U.S. intervention. Some of the most prominent Americans pushing for greater involvement in Europe, even if it meant war, were affiliated with the **Popular Front**. Wary of German and Japanese aggression, the Soviet Union instructed Communists in Western Europe and the United States to join with liberals in a broad coalition opposing fascism. In the United States, the Popular Front drew from a wide range of social groups, including the American Communist Party (which had increased its membership to between fifty and seventy thousand), African American civil rights activists, trade unionists, left-wing writers and intellectuals, and even a few New Deal administrators. Many supporters in the United States grew uneasy with the Popular Front because of the brutal political repression in the Soviet Union under Joseph Stalin. Nevertheless, Popular Front activists were among a small but vocal group of Americans encouraging Roosevelt to take a stronger stand against European fascism.

**The Failure of Appeasement**   Encouraged by the weak worldwide response to the invasions of China, Ethiopia, and the Rhineland, and emboldened by British and French neutrality during the Spanish Civil War, Hitler grew more aggressive in 1938. He sent troops to annex German-speaking Austria while making clear his intention to seize part of Czechoslovakia. Because Czechoslovakia had an alliance with France, war seemed imminent. But at the **Munich Conference** in September 1938, Britain and France capitulated, agreeing to let Germany annex the Sudetenland — a German-speaking border area of Czechoslovakia — in return for Hitler's pledge to seek no more territory. The agreement, declared British prime minister Neville Chamberlain, guaranteed "peace for our time." Hitler drew a different conclusion, telling his generals: "Our enemies are small fry. I saw them in Munich."

Within six months, Hitler's forces had overrun the rest of Czechoslovakia and were threatening to march into Poland. Realizing that their policy of appeasement — capitulating to Hitler's demands — had been disastrous, Britain and France warned Hitler that further aggression meant war. Then, in August 1939, Hitler and Stalin shocked the world by signing a mutual nonaggression pact. For

Hitler, this pact was crucial, as it meant that Germany would not have to wage a two-front war against Britain and France in the west and the Soviet Union in the east. On September 1, 1939, Hitler launched a blitzkrieg against Poland. Two days later, Britain and France declared war on Germany. World War II had officially begun.

Two days after the European war started, the United States declared its neutrality. But President Roosevelt made no secret of his sympathies. When war broke out in 1914, Woodrow Wilson had told Americans to be neutral "in thought as well as in action." FDR, by contrast, now said: "This nation will remain a neutral nation, but I cannot ask that every American remain neutral in thought as well." The overwhelming majority of Americans—some 84 percent, according to a poll in 1939—supported Britain and France rather than Germany, but most wanted America to avoid another European war.

At first, the need for U.S. intervention seemed remote. After Germany conquered Poland in September 1939, calm settled over Europe. Then, on April 9, 1940, German forces invaded Denmark and Norway. In May, the Netherlands, Belgium, and Luxembourg fell to the swift German army. The final shock came in mid-June, when France too surrendered. Britain now stood alone against Hitler's plans for domination of Europe.

**Isolationists and Interventionists**   What *Time* magazine would later call America's "thousand-step road to war" had already begun. After a bitter battle in Congress in 1939, Roosevelt won a change in the neutrality laws to allow the Allies to buy arms as well as nonmilitary goods on a cash-and-carry basis. Interventionists, led by journalist William Allen White and his **Committee to Defend America by Aiding the Allies**, became increasingly vocal in 1940 as war escalated in Europe. In response, isolationists formed the **America First Committee** (AFC), with well-respected figures such as Lindbergh and Senator Nye urging the nation to stay out of the war. The AFC held rallies across the United States, and its posters, brochures, and broadsides warning against American involvement in Europe suffused many parts of the country, especially the Midwest.

Because of the America Firsters' efforts, Roosevelt proceeded cautiously in 1940 as he moved the United States closer to involvement. The president did not want war, but he believed that most Americans "greatly underestimate the serious implications to our own future," as he confided to White. In May, Roosevelt created the National Defense Advisory Commission and brought two prominent Republicans, Henry Stimson and Frank Knox, into his cabinet as secretaries of war and the navy, respectively. During the summer, the president traded fifty World War I destroyers to Great Britain in exchange for the right to build military bases on British possessions in the Atlantic, circumventing neutrality laws by using an executive order to complete the deal. In October 1940, a bipartisan vote in Congress approved a large increase in defense spending and instituted the first peacetime draft in American history. "We must be the great arsenal of democracy," FDR declared.

As the war in Europe and the Pacific expanded, the United States was preparing for the 1940 presidential election. The crisis had convinced Roosevelt to seek an unprecedented third term. The Republicans nominated Wendell Willkie of Indiana, a former Democrat who supported many New Deal policies. The two parties' platforms differed only slightly. Both pledged aid to the Allies, and both candidates promised not to "send an American boy into the shambles of a European war," as Willkie put it. Willkie's spirited campaign resulted in a closer election than that of 1932 or 1936. Nonetheless, Roosevelt won 55 percent of the popular vote.

Having been reelected, Roosevelt now undertook to persuade Congress to increase aid to Britain, whose survival he viewed as key to American security. In January 1941, he delivered one of the most important speeches of his career. Defining "four essential human freedoms" — freedom of speech, freedom of religion, freedom from want, and freedom from fear — Roosevelt cast the war as a noble defense of democratic societies. He then linked the fate of democracy in Western Europe with the new welfare state at home. Sounding a decidedly New Deal note, Roosevelt pledged to end "special privileges for the few" and to preserve "civil liberties for all." Like President Wilson's speech championing national self-determination at the close of World War I, Roosevelt's **"Four Freedoms"** speech outlined a liberal international order with appeal well beyond its intended European and American audiences.

Two months later, in March 1941, with Britain no longer able to pay cash for arms, Roosevelt persuaded Congress to pass the **Lend-Lease Act**. The legislation authorized the president to "lease, lend, or otherwise dispose of" arms and equipment to Britain or any other country whose defense was considered vital to the security of the United States. When Hitler abandoned his nonaggression pact with Stalin and invaded the Soviet Union in June 1941, the United States extended lend-lease to the Soviets. The implementation of lend-lease marked the unofficial entrance of the United States into the European war.

Roosevelt underlined his support for the Allied cause by meeting in August 1941 with British prime minister Winston Churchill (who had succeeded Chamberlain in 1940). Their joint press release, which became known as the **Atlantic Charter**, provided the ideological foundation of the Western cause. Drawing from Wilson's Fourteen Points and Roosevelt's Four Freedoms, the charter called for economic cooperation, national self-determination, and guarantees of political stability after the war to ensure "that all men in all the lands may live out their lives in freedom from fear and want." It would become the basis for a new American-led transatlantic alliance after the war's conclusion. Its promise of national self-determination, however, set up potential conflict in Asia and Africa, where European powers would be reluctant to abandon their colonial holdings.

In the fall of 1941, the reality of U.S. involvement in the war drew closer. By September, Nazi U-boats and the American navy were exchanging fire in the Atlantic. With isolationists still a potent force, Roosevelt hesitated to declare war and insisted that the United States would defend itself only against a direct attack. But behind the scenes, the president and his close advisors considered war inevitable.

## The Attack on Pearl Harbor

The crucial provocation came not from Germany but from Japan. After Japan invaded China in 1937, Roosevelt had denounced "the present reign of terror and international lawlessness" and suggested that aggressors be "quarantined" by peaceful nations. Despite such rhetoric, the United States refused to intervene later that year when Japanese troops sacked the city of Nanjing, massacred 300,000 Chinese residents, and raped thousands of women.

With China weakened as a counterweight, Japan's military and imperial ambitions expanded. In 1940, General Hideki Tojo became war minister. After concluding a formal military alliance with Germany and Italy that year, Tojo dispatched Japanese troops to occupy the northern part of the French colony of Indochina (present-day Vietnam, Cambodia, and Laos). Tojo's goal, supported by Emperor Hirohito, was to create a "Greater East Asia Co-Prosperity Sphere" under Japan's control, stretching from the Korean Peninsula south to Indonesia. Like Germany and Italy, Japan sought to match the overseas empires of Britain, France, Holland, and the United States.

When Japanese troops staged a full-scale invasion of Indochina in July 1941, Roosevelt froze Japanese assets in the United States and stopped all trade with Japan. This included vital oil shipments that accounted for almost 80 percent of Japanese consumption. In October 1941, General Tojo became prime minister and accelerated secret preparations for war against the United States. By November, American military intelligence knew that Japan was planning an attack but did not know where it would occur.

Early on Sunday morning, December 7, 1941, Japanese bombers attacked **Pearl Harbor** in Hawaii, killing more than 2,400 Americans. They destroyed or heavily damaged eight battleships, three cruisers, three destroyers, and almost two hundred airplanes. Although the assault was devastating, it united the American people. Calling December 7th "a date which will live in infamy," President Roosevelt asked Congress for a declaration of war against Japan. The Senate voted unanimously for war, and the House concurred by a vote of 388 to 1. The lone dissenter was Jeannette Rankin of Montana, a committed pacifist—she also voted against entry into World War I—and the first female member of Congress. Three days later, Germany and Italy declared war on the United States, which in turn declared war on the Axis powers. The long shadows of two wars, one in Europe and one in Asia, had at long last converged over the United States.

| IN YOUR OWN WORDS | Explain the steps by which the United States became involved in World War II. |
|---|---|

# Organizing for a Global War

The task of fighting on a global scale dramatically increased the power of the federal government. Shifting from civilian to military production, raising an army, and assembling the necessary workforce required a massive expansion in government authority. When Congress passed the **War Powers Act** in December 1941, it gave President Roosevelt unprecedented control over all aspects of the war effort. Necessary to fight the war, this act marked the beginning of what some historians call the imperial presidency: the far-reaching use (and sometimes abuse) of executive authority during the second half of the twentieth century.

## Financing the War

Defense mobilization, not the New Deal of the 1930s, ended the Great Depression. Between 1940 and 1945, the annual gross national product doubled, and after-tax profits of American businesses nearly doubled. Federal spending on war production powered this advance. By late 1943, two-thirds of the economy was directly involved in the war effort, and war-related production jumped from just 2 percent of GNP to 40 percent. The government paid for these military expenditures by raising taxes and borrowing money. The **Revenue Act** of 1942 expanded the number of people paying income taxes from 3.9 million to 42.6 million. Taxes on personal incomes and business profits paid half the cost of the war. The government borrowed the rest, both from wealthy Americans and from ordinary citizens, who invested in treasury bonds (war bonds).

Financing and coordinating the war effort required far-reaching cooperation between government and private business. The number of civilians employed by the government increased almost fourfold, to 3.8 million—a far higher rate of growth than that during the New Deal. The powerful War Production Board (WPB) awarded defense contracts, allocated scarce resources—such as rubber, copper, and oil—for military uses, and persuaded businesses to convert to military production. For example, it encouraged Ford and General Motors to build tanks rather than cars by granting generous tax advantages for re-equipping existing factories and building new ones. In other instances, the board approved "cost-plus" contracts, which guaranteed corporations a profit and allowed them to keep new steel mills, factories, and shipyards after the war. Such government subsidies of defense industries would intensify during the Cold War and continue to this day. These corporations would form the core of what became known as the nation's "military-industrial complex" during the Cold War (Chapter 24).

To secure maximum production, the WPB preferred to deal with major enterprises rather than with small businesses. The nation's fifty-six largest corporations received three-fourths of the war contracts; the top ten received one-third. The best-known contractor was Henry J. Kaiser. Already highly successful from building roads in California and the Hoover and Grand Coulee dams, Kaiser went from government construction work to navy shipbuilding. At his shipyard in Richmond, California, he revolutionized ship construction by applying Henry Ford's techniques of mass production. To meet wartime production schedules, Kaiser broke the work process down into small, specialized tasks that newly trained workers could do easily. Soon, each of his work crews was building a "Liberty Ship," a large vessel to carry cargo and troops to the war zone, every two weeks. The press dubbed him the Miracle Man.

Central to Kaiser's success were his close ties to federal agencies. The government financed the great dams that he built during the depression, and the Reconstruction Finance Corporation lent him $300 million to build shipyards and manufacturing plants during the war. Working together in this way, American business and government turned out a prodigious supply of military hardware: 86,000 tanks; 296,000 airplanes; 15 million rifles and machine guns; 64,000 landing craft; and 6,500 cargo ships and naval vessels. The American way of war, wrote the Scottish historian D. W. Brogan in 1944, was "mechanized like the American farm and kitchen." America's industrial might, as much as or more than its troops, proved the decisive factor in winning World War II.

## Mobilizing the American Fighting Force

The expanding federal bureaucracy also had a human face. To fight the war, the government mobilized tens of millions of soldiers, civilians, and workers—coordinated on a scale unprecedented in U.S. history. During World War II, the armed forces of the United States enlisted more than sixteen million men and women. In no other military conflict have so many American citizens served in the armed services. They came from every region and economic station: black sharecroppers from Alabama; white farmers from the Midwest; the sons and daughters of European, Mexican, and Caribbean immigrants; Native men from Navajo and Choctaw reservations and other tribal communities; women from every state in the nation; even Hollywood celebrities. From urban, rural, and suburban areas, from working-class and middle-class backgrounds—they all served in the military.

In contrast to its otherwise democratic character, the American army segregated the nearly one million African Americans in uniform. The National Association for the Advancement of Colored People (NAACP) and other civil rights groups reprimanded the government, saying, "A Jim Crow army cannot fight for a free world," but the military continued to separate black soldiers and assign them menial duties. The poet Langston Hughes observed the irony: "We are elevator boys, janitors, red caps, maids—a race in uniform." The military uniform, Hughes implied, was not assigned to African Americans so readily. Native Americans and Mexican Americans, on the other hand, were never officially segregated; they rubbed elbows with the sons of European immigrants and native-born soldiers from all regions of the country.

Among the most instrumental soldiers were the Native American "**code talkers.**" In the Pacific theater, native Navajo speakers communicated orders to fleet commanders. Japanese intelligence could not decipher the code because it was based on the Navajo language, which fewer than fifty non-Navajos in the world understood. At the battle of Iwo Jima, for instance—one of the war's fiercest—Navajo code talkers, working around the clock, sent and received more than eight hundred messages without error. In the European theater, army commanders used Comanche, Choctaw, and Cherokee speakers to thwart the Nazis and exchange crucial military commands on the battlefield. No Axis nation ever broke these Native American codes.

Approximately 350,000 American women enlisted in the military. About 140,000 served in the Women's Army Corps (WAC), and 100,000 served in the navy's Women Accepted for Volunteer Emergency Service (WAVES). One-third of the nation's registered nurses, almost 75,000 overall, volunteered for military duty. In addition, about 1,000 Women's Airforce Service Pilots (WASPs) ferried planes and supplies in noncombat areas. The armed forces limited the duties assigned to women, however. Female officers could not command men, and WACs and WAVES were barred from combat duty, although nurses of both sexes served close to the front lines, risking capture or death. Most of the jobs that women did in the military—clerical work, communications, and health care—resembled women's jobs in civilian life.

Historians still debate how to characterize the World War II American military. As an army of "citizen-soldiers," it represented a wide stratum of society. Military service gave a generation of men a noble purpose, following a decade of economic depression. And its ethic of patriotism further advanced the children of immigrants into mainstream American life. Yet the military embodied the tensions and contradictions of American society as well. The draft revealed appalling levels of health, fitness, and education among millions of Americans, spurring reformers to call for improved literacy and nutrition. Women's integration into the military was marked by deep anxieties about the threat to "womanhood" allegedly posed by service. The American army was like the nation itself. United in wartime purpose, the military reflected the strengths and weaknesses of a diverse, fractious society.

## Workers and the War Effort

As millions of working-age citizens joined the military, the nation faced a critical labor shortage. Consequently, many women and African Americans joined the industrial workforce, taking jobs unavailable to them before the conflict. Unions, benefitting from the demand for labor, negotiated higher wages and improved conditions for America's workers. By 1943, with the economy operating at full capacity, the breadlines and double-digit unemployment of the 1930s were a memory.

**Rosie the Riveter**    Government officials and corporate recruiters urged women to take jobs in defense industries, creating a new image of working women. "Longing won't bring him back sooner . . . GET A WAR JOB!" one poster urged, while artist Norman Rockwell's famous "Rosie the Riveter" illustration beckoned to women

**Rosie the Riveter** Women workers install fixtures and assemblies to a tail fuselage section of a B-17 bomber at the Douglas Aircraft Company plant in Long Beach, California. To entice women to become war workers, the War Manpower Commission created the image of "Rosie the Riveter," later immortalized in posters and by a Norman Rockwell illustration on the cover of the *Saturday Evening Post.* A popular 1942 song celebrating Rosie went: "Rosie's got a boyfriend, Charlie / Charlie, he's a marine / Rosie is protecting Charlie / Working overtime on the riveting machine." Even as women joined the industrial workforce in huge numbers (half a million in the aircraft industry alone), they were understood as fulfilling a nurturing, protective role. Library of Congress.

from the cover of the *Saturday Evening Post*. The government directed its publicity at housewives, but many working women gladly abandoned low-paying "women's jobs" as domestic servants or secretaries for higher-paying work in the defense industry. Suddenly, the nation's factories were full of women working as airplane riveters, ship welders, and drill-press operators. Women made up 36 percent of the labor force in 1945, compared with 24 percent at the beginning of the war. War work did not free women from traditional expectations and limitations, however. Women often faced sexual harassment on the job and usually received lower wages than men did. In ship-yards, women with the most seniority and responsibility earned $6.95 a day, whereas the top men made as much as $22.

Wartime work was thus bittersweet for women, because it combined new oppor-tunities with old constraints. The majority labored in low-wage service jobs. Child care was often unavailable, despite the largest government-sponsored child-care program in history. When the men returned from war, Rosie the Riveter was usually out of a job. Government propaganda now encouraged women back into the home—where, it was implied, their true calling lay in raising families. But many married women refused, or could not afford, to put on aprons and stay home. Women's participation in the paid labor force rebounded by the late 1940s and continued to rise over the rest of the twentieth century, bringing major changes in family life (Chapter 25).

**Wartime Civil Rights**    Among African Americans, a new militancy emerged during the war. Pointing to parallels between anti-Semitism in Germany and racial discrimination in the United States, black leaders waged the Double V campaign: calling for victory over Nazism abroad and racism at home. "This is a war for freedom. Whose freedom?" the renowned black leader W. E. B. Du Bois asked. If it meant "the freedom of Negroes in the Southern United States," Du Bois answered, "my gun is on my shoulder."

Even before Pearl Harbor, black activism was on the rise. In 1940, only 240 of the nation's 100,000 aircraft workers were black, and most of them were jani-tors. African American leaders demanded that the government require defense con-tractors to hire more black workers. When the Roosevelt administration took no action, A. Philip Randolph, head of the Brotherhood of Sleeping Car Porters, the largest black labor union in the country, announced plans for a march on Washing-ton in the summer of 1941.

Roosevelt was not a strong supporter of African American equality, but he wanted to avoid public protest and a disruption of the nation's war preparations. So the president made a deal: he issued **Executive Order 8802**, and in June 1941 Randolph canceled the march. The order prohibited "discrimination in the employ-ment of workers in defense industries or government because of race, creed, color, or national origin" and established the Fair Employment Practice Committee (FEPC). Mary McLeod Bethune called the wartime FEPC "a refreshing shower in a thirsty land." This federal commitment to black employment rights was unprecedented but limited: it did not affect segregation in the armed forces, and the FEPC could not enforce compliance with its orders.

Nevertheless, wartime developments laid the groundwork for the civil rights rev-olution of the 1950s and 1960s. The NAACP grew ninefold, to 450,000 members, by 1945. In Chicago, James Farmer helped to found the Congress of Racial Equality (CORE) in 1942, a group that would become known nationwide in the 1960s for its direct action protests such as sit-ins. The FEPC inspired black organizing against employment discrimination in hundreds of cities and workplaces. Behind this combination of government action and black militancy, the civil rights movement would advance on multiple fronts in the postwar years.

Mexican Americans, too, challenged long-standing practices of discrimination and exclusion. Throughout much of the Southwest, it was still common for signs to read "No Mexicans Allowed," and Mexican American workers were confined to menial, low-paying jobs. Several organizations, including the League of United Latin American Citizens (LULAC) and the Spanish-Speaking People's Congress, pressed the government and private employers to end anti-Mexican discrimination. Mexican American workers themselves, often in Congress of Industrial Organizations (CIO) unions such as the Cannery Workers and Shipyard Workers, also led efforts to enforce the FEPC's equal employment mandate.

Exploitation persisted, however. To meet wartime labor demands, the U.S. government brought tens of thousands of Mexican contract laborers into the United States under the **Bracero Program**. Paid little and treated poorly, the braceros (who took their name from the Spanish *brazo*, "arm") highlighted the oppressive conditions of farm labor in the United States. After the war, the federal government continued to participate in labor exploitation, bringing hundreds of thousands of Mexicans into the country to perform low-wage agricultural work. Future Mexican American civil rights leaders Dolores Huerta and Cesar Chavez began to fight this labor system in the 1950s.

**Organized Labor**    During the war, unions solidified their position as the most powerful national voice for American workers and extended gains made during the New Deal. By 1945, almost 15 million workers belonged to a union, up from 9 million in 1939. Representatives of the major unions made a no-strike pledge for the duration of the war, and Roosevelt rewarded them by creating the National War Labor Board (NWLB), composed of representatives of labor, management, and the public. The NWLB established wages, hours, and working conditions and had the authority to seize manufacturing plants that did not comply.

Despite these arrangements, unions faced a sometimes hostile Congress. Frustrated with limits on wage increases and the no-strike pledge, in 1943 more than half a million United Mine Workers went out on strike, demanding a higher wage increase than that recommended by the NWLB. Congress responded by passing (over Roosevelt's veto) the Smith-Connally Labor Act of 1943, which allowed the president to prohibit strikes in defense industries and forbade political contributions by unions. Although organized labor would emerge from World War II more powerful than at any time in U.S. history, its business and corporate opponents, too, would emerge from the war with new strength.

## Politics in Wartime

In his 1944 State of the Union address, FDR called for a second Bill of Rights, one that would guarantee all Americans access to education and jobs, adequate food and clothing, and decent housing and medical care. Like his Four Freedoms speech, this was a call to extend the New Deal by broadening the rights to individual security and welfare guaranteed by the government. The answer to his call, however, would have to wait for the war's conclusion. Congress created new government benefits only for military veterans, known as GIs (short for "government issue"). The **Servicemen's Readjustment Act** (1944), an extraordinarily influential program popularly known as the "GI Bill of Rights," provided education, job training, medical care, pensions, and home loans for men and women who had served in the armed forces (Chapter 25).

The president's call for social legislation sought to reinvigorate the New Deal political coalition. In the election of 1944, Roosevelt again headed the Democratic ticket. But party leaders, aware of FDR's health problems and fearing that Vice President Henry Wallace's outspoken support for labor and civil rights would alienate moderate voters, dropped him from the ticket. In his place, they chose Senator Harry S. Truman of Missouri, a plain-spoken — some even thought drab — politician with little national experience. The Republicans nominated Governor Thomas E. Dewey of New York. Dewey, who accepted the general principles of welfare-state liberalism domestically and favored internationalism in foreign affairs, attracted some of Roosevelt's supporters. But a majority of voters preferred political continuity, and Roosevelt was reelected with 53.5 percent of the nationwide vote. The Democratic coalition retained its hold on government power, and the era of Republican political dominance (1896–1932) slipped further into the past.

| IN YOUR OWN WORDS | What aspects of the economy and American society were affected by mobilization for war? |
|---|---|

# Life on the Home Front

The United States escaped the physical devastation that ravaged Europe and East Asia, but the war profoundly changed the country. Americans welcomed wartime prosperity but shuddered when they saw a Western Union boy on his bicycle, fearing that he carried a War Department telegram reporting the death of someone's son, husband, or father. Citizens also grumbled about annoying wartime regulations and rationing but accepted that their lives would be different "for the duration."

## "For the Duration"

Spurred by both government propaganda and a desire to serve the war cause, people on the home front took on wartime responsibilities. They worked on civilian defense committees, recycled old newspapers and scrap metal, and served on local rationing and draft boards. About twenty million backyard "victory gardens" produced 40 percent of the nation's vegetables. Various federal agencies encouraged these efforts, especially the Office of War Information (OWI), which disseminated news and promoted patriotism. The OWI urged advertising agencies to link their clients' products to the war effort, arguing that patriotic ads would not only sell goods but also "invigorate, instruct and inspire" citizens.

Popular culture, especially the movies, reinforced connections between the home front and the war effort. Hollywood producers, directors, and actors offered their talents to the War Department. Director Frank Capra created a documentary series titled *Why We Fight* to explain war aims to conscripted soldiers. Movie stars such as John Wayne and Spencer Tracy portrayed heroic American fighting men in numerous films, such as *Guadalcanal Diary* (1943) and *Thirty Seconds over Tokyo* (1944). In this pretelevision era, newsreels accompanying the feature films kept the public up-to-date on the war, as did on-the-spot radio broadcasts by Edward R. Murrow and Mary Marvin Breckenridge, the first female radio correspondent for CBS.

For many Americans, the major inconvenience during the war years was the shortage of consumer goods. Beginning in 1942, federal agencies subjected almost everything Americans ate, wore, or used to rationing or regulation. The first major scarcity was rubber. The Japanese conquest of Malaysia and Dutch Indonesia cut off 97 percent of America's imports of that essential raw material. To conserve rubber for the war effort, the government rationed tires, so many of the nation's 30 million car owners put their cars in storage. As more people walked, they wore out their shoes. In 1944, shoes were rationed to two pairs per person a year. By 1943, the government was rationing meat, butter, sugar, and other foods. Most citizens cooperated with the complicated rationing system, but at least one-quarter of the population bought items on the black market, especially meat, gasoline, cigarettes, and nylon stockings.

## Migration and the Wartime City

The war determined where people lived. When men entered the armed services, their families often followed them to military bases or points of debarkation. Civilians moved to take high-paying defense jobs. About 15 million Americans changed residences during the war years, half of them moving to another state. One of them was Peggy Terry, who grew up in Paducah, Kentucky; worked in a shell-loading plant in nearby Viola; and then moved to a defense plant in Michigan. There, she recalled, "I met all those wonderful Polacks [Polish Americans]. They were the first people I'd ever known that were any different from me. A whole new world just opened up."

As the center of defense production for the Pacific war, California experienced the largest share of wartime migration. The state welcomed 2.5 million new residents and grew by 35 percent during the war. "The Second Gold Rush Hits the West," announced the *San Francisco Chronicle* in 1943. One-tenth of all federal dollars spent on the war flowed into California, and the state's factories turned out one-sixth of all war materials. People went where the defense jobs were: to Los Angeles, San Diego, and cities around San Francisco Bay. Some towns grew practically overnight; within two years of the opening of the Kaiser Corporation shipyard in Richmond, California, the town's population quadrupled. Other industrial states—notably New York, Illinois, Michigan, and Ohio—also attracted both federal dollars and migrants on a large scale.

The growth of war industries accelerated patterns of rural-urban migration. Cities grew dramatically, as factories, shipyards, and other defense plants drew millions of citizens from small towns and rural areas. This new mobility, coupled with people's distance from their hometowns, loosened the authority of traditional institutions and made wartime cities vibrant and lively. Around-the-clock work shifts kept people on the streets night and day, and bars, jazz clubs, dance halls, and movie theaters proliferated, fed by the ready cash of war workers.

**Racial Conflict**   Migration and more fluid social boundaries meant that people of different races and ethnicities mixed in the booming cities. Over one million African Americans left the rural South for California, Illinois, Michigan, Ohio, and Pennsylvania — a continuation of the Great Migration earlier in the century (Chapters 20 and 21). In a repeat of the events of World War I, as blacks and whites competed for jobs and housing, racial conflicts broke out in more than a hundred cities in 1943. Detroit saw the worst violence. In June 1943, a riot incited by southern-born whites and Polish Americans against African Americans left thirty-four people dead and hundreds injured.

Racial conflict struck the West as well. In Los Angeles, male Mexican American teenagers formed *pachuco* (youth) gangs. Many dressed in "**zoot suits**" — broad-brimmed felt hats, thigh-length jackets with wide lapels and padded shoulders, pegged trousers, and clunky shoes. Pachucas (young women) favored long coats, huarache sandals, and pompadour hairdos. Other working-class teenagers in Los Angeles and elsewhere took up the zoot-suit style to emphasize their rejection of middle-class values. To many adults, the zoot suit symbolized juvenile delinquency. Rumors circulating in Los Angeles in June 1943 that a pachuco gang had beaten an Anglo (white) sailor set off a four-day riot in which hundreds of Anglo service-men roamed through Mexican American neighborhoods and attacked zoot-suiters, taking special pleasure in slashing their pegged pants. In a stinging display of bias, Los Angeles police officers arrested only Mexican American youth, and the City Council passed an ordinance outlawing the wearing of the zoot suit.

**Gay and Lesbian Communities**   Wartime migration to urban centers created new opportunities for gay men and women to establish communities. Religious and social conventions against gays and lesbians kept the majority of them silent about their sexuality. During the war, however, cities such as New York, San Francisco, Los Angeles, Chicago, and even Kansas City, Buffalo, and Dallas developed vibrant gay neighborhoods, sustained by a sudden influx of migrants and the relatively open war-time atmosphere. These communities became centers of the gay rights movement of the 1960s and 1970s (Chapter 28).

The military tried to screen out homosexuals but had limited success. Once in the service, homosexuals found opportunities to participate in a gay culture often more extensive than that in civilian life. In the last twenty years, historians have documented thriving communities of gay and lesbian soldiers in the World War II military. Some "came out under fire," as one historian put it, but most kept their sexuality hidden from authorities because army officers, doctors, and psychiatrists treated homosexuality as a psychological disorder that was grounds for dishonorable discharge.

## Japanese Removal

Unlike World War I, which evoked widespread harassment of German Americans, World War II produced relatively little condemnation of European Americans. Despite the presence of small but vocal groups of Nazi sympathizers and Mussolini supporters, German American and Italian American communities were largely left in peace during the war; federal officials held only about five thousand potentially dangerous German and Italian aliens. The relocation and temporary imprisonment of Japanese immigrants and Japanese American citizens was a glaring exception to this otherwise tolerant policy. Immediately after the attack on Pearl Harbor, the West Coast remained calm. Then, as residents began to fear spies, sabotage, and further attacks, California's long history of racial animosity toward Asian immigrants surfaced. Local politicians and newspapers whipped up hysteria against Japanese Americans, who numbered only about 112,000, had no political power, and lived primarily in small enclaves in the Pacific coast states.

Early in 1942, President Roosevelt responded to anti-Japanese fears by issuing **Executive Order 9066**, which authorized the War Department to force Japanese Americans from their West Coast homes and hold them in relocation camps for the duration of the war. Although there was no disloyal or seditious activity among the evacuees, few public leaders opposed the plan. "A Jap's a Jap," snapped General John DeWitt, the officer charged with defense of the West Coast. "It makes no difference whether he is an American citizen or not."

The relocation plan shocked Japanese Americans, more than two-thirds of whom were Nisei; that is, their parents were immigrants (Isei), but they were native-born American citizens. Army officials gave families only a few days to dispose of their property. Businesses that had taken a lifetime to build were liquidated overnight. The War Relocation Authority moved the prisoners to hastily built camps in desolate areas in California, Arizona, Utah, Colorado, Wyoming, Idaho, and Arkansas (Map 23.1). Ironically, the Japanese Americans who made up one-third of the population of

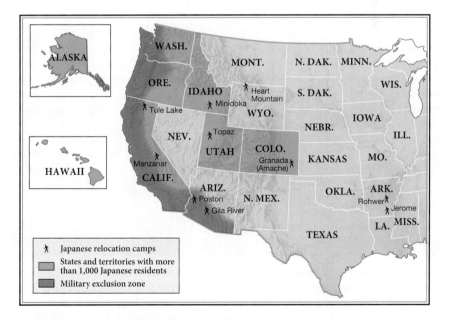

**MAP 23.1  Japanese Relocation Camps**
In 1942, the government ordered 112,000 Japanese Americans living on the West Coast into internment camps in the nation's interior because of their supposed threat to public safety. Some of the camps were as far away as Arkansas. The federal government rescinded the mass evacuation order in December 1944, but 44,000 people still remained in the camps when the war ended in August 1945.

Hawaii, and presumably posed a greater threat because of their proximity to Japan, were not imprisoned. They provided much of the unskilled labor in the island territory, and the Hawaiian economy could not have functioned without them.

Cracks soon appeared in the relocation policy. An agricultural labor shortage led the government to furlough seasonal farmworkers from the camps as early as 1942. About 4,300 students were allowed to attend colleges outside the West Coast military zone. Other internees were permitted to join the armed services. The 442nd Regimental Combat Team, a unit composed almost entirely of Nisei volunteers, served with distinction in Europe.

Gordon Hirabayashi was among the Nisei who actively resisted incarceration. A student at the University of Washington, Hirabayashi was a religious pacifist who had registered with his draft board as a conscientious objector. He refused to report for evacuation and turned himself in to the FBI. "I wanted to uphold the principles of the Constitution," Hirabayashi later stated, "and the curfew and evacuation orders which singled out a group on the basis of ethnicity violated them." Tried and convicted in 1942, he appealed his case to the Supreme Court in *Hirabayashi v. United States* (1943). In that case and in *Korematsu v. United States* (1944), the Court allowed the removal of Japanese Americans from the West Coast on the basis of "military necessity" but avoided ruling on the constitutionality of the incarceration program. The Court's decision underscored the fragility of civil liberties in

**Behind Barbed Wire**  As part of the forced relocation of 112,000 Japanese Americans, Los Angeles photographer Toyo Miyatake and his family were sent to Manzanar, a camp in the California desert east of the Sierra Nevada. Miyatake secretly began shooting photographs of the camp with a handmade camera. Eventually, Miyatake received permission from the authorities to document life in the camp—its births, weddings, deaths, and high school graduations. To communicate the injustice of internment, he also took staged photographs, such as this image of three young boys behind barbed wire with a watchtower in the distance. For Miyatake, the image gave new meaning to the phrase "prisoners of war." *The Denver Post* via Getty Images.

wartime. Congress issued a public apology in 1988 and awarded $20,000 to each of the eighty-two thousand surviving Japanese Americans who had once been internees.

| IN YOUR OWN WORDS | Describe both the short-term and the lasting domestic social changes the war produced. |
| --- | --- |

# Fighting and Winning the War

World War II was a war for control of the world. Had the Axis powers triumphed, Germany would have dominated, either directly or indirectly, all of Europe and much of Africa and the Middle East; Japan would have controlled most of East and Southeast Asia. To prevent this outcome, which would have crippled democracy in Europe and restricted American power to the Western Hemisphere, the Roosevelt administration took the United States to war. The combination of American intervention, the perseverance of Britain, and the profound civilian and military sacrifices of the Soviet Union decided the outcome of the conflict and shaped the character of the postwar world.

## Wartime Aims and Tensions

Great Britain, the United States, and the Soviet Union were the key actors in the Allied coalition. China, France, and other nations played crucial but smaller roles. The leaders who became known as the Big Three—Prime Minister Winston Churchill of Great Britain, President Franklin Roosevelt, and Premier Joseph Stalin of the Soviet Union—set military strategy. However, Stalin was not a party to the Atlantic Charter, which Churchill and Roosevelt had signed in August 1941, and disagreed fundamentally with some of its precepts, such as a capitalist international trading system. The Allies also disagreed about military strategy and timing. The Big Three made defeating Germany (rather than Japan) the top military priority, but they differed over how best to do it. In 1941, a massive German force had invaded the Soviet Union and reached the outskirts of Leningrad, Moscow, and Stalingrad before being halted in early 1942 by hard-pressed Russian troops. To relieve pressure on the Soviet army, Stalin wanted the British and Americans to open a second front with a major invasion of Germany through France.

Roosevelt informally assured Stalin that the Allies would comply in 1942, but Churchill opposed an early invasion, and American war production was not yet sufficient to support it. For eighteen months, Stalin's pleas went unanswered, and the Soviet Union bore the brunt of the fighting; in the 1943 Battle of Kursk alone, the Soviet army suffered 860,000 casualties, several times what the Allies would suffer for the first two months of the European campaign after D-Day. Then, at a conference of the Big Three in Tehran, Iran, in November 1943, Churchill and Roosevelt agreed to open a second front in France within six months in return for Stalin's promise to join the fight against Japan. Both sides adhered to this agreement, but the long delay angered Stalin, who became increasingly suspicious of American and British intentions.

## The War in Europe

Throughout 1942, the Allies suffered one defeat after another. German armies pushed deep into Soviet territory, advancing through the wheat farms of the Ukraine and the rich oil region of the Caucasus. Simultaneously, German forces began an offensive in North Africa aimed at seizing the Suez Canal. In the Atlantic, U-boats devastated American convoys carrying oil and other vital supplies to Britain and the Soviet Union.

Over the winter of 1942–1943, however, the tide began to turn in favor of the Allies. In the epic Battle of Stalingrad, Soviet forces halted the German advance, and by early 1944 Stalin's troops had driven the German army out of the Soviet Union (Map 23.2). Meanwhile, as Churchill's temporary substitute for a second front in France, the Allies launched a counteroffensive in North Africa. Between

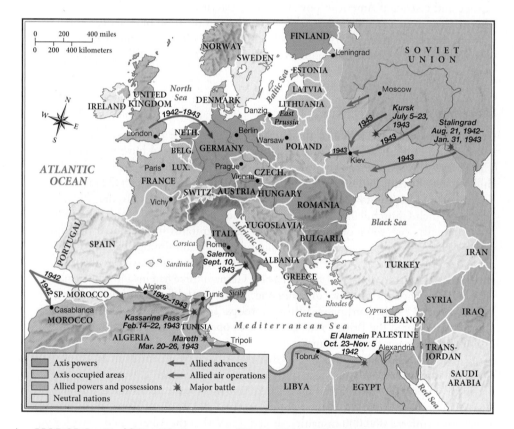

**MAP 23.2   World War II in Europe and North Africa, 1941–1943**
Hitler's Germany reached its greatest extent in 1942, by which time Nazi forces had occupied Norway, France, North Africa, central Europe, and much of western Russia. The tide of battle turned in late 1942 when the German advance stalled at Leningrad and Stalingrad. By early 1943, the Soviet army had launched a massive counterattack at Stalingrad, and Allied forces had driven the Germans from North Africa and launched an invasion of Sicily and the Italian mainland.

November 1942 and May 1943, Allied troops under the leadership of General Dwight D. Eisenhower and General George S. Patton defeated the German Afrika Korps, led by General Erwin Rommel.

From Africa, the Allied command followed Churchill's strategy of attacking the Axis through its "soft underbelly": the Italian peninsula. Faced with an Allied invasion, the Italian king ousted Mussolini's fascist regime in July 1943. But German troops, who far outmatched the Allies in skill and organization, took control of Italy and strenuously resisted the Allied invasion. American and British divisions took Rome only in June 1944 and were still fighting German forces in northern Italy when the European war ended in May 1945 (Map 23.3). Churchill's southern strategy proved a time-consuming and costly mistake.

**D-Day**   The long-promised invasion of France came on **D-Day**, June 6, 1944. That morning, the largest armada ever assembled moved across the English Channel

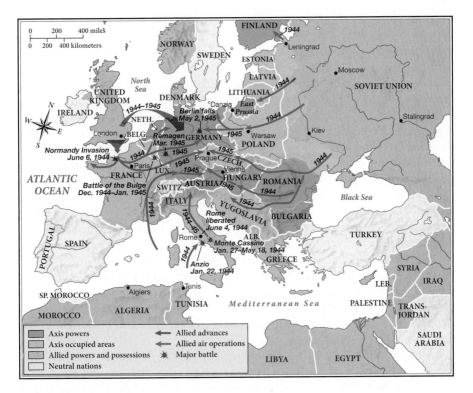

**MAP 23.3  World War II in Europe, 1944–1945**

By the end of 1943, the Russian army had nearly pushed the Germans out of the Soviet Union, and by June 1944, when the British and Americans finally invaded France, the Russians had liberated eastern Poland and most of southeastern Europe. By the end of 1944, British and American forces were ready to invade Germany from the west, and the Russians were poised to do the same from the east. Germany surrendered on May 7, 1945.

under the command of General Eisenhower. When American, British, and Canadian soldiers hit the beaches of Normandy, they suffered terrible casualties but secured a beachhead. Over the next few weeks, more than 1.5 million soldiers and thousands of tons of military supplies and equipment flowed into France. Much to the Allies' advantage, they never faced more than one-third of Hitler's Wehrmacht (armed forces), because the Soviet Union continued to hold down the Germans on the Eastern Front. In August, Allied troops liberated Paris; by September, they had driven the Germans out of most of France and Belgium. Meanwhile, long-range Allied bombers attacked German cities such as Hamburg and Dresden as well as military and industrial targets. The air campaign killed some 305,000 civilians and soldiers and injured another 780,000 — a grisly reminder of the war's brutality.

The Germans were not yet ready to give up, however. In December 1944, they mounted a final offensive in Belgium, the so-called Battle of the Bulge, before being pushed back across the Rhine River into Germany. American and British troops drove toward Berlin from the west, while Soviet troops advanced east through Poland. On April 30, 1945, as Russian troops massed outside Berlin, Hitler committed suicide; on May 7, Germany formally surrendered.

**The Holocaust** When Allied troops advanced into Poland and Germany in the spring of 1945, they came face-to-face with Hitler's "final solution" for the Jewish population of Germany and the German-occupied countries: the extermination camps in which 6 million Jews had been put to death, along with another 6 million Poles, Slavs, Gypsies, homosexuals, and other "undesirables." Photographs of the Nazi death camps at Buchenwald, Dachau, and Auschwitz showed bodies stacked like cordwood and survivors so emaciated that they were barely alive. Published in *Life* and other mass-circulation magazines, the photographs of the **Holocaust** horrified the American public and the world.

The Nazi persecution of German Jews in the 1930s was widely known in the United States. But when Jews had begun to flee Europe, the United States refused to relax its strict immigration laws to take them in. In 1939, when the SS *St. Louis*, a German ocean liner carrying nearly a thousand Jewish refugees, sought permission from President Roosevelt to dock at an American port, FDR had refused. Its passengers' futures uncertain, the *St. Louis* was forced to return to Europe, where many would later be deported to Auschwitz and other extermination camps. American officials, along with those of most other nations, continued this exclusionist policy during World War II as the Nazi regime extended its control over millions of Eastern European Jews.

Various factors inhibited American action, but the most important was widespread anti-Semitism: in the State Department, Christian churches, and the public at large. The legacy of the immigration restriction legislation of the 1920s and the isolationist attitudes of the 1930s also discouraged policymakers from assuming responsibility for the fate of the refugees. Taking a narrow view of the national interest, the State Department allowed only 21,000 Jewish refugees to enter the United States during the war. But the War Refugee Board, which President Roosevelt established in 1944 at the behest of Secretary of the Treasury Henry Morgenthau, helped move 200,000 European Jews to safe havens in other countries.

## The War in the Pacific

Waging the war against Japan was every bit as arduous as the campaign against Germany. After crippling the American battle fleet at Pearl Harbor, the Japanese quickly expanded into the South Pacific, with seaborne invasions of Hong Kong, Wake Island, and Guam. Japanese forces then advanced into Southeast Asia, conquering the Solomon Islands, Burma, and Malaya and threatening Australia and India. By May 1942, they had forced the surrender of U.S. forces in the Philippine Islands.

At that dire moment, American naval forces scored two crucial victories. These were possible because the attack on Pearl Harbor had destroyed several American battleships but left all aircraft carriers unscathed. In the Battle of the Coral Sea, off southern New Guinea in May 1942, they halted the Japanese offensive against Australia. Then, in June, at the Battle of Midway Island, the American navy severely damaged the Japanese fleet. In both battles, planes launched from American aircraft carriers provided the margin of victory. The U.S. military command, led by General Douglas MacArthur and Admiral Chester W. Nimitz, now took the offensive in the Pacific. For the next eighteen months, American forces advanced slowly toward Japan, taking one island after another in the face of determined Japanese resistance. In October 1944, MacArthur and Nimitz began the reconquest of the Philippines by winning the Battle of Leyte Gulf, a massive naval encounter in which the Japanese lost practically their entire fleet (Map 23.4).

By early 1945, victory over Japan was in sight. Japanese military forces had suffered devastating losses, and American bombing of the Japanese homeland had killed somewhere between 300,000 and 900,000 civilians and crippled the nation's economy. The bloodletting on both sides was horrendous. On the small islands of Iwo Jima and Okinawa, tens of thousands of Japanese soldiers fought to the death, killing 13,000 U.S. Marines and wounding 46,000 more. Desperate to halt the American advance and short on ammunition, Japanese pilots flew suicidal kamikaze missions, crashing their bomb-laden planes into American ships.

Among the grim realities of war in the Pacific was the conflict's racial overtones. The attack on Pearl Harbor reawakened the long tradition of anti-Asian sentiment in the United States. In the eyes of many Americans, the Japanese were "yellow monkeys," an inferior race whose humanity deserved minimal respect. Racism was evident among the Japanese as well. Their brutal attacks on China (including the rape of Nanjing), their forcing of Korean "comfort women" to have sex with Japanese soldiers, and their treatment of American prisoners in the Philippines flowed from their own sense of racial superiority. Anti-Japanese attitudes in the United States would subside in the 1950s as the island nation became a trusted ally. But racism would again play a major role in the U.S. war in Vietnam in the 1960s.

As the American navy advanced on Japan in the winter of 1945, President Roosevelt returned to the United States from the Yalta Conference, a major meeting of the Big Three at Yalta, a resort town on the Black Sea (Chapter 24). The sixty-three-year-old president was a sick man, visibly exhausted by his 14,000-mile trip and suffering from heart failure and high blood pressure. On April 12, 1945, during a short visit to his vacation home in Warm Springs, Georgia, Roosevelt suffered a cerebral hemorrhage and died.

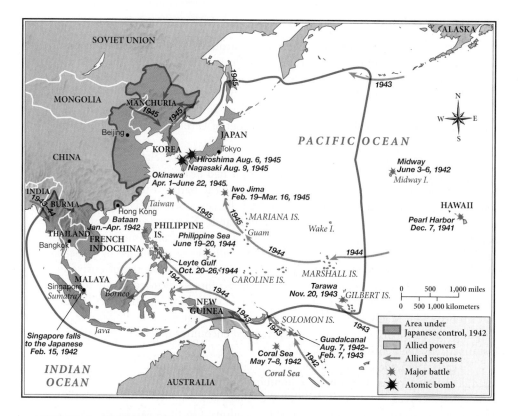

**MAP 23.4   World War II in the Pacific**

After the attacks on Pearl Harbor in December 1941, the Japanese rapidly extended their domination in the Pacific. The Japanese flag soon flew as far east as the Marshall and Gilbert islands and as far south as the Solomon Islands and parts of New Guinea. Japan also controlled the Philippines, much of Southeast Asia, and parts of China, including Hong Kong. By mid-1942, American naval victories at the Coral Sea and Midway stopped further Japanese expansion. Allied forces retook the islands of the central Pacific in 1943 and 1944 and ousted the Japanese from the Philippines early in 1945. Carrier-launched planes had started bombing Japan itself in 1942, but the capture of these islands gave U.S. bombers more bases from which to strike Japanese targets. As the Soviet army invaded Japanese-occupied Manchuria in August 1945, U.S. planes took off from one of the newly captured Mariana Islands to drop the atomic bombs on Hiroshima and Nagasaki. The Japanese offered to surrender on August 10.

## The Atomic Bomb and the End of the War

When Harry Truman assumed the presidency, he learned for the first time about the top-secret **Manhattan Project**, which was on the verge of testing a new weapon: the atomic bomb. Working at the University of Chicago in December 1942, Enrico Fermi and Leo Szilard, refugees from fascist Italy and Nazi Germany, produced the first controlled atomic chain reaction using highly processed uranium. With the aid of German-born refugee Albert Einstein, the greatest theorist of modern physics and a scholar at Princeton, they persuaded Franklin Roosevelt to develop an atomic weapon, warning that German scientists were also working on such nuclear reactions.

The Manhattan Project cost $2 billion, employed 120,000 people, and involved the construction of thirty-seven installations in nineteen states — with all of its activity hidden from Congress, the American people, and even Vice President Truman. Directed by Lieutenant General Leslie R. Groves Jr. and scientist J. Robert Oppenheimer, the nation's top physicists assembled the first bomb in Los Alamos, New Mexico, and successfully tested it on July 16, 1945. Overwhelmed by its frightening power, as he witnessed the first mushroom cloud, Oppenheimer recalled the words from the Bhagavad Gita, one of the great texts of Hindu scripture: "I am become Death, the Destroyer of Worlds."

Three weeks later, President Truman ordered the dropping of atomic bombs on two Japanese cities: Hiroshima on August 6 and Nagasaki on August 9. Truman's rationale for this order — and the implications of his decision — have long been the subject of scholarly and popular debate. The principal justification was straightforward: Truman and his American advisors, including Secretary of War Henry Stimson and Army Chief of Staff General George Marshall, believed that Japan's military leaders would never surrender unless their country faced national ruin. Moreover, at the Potsdam Conference on the outskirts of Berlin in July 1945, the Allies had agreed that only the "unconditional surrender" of Japan was acceptable — the same terms under which Germany and Italy had been defeated. To win such a surrender, an invasion of Japan itself seemed necessary. Stimson and Marshall told Truman that such an invasion would produce between half a million and a million Allied casualties.

Before giving the order to drop the atomic bomb, Truman considered other options. His military advisors rejected the most obvious alternative: a nonlethal demonstration of the bomb's awesome power, perhaps on a remote Pacific island. If the demonstration failed — not out of the question, as the bomb had been tested only once — it would embolden Japan further. A detailed advance warning designed to scare Japan into surrender was also rejected. Given Japan's tenacious fighting in the Pacific, the Americans believed that only massive devastation or a successful invasion would lead Japan's military leadership to surrender. After all, the deaths of more than 100,000 Japanese civilians in the U.S. firebombing of Tokyo and other cities in the spring of 1945 had brought Japan no closer to surrender.

In any event, the atomic bombs achieved the immediate goal. The deaths of 100,000 people at Hiroshima and 60,000 at Nagasaki prompted the Japanese government to surrender unconditionally on August 15 and to sign a formal agreement on September 2, 1945. Fascism had been defeated, thanks to a fragile alliance between the capitalist nations of the West and the communist government of the Soviet Union. The coming of peace would strain and then destroy the victorious coalition. Even as the global war came to an end, the early signs of the coming Cold War were apparent, as were the stirrings of independence in the European colonies.

## The Toll of the War

After the battle of Iwo Jima, one of the fiercest and bloodiest of the Pacific war, a rabbi chaplain in the Marine Corps delivered the eulogy for the fallen. "This shall not be in vain," he said, surveying a battlefield that witnessed the deaths of nearly

30,000 American and Japanese soldiers. Speaking of American losses, he said, "from the suffering and sorrow of those who mourn this, will come—we promise—the birth of a new freedom for the sons of man everywhere." The toll of "suffering and sorrow" from World War II was enormous. Worldwide, more than 50 million soldiers and civilians were killed, nearly 2.5 percent of the globe's population. The Holocaust took the lives of 6 million European Jews, 2.6 million from Poland alone. Nearly 100 million additional soldiers and civilians were wounded, and 30 million people across the globe were rendered homeless. It was one of the most wrenching, disruptive, and terrible wars in human history.

Alongside the human toll stood profound economic and political transformations. Hundreds of cities in Europe and Asia had been bombed. Some of them, like Dresden, Warsaw, Hamburg, and Hiroshima, had been simply obliterated. Much of the industrial infrastructure of Germany and Japan, two of the world's most important industrial economies before the war, lay in ruins. Moreover, despite emerging as one of the victors, Britain was no longer a global power. The independence movement in India was only the most obvious sign of its waning influence. Indeed, throughout the colonized world in Asia and Africa, people had taken the Atlantic Charter, and FDR's insistence that this was a war for *democracy*, seriously. For them, resumption of European imperialism was unacceptable, and the war represented a step toward national self-determination.

In the United States, too, the toll of war was great. More than 400,000 lives were lost, and nearly 300,000 American soldiers were wounded. Yet millions returned home, and in the coming decades veterans would play a central role in national life. Incredibly, in 1950 World War II veterans made up one-third of all American men over the age of nineteen. Only the Civil War involved a comparable commitment of military service from a generation. Americans paid dearly for that commitment—though not, it must be noted, as dearly as other peoples in Europe and Asia—and the legacies of the war shaped families, politics, and foreign policy for the remainder of the century.

> **IN YOUR OWN WORDS**    How did Allied strategy against the Axis powers evolve between 1941 and 1945?

# Summary

The rise of fascism in Germany, Italy, and Japan led to the outbreak of World War II. Initially, the American public opposed U.S. intervention. But by 1940, President Roosevelt was mobilizing support for the military and preparing the country for war. The Japanese attack on Pearl Harbor in December 1941 brought the nation fully into the conflict. War mobilization dramatically expanded the federal government and led to substantial economic growth. It also boosted geographical and social mobility as women, rural whites, and southern blacks found employment in new defense plants across the country. Government rules assisted both the labor movement and the African American campaign for civil rights. However, religious and racial animosity caused the exclusion of Jewish refugees and the internment of 112,000 Japanese Americans.

By 1942, Germany and Japan seemed to be winning the war. But in 1943, the Allies took the offensive — with advances by the Soviet army in Europe and the American navy in the Pacific — and by the end of 1944, Allied victory was all but certain. Germany finally surrendered in May 1945, and Japan surrendered in August, after the atomic bombing of the Japanese cities Hiroshima and Nagasaki. The United States emerged from the war with an undamaged homeland, sole possession of the atomic bomb, and a set of unresolved diplomatic disputes with the Soviet Union that would soon lead to the four-decade-long Cold War. Federal laws and practices established during the war — the universal income tax, a huge military establishment, and multibillion-dollar budgets, to name but a few — became part of American life. So, too, did the active participation of the United States in international politics and alliances, an engagement intensified by the unresolved issues of the wartime alliance with the Soviet Union and the postwar fate of colonized nations.

# Chapter 23 Review

## KEY TERMS

**Identify and explain the significance of each term below.**

fascism (p. 667)
National Socialist (Nazi) Party (p. 667)
Rome-Berlin Axis (p. 668)
Neutrality Act of 1935 (p. 668)
Popular Front (p. 669)
Munich Conference (p. 669)
Committee to Defend America by Aiding the Allies (p. 670)
America First Committee (p. 670)
Four Freedoms (p. 671)
Lend-Lease Act (p. 671)
Atlantic Charter (p. 671)

Pearl Harbor (p. 672)
War Powers Act (p. 672)
Revenue Act (p. 673)
code talkers (p. 674)
Executive Order 8802 (p. 676)
Bracero Program (p. 677)
Servicemen's Readjustment Act (p. 678)
zoot suits (p. 680)
Executive Order 9066 (p. 681)
D-Day (p. 685)
Holocaust (p. 686)
Manhattan Project (p. 688)

## REVIEW QUESTIONS

**Answer these questions to demonstrate your understanding of the chapter's main ideas.**

1. Explain the steps by which the United States became involved in World War II.
2. What aspects of the economy and American society were affected by mobilization for war?

3. Describe both the short-term and the lasting domestic social changes the war produced.
4. How did Allied strategy against the Axis powers evolve between 1941 and 1945?
5. Review the events listed under "America in the World" on the thematic timeline on page 581. How did World War II change the relationship between the United States and the rest of the world in the first half of the twentieth century?

## CHRONOLOGY

**As you read, ask yourself why this chapter begins and ends with these dates and identify the links among related events.**

| | |
|---|---|
| **1933** | • Adolf Hitler becomes chancellor of Germany |
| **1935** | • Italy invades Ethiopia |
| **1935–1939** | • U.S. Neutrality Acts |
| **1936** | • Germany reoccupies Rhineland demilitarized zone |
| | • Rome-Berlin Axis established |
| **1937** | • Japan invades China |
| **1938** | • Munich Conference |
| **1939** | • German-Soviet nonaggression pact |
| | • Germany invades Poland |
| | • Britain and France declare war on Germany |
| **1940** | • Germany, Italy, and Japan form alliance |
| **1941** | • Germany invades Soviet Union |
| | • Lend-Lease Act and Atlantic Charter established |
| | • Japanese attack Pearl Harbor (December 7) |
| **1942** | • Executive Order 9066 imprisons Japanese and Japanese Americans |
| | • Battles of Coral Sea and Midway halt Japanese advance |
| **1942–1945** | • Rationing of scarce goods |
| **1943** | • Race riots in Detroit and Los Angeles |
| **1944** | • D-Day: Allied landing in France (June 6) |

**1945**
- Yalta Conference (February)
- Germany surrenders (May 7)
- United Nations founded
- Potsdam Conference (July–August)
- United States drops atomic bombs on Hiroshima and Nagasaki (August 6 and 9)
- Japan surrenders (August 10)

# PART 8

Between 1945 and 1980, the United States became the world's leading economic and military power. The dates we've chosen to bookend the period reflect two turning points. In 1945, the United States and its allies emerged victorious from World War II. In 1980, American voters turned away from the robust liberalism of the postwar years and elected a president, Ronald Reagan, backed by a conservative political movement. Each turning point, one international and the other domestic, marked the rise of new developments in American history—and thus our periodization endeavors to capture in these decades a narrative of global power and expanding political liberalism.

Internationally, after 1945 a prolonged period of tension and conflict known as the Cold War drew the United States into an engagement in world affairs unprecedented in the nation's history. Domestically, three decades of sustained economic growth, whose benefits were widely, though imperfectly, distributed, expanded the middle class and brought into being a mass consumer society. These developments were intertwined with the predominance of liberalism in American politics and public policy. One might think of an "age of liberalism" in this era, encompassing the social-welfare liberalism that was a legacy of the New Deal and the rights liberalism of the 1960s.

Global leadership abroad and economic prosperity at home were conditioned on further expansions in government power. How that power was used proved controversial. Following World War II, a national security state emerged to investigate so-called subversives in the United States and to destabilize foreign governments abroad. Meanwhile, American troops went to war in Korea and Vietnam. At home, African Americans, women, the poor, and other social groups called for greater equality and sought new government initiatives to make that equality a reality. Here, in brief, are the three key dimensions of this convulsive, turbulent era.

## Global Leadership and the Cold War

When the United States officially joined the combatants of World War II, it entered into an alliance with England and the Soviet Union. That alliance proved impossible to sustain after 1945, as the U.S. and the Soviet Union became competitors to shape postwar Europe, East Asia, and the developing world. The resulting Cold War lasted four decades, during which the U.S. extended its political and military reach onto every continent. Under the presidency of Harry S. Truman, American officials developed the policy of containment—a combination of economic, diplomatic, and military actions to limit the expansion of communism—that subsequent presidents embraced and expanded.

Intervention abroad was a hallmark of the Cold War. Most American interventions took place in developing countries and in recently independent, decolonized

# The Modern State and the Age of Liberalism 1945–1980

nations. In the name of preventing the spread of communism, the U.S. intervened directly or indirectly in China, Iran, Guatemala, Cuba, Indonesia, and the Dominican Republic, among many other nations, and fought major wars in Korea and Vietnam. This new global role for the United States inspired support but also spurred detractors.

## The Age of Liberalism

In response to the Great Depression, the New Deal expanded federal responsibility for the social welfare of ordinary citizens. Legislators from both parties embraced liberal ideas about the role of government and undertook such measures as the GI Bill, subsidies for home ownership, and investment in infrastructure and education. Poverty, however, affected one-third of Americans in the 1960s, and racial discrimination denied millions of nonwhites full citizenship. Lack of opportunity became a driving force in the civil rights movement and in the Great Society under President Lyndon Johnson.

Inspired by African American civil rights, other social movements sought equality based on gender, sexuality, ethnicity, and other identities. If "New Deal liberalism" had focused on social welfare, this "rights liberalism" focused on protecting people from discrimination and ensuring equal citizenship. These struggles resulted in new laws, such as the Civil Rights Act of 1964 and the Voting Rights Act of 1965. Conservative opponents, however, mobilized in the 1960s against what they saw as the excesses of liberal activism. The resulting conflict began to reshape politics in the 1970s and laid the groundwork for a new conservative movement.

## Mass Consumption and the Middle Class

The postwar American economy was driven by mass consumption and suburbanization. Rising wages and increased access to higher education raised living standards and allowed more Americans than ever to afford consumer goods. Suburbs and the Sunbelt led the nation in population growth. But the new prosperity had mixed results. Cities declined and new racial and ethnic ghettos formed. Mass consumption raised concerns that the nation's rivers, streams, air, and open land were being damaged, and an environmental movement arose in response. And prosperity itself proved short-lived. By the 1970s, deindustrialization had eroded much of the nation's once prosperous industrial base.

A defining characteristic of the postwar decades was the growth of the American middle class predicated on numerous demographic changes. Women worked more outside the home and spurred a new feminism. Children enjoyed more purchasing power, and a "teen culture" arose on television, in popular music, and in film. The family became politicized, too, and by the late 1970s, liberals and conservatives were divided over how best to address the nation's family life.

## Thematic Understanding

This timeline arranges some of the important events of this period into seven themes. Consider the entries under "America in the World" and "Politics and Power" across all four decades. What connections were there between international developments and domestic politics in this era of the Cold War? Under "American and National Identity" and "Culture and Society," consider how the civil rights movement shaped these decades.

| | AMERICAN AND NATIONAL IDENTITY | POLITICS AND POWER | WORK, EXCHANGE, AND TECHNOLOGY |
|---|---|---|---|
| **1940** | • "To Secure These Rights" (1947)<br>• Desegregation of armed services (1948) | • GI Bill (1944)<br>• Loyalty-Security Program (1947)<br>• Truman reelected (1948) | • Bretton Woods system established (1944)<br>• Baby boom establishes new consumer generation |
| **1950** | • *Brown v. Board of Education* (1954)<br>• Montgomery Bus Boycott (1955)<br>• Little Rock desegregation battle (1957) | • Cold War liberalism<br>• McCarthyism and Red Scare<br>• Eisenhower's presidency (1953–1961) | • Labor-Management Accord struck in major industries (1950s)<br>• National Defense Education Act (1958) spurs development of technology |
| **1960** | • Greensboro sit-ins (1960)<br>• *The Feminine Mystique* (1963)<br>• Civil Rights and Voting Rights Acts (1964–1965) | • John F. Kennedy assassinated (1963)<br>• Lyndon B. Johnson's landslide victory (1964)<br>• War on Poverty; Great Society | • Economic boom<br>• Government spending on Vietnam and Great Society<br>• Medicare and Medicaid created (1965) |
| **1970** | • Equal Rights Amendment (1972)<br>• *Roe v. Wade* (1973)<br>• Siege at Wounded Knee (1973)<br>• *Bakke v. University of California* (1978) | • Richard Nixon's landslide victory (1972)<br>• Jimmy Carter elected president (1976)<br>• Moral Majority founded (1979) | • Energy crisis (1973)<br>• Inflation surges, while economy stagnates (stagflation)<br>• Deindustrialization<br>• Tax revolt in California (1978) |

| CULTURE AND SOCIETY | MIGRATION AND SETTLEMENT | GEOGRAPHY AND THE ENVIRONMENT | AMERICA IN THE WORLD | |
|---|---|---|---|---|
| • World War II migrations produce vibrant, diverse cities<br>• Bebop jazz<br>• Advent of television (1940s–1950s) | • War production and expansion of military reshape the Sunbelt<br>• Wartime migration to northern and western cities | • First Levittown opens (1947)<br>• FHA and VA subsidize suburbanization | • Truman Doctrine<br>• Marshall Plan (1948)<br>• Containment strategy emerges<br>• NATO founded (1949) | 1940 |
| • Emergence of rock 'n' roll and youth culture<br>• Disneyland opens (1955)<br>• McDonald's restaurants give rise to fast food | • Bracero program revived (1951)<br>• Surging middle-class migration to suburbs<br>• Racial segregation in cities and suburbs reinforced<br>• Migration to Sunbelt (1950s–1970s) | • National Interstate and Defense Highways Act (1956)<br>• Growth of suburbia and Sunbelt | • NSC-68 (1950)<br>• Korean War (1950–1953)<br>• Geneva Accords in Vietnam (1954) | 1950 |
| • Civil rights movement merges protest and gospel music<br>• Major antiwar protests (1965–1969)<br>• Counterculture<br>• Stonewall Inn riot (1969) | • Immigration and Nationality Act of 1965<br>• Immigration from Asia, Latin America, and Africa increases (1960s–1990s)<br>• Rustbelt begins to lose population | • Great Society environmental initiatives<br>• Urban riots (1964–1968)<br>• Kerner Commission Report (1968) | • Cuban missile crisis (1962)<br>• Gulf of Tonkin Resolution (1964)<br>• Johnson sends ground troops to Vietnam; war escalates (1965) | 1960 |
| • Women's and gay rights movements<br>• Cultural and political conflict over the nuclear family<br>• Evangelical Christian resurgence | • Vietnamese refugees arrive in U.S.<br>• Rustbelt population decline and Sunbelt population growth produce regional realignment in congressional power (1970s–1990s) | • First Earth Day (1970)<br>• Environmental Protection Agency established (1970)<br>• Endangered Species Act (1973)<br>• Three Mile Island accident (1979) | • Nixon invades Cambodia (1970)<br>• Paris Accords end Vietnam War (1973)<br>• Camp David Accords (1978)<br>• Iranian Revolution (1979) and hostage crisis (1979–1981) | 1970 |

# 24

# Cold War America

## 1945–1963

### IDENTIFY THE BIG IDEA

In the first two decades of the Cold War, how did competition on the international stage and a climate of fear at home affect politics, society, and culture in the United States?

**IN THE AUTUMN OF 1950, A LITTLE-KNOWN CALIFORNIA CONGRESSMAN** running for the Senate named Richard M. Nixon stood before reporters in Los Angeles. His opponent, Helen Gahagan Douglas, was a Hollywood actress and a New Deal Democrat. Nixon told the gathered reporters that Douglas had cast "Communist-leaning" votes and that she was "pink right down to her underwear." Gahagan's voting record was not much different from Nixon's. But tarring her with communism made her seem un-American, and Nixon defeated the "pink lady" (meaning nearly *red*, or communist) with nearly 60 percent of the vote.

A few months earlier, U.S. tanks and planes had arrived in French Indochina. A French colony since the nineteenth century, Indochina (present-day Vietnam, Laos, and Cambodia) was home to an independence movement led by Ho Chi Minh and supported by the Soviet Union and China. In the summer of 1950, President Harry S. Truman authorized $15 million worth of military supplies to aid France, which was fighting Ho's army to keep possession of its Indochinese empire. "Neither national independence nor democratic evolution exists in any area dominated by Soviet imperialism," Secretary of State Dean Acheson warned ominously as he announced U.S. support for French imperialism.

Connecting these coincidental historical moments, one domestic and the other international, was a decades-old force in American life that gained renewed strength after World War II: anticommunism. The events

**The Perils of the Cold War** Americans, like much of the world, lived under the threat of nuclear warfare during the tense years of the Cold War between the United States and the Soviet Union. This 1951 civil defense poster, with the message "It *can* happen Here," suggests that Americans should be prepared for such a dire outcome. swin ink 2/Corbis via Getty Images.

in Los Angeles and Vietnam, however different on the surface, were part of the Cold War: the global geopolitical struggle between the capitalist, democratic United States and the communist, authoritarian Soviet Union. Beginning in Europe as World War II ended and extending to Asia, Latin America, the Middle East, and Africa by the mid-1950s, the Cold War reshaped international relations and dominated global politics for more than forty years.

In the United States, the Cold War fostered suspicion of "subversives" in government, education, and the media. The arms race that developed between the two superpowers prompted Congress to boost military expenditures. The resulting military-industrial complex enhanced the power of the corporations that built planes, munitions, and electronic devices. In politics, the Cold War stifled liberal initiatives as the New Deal coalition tried to advance its domestic agenda in the shadow of anticommunism. In these ways, the line between the international and the domestic blurred—and that blurred line was another enduring legacy of the Cold War.

# Containment in a Divided Global Order

The Cold War began on the heels of World War II and ended in 1991 with the dissolution of the Soviet Union. While it lasted, this conflict placed two far-reaching questions at the center of global history: Would capitalism or communism shape the nations of Europe and Asia? And how would the European colonies in Asia, the Middle East, and Africa gain their independence and take their places on the world stage? Cold War rivalry framed the possible answers to both questions as it drew the United States into a prolonged engagement with world affairs unprecedented in the nation's history.

## Origins of the Cold War

World War II set the basic conditions for the Cold War. With Germany and Japan defeated and Britain and France weakened by years of war, only two geopolitical powers remained standing in 1945. Even had nothing divided them, the United States and the Soviet Union would have jostled each other as they moved to fill the postwar power vacuum. But, of course, the two countries were divided—by geography, history, ideology, and strategic interest. Little united them other than their commitment to defeating the Axis powers. President Franklin Roosevelt understood that maintaining the U.S.-Soviet alliance was essential for postwar global stability. But he also believed that permanent peace and long-term U.S. interests depended on the Wilsonian principles of collective security, self-determination, and free trade (Chapter 20).

**Yalta**   At the **Yalta Conference** of February 1945, Wilsonian principles yielded to U.S.-Soviet power realities. As Allied forces neared victory in Europe and advanced toward Japan in the Pacific, Roosevelt, Churchill, and Stalin met in Yalta, a resort on the Black Sea in southern Ukraine. Roosevelt focused on maintaining Allied unity and securing Joseph Stalin's commitment to enter the war against Japan. But the fate of Eastern Europe divided the Big Three. Stalin insisted that Russian national security required pro-Soviet governments in Eastern European nations. Roosevelt pressed for an agreement, the "Declaration on Liberated Europe," that guaranteed self-determination and democratic elections in Poland and neighboring countries, such as Romania and Hungary. However, given the presence of Soviet troops in those nations, FDR had to accept a lesser pledge from Stalin: to hold "free and unfettered elections" at a future time. The three leaders also formalized their commitment to divide Germany into four zones, each controlled by one of the four Allied powers (including France), and to similarly partition the capital city, Berlin, which was located in the Soviet zone.

At Yalta, the Big Three also agreed to establish an international body to replace the discredited League of Nations. Based on plans drawn up at the 1944 Dumbarton Oaks conference in Washington, D.C., the new organization, to be known as the **United Nations**, would have both a General Assembly, in which all nations would be represented, and a Security Council composed of the five major Allied powers — the United States, Britain, France, China, and the Soviet Union — and seven other nations elected on a rotating basis. The Big Three determined that the five permanent members of the Security Council should have veto power over decisions of the General Assembly. They announced that the United Nations would convene for the first time in San Francisco on April 25, 1945.

**Potsdam**    Following the Yalta Conference, developments over the ensuing year further hardened relations between the Soviets on one side and the Americans and British on the other. At the **Potsdam Conference** outside Berlin in July 1945, Harry Truman replaced the deceased Roosevelt. Inexperienced in world affairs and thrown into enormously complicated negotiations, Truman's instinct was to stand up to Stalin. "Unless Russia is faced with an iron fist and strong language," he said, "another war is in the making." But Truman was in no position to shape events in Eastern Europe, where Soviet-imposed governments in Poland, Hungary, and Romania were backed by the Red Army and could not be eliminated by Truman's bluster. In Poland and Romania, in particular, Stalin was determined to establish communist governments, punish wartime Nazi collaborators, and win boundary concessions that augmented Soviet territory.

Yalta and Potsdam thus set the stage for communist rule to descend over Eastern Europe. The elections called for at Yalta eventually took place in Finland, Hungary, Bulgaria, and Czechoslovakia, with varying degrees of democratic openness. Nevertheless, Stalin got the client regimes he desired in those countries and would soon exert near-complete control over their governments. Stalin's unwillingness to honor self-determination for nations in Eastern Europe was, from the American point of view, the precipitating event of the Cold War.

Germany represented the biggest challenge of all. American officials at Potsdam believed that a revived German economy was essential to ensuring the prosperity of democratic regimes throughout Western Europe — and to keeping ordinary Germans from turning again to Nazism. In contrast, Stalin hoped merely to extract reparations from Germany in the form of industrial machines and goods. In exchange for

American recognition of a new German-Polish border, Truman and Secretary of State James Byrnes convinced the Soviet leader to accept German reparations only from the Soviet zone, which was largely rural and promised little wealth or German industry to plunder. The Yalta and Potsdam agreements paved the way for the division of Germany into East and West (Map 24.1).

Yalta and Potsdam demonstrated that in private negotiations the United States and the Soviet Union had starkly different objectives. Public utterances only intensified those differences. In February 1946, Stalin delivered a speech in which he insisted that, according to Marxist-Leninist principles, "the unevenness of development of the capitalist countries" was likely to produce "violent disturbance" and even another war. He seemed to blame any future war on the capitalist West. Churchill responded in kind a month later. While visiting Truman in Missouri to be honored for his wartime leadership, Churchill accused Stalin of raising an "iron curtain" around Eastern Europe and allowing "police government" to rule its people. He went

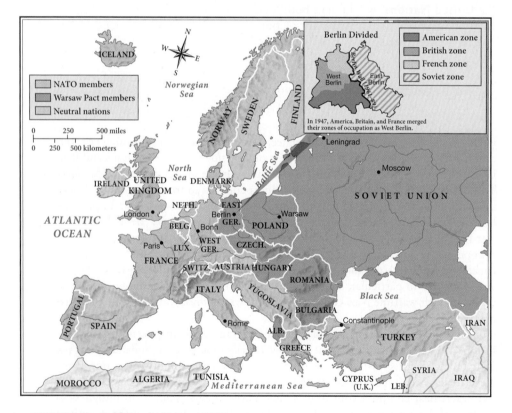

**MAP 24.1   Cold War in Europe, 1955**

This map vividly shows the Cold War division of Europe. The NATO countries (colored light green) are allies of the United States; the Warsaw Pact countries (in dark green) are allied to the USSR. In 1955, West Germany had just been admitted to NATO, completing Europe's stabilization into two rival camps. But Berlin remained divided, and one can see from its location deep in East Germany why the former capital was always a flash point in Cold War controversies.

further, claiming that "a fraternal association of English-speaking peoples," and not Russians, ought to set the terms of the postwar world.

The cities and fields of Europe had thus barely ceased to run with the blood of World War II before they were menaced again by the tense standoff between the Soviet Union and the United States. With Stalin intent on establishing client states in Eastern Europe and the United States equally intent on reviving Germany and ensuring collective security throughout Europe, the points of agreement were few and far between. Among the Allies, anxiety about a Nazi victory in World War II had been quickly replaced by fear of a potentially more cataclysmic war with the Soviet Union.

## The Containment Strategy

In the late 1940s, American officials developed a clear strategy toward the Soviet Union that would become known as **containment**. Convinced that the USSR was methodically expanding its reach, the United States would counter by limiting Soviet influence to Eastern Europe while reconstituting democratic governments in Western Europe. In 1946–1947, three specific issues worried Truman and his advisors. First, the Soviet Union was pressing Iran for access to oil and Turkey for access to the Mediterranean. Second, a civil war was roiling in Greece, between monarchists backed by England and insurgents supported by the Greek and Yugoslavian Communist parties. Third, as European nations suffered through terrible privation in 1946 and 1947, Communist parties gained strength, particularly in France and Italy. All three developments, as seen from the United States, threatened to expand the influence of the Soviet Union beyond Eastern Europe.

**Toward an Uneasy Peace**   In this anxious context, the strategy of containment emerged in a series of incremental steps between 1946 and 1949. In February 1946, American diplomat George F. Kennan first proposed the idea in an 8,000-word cable—a confidential message within the U.S. State Department—from his post at the U.S. embassy in Moscow. Kennan argued that the Soviet Union was an "Oriental despotism" and that communism was merely the "fig leaf" justifying Soviet aggression. A year after writing this cable (dubbed the Long Telegram), he published an influential *Foreign Affairs* article, arguing that the West's only recourse was to meet the Soviets "with unalterable counter-force at every point where they show signs of encroaching upon the interests of a peaceful and stable world." Kennan called for "long-term, patient but firm and vigilant containment of Russian expansive tendencies." *Containment*, the key word, came to define America's evolving strategic stance toward the Soviet Union.

Kennan contended that the Soviet system was unstable and would eventually collapse. Containment would work, he reasoned, as long as the United States and its allies opposed Soviet expansion anywhere in the world. Kennan's attentive readers included Stalin himself, who quickly obtained a copy of the classified Long Telegram. The Soviet leader saw the United States as an imperialist aggressor determined to replace Great Britain as the world's dominant capitalist power. Just as Kennan thought that the Soviet system was despotic and unsustainable, Stalin believed that the West suffered from its own fatal weaknesses. Neither side completely understood or trusted the other, and each projected its worst fears onto the other.

In fact, Britain's influence in the world was declining. Exhausted by the war, facing budget deficits and a collapsing economy at home, and confronted with growing independence movements throughout its empire, particularly in India led by Mohandas Gandhi, Britain was waning as a global power. "The reins of world leadership are fast slipping from Britain's competent but now very weak hands," read a U.S. State Department report. "These reins will be picked up either by the United States or by Russia." The United States was wedded to the notion — dating to the Wilson administration — that communism and capitalism were incompatible on the world stage. With Britain faltering, American officials saw little choice but to fill its shoes.

It did not take long for the reality of Britain's decline to resonate across the Atlantic. In February 1947, London informed Washington that it could no longer afford to support the anticommunists in the Greek civil war. Truman worried that a communist victory in Greece would lead to Soviet domination of the eastern Mediterranean and embolden Communist parties in France and Italy. In response, the president announced what became known as the **Truman Doctrine**. In a speech on March 12, he asserted an American responsibility "to support free peoples who are resisting attempted subjugation by armed minorities or by outside pressures." To that end, Truman proposed large-scale assistance for Greece and Turkey (then involved in a dispute with the Soviet Union over the Dardanelles, a strait connecting the Aegean Sea and the Sea of Marmara). "If we falter in our leadership, we may endanger the peace of the world," Truman declared. Congress quickly approved Truman's request for $300 million in aid to Greece and $100 million for Turkey.

Soviet expansionism was but one part of a larger story. Europe was sliding into economic chaos. Already devastated by the war, in 1947 the continent suffered the worst winter in memory. People were starving, wages were stagnant, and the consumer market had collapsed. For both humanitarian and practical reasons, Truman's advisors believed something had to be done. A global depression might ensue if the European economy, the largest foreign market for American goods, did not recover. Worse, unemployed and dispirited Western Europeans might fill the ranks of the Communist Party, threatening political stability. Secretary of State George C. Marshall came up with a remarkable proposal: a massive infusion of American capital to rebuild the European economy. In a June 1947 speech, Marshall urged the nations of Europe to work out a comprehensive recovery program based on U.S. aid.

This pledge of financial assistance required approval by Congress, where the plan ran into opposition. Republicans castigated the **Marshall Plan** as a huge "international WPA." But in the midst of the congressional stalemate, on February 25, 1948, Stalin supported a communist-led coup in Czechoslovakia. Congress rallied and voted overwhelmingly to approve the Marshall Plan. Over the next four years, the United States contributed nearly $13 billion to a highly successful recovery effort that benefitted both Western Europe and the United States. European industrial production increased by 64 percent, and the appeal of Communist parties waned in the West. Markets for American goods grew stronger and fostered economic interdependence between Europe and the United States. Notably, however, the Marshall Plan intensified Cold War tensions. U.S. officials invited the Soviets to participate but insisted on restrictions that virtually guaranteed Stalin's refusal. An embittered Stalin rejected participation and ordered Soviet client states to do so as well.

**East and West in the New Europe**    The flash point for a hot war remained Germany, the most important industrial economy and the key strategic nation in Europe. When no agreement could be reached with the Soviet Union to unify the four zones of occupation into a single state, the Western allies consolidated their three zones in 1947. They then prepared to establish an independent federal German republic. Marshall Plan funds would jump-start economic recovery. Some of those funds were slated for West Berlin, in hopes of making the city a capitalist showplace 100 miles inside the Soviet zone.

Stung by the West's intention to create a German republic, in June 1948 Stalin blockaded all traffic to West Berlin. Instead of yielding, as Stalin had expected, Truman and the British were resolute. "We are going to stay, period," Truman said plainly. Over the next year, American and British pilots improvised the Berlin Airlift, which flew 2.5 million tons of food and fuel into the Western zones of the city—nearly a ton for each resident. General Lucius D. Clay, the American commander in Berlin, was nervous and on edge, "drawn as tight as a steel spring," according to U.S. officials. But after a prolonged stalemate, Stalin backed down: on May 12, 1949, he lifted the blockade. Until the Cuban missile crisis in 1962, the Berlin crisis was the closest the two sides came to actual war, and West Berlin became a symbol of resistance to communism.

The crisis in Berlin persuaded Western European nations to forge a collective security pact with the United States. In April 1949, for the first time since the end of the American Revolution, the United States entered into a peacetime military alliance, the **North Atlantic Treaty Organization (NATO)**. Under the NATO pact, twelve nations—Belgium, Canada, Denmark, France, Great Britain, Iceland, Italy, Luxembourg, the Netherlands, Norway, Portugal, and the United States—agreed that "an armed attack against one or more of them in Europe or North America shall be considered an attack against them all." In May 1949, those nations also agreed to the creation of the Federal Republic of Germany (West Germany), which eventually joined NATO in 1955. In response, the Soviet Union established the German Democratic Republic (East Germany); the Council for Mutual Economic Assistance (COMECON); and, in 1955, the **Warsaw Pact**, a military alliance for Eastern Europe that included Albania, Bulgaria, Czechoslovakia, East Germany, Hungary, Poland, Romania, and the Soviet Union. In these parallel steps, the two superpowers formalized the Cold War through a massive division of the continent.

By the early 1950s, West and East were the stark markers of the new Europe. As Churchill had observed in 1946, the line dividing the two stretched "from Stettin in the Baltic to Trieste in the Adriatic," cutting off tens of millions of Eastern Europeans from the rest of the continent. Stalin's tactics had often been ruthless, but they were not without reason. The Soviet Union acted out of the sort of self-interest that had long defined powerful nations—ensuring a defensive perimeter of allies, seeking access to raw materials, and pressing the advantage that victory in war allowed.

**NSC-68**    Atomic developments, too, played a critical role in the emergence of the Cold War. As the sole nuclear power at the end of World War II, the United States entertained the possibility of international control of nuclear technology but did not wish to lose its advantage over the Soviet Union. When the American Bernard

Baruch proposed United Nations oversight of atomic energy in 1946, for instance, the plan assured the United States of near-total control of the technology, which further increased Cold War tensions. America's brief tenure as sole nuclear power ended in September 1949, however, when the Soviet Union detonated an atomic bomb. Truman then turned to the U.S. National Security Council (NSC), established by the National Security Act of 1947, for a strategic reassessment.

In April 1950, the NSC delivered its report, known as **NSC-68**. Bristling with alarmist rhetoric, the document marked a decisive turning point in the U.S. approach to the Cold War. The report's authors described the Soviet Union not as a typical great power but as one with a "fanatic faith" that seeks to "impose its absolute authority." Going beyond even the stern language used by George Kennan, NSC-68 cast Soviet ambitions as nothing short of "the domination of the Eurasian landmass."

To prevent that outcome, the report proposed "a bold and massive program of rebuilding the West's defensive potential to surpass that of the Soviet world." This included the development of a hydrogen bomb, a thermonuclear device that would be a thousand times more destructive than the atomic bombs dropped on Japan, as well as dramatic increases in conventional military forces. Critically, NSC-68 called for Americans to pay higher taxes to support the new military program and to accept whatever sacrifices were necessary to achieve national unity of purpose against the Soviet enemy. Many historians see the report as having "militarized" the American approach to the Cold War, which had to that point relied largely on economic measures such as aid to Greece and the Marshall Plan. Truman was reluctant to commit to a major defense buildup, fearing that it would overburden the national budget. But shortly after NSC-68 was completed, events in Asia led him to reverse course.

## Containment in Asia

As with Germany, American officials believed at the conclusion of World War II that restoring Japan's economy, while limiting its military influence, would ensure prosperity and contain communism in East Asia. After dismantling Japan's military, American occupation forces under General Douglas MacArthur drafted a democratic constitution and paved the way for the restoration of Japanese sovereignty in 1951. Considering the scorched-earth war that had just ended, this was a remarkable achievement, thanks partly to the imperious MacArthur but mainly to the Japanese, who embraced peace and accepted U.S. military protection. However, events on the mainland of Asia proved much more difficult for the United States to shape to its advantage.

**Civil War in China**   A civil war had been raging in China since the 1930s as Communist forces led by Mao Zedong (Mao Tse-tung) fought Nationalist forces under Jiang Jieshi (Chiang Kai-shek). Fearing a Communist victory, between 1945 and 1949 the United States provided $2 billion to Jiang's army. Pressing Truman to "save" China, conservative Republican Ohio senator Robert A. Taft predicted that "the Far East is ultimately even more important to our future peace than is Europe." By 1949, Mao's forces held the advantage. Truman reasoned that to save Jiang, the United States would have to intervene militarily. Unwilling to do so, he cut off aid and left the Nationalists to their fate. The People's Republic of China was formally established under Mao on October 1, 1949, and the remnants of Jiang's forces fled to Taiwan.

Truman expected Mao to take an independent line, as the Communist leader Tito had just done in Yugoslavia. The new Chinese leader, however, aligned himself with the Soviet Union, partly out of fear that the United States would re-arm the Nationalists and invade the mainland. As attitudes hardened, many Americans viewed Mao's success as a defeat for the United States. The pro-Nationalist "China lobby" held Truman's State Department responsible for the "loss" of China. Sensitive to these charges, the Truman administration refused to recognize "Red China" and blocked China's admission to the United Nations. But the United States pointedly declined to guarantee Taiwan's independence, and in fact accepted the outcome on the mainland. (Since 1982, however, the United States has recognized Taiwanese sovereignty.)

**The Korean War**　The United States took a stronger stance in Korea. Truman and Stalin had agreed at the close of World War II to occupy the Korean peninsula jointly, temporarily dividing the former Japanese colony at the 38th parallel. As tensions rose in Europe, the 38th parallel hardened into a permanent demarcation line. The Soviets supported a Communist government, led by Kim Il Sung, in North Korea; the United States backed a right-wing Nationalist, Syngman Rhee, in South

**The Korean War**　As a result of President Truman's 1948 Executive Order 9981, for the first time in the nation's history all troops in the Korean War served in racially integrated combat units. This photo taken during the Battle of Ch'ongch'on in 1950 shows a sergeant and his men of the 2nd Infantry Division. National Archives.

Korea. The two sides had waged low-level war since 1945, and both leaders were spoiling for a more definitive fight. However, neither Kim nor Rhee could launch an all-out offensive without the backing of his sponsor. Washington repeatedly said no, and so did Moscow. But Kim continued to press Stalin to permit him to reunify the nation. Convinced by the North Koreans that victory would be swift, the Soviet leader finally relented in the late spring of 1950.

On June 25, 1950, the North Koreans launched a surprise attack across the 38th parallel (Map 24.2). Truman immediately asked the UN Security Council to authorize a "police action" against the invaders. The Soviet Union was boycotting the Security Council to protest China's exclusion from the United Nations and therefore

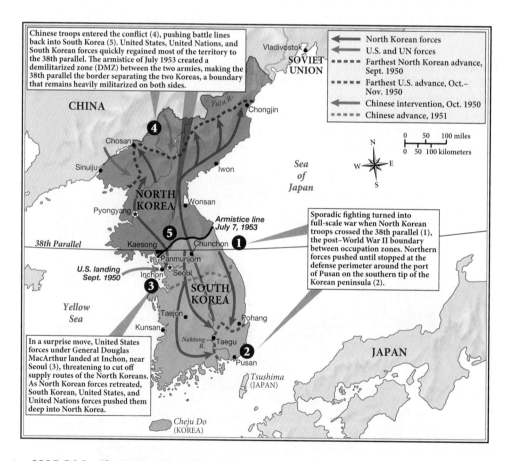

**MAP 24.2   The Korean War, 1950–1953**

The Korean War, which the United Nations officially deemed a "police action," lasted three years and cost the lives of more than 36,000 U.S. troops. South and North Korean deaths were estimated at more than 900,000. Although hostilities ceased in 1953, the South Korean Military (with U.S. military assistance) and the North Korean Army continue to face each other across the demilitarized zone, more than sixty years later.

could not veto the request. With the Security Council's approval of a "peacekeeping force," Truman ordered U.S. troops to Korea. The rapidly assembled UN army in Korea was overwhelmingly American, with General Douglas MacArthur in command. At first, the North Koreans held a distinct advantage, but MacArthur's surprise amphibious attack at Inchon gave the UN forces control of Seoul, the South Korean capital, and almost all the territory up to the 38th parallel.

The impetuous MacArthur then ordered his troops across the 38th parallel and led them all the way to the Chinese border at the Yalu River. It was a major blunder, certain to draw China into the war. Sure enough, a massive Chinese counterattack forced UN forces into headlong retreat back down the Korean peninsula. Then stalemate set in. With weak public support for the war in the United States, Truman and his advisors decided to work for a negotiated peace. MacArthur disagreed and denounced the Korean stalemate, declaring, "There is no substitute for victory." On April 11, 1951, Truman relieved MacArthur of his command. Truman's decision was highly unpopular, especially among conservative Republicans, but he had likely saved the nation from years of costly warfare with China.

Notwithstanding MacArthur's dismissal, the war dragged on for more than two years. An armistice in July 1953, pushed by the newly elected president, Dwight D. Eisenhower, left Korea divided at the original demarcation line. North Korea remained firmly allied with the Soviet Union; South Korea signed a mutual defense treaty with the United States. It had been the first major proxy war between the Soviet Union and United States, in which they took sides in a civil conflict without directly confronting one another militarily. It would not be the last.

The Korean War had far-reaching consequences. Truman's decision to commit troops without congressional approval set a precedent for future undeclared wars. His refusal to unleash atomic bombs, even when American forces were reeling under a massive Chinese attack, set ground rules for Cold War conflict. The war also expanded American involvement in Asia, transforming containment into a truly global policy. Finally, the Korean War ended Truman's resistance to a major military buildup (Map 24.3). Defense expenditures grew from $13 billion in 1950, roughly one-third of the federal budget, to $50 billion in 1953, nearly two-thirds of the budget. American foreign policy had become more global, more militarized, and more expensive. Even in times of peace, the United States now functioned in a state of permanent military mobilization.

**The Munich Analogy**   Behind much of U.S. foreign policy in the first two decades of the Cold War lay the memory of appeasement (Chapter 23). The generation of politicians and officials who designed the containment strategy had come of age in the era of Munich, the conference in 1938 at which the Western democracies had appeased Hitler by offering him part of Czechoslovakia, paving the road to World War II. Applying the lessons of Munich, American presidents believed that "appeasing" Stalin (and subsequent Soviet rulers Nikita Khrushchev and Leonid Brezhnev) would have the same result: wider war. Thus in Germany, Greece, and Korea, and later in Iran, Guatemala, and Vietnam, the United States staunchly resisted the Soviets — or what it perceived as Soviet influence. The Munich analogy strengthened the U.S. position in a number of strategic conflicts, particularly over the fate of

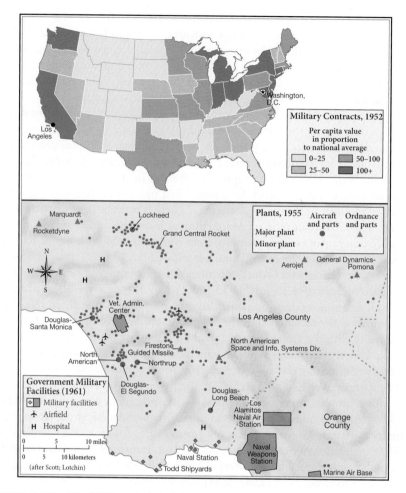

## MAP 24.3   The Military-Industrial Complex

Defense spending gave a big boost to the Cold War economy, but, as the upper map suggests, the benefits were by no means equally distributed. The big winners were the Middle Atlantic states, the industrialized Upper Midwest, Washington State (with its aircraft and nuclear plants), and California. The epicenter of California's military-industrial complex was Los Angeles, which, as is evident in the lower map, was studded with military facilities and major defense contractors like Douglas Aircraft, Lockheed, and General Dynamics. There was work aplenty for engineers and rocket scientists.

Germany. But it also drew Americans into armed conflicts—and convinced them to support repressive, right-wing regimes—that compromised, as much as supported, stated American principles.

| IN YOUR OWN WORDS | What primary factors caused the Cold War? |

# Cold War Liberalism

As president, Harry Truman cast himself in the mold of his predecessor, Franklin Roosevelt, and hoped to seize the possibilities afforded by victory in World War II to expand the New Deal at home. But the crises in postwar Europe and Asia, combined with the swift rise of anticommunism in the United States, forced him to take a different path. In the end, Truman went down in history as a Cold Warrior rather than a New Dealer. The Cold War consensus that he ultimately embraced—the notion that resisting communism at home and abroad represented America's most important postwar objective—shaped the nation's life and politics for decades to come.

## Truman and the End of Reform

Truman and the Democratic Party of the late 1940s and early 1950s forged what historians call **Cold War liberalism**. They preserved the core programs of the New Deal welfare state, developed the containment policy to oppose Soviet influence throughout the world, and fought so-called subversives at home. But there would be no second act for the New Deal. The Democrats adopted this combination of moderate liberal policies and anticommunism—Cold War liberalism—partly by choice and partly out of necessity. A few high-level espionage scandals and the Communist victories in Eastern Europe and China reenergized the Republican Party, which forced Truman and the Democrats to retreat to what historian Arthur Schlesinger called the "vital center" of American politics. However, Americans on both the progressive left and the conservative right accepted this development only reluctantly. Cold War liberalism was a practical centrist program for a turbulent era. But it would not last.

Organized labor remained a key force in the Democratic Party and played a central role in championing Cold War liberalism. Stronger than ever, union membership swelled to more than 14 million by 1945. Determined to make up for their wartime sacrifices, unionized workers made aggressive demands and mounted major strikes in the automobile, steel, and coal industries after the war, as they had after World War I. Republicans responded. They gained control of the House in a sweeping repudiation of Democrats in 1946 and promptly passed—over Truman's veto—the **Taft-Hartley Act** (1947), an overhaul of the 1935 National Labor Relations Act.

Taft-Hartley brought changes in procedures and language that, over time, weakened the right of workers to organize and engage in collective bargaining. Unions especially disliked Section 14b, which allowed states to pass "right-to-work" laws prohibiting the union shop. Additionally, the law forced unions to purge communists, who had been among the most successful labor organizers in the 1930s, from their ranks. Trade unions would continue to support the Democratic Party, but the labor movement would not crack the largely non-union South and would not penetrate the many American industries that remained unorganized. In that sense, Taft-Hartley effectively "contained" the labor movement.

**The 1948 Election**  Democrats would have dumped Truman in 1948 had they found a better candidate. But the party fell into disarray. The left wing split off and formed the Progressive Party, nominating Henry A. Wallace, an avid New Dealer whom Truman had fired as secretary of commerce in 1946 because Wallace opposed America's actions in the Cold War. A right-wing challenge came from the South. When northern liberals such as Mayor Hubert H. Humphrey of Minneapolis pushed through a strong civil rights platform at the Democratic convention, the southern delegations bolted and, calling themselves Dixiecrats, nominated for president South Carolina governor Strom Thurmond, an ardent supporter of racial segregation. The Republicans meanwhile renominated Thomas E. Dewey, the politically moderate governor of New York who had run a strong campaign against FDR in 1944.

Truman surprised everyone. He launched a strenuous cross-country speaking tour and hammered away at the Republicans for opposing progressive legislation and, in general, for running a "do-nothing" Congress. By combining these issues with attacks on the Soviet menace abroad, Truman began to salvage his troubled campaign. At his rallies, enthusiastic listeners shouted, "Give 'em hell, Harry!" Truman won, receiving 49.6 percent of the vote to Dewey's 45.1 percent (Map 24.4).

This remarkable election foreshadowed coming political turmoil. Truman occupied the center of FDR's sprawling New Deal coalition. On his left were progressives, civil rights advocates, and peace activists critical of the Cold War. On his right were segregationist southerners, who opposed civil rights and were allied with Republicans on many economic and foreign policy issues. In 1948, Truman performed a delicate balancing act, largely retaining the support of Jewish and Catholic voters in the big cities, black voters in the North, and union voters across the country. But Thurmond's strong showing—he carried four states in the Deep South—demonstrated the fragility of the Democratic coalition and prefigured the revolt of the party's southern wing in the 1960s. As he tried to manage contending forces in his own party, Truman faced mounting pressure from Republicans to denounce radicals at home and to take a tough stand against the Soviet Union.

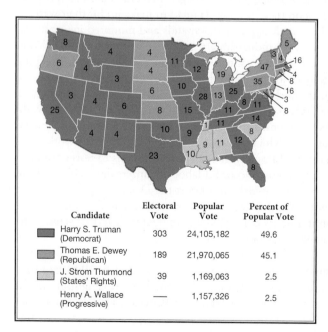

| Candidate | Electoral Vote | Popular Vote | Percent of Popular Vote |
|---|---|---|---|
| Harry S. Truman (Democrat) | 303 | 24,105,182 | 49.6 |
| Thomas E. Dewey (Republican) | 189 | 21,970,065 | 45.1 |
| J. Strom Thurmond (States' Rights) | 39 | 1,169,063 | 2.5 |
| Henry A. Wallace (Progressive) | — | 1,157,326 | 2.5 |

**MAP 24.4  The Presidential Election of 1948** Truman's electoral strategy in 1948 was to concentrate his campaign in areas where the Democrats had their greatest strength. In an election with a low turnout, Truman held on to enough support from Roosevelt's New Deal coalition of blacks, union members, and farmers to defeat Dewey by more than 2 million votes.

**The Fair Deal**    Despite having to perform a balancing act, Truman and progressive Democrats forged ahead. In 1949, reaching ambitiously to extend the New Deal, Truman proposed the **Fair Deal**: national health insurance, civil rights legislation, aid to education, a housing program, expansion of Social Security, a higher minimum wage, and a new agricultural program. In its attention to civil rights, the Fair Deal reflected the growing influence of African Americans in the Democratic Party. Congress, however, remained a huge stumbling block, and the Fair Deal fared poorly. The same conservative coalition that had blocked Roosevelt's initiatives in his second term stymied Truman's as well. Cold War pressure shaped political arguments about domestic social programs, while the nation's growing paranoia over internal subversion weakened support for bold extensions of the welfare state. Truman's proposal for national health insurance, for instance, was a popular idea, with strong backing from organized labor. But it was denounced as "socialized medicine" by the American Medical Association and the insurance industry. In the end, the Fair Deal's only significant breakthrough, other than improvements to the minimum wage and Social Security, was the National Housing Act of 1949, which authorized the construction of 810,000 low-income units.

## Red Scare: The Hunt for Communists

Cold War liberalism was premised on the grave domestic threat posed, many believed, by Communists and Communist sympathizers. Was there significant Soviet penetration of the American government? Records opened after the 1991 disintegration of the Soviet Union, including the Venona Papers made available in 1995 by the National Security Agency, indicate that there was. Among American suppliers of information to Moscow were FDR's assistant secretary of the treasury, Harry Dexter White; FDR's administrative aide Laughlin Currie; a strategically placed midlevel group in the State Department; key scientists and technicians working on the Manhattan Project; and several hundred more, some identified only by code name, working in a range of government departments and agencies.

How are we to explain this? Many of these enlistees in the Soviet cause had been bright young New Dealers in the mid-1930s, when the Soviet-backed Popular Front suggested that the lines separating liberalism, progressivism, and communism were permeable (Chapter 23). At that time, the United States was not at war and never expected to be. And when war did come, the Soviet Union was an American ally. For critics of the informants, however, there remained the time between the Nazi-Soviet Pact and the German invasion of the Soviet Union, a nearly two-year period during which cooperation with the Soviet Union could be seen in a less positive light. Moreover, passing secrets to another country, even a wartime ally, was simply indefensible to many Americans — particularly when it came to atomic secrets. The lines between U.S. and Soviet interests blurred for some; for others, they remained clear and definite.

After World War II, however, most suppliers of information to the Soviets apparently ceased spying. For one thing, the professional apparatus of Soviet spying in the United States was disrupted by American counterintelligence work. For another, most of the well-connected amateur spies moved on to other careers. Historians have thus developed a healthy skepticism that there was much Soviet espionage in the United States after 1947, but this was not how many Americans saw it at the time. Legitimate suspicions and real fears, along with political opportunism, combined to fuel the national Red Scare, which was longer and more far-reaching than the one that followed World War I (Chapter 21).

**Loyalty-Security Program**   To insulate his administration against charges of Communist infiltration, Truman issued Executive Order 9835 on March 21, 1947, which created the **Loyalty-Security Program**. The order permitted officials to investigate any employee of the federal government (some 2.5 million people) for "subversive" activities. Representing a profound centralization of power, the order sent shock waves through every federal agency. Truman intended the order to apply principally to actions designed to harm the United States (sabotage, treason, etc.), but it was broad enough to allow anyone to be accused of subversion for the slightest reason — for marching in a Communist-led demonstration in the 1930s, for instance, or signing a petition endorsing public housing. Along with suspected political subversives, more than a thousand gay men and lesbians were dismissed from federal employment in the 1950s, victims of an obsessive search for anyone deemed "unfit" for government work.

Following Truman's lead, many state and local governments, universities, political organizations, churches, and businesses undertook their own antisubversion campaigns, which often included loyalty oaths. In the labor movement, charges of Communist domination led to the expulsion of a number of unions by the Congress of Industrial Organizations (CIO) in 1949. Civil rights organizations such as the National Association for the Advancement of Colored People (NAACP) and the National Urban League also expelled Communists and "fellow travelers," or Communist sympathizers. Thus the Red Scare spread from the federal government to the farthest reaches of American organizational, economic, and cultural life.

**HUAC**   The Truman administration had legitimized the vague and malleable concept of "disloyalty." Others proved willing to stretch the concept even further, beginning with the **House Un-American Activities Committee (HUAC)**, which Congressman Martin Dies of Texas and other conservatives had launched in 1938. In 1947, HUAC helped spark the Red Scare by holding widely publicized hearings on alleged Communist infiltration in the movie industry. A group of writers and directors dubbed the Hollywood Ten went to jail for contempt of Congress after they refused to testify about their past associations. Hundreds of other actors, directors, and writers whose names had been mentioned in the HUAC investigation were unable to get work, victims of an unacknowledged but very real blacklist honored by industry executives.

Other HUAC investigations had greater legitimacy. One that intensified the anticommunist crusade in 1948 involved Alger Hiss, a former New Dealer and State Department official who had accompanied Franklin Roosevelt to Yalta. A former Communist, Whitaker Chambers, claimed that Hiss was a member of a secret Communist cell operating in the government and had passed him classified documents in the 1930s. Hiss denied the allegations, but California Republican congressman Richard Nixon doggedly pursued the case against him. In early 1950, Hiss was found guilty not of spying but of lying to Congress about his Communist affiliations and was sentenced to five years in federal prison. Many Americans doubted at the time that Hiss was a spy. But the Venona transcripts in the 1990s corroborated a great deal of Chambers's testimony, and though no definitive proof has emerged, many historians now recognize the strong circumstantial evidence against Hiss.

**McCarthyism** The meteoric career of Senator Joseph McCarthy of Wisconsin marked first the apex and then the finale of the Red Scare. In February 1950, McCarthy delivered a bombshell during a speech in Wheeling, West Virginia: "I have here in my hand a list of 205 . . . a list of names that were made known to the Secretary of State as being members of the Communist Party and who nevertheless are still working and shaping policy in the State Department." McCarthy later reduced his numbers, gave different figures in different speeches, and never released any names or proof. But he had gained the attention he sought.

For the next four years, from his position as chair of the Senate Permanent Subcommittee on Investigations, McCarthy waged a virulent smear campaign. Critics who disagreed with him exposed themselves to charges of being "soft" on communism. Truman called McCarthy's charges "slander, lies, [and] character assassination" but could do nothing to curb him. Republicans, for their part, refrained from publicly challenging their most outspoken senator and, on the whole, were content to reap the political benefits. McCarthy's charges almost always targeted Democrats.

**The Army-McCarthy Hearings** These 1954 hearings contributed to the downfall of Senator Joseph McCarthy by exposing his reckless accusations and bullying tactics to the huge television audience that tuned in each day. Some of the most heated exchanges took place between McCarthy (center) and Joseph Welch (seated, left), the lawyer representing the army. When the gentlemanly Welch finally asked, "Have you no sense of decency sir, at long last? Have you left no sense of decency?" he fatally punctured McCarthy's armor. The audience broke into applause because someone had finally had the courage to stand up to the senator from Wisconsin. Bettmann/Getty Images.

Despite McCarthy's failure to identify a single Communist in government, several national developments gave his charges credibility with the public. The dramatic 1951 espionage trial of Julius and Ethel Rosenberg, followed around the world, fueled McCarthy's allegations. Convicted of passing atomic secrets to the Soviet Union, the Rosenbergs were executed in 1953. As in the Hiss case, documents released decades later provided some evidence of Julius Rosenberg's guilt, though not Ethel's. Their execution nevertheless remains controversial — in part because some felt that anti-Semitism played a role in their sentencing. Also fueling McCarthy's charges were a series of trials of American Communists between 1949 and 1955 for violation of the 1940 Smith Act, which prohibited Americans from advocating the violent overthrow of the government. Though civil libertarians and two Supreme Court justices vigorously objected, dozens of Communist Party members were convicted. McCarthy was not involved in either the Rosenberg trial or the Smith Act convictions, but these sensational events gave his wild charges some credence.

In early 1954, McCarthy overreached by launching an investigation into subversive activities in the U.S. Army. When lengthy hearings — the first of their kind broadcast on the new medium of television — brought McCarthy's tactics into the nation's living rooms, support for him plummeted. In December 1954, the Senate voted 67 to 22 to censure McCarthy for unbecoming conduct. He died from an alcohol-related illness three years later at the age of forty-eight, his name forever attached to a period of political repression of which he was only the most flagrant manifestation.

## The Politics of Cold War Liberalism

As election day 1952 approached, the nation was embroiled in the tense Cold War with the Soviet Union and fighting a "hot" war in Korea. Though Americans gave the Republicans victory, radical change was not in the offing. The new president, Dwight D. Eisenhower, embraced what his supporters called modern Republicanism, an updated GOP approach that aimed at moderating, not dismantling, the New Deal. Eisenhower Republicans were as much successors of FDR as of Herbert Hoover. Foreign policy revealed a similar continuity. Like their predecessors, Republicans saw the world in Cold War polarities.

Despite Eisenhower's popularity as the former commander of Allied forces in Europe, divisions in the party persisted. Conservative party activists preferred Robert A. Taft of Ohio, the Republican leader in the Senate who was an outspoken opponent of the New Deal. As a close friend of business, he opposed labor unions. Though an ardent anticommunist, the isolationist-minded Taft criticized Truman's aggressive containment policy and opposed U.S. participation in NATO. Taft ran for president three times, and though he was never the Republican nominee, he won the loyalty of conservative Americans who saw the welfare state as wasteful spending and international affairs as dangerous foreign entanglements.

In contrast, moderate Republicans looked to Eisenhower and even to more liberal-minded party leaders like Nelson Rockefeller, who supported international initiatives such as the Marshall Plan and NATO and were willing to tolerate labor unions and the welfare state. Eisenhower was a man without a political past. Believing that democracy required the military to stand aside, he had never voted. Rockefeller, the scion of one of the richest families in America, was a Cold War internationalist.

He served in a variety of capacities under Eisenhower, including as an advisor on foreign affairs. Having made his political name, Rockefeller was elected the governor of New York in 1959 and became the de facto leader of the liberal wing of the Republican Party.

For eight years, between 1952 and 1960, Eisenhower steered a precarious course from the middle of the party, with conservative Taft Republicans on one side and liberal Rockefeller Republicans on the other. His popularity temporarily kept the two sides at bay, though more ardent conservatives considered him a closet New Dealer. "Ike," as he was widely known, proved willing to work with the mostly Democratic-controlled Congresses of those years. Eisenhower signed bills increasing federal outlays for veterans' benefits, housing, highway construction (Chapter 25), and Social Security, and he increased the minimum wage from 75 cents an hour to $1. Like Truman, Eisenhower accepted some government responsibility for the economic security of individuals, part of a broad consensus in American politics in these years.

**America Under Eisenhower**   The global power realities that had called forth containment guided Eisenhower's foreign policy. New developments, however, altered the tone of the Cold War. Stalin's death in March 1953 precipitated an intraparty struggle in the Soviet Union that lasted until 1956, when Nikita Khrushchev emerged as Stalin's successor. Khrushchev soon startled Communists around the world by denouncing Stalin and detailing his crimes and blunders. He also surprised many Americans by calling for "peaceful coexistence" with the West. But the new Soviet leader had his limits, and when Hungarians rose up in 1956 to demand independence from Moscow, Khrushchev crushed the incipient revolution.

With no end to the Cold War in sight, Eisenhower focused on limiting the cost of containment. The president hoped to economize by relying on a nuclear arsenal and deemphasizing expensive conventional forces. Under this **"New Look"** defense policy, the Eisenhower administration stepped up production of the hydrogen bomb and developed long-range bombing capabilities. The Soviets, however, matched the United States weapon for weapon. By 1958, both nations had intercontinental ballistic missiles. When an American nuclear submarine launched an atomic-tipped Polaris missile in 1960, Soviet engineers raced to produce an equivalent weapon. This arms race was another critical feature of the Cold War. American officials believed the best deterrent to Soviet aggression was the threat of an all-out nuclear response by the United States, which was dubbed "massive retaliation" by Secretary of State Dulles.

Although confident in the international arena, Eisenhower started out as a novice in domestic affairs. Doing his best to set a less confrontational tone after the rancorous Truman years, he was reluctant to speak out against Joe McCarthy, and he was not a leader on civil rights. Democrats meanwhile maintained a strong presence in Congress but proved weak in presidential elections in the 1950s. In the two presidential contests of the decade, 1952 and 1956, Eisenhower defeated the admired but politically ineffectual liberal Adlai Stevenson. In the 1952 election, Stevenson was hampered by the unpopularity of the Truman administration. The deadlocked Korean War and a series of scandals that Republicans dubbed "the mess in Washington" combined to give the war-hero general an easy victory. In 1956, Ike won an even more impressive victory over Stevenson, an eloquent and sophisticated spokesman for liberalism but no match for Eisenhower's popularity with the public.

During Eisenhower's presidency, new political forces on both the right and the left had begun to stir. But they had not yet fully transformed the party system itself. Particularly at the national level, Democrats and Republicans seemed in broad agreement about the realities of the Cold War and the demands of a modern, industrial economy and welfare state. Indeed, respected commentators in the 1950s declared "the end of ideology" and wondered if the great political clashes that had wracked the 1930s were gone forever. Below the apparent calm of national party politics, however, lay profound differences among Americans over the direction of the nation. Those differences would starkly divide the country in the 1960s and bring an end to the brief and fragile Cold War consensus (Chapters 26 and 27).

> **IN YOUR OWN WORDS**    What were the components of Cold War liberalism, and why did the Democratic Party embrace them?

# Containment in the Postcolonial World

As the Cold War took shape, the world scene was changing at a furious pace. New nations were emerging across Asia, Africa, and the Middle East, created in the wake of successful anticolonial movements whose origins dated to before World War II. Between 1947 and 1962, the British, French, Dutch, and Belgian empires all but disintegrated in a momentous collapse of European global power. FDR had favored the idea of national self-determination, often to the fury of his British and French allies. He expected emerging democracies to be new partners in an American-led, free-market world system. But colonial revolts produced many independent- or socialist-minded regimes in the so-called Third World, as well. *Third World* was a term that came into usage after World War II to describe developing or ex-colonial nations in Asia, Africa, Latin America, and the Middle East that were not aligned with the Western capitalist countries led by the United States or the socialist states of Eastern Europe led by the Soviet Union.

## The Cold War and Colonial Independence

Insisting that all nations had to choose sides in the Cold War, the United States drew as many countries as possible into collective security agreements, with the NATO alliance in Europe as a model. Secretary of State John Foster Dulles orchestrated the creation of the Southeast Asia Treaty Organization (SEATO), which in 1954 linked the United States and its major European allies with Australia, New Zealand, Pakistan, the Philippines, and Thailand. An extensive system of defense alliances eventually tied the United States to more than forty other countries (Map 24.5). The United States also sponsored a strategically instrumental alliance between Iraq and Iran, on the southern flank of the Soviet Union.

Despite American rhetoric, the United States was often concerned less with democracy than with stability. The Truman and Eisenhower administrations tended to support governments, no matter how repressive, that were overtly anticommunist. Some of America's staunchest allies — the Philippines, South Korea, Iran, Cuba, South Vietnam, and Nicaragua — were governed by dictatorships or right-wing regimes that lacked broad-based support. Moreover, Eisenhower's secretary of state

Dulles often resorted to covert operations against governments that, in his opinion, were too closely aligned with the Soviets.

For these covert tasks, Dulles turned to the newly created (1947) Central Intelligence Agency (CIA), run by his brother, Allen Dulles. When Iran's democratically elected nationalist premier, Mohammad Mossadegh, seized British oil properties in 1953, CIA agents helped depose him and installed the young Mohammad Reza Pahlavi as shah of Iran. Iranian resentment of the coup, followed by twenty-five years of U.S. support for the shah, provided fuel for the 1979 Iranian Revolution (Chapter 29). In 1954, the CIA also engineered a coup in Guatemala against the democratically elected president, Jacobo Arbenz Guzmán, who had seized land owned by the American-owned United Fruit Company. Arbenz Guzmán offered to pay United Fruit the declared value of the land, but the company rejected the offer and sought help from the U.S. government. Eisenhower specifically approved those CIA efforts and expanded the agency's mandate from gathering intelligence to intervening in the affairs of sovereign states.

**Vietnam**   But when covert operations failed or proved impractical, the American approach to emerging nations could entangle the United States in deeper, more intractable conflicts. One example was already unfolding on a distant stage, in a small country unknown to most Americans: Vietnam. In August 1945, at the close of World War II, the Japanese occupiers of Vietnam surrendered to China in the north of the country and to Britain in the south. The Vietminh, the nationalist movement that had led the resistance against the Japanese (and the French, prior to 1940), seized control in the north. But their leader, Ho Chi Minh, was a Communist, and this single fact outweighed American and British commitment to self-determination. When France moved to restore its control over the country, the United States and Britain sided with their European ally. President Truman rejected Ho's plea to support the Vietnamese struggle for nationhood, and France rejected Ho's offer of a negotiated independence. Shortly after France returned, in late 1946, the Vietminh resumed their war of national liberation.

Eisenhower picked up where Truman left off. If the French failed, Eisenhower argued, all non-Communist governments in the region would fall like dominoes. This so-called **domino theory**—which represented an extension of the containment doctrine—guided U.S. policy in Southeast Asia for the next twenty years. The United States eventually provided most of the financing for the French war, but money was not enough to defeat the determined Vietminh, who were fighting for the liberation of their country. After a fifty-six-day siege in early 1954, the French were defeated at the huge fortress of Dien Bien Phu. The result was the 1954 Geneva Accords, which partitioned Vietnam temporarily at the 17th parallel and called for elections within two years to unify the strife-torn nation.

The United States rejected the Geneva Accords and set about undermining them. With the help of the CIA, a pro-American government took power in South Vietnam in June 1954. Ngo Dinh Diem, an anticommunist Catholic living in exile in the United States, returned to Vietnam as premier. The next year, in a rigged election, Diem became president of an independent South Vietnam. Facing certain defeat by the popular Ho Chi Minh, Diem called off the scheduled reunification elections. The Eisenhower administration propped up Diem with an average of $200 million a year in aid and a contingent of 675 American military advisors. This support was just the beginning.

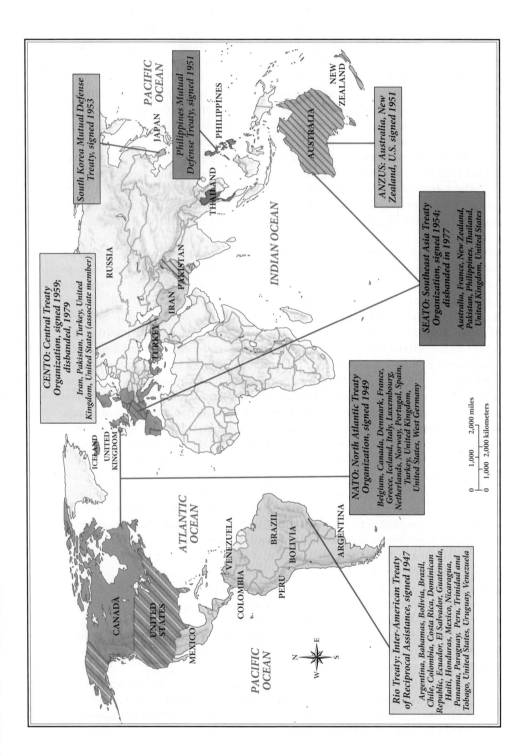

CENTO: Central Treaty Organization, signed 1959; disbanded, 1979

Iran, Pakistan, Turkey, United Kingdom, United States (associate member)

South Korea Mutual Defense Treaty, signed 1953

Philippines Mutual Defense Treaty, signed 1951

ANZUS: Australia, New Zealand, U.S. signed 1951

SEATO: Southeast Asia Treaty Organization, signed 1954; disbanded in 1977

Australia, France, New Zealand, Pakistan, Philippines, Thailand, United Kingdom, United States

NATO: North Atlantic Treaty Organization, signed 1949

Belgium, Canada, Denmark, France, Greece, Iceland, Italy, Luxembourg, Netherlands, Norway, Portugal, Spain, Turkey, United Kingdom, United States, West Germany

Rio Treaty: Inter-American Treaty of Reciprocal Assistance, signed 1947

Argentina, Bahamas, Bolivia, Brazil, Chile, Colombia, Costa Rica, Dominican Republic, Ecuador, El Salvador, Guatemala, Haiti, Honduras, Mexico, Nicaragua, Panama, Paraguay, Peru, Trinidad and Tobago, United States, Uruguay, Venezuela

PACIFIC OCEAN

ATLANTIC OCEAN

INDIAN OCEAN

PACIFIC OCEAN

RUSSIA

JAPAN

PHILIPPINES

THAILAND

PAKISTAN

IRAN

TURKEY

ICELAND

UNITED KINGDOM

CANADA

UNITED STATES

MEXICO

COLOMBIA

VENEZUELA

PERU

BOLIVIA

BRAZIL

ARGENTINA

AUSTRALIA

NEW ZEALAND

0     1,000     2,000 miles

0   1,000  2,000 kilometers

**The Middle East** If Vietnam was still of minor concern, the same could not be said of the Middle East, an area rich in oil and political complexity. The most volatile area was Palestine, populated by Arabs but also historically the ancient land of Israel and coveted by the Zionist movement as a Jewish national homeland. After World War II, many survivors of the Nazi extermination camps resettled in Palestine, which was still controlled by Britain under a World War I mandate. On November 29, 1947, the UN General Assembly voted to partition Palestine between Jewish and Arab sectors. When the British mandate ended in 1948, Palestinian leaders rejected the partition as a violation of their right to self-determination. When Zionist leaders proclaimed the state of Israel, a coalition of Arab nations known as the Arab League invaded, but Israel survived. Many Palestinians fled or were driven from their homes during the fighting. The Arab defeat left these people permanently stranded in refugee camps. President Truman recognized the new state immediately, which won him crucial support from Jewish voters in the 1948 election but alienated the Arab world.

Southeast of Palestine, Egypt began to assert its presence in the region. Having gained independence from Britain several decades earlier, Egypt remained a monarchy until 1952, when Gamal Abdel Nasser led a military coup that established a constitutional republic. Caught between the Soviet Union and the United States, Nasser sought an independent route: a pan-Arab socialism designed to end the Middle East's colonial relationship with the West. When negotiations with the United States over Nasser's plan to build a massive hydroelectric dam on the Nile broke down in 1956, he nationalized the Suez Canal, which was the lifeline for Western Europe's oil. Britain and France, in alliance with Israel, attacked Egypt and seized the canal. Concerned that the invasion would encourage Egypt to turn to the Soviets for help, Eisenhower urged France and Britain to pull back and applied additional pressure through the UN General Assembly. When the Western nations backed down, however, Egypt reclaimed the Suez Canal and built the Aswan Dam on the Nile with Soviet support. Eisenhower had likely avoided a larger war, but the West lost a potential ally in Nasser.

In early 1957, concerned about Soviet influence in the Middle East, the president announced the **Eisenhower Doctrine**, which stated that American forces would assist any nation in the region that required aid "against overt armed aggression from any nation controlled by International Communism." Invoking the doctrine later that year, Eisenhower helped King Hussein of Jordan put down a Nasser-backed revolt and propped up a pro-American government in Lebanon. The Eisenhower Doctrine was further evidence that the United States had extended the global reach

**< MAP 24.5  American Global Defense Treaties in the Cold War Era**
The advent of the Cold War led to a major shift in American foreign policy — the signing of mutual defense treaties. Dating back to George Washington's call "to steer clear of permanent alliances with any portion of the foreign world," the United States had avoided treaty obligations that entailed the defense of other nations. As late as 1919, the U.S. Senate had rejected the principle of "collective security," the centerpiece of the League of Nations established by the Treaty of Versailles that ended World War I. But after World War II, in response to fears of Soviet global expansion, the United States entered defense alliances with much of the non-Communist world.

of containment, in this instance accentuated by the strategic objective of protecting the West's access to steady supplies of oil.

## John F. Kennedy and the Cold War

Charisma, style, and personality—these, more than platforms and issues, defined a new brand of politics in the early 1960s. This was John F. Kennedy's natural environment. Kennedy, a Harvard alumnus, World War II hero, and senator from Massachusetts, had inherited his love of politics from his grandfathers—colorful, and often ruthless, Irish Catholic politicians in Boston. Ambitious and deeply aware of style, the forty-three-year-old Kennedy made use of his many advantages to become, as novelist Norman Mailer put it, "our leading man." His one disadvantage—that he was Catholic in a country that had never elected a Catholic president—he masterfully neutralized. And thanks to both media advisors and his youthful attractiveness, Kennedy projected a superb television image.

At heart, Kennedy was a Cold Warrior who had come of age politically in the era of Munich, Yalta, and McCarthyism. He projected an air of idealism, but his years in the Senate (1953–1960) had proved him to be a conventional Cold War politician. Once elected president, Kennedy would shape the nation's foreign policy by drawing both on his ingenuity and on old-style Cold War power politics.

**The Election of 1960 and the New Frontier**   Kennedy's Republican opponent in the 1960 presidential election, Eisenhower's vice president, Richard Nixon, was a seasoned politician and Cold Warrior himself. The great innovation of the 1960 campaign was a series of four nationally televised debates. Nixon, less photogenic than Kennedy, looked sallow and unshaven under the intense studio lights. Voters who heard the first debate on the radio concluded that Nixon had won, but those who viewed it on television favored Kennedy. Despite the edge Kennedy enjoyed in the debates, he won only the narrowest of electoral victories, receiving 49.7 percent of the popular vote to Nixon's 49.5 percent. Kennedy attracted Catholics, African Americans, and the labor vote; his vice-presidential running mate, Texas senator Lyndon Baines Johnson, helped bring in southern Democrats. Yet only 120,000 votes separated the two candidates, and a shift of a few thousand votes in key states would have reversed the outcome.

Kennedy brought to Washington a cadre of young, ambitious newcomers, including Robert McNamara, a renowned systems analyst and former head of Ford Motor Company, as secretary of defense. A host of trusted advisors and academics flocked to Washington to join the New Frontier—Kennedy's term for the challenges the country faced. Included on the team as attorney general was Kennedy's younger brother Robert, who had made a name as a hard-hitting investigator of organized crime. Relying on an old American trope, Kennedy's New Frontier suggested masculine toughness and adventurism and encouraged Americans to again think of themselves as exploring uncharted terrain. That terrain proved treacherous, however, as the new administration immediately faced a crisis.

**Crises in Cuba and Berlin**   In January 1961, the Soviet Union announced that it intended to support "wars of national liberation" wherever in the world they occurred. Kennedy took Soviet premier Khrushchev at his word, especially regarding Cuba, where in 1959 Fidel Castro had overthrown the right-wing dictator Fulgencio Batista and declared a revolution. Determined to keep Cuba out of the Soviet orbit, Kennedy followed through on Eisenhower administration plans to dispatch Cuban exiles to launch an anti-Castro uprising. The invaders, trained by the CIA, were ill-prepared for their task. On landing at Cuba's **Bay of Pigs** on April 17, 1961, the force of 1,400 was crushed by Castro's troops. Kennedy prudently rejected CIA pleas for a U.S. air strike. Accepting defeat, Kennedy went before the American people and took full responsibility for the fiasco (Map 24.6).

Already strained by the Bay of Pigs incident, U.S.-Soviet relations deteriorated further in June 1961 when Khrushchev stopped movement between Communist-controlled East Berlin and the city's Western sector. Kennedy responded by dispatching 40,000 more troops to Europe. In mid-August, to stop the exodus of East

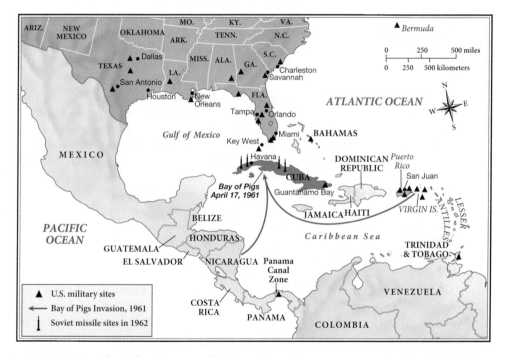

**MAP 24.6   The United States and Cuba, 1961–1962**

Fidel Castro's 1959 Communist takeover of Cuba brought Cold War tensions to the Caribbean. In 1961, the United States tried unsuccessfully to overthrow Castro's regime by sponsoring the Bay of Pigs invasion of Cuban exiles launched from Nicaragua and other points in the Caribbean. In 1962, the United States confronted the Soviet Union over Soviet construction of nuclear missile sites in Cuba. After President Kennedy ordered a naval blockade of the island, the Soviets backed down from the tense standoff and removed the missiles. Despite the 1991 dissolution of the Soviet Union and the official end of the Cold War, the United States continued to view Cuba, governed by Raúl Castro, Fidel's brother, since 2008 as an enemy nation until 2016, when President Barack Obama began the process of normalizing relations between the two countries.

Germans fleeing to the West, the Communist regime began constructing the Berlin Wall, policed by border guards under shoot-to-kill orders. Kennedy again responded, though this time rhetorically, by delivering a speech in Berlin criticizing the wall in June 1963. Until the 12-foot-high concrete barrier came down in 1989, it served as the supreme symbol of the Cold War.

Perhaps the most perilous Cold War confrontation came in October 1962. In a somber televised address on October 22, Kennedy revealed that U.S. reconnaissance planes had spotted Soviet-built bases for intermediate-range ballistic missiles in Cuba. Some of those weapons had already been installed, and more were on the way. Kennedy announced that the United States would impose a "quarantine on all offensive military equipment" bound for Cuba. As the world held its breath waiting to see if the conflict would escalate into war, on October 25 ships carrying Soviet missiles turned back. After a week of tense negotiations, both sides made concessions: Kennedy pledged not to invade Cuba, and Khrushchev promised to dismantle the missile bases. Kennedy also secretly ordered U.S. missiles to be removed from Turkey, at Khrushchev's insistence. The risk of nuclear war, greater during the **Cuban missile crisis** than at any other time in the Cold War, prompted a slight thaw in U.S.-Soviet relations. As National Security Advisor McGeorge Bundy put it, both sides were chastened by "having come so close to the edge."

**Kennedy and the World**     Kennedy also launched a series of bold nonmilitary initiatives. One was the **Peace Corps**, which embodied a call to public service put forth in his inaugural address ("Ask not what your country can do for you, but what you can do for your country"). Thousands of men and women agreed to devote two or more years as volunteers for projects such as teaching English to Filipino schoolchildren or helping African villagers obtain clean water. Exhibiting the idealism of the early 1960s, the Peace Corps was also a low-cost Cold War weapon—and an extension of American "soft power" (Chapter 21)—intended to show the developing world that there was an alternative to communism. Kennedy championed space exploration, as well. In a 1962 speech, he proposed that the nation commit itself to landing a man on the moon within the decade. The Soviets had already beaten the United States into space with the 1957 *Sputnik* satellite and the 1961 flight of cosmonaut Yuri Gagarin. Capitalizing on America's fascination with space, Kennedy persuaded Congress to increase funding for the government's space agency, the National Aeronautics and Space Administration (NASA), enabling the United States to pull ahead of the Soviet Union. Kennedy's ambition was realized when U.S. astronauts arrived on the moon in 1969.

## Making a Commitment in Vietnam

When Kennedy became president, he inherited Eisenhower's commitment in Vietnam, which he saw in Cold War terms. But rather than practicing brinksmanship—threatening nuclear war to stop communism—Kennedy sought what at the time seemed a more intelligent and realistic, if nevertheless interventionist, approach. In 1961, he increased military aid to the South Vietnamese and expanded the role of U.S. Special Forces ("Green Berets"), who would train the South Vietnamese army in unconventional, small-group warfare tactics.

South Vietnam's corrupt and repressive Diem regime, propped up by Eisenhower since 1954, was losing ground in spite of American aid. By 1961, Diem's opponents, with backing from North Vietnam, had formed a revolutionary movement known as the National Liberation Front (NLF). NLF guerrilla forces—the Vietcong—found allies among peasants alienated by Diem's "strategic hamlet" program, which had uprooted entire villages and moved villagers into barbed-wire compounds. Furthermore, Buddhists charged Diem, a Catholic, with religious persecution. Starting in May 1963, militant Buddhists staged dramatic demonstrations, including self-immolations (burning to death) recorded by reporters covering the activities of the 16,000 U.S. military personnel then in Vietnam.

The self-immolations, broadcast on television to a shocked global audience, powerfully illustrated the dilemmas of American policy in Vietnam. To ensure a stable southern government and prevent victory for Ho Chi Minh and the North, the United States had to support Diem's authoritarian regime. But the regime's repression of its political opponents made Diem more unpopular. He was assassinated on November 3, 1963. Whether one supported U.S. involvement in Vietnam or not, the elemental paradox remained unchanged: in its efforts to achieve victory over the North, the United States brought defeat ever closer.

| **IN YOUR OWN WORDS** | What objectives guided U.S. foreign policy in the so-called Third World during the Cold War? |

# Summary

The Cold War began as a conflict between the United States and the Soviet Union over Eastern Europe and the fate of post–World War II Germany. Early in the conflict, the United States adopted a strategy of containment, which quickly expanded to Asia after China became a communist state under Mao Zedong. The first effect of that expansion was the Korean War, after which, under Dwight D. Eisenhower, containment of communism became America's guiding principle across the developing world—often called the Third World. Cold War tensions relaxed in the late 1950s but erupted again under John F. Kennedy with the Cuban missile crisis, the building of the Berlin Wall, and major increases in American military assistance to South Vietnam. Cold War imperatives between 1945 and the early 1960s meant a major military buildup, a massive nuclear arms race, and unprecedented entanglements across the globe.

On the domestic front, Harry S. Truman started out with high hopes for an expanded New Deal, only to be confounded by resistance from Congress and the competing demands of the Cold War. The greatest Cold War–inspired development was a climate of fear over internal subversion by Communists that gave rise to McCarthyism. Truman's successor, Eisenhower, brought the Republicans back into power. Although personally conservative, Eisenhower actually proved a New Dealer in disguise. When Eisenhower left office and Kennedy became president, it seemed that a "liberal consensus" prevailed, with old-fashioned, *laissez faire* conservatism mostly marginalized in American political life.

# Chapter 24 Review

## KEY TERMS

**Identify and explain the significance of each term below.**

Yalta Conference (p. 700)
United Nations (p. 701)
Potsdam Conference (p. 701)
containment (p. 703)
Truman Doctrine (p. 704)
Marshall Plan (p. 704)
North Atlantic Treaty Organization
    (NATO) (p. 705)
Warsaw Pact (p. 705)
NSC-68 (p. 706)
Cold War liberalism (p. 711)

Taft-Hartley Act (p. 711)
Fair Deal (p. 713)
Loyalty-Security Program (p. 714)
House Un-American Activities
    Committee (HUAC) (p. 714)
"New Look" (p. 717)
domino theory (p. 719)
Eisenhower Doctrine (p. 721)
Bay of Pigs (p. 723)
Cuban missile crisis (p. 724)
Peace Corps (p. 724)

## REVIEW QUESTIONS

**Answer these questions to demonstrate your understanding of the chapter's main ideas.**

1. What primary factors caused the Cold War?
2. What were the components of Cold War liberalism, and why did the Democratic Party embrace them?
3. What objectives guided U.S. foreign policy in the so-called Third World during the Cold War?
4. Review the events listed under "Politics and Power" and "American and National Identity" on the thematic timelines on pages 580 and 696. Radicalism played a significant role in American history between 1890 and 1945. What radical politics took root in the United States during this time, and how did the government, the business community, and different social groups respond to that radicalism?

## CHRONOLOGY

**As you read, ask yourself why this chapter begins and ends with these dates and identify the links among related events.**

| | |
|---|---|
| **1945** | • End of World War II; Yalta and Potsdam conferences |
| | • Senate approves U.S. participation in United Nations |
| **1946** | • George F. Kennan outlines containment policy |
| | • U.S. sides with French in war between French and Vietminh over control of Vietnam |

| | |
|---|---|
| **1947** | • Truman Doctrine |
| | • House Un-American Activities Committee (HUAC) investigates film industry |
| **1948** | • Communist coup in Czechoslovakia |
| | • Marshall Plan aids economic recovery in Europe |
| | • State of Israel created |
| | • Stalin blockades West Berlin; Berlin Airlift begins |
| **1949** | • North Atlantic Treaty Organization (NATO) founded |
| | • Soviet Union detonates atomic bomb |
| | • Mao Zedong establishes People's Republic of China |
| **1950–1953** | • Korean War |
| **1950** | • NSC-68 leads to nuclear buildup |
| | • Joseph McCarthy announces "list" of Communists in government |
| **1952** | • Dwight D. Eisenhower elected president |
| **1954** | • Army-McCarthy hearings on army subversion |
| | • Geneva Accords partition Vietnam |
| **1956** | • Nikita Khrushchev emerges as Stalin's successor |
| | • Suez Canal crisis |
| **1960** | • John F. Kennedy elected president |
| **1961** | • Kennedy orders the first contingent of Special Forces ("Green Berets") to Vietnam |
| **1963** | • Ngo Dinh Diem assassinated in South Vietnam |

# 25

# Triumph of the Middle Class

## 1945–1963

### IDENTIFY THE BIG IDEA

Why did consumer culture become such a fixture of American life in the postwar decades, and how did it affect politics and society?

**AT THE HEIGHT OF THE COLD WAR, IN 1959, U.S. VICE PRESIDENT** Richard Nixon debated Soviet premier Nikita Khrushchev on the merits of Pepsi-Cola, TV dinners, and electric ovens. Face-to-face at the opening of an American exhibition in Moscow, Nixon and Khrushchev strolled through a model American home, assembled to demonstrate the consumer products available to the typical citizen of the United States. Nixon explained to Khrushchev that although the Soviet Union may have superior rockets, the United States was ahead in other areas, such as color television.

This was Cold War politics by other means—a symbolic contest over which country's standard of living was higher. What was so striking about the so-called **kitchen debate** was Nixon's insistence, to a disbelieving Khrushchev, that a modern home filled with shiny new toasters, televisions, and other consumer products was accessible to the average American worker. "Any steelworker could buy this house," Nixon told the Soviet leader. The kitchen debate settled little in the geopolitical rivalry between the United States and the Soviet Union. But it speaks to us across the decades because it reveals how Americans had come to see themselves by the late 1950s: as home owners and consumers, as a people for whom the middle-class American Dream was a commercial aspiration.

The real story of the postwar period was the growing number of Americans who embraced that aspiration. In the two decades following the end of World War II, a new middle class was born in the United States. *Fortune* magazine estimated that in the 1950s, the middle class—which

*Fortune* defined as families with more than $5,000 in annual earnings after taxes (about $45,000 today)—was increasing at the rate of 1.1 million people per year. Riding a wave of rising incomes, American dominance in the global economy, and Cold War federal spending, the postwar middle class enjoyed the highest standard of living in the world.

However, the success of the middle class could not hide deeper troubles. This was an era of neither universal conformity nor diminishing social strife. Jim Crow laws, contradictions in women's lives, a rebellious youth culture, and changing sexual mores were only the most obvious sources of social tension. Suburban growth came at the expense of cities, hastening urban decay and exacerbating racial segregation. Nor was prosperity ever as widespread as the Moscow exhibit implied. The suburban lifestyle was beyond the reach of the working poor, the elderly, immigrants, Mexican Americans, and most African Americans—indeed, the majority of the country. Such contradictions were felt acutely by many Americans but largely ignored by the majority of the country. Not until the 1960s did uneven prosperity become the subject of national debate.

# Postwar Prosperity and the Affluent Society

The United States enjoyed enormous economic advantages at the close of World War II. While the Europeans and Japanese were still clearing the war's rubble, America stood poised to enter a postwar boom. As the only major industrial nation not devastated by war, the United States enjoyed an unprecedented global position. The American economy also benefitted from an expanding internal market and heavy investment in research and development. Two additional factors stood out: First, for the first time in the nation's history, employers generally accepted collective bargaining, which for workers translated into rising wages, expanding benefits, and an increasing rate of home ownership. Second, the federal government's outlays for military and domestic programs gave a huge boost to the economy.

## Economy: From Recovery to Dominance

*Life* magazine publisher Henry Luce was so confident in the nation's growing power that during World War II he had predicted the dawning of the "American century." In economic terms, Luce envisioned U.S. corporations, banks, and manufacturers dominating global markets. That vision came to pass after the war. The preponderance of American economic muscle in the postwar decades, however, was not simply an artifact of the world war—it was not an inevitable development. Several key elements came together, internationally and at home, to propel three decades of unprecedented economic growth.

**The Bretton Woods System**    American global supremacy rested partly on the economic institutions created at an international conference in **Bretton Woods**, New Hampshire, in July 1944. The first of those institutions was the **World Bank**,

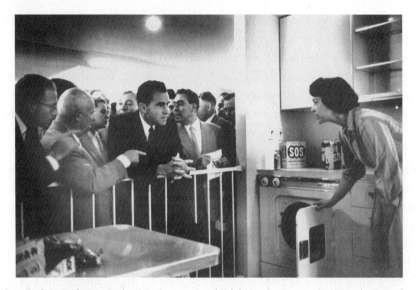

**The Kitchen Debate**  At the American National Exhibition in Moscow in 1959, the United States put on display the technological wonders of American home life. When Vice President Richard Nixon visited, he and Soviet premier Nikita Khrushchev got into a heated debate over the relative merits of their rival systems, with the up-to-date American kitchen as a case in point. This photograph shows the debate in progress. Khrushchev is the bald man pointing his finger. To Nixon's left stands Leonid Brezhnev, who would be Khrushchev's successor.  Howard Sochurek/Getty Images.

founded to provide loans for the reconstruction of war-torn Europe as well as for the development of former colonized nations—the so-called Third World or developing world. A second institution, the **International Monetary Fund (IMF)**, was set up to stabilize currencies and provide a predictable monetary environment for trade, with the U.S. dollar serving as the benchmark. The World Bank and the IMF formed the cornerstones of the Bretton Woods system, which guided the global economy after the war. The chief idea of the Bretton Woods system was to make American capital available, on cheap terms, to nations that adopted free-trade capitalist economies.

The Bretton Woods system was joined in 1947 by the first General Agreement on Tariffs and Trade (GATT), which established an international framework for overseeing trade rules and practices. Together, the Bretton Woods system and GATT served America's conception of an open-market global economy and complemented the nation's ambitious diplomatic aims in the Cold War. Critics charged, rightly, that Bretton Woods and GATT favored the United States at the expense of recently independent countries, because the United States could dictate lending and trading terms and stood to benefit as nations purchased more American goods. But the system provided needed economic stability.

**The Military-Industrial Complex**  A second engine of postwar prosperity was defense spending. In his final address to the nation in 1961, President Dwight D. Eisenhower spoke about the power of what he called the **military-industrial complex**, which by then employed 3.5 million Americans. Even though his administration had fostered this defense establishment, Eisenhower feared its implications: "We must guard against the acquisition of unwarranted influence, whether sought or unsought, by the military-industrial complex," he warned. This complex had its roots in the business-government partnerships of World War II (Chapter 23). After 1945, though the country was nominally at peace, the economy and the government operated in a state of perpetual readiness for war.

Based at the sprawling Pentagon in Arlington, Virginia, the Defense Department evolved into a massive bureaucracy. In the name of national security, defense-related industries entered into long-term relationships with the Pentagon. Some companies did so much business with the government that they in effect became private divisions of the Defense Department. Over 60 percent of the income of Boeing, General Dynamics, and Raytheon, for instance, came from military contracts, and the percentages were even higher for Lockheed and Republic Aviation. In previous peacetime years, military spending had constituted only 1 percent of gross domestic product (GDP); now it represented 10 percent. Economic growth was increasingly dependent on a robust defense sector.

As permanent mobilization took hold, science, industry, and government became intertwined. Cold War competition for military supremacy spawned both an arms race and a space race as the United States and the Soviet Union each sought to develop more explosive bombs and more powerful rockets. Federal spending underwrote 90 percent of the cost of research for aviation and space, 65 percent for electricity and electronics, 42 percent for scientific instruments, and even 24 percent for automobiles. With the government footing the bill, corporations lost little time in transforming new technology into useful products. Backed by the Pentagon, for instance, IBM and Sperry Rand pressed ahead with research on integrated circuits, which later spawned the computer revolution.

When the Soviet Union launched the world's first satellite, *Sputnik*, in 1957, the startled United States went into high gear to catch up in the Cold War space competition. Alarmed that the United States was falling behind in science and technology, Eisenhower persuaded Congress to appropriate additional money for college scholarships and university research. The **National Defense Education Act** of 1958 funneled millions of dollars into American universities, helping institutions such as the University of California at Berkeley, Stanford University, the Massachusetts Institute of Technology, and the University of Michigan become the leading research centers in the world.

**Corporate Power**　Despite its massive size, the defense industry was only one part of the nation's economy. For over half a century, the consolidation of economic power into large corporate firms had characterized American capitalism. In the postwar decades, that tendency accelerated. By 1970, the top four U.S. automakers produced 91 percent of all motor vehicles sold in the country; the top four firms in tires produced 72 percent; those in cigarettes, 84 percent; and those in detergents, 70 percent. Eric Johnston, former president of the American Chamber of Commerce, declared that "we have entered a period of accelerating bigness in all aspects of American life." Expansion into foreign markets also spurred corporate growth. During the 1950s, U.S. exports nearly doubled, giving the nation a trade surplus of close to $5 billion in 1960. By the 1970s, such firms as Coca-Cola, Gillette, IBM, and Mobil made more than half their profits abroad.

To staff their bureaucracies, the postwar corporate giants required a huge white-collar army. A new generation of corporate chieftains emerged, operating in a complex environment that demanded long-range forecasting. Postwar corporate culture inspired numerous critics, who argued that the obedience demanded of white-collar workers was stifling creativity and blighting lives. The sociologist William Whyte painted a somber picture of "organization men" who left the home "spiritually as well as physically to take the vows of organization life." Andrew Hacker, in *The Corporation Take-Over* (1964), warned that a small handful of such organization men "can draw up an investment program calling for the expenditure of several billions of dollars" and thereby "determine the quality of life for substantial segments of society."

Many of these "investment programs" relied on mechanization, or automation—another important factor in the postwar boom. From 1947 to 1975, worker productivity more than doubled across the whole of the economy. American factories replaced manpower with machines, substituting cheap fossil energy for human muscle. As industries mechanized, they could turn out products more efficiently and at lower cost. Mechanization did not come without social costs, however. Over the course of the postwar decades, millions of high-wage manufacturing jobs were lost as machines replaced workers, affecting entire cities and regions. Corporate leaders approved, but workers and their union representatives were less enthusiastic. "How are you going to sell cars to all of these machines?" wondered Walter Reuther, president of the United Auto Workers (UAW).

**The Economic Record**   The American economy produced an extraordinary postwar record. Annual GDP jumped from $213 billion in 1945 to more than $500 billion in 1960; by 1970, it exceeded $1 trillion. This sustained economic growth helped produce a 25 percent rise in real income for ordinary Americans between 1946 and 1959. Even better, the new prosperity featured low inflation. After a burst of high prices in the immediate postwar period, inflation slowed to 2 to 3 percent annually, and it stayed low until the escalation of the Vietnam War in the mid-1960s. Feeling secure about the future, Americans were eager to spend and rightly felt that they were better off than ever before. In 1940, 43 percent of American families owned their homes; by 1960, 62 percent did. In that period, moreover, income inequality dropped sharply. The share of total income going to the top tenth—the richest Americans—declined by nearly one-third from the 45 percent it had been in 1940. American society had become not only more prosperous but also more egalitarian.

However, the picture was not as rosy at the bottom, where tenacious poverty accompanied the economic boom. In *The Affluent Society* (1958), which analyzed the nation's successful, "affluent" middle class, economist John Kenneth Galbraith argued that the poor were only an "afterthought" in the minds of economists and politicians, who largely celebrated the new growth. As Galbraith noted, one in thirteen families at the time earned less than $1,000 a year (about $8,300 in today's dollars). Four years later, in *The Other America* (1962), the left-wing social critic Michael Harrington chronicled "the economic underworld of American life," and a U.S. government study, echoing a well-known sentence from Franklin Roosevelt's second inaugural address ("I see one-third of a nation ill-housed, ill-clad, ill-nourished"), declared "one-third of the nation" to be poorly paid, poorly educated, and poorly housed. It appeared that in economic terms, as the top and the middle converged, the bottom remained far behind.

## A Nation of Consumers

The most breathtaking development in the postwar American economy was the dramatic expansion of the domestic consumer market. The sheer quantity of consumer goods available to the average person was without precedent. In some respects, the postwar decades seemed like the 1920s all over again, with an abundance of new gadgets and appliances, a craze for automobiles, and new types of mass media. Yet there was a significant difference: in the 1950s, consumption became associated with citizenship. Buying things, once a sign of personal indulgence, now meant participating fully in American society and, moreover, fulfilling a social responsibility. What the suburban family consumed, asserted *Life* magazine in a photo essay, would help to ensure "full employment and improved living standards for the rest of the nation."

**The GI Bill**   The new ethic of consumption appealed to the postwar middle class, the driving force behind the expanding domestic market. Middle-class status was more accessible than ever before because of the Servicemen's Readjustment Act of 1944, popularly known as the GI Bill. In the immediate postwar years, more than half of all U.S. college students were veterans attending class on the government's dime. By the middle of the 1950s, 2.2 million veterans had attended college and another 5.6 million had attended trade school with government financing. Before the GI Bill, commented one veteran, "I looked upon college education as likely as my owning a Rolls-Royce with a chauffeur."

Government financing of education helped make the U.S. workforce the best educated in the world in the 1950s and 1960s. American colleges, universities, and trade schools grew by leaps and bounds to accommodate the flood of students — and expanded again when the children of those students, the baby boomers, reached college age in the 1960s. At Rutgers University, enrollment went from 7,000 before the war to 16,000 in 1947; at the University of Minnesota, from 15,000 to more than 27,000. The GI Bill trained nearly half a million engineers; 200,000 doctors, dentists, and nurses; and 150,000 scientists (among many other professions). Better education meant higher earning power, and higher earning power translated into the consumer spending that drove the postwar economy. One observer of the GI Bill was so impressed with its achievements that he declared it responsible for "the most important educational and social transformation in American history."

The GI Bill stimulated the economy and expanded the middle class in another way: by increasing home ownership. Between the end of World War II and 1966, one of every five single-family homes built in the United States was financed through a GI Bill mortgage — 2.5 million new homes in all. In cities and suburbs across the country, the **Veterans Administration** (VA), which helped former soldiers purchase new homes with no down payment, sparked a building boom that created jobs in the construction industry and fueled consumer spending in home appliances and automobiles. Education and home ownership were more than personal triumphs for the families of World War II veterans (and Korean and Vietnam War veterans, after a new GI Bill was passed in 1952). They were financial *assets* that helped lift more Americans than ever before into a mass-consumption-oriented middle class.

**Trade Unions**   Organized labor also expanded the ranks of the middle class. For the first time ever, trade unions and **collective bargaining** became major factors in the nation's economic life. In the past, organized labor had been confined to a narrow band of craft trades and a few industries, primarily coal mining, railroading, and the building and metal trades. The power balance shifted during the Great Depression, and by the time the dust settled after World War II, labor unions overwhelmingly represented America's industrial workforce (Figure 25.1). By the beginning of the 1950s, the nation's major industries, including auto, steel, clothing, chemicals, and virtually all consumer product manufacturing, were operating with union contracts.

   That outcome did not arrive without a battle. Unions staged major strikes in nearly all American industries in 1945 and 1946, much as they had done after World War I. Head of the UAW Walter Reuther and CIO president Philip Murray declared that employers could afford a 30 percent wage increase, which would fuel postwar consumption. When employers, led by the giant General Motors, balked at that demand, the two sides seemed set for a long struggle. Between 1947 and 1950, however, a broad "labor-management accord" gradually emerged across most industries. This was not industrial peace — the country still experienced many strikes — but a general acceptance of collective bargaining as the method for setting the terms

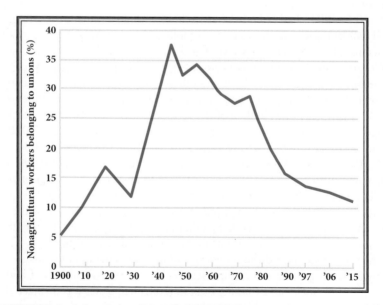

**FIGURE 25.1   Labor Union Strength, 1900–2015**
Labor unions reached their peak strength immediately after World War II, when they represented close to 40 percent of the nonfarm workforce. Although there was some decline after the mid-1950s, unions still represented nearly 30 percent in 1973. Thereafter, between the 1970s and the 2010s, their decline was precipitous. AFL-CIO Information Bureau, Washington, D.C.

of employment. The result was rising real income. The average worker with three dependents gained 18 percent in spendable real income in the 1950s.

In addition, unions delivered greater leisure (more paid holidays and longer vacations) and, in a startling departure, a social safety net. In postwar Europe, America's allies were constructing welfare states. But having lost the bruising battle in Washington for national health care during Truman's presidency, American unions turned to the bargaining table. By the end of the 1950s, union contracts commonly provided pension plans and company-paid health insurance. Collective bargaining, the process of trade unions and employers negotiating workplace contracts, had become, in effect, the American alternative to the European welfare state and, as Reuther boasted, the passport into the middle class.

This impressive labor-management accord, however, was never as durable or universal as it seemed. Vulnerabilities lurked. For one thing, the sheltered domestic markets — the essential condition for generous contracts, because without competition firms were not pressured to lower wages — were quite fragile. In certain industries, the lead firms were already losing market share. Second, generally overlooked were the many unorganized workers with no middle-class passport — those consigned to unorganized industries, casual labor, or low-wage jobs in the service sector. A final vulnerability was the most basic: the abiding antiunionism of American employers. At heart, business regarded the labor-management accord as a negotiated truce, not a permanent peace. The postwar labor-management accord turned out to be a transitory event, not a permanent condition of American economic life.

**Houses, Cars, and Children**   Increased educational levels, growing home ownership, and higher wages all enabled more Americans than ever before to become members of what one historian has called a "consumer republic." But what did they buy? The postwar emphasis on nuclear families and suburbs provides the answer. In the emerging suburban nation, three elements came together to create patterns of consumption that would endure for decades: houses, cars, and children.

A feature in a 1949 issue of *McCall's*, a magazine targeting middle-class women, illustrates the connections. "I now have three working centers," a typical housewife explains. "The baby center, a baking center and a cleaning center." Accompanying illustrations reveal the interior of the brand-new house, stocked with the latest consumer products: accessories for the baby's room; a new stove, oven, and refrigerator; and a washer and dryer, along with cleaning products and other household goods. The article does not mention automobiles, but the photo of the house's exterior makes the point clear: father drives home from work in a new car.

Consumption for the home, including automobiles, drove the postwar American economy as much as, or more than, the military-industrial complex did. If we think like advertisers and manufacturers, we can see why. Between 1945 and 1970, more than 25 million new houses were built in the United States. Each required its own supply of new appliances, from refrigerators to lawn mowers. In 1955 alone, Americans purchased 4 million new refrigerators, and between 1940 and 1951 the sale of power mowers increased from 35,000 per year to more than 1 million. Moreover, as American industry discovered planned obsolescence — the encouragement of consumers to replace appliances and cars every few years — the home became a site of perpetual consumer desire.

Children also encouraged consumption. The baby boomers born between World War II and the late 1950s have consistently, throughout every phase of their lives, been the darlings of American advertising and consumption. When they were infants, companies focused on developing new baby products, from disposable diapers to instant formula. When they were toddlers and young children, new television programs, board games, fast food, TV dinners, and thousands of different kinds of toys came to market to supply the rambunctious youth. When they were teenagers, rock music, Hollywood films, and a constantly marketed "teen culture"—with its appropriate clothing, music, hairstyles, and other accessories—bombarded them. Remarkably, in 1956, middle-class American teenagers on average had a weekly income of more than $10, close to the weekly disposable income of an entire family a generation earlier.

**Television**    The emergence of commercial television in the United States was swift and overwhelming. In the realm of technology, only the automobile and the personal computer were its equal in transforming everyday life in the twentieth century. In 1947, there were 7,000 TV sets in American homes. A year later, the CBS and NBC radio networks began offering regular programming, and by 1950 Americans owned 7.3 million sets. Ten years later, 87 percent of American homes had at least one television set. Having conquered the home, television would soon become the principal mediator between the consumer and the marketplace.

Television advertisers mastered the art of manufacturing consumer desire. TV stations, like radio stations before them, depended entirely on advertising for profits. The first television executives understood that as long as they sold viewers to advertisers they would stay on the air. Early corporate-sponsored shows (such as *General Electric Theater* and *U.S. Steel Hour*) and simple product jingles (such as "No matter what the time or place, let's keep up with that happy pace. 7-Up your thirst away!") gave way by the early 1960s to slick advertising campaigns that used popular music, movie stars, sports figures, and stimulating graphics to captivate viewers.

By creating powerful visual narratives of comfort and plenty, television revolutionized advertising and changed forever how products were sold to American, and global, consumers. On *Queen for a Day*, a show popular in the mid-1950s, women competed to see who could tell the most heartrending story of tragedy and loss. The winner was lavished with household products: refrigerators, toasters, ovens, and the like. In a groundbreaking advertisement for Anacin aspirin, a tiny hammer pounded inside the skull of a headache sufferer. Almost overnight, sales of Anacin increased by 50 percent.

By the late 1950s, what Americans saw on television, both in the omnipresent commercials and in the programming, was an overwhelmingly white, Anglo-Saxon, Protestant world of nuclear families, suburban homes, and middle-class life. A typical show was *Father Knows Best*, starring Robert Young and Jane Wyatt. Father left home each morning wearing a suit and carrying a briefcase. Mother was a stereotypical full-time housewife, prone to bad driving and tears. *Leave It to Beaver*, another immensely popular series about suburban family life, embodied similar late-fifties themes. Earlier in the decade, however, television featured grittier realities. *The Honeymooners*, starring Jackie Gleason as a Brooklyn bus driver, and *The Life of Riley*, a situation comedy featuring a California aircraft worker, treated working-class lives. Two other early-fifties television series, *Beulah*, starring Ethel Waters and then Louise Beavers as an African American maid, and the comedic *Amos 'n' Andy*, were the only shows featuring black actors in major roles. Television was never a showcase for the breadth of American society, but in the second half of the 1950s broadcasting lost much of its ethnic, racial, and class diversity and became a vehicle for the transmission of a narrow range of middle-class tastes and values.

## Youth Culture

One of the most striking developments in American life in the postwar decades was the emergence of the **teenager** as a cultural phenomenon. In 1956, only partly in jest, the CBS radio commentator Eric Sevareid questioned "whether the teenagers will take over the United States lock, stock, living room, and garage." Sevareid was grumbling about American youth culture, a phenomenon first noticed in the 1920s and with its roots in the lengthening years of education, the role of peer groups, and the consumer tastes of young people. Market research revealed a distinct teen market to be exploited. *Newsweek* noted with awe in 1951 that the aggregate of the weekly spending money of teenagers was enough to buy 190 million candy bars, 130 million soft drinks, and 230 million sticks of gum. Increasingly, advertisers targeted the young, both to capture their spending money and to exploit their influence on family purchases.

**Teenagers** These teenage girls and boys are being restrained by police outside an Elvis Presley concert in Florida in 1956. Elvis, who was instrumental in popularizing rock 'n' roll music among white middle-class teenagers in the mid-1950s, was one example of a broader phenomenon: the creation of the "teenager" as a distinct demographic, cultural category and, perhaps most significantly, consumer group. Beginning in the 1950s, middle-class teenagers had money to spend, and advertisers and other entrepreneurs—such as the music executives who marketed Elvis or the Hollywood executives who invented the "teen film"—sought ways to win their allegiance and their dollars. Charles Trainor/The LIFE Images Collection/Getty Images.

Hollywood movies played a large role in fostering a teenage culture. Young people made up the largest audience for motion pictures, and Hollywood studios learned over the course of the 1950s to cater to them. The success of films such as *The Wild One* (1953), starring Marlon Brando; *Blackboard Jungle* (1955), with Sidney Poitier; and *Rebel Without a Cause* (1955), starring James Dean, convinced movie executives that films directed at teenagers were worthy investments. "What are you rebelling against?" Brando is asked in *The Wild One*. "Whattaya got?" he replies. By the early 1960s, Hollywood had retooled its business model, shifting emphasis away from adults and families, the industry's primary audience since its rise in the 1920s, to teenagers. The "teenpic" soon included multiple genres: horror, rock 'n' roll, dangerous youth, and beach party, among others.

**Rock 'n' Roll**    What really defined the youth culture, however, was its music. Rejecting the romantic ballads of the 1940s, teenagers discovered rock 'n' roll, which originated in African American rhythm and blues. The Cleveland disc jockey Alan Freed took the lead in introducing white America to the black-created sound by playing what were called "race" records. "If I could find a white man who had the Negro sound and the Negro feel, I could make a billion dollars," a record company owner is quoted as saying. The performer who fit that bill was Elvis Presley, who rocketed into instant celebrity in 1956 with his hit records "Hound Dog" and "Heartbreak Hotel," covers of songs originally recorded by black artists such as Big Mama Thornton. Between 1953 and 1959, record sales increased from $213 million to $603 million, with rock 'n' roll as the driving force.

Many unhappy adults saw in rock 'n' roll music an invitation to interracial dating, rebellion, and a more flagrant sexuality. The media featured hundreds of stories on problem teens, and denunciations of the new music poured forth from many corners. Such condemnation only deflected off the new youth culture or, if anything, increased its popularity. Both Hollywood and the music industry had learned that youth rebellion sold tickets.

**Cultural Dissenters**    Youth rebellion was only one aspect of a broader discontent with the sometimes saccharine consumer culture of the postwar years. Many artists, writers, and jazz musicians embarked on powerful new experimental projects in a remarkable flowering of intensely personal, introspective art forms. During and just after World War II, black musicians developed a hard-driving improvisational style known as bebop. Whether the "hot" bebop of saxophonist Charlie Parker or the more subdued "cool" sound of the influential trumpeter Miles Davis, postwar jazz was cerebral, intimate, and individualistic. As such, it stood in stark contrast to the commercialized, dance-oriented "swing" bands of the 1930s and 1940s.

Black jazz musicians found eager fans not only in the African American community but also among young white **Beats**, a group of writers and poets centered in New York and San Francisco who disdained middle-class materialism. In his poem "Howl" (1956), which became a manifesto of the Beat generation, Allen Ginsberg lamented: "I saw the best minds of my generation destroyed by madness, starving hysterical naked, dragging themselves through the negro streets at dawn looking for an angry fix." In works such as Jack Kerouac's novel *On the Road* (1957), the Beats glorified spontaneity, sexual adventurism, drug use, and spirituality. The Beats were apolitical, but their cultural rebellion would, in the 1960s, inspire a new generation of young rebels disenchanted with both the political and cultural status quo.

## Religion and the Middle Class

In an age of anxiety about nuclear annihilation and the spread of "godless communism," Americans yearned for a reaffirmation of faith. Church membership jumped from 49 percent of the population in 1940 to 70 percent in 1960. People flocked to the evangelical Protestant denominations, beneficiaries of a remarkable new crop of preachers. Most eloquent was the young Reverend Billy Graham, who made brilliant use of television, radio, and advertising. Hundreds of thousands of Americans attended his massive 1949 revival in Los Angeles and his 1957 crusade at Madison Square Garden in New York, establishing Graham as the nation's leading evangelical.

Rather than clashing with the new middle-class ethic of consumption, the religious reawakening was designed to mesh with it. Preachers such as Graham told Americans that so long as they lived moral lives, they deserved the material blessings of modern life. No one was more influential in this regard than the minister and author Norman Vincent Peale, whose best-selling book *The Power of Positive Thinking* (1952) embodied the therapeutic use of religion as an antidote to life's trials and tribulations. Peale taught that with faith in God and "positive thinking," anyone could overcome obstacles and become a success. Graham, Peale, and other 1950s evangelicals laid the foundation for the rise of the televangelists, who created popular television ministries in the 1970s.

The postwar purveyors of religious faith cast Americans as a righteous people opposed to communist atheism. When Julius and Ethel Rosenberg were sentenced to death in 1953, the judge criticized them for "devoting themselves to the Russian ideology of denial of God." Cold War imperatives drew Catholics, Protestants, and Jews into an influential ecumenical movement that downplayed doctrinal differences. The phrase "under God" was inserted into the Pledge of Allegiance in 1954, and U.S. coins carried the words "In God We Trust" after 1956. These religious initiatives struck a distinctly moderate tone, however, in comparison with the politicized evangelism that emerged in the 1960s and 1970s (Chapter 28).

| IN YOUR OWN WORDS | What explains the growth of the American economy after World War II? |
|---|---|

# The American Family in the Era of Containment

Marriage, family structure, and gender roles had been undergoing significant changes since the turn of the twentieth century (Chapter 17). Beginning in the nineteenth century, middle-class Americans increasingly saw marriage as "companionate," that is, based on romantic love and a lifetime of shared friendship. *Companionate* did not mean *equal*. In the mid-twentieth century, family life remained governed by notions of gender inequality, in which men provided economic support and controlled the family's financial resources, while women cared for children and occupied a secondary position in public life.

The resurgent postwar American middle class was preoccupied with the virtues of this paternalist, or patriarchal, vision of family life. Everyone from professional psychologists to television advertisers and every organization from schools to the popular press celebrated nuclear families. Children were prized, and women's caregiving roles were valorized. This view of family life, and especially its emphasis on female "domesticity," was bolstered by Cold War politics. Americans who deviated from prevailing gender and familial norms were not only viewed with scorn but were also sometimes thought to be subversive and politically dangerous.

Yet the model of domesticity so highly esteemed in the postwar middle class hid deeper, longer-term changes in the way marriage, gender roles, women's work, and even sex were understood. To comprehend the postwar decades, we have to keep in mind that while domesticity remained the ideal, in people's daily lives a sometimes different reality held true.

## The Baby Boom

A popular 1945 song was called "Gotta Make Up for Lost Time," and Americans did just that. Two things were noteworthy about the families they formed after World War II: First, marriages were remarkably stable. Not until the mid-1960s did the divorce rate begin to rise sharply. Second, married couples were intent on having babies. Everyone expected to have several children—it was part of adulthood, almost a citizen's responsibility. After a century and a half of decline, the birthrate shot up. More babies were born in the six years between 1948 and 1953 than in the previous thirty years (Figure 25.2). Far from "normal," all these developments were anomalies, temporary reversals of long-standing demographic trends. From the perspective of the whole of the twentieth century, the 1950s and early 1960s stand out as exceptions to declining birthrates, rising divorce rates, and the steadily rising marriage age.

One of the reasons for the **baby boom** was a drop in the average marriage age—down to twenty-two for men and twenty for women. Younger parents meant a bumper crop of children. Women who came of age in the 1930s averaged

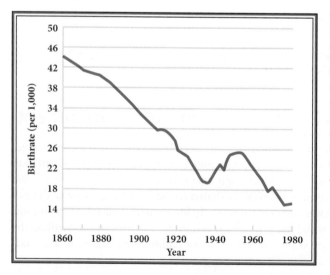

**FIGURE 25.2 The American Birthrate, 1860–1980**
When birthrates are viewed over more than a century, the postwar baby boom is clearly only a temporary reversal of the long-term downward trend in the American birthrate.

2.4 children; their counterparts in the 1950s averaged 3.2 children. Such a dramatic turnaround reflected couples' decisions during the Great Depression to limit child-bearing and couples' contrasting decisions in the postwar years to have more children. The baby boom peaked in 1957 and remained at a high level until the early 1960s. The passage of time revealed the ever-widening impact of the baby boom. When baby boomers competed for jobs during the 1970s, the labor market became tight. When career-oriented baby boomers belatedly began having children in the 1980s, the birthrate jumped. And in our own time, as baby boomers begin retiring, huge funding problems threaten to engulf Social Security and Medicare. The intimate decisions of so many couples after World War II continued to shape American life well into the twenty-first century.

Baby boom children benefitted from a host of important advances in public health and medical practice in the postwar years. Formerly serious illnesses became merely routine after the introduction of such "miracle drugs" as penicillin (introduced in 1943), streptomycin (1945), and cortisone (1946). When Dr. Jonas Salk perfected a polio vaccine in 1954, he became a national hero. The free distribution of Salk's vaccine in the nation's schools, followed in 1961 by Dr. Albert Sabin's oral polio vaccine, demonstrated the potential of government-sponsored public health programs.

**Dr. Benjamin Spock**    To keep baby boom children healthy and happy, middle-class parents increasingly relied on the advice of experts. Dr. Benjamin Spock's *Common Sense Book of Baby and Child Care* sold 1 million copies every year after its publication in 1946. Spock urged mothers to abandon the rigid feeding and baby-care schedules of an earlier generation. New mothers found Spock's commonsense approach liberating. "Your little paperback is still in my cupboard, with loose pages, rather worn from use because I brought up two babies using it as my 'Bible,'" a California housewife wrote to Spock.

Despite his commonsense approach to child rearing, Spock was part of a generation of psychological experts whose advice often failed to reassure women. If mothers were too protective, Spock and others argued, they might hamper their children's preparation for adult life. On the other hand, mothers who wanted to work outside the home felt guilty because Spock recommended that they be constantly available for their children. As American mothers aimed for the perfection demanded of them seemingly at every turn, many began to question these mixed messages. Some of them would be inspired by the resurgence of feminism in the 1960s.

## Women, Work, and Family

Two powerful forces shaped women's relationships to work and family life in the postwar decades. One was the middle-class domestic ideal, in which women were expected to raise children, attend to other duties in the home, and devote themselves to their husbands' happiness. So powerful was this ideal that in 1957 the *Ladies' Home Journal* entitled an article, "Is College Education Wasted on Women?" The second force was the job market. Most working-class women had to earn a paycheck to help their family. And despite their education, middle-class women found that jobs in the professions and business were dominated by men and often closed to them. For both groups, the market offered mostly "women's jobs"—in teaching, nursing, and other areas of the growing service sector—and little room for advancement.

The idea that a woman's place was in the home was, of course, not new. The postwar obsession with femininity and motherhood bore a remarkable similarity to the nineteenth century's notion of domesticity. The updated version drew on new elements of twentieth-century science and culture. Psychologists equated motherhood with "normal" female identity and suggested that career-minded mothers needed therapy. "A mother who runs out on her children to work—except in cases of absolute necessity—betrays a deep dissatisfaction with motherhood or with her marriage," wrote one leading psychiatrist. Television shows and movies depicted career women as social misfits. The postwar consumer culture also emphasized women's domestic role as purchasing agents for home and family. "Can a woman ever feel right cooking on a dirty range?" asked one advertisement.

Despite the postwar domestic ideal, financial necessity increasingly took women outside their homes and into the workforce. In 1954, married women made up half of all women workers. Six years later, the 1960 census reported a stunning fact: the number of mothers who worked had increased four times, and over one-third of these women had children between the ages of six and seventeen. In that same year, 30 percent of wives worked, and by 1970, it was 40 percent. For working-class women, in particular, the economic needs of their families demanded that they work outside the home. Contrary to stereotypes, women's paid work often helped lift many families into the middle class.

Despite rising employment rates, occupational segmentation still haunted women. Until 1964, the classified sections of newspapers separated employment ads into "Help Wanted Male" and "Help Wanted Female." More than 80 percent of all employed women did stereotypical women's work as sales clerks, health-care technicians, waitresses, stewardesses, domestic servants, receptionists, telephone operators,

**Middle Class Domesticity** The nuclear family, meaning a married couple plus children, stood at the heart of middle-class American culture in the postwar years. The "domestic ideal" held that men worked for wages and women labored in the home. A new generation of Americans, including many African Americans, aspired to this cultural ideal, which came within reach for many for the first time. Here a couple and their children look over blueprints of their new home in the early 1960s. ClassicStock. com/Superstock.

and secretaries. In 1960, only 3 percent of lawyers and 6 percent of physicians were women; on the flip side, 97 percent of nurses and 85 percent of librarians were women. Along with women's jobs went women's pay, which averaged 60 percent of men's pay in 1963.

American society steadfastly upheld the domestic ideal even as so many women entered the workforce. When mothers took jobs outside the home, they still bore full responsibility for child care and household management, contributing to the "double day" of paid work and family work. As one overburdened woman noted, she now had "two full-time jobs instead of just one—underpaid clerical worker and unpaid housekeeper." Meanwhile, the pressures of the Cold War made strong nuclear families with breadwinning fathers and domesticated mothers symbols of a healthy nation. Americans wanted to believe they upheld the domestic ideal even if it did not perfectly describe the reality of their lives.

## Challenging Middle-Class Morality

In many ways, the two decades between 1945 and 1965 were a period of cultural conservatism that reflected the values of domesticity. At the dawn of the 1960s, going steady as a prelude to marriage was the fad in high school. College women had curfews and needed permission to see a male visitor. Americans married young; more than half of those who married in 1963 were under the age of twenty-one. After the birth control pill came on the market in 1960, few doctors prescribed it to unmarried women, and even married women did not enjoy unfettered access to contraception until the Supreme Court ruled it a "privacy" right in the 1965 decision *Griswold v. Connecticut.*

**Alfred Kinsey**   Beneath the surface of middle-class morality, Americans were less repressed than confused. They struggled to reconcile new freedoms with older moral traditions. This was especially true with regard to sex. Two controversial studies by an unassuming Indiana University zoologist named Alfred Kinsey forced questions about sexuality into the open. Kinsey and his research team published *Sexual Behavior in the Human Male* in 1948 and followed it up in 1953 with *Sexual Behavior in the Human Female*—an 842-page book that sold 270,000 copies in the first month after its publication. Taking a scientific, rather than moralistic, approach, Kinsey, who became known as "the sex doctor," documented the full range of sexual experiences of thousands of Americans. He broke numerous taboos, discussing such topics as homosexuality and marital infidelity in the detached language of science.

Both studies confirmed that a sexual revolution, although a largely hidden one, had already begun to transform American society by the early 1950s. Kinsey estimated that 85 percent of men had had sex prior to marriage and that more than 25 percent of married women had had sex outside of marriage by the age of forty. These were shocking public admissions in the late 1940s and early 1950s, and "hotter than the Kinsey report" became a national figure of speech. Kinsey was criticized by statisticians—because his samples were not randomly selected—and condemned even more fervently by religious leaders, who charged him with encouraging promiscuity and adultery. But his research opened a national conversation that helped Americans learn to talk more openly about sex.

**The Homophile Movement**   Among the most controversial of Kinsey's claims was that homosexuality was far more prevalent than most Americans believed. Although the American Psychiatric Association officially defined homosexuality as a mental illness, Kinsey's research found that 37 percent of men had engaged in some form of homosexual activity by early adulthood, as had 13 percent of women. Even more important, Kinsey claimed that 10 percent of American men were *exclusively* homosexual. These claims came as little surprise, but great encouragement, to a group of gay and lesbian activists who called themselves "homophiles." Organized primarily in the Mattachine Society (the first gay rights organization in the country, founded in 1951) and the Daughters of Bilitis (a lesbian organization founded in 1955), homophiles were a small but determined collection of activists who sought equal rights for gays and lesbians. "The lesbian is a woman endowed with all the attributes of any other woman," wrote the pioneer lesbian activist Del Martin in 1956. "The salvation of the lesbian lies in her acceptance of herself without guilt or anxiety."

Building on the urban gay and lesbian communities that had coalesced during World War II, homophiles sought to change American attitudes about same-sex love. They faced daunting obstacles, since same-sex sexual relations were illegal in every state and scorned, or feared, by most Americans. To combat prejudice and change the laws, homophile organizations cultivated a respectable, middle-class image. Members were encouraged to avoid bars and nightclubs, to dress in conservative shirts and ties (for men) and modest skirts and blouses (for women), and to seek out professional psychologists who would attest to their "normalcy." Only in the 1960s did homophiles begin to talk about the "homophile vote" and their "rights as citizens," laying the groundwork for the gay rights movement of the 1970s.

**Media and Morality**   The homophile movement remained unknown to most Americans. But other challenges to traditional morality received national media attention, and the media themselves became a controversial source of these challenges. Concerned that excessive crime, violence, and sex in comic books were encouraging juvenile delinquency, the U.S. Senate held nationally televised hearings in 1954. The Senate's final report, written largely by the Tennessee Democrat Estes Kefauver, complained of the "scantily clad women" and "penchant for violent death" common in comic books aimed at teenagers. Kefauver's report forced the comics industry to tame its wildest practices but did little to slow the growing frankness about both sex and violence in the nation's print media and films.

A magazine entrepreneur from Chicago named Hugh Hefner played a leading role in that growing frankness. Hefner founded *Playboy* magazine in 1953, in which he created a countermorality to domesticity: a fictional world populated by "hip" bachelor men and sexually available women. Hefner's imagined bachelors condemned marriage and lived in sophisticated apartments filled with the latest stereo equipment and other consumer products. While domesticated fathers bought lawn mowers and patio furniture, Hefner's magazine encouraged men to spend money on clothing and jazz albums for themselves, and for the "scantily clad women" that filled its pages. Hefner and his numerous imitators became powerful purveyors of sex in the media. But Hefner was the exception that proved the rule: marriage, not swinging bachelorhood, remained the destination for the vast majority of men. Millions of men read *Playboy*, but few adopted its fantasy lifestyle.

| IN YOUR OWN WORDS | What was the domestic ideal, and how did Americans embrace it in the postwar decades? |
|---|---|

# A Suburban Nation

Prosperity — how much an economy produces, how much people earn — is more easily measured than is quality of life. During the 1950s, however, the American definition of the good life emerged with exceptional distinctness: a high value on consumption, a devotion to family and domesticity, and a preference for suburban living. In this section, we consider the third dimension of that definition: suburbanization. What drove the nation to abandon its cities for the suburbs, and what social and political consequences did this shift have?

## The Postwar Housing Boom

Migration to the suburbs had been going on for a hundred years, but never before on the scale that the country experienced after World War II. Within a decade, farmland on the outskirts of cities filled up with tract housing and shopping malls. Entire counties that had once been rural — such as San Mateo, south of San Francisco, or Passaic and Bergen in New Jersey, west of Manhattan — went suburban. By 1960, one-third of Americans lived in suburbs. Home construction, having ground to a halt during the Great Depression, surged after the war. One-fourth of the country's entire housing stock in 1960 had not even existed a decade earlier.

**William J. Levitt and the FHA**   Two unique postwar developments remade the national housing market and gave it a distinctly suburban shape. First, an innovative Long Island building contractor, William J. Levitt, revolutionized suburban housing by applying mass-production techniques and turning out new homes at a dizzying speed. Levitt's basic four-room house, complete with kitchen appliances, was priced at $7,990 when homes in the first Levittown went on sale in 1947 (about $86,000 today). Levitt did not need to advertise; word of mouth brought buyers flocking to his developments (all called Levittown) in New York, Pennsylvania, and New Jersey. Dozens of other developers were soon snapping up cheap farmland and building subdivisions around the country.

Even at $7,990, Levitt's homes would have been beyond the means of most young families had the traditional home-financing standard — a down payment of half the full price and ten years to pay off the balance — still prevailed. That is where the second postwar development came in. The Federal Housing Administration (FHA) and the Veterans Administration (VA) — that is, the federal government — brought the home mortgage market within the reach of a broader range of Americans than ever before. After the war, the FHA insured thirty-year mortgages with as little as 5 percent down and interest at 2 or 3 percent. The VA was even more generous, requiring only a token $1 down for qualified ex-GIs. FHA and VA mortgages best explain why, after hovering around 45 percent for the previous half century, home ownership jumped to 60 percent by 1960.

What purchasers of suburban houses got, in addition to a good deal, were homogeneous communities. Levitt's houses came with restrictive covenants prohibiting occupancy "by members of other than the Caucasian Race." (Restrictive covenants often applied to Jews and, in California, Asian Americans as well.) Levittowns were hardly alone. Suburban developments from coast to coast exhibited the same age, class, and racial homogeneity. In *Shelley v. Kraemer* (1948), the Supreme Court outlawed restrictive covenants, but racial discrimination in housing changed little. The practice persisted long after *Shelley*, because the FHA and VA continued the policy of redlining: refusing mortgages to African Americans and members of other minority groups seeking to buy in white neighborhoods. Indeed, no federal law—or even Court decisions like *Shelley*—actually prohibited racial discrimination in housing until Congress passed the Fair Housing Act in 1968.

**Interstate Highways**    Without automobiles, suburban growth on such a massive scale would have been impossible. Planners laid out subdivisions on the assumption that everybody would drive. And they did—to get to work, to take the children to Little League, to shop. With gas plentiful and cheap (15 cents a gallon), no one cared about the fuel efficiency of their V-8 engines or seemed to mind the elaborate tail fins and chrome that weighed down their cars. In 1945, Americans owned twenty-five million cars; by 1965, just two decades later, the number had tripled to seventy-five million. American oil consumption followed course, tripling as well between 1949 and 1972.

More cars required more highways, and the federal government obliged. In 1956, in a move that drastically altered America's landscape and driving habits, the **National Interstate and Defense Highways Act** authorized $26 billion over a ten-year period for the construction of a nationally integrated highway system—42,500 miles (Map 25.1). Cast as a Cold War necessity because broad highways made evacuating crowded cities easier in the event of a nuclear attack, the law changed American cities forever. An enormous public works program surpassing anything undertaken during the New Deal, and enthusiastically endorsed by the Republican president, Dwight Eisenhower, federal highways made possible the massive suburbanization of the nation in the 1960s. Interstate highways rerouted traffic away from small towns, bypassed well-traveled main roads such as the cross-country Route 66, and cut wide swaths through old neighborhoods in the cities.

**Fast Food and Shopping Malls**    Americans did not simply fill their new suburban homes with the latest appliances and gadgets; they also pioneered entirely new forms of consumption. Through World War II, downtowns had remained the center of retail sales and restaurant dining with their grand department stores, elegant eateries, and low-cost diners. As suburbanites abandoned big-city centers in the 1950s, ambitious entrepreneurs invented two new commercial forms that would profoundly shape the rest of the century: the shopping mall and the fast-food restaurant.

By the late 1950s, the suburban shopping center had become as much a part of the American landscape as the Levittowns and their imitators. A major developer of

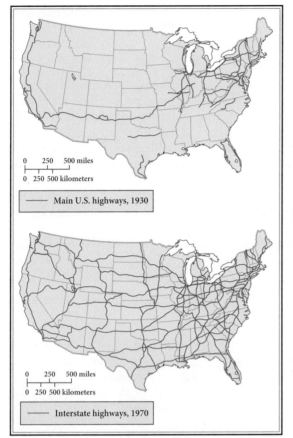

**MAP 25.1 Connecting the Nation: The Interstate Highway System, 1930 and 1970**

The 1956 National Interstate and Defense Highways Act paved the way for an extensive network of federal highways throughout the nation. The act not only pleased American drivers and enhanced their love affair with the automobile but also benefitted the petroleum, construction, trucking, real estate, and tourist industries. The new highway system promoted the nation's economic integration, facilitated the growth of suburbs, and contributed to the erosion of America's distinct regional identities.

shopping malls in the Northeast called them "today's village green," and noted that "the fountain in the mall has replaced the downtown department clock as the gathering place for young and old alike." By centralizing the otherwise dispersed world of suburban consumption, shopping malls brought "the market to the people instead of people to the market," commented the *New York Times*. In 1939, the suburban share of total metropolitan retail trade in the United States was a paltry 4 percent. By 1961, it was an astonishing 60 percent in the nation's ten largest metropolitan regions.

No one was more influential in creating suburban patterns of consumption than a Chicago-born son of Czech immigrants named Ray Kroc. A former jazz musician and traveling salesman, Kroc found his calling in 1954 when he acquired a single franchise of the little-known McDonald's Restaurant, based in San Bernardino, California. In 1956, Kroc invested in twelve more franchises and by 1958 owned seventy-nine. Three years later, Kroc bought the company from the McDonald brothers and proceeded to turn it into the largest chain of restaurants in the world. Based on inexpensive, quickly served hamburgers that hungry families could eat in the restaurant, in their cars, or at home, Kroc's vision transformed the way Americans consumed food. "Drive-in" or "fast" food became a staple of the American diet in the subsequent decades. By the year 2000, fast food was a $100 billion industry, and more children recognized Ronald McDonald, the clown in McDonald's television commercials, than Santa Claus.

## Rise of the Sunbelt

Suburban living, although a nationwide phenomenon, was most at home in the **Sunbelt** (the southern and southwestern states), where taxes were low, the climate was mild, and open space allowed for sprawling subdivisions (Map 25.2). Florida added 3.5 million people, many of them retired, between 1940 and 1970. Texas profited from expanding petrochemical and defense industries. Most dramatic was California's growth, spurred especially by the state's booming defense-related aircraft and electronics industries. By 1970, California contained one-tenth of the nation's population and surpassed New York as the most populous state. By the end of the century, if California had been a nation its economy would have ranked among the top ten largest in the world.

A distinctive feature of Sunbelt suburbanization was its close relationship to the military-industrial complex. Building on World War II expansion, military bases

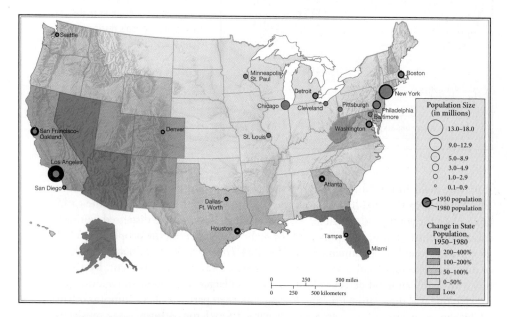

**MAP 25.2   Shifting Population Patterns, 1950–1980**
This map shows the two major, somewhat overlapping, patterns of population movement between 1950 and 1980. Most striking is the rapid growth of the Sunbelt states. All the states experiencing increases of over 100 percent in that period are in the Southwest, plus Florida. The second pattern involves the growth of metropolitan areas, defined as a central city or urban area and its suburbs. The central cities were themselves mostly not growing, however. The metropolitan growth shown in this map was accounted for by the expanding suburbs. And because Sunbelt growth was primarily suburban growth, that's where we see the most rapid metropolitan growth, with Los Angeles the clear leader.

proliferated in the South and Southwest in the postwar decades, especially in Florida, Texas, and California. In some instances, entire metropolitan regions—such as San Diego County, California, and the Houston area in Texas—expanded in tandem with nearby military outposts. Moreover, the aerospace, defense, and electronics industries were based largely in Sunbelt metropolitan regions. With government contracts fueling the economy and military bases providing thousands of jobs, Sunbelt politicians had every incentive to support vigorous defense spending by the federal government.

Sunbelt suburbanization was best exemplified by Orange County, California. Southwest of Los Angeles, Orange County was until the 1940s mostly just that—a land of oranges, groves of them. But during World War II, boosters attracted new bases and training facilities for the marines, navy, and air force (at the time the army air corps). Cold War militarization and the Korean War kept those bases humming, and Hughes Aircraft, Ford Aeronautics, and other defense-related manufacturers built new plants in the sunny, sprawling groves. So did subdivision developers, who built so many new homes that the population of the county jumped from 130,760 in 1940 to 703,925 in 1960. Casting his eye on all this development in the early 1950s, an entrepreneurial filmmaker and cartoonist named Walt Disney chose Anaheim in Orange County as the place for a massive new amusement park. Disneyland was to the new generation of suburbanites what Coney Island had been to an earlier generation of urbanites.

## Two Societies: Urban and Suburban

While middle-class whites flocked to the suburbs, an opposite stream of working-class migrants, many of them southern African Americans, moved into the cities. In the 1950s, the nation's twelve largest cities lost 3.6 million whites while gaining 4.5 million nonwhites. These urban newcomers inherited a declining economy and a decaying infrastructure. To those enjoying prosperity, the "other America," as the social critic Michael Harrington called it, remained largely invisible. In 1968, however, a report by the National Advisory Commission on Civil Disorders (informally known as the **Kerner Commission** and formed by the president to investigate the causes of the 1967 urban riots), delivered to President Lyndon Johnson, warned that "our nation is moving toward two societies, one black, one white, separate and unequal."

American cities had long been the home of poverty, slum housing, and the hardships and cultural dislocations brought on by immigration from overseas or migration from rural areas. But postwar American cities, especially those in the industrial Northeast and Midwest, experienced these problems with new intensity. By the 1950s, the manufacturing sector was contracting, and mechanization was eliminating thousands upon thousands of unskilled and semiskilled jobs, the kind traditionally taken up by new urban residents. The disappearing jobs were the ones "in which [African Americans] are disproportionately concentrated," noted the civil rights activist Bayard Rustin.

**The Urban Crisis**   The intensification of poverty, the deterioration of older housing stock, and the persistence of racial segregation produced what many at the time called the urban crisis. Unwelcome in the shiny new suburbs built by men such as William J. Levitt, African Americans found low-paying jobs in the city and lived in aging, slumlike apartment buildings. Despite a thriving black middle class—indeed, larger than ever before—for those without resources, upward mobility remained elusive. Racism in institutional forms frustrated African Americans at every turn: housing restrictions, increasingly segregated schools, and an urban infrastructure that stood underfunded and decaying as whites left for the suburbs.

Housing and job discrimination were compounded by the frenzy of urban renewal that hit black neighborhoods in the 1950s and early 1960s. Seeking to revitalize declining city centers, politicians and real estate developers proposed razing blighted neighborhoods to make way for modern construction projects that would appeal to the fleeing middle class. In Boston, almost one-third of the old city—including the historic West End, a long-established Italian neighborhood—was demolished to make way for a new highway, high-rise housing, and government and commercial buildings. In San Francisco, some 4,000 residents of the Western Addition, a predominantly black neighborhood, lost out to an urban renewal program that built luxury housing, a shopping center, and an express boulevard. Between 1949 and 1967, urban renewal nationwide demolished almost 400,000 buildings and displaced 1.4 million people.

The urban experts believed they knew what to do with the dislocated: relocate them to federally funded housing projects, an outgrowth of New Deal housing policy, now much expanded. However well intended, these grim projects too often took the form of cheap high-rises that isolated their inhabitants from surrounding neighborhoods. The impact was felt especially strongly among African Americans, who often found that public housing increased racial segregation and concentrated the poor. The Robert Taylor Homes in Chicago, with twenty-eight buildings of sixteen stories each, housed 20,000 residents, almost all of them black. Despite the planners' wish to build decent affordable apartments, the huge complex became a notorious breeding ground for crime and hopelessness.

**Urban Immigrants**   Despite the evident urban crisis, cities continued to attract immigrants from abroad. Since the passage of the National Origins Act of 1924 (Chapter 21), U.S. immigration policy had aimed mainly at keeping foreigners out. But World War II and the Cold War began slowly to change American policy. The Displaced Persons Act of 1948 permitted the entry of approximately 415,000 Europeans, many of them Jewish refugees. In a gesture to an important war ally, the Chinese Exclusion Act was repealed in 1943. More far-reaching was the 1952 McCarran-Walter Act, which ended the exclusion of Japanese, Koreans, and Southeast Asians.

After the national-origins quota system went into effect in 1924, Mexico replaced Eastern and Southern Europe as the nation's labor reservoir. During World War II, the federal government introduced the Bracero Program to ease wartime labor shortages (Chapter 23) and then revived it in 1951, during the Korean War. The federal government's ability to force workers to return to Mexico, however, was strictly limited. The Mexican immigrant population continued to grow, and by the time the Bracero Program ended in 1964, many of that group—an estimated 350,000—had settled permanently in the United States. Braceros were joined by other Mexicans from small towns and villages, who immigrated to the United States to escape poverty or to earn money to return home and purchase land for farming.

As generations of immigrants had before them, Mexicans gravitated to major cities. Mostly, they settled in Los Angeles, Long Beach, San Jose, El Paso, and other southwestern cities. But many also went north, augmenting well-established Mexican American communities in Chicago, Detroit, Kansas City, and Denver. Although still important to American agriculture, Mexican Americans were employed in substantial numbers as industrial and service workers by 1960.

Another major group of Spanish-speaking migrants came from Puerto Rico. American citizens since 1917, Puerto Ricans enjoyed an unrestricted right to move to the mainland United States. Migration increased dramatically after World War II, when mechanization of the island's sugarcane agriculture left many Puerto Ricans jobless. Airlines began to offer cheap direct flights between San Juan and New York City. With the fare at about $50 (two weeks' wages), Puerto Ricans became America's first immigrants to arrive en masse by air. Most Puerto Ricans went to New York, where they settled first in East ("Spanish") Harlem and then scattered in neighborhoods across the city's five boroughs. This massive migration, which increased the Puerto Rican population to 613,000 by 1960, transformed the ethnic composition of the city. More Puerto Ricans now lived in New York City than in San Juan.

Cuban refugees constituted the third largest group of Spanish-speaking immigrants. In the six years after Fidel Castro's seizure of power in 1959 (Chapter 24), an estimated 180,000 people fled Cuba for the United States. The Cuban refugee community grew so quickly that it turned Miami into a cosmopolitan, bilingual city almost overnight. Unlike other urban migrants, Miami's Cubans quickly prospered, in large part because they had arrived with money and middle-class skills.

Spanish-speaking immigrants — whether Mexican, Puerto Rican, or Cuban — created huge barrios in major American cities, where bilingualism flourished, the Catholic Church shaped religious life, and families sought to join the economic mainstream. Though distinct from one another, these Spanish-speaking communities remained largely segregated from white, or Anglo, neighborhoods and suburbs as well as from African American districts.

| IN YOUR OWN WORDS | What were the major forces that contributed to postwar suburbanization? |

# Summary

We have explored how, at the same time it became mired in the Cold War, the United States entered an unparalleled era of prosperity in which a new middle class came into being. Indeed, the Cold War was one of the engines of prosperity. The postwar economy was marked by the dominance of big corporations and defense spending.

After years of depression and war-induced insecurity, Americans turned inward toward religion, home, and family. Postwar couples married young, had several children, and — if they were white and middle class — raised their children in a climate of suburban comfort and consumerism. The profamily orientation of the 1950s celebrated traditional gender roles, even though millions of women entered the workforce in those years. Not everyone, however, shared in the postwar prosperity. Postwar cities increasingly became places of last resort for the nation's poor. Black migrants, unlike earlier immigrants, encountered an urban economy that had little use for them. Without opportunity, and faced with pervasive racism, many of them were on their way to becoming an American underclass, even as sparkling new suburbs emerged outside cities to house the new middle class. Many of the smoldering contradictions of the postwar period—Cold War anxiety in the midst of suburban domesticity, tensions in women's lives, economic and racial inequality—helped spur the protest movements of the 1960s.

# Chapter 25 Review

## KEY TERMS

**Identify and explain the significance of each term below.**

kitchen debate (p. 728)

Bretton Woods (p. 729)

World Bank (p. 729)

International Monetary Fund (IMF) (p. 730)

military-industrial complex (p. 730)

*Sputnik* (p. 731)

National Defense Education Act (p. 731)

*The Affluent Society* (p. 732)

*The Other America* (p. 732)

Veterans Administration (p. 733)

collective bargaining (p. 734)

teenager (p. 737)

Beats (p. 738)

baby boom (p. 740)

*Shelley v. Kraemer* (p. 746)

National Interstate and Defense Highways Act (p. 746)

Sunbelt (p. 748)

Kerner Commission (p. 749)

## REVIEW QUESTIONS

**Answer these questions to demonstrate your understanding of the chapter's main ideas.**

1. What explains the growth of the American economy after World War II?
2. What was the domestic ideal, and how did Americans embrace it in the postwar decades?
3. What were the major forces that contributed to postwar suburbanization?
4. Review the events listed under "America in the World" and "Work, Exchange, and Technology" for the periods 1930–1945 and 1945–1960 on the thematic timelines on pages 580–581 and 696–697, respectively. Explain how the United States began the 1930s in deep depression with unemployment near 25 percent and ended the 1950s with an expanded middle class and a consumption-driven economy.

## CHRONOLOGY

**As you read, ask yourself why this chapter begins and ends with these dates and identify the links among related events.**

| | |
|---|---|
| **1944** | • Bretton Woods economic conference |
| | • World Bank and International Monetary Fund (IMF) founded |
| | • GI Bill (Servicemen's Readjustment Act) |
| **1946** | • First edition of Dr. Spock's *Common Sense Book of Baby and Child Care* |
| **1947** | • First Levittown built |
| **1948** | • Beginning of network television |
| | • *Shelley v. Kraemer* |
| | • Alfred Kinsey's *Sexual Behavior in the Human Male* published |
| **1949** | • Billy Graham revival in Los Angeles |
| **1951** | • Bracero Program revived |
| | • Mattachine Society founded |
| **1952** | • McCarran-Walter Act |
| **1953** | • Kinsey's *Sexual Behavior in the Human Female* published |
| **1954** | • Ray Kroc buys the first McDonald's franchise |
| **1955** | • Daughters of Bilitis founded |
| **1956** | • National Interstate and Defense Highways Act |
| | • Elvis Presley's breakthrough records |
| | • Allen Ginsberg's poem "Howl" published |
| **1957** | • Peak of postwar baby boom |
| **1961** | • Eisenhower warns nation against military-industrial complex |
| **1965** | • *Griswold v. Connecticut* |

# Walking into Freedom Land: The Civil Rights Movement

## 1941–1973

**IDENTIFY THE BIG IDEA**

How did the civil rights movement evolve over time, and how did competing ideas and political alliances affect its growth and that of other social movements?

**IN JUNE 1945, AS WORLD WAR II WAS COMING TO AN END,** Democratic senator James O. Eastland of Mississippi stood on the floor of the U.S. Senate and brashly proclaimed that "the Negro race is an inferior race." Raising his arms, his tie askew from vigorous gesturing, Eastland ridiculed black troops. "The Negro soldier was an utter and dismal failure in combat," he said.

Eastland's assertions were untrue. Black soldiers had served honorably; many won medals for bravery in combat. All-black units, such as the 761st "Black Panther" Tank Battalion and the famous Tuskegee Airmen, were widely praised by military commanders. But segregationists like Eastland were a nearly unassailable force in Congress, able to block civil rights legislation and shape national opinion.

In the 1940s, two generations after W. E. B. Du Bois famously wrote that "the problem of the twentieth century is the problem of the color line," few white Americans believed wholeheartedly in racial equality. Racial segregation remained entrenched across the country. Much of the Deep South, like Eastland's Mississippi, was a "closed society": black people had no political rights and lived on the margins of white society, impoverished and exploited. Northern cities proved more hospitable to African Americans, but schools, neighborhoods, public amenities like swimming pools, and many businesses remained segregated and unequal in the North as well.

Across the nation, however, winds of change were gathering. Between World War II and the 1970s, slowly at first, and then with greater urgency in the 1960s, the civil rights movement swept aside systematic racial segregation. It could not sweep away racial inequality in its entirety, but the movement constituted a "second Reconstruction" in which black activism reshaped the nation's laws and practices. Civil rights was the paradigmatic social movement of the twentieth century. Its model of nonviolent protest and its calls for self-determination inspired the New Left, feminism, the Chicano movement, the gay rights movement, the American Indian movement, and many others.

The black-led civil rights movement, joined at key moments by Latinos, Asian Americans, and Native Americans, redefined American *liberalism*. In the 1930s, New Deal liberalism had established a welfare state to protect citizens from economic hardship. The civil rights movement forged a new **rights liberalism**: the idea that individuals deserve state protection from discrimination. This version of liberalism focused on identities—such as race or gender, and eventually sexuality—rather than general social welfare. Rights liberalism proved to be both a necessary expansion of the nation's ideals and a wellspring of political backlash. Indeed, the quest for racial justice would contribute to a crisis of liberalism itself.

# The Emerging Civil Rights Struggle, 1941–1957

As it took shape during World War II and the early Cold War, the campaign against racial injustice proceeded along two tracks: at the grass roots and in government institutions (federal courts, state legislatures, and ultimately the U.S. Congress). Labor unions, churches, and organizations such as the Congress of Racial Equality (CORE) inspired hundreds of thousands of ordinary citizens to join the movement. But grassroots protest was not African Americans' only weapon. They also had the Bill of Rights and the Reconstruction amendments to the Constitution. Civil rights lived in those documents—especially in the Fourteenth Amendment, which guaranteed equal protection under the law to all U.S. citizens, and in the Fifteenth, which guaranteed the right to vote regardless of "race, color, or previous condition of servitude"—but had been ignored or violated for nearly a century. The task was to restore the Constitution's legal force. Neither track, grassroots or legal, was entirely independent of the other. Together, they were the foundation of the fight for racial equality in the postwar decades.

## Life Under Jim Crow

Racial segregation and economic exploitation defined the lives of the majority of African Americans in the postwar decades. Numbering 15 million in 1950, African Americans were approximately 10 percent of the U.S. population. In the South, however, they constituted between 30 and 50 percent of the population of several states, such as South Carolina and Mississippi. Segregation, commonly known as Jim Crow (Chapter 17), prevailed in every aspect of life in the southern states, where two-thirds of all African Americans lived in 1950. African Americans could not eat in restaurants patronized by whites or use the same waiting rooms at bus stations. All forms of public transportation were rigidly segregated by custom or by law. Public parks and libraries were segregated. Even drinking fountains were labeled "White" and "Colored."

This system of segregation underlay economic and political structures that further marginalized and disempowered black citizens. Virtually no African Americans were allowed to work for city or state government, and the best jobs in the private sector were reserved for whites. Black workers labored "in the back," cleaning, cooking, stocking shelves, and loading trucks for the lowest wages. Rural African Americans labored in a sharecropping system that kept them stuck in poverty, often prevented them from obtaining an education, and offered no avenue of escape. Politically, less than 20 percent of eligible black voters were allowed to vote, the result of poll taxes, literacy tests, intimidation, fraud, and the "white primary" (elections in which only whites could vote). This near-total disfranchisement gave whites power disproportionate to their numbers—black people were one-third of the residents of Mississippi, South Carolina, and Georgia but had basically no political voice in those states.

**Segregation in Virginia, 1962** As the law of the land in most southern states, racial segregation (known as Jim Crow) required the complete separation of blacks and whites in most public spaces. The "white only" sign on a restaurant door shown in this 1962 photograph in Hampton, Virginia, was typical. Everything from restaurants, drinking fountains, and public waiting areas to libraries, public parks, schools, restrooms, and even cola vending machines was subject to strict racial segregation. © Bruce Davidson/Magnum Photos.

In the North, racial segregation in everyday life was less acute but just as tangible. Northern segregation took the form of a spatial system in which whites increasingly lived in suburbs or on the outskirts of cities, while African Americans were concentrated in declining downtown neighborhoods. The result was what many called ghettos: all-black districts characterized by high rents, low wages, and inadequate city services. Employment discrimination and their exclusion from job training left many African Americans without any means of support. Few jobs other than the most menial were open to African Americans; journalists, accountants, engineers, and other highly educated men from all-black colleges and universities often labored as railroad porters or cooks because jobs commensurate with their skills remained for whites only. These conditions produced a self-perpetuating cycle that kept far too many black citizens trapped on the social margins.

To be certain, African Americans found a measure of freedom in the North and West compared to the South. They could vote, participate in politics, and, at least after the early 1960s, enjoy equal access to public accommodations. But we err in thinking that racial segregation was only a southern condition or that poverty and racial discrimination were not also deeply entrenched in the North and West. In northern cities such as Detroit, Chicago, and Philadelphia, for instance, white home owners in the 1950s used various tactics—from police harassment to thrown bricks, burning crosses, bombs, and mob violence—to keep African Americans from living near them. Moreover, as we saw in Chapter 25, Federal Housing Administration (FHA) and bank redlining excluded African American home buyers from the all-white suburbs emerging around major cities. Racial segregation was a national, not regional, problem.

## Origins of the Civil Rights Movement

Since racial injustice had been part of American life for hundreds of years, why did the civil rights movement arise when it did? After all, the National Association for the Advancement of Colored People (NAACP), founded in 1909, had begun challenging racial segregation in a series of court cases in the 1930s. And other organizations, such as Marcus Garvey's Universal Negro Improvement Association in the 1920s, had attracted significant popular support (Chapter 21). These precedents were important, but several factors came together in the middle of the twentieth century to make a broad movement possible.

An important influence was World War II. "The Jewish people and the Negro people both know the meaning of Nordic supremacy," wrote the African American poet Langston Hughes in 1945. In the war against fascism, the Allies sought to discredit racist Nazi ideology. Committed to fighting racism abroad, Americans increasingly condemned racism at home. The Cold War placed added pressure on U.S. officials. "More and more we are learning how closely our democracy is under observation," President Harry S. Truman commented in 1947. To inspire other nations in the global standoff with the Soviet Union, Truman explained, "we must correct the remaining imperfections in our practice of democracy."

Among the most consequential factors was the growth of the black middle class. Historically small, the black middle class experienced robust growth after World War II. Its ranks produced most of the civil rights leaders: ministers, teachers, trade unionists, attorneys, and other professionals. Churches, for centuries a sanctuary for black Americans, were especially important. Moreover, in the 1960s African American college students—part of the largest expansion of college enrollment in U.S. history—joined the movement, adding new energy and fresh ideas. With access to education and media, this new middle class had more resources than ever before. Less dependent on white patronage, and therefore less vulnerable to white retaliation, middle-class African Americans were in a position to lead a movement for change.

Still other influences assisted the movement. White labor leaders were generally more equality-minded than the rank and file, but the United Auto Workers, the United Steelworkers, and the Communications Workers of America, among many other progressive trade unions, were reliable allies at the national level. The new medium of television, too, played a crucial role. When television networks covered early desegregation struggles—at Little Rock High School in 1957, for instance—Americans across the country saw the violence of white supremacy firsthand. None of these factors alone was decisive. None ensured an easy path. The civil rights movement faced enormous resistance and required dauntless courage and sacrifice from thousands upon thousands of activists for more than three decades. Ultimately, however, the movement changed the nation for the better and improved the lives of millions of Americans.

## World War II: The Beginnings

During the war fought "to make the world safe for democracy," the United States was far from ready to extend full equality to its own black citizens. Black workers faced discrimination in wartime employment, and the more than 1 million black troops who served in World War II were placed in segregated units commanded solely by whites. Both at home and abroad, World War II "immeasurably magnified the Negro's awareness of the disparity between the American profession and practice of democracy," NAACP president Walter White observed.

**Executive Order 8802**   On the home front, activists pushed two strategies. First, A. Philip Randolph, whose **Brotherhood of Sleeping Car Porters** was the most prominent black trade union, called for a march on Washington in early 1941. Randolph planned to bring 100,000 protesters to the nation's capital to call for equal opportunity for black workers in war jobs—then just beginning to expand with President Franklin Roosevelt's pledge to supply the Allies with materiel. To avoid a divisive protest, FDR issued Executive Order 8802 in June of that year, prohibiting racial discrimination in defense industries, and Randolph agreed to cancel the march. The resulting Fair Employment Practice Committee (FEPC) had few enforcement powers, but it set an important precedent: federal action. Randolph's efforts showed that white leaders and institutions could be swayed by concerted African American pressure. It would be a critical lesson for the movement.

**The Double V Campaign**   A second strategy jumped from the pages of the *Pittsburgh Courier*, one of the foremost African American newspapers of the era. It was the brainchild of an ordinary cafeteria worker from Kansas. In a 1942 letter to the editor, James G. Thompson urged that "colored Americans adopt the double VV for a double victory"—victory over fascism abroad and victory over racism at home. Edgar Rouzeau, editor of the paper's New York office, agreed: "Black America must fight two wars and win in both." Instantly dubbed the Double V Campaign, Thompson's notion, with Rouzeau's backing, spread like wildfire through black communities across the country. African Americans would demonstrate their loyalty and citizenship by fighting the Axis powers. But they would also demand, peacefully but emphatically, the defeat of racism at home. "The suffering and privation may be great," Rouzeau told his readers, "but the rewards loom even greater."

The Double V met considerable resistance. In war industries, factories periodically shut down in Chicago, Baltimore, Philadelphia, and other cities because of "hate strikes": the refusal of white workers to labor alongside black workers. Detroit was especially tense. Referring to the potential for racial strife, *Life* magazine reported in 1942 that "Detroit is Dynamite. . . . It can either blow up Hitler or blow up America." In 1943, it nearly did the latter. On a hot summer day, whites from the city's ethnic European neighborhoods taunted and beat African Americans in a local park. Three days of rioting ensued in which thirty-four people were killed, twenty-five of them black. Federal troops were called in to restore order.

Despite such incidents, and to some degree because of them, a generation was spurred into action during the war years. In New York City, employment discrimination on the city's transit lines prompted one of the first bus boycotts in the nation's history, led in 1941 by Harlem minister Adam Clayton Powell Jr. In Chicago, James Farmer and three other members of the Fellowship of Reconciliation (FOR), a nonviolent peace organization, founded the **Congress of Racial Equality (CORE)** in 1942. FOR and CORE embraced the philosophy of nonviolent direct action espoused by Mahatma Gandhi of India. Another FOR member in New York and proponent of direct action, Bayard Rustin, led one of the earliest challenges to southern segregation, the 1947 Journey of Reconciliation. Meanwhile, after the war, hundreds of thousands of African American veterans used the GI Bill to go to college, trade school, or graduate school, placing themselves in a position to push against segregation. At the war's end, Powell affirmed that "the black man . . . is ready to throw himself into the struggle to make the dream of America become flesh and blood, bread and butter."

## Cold War Civil Rights

Demands for justice persisted in the early years of the Cold War. African American efforts were propelled by symbolic victories—as when Jackie Robinson broke through the color line in major league baseball by joining the Brooklyn Dodgers in 1947—but the growing black vote in northern cities proved more consequential. During World War II, more than a million African Americans migrated to northern and western cities, where they joined the Democratic Party of Franklin Roosevelt and the New Deal (Map 26.1). This newfound political leverage awakened northern liberals, many of whom became allies of civil rights advocates. Ultimately, however, the Cold War produced mixed results, as the nation's growing anticommunism opened some avenues for civil rights while closing others.

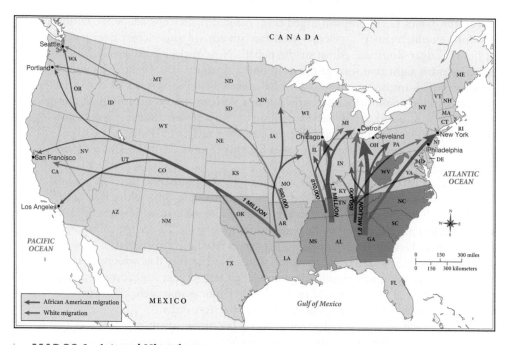

**MAP 26.1   Internal Migrations**
The migration of African Americans from the South to other regions of the country produced one of the most remarkable demographic shifts of the mid-twentieth century. Between World War I—which marked the start of the Great Migration—and the 1970s, more than 6 million African Americans left the South. Where they settled in the North and West, they helped change the politics of entire cities and even states. Seeking black votes, which had become a key to victory in major cities, liberal Democrats and Republicans alike in New York, Illinois, California, and Pennsylvania, for instance, increasingly made civil rights part of their platform. In this way, migration advanced the political cause of black equality.

**Civil Rights and the New Deal Coalition**   African American leaders were uncertain what to expect from President Truman, inheritor of the New Deal coalition but not opposed to using racist language himself. Though he did not immediately support social equality for African Americans, Truman supported civil rights because he believed in equality before the law. Moreover, he understood the growing importance of the small but often decisive black vote in key northern states such as New York, Illinois, Pennsylvania, and Michigan. Civil rights activists Randolph and Powell—along with vocal white liberals such as Hubert Humphrey, the mayor of Minneapolis, and members of Americans for Democratic Action (ADA), a liberal organization—pressed Truman to act.

With no support for civil rights in Congress, Truman turned to executive action. In 1946, he appointed the Presidential Committee on Civil Rights, whose 1947 report, **"To Secure These Rights,"** called for robust federal action to ensure black equality. With the report's recommendations in mind, in 1948 Truman issued an executive order desegregating employment in federal agencies and, under pressure from Randolph's Committee Against Jim Crow in Military Service, desegregated the armed forces. Truman then sent a message to Congress asking that every one of the report's recommendations—including the abolition of poll taxes and the restoration of the Fair Employment Practice Committee—be made into law. It was the most aggressive and politically bold call for racial equality by the leader of a major political party since Reconstruction.

Truman's boldness was too much for southern Democrats. Under the leadership of Strom Thurmond, governor of South Carolina, white Democrats from the South formed the **States' Rights Democratic Party**, known popularly as the Dixiecrats, for the 1948 election (Chapter 24). This brought into focus an internal struggle developing within the Democratic Party and its still-formidable New Deal coalition. Would the civil rights aims of the party's liberal wing alienate southern white Democrats, as well as many suburban whites in the North? It was the first hint of the discord that would eventually divide the Democratic Party in the 1960s.

**Race and Anticommunism**    The Cold War both helped and impeded the civil rights movement. In a time of growing fear of communist expansionism, Truman worried about America's image in the world. He reminded Americans that when whites and blacks "fail to live together in peace," that failure harmed "the cause of democracy itself in the whole world." Indeed, the Soviet Union used American racism to discredit the United States abroad. "We cannot escape the fact that our civil rights record has been an issue in world politics," the Committee on Civil Rights wrote. International tensions between the United States and the Soviet Union thus appeared to strengthen the hand of civil rights leaders, because America needed to demonstrate to the rest of the world that its racial climate was improving.

However, the Cold War, McCarthyism, and the hunt for subversives at home also held the civil rights movement back. Civil rights opponents charged that racial integration was "communistic," and the NAACP was banned in many southern states as an "anti-American" organization. Black Americans who spoke favorably of the Soviet Union, such as the actor and singer Paul Robeson, or had been "fellow travelers" in the 1930s, such as the pacifist Rustin, were persecuted. Robeson, whose career was destroyed by such accusations, told House Un-American Activities Committee (HUAC) interrogators, "My father was a slave, and my people died to build this country, and I am going to . . . have a part of it just like you." The fate of people like Robeson showed that the Cold War could work *against* the civil rights cause just as easily as for it.

## Mexican Americans and Japanese Americans

African Americans were the most prominent, but not the only, group in American society to organize against racial injustice in the 1940s. In the Southwest, from Texas to California, Mexican immigrants and Mexican Americans endured a "caste" system not unlike the Jim Crow system in the South. In Texas, for instance, poll taxes kept most Mexican American citizens from voting. Decades of discrimination by employers in agriculture and manufacturing—made possible by the constant supply of cheap labor from across the border—suppressed wages and kept the majority of Mexican Americans barely above poverty. Many lived in *colonias* or barrios, neighborhoods separated from Anglos and often lacking sidewalks, reliable electricity and water, and public transportation.

Developments within the Mexican American community set the stage for fresh challenges to these conditions in the 1940s. Labor activism, especially in Congress of Industrial Organizations (CIO) unions with large numbers of Mexican Americans, improved wages and working conditions in some industries and produced a new generation of leaders. More than 400,000 Mexican Americans also served in World War II. Having fought for their country, many returned to the United States determined to challenge their second-class citizenship. Additionally, a new Mexican American middle class began to take shape in major cities such as Los Angeles, San Antonio, El Paso, and Chicago, which, like the African American middle class, gave leaders and resources to the cause.

In Texas and California, Mexican Americans created new civil rights organizations in the postwar years. In Corpus Christi, Texas, World War II veterans founded the **American GI Forum** in 1948 to protest the poor treatment of Mexican American soldiers and veterans. Activists in Los Angeles created the **Community Services Organization (CSO)** the same year. Both groups arose to address specific local injustices (such as the segregation of military cemeteries), but they quickly broadened their scope to encompass political and economic justice for the larger community. Among the first young activists to work for the CSO were Cesar Chavez and Dolores Huerta, who would later found the United Farm Workers (UFW) and inspire the Chicano movement of the 1960s.

Activists also pushed for legal change. In 1947, five Mexican American fathers in California sued a local school district for placing their children in separate "Mexican" schools. The case, *Mendez v. Westminster School District*, never made it to the U.S. Supreme Court. But the Ninth Circuit Court ruled such segregation unconstitutional, laying the legal groundwork for broader challenges to racial inequality. Among those filing briefs in the case was the NAACP's Thurgood Marshall, who was then developing the legal strategy to strike at racial segregation in the South. In another significant legal victory, the Supreme Court ruled in 1954 — just two weeks before the landmark *Brown v. Board of Education* decision — that Mexican Americans constituted a "distinct class" that could claim constitutional protection from discrimination.

Also on the West Coast, Japanese Americans accelerated their legal challenge to discrimination. Undeterred by rulings in the *Hirabayashi* (1943) and *Korematsu* (1944) cases upholding wartime imprisonment (Chapter 23), the Japanese American Citizens League (JACL) filed lawsuits in the late 1940s to regain property lost during the war. The JACL also challenged the constitutionality of California's Alien Land Law, which prohibited Japanese immigrants from owning land, and successfully lobbied Congress to enable those same immigrants to become citizens — a right they were denied for fifty years. These efforts by Mexican and Japanese Americans enlarged the sphere of civil rights and laid the foundation for a broader notion of racial equality in the postwar years.

## Fighting for Equality Before the Law

With civil rights legislation blocked in Congress by southern Democrats throughout the 1950s, activists looked in two different directions for a breakthrough: to northern state legislatures and to the federal courts. School segregation remained a stubborn problem in northern states, but the biggest obstacle to black progress there was persistent job and housing discrimination. The states with the largest African American populations, and hence the largest share of black Democratic Party voters, became testing grounds for state legislation to end such discriminatory practices.

Winning antidiscrimination legislation depended on coalition politics. African American activists forged alliances with trade unions and liberal organizations such as the American Friends Service Committee (a Quaker group), among many others. Progress was slow and often occurred only after long periods of unglamorous struggle to win votes in state capitals such as Albany, New York; Springfield, Illinois; and Lansing, Michigan. The first fair employment laws had come in New York and New Jersey in 1945. A decade passed, however, before other states with significant black populations passed similar legislation. Antidiscrimination laws in housing were even more difficult to pass, with most progress not coming until the 1960s. These legislative campaigns in northern states received little national attention, but they were instrumental in laying the groundwork for legal equality outside the South.

**Thurgood Marshall**   Because the vast majority of southern African Americans were prohibited from voting, state legislatures there were closed to the kind of organized political pressure possible in the North. Thus activists looked to federal courts for leverage. In the late 1930s, NAACP lawyers Thurgood Marshall, Charles Hamilton Houston, and William Hastie had begun preparing the legal ground in a series of cases challenging racial discrimination. The key was prodding the U.S. Supreme Court to use the Fourteenth Amendment's "equal protection" clause to overturn its 1896 ruling in *Plessy v. Ferguson*, which upheld racial segregation under the "separate but equal" doctrine.

Marshall was the great-grandson of slaves. Of modest origins, his parents instilled in him a faith in law and the Constitution. After his 1930 graduation from Lincoln University, a prestigious African American institution near Philadelphia, Marshall applied to the University of Maryland Law School. Denied admission because the school did not accept black applicants, he enrolled at all-black Howard University. There Marshall met Houston, a law school dean, and the two forged a friendship and intellectual partnership that would change the face of American legal history. Marshall, with Houston's and Hastie's critical strategic input, would argue most of the NAACP's landmark cases. (In 1967, President Johnson appointed Marshall to the Supreme Court—the first African American to have that honor.)

Marshall, Houston, Hastie, and six other attorneys filed suit after suit, deliberately selecting each case from dozens of possibilities. The strategy was slow and time-consuming, but progress came. In 1936, Marshall and Houston won a state case that forced the University of Maryland Law School to admit qualified African Americans—a ruling of obvious significance to Marshall. Eight years later, in *Smith v. Allwright* (1944), Marshall convinced the U.S. Supreme Court that all-white primaries were unconstitutional. In 1950, with Marshall once again arguing the case, the Supreme Court ruled in *McLaurin v. Oklahoma* that universities could not segregate black students from others on campus. None of these cases produced swift

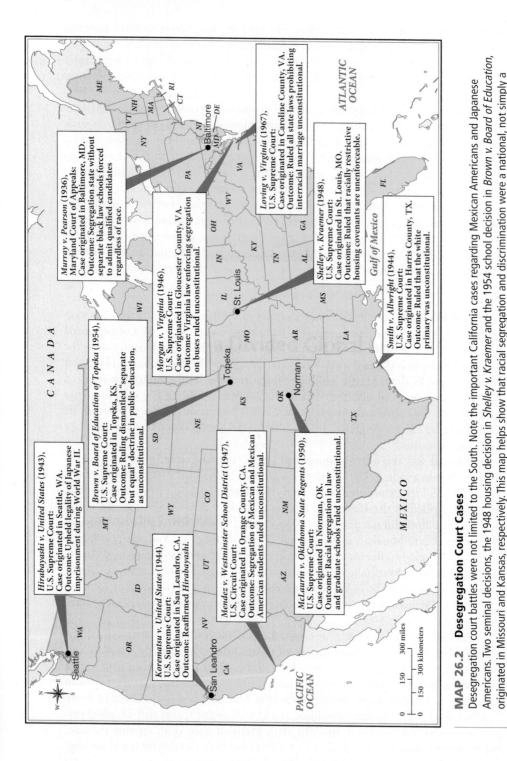

*Hirabayashi v. United States* (1943),
U.S. Supreme Court:
Case originated in Seattle, WA.
Outcome: Upheld legality of Japanese
imprisonment during World War II.

*Korematsu v. United States* (1944),
U.S. Supreme Court:
Case originated in San Leandro, CA.
Outcome: Reaffirmed *Hirabayashi*.

*Mendez v. Westminster School District* (1947),
U.S. Circuit Court:
Case originated in Orange County, CA.
Outcome: Segregation of Mexican and Mexican
American students ruled unconstitutional.

*McLaurin v. Oklahoma State Regents* (1950),
U.S. Supreme Court:
Case originated in Norman, OK.
Outcome: Racial segregation in law
and graduate schools ruled unconstitutional.

*Brown v. Board of Education of Topeka* (1954),
U.S. Supreme Court:
Case originated in Topeka, KS.
Outcome: Ruling dismantled "separate
but equal" doctrine in public education,
as unconstitutional.

*Murray v. Pearson* (1936),
Maryland Court of Appeals:
Case originated in Baltimore, MD.
Outcome: Segregation state without
separate black law schools forced
to admit qualified candidates
regardless of race.

*Morgan v. Virginia* (1946),
U.S. Supreme Court:
Case originated in Gloucester County, VA.
Outcome: Virginia law enforcing segregation
on buses ruled unconstitutional.

*Loving v. Virginia* (1967),
U.S. Supreme Court:
Case originated in Caroline County, VA.
Outcome: Ruled all state laws prohibiting
interracial marriage unconstitutional.

*Shelley v. Kraemer* (1948),
U.S. Supreme Court:
Case originated in St. Louis, MO.
Outcome: Ruled that racially restrictive
housing covenants are unenforceable.

*Smith v. Allwright* (1944),
U.S. Supreme Court:
Case originated in Harris County, TX.
Outcome: Ruled that the white
primary was unconstitutional.

## MAP 26.2 Desegregation Court Cases

Desegregation court battles were not limited to the South. Note the important California cases regarding Mexican Americans and Japanese Americans. Two seminal decisions, the 1948 housing decision in *Shelley v. Kraemer* and the 1954 school decision in *Brown v. Board of Education*, originated in Missouri and Kansas, respectively. This map helps show that racial segregation and discrimination were a national, not simply a southern, problem.

changes in the daily lives of most African Americans, but they confirmed that civil rights attorneys were on the right track.

*Brown v. Board of Education*    The NAACP's legal strategy achieved its ultimate validation in a case involving Linda Brown, a black pupil in Topeka, Kansas, who had been forced to attend a distant segregated school rather than the nearby white elementary school. In his argument before the court in ***Brown v. Board of Education of Topeka*** (1954), Marshall contended that such segregation was unconstitutional because it denied Linda Brown the "equal protection of the laws" guaranteed by the Fourteenth Amendment (Map 26.2). In a unanimous decision on May 17, 1954, the Supreme Court agreed, overturning the "separate but equal" doctrine at last. Writing for the Court, the new chief justice, Earl Warren, wrote: "We conclude that in the field of public education the doctrine of 'separate but equal' has no place. Separate educational facilities are inherently unequal." In an implementing 1955 decision known as *Brown II*, the Court declared that desegregation should proceed "with all deliberate speed."

In the South, however, Virginia senator Harry F. Byrd issued a call for "massive resistance." Calling May 17 "Black Monday," the Mississippi segregationist Tom P. Brady invoked the language of the Cold War to discredit the decision, assailing the "totalitarian government" that had rendered the decision in the name of "socialism and communism." That year, half a million southerners joined White Citizens' Councils dedicated to blocking school integration. Some whites revived the old tactics of violence and intimidation, swelling the ranks of the Ku Klux Klan to levels not seen since the 1920s. The "Southern Manifesto," signed in 1956 by 101 members of Congress, denounced the *Brown* decision as "a clear abuse of judicial power" and encouraged local officials to defy it. The white South had declared all-out war on *Brown*.

Enforcement of the Supreme Court's decision was complicated further by Dwight Eisenhower's presence in the White House — the president was no champion of civil rights. Eisenhower accepted the *Brown* decision as the law of the land, but he thought it a mistake. Ike was especially unhappy about the prospect of committing federal power to enforce the decision. A crisis in Little Rock, Arkansas, forced his hand. In September 1957, when nine black students attempted to enroll at the all-white Central High School, Governor Orval Faubus called out the National Guard to bar them. Angry white mobs appeared daily to taunt the students, chanting "Go back to the jungle." As the vicious scenes played out on television night after night, Eisenhower finally acted. He sent 1,000 federal troops to Little Rock and nationalized the Arkansas National Guard, ordering them to protect the black students. Eisenhower thus became the first president since Reconstruction to use federal troops to enforce the rights of African Americans. But Little Rock also showed that southern officials had more loyalty to local custom than to the law — a repeated problem in the post-*Brown* era.

> **IN YOUR OWN WORDS**    What factors best explain why and how the civil rights movement developed between 1941 and 1954?

# Forging a Protest Movement, 1955–1965

By declaring racial segregation integral to the South's "habits, traditions, and way of life," the Southern Manifesto signaled that many whites would not readily accept black equality. As the battle over desegregating Little Rock High School had shown, the unwillingness of local officials to enforce *Brown* could render the decision invalid in practice. If legal victories would not be enough, citizens themselves, black and white, would have to take to the streets and demand justice. Following the *Brown* decision, they did just that, forging a protest movement unique in the history of the United States.

## Nonviolent Direct Action

*Brown* had been the law of the land for barely a year when a single act of violence struck at the heart of black America. A fourteen-year-old African American from the South Side of Chicago, Emmett Till, was visiting relatives in Mississippi in the summer of 1955. Seen talking to a white woman in a grocery store, Till was tortured and murdered under cover of night. His mutilated body was found at the bottom of a river, tied with barbed wire to a heavy steel cotton gin fan. Photos of Till's body in *Jet* magazine brought national attention to the heinous crime.

Two white men were arrested for Till's murder. During the trial, followed closely in black communities across the country, the lone witness to Till's kidnapping — his uncle, Mose Wright — identified both killers. Feeling "the blood boil in hundreds of white people as they sat glaring in the courtroom," Wright said, "it was the first time in my life I had the courage to accuse a white man of a crime." Despite Wright's eyewitness testimony, the all-white jury found the defendants innocent. This miscarriage of justice — later, the killers even admitted their guilt in a *Look* magazine article — galvanized an entire generation of African Americans; no one who lived through the Till incident ever forgot it.

**Montgomery Bus Boycott**   In the wake of the Till murder, civil rights advocates needed some good news. They received it three months later, as southern black leaders embraced an old tactic put to new ends: nonviolent direct action. On December 1, 1955, Rosa Parks, a civil rights activist in Montgomery, Alabama, refused to give up her seat on a bus to a white man. She was arrested and charged with violating a local segregation ordinance. Parks's act was not the spur-of-the-moment decision that it seemed: a longtime NAACP member, she and other female civil rights activists in Montgomery had been contemplating such an act for some time. Parks's arrest became the focal point for the black community's challenge against segregated buses, which were a powerful symbol of the city's racial hierarchy.

Soon after Parks's arrest, the black community turned for leadership to the Reverend Martin Luther King Jr., the recently appointed pastor of Montgomery's Dexter Street Baptist Church. The son of a prominent Atlanta minister, King embraced the teachings of Mahatma Gandhi. Working closely, but behind the scenes, with Bayard Rustin, King deepened his investment in nonviolent philosophy and the practice of direct action, which Rustin and others in the Fellowship of Reconciliation had first used in the 1940s. King and other black ministers endorsed a plan proposed by a local black women's organization to boycott Montgomery's bus system. The **Montgomery Bus Boycott** was inspired by similar boycotts that had taken place in Harlem in 1941 and Baton Rouge, Louisiana, in 1953.

For the next 381 days, Montgomery's African Americans formed car pools or walked to work. "Darling, it's empty!" Coretta Scott King exclaimed to her husband as a bus normally filled with black riders rolled by their living room window on the first day of the boycott. The transit company neared bankruptcy, and downtown stores complained about the loss of business. But only after the Supreme Court ruled in November 1956 that bus segregation was unconstitutional did the city of Montgomery finally comply. "My feets is tired, but my soul is rested," said one woman boycotter.

The Montgomery Bus Boycott catapulted King to national prominence. In 1957, along with the Reverend Ralph Abernathy and dozens of black ministers from across the South, he founded the **Southern Christian Leadership Conference (SCLC)** in Atlanta. The black church, long the center of African American social and cultural life, now lent its moral and organizational strength to the civil rights movement. Black churchwomen were a tower of strength, transferring the skills they had honed during years of church work to the fight for civil rights. The SCLC quickly joined the NAACP at the leading edge of the movement for racial justice.

**Greensboro Sit-Ins**    The battle for civil rights entered a new phase in Greensboro, North Carolina, on February 1, 1960, when four black college students took seats at the whites-only lunch counter at the local Woolworth's drugstore, which had a diner-style lunch counter, as most southern drugstores in that era did. This simple act was entirely the brainchild of the four students, who had discussed it in their dorm rooms over several preceding nights. A New York–based spokesman for Woolworth's said the chain would "abide by local custom," which meant refusing to serve African Americans at the lunch counter. The students were determined to "sit in" until they were served. For three weeks, hundreds of students inspired by the original foursome took turns sitting at the counters, quietly eating, doing homework, or reading. Taunted and beaten by groups of whites, pelted with food and other debris, the black students — often occupying more than sixty of the sixty-six seats — held strong. Although many were arrested, the tactic worked: the Woolworth's lunch counter was desegregated, and sit-ins quickly spread to other southern cities.

**Ella Baker and SNCC**    Inspired by the developments in Greensboro and elsewhere, Ella Baker, an administrator with the SCLC, helped organize the **Student Nonviolent Coordinating Committee** (**SNCC**, pronounced "Snick") in 1960 to facilitate student sit-ins. Rolling like a great wave across the Upper South, from North Carolina into Virginia, Maryland, and Tennessee, sit-ins had been launched by students in 126 cities by the end of the year. More than 50,000 people participated, and 3,600 went to jail. The sit-ins drew black college students into the movement in significant numbers for the first time. Northern students formed solidarity committees and raised money for bail. SNCC quickly emerged as the most important student protest organization in the country and inspired a generation of students on college campuses across the nation.

**Ella Baker**  Born in Virginia and educated at Shaw University in Raleigh, North Carolina, Ella Baker was one of the foremost theorists of grassroots, participatory democracy in the United States. Active all her life in the black freedom movement, in 1960 Baker cofounded the Student Nonviolent Coordinating Committee (SNCC). Her advocacy of leadership by ordinary, nonelite people often led her to disagree with the top-down movement strategy of Martin Luther King Jr. and other ministers of the Southern Christian Leadership Conference (SCLC).  AP Photo/Jack Harris.

Baker took a special interest in these students because she found them receptive to her notion of participatory democracy. The granddaughter of slaves, Baker had moved to Harlem in the 1930s, where she worked for New Deal agencies and then the NAACP. She believed in nurturing leaders from the grass roots, encouraging ordinary people to stand up for their rights rather than depend on charismatic figureheads. "My theory is, strong people don't need strong leaders," she once said. Nonetheless, Baker nurtured a generation of young activists in SNCC, including Stokely Carmichael, Anne Moody, John Lewis, and Diane Nash, who went on to become some of the most important civil rights leaders in the United States.

**Freedom Rides**    Emboldened by SNCC's sit-in tactics, in 1961 the Congress of Racial Equality (CORE) organized a series of what were called Freedom Rides on interstate bus lines throughout the South. The aim was to call attention to blatant violations of recent Supreme Court rulings that had declared segregation in interstate commerce unconstitutional. The activists who signed on — mostly young, both black and white — knew that they were taking their lives in their hands. They found courage in song, as civil rights activists had begun to do across the country, with lyrics such as "I'm taking a ride on the Greyhound bus line. . . . Hallelujah, I'm traveling down freedom's main line!"

Courage they needed. Club-wielding Klansmen attacked the buses when they stopped in small towns. Outside Anniston, Alabama, one bus was firebombed; the Freedom Riders escaped only moments before it exploded. Some riders were then brutally beaten. Freedom Riders and news reporters were also viciously attacked by

Klansmen in Birmingham and Montgomery. Despite the violence, state authorities refused to intervene. "I cannot guarantee protection for this bunch of rabble rousers," declared Governor John Patterson of Alabama.

Once again, local officials' refusal to enforce the law left the fate of the Freedom Riders in Washington's hands. The new president, John F. Kennedy, was cautious about civil rights. Despite a campaign commitment, he failed to deliver on a civil rights bill. Elected by a thin margin, Kennedy believed that he could ill afford to lose the support of powerful southern senators. But civil rights was unlike other domestic issues. Its fate was going to be decided not in the halls of Congress, but on the streets of southern cities. Although President Kennedy discouraged the Freedom Rides, beatings shown on the nightly news forced Attorney General Robert Kennedy to dispatch federal marshals. Civil rights activists thus learned the tactical value of nonviolent protest that provoked violent white resistance.

The victories so far had been limited, but the groundwork had been laid for a civil rights offensive that would transform the nation. The NAACP's legal strategy had been followed by the emergence of a major protest movement. And now civil rights leaders focused their attention on Congress.

## Legislating Civil Rights, 1963–1965

The first civil rights law in the nation's history came in 1866 just after the Civil War. Its provisions were long ignored (Chapter 14). A second law was passed during Reconstruction in 1875, but it was declared unconstitutional by the Supreme Court. For nearly ninety years, new civil rights legislation was blocked or filibustered by southern Democrats in Congress. Only a weak, largely symbolic act was passed in 1957 during the Eisenhower administration. But by the early 1960s, with legal precedents in their favor and nonviolent protest awakening the nation, civil rights leaders believed the time had come for a serious civil rights bill. The challenge was getting one through a still-reluctant Congress.

**The Battle for Birmingham**   The road to such a bill began when Martin Luther King Jr. called for demonstrations in "the most segregated city in the United States": Birmingham, Alabama. King and the SCLC needed a concrete victory in Birmingham to validate their strategy of nonviolent direct action. In May 1963, thousands of black marchers protested employment discrimination in Birmingham's department stores. Eugene "Bull" Connor, the city's public safety commissioner, ordered the city's police troops to meet the marchers with violent force: snarling dogs, electric cattle prods, and high-pressure fire hoses. Television cameras captured the scene for the evening news.

While serving a jail sentence for leading the march, King, scribbling in pencil on any paper he could find, composed one of the classic documents of nonviolent direct action: "Letter from Birmingham Jail." "Why direct action?" King asked. "There is a type of constructive, nonviolent tension that is necessary for growth," he began his answer. The civil rights movement sought, King continued, "to create such a crisis and establish such a creative tension." Grounding his appeal in equal parts Christian brotherhood and democratic liberalism, King argued that Americans confronted a moral choice: they could "preserve the evil system of segregation" or take the side of "those great wells of democracy . . . the Constitution and the Declaration of Independence."

Outraged by the brutality in Birmingham and embarrassed by King's imprisonment for leading a nonviolent march, President Kennedy decided that it was time to act. On June 11, 1963, after newly elected Alabama governor George Wallace barred two black students from the state university, Kennedy went on television to denounce racism and promise a new civil rights bill. Many black leaders felt Kennedy's action was long overdue, but they nonetheless hailed this "Second Emancipation Proclamation." That night, Medgar Evers, president of the Mississippi chapter of the NAACP, was shot in the back in his driveway in Jackson by a white supremacist. Evers's martyrdom became a spur to further action (Map 26.3).

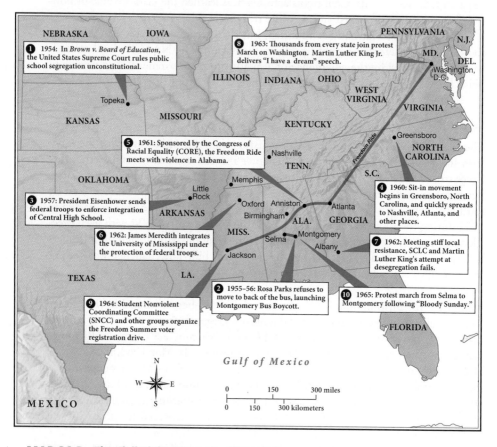

### MAP 26.3   The Civil Rights Struggle, 1954–1965

In the postwar battle for black civil rights, the first major victory was the NAACP litigation of *Brown v. Board of Education*, which declared public school segregation unconstitutional. As indicated on this map, the struggle then quickly spread, raising other issues and seeding new organizations. Other organizations quickly joined the battle and shifted the focus away from the courts to mass action and organization. The year 1965 marked the high point, when violence against the Selma, Alabama, marchers spurred the passage of the Voting Rights Act.

**The March on Washington**   To marshal support for Kennedy's bill, civil rights leaders took advantage of a long-planned event set for that August. It was the massive demonstration in Washington that had first been proposed by A. Philip Randolph in 1941. Working with Bayard Rustin, Randolph revived the idea and in early 1963 called for a march to mark the centennial of the Emancipation Proclamation. Under the leadership of Randolph and Rustin, thousands of volunteers across the country coordinated car pools, "freedom buses," and "freedom trains," and on August 28, 1963, delivered a quarter of a million people to the Lincoln Memorial for the **March on Washington**, officially named the March on Washington for Jobs and Freedom.

Although Randolph and Rustin planned the event, Martin Luther King Jr. was the public face of the march. It was King's dramatic "I Have a Dream" speech, beginning with his admonition that too many black people lived "on a lonely island of poverty" and ending with the exclamation from a traditional black spiritual— "Free at last! Free at last! Thank God almighty, we are free at last!" — that captured the nation's imagination. The sight of 250,000 blacks and whites marching solemnly together marked the high point of the civil rights movement and confirmed King's position as the leading spokesperson for the cause.

To have any chance of getting the civil rights bill through Congress, King, Randolph, and Rustin knew they had to sustain this broad coalition of blacks and whites. They could afford to alienate no one. Reflecting a younger, more militant set of activists, however, SNCC member John Lewis had prepared a provocative speech for that afternoon. In his original draft of the speech, Lewis wrote, "The time will come when we will not confine our marching to Washington. We will march through the South, through the Heart of Dixie, the way Sherman did." Signaling a growing restlessness among black youth, Lewis warned: "We shall fragment the South into a thousand pieces and put them back together again in the image of democracy." Fearing the speech would alienate white supporters, Rustin and others implored Lewis to tone down his rhetoric. With only minutes to spare before he stepped up to the podium, Lewis agreed. He delivered a more conciliatory speech, but his conflict with march organizers signaled an emerging rift in the movement.

Although the March on Washington galvanized public opinion, it changed few congressional votes. Southern senators continued to block Kennedy's legislation. Georgia senator Richard Russell, a leader of the opposition, refused to support any bill that would in his words "bring about social equality and intermingling and amalgamation of the races." Then, tragedies began to pile up, one on another. In September, white supremacists bombed a Baptist church in Birmingham, killing four black girls in Sunday school. Less than two months later, Kennedy himself lay dead, the victim of assassination.

On assuming the presidency, Lyndon Johnson made passing the civil rights bill a priority. A southerner and former Senate majority leader, Johnson was renowned for his fierce persuasive style and tough political bargaining. By appealing to the white South's conscience, invoking the memory of the slain JFK, and practicing his own brand of hardball politics, Johnson overcame the filibuster. In June 1964, Congress approved the most far-reaching civil rights law since Reconstruction. The keystone of the **Civil Rights Act of 1964**, Title VII, outlawed discrimination in employment on the basis of race, religion, national origin, and sex. Another section guaranteed equal access to public accommodations and schools. The law granted new enforcement powers to the U.S. attorney general and established the Equal Employment Opportunity Commission to implement the prohibition against job discrimination.

**Freedom Summer**    The Civil Rights Act was a law with real teeth, but it left untouched the obstacles to black voting. So protesters went back into the streets. In 1964, in what came to be known as Freedom Summer, black organizations mounted a major campaign in Mississippi. The effort drew several thousand volunteers from across the country, including nearly one thousand white college students from the North. Led by the charismatic SNCC activist Robert "Bob" Moses, the four major civil rights organizations (SNCC, CORE, NAACP, and SCLC) spread out across the state. They established freedom schools for black children and conducted a major voter registration drive. Yet so determined was the opposition that only about twelve hundred black voters were registered that summer, at a cost of four murdered civil rights workers and thirty-seven black churches bombed or burned.

The murders strengthened the resolve of the **Mississippi Freedom Democratic Party** (MFDP), which had been founded during Freedom Summer. Banned from the "whites only" Mississippi Democratic Party, MFDP leaders were determined to attend the 1964 Democratic National Convention in Atlantic City, New Jersey, as the legitimate representatives of their state. Inspired by Fannie Lou Hamer, a former sharecropper turned civil rights activist, the MFDP challenged the most powerful figures in the Democratic Party, including President Johnson himself. "Is this America?" Hamer asked party officials when she demanded that the MFDP, and not the all-white Mississippi delegation, be recognized by the convention. Democratic leaders, however, seated the white Mississippi delegation and refused to recognize the MFDP. Demoralized and convinced that the Democratic Party would not change, Bob Moses told television reporters: "I will have nothing to do with the political system any longer." Freedom Summer began with optimism but ended with bitter disappointment.

**Selma and the Voting Rights Act**    Martin Luther King Jr. and the SCLC did not share Moses's skepticism. They believed that another confrontation with southern injustice could provoke further congressional action. In March 1965, James Bevel of the SCLC called for a march from Selma, Alabama, to the state capital, Montgomery, to protest the murder of a voting-rights activist. As soon as the six hundred marchers left Selma, crossing over the Edmund Pettus Bridge, mounted state troopers attacked them with tear gas and clubs. The scene was shown on national television that night, and the day became known as Bloody Sunday. Calling the episode "an American tragedy," President Johnson went back to Congress.

The **Voting Rights Act of 1965**, which was signed by President Johnson on August 6, outlawed the literacy tests and other devices that prevented African Americans from registering to vote, and authorized the attorney general to send federal examiners to register voters in any county where registration was less than 50 percent. Together with the Twenty-Fourth Amendment (ratified in 1964), which outlawed the poll tax in federal elections, the Voting Rights Act enabled millions of African Americans to vote for the first time since Reconstruction.

In the South, the results were stunning. In 1960, only 20 percent of black citizens had been registered to vote; by 1971, registration reached 62 percent (see Map 26.4).

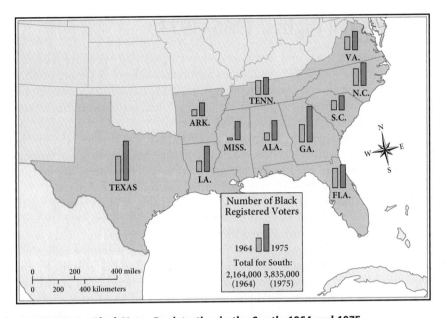

**MAP 26.4   Black Voter Registration in the South, 1964 and 1975**
After passage of the Voting Rights Act of 1965, black registration in the South increased dramatically. The bars on the map show the number of African Americans registered in 1964, before the act was passed, and in 1975, after it had been in effect for ten years. States in the Deep South, such as Mississippi, Alabama, and Georgia, had the biggest increases.

Moreover, across the nation the number of black elected officials began to climb, almost quadrupling from 1,400 to 4,900 between 1970 and 1980 and doubling again by the early 1990s. Most of those elected held local offices—from sheriff to county commissioner—but nonetheless embodied a shift in political representation nearly unimaginable a generation earlier. As Hartman Turnbow, a Mississippi farmer who risked his life to register in 1964, later declared, "It won't never go back where it was."

Something else would never go back either: the liberal New Deal coalition. By the second half of the 1960s, the liberal wing of the Democratic Party had won its battle with the conservative, segregationist wing. Democrats had embraced the civil rights movement and made black equality a cornerstone of a new "rights" liberalism. But over the next generation, between the 1960s and the 1980s, southern whites and many conservative northern whites would respond by switching to the Republican Party. Strom Thurmond, the segregationist senator from South Carolina, symbolically led the revolt by renouncing the Democratic Party and becoming a Republican in 1964. The New Deal coalition—which had joined working-class whites, northern African Americans, urban professionals, and white southern segregationists together in a fragile political alliance since the 1930s—was beginning to crumble.

| IN YOUR OWN WORDS | How did the civil rights movement achieve its major legal and legislative victories between 1954 and 1965? |
|---|---|

# Beyond Civil Rights, 1966–1973

Supreme Court decisions and new laws do not automatically produce changes in society. But in the mid-1960s, civil rights advocates confronted a more profound issue: perhaps even protests were not enough. In 1965, Bayard Rustin wrote of the need to move "from protest to politics" in order to build institutional black power. Some black leaders, such as the young SNCC activists Stokely Carmichael, Frances Beal, and John Lewis, grew frustrated with the slow pace of reform and the stubborn resistance of whites. Still others believed that addressing black poverty and economic disadvantage remained the most important objective. Neither new laws nor long marches appeared capable of meeting these varied and complex challenges.

The conviction that civil rights alone were incapable of guaranteeing equality took hold in many communities of color in this period. African Americans were joined by Mexican Americans, Puerto Ricans, and American Indians. They came at the problem of inequality from different perspectives, but each group asked a similar question: As crucial as legal equality was, how much did it matter if most people of color remained in or close to poverty, if white society still regarded nonwhites as inferior, and if the major social and political institutions in the country were run by whites? Black leaders and representatives of other nonwhite communities increasingly asked themselves this question as they searched for ways to build on the achievements of the civil rights decade of 1954–1965.

## Black Nationalism

Seeking answers to these questions led many African Americans to embrace **black nationalism**. The philosophy of black nationalism signified many things in the 1960s. It could mean everything from pride in one's community to total separatism, from building African American–owned businesses to wearing dashikis in honor of African traditions. Historically, nationalism had emphasized black pride, "self-help" (African Americans creating their own community institutions), and black people's right to shape their own destiny. In the late nineteenth century, Frederick Douglass stood as a primary inspiration, and nationalists founded the Back to Africa movement. In the 1920s the nationalist Marcus Garvey inspired African Americans to take pride in their racial heritage (Chapter 21).

In the early 1960s, the leading exponent of black nationalism was the **Nation of Islam**, which fused a rejection of Christianity with a strong philosophy of self-improvement. Black Muslims, as they were known, adhered to a strict code of personal behavior; men were recognizable by their dark suits, white shirts, and ties, women by their long dresses and head coverings. Black Muslims preached an apocalyptic brand of Islam, anticipating the day when Allah would banish the white "devils" and give the black nation justice. Although its full converts numbered only about ten thousand, the Nation of Islam had a wide popular following among African Americans in northern cities.

**Malcolm X**   The most charismatic Black Muslim was Malcolm X (the *X* stood for his African family name, lost under slavery). A spellbinding speaker, Malcolm X preached a philosophy of militant separatism, although he advocated violence only for self-defense. Hostile to mainstream civil rights organizations, he caustically referred to the 1963 March on Washington as the "Farce on Washington." Malcolm X said plainly, "I believe in the brotherhood of man, all men, but I don't believe in brotherhood with anybody who doesn't want brotherhood with me." Malcolm X had little interest in changing the minds of hostile whites. Strengthening the black community, he believed, represented a surer path to freedom and equality.

In 1964, after a power struggle with founder Elijah Muhammad, Malcolm X broke with the Nation of Islam. While he remained a black nationalist, he moderated his antiwhite views and began to talk of a class struggle uniting poor whites and blacks. Following an inspiring trip to the Middle East, where he saw Muslims of all races worshipping together, Malcolm X formed the Organization of Afro-American Unity to promote black pride and to work with traditional civil rights groups. But he got no further. On February 21, 1965, Malcolm X was assassinated while delivering a speech in Harlem. Three Black Muslims were later convicted of his murder.

**Black Power**    A more secular brand of black nationalism emerged in 1966 when SNCC and CORE activists, following the lead of Stokely Carmichael, began to call for black self-reliance under the banner of Black Power. Advocates of Black Power asked fundamental questions: If alliances with whites were necessary to achieve racial justice, as King believed they were, did that make African Americans dependent on the good intentions of whites? If so, could black people trust those good intentions in the long run? Increasingly, those inclined toward Black Power believed that African Americans should build economic and political power in their own communities. Such power would translate into a less dependent relationship with white America. "For once," Carmichael wrote, "black people are going to use the words they want to use—not the words whites want to hear."

Spurred by the Black Power slogan, African American activists turned their attention to the poverty and social injustice faced by so many black people. President Johnson had declared the War on Poverty, and black organizers joined, setting up day care centers, running community job training programs, and working to improve housing and health care in urban neighborhoods. In major cities such as Philadelphia, New York, Chicago, and Pittsburgh, activists sought to open jobs in police and fire departments and in construction and transportation to black workers, who had been excluded from these occupations for decades. Others worked to end police harassment—a major problem in urban black communities—and to help black entrepreneurs receive small-business loans. CORE leader Floyd McKissick explained, "Black Power is not Black Supremacy; it is a united Black Voice reflecting racial pride."

The attention to racial pride led some African Americans to reject white society and to pursue more authentic cultural forms. In addition to focusing on economic disadvantage, Black Power emphasized black pride and self-determination. Those subscribing to these beliefs wore African clothing, chose natural hairstyles, and celebrated black history, art, and literature. The Black Arts movement thrived, and musical tastes shifted from the crossover sounds of Motown to the soul music of Philadelphia, Memphis, and Chicago.

**Black Panther Party**    One of the most radical nationalist groups was the **Black Panther Party**, founded in Oakland, California, in 1966 by two college students, Huey Newton and Bobby Seale. A militant organization dedicated to protecting African Americans from police violence, the Panthers took their cue from the

**The Black Panther Party** One of the most radical organizations of the 1960s, the Black Panther Party was founded in 1966 by Bobby Seale and Huey Newton (shown together in the photograph on the left) in Oakland, California. Its members carried weapons, advocated socialism, and fought police brutality in black communities, but they also ran into their own trouble with the law. Nevertheless, the party had great success in reaching ordinary people, often with programs targeted at the poor. On the right, party members distribute a free meal to the public in New Haven, Connecticut, in 1969. LEFT: © Bruno Barbey/ Magnum Photos. RIGHT: David Fenton/Getty Images.

slain Malcolm X. They vehemently opposed the Vietnam War and declared their affinity for Third World revolutionary movements and armed struggle (Map 26.5). In their manifesto, "What We Want, What We Believe," the Panthers outlined their Ten Point Program for black liberation.

The Panthers' organization spread to other cities in the late 1960s, where members undertook a wide range of community-organizing projects. Their free breakfast program for children and their testing program for sickle-cell anemia, an inherited disease with a high incidence among African Americans, were especially popular. However, the Panthers' radicalism and belief in armed self-defense resulted in violent clashes with police. Newton was charged with murdering a police officer, several Panthers were killed by police, and dozens went to prison. Moreover, under its domestic counterintelligence program, the Federal Bureau of Investigation (FBI) had begun disrupting party activities.

**Young Lords** Among those inspired by the Black Panthers were Puerto Ricans in New York. Their vehicle was the **Young Lords Organization** (YLO), later renamed the Young Lords Party. Like the Black Panthers, YLO activists sought

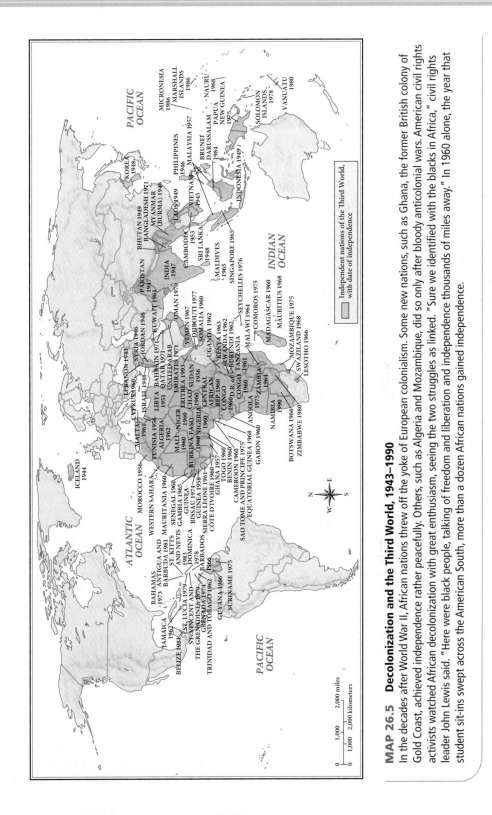

**MAP 26.5　Decolonization and the Third World, 1943–1990**

In the decades after World War II, African nations threw off the yoke of European colonialism. Some new nations, such as Ghana, the former British colony of Gold Coast, achieved independence rather peacefully. Others, such as Algeria and Mozambique, did so only after bloody anticolonial wars. American civil rights activists watched African decolonization with great enthusiasm, seeing the two struggles as linked. "Sure we identified with the blacks in Africa," civil rights leader John Lewis said. "Here were black people, talking of freedom and liberation and independence thousands of miles away." In 1960 alone, the year that student sit-ins swept across the American South, more than a dozen African nations gained independence.

self-determination for Puerto Ricans, both those in the United States and those on the island in the Caribbean. In practical terms, the YLO focused on improving neighborhood conditions: city garbage collection was notoriously poor in East Harlem, where most Puerto Ricans lived, and slumlords had allowed the housing to become squalid. Women in the YLO were especially active, protesting sterilization campaigns against Puerto Rican women and fighting to improve access to health care. As was true of so many nationalist groups, immediate victories for the YLO were few, but their dedicated community organizing produced a generation of leaders (many of whom later went into politics) and awakened community consciousness.

**The New Urban Politics**     Black Power also inspired African Americans to work within the political system. By the mid-1960s, black residents neared 50 percent of the population in several major American cities — such as Atlanta, Cleveland, Detroit, and Washington, D.C. Black Power in these cities was not abstract; it counted in real votes. Residents of Gary, Indiana, and Cleveland, Ohio, elected the first black mayors of large cities in 1967. Richard Hatcher in Gary and Carl Stokes in Cleveland helped forge a new urban politics in the United States. Their campaign teams registered thousands of black voters and made alliances with enough whites to create a working majority. Many saw Stokes's victory, in particular, as heralding a new day. As one of Stokes's campaign staffers said: "If Carl Stokes could run for mayor in the eighth largest city in America, then maybe who knows. We could be senators. We could be anything we wanted."

Having met with some political success, black leaders gathered in Gary for the 1972 National Black Political Convention. In a meeting that brought together radicals, liberals, and centrists, debate centered on whether to form a third political party. Hatcher recalled that many in attendance believed that "there was going to be a black third party." In the end, however, delegates decided to "give the Democratic Party one more chance." Instead of creating a third party, the convention issued the National Black Political Agenda, which included calls for community control of schools in black neighborhoods, national health insurance, and the elimination of the death penalty.

Democrats failed to enact the National Black Political Agenda, but African Americans were increasingly integrated into American political institutions. By the end of the century, black elected officials had become commonplace in major American cities. There were forty-seven African American big-city mayors by the 1990s, and blacks had led most of the nation's most prominent cities: Atlanta, Chicago, Detroit, Los Angeles, New York, Philadelphia, and Washington, D.C. These politicians had translated black power not into a wholesale rejection of white society but into a revitalized liberalism that would remain an indelible feature of urban politics for the rest of the century.

## Urban Disorder

Black Power was not, fundamentally, a violent political ideology. But violence did play a decisive role in the politics of black liberation in the mid-1960s. Too many Americans, white and black, had little knowledge or understanding of the rage that existed just below the surface in many poor northern black neighborhoods. That rage boiled over in a wave of riots that struck the nation's cities in mid-decade. The first "long hot summer" began in July 1964 in New York City when police shot a black criminal suspect in Harlem. Angry youths looted and rioted there for a week. Over the next four years, the volatile issue of police brutality set off riots in dozens of cities.

In August 1965, the arrest of a young black motorist in the Watts section of Los Angeles sparked six days of rioting that left thirty-four people dead. "There is a different type of Negro emerging," one riot participant told investigators. "They are not going to wait for the evolutionary process for their rights to be a man." The riots of 1967, however, were the most serious, engulfing twenty-two cities in July and August. Forty-three people were killed in Detroit alone, nearly all of them black, and $50 million worth of property was destroyed. President Johnson called in the National Guard and U.S. Army troops, many of them having just returned from Vietnam, to restore order.

Johnson, who believed that the Civil Rights Act and the Voting Rights Act had immeasurably helped African Americans, was stunned by the rioting. Despondent at the news from Watts, "he refused to look at the cables from Los Angeles," recalled one aide. Virtually all black leaders condemned the rioting, though they understood its origins in poverty and deprivation. At a meeting in Watts, Martin Luther King Jr. admitted that he had "failed to take the civil rights movement to the masses of the people." His appearance appeased few. "We don't need your dreams; we need jobs!" one heckler shouted at King.

Following the gut-wrenching riots in Detroit and Newark in 1967, Johnson appointed a presidential commission, headed by Illinois governor Otto Kerner, to investigate the causes of the violence. Released in 1968, the Kerner Commission Report was a searing look at race in America, the most honest and forthright government document about race since the Presidential Committee on Civil Rights' 1947 report "To Secure These Rights." "Our nation is moving toward two societies," the Kerner Commission Report concluded, "one black, one white — separate and unequal." The report did not excuse the brick-throwing, firebombing, and looting of the previous summers, but it placed the riots in sociological context. Shut out of white-dominated society, impoverished African Americans felt they had no stake in the social order.

Stirred by turmoil in the cities, and seeing the limitations of his civil rights achievements, Martin Luther King Jr. began to expand his vision beyond civil rights to confront the deep-seated problems of poverty and racism in America as a whole. He criticized President Johnson and Congress for prioritizing the war in Vietnam over the fight against poverty at home, and he planned a massive movement called the Poor People's Campaign to fight economic injustice. To advance that cause, he went to Memphis, Tennessee, to support a strike by predominantly black sanitation workers. There, on April 4, 1968, he was assassinated by escaped white convict James Earl Ray. King's death set off a further round of urban rioting, with major violence breaking out in more than a hundred cities.

Tragically, King was murdered before achieving the transformations he sought: an end to racial injustice and a solution to poverty. The civil rights movement had helped set in motion permanent, indeed revolutionary, changes in American race relations. Jim Crow segregation ended, federal legislation ensured black Americans' most basic civil rights, and the white monopoly on political power in the South was broken. However, by 1968, the fight over civil rights had also divided the nation. The Democratic Party was splitting, and a new conservatism was gaining strength. Many whites felt that the issue of civil rights was receiving too much attention, to the detriment of other national concerns. The riots of 1965, 1967, and 1968 further alienated many whites, who blamed the violence on the inability of Democratic officials to maintain law and order.

## Rise of the Chicano Movement

Mexican Americans had something of a counterpart to Martin Luther King Jr.: Cesar Chavez. In Chavez's case, however, economic struggle in community organizations and the labor movement had shaped his approach to mobilizing society's disadvantaged. He and Dolores Huerta had worked for the Community Service Organization (CSO), a California group founded in the 1950s to promote Mexican political participation and civil rights. Leaving that organization in 1962, Chavez concentrated on the agricultural region around Delano, California. With Huerta, he organized the **United Farm Workers (UFW)**, a union for migrant workers.

Huerta was a brilliant organizer, but the deeply spiritual and ascetic Chavez embodied the moral force behind what was popularly called La Causa. A 1965 grape pickers' strike led the UFW to call a nationwide boycott of table grapes, bringing Chavez huge publicity and backing from the AFL-CIO. In a bid for attention to the struggle, Chavez staged a hunger strike in 1968, which ended dramatically after twenty-eight days with Senator Robert F. Kennedy at his side to break the fast. Victory came in 1970 when California grape growers signed contracts recognizing the UFW.

Mexican Americans shared many economic circumstances with African Americans — especially access to jobs — but they also had unique concerns: the status of the Spanish language in schools, for instance, and immigration policy. Mexican Americans had been politically active since the 1940s, aiming to surmount factors that obstructed their political involvement: poverty, language barriers, and discrimination. Their efforts began to pay off in the 1960s, when the Mexican American Political Association (MAPA) mobilized support for John F. Kennedy and worked successfully with other organizations to elect Mexican American candidates such as Edward Roybal of California and Henry González of Texas to Congress. Two other organizations, the **Mexican American Legal Defense and Education Fund (MALDEF)** and the Southwest Voter Registration and Education Project, carried the fight against discrimination to Washington, D.C., and mobilized Mexican Americans into an increasingly powerful voting bloc.

Younger Mexican Americans grew impatient with civil rights groups such as MAPA and MALDEF, however. The barrios of Los Angeles and other western cities produced the militant Brown Berets, modeled on the Black Panthers (who wore black berets). Rejecting their elders' assimilationist approach (that is, a belief in adapting to Anglo society), fifteen hundred Mexican American students met in Denver in 1969 to hammer out a new political and cultural agenda. They proclaimed a new term, *Chicano* (and its feminine form, *Chicana*), to replace *Mexican American*, and later organized a political party, **La Raza Unida** (People United), to promote Chicano interests. Young Chicana feminists formed a number of organizations, including Las Hijas (The Daughters), that organized women both on college campuses and in the barrios. In California and many southwestern states, students staged demonstrations to press for bilingual education, the hiring of more Chicano teachers, and the creation of Chicano studies programs. By the 1970s, dozens of such programs were offered at universities throughout the region.

## The American Indian Movement

American Indians, inspired by the Black Power and Chicano movements, organized to address their unique circumstances. Numbering nearly 800,000 in the 1960s, native people were exceedingly diverse—divided by language, tribal history, region, and degree of integration into American life. As a group, they shared a staggering unemployment rate—ten times the national average—and were the worst off in housing, disease rates, and access to education. Native people also had an often troubling relationship with the federal government. In the 1960s, the prevailing spirit of protest swept through Native communities. Young militants challenged their elders in the National Congress of American Indians. Beginning in 1960, the National Indian Youth Council (NIYC), under the slogan "For a Greater Indian America," promoted the ideal of Native Americans as a single ethnic group. The effort to both unite Indians and celebrate individual tribal culture proved a difficult balancing act.

The NIYC had substantial influence within tribal communities, but two other organizations, the militant Indians of All Tribes (IAT) and the **American Indian Movement (AIM)**, attracted more attention in the larger society. These groups embraced the concept of Red Power, and beginning in 1968 they staged escalating protests to draw attention to Indian concerns, especially the concerns of urban Indians, many of whom had been encouraged, or forced, to leave reservations by the federal government in earlier decades. In 1969, members of the IAT occupied the deserted federal penitentiary on Alcatraz Island in San Francisco Bay and proclaimed: "We will purchase said Alcatraz Island for twenty-four dollars in glass beads and red cloth, a precedent set by the white man's purchase of a similar island [Manhattan] about 300 years ago." In 1972, AIM members joined the Trail of Broken Treaties, a march sponsored by a number of Indian groups. When AIM activists seized the headquarters of the hated Bureau of Indian Affairs in Washington, D.C., and ransacked the building, older tribal leaders denounced them.

However, AIM managed to focus national media attention on Native American issues with a siege at Wounded Knee, South Dakota, in February 1973. The site of the infamous 1890 massacre of the Sioux by the U.S. military, Wounded Knee was situated on the Pine Ridge Reservation, where young AIM activists had cultivated ties to sympathetic elders. For more than two months, AIM members occupied a small collection of buildings, surrounded by a cordon of FBI agents and U.S. marshals. Several gun battles left two dead, and the siege was finally brought to a negotiated end. Although upsetting to many white onlookers and Indian elders alike, AIM protests attracted widespread mainstream media coverage and spurred government action on tribal issues.

| IN YOUR OWN WORDS | What social conditions prompted many Americans to seek remedies beyond formal legal equality on the basis of race? How successful were those remedies? |

# Summary

African Americans and others who fought for civil rights from World War II through the early 1970s sought equal rights and economic opportunity. That quest was also inspired by various forms of nationalism that called for self-determination for minority groups. For most of the first half of the twentieth century, African Americans faced a harsh Jim Crow system in the South and a segregated, though more open, society in the North. Segregation was maintained by a widespread belief in black inferiority and by a southern political system that denied African Americans the vote. In the Southwest and West, Mexican Americans, Native Americans, and Americans of Asian descent faced discriminatory laws and social practices that marginalized them.

The civil rights movement attacked racial inequality in three ways. First, the movement sought equality under the law for all Americans, regardless of race. This required patient work through the judicial system and the more arduous task of winning congressional legislation, such as the Civil Rights Act of 1964 and the Voting Rights Act of 1965. Second, grassroots activists, using nonviolent protest, pushed all levels of government (from city to federal) to abide by Supreme Court decisions (such as *Brown v. Board of Education*) and civil rights laws. Third, the movement worked to open economic opportunity for minority populations. This was embodied in the 1963 March on Washington for Jobs and Freedom. Ultimately, the civil rights movement successfully established the principle of legal equality, but it faced more difficult problems in fighting poverty and creating widespread economic opportunity.

The limitations of the civil rights model led black activists — along with Mexican Americans, Native Americans, and others — to adopt a more nationalist stance after 1966. Nationalism stressed the creation of political and economic power in communities of color, the celebration of racial heritage, and the rejection of white cultural standards.

# Chapter 26 Review

## KEY TERMS

**Identify and explain the significance of each term below.**

rights liberalism (p. 755)

Brotherhood of Sleeping Car Porters (p. 758)

Congress of Racial Equality (CORE) (p. 759)

"To Secure These Rights" (p. 760)

States' Rights Democratic Party (p. 761)

American GI Forum (p. 762)

Community Services Organization (CSO) (p. 762)

*Brown v. Board of Education of Topeka* (p. 765)

Montgomery Bus Boycott (p. 767)

Southern Christian Leadership Conference (SCLC) (p. 767)

Student Nonviolent Coordinating Committee (SNCC) (p. 767)

March on Washington (p. 771)

Civil Rights Act of 1964 (p. 771)

Mississippi Freedom Democratic Party
  (p. 772)

Voting Rights Act of 1965 (p. 772)

black nationalism (p. 774)

Nation of Islam (p. 774)

Black Panther Party (p. 775)

Young Lords Organization (p. 776)

United Farm Workers (UFW) (p. 780)

Mexican American Legal Defense
  and Education Fund (MALDEF)
  (p. 780)

La Raza Unida (p. 780)

American Indian Movement
  (AIM) (p. 781)

## REVIEW QUESTIONS

**Answer these questions to demonstrate your understanding of the chapter's main ideas.**

1. What factors best explain why and how the civil rights movement developed between 1941 and 1954?
2. How did the civil rights movement achieve its major legal and legislative victories between 1954 and 1965?
3. What social conditions prompted many Americans to seek remedies beyond formal legal equality on the basis of race? How successful were those remedies?
4. One of the most significant themes of the period from 1945 to the 1980s is the growth of the power of the federal government. (See "Politics and Power" and "American and National Identity" on the thematic timeline on p. 696.) In what ways is the civil rights movement also part of that story?

## CHRONOLOGY

**As you read, ask yourself why this chapter begins and ends with these dates and identify the links among related events.**

| | |
|---|---|
| **1941** | • A. Philip Randolph proposes march on Washington |
| | • Roosevelt issues Executive Order 8802 |
| **1942** | • Double V Campaign launched |
| | • Congress of Racial Equality (CORE) founded |
| **1947** | • "To Secure These Rights" published |
| | • Jackie Robinson integrates major league baseball |
| | • *Mendez v. Westminster School District* |
| **1948** | • States' Rights Democratic Party (Dixiecrats) founded |

| | |
|---|---|
| **1954** | • *Brown v. Board of Education of Topeka* |
| **1955** | • Emmett Till murdered (August) |
| | • Montgomery Bus Boycott begins (December) |
| **1956** | • Southern Manifesto issued against *Brown* ruling |
| **1957** | • Desegregation of Little Rock Central High School |
| | • Southern Christian Leadership Conference (SCLC) founded |
| **1960** | • Greensboro, North Carolina, sit-ins (February) |
| | • Student Nonviolent Coordinating Committee (SNCC) founded (April) |
| **1961** | • Freedom Rides (May) |
| **1963** | • Demonstrations in Birmingham, Alabama |
| | • March on Washington for Jobs and Freedom (August) |
| **1964** | • Civil Rights Act passed by Congress |
| | • Freedom Summer |
| **1965** | • Voting Rights Act passed by Congress |
| | • Malcolm X assassinated (February 21) |
| | • Riot in Watts neighborhood of Los Angeles (August) |
| **1966** | • Black Panther Party founded |
| **1967** | • Riots in Detroit and Newark |
| **1968** | • Martin Luther King Jr. assassinated (April 4) |
| **1969** | • Young Lords founded |
| | • American Indian Occupation of Alcatraz |
| **1972** | • National Black Political Convention |
| | • "Trail of Broken Treaties" protest |

# 27

# Uncivil Wars: Liberal Crisis and Conservative Rebirth

## 1961–1972

**IDENTIFY THE BIG IDEA**

What were liberalism's social and political achievements in the 1960s, and how did debates over liberal values contribute to conflict at home and reflect war abroad?

**THE CIVIL RIGHTS MOVEMENT STIRRED AMERICAN LIBERALS AND** pushed them to launch bold new government initiatives to advance racial equality. That progressive spirit inspired an expansive reform agenda that came to include women's rights, new social programs for the poor and the aged, job training, environmental laws, and other educational and social benefits for the middle class. All told, Congress passed more liberal legislation between 1964 and 1972 than in any period since the 1930s. The great bulk of it came during the 1965–1966 legislative session, one of the most active in American history. Liberalism was at high tide.

It did not stay there long. Liberalism quickly came under assault from two directions. First, young, left-leaning activists became frustrated with slow progress on civil rights and rebelled against the Vietnam War. Some of them had been among the young idealists inspired by President John F. Kennedy's inaugural address and the civil rights movement. Now they rejected everything that Cold War liberalism stood for. Their rebellion was symbolized by protests at the 1968 Democratic National Convention in Chicago, where police teargassed and clubbed antiwar demonstrators, who chanted (as the TV cameras rolled), "The whole world is watching!" Inside the convention hall, the proceedings were chaotic, the atmosphere poisonous, the delegates bitterly divided over Vietnam.

A second assault on liberalism came from conservatives, who found their footing after being marginalized during the 1950s. Conservatives opposed the dramatic expansion of the federal government under President Lyndon B. Johnson and disdained the "permissive society" they believed liberalism had encouraged. Advocating law and order, belittling welfare, and resisting key civil rights reforms, conservatives leaped back to political life in the sixties. Their champion was Barry Goldwater, a Republican senator from Arizona, who warned that "a government big enough to give you everything you want is also big enough to take away everything you have."

The clashing of left, right, and center made the years between the inauguration of President Kennedy in 1961 and the landslide reelection of Richard Nixon in 1972 one of the most contentious, complicated, and explosive eras in American history. There were thousands of marches and demonstrations; massive new federal programs aimed at achieving civil rights, ending poverty, and extending the welfare state; and new voices among women, African Americans, Latinos, and gay men and lesbians demanding to be heard. With heated, vitriolic rhetoric on all sides, these developments overlapped with political assassinations and violence both overseas and at home. In this chapter, we undertake to explain how the rekindling of liberal reform under the twin auspices of the civil rights movement and the leadership of President Johnson gave way to a profound liberal crisis and the resurgence of conservatism.

# Liberalism at High Tide

In May 1964, Lyndon B. Johnson, president for barely six months, delivered the commencement address at the University of Michigan, where he offered a grand and inspirational vision of a new liberal age. "We have the opportunity to move not only toward the rich society and the powerful society," Johnson continued, "but upward to the **Great Society**." As the graduates listened, Johnson spelled out what he meant: "The Great Society rests on abundance and liberty for all. It demands an end to poverty and racial injustice." Even this, Johnson declared, was just the beginning. He would push to renew American education, rebuild the cities, and restore the natural environment. Ambitious, even audacious, Johnson's vision was a New Deal for a new era. A tragic irony, however, was that he held the presidency at all.

## John F. Kennedy's Promise

In 1961, three years before Johnson's Great Society speech, John F. Kennedy declared at his presidential inauguration: "Let the word go forth from this time and place, to friend and foe alike, that the torch has been passed to a new generation of Americans." He challenged his fellow citizens to "ask what you can do for your country," a call to service that inspired many Americans. The British journalist Henry Fairley called Kennedy's activism "the politics of expectation." Over time, the expectations

Kennedy embodied, combined with his ability to inspire a younger generation, encouraged the emerging spirit of liberal reform.

Kennedy's legislative record did not live up to his promising image. This was not entirely his fault; congressional partisanship and resistance stymied many presidents in the twentieth century. Kennedy's domestic advisors devised bold plans for health insurance for the aged, a new antipoverty program, and a tax cut. After enormous pressure from Martin Luther King Jr. and other civil rights leaders—and pushed by the demonstrations in Birmingham, Alabama, in 1963—they added a civil rights bill. None of these initiatives went anywhere in the Senate, where powerful conservative interests practiced an old legislative art: delay, delay, delay. All Kennedy's bills were at a virtual standstill when tragedy struck.

On November 22, 1963, Kennedy was in Dallas, Texas, on a political trip. As he and his wife, Jacqueline, rode in an open car past the Texas School Book Depository, he was shot through the head and neck by a sniper. He died within the hour. (The accused killer, twenty-four-year-old Lee Harvey Oswald, was himself killed while in custody a few days later by an assassin, a Dallas nightclub owner named Jack Ruby.) Before Air Force One left Dallas to take the president's body back to Washington, a grim-faced Lyndon Johnson was sworn in as Kennedy's successor.

Kennedy's youthful image, the trauma of his assassination, and the nation's sense of loss contributed to a powerful Kennedy mystique. His canonization after death capped what had been an extraordinarily stage-managed presidency. An admiring country saw in Jack and Jackie Kennedy an ideal American marriage (though JFK was, in fact, an obsessive womanizer); in Kennedy the epitome of robust good health (though he was actually afflicted by Addison's disease); and in the Kennedy White House a glamorous world of high fashion and celebrity. No other presidency ever matched the Kennedy aura, but every president after him embraced the idea that image mattered as much as reality in conducting a politically effective presidency.

## Lyndon B. Johnson and the Great Society

In many ways, Lyndon Johnson was the opposite of Kennedy. A seasoned Texas politician and longtime Senate leader, Johnson was most at home in the back rooms of power. He was a rough-edged character who had scrambled his way up, with few scruples, to wealth and political eminence. But he never forgot his modest, hill-country origins or lost his sympathy for the downtrodden. Johnson lacked Kennedy's style, but he rose to the political challenge after Kennedy's assassination, applying his astonishing energy and negotiating skills to revive several of Kennedy's stalled programs, and many more of his own, in the ambitious Great Society.

On assuming the presidency, Johnson promptly pushed for civil rights legislation as a memorial to his slain predecessor. His motives were complex. As a southerner who had previously opposed civil rights for African Americans, Johnson wished to prove that he was more than a regional figure—he would be the president of all the people. He also wanted to make a mark on history, telling Martin Luther King Jr. and other black leaders to lace up their sneakers because he would move so fast on civil rights they would be running to catch up. Politically, the choice was risky. Johnson would please the Democratic Party's liberal wing, but because most northern African Americans already voted Democratic, the party would gain few

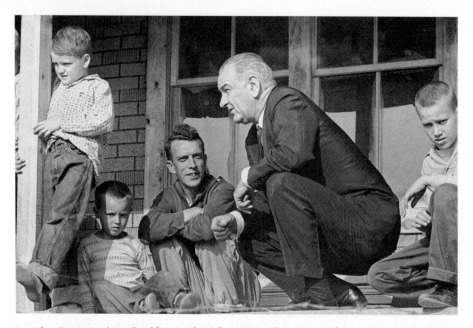

**The Great Society** President Lyndon Johnson toured poverty-stricken regions of the country in 1964. Here he visits with Tom Fletcher, a father of eight children in Martin County, Kentucky. Johnson envisioned a dramatic expansion of liberal social programs, both to assist the needy and to strengthen the middle class, that he called the Great Society. Bettmann/Getty Images.

additional votes. Moreover, southern white Democrats would likely revolt, dividing the party at a time when Johnson's legislative agenda most required unanimity. But Johnson pushed ahead, and the 1964 Civil Rights Act stands, in part, as a testament to the president's political risk-taking.

More than civil rights, what drove Johnson hardest was his determination to "end poverty in our time." The president called it a national disgrace that in the midst of plenty, one-fifth of all Americans — hidden from most people's sight in Appalachia, urban ghettos, migrant labor camps, and Indian reservations — lived in poverty. But, Johnson declared, "for the first time in our history, it is possible to conquer poverty."

The **Economic Opportunity Act** of 1964, which created a series of programs to reach these Americans, was the president's answer — what he called the War on Poverty. This legislation included several different initiatives. Head Start provided free nursery schools to prepare disadvantaged preschoolers for kindergarten. The Job Corps and Upward Bound provided young people with training and employment. Volunteers in Service to America (VISTA), modeled on the Peace Corps, offered technical assistance to the urban and rural poor. An array of regional development programs focused on spurring economic growth in impoverished areas. On balance, the 1964 legislation provided services to the poor rather than jobs, leading some critics to charge the War on Poverty with doing too little.

**The 1964 Election**   With the Civil Rights Act passed and his War on Poverty initiatives off the ground, Johnson turned his attention to the upcoming presidential election. Not content to govern in Kennedy's shadow, he wanted a national mandate of his own. Privately, Johnson saw himself less as akin Kennedy than as the heir of Franklin Roosevelt, whose political skills he had long admired, and the expansive liberalism of the 1930s. He reminded his advisors never to forget "the meek and the humble and the lowly," because "President Roosevelt never did."

In the 1964 election, Johnson faced Republican Barry Goldwater of Arizona. An archconservative, Goldwater ran on an anticommunist, antigovernment platform, offering "a choice, not an echo"—meaning he represented a genuinely conservative alternative to liberalism rather than the echo of liberalism offered by the moderate wing of the Republican Party (Chapter 24). Goldwater campaigned against the Civil Rights Act of 1964 and promised a more vigorous Cold War foreign policy. Among those supporting him was former actor Ronald Reagan, whose speech on behalf of Goldwater at the Republican convention, called "A Time for Choosing," made him a rising star in the party.

But Goldwater's strident foreign policy alienated voters. "Extremism in the defense of liberty is no vice," he told Republicans at the convention. Moreover, there remained strong national sentiment for Kennedy. Telling Americans that he was running to fulfill Kennedy's legacy, Johnson and his running mate, Hubert H. Humphrey of Minnesota, won in a landslide (Map 27.1). In the long run, Goldwater's candidacy marked the beginning of a grassroots conservative revolt that would eventually transform the Republican Party. In the short run, however, Johnson's sweeping victory gave him a popular mandate and, equally important, congressional majorities that rivaled FDR's in 1935—just what he and liberal Democrats needed to push the Great Society forward.

**MAP 27.1   The Presidential Election of 1964**
This map reveals how one-sided was the victory of Lyndon Johnson over Barry Goldwater in 1964. Except for Arizona, his home state, Goldwater won only five states in the Deep South—not of much immediate consolation to him, but a sure indicator that the South was cutting its historic ties to the Democratic Party. Moreover, although soundly rejected in 1964, Goldwater's far-right critique of "big government" laid the foundation for a Republican resurgence in the 1980s.

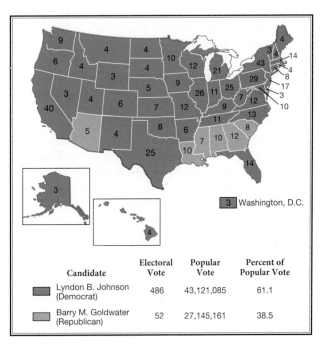

| Candidate | Electoral Vote | Popular Vote | Percent of Popular Vote |
|---|---|---|---|
| Lyndon B. Johnson (Democrat) | 486 | 43,121,085 | 61.1 |
| Barry M. Goldwater (Republican) | 52 | 27,145,161 | 38.5 |

**Great Society Initiatives**    One of Johnson's first successes was breaking a congressional deadlock on education and health care. Passed in April 1965, the Elementary and Secondary Education Act authorized $1 billion in federal funds for teacher training and other educational programs. Standing in his old Texas schoolhouse, Johnson, a former teacher, said: "I believe no law I have signed or will ever sign means more to the future of America." Six months later, Johnson signed the Higher Education Act, providing federal scholarships for college students. Johnson also had the votes he needed to achieve some form of national health insurance. That year, he won passage of two new programs: **Medicare**, a health plan for the elderly funded by a surcharge on Social Security payroll taxes, and **Medicaid**, a health plan for the poor paid for by general tax revenues and administered by the states.

The Great Society's agenda included environmental reform as well: an expanded national park system, improvement of the nation's air and water, protection for endangered species, stronger land-use planning, and highway beautification. Hardly pausing for breath, Johnson oversaw the creation of the Department of Housing and Urban Development (HUD); won funding for hundreds of thousands of units of public housing; made investments in urban rapid transit such as the new Washington, D.C., Metro and the Bay Area Rapid Transit (BART) system in San Francisco; ushered child safety and consumer protection laws through Congress; and helped create the National Endowment for the Arts and the National Endowment for the Humanities to support the work of artists, writers, and scholars.

It even became possible, at this moment of reform zeal, to tackle the nation's discriminatory immigration policy. The Immigration Act of 1965 abandoned the quota system that favored northern Europeans, replacing it with numerical limits that did not discriminate among nations. To promote family reunification, the law also stipulated that close relatives of legal residents in the United States could be admitted outside the numerical limits, an exception that especially benefitted Asian and Latin American immigrants. Since 1965, as a result, immigrants from those regions have become increasingly prominent in American society (Chapter 30).

**Assessing the Great Society**    The Great Society enjoyed mixed results. The proportion of Americans living below the poverty line dropped from 20 percent to 13 percent between 1963 and 1968. Medicare and Medicaid, the most enduring of the Great Society programs, helped millions of elderly and poor citizens afford necessary health care. Further, as millions of African Americans moved into the middle class, the black poverty rate fell by half. Liberals believed they were on the right track.

Conservatives, however, gave more credit for these changes to the decade's booming economy than to government programs. Indeed, conservative critics accused Johnson and other liberals of believing that every social problem could be solved with a government program. In the final analysis, the Great Society dramatically improved the financial situation of the elderly, reached millions of children, and increased the racial diversity of American society and workplaces. However, entrenched poverty remained, racial segregation in the largest cities worsened, and the national distribution of wealth remained highly skewed. In relative terms, the bottom 20 percent remained as far behind as ever. In these arenas, the Great Society made little progress.

# Rebirth of the Women's Movement

In the new era of liberal reform the women's movement reawakened. Inspired by the civil rights movement and legislative advances under the Great Society, but frustrated by the lack of attention both gave to women, feminists entered the political fray and demanded not simply inclusion, but a rethinking of national priorities.

**Labor Feminists**   The women's movement had not languished entirely in the postwar years. Feminist concerns were kept alive in the 1950s and early 1960s by working women, who campaigned for such policies as maternity leave and equal pay for equal work. One historian has called these women "labor feminists," because they belonged to trade unions and fought for equality and dignity in the workplace. "It became apparent to me why so many employers could legally discriminate against women—because it was written right into the law," said one female labor activist. Trade-union women were especially critical in pushing for, and winning, congressional passage of the 1963 **Equal Pay Act**, which established the principle of equal pay for equal work.

Labor feminists were responding to the times. More women—including married women (40 percent by 1970) and mothers with young children (30 percent by 1970)—were working outside the home than ever before. But they faced a labor market that undervalued their contributions. Moreover, most working women faced the "double day": they were expected to earn a paycheck and then return home to domestic labor. One woman put the problem succinctly: "The working mother has no 'wife' to care for her children."

**Betty Friedan and the National Organization for Women**   When Betty Friedan's indictment of suburban domesticity, *The Feminine Mystique*, appeared in 1963, it targeted a different audience: college-educated, middle-class women who found themselves not working for wages but rather stifled by their domestic routine. Tens of thousands of women read Friedan's book and thought, "She's talking about me." *The Feminine Mystique* became a runaway best-seller. Friedan persuaded middle-class women that they needed more than the convenience foods, improved diapers, and better laundry detergents that magazines and television urged them to buy. To live rich and fulfilling lives, they needed education and work outside the home.

Paradoxically, the domesticity described in *The Feminine Mystique* was already crumbling. After the postwar baby boom, women were again having fewer children, aided now by the birth control pill, first marketed in 1960. And as states liberalized divorce laws, more women were divorcing. Educational levels were also rising: by 1970, women made up 42 percent of the college population. All of these changes undermined traditional gender roles and enabled many women to embrace *The Feminine Mystique*'s liberating prescriptions.

Government action also made a difference. In 1961, Kennedy had appointed the **Presidential Commission on the Status of Women**, which issued a 1963 report documenting job and educational discrimination. A bigger breakthrough came when Congress added the word *sex* to the categories protected against discrimination in the Civil Rights Act of 1964. Women suddenly had a powerful legal tool for fighting gender discrimination.

To force compliance with the new act, Friedan and others, including many labor feminists from around the country, founded the **National Organization for Women (NOW)** in 1966. Modeled on the NAACP, NOW intended to be a civil rights organization for women, with the aim of bringing "women into full participation in . . . American society now, exercising all the privileges and responsibilities thereof in truly equal partnership with men." Under Friedan's leadership, membership grew to fifteen thousand by 1971, and NOW became a powerful voice for equal rights.

One of the ironies of the 1960s was the enormous strain that all of this liberal activism placed on the New Deal coalition. Faced with often competing demands from the civil rights movement, feminists, the poor, labor unions, conservative southern Democrats, the suburban middle class, and urban political machines, the old Rooseveltian coalition had begun to fray. Johnson hoped that the New Deal coalition was strong enough to negotiate competing demands among its own constituents while simultaneously resisting conservative attacks. In 1965, that still seemed possible. It would not remain so for long.

| IN YOUR OWN WORDS | What explains the surge in liberal politics and social policy in the early 1960s? |
| --- | --- |

# The Vietnam War Begins

As the accelerating rights revolution placed strain on the Democratic coalition, the war in Vietnam divided the country. In a CBS interview before his death, Kennedy remarked that it was up to the South Vietnamese whether "their war" would be won or lost. But the young president had already placed the United States on a course that would make retreat difficult. Like other U.S. presidents, Kennedy believed that giving up in Vietnam would weaken America's "credibility." Withdrawal "would be a great mistake," he said.

It is impossible to know how JFK would have managed Vietnam had he lived. What is known is that in the fall of 1963, Kennedy had lost patience with Ngo Dinh Diem, the dictatorial head of South Vietnam whom the United States had supported since 1955 (Chapter 24). The president let it be known in Saigon that the United States would support a military coup. Kennedy's hope was that if Diem, reviled throughout the South because of his brutal repression of political opponents, could be replaced by a popular general or other military figure, a stable government would emerge—one strong enough to repel the South Vietnam National Liberation Front (NLF), or Vietcong.

That calculation proved overly optimistic. Emboldened by Kennedy's approval of their plan, a handful of South Vietnamese generals overthrew Diem on November 1, and then brutally killed him and his brother. Rather than stability, the coup brought chaos. South Vietnam fell into a period of turmoil marked by the increasing ungovernability of both the cities and countryside. Kennedy himself was assassinated in late November and would not live to see the grim results of Diem's murder: American engagement in a long and costly civil conflict in the name of fighting communism.

## Escalation Under Johnson

Just as Kennedy had inherited Vietnam from Eisenhower, so Lyndon Johnson inherited Vietnam from Kennedy. Johnson's inheritance was more burdensome, however, for by now only massive American intervention could prevent the collapse of South Vietnam (Map 27.2). Johnson, like Kennedy, was a subscriber to the Cold War tenets of global containment. "I am not going to lose Vietnam," he vowed on taking office. "I am not going to be the President who saw Southeast Asia go the way China went" (Chapter 24).

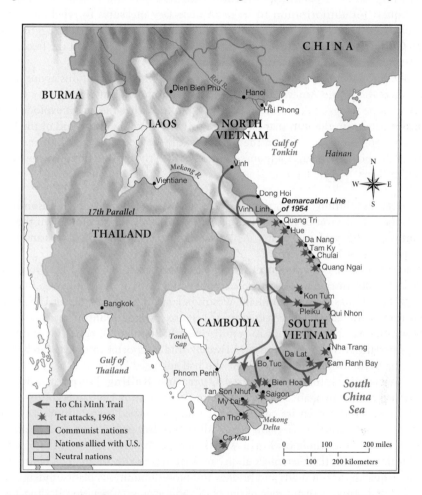

**MAP 27.2   The Vietnam War, 1968**
The Vietnam War was a guerrilla war, fought in skirmishes rather than set-piece battles. Despite repeated airstrikes, the United States was never able to halt the flow of North Vietnamese troops and supplies down the Ho Chi Minh Trail, which wound through Laos and Cambodia. In January 1968, Vietcong forces launched the Tet offensive, a surprise attack on cities and provincial centers across South Vietnam. Although the attackers were pushed back with heavy losses, the Tet offensive revealed the futility of American efforts to suppress the Vietcong guerrillas and marked a turning point in the war.

**Gulf of Tonkin**   It did not take long for Johnson to place his stamp on the war. During the summer of 1964, the president got reports that North Vietnamese torpedo boats had fired on the U.S. destroyer *Maddox* in the Gulf of Tonkin. In the first attack, on August 2, the damage inflicted was limited to a single bullet hole; a second attack, on August 4, later proved to be only misread radar sightings. To Johnson, it didn't matter if the attack was real or imagined; the president believed a wider war was inevitable and issued a call to arms, sending his national approval rating from 42 to 72 percent. In the entire Congress, only two senators voted against his request for authorization to "take all necessary measures to repel any armed attack against the forces of the United States and to prevent further aggression." The **Gulf of Tonkin Resolution**, as it became known, gave Johnson the freedom to conduct operations in Vietnam as he saw fit.

Despite his congressional mandate, Johnson was initially cautious about revealing his plans to the American people. "I had no choice but to keep my foreign policy in the wings . . . ," Johnson later said. "I knew that the day it exploded into a major debate on the war, that day would be the beginning of the end of the Great Society." So he ran in 1964 on the pledge that there would be no escalation — no "American boys" fighting Vietnam's fight, he said. Privately, he doubted the pledge could be kept.

**American Escalation**   With the 1964 election safely behind him, Johnson began an American takeover of the war in Vietnam. The escalation, beginning in the early months of 1965, took two forms: deployment of American ground troops and intensive bombing of North Vietnam.

On March 8, 1965, the first marines waded ashore at Da Nang. By 1966, more than 380,000 American soldiers were stationed in Vietnam; by 1967, 485,000; and by 1968, 536,000. General William Westmoreland, the commander of U.S. forces, and Robert McNamara, the secretary of defense, pushed Johnson to Americanize the ground war in an attempt to stabilize South Vietnam. "I can't run and pull a Chamberlain at Munich," Johnson privately told a reporter in early March 1965, referring to the British prime minister who had appeased Hitler in 1938.

Meanwhile, Johnson authorized **Operation Rolling Thunder**, a massive bombing campaign against North Vietnam that began in 1965 and continued for three years. Over the entire course of the war, the United States dropped twice as many tons of bombs on Vietnam as the Allies had dropped in both Europe and the Pacific during the whole of World War II. To McNamara's surprise, the bombing had little effect on the Vietcong's ability to wage war in the South. The North Vietnamese quickly rebuilt roads and bridges and moved munitions plants underground. Instead of destroying the morale of the North Vietnamese, Operation Rolling Thunder hardened their will to fight. The massive commitment of ground troops and air power devastated Vietnam's countryside, however. After one harsh but not unusual engagement, a commanding officer reported that "it became necessary to destroy the town in order to save it" — a statement that came to symbolize the terrible logic of the war.

The Johnson administration gambled that American superiority in personnel and weaponry would ultimately triumph. This strategy was inextricably tied to political considerations. For domestic reasons, policymakers searched for an elusive middle ground between all-out invasion of North Vietnam, which included the possibility of war with China, and disengagement. "In effect, we are fighting a war of attrition," said General Westmoreland. "The only alternative is a war of annihilation."

## Public Opinion and the War

Johnson gradually grew more confident that his Vietnam policy had the support of the American people. Both Democrats and Republicans approved Johnson's escalation in Vietnam, and so did public opinion polls in 1965 and 1966. But then opinion began to shift.

Every night, Americans saw the carnage of war on their television screens, including images of dead and wounded Americans. One such incident occurred in the first months of fighting in 1965. Television reporter Morley Safer witnessed a marine unit burning the village of Cam Ne to the ground. "Today's operation is the frustration of Vietnam in miniature," Safer explained. America can "win a military victory here, but to a Vietnamese peasant whose home is [destroyed] it will take more than presidential promises to convince him that we are on his side."

With such firsthand knowledge of the war, journalists began to write about a "credibility gap." The Johnson administration, they charged, was concealing bad news about the war's progress. In February 1966, television coverage of hearings by the Senate Foreign Relations Committee (chaired by J. William Fulbright, an outspoken critic of the war) raised further questions about the administration's policy. Johnson complained to his staff in 1966 that "our people can't stand firm in the face of heavy losses, and they can bring down the government." Economic problems put Johnson even more on the defensive. The Vietnam War cost taxpayers $27 billion in 1967, pushing the federal deficit from $9.8 billion to $23 billion. By then, military spending had set in motion the inflationary spiral that would plague the U.S. economy throughout the 1970s.

Out of these troubling developments, an antiwar movement began to crystallize. Little opposition had materialized in 1964, even after Johnson won passage of the Tonkin Resolution. But following the escalation in 1965, groups of students, clergy, civil rights advocates, antinuclear proponents, and even Dr. Benjamin Spock, whose book on child care had helped raise many of the younger activists, began to protest. Their launchpad was an April march of 15,000 people in Washington, D.C., that included a picket line around the White House and speeches denouncing what antiwar activist Paul Potter called "this mad war." Despite their diversity, these opponents of the war shared a skepticism about U.S. policy in Vietnam. They charged variously that intervention was antithetical to American ideals; that an independent, anticommunist South Vietnam was unattainable; and that no American objective justified the suffering that was being inflicted on the Vietnamese people.

## The Student Movement

College students, many of them inspired by the civil rights movement, had already begun to organize and agitate for social change prior to the first antiwar march in 1965. In Ann Arbor, Michigan, they founded **Students for a Democratic Society (SDS)** in 1960. Two years later, they held the first national SDS convention in Port Huron, Michigan. Tom Hayden penned a manifesto, the **Port Huron Statement**, expressing students' disillusionment with the nation's consumer culture and the gulf between rich and poor. "We are people of this generation," Hayden wrote, "bred in at least modest comfort, housed now in universities, looking uncomfortably to the world we inherit." Hayden and SDS sought to shake up what they saw as a complacent nation.

**The New Left**   The founders of SDS referred to their movement as the **New Left** to distinguish themselves from the Old Left—communists and socialists of the 1930s and 1940s. As New Left influence spread, it hit major university towns first—places such as Madison, Wisconsin, and Berkeley, California. One of the first notable demonstrations erupted in the fall of 1964 at the University of California at Berkeley after administrators banned student political activity on university grounds. In protest, student organizations formed the Free Speech Movement and organized a sit-in at the administration building. Some students had just returned from Freedom Summer in Mississippi, radicalized by their experience. One such student, Mario Savio, spoke for many when he compared the conflict in Berkeley to the civil rights struggle in the South: "The same rights are at stake in both places—the right to participate as citizens in a democratic society and to struggle against the same enemy."

Emboldened by the Berkeley movement, students across the nation were soon protesting their universities' academic policies and then, beginning in 1965, the Vietnam War. Students were on the front lines as the campaign against the war escalated. The 1967 Mobilization to End the War brought 100,000 protesters into the streets of San Francisco, while more than 250,000 followed Martin Luther King Jr. from Central Park to the United Nations in New York. Another 100,000 marched on the Pentagon. President Johnson absorbed the blows and counterpunched—"The enemy's hope for victory . . . is in our division, our weariness, our uncertainty," he proclaimed—but it had become clear that Johnson's war, as many began calling it, was no longer uniting the country.

One spur to student protest was the military's Selective Service System, which in 1967 abolished automatic student deferments. To avoid the draft, some young men enlisted in the National Guard or applied for conscientious objector status; others left the country, most often for Canada or Sweden. In public demonstrations, opponents of the war burned their draft cards, picketed induction centers, and on a few occasions broke into Selective Service offices and destroyed records. Antiwar demonstrators numbered in the tens or, at most, hundreds of thousands—a small fraction of American youth—but they were vocal, visible, and determined.

**Young Americans for Freedom**   The New Left was not the only political force on college campuses. Conservative students were less noisy but equally numerous. For them, the 1960s was not about protesting Vietnam, staging student strikes, and idolizing Black Power. Inspired by the group **Young Americans for Freedom (YAF)**, conservative students asserted their faith in "God-given free will" and their concern that the federal government "accumulates power which tends to diminish order and liberty." The YAF, the largest student political organization in the country, defended free enterprise and supported the war in Vietnam. Its founding principles were outlined in "The **Sharon Statement**," drafted (in Sharon, Connecticut) two years before the Port Huron Statement. Young conservatives, many of whom would play important roles in the Reagan administration in the 1980s, rallied to the YAF's call.

**The Counterculture**    While the New Left organized against the political and economic system and the YAF defended it, many other young Americans embarked on a general revolt against authority and middle-class respectability. The "hippie"—identified by ragged blue jeans or army fatigues, flowing skirts, shirts, and blouses, beads, and long unkempt hair—symbolized the new **counterculture**. With roots in the 1950s Beat culture of New York's Greenwich Village and San Francisco's North Beach, the 1960s counterculture was composed largely of white youth alienated from the staid predictability and formality of an older generation. Seeking an ethic of personal freedom and authenticity, they initially turned to folk music for inspiration. Pete Seeger set the tone for the era's idealism with songs such as the 1961 antiwar ballad "Where Have All the Flowers Gone?" In 1963, the year of the civil rights demonstrations in Birmingham and President Kennedy's assassination, Bob Dylan's "Blowin' in the Wind" reflected the impatience of people whose faith in America was wearing thin. Judy Collins and Joan Baez emerged alongside Dylan and pioneered a folk sound that inspired a generation of female musicians.

By the mid-1960s, other winds of change in popular music came from the Beatles, four working-class Brits whose awe-inspiring music, by turns lyrical and

**The Counterculture**   The three-day outdoor Woodstock concert in August 1969 was a defining moment in the rise of the counterculture. The event attracted 400,000 young people, like those pictured here, to Bethel, New York, for a weekend of music, drugs, and sex. The counterculture was distinct from the New Left and was less a political movement than a shifting set of cultural styles, attitudes, and practices. It rejected conformity of all kinds and placed rebellion and contrariness among its highest values. Another concept held dear by the counterculture was, simply, "love." In an era of military violence abroad and police violence at home, many in the counterculture hoped that "peace and love" would prevail instead. Bill Eppridge/The LIFE Picture Collection/Getty Images.

driving, spawned a commercial and cultural phenomenon known as Beatlemania. American youths' embrace of the Beatles, as well as even more rebellious bands such as the Rolling Stones, the Who, and the Doors, deepened the generational divide between young people and their elders. So did the recreational use of drugs—especially marijuana and the hallucinogen popularly known as LSD or acid—which was celebrated in popular music in the second half of the 1960s.

For a brief time, adherents of the counterculture believed that a new age was dawning. In 1967, the "world's first Human Be-In" drew 20,000 people to Golden Gate Park in San Francisco. That summer—known as the Summer of Love—San Francisco's Haight-Ashbury, New York's East Village, Chicago's Uptown neighborhoods, and the Sunset Strip in Los Angeles swelled with young dropouts, drifters, and teenage runaways whom the media dubbed "flower children." Although most young people had little interest in all-out revolt, media coverage made it seem as though all of American youth was rejecting the nation's social and cultural norms.

> **IN YOUR OWN WORDS**    What led President Johnson to escalate the war in Vietnam, and how did Americans respond?

# Days of Rage, 1968–1972

By 1968, a sense of crisis gripped the country. Riots in the cities, campus unrest, and a nose-thumbing counterculture escalated into a general youth rebellion that seemed on the verge of tearing America apart. Calling 1968 "the watershed year for a generation," SDS founder Tom Hayden wrote that it "started with legendary events, then raised hopes, only to end by immersing innocence in tragedy." It was perhaps the most shocking year in all the postwar decades. Violent clashes both in Vietnam and back home in the United States combined with political assassinations to produce a palpable sense of despair and hopelessness.

## War Abroad, Tragedy at Home

President Johnson had gambled in 1965 on a quick victory in Vietnam, before the political cost of escalation came due. But there was no quick victory. North Vietnamese and Vietcong forces fought on, the South Vietnamese government repeatedly collapsed, and American casualties mounted. By early 1968, the death rate of U.S. troops had reached several hundred a week. Johnson and his generals kept insisting that there was "light at the end of the tunnel." Facts on the ground showed otherwise.

**The Tet Offensive**   On January 30, 1968, the Vietcong unleashed a massive, well-coordinated assault in South Vietnam. Timed to coincide with Tet, the Vietnamese new year, the offensive struck thirty-six provincial capitals and five of the six major cities, including Saigon, where the Vietcong nearly overran the U.S. embassy. In strictly military terms, the Tet offensive was a failure, with very heavy Vietcong losses. But psychologically, the effect was devastating. Television brought into American homes shocking live images: the American embassy under siege and the Saigon police chief placing a pistol to the head of a Vietcong suspect and executing him.

The **Tet offensive** made a mockery of official pronouncements that the United States was winning the war. How could an enemy on the run manage such a large-scale, complex, and coordinated attack? Just before Tet, a Gallup poll found that 56 percent of Americans considered themselves "hawks" (supporters of the war), while only 28 percent identified with the "doves" (war opponents). Three months later, doves outnumbered hawks 42 to 41 percent. Without embracing the peace movement, many Americans simply concluded that the war was unwinnable.

The Tet offensive undermined Johnson and discredited his war policies. When the 1968 presidential primary season got under way in March, antiwar senators Eugene McCarthy of Minnesota and Robert Kennedy of New York, JFK's brother, challenged Johnson for the Democratic nomination. Discouraged, perhaps even physically exhausted, on March 31 Johnson stunned the nation by announcing that he would not seek reelection.

**Political Assassinations**　　Americans had barely adjusted to the news that a sitting president would not stand for reelection when, on April 4, James Earl Ray shot and killed Martin Luther King Jr. in Memphis. Riots erupted in more than a hundred cities. The worst of them, in Baltimore, Chicago, and Washington, D.C., left dozens dead and hundreds of millions of dollars in property damaged or destroyed. The violence on the streets of Saigon had found an eerie parallel on the streets of the United States.

One city that did not erupt was Indianapolis. There, Robert Kennedy, in town campaigning in the Indiana primary, gave a quiet, somber speech to the black community on the night of King's assassination. Americans could continue to move toward "greater polarization," Kennedy said, "black people amongst blacks, white amongst whites," or "we can replace that violence . . . with an effort to understand, compassion and love." Kennedy sympathized with African Americans' outrage at whites, but he begged them not to strike back in retribution. Impromptu and heart-felt, Kennedy's speech was a plea to follow King's nonviolent example, even as the nation descended into greater violence.

But two months later, having emerged as the front-runner for the Democratic presidential nomination, Kennedy, too, would be gone. On June 5, as he was celebrating his victory in the California primary over Eugene McCarthy, Kennedy was shot dead by a young Palestinian named Sirhan Sirhan. Amid the national mourning for yet another political murder, one newspaper columnist declared that "the country does not work anymore." *Newsweek* asked, "Has violence become a way of life?" Kennedy's assassination was a calamity for the Democratic Party because only he had seemed able to surmount the party's fissures over Vietnam. In the space of eight weeks, American liberals had lost their two most important national figures, King and Kennedy. The third, Johnson, was unpopular and politically damaged. Without these unifying leaders, the crisis of liberalism had become unmanageable.

## The Antiwar Movement and the 1968 Election

Before their deaths, Martin Luther King Jr. and Robert Kennedy had spoken eloquently against the Vietnam War. To antiwar activists, however, bold speeches and marches had not produced the desired effect. "We are no longer interested in merely protesting the war," declared one. "We are out to stop it." They sought nothing short of an immediate American withdrawal. Their anger at Johnson and the Democratic Party—fueled by news of the Tet offensive, the murders of King and Kennedy, and the general youth rebellion—had radicalized the movement.

**Democratic Convention**   In August, at the **1968 Democratic National Convention** in Chicago, the political divisions generated by the war consumed the party. Thousands of protesters descended on the city. The most visible group, led by Jerry Rubin and Abbie Hoffman, a remarkable pair of troublemakers, claimed to represent the Youth International Party (whose members were known as "Yippies"). To mock those inside the convention hall, they nominated a live pig, Pigasus, for president. The Yippies' stunts were geared toward maximum media exposure. But a far larger and more serious group of activists had come to Chicago to demonstrate against the war as well—and they staged what many came to call the Siege of Chicago.

Democratic mayor Richard J. Daley ordered the police to break up the demonstrations. Several nights of skirmishes between protesters and police culminated on the evening of the nominations. In what an official report later described as a "police riot," police officers attacked protesters with tear gas and clubs. As the nominating speeches proceeded, television networks broadcast scenes of the riot, cementing a popular impression of the Democrats as the party of disorder. "They are going to be spending the next four years picking up the pieces," one Republican said gleefully. Inside the hall, the party dispiritedly nominated Hubert H. Humphrey, Johnson's vice president. The delegates approved a middle-of-the-road platform that endorsed continued fighting in Vietnam while urging a diplomatic solution to the conflict.

**Richard Nixon**   On the Republican side, Richard M. Nixon had engineered a remarkable political comeback. After losing the presidential campaign in 1960 and the California gubernatorial race in 1962, he won the Republican presidential nomination in 1968. Sensing weakness in the Democratic Party, Nixon and his advisors believed there were two groups of voters whose long political loyalty to Democrats was wavering: working-class white voters in the North and southern whites of all social classes.

Offended by the antiwar movement and the counterculture, and disturbed by urban riots, northern blue-collar voters, especially Catholics, had drifted away from the Democratic Party. Growing up in the Great Depression, these families were admirers of FDR and perhaps even had his picture on their living-room wall. But times had changed over three decades. To show how much they had changed, the social scientists Ben J. Wattenberg and Richard Scammon profiled blue-collar workers in their study *The Real Majority* (1970). Wattenberg and Scammon asked their readers to consider people such as a forty-seven-year-old working-class woman from Dayton, Ohio: "[She] is afraid to walk the streets alone at night. . . . She has a mixed view about blacks and civil rights." Moreover, they wrote, "she is deeply distressed that her son is going to a community junior college where LSD was found on campus." Such northern blue-collar families were once reliable Democratic voters, but their political loyalties were increasingly up for grabs—a fact Republicans knew well.

**George Wallace**   Working-class anxieties over student protests and urban riots were first exploited by the controversial governor of Alabama, George C. Wallace. Running in 1968 as a third-party presidential candidate, Wallace traded on his fame as a segregationist governor. He had tried to stop the federal government from desegregating the University of Alabama in 1963, and he was equally obstructive during the Selma crisis of 1965. Appealing to whites in both the North and the South, Wallace called for "law and order" and attacked welfare programs; he claimed that mothers on public assistance were, thanks to Johnson's Great Society, "breeding children as a cash crop."

Wallace's hope was that by carrying the South, he could deny a major candidate an electoral majority and force the election into the House of Representatives. He fell short of that objective, finishing with just 13.5 percent of the popular vote. But he had defined hot-button issues — liberal elitism, welfare policies, and law and order — that became hallmarks for the next generation of mainstream conservatives.

**Nixon's Strategy**   Nixon offered a subtler version of Wallace's populism in a two-pronged approach to the campaign. He adopted what his advisors called the "southern strategy," which aimed at attracting southern white voters still smarting over the civil rights gains by African Americans. Nixon won over the key southerner, Democrat-turned-Republican senator Strom Thurmond of South Carolina, the 1948 Dixiecrat presidential nominee. Nixon informed Thurmond that while formally he had to support civil rights, his administration would go easy on enforcement. He also campaigned against the antiwar movement, urban riots, and protests, calling for a strict adherence to "law and order." He pledged to represent the "quiet voice" of the "great majority of Americans, the forgotten Americans, the nonshouters, the nondemonstrators." Here Nixon was speaking not just to the South, but to the many millions of anxious suburban voters across the country concerned that social disorder had gripped the nation.

These political strategies — southern and suburban — worked. Nixon received 43.4 percent of the vote to Humphrey's 42.7 percent, defeating him by a scant 500,000 votes out of the 73 million that were cast (Map 27.3). But the numerical closeness of the race could not disguise the devastating blow to the Democrats. Humphrey received almost 12 million fewer votes than Johnson had in 1964. The white South largely abandoned the Democratic Party, an exodus that would accelerate in the 1970s. In the North, meanwhile, Nixon and Wallace made significant inroads among traditionally Democratic voters. The result was that New Deal Democrats lost the unity of purpose that had served them for thirty years. A nation exhausted by months of turmoil and violence had chosen a new direction. Nixon's victory in 1968 foreshadowed — and helped propel — a national electoral realignment in the coming decade.

## The Nationalist Turn

Vietnam and the increasingly radical youth rebellion intersected with the turn toward racial and ethnic nationalism by young African American and Chicano activists. As we saw in Chapter 26, the Black Power and Chicano movements broke with the liberal "rights" politics of an older generation of leaders. These new activists expressed fury at the poverty and white racism that were beyond the reach of civil rights laws; they also saw Vietnam as an unjust war against other people of color.

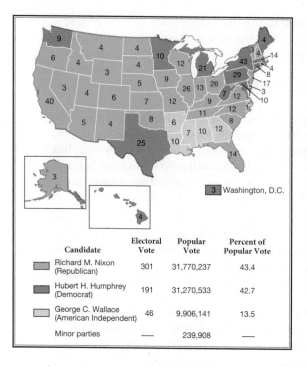

| Candidate | Electoral Vote | Popular Vote | Percent of Popular Vote |
|---|---|---|---|
| Richard M. Nixon (Republican) | 301 | 31,770,237 | 43.4 |
| Hubert H. Humphrey (Democrat) | 191 | 31,270,533 | 42.7 |
| George C. Wallace (American Independent) | 46 | 9,906,141 | 13.5 |
| Minor parties | — | 239,908 | — |

**MAP 27.3  The Presidential Election of 1968**

With Lyndon B. Johnson's surprise withdrawal and the assassination of the party's most charismatic contender, Robert Kennedy, the Democrats faced the election of 1968 in disarray. Governor George Wallace of Alabama, who left the Democrats to run as a third-party candidate, campaigned on the backlash against the civil rights movement. As late as mid-September Wallace held the support of 21 percent of the voters. But in November he received only 13.5 percent of the vote, winning five southern states. Republican Richard M. Nixon, who like Wallace emphasized "law and order" in his campaign, defeated Hubert H. Humphrey with only 43.4 percent of the popular vote, but it was now clear, given that Wallace's southern support would otherwise have gone to Nixon, that the South had shifted decisively to the Republican side.

In this spirit, the **Chicano Moratorium Committee** organized demonstrations against the war. Chanting "Viva la Raza, Afuera Vietnam" ("Long live the Chicano people, Get out of Vietnam"), 20,000 Mexican Americans marched in Los Angeles in August 1970. At another rally, Cesar Chavez said: "For the poor it is a terrible irony that they should rise out of their misery to do battle against other poor people." He and other Mexican American activists charged that the draft was biased against those who had little—like most wars in history, Vietnam was, in the words of one retired army colonel, "a poor boy's fight."

Among African Americans, the Black Panther Party and the National Black Antiwar Antidraft League spoke out against the war. "Black Americans are considered to be the world's biggest fools," Eldridge Cleaver of the Black Panther Party wrote in his typically acerbic style, "to go to another country to fight for something they don't have for themselves." Muhammad Ali, the most famous boxer in the world, refused his army induction. Sentenced to prison, Ali was eventually acquitted on appeal. But his action cost him his heavyweight title, and for years he was not allowed to box professionally in the United States.

## Women's Liberation and Black and Chicana Feminism

Among women, 1968 also marked a break with the past. The late 1960s spawned new expressions of feminism: **women's liberation** and black and Chicana feminisms. Activists for the former were primarily younger, college-educated women fresh from the New Left, antiwar, and civil rights movements. Those movements' male leaders, they discovered, considered women little more than pretty helpers who typed memos and fetched coffee. Women who tried to raise feminist issues at civil rights and anti-war events were shouted off the platform with jeers such as "Move on, little girl, we have more important issues to talk about here than women's liberation."

Fed up with second-class status, and well versed in the tactics of organization and protest, women radicals broke away and organized on their own. Unlike the National Organization for Women (NOW), the women's liberation movement was loosely structured, comprising an alliance of collectives in New York, San Francisco, Boston, and other big cities and college towns. "Women's lib," as it was dubbed by a skeptical media, went public in 1968 at the Miss America pageant. Demonstrators carried posters of women's bodies labeled as slabs of beef—implying that society treated them as meat. Mirroring the identity politics of Black Power activists and the self-dramatization of the counterculture, women's liberation sought an end to the denigration and exploitation of women. "Sisterhood is powerful!" read one women's liberationist manifesto. The national Women's Strike for Equality in August 1970 brought hundreds of thousands of women into the streets of the nation's cities for marches and demonstrations.

By that year, new terms such as *sexism* and *male chauvinism* had become part of the national vocabulary. As converts flooded in, two branches of the women's movement began to converge. Radical women realized that key feminist goals—child care, equal pay, and reproduction rights—could best be achieved in the political arena. At the same time, more traditional activists, often known as "liberal feminists" and exemplified by Betty Friedan, developed a broader view of women's oppression. They came to understand that women required more than equal opportunity: the culture that regarded women as nothing more than sexual objects and helpmates to men had to change as well. Although still largely white and middle class, feminists began to think of themselves as part of a broad social crusade.

"Sisterhood" did not unite all women, however. Black and Latina women continued to work within the larger framework of the civil rights movement, their feminism linked to the crusade for racial justice. New groups such as the Combahee River Collective and the National Black Feminist Organization arose to speak for the concerns of black women. They criticized sexism but were reluctant to break completely with black men and the struggle for racial equality. Mexican American feminists, or Chicana feminists as they called themselves, came from Catholic backgrounds in which motherhood and family were held in high regard. "We want to walk hand in hand with the Chicano brothers, with our children, our *viejitos* [elders], our Familia de la Raza," one Chicana feminist wrote. Black and Chicana feminists embraced the larger movement for women's rights but carried on their own struggles to address specific needs in their communities.

One of the most important contributions of all the new feminisms was to raise awareness about what feminist Kate Millett called sexual politics. Liberationists, along with black and Chicana feminists, argued that unless women had control over their own bodies, they could not freely shape their destinies. They campaigned for reproductive rights, especially access to abortion, and railed against a culture that blamed women for their own sexual assault and turned a blind eye to sexual harassment in the workplace.

Meanwhile, women's opportunities expanded dramatically in higher education. Dozens of formerly all-male bastions such as Yale, Princeton, and the U.S. military academies admitted women undergraduates for the first time. Colleges started women's studies programs, which eventually numbered in the hundreds, and the proportion of women attending graduate and professional schools rose markedly. With the adoption of **Title IX** in 1972, Congress broadened the 1964 Civil Rights Act to include educational institutions, prohibiting colleges and universities that received federal funds from discriminating on the basis of sex. By requiring comparable funding for sports programs, Title IX made women's athletics a real presence on college campuses.

Women also became increasingly visible in public life. Congresswomen Bella Abzug and Shirley Chisholm joined Betty Friedan and Gloria Steinem, the founder of *Ms.* magazine, to create the National Women's Political Caucus in 1971. Abzug and Chisholm, both from New York, joined Congresswomen Patsy Mink from Hawaii and Martha Griffiths from Michigan to sponsor equal rights legislation. Congress authorized child-care tax deductions for working parents in 1972 and in 1974 passed the Equal Credit Opportunity Act, which enabled married women to get credit, including credit cards and mortgages, in their own names.

## Stonewall and Gay Liberation

The liberationist impulse transformed the gay rights movement as well. Homophile activists in the 1960s (Chapter 25) had pursued rights by protesting, but they adopted the respectable dress and behavior they knew straight society demanded. Meanwhile, the vast majority of gay men, lesbians, and transgender persons remained "in the closet." So many were closeted because homosexuality was considered immoral and was even illegal in the vast majority of states — sodomy statutes outlawed same-sex relations, and police used other morals laws to harass and arrest gay men and lesbians. In the late 1960s, however, inspired by the Black Power and women's movements, gay activists increasingly demanded immediate and unconditional recognition of their rights. A gay newspaper in New York bore the title *Come Out!*

The new gay liberation found multiple expressions in major cities across the country, but a defining event occurred in New York's Greenwich Village. Police had raided gay bars for decades, making arrests, publicizing the names of patrons, and harassing customers simply for being gay. When a local gay bar called the **Stonewall Inn** was raided by police in the summer of 1969, however, its patrons rioted for two days, setting the establishment on fire and battling with police in the narrow streets of the Village. Decades of police repression had taken their toll. Few commentators excused the violence, and the Stonewall riots were not repeated, but activists celebrated them as a symbolic demand for full citizenship. The gay liberation movement grew quickly after Stonewall. Local gay, lesbian, and transgender organizations proliferated, and activists began pushing for nondiscrimination ordinances and consensual sex laws at the state level. By 1975, the National Gay Task Force and other national organizations were lobbying Congress, serving as media watchdogs, and advancing suits in the courts. Despite all the activity, progress was slow; in most arenas of American life, gay men, lesbians, and transgender people did not enjoy the same legal protections and rights as other Americans.

| IN YOUR OWN WORDS | What factors best explain the rising militancy of social change and protest movements in 1968 and afterward? |

# Rise of the Silent Majority

Vietnam abroad and the antiwar movement at home tore at the fabric of the Democratic coalition. Lyndon Johnson could not stitch the party back together. Richard Nixon, in contrast, showed himself adept at taking advantage of the nation's unrest through carefully timed speeches and displays of moral outrage. A centrist by nature and temperament, Nixon was not part of the conservative Goldwater wing of the Republican Party. Though he was an ardent anticommunist like Goldwater, Nixon also shared some of Eisenhower's traits, including a basic acceptance of government's role in economic matters. Nixon is thus most profitably viewed as a transitional figure, a national politician who formed a bridge between the liberal postwar era and the much more conservative decades that followed the 1970s.

In late 1969, following a massive antiwar rally in Washington, President Nixon gave a televised speech in which he referred to his supporters as the **silent majority**. It was classic Nixonian rhetoric. In a single phrase, he summed up a generational and cultural struggle, placing himself on the side of ordinary Americans against the rabble-rousers and troublemakers. It was an oversimplification, but the label *silent majority* stuck, and Nixon had defined a political phenomenon. For the remainder of his presidency, Nixon projected himself to the public as the defender of a reasonable middle ground under assault from the radical left.

## Nixon in Vietnam

In Vietnam, Nixon picked up where Johnson had left off. Cold War assumptions continued to dictate presidential policy. Abandoning Vietnam, Nixon insisted, would damage America's "credibility" and make the country seem "a pitiful, helpless giant." Nixon wanted peace, but only "peace with honor." The North Vietnamese were not about to oblige him. The only reasonable outcome, from their standpoint, was a unified Vietnam under their control.

**Vietnamization and Cambodia**    To neutralize criticism at home, Nixon began delegating the ground fighting to the South Vietnamese. Under this new policy of **Vietnamization**, American troop levels dropped from 543,000 in 1968 to 334,000 in 1971 to barely 24,000 by early 1973. American casualties dropped correspondingly. But the killing in Vietnam continued. As Ellsworth Bunker, the U.S. ambassador to Vietnam, noted cynically, it was just a matter of changing "the color of the bodies."

Far from abating, however, the antiwar movement intensified. First, in November 1969, half a million demonstrators staged a huge protest in Washington called the Vietnam Moratorium, one of the largest protests ever held in the capital. Then, on April 30, 1970, as part of a secret bombing campaign against Vietcong supply lines, American troops destroyed enemy bases in neutral Cambodia. When news of the invasion of Cambodia came out, American campuses exploded in outrage—and, for the first time, students died. On May 4, 1970, at Kent State University in Ohio, panicky National Guardsmen fired into an antiwar rally, wounding eleven students and killing four. (At least 61 shots were fired in about 13 seconds; of the 13 people hit, the nearest was 60 feet from the Guardsmen.) Less than two weeks later, at

**"I Want Out"** Protest movements of all kinds shook the foundations of American society and national politics in the 1960s. No issue was more controversial and divisive than the war in Vietnam. Private Collection/Peter Newark American Pictures/Bridgeman Images.

Jackson State College in Mississippi, Guardsmen stormed a dormitory, killing two black students. More than 450 colleges closed in protest. Across the country, the spring semester was essentially canceled.

**My Lai Massacre**    Meanwhile, one of the worst atrocities of the war had become public. In 1968, U.S. Army troops had executed nearly five hundred people in the South Vietnamese village of **My Lai**, including a large number of women and children. The massacre was known only within the military until 1969, when journalist Seymour Hersh broke the story and photos of the massacre appeared in *Life* magazine, discrediting the United States around the world. Americans, *Time* observed, "must stand in the larger dock of guilt and human conscience." Although high-ranking officers participated in the My Lai massacre and its cover-up, only one soldier, a low-ranking second lieutenant named William Calley, was convicted.

Believing that Calley had been made a fall guy for official U.S. policies that inevitably brought death to innocent civilians, a group called Vietnam Veterans Against the War publicized other atrocities committed by U.S. troops. In a controversial protest in 1971, they returned their combat medals at demonstrations outside the U.S. Capitol, literally hurling them onto the Capitol steps. "Here's my merit badge for murder," one vet said. Supporters of the war called these veterans cowardly and un-American, but their heartfelt antiwar protest exposed the deep personal torment that Vietnam had caused many soldiers.

**Détente**    As protests continued at home, Nixon pursued two strategies to achieve his declared "peace with honor," one diplomatic and the other military. First, he sought **détente** (a lessening of tensions) with the Soviet Union and a new openness with China. In a series of meetings between 1970 and 1972, Nixon and Soviet premier Leonid Brezhnev resolved tensions over Cuba and Berlin and signed the first Strategic Arms Limitation Treaty (SALT I), the latter a symbolic step toward ending the Cold War arms race. Heavily influenced by his national security advisor, the Harvard professor Henry Kissinger, Nixon believed that he could break the Cold War impasse that had kept the United States from productive dialogue with the Soviet Union.

Then, in 1972, Nixon visited China, becoming the first sitting U.S. president to do so. In a televised weeklong trip, the president pledged better relations with China and declared that the two nations — one capitalist, the other communist — could peacefully coexist. This was the man who had risen to prominence in the 1950s by railing against the Democrats for "losing" China and by hounding Communists and fellow travelers. Indeed, the president's impeccable anticommunist credentials gave him the political cover to travel to Beijing. Praised for his efforts to lessen Cold War tensions, Nixon also had tactical objectives in mind. He hoped that by befriending both the Soviet Union and China, he could play one against the other and strike a better deal over Vietnam at the ongoing peace talks in Paris. His second strategy, however, would prove less praiseworthy and cost more lives.

**Exit America**    In April 1972, in an attempt to strengthen his negotiating position, Nixon ordered large-scale bombing raids against North Vietnam. A month later, he approved the mining of North Vietnamese ports, something Johnson had never dared to do. The North Vietnamese were not isolated, however: supplies from China and the Soviet Union continued, and the Vietcong fought on.

With the 1972 presidential election approaching, Nixon sent Kissinger back to the Paris peace talks, which had been initiated under Johnson. In a key concession, Kissinger accepted the presence of North Vietnamese troops in South Vietnam. North Vietnam then agreed to an interim arrangement whereby the South Vietnamese government in Saigon would stay in power while a special commission arranged a final settlement. With Kissinger's announcement that "peace is at hand," Nixon got the election lift he wanted, but the agreement was then sabotaged by General Nguyen Van Thieu, the South Vietnamese president. So Nixon, in one final spasm of bloodletting, unleashed the two-week "Christmas bombing," the most intense of the entire war. On January 27, 1973, the two sides signed the Paris Peace Accords.

Nixon hoped that with massive U.S. aid the Thieu regime might survive. But Congress was in revolt. It refused appropriations for bombing Cambodia after August 15, 1973, and gradually cut back aid to South Vietnam. In March 1975, North Vietnamese forces launched a final offensive, and on April 30, Vietnam was reunited. Saigon, the South Vietnamese capital, was renamed Ho Chi Minh City, after the founding father of the communist regime.

The collapse of South Vietnam in 1975 produced a powerful, and tragic, historical irony: an outcome little different from what would likely have resulted from the unification vote in 1954 (Chapter 24). In other words, America's most disastrous military adventure of the twentieth century barely altered the geopolitical realities in Southeast Asia. The Hanoi regime called itself communist but never intended to be a satellite of any country, least of all China, Vietnam's ancient enemy.

The price paid for the Vietnam War was steep. America's Vietnamese friends lost jobs and property, spent years in "reeducation" camps, or had to flee the country. Millions of Vietnamese died in more than a decade of war, which included some of the most intensive aerial bombing of the twentieth century. In bordering Cambodia, the maniacal Khmer Rouge, followers of Cambodia's ruling Communist Party, took power and murdered 1.7 million people in bloody purges. And in the United States, more than 58,000 Americans had given their lives, and 300,000 had been wounded. On top of the war's $150 billion price tag, slow-to-heal internal wounds divided the country, and Americans increasingly lost confidence in their political leaders.

## The Silent Majority Speaks Out

Nixon placed himself on the side of what he called "the nonshouters, the nondemonstrators." But moderate and conservative Americans were not in the mood to simply remain silent. They increasingly spoke out. During Nixon's first presidential term, those opposed to the direction liberalism had taken since the early 1960s focused their discontent on what they believed to be the excesses of the "rights revolution"—the enormous changes in American law and society initiated by the civil rights movement and advanced by feminists and others thereafter.

**Law and Order and the Supreme Court**     The rights revolution had found an ally in an unexpected place: the U.S. Supreme Court. The decision that stood as a landmark in the civil rights movement, *Brown v. Board of Education* (1954), triggered a larger judicial revolution. Following *Brown*, the Court increasingly agreed to hear human rights and civil liberties cases—as opposed to its previous focus on property-related suits. Surprisingly, this shift was led by the man whom President Dwight Eisenhower had appointed chief justice in 1953: Earl Warren. A popular Republican governor of California, Warren surprised many, including Eisenhower himself, with his robust advocacy of civil rights and civil liberties. The **Warren Court** lasted from 1954 until 1969 and established some of the most far-reaching liberal jurisprudence in U.S. history.

Right-wing activists fiercely opposed the Warren Court, which they accused of "legislating from the bench" and contributing to social breakdown. They pointed, for instance, to the Court's rulings that people who are arrested have a constitutional right to counsel (1963, 1964) and, in *Miranda v. Arizona* (1966), that arrestees have to be informed by police of their right to remain silent. Compounding conservatives' frustration was a series of decisions that liberalized restrictions on pornography. Trying to walk the fine line between censorship and obscenity, the Court ruled in *Roth v. United States* (1957) that obscene material had to be "utterly without redeeming social importance" to be banned. The "social importance" test, however, proved nearly impossible to define and left wide latitude for pornography to flourish.

That constitutional test was finally abandoned in 1972, when the Court ruled in *Miller v. California* that "contemporary community standards" were the rightful measure of obscenity. But *Miller*, too, little slowed the proliferation of pornographic magazines, films, and live shows in the 1970s. Conservatives found these decisions especially distasteful, since the Court had also ruled that religious ritual of any kind in public schools—including prayers and Bible reading—violated the constitutional separation of church and state. To many religious Americans, the Court had taken the side of immorality over Christian values.

Supreme Court critics blamed rising crime rates and social breakdown on the Warren Court's liberal judicial record. Every category of crime was up in the 1970s, but especially disconcerting was the doubling of the murder rate since the 1950s and the 76 percent increase in burglary and theft between 1967 and 1976. Sensational crimes had always grabbed headlines, but now "crime" itself preoccupied politicians, the media, and the public. However, no one could establish a direct causal link between increases in crime and Supreme Court decisions, given a myriad of other social factors, including drugs, income inequality, enhanced statistical record-keeping, and the proliferation of guns. But when many Americans looked at their cities in the 1970s, they saw pornographic theaters, X-rated bookstores, and rising crime rates. Where, they wondered, was law and order?

**Busing** Another major civil rights objective—desegregating schools—produced even more controversy and fireworks. For fifteen years, southern states, by a variety of stratagems, had fended off court directives that they desegregate "with all deliberate speed." In 1968, only about one-third of all black children in the South attended schools with whites. At that point, the federal courts got serious and, in a series of stiff decisions, ordered an end to "dual school systems."

Where schools remained highly segregated, the courts increasingly endorsed the strategy of busing students to achieve integration. Plans differed across the country. In some states, black children rode buses from their neighborhoods to attend previously all-white schools. In others, white children were bused to black or Latino neighborhoods. In an important 1971 decision, *Swan v. Charlotte-Mecklenburg*, the Supreme Court upheld a countywide busing plan for Charlotte-Mecklenburg, a North Carolina school district. Despite local opposition, desegregation proceeded, and many cities in the South followed suit. By the mid-1970s, 86 percent of southern black children were attending school with whites. (In recent years, this trend toward desegregation has reversed.)

In the North, where segregated schooling was also a fact of life—arising from suburban residential patterns—busing orders proved less effective. Detroit dramatized the problem. To integrate Detroit schools would have required merging city and suburban school districts. A lower court ordered just such a merger in 1971, but in *Milliken v. Bradley* (1974), the Supreme Court reversed the ruling, requiring busing plans to remain within the boundaries of a single school district. Without including the largely white suburbs in busing efforts, however, achieving racial balance in Detroit, and other major northern cities, was all but impossible. Postwar suburbanization had produced in the North what law had mandated in the South: entrenched racial segregation of schools.

As the 1972 election approached, President Nixon took advantage of rising discontent over "law and order" and busing. In so doing, he was the political beneficiary of a growing reaction against liberalism that had begun to take hold between 1968 and the early 1970s.

## The 1972 Election

Political realignments have been infrequent in American history. One occurred between 1932 and 1936, when many Republicans, despairing over the Great Depression, had switched sides and voted for FDR. The years between 1968 and 1972 were another such pivotal moment. This time, Democrats were the ones who abandoned their party.

After the 1968 elections, the Democrats fell into disarray. Bent on sweeping away the party's old guard, reformers took over, adopting new rules that granted women, African Americans, and young people delegate seats at the convention "in reasonable relation to their presence in the population." In the past, an alliance of urban machines, labor unions, and white ethnic groups—the heart of the New Deal coalition—dominated the presidential nominating process. But at the 1972 convention, few of the party faithful qualified as delegates under the changed rules. The crowning insult came when the convention rejected the credentials of Chicago mayor Richard Daley and his delegation, seating instead an Illinois delegation led by Jesse Jackson, a firebrand young black minister and former aide to Martin Luther King Jr.

Capturing the party was one thing; beating the Republicans was quite another. These party reforms opened the door for George McGovern, a liberal South Dakota senator and favorite of the antiwar and women's movements, to capture the nomination. But McGovern took a number of missteps, including failing to mollify key party backers such as the AFL-CIO, which, for the first time in memory, refused to endorse the Democratic ticket. A weak campaigner, McGovern was also no match for Nixon, who pulled out all the stops. Using the advantages of incumbency, Nixon gave the economy a well-timed lift and proclaimed (prematurely) a cease-fire in

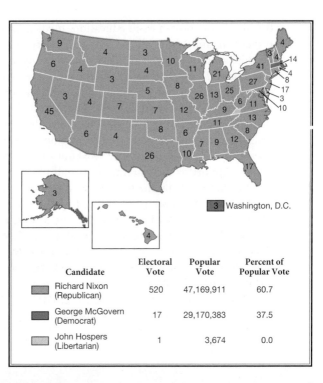

**MAP 27.4　The Presidential Election of 1972**

In one of the most lopsided presidential elections of the twentieth century, Republican Richard Nixon defeated Democrat George McGovern in a landslide in 1972. It was a reversal of the 1964 election, just eight years before, in which Republican Barry Goldwater had been defeated by a similar margin. Nixon hoped that his victory signaled what Kevin Phillips called "the emerging Republican majority," but the president's missteps and criminal actions in the Watergate scandal would soon bring an end to his tenure in office.

| 3 | Washington, D.C. |

| Candidate | Electoral Vote | Popular Vote | Percent of Popular Vote |
|---|---|---|---|
| Richard Nixon (Republican) | 520 | 47,169,911 | 60.7 |
| George McGovern (Democrat) | 17 | 29,170,383 | 37.5 |
| John Hospers (Libertarian) | 1 | 3,674 | 0.0 |

Vietnam. Nixon's appeal to the "silent majority"—people who "care about a strong United States, about patriotism, about moral and spiritual values"—was by now well honed.

Nixon won in a landslide, receiving nearly 61 percent of the popular vote and carrying every state except Massachusetts and the District of Columbia (Map 27.4). The returns revealed how fractured traditional Democratic voting blocs had become. McGovern received only 38 percent of the big-city Catholic vote and lost 42 percent of self-identified Democrats overall. The 1972 election marked a pivotal moment in the country's shift to the right. Yet observers legitimately wondered whether the 1972 election results proved the popularity of conservatism or merely showed that the country had grown weary of liberalism and the changes it had wrought in national life.

> **IN YOUR OWN WORDS**　What social issues divided Americans in the early 1970s, and how did those divisions affect the two major political parties?

# Summary

In this chapter, we saw that the combined pressures of the Vietnam War and racial, gender, and cultural conflict fractured and split the New Deal coalition. Following John Kennedy's assassination in 1963, Lyndon Johnson advanced the most ambitious liberal reform program since the New Deal, securing not only civil rights legislation but also many programs in education, medical care, transportation, environmental protection, and, above all, his War on Poverty. But the Great Society fell short of its promise as Johnson escalated American involvement in Vietnam.

The war bitterly divided Americans. Galvanized by the carnage of war and the draft, the antiwar movement spread rapidly among young people, and the spirit of rebellion spilled beyond the war. The New Left took the lead among college students, while the more apolitical counterculture preached liberation through sex, drugs, music, and personal transformation. Women's liberationists broke from the New Left and raised new concerns about society's sexism. Conservative students rallied in support of the war and on behalf of conservative principles, but they were often drowned out by the more vocal and demonstrative liberals and radicals.

In 1968, the nation was rocked by the assassinations of Martin Luther King Jr. and Robert F. Kennedy, as well as by a wave of urban riots, fueling a growing popular desire for law and order. Adding to the national disquiet was the Democratic National Convention that summer, which was divided by the Vietnam War and besieged by street riots outside. The stage was set for a new cycle of conservative politics to take hold of the country and a resurgence of the Republican Party under Richard Nixon between 1968 and 1972. President Nixon ended the war in Vietnam, but only after four more years and many more casualties.

# Chapter 27 Review

## KEY TERMS

**Identify and explain the significance of each term below.**

Great Society (p. 786)
Economic Opportunity Act (p. 788)
Medicare and Medicaid (p. 790)
Equal Pay Act (p. 791)
*The Feminine Mystique* (p. 791)
Presidential Commission on the Status of Women (p. 791)
National Organization for Women (NOW) (p. 792)
Gulf of Tonkin Resolution (p. 794)
Operation Rolling Thunder (p. 794)
Students for a Democratic Society (SDS) (p. 795)
Port Huron Statement (p. 795)
New Left (p. 796)
Young Americans for Freedom (YAF) (p. 796)

Sharon Statement (p. 796)
counterculture (p. 797)
Tet offensive (p. 799)
1968 Democratic National Convention (p. 800)
Chicano Moratorium Committee (p. 802)
women's liberation (p. 802)
Title IX (p. 804)
Stonewall Inn (p. 804)
silent majority (p. 805)
Vietnamization (p. 805)
My Lai (p. 807)
détente (p. 807)
Warren Court (p. 809)

## REVIEW QUESTIONS

**Answer these questions to demonstrate your understanding of the chapter's main ideas.**

1. What explains the surge in liberal politics and social policy in the early 1960s?
2. What led President Johnson to escalate the war in Vietnam, and how did Americans respond?
3. What factors best explain the rising militancy of social change and protest movements in 1968 and afterward?
4. What social issues divided Americans in the early 1970s, and how did those divisions affect the two major political parties?
5. Look at the events listed under "America in the World" on the thematic timeline on page 697. American global leadership is a major theme of Part 8. How did the global role of the United States shift in the 1960s?

## CHRONOLOGY

**As you read, ask yourself why this chapter begins and ends with these dates and identify the links among related events.**

| | |
|---|---|
| **1961** | • John F. Kennedy inaugurated as president |
| **1963** | • John F. Kennedy assassinated; Lyndon B. Johnson assumes presidency |
| **1964** | • Civil Rights Act |
| | • Economic Opportunity Act inaugurates War on Poverty |
| | • Free Speech Movement at Berkeley |
| | • Gulf of Tonkin Resolution |
| **1965** | • Immigration Act abolishes national quota system |
| | • Medicare and Medicaid programs established |
| | • Operation Rolling Thunder escalates bombing campaign (March) |
| | • First U.S. combat troops arrive in Vietnam |
| **1967** | • Counterculture's "Summer of Love" |
| | • 100,000 march in antiwar protest in Washington, D.C. (October) |
| **1968** | • Tet offensive begins (January) |
| | • Martin Luther King Jr. and Robert F. Kennedy assassinated |
| | • Women's liberation protest at Miss America pageant |

|      |   |
|------|---|
|      | • Riot at Democratic National Convention in Chicago (August) |
|      | • Richard Nixon elected president |
| **1969** | • Stonewall riots (June) |
| **1970** | • National Women's Strike for Equality |
| **1971** | • *Swan v. Charlotte-Mecklenburg* approves countywide busing |
| **1972** | • Nixon visits China (February) |
|      | • Nixon wins a second term (November 7) |
| **1973** | • Paris Peace Accords end Vietnam War |
| **1974** | • *Milliken v. Bradley* limits busing to school district boundaries |
| **1975** | • Vietnam reunified under Communist rule |

# 28

# The Search for Order in an Era of Limits

## 1973–1980

### IDENTIFY THE BIG IDEA

How did the legacy of social changes in the 1960s—such as civil rights, shifting gender roles, and challenges to the family—continue to reverberate in the 1970s, leading to both new opportunities and political clashes?

**EARLY IN 1971, A NEW FICTIONAL CHARACTER APPEARED ON NATIONAL** television. Archie Bunker was a gruff blue-collar worker who berated his wife and bemoaned his daughter's marriage to a bearded hippie. Prone to bigoted and insensitive remarks, Archie and his wife Edith sang "Those Were the Days" at the opening of each episode of *All in the Family*, a half-hour comedy. The song celebrated a bygone era, when "girls were girls and men were men." Disdainful of the liberal social movements of the 1960s, Archie professed a conservative, hardscrabble view of the world.

Archie Bunker became a folk hero to many conservative Americans in the 1970s; he said what they felt. But his significance went beyond his politics. *All in the Family* gave voice to a national search for order. His feminist daughter, liberal son-in-law, and black neighbors brought a changing world into Archie's modest home in Queens, New York. Not all Americans were as resistant to change as Archie. Most were ordinary, middle-of-the-road people confronting the aftermath of the tumultuous late 1960s and early 1970s. The social movements of those years challenged Americans to think in new ways about race, gender roles, sexual morality, and the family. Vietnam and the Watergate scandal had compounded matters by producing a crisis of political authority. An "old order" had seemingly collapsed. But what would take its place was not yet clear.

Alongside cultural dislocation and political alienation, the country confronted economic setbacks. In 1973, inflation began to climb at a pace unprecedented in the post–World War II decades, and economic growth slowed. An energy crisis, aggravated by U.S. foreign policy in the Middle East, produced fuel shortages. Foreign competition in manufacturing brought less expensive, and often more reliable, goods into the U.S. market from nations such as Japan and West Germany. As a result, more American plants closed. The great economic ride enjoyed by the United States since World War II was coming to an end.

What distinguishes the period between the energy crisis (1973) and the election of Ronald Reagan to the presidency (1980) is the collective national search for order in the midst of rapid social change, political realignment, and economic crisis. Virtually all the verities and touchstones of the post-war decades — Cold War liberalism, rising living standards, and the nuclear family — had come into question, and most Americans agreed on the urgency to act. For some, this search demanded new forms of liberal experimentation. For others, it led instead to the conservatism of the emerging New Right.

# An Era of Limits

The economic downturn of the early 1970s was the deepest slump since the Great Depression. Every major economic indicator — employment, productivity, growth — turned negative, and by 1973 the economy was in a tailspin. Inflation, brought on in part by military spending on the war in Vietnam, proved especially difficult to control. When a Middle East embargo cut oil supplies in 1973, prices climbed even more. Unemployment remained high and productivity growth low until 1982. Overall, the 1970s represented the worst economic decade of the postwar period — what California governor Jerry Brown called an "era of limits."

In this time of distress, Americans were forced to consider other limits to the growth and expansion that had long been markers of national progress. The environmental movement brought attention to the toxic effects of modern industrial capitalism on the natural world. As the urban crisis grew worse, several major cities verged on bankruptcy. Finally, political limits were reached as well: none of the presidents of the 1970s could reverse the nation's economic slide, though each spent years trying.

## Energy Crisis

Modern economies run on oil. If the oil supply is drastically reduced, woe follows. Something like that happened to the United States in the 1970s. Once the world's leading oil producer, the United States had become heavily dependent on inexpensive imported oil, mostly from the Persian Gulf. French, British, and American companies extracted the oil, a legacy of European colonialism, but they did so under profit-sharing agreements with the Persian Gulf states. In 1960, these nations and other oil-rich developing countries, such as Venezuela, formed a cartel (a business association formed to control prices), the **Organization of Petroleum Exporting Countries (OPEC)**.

Conflict between Israel and the neighboring Arab states of Egypt, Syria, and Jordan prompted OPEC to take political sides between 1967 and 1973. Following Israel's victory in the 1967 Six-Day War, Israeli-Arab tensions in the region grew closer to boiling over with each passing year. In the 1973 Yom Kippur War, Egypt and Syria invaded Israel to regain territory lost in the 1967 conflict. Israel prevailed, but only after being resupplied by an emergency American airlift. In response to U.S. support for Israel, the Arab states in OPEC declared an oil embargo in October 1973. Gas prices in the United States quickly jumped by 40 percent and heating oil prices by 30 percent. Demand outpaced supply, and Americans found themselves parked for hours in mile-long lines at gasoline stations for much of the winter of 1973–1974. Oil had become a political weapon, and the West's vulnerability stood revealed.

The United States scrambled to meet its energy needs in the face of the oil shortage. Just two months after the OPEC embargo began, Congress imposed a national speed limit of 55 miles per hour to conserve fuel. Americans began to buy smaller, more fuel-efficient cars such as Volkswagens, Toyotas, and Datsuns (later Nissans)—while sales of Detroit-made cars (now nicknamed "gas guzzlers") slumped. With one of every six jobs in the country generated directly or indirectly by the auto industry, the effects rippled across the economy. Compounding the distress was the raging inflation set off by the oil shortage; prices of basic necessities, such as bread, milk, and canned goods, rose by nearly 20 percent in 1974 alone. "THINGS WILL GET WORSE," one newspaper headline warned, "BEFORE THEY GET WORSE."

## Environmentalism

The **energy crisis** drove home the realization that the earth's resources are not limitless. Such a notion was also at the heart of the era's revival of **environmentalism**. The environmental movement was an offshoot of sixties activism, but it had numerous historical precedents: the preservationist, conservationist, and wilderness movements of the late nineteenth century; the conservationist ethos of the New Deal; and anxiety about nuclear weapons and overpopulation in the 1940s. Three of the nation's leading environmental organizations—the Sierra Club, the Wilderness Society, and the Natural Resources Council—were founded in 1892, 1935, and 1942, respectively. Environmental activists in the 1970s expanded on this long history through renewed efforts to ensure a healthy environment and access to unspoiled nature.

The movement had received a hefty boost back in 1962 when biologist Rachel Carson published **Silent Spring**, a stunning analysis of the pesticide DDT's toxic impact on the human and natural food chains. A succession of galvanizing developments followed in the late 1960s. The Sierra Club successfully fought two dams in

1966 that would have flooded the Grand Canyon. And in 1969, three major events spurred the movement: an offshore drilling rig spilled millions of gallons of oil off the coast of Santa Barbara; the Cuyahoga River near Cleveland burst into flames because of the accumulation of flammable chemicals on its surface; and Friends of the Everglades protested the construction of an airport that threatened plants and wildlife in Florida. With these events serving as catalysts, environmentalism became a certifiable mass movement on the first **Earth Day**, April 22, 1970, when 20 million people gathered in communities across the country to express their support for a cleaner, healthier planet.

**Environmental Protection Agency**    Earlier that year, on the heels of the Santa Barbara oil spill, Congress passed the National Environmental Policy Act, which created the **Environmental Protection Agency (EPA)**. A bipartisan bill with broad support, including that of President Nixon, the law required developers to file environmental impact statements assessing the effect of their projects on ecosystems.

**Environmental Crisis in Cleveland**  On June 22, 1969, a large section of the Cuyahoga River near Cleveland on the southern shore of Lake Erie caught fire and burned for hours. Accumulated oil and other chemicals from nearby factories and refineries produced this "burning river," which received national attention and sparked renewed scrutiny of pollution and environmental degradation. Pictured here are firefighters battling an earlier fire on the same river in 1952. Between 1968 and the June 1969 blaze, there were a total of nine fires on the Cuyahoga. Together, the fires were among a series of environmental catastrophes that helped spur grassroots activism in support of new federal legislation devoted to clean air, clean water, and natural resource protection.  Bettmann/Getty Images.

A spate of new laws followed: the Clean Air Act (1970), the Occupational Health and Safety Act (1970), the Water Pollution Control Act (1972), and the Endangered Species Act (1973).

The Democratic majority in Congress and the Republican president generally found common ground on these issues, and *Time* magazine wondered if the environment was "the gut issue that can unify a polarized nation." Despite the broad popularity of the movement, however, *Time*'s prediction was not borne out. Corporations opposed environmental regulations, as did many of their workers, who believed that tightened standards threatened their jobs. "IF YOU'RE HUNGRY AND OUT OF WORK, EAT AN ENVIRONMENTALIST," read one labor union bumper sticker. By the 1980s, environmentalism starkly divided Americans, with proponents of unfettered economic growth on one side and environmental activists preaching limits on the other.

**Nuclear Power**　An early foreshadowing of those divisions came in the brewing controversy over nuclear power. Electricity from the atom—what could be better? That was how Americans had greeted the arrival of power-generating nuclear technology in the 1950s. By 1974, U.S. utility companies were operating forty-two nuclear power plants, with a hundred more planned. Given the oil crisis, nuclear energy might have seemed a godsend; unlike coal- or oil-driven plants, nuclear operations produced no air pollutants.

Environmentalists, however, publicized the dangers of nuclear power plants: a reactor meltdown would be catastrophic, and so, in slow motion, would the dumping of radioactive waste, which would generate toxic levels of radioactivity for hundreds of years. These fears seemed to be confirmed in March 1979, when the reactor core at the **Three Mile Island** nuclear plant near Harrisburg, Pennsylvania, came close to meltdown. More than 100,000 people fled their homes. A prompt shutdown saved the plant, but the near catastrophe enabled environmentalists to win the battle over nuclear energy. After the incident at Three Mile Island, no new nuclear plants were authorized, though a handful with existing authorization were built in the 1980s. Today, nuclear reactors account for 20 percent of all U.S. power generation—substantially less than several European nations, but still fourth in the world.

## Economic Transformation

In addition to the energy crisis, the economy was beset by a host of longer-term problems. Government spending on the Vietnam War and the Great Society made for a growing federal deficit and spiraling inflation. In the industrial sector, the country faced more robust competition from West Germany and Japan. America's share of world trade dropped from 32 percent in 1955 to 18 percent in 1970 and was headed downward. As a result, in a blow to national pride, nine Western European countries had surpassed the United States in per capita gross domestic product (GDP) by 1980.

Many of these economic woes highlighted a broader, multigenerational transformation in the United States: from an economy based on industrial manufacturing to one based on provision of services. That transformation, which continues to this day, meant that the United States began to produce fewer automobiles, appliances, and televisions and more financial services, health-care services, and management consulting services — not to mention many millions of low-paying jobs in the restaurant, retail, and tourist industries.

In the 1970s, the U.S. economy was hit simultaneously by unemployment, stagnant consumer demand, and inflation — a combination called **stagflation** — which contradicted a basic principle taught by economists: prices were not supposed to rise in a stagnant economy. For ordinary Americans, stagflation meant a noticeable decline in purchasing power, as discretionary income per worker dropped 18 percent between 1973 and 1982. None of the three presidents of the decade — Richard Nixon, Gerald Ford, and Jimmy Carter — had much luck tackling stagflation. Nixon's New Economic Policy was perhaps the most radical attempt. Nixon imposed temporary price and wage controls in 1971 in an effort to curb inflation. Then he took an even bolder step: removing the United States from the gold standard, which allowed the dollar to float in international currency markets and effectively ended the Bretton Woods monetary system established after World War II. The underlying weaknesses in the U.S. economy remained, however, and neither Ford nor Carter had more luck finding a solution. The fruitless search for a new economic order was a hallmark of 1970s politics.

**Deindustrialization**    America's economic woes struck hardest at the industrial sector, which suddenly — shockingly — began to be dismantled. Worst hit was the steel industry, which for seventy-five years had been the economy's crown jewel. Unscathed by World War II, U.S. steel producers had enjoyed an open, hugely profitable market since the 1940s. But lack of serious competition left them without incentives to replace outdated plants and equipment. When West Germany and Japan rebuilt their steel industries, these facilities incorporated the latest technology. Foreign steel flooded into the United States during the 1970s, and the American industry was simply overwhelmed. Formerly titanic steel companies began a massive dismantling; virtually the entire Pittsburgh region, once a national hub of steel production, lost its heavy industry in a single generation. By the mid-1980s, downsizing, automation, and investment in new technologies made the American steel industry competitive again — but it was a shadow of its former self.

The steel industry was the prime example of what became known as **deindustrialization**. The country was in the throes of an economic transformation that left it largely stripped of its industrial base. Steel was hardly alone. A swath of the Northeast and Midwest, the country's manufacturing heartland, became the nation's **Rust Belt** (Map 28.1), strewn with abandoned plants and distressed communities. The automobile, tire, textile, and other consumer durable industries (appliances, electronics, furniture, and the like) all started shrinking in the 1970s. In 1980, *Business Week* bemoaned "plant closings across the continent" and called for the "*reindustrialization of America.*"

**Organized Labor in Decline**    Deindustrialization threw many tens of thousands of blue-collar workers out of well-paid union jobs. One study followed 4,100 steelworkers left jobless by the 1977 shutdown of the Campbell Works of the Youngstown Sheet & Tube Co. Two years later, 35 percent had retired early at half pay; 10 percent

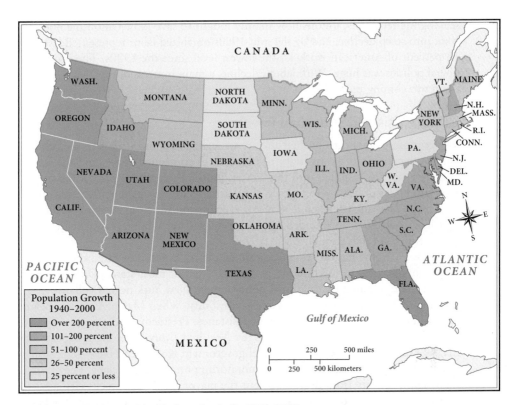

**MAP 28.1 From Rust Belt to Sunbelt, 1940–2000**
One of the most significant developments of the post–World War II era was the growth of the Sunbelt. Sparked by federal spending for military bases, the defense industry, and the space program, states of the South and Southwest experienced an economic boom in the 1950s. This growth was further enhanced in the 1970s, as the heavily industrialized regions of the Northeast and Midwest declined and migrants from what was quickly dubbed the Rust Belt headed to the South and West in search of jobs.

had moved; 15 percent were still jobless, with unemployment benefits long gone; and 40 percent had found local work, but mostly in low-paying, service-sector jobs. In another instance, between 1978 and 1981, eight Los Angeles companies—including such giants as Ford, Uniroyal, and U.S. Steel—closed factories employing 18,000 workers. These Ohio and California workers, like hundreds of thousands of their counterparts across the nation, had fallen from their perch in the middle class.

Deindustrialization dealt an especially harsh blow to the labor movement, which had facilitated the postwar expansion of that middle class. In the early 1970s, as inflation hit, the number of strikes surged; 2.4 million workers participated in work stoppages in 1970 alone. However, industry argued that it could no longer afford union demands, and labor's bargaining power produced fewer and fewer concrete results. In these hard years, the much-vaunted labor-management accord of the 1950s, which raised profits and wages by passing costs on to consumers, went bust. Instead of seeking higher wages, unions now mainly fought to save jobs. Union membership went into steep decline, and by the mid-1980s organized labor represented less than 18 percent of American workers, the lowest level since the 1920s. The impact on liberal politics was huge. With labor's decline, a main buttress of the New Deal coalition was coming undone.

## Urban Crisis and Suburban Revolt

The economic downturn pushed already struggling American cities to the brink of fiscal collapse. Middle-class flight to the suburbs continued apace, and the "urban crisis" of the 1960s spilled into the "era of limits." Facing huge price inflation and mounting piles of debt—to finance social services for low-income residents and to replace disappearing tax revenue—nearly every major American city struggled to pay its bills in the 1970s. Surrounded by prosperous postwar suburbs, central cities seemingly could not catch a break.

New York, the nation's financial capital and its largest city, fared the worst. Its annual budget was in the billions, larger than that of most states. Unable to borrow on the tightening international bond market, New York neared collapse in the summer of 1975; bankruptcy was a real possibility. When Mayor Abraham Beame appealed to the federal government for assistance, President Ford refused. "Ford to City: Drop Dead" read the headline in the *New York Daily News*. Fresh appeals ultimately produced a solution: the federal government would lend New York money, and banks would declare a three-year moratorium on municipal debt. The arrangement saved the city from defaulting, but the mayor was forced to cut city services, freeze wages, and lay off workers. One pessimistic observer declared that "the banks have been saved, and the city has been condemned."

Cities faced declining fortunes in these years for many reasons, but one key was the continued loss of residents and businesses to nearby suburbs. In the 1970s alone, 13 million people (6 percent of the total U.S. population) moved to the suburbs. New suburban shopping centers opened weekly across the country, and other businesses—such as banks, insurance companies, and technology firms—increasingly sought suburban locations. More and more, people lived *and* worked in suburbs. In the San Francisco Bay area, 75 percent of all daily commutes were suburb-to-suburb, and 78 percent of New York's suburban residents worked in nearby suburbs. The 1950s "organization man," commuting downtown from his suburban home, had been replaced by the engineer, teacher, nurse, student, and carpenter who lived in one suburb and worked in another.

Beyond city limits, suburbanization and the economic crisis combined powerfully in what became known as the **tax revolt**, a dramatic reversal of the postwar spirit of generous public investment. The premier example was California. Inflation pushed real estate values upward, and property taxes skyrocketed. Hardest hit were suburban property owners, along with retirees and others on fixed incomes, who suddenly faced unaffordable tax bills. Into this dire situation stepped Howard Jarvis, a conservative anti–New Dealer and a genius at mobilizing grassroots discontent. In 1978, Jarvis proposed **Proposition 13**, an initiative that would roll back property taxes, cap future increases for present owners, and require that all tax measures have a two-thirds majority in the legislature. Despite opposition by virtually the entire state leadership, including politicians from both parties, Californians voted overwhelmingly for Jarvis's measure.

Proposition 13 hobbled public spending in the nation's most populous state. Per capita funding of California public schools, once the envy of the nation, plunged from the top tier to the bottom, where it was second only to Mississippi. Moreover, Proposition 13's complicated formula benefited middle-class and wealthy home owners at the expense of less-well-off citizens, especially those who depended heavily on public services. Businesses, too, came out ahead, because commercial property got the same protection as residential property. More broadly, Proposition 13 inspired tax revolts across the country and helped conservatives define an enduring issue: low taxes.

In addition to public investment, another cardinal marker of New Deal and Great Society liberalism had been a remarkable decline in income inequality. In the 1970s, that trend reversed, and the wealthiest Americans, those among the top 10 percent, began to pull ahead again. As corporations restructured to boost profits during the 1970s slump, they increasingly laid off high-wage workers, paid the remaining workers less, and relocated overseas. Thus upper-class Americans benefitted, while blue-collar families who had been lifted into the middle class during the postwar boom increasingly lost out. An unmistakable trend was apparent by the end of the 1970s. The U.S. labor market was dividing in two: a vast, low-wage market at the bottom and a much narrower high-wage market at the top, with the middle squeezed smaller and smaller.

| **IN YOUR OWN WORDS** | What limits did the American economy experience in the 1970s? |
| --- | --- |

# Politics in Flux, 1973–1980

A search for order characterized national politics in the 1970s as well. It began with a scandal. Misbehavior is endemic to politics. Yet what became known as the Watergate affair — or simply **Watergate** — implicated President Richard Nixon in illegal behavior severe enough to bring down his presidency. Liberals benefitted from Nixon's fall in the short term, but their long-term retreat continued. Politics remained in flux because while liberals were on the defensive, conservatives had not yet put forth a clear alternative.

## Watergate and the Fall of a President

On June 17, 1972, something strange happened at Washington's Watergate office/apartment/hotel complex. Early that morning, five men carrying wiretapping equipment were apprehended there attempting to break into the headquarters of the Democratic National Committee (DNC). Queried by the press, a White House spokesman dismissed the episode as "a third-rate burglary attempt." Pressed further, Nixon himself denied any White House involvement in "this very bizarre incident."

In fact, the two masterminds of the break-in, G. Gordon Liddy and E. Howard Hunt, were former FBI and CIA agents currently working for Nixon's Committee to Re-elect the President (CREEP).

The Watergate burglary was no isolated incident. It was part of a broad pattern of abuse of power by a White House obsessed with its political enemies. Liddy and Hunt were on the White House payroll, part of a clandestine squad hired to stop leaks to the press. But they were soon arranging illegal wiretaps at DNC headquarters, part of a campaign of "dirty tricks" against the Democrats. Nixon's siege mentality best explains his fatal misstep. He could have dissociated himself from the break-in by firing his guilty aides or even just by letting justice take its course. But it was election time, and Nixon did not trust his political future to such a strategy. Instead, he arranged hush money for the burglars and instructed the CIA to stop an FBI investigation into the affair. This was obstruction of justice, a criminal offense.

Nixon kept the lid on until after the election, but in early 1973, one of the Watergate burglars began to talk. In the meantime, two reporters at the *Washington Post*, Carl Bernstein and Bob Woodward, uncovered CREEP's links to key White House aides. In May 1973, a Senate investigating committee began holding nationally televised hearings, at which administration officials implicated Nixon in the illegal cover-up. The president kept investigators at bay for a year, but in June 1974, the House Judiciary Committee began to consider articles of impeachment. Certain of being convicted by the Senate, Nixon became, on August 9, 1974, the first U.S. president to resign his office. The next day, Vice President Gerald Ford was sworn in as president. Ford, the Republican minority leader in the House of Representatives, had replaced Vice President Spiro Agnew, who had himself resigned in 1973 for accepting kickbacks while governor of Maryland. A month after he took office, Ford stunned the nation by granting Nixon a "full, free, and absolute" pardon.

Congress pushed back, passing a raft of laws inspired by the abuses of the Nixon administration and designed to limit the power of future presidents: the **War Powers Act** (1973), which reined in the president's ability to deploy U.S. forces without congressional approval; amendments strengthening the **Freedom of Information Act** (1974), which gave citizens access to federal records; the **Ethics in Government Act** (1978); and the Foreign Intelligence Surveillance Act (1978), which prohibited domestic wiretapping without a warrant.

Popular disdain for politicians, evident in declining voter turnout, deepened with Nixon's resignation in 1974. "Don't vote," read one bumper sticker in 1976. "It only encourages them." Watergate not only damaged short-term Republican prospects but also shifted the party's balance to the right. Despite mastering the populist appeal to the "silent majority," the moderate Nixon was never beloved by conservatives. His relaxation of tensions with the Soviet Union and his visit to communist China, in particular, won him no friends on the right. His disgraceful exit benefitted the more conservative Republicans, who proceeded to reshape the party in their image.

**Watergate Babies**    As for the Democrats, Watergate granted them a reprieve, a second chance at recapturing their eroding base. Democratic candidates in the 1974 midterm elections made Watergate and Ford's pardon of Nixon their top issues. It worked. Seventy-five new Democratic members of the House came to Washington in 1975, many of them under the age of forty-five, and the press dubbed them Watergate babies.

Young and reform-minded, the Watergate babies solidified huge Democratic majorities in both houses of Congress and quickly set to work. They eliminated the House Un-American Activities Committee (HUAC), which had investigated alleged Communists in the 1940s and 1950s and antiwar activists in the 1960s. In the Senate, Democrats reduced the number of votes needed to end a filibuster from 67 to 60 — a move intended to weaken the power of the minority to block legislation. In both houses, Democrats dismantled the existing committee structure, which had entrenched power in the hands of a few elite committee chairs. Overall, the Watergate babies helped to decentralize power in Washington and bring greater transparency to American government.

In one of the great ironies of American political history, however, the post-Watergate reforms made government *less* efficient and *more* susceptible to special interests — the opposite of what had been intended. Under the new committee structure, smaller subcommittees proliferated, and the size of the congressional staff doubled to more than 20,000. A diffuse power structure actually gave lobbyists more places to exert influence. As the power of committee chairs weakened, influence shifted to party leaders, such as the Speaker of the House and the Senate majority leader. With little incentive to compromise, the parties grew more rigid, and bipartisanship became rare. Finally, filibustering, a seldom-used tactic largely employed by anti–civil rights southerners, increased in frequency. The Congress that we have come to know today — with its partisan rancor, its army of lobbyists, and its slow-moving response to public needs — came into being in the 1970s.

**Political Realignment**    Despite Democratic gains in 1974, the electoral realignment that had begun with Richard Nixon's presidential victories in 1968 and 1972 continued. As liberals proved unable to stop runaway inflation or speed up economic growth, conservatives gained greater traction with the public. The postwar liberal economic formula — sometimes known as the Keynesian consensus — consisted of micro-adjustments to the money supply coupled with federal spending. When that formula failed to restart the economy in the mid-1970s, conservatives in Congress used this opening to articulate alternatives, especially economic deregulation and tax cuts (Chapter 29).

On a grander scale, deindustrialization in the Northeast and Midwest and continued population growth in the Sunbelt were changing the political geography of the country. Power was shifting, incrementally but perceptibly, toward the West and South. As states with strong trade unions at the center of the postwar liberal political coalition — such as New York, Illinois, and Michigan — lost industry, jobs, and people, states with traditions of libertarian conservatism — such as California, Arizona, Florida, and Texas — gained greater political clout. The full impact of this shifting political geography would not be felt until the 1980s and 1990s, but its effects had become apparent by the mid-1970s.

## Jimmy Carter: The Outsider as President

"Jimmy who?" was how journalists first responded when James Earl Carter, who had been a naval officer, a peanut farmer, and the governor of Georgia, emerged from the pack to win the Democratic presidential nomination in 1976. When Carter told his mother that he intended to run for president, she had asked, "President of what?" Trading on Watergate and his down-home image, Carter pledged to restore morality to the White House. "I will never lie to you," he promised voters. Carter played up his credentials as a Washington outsider, although he selected Senator Walter F. Mondale of Minnesota as his running mate to ensure his ties to traditional Democratic voting blocs. Ford still might have prevailed, but his pardon of Nixon likely cost him enough votes in key states to swing the election to the Democratic candidate. Carter won with 50 percent of the popular vote to Ford's 48 percent.

For a time, Carter got some mileage as an outsider—the common man who walked to the White House after the inauguration and delivered fireside chats in a cardigan sweater. The fact that he was a born-again Christian also played well. But Carter's inexperience began to show. He responded to feminists, an important Democratic constituency, by establishing a new women's commission in his administration. But later he dismissed the commission's concerns and became embroiled in a public fight with prominent women's advocates. Most consequentially, his outsider strategy made for chilly relations with congressional leaders. Disdainful of the Democratic establishment, Carter relied heavily on inexperienced advisors from Georgia. And as a detail-oriented micromanager, he exhausted himself over the fine points of policy better left to his aides.

**Jimmy Carter** President Jimmy Carter is seen here at his home in Plains, Georgia, in 1975, soon after he'd declared himself a candidate for the Democratic presidential nomination. Carter was content to portray himself as a political outsider, an ordinary American who could restore trust to Washington after the Watergate scandal. A thoughtful man and a born-again Christian, Carter nonetheless proved unable to solve the complex economic problems, especially high inflation, and international challenges of the late 1970s. AP Photo.

On the domestic front, Carter's big challenge was managing the economy. The problems that he faced defied easy solution. Most confounding was stagflation. If the government focused on inflation — forcing prices down by raising interest rates — unemployment became worse. If the government tried to stimulate employment, inflation became worse. None of the levers of government economic policy seemed to work. At heart, Carter was an economic conservative. He toyed with the idea of an "industrial policy" to bail out the ailing manufacturing sector, but he moved instead in a free-market direction by lifting the New Deal–era regulation of the airline, trucking, and railroad industries. **Deregulation** stimulated competition and cut prices, but it also drove firms out of business and hurt unionized workers.

The president's efforts failed to reignite economic growth. Then, the Iranian Revolution (see Chapter 29) curtailed oil supplies, and gas prices jumped again. In a major TV address, Carter lectured Americans about the nation's "crisis of the spirit." He called energy conservation "the moral equivalent of war" — or, in the media's shorthand, "MEOW," which aptly captured the nation's assessment of Carter's sermonizing. By then, his approval rating had fallen below 30 percent. And it was no wonder, given an inflation rate over 11 percent, failing industries, and long lines at the pumps. It seemed the worst of all possible economic worlds, and the first-term president could not help but worry about the political costs to him and his party.

| **IN YOUR OWN WORDS** | In what ways was the period between 1973 and 1980 a transitional one in American politics? |
|---|---|

# Reform and Reaction in the 1970s

Having lived through a decade of profound social and political upheaval — the Vietnam War, protests, riots, Watergate, recession — many Americans were exhausted and cynical by the mid-1970s. But while some retreated to private concerns, others took reform in new directions. Civil rights battles continued, the women's movement achieved some of its most far-reaching aims, and gay rights blossomed. These movements pushed the "rights revolution" of the 1960s deeper into American life. Others, however, pushed back. Social conservatives responded by forming their own organizations and resisting the emergence of what they saw as a permissive society.

## Civil Rights in a New Era

When Congress banned job discrimination in the 1964 Civil Rights Act, the law required only that employers hire without regard to "race, color, religion, sex, or national origin." But after centuries of slavery and decades of segregation, would nondiscrimination bring African Americans into the economic mainstream? Many liberals thought not. They believed that government, universities, and private employers needed to take positive steps to open their doors to a wider, more diverse range of Americans — including those from other historically underrepresented groups and women.

Among the most significant efforts to address the legacy of exclusion was **affirmative action**—procedures designed to take into account the disadvantaged position of Americans from historically underrepresented groups after centuries of discrimination. First advanced by the Kennedy administration in 1961, affirmative action received a boost under President Lyndon Johnson, whose Labor Department fashioned a series of plans in the late 1960s to encourage government contractors to recruit underrepresented racial groups. Women were added under the last of these plans, when pressure from the women's movement highlighted the problem of sex discrimination. By the early 1970s, affirmative action had been refined by court rulings that identified acceptable procedures: hiring and enrollment goals, special recruitment and training programs, and set-asides (specially reserved slots) for both underrepresented racial groups and women.

Affirmative action, however, did not please many whites, who felt that the deck was being stacked against them. Much of the dissent came from conservative groups that had opposed civil rights all along. They charged affirmative action advocates with "reverse discrimination." Legal challenges abounded, as employees, students, and university applicants went to court to object to these new procedures. Some liberal groups sought a middle position. In a widely publicized 1972 letter, Jewish organizations, seared by the memory of quotas that once kept Jewish students out of elite colleges, came out against all racial quotas but nonetheless endorsed "rectifying the imbalances resulting from past discrimination."

A major shift in affirmative action policy came in 1978. Allan Bakke, a white man, sued the University of California at Davis Medical School for rejecting him in favor of less-qualified minority-group candidates. Headlines across the country sparked anti–affirmative action protest marches on college campuses and vigorous discussion on television and radio and in the White House. Ultimately, the Supreme Court rejected the medical school's quota system, which set aside 16 of 100 places for "disadvantaged" students. The Court ordered Bakke admitted but indicated that a more flexible affirmative action plan, in which race could be considered along with other factors, would still pass constitutional muster. *Bakke v. University of California* thus upheld affirmative action but, by rejecting a quota system, also called it into question. Future court rulings and state referenda, in the 1990s and 2000s, would further limit the scope of affirmative action. In particular, California voters passed Proposition 209 in 1996, prohibiting public institutions from using affirmative action to increase diversity in employment and education.

## The Women's Movement and Gay Rights

Unlike the civil rights movement, whose signal achievements came in the 1960s, the women's and gay rights movements flourished in the 1970s. With three influential wings—radical, liberal, and "Third World"—the women's movement inspired both grassroots activism and legislative action across the nation. For their part, gay activists faced a unique set of challenges: they needed to convince Americans that same-sex relationships were natural and that gay men and lesbians deserved the same protection of the law as all other citizens. Neither movement achieved all of its aims in this era, but each laid a strong foundation for the future.

**Women's Activism**    In the first half of the 1970s, the women's liberation movement reached its historic peak. Taking a dizzying array of forms—from lobbying legislatures to marching in the streets and establishing all-female collectives—women's liberation inspired activism on the scale of the earlier black-led civil rights movement. Women's centers, as well as women-run child-care facilities, began to spring up in cities and towns. A feminist art and poetry movement flourished. Women challenged the admissions policies of all-male colleges and universities—opening such prestigious universities as Yale and Columbia and nearly bringing an end to male-only institutions of higher education. Female scholars began to transform higher education: by studying women's history, by increasing the number of women on college and university faculties, and by founding women's studies programs.

Women's liberationists drew new attention to, and thereby politicized, the female body. Inspired by the Boston collective that first published *Our Bodies, Ourselves*—a groundbreaking book on women's health—the women's health movement founded dozens of medical clinics, encouraged women to become physicians, and educated millions of women about their bodies. To reform antiabortion laws, activists pushed for remedies in more than thirty state legislatures. Women's liberationists established rape crisis centers around the nation and lobbied state legislatures and Congress to reform rape laws. Many of these endeavors and movements began as shoestring operations in living rooms and kitchens: *Our Bodies, Ourselves* was first published as a 35-cent mimeographed booklet, and the antirape movement began in small consciousness-raising groups that met in churches and community centers. By the end of the decade, however, all of these causes had national organizations and touched the lives of millions of American women.

**Equal Rights Amendment**    Buoyed by this flourishing of activism, the women's movement renewed the fight for an **Equal Rights Amendment (ERA)** to the Constitution. First introduced in 1923, the ERA stated, in its entirety, "Equality of rights under the law shall not be denied or abridged by the United States or any State on the basis of sex." Vocal congressional women from the Democratic Party, such as Patsy Mink (Hawaii), Bella Abzug (New York), and Shirley Chisholm (New York), found enthusiastic male allies—among both Democrats and Republicans—and Congress adopted the amendment in 1972. Within just two years, thirty-four of the necessary thirty-eight states had ratified it, and the ERA appeared headed for adoption. But then, progress abruptly halted (Map 28.2).

Credit for putting the brakes on ERA ratification goes chiefly to a remarkable woman: Phyllis Schlafly, a lawyer long active in conservative causes. Despite her own flourishing career, Schlafly advocated traditional roles for women. The ERA, she proclaimed, would create an unnatural "unisex society," with women drafted into the army and forced to use single-sex restrooms. Abortion, she alleged, could never be prohibited by law. Led by Schlafly's organization, **STOP ERA** (founded in 1972), thousands of women mobilized, showing up at statehouses with home-baked bread and apple pies. As labels on baked goods at one anti-ERA rally expressed it: "My heart and hand went into this dough / For the sake of the family please vote no." It was a message that resonated widely, especially among those troubled by the rapid pace of social change. The ERA never was ratified, despite a congressional extension of the deadline to June 30, 1982.

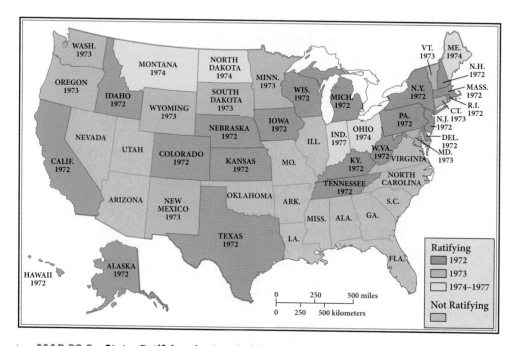

**MAP 28.2    States Ratifying the Equal Rights Amendment, 1972–1977**

The ratifying process for the Equal Rights Amendment (ERA) went smoothly in 1972 and 1973 but then stalled. The turning point came in 1976, when ERA advocates lobbied extensively, particularly in Florida, North Carolina, and Illinois, but failed to sway the conservative legislatures in those states. After Indiana ratified in 1977, the amendment still lacked three votes toward the three-fourths majority needed for adoption. Efforts to revive the ERA in the 1980s were unsuccessful, and it became a dead issue.

*Roe v. Wade*   In addition to the ERA, the women's movement had identified another major goal: winning reproductive rights. Activists pursued two tracks: legislative and judicial. In the early 1960s, abortion was illegal in virtually every state. A decade later, thanks to intensive lobbying by women's organizations, liberal ministers, and physicians, a handful of states, such as New York, Hawaii, California, and Colorado, adopted laws making legal abortions easier to obtain. But progress after that was slow, and women's advocates turned to the courts. There was reason to be optimistic. The Supreme Court had first addressed reproductive rights in a 1965 case, *Griswold v. Connecticut. Griswold* struck down an 1879 state law prohibiting the possession of contraception as a violation of married couples' constitutional "right of privacy." Following the logic articulated in *Griswold,* the Court gradually expanded the right of privacy in a series of cases in the late 1960s and early 1970s.

Those cases culminated in ***Roe v. Wade*** (1973). In that landmark decision, the justices nullified a Texas law that prohibited abortion under any circumstances, even when the woman's health was at risk, and laid out a new national standard: abortions performed during the first trimester were protected by the right of privacy. At the time and afterward, some legal authorities questioned whether the Constitution recognized any such privacy right and criticized the Court's seemingly arbitrary first-trimester timeline. Nevertheless, the Supreme Court chose to move forward, transforming a traditionally state-regulated policy into a national, constitutionally protected right.

For the women's movement, *Roe v. Wade* represented a triumph. For evangelical and fundamentalist Christians, Catholics, and conservatives generally, it was a bitter pill. In their view, abortion was, unequivocally, the taking of a human life. These Americans, represented by groups such as the National Right to Life Committee, did not believe that something they regarded as immoral and sinful could be the basis for women's equality. Women's advocates responded that illegal abortions—common prior to *Roe*—were often unsafe procedures that resulted in physical harm to women and even death. *Roe* polarized what was already a sharply divided public and mobilized conservatives to seek a Supreme Court reversal or, short of that, to pursue legislation that would strictly limit the conditions under which abortions could be performed. In 1976, they convinced Congress to deny Medicaid funds for abortions, an opening round in a campaign against *Roe v. Wade* that continues today.

**Harvey Milk**    The gay rights movement had achieved notable victories as well. These, too, proved controversial. By the mid-1970s, more than a dozen cities had passed gay rights ordinances protecting gay men and lesbians from employment and housing discrimination. One such ordinance in Dade County (Miami), Florida, sparked a protest led by Anita Bryant, a conservative Baptist and a television celebrity. Her "Save Our Children" campaign in 1977, which garnered national media attention, resulted in the repeal of the ordinance and symbolized the emergence of a conservative religious movement opposed to gay rights.

Across the country from Miami, developments in San Francisco looked promising for gay rights advocates, then turned tragic. No one embodied the combination of gay liberation and hard-nosed politics better than a San Francisco camera-shop owner named Harvey Milk. A closeted businessman in New York until he was forty, Milk arrived in San Francisco in 1972 and threw himself into city politics. Fiercely independent, he ran as an openly gay candidate for city supervisor (city council) twice and the state assembly once, both times unsuccessfully.

By mobilizing the "gay vote" into a powerful bloc, Milk finally won a supervisor seat in 1977. He was not the first openly gay elected official in the country—Kathy Kozachenko of Michigan and Elaine Noble of Massachusetts share that distinction—but he became a national symbol of emerging gay political power. Tragically, after he helped to win passage of a gay rights ordinance in San Francisco, he was assassinated in 1978—along with the city's mayor, George Moscone—by a disgruntled former supervisor named Dan White. When White was convicted of manslaughter rather than murder, five thousand gays and lesbians in San Francisco marched on city hall.

## After the Warren Court

In response to what conservatives considered the liberal judicial revolution under the Warren Court, Nixon came into the presidency promising to appoint "strict constructionists" (conservative-minded justices) to the bench. In three short years, between 1969 and 1972, he was able to appoint four new justices to the Supreme Court, including the new chief justice, Warren Burger. Burger and his conservative colleagues did not, suprisingly, immediately seek to overturn Warren Court precedents. Indeed, in *Roe v. Wade* the Burger Court extended the "right of privacy" developed under Warren to include women's access to abortion. As we saw above, few Supreme Court decisions in the twentieth century have disappointed conservatives more. Other decisions advanced women's rights further. In 1976, the Court ruled that arbitrary distinctions based on sex in the workplace and other arenas were unconstitutional, and in 1986 that sexual harassment violated the Civil Rights Act. These rulings helped women break employment barriers in the subsequent decades.

In a variety of cases, however, the Burger Court chose a centrist course, particularly in cases regarding criminal law. After first striking down all existing capital punishment laws, in *Furman v. Georgia* (1972), the court shortly restored them, in *Gregg v. Georgia* (1976). Rather than overturning the Warren Court's rulings on the rights of suspected criminals (such as the 1966 decision in *Miranda v. Arizona*), which were deeply unpopular among conservatives, the Burger Court instead limited their reach. Overall, despite its reputation for centrist restraint, the Burger Court helped to ratify the "law and order" politics embraced by many Americans in the years following the 1960s.

In keeping with such centrism, in all of their rulings on privacy rights the Burger Court was reluctant to move ahead of public attitudes toward homosexuality. Gay men and lesbians still had no legal recourse if state laws prohibited same-sex relations. In a controversial 1986 case, *Bowers v. Hardwick*, the Supreme Court upheld a Georgia sodomy statute that criminalized same-sex sexual acts. The majority opinion held that homosexuality was contrary to "ordered liberty" and that extending sexual privacy to gays and lesbians "would be to cast aside millennia of moral teaching." Not until 2003 (*Lawrence v. Texas*) would the Court overturn that decision, recognizing for all Americans the right to sexual privacy.

| IN YOUR OWN WORDS | How did controversies over new individual rights shape the politics of the 1970s? |
|---|---|

# The American Family on Trial

In 1973, the Public Broadcasting System (PBS) aired a twelve-part television series that followed the life of a real American family. Producers wanted the show, called simply *An American Family*, to document how a middle-class white family coped with the stresses of a changing society. They did not anticipate that the family would dissolve in front of their cameras. Tensions and arguments raged, and in the final episode, Bill, the husband and father (who had had numerous extramarital affairs), moved out. By the time the show aired, the couple was divorced and Pat, the former wife, had become a single working mother with five children.

*An American Family* captured a traumatic moment in the twentieth-century history of the family. Between 1965 and 1985, the divorce rate doubled, and children born in the 1970s had a 40 percent chance of spending part of their youth in a single-parent household. As wages stagnated and inflation pushed prices up, more and more families depended on two incomes for survival. Furthermore, the women's movement and the counterculture had called into question traditional sex roles — father as provider and mother as homemaker — and middle-class baby boomers rebelled against what they saw as the puritanical sexual values of their parents' generation. In the midst of such rapid change, where did the family stand?

## Working Families in the Age of Deindustrialization

One of the most striking developments of the 1970s and 1980s was the relative stagnation of wages. After World War II, hourly wages had grown steadily ahead of inflation, giving workers more buying power with each passing decade. By 1973, that trend had stopped in its tracks. The decline of organized labor, the loss of manufacturing jobs, and runaway inflation all played a role in the reversal. Hardest hit were blue-collar and pink-collar workers and those without college degrees.

**Women Enter the Workforce**    Millions of wives and mothers had worked for wages for decades. But many Americans still believed in the "family wage": a breadwinner income, earned by men, sufficient to support a family. After 1973, fewer and fewer Americans had access to that luxury. Between 1973 and the early 1990s, every major income group except the top 10 percent saw their real earnings (accounting for inflation) either remain the same or decline. Over this period, the typical worker saw a 10 percent drop in real wages. To keep their families from falling behind, women streamed into the workforce. Between 1950 and 1994, the proportion of women ages twenty-five to fifty-four working for pay increased from 37 to 75 percent. Much of that increase occurred in the 1970s. Americans were fast becoming dependent on the two-income household.

The numbers tell two different stories of American life in these decades. On one hand, the trends unmistakably show that women, especially in blue-collar and pink-collar families, *had* to work for wages to sustain their family's standard of living: to buy a car, pay for college, afford medical bills, support an aging parent, or simply pay the rent. Moreover, the number of single women raising children nearly doubled between 1965 and 1990. Women's paid labor was making up for the declining earning power or the absence of men in American households. On the other hand, women's real income overall grew during the same period. This increase reflected the opening of professional jobs to educated baby boom women. As older barriers began to fall, women poured into law and medicine, business and government, and, though more slowly, the sciences and engineering. Beneficiaries of feminism, these women pursued careers of which their mothers had only dreamed.

**Workers in the National Spotlight**    For a brief period in the 1970s, the trials of working men and women made a distinct imprint on national culture. Reporters wrote of the "blue-collar blues" associated with plant closings and the hard-fought strikes of the decade. A 1972 strike at the Lordstown, Ohio, General Motors plant captivated the nation. Holding out not for higher wages but for better working conditions — the

***Good Times*** The popular 1970s sitcom *Good Times* examined how the "blue-collar blues" affected a working-class black family struggling to make ends meet in tough economic times. The show's theme song spoke of "temporary layoffs . . . easy credit ripoffs . . . scratchin' and surviving." Its actors, many of them classically trained, brought a realistic portrait of working-class African American life to television. Bettmann/Getty Images.

plant had the most complex assembly line in the nation—Lordstown strikers spoke out against what they saw as an inhumane industrial system. Across the nation, the number of union-led strikes surged, even as the number of Americans in the labor movement continued to decline. In Lordstown and most other sites of strikes and industrial conflict, workers won a measure of public attention but typically gained little economic ground.

When Americans turned on their televisions in the mid-1970s, the most popular shows reflected the "blue-collar blues" of struggling families. *All in the Family* was joined by *The Waltons*, set during the Great Depression. *Good Times, Welcome Back, Kotter,* and *Sanford and Son* dealt with poverty in the inner city. *The Jeffersons* featured an upwardly mobile black couple struggling to leave their working-class roots behind. *Laverne and Shirley* focused on young working women in the 1950s and *One Day at a Time* on working women in the 1970s making do after divorce. The most-watched television series of the decade, 1977's eight-part *Roots*, explored the history of slavery and the survival of African American culture and family roots despite the oppressive labor system. Not since the 1930s had American culture paid such close attention to working-class life.

The decade also saw the rise of musicians such as Bruce Springsteen, Johnny Paycheck, and John Cougar (Mellencamp), who became stars by turning the hardscrabble lives of people in small towns and working-class communities into rock anthems that filled arenas. Springsteen wrote songs about characters who "sweat it out in the streets of a runaway American dream," and, to the delight of his audience, Paycheck famously sang, "Take this job and shove it!" Meanwhile, on the streets of Harlem and the South Bronx in New York, young working-class African American men experimenting with dance and musical forms invented break dancing and rap music — styles that expressed both the hardship and the creativity of working-class black life in the deindustrialized American city.

## Navigating the Sexual Revolution

The economic downturn was not the only force that placed stress on American families in this era. Another such force was what many came to call the "sexual revolution." Hardly revolutionary, sexual attitudes in the 1970s were, in many ways, a logical evolution of developments in the first half of the twentieth century. Beginning in the 1910s, Americans increasingly viewed sex as a component of personal happiness, distinct from reproduction. Attitudes toward sex grew even more lenient in the postwar decades, a fact reflected in the Kinsey studies of the 1940s and 1950s. By the 1960s, sex before marriage had grown more socially acceptable — an especially profound change for women — and frank discussions of sex in the media and popular culture had grown more common.

In that decade, three developments dramatically accelerated this process: the introduction of the birth control pill, the rise of the baby-boomer-led counterculture, and the influence of feminism. First made available in the United States in 1960, the birth control pill gave women an unprecedented degree of control over reproduction. By 1965, more than 6 million American women were taking advantage of this pharmaceutical advance. Rapid shifts in attitude accompanied the technological breakthrough. Middle-class baby boomers embraced a sexual ethic of greater freedom and, in many cases, a more casual approach to sex outside marriage. "I just feel I am expressing myself the way I feel at that moment in the most natural way," a female California college student, explaining her sex life, told a reporter in 1966. The rebellious counterculture encouraged this attitudinal shift by associating a puritanical view of sex with their parents' generation.

Finally, women's rights activists reacted to the new emphasis on sexual freedom in at least two distinct ways. Many feminists felt that the sexual revolution was by and for men: the emphasis on casual sex seemed to perpetuate male privilege — the old double standard; sexual harassment was all too common in the workplace; and the proliferation of pornography continued to commercialize women as sex objects. On the other hand, they remained optimistic that the new sexual ethic could free women from those older moral constraints. They called for a revolution in sexual *values*, not simply behavior, that would end exploitation and grant women the freedom to explore their sexuality on equal terms with men.

**Sex and Popular Culture**　In the 1970s, popular culture was suffused with discussions of the sexual revolution. Mass-market books with titles such as *Everything You Always Wanted to Know About Sex*, *Human Sexual Response*, and *The Sensuous Man* shot up the best-seller list. William Masters and Virginia Johnson became the most famous sex researchers since Alfred Kinsey by studying couples in the act of lovemaking. In 1972, English physician Alex Comfort published *The Joy of Sex*, a guidebook for couples that became one of the most popular books of the decade. Comfort made certain to distinguish his writing from pornographic exploitation. "Sex is the one place where we today can learn to treat people as people," he wrote.

Hollywood took advantage of the new sexual ethic by making films with explicit erotic content that pushed the boundaries of middle-class taste. Films such as *Midnight Cowboy* (1969), *Carnal Knowledge* (1971), and *Shampoo* (1974), the latter starring Hollywood's leading ladies' man, Warren Beatty, led the way. Throughout the decade, and into the 1980s, the Motion Picture Association of America (MPAA) scrambled to keep its guide for parents — the system of rating pictures G, PG, R, and X (and, after 1984, PG-13) — in tune with Hollywood's advancing sexual revolution.

On television, the popularity of social problem shows, such as *All in the Family*, and the fear of losing advertising revenue moderated the portrayal of sex in the early 1970s. However, in the second half of the decade networks both exploited and criticized the new sexual ethic. In frivolous, lighthearted shows such as the popular *Charlie's Angels*, *Three's Company*, and *The Love Boat*, heterosexual couples explored the often confusing, and usually comical, landscape of sexual morality. At the same time, between 1974 and 1981, the major networks produced more than a dozen made-for-TV movies about children in sexual danger — a sensationalized warning to parents of the potential threats to children posed by a less strict sexual morality.

**Middle-Class Marriage**     Many Americans worried that the sexual revolution threatened marriage itself. The notion of marriage as romantic companionship had defined middle-class norms since the nineteenth century. It was also quite common throughout most of the twentieth century for Americans to see sexual satisfaction as a healthy part of the marriage bond. But what defined a healthy marriage in an age of rising divorce rates, changing sexual values, and feminist critiques of the nuclear family? Only a small minority of Americans rejected marriage outright; most continued to create monogamous relationships codified in marriage. But many came to believe that they needed help as marriage came under a variety of economic and psychological stresses.

A therapeutic industry arose in response. Churches and secular groups alike established marriage seminars and counseling services to assist couples in sustaining a healthy marriage. A popular form of 1960s psychotherapy, the "encounter group," was adapted to marriage counseling: couples met in large groups to explore new methods of communicating. One of the most successful of these organizations, Marriage Encounter, was founded by the Catholic Church. It expanded into Protestant and Jewish communities in the 1970s and became one of the nation's largest counseling organizations. Such groups embodied another long-term shift in how middle-class Americans understood marriage. Spurred by both feminism and psychotherapeutic models that stressed self-improvement, Americans increasingly defined marriage not simply by companionship and sexual fidelity but also by the deeply felt emotional connection between two people.

## Religion in the 1970s: The New Evangelicalism

For three centuries, American society has been punctuated by intense periods of religious revival—some of which historians have called Great Awakenings (Chapters 4 and 10). These periods have seen a rise in church membership, the appearance of charismatic religious leaders, and the increasing influence of religion, usually of the evangelical variety, on society and politics. One such surge in religiosity and evangelical fervor took shape between the 1960s and 1980s. The "New Evangelicalism" of those decades had many elements, but one of its central features was a growing concern with the family.

In the 1950s and 1960s, many mainstream Protestants had embraced the reform spirit of the age. Some of the most visible Protestant leaders were social activists who condemned racism and opposed the Vietnam War. Organizations such as the National Council of Churches—along with many progressive Catholics and Jews—joined with Martin Luther King Jr. and other African American ministers in the long battle for civil rights. Many mainline Protestant churches, among them the Episcopal, Methodist, and Congregationalist denominations, practiced a version of the "Social Gospel," the reform-minded Christianity of the early twentieth century.

**Evangelical Resurgence**   Meanwhile, **evangelicalism** survived at the grass roots. Evangelical Protestant churches emphasized an intimate, personal salvation (being "born again"); focused on a literal interpretation of the Bible; and regarded the death and resurrection of Jesus as the central message of Christianity. These tenets distinguished evangelicals from mainline Protestants as well as from Catholics and Jews, and they flourished in a handful of evangelical colleges, Bible schools, and seminaries in the postwar decades.

No one did more to keep the evangelical fire burning than Billy Graham. A graduate of the evangelical Wheaton College in Illinois, Graham cofounded Youth for Christ in 1945 and then toured the United States and Europe preaching the gospel. Following a stunning 1949 tent revival in Los Angeles that lasted eight weeks, Graham shot to national fame. His success in Los Angeles led to a popular radio program, but he continued to travel relentlessly, conducting old-fashioned revival meetings he called crusades. A massive sixteen-week 1957 crusade held in New York City's Madison Square Garden made Graham, along with the conservative Catholic priest Fulton Sheen, one of the nation's most visible religious leaders.

Graham and other evangelicals in the 1950s and 1960s laid the groundwork for the New Evangelicalism. But it was a startling combination of events in the late 1960s and early 1970s that dramatically magnified the evangelical revival. First, rising divorce rates, social unrest, and challenges to prevailing values led people to seek the stability of faith. Second, many Americans regarded feminism, the counterculture, sexual freedom, homosexuality, pornography, and legalized abortion not as distinct issues, but as a collective sign of moral decay in society. To seek answers and find order, more and more people turned to evangelical ministries, especially Southern Baptist, Pentecostal, and Assemblies of God churches.

Numbers tell part of the story. As mainline churches lost about 15 percent of their membership between 1970 and 1985, evangelical church membership soared. The Southern Baptist Convention, the largest Protestant denomination, grew by 23 percent, while the Assemblies of God grew by an astounding 300 percent. *Newsweek* magazine declared 1976 "The Year of the Evangelical," and that November the nation made Jimmy Carter the nation's first evangelical president. In a national Gallup poll, a robust one-third of Americans answered yes when asked, "Would you describe yourself as a 'born again' or evangelical Christian?"

Much of this astonishing growth came from the creative use of television. A new generation of preachers brought religious conversion directly into Americans' living rooms through television. These so-called televangelists built huge media empires through small donations from millions of avid viewers—not to mention advertising. Jerry Falwell's *Old Time Gospel Hour*, Pat Robertson's *700 Club*, and Jim and Tammy Bakker's *PTL (Praise the Lord) Club* were the leading pioneers in this televised race for American souls, but another half dozen—including Oral Roberts and Jimmy Swaggart—followed them onto the airwaves. Together, they made the 1970s and 1980s the era of Christian broadcasting.

**Religion and the Family**   Of primary concern to evangelical Christians was the family. Drawing on selected Bible passages, evangelicals believed that the nuclear family, and not the individual, represented the fundamental unit of society. The family itself was organized along paternalist lines: father was breadwinner and disciplinarian; mother was nurturer and supporter. "Motherhood is the highest form of femininity," the evangelical author Beverly LaHaye wrote in an influential book on Christian women. Another popular Christian author declared, "A church, a family, a nation is only as strong as its men."

Evangelicals spread their message about the Christian family through more than the pulpit and television. They founded publishing houses, wrote books, established foundations, and offered seminars. Helen B. Andelin, for instance, a California housewife, produced a homemade book called *Fascinating Womanhood* that eventually sold more than 2 million copies. She used the book as the basis for her classes, which by the early 1970s had been attended by 400,000 women and boasted 11,000 trained teachers. *Fascinating Womanhood* led evangelical women in the opposite direction of feminism. Whereas the latter encouraged women to be independent and to seek equality with men, Andelin taught that "submissiveness will bring a strange but righteous power over your man." Andelin was but one of dozens of evangelical authors and educators who encouraged women to defer to men.

Evangelical Christians held that strict gender roles in the family would ward off the influences of an immoral society. Christian activists were especially concerned with sex education in public schools, the proliferation of pornography, legalized abortion, and the rising divorce rate. For them, the answer was to strengthen what they called "traditional" family structures. By the early 1980s, Christians could choose from among hundreds of evangelical books, take classes on how to save a marriage or how to be a Christian parent, attend evangelical churches and Bible study courses, watch evangelical ministers on television, and donate to foundations that promoted "Christian values" in state legislatures and the U.S. Congress.

Wherever one looked in the 1970s and early 1980s, American families were under strain. Nearly everyone agreed that the waves of social liberalism and economic transformation that swept over the nation in the 1960s and 1970s had destabilized society and, especially, family relationships. But Americans did not agree about how to *re*stabilize families. Indeed, different approaches to the family would further divide the country in the 1980s and 1990s, as the New Right would increasingly make "family values" a political issue.

| IN YOUR OWN WORDS | What were the major sources of anxiety about the American family in the decade after the 1960s? |
|---|---|

## Summary

For much of the 1970s, Americans struggled with economic problems, including inflation, energy shortages, income stagnation, and deindustrialization. These challenges highlighted the limits of postwar prosperity and forced Americans to consider lowering their economic expectations. A movement for environmental protection, widely supported, led to new laws and an awareness of nature's limits, and the energy crisis highlighted the nation's dependence on resources from abroad, especially oil.

In the midst of this gloomy economic climate, Americans also sought political and cultural resolutions to the upheavals of the 1960s. In politics, the Watergate scandal led to a brief period of political reform. Meanwhile, the battle for civil rights entered a second stage, expanding to encompass women's rights, gay rights, and the rights of alleged criminals and prisoners and, in the realm of racial justice, focusing on the problem of producing concrete results rather than legislation. Many liberals cheered these developments, but another effect was to strengthen a new, more conservative social mood that began to challenge liberal values in politics and society more generally. Finally, we considered the multiple challenges faced by the American family in the 1970s and how a perception that the family was in trouble helped to spur an evangelical religious revival that would shape American society for decades to come.

# Chapter 28 Review

## KEY TERMS

**Identify and explain the significance of each term below.**

Organization of Petroleum Exporting Countries (OPEC) (p. 817)
energy crisis (p. 817)
environmentalism (p. 817)
*Silent Spring* (p. 817)
Earth Day (p. 818)
Environmental Protection Agency (EPA) (p. 818)
Three Mile Island (p. 819)
stagflation (p. 820)
deindustrialization (p. 820)
Rust Belt (p. 820)
tax revolt (p. 822)

Proposition 13 (p. 822)
Watergate (p. 823)
War Powers Act (p. 824)
Freedom of Information Act (p. 824)
Ethics in Government Act (p. 824)
deregulation (p. 827)
affirmative action (p. 828)
*Bakke v. University of California* (p. 828)
Equal Rights Amendment (ERA) (p. 829)
STOP ERA (p. 829)
*Roe v. Wade* (p. 830)
evangelicalism (p. 837)

## REVIEW QUESTIONS

**Answer these questions to demonstrate your understanding of the chapter's main ideas.**

1. What limits did the American economy experience in the 1970s?

2. In what ways was the period between 1973 and 1980 a transitional one in American politics?

3. How did controversies over new individual rights shape the politics of the 1970s?

4. What were the major sources of anxiety about the American family in the decade after the 1960s?

5. Examine the category "Work, Exchange, and Technology" on the thematic timeline on page 696. How did economic developments in the 1970s reverse the course the national economy had been on since World War II? More broadly, can you identify events in each of the timeline categories that made the 1970s a decade of important historical transition?

## CHRONOLOGY

**As you read, ask yourself why this chapter begins and ends with these dates and identify the links among related events.**

| | |
|---|---|
| **1970** | • Earth Day first observed |
| | • Environmental Protection Agency established |
| **1972** | • Equal Rights Amendment passed by Congress |
| | • Phyllis Schlafly founds STOP ERA |
| | • *Furman v. Georgia* outlaws death penalty |
| | • Watergate break-in (June) |
| **1973** | • *Roe v. Wade* legalizes abortion |
| | • Endangered Species Act |
| | • OPEC oil embargo; gas shortages |
| | • Period of high inflation begins |
| | • War Powers Act |
| **1974** | • Nixon resigns over Watergate |
| | • Congress imposes 55 miles-per-hour speed limit |
| **1975** | • New York City nears bankruptcy |
| | • "Watergate babies" begin congressional reform |
| **1976** | • Jimmy Carter elected president |
| **1978** | • Proposition 13 reduces California property taxes |
| | • *Bakke v. University of California* limits affirmative action |
| | • Harvey Milk assassinated in San Francisco |
| **1979** | • Three Mile Island nuclear accident |

# PART 9

For historians, the recent past can be a challenge to assess. Insufficient time has passed for scholars to weigh the significance of events and to determine which developments will have a lasting effect and which are more fleeting. Nevertheless, scholars generally agree on the era's three most significant developments: the resurgence of political conservatism, the end of the Cold War, and the globalization of communications and the economy. The first of these, as we showed in Part 8, was decades in the making. Conservatism had leaped back to life in the 1960s, but not until the 1980s did American conservatives have the political muscle to reshape national politics in fundamental respects. Conservatism's resurgence occasioned a wide-ranging and divisive internal debate among Americans over what the nation's common values and priorities should be.

The second two developments began to reshape the place of the United States in the world. With the collapse of European communism after 1989, the Cold War came to an end, leaving the U.S. as the world's dominant military power. But military dominance coexisted with shrinking economic influence. What *Time* magazine publisher Henry Luce in 1941 had named the American Century—in his call for the U.S. to assume global leadership after World War II—came to an end in the last quarter of the twentieth century. The U.S. remained the world's largest economy but faced rising competition from a united Europe and a surging China. These decades stand as an era of transition away from the bipolar world of the Cold War.

Contemporary events continue to unfold, and thus Part 9 remains necessarily a work-in-progress. We've emphasized how through equal parts conflict, struggle, and ingenuity, Americans collectively forged a new era in national history after the 1980s.

## Conservative Ascendancy

In the 1980s, the conservatism of Ronald Reagan and the New Right, consolidated in the Republican Party, challenged the liberalism of the 1960s and 1970s. Conservatives reduced the regulatory power of the federal government, eroded the welfare state of the New Deal and the Great Society, and expanded the military. Evangelical Christians and conservative lawmakers challenged abortion rights, feminism, and gay rights, setting off a "culture war" that sharply divided Americans.

Even as the Reagan coalition brought an end to decades of liberal government activism, much of the legacy of the New Deal was preserved: Medicare, Medicaid, and Social Security grew as a proportion of the federal budget. Conservatives shaped U.S. foreign policy, however, dramatically increasing the defense budget and, under George W. Bush, asserting a new doctrine of "preemptive war." By the election of 2016, national politics seemed as divided as ever. Republican Donald Trump won the presidency, and voters returned a conservative majority to Congress. Polls showed that Americans embraced a moderate liberalism, but the national political system had moved firmly into conservative hands.

## End of the Cold War and Rising Conflict in the Middle East

Under Reagan's direction, the U.S. increased military spending and returned to the sharp Cold War rhetoric of earlier decades. Yet in the second half of the 1980s, as internal reforms swept through the Soviet Union, Reagan engaged in productive dialogue with the Soviet leader Mikhail Gorbachev. Then in 1991, the Soviet Union stunningly collapsed and the U.S. emerged as the lone military "superpower" in the world. Absent a clear Cold War enemy, it intervened in civil wars, worked to disrupt terrorist activities, and provided humanitarian aid — but guided more by pragmatism than by principle.

The foremost region that occupied U.S. attention was the Middle East, where strategic interest in oil remained paramount. Between 1991 and 2016, the U.S. fought three wars in the region — two in Iraq and one in Afghanistan — and became even more deeply embedded in its politics. The end of the Cold War thus expanded the U.S. role in the Middle East and renewed debates about the proper American role in the world.

## Global Capitalism and Increasing Social Inequality

The post–World War II expansion of the American economy ended in the 1970s, when wages stagnated and inflation skyrocketed. In the 1980s and 1990s, however, productivity grew, military spending boosted production, and new industries — such as computer technology — emerged. These developments led to renewed economic growth. More and more, though, the economy produced *services* rather than *goods* — as Americans increasingly bought the latter from overseas.

The fall of communism had made possible this global expansion of capitalism, as multinational corporations moved production to low-wage countries. Governments across the world facilitated this process by creating new trading zones such as the European Union (EU) and the North American Free Trade Agreement (NAFTA). Conservative tax policies, deindustrialization, the decline of unions, and globalization all contributed to a widening inequality between the wealthiest Americans and the middle class and poor. Globalization thus brought both new economic opportunities and renewed economic insecurity.

## Thematic Understanding

This timeline arranges some of the important events of this period into themes. Consider the entries under "Culture and Society" and "Migration and Settlement." What were the major events of the "culture wars," and how did American attitudes and public policy change over the decades between the 1980s and the 2010s? Next, examine the entries under "American and National Identity" and "America in the World." How did globalization reshape the United States in these decades? How did the U.S. actions affect other regions, particularly the Middle East?

| | AMERICAN AND NATIONAL IDENTITY | POLITICS AND POWER | WORK, EXCHANGE, AND TECHNOLOGY |
|---|---|---|---|
| 1980 | • Ronald Reagan campaigns for presidency (1980), says United States is "greatest country in the world" <br> • Reagan campaigns for reelection (1984) with theme of "It's morning in America" | • New Right helps elect Ronald Reagan president <br> • Iran-Contra scandal (1985–1987) <br> • George H. W. Bush elected president (1988) | • Recession (1981–1982) followed by strong growth (1982–1987) <br> • Reagan tax cut (1981) <br> • Apple IIe personal computer introduced (1983) <br> • National debt triples (1981–1989) |
| 1990 | • Americans debate multiculturalism <br> • World Trade Organization (WTO) protests in Seattle against globalization (1999) | • Bill Clinton elected president (1992) <br> • Republican resurgence (1994) <br> • Welfare reform (1996) <br> • Clinton impeached and acquitted (1998–1999) | • Internet gains in popularity <br> • Recession (1990–1991) <br> • NAFTA ratified (1993) <br> • Debt reduction under Bill Clinton |
| 2000 | • "War on terror" becomes fixture in American discourse <br> • USA PATRIOT Act authorizes new domestic surveillance to combat terrorism <br> • Abu Ghraib (2004) revelations document U.S. torture practices | • George W. Bush wins presidency in contested election (2000) <br> • USA PATRIOT Act (2001) <br> • Barack Obama elected first African American president (2008) | • Great Recession (2007–2010) <br> • President Bush asks for and receives bank bailout from Congress (2008) <br> • Unemployment hits 10 percent |
| 2010 | • Presidential candidates debate whether United States is declining as a nation and the role of international trade and immigration (2016) | • Health-care reform (2010) <br> • Tea Party helps Republicans regain control of House of Representatives <br> • Barack Obama reelected president (2012) <br> • Donald Trump elected president (2016) | • Financial industry accounts for largest share of GDP among all industry sectors |

| CULTURE AND SOCIETY | MIGRATION AND SETTLEMENT | GEOGRAPHY AND THE ENVIRONMENT | AMERICA IN THE WORLD | |
|---|---|---|---|---|
| • HIV/AIDS crisis prompts national conversation about homosexuality<br>• Renewed emphasis on material success and the "rich and famous"<br>• *Webster v. Reproductive Health Services* (1989) | • Rise in Latino and Asian immigration<br>• Californians vote to establish English as official language (1986) | • Reagan appoints the antienvironmentalist James Watt as secretary of interior | • Reagan begins arms buildup<br>• United States arms Contras in Nicaragua<br>• Berlin Wall comes down (1989) | 1980 |
| • Pat Buchanan declares "culture war" (1992)<br>• Proposition 209 ends affirmative action in California universities (1996)<br>• Defense of Marriage Act (1998) | • California bans bilingual education in public schools (1998) | • New states emerge in central Asia from dissolution of Soviet Union (1989–1991)<br>• Oil at center of Gulf War<br>• European Union created (1992) | • Persian Gulf War (1990–1991)<br>• USSR breaks apart; end of Cold War<br>• World Trade Center bombed (1993)<br>• NATO begins peacekeeping efforts in Bosnia (1995) | 1990 |
| • *Lawrence v. Texas* (2003)<br>• Massachusetts becomes first state to legalize same-sex marriage (2004); nine states follow by 2012 | • California, Texas, Hawaii, and New Mexico become "majority-minority" states (where the majority of the population is composed of different nonwhite groups) | • Kyoto Protocol international treaty on climate change signed by 84 nations (2005) but not by United States | • Al Qaeda attacks World Trade Center and Pentagon (2001)<br>• United States and allies invade Afghanistan (2002)<br>• United States invades Iraq (2003) | 2000 |
| • *Obergefell v. Hodges* (2015) upholds same-sex marriage as legal in all states | • Obama's 2012 electoral coalition heavily African American, Hispanic, Asian American, female, and young<br>• President Donald Trump bans immigrants from six majority-Muslim countries (2017) | • President Obama issues Clean Power Plan through executive action (2015)<br>• President Trump rescinds portions of the Clean Power Plan and orders reconsideration of the remainder (2017) | • Arab Spring (2010–2012)<br>• Osama bin Laden killed (2011)<br>• Last combat troops withdrawn from Iraq (2011)<br>• Syrian civil war and refugee crisis (2011–present) | 2010 |

# 29

## Conservative America in the Ascent

### 1980–1991

**IDENTIFY THE BIG IDEA**

What factors made the rise of the New Right possible, and what ideas about freedom and citizenship did conservatives articulate in the 1980s?

**THE DECADE OF THE 1970S SAW AMERICANS DIVIDED BY THE VIETNAM** War, wearied by social unrest, and unmoored by economic drift. As a result, many ordinary citizens developed a deep distrust of the muscular Great Society liberalism of the 1960s. Seizing political advantage amid the trauma and divisions, a revived Republican Party, led by a political movement known as the New Right, offered the nation a fresh way forward: economic deregulation, low taxes, Christian morality, and a reenergized Cold War foreign policy. The election of President Ronald Reagan in 1980 symbolized the ascendance of this new political formula, and the president himself helped shape the era.

The New Right revived confidence in "free markets" and called for a smaller government role in economic regulation and social welfare. Reagan famously said, "Government is not the solution to our problem; government *is* the problem." Like the New Right generally, Reagan was profoundly skeptical of the liberal ideology that had informed American public policy since Franklin D. Roosevelt's New Deal. His presidency combined an economically conservative domestic agenda with aggressive anticommunism abroad. Reagan's foreign policy reignited tensions with the Soviet Union, and then, unexpectedly, the president helped orchestrate a thawing of U.S.-Soviet relations, laying the groundwork for the end of the Cold War.

Reagan defined the conservative ascendancy of the 1980s, but he did not create the New Right groundswell that brought him into office. Grassroots conservative activists in the 1960s and 1970s built a formidable right-wing movement that awaited an opportune political moment to contend for national power. That moment came in 1980, when Democratic president Jimmy Carter's popularity plummeted as a result of his mismanagement of two national crises. Raging inflation and the Iranian seizure of U.S. hostages in Tehran undid Carter and provided an opening for the New Right, which would shape the nation's politics for the remainder of the twentieth century and the first decades of the twenty-first.

# The Rise of the New Right

The Great Depression and World War II discredited the traditional conservative program of limited government at home and diplomatic isolationism abroad. Nevertheless, a right-wing faction survived within the Republican Party. Its adherents continued to oppose the New Deal but reversed their earlier isolationism. In the postwar decades, conservatives pushed for military interventions against communism in Europe, Asia, and the developing world while calling for the broadest possible investigation of subversives at home (Chapter 24).

However, conservatives failed to devise policies that could win the allegiance of American voters in the two decades after World War II. Republicans by and large continued to favor party moderates, such as Dwight Eisenhower, Thomas Dewey, and Nelson Rockefeller. These were politicians, often called liberal Republicans, who supported much of the New Deal, endorsed the containment policy overseas, and steered a middle course through the volatile social and political changes of the postwar era. The conservative faction held out hope, however, that it might one day win the loyalty of a majority of Republicans and remake the party in its image. In the 1960s and 1970s, these conservatives invested their hopes for national resurgence in two dynamic figures: Barry Goldwater and Ronald Reagan. Together, the two carried the conservative banner until the national electorate grew more receptive to right-wing appeals.

## Barry Goldwater and Ronald Reagan: Champions of the Right

The personal odyssey of Ronald Reagan embodies the story of New Right Republican conservatism. Before World War II, Reagan was a well-known movie actor as well as a New Deal Democrat and admirer of Roosevelt. However, he turned away from liberalism, partly from self-interest (he disliked paying high taxes) and partly on principle. As head of the Screen Actors Guild from 1947 to 1952, Reagan had to deal with its Communist members, who formed the extreme left wing of the American labor movement. Dismayed by their hardline tactics and goals, he became a militant anticommunist. After nearly a decade as a spokesperson for the General Electric Corporation, Reagan joined the Republican Party in the early 1960s and began speaking for conservative causes and candidates.

One of those candidates was the forthright conservative Barry Goldwater, a Republican senator from Arizona. Confident in their power, centrist Republicans did not anticipate that grassroots conservatives could challenge the party's old guard and nominate one of their own for president: Goldwater himself. Understanding how they did so in 1964 brings us closer to comprehending the forces that propelled Reagan to the presidency a decade and a half later. Indeed, Reagan the politician came to national attention in 1964 with a televised speech at the Republican convention supporting Goldwater for the presidency. In a dramatic address titled "A Time for Choosing," Reagan warned that if we "trade our freedom for the soup kitchen of the welfare state," the nation would "take the first step into a thousand years of darkness."

**The Conscience of a Conservative**   Like Reagan, Goldwater came from the Sunbelt, home to a libertarian spirit of limited government and great personal freedom. His 1960 book, ***The Conscience of a Conservative***, set forth an uncompromising conservatism. In direct and accessible prose, Goldwater attacked the New Deal state, arguing that "the natural tendency of government [is] to expand in the direction of absolutism." The problem with the Republican Party, as he saw it, was that Eisenhower had been too accommodating to liberalism. When Ike told reporters that he was "liberal when it comes to human problems," Goldwater privately fumed.

*The Conscience of a Conservative* spurred a Republican grassroots movement in support of Goldwater. By distributing his book widely and mobilizing activists at state party conventions, conservatives hoped to create such a groundswell of support

**Barry Goldwater**  Barry Goldwater was a three-term senator from Arizona before he ran for the presidency in 1964 (this photo was taken during the campaign). Goldwater's conservative influence on the Republican Party was considerable and laid the political groundwork for the rise of Ronald Reagan a decade and a half later. Everett Collection Inc./Alamy Stock Photo.

that Goldwater could be "drafted" to run for president in 1964, something he reportedly did not wish to do. Meanwhile, Goldwater further enchanted conservatives with another book, *Why Not Victory?*, in which he criticized the containment policy—the strategy of preventing the spread of communism followed by both Democrats and Republicans since 1947 (Chapter 24). It was, he complained, a policy of "timidly refusing to draw our own lines against aggression . . . unmarked by pride or the prospect of victory." Here was a politician saying exactly what conservatives wanted to hear.

**Grassroots Conservatives**    Because moderates dominated the Republican Party leadership, winning the 1964 nomination for Goldwater required conservative activists to build their campaign from the bottom up. They found thousands upon thousands of Americans willing to hit the streets on behalf of their political hero. Organizations such as the John Birch Society, Young Americans for Freedom, and the Liberty Lobby supplied an army of eager volunteers. They came from such conservative strongholds as Orange County, California, and the fast-growing suburbs of Phoenix, Dallas, Houston, Atlanta, and other Sunbelt metropolises. A critical boost came in the early spring of 1964, when conservatives outmaneuvered moderates at the state convention of the California Republican Party, which then enthusiastically endorsed Goldwater. The fight had been bruising, and one moderate Republican warned that "sinister forces are at work to take over the whole Republican apparatus in California."

Another spur to Goldwater backers was the appearance of a book by Phyllis Schlafly, who was then a relatively unknown conservative activist from the Midwest. Like Goldwater's own book, Schlafly's *A Choice Not an Echo* accused moderate Republicans of being Democrats in disguise (that is, an "echo" of Democrats). Schlafly, who reappeared in the national spotlight in the early 1970s to help halt the ratification of the Equal Rights Amendment, denounced the "Rockefeller Republicans" of the Northeast and encouraged the party to embrace a defiant conservatism. Contrasting Goldwater's "grassroots Republicans" with Rockefeller's "kingmakers," Schlafly hoped to "forestall another defeat like 1940, 1944, 1948, and 1960," Democratic victories all.

The conservative groundswell won the Republican nomination for Goldwater. However, his strident tone and militarist foreign policy were too much for a nation mourning the death of John F. Kennedy and still committed to liberalism. Democrat Lyndon B. Johnson defeated Goldwater in a historic landslide (Chapter 27). Many believed that Goldwater conservatism would wither and die, but instead the nearly four million volunteers who had campaigned for the Arizona senator swung their support to Ronald Reagan and built toward the future. Skilled conservative political operatives such as Richard Viguerie, a Louisiana-born Catholic and antiabortion activist, applied new computer technology to political campaigning. Viguerie took a list of 12,000 Goldwater contributors and used computerized mailing lists, which were new at the time, to solicit campaign funds, rally support for conservative causes, and get out the vote on election day. Conservatism was down but not out.

Backed financially by wealthy southern Californians and supported by Goldwaterites, Reagan won California's governorship in 1966 and again in 1970. His impassioned rhetoric supporting limited government and law and order—referring to campus radicals, he vowed to "clean up the mess in Berkeley"—won broad support among citizens of the nation's most populous state. More significantly, it made him a force in national politics. His supporters believed that he was in line to succeed Nixon as the next Republican president. The Watergate scandal intervened, however, discrediting Nixon and making Gerald Ford the incumbent. After narrowly losing a campaign against Ford for the Republican presidential nomination in 1976, Reagan was forced to bide his time. When Ford lost to Carter in that year's election, as the party's brightest star Reagan was a near lock to be the nominee in 1980.

## Free-Market Economics and Religious Conservatism

The last phase of Reagan's rise was the product of several additional developments within the New Right. The burgeoning conservative movement increasingly resembled a three-legged stool. Each leg represented an ideological position and a popular constituency: anticommunism, free-market economics, and religious traditionalism. Uniting all three in a political coalition was no easy feat. Religious traditionalists demanded strong government action to implement their faith-based agenda, while economic conservatives favored limited government and free markets. Both groups, however, were ardent anticommunists — free marketeers loathed the state-directed Soviet economy, and religious conservatives despised the "godless" secularism of the Soviet state. In the end, the success of the New Right would come to depend on balancing the interests of economic and moral conservatives.

Since the 1950s, William F. Buckley, the founder and editor of the conservative magazine *National Review*, and Milton Friedman, the Nobel Prize–winning economist at the University of Chicago, had been the most prominent conservative intellectuals. Convinced that "the growth of government must be fought relentlessly," Buckley used the *National Review* to criticize liberal policy. For his part, Friedman became a national conservative icon with the publication of *Capitalism and Freedom* (1962), in which he argued that "economic freedom is . . . an indispensable means toward the achievement of political freedom." Friedman's free-market ideology, along with that of Friedrich von Hayek, another University of Chicago economist, was taken up by wealthy conservatives, who funded think tanks during the 1980s to disseminate market-based public policy ideas. The Heritage Foundation, the American Enterprise Institute, and the Cato Institute issued policy proposals and attacked liberal legislation and the stranglehold of economic regulation they believed it represented. Followers of Buckley and Friedman envisioned themselves as crusaders working against what one conservative called "the despotic aspects of egalitarianism."

The most striking addition to the conservative coalition was the **Religious Right**. Until the 1970s, politics was an earthly concern of secondary interest to most fundamentalist and evangelical Protestants. But the perception that American society had become immoral, combined with the influence of a new generation of popular ministers, gave politics a new urgent relevance. Conservative Protestants and Catholics joined together in a tentative alliance, as the Religious Right condemned divorce, abortion, premarital sex, and feminism. The route to a moral life and to "peace, pardon, purpose, and power," as one evangelical activist said, was "to plug yourself into the One, the Only One [God]."

Charismatic televangelists such as Pat Robertson and Jerry Falwell emerged as the champions of a morality-based political agenda during the late 1970s. Falwell, founder of Liberty University and host of the *Old Time Gospel Hour* television program, established the Moral Majority in 1979. With 400,000 members and $1.5 million in contributions in its first year, it would be the organizational vehicle for transforming the new evangelicalism into a religious political movement. Falwell made no secret of his views: "If you want to know where I am politically," he told reporters, "I thought Goldwater was too liberal." Falwell was not alone. Phyllis Schlafly's STOP ERA, which became Eagle Forum in 1975, continued to advocate for conservative public policy; Focus on the Family was founded in 1977; and a succession of conservative organizations would emerge in the 1980s, including the Family Research Council.

The conservative message preached by Barry Goldwater and Ronald Reagan had appealed to few American voters in 1964. Then came the series of events that undermined support for the liberal agenda of the Democratic Party: the failed war in Vietnam; a judiciary that legalized abortion and pornography, enforced school busing, and curtailed public expression of religion; urban riots; and a stagnating economy. By the late 1970s, the New Right had developed a conservative message that commanded much greater popular support than Goldwater's program had. Religious and free-market conservatives joined with traditional anticommunist hard-liners — alongside whites opposed to black civil rights, affirmative action, and busing — in a broad coalition that attacked welfare-state liberalism, social permissiveness, and an allegedly weak and defensive foreign policy. Ronald Reagan expertly appealed to all of these conservative constituencies and captured the Republican presidential nomination in 1980. It had taken almost two decades, but the New Right appeared on the verge of winning the presidency.

## The Carter Presidency

First, the Republican Party had to defeat incumbent president Jimmy Carter. Carter's outsider status and his disdain for professional politicians had made him the ideal post-Watergate president. But his ineffectiveness and missteps as an executive also made him the perfect foil for Ronald Reagan.

Carter had an idealistic vision of American leadership in world affairs. He presented himself as the anti-Nixon, a world leader who rejected Henry Kissinger's "realism" in favor of human rights and peacemaking. "Human rights is the soul of our foreign policy," Carter asserted, "because human rights is the very soul of our sense of nationhood." He established the Office of Human Rights in the State Department and withdrew economic and military aid from repressive regimes in Argentina, Uruguay, and Ethiopia — although, in realist fashion, he still funded equally repressive U.S. allies such as the Philippines, South Africa, and Iran. In Latin America, Carter eliminated a decades-old symbol of Yankee imperialism by signing a treaty on September 7, 1977, turning control of the Panama Canal over to Panama (effective December 31, 1999). Carter's most important efforts came in forging an enduring, although in retrospect limited, peace in the intractable Arab-Israeli conflict. In 1978, he invited Israeli prime minister Menachem Begin and Egyptian president Anwar el-Sadat to Camp David, where they crafted a "framework for peace," under which Egypt recognized Israel and received back the Sinai Peninsula, which Israel had occupied since 1967.

Carter deplored what he called the "inordinate fear of communism," but his efforts at improving relations with the Soviet Union foundered. His criticism of the Kremlin's record on human rights offended Soviet leader Leonid Brezhnev and slowed arms reduction negotiations. When, in 1979, Carter finally signed the second Strategic Arms Limitations Treaty (SALT II), limiting bombers and missiles, Senate hawks objected. Then, when the Soviet Union invaded Afghanistan that December, Carter suddenly endorsed the hawks' position and treated the invasion as the "gravest threat to world peace since World War II." After ordering an embargo on wheat shipments to the Soviet Union and withdrawing SALT II from Senate consideration, Carter called for increased defense spending and declared an American boycott of the 1980 Summer Olympics in Moscow. In a fateful decision, he and Congress began providing covert assistance to anti-Soviet fighters in Afghanistan, some of whom, including Osama bin Laden, would emerge decades later as anti-American Islamic radicals.

**Hostage Crisis**    Carter's ultimate undoing came in Iran, however. The United States had long counted Iran as a faithful ally, a bulwark against Soviet expansion into the Middle East and a steady source of oil. Since the 1940s, Iran had been ruled by Mohammad Reza Shah Pahlavi. Ousted by a democratically elected parliament in the early 1950s, the shah (king) sought and received the assistance of the U.S. Central Intelligence Agency (CIA), which helped him reclaim power in 1953. American intervention soured Iranian views of the United States for decades. Early in 1979, a revolution drove the shah into exile and brought a fundamentalist Shiite cleric, the Ayatollah Ruhollah Khomeini, to power (Shiites represent one branch of Islam, Sunnis the other). When the United States admitted the deposed shah into the country for cancer treatment, Iranian students seized the U.S. embassy in Tehran, taking sixty-six Americans hostage. The captors demanded that the shah be returned to Iran for trial. Carter refused. Instead, he suspended arms sales to Iran and froze Iranian assets in American banks.

For the next fourteen months, the **hostage crisis** paralyzed Carter's presidency. Night after night, humiliating pictures of blindfolded American hostages appeared on television newscasts. An attempt to mount a military rescue in April 1980 had to be aborted because of equipment failures in the desert. Several months later, however, a stunning development changed the calculus on both sides: Iraq, led by Saddam Hussein, invaded Iran, officially because of a dispute over deep-water ports but also to prevent the Shiite-led Iranian Revolution from spreading across the border into Sunni-run Iraq. Desperate to focus his nation's attention on Iraq's invasion, Khomeini began to talk with the United States about releasing the hostages. Difficult negotiations dragged on past the American presidential election in November 1980, and the hostages were finally released the day after Carter left office—a final indignity endured by a well-intentioned but ineffectual president.

**The Election of 1980**    President Carter's sinking popularity hurt his bid for reelection. When the Democrats barely renominated him over his liberal challenger, Edward (Ted) Kennedy of Massachusetts, Carter's approval rating was historically low: a mere 21 percent of Americans believed that he was an effective president. The reasons were clear. Economically, millions of citizens were feeling the pinch from stagnant wages, high inflation, crippling mortgage rates, and an unemployment rate of nearly 8 percent. In international affairs, the nation blamed Carter for his weak response to Soviet expansion and the Iranians' seizure of American diplomats.

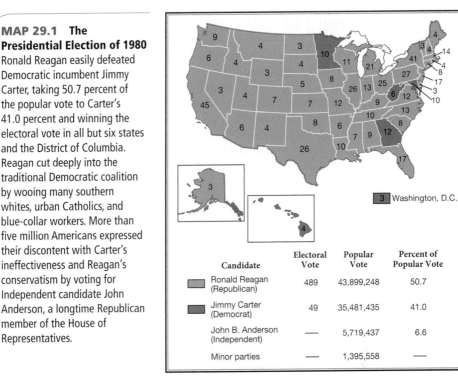

**MAP 29.1** **The Presidential Election of 1980** Ronald Reagan easily defeated Democratic incumbent Jimmy Carter, taking 50.7 percent of the popular vote to Carter's 41.0 percent and winning the electoral vote in all but six states and the District of Columbia. Reagan cut deeply into the traditional Democratic coalition by wooing many southern whites, urban Catholics, and blue-collar workers. More than five million Americans expressed their discontent with Carter's ineffectiveness and Reagan's conservatism by voting for Independent candidate John Anderson, a longtime Republican member of the House of Representatives.

| Candidate | Electoral Vote | Popular Vote | Percent of Popular Vote |
|---|---|---|---|
| Ronald Reagan (Republican) | 489 | 43,899,248 | 50.7 |
| Jimmy Carter (Democrat) | 49 | 35,481,435 | 41.0 |
| John B. Anderson (Independent) | — | 5,719,437 | 6.6 |
| Minor parties | — | 1,395,558 | — |

With Carter on the defensive, Reagan remained upbeat and decisive. "This is the greatest country in the world," Reagan reassured the nation in his warm baritone voice. "We have the talent, we have the drive. . . . All we need is the leadership." To emphasize his intention to be a formidable international leader, Reagan hinted that he would take strong action to win the return of the hostages held in Iran. To signal his rejection of liberal policies, he declared his opposition to affirmative action and forced busing and promised to "get the government off our backs." Most important, Reagan effectively appealed to the many Americans who felt financially insecure. In a televised debate with Carter, Reagan emphasized the hardships facing working- and middle-class Americans in an era of stagflation and asked them: "Are you better off today than you were four years ago?"

In November, the voters gave a clear answer. They repudiated Carter, giving him only 41.0 percent of the vote. Independent candidate John Anderson garnered 6.6 percent (with a few minor candidates receiving fractions of a percent), and Reagan won with 50.7 percent of the popular vote (Map 29.1). Moreover, the Republicans elected thirty-three new members of the House of Representatives and twelve new senators, which gave them control of the U.S. Senate for the first time since 1954. The New Right's long road to national power had culminated in an election victory that signaled a new political alignment in the country.

**IN YOUR OWN WORDS**      What were the major characteristics of the political movement that backed Ronald Reagan, known as the New Right?

# The Dawning of the Conservative Age

By the time Ronald Reagan took office in 1981, conservatism commanded wider popular support than at any time since the 1920s. As the New Deal Democratic coalition continued to fragment, the Republican Party accelerated the realignment of the American electorate that had begun during the 1960s. Conservatism's ascendancy did more than realign the nation politically. Its emphasis on free markets, low taxes, and individual success shaped the nation's culture and inaugurated an era of conservative individualism. Reagan exhorted Americans, "Let the men and women of the marketplace decide what they want."

## The Reagan Coalition

Reagan's decades in public life, especially his years working for General Electric, had equipped him to articulate conservative ideas in easily understandable aphorisms. Speaking against the growing size and influence of government, Reagan said, "Concentrated power has always been the enemy of liberty." In a humorous version of the same sentiment, the president said, "The nine most terrifying words in the English language are: 'I'm from the government, and I'm here to help.'"

Under his leadership, the core of the Republican Party remained the relatively affluent, white, Protestant voters who supported balanced budgets, opposed government activism, feared communism, and believed in a strong national defense. Reagan Republicanism also attracted middle-class suburbanites and migrants to the Sunbelt

**President Reagan at His Ranch in Southern California** Images of Reagan quickly became vital for the White House to deliver its message of conservative reform to the American people. This photo was taken by a White House photographer. Ronald Reagan Presidential Library.

states who endorsed the conservative agenda of combating crime and limiting social-welfare spending. Suburban growth in particular, a phenomenon that reshaped metropolitan areas across the country in the 1960s and 1970s, benefitted conservatives politically. Suburban traditions of privatization and racial homogeneity, combined with the amenities of middle-class comfort, inclined the residents of suburban cities toward conservative public policies.

This emerging **Reagan coalition** was joined by a large and electorally key group of former Democrats that had been gradually moving toward the Republican Party since 1964: southern whites. Reagan capitalized on the "southern strategy" developed by Richard Nixon's advisors in the late 1960s. Many southern whites had lost confidence in the Democratic Party for a wide range of reasons, but one factor stood out: the party's support for civil rights. When Reagan came to Philadelphia, Mississippi, to deliver his first official speech as the Republican presidential nominee, his ringing endorsement of "states' rights" sent a clear message: he endorsed twenty-five years of southern opposition to federal civil rights legislation. Some of Reagan's advisors had warned him not to go to Philadelphia, the site of the tragic murder of three civil rights workers in 1964, but Reagan believed the opportunity to launch his campaign on a "states' rights" note was too important. After 1980, southern whites would remain a cornerstone of the Republican coalition.

The Religious Right proved crucial to the Republican ascendance as well. Falwell's **Moral Majority** claimed that it had registered two million new voters for the 1980 election, and the Republican Party's platform reflected its influence. That platform called for a constitutional ban on abortion, voluntary prayer in public schools, and a mandatory death penalty for certain crimes. Republicans also demanded an end to court-mandated busing to achieve racial integration in schools, and, for the first time in forty years, opposed the Equal Rights Amendment. Within the Republican Party, conservatism had triumphed.

Reagan's broad coalition attracted the allegiance of another group dissatisfied with the direction of liberalism in the 1970s: blue-collar voters, a high number of Catholics among them, alarmed by antiwar protesters and rising welfare expenditures and hostile to feminist demands. Some observers saw these voters, which many called **Reagan Democrats**, as coming from the "silent majority" that Nixon had swung into the Republican fold in 1968 and 1972. They lived in heavily industrialized midwestern states such as Michigan, Ohio, and Illinois and had been a core part of the Democratic coalition for three decades. Reagan's victory in the 1980s thus hinged on both a revival of right-wing conservative activism and broad dissatisfaction with liberal Democrats—a dissatisfaction that had been building since 1968 but had been interrupted by the post-Watergate backlash against the Republican Party.

## Conservatives in Power

The new president kept his political message clear and uncomplicated. "What I want to see above all," he remarked, "is that this country remains a country where someone can always get rich." Standing in the way, Reagan believed, was government. In his first year in office, Reagan and his chief advisor, James A. Baker III, quickly set new governmental priorities. To roll back the expanded liberal state, they launched a three-pronged assault on federal taxes, social-welfare spending, and the regulatory bureaucracy. To prosecute the Cold War, they advocated a vast increase in defense spending and an end to détente with the Soviet Union. And to match the resurgent economies of Germany and Japan, they set out to restore American leadership of the world's capitalist societies and to inspire renewed faith in "free markets."

**Reaganomics**    To achieve its economic objectives, the new administration advanced a set of policies, quickly dubbed **Reaganomics**, to increase the production (and thus the supply) of goods. The theory underlying **supply-side economics**, as this approach was called, emphasized investment in productive enterprises. According to supply-side theorists, the best way to bolster investment was to reduce the taxes paid by corporations and wealthy Americans, who could then use these funds to expand production.

Supply-siders maintained that the resulting economic expansion would increase government revenues and offset the loss of tax dollars stemming from the original tax cuts. Meanwhile, the increasing supply would generate its own demand, as consumers stepped forward to buy ever more goods. Supply-side theory presumed—in fact, gambled—that future tax revenues would make up for present tax cuts. The idea had a growing list of supporters in Congress, led by an ex-professional football player from Buffalo named Jack Kemp. Kemp praised supply-side economics as "an alternative to the slow-growth, recession-oriented policies of the [Carter] administration."

Reagan took advantage of Republican control of the Senate, as well as high-profile allies such as Kemp, to win congressional approval of the 1981 **Economic Recovery Tax Act (ERTA)**, a massive tax cut that embodied supply-side principles. The act reduced income tax rates for most Americans by 23 percent over three years. For the wealthiest Americans—those with millions to invest—the highest marginal tax rate dropped from 70 to 50 percent. The act also slashed estate taxes, levies on inheritances instituted during the Progressive Era to prevent the transmission of huge fortunes from one generation to the next. Finally, the new legislation trimmed the taxes paid by business corporations by $150 billion over a period of five years. As a result of ERTA, by 1986 the annual revenue of the federal government had been cut by $200 billion (nearly half a trillion in 2010 dollars).

David Stockman, Reagan's budget director, hoped to match this reduction in tax revenue with a comparable cutback in federal expenditures. To meet this ambitious goal, he proposed substantial cuts in Social Security and Medicare. But Congress, and even the president himself, rejected his idea; they were not willing to antagonize middle-class and elderly voters who viewed these government entitlements as sacred. As conservative columnist George Will noted ironically, "Americans are conservative. What they want to conserve is the New Deal." After defense spending, Social Security and Medicare were by far the nation's largest budget items; reductions in other programs would not achieve the savings the administration desired. This contradiction between New Right Republican ideology and political reality would continue to frustrate the party into the twenty-first century.

A more immediate embarrassment confronted conservatives, however. In a 1982 *Atlantic* article, Stockman admitted that supply-side theory was based on faith, not economics. To produce optimistic projections of higher tax revenue in future years, Stockman had manipulated the figures. Worse, Stockman told the *Atlantic* reporter candidly that supply-side theory was based on a long-discredited idea: the "trickle-down" notion that helping the rich would eventually benefit the lower and middle classes. Stockman had drawn back the curtain, much to Republicans' consternation, on the flawed reasoning of supply-side theory. But it was too late. The plan had passed Congress, and since Stockman could not cut major programs such as Social Security and Medicare, he had few options to balance the budget.

As the administration's spending cuts fell short, the federal budget deficit increased dramatically. Military spending contributed a large share of the growing **national debt**. But President Reagan remained undaunted. "Defense is not a budget item," he declared. "You spend what you need." Reagan and Defense Secretary Caspar Weinberger pushed through Congress a five-year, $1.2 trillion military spending program in 1981. During Reagan's presidency, military spending accounted for one-fourth of all federal expenditures and contributed to rising annual budget deficits (the amount overspent by the government in a single year) and a skyrocketing national debt (the cumulative total of all budget deficits). By the time Reagan left office, the total federal debt had tripled, rising from $930 billion in 1981 to $2.8 trillion in 1989. The rising annual deficits of the 1980s contradicted Reagan's pledge of fiscal conservatism (Figure 29.1).

**Deregulation**    Advocates of Reaganomics asserted that excessive regulation by federal agencies impeded economic growth. **Deregulation** of prices in the trucking, airline, and railroad industries had begun under President Carter in the late 1970s,

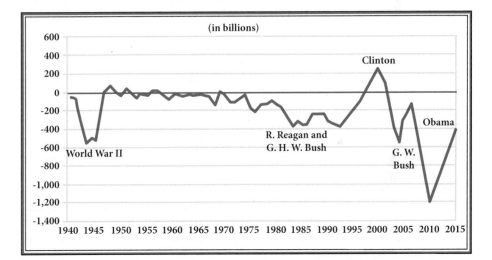

**FIGURE 29.1    The Annual Federal Budget Deficit (or Surplus), 1940–2015**
During World War II, the federal government incurred an enormous budget deficit. But between 1946 and 1965, it ran either an annual budget surplus or incurred a relatively small debt. The annual deficits rose significantly during the Vietnam War and the stagflation of the 1970s, but they really exploded between 1982 and 1994, in the budgets devised by the Ronald Reagan and George H. W. Bush administrations, and again between 2002 and 2005, in those prepared by George W. Bush. The Republican presidents increased military spending while cutting taxes, a budgetary policy that produced deficits.

but Reagan expanded the mandate to include cutting back on government protections of consumers, workers, and the environment. Some of the targeted federal bureaucracies, such as the U.S. Department of Labor, had risen to prominence during the New Deal; others, such as the Occupational Safety and Health Administration (OSHA) and the Environmental Protection Agency (EPA), had been created during the Johnson and Nixon administrations. Although these agencies provided many services to business corporations, they also increased their costs — by protecting the rights of workers, mandating safety improvements in factories, and requiring expensive equipment to limit the release of toxic chemicals into the environment. To reduce the reach of federal regulatory agencies, the Reagan administration in 1981 cut their budgets, by an average of 12 percent.

Reagan also rendered regulatory agencies less effective by staffing them with leaders who were opposed to the agencies' missions. James Watt, an outspoken conservative who headed the Department of the Interior, attacked environmentalism as "a left-wing cult." Acting on his free-enterprise principles, Watt opened public lands for use by private businesses — oil and coal corporations, large-scale ranchers, and timber companies. Anne Gorsuch Burford, whom Reagan appointed to head the EPA, likewise disparaged environmentalists and refused to cooperate with Congress to clean up toxic waste sites under a program known as the Superfund. The Sierra Club and other environmental groups aroused enough public outrage about these appointees that the administration changed its position. During President Reagan's second term, he significantly increased the EPA's budget and added acreage to the National Wilderness Preservation System and animals and plants to the endangered species lists.

Ultimately, as these adjustments demonstrate, politics in the United States remained "the art of the possible." Savvy politicians know when to advance and when to retreat. Having attained two of his prime goals — a major tax cut and a dramatic increase in defense spending — Reagan did not seriously attempt to scale back big government and the welfare state. When he left office in 1989, federal spending stood at 22.1 percent of the gross domestic product (GDP) and federal taxes at 19 percent of GDP, both virtually the same as in 1981. In the meantime, though, in addition to the tripling of the federal debt, the number of government workers had increased from 2.9 to 3.1 million. This outcome — because it cut against the president's rhetoric about balancing budgets and downsizing government — elicited harsh criticism from some conservative commentators. "There was no Reagan Revolution," one conservative stated flatly. A former Reagan aide offered a more balanced assessment: "Ronald Reagan did far less than he had hoped . . . and a hell of a lot more than people thought he would."

**Remaking the Judiciary**     Even if he did not achieve everything many of his supporters desired, Reagan left an indelible imprint on politics, public policy, and American culture. One place this imprint was felt in far-reaching ways was the judiciary, where Reagan and his attorney general, Edwin Meese, aimed at reversing the liberal judicial philosophy that had prevailed since the 1950s. During his two terms, Reagan appointed 368 federal court judges — most of them with conservative credentials — and three Supreme Court justices: Sandra Day O'Connor (1981), Antonin Scalia (1986), and Anthony Kennedy (1988). Ironically, O'Connor and Kennedy turned out to be far less devoted to New Right conservatism than Reagan and his supporters imagined. O'Connor, the first woman to serve on the Court, shaped its decision making as a swing vote between liberals and conservatives. Kennedy also emerged as a judicial moderate, leaving Scalia as Reagan's only genuinely conservative appointee.

But Reagan also elevated Justice William Rehnquist, a conservative Nixon appointee, to the position of chief justice. Under Rehnquist's leadership (1986–2005), the Court's conservatives took an activist stance, limiting the reach of federal laws, ending court-ordered busing, and endorsing constitutional protection of property rights. However, on controversial issues such as individual liberties, abortion rights, affirmative action, and the rights of criminal defendants, the presence of O'Connor ensured that the Court adopted a more centrist position. As a result, the justices scaled back, but did not usually overturn, the liberal rulings of the Warren and Burger Courts. In the controversial *Webster v. Reproductive Health Services* (1989), for instance, Scalia pushed for the justices to overturn the abortion-rights decision in *Roe v. Wade* (1973). O'Connor refused, but she nonetheless approved the constitutional validity of state laws that limited the use of public funds and facilities for abortions. A more conservative federal judiciary would remain a significant institutional legacy of the Reagan presidency.

**HIV/AIDS**    Another conservative legacy was the slow national response to one of the worst disease epidemics of the postwar decades. The human immunodeficiency virus (HIV), a deadly (though slow-acting) pathogen, developed in Africa when a chimpanzee virus jumped to humans; immigrants carried it to Haiti and then to the United States during the 1970s. In 1981, American physicians identified HIV as a new virus — one that caused a disease known as acquired immunodeficiency syndrome (AIDS). Hundreds of gay men, who were prominent among the earliest carriers of the virus, were dying of AIDS. Within two decades, **HIV/AIDS** had spread worldwide, infected more than 50 million people of both sexes, and killed more than 20 million.

Within the United States, AIDS took nearly one hundred thousand lives in the 1980s — more than were lost in the Korean and Vietnam Wars combined. However, because its most prominent early victims were gay men, President Reagan, emboldened by New Right conservatives, hesitated in declaring a national health emergency. Some of Reagan's advisors asserted that this "gay disease" might even be God's punishment of homosexuals. Between 1981 and 1986, as the epidemic spread, the Reagan administration took little action — worse, it prevented the surgeon general, C. Everett Koop, from speaking forthrightly to the nation about the disease. Pressed by gay activists and prominent health officials from across the country, in Reagan's last years in office the administration finally began to devote federal resources to treatment for HIV and AIDS patients and research into possible vaccines. But the delay had proved costly, inhumane, and embarrassing.

## Morning in America

During his first run for governor of California in 1966, Reagan held a revelatory conversation with a campaign consultant. "Politics is just like the movies," Reagan told him. "You have a hell of an opening, coast for a while, and then have a hell of a close." Reagan indeed had a "hell of an opening." Following a lavish, spectacular inauguration, he quickly won passage of his tax reduction bill and launched his plan to bolster the Pentagon. But then a long "coasting" period descended on his presidency, during which he retreated on tax cuts and navigated a major foreign policy scandal. Finally, toward the end of his two-term presidency, Reagan found his "hell of a close," leaving office as major reforms—which he encouraged from afar—had begun to tear apart the Soviet Union and bring an end to the Cold War. Through all the ups and downs, Reagan remained a master of the politics of symbolism, championing a resurgent American economy and reassuring the country that the pursuit of wealth was noble and that he had the reins of the nation firmly in hand.

Reagan came to symbolize the tax-cutting president, but economic conditions forced him to reverse course on taxes early in his first term. High interest rates set by the Federal Reserve Board had cut the runaway inflation of the Carter years. But these rates—as high as 18 percent—sent the economy into a recession in 1981–1982 that put 10 million Americans out of work and shuttered 17,000 businesses. Unemployment neared 10 percent, the highest rate since the Great Depression. These troubles, combined with the booming deficit, forced Reagan to negotiate a tax increase with Congress in 1982—to the loud complaints of supply-side diehards. The president's job rating plummeted, and in the 1982 midterm elections Democrats picked up twenty-six seats in the House of Representatives and seven state governorships.

**Election of 1984**   Fortunately for Reagan, the economy had recovered by 1983, restoring the president's job approval rating just in time for the 1984 presidential election. During the campaign, Reagan emphasized the economic resurgence, touring the country promoting his tax policies and the nation's new prosperity. The Democrats nominated former vice president Walter Mondale of Minnesota. With strong ties to labor unions, a variety of ethnic and racial groups, and party leaders, Mondale epitomized the New Deal coalition. He selected Representative Geraldine Ferraro of New York as his running mate—the first woman to run on the presidential ticket of a major political party. Neither Ferraro's presence nor Mondale's credentials made a difference, however: Reagan won a landslide victory, losing only Minnesota and the District of Columbia. Still, Democrats retained their majority in the House and, in the 1986 midterm elections, regained control of the Senate.

Reagan's 1984 campaign slogan, "It's Morning in America," projected the image of a new day dawning on a confident people. In Reagan mythology, the United States was an optimistic nation of small towns, close-knit families, and kindly neighbors. "The success story of America," he once said, "is neighbor helping neighbor." The mythology may not have reflected the *actual* nation—which was overwhelmingly urban and suburban, and in which the hard knocks of capitalism held down more than opportunity elevated—but that mattered little. Reagan's remarkable ability to produce positive associations and feelings, alongside robust economic growth after the 1981–1982 recession, helped make the 1980s a decade characterized by both backward-looking nostalgia and a future-oriented, aggressive capitalism.

**Return to Prosperity**   Between 1945 and the 1970s, the United States was the world's leading exporter of agricultural products, manufactured goods, and investment capital. Then American manufacturers lost market share, undercut by cheaper and better-designed products from West Germany and Japan. By 1985, for the first time since 1915, the United States registered a negative balance of international payments. It now imported more goods and capital than it exported. The country became a debtor (rather than a creditor) nation. The rapid ascent of the Japanese economy to become the world's second largest was a key factor in this historic reversal. More than one-third of the American annual trade deficit of $138 billion in the 1980s was from trade with Japan, whose corporations exported huge quantities of electronic goods and made nearly one-quarter of all cars bought in the United States.

Meanwhile, American businesses grappled with a worrisome decline in productivity. Between 1973 and 1992, American productivity (the amount of goods or services per hour of work) grew at the meager rate of 1 percent a year—a far cry from the post–World War II rate of 3 percent. Because managers wanted to cut costs, the wages of most employees stagnated. Further, because of foreign competition, the number of high-paying, union-protected manufacturing jobs shrank. By 1985, more people in the United States worked for McDonald's slinging Big Macs than rolled out rails, girders, and sheet steel in the nation's steel industry.

A brief return to competitiveness in the second half of the 1980s masked the steady long-term transformation of the economy that had begun in the 1970s. The nation's heavy industries—steel, autos, chemicals—continued to lose market share to global competitors. Nevertheless, the U.S. economy grew at the impressive average rate of 2 to 3 percent per year for much of the late 1980s and 1990s (with a short recession in 1990–1991). What had changed was the direction of growth and its beneficiaries. Increasingly, financial services, medical services, and computer technology—**service industries**, broadly speaking—were the leading sectors of growth. This shift in the underlying foundation of the American economy, from manufacturing to service, from making *things* to producing *services*, would have long-term consequences for the global competitiveness of U.S. industries and the value of the dollar.

**Culture of Success**    The economic growth of the second half of the 1980s popularized the materialistic values championed by the free marketeers. Every era has its capitalist heroes, but Americans in the 1980s celebrated wealth accumulation in ways unseen since the 1920s. When the president christened self-made entrepreneurs "the heroes for the eighties," he probably had people like Lee Iacocca in mind. Born to Italian immigrants and trained as an engineer, Iacocca rose through the ranks to become president of the Ford Motor Corporation. In 1978, he took over the ailing Chrysler Corporation and made it profitable again—by securing a crucial $1.5 billion loan from the U.S. government, pushing the development of new cars, and selling them on TV. His patriotic commercials in the 1980s echoed Reagan's rhetoric: "Let's make American mean something again."

If Iacocca symbolized a resurgent corporate America, high-profile financial wheeler-dealers also captured Americans' imagination. One was Ivan Boesky, a white-collar criminal convicted of insider trading (buying or selling stock based on information from corporate insiders). "I think greed is healthy," Boesky told a business school graduating class. Boesky inspired the fictional character Gordon Gekko, who proclaimed "Greed is good!" in the 1987 film *Wall Street*. A new generation of Wall Street executives, of which Boesky was one example, pioneered the leveraged buyout (LBO). In a typical LBO, a financier used heavily leveraged (borrowed) capital to buy a company, quickly restructured that company to make it appear spectacularly profitable, and then sold it at a higher price.

Americans had not set aside the traditional work ethic, but the Reagan-era public was fascinated with money and celebrity. (The documentary television show *Lifestyles of the Rich and Famous* began its run in 1984.) One of the most enthralling of the era's money moguls was Donald Trump, a real estate developer who craved publicity. In 1983, the flamboyant Trump built the equally flamboyant Trump Towers in New York City. At the entrance of the $200 million apartment building stood two enormous bronze *T*'s, a display of self-promotion reinforced by the media. Calling him "The Donald," a nickname used by Trump's first wife, TV reporters and magazines commented relentlessly on his marriages, divorces, and glitzy lifestyle. Trading on his celebrity as much as his business acumen, Trump would in later decades forge a career on reality television and, in one of the most unexpected political developments of the early twentieth-first century, win the Republican nomination for president in 2016 and ascend to the presidency itself.

**The Computer Revolution**    While Trump grabbed headlines and made splashy real estate investments, a handful of quieter, less flashy entrepreneurs was busy changing the face of the American economy. Bill Gates, Paul Allen, Steve Jobs, and Steve Wozniak were four entrepreneurs who pioneered the computer revolution in the late 1970s and 1980s. They took a technology that had been used exclusively for large-scale enterprises — the military and multinational corporations — and made it accessible to individual consumers. Scientists had devised the first computers for military purposes during World War II. Cold War military research subsequently funded the construction of large mainframe computers. But government and private-sector first-generation computers were bulky, cumbersome machines that had to be placed in large air-conditioned rooms.

Between the 1950s and the 1970s, concluding with the development of the microprocessor in 1971, each generation of computers grew faster and smaller. By the mid-1970s, a few microchips the size of the letter *O* on this page provided as much processing power as a World War II–era computer. The day of the personal computer (PC) had arrived. Working in the San Francisco Bay Area, Jobs and Wozniak founded Apple Computers in 1976 and within a year were producing small, individual computers that could be easily used by a single person. When Apple enjoyed success, other companies scrambled to get into the market. International Business Machines (IBM) offered its first personal computer in 1981, but Apple Corporation's 1984 Macintosh computer (later shortened to "Mac") became the first runaway commercial success for a personal computer.

Meanwhile, two former high school classmates, Gates, age nineteen, and Allen, age twenty-one, had set a goal in the early 1970s of putting "a personal computer on every desk and in every home." They recognized that software was the key. In 1975, they founded the Microsoft Corporation, whose MS-DOS and Windows operating systems soon dominated the software industry. By 2000, the company's products ran nine out of every ten personal computers in the United States and a majority of those around the world. Gates and Allen became billionaires, and Microsoft exploded into a huge company with 57,000 employees and annual revenues of $38 billion. In three decades, the computer had moved from a few military research centers to thousands of corporate offices and then to millions of people's homes. Ironically, in an age that celebrated free-market capitalism, government research and government funding had played an enormous role in the development of the most important technology since television.

| IN YOUR OWN WORDS | What were the major political successes and failures of the Reagan coalition? |
|---|---|

# The End of the Cold War

Ronald Reagan entered office determined to confront the Soviet Union diplomatically and militarily. Backed by Republican and Democratic hard-liners alike, Reagan unleashed some of the harshest Cold War rhetoric since the 1950s, labeling the Soviet Union an "evil empire" and vowing that it would end up "on the ash heap of history." In a remarkable turnaround, however, by his second term Reagan had decided that this goal would be best achieved by actively cooperating with Mikhail Gorbachev, the reform-minded Russian Communist leader. The downfall of the Soviet Union in 1991 ended the nearly fifty-year-long Cold War, but a new set of foreign challenges quickly emerged.

## U.S.-Soviet Relations in a New Era

When Reagan assumed the presidency in 1981, he broke with his immediate predecessors—Richard Nixon, Gerald Ford, and Jimmy Carter—in Cold War strategy. Nixon regarded himself as a "realist" in foreign affairs. That meant, above all, advancing the national interest without regard to ideology. Nixon's policy of détente with the Soviet Union and China embodied this realist view (Chapter 27). President Carter endorsed détente and continued to push for relaxing Cold War tensions. This worked for a time, but the Soviet invasion of Afghanistan empowered hard-liners in the U.S. Congress and forced Carter to take a tougher line—which he did with the Olympic boycott and grain embargo. This was the relationship Reagan inherited in 1981: a decade of détente that had produced a noticeable relaxation of tensions with the communist world, followed by a year of tense standoffs over Soviet advances into Central Asia, which threatened U.S. interests in the Middle East.

**Reagan's Cold War Revival**   Conservatives did not support détente. Neither did they care much for the containment policy that had guided U.S. Cold War strategy since 1947. Reagan and his advisors wanted to *defeat*, not merely contain, the Soviet Union. His administration pursued a two-pronged strategy toward that end. First, it abandoned détente and set about rearming America. Reagan's military budgets authorized new weapons systems, dramatically expanded military bases, and significantly expanded the nation's nuclear arsenal. This buildup in American military strength, reasoned Secretary of Defense Caspar Weinberger, would force the Soviets into an arms race that would strain their economy and cause domestic unrest. The Reagan administration also proposed the Strategic Arms Reduction Talks (START) with the Soviet Union, in which the United States put forward a plan calculated to increase American advantage in sea- and air-based nuclear systems over the Soviet's ground-based system.

Second, the president supported CIA initiatives to roll back Soviet influence in the developing world by funding anticommunist movements in Angola, Mozambique, Afghanistan, and Central America. To accomplish this objective, Reagan supported repressive, right-wing regimes. Nowhere was this more conspicuous in the 1980s than in the Central American countries of Guatemala, Nicaragua, and El Salvador. Conditions were unique in each country but held to a pattern: the United States sided with military dictatorships and oligarchies if democratically elected governments or left-wing movements sought support from the Soviet Union. In Guatemala, this approach produced a brutal military rule—thousands of opponents of the government were executed or kidnapped. In Nicaragua, Reagan actively encouraged a coup against the left-wing Sandinista government. And in El Salvador, the U.S.-backed government maintained secret "death squads," which murdered members of the opposition. In each case, Reagan blocked Soviet influence, but the damage done to local communities and to the international reputation of the United States, as in Vietnam, was great.

**Iran-Contra**    Reagan's determination to oppose left-wing movements in Central America engulfed his administration in a major scandal during the president's second term. For years, Reagan had denounced Iran as an "outlaw state" and a supporter of terrorism. But in 1985, he wanted its help. To win its assistance in freeing two dozen American hostages held by Hezbollah, a pro-Iranian Shiite group in Lebanon, the administration sold arms to Iran without public or congressional knowledge. While this secret arms deal was diplomatically and politically controversial, the use of the resulting profits in Nicaragua was explicitly illegal. To overthrow the democratically elected **Sandinistas**, whom the president accused of threatening U.S. business interests, Reagan ordered the CIA to assist an armed opposition group called the **Contras** (Map 29.2). Although Reagan praised the Contras as "freedom fighters," Congress worried that the president and other executive branch agencies were assuming war-making powers that the Constitution reserved to the legislature. In 1984, Congress banned the CIA and all other government agencies from providing any military support to the Contras.

Oliver North, a lieutenant colonel in the U.S. Marines and an aide to the National Security Council, defied that ban. With the tacit or explicit consent of high-ranking administration officials, including the president, North used the profits from the Iranian arms deal to assist the Contras. When asked whether he knew of North's illegal actions, Reagan replied, "I don't remember." The **Iran-Contra affair** came to public light in 1986, resulting in the prosecution of North and several other officials and weakening Reagan domestically—he proposed no bold domestic policy initiatives in his last two years. But the president remained steadfastly engaged in international affairs, where events were unfolding that would bring a dramatic close to the Cold War.

**Gorbachev and Soviet Reform**    The Soviet system of state socialism and central economic planning had transformed Russia from an agricultural to an industrial society between 1917 and the 1950s. But it had done so inefficiently. Lacking the

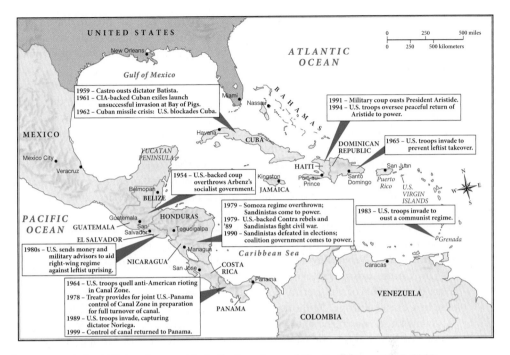

### MAP 29.2 U.S. Involvement in Latin America and the Caribbean, 1954–2000

Ever since the Monroe Doctrine (1823), the United States has claimed a special interest in Latin America. During the Cold War, U.S. foreign policy throughout Latin America focused on containing instability and the appeal of communism in a region plagued by poverty and military dictatorships. Providing foreign aid was one approach to addressing social and economic needs, but the United States frequently intervened with military forces (or by supporting military coups) to remove unfriendly or socialist governments. The Reagan administration's support of the Contra rebels in Nicaragua, some of which was contrary to U.S. law, was one of those interventions.

incentives of a market economy, most enterprises hoarded raw materials, employed too many workers, and did not develop new products. Except in military weaponry and space technology, the Russian economy fell further and further behind those of capitalist societies, and most people in the Soviet bloc endured a low standard of living. Moreover, the Soviet invasion of Afghanistan in 1979, like the American war in Vietnam, turned out to be a major blunder—an unwinnable war that cost vast amounts of money, destroyed military morale, and undermined popular support of the government.

Mikhail Gorbachev, a relatively young Russian leader who became general secretary of the Communist Party in 1985, recognized the need for internal economic reform and an end to the war in Afghanistan. An iconoclast in Soviet terms, Gorbachev introduced policies of *glasnost* (openness) and *perestroika* (economic restructuring), which encouraged widespread criticism of the rigid institutions and authoritarian controls of the Communist regime. To lessen tensions with the United States, Gorbachev met with Reagan in 1985, and the two leaders established a warm personal rapport. By 1987, they had agreed to eliminate all intermediate-range nuclear missiles based in Europe. A year later, Gorbachev ordered Soviet troops out of Afghanistan, and Reagan replaced many of his hardline advisors with policymakers who favored a renewal of détente.

Reagan's sudden reversal with regard to the Soviet Union remains one of the most intriguing aspects of his presidency. Many conservatives worried that their cowboy-hero president had been duped by a duplicitous Gorbachev, but Reagan's gamble paid off: the easing of tensions with the United States allowed the Soviet leader to press forward with his domestic reforms.

As Gorbachev's efforts revealed the flaws of the Soviet system, the peoples of Eastern and Central Europe demanded the ouster of their Communist governments. In Poland, the Roman Catholic Church and its pope — Polish-born John Paul II — joined with Solidarity, the trade-union movement, to overthrow the pro-Soviet regime. In 1956 and 1964, Russian troops had quashed similar popular uprisings in Hungary and East Germany. Now they did not intervene, and a series of peaceful uprisings —"Velvet Revolutions" — created a new political order throughout the region. Communism's fall even reached into Germany, the birthplace of the Cold War: destruction of the Berlin Wall in 1989 symbolized the end of Communist rule in Central Europe. Millions of television viewers worldwide watched jubilant Germans knock down the hated wall that had divided the city since 1961 — a vivid symbol of communist repression and the Cold War division of Europe. A new geopolitical order in Europe was in the making.

Alarmed by the reforms, Soviet military leaders seized power in August 1991 and arrested Gorbachev. But widespread popular opposition led by Boris Yeltsin, the president of the Russian Republic, thwarted their efforts to oust Gorbachev from office. This failure broke the dominance of the Communist Party. Inspired by the Velvet Revolutions and the weakening of the Communist Party, several Soviet Republics (Estonia, Latvia, Lithuania, Ukraine, and Belarus) broke away as independent nation-states. Finally, on December 25, 1991, the Union of Soviet Socialist Republics formally dissolved to make way for an eleven-member Commonwealth of Independent States (CIS) (Map 29.3). The remarkable and total collapse of the Soviet Union was the result of internal weaknesses of the Communist economy. External pressure from the United States played an important, though secondary, role.

"Nobody — no country, no party, no person — 'won' the cold war," concluded George Kennan, the architect in 1947 of the American policy of containment. The Cold War's cost was enormous, and both sides benefitted greatly from its end. For more than forty years, the United States had fought a bitter economic and ideological battle against its communist foe, a struggle that exerted an enormous impact on American society. Taxpayers had spent some $4 trillion on nuclear weapons and trillions more on conventional arms, placing the United States on a permanent war footing and creating a massive military-industrial complex. The physical and psychological costs were equally high, including anticommunist witch-hunts and a constant fear of nuclear annihilation. Most Americans had no qualms about proclaiming victory, however, and conservative advocates of free-market capitalism celebrated the outcome. The collapse of communism in Eastern Europe and the disintegration of the Soviet Union itself, they argued, demonstrated that they had been right all along.

**MAP 29.3**    **The Collapse of the Soviet Union and the Creation of Independent States, 1989–1991**

The collapse of Soviet communism dramatically altered the political landscape of Central Europe and Central Asia. The Warsaw Pact, the USSR's answer to NATO, vanished. West and East Germany reunited, and the nations created by the Versailles treaty of 1919 — Estonia, Latvia, Lithuania, Poland, Czechoslovakia, Hungary, and Yugoslavia — reasserted their independence or split into smaller, ethnically defined nations. The Soviet republics bordering Russia, from Belarus in the west to Kyrgyzstan in the east, also became independent states, while remaining loosely bound with Russia in the Commonwealth of Independent States (CIS).

## A New Political Order at Home and Abroad

Ronald Reagan's role in facilitating the end of the Cold War was among his most important achievements. Overall, his presidency left a mixed legacy. Despite his pledge to get the federal government "off our backs," he could not ultimately reduce its size or scope. Social Security and other entitlement programs remained untouched, and increased military spending outweighed cuts in other programs. Determined not to divide the country, Reagan did not actively push controversial policies espoused by the Religious Right. He called for tax credits for private religious schools, restrictions on abortions, and a constitutional amendment to permit prayer in public schools, but he did not expend his political capital to secure these measures.

While Reagan failed to roll back the social welfare and regulatory state of the New Deal–Great Society era, he changed the dynamic of American politics. The Reagan presidency restored popular belief that the nation — and individual Americans — could enjoy increasing prosperity. And his antigovernment rhetoric won many adherents, as did his bold and fiscally aggressive tax cuts. Social-welfare liberalism, ascendant since 1933, remained intact but was now on the defensive — led by Reagan, conservatives had changed the political conversation.

**Election of 1988**   George H. W. Bush, Reagan's vice president and successor, was not beloved by conservatives, who did not see him as one of their own. But he possessed an insider's familiarity with government and a long list of powerful allies, accumulated over three decades of public service. Bush's route to the White House reflected the post-Reagan alignments in American politics. In the primaries, he faced a spirited challenge from Pat Robertson, the archconservative televangelist whose influence and profile had grown during Reagan's two terms. After securing the presidential nomination, which he won largely because of his fierce loyalty to Reagan, Bush felt compelled to select as his vice-presidential running mate an unknown and inexperienced Indiana senator, Dan Quayle. Bush hoped that Quayle would help secure the Christian "**family values**" vote upholding the traditional nuclear family and Christian morality. Robertson's challenge and Quayle's selection showed that the Religious Right had become a major force in Republican politics.

On the Democratic side, Jesse Jackson became the first African American to challenge for a major-party nomination, winning eleven states in primary and caucus voting. However, the much less charismatic Massachusetts governor, Michael Dukakis, emerged as the Democratic nominee. Dukakis, a liberal from the Northeast, proved unable to win back the constituencies Democrats had lost in the 1970s: southern whites, midwestern blue-collar Catholics, and middle-class suburbanites. Indeed, Bush's campaign manager, Lee Atwater, baited Dukakis by calling him a "card-carrying liberal," a not-so-subtle reference to J. Edgar Hoover's 1958 phrase "card-carrying communist." Bush won with 53 percent of the vote, a larger margin of victory than Reagan's in 1980. The election confirmed a new pattern in presidential politics that would last through the turn of the twenty-first century: every four years, Americans would refight the battles of the 1960s, with liberals on one side and conservatives on the other.

**Middle East**   The end of the Cold War left the United States as the world's only military superpower and raised the prospect of what President Bush called a "new world order" dominated by the United States and its European and Asian allies. American officials and diplomats presumed that U.S. interests should prevail in this new environment, but they now confronted an array of regional, religious, and ethnic conflicts that defied easy solutions. None were more pressing or more complex than those in the Middle East — the oil-rich lands stretching from Iran to Algeria. Middle Eastern conflicts would dominate the foreign policy of the United States for the next two decades, replacing the Cold War at the center of American geopolitics.

After Carter's success negotiating the 1979 Egypt-Israel treaty at Camp David, there were few bright spots in U.S. Middle Eastern diplomacy. In 1982, the Reagan administration supported Israel's invasion of Lebanon, a military operation intended to destroy the Palestine Liberation Organization (PLO). But when Lebanese militants, angered at U.S. intervention on behalf of Israel, killed 241 American marines, Reagan abruptly withdrew the forces. Three years later, Palestinians living in the Gaza Strip and along the West Bank of the Jordan River — territories occupied by Israel since 1967 — mounted an intifada, a civilian uprising against Israeli authority. In response, American diplomats stepped up their efforts to persuade the PLO and

Arab nations to accept the legitimacy of Israel and to convince the Israelis to allow the creation of a Palestinian state. Neither initiative met with much success. Unable, or unwilling, to solve the region's most intractable problems and burdened by a history of support for undemocratic regimes in Middle Eastern countries, the United States was not seen by residents of the region as an honest broker.

**Persian Gulf War** American interest in a reliable supply of oil from the region led the United States into a short but consequential war in the Persian Gulf in the early 1990s. Ten years earlier, in September 1980, the revolutionary Shiite Islamic nation of Iran, headed by Ayatollah Khomeini, came under attack from Iraq, a secular state headed by the dictator Saddam Hussein. The fighting was intense and long lasting—a war of attrition that claimed a million casualties. Reagan supported Hussein with military intelligence and other aid—in order to maintain supplies of Iraqi oil, undermine Iran, and preserve a balance of power in the Middle East. Finally, in 1988, an armistice ended the inconclusive war, with both sides still claiming the territory that sparked the conflict.

Two years later, in August 1990, Hussein went to war to expand Iraq's boundaries and oil supply. Believing (erroneously) that he still had the support of the United States, Hussein sent in troops and quickly conquered Kuwait, Iraq's small, oil-rich neighbor, and threatened Saudi Arabia, the site of one-fifth of the world's known oil reserves and an informal ally of the United States. To preserve the balance of power

**Men—and Women—at War** A U.S. soldier with Norman Schwarzkopf, commander of coalition forces in the Persian Gulf War. Women comprised approximately 10 percent of American troops in that conflict. In the last decades of the twentieth century, women increasingly chose military careers and were more frequently assigned to combat zones.
David Turnley/Corbis/VCG via Getty Images.

in the region favored by the United States, President George H. W. Bush sponsored a series of resolutions in the United Nations Security Council calling for Iraq to withdraw from Kuwait. When Hussein refused, Bush successfully prodded the UN to authorize the use of force, and the president organized a military coalition of thirty-four nations. Dividing mostly along party lines, the Republican-led House of Representatives authorized American participation by a vote of 252 to 182, and the Democratic-led Senate agreed by the close margin of 52 to 47.

The coalition forces led by the United States quickly won the **Persian Gulf War** for the "liberation of Kuwait." To avoid a protracted struggle and retain French and Russian support for the UN coalition, Bush decided against occupying Iraq and removing Saddam Hussein from power. Instead, he won passage of UN Resolution 687, which imposed economic sanctions against Iraq unless it allowed unfettered inspection of its weapons systems, destroyed all biological and chemical arms, and unconditionally pledged not to develop nuclear weapons. The military victory, the low incidence of American casualties, and the quick withdrawal produced a euphoric reaction at home. "By God, we've kicked the Vietnam syndrome once and for all," Bush announced, and his approval rating shot up precipitously. But Saddam Hussein remained a formidable power in the region, and in March 2003, he would become the pretext for Bush's son, President George W. Bush, to initiate another war in Iraq—one that would be much more protracted, expensive, and bloody for Americans, Iraqis, and the entire Middle East (Chapter 30).

Thus the end of the Cold War brought not peace, but a deeper American involvement in the Middle East. For half a century, the United States and the Soviet Union had tried to divide the world into two rival economic and ideological blocs: communist and capitalist. The next decades promised many new struggles, one of them between a Western-led agenda of economic and cultural globalization and an anti-Western ideology of Muslim and Arab regionalism. Still more post–Cold War shifts were coming into view as well. One was the spectacular emergence of the European Union as a massive united trading bloc, economic engine, and global political force. Another was the equally spectacular economic growth in China, which was just beginning to take off in the early 1990s. The post–Cold War world promised to be a *multi*polar one, with centers of power in Europe, the United States, and East Asia, and seemingly intractable conflict in the Middle East.

| IN YOUR OWN WORDS | What were the aims of U.S. foreign policy during the waning years of the Cold War and in its immediate aftermath? |
|---|---|

## Summary

This chapter examined two central developments of the years 1980–1991: the rise of the New Right in U.S. politics and the end of the Cold War. Each development set the stage for a new era in American life, one that stretches to our own day. Domestically, the New Right, which had been building in strength since the mid-1960s, criticized the liberalism of the Great Society and the permissiveness that conservative activists associated with feminism and the sexual revolution. Shifting their allegiance from Barry Goldwater to Ronald Reagan, right-wing Americans built a conservative movement from the ground up and in 1980 elected Reagan president. Advocating free-market economics, lower taxes, and fewer government regulations, Reagan became a champion of the New Right. His record as president was more mixed than his rhetoric would suggest, however. Reagan's initial tax cuts were followed by tax hikes. Moreover, he frequently dismayed the Christian Right by not pursuing their interests forcefully enough—especially regarding abortion and school prayer.

Reagan played a role in the ending of the Cold War. His massive military buildup in the early 1980s strained an already overstretched Soviet economy, which struggled to keep pace. Reagan then agreed to meet with Soviet leader Mikhail Gorbachev in several summits between 1985 and 1987. More important than Reagan's actions, however, were inefficiencies and contradictions in the Soviet economic structure itself. Combined with the forced military buildup and the disastrous war in Afghanistan, these strains led Gorbachev to institute the first significant reforms in Soviet society in half a century. The reforms stirred popular criticism of the Soviet Union, which formally collapsed in 1991. Beginning the same year with the Gulf War against Iraq, the United States became embroiled in what would become a decades-long series of wars in the Middle East.

# Chapter 29 Review

## KEY TERMS

Identify and explain the significance of each term below.

*The Conscience of a Conservative* (p. 848)

*National Review* (p. 850)

Religious Right (p. 850)

hostage crisis (p. 852)

Reagan coalition (p. 855)

Moral Majority (p. 855)

Reagan Democrats (p. 855)

supply-side economics (Reaganomics) (p. 856)

Economic Recovery Tax Act (ERTA) (p. 856)

national debt (p. 857)

deregulation (p. 857)

HIV/AIDS (p. 859)

service industries (p. 861)

Sandinistas (p. 864)

Contras (p. 864)

Iran-Contra affair (p. 864)

*glasnost* (p. 865)

*perestroika* (p. 865)

family values (p. 868)

Persian Gulf War (p. 870)

## REVIEW QUESTIONS

Answer these questions to demonstrate your understanding of the chapter's main ideas.

1. What were the major characteristics of the political movement that backed Ronald Reagan, known as the New Right?

2. What were the major political successes and failures of the Reagan coalition?

3. What were the aims of U.S. foreign policy during the waning years of the Cold War and in its immediate aftermath?

4. Review the events listed on the thematic timeline on pages 844–845. In what ways was the New Right "reactive," responding to liberalism, and in what ways was it "proactive," asserting its own agenda?

## CHRONOLOGY

As you read, ask yourself why this chapter begins and ends with these dates and identify the links among related events.

**1981**
- Ronald Reagan becomes president
- Republicans gain control of Senate
- Economic Recovery Tax Act (ERTA) cuts taxes

|  |  |
|---|---|
| **1981– 1989** | • Military expenditures increase sharply |
|  | • Reagan cuts budgets of regulatory agencies |
|  | • Sandra Day O'Connor appointed to the Supreme Court |
|  | • National debt triples |
|  | • Emergence of New Right think tanks: Heritage Foundation, American Enterprise Institute, and the Cato Institute |
|  | • United States assists Iraq in war against Iran (1980–1988) |
| **1985** | • Mikhail Gorbachev takes power in Soviet Union |
| **1986** | • Iran-Contra scandal weakens Reagan presidency |
|  | • William Rehnquist named chief justice |
| **1987** | • United States and USSR agree to limit missiles in Europe |
| **1988** | • George H. W. Bush elected president |
| **1989** | • Destruction of Berlin Wall |
|  | • "Velvet Revolutions" in Eastern Europe |
|  | • *Webster v. Reproductive Health Services* limits abortion services |
| **1990–1991** | • Persian Gulf War |
| **1991** | • Dissolution of Soviet Union ends Cold War |

# 30

# Confronting Global and National Dilemmas

## 1989 TO THE PRESENT

**IDENTIFY THE BIG IDEA**

How has the post–Cold War era of globalization affected American politics, economics, and society?

**ON THE MORNING OF SEPTEMBER 11, 2001, TWO COMMERCIAL** airliners were deliberately flown into the World Trade Center in lower Manhattan. Millions of Americans, and many more people worldwide, watched live on television and the Internet as the towers burned and collapsed. Simultaneously, a third plane was flown into the Pentagon, and a fourth hijacked plane crashed in rural Pennsylvania. It took Federal Bureau of Investigation officials only a few hours to determine the identity of most of the hijackers, as well as the organization behind the murderous attacks, a radical Islamic group known as **Al Qaeda**.

The attacks were made possible by the new era of globalization. Of the nineteen hijackers, fifteen were from Saudi Arabia, two were from the United Arab Emirates, one was from Egypt, and one was from Lebanon. Many had trained in Afghanistan, in guerrilla warfare camps operated by Osama bin Laden, Al Qaeda's leader. Four had gone to flight school in the United States itself. Several had lived and studied in Germany. They communicated with one another and with planners in Afghanistan through e-mail, Web sites, and cell phones. The most conspicuous crime of the twenty-first century, which left 2,900 people dead and sent waves of shock and anxiety through the American public, would have been impossible without the openness and interconnectivity that are central features of globalization.

The emergence in the Middle East of a radical Islamic movement willing to use terrorism to inflict major damage on the United States and the West testified to the altered realities of global politics. The simple Cold War duality—communism versus capitalism—had for decades obscured regional, ethnic, and religious loyalties and conflicts. Absent the global Cold War rivalry, those loyalties and conflicts moved to center stage. For the United States, the period between the end of the Cold War and the present has been defined by twin dilemmas. The first relates to **globalization**. How would the United States engage in global trade and commerce? How would it engage with the emerging economic strength of Europe and Asia? And how would it conceptualize and address new threats to the nation and to global stability? The second dilemma relates to domestic politics and the economy. In an era of conservative ideological dominance, how would Americans reconcile their political differences, and how would the nation continue to ensure economic opportunity and security for its citizens? As profound geopolitical changes shook the world, these were, as the chapter title suggests, Americans' dilemmas in a global society.

## America in the Global Economy

In the decade following the collapse of the Soviet Union and the end of the Cold War, Americans rediscovered a long-standing truth: the United States was not an island but was linked in countless ways to a global economy and society. Economic prosperity in the post–World War II decades had obscured for Americans this fundamental reality. Globalization was not itself new—think of the Atlantic economy of the eighteenth century linking Europe, the Americas, and Africa—but a new and distinct era of global integration emerged at the turn of the twenty-first century. This current era has seen the rapid spread of capitalism around the world, huge increases in global trade and commerce, and a diffusion of communications technology, including the Internet, linking the world's people to one another in ways unimaginable a generation earlier.

Suddenly, the United States faced a dizzying array of opportunities and challenges, both at home and abroad. "Profound and powerful forces are shaking and remaking our world," said a young President Bill Clinton in his first inaugural address in 1993. "The urgent question of our time is whether we can make change our friend and not our enemy." For many, globalization indeed looked like an enemy. In late 1999, more than 50,000 protesters took to the streets of Seattle, Washington, immobilizing a wide swath of the city's downtown. Police, armed with pepper spray and arrayed in riot gear, worked feverishly to clear the clogged streets, get traffic moving, and usher well-dressed government ministers from around the world into a conference hall. Protesters jeered, chanted, and held hundreds of signs and banners aloft. A radical contingent joined the otherwise peaceful march, and a handful of them began breaking the windows of the chain stores they saw as symbols of global capitalism: Starbucks, Gap, Old Navy.

What aroused such passion in the so-called battle of Seattle was a meeting of the **World Trade Organization (WTO)**, one of the principal institutions pushing unrestrained global trade. Protestors raised a question both fundamental and easily misunderstood: In whose interest was the global economy structured? Many of the Seattle activists took inspiration from the five-point "Declaration for Global Democracy," issued by the human rights organization Global Exchange during the WTO's Seattle meeting. "Global trade and investment," the declaration demanded, "must not be ends in themselves but rather the instruments for achieving equitable and sustainable development, including protections for workers and the environment." This was precisely what the demonstrators charged the WTO with failing to do. The declaration also addressed inequality among nations, calling attention to who benefitted from globalization and who did not.

## The Rise of the European Union and China

During the Cold War, the United States and the Soviet Union oversaw what observers called a bipolar world—two powerful poles, one capitalist and the other communist, around which global geopolitics were organized. Since the early 1990s, however, a multipolar world has emerged—with centers of power in Europe, Japan, China, and the United States, along with rising regional powers such as India and Brazil.

In 1992, the nations of Western Europe created the European Union (EU) and moved toward the creation of a single federal state, somewhat like the United States. By the first decades of the twenty-first century, the European Union included twenty-eight countries and 500 million people—collectively, the third largest population in the world, behind China and India—and accounted for a fifth of all global imports and exports. In 2002, the EU introduced a single currency, the euro, which soon rivaled the dollar and the Japanese yen as a major international currency (Map 30.1). The EU has remained an economic juggernaut and trading rival of the United States, but following the Great Recession of 2007–2008, it pursued a policy of austerity largely unpopular outside of Germany, its dominant economic member. In a stunning referendum in 2016, the voters of the United Kingdom rejected EU membership on the grounds that it compromised national sovereignty and permitted unregulated immigration. Whatever its future, the EU has presented a number of new dilemmas for American officials, especially economic competition and the strength of the EU currency.

China has also presented dilemmas. A vast nation of 1.3 billion people that was the world's fastest-rising economic power in the first decade of the twenty-first century, China *quadrupled* its gross domestic product (GDP) between 2000 and 2008. Economic growth rates during those years were consistently near 10 percent—higher than the United States achieved during its periods of furious economic growth in the 1950s and 1960s. Although still governed by the Communist Party, China embraced capitalism, and its factories produced inexpensive products that Americans eagerly purchased—everything from children's toys and television sets to clothing, household appliances, and video games. To maintain this symbiotic relationship, China deliberately kept its currency weak against the American dollar, ensuring that its exports remained cheap in the United States.

Although this relationship has been beneficial to American consumers in the short run, its implications for the future may be less promising. Two such implications

**WTO Demonstration, Seattle, 1999**  In November 1999, an estimated 50,000 to 100,000 people from many states and foreign nations staged a major protest at a World Trade Organization (WTO) meeting in Seattle. The goals of the protesters were diffuse; many feared that the trend toward a system of free (capitalist-run) trade would primarily benefit multinational corporations and would hurt both developing nations and the working classes in the industrialized world. Protests have continued at subsequent meetings of the WTO and the World Bank.  Hector Mata/AFP/Getty Images.

stand out. First, as more and more goods that Americans buy are produced in China, the manufacturing base in the United States continues to shrink, costing jobs and adversely affecting communities. Second, until quite recently China kept its currency low against the dollar primarily by purchasing American debt. China now owns 7 percent of total U.S. debt, making it the largest foreign holder alongside Japan. Many economists believe that it is unwise to allow a single country to wield so much influence over the U.S. currency supply. Should this relationship continue unchanged, Americans may find their manufacturing sector contracting even more severely in the coming decades.

## A New Era of Globalization

Americans have long depended on foreign markets to which they export their goods and have long received imported products and immigrants from other countries. But the *intensity* of international exchange has varied over time. The end of the Cold War shattered barriers that had restrained international trade and impeded capitalist development of vast areas of the world. New communications systems—satellites, fiber-optic cables, global positioning networks—were shrinking the world's physical

**MAP 30.1   Growth of the European Community, 1951–2016**
The European Community (EU) began in the 1950s as a loose organization of Western
European nations. Over the course of the following decades, it created stronger common
institutions, such as the European Parliament in Strasbourg, the EU Commission in Brussels,
and the Court of Justice in Luxembourg. With the collapse of communism, the EU expanded to
include the nations of Eastern and Central Europe. It now includes twenty-eight nations and
over 500 million people. Many states have applied for membership and are awaiting official
ascension into the union, while in 2016 the United Kingdom voted to exit the EU.

spaces to a degree unimaginable at the beginning of the twentieth century. Perhaps
most important, global financial markets became integrated to an unprecedented
extent, allowing investment capital to "flow" into and out of nations and around the
world in a matter of moments.

**International Organizations and Corporations**   International organizations, many
of them created in the wake of World War II, set the rules for capitalism's worldwide
expansion: the World Bank, the International Monetary Fund (IMF), and the General
Agreement on Tariffs and Trade (GATT). During the final decades of the Cold War,
the leading capitalist industrial nations formed the Group of Seven (G7) to manage
global economic policy. Russia joined in 1997, creating the **Group of Eight (G8)**.

The G8 nations—the United States, Britain, Germany, France, Italy, Japan, Canada, and Russia—largely controlled the major international financial organizations (Russia was suspended from the G8 in 2014). In 1995, GATT evolved into the World Trade Organization (WTO), with nearly 150 participating nations that regulate and formalize trade agreements with member states.

As globalization accelerated, so did the integration of regional economies. To offset the economic clout of the European bloc, in 1993 the United States, Canada, and Mexico signed the **North American Free Trade Agreement (NAFTA)**. This treaty, as ratified by the U.S. Congress, envisioned the eventual creation of a free-trade zone covering all of North America. In East Asia, the capitalist nations of Japan, South Korea, Taiwan, and Singapore consulted on economic policy; as China developed a quasi-capitalist economy and became a major exporter of manufactures, its Communist-led government joined their deliberations.

International organizations set the rules, but globalization was made possible by the proliferation of **multinational corporations** (MNCs). In 1970, there were 7,000 corporations with offices and factories in multiple countries; by 2000, the number had exploded to 63,000. Many of the most powerful MNCs were, and continue to be, based in the United States. Walmart, the biggest American retailer, is also one of the world's largest corporations, with 6,000 stores in other nations and more than $475 billion in sales in 2015. Apple, maker of the iPhone and iPad, grew spectacularly in the 2000s and now has more than $170 billion in annual global sales. The McDonald's restaurant chain had 1,000 outlets outside the United States in 1980; twenty years later, there were nearly 13,000, and "McWorld" had become a popular shorthand term for globalization.

Globalization was driven by more than a quest for new markets. Corporations also sought ever-cheaper sources of labor. Many American MNCs closed their factories in the United States and outsourced manufacturing jobs to plants in Mexico, Eastern Europe, and especially Asia. The athletic sportswear firm Nike was a prime example. By 2005, Nike had established 700 factories worldwide that employed more than 650,000 workers, most of whom received low wages, endured harsh working conditions, and had no health or pension benefits. Highly skilled jobs were outsourced as well.

**Financial Deregulation**   One of the principal differences between this new era of globalization and previous eras has been the opening of national financial and currency markets to investment from around the world. The United States and Britain led the way. Both countries came under the sway of powerful political forces in the 1980s calling for the total deregulation of banks, brokerage houses, investment firms, and financial markets—letting the free market replace government oversight. Together, the United States and Britain led a quiet revolution in which investment markets around the world were gradually set free.

Financial deregulation led to spectacular profits for investors but produced a more fragile, crash-prone global economy. On the profit side, financial-industry profits in the United States rose from less than 10 percent of total business profits in the 1950s to more than 40 percent beginning in the 1990s. But the costs were becoming clear as well: the bankruptcy of the American savings and loan industry in the 1980s; the "lost decade" in Japan in the 1990s; the near bankruptcy of Russia in the late 1990s and of Argentina in 2001; the 1997 Asian financial crisis, centered in Thailand and Indonesia; and the Great Recession, which affected the entire global economy in 2008. These and other episodes dramatized the extraordinary risks that financial globalization has introduced.

## Revolutions in Technology

The technological advances of the 1980s and 1990s changed the character of everyday life for millions of Americans, linking them with a global information and media environment unprecedented in world history. Not since television was introduced to American homes in the years following World War II had technology so profoundly changed the way people lived their lives. Personal computers, cell phones and smartphones, the Internet and the World Wide Web, and other electronic devices and systems altered work, leisure, and access to knowledge in stunning ways. Like unimpeded trade, these advances in communications and personal technologies enhanced globalization.

During the 1990s, personal computers, which had emerged in the late 1970s, grew even more significant with the spread of the Internet and the World Wide Web. Like the computer itself, the Internet was the product of military-based research. During the late 1960s, the U.S. Department of Defense, in conjunction with the Massachusetts Institute of Technology, began developing a decentralized computer network, the **Advanced Research Projects Agency Network (ARPANET)**. The Internet, which grew out of the ARPANET, was soon used by government scientists, academic specialists, and military contractors to exchange data, information, and electronic mail (e-mail). By the 1980s, the Internet had spread to universities, businesses, and the general public. The debut in 1991 of the graphics-based **World Wide Web** — a collection of servers that allowed access to millions of documents, pictures, and other materials — enhanced the popular appeal and commercial possibilities of the Internet. By 2011, 78 percent of all Americans and more than two billion people worldwide used the Internet to send messages, view information, and buy and sell products and services.

> **IN YOUR OWN WORDS**    How did globalization redefine the relationship of the United States to the rest of the world after the end of the Cold War?

# Politics and Partisanship in a Contentious Era

Standing at the podium at the 1992 Republican National Convention, his supporters cheering by the thousands, Patrick Buchanan did not mince words. Buchanan was a former speechwriter for President Richard Nixon and a White House aide to President Ronald Reagan. Despite having lost the nomination for president, Buchanan still hoped to shape the party's message to voters. This election, he told the audience — including millions watching on television — "is about what we stand for as Americans." Citing Democratic support for abortion rights and the rights of lesbians and gay men, Buchanan claimed there was "a religious war going on in our country for the soul of America." He also called it "a cultural war," and his address became known as the "**culture war**" speech.

Buchanan's war was another name for a long-standing political struggle, dating to the 1920s, between religious traditionalists and secular liberals (Chapter 21). This time, however, Americans struggled over these questions in the long shadow of the 1960s, which had taken on an exaggerated meaning in the nation's politics. Against the backdrop of globalization, American politics in the 1990s and early 2000s careened back and forth between contests over divisive social issues and concern over the nation's economic future.

## An Increasingly Plural Society

Exact estimates vary, but demographers predict that at some point between 2040 and 2050 the United States will become a "majority-minority" nation: no single ethnic or racial group will be in the numerical majority. This was already the case in four states by 2010—California, Texas, Hawaii, and New Mexico—where African Americans, Latinos, and Asians together constituted a majority of the state's residents. As this unmistakable trend became apparent in the 1990s, it fueled renewed debates over ethnic and racial identity and over public policies such as affirmative action.

**New Immigrants** According to the Census Bureau, the population of the United States grew from 203 million in 1970 to 280 million in 2000. Of that 77-million-person increase, immigrants accounted for 28 million, with documented entrants numbering 21 million and undocumented entrants adding another 7 million. As a result, by 2010, 27 percent of California's population was foreign-born, as was 20 percent of New York's and 17 percent each of New Jersey's and Florida's (these percentages declined somewhat in the 2010 Census). Relatively few immigrants came from Europe, which had dominated immigration to the United States between 1880 and 1924. The overwhelming majority—some 25 million—now came from Latin America (16 million) and East Asia (9 million) (Map 30.2).

This extraordinary inflow of immigrants was the unintended result of the **Immigration and Nationality Act** of 1965, one of the less well-known but most influential pieces of Great Society legislation (Chapter 27). Known as the Hart-Celler

**New Immigrants** In the early years of the 2000s, more immigrants lived in the United States than at any time since the first decades of the twentieth century. Most came from Asia, Latin America, and Africa. Many, like those pictured here, started small businesses that helped revive the economies of urban and suburban neighborhoods across the country. Blend Images/ SuperStock.

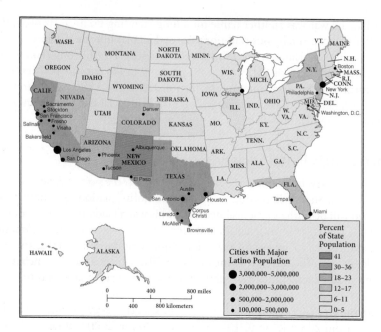

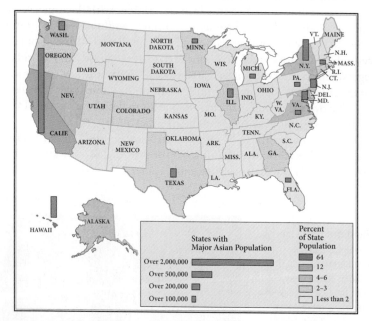

## MAP 30.2   Latino and Asian Populations, 2000

In 2000, people of Latin American descent made up more than 11 percent of the American population, and they now outnumber African Americans as the largest minority group. Asian Americans accounted for an additional 4 percent of the population. Demographers predict that by the year 2050 only about half of the U.S. population will be composed of non-Latino whites. Note the high percentage of Latinos and Asians in California and certain other states.

Act, the legislation eliminated the 1924 quota system, which had favored Northern Europe. In its place, Congress created a more equal playing field among nations and a slightly higher total limit on immigration. The legislation also eased the entry of immigrants who possessed skills in high demand in the United States. Finally, a provision with far-reaching implications was included in the new law: immediate family members of those legally resident in the United States were admitted outside of the total numerical limit.

American residents from Latin America and the Caribbean were best positioned to take advantage of the family provision. Millions of Mexicans came to the United States to join their families, and U.S. residents from El Salvador and Guatemala — tens of thousands of whom had arrived seeking sanctuary or asylum during the civil wars of the 1980s — and the Dominican Republic now brought their families to join them. Nationally, there were now more Latinos than African Americans. Many of these immigrants profoundly shaped the emerging global economy by sending substantial portions of their earnings, called remittances, back to family members in their home countries. In 2015, for instance, workers in the United States sent $25 billion to Mexico, a massive remittance flow that constituted Mexico's third largest source of foreign exchange.

Asian immigrants came largely from China, the Philippines, South Korea, India, and Pakistan. In addition, 700,000 refugees came to the United States from Southeast Asia (Vietnam, Laos, and Cambodia) after the Vietnam War. This immigration signaled more than new flows of people into the United States. Throughout much of its history, the United States had oriented itself toward the Atlantic. Indeed, at the end of the nineteenth century, American secretary of state John Hay observed, "The Mediterranean is the ocean of the past; the Atlantic the ocean of the present." He added, presciently, "The Pacific [is] the ocean of the future." By the last decades of the twentieth century, Hay's future had arrived. As immigration from Asia increased, as Japan and China grew more influential economically, and as more and more transnational trade crossed the Pacific, commentators on both sides of the ocean began speaking of the Pacific Rim as an important new region.

**Multiculturalism and Its Critics**   Most new immigrants arrived under the terms of the 1965 law. But those who entered without legal documentation stirred political controversy. After twenty years under the new law, there were between three and five million immigrants without legal status. In 1986, to remedy this situation, Congress passed the Immigration Reform and Control Act. The law granted citizenship to many of those who had arrived outside the law's numerical limits, provided incentives for employers not to hire undocumented immigrants, and increased surveillance along the border with Mexico.

Immigration critics persisted, however. In 1992, Patrick Buchanan warned Americans that their country was "undergoing the greatest invasion in its history, a migration of millions of illegal aliens a year from Mexico." Many states took immigration matters into their own hands. In 1994, for instance, Californians approved Proposition 187, a ballot initiative that barred undocumented immigrants from public schools, nonemergency care at public health clinics, and all other state social services (after five years in federal court, the controversial measure was ruled unconstitutional). Two decades later, in 2016, immigration's critics massed behind

Republican presidential nominee Donald Trump, who repeatedly pledged to "build a wall" between the U.S. and Mexico and to deport the approximately 11 million undocumented immigrants who resided in the country.

Debates over post-1965 immigration looked a great deal like conflicts in the early decades of the century. Then, many native-born white Protestants worried that the largely Jewish and Catholic immigrants from Southern and Eastern Europe, along with African American migrants leaving the South, could not assimilate and threatened the "purity" of the nation. Although the conflicts looked the same, the cultural paradigm had shifted. In the earlier era, the *melting pot*—a term borrowed from the title of a 1908 play—became the metaphor for how American society would accommodate its newfound diversity. Some native-born Americans found solace in the melting-pot concept because it implied that a single "American" culture would predominate. In the 1990s, however, a different concept, **multiculturalism**, emerged to define social diversity. Americans, this concept suggested, were not a single people into whom others melted; rather, they comprised a diverse set of ethnic and racial groups living and working together. A shared set of public values held the multicultural society together, even as different groups maintained unique practices and traditions.

Critics, however, charged that multiculturalism sowed division and conferred preferential treatment on minority groups. Many government policies, as well as a large number of private employers, for instance, continued to support affirmative action programs designed to bring African Americans and Latinos into public- and private-sector jobs and universities in larger numbers. Conservatives argued that such governmental programs were deeply flawed because they promoted "reverse discrimination" against white men and women and resulted in the selection and promotion of less qualified applicants for jobs and educational advancement.

California stood at the center of the debate. In 1995, under pressure from Republican governor Pete Wilson, the regents of the University of California scrapped their entire affirmative action admissions policy. A year later, California voters approved **Proposition 209**, which outlawed affirmative action in state employment and public education. At the height of the 1995 controversy, President Bill Clinton delivered a major speech defending affirmative action. He reminded Americans that Richard Nixon, a Republican president, had endorsed affirmative action, and he concluded by saying the nation should "mend it," not "end it." However, as in the *Bakke* decision of the 1970s (Chapter 28), it was the U.S. Supreme Court that spoke loudest on the subject. In two parallel 2003 cases, the Court invalidated one affirmative action plan at the University of Michigan but allowed racial preference policies that promoted a "diverse" student body. Thus diversity became the law of the land, the constitutionally acceptable basis for affirmative action. The policy had been narrowed but preserved.

Additional anxieties about a multicultural nation centered on language. In 1998, Silicon Valley software entrepreneur Ron Unz sponsored a California initiative calling for an end to bilingual education in public schools. Unz argued that bilingual education had failed because it did not adequately prepare Spanish-speaking students to succeed in an English-speaking society. The state's white, Anglo residents largely approved of the measure; most Mexican American, Asian American, and civil rights organizations opposed it. When Unz's measure, Proposition 227, passed with a 61 percent majority, it seemed to confirm the limits of multiculturalism in the nation's most diverse state.

## Clashes over "Family Values"

If the promise of a multicultural nation was one contested political issue, another was American families. New Right conservatives charged that the "abrasive experiments of two liberal decades," as a Reagan administration report put it, had eroded respect for marriage and what they had called, since the 1970s, "family values." They pointed to the 40 percent rate of divorce among whites and the nearly 60 percent rate of out-of-wedlock pregnancies among African Americans. To conservatives, there was a wide range of culprits: legislators who enacted liberal divorce laws, funded child care, and allowed welfare payments to unmarried mothers, as well as judges who condoned abortion and banished religious instruction from public schools.

**Abortion**   Abortion was central to the battles between feminists and religious conservatives and a defining issue between Democrats and Republicans. Feminists who described themselves as prochoice viewed the issue from the perspective of the pregnant woman; they argued that the right to a legal, safe abortion was crucial to her autonomy over her body and life. Conversely, religious conservatives, who pronounced themselves prolife, viewed abortion from the perspective of the unborn fetus and claimed that its rights trumped those of the mother. That is where the debate had stood since the U.S. Supreme Court's 1973 decision in *Roe v. Wade*.

By the 1980s, fundamentalist Protestants had assumed leadership of the antiabortion movement, which became increasingly confrontational and politically powerful. In 1987, the religious activist Randall Terry founded **Operation Rescue**, which mounted protests outside abortion clinics and harassed their staffs and clients. While such vocal protests took shape outside clinics, antiabortion activists also won state laws that limited public funding for abortions, required parental notification before minors could obtain abortions, and mandated waiting periods before any woman could undergo an abortion procedure. Such laws further restricted women's reproductive choices.

**Gay Rights**   The issue of homosexuality stirred equally deep passions. As more gay men and women came out of the closet in the years after Stonewall (Chapter 27), they demanded legal protections from discrimination in housing, education, and employment. Public opinion about these demands varied by region, but by the 1990s, many cities and states had banned discrimination on the basis of sexual orientation. Gay rights groups also sought legal rights for same-sex couples — such as the eligibility for workplace health-care coverage — that were akin to those enjoyed by married heterosexuals. In later years, activists pushed to have transgender persons included in such protections. Many of the most prominent national gay rights organizations, such as the Human Rights Campaign, focused on full marriage equality: a legal recognition of same-sex marriage that was on par with opposite-sex marriages.

The Religious Right had long condemned homosexuality as morally wrong, and public opinion remained sharply divided. In 1992, Colorado voters approved an amendment to the state constitution that prevented local governments from enacting ordinances protecting gays and lesbians — a measure that the Supreme Court subsequently overturned as unconstitutional. That same year, however, Oregon voters defeated a more radical initiative that would have prevented the state from using any funds "to promote, encourage or facilitate" homosexuality. In 1998, Congress entered the fray by enacting the **Defense of Marriage Act,** which allowed states to refuse to recognize gay marriages or civil unions formed in other jurisdictions. Following the lead of Massachusetts, which legalized same-sex marriage in 2004, in the first decades of the twenty-first century, ten states approved gay unions: California, Connecticut, Iowa, Maine, Maryland, New Hampshire, New York, Vermont, Washington, and Rhode Island. Then, in *Obergefell v. Hodges* in 2015, the Supreme Court ruled that states could not prohibit same-sex marriage under the constitution. Remarkably, in a generation, marriage equality had prevailed.

**Culture Wars and the Supreme Court**  Divisive rights issues increasingly came before the U.S. Supreme Court. Abortion led the way, with abortion rights activists challenging the constitutionality of the new state laws limiting access to the procedure. In *Webster v. Reproductive Health Services* (1989), the Supreme Court upheld the authority of state governments to limit the use of public funds and facilities for abortions. Then, in the important case of *Planned Parenthood of Southeastern Pennsylvania v. Casey* (1992), the Court upheld a law requiring a twenty-four-hour waiting period prior to an abortion. Surveying these and other decisions, a reporter suggested that 1989 was "the year the Court turned right," with a conservative majority ready and willing to limit or invalidate liberal legislation and legal precedents.

This observation was only partly correct. The Court was not yet firmly conservative. Although the *Casey* decision upheld certain restrictions on abortions, it affirmed the "essential holding" in *Roe v. Wade* (1973) that women had a constitutional right to control their reproduction. Justice David Souter, appointed to the Court by President George H. W. Bush in 1990, voted with Reagan appointees Sandra Day O'Connor and Anthony Kennedy to uphold *Roe.* Souter, like O'Connor, emerged as an ideologically moderate justice on a range of issues. Moreover, in a landmark decision, *Lawrence v. Texas* (2003), the Supreme Court limited the power of states to prohibit private homosexual activity between consenting adults and, more recently, in *Windsor v. United States* (2013) declared the Defense of Marriage Act unconstitutional. The Court had crept incrementally, rather than lurched, to the right while signaling its continued desire to remain within the broad mainstream of American public opinion, particularly on the issues of reproduction and marriage equality.

## Bill Clinton and the New Democrats

The culture wars contributed to a new, divisive partisanship in national politics. Rarely in the twentieth century had the two major parties so adamantly refused to work together. Also rare was the vitriolic rhetoric that politicians used to describe their opponents. The fractious partisanship was filtered through — or, many would argue, created by — the new twenty-four-hour cable news television networks, such as Fox News and CNN. Commentators on these channels, finding that nothing drew viewers like aggressive partisanship, increasingly abandoned their roles as conveyors of information and became entertainers and provocateurs.

That divisiveness was a hallmark of the presidency of William (Bill) Jefferson Clinton. In 1992, Clinton, the governor of Arkansas, styled himself a New

Democrat who would bring Reagan Democrats and middle-class voters back to the party. Only forty-six, he was an energetic, ambitious policy wonk—extraordinarily well informed about the details of public policy. To win the Democratic nomination in 1992, Clinton had to survive charges that he embodied the permissive social values conservatives associated with the 1960s: namely, that he dodged the draft to avoid service in Vietnam, smoked marijuana, and cheated repeatedly on his wife. The charges were damaging, but Clinton adroitly talked his way into the presidential nomination: he had charisma and a way with words. When he chose Albert A. Gore, a senator from Tennessee, as his running mate, they became the first baby boom national ticket as well as the nation's first all-southern major-party ticket.

President George H. W. Bush won renomination over his lone opponent Pat Buchanan. The Democrats mounted an aggressive campaign that focused on Clinton's domestic agenda: he promised a tax cut for the middle class, universal health insurance, and a reduction of the huge Republican budget deficit. It was an audacious combination of traditional social-welfare liberalism and fiscal conservatism. For his part, Bush could not overcome voters' discontent with the weak economy and conservatives' disgust at his tax hikes. He received only 38.0 percent of the popular vote as millions of Republicans cast their ballots for independent businessman Ross Perot, who won more votes (19.0 percent) than any independent candidate since Theodore Roosevelt in 1912. With 43.7 percent of the vote, Clinton won the election (Map 30.3). Among all post–World War II presidents, only Richard Nixon (in 1969) entered the White House with a comparably small share of the national vote.

**MAP 30.3   The Presidential Election of 1992**

The first national election after the end of the Cold War focused on the economy, which had fallen into a recession in 1991. The first-ever all-southern Democratic ticket of Bill Clinton (Arkansas) and Al Gore (Tennessee) won support across the country but won the election with only 43.7 percent of the popular vote. The Republican candidate, President George H. W. Bush, ran strongly in his home state of Texas and the South, an emerging Republican stronghold. Independent candidate H. Ross Perot, a wealthy technology entrepreneur, polled an impressive 19.0 percent of the popular vote by capitalizing on voter dissatisfaction with the huge federal deficits of the Reagan-Bush administrations.

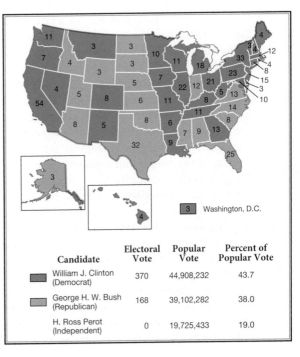

| Candidate | Electoral Vote | Popular Vote | Percent of Popular Vote |
|---|---|---|---|
| William J. Clinton (Democrat) | 370 | 44,908,232 | 43.7 |
| George H. W. Bush (Republican) | 168 | 39,102,282 | 38.0 |
| H. Ross Perot (Independent) | 0 | 19,725,433 | 19.0 |

**New Democrats and Public Policy**   Clinton tried to steer a middle course through the nation's increasingly divisive partisanship. On his left was the Democratic Party's weakened but still vocal liberal wing. On his right were party moderates influenced by Reagan-era notions of reducing government regulation and the welfare state. Clinton's "third way," as he dubbed it, called for the new president to tailor his proposals to satisfy these two quite different — and often antagonistic — political constituencies. Clinton had notable successes as well as spectacular failures pursuing this course.

The spectacular failure came first. Clinton's most ambitious social-welfare goal was to provide a system of health care that would cover all Americans and reduce the burden of health-care costs on the larger economy. It was an objective that had eluded every Democratic president since Harry Truman. Recognizing the potency of Reagan's attack on "big government," Clinton's health-care task force — led by First Lady Hillary Clinton — proposed a system of "managed competition." Private insurance companies and market forces were to rein in health-care expenditures. The cost of this system would fall heavily on employers, and many smaller businesses campaigned strongly against it. So did the health insurance industry and the American Medical Association, powerful lobbies with considerable influence in Washington. By mid-1994, Democratic leaders in Congress declared that the Clintons' universal health-care proposal was dead. Forty million Americans, or 15 percent of the population, remained without health insurance coverage.

More successful was Clinton's plan to reduce the budget deficits of the Reagan-Bush presidencies. In 1993, he secured a five-year budget package that would reduce the federal deficit by $500 billion. Republicans unanimously opposed the proposal because it raised taxes on corporations and wealthy individuals, and liberal Democrats complained because it limited social spending. But shared sacrifice led to shared rewards. By 1998, Clinton's fiscal policies had balanced the federal budget and begun to pay down the federal debt — at a rate of $156 billion a year between 1999 and 2001. As fiscal sanity returned to Washington, the economy boomed, thanks in part to the low interest rates stemming from deficit reduction.

**The Republican Resurgence**   The midterm election of 1994 confirmed that the Clinton presidency had not produced an electoral realignment: conservatives still had a working majority. In a well-organized campaign, in which grassroots appeals to the New Right dominated, Republicans gained fifty-two seats in the House of Representatives, giving them a majority for the first time since 1954. They also retook control of the Senate and captured eleven governorships. Leading the Republican charge was Representative Newt Gingrich of Georgia, who revived calls for significant tax cuts, reductions in welfare programs, anticrime initiatives, and cutbacks in federal regulations. These initiatives, which Gingrich promoted under the banner of a "**Contract with America**," had been central components of the conservative-backed Reagan Revolution of the 1980s, but Gingrich believed that under the presidency of George H. W. Bush Republicans had not emphasized them enough.

In response to the massive Democratic losses in 1994, Clinton moved to the right. Claiming in 1996 that "the era of big government is over," he avoided expansive social-welfare proposals for the remainder of his presidency and sought Republican support for a centrist New Democrat program. The signal piece of that program was reforming the welfare system, a measure that saved relatively little money but carried a big ideological message. Many taxpaying Americans believed — with some supporting evidence — that the Aid to Families with Dependent Children (AFDC) program encouraged female recipients to remain on welfare rather than seek employment. In August 1996, the federal government abolished AFDC, achieving a long-standing goal of conservatives when Clinton signed the **Personal Responsibility and Work Opportunity Reconciliation Act**. Liberals were furious with the president.

**Clinton's Impeachment**    Following a relatively easy victory in the 1996 election, Clinton's second term unraveled when a sex scandal led to his impeachment. Clinton denied having had a sexual affair with Monica Lewinsky, a former White House intern, and Republicans concluded that Clinton had committed perjury and obstructed justice and that these actions were grounds for impeachment. Viewed historically, Americans have usually defined "high crimes and misdemeanors" — the constitutional standard for impeachment — as involving a serious abuse of public trust that endangered the republic. In 1998, conservative Republicans favored a much lower standard because of their total opposition to the Clinton presidency. On December 19, the House of Representatives narrowly approved two articles of impeachment. Only a minority of Americans supported the House's action; according to a CBS News poll, 38 percent favored impeachment while 58 percent opposed it. Chastened by the lack of public support, in early 1999 Republicans in the Senate fell well short of the two-thirds majority they needed to remove the president. But like Andrew Johnson, the only other president to be tried by the Senate, Clinton and the Democratic Party paid a high price for his acquittal. Preoccupied with defending himself, the president was unable to fashion a Democratic alternative to the Republicans' domestic agenda.

## Post–Cold War Foreign Policy

Politically weakened after 1994, Clinton believed he could nonetheless make a difference on the international stage. There, post–Cold War developments gave him historic opportunities. The 1990s was a decade of stunning change in Europe and Central Asia. A great arc of newly independent states emerged as the Soviet empire collapsed. The majority of the 142 million people living in the former Soviet states were poor, but the region had a sizable middle class and was rich in natural resources, especially oil and natural gas.

Among the challenges for the United States was the question of whether to support the admission of some of the new states into the North Atlantic Treaty Organization (NATO) (Chapter 24). Many observers believed, with ample justification, that extending the NATO alliance into Eastern Europe, right up to Russia's western border, would damage U.S.-Russian relations. However, Czechoslovakia, Poland, and Hungary were also eager to become NATO members — three nations that Stalin had decisively placed in the Soviet sphere of influence at the close of World War II. Clinton encouraged NATO admission for those three countries but stopped short of advocating a broader expansion of the alliance. Nonetheless, by 2010, twelve new nations — most of them in Eastern Europe — had been admitted to the NATO alliance. Nothing symbolized the end of the Cold War more than the fact that ten of those nations were former members of the Warsaw Pact. As some observers had feared, however, NATO's expansion damaged U.S.-Russian relations. Russia's leader since 2000, Vladimir Putin, has made no secret of his disdain for the West's encroachment.

**The Breakup of Yugoslavia**　Two of the new NATO states, Slovenia and Croatia, emerged from an intractable set of conflicts that led to the dissolution of the communist nation of Yugoslavia. In 1992, the heavily Muslim province of Bosnia-Herzegovina declared its independence, but its substantial Serbian population refused to live in a Muslim-run multiethnic state. Slobodan Milosevic, an uncompromising Serbian nationalist, launched a ruthless campaign of "ethnic cleansing" to create a Serbian state. In November 1995, Clinton organized a NATO-led bombing campaign and peacekeeping effort, backed by 20,000 American troops, that ended the Serbs' vicious expansionist drive. Four years later, a new crisis emerged in Kosovo, another province of the Serbian-dominated Federal Republic of Yugoslavia. Again led by the United States, NATO intervened with air strikes and military forces to preserve Kosovo's autonomy. By 2008, seven independent nations had emerged from the wreckage of Yugoslavia.

**America and the Middle East**　No post–Cold War development proved more challenging than the emergence of radical Islamic movements in the Middle East. Muslim nations there had a long list of grievances against the West. Colonialism — both British and French — in the early decades of the twentieth century had been thoroughly exploitive. A U.S.-sponsored overthrow of Iran's government in 1953 — and twenty-five years of American support for the Iranian shah — was also a sore point. America's support for Israel in the 1967 Six-Day War and the 1973 Yom Kippur War and its near-unconditional backing of Israel in the 1980s were particularly galling to Muslims. The region's religious and secular moderates complained about these injustices, but many of them had political and economic ties to the West that constrained their criticism.

This situation left an opening for radical Islamic fundamentalists to build a movement based on fanatical opposition to Western imperialism and consumer culture. These groups interpreted the American presence in Saudi Arabia as signaling new U.S. colonial ambitions in the region. Clinton had inherited from President George H. W. Bush a defeated Iraq and a sizable military force — about 4,000 Air Force personnel — in Saudi Arabia. Clinton also enforced a UN-sanctioned embargo on trade with Iraq, a policy designed to constrain Saddam Hussein's military that ultimately denied crucial goods to the civilian population. Spurred by their opposition to U.S. intervention in the region, Muslim fundamentalists soon began targeting Americans. In 1993, radical Muslim immigrants set off a bomb beneath the World Trade Center in New York City, killing six people and injuring more than a thousand. Terrorists used truck bombs to blow up U.S. embassies in Kenya and Tanzania in 1998, and they bombed the USS *Cole* in the Yemeni port of Aden in 2000.

The Clinton administration knew these attacks were the work of Al Qaeda, a network of radical Islamic terrorists organized by the wealthy Saudi exile Osama bin Laden. In February 1998, bin Laden had issued a call for a global struggle — a "Jihad against Jews and Crusaders," in which it was said to be the duty of every Muslim to kill Americans and their allies. After the embassy attacks, Clinton ordered air strikes on Al Qaeda bases in Afghanistan, where an estimated 15,000 operatives had been trained since 1990. The strikes failed to disrupt this growing terrorist network, and when Clinton left office, the Central Intelligence Agency (CIA), the State Department, and the Pentagon were well aware of the potential threat posed by bin Laden's followers. That was where things stood on September 10, 2001.

| **IN YOUR OWN WORDS** | What were the sources of domestic division in the United States after 1988, and how did they reshape the political landscape? |
|---|---|

# Into a New Century

In the second decade of the new century, Americans can reflect on three significant developments that have profoundly shaped their own day: the long war in the Middle East that began with the terrorist attack on September 11, 2001; the election of the nation's first African American president in 2008, Barack Obama (reelected in 2012); and the election of the brazenly contrarian businessman and television personality, Donald Trump, as president on November 8, 2016. Too little time has passed for us to assess exactly how these events will help to define the twenty-first century, but all three have indelibly marked our present.

## The Ascendance of George W. Bush

The 2000 presidential election briefly offered the promise of a break with the intense partisanship of the final Clinton years. The Republican nominee, George W. Bush, the son of President George H. W. Bush, cast himself as a "uniter, not a divider" against his opponent, Al Gore, Clinton's vice president. The election of 2000 would join those of 1876 and 1960 as the closest and most contested in American history. Gore won the popular vote, amassing 50.9 million votes to Bush's 50.4 million, but fell short in the electoral college, 267 to 271.

Late on election night, the vote tally in Florida gave Bush the narrowest of victories. As was their legal prerogative, the Democrats demanded hand recounts in several counties. A month of tumult followed, until the U.S. Supreme Court, splitting directly along conservative-liberal lines, ordered the recount stopped and let Bush's victory stand. Recounting ballots without a consistent standard to determine "voter intent," the Court reasoned, violated the rights of Floridian voters under the Fourteenth Amendment's equal protection clause. As if acknowledging the frailty of this argument, the Court declared that *Bush v. Gore* was not to be regarded as precedent. But in a dissenting opinion, Justice John Paul Stevens warned that the transparently partisan decision undermined "the Nation's confidence in the judge as an impartial guardian of the rule of law."

Although Bush had positioned himself as a moderate, countertendencies drove his administration. His vice president, the uncompromising conservative Richard (Dick) Cheney, became, with Bush's consent, virtually a copresident. Bush also brought into the administration his campaign advisor, Karl Rove, who argued that a permanent Republican majority could be built on the party's conservative base. On Capitol Hill, Rove's hard line was reinforced by Tom DeLay, the House majority leader, who in 1995 had declared "all-out war" on the Democrats. To win that war, DeLay pushed congressional Republicans to endorse a fierce partisanship. The Senate, although more collegial, went through a similar hardening process. After 2002, with Republicans in control of both Congress and the White House, bipartisan law-making came to an end.

**Tax Cuts**     The domestic issue that most engaged President Bush, as it had Ronald Reagan, was taxes. Bush's **Economic Growth and Tax Relief Act** of 2001 had something for everyone. It slashed income tax rates, extended the earned income credit for the poor, and marked the estate tax to be phased out by 2010. A second round of cuts in 2003 targeted dividend income and capital gains. Bush's signature cuts — those favoring big estates and well-to-do owners of stocks and bonds — skewed the distribution of tax benefits upward and pushed far beyond those of any other postwar president, even Reagan.

Critics warned that such massive tax cuts would plunge the federal government into debt. By 2006, federal expenditures had jumped 33 percent, at a faster clip than under any president since Lyndon Johnson. Huge increases in health-care costs were the main culprit. Two of the largest federal programs, Medicare and Medicaid — health care for the elderly and the poor, respectively — could not contain runaway medical costs. Midway through Bush's second term, the national debt stood at over $8 trillion — much of it owned by foreign investors, who also financed the nation's huge trade deficit. On top of that, staggering Social Security and Medicare obligations were beginning to come due for retiring baby boomers, burdens the tax cuts passed on to future generations.

**September 11, 2001**     As a candidate in 2000, George W. Bush had said little about foreign policy. He had assumed that his administration would rise or fall on his domestic program. But nine months into his presidency, an altogether different political scenario unfolded. On a sunny September morning, nineteen Al Qaeda terrorists hijacked four commercial jets and flew two of them into New York City's World Trade Center, destroying its twin towers and killing nearly 2,900 people. A third plane crashed into the Pentagon, near Washington, D.C. The fourth, presumably headed for the White House or possibly the U.S. Capitol, crashed in Pennsylvania when the passengers fought back and thwarted the hijackers. As an outburst of patriotism swept the United States in the wake of the September 11 attacks, George W. Bush proclaimed a "war on terror" and vowed to carry the battle to Al Qaeda.

Operating out of Afghanistan, where they had been harbored by the fundamentalist Taliban regime, the elusive Al Qaeda briefly offered a clear target. In October 2001, while Afghani allies carried the ground war, American planes attacked the enemy. By early 2002, this lethal combination had ousted the Taliban, destroyed Al Qaeda's training camps, and killed or captured many of its operatives. However, the big prize, Al Qaeda leader Osama bin Laden, had retreated to a mountain hide-out. Inexplicably, U.S. forces failed to press the attack, and bin Laden escaped over the border into Pakistan.

**September 11, 2001**
Photographers at the scene after a plane crashed into the north tower of New York City's World Trade Center on September 11 found themselves recording a defining moment in the nation's history. When a second airliner approached and then slammed into the building's south tower at 9:03 A.M., the nation knew this was no accident. The United States was under attack. Of the nearly 2,900 people killed on that day, 2,600 died at the World Trade Center. Spencer Platt/ Getty Images.

**The Invasion of Iraq**   On the domestic side, Bush declared the terrorist threat too big to be contained by ordinary law-enforcement means. He wanted the government's powers of domestic surveillance placed on a wartime footing. With little debate, in 2001 Congress passed the **USA PATRIOT Act**, granting the administration sweeping authority to monitor citizens and apprehend suspected terrorists. On the international front, Bush used the war on terror as the premise for a new policy of preventive war. Under international law, only an imminent threat justified a nation's right to strike first, but with what became known as the Bush doctrine, the United States lowered the bar. It reserved for itself the right to act in "anticipatory self-defense." In 2002, President Bush singled out Iran, North Korea, and Iraq—"an axis of evil"—as the targeted states.

Of the three, Iraq was the preferred mark. Officials in the Pentagon regarded Iraq as unfinished business, left over from the Gulf War of 1991. More grandly, Bush administration officials saw in Iraq an opportunity to fulfill what they believed to be America's mission to democratize the world. Iraqis, they contended, would abandon the tyrant Saddam Hussein and embrace democracy if given the chance. The democratizing effect would spread across the Middle East, toppling or reforming other unpopular Arab regimes and stabilizing the region. That, in turn, would secure the Middle East's oil supply, whose fragility Hussein's 1990 invasion of Kuwait had made all too clear. It was the oil, in the end, that was of vital interest to the United States (Map 30.4).

None of these considerations, either singly or together, met Bush's declared threshold for preventive war. So the president reluctantly acceded to the demand by anxious European allies that the United States go to the UN Security Council,

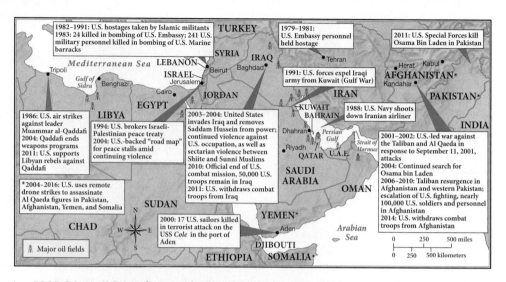

**MAP 30.4   U.S. Involvement in the Middle East, 1979–2016**
The United States has long played an active role in the Middle East, driven by the strategic importance of that region and, most important, by America's need to ensure a reliable supply of oil from the Persian Gulf states. This map shows the highlights of that troubled involvement, from the Tehran embassy hostage taking in 1979 to the invasion and occupation of both Iraq and Afghanistan. President Obama withdrew most combat troops from Iraq in 2011 and from Afghanistan in 2014, but U.S. involvement in the region, in the form of drone strikes, material assistance to various states and factions, and other forms of diplomatic and military assistance continues.

which demanded that Saddam Hussein allow the return of the UN weapons inspectors expelled in 1998. Hussein surprisingly agreed. Anxious to invade Iraq for its own reasons, the Bush administration insisted that Hussein's regime constituted a "grave and gathering danger" and ignored further UN deliberations. American forces invaded in March 2003 in what newspapers in France, which refused to cooperate with its longtime ally, called simply "Bush's war." America's one major ally in the rush to war was Great Britain. Relations with France and Germany became poisonous. Even neighboring Mexico and Canada condemned the invasion, and Turkey, a key military ally, refused transit permission, ruining the army's plan for a northern thrust into Iraq. As for the Arab world, it exploded in anti-American demonstrations.

Within three weeks, American troops had taken the Iraqi capital. The regime collapsed, and its leaders went into hiding (Saddam Hussein was captured nine months later). But despite meticulous military planning, the Pentagon had made no provision for postconflict operations. The war shattered the infrastructure of Iraq's cities, leaving them without reliable supplies of electricity and water. In the midst of this turmoil, an insurgency began, sparked by Sunni Muslims, a minority religious faction who had nonetheless dominated Iraq under Hussein's Baathist regime. Iraq's Shiite majority, long oppressed by Hussein, at first welcomed the Americans, but extremist Shiite elements soon turned hostile, and U.S. forces found themselves under fire from both sides. With the borders unguarded, Al Qaeda supporters flocked in from all over the Middle East, eager to do battle with the infidel Americans.

Blinded by their own nationalism, dominant nations tend to underestimate the strength of religious and national identities in other people. Although it was hard for Bush administration officials to believe, Iraqis of all stripes viewed the U.S. forces as invaders. Moreover, in a war against insurgents, no occupation force comes out with clean hands. In 2004 in Iraq, that painful truth burst forth graphically in photographs showing American guards at Baghdad's **Abu Ghraib prison** abusing and torturing suspected insurgents. The ghastly images shocked the world. For Muslims, they offered final proof of American treachery. At that low point, in 2004, the United States had spent upward of $100 billion. More than 1,000 American soldiers had died, and 10,000 others had been wounded, many maimed for life. But if the United States pulled out, Iraq would descend into chaos. So, as Bush took to saying, the United States had to "stay the course."

**The 2004 Election**   As the 2004 presidential election approached, Karl Rove, Bush's top advisor, theorized that stirring the culture wars and emphasizing patriotism and Bush's war on terror would mobilize conservatives to vote for Bush. Rove encouraged activists to place antigay initiatives on the ballot in key states to draw conservative voters to the polls; in all, eleven states would pass ballot initiatives that wrote bans on gay marriage equality into state constitutions that year. The Democratic nominee, Senator John Kerry of Massachusetts, was a Vietnam hero, twice wounded and decorated for bravery—in contrast to the president, who had spent the Vietnam years in the Texas Air National Guard. But when Kerry returned from service in Vietnam, he had joined the antiwar group Vietnam Veterans Against the War and in 1971 had delivered a blistering critique of the war to the Senate Armed Services Committee. In the logic of the culture wars, this made him vulnerable to charges of being weak and unpatriotic. Nearly 60 percent of eligible voters—the highest percentage since 1968—went to the polls. Bush beat Kerry, with 286 electoral votes to Kerry's 252. In exit polls, Bush did well among voters for whom moral "values" and national security were top concerns. Voters told interviewers that Bush, a wartime president, made them feel "safer."

## Violence Abroad and Economic Collapse at Home

George Bush's second term was defined by crisis management. In 2005, Hurricane Katrina—one of the deadliest hurricanes in the nation's history—devastated New Orleans. Chaos ensued as floodwaters breached earthen barricades surrounding the city. Many residents remained without food, drinking water, or shelter for days following the storm, and deaths mounted—the final death toll stood at more than 2,000. Initial emergency responses to the catastrophe by federal and local authorities were uncoordinated and inadequate. Because the hardest-hit parts of the city were poor and African American, Katrina had revealed the poverty and vulnerability, alongside decaying and vulnerable infrastructure, at the heart of American cities.

The run of crises did not abate after Katrina. Increasing violence and a rising insurgency in Iraq made the war there even more unpopular in the United States. In 2007, changes in U.S. military strategy helped quell some of the worst violence, but the war dragged into its fifth and sixth years under Bush. Then, in 2008, the American economy began to stumble. By the fall, the Dow Jones Industrial Average had lost half its total value, and major banks, insurance companies, and financial institutions were on the verge of collapse. The entire automobile industry was near bankruptcy. Millions of Americans lost their jobs, and the unemployment rate surged to 10 percent. Housing prices dropped by as much as 40 percent in some parts of the country, and millions of Americans defaulted on their mortgages. The United States had entered the worst economic recession since the 1930s, what soon became known as the Great Recession — technically, the recession had begun in 2007, but its major effects were not felt until the fall of 2008.

The 2008 presidential election took shape in that perilous context. In a historically remarkable primary season, the Democratic nomination was contested between the first woman and the first African American to be viable presidential contenders, Hillary R. Clinton and Barack H. Obama. In a close-fought contest, Obama emerged by early summer as the nominee.

Meanwhile, the Bush administration confronted an economy in free fall. In September, less than two months before the election, Secretary of the Treasury Henry Paulson urged Congress to pass the Emergency Economic Stabilization Act, commonly referred to as the bailout of the financial sector. Passed in early October, the act dedicated $700 billion to rescuing many of the nation's largest banks and brokerage houses. Between Congress's actions and the independent efforts of the Treasury Department and the Federal Reserve, the U.S. government invested close to $1 trillion in saving the nation's financial system.

## Reform and Stalemate in the Obama Years

During his campaign for the presidency against Republican senator John McCain, Barack Obama, a Democratic senator from Illinois, established himself as a unique figure in American politics. The son of an African immigrant-student and a young white woman from Kansas, Obama was raised in Hawaii and Indonesia, and he easily connected with an increasingly multiracial America. A generation younger than Bill Clinton and George W. Bush, Obama (born in 1961) seemed at once a product of the 1960s, especially civil rights gains, and outside its heated conflicts. He took the oath of office of the presidency on January 21, 2009, amid the deepest economic recession since the Great Depression and with the United States mired in two wars in the Middle East. From the podium, the new president recognized the crises and, striking an optimistic tone, encouraged the country to "begin again the work of remaking America."

**"Remaking America"**   A nation that a mere two generations ago would not allow black Americans to dine with white Americans had elected a black man to the highest office. Obama himself was less taken with this historic accomplishment — which was also part of his deliberate strategy to downplay race — than with developing a plan to deal with the nation's innumerable challenges, at home and abroad. With explicit comparisons to Franklin Roosevelt, Obama used the "first hundred days" of his presidency to lay out an ambitious agenda: an economic stimulus package of federal spending to invigorate the economy; plans to draw down the war in Iraq and refocus American military efforts in Afghanistan; a reform of the nation's health insurance system; and new federal laws to regulate Wall Street.

Remarkably, the president accomplished much of that agenda. The Democratic-controlled Congress elected alongside Obama passed the **American Recovery and Reinvestment Act**, an economic stimulus bill that provided $787 billion to state and local governments—one of the largest single packages of government spending in American history. Congress next passed the Wall Street Reform and Consumer Protection Act, a complex law that added new regulations limiting the financial industry and new consumer protections. The president's signal accomplishment, however, was the first major reform of the nation's health-care system since the introduction of Medicare in 1965: the **Patient Protection and Affordable Care Act**, signed into law by Obama on March 23, 2010. Political opposition and the powerful lobbying of the private health insurance industry ensured that the new law contained enough compromises that few could predict its long-term impact.

Following the legislative accomplishments of his first two years in office, President Obama faced a divided Congress. During the fierce debate over health-care reform, a coalition of far-right groups, known collectively as the Tea Party, emerged to catalyze Republican opposition to the president. Democrats lost their majority in the House of Representatives in 2010 and in the Senate in 2014. With **Tea Party**–backed Republicans leading the way, the GOP refused to consider virtually any Democratic legislation. In the face of the legislative stalemate, Obama turned to executive authority to advance his broader, cautiously liberal, agenda. In 2011, for instance, the president ordered that gay men and lesbians be allowed to serve openly in the armed forces, a reversal of decades of military policy. He made two appointments to the Supreme Court: Sonia Sotomayor in 2009, the first Latina to serve on the high court, and Elena Kagan in 2010. Both are committed liberals. And in 2015, Obama directed the Environmental Protection Agency (EPA) to adopt the Clean Power Plan to combat greenhouse gases (an action blocked by a Supreme Court stay and further limited by President Trump).

**Climate Change**   Obama took the executive action on climate change because of congressional inaction on that issue. A scientific consensus has existed for decades that the production of energy through the burning of carbon-based substances (especially petroleum and coal) increases the presence of greenhouse gases in the atmosphere, warming the earth. Increasing temperatures have begun to produce dramatically new weather patterns and promise rising sea levels in this century, developments that threaten agriculture, the global distributions of plant and animal life, and whole cities and regions at or near the current sea level. How to halt, or at least mitigate, climate change has been one of the most pressing public policy issues of the twenty-first century.

Arriving at the scientific consensus on climate change has proven easier than developing government policies to address it. This has been especially true in the United States, where oil company lobbyists, defenders of free-market capitalism, and conservatives who deny global warming altogether have been instrumental in blocking action. For instance, the United States is not a signatory to the major international treaty—the so-called Kyoto Protocol—designed to reduce carbon emissions. Legislative proposals have not fared better. Cap-and-trade legislation, so named because it places a cap on individual polluters' emissions but allows those companies to trade for more emission allowances from low polluters, has stalled in Congress.

Another proposal, a tax on carbon emissions, has likewise gained little political support. There is little doubt, however, that global climate change, and the role of the United States in both causing and mitigating it, will remain among the most critical questions of the next decades.

**War and Instability in the Middle East**   Even as he pursued an ambitious domestic agenda, Obama faced two wars in the Middle East that he inherited from his predecessor. Determined to end American occupation of Iraq, in 2010 the president began to draw down troops stationed there, and the last convoy of U.S. soldiers departed in late 2011. The nine-year war in Iraq, begun to find alleged weapons of mass destruction, had followed a long and bloody arc to its end. That same year, in May, U.S. Special Forces found and killed Osama bin Laden in Pakistan, where he had been hiding for many years, an action for which the president won a great deal of praise domestically. More controversial has been the president's use of "drone" strikes to assassinate Al Qaeda leaders and other U.S. enemies in Afghanistan, Pakistan, and elsewhere in the region.

Whatever the nature of the president's efforts, disengaging from Afghanistan proved difficult. Early in his first term, and despite his campaign promise to end the war there, the president ordered an additional 30,000 American troops to prevent further Taliban victories. The surge temporarily stabilized the country, but securing long-term political and military stability eluded Obama in the long run, and he left office in 2017 having been unable to withdraw the remaining 8,000 to 10,000 U.S. troops stationed there.

Meanwhile, a host of events in the Middle East deepened the region's volatility. In late 2010, a series of multicountry demonstrations and protests, dubbed the Arab Spring, toppled autocratic rulers in Egypt, Tunisia, Libya, and Yemen. Obama and the U.S. State Department cautiously supported the uprisings but were unable to significantly shape events thereafter. In Syria, for instance, the Arab Spring insurgency produced a brutal civil war that has resulted in hundreds of thousands of deaths, nearly five million refugees, and the internal displacement of nearly six million Syrian citizens. Syria has also been plagued by the Islamic State, an ultraviolent, fundamentalist Sunni group that emerged in the chaos of war-torn Iraq. It has conquered territory and sown instability and fear among populations across northern Iraq and northern Syria since 2011. Between 2001, when the war against the Taliban began in Afghanistan, and 2016, when the Syrian refugee crisis and the Islamic State dominated headlines, the United States demonstrated that it could make war far more readily and easily than it could control the events that followed.

**Domestic Crisis**   Much as in the era of the Vietnam War, violence abroad came to have an eerie echo at home. African Americans have long endured, and have long resisted, police brutality, in cycles of pain and protest dating to the nineteenth century. One such cycle began in 2014 with the killing of an unarmed black teenager named Michael Brown in Ferguson, Missouri. Weeks of demonstrations followed, as black activists, joined by many white and Latino supporters, converged on Ferguson from around the country. Many groups and leaders articulated calls for police reform and a renewed struggle against racism.

Amid this increased activism, an organization called Black Lives Matter (BLM) emerged at the fore of a broader movement. Formed two years earlier, in response to the 2012 killing of Trayvon Martin, an unarmed black teenager, by a civilian neighborhood watch captain, BLM put forth a comprehensive agenda of police reform, economic justice, political empowerment, and, echoing Black Power activists from the 1960s, black community control. Between 2014 and 2016, BLM and other activists staged protests in more than one hundred American cities, as the shooting and/or killing of black men by police came to the public's attention through cell phone, surveillance, and police videos. Many activists stressed that the ongoing crisis disproved the notion that electing a black president represented a fundamental transformation in American racial history. Indeed, many activists claimed that the Tea Party's opposition to the president was racially charged. Evidence for such a claim could be found in the appearance of "go back to Kenya" signs directed at Obama at Tea Party rallies or in the so-called "birther" movement, which questioned the president's U.S. citizenship.

**The 2016 Election**   From one political vantage point, President Obama and the Democratic Party looked like the beneficiaries of an electoral shift in a liberal direction. Between 1992 and 2012, Democrats won the popular vote in five of the six presidential elections, and in 2008 Obama won a greater share of the popular vote (53 percent) than any Democratic nominee since Lyndon Johnson in 1964. He won the support of 93 percent of African Americans, 71 percent of Hispanics, 73 percent of Asian Americans, 55 percent of women, and 60 percent of Americans under the age of thirty. His coalition was multiracial, heavily female, and young.

That coalition appears strong enough to win popular majorities for Democratic presidential nominees into the foreseeable future. Yet the nation's peculiar constitutional method of awarding the presidency through the electoral college allows for the possibility, as in 2000 and again in 2016, that a candidate with the lower national vote total can win. Moreover, the Constitution's awarding of two senators to each state regardless of population means that a fiercely conservative state with a small population, like North Dakota, has as much influence in the U.S. Senate as a fiercely liberal state with a massive population, like California. In that context, the Democratic coalition has struggled to sustain Senate majorities. Furthermore, changes in House districts after the 2010 Census have further disadvantaged Democrats. In 2012, Democratic candidates for the House of Representatives won more votes nationally than Republican candidates did (59.6 million to 58.2 million), but Republicans still won a majority of seats. Thus, heading into the 2016 election, the long-term fate of the liberal Obama coalition remained unclear.

Few historians can predict the future of the Obama coalition, but in the short term the outcome of the 2016 presidential election proved to be a stunning surprise to many Americans. First, the presidential campaign itself looked nothing like recent contests. The Republican nominee was Donald Trump, a political novice who had never held elective office and who defeated a series of more experienced, and traditionally conservative, politicians for the Republican nomination. A Manhattan real estate developer and symbol of the "rich and famous" celebrity culture of the 1980s, Trump was primarily known for building a series of failed casinos in Atlantic City, New Jersey, and for starring in the reality television show *The Apprentice*. As a candidate, Trump secured ample media coverage with disparaging remarks about immigrants and his oft-recited promise to "build a wall" along the U.S.-Mexico border, alongside other nationalist slogans. His speeches, impromptu and off-the-cuff, railed against globalization, President Obama, the media, the political establishment, and the Democratic nominee, Hillary Clinton.

Clinton had secured the Democratic nomination after a spirited primary campaign against the social-democratic Bernie Sanders, a U.S. senator from Vermont. The first woman to lead a major-party ticket for U.S. president, Clinton boasted a resume with decades of high-level political service, including eight years as First Lady, eight years as a U.S. senator, and four years as secretary of state. In the general election campaign against Trump, Clinton emphasized this experience and proposed detailed plans of action on a wide range of issues, including climate change, criminal justice reform, workers' rights, early childhood education, tax reform, the nation's deteriorating infrastructure, and many more. For its part, the Trump campaign issued no specific proposals and instead ran a populist campaign that featured few substantive issues—the exception being global trade policy—and relied on inaccurate claims about the threat of immigration and urban crime along with promises to restore a romanticized American past. Trump remained a viable presidential candidate despite revelations that many observers believed were disqualifying: that he likely avoided paying federal income taxes for decades, for instance, and his bragging in a 2005 video about sexually assaulting women.

National polls predicted a close election, with many indicating a likely Clinton victory. But in one of the most surprising presidential elections in more than a generation, Trump achieved an electoral college majority and won the presidency. As in 2000, the Democratic nominee, Clinton, won the popular vote (by more than 2.8 million votes) but could not secure a majority in enough key states to emerge victorious. Between Trump's election in November 2016 and his inauguration on January 20, 2017, Americans debated the meaning of that victory, the fate of the Obama coalition, and the capacity of the nation's governing institutions to successfully address the major national and global challenges of the twenty-first century. As we go to press, history is unfolding at a furious pace, as President Trump has begun his administration with a series of unprecedented executive orders, while anti-Trump protests, both massive and small-scale, roil American cities.

> **IN YOUR OWN WORDS**    How did wars abroad and political contest at home shape the United States in the first decades of the twenty-first century?

# Summary

This chapter has stressed how globalization—the worldwide flow of capital, goods, and people—entered a new phase after the end of the Cold War. The number of multinational corporations, many of them based in the United States, increased dramatically, and people, goods, and investment capital moved easily across political boundaries. Financial markets, in particular, grew increasingly open and interconnected across the globe. Technological innovations strengthened the American economy and transformed daily life. The computer revolution and the spread of the Internet changed the ways in which Americans shopped, worked, learned, and stayed in touch with family and friends. Globalization also facilitated the immigration of millions of Asians and Latin Americans into the United States.

In the decades since 1989, American life has been characterized by the dilemmas presented by the twin issues of globalization and divisive cultural politics. Conservatives spoke out strongly, and with increasing effectiveness, against multiculturalism and what they viewed as serious threats to "family values." Debates over access to abortion, affirmative action, and the legal rights of homosexuals intensified. The terrorist attacks of September 11, 2001, diverted attention from this increasingly bitter partisanship, but that partisanship was revived after President Bush's decision to invade Iraq (a nation not involved in the events of 9/11) in 2003 led to a protracted war. When Barack Obama was elected in 2008, the first African American president in the nation's history, he inherited two wars and the Great Recession, the most significant economic collapse since the 1930s. His, and the nation's, efforts to address these and other pressing issues enjoyed initial success before stalling in a deepening partisan stalemate, especially after his reelection in 2012. Finally, bringing matters nearly to the present, the election of the celebrity businessman Donald Trump to the presidency in 2016 confirmed that globalization and domestic cultural divisions remain at the core of American politics. Trump won the election (over Democrat Hillary Clinton), as George W. Bush had in 2000, while losing the popular vote, giving his presidency a fragile legitimacy and leaving the country as divided politically as it has been since the 1960s.

# Chapter 30 Review

## KEY TERMS

**Identify and explain the significance of each term below.**

Al Qaeda (p. 874)

globalization (p. 875)

World Trade Organization (WTO) (p. 876)

Group of Eight (G8) (p. 878)

North American Free Trade Agreement (NAFTA) (p. 879)

multinational corporations (p. 879)

Advanced Research Projects Agency Network (ARPANET) (p. 880)

World Wide Web (p. 880)

culture war (p. 880)

Immigration and Nationality Act (p. 881)

multiculturalism (p. 884)

Proposition 209 (p. 884)

Operation Rescue (p. 885)

Defense of Marriage Act (p. 886)

*Webster v. Reproductive Health Services* (p. 886)

*Planned Parenthood of Southeastern Pennsylvania v. Casey* (p. 886)

*Lawrence v. Texas* (p. 886)

Contract with America (p. 888)

Personal Responsibility and Work Opportunity Reconciliation Act (p. 889)

Economic Growth and Tax Relief Act (p. 892)

USA PATRIOT Act (p. 893)

Abu Ghraib prison (p. 895)

American Recovery and Reinvestment Act (p. 897)

Patient Protection and Affordable Care Act (p. 897)

Tea Party (p. 897)

## REVIEW QUESTIONS

**Answer these questions to demonstrate your understanding of the chapter's main ideas.**

1. How did globalization redefine the relationship of the United States to the rest of the world after the end of the Cold War?

2. What were the sources of domestic division in the United States after 1988, and how did they reshape the political landscape?

3. How did wars abroad and political contest at home shape the United States in the first decades of the twenty-first century?

4. Review the events included on the thematic timeline on pages 844–845. In what ways does the period between 1992 (Bill Clinton's election) and 2016 (Donald Trump's election) suggest a postliberal era in American politics? In what ways was the conservative resurgence under Reagan preserved, and in what ways was it not?

## CHRONOLOGY

**As you read, ask yourself why this chapter begins and ends with these dates and then identify the links among related events.**

| | |
|---|---|
| **1992** | • Democratic moderate Bill Clinton elected president |
| | • *Planned Parenthood of Southeastern Pennsylvania v. Casey* |
| **1993** | • North American Free Trade Agreement (NAFTA) |
| | • Clinton budget plan balances federal budget and begins to pay down federal debt |
| **1994** | • Clinton health insurance reform effort fails |
| | • Republicans gain control of Congress |
| **1995** | • U.S. troops enforce peace in Bosnia |
| **1996** | • Personal Responsibility and Work Opportunity Reconciliation Act reforms welfare system |
| **1998** | • Bill Clinton impeached by House of Representatives |
| | • Defense of Marriage Act |
| **1999** | • Clinton acquitted by Senate |
| | • World Trade Organization (WTO) protests |
| **2000** | • George W. Bush wins contested presidential election |
| **2001** | • Bush tax cuts |
| | • September 11: Al Qaeda terrorists attack World Trade Center and Pentagon |
| | • Congress passes USA PATRIOT Act |
| **2002** | • United States unseats Taliban in Afghanistan |
| | • President Bush declares Iran, North Korea, and Iraq an "axis of evil" |
| **2003** | • United States invades Iraq in March |
| **2004** | • Torture at Abu Ghraib prison becomes public |
| | • President Bush wins reelection |
| **2007** | • Great Recession begins |
| **2008** | • Barack Obama elected president |
| **2009** | • American Recovery and Reinvestment Act |
| **2010** | • Patient Protection and Affordable Care Act |
| **2011** | • Osama bin Laden killed by U.S. forces |
| | • Last U.S. combat troops withdrawn from Iraq |
| **2014** | • Shooting of Michael Brown and demonstrations in Ferguson, Missouri |
| **2015** | • Obama introduces Clean Power Plan |
| **2016** | • Donald Trump elected president |

# Documents

## The Declaration of Independence

### In Congress, July 4, 1776,

### The Unanimous Declaration of the Thirteen United States of America

When in the Course of human events, it becomes necessary for one people to dissolve the political bands which have connected them with another, and to assume among the Powers of the earth, the separate and equal station to which the Laws of Nature and of Nature's God entitle them, a decent respect to the opinions of mankind requires that they should declare the causes which impel them to the separation.

We hold these truths to be self-evident, that all men are created equal, that they are endowed by their Creator with certain unalienable rights, that among these are Life, Liberty, and the pursuit of Happiness. That to secure these rights, Governments are instituted among Men, deriving their just powers from the consent of the governed. That whenever any Form of Government becomes destructive of these ends, it is the Right of the People to alter or to abolish it, and to institute new Government, laying its foundation on such principles and organizing its powers in such form, as to them shall seem most likely to effect their Safety and Happiness. Prudence, indeed, will dictate that Governments long established should not be changed for light and transient causes; and accordingly all experience hath shown, that mankind are more disposed to suffer, while evils are sufferable, than to right themselves by abolishing the forms to which they are accustomed. But when a long train of abuses and usurpations, pursuing invariably the same Object evinces a design to reduce them under absolute Despotism, it is their right, it is their duty, to throw off such Government, and to provide new Guards for their future security.— Such has been the patient sufferance of these Colonies; and such is now the necessity which constrains them to alter their former Systems of Government. The history of the present King of Great Britain is a history of repeated injuries and usurpations, all having in direct object the establishment of an absolute Tyranny over these States. To prove this, let Facts be submitted to a candid world.

He has refused his Assent to Laws, the most wholesome and necessary for the public good.

He has forbidden his Governors to pass Laws of immediate and pressing importance, unless suspended in their operation till his Assent should be obtained; and, when so suspended, he has utterly neglected to attend to them.

He has refused to pass other Laws for the accommodation of large districts of people, unless those people would relinquish the right of Representation in the Legislature, a right inestimable to them and formidable to tyrants only.

He has called together legislative bodies at places unusual, uncomfortable, and distant from the depository of their public Records, for the sole purpose of fatiguing them into compliance with his measures.

He has dissolved Representative Houses repeatedly, for opposing with manly firmness his invasions on the rights of the people.

He has refused for a long time, after such dissolutions, to cause others to be elected; whereby the Legislative powers, incapable of Annihilation, have returned to the People at large for their exercise; the State remaining in the mean time exposed to all the dangers of invasion from without and convulsions within.

He has endeavoured to prevent the population of these States; for that purpose obstructing the Laws of Naturalization of Foreigners; refusing to pass others to encourage their migrations hither, and raising the conditions of new Appropriations of Lands.

He has obstructed the Administration of Justice, by refusing his Assent to Laws for establishing Judiciary powers.

He has made Judges dependent on his Will alone, for the tenure of their offices, and the amount and payment of their salaries.

He has erected a multitude of New Offices, and sent hither swarms of Officers to harass our People, and eat out their substance.

He has kept among us, in times of peace, Standing Armies without the Consent of our legislature.

He has affected to render the Military independent of and superior to the Civil Power.

He has combined with others to subject us to a jurisdiction foreign to our constitution, and unacknowledged by our laws; giving his Assent to their Acts of pretended Legislation:

For quartering large bodies of armed troops among us:

For protecting them, by a mock Trial, from Punishment for any Murders which they should commit on the Inhabitants of these States:

For cutting off our Trade with all parts of the world:

For imposing taxes on us without our Consent:

For depriving us, in many cases, of the benefits of Trial by jury:

For transporting us beyond Seas to be tried for pretended offences:

For abolishing the free System of English Laws in a neighbouring Province, establishing therein an Arbitrary government, and enlarging its Boundaries so as to render it at once an example and fit instrument for introducing the same absolute rule into these Colonies:

For taking away our Charters, abolishing our most valuable Laws, and altering fundamentally the Forms of our Governments:

For suspending our own Legislatures, and declaring themselves invested with Power to legislate for us in all cases whatsoever.

He has abdicated Government here, by declaring us out of his Protection and waging War against us.

He has plundered our seas, ravaged our Coasts, burnt our towns, and destroyed the lives of our people.

He is at this time transporting large armies of foreign mercenaries to compleat the works of death, desolation, and tyranny, already begun with circumstances of Cruelty & perfidy scarcely paralleled in the most barbarous ages, and totally unworthy the Head of a civilized nation.

He has constrained our fellow Citizens taken Captive on the high Seas to bear Arms against their Country, to become the executioners of their friends and Brethren, or to fall themselves by their Hands.

He has excited domestic insurrections amongst us, and has endeavoured to bring on the inhabitants of our frontiers, the merciless Indian Savages, whose known rule of warfare, is an undistinguished destruction of all ages, sexes, and conditions.

In every stage of these Oppressions We have Petitioned for Redress in the most humble terms: Our repeated Petitions have been answered only by repeated injury. A Prince, whose character is thus marked by every act which may define a Tyrant, is unfit to be the ruler of a free people.

Nor have We been wanting in attention to our British brethren. We have warned them from time to time of attempts by their legislature to extend an unwarrantable jurisdiction over us. We have reminded them of the circumstances of our emigration and settlement here. We have appealed to their native justice and magnanimity, and we have conjured them by the ties of our common kindred to disavow these usurpations, which would inevitably interrupt our connections and correspondence. They too have been deaf to the voice of justice and of consanguinity. We must, therefore, acquiesce in the necessity, which denounces our Separation, and hold them, as we hold the rest of mankind, Enemies in War, in Peace Friends.

We, therefore, the Representatives of the United States of America, in General Congress, Assembled, appealing to the Supreme Judge of the world for the rectitude of our intentions, do, in the Name, and by Authority of the good People of these Colonies, solemnly publish and declare, That these United Colonies are, and of Right ought to be FREE AND INDEPENDENT STATES; that they are Absolved from all Allegiance to the British Crown, and that all political connection between them and the State of Great Britain, is and ought to be totally dissolved; and that as Free and Independent States, they have full Power to levy War, conclude Peace, contract Alliances, establish Commerce, and to do all other Acts and Things which Independent States may of right do. And for the support of this Declaration, with a firm reliance on the Protection of Divine Providence, we mutually pledge to each other our Lives, our Fortunes, and our sacred Honor.

### John Hancock

| | | |
|---|---|---|
| Button Gwinnett | Wm. Paca | Robt. Morris |
| Lyman Hall | Thos. Stone | Benjamin Rush |
| Geo. Walton | Charles Carroll of | Benja. Franklin |
| Wm. Hooper | Carrollton | John Morton |
| Joseph Hewes | George Wythe | Geo. Clymer |
| John Penn | Richard Henry Lee | Jas. Smith |
| Edward Rutledge | Th. Jefferson | Geo. Taylor |
| Thos. Heyward, Junr. | Benja. Harrison | James Wilson |
| Thomas Lynch, Junr. | Thos. Nelson, Jr. | Geo. Ross |
| Arthur Middleton | Francis Lightfoot Lee | Caesar Rodney |
| Samuel Chase | Carter Braxton | Geo. Read |

Thos. M'Kean
Wm. Floyd
Phil. Livingston
Frans. Lewis
Lewis Morris
Richd. Stockton
John Witherspoon
Fras. Hopkinson

John Hart
Abra. Clark
Josiah Bartlett
Wm. Whipple
Matthew Thornton
Saml. Adams
John Adams
Robt. Treat Paine

Elbridge Gerry
Step. Hopkins
William Ellery
Roger Sherman
Sam'el Huntington
Wm. Williams
Oliver Wolcott

# The Constitution of the United States of America

## Agreed to by Philadelphia Convention, September 17, 1787
## Implemented March 4, 1789

We the People of the United States, in Order to form a more perfect Union, establish Justice, insure domestic Tranquility, provide for the common defence, promote the general Welfare, and secure the Blessings of Liberty to ourselves and our Posterity, do ordain and establish this Constitution for the United States of America.

### Article I

**Section 1.** All legislative Powers herein granted shall be vested in a Congress of the United States, which shall consist of a Senate and a House of Representatives.

**Section 2.** The House of Representatives shall be composed of Members chosen every second Year by the People of the several States, and the Electors in each State shall have the Qualifications requisite for Electors of the most numerous Branch of the State Legislature.

No Person shall be a Representative who shall not have attained to the Age of twenty-five Years, and been seven Years a Citizen of the United States, and who shall not, when elected, be an Inhabitant of that State in which he shall be chosen.

Representatives and direct Taxes shall be apportioned among the several States which may be included within this Union, according to their respective Numbers, *which shall be determined by adding to the whole Number of free Persons, including those bound to Service for a Term of Years, and excluding Indians not taxed, three fifths of all other Persons.** The actual Enumeration shall be made within three Years after the first Meeting of the Congress of the United States, and within every subsequent Term of ten Years, in such Manner as they shall by Law direct. The Number of Representatives shall not exceed one for every thirty Thousand, but each State shall have at Least one Representative; and *until such enumeration shall be made, the State of New Hampshire shall be entitled to chuse three, Massachusetts eight, Rhode Island and Providence Plantations one, Connecticut five, New York six, New Jersey four, Pennsylvania eight, Delaware one, Maryland six, Virginia ten, North Carolina five, South Carolina five, and Georgia three.*

When vacancies happen in the Representation from any State, the Executive Authority thereof shall issue Writs of Election to fill such Vacancies.

The House of Representatives shall chuse their Speaker and other Officers; and shall have the sole Power of Impeachment.

**Section 3.** The Senate of the United States shall be composed of two Senators from each State, *chosen by the Legislature thereof,*† for six Years; and each Senator shall have one Vote.

---

*Note:* The Constitution became effective March 4, 1789. Provisions in italics are no longer relevant or have been changed by constitutional amendment.
*Changed by Section 2 of the Fourteenth Amendment.
†Changed by Section 1 of the Seventeenth Amendment.

*Immediately after they shall be assembled in Consequence of the first Election, they shall be divided as equally as may be into three Classes. The Seats of the Senators of the first Class shall be vacated at the Expiration of the second Year, of the second Class at the Expiration of the fourth Year, and of the third Class at the Expiration of the sixth Year, so that one-third may be chosen every second Year; and if Vacancies happen by Resignation, or otherwise, during the Recess of the Legislature of any State, the Executive thereof may make temporary Appointments until the next Meeting of the Legislature, which shall then fill such Vacancies.*\*

No person shall be a Senator who shall not have attained to the Age of thirty Years, and been nine Years a Citizen of the United States, and who shall not, when elected, be an Inhabitant of that State for which he shall be chosen.

The Vice President of the United States shall be President of the Senate, but shall have no Vote, unless they be equally divided.

The Senate shall chuse their other Officers, and also a President pro tempore, in the absence of the Vice President, or when he shall exercise the Office of President of the United States.

The Senate shall have the sole Power to try all Impeachments. When sitting for that Purpose, they shall be on Oath or Affirmation. When the President of the United States is tried, the Chief Justice shall preside: And no Person shall be convicted without the Concurrence of two-thirds of the Members present.

Judgment in Cases of Impeachment shall not extend further than to removal from Office, and disqualification to hold and enjoy any Office of honor, Trust or Profit under the United States: but the Party convicted shall nevertheless be liable and subject to Indictment, Trial, Judgment and Punishment, according to Law.

**Section 4.** The Times, Places and Manner of holding Elections for Senators and Representatives, shall be prescribed in each State by the Legislature thereof; but the Congress may at any time by Law make or alter such Regulations, except as to the Places of Chusing Senators.

The Congress shall assemble at least once in every Year, and such Meeting *shall be on the first Monday in December, unless they shall by Law appoint a different Day.*†

**Section 5.** Each House shall be the Judge of the Elections, Returns and Qualifications of its own Members, and a Majority of each shall constitute a Quorum to do Business; but a smaller number may adjourn from day to day, and may be authorized to compel the Attendance of absent Members, in such Manner, and under such Penalties, as each House may provide.

Each House may determine the Rules of its Proceedings, punish its Members for disorderly Behavior, and, with the Concurrence of two-thirds, expel a Member.

Each House shall keep a Journal of its Proceedings, and from time to time publish the same, excepting such Parts as may in their Judgment require Secrecy; and the Yeas and Nays of the Members of either House on any question shall, at the Desire of one-fifth of those Present, be entered on the Journal.

Neither House, during the Session of Congress, shall, without the Consent of the other, adjourn for more than three days, nor to any other Place than that in which the two Houses shall be sitting.

---

\*Changed by Clause 2 of the Seventeenth Amendment.
†Changed by Section 2 of the Twentieth Amendment.

**Section 6.** The Senators and Representatives shall receive a Compensation for their Services, to be ascertained by Law, and paid out of the Treasury of the United States. They shall in all Cases, except Treason, Felony and Breach of the Peace, be privileged from Arrest during their Attendance at the Session of their respective Houses, and in going to and returning from the same; and for any Speech or Debate in either House, they shall not be questioned in any other Place.

No Senator or Representative shall, during the Time for which he was elected, be appointed to any civil Office under the Authority of the United States, which shall have been created, or the Emoluments whereof shall have been increased, during such time; and no Person holding any Office under the United States, shall be a Member of either House during his Continuance in Office.

**Section 7.** All Bills for raising Revenue shall originate in the House of Representatives; but the Senate may propose or concur with Amendments as on other Bills.

Every Bill which shall have passed the House of Representatives and the Senate, shall, before it becomes a Law, be presented to the President of the United States; If he approve he shall sign it, but if not he shall return it, with his Objections to that House in which it shall have originated, who shall enter the Objections at large on their Journal, and proceed to reconsider it. If after such Reconsideration two-thirds of that House shall agree to pass the Bill, it shall be sent, together with the Objections, to the other House, by which it shall likewise be reconsidered, and if approved by two-thirds of that House, it shall become a Law. But in all such Cases the Votes of both Houses shall be determined by Yeas and Nays, and the Names of the Persons voting for and against the Bill shall be entered on the Journal of each House respectively. If any Bill shall not be returned by the President within ten Days (Sundays excepted) after it shall have been presented to him, the Same shall be a Law, in like Manner as if he had signed it, unless the Congress by their Adjournment prevent its Return, in which Case it shall not be a Law.

Every Order, Resolution, or Vote to which the Concurrence of the Senate and the House of Representatives may be necessary (except on a question of Adjournment) shall be presented to the President of the United States; and before the Same shall take Effect, shall be approved by him, or being disapproved by him, shall be repassed by two-thirds of the Senate and House of Representatives, according to the Rules and Limitations prescribed in the Case of a Bill.

**Section 8.** The Congress shall have Power To lay and collect Taxes, Duties, Imposts and Excises, to pay the Debts and provide for the common Defence and general Welfare of the United States; but all Duties, Imposts and Excises shall be uniform throughout the United States;

To borrow Money on the credit of the United States;

To regulate Commerce with foreign Nations, and among the several States, and with the Indian Tribes;

To establish an uniform Rule of Naturalization, and uniform Laws on the subject of Bankruptcies throughout the United States;

To coin Money, regulate the Value thereof, and of foreign Coin, and fix the Standard of Weights and Measures;

To provide for the Punishment of counterfeiting the Securities and current Coin of the United States;

To establish Post Offices and post Roads;

To promote the Progress of Science and useful Arts, by securing for limited Times to Authors and Inventors the exclusive Right to their respective Writings and Discoveries;

To constitute Tribunals inferior to the supreme Court;

To define and punish Piracies and Felonies committed on the high Seas, and Offenses against the Law of Nations;

To declare War, grant Letters of Marque and Reprisal, and make Rules concerning Captures on Land and Water;

To raise and support Armies, but no Appropriation of Money to that Use shall be for a longer Term than two Years;

To provide and maintain a Navy;

To make Rules for the Government and Regulation of the land and naval Forces;

To provide for calling forth the Militia to execute the Laws of the Union, suppress Insurrections and repel Invasions;

To provide for organizing, arming, and disciplining the Militia, and for governing such Part of them as may be employed in the Service of the United States, reserving to the States respectively, the Appointment of the Officers, and the Authority of training the Militia according to the discipline prescribed by Congress;

To exercise exclusive Legislation in all Cases whatsoever, over such District (not exceeding ten Miles square) as may, by Cession of particular States, and the acceptance of Congress, become the Seat of Government of the United States, and to exercise like Authority over all Places purchased by the Consent of the Legislature of the State in which the Same shall be, for the Erection of Forts, Magazines, Arsenals, dock-Yards, and other needful Buildings; — And

To make all Laws which shall be necessary and proper for carrying into Execution the foregoing Powers, and all other Powers vested by this Constitution in the Government of the United States, or in any Department or Officer thereof.

**Section 9.** The Migration or Importation of such Persons as any of the States now existing shall think proper to admit, shall not be prohibited by the Congress prior to the Year one thousand eight hundred and eight but a tax or duty may be imposed on such Importation, not exceeding ten dollars for each Person.

The privilege of the Writ of Habeas Corpus shall not be suspended, unless when in Cases of Rebellion or Invasion the public Safety may require it.

No Bill of Attainder or ex post facto Law shall be passed.

*No capitation, or other direct, Tax shall be laid, unless in Proportion to the Census or Enumeration herein before directed to be taken.** 

No Tax or Duty shall be laid on Articles exported from any State.

No Preference shall be given by any Regulation of Commerce or Revenue to the Ports of one State over those of another: nor shall Vessels bound to, or from, one State, be obliged to enter, clear, or pay Duties in another.

No Money shall be drawn from the Treasury, but in Consequence of Appropriations made by law; and a regular Statement and Account of the Receipts and Expenditures of all public Money shall be published from time to time.

No Title of Nobility shall be granted by the United States: And no Person holding any Office of Profit or Trust under them, shall, without the Consent of the

---

*Changed by the Sixteenth Amendment.

Congress, accept of any present, Emolument, Office, or Title, of any kind whatever, from any King, Prince, or foreign State.

**Section 10.** No State shall enter into any Treaty, Alliance, or Confederation; grant Letters of Marque and Reprisal; coin Money; emit Bills of Credit; make any Thing but gold and silver Coin a Tender in Payment of Debts; pass any Bill of Attainder, ex post facto Law, or Law impairing the Obligation of Contracts, or grant any Title of Nobility.

No State shall, without the Consent of the Congress, lay any Imposts or Duties on Imports or Exports, except what may be absolutely necessary for executing its inspection Laws: and the net Produce of all Duties and Imposts, laid by any State on Imports or Exports, shall be for the Use of the Treasury of the United States; and all such Laws shall be subject to the Revision and Control of the Congress.

No State shall, without the Consent of the Congress, lay any duty of Tonnage, keep Troops, or Ships of War in time of Peace, enter into any Agreement or Compact with another State, or with a foreign Power, or engage in War, unless actually invaded, or in such imminent Danger as will not admit of delay.

## Article II

**Section 1.** The executive Power shall be vested in a President of the United States of America. He shall hold his Office during the Term of four Years, and, together with the Vice President, chosen for the same Term, be elected, as follows:

Each State shall appoint, in such Manner as the Legislature thereof may direct, a Number of Electors, equal to the whole Number of Senators and Representatives to which the State may be entitled in the Congress; but no Senator or Representative, or Person holding an Office of Trust or Profit under the United States, shall be appointed an Elector.

*The Electors shall meet in their respective States, and vote by Ballot for two Persons, of whom one at least shall not be an Inhabitant of the same State with themselves. And they shall make a List of all the Persons voted for, and of the Number of Votes for each; which List they shall sign and certify, and transmit sealed to the Seat of the Government of the United States, directed to the President of the Senate. The President of the Senate shall, in the Presence of the Senate and House of Representatives, open all the Certificates, and the Votes shall then be counted. The Person having the greatest Number of Votes shall be the President, if such Number be a Majority of the whole Number of Electors appointed; and if there be more than one who have such Majority, and have an equal Number of Votes, then the House of Representatives shall immediately chuse by Ballot one of them for President; and if no Person have a Majority, then from the five highest on the List the said House shall in like Manner chuse the President. But in chusing the President, the Votes shall be taken by States, the Representation from each State having one Vote; a quorum for this Purpose shall consist of a Member or Members from two thirds of the States, and a Majority of all the States shall be necessary to a Choice. In every Case, after the Choice of the President, the Person having the greatest Number of Votes of the Electors shall be the Vice President. But if there should remain two or more who have equal Votes, the Senate shall chuse from them by Ballot the Vice President.\**

The Congress may determine the Time of chusing the Electors, and the Day on which they shall give their Votes; which Day shall be the same throughout the United States.

---

*Superseded by the Twelfth Amendment.

No Person except a natural born Citizen, or a Citizen of the United States, at the time of the Adoption of this Constitution, shall be eligible to the Office of President; neither shall any Person be eligible to that Office who shall not have attained to the Age of thirty five Years, and been fourteen Years a Resident within the United States.

In Case of the Removal of the President from Office, or of his Death, Resignation, or Inability to discharge the Powers and Duties of the said Office, the same shall devolve on the Vice President, *and the Congress may by Law provide for the Case of Removal, Death, Resignation, or Inability, both of the President and Vice President, declaring what Officer shall then act as President, and such Officer shall act accordingly, until the Disability be removed, or a President shall be elected.*\*

The President shall, at stated Times, receive for his Services a Compensation, which shall neither be increased nor diminished during the Period for which he shall have been elected, and he shall not receive within that Period any other Emolument from the United States, or any of them.

Before he enter on the Execution of his Office, he shall take the following Oath or Affirmation:—"I do solemnly swear (or affirm) that I will faithfully execute the Office of President of the United States, and will to the best of my Ability, preserve, protect and defend the Constitution of the United States."

**Section 2.** The President shall be Commander in Chief of the Army and Navy of the United States, and of the Militia of the several States, when called into the actual Service of the United States; he may require the Opinion, in writing, of the principal Officer in each of the executive Departments, upon any Subject relating to the Duties of their respective Offices, and he shall have Power to Grant Reprieves and Pardons for Offences against the United States, except in Cases of Impeachment.

He shall have Power, by and with the Advice and Consent of the Senate, to make Treaties, provided two thirds of the Senators present concur; and he shall nominate, and by and with the Advice and Consent of the Senate, shall appoint Ambassadors, other public Ministers and Consuls, Judges of the supreme Court, and all other Officers of the United States, whose Appointments are not herein otherwise provided for, and which shall be established by Law: but the Congress may by Law vest the Appointment of such inferior Officers, as they think proper, in the President alone, in the Courts of Law, or in the Heads of Departments.

The President shall have Power to fill up all Vacancies that may happen during the Recess of the Senate, by granting Commissions which shall expire at the End of their next Session.

**Section 3.** He shall from time to time give to the Congress Information of the State of the Union, and recommend to their Consideration such Measures as he shall judge necessary and expedient; he may, on extraordinary Occasions, convene both Houses, or either of them, and in Case of Disagreement between them, with Respect to the Time of Adjournment, he may adjourn them to such Time as he shall think proper; he shall receive Ambassadors and other public Ministers; he shall take Care that the Laws be faithfully executed, and shall Commission all the Officers of the United States.

---

\*Modified by the Twenty-Fifth Amendment.

**Section 4.** The President, Vice President and all civil Officers of the United States, shall be removed from Office on Impeachment for, and Conviction of, Treason, Bribery, or other high Crimes and Misdemeanors.

## Article III

**Section 1.** The judicial Power of the United States, shall be vested in one supreme Court, and in such inferior Courts as the Congress may from time to time ordain and establish. The Judges, both of the supreme and inferior Courts, shall hold their Offices during good Behaviour, and shall, at stated Times, receive for their Services a Compensation, which shall not be diminished during their Continuance in Office.

**Section 2.** The judicial Power shall extend to all Cases, in Law and Equity, arising under this Constitution, the Laws of the United States, and Treaties made, or which shall be made, under their Authority;—to all Cases affecting Ambassadors, other public Ministers and Consuls;—to all Cases of admiralty and maritime Jurisdiction;—to Controversies to which the United States shall be a Party;—to Controversies between two or more States;—*between a State and Citizens of another State;** —between Citizens of different States;—between Citizens of the same State claiming Lands under Grants of different States, and between a State, or the Citizens thereof, and foreign States, Citizens or Subjects.

In all Cases affecting Ambassadors, other public Ministers and Consuls, and those in which a State shall be Party, the supreme Court shall have original Jurisdiction. In all the other Cases before mentioned, the supreme Court shall have appellate Jurisdiction, both as to Law and Fact, with such Exceptions, and under such Regulations as the Congress shall make.

The trial of all Crimes, except in Cases of Impeachment, shall be by Jury; and such Trial shall be held in the State where said Crimes shall have been committed; but when not committed within any State, the Trial shall be at such Place or Places as the Congress may by Law have directed.

**Section 3.** Treason against the United States, shall consist only in levying War against them, or in adhering to their Enemies, giving them Aid and Comfort. No Person shall be convicted of Treason unless on the Testimony of two Witnesses to the same overt Act, or on Confession in open Court.

The Congress shall have Power to declare the Punishment of Treason, but no Attainder of Treason shall work Corruption of Blood, or Forfeiture except during the Life of the Person attainted.

## Article IV

**Section 1.** Full Faith and Credit shall be given in each State to the public Acts, Records, and judicial Proceedings of every other State. And the Congress may by general Laws prescribe the Manner in which such Acts, Records, and Proceedings shall be proved, and the Effect thereof.

**Section 2.** The Citizens of each State shall be entitled to all Privileges and Immunities of Citizens in the several States.

A Person charged in any State with Treason, Felony, or other Crime, who shall flee from Justice, and be found in another State, shall on demand of the executive

---

*Restricted by the Eleventh Amendment.

Authority of the State from which he fled, be delivered up, to be removed to the State having Jurisdiction of the Crime.

*No Person held to Service or Labour in one State, under the Laws thereof, escaping into another, shall, in Consequence of any Law or Regulation therein, be discharged from such Service or Labour, but shall be delivered up on Claim of the Party to whom such Service or Labour may be due.*\*

**Section 3.** New States may be admitted by the Congress into this Union; but no new State shall be formed or erected within the Jurisdiction of any other State; nor any State be formed by the Junction of two or more States, or parts of States, without the Consent of the Legislatures of the States concerned as well as of the Congress.

The Congress shall have Power to dispose of and make all needful Rules and Regulations respecting the Territory or other Property belonging to the United States; and nothing in this Constitution shall be so construed as to Prejudice any Claims of the United States, or of any particular State.

**Section 4.** The United States shall guarantee to every State in this Union a Republican Form of Government, and shall protect each of them against Invasion; and on Application of the Legislature, or of the Executive (when the Legislature cannot be convened) against domestic Violence.

## Article V

The Congress, whenever two-thirds of both Houses shall deem it necessary, shall propose Amendments to this Constitution, or, on the Application of the Legislatures of two-thirds of the several States, shall call a Convention for proposing Amendments, which, in either Case, shall be valid to all Intents and Purposes, as Part of this Constitution, when ratified by the Legislatures of three-fourths of the several States, or by Conventions in three-fourths thereof, as the one or the other Mode of Ratification may be proposed by the Congress; *Provided that no Amendment which may be made prior to the Year One thousand eight hundred and eight shall in any Manner affect the first and fourth Clauses in the Ninth Section of the first Article; and* that no State, without its Consent, shall be deprived of its equal Suffrage in the Senate.

## Article VI

All Debts contracted and Engagements entered into, before the Adoption of this Constitution, shall be as valid against the United States under this Constitution, as under the Confederation.

This Constitution, and the Laws of the United States which shall be made in Pursuance thereof; and all Treaties made, or which shall be made, under the Authority of the United States, shall be the supreme Law of the Land; and the Judges in every State shall be bound thereby, any Thing in the Constitution or Laws of any State to the Contrary notwithstanding.

The Senators and Representatives before mentioned, and the Members of the several State Legislatures, and all executive and judicial Officers, both of the United States and of the several States, shall be bound by Oath or Affirmation, to support this Constitution; but no religious Test shall ever be required as a Qualification to any Office or public Trust under the United States.

---

\*Superseded by the Thirteenth Amendment.

## Article VII

The Ratification of the Conventions of nine States shall be sufficient for the Establishment of this Constitution between the States so ratifying the Same.

Done in Convention by the Unanimous Consent of the States present the Seventeenth Day of September in the Year of our Lord one thousand seven hundred and Eighty seven and of the Independence of the United States of America the Twelfth. In Witness whereof We have hereunto subscribed our Names.

Go. Washington
President and deputy from Virginia

*New Hampshire*
John Langdon
Nicholas Gilman

*Massachusetts*
Nathaniel Gorham
Rufus King

*Connecticut*
Wm. Saml. Johnson
Roger Sherman

*New York*
Alexander Hamilton

*New Jersey*
Wil. Livingston
David Brearley
Wm. Paterson
Jona. Dayton

*Pennsylvania*
B. Franklin
Thomas Mifflin
Robt. Morris
Geo. Clymer
Thos. FitzSimons
Jared Ingersoll
James Wilson
Gouv. Morris

*Delaware*
Geo. Read
Gunning Bedford jun
John Dickinson
Richard Bassett
Jaco. Broom

*Maryland*
James McHenry
Dan. of St. Thos. Jenifer
Danl. Carroll

*Virginia*
John Blair
James Madison, Jr.

*North Carolina*
Wm. Blount
Richd. Dobbs Spaight
Hu Williamson

*South Carolina*
J. Rutledge
Charles Cotesworth
    Pinckney
Charles Pinckney
Pierce Butler

*Georgia*
William Few
Abr. Baldwin

# Amendments to the Constitution (Including the Six Unratified Amendments)

### Amendment I [1791]*
Congress shall make no law respecting an establishment of religion, or prohibiting the free exercise thereof; or abridging the freedom of speech, or of the press; or the right of the people peaceably to assemble, and to petition the Government for a redress of grievances.

### Amendment II [1791]
A well regulated Militia, being necessary to the security of a free State, the right of the people to keep and bear Arms shall not be infringed.

### Amendment III [1791]
No Soldier shall, in time of peace, be quartered in any house, without the consent of the Owner, nor in time of war, but in a manner to be prescribed by law.

### Amendment IV [1791]
The right of the people to be secure in their persons, houses, papers, and effects, against unreasonable searches and seizures, shall not be violated, and no Warrants shall issue, but upon probable cause, supported by Oath or affirmation, and particularly describing the place to be searched, and the persons or things to be seized.

### Amendment V [1791]
No person shall be held to answer for a capital or otherwise infamous crime, unless on a presentment or indictment of a Grand Jury, except in cases arising in the land or naval forces, or in the Militia, when in actual service in time of War or public danger; nor shall any person be subject for the same offence to be twice put in jeopardy of life or limb; nor shall be compelled in any criminal case to be a witness against himself, nor be deprived of life, liberty, or property, without due process of law; nor shall private property be taken for public use, without just compensation.

### Amendment VI [1791]
In all criminal prosecutions, the accused shall enjoy the right to a speedy and public trial, by an impartial jury of the State and district wherein the crime shall have been committed, which district shall have been previously ascertained by law, and to be informed of the nature and cause of the accusation; to be confronted with the witnesses against him; to have compulsory process for obtaining witnesses in his favor, and to have the Assistance of Counsel for his defence.

### Amendment VII [1791]
In suits at common law, where the value in controversy shall exceed twenty dollars, the right of trial by jury shall be preserved, and no fact tried by a jury, shall be otherwise reexamined in any Court of the United States, than according to the Rules of the common law.

*The dates in brackets indicate when the amendment was ratified.

## Amendment VIII [1791]

Excessive bail shall not be required, nor excessive fines imposed, nor cruel and unusual punishments inflicted.

## Amendment IX [1791]

The enumeration in the Constitution, of certain rights, shall not be construed to deny or disparage others retained by the people.

## Amendment X [1791]

The powers not delegated to the United States by the Constitution, nor prohibited by it to the States, are reserved to the States respectively, or to the people.

### Unratified Amendment

*Reapportionment Amendment (proposed by Congress September 25, 1789, along with the Bill of Rights)*

*After the first enumeration required by the first article of the Constitution, there shall be one Representative for every thirty thousand, until the number shall amount to one hundred, after which the proportion shall be so regulated by Congress, that there shall be not less than one hundred Representatives, nor less than one Representative for every forty thousand persons, until the number of Representatives shall amount to two hundred; after which the proportion shall be so regulated by Congress, that there shall not be less than two hundred Representatives, nor more than one Representative for every fifty thousand persons.*

## Amendment XI [1795]

The Judicial power of the United States shall not be construed to extend to any suit in law or equity, commenced or prosecuted against one of the United States by Citizens of another State, or by Citizens or subjects of any foreign state.

## Amendment XII [1804]

The Electors shall meet in their respective States and vote by ballot for President and Vice-President, one of whom, at least, shall not be an inhabitant of the same State with themselves; they shall name in their ballots the person voted for as President, and in distinct ballots the person voted for as Vice-President, and they shall make distinct lists of all persons voted for as President, and of all persons voted for as Vice-President, and of the number of votes for each, which lists they shall sign and certify, and transmit sealed to the seat of government of the United States, directed to the President of the Senate;—the President of the Senate shall, in the presence of the Senate and House of Representatives, open all the certificates and the votes shall then be counted;—The person having the greatest number of votes for President, shall be the President, if such number be a majority of the whole number of Electors appointed; and if no person have such majority, then from the persons having the highest numbers not exceeding three on the list of those voted for as President, the House of Representatives shall choose immediately, by ballot, the President. But in choosing the President, the votes shall be taken by States, the representation from each State having one vote; a quorum for this purpose shall consist of a member or members from two-thirds of the States, and a majority of all the States shall be necessary to a choice. And if the House of Representatives shall not choose a President whenever the right of choice shall devolve upon them, before *the fourth day* *of March* next following, then the Vice-President shall act as President, as in the case of the death or other constitutional disability of the President.* — The person having the greatest number of votes as Vice-President, shall be the Vice-President, if such number be a majority of the whole number of Electors appointed; and if no person have a majority, then from the two highest numbers on the list, the Senate shall choose the Vice-President; a quorum for the purpose shall consist of two-thirds of the whole number of Senators, and a majority of the whole number shall be necessary to a choice. But no person constitutionally ineligible to the office of President shall be eligible to that of Vice-President of the United States.

### Unratified Amendment
### Titles of Nobility Amendment (proposed by Congress May 1, 1810)

*If any citizen of the United States shall accept, claim, receive or retain any title of nobility or honor or shall, without the consent of Congress, accept and retain any present, pension, office or emolument of any kind whatever, from any emperor, king, prince or foreign power, such person shall cease to be a citizen of the United States, and shall be incapable of holding any office of trust or profit under them, or either of them.*

### Unratified Amendment
### Corwin Amendment (proposed by Congress March 2, 1861)

*No amendment shall be made to the Constitution which will authorize or give to Congress the power to abolish or interfere, within any State, with the domestic institutions thereof, including that of persons held to labor or service by the laws of said State.*

### Amendment XIII [1865]

**Section 1.** Neither slavery nor involuntary servitude, except as a punishment for crime whereof the party shall have been duly convicted, shall exist within the United States, or any place subject to their jurisdiction.

**Section 2.** Congress shall have power to enforce this article by appropriate legislation.

### Amendment XIV [1868]

**Section 1.** All persons born or naturalized in the United States, and subject to the jurisdiction thereof, are citizens of the United States and of the State wherein they reside. No State shall make or enforce any law which shall abridge the privileges or immunities of citizens of the United States; nor shall any State deprive any person of life, liberty, or property, without due process of law; nor deny to any person within its jurisdiction the equal protection of the laws.

**Section 2.** Representatives shall be apportioned among the several States according to their respective numbers, counting the whole number of persons in each State, excluding Indians not taxed. But when the right to vote at any election for the choice of electors for President and Vice-President of the United States, Representatives in Congress, the Executive and Judicial officers of a State, or the

---

*Superseded by Section 3 of the Twentieth Amendment.

members of the Legislature thereof, is denied to any of the *male* inhabitants of such State, being *twenty-one* years of age and citizens of the United States, or in any way abridged, except for participation in rebellion, or other crime, the basis of representation therein shall be reduced in the proportion which the number of such *male* citizens shall bear to the whole number of *male* citizens *twenty-one* years of age in such State.

**Section 3.** No person shall be a Senator or Representative in Congress, or Elector of President and Vice-President, or hold any office, civil or military, under the United States, or under any State, who, having previously taken an oath, as a member of Congress, or as an officer of the United States, or as a member of any State legislature, or as an executive or judicial officer of any State, to support the Constitution of the United States, shall have engaged in insurrection or rebellion against the same, or given aid or comfort to the enemies thereof. Congress may, by a vote of two-thirds of each house, remove such disability.

**Section 4.** The validity of the public debt of the United States, authorized by law, including debts incurred for payment of pensions and bounties for services in suppressing insurrection or rebellion, shall not be questioned. But neither the United States nor any State shall assume or pay any debt or obligation incurred in aid of insurrection or rebellion against the United States, or any claim for the loss or emancipation of any slave; but all such debts, obligations, and claims shall be held illegal and void.

**Section 5.** The Congress shall have power to enforce, by appropriate legislation, the provisions of this article.

### Amendment XV [1870]

**Section 1.** The right of citizens of the United States to vote shall not be denied or abridged by the United States or by any State on account of race, color, or previous condition of servitude—

**Section 2.** The Congress shall have power to enforce this article by appropriate legislation.

### Amendment XVI [1913]

The Congress shall have power to lay and collect taxes on incomes, from whatever source derived, without apportionment among the several States, and without regard to any census or enumeration.

### Amendment XVII [1913]

**Section 1.** The Senate of the United States shall be composed of two Senators from each State, elected by the people thereof, for six years; and each Senator shall have one vote. The electors in each State shall have the qualifications requisite for electors of [voters for] the most numerous branch of the State legislatures.

**Section 2.** When vacancies happen in the representation of any State in the Senate, the executive authority of such State shall issue writs of election to fill such vacancies: Provided, that the Legislature of any State may empower the executive thereof to make temporary appointments until the people fill the vacancies by election as the Legislature may direct.

**Section 3.** *This amendment shall not be so construed as to affect the election or term of any Senator chosen before it becomes valid as part of the Constitution.*

## Amendment XVIII [1919; repealed 1933 by Amendment XXI]

**Section 1.** *After one year from the ratification of this article the manufacture, sale, or transportation of intoxicating liquors within, the importation thereof into, or the exportation thereof from the United States and all territory subject to the jurisdiction thereof, for beverage purposes, is hereby prohibited.*

**Section 2.** *The Congress and the several States shall have concurrent power to enforce this article by appropriate legislation.*

**Section 3.** *This article shall be inoperative unless it shall have been ratified as an amendment to the Constitution by the legislatures of the several States, as provided by the Constitution, within seven years from the date of the submission thereof to the States by the Congress.*

## Amendment XIX [1920]

**Section 1.** The right of citizens of the United States to vote shall not be denied or abridged by the United States or by any State on account of sex.

**Section 2.** Congress shall have the power to enforce this article by appropriate legislation.

## Unratified Amendment
## Child Labor Amendment
## (proposed by Congress June 2, 1924)

**Section 1.** *The Congress shall have power to limit, regulate, and prohibit the labor of persons under eighteen years of age.*

**Section 2.** *The power of the several States is unimpaired by this article except that the operation of State laws shall be suspended to the extent necessary to give effect to legislation enacted by Congress.*

## Amendment XX [1933]

**Section 1.** The terms of the President and Vice-President shall end at noon on the 20th day of January, and the terms of Senators and Representatives at noon on the 3rd day of January, of the years in which such terms would have ended if this article had not been ratified; and the terms of their successors shall then begin.

**Section 2.** The Congress shall assemble at least once in every year, and such meeting shall begin at noon on the 3rd day of January, unless they shall by law appoint a different day.

**Section 3.** If, at the time fixed for the beginning of the term of the President, the President-elect shall have died, the Vice-President-elect shall become President. If a President shall not have been chosen before the time fixed for the beginning of his term, or if the President-elect shall have failed to qualify, then the Vice-President-elect shall act as President until a President shall have qualified; and the Congress may by law provide for the case wherein neither a President-elect nor a Vice-President-elect shall have qualified, declaring who shall then act as President, or the manner in which one who is to act shall be selected, and such person shall act accordingly until a President or Vice-President shall have qualified.

**Section 4.** The Congress may by law provide for the case of the death of any of the persons from whom the House of Representatives may choose a President whenever the right of choice shall have devolved upon them, and for the case of the death of any of the persons from whom the Senate may choose a Vice-President whenever the right of choice shall have devolved upon them.

**Section 5.** Sections 1 and 2 shall take effect on the 15th day of October following the ratification of this article.

**Section 6.** This article shall be inoperative unless it shall have been ratified as an amendment to the Constitution by the Legislatures of three-fourths of the several States within seven years from the date of its submission.

## Amendment XXI [1933]

**Section 1.** The eighteenth article of amendment to the Constitution of the United States is hereby repealed.

**Section 2.** The transportation or importation into any State, Territory, or Possession of the United States for delivery or use therein of intoxicating liquors, in violation of the laws thereof, is hereby prohibited.

**Section 3.** This article shall be inoperative unless it shall have been ratified as an amendment to the Constitution by conventions in the several States, as provided in the Constitution, within seven years from the date of the submission thereof to the States by the Congress.

## Amendment XXII [1951]

**Section 1.** No person shall be elected to the office of the President more than twice, and no person who has held the office of President, or acted as President, for more than two years of a term to which some other person was elected President shall be elected to the office of President more than once. But this article shall not apply to any person holding the office of President when this Article was proposed by the Congress, and shall not prevent any person who may be holding the office of President, or acting as President, during the term within which this Article becomes operative from holding the office of President or acting as President during the remainder of such term.

**Section 2.** This article shall be inoperative unless it shall have been ratified as an amendment to the Constitution by the legislatures of three-fourths of the several States within seven years from the date of its submission to the States by the Congress.

## Amendment XXIII [1961]

**Section 1.** The District constituting the seat of Government of the United States shall appoint in such manner as the Congress may direct: A number of electors of President and Vice-President equal to the whole number of Senators and Representatives in Congress to which the District would be entitled if it were a State, but in no event more than the least populous State; they shall be in addition to those appointed by the States, but they shall be considered for the purposes of the election of President and Vice-President, to be electors appointed by a State; and they shall meet in the District and perform such duties as provided by the twelfth article of amendment.

**Section 2.** The Congress shall have the power to enforce this article by appropriate legislation.

## Amendment XXIV [1964]

**Section 1.** The right of citizens of the United States to vote in any primary or other election for President or Vice-President, for electors for President or Vice-President, or for Senator or Representative in Congress, shall not be denied or abridged by the United States or any State by reason of failure to pay any poll tax or other tax.

**Section 2.** The Congress shall have the power to enforce this article by appropriate legislation.

## Amendment XXV [1967]

**Section 1.** In case of the removal of the President from office or of his death or resignation, the Vice-President shall become President.

**Section 2.** Whenever there is a vacancy in the office of the Vice-President, the President shall nominate a Vice-President who shall take office upon confirmation by a majority vote of both Houses of Congress.

**Section 3.** Whenever the President transmits to the President pro tempore of the Senate and the Speaker of the House of Representatives his written declaration that he is unable to discharge the powers and duties of his office, and until he transmits to them a written declaration to the contrary, such powers and duties shall be discharged by the Vice-President as Acting President.

**Section 4.** Whenever the Vice-President and a majority of either the principal officers of the executive departments or of such other body as Congress may by law provide, transmit to the President pro tempore of the Senate and the Speaker of the House of Representatives their written declaration that the President is unable to discharge the powers and duties of his office, the Vice-President shall immediately assume the powers and duties of the office as Acting President.

Thereafter, when the President transmits to the President pro tempore of the Senate and the Speaker of the House of Representatives his written declaration that no inability exists, he shall resume the powers and duties of his office unless the Vice-President and a majority of either the principal officers of the executive department[s] or of such other body as Congress may by law provide, transmit within four days to the President pro tempore of the Senate and the Speaker of the House of Representatives their written declaration that the President is unable to discharge the powers and duties of his office. Thereupon Congress shall decide the issue, assembling within forty-eight hours for that purpose if not in session. If the Congress, within twenty-one days after receipt of the latter written declaration, or, if Congress is not in session, within twenty-one days after Congress is required to assemble, determines by two-thirds vote of both Houses that the President is unable to discharge the powers and duties of his office, the Vice-President shall continue to discharge the same as Acting President; otherwise, the President shall resume the powers and duties of his office.

## Amendment XXVI [1971]

**Section 1.** The right of citizens of the United States, who are eighteen years of age or older, to vote shall not be denied or abridged by the United States or by any State on account of age.

**Section 2.** The Congress shall have power to enforce this article by appropriate legislation.

### Unratified Amendment
### Equal Rights Amendment (proposed by Congress March 22, 1972; seven-year deadline for ratification extended to June 30, 1982)

**Section 1.** *Equality of rights under the law shall not be denied or abridged by the United States or by any State on account of sex.*

**Section 2.** *The Congress shall have the power to enforce, by appropriate legislation, the provisions of this article.*

**Section 3.** *This amendment shall take effect two years after the date of ratification.*

## Unratified Amendment
### District of Columbia Statehood Amendment (proposed by Congress August 22, 1978)

**Section 1.** *For purposes of representation in the Congress, election of the President and Vice President, and article V of this Constitution, the District constituting the seat of government of the United States shall be treated as though it were a State.*

**Section 2.** *The exercise of the rights and powers conferred under this article shall be by the people of the District constituting the seat of government, and as shall be provided by Congress.*

**Section 3.** *The twenty-third article of amendment to the Constitution of the United States is hereby repealed.*

**Section 4.** *This article shall be inoperative, unless it shall have been ratified as an amendment to the Constitution by the legislatures of three-fourths of the several states within seven years from the date of its submission.*

## Amendment XXVII [1992]

No law varying the compensation for the services of the Senators and Representatives, shall take effect, until an election of Representatives shall have intervened.

# Glossary

**1968 Democratic National Convention:** A convention held in Chicago during which numerous antiwar demonstrators outside the convention hall were tear-gassed and clubbed by police. Inside the convention hall, the delegates were bitterly divided over Vietnam. (p. 800)

**abolitionism:** The social reform movement to end slavery immediately and without compensation that began in the United States in the 1830s. (p. 311)

**Abu Ghraib prison:** A prison just outside Baghdad, Iraq, where American guards were photographed during the Iraq War abusing and torturing suspected insurgents. (p. 895)

**Adams-Onís Treaty:** An 1819 treaty in which John Quincy Adams persuaded Spain to cede the Florida territory to the United States. In return, the American government accepted Spain's claim to Texas and agreed to a compromise on the western boundary for the state of Louisiana. (p. 223)

**Advanced Research Projects Agency Network (ARPANET):** A decentralized computer network developed in the late 1960s by the U.S. Department of Defense in conjunction with the Massachusetts Institute of Technology. The Internet grew out of the ARPANET. (p. 880)

**affirmative action:** Policies established in the 1960s and 1970s by governments, businesses, universities, and other institutions to overcome the effects of past discrimination against specific groups such as racial and ethnic minorities and women. Measures to ensure equal opportunity include setting goals for the admission, hiring, and promotion of minorities; considering minority status when allocating resources; and actively encouraging victims of past discrimination to apply for jobs and other resources. (p. 828)

*The Affluent Society:* A 1958 book by John Kenneth Galbraith that analyzed the nation's successful middle class and argued that the poor were only an "afterthought" in the minds of economists and politicians. (p. 732)

**African Methodist Episcopal Church:** Church founded in 1816 by African Americans who were discriminated against by white Protestants. The church spread across the Northeast and Midwest and even founded a few congregations in the slave states of Missouri, Kentucky, Louisiana, and South Carolina. (p. 310)

**Agricultural Adjustment Act:** New Deal legislation passed in May 1933 that aimed at cutting agricultural production to raise crop prices and thus farmers' income. (p. 643)

**Alamo:** The 1836 defeat by the Mexican army of the Texan garrison defending the Alamo in San Antonio. Newspapers urged Americans to "Remember the Alamo," and American adventurers, lured by offers of land grants, flocked to Texas to join the rebel forces. (p. 329)

**Algonquian cultures/languages:** A Native American language family whose speakers were widespread in the eastern woodlands, Great Lakes, and subarctic regions of eastern North America. The Algonquian language family should not be confused with the Algonquins, who were a single nation inhabiting the St. Lawrence Valley at the time of first contact. (p. 11)

**Al Qaeda:** A network of radical Islamic terrorists organized by Osama bin Laden, who issued a call for holy war against Americans and their allies. Members of Al Qaeda were responsible for the 9/11 terrorist attacks. (p. 874)

**America First Committee:** A committee organized by isolationists in 1940 to oppose the entrance of the United States into World War II. The membership of the committee included senators, journalists, and publishers and such well-respected figures as the aviator Charles Lindbergh. (p. 670)

**American Anti-Slavery Society:** The first interracial social justice movement in the United States, which advocated the immediate, unconditional end of slavery on the basis of human rights, without compensation to slave masters. (p. 311)

**American Civil Liberties Union:** An organization formed during the Red Scare to protect free speech rights. (p. 623)

**American Colonization Society:** Founded by Henry Clay and other prominent citizens in 1817, the society argued that slaves had to be freed and then resettled, in Africa or elsewhere. (p. 270)

**American exceptionalism:** The idea that the United States has a unique destiny to foster democracy and civilization on the world stage. (p. 584)

**American Federation of Labor:** Organization created by Samuel Gompers in 1886 that coordinated the activities of craft unions and called for direct negotiation with employers in order to achieve benefits for skilled workers. Like other trade unions, the AFL called for the closed shop—all employees had to be union members—to keep out low-wage competition and strengthen unions' bargaining power with employers. (p. 494)

**American GI Forum:** A group founded by World War II veterans in Corpus Christi, Texas, in 1948 to protest the poor treatment of Mexican American soldiers and veterans. (p. 762)

**American Indian Movement (AIM):** Organization established in 1968 to address the problems Indians faced in American cities, including poverty and police harassment. AIM organized Indians to end relocation and termination policies and to win greater control over their cultures and communities. (p. 781)

**American Liberty League:** A group of Republican business leaders and conservative Democrats who banded together to fight what they called the "reckless spending" and "socialist" reforms of the New Deal. (p. 645)

**American, or Know-Nothing, Party:** An anti-immigrant, anti-Catholic political party formed in 1851 that arose in response to mass immigration in the 1840s, especially from Ireland and Germany. In 1854, the party gained control of the state governments of Massachusetts and Pennsylvania. (p. 368)

**American Plan:** Strategy by American business in the 1920s to keep workplaces free of unions, which included refusing to negotiate with trade unions and requiring workers to sign contracts (known as "yellow dog" contracts) pledging not to join a union. (p. 614)

**American Protective Association:** A powerful political organization of militant Protestants, which for a brief period in the 1890s counted more than two million members. In its virulent anti-Catholicism and calls for restrictions on immigrants, the APA prefigured the revived Ku Klux Klan of the 1920s. (p. 502)

**American Recovery and Reinvestment Act:** An economic stimulus bill passed in 2009, in response to the Great Recession, that provided $787 billion to state and local governments for schools, hospitals, and transportation projects. It was one of the largest single packages of government spending in American history. (p. 897)

**American Renaissance:** A literary explosion during the 1840s inspired in part by Emerson's ideas on the liberation of the individual. (p. 298)

**American System:** The mercantilist system of national economic development advocated by Henry Clay and adopted by John Quincy Adams, with a national bank to manage the nation's financial system; protective tariffs to provide revenue and encourage industry; and a nationally funded network of roads, canals, and railroads. (p. 273)

**American Woman Suffrage Association:** A women's suffrage organization led by Lucy Stone, Henry Blackwell, and others who remained loyal to the Republican Party, despite its failure to include women's voting rights in the Reconstruction amendments. Stressing the urgency of voting rights for African American men, AWSA leaders held out hope that once Reconstruction had been settled, it would be women's turn. (p. 423)

**anarchism:** The advocacy of a stateless society achieved by revolutionary means. Feared for their views, anarchists became scapegoats for the 1886 Haymarket Square bombing. (p. 491)

**Antifederalists:** Opponents of ratification of the Constitution. Antifederalists feared that a powerful and distant central government would be out of touch with the needs of citizens. They also complained that it failed to guarantee individual liberties in a bill of rights. (p. 191)

**Antiquities Act:** A 1906 act that allowed the U.S. president to use executive powers to set aside, as federal monuments, sites of great environmental or cultural significance. Theodore Roosevelt, the first president to invoke the act's powers, used them to preserve the Grand Canyon. (p. 513)

**Articles of Confederation:** The written document defining the structure of the government from 1781 to 1788, under which the Union was a confederation of equal states, with no executive and limited powers, existing mainly to foster a common defense. (p. 182)

**artisan republicanism:** An ideology that celebrated small-scale producers, men and women who owned their own shops (or farms). It defined the ideal republican society as one constituted by, and dedicated to the welfare of, independent workers and citizens. (p. 253)

**associated state:** A system of voluntary business cooperation with government. The Commerce Department helped create two thousand trade associations representing companies in almost every major industry. (p. 616)

**Atlanta Compromise:** An 1895 address by Booker T. Washington that urged whites and African Americans to work together for the progress of all. Delivered at the Cotton States Exposition in Atlanta, the speech was widely interpreted as approving racial segregation. (p. 516)

**Atlantic Charter:** A press release by President Roosevelt and British prime minister Winston Churchill in August 1941 calling for economic cooperation, national self-determination, and guarantees of political stability after the war. (p. 671)

**baby boom:** The surge in the American birthrate between 1945 and 1965, which peaked in 1957 with 4.3 million births. (p. 740)

***Bakke v. University of California:*** The 1978 Supreme Court ruling that limited affirmative action by rejecting a quota system. (p. 828)

**Bank of the United States:** A bank chartered in 1790 and jointly owned by private stockholders and the national government. Alexander Hamilton argued that the bank would provide stability to the specie-starved American economy by making loans to merchants, handling government funds, and issuing bills of credit. (p. 200)

**Battle of Little Big Horn:** The 1876 battle begun when American cavalry under George Armstrong Custer attacked an encampment of Sioux, Arapaho, and Cheyenne Indians who were resisting removal to a reservation. Custer's force was annihilated, but with whites calling for U.S. soldiers to retaliate, the Native American military victory was short-lived. (p. 463)

**Battle of Long Island (1776):** First major engagement of the new Continental army, defending against 32,000 British troops outside of New York City. (p. 167)

**Battle of Saratoga (1777):** A multistage battle in New York ending with the surrender of British general John Burgoyne. The victory ensured the diplomatic success of American representatives in Paris, who won a military alliance with France. (p. 170)

**Battle of Tippecanoe:** An attack on Shawnee Indians at Prophetstown on the Tippecanoe River in 1811 by American forces headed by William Henry Harrison, Indiana's territorial governor. The governor's troops traded heavy casualties with the confederacy's warriors and then destroyed the holy village. (p. 217)

**Battle of Yorktown (1781):** A battle in which French and American troops and a French fleet trapped the British army under the command of General Charles Cornwallis at Yorktown, Virginia. The Franco-American victory broke the resolve of the British government. (p. 177)

**Bay of Pigs:** A failed U.S.-sponsored invasion of Cuba in 1961 by anti-Castro forces who planned to overthrow Fidel Castro's government. (p. 723)

**Bear Flag Republic:** A short-lived republic created in California by American emigrants to sponsor a rebellion against Mexican authority in 1846. The army of the Bear Flag Republic was quickly absorbed into the California Battalion of the U.S. Army under the command of John C. Frémont. (p. 345)

**Beats:** A small group of literary figures based in New York City and San Francisco in the 1950s who rejected mainstream culture and instead celebrated personal freedom, which often included drug consumption and casual sex. (p. 738)

**Beecher-Tilton scandal:** A trial, triggered by revelations made by free love advocate and journalist Victoria Woodhull, that exposed unconventional sexual relationships among a leading New York abolitionist pastor and his congregants, discrediting radical Reconstruction by associating some of its advocates with alleged sexual immorality. (p. 423)

**Benevolent Empire:** A web of reform organizations, heavily Whig in their political orientation, built by evangelical Protestant men and women influenced by the Second Great Awakening. (p. 297)

**Bill of Rights:** The first ten amendments to the Constitution, officially ratified by 1791. The amendments safeguarded fundamental personal rights, including freedom of speech and religion, and mandated legal procedures, such as trial by jury. (p. 199)

**Black Codes:** Laws passed by southern states after the Civil War that denied ex-slaves the civil rights enjoyed by whites, punished vague crimes such as "vagrancy" or failing to have a labor contract, and tried to force African Americans back to plantation labor systems that closely mirrored those in slavery times. (p. 418)

**black nationalism:** A major strain of African American thought that emphasized black racial pride and autonomy. Present in black communities for centuries, it periodically came to the fore, as in Marcus Garvey's pan-Africanist movement in the early twentieth century and in various organizations in the 1960s and 1970s, such as the Nation of Islam and the Black Panther Party. (p. 774)

**Black Panther Party:** A militant organization dedicated to protecting African Americans from police violence, founded in Oakland, California, in 1966 by Huey Newton and Bobby Seale. In the late 1960s the organization spread to other cities, where members undertook a wide range of community-organizing projects, but the Panthers' radicalism and belief in armed self-defense resulted in violent clashes with police. (p. 775)

**black Protestantism:** A form of Protestantism that was devised by Christian slaves in the Chesapeake and spread to the Cotton South as a result of the domestic slave trade. It emphasized the evangelical message of emotional conversion, ritual baptism, communal spirituality, and the idea that blacks were "children of God" and should be treated accordingly. (p. 334)

**blues:** A form of American music that originated in the Deep South, especially from the black workers in the cotton fields of the Mississippi Delta. (p. 534)

**Bonus Army:** A group of fifteen thousand to twenty thousand unemployed World War I veterans who set up camps near the Capitol building in 1932 to demand immediate payment of pension awards due to be paid in 1945. (p. 640)

**Bracero Program:** Officially the Mexican Farm Labor Agreement (signed with Mexico), a federal program that brought hundreds of thousands of Mexican agricultural workers to the United States during and after World War II. The program continued until 1964 and was a major spur of Mexican immigration to the United States. (p. 677)

**Bretton Woods:** An international conference in New Hampshire in July 1944 that established the World Bank and the International Monetary Fund (IMF). (p. 729)

**Brotherhood of Sleeping Car Porters:** A prominent black trade union of railroad car porters working for the Pullman Company. (p. 758)

**Brown v. Board of Education of Topeka:** Supreme Court ruling of 1954 that overturned the "separate but equal" precedent established in *Plessy v. Ferguson* in 1896. The Court declared that separate educational facilities were inherently unequal and thus violated the Fourteenth Amendment. (p. 765)

**Burlingame Treaty:** An 1868 treaty that guaranteed the rights of U.S. missionaries in China and set official terms for the emigration of Chinese laborers to work in the United States. (p. 445)

**Californios:** The elite Mexican ranchers in the province of California. (p. 341)

**casta system:** A hierarchical system of racial classification developed by colonial elites in Latin America to make sense of the complex patterns of racial mixing that developed there. (p. 37)

**caucus:** A meeting held by a political party to choose candidates, make policies, and enforce party discipline. (p. 267)

**chain migration:** A pattern by which immigrants find housing and work and learn to navigate a new environment, and then assist other immigrants from their family or home area to settle in the same location. (p. 366)

**chattel principle:** A system of bondage in which a slave has the legal status of property and so can be bought and sold. (p. 250)

**chattel slavery:** A system of bondage in which a slave has the legal status of property and so can be bought and sold like property. (p. 35)

**Chicago school:** A school of architecture dedicated to the design of buildings whose form expressed, rather than masked, their structure and function. (p. 528)

**Chicano Moratorium Committee:** Group founded by activist Latinos to protest the Vietnam War. (p. 802)

**Chinese Exclusion Act:** The 1882 law that barred Chinese laborers from entering the United States. It continued in effect until the 1940s. (p. 487)

**Christianity:** A religion that holds the belief that Jesus Christ was himself divine. For centuries, the Roman Catholic Church was the great unifying institution in Western Europe, and it was from Europe that Christianity spread to the Americas. (p. 19)

**Church of Jesus Christ of Latter-day Saints, or Mormons:** Founded by Joseph Smith in 1830. After Smith's death at the hands of an angry mob, in 1846 Brigham Young led many followers of Mormonism to lands in present-day Utah. (p. 304)

**"City Beautiful" movement:** A turn-of-the-twentieth-century movement that advocated landscape beautification, playgrounds, and more and better urban parks. (p. 542)

**Civilian Conservation Corps:** Federal relief program that provided jobs to millions of unemployed young men who built thousands of bridges, roads, trails, and other structures in state and national parks, bolstering the national infrastructure. (p. 644)

**Civil Rights Act of 1866:** Legislation passed by Congress that nullified the Black Codes and affirmed that African Americans should have equal benefit of the law. (p. 419)

**Civil Rights Act of 1875:** A law that required "full and equal" access to jury service and to transportation and public accommodations, irrespective of race. (p. 433)

**Civil Rights Act of 1964:** Law that responded to demands of the civil rights movement by making discrimination in employment, education, and public accommodations illegal. It was the strongest such measure since Reconstruction and included a ban on sex discrimination in employment. (p. 771)

***Civil Rights Cases:*** A series of 1883 Supreme Court decisions that struck down the Civil Rights Act of 1875, rolling back key Reconstruction laws and paving the way for later decisions that sanctioned segregation. (p. 438)

**classical liberalism or laissez-faire:** The political ideology of individual liberty, private property, a competitive market economy, free trade, and limited government. The ideal is a *laissez faire* or "let alone" policy, in which government does the least possible, particularly in reference to economic policies such as tariffs and incentives for industrial development. Attacking corruption and defending private property, late-nineteenth-century liberals generally called for elite governance and questioned the advisability of full democratic participation. (pp. 285, 435, 649)

**Clayton Antitrust Act:** A 1914 law that strengthened federal definitions of "monopoly" and gave more power to the Justice Department to pursue antitrust cases; it also specified that labor unions could not generally be prosecuted for "restraint of trade," ensuring that antitrust laws would apply to corporations rather than unions. (p. 572)

**coastal trade:** The domestic slave trade with routes along the Atlantic coast that sent thousands of slaves to sugar plantations in Louisiana and cotton plantations in the Mississippi Valley. (p. 248)

**code talkers:** Native American soldiers trained to use native languages to send messages in battle during World War II. Neither the Japanese nor the Germans could decipher the codes used by these Navajo, Comanche, Choctaw, and Cherokee speakers, and the messages they sent gave the Allies great advantage in the battle of Iwo Jima, among many others. (p. 674)

**Coercive Acts:** Four British acts of 1774 meant to punish Massachusetts for the destruction of three shiploads of tea. Known in America as the Intolerable Acts, they led to open rebellion in the northern colonies. (p. 152)

**Cold War liberalism:** A combination of moderate liberal policies that preserved the programs of the New Deal welfare state and forthright anticommunism that vilified the Soviet Union abroad and radicalism at home. Adopted by President Truman and the Democratic Party during the late 1940s and early 1950s. (p. 711)

**collective bargaining:** A process of negotiation between labor unions and employers, which after World War II translated into rising wages, expanding benefits, and an increasing rate of home ownership. (p. 734)

**Columbian Exchange:** The massive global exchange of living things, including people, animals, plants, and diseases, between the Eastern and Western Hemispheres that began after the voyages of Columbus. (p. 37)

**committees of correspondence:** A communications network established among towns in the colonies, and among colonial assemblies, between 1772 and 1773 to provide for rapid dissemination of news about important political developments. (p. 151)

**Committee to Defend America by Aiding the Allies:** A group of interventionists who believed in engaging with, rather than withdrawing from, international developments. Interventionists became increasingly vocal in 1940 as war escalated in Europe. (p. 670)

**Commonwealth System:** The republican system of political economy created by state governments by 1820, whereby states funneled aid to private businesses whose projects would improve the general welfare. (p. 235)

**Community Services Organization (CSO):** A Latino civil rights group founded in Los Angeles in 1947 that trained many Latino politicians and community activists, including Cesar Chavez and Dolores Huerta. (p. 762)

**competency:** The ability of a family to keep a household solvent and independent and to pass that ability on to the next generation. (p. 104)

**Compromise of 1850:** Laws passed in 1850 that were meant to resolve the dispute over the status of slavery in the territories. Key elements included the admission of California as a free state and a new Fugitive Slave Act. (p. 361)

**Comstock Act:** An 1873 law that prohibited circulation of "obscene literature," defined as including most information on sex, reproduction, and birth control. (p. 514)

**Comstock Lode:** A vein of silver ore discovered in Nevada in 1859, leading to one of the West's most important mining booms. The lode was so rich that a Confederate expedition tried unsuccessfully to capture it during the Civil War; its output significantly altered the ratio of silver in circulation, leading to changes in monetary policy. (p. 450)

**Congress of Racial Equality (CORE):** Civil rights organization founded in 1942 in Chicago by James Farmer and other members of the Fellowship of Reconciliation (FOR) that espoused nonviolent direct action. In 1961 CORE organized a series of what were called Freedom Rides on interstate bus lines throughout the South to call attention to blatant violations of recent Supreme Court rulings against segregation in interstate commerce. (p. 759)

***The Conscience of a Conservative:*** A 1960 book that set forth an uncompromising conservatism and inspired a Republican grassroots movement in support of its author, Barry Goldwater. (p. 848)

**conscience Whigs:** Whig politicians who opposed the U.S.-Mexico War on moral grounds, maintaining that the purpose of the war was to expand and perpetuate control of the national government. (p. 355)

**constitutional monarchy:** A monarchy limited in its rule by a constitution. (p. 79)

**consumer credit:** New forms of borrowing, such as auto loans and installment plans, that flourished in the 1920s but helped trigger the Great Depression. (p. 618)

**consumer revolution:** An increase in consumption in English manufactures in Britain and the British colonies fueled by the Industrial Revolution. Although the consumer revolution raised living standards, it landed many consumers — and the colonies as a whole — in debt. (p. 125)

**containment:** The basic U.S. policy of the Cold War, which sought to contain communism within its existing geographic boundaries. Initially, containment focused on the Soviet Union and Eastern Europe, but in the 1950s it came to include China, North Korea, and other parts of the developing world. (p. 703)

**Continental Association:** An association established in 1774 by the First Continental Congress to enforce a boycott of British goods. (p. 155)

**Continental Congress:** September 1774 gathering of colonial delegates in Philadelphia to discuss the crisis precipitated by the Coercive Acts. The Congress produced a declaration of rights and an agreement to impose a limited boycott of trade with Britain. (p. 152)

**"contrabands":** Slaves who fled plantations and sought protection behind Union lines during the Civil War. (p. 392)

**Contract with America:** Initiatives by Representative Newt Gingrich of Georgia for significant tax cuts, reductions in welfare programs, anticrime measures, and cutbacks in federal regulations. (p. 888)

**Contras:** An opposition group in Nicaragua that President Reagan ordered the CIA to assist. While Congress banned the CIA and all other government agencies from providing any military support to the Contras, a lieutenant colonel in the U.S. Marines, Oliver North, used the profits from the Iranian arms deal to assist the Contras, resulting in the Iran-Contra affair. (p. 864)

**convict leasing:** Notorious system, begun during Reconstruction, whereby southern state officials allowed private companies to hire out prisoners to labor under brutal conditions in mines and other industries. (p. 431)

**corrupt bargain:** A term used by Andrew Jackson's supporters for the appointment by President John Quincy Adams of Henry Clay as his secretary of state, the traditional stepping-stone to the presidency. Clay had used his influence as Speaker of the House to elect Adams rather than Jackson in the election in 1824. (p. 273)

**cotton complex:** The economic system that developed in the first half of the nineteenth century binding together southern cotton production with northern cloth-making, shipping, and capital. (p. 240)

**counterculture:** A culture embracing values or lifestyles opposing those of the mainstream culture. Became synonymous with hippies, people who opposed and rejected conventional standards of society and advocated extreme liberalism in their sociopolitical attitudes and lifestyles. (p. 797)

**Counter-Reformation:** A reaction in the Catholic Church triggered by the Reformation that sought change from within and created new monastic and missionary orders, including the Jesuits (founded in 1540), who saw themselves as soldiers of Christ. (p. 21)

**Covenant Chain:** The alliance of the Iroquois, first with the colony of New York, then with the British Empire and its other colonies. The Covenant Chain became a model for relations between the British Empire and other Native American peoples. (p. 81)

**covenant of grace:** The Christian idea that God's elect are granted salvation as a pure gift of grace. This doctrine holds that nothing people do can erase their sins or earn them a place in heaven. (p. 56)

**covenant of works:** The Christian idea that God's elect must do good works in their earthly lives to earn their salvation. (p. 56)

**coverture:** A principle in English law that placed wives under the protection and authority of their husbands, so that they did not have independent legal standing. (p. 104)

**Crédit Mobilier:** A sham corporation set up by shareholders in the Union Pacific Railroad to secure government grants at an enormous profit. Organizers of the scheme protected it from investigation by providing gifts of its stock to powerful members of Congress. (p. 435)

**"Crime of 1873":** A term used by those critical of an 1873 law directing the U.S. Treasury to cease minting silver dollars, retire Civil War–era greenbacks, and replace them with notes backed by the gold standard from an expanded system of national banks. (p. 449)

**Crusades:** A series of wars undertaken by Christian armies between A.D. 1096 and 1291 to reverse the Muslim advance in Europe and win back the holy lands where Christ had lived. (p. 21)

**Cuban missile crisis:** The 1962 nuclear standoff between the Soviet Union and the United States when the Soviets attempted to deploy nuclear missiles in Cuba. (p. 724)

**culture war:** A term used by Patrick Buchanan in 1992 to describe a long-standing political struggle, dating to the 1920s, between religious traditionalists and secular liberals. Social issues such as abortion rights and the rights of lesbians and gay men divided these groups. (p. 880)

**currency tax:** A hidden tax on the farmers and artisans who accepted Continental bills in payment for supplies and on the thousands of soldiers who took them as pay. Because of rampant inflation, Continental currency lost much of its value during the war—thus, the implicit tax on those who accepted it as payment. (p. 178)

**Dawes Severalty Act:** The 1887 law that gave Native Americans severalty (individual ownership of land) by dividing reservations into homesteads. The law was a disaster for Native peoples, resulting over several decades in the loss of 66 percent of lands held by Indians at the time of the law's passage. (p. 461)

**D-Day:** June 6, 1944, the date of the Allied invasion of northern France. D-Day was the largest amphibious assault in world history. The invasion opened a second front against the Germans and moved the Allies closer to victory in Europe. (p. 685)

**Declaration of Independence:** A document containing philosophical principles and a list of grievances that declared separation from Britain. Adopted by the Second Continental Congress on July 4, 1776, it ended a period of intense debate with moderates still hoping to reconcile with Britain. (p. 161)

**Declaratory Act of 1766:** Law issued by Parliament to assert Parliament's unassailable right to legislate for its British colonies "in all cases whatsoever," putting Americans on notice that the simultaneous repeal of the Stamp Act changed nothing in the imperial powers of Britain. (p. 146)

**Defense of Marriage Act:** A law enacted by Congress in 1998 that allowed states to refuse to recognize gay marriages or civil unions formed in other jurisdictions. The Supreme Court ruled that DOMA was unconstitutional in 2013. (p. 886)

**deindustrialization:** The dismantling of manufacturing—especially in the automobile, steel, and consumer-goods industries—in the decades after World War II, representing a reversal of the process of industrialization that had dominated the American economy from the 1870s through the 1940s. (p. 820)

**deism:** The Enlightenment-influenced belief that the Christian God created the universe and then left it to run according to natural laws. (p. 114)

**demographic transition:** The sharp decline in birthrate in the United States beginning in the 1790s that was caused by changes in cultural behavior, including the use of birth control. The migration of thousands of young men to the trans-Appalachian West was also a factor in this decline. (p. 268)

**deregulation:** The limiting of regulation by federal agencies. Deregulation of prices in the trucking, airline, and railroad industries had begun under President Carter in the late 1970s, and Reagan expanded it to include cutting back on government protections of consumers, workers, and the environment. (p. 827)

**deskilling:** The elimination of skilled labor under a new system of mechanized manufacturing, in which workers completed discrete, small-scale tasks rather than crafting an entire product. With deskilling, employers found they could pay workers less and replace them more easily. (p. 481)

**détente:** The easing of conflict between the United States and the Soviet Union during the Nixon administration, which was achieved by focusing on issues of common concern, such as arms control and trade. (p. 807)

**dollar diplomacy:** Policy emphasizing the connection between America's economic and political interests overseas. Business would gain from diplomatic efforts on its behalf, while the strengthened American economic presence overseas would give added leverage to American diplomacy. (p. 615)

**domesticity:** A middle-class ideal of "separate spheres" that celebrated women's special mission as homemakers, wives, and mothers who exercised a Christian influence on their families and communities; it excluded women from professional careers, politics, and civic life. (p. 314)

**Dominion of New England:** A royal province created by King James II in 1686 that would have absorbed Connecticut, Rhode Island, Massachusetts Bay, Plymouth, New York, and New Jersey into a single, vast colony and eliminated their assemblies and other chartered rights. James's plan was canceled by the Glorious Revolution in 1688, which removed him from the throne. (p. 77)

**domino theory:** President Eisenhower's theory of containment, which warned that the fall of a non-Communist government to communism in Southeast Asia would trigger the spread of communism to neighboring countries. (p. 719)

**draft (conscription):** The system for selecting individuals for conscription, or compulsory military service, first implemented during the Civil War. (p. 397)

**draft riots:** Violent protests against military conscription that occurred in the North, most dramatically in New York City; led by working-class men who could not buy exemption from the draft. (p. 398)

***Dred Scott* decision:** The 1857 Supreme Court decision that ruled the Missouri Compromise unconstitutional. The Court ruled against slave Dred Scott, who claimed that travels with his master into free states and territories made him and his family free. The decision also denied the federal government the right to exclude slavery from the territories and declared that African Americans were not citizens. (p. 371)

**Dunmore's War:** A 1774 war led by Virginia's royal governor, the Earl of Dunmore, against the Ohio Shawnees, who had a long-standing claim to Kentucky as a hunting ground. The Shawnees were defeated and Dunmore and his militia forces claimed Kentucky as their own. (p. 158)

**dust bowl:** An area including the semiarid states of Oklahoma, Texas, New Mexico, Colorado, Arkansas, and Kansas that experienced a severe drought and large dust storms from 1930 to 1941. (p. 657)

**Earth Day:** An annual event honoring the environment that was first celebrated on April 22, 1970, when 20 million citizens gathered in communities across the country to express their support for a cleaner, healthier planet. (p. 818)

**eastern woodlands:** A culture area of Native Americans that extended from the Atlantic Ocean westward to the Great Plains, and from the Great Lakes to the Gulf of Mexico. The eastern woodlands could be subdivided into the southeastern and northeastern woodlands. Eastern woodlands peoples were generally semisedentary, with agriculture based on maize, beans, and squash. Most, but not all, were chiefdoms. (p. 11)

**Economic Growth and Tax Relief Act:** Legislation introduced by President George W. Bush and passed by Congress in 2001 that slashed income tax rates, extended the earned income credit for the poor, and marked the estate tax to be phased out by 2010. (p. 892)

**Economic Opportunity Act:** A 1964 act that created a series of programs, including Head Start to prepare disadvantaged preschoolers for kindergarten and the Job Corps and Upward Bound to provide young people with training and employment, aimed at alleviating poverty and spurring economic growth in impoverished areas. (p. 788)

**Economic Recovery Tax Act (ERTA):** Legislation introduced by President Reagan and passed by Congress in 1981 that authorized the largest reduction in taxes in the nation's history. (p. 856)

**Eighteenth Amendment:** The ban on the manufacture and sale of alcohol that went into effect in January 1920. Also called "prohibition," the amendment was repealed in 1933. (p. 622)

**Eisenhower Doctrine:** President Eisenhower's 1957 declaration that the United States would actively combat communism in the Middle East. (p. 721)

**Emancipation Proclamation:** President Abraham Lincoln's proclamation issued on January 1, 1863, that legally abolished slavery in all states that remained out of the Union. While the Emancipation Proclamation did not immediately free a single slave, it signaled an end to the institution of slavery. (p. 393)

**Embargo Act of 1807:** An act of Congress that prohibited U.S. ships from traveling to foreign ports and effectively banned overseas trade in an attempt to deter Britain from halting U.S. ships at sea. The embargo caused grave hardships for Americans engaged in overseas commerce. (p. 216)

***encomienda:*** A grant of Indian labor in Spanish America given in the sixteenth century by the Spanish kings to prominent men. *Encomenderos* extracted tribute from these Indians in exchange for granting them protection and Christian instruction. (p. 36)

**energy crisis:** A period of fuel shortages in the United States after the Arab states in the Organization of Petroleum Exporting Countries (OPEC) declared an oil embargo in October 1973. (p. 817)

**Enforcement Laws:** Acts passed in Congress in 1870 and signed by President U. S. Grant that were designed to protect freedmen's rights under the Fourteenth and Fifteenth Amendments. Authorizing federal prosecutions, military intervention, and martial law to suppress terrorist activity, the Enforcement Laws largely succeeded in shutting down Klan activities. (p. 437)

**English common law:** The centuries-old body of legal rules and procedures that protected the lives and property of the British monarch's subjects. (p. 144)

**Enlightenment:** An eighteenth-century philosophical movement that emphasized the use of reason to reevaluate previously accepted doctrines and traditions and the power of reason to understand and shape the world. (p. 112)

**environmentalism:** Activist movement begun in the 1960s that was concerned with protecting the environment through activities such as conservation, pollution control measures, and public awareness campaigns. In response to the new environmental consciousness, the federal government staked out a broad role in environmental regulation in the 1960s and 1970s. (p. 817)

**Environmental Protection Agency (EPA):** Federal agency created by Congress and President Nixon in 1970 to enforce environmental laws, conduct environmental research, and reduce human health and environmental risks from pollutants. (p. 818)

**Equal Pay Act:** Law passed in 1963 that established the principle of equal pay for equal work. Trade-union women were especially critical in pushing for, and winning, congressional passage of the law. (p. 791)

**Equal Rights Amendment (ERA):** Constitutional amendment passed by Congress in 1972 that would require equal treatment of men and women under federal and state law. Facing fierce opposition from the New Right and the Republican Party, the ERA was defeated as time ran out for state ratification in 1982. (p. 829)

**Erie Canal:** A 364-mile waterway connecting the Hudson River and Lake Erie. The Erie Canal brought prosperity to the entire Great Lakes region, and its benefits prompted civic and business leaders in Philadelphia and Baltimore to propose canals to link their cities to the Midwest. (p. 236)

**Ethics in Government Act:** Passed in the wake of the Watergate scandal, the 1978 act that forced political candidates to disclose financial contributions and limited the lobbying activities of former elected officials. (p. 824)

**eugenics:** An emerging "science" of human breeding in the late nineteenth century that argued that mentally deficient people should be prevented from reproducing. (p. 500)

**evangelicalism:** The trend in Protestant Christianity that stresses salvation through conversion, repentance of sin, and adherence to scripture; it also stresses the importance of preaching over ritual. (p. 837)

**Executive Order 8802:** An order signed by President Roosevelt in 1941 that prohibited "discrimination in the employment of workers in defense industries or government because of race, creed, color, or national origin" and established the Fair Employment Practices Commission (FEPC). (p. 676)

**Executive Order 9066:** An order signed by President Roosevelt in 1942 that authorized the War Department to force Japanese Americans from their West Coast homes and hold them in relocation camps for the rest of the war. (p. 681)

**Exodusters:** African Americans who walked or rode out of the Deep South following the Civil War, many settling on farms in Kansas in hopes of finding peace and prosperity. (p. 454)

**Fair Deal:** The domestic policy agenda announced by President Harry S. Truman in 1949. Including civil rights, health care, and education reform, Truman's initiative was only partially successful in Congress. (p. 713)

**Fair Labor Standards Act:** One of the final major laws of the New Deal, it outlawed child labor, made the 40-hour workweek standard (and mandated overtime pay), and established a national minimum wage. (p. 651)

**family values:** Values promoted by the Religious Right, including support for the traditional nuclear family and opposition to same-sex marriage and abortion. (p. 868)

**Farmers' Alliance:** A rural movement founded in Texas during the depression of the 1870s that spread across the plains states and the South. The Farmers' Alliance advocated cooperative stores and exchanges that would circumvent middlemen, and it called for greater government aid to farmers and stricter regulation of railroads. (p. 492)

**fascism:** An authoritarian system of government characterized by dictatorial rule, extreme nationalism, disdain for civil society, and a conviction that imperialism and warfare are the principal means by which nations attain greatness. The United

States went to war against fascism when it faced Nazi Germany under Adolf Hitler and Italy under Benito Mussolini during World War II. (p. 667)

**Federal Housing Administration:** An agency established by the Federal Housing Act of 1934 that refinanced home mortgages for mortgage holders facing possible foreclosure. (p. 644)

**Federalist No. 10:** An essay by James Madison in *The Federalist* (1787–1788) that challenged the view that republican governments only worked in small polities; it argued that a geographically expansive national government would better protect republican liberty. (p. 192)

**Federalists:** Supporters of the Constitution of 1787, which created a strong central government; their opponents, the Antifederalists, feared that a strong central government would corrupt the nation's newly won liberty. (p. 191)

**Federal Reserve Act:** The central bank system of the United States, created in 1913. The Federal Reserve helps set the money supply level, thus influencing the rate of growth of the U.S. economy, and seeks to ensure the stability of the U.S. monetary system. (p. 572)

**Federal Writers' Project:** A program under the Works Progress Administration (WPA) from 1935 to 1939 in which historians, teachers, editors, novelists, poets, and playwrights were employed by the federal government to produce a variety of materials—this included, for example, interviews with hundreds of former slaves; a major survey of American foodways; and state-by-state guidebooks to history, geography, and culture. (p. 660)

**Female Moral Reform Society:** An organization led by middle-class Christian women who viewed prostitutes as victims of male lust and sought to expose their male customers while "rescuing" sex workers and encouraging them to pursue respectable trades. (p. 315)

***The Feminine Mystique:*** The title of an influential book written in 1963 by Betty Friedan critiquing the ideal whereby women were encouraged to confine themselves to roles within the domestic sphere. (p. 791)

**feminism:** The ideology that women should enter the public sphere not only to work on behalf of others, but also for their own equal rights and advancement. Feminists moved beyond advocacy of women's voting rights to seek greater autonomy in professional careers, property rights, and personal relationships. (p. 521)

**Fetterman massacre:** A massacre in December 1866 in which 1,500 Sioux warriors lured Captain William Fetterman and 80 soldiers from a Wyoming fort and attacked them. With the Fetterman massacre the Sioux succeeded in closing the Bozeman Trail, the main route into Montana. (p. 459)

**Fifteenth Amendment:** Constitutional amendment ratified in 1870 that forbade states to deny citizens the right to vote on grounds of race, color, or "previous condition of servitude." (p. 422)

**"Fifty-four forty or fight!":** Democratic candidate Governor James K. Polk's slogan in the election of 1844 calling for American sovereignty over the entire Oregon

Country, which stretched from California to Russian-occupied Alaska and at the time was shared with Great Britain. (p. 344)

**filibustering:** Private paramilitary campaigns, mounted particularly by southern proslavery advocates in the 1850s, to seize additional territory in the Caribbean or Latin America in order to establish control by U.S.-born leaders, with an expectation of eventual annexation by the United States. (p. 365)

**fireside chats:** A series of informal radio addresses Franklin Roosevelt made to the nation in which he explained New Deal initiatives. (p. 642)

**flapper:** A young woman of the 1920s who defied conventional standards of conduct by wearing short skirts and makeup, freely spending the money she earned on the latest fashions, dancing to jazz, and flaunting her liberated lifestyle. (p. 618)

**Foreign Miner's Tax:** A discriminatory tax, adopted in 1850 in California Territory, that forced Chinese and Latin American immigrant miners to pay high taxes for the right to prospect for gold. The tax effectively drove these miners from the goldfields. (p. 358)

**Four Freedoms:** Identified by President Franklin D. Roosevelt as the most basic human rights: freedom of speech, freedom of religion, freedom from want, and freedom from fear. The president used these ideas of freedom to justify support for England during World War II, which in turn pulled the United States into the war. (p. 671)

**Fourierist socialism:** A system of social and economic organization proposed by French thinker Charles Fourier, which was based on common ownership of goods and shared labor by members of a community. A number of nineteenth-century American utopian communities tried to put Fourierist principles into practice. (p. 302)

**Four-Minute Men:** Name given to thousands of volunteers enlisted by the Committee on Public Information to deliver short prowar speeches at movie theaters to galvanize public support for the war. Their work, as part of the broader objectives of the CPI, helped create a political climate intolerant of dissent. (p. 600)

**Fourteen Points:** Principles for a new world order proposed in 1919 by President Woodrow Wilson as a basis for peace negotiations at Versailles. Among them were open diplomacy, freedom of the seas, free trade, territorial integrity, arms reduction, national self-determination, and creation of the League of Nations. (p. 603)

**Fourteenth Amendment:** Constitutional amendment ratified in 1868 that made all native-born or naturalized persons U.S. citizens and prohibited states from abridging the rights of national citizens, thus giving primacy to national rather than state citizenship. (p. 419)

**franchise:** The right to vote. Between 1820 and 1860, most states revised their constitutions to extend the vote to all adult white males. Black adult men gained the right to vote with the passage of the Fourteenth Amendment (1868). The Nineteenth Amendment (1920) granted adult women the right to vote. (p. 265)

**Free African Societies:** Organizations in northern free black communities that sought to help community members and work against racial discrimination, inequality, and political slavery. (p. 310)

**Freedmen's Bureau:** Government organization created in March 1865 to aid displaced blacks and other war refugees. Active until the early 1870s, it was the first federal agency in history that provided direct payments to assist those in poverty and to foster social welfare. (p. 419)

**Freedom of Information Act:** Passed in the wake of the Watergate scandal, the 1974 act that gave citizens access to federal records. (p. 824)

**freeholds:** Land owned in its entirety, without feudal dues or landlord obligations. Freeholders had the legal right to improve, transfer, or sell their landed property. (p. 45)

**free silver:** A policy of loosening the money supply by expanding federal coinage to include silver as well as gold. Advocates of the policy thought it would encourage borrowing and stimulate industry, but the defeat of Democratic presidential candidate William Jennings Bryan ended the "free silver" movement and gave Republicans power to retain the gold standard. (p. 558)

**free soil movement:** A political movement that opposed the expansion of slavery. In 1848 the free soilers organized the Free Soil Party, which depicted slavery as a threat to republicanism and to the Jeffersonian ideal of a freeholder society, arguments that won broad support among aspiring white farmers. (p. 357)

**French Revolution:** A 1789 revolution in France that was initially welcomed by most Americans because it abolished feudalism and established a constitutional monarchy, but eventually came to seem too radical to many. (p. 202)

**fundamentalism:** A term adopted by Protestants, between the 1890s and the 1910s, who rejected modernism and historical interpretations of scripture and asserted the literal truth of the Bible. Fundamentalists have historically seen secularism and religious relativism as markers of sin that will be punished by God. (p. 503)

**gag rule:** A procedure in the House of Representatives from 1836 to 1844 by which antislavery petitions were automatically tabled when they were received so that they could not become the subject of debate. (p. 313)

**gang-labor system:** A system of work discipline used on southern cotton plantations in the mid-nineteenth century in which white overseers or black drivers supervised gangs of enslaved laborers to achieve greater productivity. (p. 258)

**gentility:** A refined style of living and elaborate manners that came to be highly prized among well-to-do English families after 1600 and strongly influenced leading colonists after 1700. (p. 92)

**Gettysburg Address:** Abraham Lincoln's November 1863 speech dedicating a national cemetery at the Gettysburg battlefield. Lincoln declared the nation's founding ideal to be that "all men are created equal," and he urged listeners to dedicate themselves out of the carnage of war to a "new birth of freedom" for the United States. (p. 403)

**Ghost Dance movement:** Religion of the late 1880s and early 1890s that combined elements of Christianity and traditional Native American religion. It fostered Plains Indians' hope that they could, through sacred dances, resurrect the great bison herds and call up a storm to drive whites back across the Atlantic. (p. 465) *glasnost:* The policy introduced by Soviet president Mikhail Gorbachev during the 1980s that involved greater openness and freedom of expression and that contributed, unintentionally, to the 1991 breakup of the Soviet Union. (p. 865)

**Glass-Steagall Act:** A 1933 law that created the Federal Deposit Insurance Corporation (FDIC), which insured deposits up to $2,500 (and now up to $250,000). The act also prohibited banks from making risky, unsecured investments with customers' deposits. (p. 642)

**globalization:** The spread of political, cultural, and economic influences and connections among countries, businesses, and individuals around the world through trade, immigration, communication, and other means. (p. 875)

**Glorious Revolution:** A quick and nearly bloodless coup in 1688 in which James II of England was overthrown by William of Orange. Whig politicians forced the new King William and Queen Mary to accept the Declaration of Rights, creating a constitutional monarchy that enhanced the powers of the House of Commons at the expense of the crown. (p. 78)

**gold standard:** The practice of backing a country's currency with its reserves of gold. In 1873 the United States, following Great Britain and other European nations, began converting to the gold standard. (p. 449)

**Gospel of Wealth:** Andrew Carnegie's argument that corporate leaders' success showed their "fitness" to lead society and that poverty demonstrated, on the contrary, lack of "fitness" to compete in the new economy. Carnegie advocated, however, that wealthy men should use their fortunes for the public good. (p. 475)

**gradual emancipation:** The practice of ending slavery in the distant future while recognizing white property rights to the slaves they owned. Generally, living slaves were not freed by gradual emancipation statutes; they applied only to slaves born after the passage of the statute, and only after they had first labored for their owners for a term of years. (p. 243)

**Granger laws:** Economic regulatory laws passed in some midwestern states in the late 1870s, triggered by pressure from farmers and the Greenback-Labor Party. (p. 490)

**Great American Desert:** A term coined by Major Stephen H. Long in 1820 to describe the grasslands of the southern plains from the ninety-fifth meridian west to the Rocky Mountains, which he believed was "almost wholly unfit for cultivation." (p. 329)

**Great Basin:** An arid basin-and-range region bounded by the Rocky Mountains on the east and the Sierra Mountains on the west. All of its water drains or evaporates within the basin. A resource-scarce environment, the Great Basin was thinly populated by Native American hunter-gatherers who ranged long distances to support themselves. (p. 14)

**Great Lakes:** Five enormous, interconnected freshwater lakes—Ontario, Erie, Huron, Michigan, and Superior—that dominate eastern North America. In the era before long-distance overland travel, they comprised the center of the continent's transportation system. (p. 13)

**Great Migration:** The migration of over 400,000 African Americans from the rural South to the industrial cities of the North during and after World War I. (p. 601)

**Great Plains:** A broad plateau region that stretches from central Texas in the south to the Canadian plains in the north, bordered on the east by the eastern woodlands and on the west by the Rocky Mountains. Averaging around 20 inches of rainfall a year, the Great Plains are primarily grasslands that support grazing but not crop agriculture. (p. 13)

**Great Railroad Strike of 1877:** A nationwide strike of thousands of railroad workers and labor allies, who protested the growing power of railroad corporations and the steep wage cuts imposed by railroad managers amid a severe economic depression that had begun in 1873. (p. 488)

**Great Society:** President Lyndon B. Johnson's domestic program, which included civil rights legislation, antipoverty programs, government subsidy of medical care, federal aid to education, consumer protection, and aid to the arts and humanities. (p. 786)

**Greenback-Labor Party:** A national political movement calling on the government to increase the money supply in order to assist borrowers and foster economic growth; "Greenbackers" also called for greater regulation of corporations and laws enforcing an eight-hour workday. (p. 490)

**greenbacks:** Paper money issued by the U.S. Treasury during the Civil War to finance the war effort. (p. 396)

**Group of Eight (G8):** An international organization of the leading capitalist industrial nations: the United States, Britain, Germany, France, Italy, Japan, Canada, and Russia. The G8 largely control the world's major international financial organizations: the World Bank, the International Monetary Fund (IMF), and the World Trade Organization (WTO). In 2014 Russia was suspended because of its invasion of Crimea. (p. 878)

**Gulf of Tonkin Resolution:** Resolution passed by Congress in 1964 in the wake of a naval confrontation in the Gulf of Tonkin between the United States and North Vietnam. It gave the president virtually unlimited authority in conducting the Vietnam War. The Senate terminated the resolution in 1970 following outrage over the U.S. invasion of Cambodia. (p. 794)

**Gullah dialect:** A Creole language that combined words from English and a variety of African languages in an African grammatical structure. Though it remained widespread in the South Carolina and Georgia lowcountry throughout the nineteenth century and is still spoken in a modified form today, Gullah did not take root in the Cotton South, where lowcountry slaves were far outnumbered. (p. 335)

**habeas corpus:** A legal writ forcing government authorities to justify their arrest and detention of an individual. During the Civil War, Lincoln suspended habeas corpus to stop protests against the draft and other anti-Union activities. (p. 389)

**Haitian Revolution:** The 1791 conflict involving diverse Haitian participants and armies from three European countries. At its end, Haiti became a free, independent nation in which former slaves were citizens. (p. 203)

**hard war:** The philosophy and tactics used by Union general William Tecumseh Sherman, by which he treated civilians as combatants. (p. 407)

**Harlem Renaissance:** A flourishing of African American artists, writers, intellectuals, and social leaders in the 1920s, centered in the neighborhoods of Harlem, New York City. (p. 627)

**Haymarket Square:** The May 4, 1886, conflict in Chicago in which both workers and policemen were killed or wounded during a labor demonstration called by local anarchists. The incident created a backlash against all labor organizations, including the Knights of Labor. (p. 491)

**headright system:** A system of land distribution, pioneered in Virginia and used in several other colonies, that granted land — usually 50 acres — to anyone who paid the passage of a new arrival. By this means, large planters amassed huge landholdings as they imported large numbers of servants and slaves. (p. 45)

**Hepburn Act:** A 1906 antitrust law that empowered the federal Interstate Commerce Commission to set railroad shipment rates wherever it believed that railroads were unfairly colluding to set prices. (p. 565)

**HIV/AIDS:** A deadly disease that killed nearly one hundred thousand people in the United States in the 1980s. (p. 859)

**Hollywood:** The city in southern California that became synonymous with the American movie industry in the 1920s. (p. 618)

**Holocaust:** Germany's campaign during World War II to exterminate all Jews living in German-controlled lands, along with other groups the Nazis deemed "undesirable." In all, some 11 million people were killed in the Holocaust, most of them Jews. (p. 686)

**Homestead Act:** The 1862 act that gave 160 acres of free western land to any applicant who occupied and improved the property. This policy led to the rapid development of the American West after the Civil War; facing arid conditions in the West, however, many homesteaders found themselves unable to live on their land. (p. 450)

**Homestead lockout:** The 1892 lockout of workers at the Homestead, Pennsylvania, steel mill after Andrew Carnegie refused to renew the union contract. Union supporters attacked the guards hired to close them out and protect strikebreakers who had been employed by the mill, but the National Guard soon suppressed this resistance and Homestead, like other steel plants, became a non-union mill. (p. 475)

**horizontal integration:** A business concept invented in the late nineteenth century to pressure competitors and force rivals to merge their companies into a conglomerate. John D. Rockefeller of Standard Oil pioneered this business model. (p. 477)

**hostage crisis:** Crisis that began in 1979 after the deposed shah of Iran was allowed into the United States following the Iranian Revolution. Iranians broke into the U.S. embassy in Tehran and took sixty-six Americans hostage. The hostage crisis lasted 444 days and contributed to President Carter's reelection defeat. (p. 852)

**household mode of production:** The system of exchanging goods and labor that helped eighteenth-century New England freeholders survive on ever-shrinking farms as available land became more scarce. (p. 106)

**House of Burgesses:** Organ of government in colonial Virginia made up of an assembly of representatives elected by the colony's inhabitants. (p. 44)

**House Un-American Activities Committee (HUAC):** Congressional committee especially prominent during the early years of the Cold War that investigated Americans who might be disloyal to the government or might have associated with communists or other radicals. (p. 714)

**Hull House:** One of the first and most famous social settlements, founded in 1889 by Jane Addams and her companion Ellen Gates Starr in an impoverished, largely Italian immigrant neighborhood on Chicago's West Side. (p. 543)

**Hundred Days:** A legendary session during the first few months of Franklin Roosevelt's administration in which Congress enacted fifteen major bills that focused primarily on four problems: banking failures, agricultural overproduction, the business slump, and soaring unemployment. (p. 642)

**hunters and gatherers:** Societies whose members gather food by hunting, fishing, and collecting wild plants rather than relying on agriculture or animal husbandry. Because hunter-gatherers are mobile, moving seasonally through their territory to exploit resources, they have neither fixed townsites nor weighty material goods. (p. 7)

**Immigration and Nationality Act:** A 1965 law that eliminated the discriminatory 1924 nationality quotas, established a slightly higher total limit on immigration, included provisions to ease the entry of immigrants with skills in high demand, and allowed immediate family members of legal residents in the United States to be admitted outside of the total numerical limit. (p. 881)

**indentured servitude:** System in which workers contracted for service for a specified period. In exchange for agreeing to work for four or five years (or more) without wages in the colonies, indentured workers received passage across the Atlantic, room and board, and status as a free person at the end of the contract period. (p. 48)

**Indian Removal Act of 1830:** Act that directed the mandatory relocation of eastern tribes to territory west of the Mississippi. Jackson insisted that his goal was to save the Indians and their culture. Indians resisted the controversial act, but in the end most were forced to comply. (p. 281)

**Indian Reorganization Act:** A 1934 law that reversed the Dawes Act of 1887. Through the law, Indians won a greater degree of religious freedom, and tribal governments regained their status as semisovereign dependent nations. (p. 655)

**individualism:** Word coined by Alexis de Tocqueville in 1835 to describe Americans as people no longer bound by social attachments to classes, castes, associations, and families. (p. 295)

**Industrial Revolution:** A burst of major inventions and economic expansion based on water and steam power and the use of machine technology that transformed certain industries, such as cotton textiles and iron, between 1790 and 1860. (p. 240)

**Industrial Workers of the World:** An umbrella union and radical political group founded in 1905, dedicated to organizing unskilled workers to oppose capitalism. Nicknamed the Wobblies, it advocated direct action by workers, including sabotage and general strikes. (p. 568)

**inland system:** The slave trade system in the interior of the country that fed slaves to the Cotton South. (p. 249)

***Insular Cases:*** A set of Supreme Court rulings in 1901 that declared that the U.S. Constitution did not automatically extend citizenship to people in acquired territories; only Congress could decide whether to grant citizenship. (p. 588)

**internal improvements:** Public works such as roads and canals. (p. 273)

**International Monetary Fund (IMF):** A fund established to stabilize currencies and provide a predictable monetary environment for trade, with the U.S. dollar serving as the benchmark. (p. 730)

**Interstate Commerce Act:** An 1887 act that created the Interstate Commerce Commission (ICC), a federal regulatory agency designed to oversee the railroad industry and prevent collusion and unfair rates. (p. 493)

**Iran-Contra affair:** Reagan administration scandal that involved the sale of arms to Iran in exchange for its efforts to secure the release of hostages held in Lebanon and the redirection—illegal because banned by American law—of the proceeds of those sales to the Nicaraguan Contras. (p. 864)

**Iroquoian cultures/languages:** A Native American language family whose speakers were concentrated in the eastern woodlands. The Iroquoian language family should not be confused with the nations of the Iroquois Confederacy, which inhabited the territory of modern-day upstate New York at the time of first contact. (p. 11)

**Iroquois Confederacy:** A league of five Native American nations—the Mohawks, Oneidas, Onondagas, Cayugas, and Senecas—probably formed around A.D. 1450. A sixth nation, the Tuscaroras, joined the confederacy around 1720. Condolence ceremonies introduced by a Mohawk named Hiawatha formed the basis for the league. Positioned between New France and New Netherland (later New York), the Iroquois played a central role in the era of European colonization. (p. 12)

**Islam:** A religion that considers Muhammad to be God's last prophet. Following the death of Muhammad in A.D. 632, the newly converted Arab peoples of North Africa used force and fervor to spread the Muslim faith into sub-Saharan Africa, India, Indonesia, Spain, and the Balkan regions of Europe. (p. 20)

**Jacobins:** A political faction in the French Revolution. Many Americans embraced the democratic ideology of the radical Jacobins and, like them, formed political clubs and began to address one another as "citizen." (p. 202)

**Jay's Treaty:** A 1795 treaty between the United States and Britain, negotiated by John Jay. The treaty accepted Britain's right to stop neutral ships. In return, it allowed Americans to submit claims for illegal seizures and required the British to remove their troops and Indian agents from the Northwest Territory. (p. 203)

**jazz:** Unique American musical form that arose in New Orleans and other parts of the South before World War I. Jazz musicians developed an ensemble improvisational style. (p. 629)

**Jim Crow:** Laws that required separation of the races, especially blacks and whites, in public facilities. This system of racial segregation in the South lasted a century, from after the Civil War until the 1960s. (p. 507)

**joint-stock corporation:** A financial organization devised by English merchants around 1550 that facilitated the colonization of North America. In these companies, a number of investors pooled their capital and received shares of stock in the enterprise in proportion to their share of the total investment. (p. 42)

**Judiciary Act of 1789:** Act that established a federal district court in each state and three circuit courts to hear appeals from the districts, with the Supreme Court having the final say. (p. 199)

**Kansas-Nebraska Act:** A controversial 1854 law that divided Indian Territory into Kansas and Nebraska, repealed the Missouri Compromise, and left the new territories to decide the issue of slavery on the basis of popular sovereignty. Far from clarifying the status of slavery in the territories, the act led to violent conflict in "Bleeding Kansas." (p. 369)

**Kerner Commission:** Informal name for the National Advisory Commission on Civil Disorders, formed by the president to investigate the causes of the 1967 urban riots. Its 1968 report warned that "our nation is moving toward two societies, one black, one white, separate and unequal." (p. 749)

**Keynesian economics:** The theory, developed by British economist John Maynard Keynes in the 1930s, that purposeful government intervention in the economy (through lowering or raising taxes, interest rates, and government spending) can affect the level of overall economic activity and thereby prevent severe depressions and runaway inflation. (p. 651)

**King Cotton:** The Confederates' belief during the Civil War that their cotton was so important to the British and French economies that those governments would recognize the South as an independent nation and supply it with loans and arms. (p. 387)

**kitchen debate:** A 1959 debate over the merits of their rival systems between U.S. vice president Richard Nixon and Soviet premier Nikita Khrushchev at the opening of an American exhibition in Moscow. (p. 728)

**Knights of Labor:** The first mass labor organization created among America's working class. Founded in 1869 and peaking in strength in the mid-1880s, the Knights of Labor attempted to bridge boundaries of ethnicity, gender, ideology, race, and occupation to build a "universal brotherhood" of all workers. (p. 490)

**Ku Klux Klan:** Secret society that first undertook violence against African Americans in the South after the Civil War but was reborn in 1915 to fight the perceived threats posed by African Americans, immigrants, radicals, feminists, Catholics, and Jews. (pp. 436, 625)

**labor theory of value:** The belief that human labor produces economic value. Adherents argued that the price of a product should be determined not by the market (supply and demand) but by the amount of work required to make it, and that most of the price should be paid to the person who produced it. (p. 255)

**land-grant colleges:** Authorized by the Morrill Act of 1862, land-grant colleges were public universities founded to broaden educational opportunities and foster technical and scientific expertise. These universities were funded by the Morrill Act, which authorized the sale of federal lands to raise money for higher education. (p. 450)

**La Raza Unida:** An organization founded in Texas in 1970 by Mexican Americans as an alternative to the two major political parties; La Raza Unida (The United Race) ran candidates for state governor and other local government positions in the 1970s. It was an expression of the Chicano/a movement's attempts to create political unity among American citizens of Mexican descent. (p. 780)

*Lawrence v. Texas:* A 2003 landmark decision by the Supreme Court that limited the power of states to prohibit private homosexual activity between consenting adults. (p. 886)

**League of Nations:** The international organization bringing together world governments to prevent future hostilities, proposed by President Woodrow Wilson in the aftermath of World War I. Although the League of Nations did form, the United States never became a member state. (p. 603)

**Lend-Lease Act:** Legislation in 1941 that enabled Britain to obtain arms from the United States without cash but with the promise to reimburse the United States when the war ended. The act reflected Roosevelt's desire to assist the British in any way possible, short of war. (p. 671)

**Liberty Party:** An antislavery political party that ran its first presidential candidate in 1844, controversially challenging both the Democrats and Whigs. (p. 313)

**Lieber Code:** Union guidelines for the laws of war, issued in April 1863. The code ruled that soldiers and prisoners must be treated equally without respect to color or race; justified a range of military actions if they were based on "necessity" that would "hasten surrender"; and outlawed use of torture. The code provided a foundation for later international agreements on the laws of war. (p. 400)

*Lochner v. New York:* A 1905 Supreme Court ruling that New York State could not limit bakers' workday to ten hours because that violated bakers' rights to make contracts. (p. 563)

**Lodge Bill:** Also known as the Federal Elections Bill of 1890, a bill proposing that whenever 100 citizens in any district appealed for intervention, a bipartisan federal board could investigate and seat the rightful winner. The defeat of the bill was a blow to those seeking to defend African American voting rights and to ensure full participation in politics. (p. 554)

*Lone Wolf v. Hitchcock:* A 1903 Supreme Court ruling that Congress could make whatever Indian policies it chose, ignoring all existing treaties. (p. 461)

**Louisiana Purchase:** The 1803 purchase of French territory west of the Mississippi River that stretched from the Gulf of Mexico to Canada. The Louisiana Purchase nearly doubled the size of the United States and opened the way for future American expansion west. The purchase required President Thomas Jefferson to exercise powers not explicitly granted to him by the Constitution. (p. 214)

**Loyalty-Security Program:** A program created in 1947 by President Truman that permitted officials to investigate any employee of the federal government for "subversive" activities. (p. 714)

**machine tools:** Cutting, boring, and drilling machines used to produce standardized metal parts, which were then assembled into products such as textile looms and sewing machines. The rapid development of machine tools by American inventors in the early nineteenth century was a factor in the rapid spread of industrialization. (p. 252)

**Maine Law:** The nation's first state law for the prohibition of liquor manufacture and sales, passed in 1851. (p. 298)

**management revolution:** An internal management structure adopted by many large, complex corporations that distinguished top executives from those responsible for day-to-day operations and departmentalized operations by function. (p. 476)

**Manhattan Project:** Top-secret project authorized by Franklin Roosevelt in 1942 to develop an atomic bomb ahead of the Germans. The Americans who worked on the project at Los Alamos, New Mexico (among other highly secretive sites around the country), succeeded in producing a successful atomic bomb by July 1945. (p. 688)

**Manifest Destiny:** A term coined by John L. O'Sullivan in 1845 to express the idea that Euro-Americans were fated by God to settle the North American continent from the Atlantic to the Pacific Ocean. (p. 338)

**manumission:** The legal act of relinquishing property rights in slaves. Worried that a large free black population would threaten the institution of slavery, the Virginia assembly repealed Virginia's 1782 manumission law in 1792. (p. 245)

*Marbury v. Madison* **(1803):** A Supreme Court case that established the principle of judicial review in finding that parts of the Judiciary Act of 1789 were in conflict with the Constitution. For the first time, the Supreme Court assumed legal authority to overrule acts of other branches of the government. (p. 212)

**March on Washington:** Officially named the March on Washington for Jobs and Freedom, on August 28, 1963, a quarter of a million people marched to the Lincoln Memorial to demand that Congress end Jim Crow racial discrimination and launch a major jobs program to bring needed employment to black communities. (p. 771)

**Market Revolution:** The dramatic increase between 1820 and 1850 in the exchange of goods and services in market transactions. The Market Revolution reflected the increased output of farms (including cotton plantations) and factories, the entrepreneurial activities of traders and merchants, and the creation of a transportation network of roads, canals, and railroads. (p. 237)

**married women's property laws:** Laws enacted between 1839 and 1860 in New York and other states that permitted married women to own, inherit, and bequeath property. (p. 317)

**Marshall Plan:** Aid program begun in 1948 to help European economies recover from World War II. (p. 704)

**maternalism:** The belief that women should contribute to civic and political life through their special talents as mothers, Christians, and moral guides. Maternalists put this ideology into action by creating dozens of social reform organizations. (p. 517)

*McCulloch v. Maryland* (1819): A Supreme Court case that asserted the dominance of national over state statutes. (p. 221)

**mechanics:** A term used in the nineteenth century to refer to skilled craftsmen and inventors who built and improved machinery and machine tools for industry. (p. 241)

**Medicaid:** A health plan for the poor passed in 1965 and paid for by general tax revenues and administered by the states. (p. 790)

**Medicare:** A health plan for the elderly passed in 1965 and funded by a surcharge on Social Security payroll taxes. (p. 790)

**mercantilism:** A system of political economy based on government regulation. Beginning in 1650, Britain enacted Navigation Acts that controlled colonial commerce and manufacturing for the enrichment of Britain. (p. 40)

**Metacom's War:** Also known as King Philip's War, it pitted a coalition of Native Americans led by the Wampanoag leader Metacom against the New England colonies in 1675–1676. A thousand colonists were killed and twelve colonial towns destroyed, but the colonies prevailed. Metacom and his allies lost some 4,500 people. (p. 62)

**Mexican American Legal Defense and Education Fund (MALDEF):** A Mexican American civil rights organization founded in 1967 and based on the model of the NAACP Legal Defense and Education Fund. MALDEF focused on legal issues and endeavored to win protections against discrimination through court decisions. (p. 780)

**Mexican cession:** Lands taken by the United States in the U.S.-Mexico War (1846–1848). (p. 354)

**middle class:** An economic group of prosperous farmers, artisans, and traders that emerged in the early nineteenth century. Its rise reflected a dramatic increase in prosperity. This surge in income, along with an abundance of inexpensive mass-produced goods, fostered a distinct middle-class urban culture. (p. 259)

**Middle Passage:** The brutal sea voyage from Africa to the Americas that took the lives of nearly 2 million enslaved Africans. (p. 86)

**military-industrial complex:** A term President Eisenhower used to refer to the military establishment and defense contractors who, he warned, exercised undue influence over the national government. (p. 730)

*Minor v. Happersett:* A Supreme Court decision in 1875 that ruled that suffrage rights were not inherent in citizenship and had not been granted by the Fourteenth Amendment, as some women's rights advocates argued. Women were citizens, the Court ruled, but state legislatures could deny women the vote if they wished. (p. 423)

**minstrel shows:** Popular theatrical entertainment begun around 1830, in which white actors in blackface presented comic routines that combined racist caricature and social criticism. (p. 308)

**Minutemen:** Colonial militiamen who stood ready to mobilize on short notice during the imperial crisis of the 1770s. These volunteers formed the core of the citizens' army that met British troops at Lexington and Concord in April 1775. (p. 158)

**miscegenation:** A derogatory word for interracial sexual relationships coined by Democrats in the 1864 election, as they claimed that emancipation would allow African American men to gain sexual access to white women and produce mixed-race children. (p. 409)

**Mississippian culture:** A Native American culture complex that flourished in the Mississippi River basin and the Southeast from around A.D. 850 to around 1700. Characterized by maize agriculture, moundbuilding, and distinctive pottery styles, Mississippian communities were complex chiefdoms usually located along the floodplains of rivers. The largest of these communities was Cahokia, in modern-day Illinois. (p. 10)

**Mississippi Freedom Democratic Party:** Party founded in Mississippi during the Freedom Summer of 1964. Its members attempted to attend the 1964 Democratic National Convention in Atlantic City, New Jersey, as the legitimate representatives of their state, but Democratic leaders refused to recognize the party. (p. 772)

**Missouri Compromise:** A series of political agreements devised by Speaker of the House Henry Clay. Maine entered the Union as a free state in 1820 and Missouri followed as a slave state in 1821, preserving a balance in the Senate between North and South and setting a precedent for future admissions to the Union. Most importantly, this bargain set the northern boundary of slavery in the lands of the Louisiana Purchase at the southern boundary of Missouri, with the exception of that state. (p. 271)

**mixed government:** John Adams's theory from *Thoughts on Government* (1776), which called for three branches of government, each representing one function: executive, legislative, and judicial. This system of dispersed authority was devised to maintain a balance of power and ensure the legitimacy of governmental procedures. (p. 180)

**modernism:** A movement that questioned the ideals of progress and order, rejected realism, and emphasized new cultural forms. Modernism became the first great literary and artistic movement of the twentieth century and remains influential today. (p. 504)

**Monroe Doctrine:** The 1823 declaration by President James Monroe that the Western Hemisphere was closed to any further colonization or interference by European powers. In exchange, Monroe pledged that the United States would not become involved in European struggles. (p. 224)

**Montgomery Bus Boycott:** Yearlong boycott of Montgomery's segregated bus system in 1955–1956 by the city's African American population. The boycott brought Martin Luther King Jr. to national prominence and ended in victory when the Supreme Court declared segregated seating on public transportation unconstitutional. (p. 767)

**Moral Majority:** A political organization established by evangelist Jerry Falwell in 1979 to mobilize conservative Christian voters on behalf of Ronald Reagan's campaign for president. (p. 855)

**mothers' pensions:** Progressive Era government support provided to mothers whose husbands had died, been disabled, or abandoned the family. Recipients had to meet standards of "respectability" defined by middle-class home visitors, but those who met approval got help in raising their young children. (p. 567)

**muckrakers:** A critical term, first applied by Theodore Roosevelt, for investigative journalists who published exposés of political scandals and industrial abuses. (p. 536)

***Muller v. Oregon:*** A 1908 Supreme Court case that upheld an Oregon law limiting women's workday to ten hours, based on the need to protect women's health for motherhood. *Muller* complicated the earlier decision in *Lochner v. New York*, laying out grounds on which states could intervene to protect workers. It divided women's rights activists, however, because some saw its provisions as discriminatory. (p. 567)

**multiculturalism:** The promotion of diversity in gender, race, ethnicity, religion, and sexual preference. This political and social policy became increasingly popular in the United States during the 1980s post–civil rights era. (p. 884)

**multinational corporations:** Corporations with offices and factories in multiple countries, which expanded to find new markets and cheaper sources of labor. Globalization was made possible by the proliferation of these multinational corporations. (p. 879)

**Munich Conference:** A conference in Munich held in September 1938 during which Britain and France agreed to allow Germany to annex the Sudetenland—a German-speaking border area of Czechoslovakia—in return for Hitler's pledge to seek no more territory. (p. 669)

***Munn v. Illinois:*** An 1877 Supreme Court case that affirmed that states could regulate key businesses, such as railroads and grain elevators, if those businesses were "clothed in the public interest." (p. 448)

**mutual aid society:** An urban aid society that served members of an ethnic immigrant group, usually those from a particular province or town. The societies functioned as fraternal clubs that collected dues from members in order to pay support in case of death or disability. (p. 529)

**My Lai:** Vietnamese village where U.S. Army troops executed nearly five hundred people in 1968, including a large number of women and children. (p. 807)

**National American Woman Suffrage Association:** Women's suffrage organization created in 1890 by the union of the National Woman Suffrage Association and the American Woman Suffrage Association. Up to national ratification of suffrage in 1920, the NAWSA played a central role in campaigning for women's right to vote. (p. 520)

**National Association for the Advancement of Colored People (NAACP):** An organization founded in 1909 by leading African American reformers and white allies as a vehicle for advocating equal rights for African Americans, especially through the courts. (p. 568)

**National Association of Colored Women:** An organization created in 1896 by African American women to provide community support. Through its local clubs, the NACW arranged for the care of orphans, founded homes for the elderly, advocated temperance, undertook public health campaigns, campaigned for women's suffrage, and raised awareness of racial injustice (such as lynching, segregated facilities, and disfranchisement). (p. 519)

**National Association of Manufacturers:** An association of industrialists and business leaders opposed to government regulation. In the era of the New Deal, the group promoted free enterprise and capitalism through a publicity campaign of radio programs, motion pictures, billboards, and direct mail. (p. 645)

**National Child Labor Committee:** A reform organization that worked (unsuccessfully) to win a federal law banning child labor. The NCLC hired photographer Lewis Hine to record brutal conditions in mines and mills where thousands of children worked. (p. 566)

**National Consumers' League:** Begun in New York, a national progressive organization that encouraged women, through their shopping decisions, to support fair wages and working conditions for industrial laborers. (p. 545)

**national debt:** The cumulative total of all budget deficits. (p. 857)

**National Defense Education Act:** A 1958 act, passed in response to the Soviet launching of the *Sputnik* satellite, that funneled millions of dollars into American universities, helping institutions such as the University of California at Berkeley and the Massachusetts Institute of Technology, among others, become the leading research centers in the world. (p. 731)

**National Interstate and Defense Highways Act:** A 1956 law authorizing the construction of a national highway system. (p. 746)

**National Municipal League:** A political reform organization that advised cities to elect small councils and hire professional city managers who would direct operations like a corporate executive. (p. 540)

**National Organization for Women (NOW):** Women's civil rights organization formed in 1966. Initially, NOW focused on eliminating gender discrimination in public institutions and the workplace, but by the 1970s it also embraced many of the issues raised by more radical feminists. (p. 792)

**National Origins Act:** A 1924 law limiting annual immigration from each country to no more than 2 percent of that nationality's percentage of the U.S. population as it had stood in 1890. The law severely limited immigration, especially from Southern and Eastern Europe. (p. 624)

**National Park Service:** A federal agency founded in 1916 that provided comprehensive oversight of the growing system of national parks. (p. 512)

**National Recovery Administration:** Federal agency established in June 1933 to promote industrial recovery during the Great Depression. It encouraged industrialists to voluntarily adopt codes that defined fair working conditions, set prices, and minimized competition. (p. 643)

*National Review:* A conservative magazine founded by editor William F. Buckley in 1955, who used it to criticize liberal policy. (p. 850)

**National Socialist (Nazi) Party:** German political party led by Adolf Hitler, who became chancellor of Germany in 1933. The party's ascent was fueled by huge World War I reparation payments, economic depression, fear of communism, labor unrest, and rising unemployment. (p. 667)

**National War Labor Board:** A federal agency founded in 1918 that established an eight-hour day for war workers (with time-and-a-half pay for overtime), endorsed equal pay for women, and supported workers' right to organize. (p. 599)

**National Woman's Party:** A political party founded in 1916 that fought for an Equal Rights Amendment to the U.S. Constitution in the early twentieth century. (p. 601)

**National Woman Suffrage Association:** A suffrage group headed by Elizabeth Cady Stanton and Susan B. Anthony that stressed the need for women to lead organizations on their own behalf. The NWSA focused exclusively on women's rights—sometimes denigrating men of color in the process—and took up the battle for a federal women's suffrage amendment. (p. 423)

**Nation of Islam:** A religion founded in the United States that became a leading source of black nationalist thought in the 1960s. Black Muslims preached an apocalyptic brand of Islam, anticipating the day when Allah would banish the white "devils" and give the black nation justice. (p. 774)

**nativism:** Opposition to immigration and to full citizenship for recent immigrants or to immigrants of a particular ethnic or national background, as expressed, for example, by anti-Irish discrimination in the 1850s and Asian exclusion laws between the 1880s and 1940s. (p. 367)

**Naturalization, Alien, and Sedition Acts:** Three laws passed in 1798 that limited individual rights and threatened the fledgling party system. The Naturalization Act lengthened the residency requirement for citizenship, the Alien Act authorized the deportation of foreigners, and the Sedition Act prohibited the publication of insults or malicious attacks on the president or members of Congress. (p. 205)

**natural rights:** The rights to life, liberty, and property. According to the English philosopher John Locke in *Two Treatises of Government* (1690), political authority was not given by God to monarchs. Instead, it derived from social compacts that people made to preserve their natural rights. (p. 113)

**Navigation Acts:** English laws passed, beginning in the 1650s and 1660s, requiring that certain English colonial goods be shipped through English ports on English ships manned primarily by English sailors in order to benefit English merchants, shippers, and seamen. (p. 76)

**Negro Leagues:** Professional baseball teams formed for and by black players, after the main national leagues began to exclude all African American players in the 1890s. Enduring until the desegregation of baseball after World War II, the leagues enabled black men to showcase athletic ability and race pride, but their working conditions and wages were much less desirable than those of players in the white leagues. (p. 510)

**neo-Europes:** Term for colonies in which colonists sought to replicate, or at least approximate, economies and social structures they knew at home. (p. 36)

**neomercantilism:** A system of government-assisted economic development embraced by republican state legislatures throughout the nation, especially in the Northeast. This system of activist government encouraged private entrepreneurs to seek individual opportunity and the public welfare through market exchange. (p. 233)

**Neutrality Act of 1935:** Legislation that sought to avoid entanglement in foreign wars while protecting trade. It imposed an embargo on selling arms to warring countries and declared that Americans traveling on the ships of belligerent nations did so at their own risk. (p. 668)

**New Jersey Plan:** Alternative to the Virginia Plan drafted by delegates from small states, retaining the confederation's single-house congress with one vote per state. It shared with the Virginia Plan enhanced congressional powers to raise revenue, control commerce, and make binding requisitions on the states. (p. 189)

**Newlands Reclamation Act:** A 1902 law, supported by President Theodore Roosevelt, that allowed the federal government to sell public lands to raise money for irrigation projects that expanded agriculture on arid lands. (p. 565)

**New Left:** A term applied to radical students of the 1960s and 1970s, distinguishing their activism from the Old Left—the communists and socialists of the 1930s and 1940s, who tended to focus on economic and labor questions rather than cultural issues. (p. 796)

**New Lights:** Evangelical preachers, many of them influenced by John Wesley, the founder of English Methodism, and George Whitefield, the charismatic itinerant preacher who brought his message to Britain's American colonies. They decried a Christian faith that was merely intellectual and emphasized the importance of a spiritual rebirth. (p. 116)

**"New Look":** The defense policy of the Eisenhower administration that stepped up production of the hydrogen bomb and developed long-range bombing capabilities. (p. 717)

**New Nationalism:** In a 1910 speech, Theodore Roosevelt called for a "New Nationalism" that promoted government intervention to enhance public welfare, including a federal child labor law, more recognition of labor rights, a national minimum wage for women, women's suffrage, and curbs on the power of federal courts to stop reform. (p. 569)

**New South:** A nickname for the former Confederate states, used by boosters to describe the region's economic diversification and growth of industrial jobs in the post–Civil War era. Because of the region's poverty, many of those industries were extractive (such as coal and timber), and some (like textiles) were low-wage and involved considerable child labor. (p. 483)

**nonimportation movement:** Colonists attempted nonimportation agreements three times: in 1766, in response to the Stamp Act; in 1768, in response to the Townshend duties; and in 1774, in response to the Coercive Acts. In each case, colonial radicals pressured merchants to stop importing British goods. In 1774 nonimportation was adopted by the First Continental Congress and enforced by the

Continental Association. American women became crucial to the movement by reducing their households' consumption of imported goods and producing large quantities of homespun cloth. (p. 147)

**North American Free Trade Agreement (NAFTA):** A 1993 treaty that eliminated all tariffs and trade barriers among the United States, Canada, and Mexico. (p. 879)

**North Atlantic Treaty Organization (NATO):** Military alliance formed in 1949 among the United States, Canada, and Western European nations to counter any possible Soviet threat. (p. 705)

**Northwest Ordinance of 1787:** A land act that provided for orderly settlement and established a process by which settled territories would become the states of Ohio, Indiana, Illinois, Michigan, and Wisconsin. It also banned slavery in the Northwest Territory. (p. 184)

**notables:** Northern landlords, slave-owning planters, and seaport merchants who dominated the political system of the early nineteenth century. (p. 265)

**NSC-68:** Top-secret government report of April 1950 warning that national survival in the face of Soviet communism required a massive military buildup. (p. 706)

**nullification:** The constitutional argument advanced by John C. Calhoun that a state legislature or convention could void a law passed by Congress. (p. 278)

**Old Lights:** Conservative ministers opposed to the passion displayed by evangelical preachers; they preferred to emphasize the importance of cultivating a virtuous Christian life. (p. 116)

**Omaha Platform:** An 1892 statement by the Populists calling for stronger government to protect ordinary Americans. (p. 556)

**one-tenth tax:** A tax adopted by the Confederacy in 1863 that required all farmers to turn over a tenth of their crops and livestock to the government for military use. The tax demonstrated the southern government's strong use of centralized power; it caused great hardship for poor families. (p. 397)

**"open door" policy:** A claim put forth by U.S. Secretary of State John Hay that all nations seeking to do business in China should have equal trade access. (p. 589)

**Operation Rescue:** A movement founded by religious activist Randall Terry in 1987 that mounted protests outside abortion clinics and harassed their staffs and clients. (p. 885)

**Operation Rolling Thunder:** Massive bombing campaign against North Vietnam authorized by President Johnson in 1965; against expectations, it ended up hardening the will of the North Vietnamese to continue fighting. (p. 794)

**Oregon Trail:** An emigrant route that originally led from Independence, Missouri, to the Willamette Valley in Oregon, a distance of some 2,000 miles. Alternate routes included the California Trail, the Mormon Trail, and the Bozeman Trail. Together they conveyed several hundred thousand migrants to the Far West in the 1840s, 1850s, and 1860s. (p. 338)

**Organization of Petroleum Exporting Countries (OPEC):** A cartel formed in 1960 by the Persian Gulf states and other oil-rich developing countries that allowed its members to exert greater control over the price of oil. (p. 817)

**Ostend Manifesto:** An 1854 manifesto that urged President Franklin Pierce to seize the slave-owning province of Cuba from Spain. Northern Democrats denounced this aggressive initiative, and the plan was scuttled. (p. 365)

**The Other America:** A 1962 book by left-wing social critic Michael Harrington, chronicling "the economic underworld of American life." His study made it clear that in economic terms the bottom class remained far behind. (p. 732)

**Palmer raids:** A series of raids led by Attorney General A. Mitchell Palmer on radical organizations that peaked in January 1920, when federal agents arrested six thousand citizens and aliens and denied them access to legal counsel. (p. 613)

**pan-Africanism:** The idea that people of African descent, in all parts of the world, have a common heritage and destiny and should cooperate in political action. (p. 630)

**Panama Canal:** A canal across the Isthmus of Panama connecting trade between the Atlantic and Pacific oceans. Built by the U.S. Army Corps of Engineers and opened in 1914, the canal gave U.S. naval vessels quick access to the Pacific and provided the United States with a commanding position in the Western Hemisphere. (p. 591)

**Panic of 1819:** First major economic crisis of the United States. Farmers and planters faced an abrupt 30 percent drop in world agricultural prices, and as farmers' income declined, they could not pay debts owed to stores and banks, many of which went bankrupt. (p. 234)

**Panic of 1837:** Triggered by a sharp reduction in English capital and credit flowing into the United States, the cash shortage caused a panic while the collapse of credit led to a depression—the second major economic crisis of the United States—that lasted from 1837 to 1843. (p. 288)

**paternalism:** The ideology held by slave owners who considered themselves committed to the welfare of their slaves. (p. 251)

**Patient Protection and Affordable Care Act:** Sweeping 2010 health-care reform bill championed by President Obama that established nearly universal health insurance by providing subsidies and compelling larger businesses to offer coverage to employees. (p. 897)

**patronage:** The power of elected officials to grant government jobs and favors to their supporters; also the jobs and favors themselves. (p. 96)

**Peace Corps:** Program launched by President Kennedy in 1961 through which young American volunteers helped with education, health, and other projects in developing countries around the world. (p. 724)

**Pearl Harbor:** A naval base in Pearl Harbor, Hawaii, that was attacked by Japanese bombers on December 7, 1941; more than 2,400 Americans were killed. The following day, President Roosevelt asked Congress for a declaration of war against Japan. (p. 672)

**peasants:** The traditional term for farmworkers in Europe. Some peasants owned land, while others leased or rented small plots from landlords. (p. 17)

**Pendleton Act:** An 1883 law establishing a nonpartisan Civil Service Commission to fill federal jobs by examination. The Pendleton Act dealt a major blow to the "spoils system" and sought to ensure that government positions were filled by trained, professional employees. (p. 553)

**Pennsylvania constitution of 1776:** A constitution that granted all taxpaying men the right to vote and hold office and created a unicameral (one-house) legislature with complete power; there was no governor to exercise a veto. Other provisions mandated a system of elementary education and protected citizens from imprisonment for debt. (p. 180)

**penny papers:** Sensational and popular urban newspapers that built large circulations by reporting crime and scandals. (p. 307)

*perestroika:* The economic restructuring policy introduced by Soviet president Mikhail Gorbachev during the 1980s that contributed, unintentionally, to the 1991 breakup of the Soviet Union. (p. 865)

**Persian Gulf War:** The 1991 war between Iraq and a U.S.-led international coalition that was sparked by the 1990 Iraqi invasion of Kuwait. A forty-day bombing campaign against Iraq followed by coalition troops storming into Kuwait brought a quick coalition victory. (p. 870)

**personal liberty laws:** Laws enacted in many northern states that guaranteed to all residents, including alleged fugitives, the right to a jury trial. (p. 364)

**Personal Responsibility and Work Opportunity Reconciliation Act:** Legislation signed by President Clinton in 1996 that replaced Aid to Families with Dependent Children, the major welfare program dating to the New Deal era, with Temporary Assistance for Needy Families, which provided grants to the states to assist the poor and which limited welfare payments to two years, with a lifetime maximum of five years. (p. 889)

**Philipsburg Proclamation:** A 1779 proclamation that declared that any slave who deserted a rebel master would receive protection, freedom, and land from Great Britain. (p. 175)

**Pietism:** A Christian revival movement characterized by Bible study, the conversion experience, and the individual's personal relationship with God. It began as an effort to reform the German Lutheran Church in the mid-seventeenth century and became widely influential in Britain and its colonies in the eighteenth century. (p. 112)

**Pilgrims:** One of the first Protestant groups to come to America, seeking a separation from the Church of England. They founded Plymouth, the first permanent community in New England, in 1620. (p. 54)

***Planned Parenthood of Southeastern Pennsylvania v. Casey:*** A 1992 Supreme Court case that upheld a law requiring a twenty-four-hour waiting period prior to an abortion. Although the decision upheld certain restrictions on abortions, it affirmed the "essential holding" in *Roe v. Wade* (1973) that women had a constitutional right to control their reproduction. (p. 886)

**plantation system:** A system of production characterized by unfree labor producing cash crops for distant markets. The plantation complex developed in sugar-producing areas of the Mediterranean world and was transferred to the Americas, where it took hold in tropical and subtropical areas, including Brazil, the West Indies, and southeastern North America. In addition to sugar, the plantation complex was adapted to produce tobacco, rice, indigo, and cotton. (p. 31)

**Platt Amendment:** A 1902 amendment to the Cuban constitution that blocked Cuba from making a treaty with any country except the United States and gave the United States the right to intervene in Cuban affairs. The amendment was a condition for U.S. withdrawal from the newly independent island. (p. 589)

*Plessy v. Ferguson:* An 1896 Supreme Court case that ruled that racially segregated railroad cars and other public facilities, if they claimed to be "separate but equal," were permissible according to the Fourteenth Amendment. (p. 507)

**plural marriage:** The practice of men taking multiple wives, which Mormon prophet Joseph Smith argued was biblically sanctioned and divinely ordained as a family system. (p. 305)

**political machine:** A highly organized group of insiders that directs a political party. As the power of notables waned in the 1820s, disciplined political parties usually run by professional politicians appeared in a number of states. (p. 267)

**political machines:** Complex, hierarchical party organizations such as New York's Tammany Hall, whose candidates remained in office on the strength of their political organization and their personal relationship with voters, especially working-class immigrants who had little alternative access to political power. (p. 537)

**Popular Front:** A small but vocal group of Americans who pushed for greater U.S. involvement in Europe. American Communist Party members, African American civil rights activists, and trade unionists, among other members of the Popular Front coalition, encouraged Roosevelt to take a stronger stand against European fascism. (p. 669)

**popular sovereignty:** The principle that ultimate power lies in the hands of the electorate. Also a plan, first promoted by Democratic candidate Senator Lewis Cass as "squatter sovereignty," then revised as "popular sovereignty" by fellow Democratic presidential aspirant Stephen Douglas, under which Congress would allow settlers in each territory to determine its status as free or slave. (pp. 161, 360)

**Port Huron Statement:** A 1962 manifesto by Students for a Democratic Society from its first national convention in Port Huron, Michigan, expressing students' disillusionment with the nation's consumer culture and the gulf between rich and poor, as well as a rejection of Cold War foreign policy, including the war in Vietnam. (p. 795)

**"positive good":** In 1837, South Carolina Senator John C. Calhoun argued on the floor of the Senate that slavery was not a necessary evil, but a positive good, "indispensable to the peace and happiness" of blacks and whites alike. (p. 251)

**Potsdam Conference:** The July 1945 conference in which American officials convinced the Soviet Union leader Joseph Stalin to accept German reparations only from the Soviet zone, or far eastern part of Germany. The agreement paved the way for the division of Germany into East and West. (p. 701)

**Presidential Commission on the Status of Women:** Commission appointed by President Kennedy in 1961, which issued a 1963 report documenting job and educational discrimination. (p. 791)

**Proclamation of Neutrality:** A proclamation issued by President George Washington in 1793, allowing U.S. citizens to trade with all belligerents in the war between France and Great Britain. (p. 202)

**producerism:** The argument that real economic wealth is created by workers who make their living by physical labor, such as farmers and craftsmen, and that merchants, lawyers, bankers, and other middlemen unfairly gain their wealth from such "producers." (p. 490)

**progressivism:** A loose term for the cause of political reformers—especially those from the elite and middle classes—who worked to improve the political system, fight poverty, conserve environmental resources, and increase government involvement in the economy. Giving their name to the "Progressive Era," such reformers were often prompted to act by fear that mass, radical protests by workers and farmers would spread, as well as by their desire to enhance social welfare and social justice. (p. 541)

**Proposition 13:** A measure passed overwhelmingly by Californians to roll back property taxes, cap future increases for present owners, and require that all tax measures have a two-thirds majority in the legislature. Proposition 13 inspired "tax revolts" across the country and helped conservatives define an enduring issue: low taxes. (p. 822)

**Proposition 209:** A proposition approved by California voters in 1996 that outlawed affirmative action in state employment and public education. (p. 884)

**proprietorship:** A colony created through a grant of land from the English monarch to an individual or group, who then set up a form of government largely independent from royal control. (p. 74)

**protective tariff:** A tax or duty on foreign producers of goods coming into or imported into the United States; tariffs gave U.S. manufacturers a competitive advantage in America's gigantic domestic market. (p. 444)

**Protestant Reformation:** The reform movement that began in 1517 with Martin Luther's critiques of the Roman Catholic Church and that precipitated an enduring schism that divided Protestants from Catholics. (p. 21)

**Public Works Administration:** A New Deal construction program established by Congress in 1933. Designed to put people back to work, the PWA built the Boulder Dam (renamed Hoover Dam) and Grand Coulee Dam, among other large public works projects. (p. 643)

**Pueblo Revolt:** Also known as Popé's Rebellion, the revolt in 1680 was an uprising of 46 Native American pueblos against Spanish rule. Spaniards were driven out of New Mexico. When they returned in the 1690s, they granted more autonomy to the pueblos they claimed to rule. (p. 62)

**Pure Food and Drug Act:** A 1906 law regulating the conditions in the food and drug industries to ensure a safe supply of food and medicine. (p. 544)

**Puritans:** Dissenters from the Church of England who wanted a genuine Reformation rather than the partial Reformation sought by Henry VIII. The Puritans' religious principles emphasized the importance of an individual's relationship with God developed through Bible study, prayer, and introspection. (p. 55)

**Quakers:** Epithet for members of the Society of Friends. Their belief that God spoke directly to each individual through an "inner light" and that neither ministers nor the Bible was essential to discovering God's Word put them in conflict with both the Church of England and orthodox Puritans. (p. 75)

**Quartering Act of 1765:** A British law passed by Parliament at the request of General Thomas Gage, the British military commander in America, that required colonial governments to provide barracks and food for British troops. (p. 142)

**race riot:** A term for an attack on African Americans by white mobs, triggered by political conflicts, street altercations, or rumors of crime. In some cases, such "riots" were not spontaneous but planned in advance by a group of leaders seeking to enforce white supremacy. (p. 531)

**Radical Republicans:** The members of the Republican Party who were bitterly opposed to slavery and to southern slave owners since the mid-1850s. With the Confiscation Act in 1861, Radical Republicans began to use wartime legislation to destroy slavery. (p. 392)

**"rain follows the plow":** An unfounded theory that settlement and farming of the Great Plains caused an increase in rainfall. (p. 454)

**Reagan coalition:** A coalition supporting Ronald Reagan that included the traditional core of Republican Party voters, middle-class suburbanites and migrants to the Sunbelt states, blue-collar Catholics, and a large contingent of southern whites, an electorally key group of former Democrats that had been gradually moving toward the Republican Party since 1964. (p. 855)

**Reagan Democrats:** Blue-collar Catholics from industrialized midwestern states such as Michigan, Ohio, and Illinois who were dissatisfied with the direction of liberalism in the 1970s and left the Democratic Party for the Republicans. (p. 855)

**realism:** A movement that called for writers and artists to picture daily life as precisely and truly as possible. (p. 503)

**Reconstruction Act of 1867:** An act that divided the conquered South into five military districts, each under the command of a U.S. general. To reenter the Union, former Confederate states had to grant the vote to freedmen and deny it to leading ex-Confederates. (p. 419)

**redemptioner:** A common type of indentured servant in the Middle colonies in the eighteenth century. Unlike other indentured servants, redemptioners did not sign a contract before leaving Europe. Instead, they found employers after arriving in America. (p. 109)

**Red Scare:** A term for anticommunist hysteria that swept the United States, first after World War I, and led to a series of government raids on alleged subversives and a suppression of civil liberties. (p. 612)

**Red Summer:** The summer and fall of 1919, in which antiblack riots by white Americans in more than two dozen cities led to hundreds of deaths. So named because of the bloody clashes. The worst occurred in Chicago, in which 38 people were killed (23 blacks, 15 whites), 537 injured, and 1,000 black families made homeless. (p. 613)

**Regulators:** Landowning protestors who organized in North and South Carolina in the 1760s and 1770s to demand that the eastern-controlled government provide western districts with more courts, fairer taxation, and greater representation in the assembly. (p. 127)

**Religious Right:** Politically active religious conservatives, especially Catholics and evangelical Christians, who became particularly vocal in the 1980s against feminism, abortion, and homosexuality and who promoted "family values." (p. 850)

**Report on Manufactures:** A proposal by treasury secretary Alexander Hamilton in 1791 calling for the federal government to urge the expansion of American manufacturing while imposing tariffs on foreign imports. (p. 201)

**Report on the Public Credit:** Alexander Hamilton's 1790 report recommending that the federal government should assume all state debts and fund the national debt — that is, offer interest on it rather than repaying it — at full value. Hamilton's goal was to make the new country creditworthy, not debt-free. (p. 199)

**republic:** A state without a monarch or prince that is governed by representatives of the people. (p. 18)

**republican aristocracy:** The Old South gentry that built impressive mansions, adopted the manners and values of the English landed gentry, and feared federal government interference with their slave property. (p. 326)

**republican motherhood:** The idea that the primary political role of American women was to instill a sense of patriotic duty and republican virtue in their children and mold them into exemplary republican citizens. (p. 268)

**Revenue Act:** A 1942 act that expanded the number of people paying income taxes from 3.9 million to 42.6 million. These taxes on personal incomes and business profits paid half the cost of World War II. (p. 673)

**revival:** A renewal of religious enthusiasm in a Christian congregation. In the eighteenth century, revivals were often inspired by evangelical preachers who urged their listeners to experience a rebirth. (p. 115)

**rights liberalism:** The conviction that individuals require government protection from discrimination. This version of liberalism was promoted by the civil rights and women's movements and focused on identities — such as race or gender — rather than the general social welfare of New Deal liberalism. (p. 755)

**Rocky Mountains:** A high mountain range that spans some 3,000 miles, the Rocky Mountains are bordered by the Great Plains on the east and the Great Basin on the west. Native peoples fished, gathered roots and berries, and hunted elk, deer, and bighorn sheep there. Silver mining boomed in the Rockies in the nineteenth century. (p. 14)

**Roe v. Wade:** The 1973 Supreme Court ruling that the Constitution protects the right to abortion, which states cannot prohibit in the early stages of pregnancy. The decision galvanized social conservatives and made abortion a controversial policy issue for decades to come. (p. 830)

**romanticism:** A European philosophy that rejected the ordered rationality of the eighteenth-century Enlightenment, embracing human passion, spiritual quest, and self-knowledge. Romanticism strongly influenced American transcendentalism. (p. 298)

**Rome-Berlin Axis:** A political and military alliance formed in 1936 between German dictator Adolf Hitler and the Italian dictator Benito Mussolini. (p. 668)

**Roosevelt Corollary:** The 1904 assertion by President Theodore Roosevelt that the United States would act as a "policeman" in the Caribbean region and intervene in the affairs of nations that were guilty of "wrongdoing or impotence" in order to protect U.S. interests in Latin America. (p. 592)

**Roosevelt recession:** A recession from 1937 to 1938 that occurred after President Roosevelt cut the federal budget. (p. 650)

**Root-Takahira Agreement:** A 1908 agreement between the United States and Japan confirming principles of free oceanic commerce and recognizing Japan's authority over Manchuria. (p. 591)

**royal colony:** In the English system, a royal colony was chartered by the crown. The colony's governor was appointed by the crown and served according to the instructions of the Board of Trade. (p. 44)

**Rural Electrification Administration:** An agency established in 1935 to promote nonprofit farm cooperatives that offered loans to farmers to install power lines. (p. 659)

**Rust Belt:** The once heavily industrialized regions of the Northeast and Midwest that went into decline after deindustrialization. By the 1970s and 1980s, these regions were full of abandoned plants and distressed communities. (p. 820)

**salutary neglect:** A term used to describe British colonial policy during the reigns of George I (r. 1714–1727) and George II (r. 1727–1760). By relaxing their supervision of internal colonial affairs, royal bureaucrats inadvertently assisted the rise of self-government in North America. (p. 96)

**Sand Creek massacre:** The November 29, 1864, massacre of more than one hundred peaceful Cheyennes, largely women and children, by John M. Chivington's Colorado militia. (p. 459)

**Sandinistas:** The democratically elected group in Nicaragua that President Reagan accused of threatening U.S. business interests. Reagan attempted to overthrow them by ordering the CIA to assist an armed opposition group called the Contras. (p. 864)

**scientific management:** A system of organizing work developed by Frederick W. Taylor in the late nineteenth century. It was designed to coax maximum output from the individual worker, increase efficiency, and reduce production costs. (p. 482)

**Scopes trial:** The 1925 trial of John Scopes, a biology teacher in Dayton, Tennessee, for violating his state's ban on teaching evolution. The trial created a nationwide media frenzy and came to be seen as a showdown between urban and rural values. (p. 623)

**Second Bank of the United States:** National bank with multiple branches chartered in 1816 for twenty years. Intended to help regulate the economy, the bank became a major issue in Andrew Jackson's reelection campaign in 1832. (p. 279)

**Second Continental Congress:** Legislative body that governed the United States from May 1775 through the war's duration. It established an army, created its own money, and declared independence once all hope for a peaceful reconciliation with Britain was gone. (p. 159)

**Second Great Awakening:** A series of evangelical Protestant revivals extending from the 1790s to the 1830s that prompted thousands of conversions and widespread optimism about Americans' capacity for progress and reform. (p. 295)

**Second Hundred Years' War:** An era of warfare beginning with the War of the League of Augsburg in 1689 and lasting until the defeat of Napoleon at Waterloo in 1815. In that time, England fought in seven major wars; the longest era of peace lasted only twenty-six years. (p. 80)

**secret ballot:** Form of voting that allows the voter to enter a choice in privacy without having to submit a recognizable ballot or to voice the choice out loud to others. (p. 330)

**Securities and Exchange Commission:** A commission established by Congress in 1934 to regulate the stock market. The commission had broad powers to determine how stocks and bonds were sold to the public, to set rules for margin (credit) transactions, and to prevent stock sales by those with inside information about corporate plans. (p. 645)

**Sedition Act of 1918:** Wartime law that prohibited any words or behavior that might promote resistance to the United States or help in the cause of its enemies. (p. 600)

**self-made man:** A nineteenth-century ideal that celebrated men who rose to wealth or social prominence from humble origins through self-discipline, hard work, and temperate habits. (p. 260)

**semisedentary societies:** Societies whose members combine slash-and-burn agriculture with hunting and fishing. Semisedentary societies often occupy large village sites near their fields in the summer, then disperse during the winter months into smaller hunting, fishing, and gathering camps, regathering again in spring to plant their crops. (p. 7)

**Seneca Falls Convention:** The first women's rights convention in the United States. Held in Seneca Falls, New York, in 1848, it resulted in a manifesto extending to women the egalitarian republican ideology of the Declaration of Independence. (p. 317)

**service industries:** Term that includes food, beverage, and tourist industries, financial and medical service industries, and computer technology industries, which were the leading sectors of U.S. growth in the second half of the 1980s. This pattern represented a shift from reliance on the heavy industries of steel, autos, and chemicals. (p. 861)

**Servicemen's Readjustment Act:** Popularly known as the GI Bill, 1944 legislation authorizing the government to provide World War II veterans with funds for education, housing, and health care, as well as loans to start businesses and buy homes. (p. 678)

**sharecropping:** The labor system by which landowners and impoverished southern farmworkers, particularly African Americans, divided the proceeds from crops harvested on the landowner's property. With local merchants providing supplies—in exchange for a lien on the crop—sharecropping pushed farmers into cash-crop production and often trapped them in long-term debt. (p. 426)

**Sharon Statement:** Drafted by founding members of the Young Americans for Freedom (YAF), this manifesto outlined the group's principles and inspired young conservatives who would play important roles in the Reagan administration in the 1980s. (p. 796)

**Shays's Rebellion:** A 1786–1787 uprising led by dissident farmers in western Massachusetts, many of them Revolutionary War veterans, protesting the taxation policies of the eastern elites who controlled the state's government. (p. 186)

***Shelley v. Kraemer:*** A 1948 Supreme Court decision that outlawed restrictive covenants on the occupancy of housing developments by African Americans, Asian Americans, and other minorities. Because the Court decision did not actually prohibit racial discrimination in housing, unfair practices against minority groups continued until passage of the Fair Housing Act in 1968. (p. 746)

**Sheppard-Towner Federal Maternity and Infancy Act:** The first federally funded health-care legislation that provided federal funds for medical clinics, prenatal education programs, and visiting nurses. (p. 620)

**Sherman Antitrust Act:** Landmark 1890 act that forbade anticompetitive business activities, requiring the federal government to investigate trusts and any companies operating in violation of the act. (p. 554)

**Sierra Club:** An organization founded in 1892 that was dedicated to the enjoyment and preservation of America's great mountains (including the Sierra Nevadas) and wilderness environments. Encouraged by such groups, national and state governments began to set aside more public lands for preservation and recreation. (p. 512)

**silent majority:** Term derived from the title of a book by Ben J. Wattenberg and Richard Scammon (called *The Real Majority*) and used by Nixon in a 1969 speech to describe those who supported his positions but did not publicly assert their voices, in contrast to those involved in the antiwar, civil rights, and women's movements. (p. 805)

***Silent Spring:*** Book published in 1962 by biologist Rachel Carson. Its analysis of the pesticide DDT's toxic impact on the human and natural food chains galvanized environmental activists. (p. 817)

***Slaughter-House Cases:*** A group of decisions begun in 1873 in which the Court began to undercut the power of the Fourteenth Amendment to protect African American rights. (p. 438)

**"slave power" conspiracy:** The political argument, made by abolitionists, free soilers, and Republicans in the pre–Civil War years, that southern slaveholders were using their unfair representative advantage under the three-fifths compromise of the Constitution, as well as their clout within the Democratic Party, to demand extreme federal proslavery policies (such as annexation of Cuba) that the majority of American voters would not support. (p. 356)

**slave society:** A society in which the institution of slavery affects all aspects of life. (p. 323)

**Smoot-Hawley Tariff:** A high tariff enacted in 1930 during the Great Depression. By taxing imported goods, Congress hoped to stimulate American manufacturing, but the tariff triggered retaliatory tariffs in other countries, which further hindered global trade and led to greater economic contraction. (p. 638)

**Social Darwinism:** An idea, actually formulated not by Charles Darwin but by British philosopher and sociologist Herbert Spencer, that human society advanced through ruthless competition and the "survival of the fittest." (p. 500)

**Social Gospel:** A movement to renew religious faith through dedication to public welfare and social justice, reforming both society and the self through Christian service. (p. 503)

**Social Security Act:** A 1935 act with three main provisions: old-age pensions for workers; a joint federal-state system of compensation for unemployed workers; and a program of payments to widowed mothers and the blind, deaf, and disabled. (p. 648)

**social settlement:** A community welfare center that investigated the plight of the urban poor, raised funds to address urgent needs, and helped neighborhood residents advocate on their own behalf. Social settlements became a nationally recognized reform strategy during the Progressive Era. (p. 543)

**soft power:** The exercise of popular cultural influence abroad, as American radio and movies became popular around the world in the 1920s, transmitting American cultural ideals overseas. (p. 619)

**Sons of Liberty:** Colonists—primarily middling merchants and artisans—who banded together to protest the Stamp Act and other imperial reforms of the 1760s. The group originated in Boston in 1765 but soon spread to all the colonies. (p. 144)

**South Atlantic System:** A new agricultural and commercial order that produced sugar, tobacco, rice, and other tropical and subtropical products for an international market. Its plantation societies were ruled by European planter-merchants and worked by hundreds of thousands of enslaved Africans. (p. 83)

**Southern Christian Leadership Conference (SCLC):** After the Montgomery Bus Boycott, Martin Luther King Jr. and other civil rights leaders formed the SCLC in 1957 to coordinate civil rights activity in the South. (p. 767)

**Special Field Order No. 15:** An order by General William T. Sherman, later reversed by policymakers, that granted confiscated land to formerly enslaved families in Georgia and South Carolina so they could farm independently. (p. 411)

**Specie Circular:** An executive order in 1836 that required the Treasury Department to accept only gold and silver in payment for lands in the national domain. (p. 288)

**spoils system:** The widespread award of public jobs to political supporters after an electoral victory. In 1829, Andrew Jackson instituted the system on the national level, arguing that the rotation of officeholders was preferable to a permanent group of bureaucrats. (p. 267)

***Sputnik:*** The world's first satellite, launched by the Soviet Union in 1957. After its launch, the United States funded research and education to catch up in the Cold War space competition. (p. 731)

**squatter:** Someone who settles on land he or she does not own or rent. Many eighteenth-century settlers established themselves on land before it was surveyed and entered for sale, requesting the first right to purchase the land when sales began. (p. 107)

**stagflation:** An economic term coined in the 1970s to describe the condition in which inflation and unemployment rise at the same time. (p. 820)

**Stamp Act Congress:** A congress of delegates from nine assemblies that met in New York City in October 1765 to protest the loss of American "rights and liberties," especially the right to trial by jury. The congress challenged the constitutionality of both the Stamp and Sugar Acts by declaring that only the colonists' elected representatives could tax them. (p. 143)

**Stamp Act of 1765:** British law imposing a tax on all paper used in the colonies. Widespread resistance to the Stamp Act prevented it from taking effect and led to its repeal in 1766. (p. 141)

**Standard Oil decision:** A 1911 Supreme Court decision that directed the breakup of the Standard Oil Company into smaller companies because its overwhelming market dominance and monopoly power violated antitrust laws. (p. 565)

**states' rights:** An interpretation of the Constitution that exalts the sovereignty of the states and circumscribes the authority of the national government. (p. 278)

**States' Rights Democratic Party:** Known popularly as the Dixiecrats, a breakaway party of white Democrats from the South that formed for the 1948 election. Its formation shed light on an internal struggle between the civil rights aims of the party's liberal wing and southern white Democrats. (p. 761)

**Stonewall Inn:** A gay bar in New York's Greenwich Village that was raided by police in 1969; the ensuing two-day riot contributed to the rapid rise of a gay liberation movement. (p. 804)

**Stono Rebellion:** Slave uprising in 1739 along the Stono River in South Carolina in which a group of slaves armed themselves, plundered six plantations, and killed more than twenty colonists. Colonists quickly suppressed the rebellion. (p. 91)

**STOP ERA:** An organization founded by Phyllis Schlafly in 1972 to fight the Equal Rights Amendment. (p. 829)

**Student Nonviolent Coordinating Committee (SNCC):** A student civil rights group founded in 1960 under the mentorship of activist Ella Baker. SNCC initially embraced an interracial and nonhierarchical structure that encouraged leadership at the grassroots level and practiced the civil disobedience principles of Martin Luther King Jr. As violence toward civil rights activists escalated nationwide in the 1960s, SNCC expelled nonblack members and promoted "black power" and the teachings of Malcolm X. (p. 767)

**Students for a Democratic Society (SDS):** An organization for social change founded by college students in 1960. (p. 795)

**Sugar Act of 1764:** British law that decreased the duty on French molasses, making it more attractive for shippers to obey the law, and at the same time raised penalties for smuggling. The act enraged New England merchants, who opposed both the tax and the fact that prosecuted merchants would be tried by British-appointed judges in a vice-admiralty court. (p. 140)

**Sunbelt:** Name applied to the Southwest and South, which grew rapidly after World War II as a center of defense industries and non-unionized labor. (p. 748)

**supply-side economics (Reaganomics):** Economic theory that tax cuts for individuals and businesses encourage investment and production (supply) and stimulate consumption (demand) because individuals can keep more of their earnings. In reality, supply-side economics created a massive federal budget deficit. (p. 856)

**Taft-Hartley Act:** Law passed by the Republican-controlled Congress in 1947 that overhauled the 1935 National Labor Relations Act, placing restrictions on organized labor that made it more difficult for unions to organize workers. (p. 711)

**talented tenth:** A term used by Harvard-educated sociologist W. E. B. Du Bois for the top 10 percent of educated African Americans, whom he called on to develop new strategies to advocate for civil rights. (p. 568)

**Tariff of Abominations:** A tariff enacted in 1828 that raised duties significantly on raw materials, textiles, and iron goods. New York senator Van Buren hoped to win the support of farmers in New York, Ohio, and Kentucky with the tariff, but it enraged the South, which had no industries that needed tariff protection and resented the higher cost of imported dutied goods. (p. 275)

**task system:** A system of labor common in the rice-growing regions of South Carolina in which a slave was assigned a daily task to complete and allowed to do as he wished upon its completion. (p. 336)

**tax revolt:** A movement to lower or eliminate taxes. California's Proposition 13, which rolled back property taxes, capped future increases for present owners, and required that all tax measures have a two-thirds majority in the legislature, was the result of one such revolt, inspiring similar movements across the country. (p. 822)

**Tea Act of May 1773:** British act that lowered the existing tax on tea and granted exemptions to the East India Company to make their tea cheaper in the colonies and entice boycotting Americans to buy it. Resistance to the Tea Act led to the passage of the Coercive Acts and imposition of military rule in Massachusetts. (p. 151)

**Tea Party:** A set of far-right opposition groups that emerged during President Obama's first term and gave voice to the extreme individualism and antigovernment sentiment traditionally associated with right-wing movements in the United States. (p. 897)

**Teapot Dome:** Nickname for scandal in which Interior Secretary Albert Fall accepted $300,000 in bribes for leasing oil reserves on public land in Teapot Dome, Wyoming. It was part of a larger pattern of corruption that marred Warren G. Harding's presidency. (p. 616)

**teenager:** A term for a young adult. American youth culture, focused on the spending power of the "teenager," emerged as a cultural phenomenon in the postwar decades. (p. 737)

**Teller Amendment:** An amendment to the 1898 U.S. declaration of war against Spain disclaiming any intention by the United States to occupy Cuba. The amendment assured the public that the United States would uphold democracy abroad as well as at home. (p. 586)

**tenancy:** The rental of property. To attract tenants in New York's Hudson River Valley, Dutch and English manorial lords granted long tenancy leases, with the right to sell improvements—houses and barns, for example—to the next tenant. (p. 103)

**tenement:** A high-density, cheap, five- or six-story housing unit designed for working-class urban populations. In the late nineteenth and early twentieth centuries, tenements became a symbol of urban immigrant poverty. (p. 531)

**Tennessee Valley Authority:** An agency funded by Congress in 1933 that integrated flood control, reforestation, electricity generation, and agricultural and industrial development in the Tennessee Valley area. (p. 658)

**Ten Percent Plan:** A plan proposed by President Abraham Lincoln during the Civil War, but never implemented, that would have granted amnesty to most ex-Confederates and allowed each rebellious state to return to the Union as soon as 10 percent of its voters had taken a loyalty oath and the state had approved the Thirteenth Amendment. (p. 417)

**Tet offensive:** Major campaign of attacks launched throughout South Vietnam in January 1968 by the North Vietnamese and Vietcong. A major turning point in the war, it exposed the credibility gap between official statements and the war's reality, and it shook Americans' confidence in the government. (p. 799)

**Three Mile Island:** A nuclear plant near Harrisburg, Pennsylvania, where a reactor core came close to a meltdown in March 1979. After the incident at Three Mile Island, no new nuclear plants were authorized in the United States, though a handful with existing authorization were built in the 1980s. (p. 819)

**Title IX:** A law passed by Congress in 1972 that broadened the 1964 Civil Rights Act to include educational institutions, prohibiting colleges and universities that received federal funds from discriminating on the basis of sex. By requiring comparable funding for sports programs, Title IX made women's athletics a real presence on college campuses. (p. 804)

**toleration:** The allowance of different religious practices. Lord Baltimore persuaded the Maryland assembly to enact the Toleration Act (1649), which granted all Christians the right to follow their beliefs and hold church services. The crown imposed toleration on Massachusetts Bay in its new royal charter of 1691. (p. 56)

**"To Secure These Rights":** The 1947 report by the Presidential Committee on Civil Rights that called for robust federal action to ensure equality for African Americans. President Truman asked Congress to make all of the report's recommendations—including the abolition of poll taxes and the restoration of the Fair Employment Practice Committee—into law, leading to discord in the Democratic Party. (p. 760)

**town meeting:** A system of local government in New England in which all male heads of households met regularly to elect selectmen, levy local taxes, and regulate markets, roads, and schools. (p. 61)

**Townsend Plan:** A plan proposed by Francis Townsend in 1933 that would give $200 a month (about $3,600 today) to citizens over the age of sixty. Townsend Clubs sprang up across the country in support of the plan, mobilizing mass support for old-age pensions. (p. 647)

**Townshend Act of 1767:** British law that established new duties on tea, glass, lead, paper, and painters' colors imported into the colonies. The Townshend duties led to boycotts and heightened tensions between Britain and the American colonies. (p. 146)

**Trail of Tears:** Forced westward journey of Cherokees from their lands in Georgia to present-day Oklahoma in 1838. Nearly a quarter of the Cherokees died en route. (p. 283)

**transcendentalism:** A nineteenth-century American intellectual movement that posited the importance of an ideal world of mystical knowledge and harmony beyond the immediate grasp of the senses. Influenced by romanticism, transcendentalists Ralph Waldo Emerson and Henry David Thoreau called for the critical examination of society and emphasized individuality, self-reliance, and nonconformity. (p. 299)

**transcontinental railroad:** The railway line completed on May 10, 1869, that connected the Central Pacific and Union Pacific lines, enabling goods to move by railway from the eastern United States all the way to California. (p. 443)

**"treat":** A form of heterosexual dating in which, given the male partner's higher wage level, he is expected to pay for food and entertainment, and the young woman is expected to provide sexual favors in return. (p. 535)

**Treaty of Ghent:** The treaty signed on Christmas Eve 1814 that ended the War of 1812. It retained the prewar borders of the United States. (p. 219)

**Treaty of Greenville:** A 1795 treaty between the United States and various Indian tribes in Ohio. American negotiators acknowledged Indian ownership of the land, and, in return for various payments, the Western Confederacy ceded most of Ohio to the United States. (p. 207)

**Treaty of Kanagawa:** An 1854 treaty in which, after a show of military force by U.S. Commodore Matthew Perry, leaders of Japan agreed to permit American ships to refuel at two Japanese ports. (p. 365)

**Treaty of Paris of 1783:** The treaty that ended the Revolutionary War. In the treaty, Great Britain formally recognized American independence and relinquished its claims to lands south of the Great Lakes and east of the Mississippi River. (p. 178)

**Treaty of Versailles:** The 1919 treaty that ended World War I. The agreement redrew the map of the world, assigned Germany sole responsibility for the war, and saddled it with a debt of $33 billion in war damages. Its long-term impact around the globe—including the creation of British and French imperial "mandates"—was catastrophic. (p. 604)

**Triangle Fire:** A devastating fire that quickly spread through the Triangle Shirtwaist Company in New York City on March 25, 1911, killing 146 people. In the wake of the tragedy, fifty-six state laws were passed dealing with such issues as fire hazards, unsafe machines, and wages and working hours for women and children. The fire also provided a national impetus for industrial reform. (p. 545)

**tribalization:** The adaptation of stateless peoples to the demands imposed on them by neighboring states. (p. 80)

**Truman Doctrine:** President Harry S. Truman's commitment to "support free peoples who are resisting attempted subjugation by armed minorities or by outside pressures." First applied to Greece and Turkey in 1947, it became the justification for U.S. intervention into several countries during the Cold War. (p. 704)

**trust:** A small group of associates that hold stock from a group of combined firms, managing them as a single entity. Trusts quickly evolved into other centralized business forms, but progressive critics continued to refer to giant firms like U.S. Steel and Standard Oil as "trusts." (p. 477)

**twenty-Negro rule:** A law adopted by the Confederate Congress that exempted one man from military conscription for every twenty slaves owned by a family. The law showed how dependence on coerced slave labor could be a military disadvantage, and it exacerbated class resentments among nonslaveholding whites who were required to serve in the army. (p. 397)

**Tydings-McDuffie Act:** A 1934 law that provided for the independence of the Philippines, after a ten-year transition period. Though it granted Philippine independence, its origins were nativist, because the law's proponents wished to classify Filipinos as "alien" and reduce their immigration to the United States. (p. 657)

**Underground Railroad:** An informal network of whites and free blacks in the South that assisted fugitive slaves to reach freedom in the North. (p. 312)

**unions:** Organizations of workers that began during the Industrial Revolution to bargain with employers over wages, hours, benefits, and control of the workplace. (p. 254)

**United Farm Workers (UFW):** A union of farmworkers founded in 1962 by Cesar Chavez and Dolores Huerta that sought to empower the mostly Mexican American migrant farmworkers who faced discrimination and exploitative conditions, especially in the Southwest. (p. 780)

**United Nations:** An international body agreed upon at the Yalta Conference and founded at a conference in San Francisco in 1945, consisting of a General Assembly, in which all nations are represented, and a Security Council of the five major Allied powers—the United States, Britain, France, China, and the Soviet Union—and seven other nations elected on a rotating basis. (p. 701)

**Universal Negro Improvement Association:** A Harlem-based group, led by charismatic, Jamaican-born Marcus Garvey, that arose in the 1920s to mobilize African American workers and champion black separatism. (p. 629)

**USA PATRIOT Act:** A 2001 law that gave the government new powers to monitor suspected terrorists and their associates, including the ability to access personal information. (p. 893)

**U.S. Fisheries Commission:** A federal bureau established in 1871 that made recommendations to stem the decline in wild fish. Its creation was an important step toward wildlife conservation and management. (p. 457)

**U.S. Sanitary Commission:** An organization that supported the Union war effort through professional and volunteer medical aid. (p. 400)

**utopias:** Communities founded by reformers and transcendentalists to help realize their spiritual and moral potential and to escape from the competition of modern industrial society. (p. 301)

**Valley Forge:** A military camp in which George Washington's army of 12,000 soldiers and hundreds of camp followers suffered horribly in the winter of 1777–1778. (p. 172)

**vaudeville theater:** A type of professional stage show popular in the 1880s and 1890s that included singing, dancing, and comedy routines; it created a form of family entertainment for the urban masses that deeply influenced later forms, such as radio shows and television sitcoms. (p. 533)

**vertical integration:** A business model in which a corporation controlled all aspects of production from raw materials to packaged products. "Robber barons," or industrial innovators such as Gustavus Swift and Andrew Carnegie, pioneered this business form at the end of the Civil War. (p. 477)

**Veterans Administration:** A federal agency that assists former soldiers. Following World War II, the VA helped veterans purchase new homes with no down payment, sparking a building boom that created jobs in the construction industry and fueling consumer spending in home appliances and automobiles. (p. 733)

**vice-admiralty court:** A maritime tribunal presided over by a royally appointed judge, with no jury. (p. 141)

**Vietnamization:** A new U.S. policy, devised under President Nixon in the early 1970s, of delegating the ground fighting to the South Vietnamese in the Vietnam War. American troop levels dropped and American casualties dropped correspondingly, but the killing in Vietnam continued. (p. 805)

**Virginia and Kentucky Resolutions:** Resolutions of 1798 condemning the Alien and Sedition Acts that were submitted to the federal government by the Virginia and Kentucky state legislatures. The resolutions tested the idea that state legislatures could judge the constitutionality of federal laws and nullify them. (p. 206)

**Virginia Plan:** A plan drafted by James Madison that was presented at the Philadelphia Constitutional Convention. It designed a powerful three-branch government, with representation in both houses of the congress tied to population; this plan would have eclipsed the voice of small states in the national government. (p. 189)

**virtual representation:** The claim made by British politicians that the interests of the American colonists were adequately represented in Parliament by merchants who traded with the colonies and by absentee landlords (mostly sugar planters) who owned estates in the West Indies. (p. 142)

**Volstead Act:** Officially the National Prohibition Act, passed by Congress in 1920 to enforce the provisions of the Eighteenth Amendment banning the sale of alcohol. (p. 622)

**Voting Rights Act of 1965:** Law passed during Lyndon Johnson's administration that empowered the federal government to intervene to ensure minorities' access to the voting booth. (p. 772)

**Wade-Davis Bill:** A bill proposed by Congress in July 1864 that required an oath of allegiance by a majority of each state's adult white men, new governments formed only by those who had never taken up arms against the Union, and permanent disenfranchisement of Confederate leaders. The plan was passed but pocket vetoed by President Abraham Lincoln. (p. 417)

**Wagner Act:** A 1935 act that upheld the right of industrial workers to join unions and established the National Labor Relations Board (NLRB), a federal agency with the authority to protect workers from employer coercion and to guarantee collective bargaining. (p. 648)

**Waltham-Lowell System:** A system of labor using young women recruited from farm families to work in factories in Lowell, Chicopee, and other sites in Massachusetts and New Hampshire. The women lived in company boardinghouses with strict rules and curfews and were often required to attend church. (p. 242)

**War Industries Board:** A federal board established in July 1917 to direct military production, including allocation of resources, conversion of factories to war production, and setting of prices. (p. 599)

**War Powers Act (1941):** The law that gave President Roosevelt unprecedented control over all aspects of the war effort during World War II. (p. 672)

**War Powers Act (1973):** A law that limited the president's ability to deploy U.S. forces without congressional approval. Congress passed the War Powers Act in 1973 as a series of laws to fight the abuses of the Nixon administration. (p. 824)

**Warren Court:** The Supreme Court under Chief Justice Earl Warren (1953–1969), which expanded the Constitution's promise of equality and civil rights. It issued landmark decisions in the areas of civil rights, criminal rights, reproductive freedom, and separation of church and state. (p. 809)

**Warsaw Pact:** A military alliance established in Eastern Europe in 1955 to counter the NATO alliance; it included Albania, Bulgaria, Czechoslovakia, East Germany, Hungary, Poland, Romania, and the Soviet Union. (p. 705)

**Watergate:** Term referring to the 1972 break-in at Democratic Party headquarters in the Watergate complex in Washington, D.C., by men working for President Nixon's reelection campaign, along with Nixon's efforts to cover it up. The Watergate scandal led to President Nixon's resignation. (p. 823)

***Webster v. Reproductive Health Services:*** A 1989 Supreme Court ruling that upheld the authority of state governments to limit the use of public funds and facilities for abortions. (p. 886)

**welfare capitalism:** A system of labor relations that stressed management's responsibility for employees' well-being. (p. 614)

**welfare state:** A term applied to industrial democracies that adopt various government-guaranteed social-welfare programs. The creation of Social Security and other measures of the Second New Deal fundamentally changed American society and established a national welfare state for the first time. (p. 648)

**Whigs:** The second national party, the Whig Party arose in 1834 when a group of congressmen contested Andrew Jackson's policies and conduct. The party identified itself with the pre-Revolutionary American and British parties—also called Whigs—that had opposed the arbitrary actions of British monarchs. (p. 285)

**Whiskey Rebellion:** A 1794 uprising by farmers in western Pennsylvania in response to enforcement of an unpopular excise tax on whiskey. (p. 202)

***Williams v. Mississippi:*** An 1898 Supreme Court ruling that allowed states to impose poll taxes and literacy tests. By 1908, every southern state had adopted such measures. (p. 559)

**Wilmot Proviso:** The 1846 proposal by Representative David Wilmot of Pennsylvania to ban slavery in territory acquired from the U.S.-Mexico War. (p. 355)

**Wisconsin Idea:** A policy promoted by Republican governor Robert La Follette of Wisconsin for greater government intervention in the economy, with reliance on experts, particularly progressive economists, for policy recommendations. (p. 566)

**Woman's Christian Temperance Union:** An organization advocating the prohibition of liquor that spread rapidly after 1879, when charismatic Frances Willard became its leader. Advocating suffrage and a host of reform activities, it launched tens of thousands of women into public life and was the first nationwide organization to identify and condemn domestic violence. (p. 518)

**Woman's Loyal National League:** An organization of Unionist women that worked to support the war effort, hoping the Union would recognize women's patriotism with voting rights after the war. (p. 401)

**women's liberation:** A new brand of feminism in the 1960s that attracted primarily younger, college-educated women fresh from the New Left, antiwar, and civil rights movements who sought to end to the denigration and exploitation of women. (p. 802)

**Women's Trade Union League:** A labor organization for women founded in New York in 1903 that brought elite, middle-class, and working-class women together as allies. The WTUL supported union organizing efforts among garment workers. (p. 545)

**Works Progress Administration:** Federal New Deal program established in 1935 that provided government-funded public works jobs to millions of unemployed Americans during the Great Depression in areas ranging from construction to the arts. (p. 649)

**World Bank:** An international bank created to provide loans for the reconstruction of war-torn Europe as well as for the development of former colonized nations in the developing world. (p. 729)

**World Trade Organization (WTO):** International economic body established in 1995 through the General Agreement on Tariffs and Trade to enforce substantial tariff and import quota reductions. (p. 876)

**World Wide Web:** A collection of interlinked computer servers that debuted in 1991, allowing access by millions to documents, pictures, and other materials. (p. 880)

**Wounded Knee:** The 1890 massacre of Sioux Indians by American cavalry at Wounded Knee Creek, South Dakota. Sent to suppress the Ghost Dance, soldiers caught up with fleeing Lakotas and killed as many as three hundred. (p. 465)

**XYZ Affair:** A 1797 incident in which American negotiators in France were rebuffed for refusing to pay a substantial bribe. The incident led the United States into an undeclared war that curtailed American trade with the French West Indies. (p. 204)

**Yalta Conference:** A meeting in Yalta of President Roosevelt, Prime Minister Churchill, and Joseph Stalin in February 1945, in which the leaders discussed the treatment of Germany, the status of Poland, the creation of the United Nations, and Russian entry into the war against Japan. (p. 700)

**yellow journalism:** A derogatory term for newspapers that specialize in sensationalistic reporting. Yellow journalism is associated with the inflammatory reporting by the Hearst and Pulitzer newspapers leading up to the Spanish-American War in 1898. (p. 536)

**Yellowstone National Park:** Established in 1872 by Congress, Yellowstone was the United States's first national park. (p. 457)

**Young Americans for Freedom (YAF):** The largest student political organization in the country, whose conservative members defended free enterprise and supported the war in Vietnam. (p. 796)

**Young Lords Organization:** An organization that sought self-determination for Puerto Ricans in the United States and in the Caribbean. Though immediate victories for the YLO were few, their dedicated community organizing produced a generation of leaders and awakened community consciousness. (p. 776)

**Young Men's Christian Association:** Introduced in Boston in 1851, the YMCA promoted muscular Christianity, combining evangelism with athletic facilities where men could make themselves "clean and strong." (p. 507)

**Zimmermann telegram:** A 1917 intercepted dispatch in which German foreign secretary Arthur Zimmermann urged Mexico to join the Central Powers and promised that if the United States entered the war, Germany would help Mexico recover Texas, New Mexico, and Arizona. Published by American newspapers, the telegram outraged the American public and help precipitate the move toward U.S. entry in the war on the Allied side. (p. 596)

**zoot suits:** Oversized suits of clothing in fashion in the 1940s, particularly among young male African Americans and Mexican Americans. In June 1943, a group of white sailors and soldiers in Los Angeles, seeking revenge for an earlier skirmish with Mexican American youths, attacked anyone they found wearing a zoot suit in what became known as the zoot-suit riots. (p. 680)

# Index

*A note about the index:* Names of individuals appear in boldface; biographical dates are included for major historical figures. Letters in parentheses following page numbers refer to: *(f)* figures, including charts and graphs; *(i)* illustrations, including photographs and artifacts; and *(m)* maps.

# About the Authors

**Rebecca Edwards** is Eloise Ellery Professor of History at Vassar College, where she teaches courses on nineteenth-century politics, the Civil War, the frontier West, and women, gender, and sexuality. She is the author of, among other publications, *Angels in the Machinery: Gender in American Party Politics from the Civil War to the Progressive Era*; *New Spirits: Americans in the "Gilded Age," 1865–1905*; and the essay "Women's and Gender History" in *The New American History*. She is currently working on a book about the role of childbearing in the expansion of America's nineteenth-century empire.

**Eric Hinderaker** is Professor of History at the University of Utah. His research explores early modern imperialism, relations between Europeans and Native Americans, military-civilian relations in the Atlantic world, and comparative colonization. His most recent book, *Boston's Massacre*, was published in 2017. His other publications include *Elusive Empires: Constructing Colonialism in the Ohio Valley, 1673–1800*; *The Two Hendricks: Unraveling a Mohawk Mystery*, which won the Herbert H. Lehman Prize for Distinguished Scholarship in New York History from the New York Academy of History; and, with Peter C. Mancall, *At the Edge of Empire: The Backcountry in British North America*.

**Robert O. Self** is Mary Ann Lippitt Professor of American History at Brown University. His research focuses on urban history, American politics, and the post-1945 United States. He is the author of *American Babylon: Race and the Struggle for Postwar Oakland*, which won four professional prizes, including the James A. Rawley Prize from the Organization of American Historians, and *All in the Family: The Realignment of American Democracy Since the 1960s*. He is currently at work on a book about the centrality of houses, cars, and children to family consumption in the twentieth-century United States.

**James A. Henretta** is Professor Emeritus of American History at the University of Maryland, College Park. His publications include *The Evolution of American Society, 1600–1815, The Origins of American Capitalism*, and an edited volume, *Republicanism and Liberalism in America and the German States, 1750–1850*. His most recent publications include two long articles, "Magistrates, Common Law Lawyers, Legislators: The Three Legal Systems of British America" and "Charles Evans Hughes and the Strange Death of Liberal America," derived from his ongoing research on the liberal state in America, and in particular New York, 1820–1975.